OCCASIONS FOR WRITING

EVIDENCE

IDEA

ESSAY

ROBERT DiYANNI

New York University

PAT C. HOY II

New York University

THOMSON

WADSWORTH

Australia * Brazil * Canada * Mexico * Singapore * Spain * United Kingdom * United States

THOMSON

★ ™

WADSWORTH

Occasions for Writing: Evidence, Idea, Essay
Robert DiYanni / Pat C. Hoy II

Publisher: *Lyn Uhl*
Development Editor: *Marita Sermolins*
Editorial Assistant: *Megan Garvey*
Technology Project Manager: *Joe Gallagher*
Managing Marketing Manager: *Mandee Eckersley*
Marketing Assistant: *Kate Remsberg*
Senior Marketing Communications Manager:
   Stacey Purviance
Senior Art Director: *Cate Rickard Barr*
Senior Content Project Manager: *Samantha Ross*
Print Buyer: *Betsy Donaghey*

Permissions Manager: *Ron Montgomery*
Photo Manager: *Sheri Blaney*
Permissions Researcher: *Marcy Lunetta*
Text/Cover Designer: *Yvo Riezebos*
Cover Printer: *Courier–Kendallville*
Production Service/Compositor: *Graphic World Inc.*
Printer: *Courier–Kendallville*
Cover Art: *Christo and Jeanne-Claude: The
   Umbrellas, Japan - U.S.A., 1984–91; Photo:
   Wolfgang Volz / laif / Redux Pictures. Copyright:
   Christo 1991–2005*

Printed in the United States of America
1 2 3 4 5 6 7 09 08 07 06

Library of Congress Control Number: 2006937801

ISBN 1-4130-1206-X

Thomson Higher Education
25 Thomson Place
Boston, MA 02210-1202
USA

For more information about our products, contact us at:
Thomson Learning Academic
Resource Center
1-800-423-0563

For permission to use material from this text or
product, submit a request online at
http://www.thomsonrights.com
Any additional questions about permissions can
be submitted by e-mail to
thomsonrights@thomson.com

Credits appear on pages 815–826, which constitute
a continuation of the copyright page.

CONTENTS

PART ONE A BRIEF GUIDE TO WRITING

APPENDIX FINDING EVIDENCE AND DOCUMENTING SOURCES

{ RHETORICAL CONTENTS

ABOUT THE AUTHORS

ROBERT DiYANNI

Robert DiYanni is the author of over 35 textbooks, including *The Scribner Handbook for Writers,* Fourth Edition (with Pat Hoy); *Modern American Prose: A Reader for Writers;* and the best-selling *Literature: Reading Fiction, Poetry, Drama* and *The Essay: An Introduction.* He received his BA from Rutgers University and his PhD from the City University of New York. He currently works for The College Board as the Director of International Services for K–12 programs. Professor DiYanni is also an adjunct professor of Humanities at New York University.

PAT C. HOY II

Pat C. Hoy II, director of the Expository Writing Program and professor of English at New York University, has also held appointments at the U.S. Military Academy and Harvard. He received his PhD from the University of Pennsylvania. Professor Hoy regularly teaches freshman composition.

Professor Hoy is the author of numerous textbooks and articles, including *The Scribner Handbook for Writers,* Fourth Edition (with Robert DiYanni). His essays have appeared in *Sewanee Review, Virginia Quarterly Review, Agni, Twentieth Century Literature, South Atlantic Review,* and *The Wall Street Journal.* Eight of his essays have been selected as "Notables" in *Best American Essays. Instincts for Survival: Essays by Pat C. Hoy II* was selected as a "Notable" selection in *Best American Essays of the Century,* edited by Joyce Carol Oates and Robert Atwan. He was awarded the 2003 Cecil Woods Jr. Prize for Nonfiction from the Fellowship of Southern Writers.

{ PREFACE

oc•ca•sion *n.* 1. reason, call, cause. 2. a favorable or appropriate time, an opportunity. 3. something that brings on or precipitates an action.

GIVING RISE TO THE OCCASION: EVIDENCE, IDEA, ESSAY

Occasions for Writing is an inviting and challenging book designed to help students learn to read critically, think rigorously, become more reflective, and write compelling essays. The book's rhythm follows a fundamental sequence: the movement *from* evidence *to* idea *to* essay. Thematically arranged readings are coupled with carefully designed assignment cycles called *Occasions for Writing*.

A careful consideration of *evidence*—which comes primarily from what students read, see, and have experienced—leads to *ideas,* and ideas lead invariably to *essays.* Each Occasion for Writing provides evidence for consideration (an essay and a series of images—photographs, paintings, advertisements, even video clips). Probing questions and exercises help students better understand each essay while encouraging them to discover connections both within the written texts and among the images.

The images that accompany the essays are provocative. They stimulate thinking and allow teachers to take advantage of students' natural tendency to respond to our culture's most ubiquitous form of communication. The images speak to us and sometimes for us, sometimes without our sense of their power. The Occasion for Writing assignment cycles lead students to a more careful examination of some of the culture's most stimulating images, but we take students to the images not only because the images speak so powerfully but also because we want students to become more aware of the power of images and of their usefulness to the persuasive writer.

Each linked to a thematic essay, the Occasions for Writing begin by showing an image (or images) that is related in explicit and implicit ways to the essay's theme. Accompanying the images is a rigorous set of writing prompts intended to move students through the thinking and writing process.

- *Preparing to Write: Occasions to Think about What You See* exercises guide students in carefully analyzing the images and writings, asking them to pay attention to characteristics such as colors, shapes, shadows, internal order, tone, and striking oddities. This intense study of the evidence will help students move into more critical thinking.

- *Moving toward Essay: Occasions to Analyze and Reflect* prompts ask students to analyze and interpret the evidence they've discovered in the essay and images, as well as in their own experiences. Students are encouraged to formulate fresh ideas for their own essays.

- *Writing Thoughtfully: Occasions for Ideas and Writing* exercises provide the foundation and direction for developing both ideas and essays. These assignments sometimes provide more information about the images and/or writings and the artist who created them. Other times, students are asked to make connections between the images and essays that set the Occasion in motion, or they are asked to use their own experiences to clarify their understanding of selected images, or essays, or both.

- *Creating Occasions* assignments complete the Occasion for Writing assignment cycle, suggesting other ways to use the evidence that students have been analyzing and interpreting in earlier exercises.

The writing that students are asked to do leads to a deeper understanding of the essays and the images. Such writing is necessarily an act of discovery and learning. One thing uncovered leads to another, so that rudimentary ideas become more complex, more interesting, as the evidence is examined more closely. That which is fundamental becomes complex primarily because the book's pedagogy slows the process of discovery and asks students to pause over the evidence, consider it in light of other related evidence, write tentatively about it, and, finally, formulate an idea worthy of the reading and writing that have led to discovery—what John Henry Newman called "acquired illumination," or knowledge. This work leads not simply to an accumulation of information; it leads as well to critical analysis of that information and to the formulation and development of a complete essay.

This process of investigation—this careful and exciting process of reading, analyzing, reflecting, formulating, and writing—provides the foundation for students' work throughout his or her college career. Investigation and research are essentially synonymous. Writing is at the core of the process, leading as it always does to discovery after discovery and to a deepening of one's understanding of the evidence itself. The idea, and then the essay that follows, are proof positive of the value and centrality of this process of investigation.

THEMES

Occasions for Writing is built on thematically grouped readings. Each of the thematic chapters (5 through 14) is built around an interesting theme, six primary full-length essays grouped in two thematic clusters, and a host of images that bring vitality to the Occasions. Students are directed to read and to see; they are encouraged to make connections, to be reflective; finally, they are asked to make something new from their reading and thinking and writing. That newness attaches itself to the idea they discover and to the essay they write.

The themes themselves may be familiar, but our treatment of them is fresh and stimulating. The selected essays in each Occasion evoke the themes; the images reinforce them; and the students' own experiences ground them. Essays, images, and experience constitute the evidence—that and whatever else the student can bring to bear on the evloving idea. Students are encouraged to make connections with readings from other courses and from their visual experiences. The Occasions for Writing assignment cycles call students into relationships with the themes, asking them to see their own experiences anew and from different perspectives. *Occasions for Writing* improves both analytical skills and the writing of essays.

ESSAYING

A profound belief in essaying informs this book's pedagogy. The three-part form of the essay is intriguing and accommodating—a writing student's most effective *silent* teacher. The process of learning to write essays, however, requires the attendance of an active teacher, one who attends the process and offers stimulating questions, encouragement, and an informed sense of the possible. Students writing essays under the influence of good teachers and good ideas invariably do what they have never done before. They write compelling essays. The thinking sets it all in motion—that and the guidance of a teacher who encourages students to test the elasticity of the essay's form while insisting that the three parts (beginning, middle, and end) work together to create a whole.

The first three chapters of the book address the qualities and characteristics of essays, allowing students to learn just what an essay is, just what one looks like, and just how essays actually come into being through trial and error, through continual revision, as the mind figures out what the idea is and how best to present it. Aristotle tells us that rhetoric itself is the ability to see the available means of persuasion in every instance that the speaker confronts. The same is true for the writer, who must learn how to make use of the essay's form to be more persuasive—to *see* what it takes to convince a particular audience that the idea and its presentation have merit. Chapters 2 and 3 present student work in detail so that students and teachers alike can see how the various Occasions can lead to fine essays. Chapter 4 teaches students how to read images and couples that process with the process of writing essays. The opening four chapters thus work together to prepare students for the Occasions for Writing assignment cycles that accompany the thematic readings.

ANTHOLOGY

Besides the 60 essays that accompany the Occasion for Writing assignment cycles, there is an anthology of 18 additional essays that provide other opportunities for writing and the creation of additional Occasions. These essays are also accompanied by a series of reading, thinking, and writing questions that lead students to more rigorous, comprehensive readings of the essays.

SUPPLEMENTS

INSTRUCTOR'S MANUAL

This exceptionally useful *Instructor's Manual* includes synopses and in-depth discussion of every essay in the textbook, ideas for initiating classroom discussion, tips for helping students use the book's visuals as springboards for their writing, and additional image and research ideas for each of the textbook's *Occasion for Writing* exercises.

ENGLISH21 ONLINE

Helps students develop the adaptive analytical skills needed for writing in the 21st century.

Through interactive instruction, English21 not only teaches students how to analyze the various "texts" that inundate their lives but also demonstrates how to use rhetorical devices in their writing. This groundbreaking online tool includes:

- Comprehensive media libraries, containing more than 500 essays, images, video clips, and audio clips.

- The Explicator, an innovative note-taking tool that promotes critical thinking skills, helping students analyze and dissect various media "texts," and generates original ideas to use in their own writing.

- An interactive "Introduction to Visual Rhetoric" that provides students with the analytical framework and essentials of visual composition necessary to analyze and write about "texts" in today's visual world.

- Guided writing sequences that help students develop analysis and synthesis skills.
- Rhetorical instruction suitable for a variety of writing occasions, including coverage of argumentation, modes, and themes.

Visit www.thomsonedu.com/english for a demonstration.

THOMSON INSITE FOR WRITING AND RESEARCH™

An online solution for both instructors and students, InSite is a groundbreaking, all-in-one tool that allows instructors the opportunity to manage the flow of papers online and allows students to submit papers and peer reviews online. Features include fully integrated discussion boards, streamlined assignment creation, advanced originality checking powered by Turnitin®, the ability for students to manage peer review and paper portfolios online, the ability for instructors to give feedback and manage grades electronically, access to the InfoTrac® College Edition online research database, and more. Visit www .thomsonedu.com/insite to view a demonstration.

TURNITIN®

This proven online plagiarism-prevention software promotes fairness in the classroom by helping students learn to correctly cite sources and enabling you to check for originality before reading and grading papers. Turnitin® quickly checks student papers against billions of pages of Internet content, published works, and student papers. Visit www.thomsonedu.com/turnitin to view a demonstration.

WRITENOTE

Now your students can "cite while they write" with WriteNote, an online writing, research, and bibliography tool from Thomson. Ideal for use in any course in which students write papers, WriteNote allows students to spend less time on the mechanics of citing sources and more time on developing strong, well-organized papers. With WriteNote, students can format bibliographies instantly because WriteNote knows the latest updates for more than 1,000 documentation styles, including such standards as MLA, APA, Chicago, and CSE. Visit www.thomsonedu.com/english to view a demonstration.

BOOK COMPANION WEBSITE

In addition to a great selection of password-protected instructor resources, the Book Companion website contains many interactive resources for students, including libraries that offer animated tutorials and information on diction, grammar, mechanics, punctuation, research, and examples of student papers. Visit www.thomsonedu.com/english/diyanni.

INFOTRAC® COLLEGE EDITION WITH INFOMARKS™

This extensive online library includes innumerable articles from thousands of magazines, journals, and other popular periodicals. InfoTrac College Edition also includes InfoWrite, which gives students access to topics such as how to write a successful paper. To take a quick tour of InfoTrac College Edition, visit www.thomsonedu.com/infotrac and select the "InfoTrac Demo." *Certain restrictions may apply.*

ACKNOWLEDGMENTS

A number of smart and dedicated people helped us develop this new book. We especially want to thank Aron Keesbury and Dickson Musslewhite, who sought us out and helped us develop the general concept for *Occasions for Writing* (and for *Frames of Mind* as well). Though Aron and Dickson moved on to other projects and responsibilities just as the actual work on Occasions was beginning, their passion for what we did together in its early stages and their genius inspired us to carry on in their absence.

Closer to the work of helping us develop the book was Marita Sermolins, Associate Development Editor, who kept us focused on the intricate details of our multifaceted work and who provided inspiring comments and suggestions all along the way. Samantha Ross, Content Production Manager, steered the book through the production process with her customary expertise. We owe both Marita and Samantha a world of thanks. We owe thanks as well to our text and photo permissions researcher, Marcy Lunetta, who worked indefatigably to search out and secure rights to a multitude of striking and thought-provoking images. We were also fortunate to have assisting us in this facet of the work Stephanie Hopkins, who helped us find stunning images and provided editorial help. Thanks are also due Mandee Eckersley, Marketing Manager, for her excellent work in managing the all-important marketing process.

James Dubinsky of Virginia Polytechnic Institute provided the exceptionally useful chapter, "An Introduction to Visual Understanding." And Dawn Lundy Martin provided the richly textured Instructor's Manual with its plethora of practical teaching suggestions. Thanks to both Jim and Dawn for their excellent work.

Like any project, *Occasions for Writing* benefited from the thoughtful suggestions of reviewers across the country. Our thanks to the following professors for their helpful suggestions:

Jess Airaudi, *Baylor University*

David Beach, *George Mason University*

Stacia Bensyl, *Missouri Western State College*

Peter Bergenstock, *Canisius College*

Mary Blanchard, *New Jersey City University*

Tina Boshca, *University of Oregon*

Marci L. Carrasquillo, *University of Oregon*

Richard Case, *James Madison University*

Craig Challender, *Longwood College*

Kory Ching, *University of Illinois, Urbana-Champaign*

Sandra Coffey, *Columbus State University*

Carla Conforto, *Pennsylvania State University*

Cynthia Davidson, *Stony Brook University*

Virigina Davis, *University of Oregon*

Laura Dearing, *Jefferson Community College*

Wayne Fulks, *Sullivan County Community College*

Ryan Futrell, *Cedarville University*

Ruth Gerik, *University of Texas, Arlington*

Lisa Gring-Pemble, *George Mason University*

Diana Gruendler, *Pennsylvania State University*

Charles Hill, *University of Wisconsin, Oshkosh*

Sandra Jamieson, *Drew University*

Brian Johnson, *Southern Connecticut State University*

Audrey Kerr, *Southern Connecticut State University*

Ginny Machann, *Blinn College*

Jayne Marek, *Franklin College*

Sarah Markgraf, *Bergen Community College*

Tori Mask, *Blinn College*

Dani McClean, *Saddleback College*

Barbara Morris, *Bergen Community College*

Mary Morse, *Rider University*

Robbi Nester, *Irvine Valley College*

Linda Norris, *Indiana University of Pennsylvania*

Karen Osborne, *Columbia College*

Anna Priddy, *Louisiana State University*

J. Lisa Ray, *Thomas Nelson Community College*

Larry Rochelle, *Johnson County Community College*

Aaron Rosenfeld, *Iona College*

David Ross, *Houston Community College*

Lisa Siefker-Bailey, *Franklin College of Indiana*

Martha Sims, *Ohio State University*

Shari Stenberg, *Creighton University*

Joyce Stoffers, *Southwestern Oklahoma State University*

Filiz Turhan-Swenson, *Suffolk County Community College*

Wendy Waisala, *Atlantic Community College*

Jennifer Wagner, *West Valley College*

Thanks also to the survey participants who helped us determine the most popular, essential, and successful themes and readings. We'd like to thank our survey participants for sharing their successes with us and enabling us to shape our book to their responses.

Allison Alison, *Southeastern Community College*

Michael Arnzen, *Seton Hall University*

Jonathan Ausubel, *Chaffey College*

Nancy Barta-Smith, *Slippery Rock University*

Scott Boltwood, *Emory & Henry College*

Loretta Brister, *Tarleton State University*

Imogene Bunch, *Christopher Newport University*

Patricia Burdette, *Ohio State University*

Minnie A. Collins, *Seattle Central Community College*

G. Michelle Collins-Sibley, *Mount Union College*

Connie Corbett-Whittier, *Friends University*

James Cotter, *Mount Saint Mary College*

Huey Crisp, *University of Arkansas, Little Rock*

Laurie Dashnau, *Houghton College*

Samir Dayal, *Bentley College*

Stacey Donohue, *Central Oregon Community College*

Harry Eiss, *Eastern Michigan University*

June Farmer, *Southern Union State Community College*

Amy Flagg, *Aims Community College*

Ryan Futrell, *Cedarville University*

Lara Gary, *Sacramento City College*

Eckhard Gerdes, *Middle Georgia College*

Risa Gorelick, *Monmouth University*

Denise Greenwood, *Albright College*

Eric Grekowicz, *University of La Verne*

Brenda Hampton, *Kirkwood Community College*

Kathryn Henkins, *Mt. San Antonio College*

Patricia A. Herb, *North Central State College*

H. Brooke Hessler, *Oklahoma City University*

Michael J. Hricik, *Westmoreland County Community College*

Lynn M. Hublou, *South Dakota State University*

Michael Hustedde, *St. Ambrose University*

Doris Jackson, *Westchester Community College*

Dawnelle Jager, *State University of New York, Syracuse*

James Kirkpatrick, *Central Piedmont Community College*

Liz Kleinfeld, *Red Rocks Community College*

Andrew Kunka, *University of South Carolina, Sumter*

Marti Lee, *Georgia Southern University*

Kelly Lowry, *Terra State Community College*

Brooke McLaughlin, *Wingate University*

Crystal O'Leary, *Middle Georgia College*

Dara Perales, *Palomar College*

Steve Price, *Monmouth College*

David Pulling, *Louisiana State University, Eunice*

Jerry Rafiki Jenkins, *Palomar College*

Ruth Reilly, *Hocking College*

Steven Reynolds, *College of the Siskiyous*

Rich Rice, *Texas Tech University*

Julie Rivera, *California State University, Long Beach*

Donnalee Rubin, *Salem State College*

Jillian Schedneck, *West Virginia University*

Heather Schell, *George Washington University*

Andrew Scott, *Ball State University*

William Stevenson, *Saddleback College*

Anne Stockdell-Giesler, *University of Tampa*

Anthony Stubbs, *Iowa Lakes Community College*

Celia Swanson, *Inver Hills Community College*

Dean Swinford, *University of North Florida*

John W. Taylor, *South Dakota State University*

Caryl Terrell-Bamiro, *Chandler-Gilbert Community College*

Pamela Turley, *Community College of Allegheny County*

Vernelle Tyler, *University of South Carolina, Aiken*

Michael Van Meter, *Central Oregon Community College*

Carl Waluconis, *Seattle Central Community College*

Michelle Weisman, *College of the Ozarks*

Mary Jo Wocken, *University of Mary*

Finally, we'd like to thank our wives, Mary DiYanni and Ann Hoy, who have stood behind this process, encouraging us just as they have done for so many, many years. Our grown sons (Michael DiYanni and Patrick and Timothy Hoy) and daughter (Karen DiYanni), long gone from the nest, continue to watch these collaborations, amazed perhaps that the work still goes on. So are we—amazed, and this time especially, especially pleased that we were fortunate enough to make this book, which we firmly believe can make a lasting difference in the lives of those who use it to enrich their thinking and their writing. There is much here to ponder, and we hope that our own enthusiasm leads to an infectious epidemic of reading, writing, and thinking, eventuating in thoughtful essays.

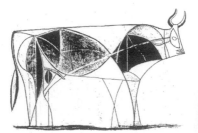

Pablo Picasso sketching for clarity: Which image best captures the essence or idea of the bull?

THE PRACTICE OF WRITING

Writing is an act of clarification. We write to reveal and explain to others what seems important to us. We write to reveal things that we have discovered from books, essays, and articles; from theatrical performances or movies; from our own lived experiences; and from our observations of the world at large.

The act of writing is always predicated on acts of inquiry. The process of inquiry and discovery is usually followed by a nagging, persistent question: How best can I reveal to my readers what I want them to know? The answer is both complicated and educational.

We write to learn. Even after we have gathered our evidence and have thought about it, there is more clarifying to be done. We hear over and over from seasoned writers that they write to clarify their thinking or to straighten it out. Writing then is done both for ourselves—as a way for us to understand more fully what we think about a given subject and a given body of evidence—and for others. We want others to *see* what we have come to see. We want to persuade them, to hold them in thrall as they read what we have written so that they will consider seriously the work that we have done as thinkers.

Writing shows others just what we are made of intellectually. It reveals how thoroughly we have considered our subject, how clearly we can express ourselves, and how excited we are about what we have learned. Writing is a personal act of expression, but it is not, when it is most effective, an autobiographical tale about ourselves. Rather it is an account of our mind's work—a reflection of what we know, what we have discovered, what we want others to know.

That is what writing is when we are essayists. The essayist has at his or her fingertips the world and develops the capacity to see within the world things of value, to notice the unusual, the secret in the commonplace, the hidden meaning in the scholarly text, the pearl of wisdom in the recollected experience. The essayist cares about such discoveries and the proper written expression of them. It is the essayist's business to persuade readers that those discoveries have real value—that we need to know about them and understand their significance.

WHY AM I WRITING ESSAYS?

Every essay that you write calls on you to make something new, something that only you can create. Each time you write an essay, you will develop an **idea** of your own from the materials that you have gathered from your research, whether that research is focused on other essays, scholarly articles, newspaper reports, laboratory data, or your own lived experiences. You and your mind are central to this writing process and the essay you create.

When you write an essay, your readers see you thinking about what you have examined, or your **evidence**—a text, images, stories, personal experiences, anything you bring to your idea—and what it means, why it is important. Your readers see your thoughts about the evidence and come to understand what you have figured out from the evidence and what meaning you have derived from it.

Learning to write the **essay** establishes the foundation for all the writing that you will be called on to do as a college student—reports; surveys and summaries of literature from any academic field; laboratory reports; response papers to books, essays, and scholarly articles. The essay, while teaching you the skills associated with each of those tasks, asks that you go beyond preliminary reading, preparation of summaries, lists of findings, and organization of reports to develop your own ideas.

Montaigne showed us in the sixteenth century that the essay is indeed a trial, an attempt to capture meaning (in French, the word *essai* means "a trial"), using whatever is at our disposal to do so—everything from our lived experiences to our most complex and sacred texts. He also taught us something about the art of meaningful digression—reaching out for the odd connections, the unexpected texts, to help us ensure that we leave nothing out of our thinking as we try to bring our readers to understand fully what we understand. The essay is an accommodating, protean form; it can adapt to our needs as writers, allowing us to make use of all that we know. It is, as Donald McQuade has reminded us, our most democratic form of literature, adaptable to our personal language and our idiosyncratic ways of thinking. But it also demands of us feats of intellectual derring-do, calling on us time and again to make sense of our evidence—the complicated texts (written, visual, and lived) that we read and study.

You will soon see that all essays have certain things in common: a three-part structure (beginning, middle, and ending); an idea, or, more properly, a network of ideas that shape and bind the many pieces of evidence together; and, finally, every good essay reveals how the mind writing it makes sense of things. Readers can actually see the writer's mind transforming evidence and making sense of it. This transforming act draws writer and readers into a relationship with one another as they consider together the essay's compelling idea. Essays do not prove, repeat, or reiterate. Instead, essays, like ideas, develop, expand, turn on themselves—and captivate the reader when the writer gets the words right. In every essay that you write, you will be trying to get your reader to see as you see, to understand as you understand. You will be trying to convince your readers that your own ideas have merit.

AN OCCASION FOR WRITING

You have perhaps come to think that only your teachers provide occasions for writing, but almost everything you see or read provides such an occasion. The best essayists seize moments from the ordinary and make of them something extraordinary. E. B. White, one of the most accomplished essayists, could write as movingly and convincingly about the death of his pig as the scientist Lewis Thomas could write of an impending nuclear disaster or the life of a cell. The seized moment—a brief conversation, the sight of a beautiful man or woman, the aftermath of a movie, the excitement of a compelling essay, a recollected experience, a wave of nostalgia, a haunting smell—these moments afford the opportunity to write, to try to figure out for yourself why that something is important.

An occasion for writing is simply an opportunity that presents itself to you, that compels you to take out your pen or sit down with your laptop to try to capture your own thinking, your own reaction, in words. Paying attention to these moments we become more curious, more inquiring. Writing, we learn to go beyond mere recollection and re-creation to try to make something of the moment, to see it through to an idea. Annie Dillard, an award-winning essayist, urges us to open ourselves up to such occasions, to learn to be more aware, to let the world impress itself upon us. These occasions come to us often, asking only that we pay attention and that we write to learn more about them.

These occasions also come to us from our teachers and from some of the textbooks that we read. As we work collaboratively within this book, you will analyze and interpret many kinds of texts, both visual and verbal. The *Occasions for Writing* ask you to read imaginatively, to consider what may seem at times odd connections between written and visual texts, and to go beyond these suggested connections to connections that only you can make. We lay out pathways—exercises and occasions for writing—but those pathways provide space for you to take detours, to read and write as only you can read and write. In this chapter, we present some key terms and essential aspects of essay writing—working definitions that will help prepare you for the writing that follows. In the next two chapters, we offer real-life examples by presenting one student's work, showing how she responds to a sequence of writing exercises that lead her to develop two different compelling essays, one **exploratory** essay that evolves from a visual image (a painting) and makes primary use of experience as evidence, the other a **persuasive, text-based** essay that depends primarily on written texts to generate, develop, and substantiate its idea. Our aim throughout is to give you a clear sense of fundamental rhetorical concepts related to the writing of essays.

USING YOUR VOICE AND
FINDING YOUR CHARACTER

As you bring ideas and evidence together, you will always be trying to compel your readers to listen carefully to what you have to tell them about your own discoveries. You will be learning to write so that your readers can actually hear your personal persuasive voice emerging from your sentences and your paragraphs. Notice that you have not one but several voices—one that converses with friends, one that addresses teachers and other scholars, others that tell stories, plead with parents, appeal to a love interest. So voice suggests not only sounds but also different inflections, different ways of talking and persuading, depending on who is listening. Over time, you will learn when and how to use your own complexities, making use of different degrees of formality as you consider your readers and their varying needs. You will learn too that different forms of the essay accommodate different degrees of formality, and you will develop a voice that can speak colloquially and effectively in some essays and a voice that speaks more formally in others. But no matter what the tone, no matter what your relationship to your evidence and your audience, you will be aiming to write so that your work carries within it traces of your own mind and personality. You will be learning to write so that others listen.

Getting others to listen requires that you be wise enough to accommodate their needs. Aristotle suggests in *On Rhetoric* that the speaker (or the writer) must anticipate the thinking of others, and he associates the ability to do so with the character of the speaker, or *ethos*. He suggests that ethos may be the most effective element of persuasion, placing it above both *logos* (logic) and *pathos* (feelings). Some might argue that *character* is an old-fashioned, outmoded word, but when we turn to the *Oxford English Dictionary* (*OED*), we find a number of crucial aspects of character that compel us, as writers, to pay attention. Character, we are reminded, refers to the "style of writing peculiar to any individual"; it also suggests the "sum of the moral and mental qualities which distinguish an individual." So when we think of the character of the writer, we are not thinking about the writer as a character in a story, but rather about the writer's thoughts, the way he or she weighs and values the evidence so that readers can clearly see the thinking and the judging that has led to particular verbal expressions, and to a particular way of seeing the world. We are also thinking of how a writer's mind can anticipate objections to the argument at hand and can persuade us by recognizing and predicting our needs.

To be a successful writer, you need to use your knowledge and personal thoughts and make your particular appeal to an audience in a way that no one else can duplicate. Writing is a personal experience that leads you to original thinking. The essay that you write will be a reflection of who you are and what you know; it will be a written record of your thoughts presented in such a way as to convince others to see as you see and to understand as you understand.

MOVING FROM EVIDENCE TO IDEA TO ESSAY

Every occasion for writing an essay calls on a writer to consider a body of evidence; develop an idea about it; and, finally, to write an essay that will explain the relationship between the evidence and the idea. **Evidence, idea, essay**—these key terms suggest how the mind moves as it first considers a body of evidence; then turns to the creation of an idea; and finally develops an essay that will express and substantiate that idea, or *thesis*.

EVIDENCE

Evidence comes from the information you gather as you investigate a topic. As you set out to make sense of the evidence and as it begins to suggest things to you, you begin to interact with it; you begin to formulate your own thoughts and opinions about the evidence you have been given or have collected yourself. The evidence eventually leads you to an idea for your own essay as you read, analyze, and reflect on what the evidence means. This is a slow, recursive process, one that requires patience and your persistence.

In the past, you have surely chosen telling examples to support your claims or ideas, or perhaps you have selected quotations from written texts that you have read. Perhaps you have even written about movies or plays and have chosen scenes to analyze so that you can reveal to your readers what you discovered as you read or watched the performance. You can find evidence for your essays from your reading (written texts of all kinds—books, essays, journal articles, newspapers, magazines), your observations (in the classroom or in the outside world), images (painting, sculpture, photographs, movies, television programs), and your own experiences and the stories you construct from them. Your own experiences are very important in the process of analyzing and reading the evidence. Often an abstract written text can be coupled with your own experience to create and help clarify the more abstract ideas and to add concreteness and depth to what might otherwise be a flat, unconvincing presentation of evidence.

Evidence is all around you and isn't necessarily as solid, or as factual, as you might think. Evidence consists of more than verifiable facts. Other scholars' interpretations of facts can serve you well. But whether you are looking at solid facts, reasoned opinions, or a host of primary sources (scholarly journals, fiction, images, laboratory experiments, your own experiences), all of these sources must be read and analyzed by you; it is from these sources that you make your own discoveries. You take advantage of what you already know, but you challenge yourself by deepening your understanding of the sources. As you think about the evidence, you will be continuously forming thoughts, opinions, and ideas that you should record as they occur to you. This preliminary thinking and writing leads to new ideas and to your essay.

You analyze and interpret your sources not to repeat what others have said but to develop your own idea, building both on what others have discovered and on what you discover. Your aim is to use various kinds of evidence to develop the interesting idea that you have begun to formulate. Your most exciting work will be to consider diverse sources and to create something new from them, something that is your very own, something that you want to pass on to others.

IDEA

You want always to communicate what you have discovered as you analyze the evidence and figure out what it means. Your idea carries that meaning to your reader; it provides a theory about the evidence. An idea is simply your sense of what the evidence means, your explanation or interpretation of the facts and sources you have gathered during your research. As an interpreter, you will help your readers understand what the evidence means. This meaning is rarely obvious to others; others will not have studied the evidence the way you have. Your readers necessarily depend on you to interpret the evidence and to explain its relationship to your idea.

The important supporting relationship that must exist in all essays between evidence and idea (or thesis) is that your own thinking is represented. You should be thinking about an idea throughout the entire writing process, because your idea constantly forms and reforms itself as you write. Rather than simply declaring a thesis in your writing—something that you intend to "prove"—you should be actively inquiring about and developing an idea. Instead of thinking deductively (moving from premises to a forced conclusion), you'll be thinking inductively (moving from a diverse body of evidence to reasoned conclusions), drawing from your evidence, inferring meaning from it.

As an inductive thinker, you know that your evidence, if it is worth thinking about at all, can never yield an iron-clad conclusion. When we reason inductively, our conclusions are never forced. We do not *prove* our points in an essay; we draw from the evidence the most reasonable conclusion we can draw and let the idea develop and deepen further as we write. We write to learn; the process itself leads to discovery and to better, more complex thinking. Over time and through multiple drafts, the thinking becomes more seasoned, more reasonable. It is as if you are brewing a stew, letting it simmer for a long period of time so that the various ingredients can come together to produce a more integrated, harmonious mixture. The tastes marry, yielding a more intense, more cohesive flavor. So too with your writing. Let it evolve, come together, intensify as your mind provides the transformation.

Static arguments that depend on a series of assertions (or premises) supported by a few examples rarely satisfy discerning readers. Readers do not get to see enough of the writer's thinking in such arguments. To be convincing, you have to let your readers see through your words why you consider your idea reliable, why you are so convinced of the truth of what you are saying that you have written an essay to reveal your thinking. Your persuasiveness depends, always, on the soundness of your inductive thinking, on how carefully you have read, analyzed, and interpreted the evidence, and on how skillfully you have presented the idea that evolves from that rigorous, meaning-making process. The fruits of that process must reveal themselves in the reflection that accompanies the evidence.

As you search for ideas in the evidence, you will necessarily seek out disagreement, controversy, or areas where a consensus is needed. Within these tensions, typically, is the core of an important idea—that which is really at stake in the debate, or discussion, of your chosen topic. There you will find many different perspectives to investigate. Somewhere at the center of that *controversy* beats the heart of an idea that you can make your own, or bring a new perspective to, through analysis, interpretation, and reflection. This idea will be your reasoned perspective on the controversy—a perspective that has been developed through a careful analysis of the gathered evidence.

You know that you have a good idea when it helps to resolve a controversy or disagreement, when you begin to hear from your readers, "Tell me more. I never thought of it that way until now. That's really interesting." You must bring the evidence to life by providing an explanation of its meaning. This explanation constitutes your idea; without the idea, there can be no essay—your vehicle for the expression of your idea.

ESSAY

The word "essay" comes from a French verb *essayer,* which means "to attempt" or "to try." An essay, then, is a trial or an attempt to develop an idea, work out its implications, and share it with others. The form of the essay itself consists of three parts: a beginning (or introduction), a middle (or body), and an end (or conclusion). Within that three-part structure an essayist makes an appeal to the readers' interests, develops an interesting idea and supports it with evidence, and provides a closing perspective on the writer's thoughts. Essayists seek consensus; they aim to induce belief.

The essay is, as O. B. Hardison, former director of the Folger Shakespeare Library, reminds us, a protean form, one that can change shape within its own fundamental three-part structure to accommodate the mind of the writer writing. It is a form that frees you to create meaning (develop those ideas) in ways that no one else can duplicate. That idiosyncratic work, the work of a particular person creating a particular set of ideas within an accommodating form, lies at the very heart of all good persuasive writing.

Most good essayists can write a spectrum of essays, ranging from the exploratory to the argumentative, from the less formal to the more formal. **Exploratory essays** depend primarily on stories of experience; those stories constitute the essay's primary evidence. The writer—whose own stories of experience reveal and substantiate the idea—often appears in these stories as a character named "I." But there is another "I" who is actually assembling these stories and using them as evidence: the discerning, writing "I" who offers his or her perspective on the meaning of the stories. In exploratory essays, the development of the idea tends to be digressive; we sense that we are seeing the writer working out the idea aloud as we watch and listen.

More formal and traditional **argumentative essays** often avoid use of the personal pronoun, omit experiential evidence, and attempt to offer a more detached perspective. The primary evidence in these essays comes almost exclusively from written and visual sources rather than from experience; the presentation of the evidence within the essay is more straightforward, somewhat more formal. The writer is, of course, also present in these essays, but that presence manifests itself primarily through the selection and ordering of evidence, the reflections that accompany the presentation of evidence, and the quality of the idea—all of which reflect the writer's mind at work.

The most interesting essays fall within this spectrum, bringing together the best of the familiar and the best of the academic. Blended essays like this allow readers to see the writer calling on experience as well as complex written texts and using all the means at her disposal to write a persuasive essay. The subject, the evidence, and the audience dictate the most important features of the essay, with the writer making rhetorical choices that are most appropriate for the occasion. The differences between exploratory and argumentative essays are less important than the commonalities between these two general types of essays. Degrees of formality and variations in patterns of development are less important than the quality and signs of thinking that we see across the entire spectrum of essays. What matters most in a good essay is that you establish a clear relationship between your evidence and your idea and that your readers can actually see you thinking about this relationship across the essay. Readers respond most positively when they sense that they are watching you make discoveries.

HOW TO REVEAL THE DISCOVERIES

The work of developing an idea and then presenting it depends on a recursive process of analysis, interpretation, and reflection. There is much to this process, but it is important to understand that the mind moves fundamentally from **evidence** to **idea** to **essay.** Within each essay the movement from evidence to idea is what the reader wants most to see and understand. Clearly, you cannot show your readers all of the steps and missteps that you take as you read and analyze the evidence, but you can preserve in the final form of your essay the most compelling analytical work that led you to your idea. Doing so is essential.

ANALYSIS

You **analyze** as a way of understanding. Analysis is primarily an effort on your part to study evidence—a book, a poem, a painting, a theory, a personality, an historical event, a performance, a political or philosophical point of view, a way of life—so that you can understand something significant about that subject and then develop an idea of your own about it. Writers use analysis first to understand and then to record and demonstrate to readers what they have learned. The writing that accompanies analysis, especially in the early stages, is a form of exploration, an effort of the mind to learn something about the thing being studied. Later, writing preserves that analytical spirit, revealing to readers significant parts of your learning process and how your thinking led to the idea presented about the evidence.

Analysis accompanies nearly every form of writing. The analytical, or sense-making, act turns description, narration, comparison/contrast, description, even analysis itself, toward a specific purpose. Analysis is ubiquitous; it turns your mind toward a common goal: the understanding of an object (your subject), or an idea about it. Storytelling, or description, or comparison and contrast linked with analysis, conspire to persuade, to convince the reader of a meaning.

INTERPRETATION

The analytical act is almost always accompanied by an **interpretive** act. As an interpreter you translate, conceptualize, and explain. An interpretive act is, therefore, both an act of conception and an explanatory act. Stephen Jay Gould, one of the most eminent scientists of the last century, reminds us that facts considered alone offer very little in the way of knowing. The scientist's primary work (and the writer's) is to interpret the facts, to translate them, to tell us what they mean. Interpretation amounts to figuring out and clarifying what the evidence only suggests.

As the writer, you collect the facts from the written text, the characteristics of a particular painting, the details of a particular story, as a part of your preliminary analysis; the second stage of the analysis calls on you to interpret—to create meaning. The act of meaning-making is your most crucial responsibility as a writer. As you interpret, you give meaning to the evidence, meaning that perhaps only you can see until you reveal it to your readers. Your primary task is to look into meaning, to think seriously and deeply about what your collected evidence is telling you. What you discover is what your reader wants to know about. What you discover constitutes your idea.

REFLECTION AND MEANING

During the third stage, you must bring evidence (the facts collected during analysis); the interpretation and the reasoning behind the interpretation; and, finally, your **reflective** thoughts about both evidence and interpretation together. This voice of reflection is your discerning voice—meditative and thoughtful—that makes sense of both analysis and interpretation, reminding us that *to* reflect is to bend back and create a new understanding of the text, the image, the experience. This new perspective amounts to an explanation and a revelation of something you have discovered—the idea that leads to the essay.

MAKING EVIDENCE AND DISCOVERY WORK TOGETHER

This analytical and conceptual work—the whole process of discovery—evolves from a lengthy process. During this process your own personal way of thinking comes to the forefront. No one else can do this work for you; no one else can figure out what the various pieces of evidence mean in the same way that you will. It is important to take risks when trying to figure out just what the evidence means and how to explain what the evidence means to a reader who knows little about the idea until he or she reads your essay.

The creation of the essay follows from this exciting work. Making the essay itself requires that you organize and order your thoughts, that you revise and clarify as you draft, and that you bring the many parts of the essay together in satisfying, harmonious ways to create a coherent whole.

The next two chapters show you more precisely how this creative work takes place. Those two chapters reveal just how an essay gets made. The work there, focusing on how one student writer creates two different essays, plays on the basic pattern of exercises that are offered throughout this book, within each of the other chapters. The *Occasions for Writing* will take you through the process that includes reading, analyzing, connecting, reflecting, and conceptualizing. Writing accompanies all of these activities. What follows is a description of the general pattern of exercises that constitute each Occasion:

- A compelling essay related to the chapter's thematic emphasis is accompanied by *Reading and Thinking* and *Thinking and Writing* exercises. These analytical exercises help you, the student writer, to better understand the author's ideas and to begin to see the importance of your own discoveries that arise from analytical thinking and exploratory, thoughtful writing.

- Images related to the thematic essay in explicit and inexplicit ways are accompanied by a distinctive set of analytical exercises. These *Preparing to Write* exercises ask you to pay particular attention to the characteristics of the image itself: what is there in terms of colors, shapes, correspondences, shadows, internal order, striking oddities. (Chapter 4 provides explicit guidance for reading and responding to images.)

- *Moving toward Essay* exercises lead to and ask for interpretation, building on the work done in the *Preparing to Write* exercises. These interpretive exercises encourage you to take risks based on the facts you have discovered about the essay and the images; they lead toward deeper analysis and the formulation of an idea. Often they will ask you to ground your discoveries by relating them to your own experiences.

- *Writing Thoughtfully* exercises lead more directly toward the creation of an essay. The exercises themselves sometimes provide more information about the images and the artist who made them; they may ask you to make connections between the image and the essay that set the occasion in motion; they sometimes ask you to make a connection of your own, one that links the printed image and essay to another essay you have read elsewhere (in another course, for example); or the exercises may ask you to use your own experiences to clarify your understanding of selected images, or the essays, or both. The work in this series of exercises provides the foundation and direction for reflection and developing both idea and essay.

- *Creating Occasions* exercises suggest other ways for using the evidence you have been analyzing and interpreting in the earlier exercises, other ways for creating a variety of essays, giving you the beginnings of a topic to explore and guiding you through the further development of that topic.

You will always produce better writing by committing yourself to the process of discovery and by taking interpretive risks as you go about figuring out what the evidence means to you. Take advantage of your classmates' thoughts; work collaboratively as you read one another's exercises and drafts. Always be on the lookout for new connections, new ways of seeing the world around you, and new ways of reading the evidence. Listen to what others say about your work. When you have assembled your evidence and have begun to read it and make sense of it, remember that no one can read it exactly the way you can. Learn to face that conceptual challenge head on and find the relationships among the pieces of evidence. The process of assembling an essay resembles the creation of a mosaic design; you are looking for a way to slide the various shards of evidence together to form a picture that no one else could create. That is the challenge.

Creating meaning provides its own heady reward. There are no right or wrong creations. What you figure out to reveal to the reader matters most, that and how you present your overall picture of meaning, the essay itself.

PASCAL ADOLPHE
JEAN DAGNAN-BOUVERET,
Ophelia (1900)

Images stir us to speak in response to them, to tell our

2

AN EXPLORATORY ESSAY:
A STUDENT'S PROCESS

Using Images and Experience as Evidence

In this chapter, we will follow one writer as she moves from a consideration of **evidence,** to the development of an **idea,** to the presentation and substantiation of that idea in the form of an **essay.**

The student essay in this chapter is set in motion by a painting; that painting also constitutes an important piece of evidence in the essay. Student Claudia Quiros uses written texts, but her primary evidence throughout the essay is stories or scenes from her own experience. Her exploratory essay develops an interesting and important idea about the unexpected benefits of anxiety in the shaping of one's identity.

The pattern of development—the sequential and recursive steps Claudia takes to create the essay—follows the same general pattern that informs the sequencing of exercises accompanying each of the *Occasions for Writing* in this book. The exercises and the questions vary from Occasion to Occasion, but they always move back and forth along the journey from **evidence** to **idea** to **essay.** In this particular case the teacher, following the general pattern, specifies a particular product. He wants his students to write an **exploratory essay,** one that depends primarily on the writer's own experiences to demonstrate and clarify her idea.

Exploratory essays follow what often seems to be a digressive pattern of storytelling, but on closer inspection we can see that the digressive pattern has a purpose. The writer moves from story to story to introduce different aspects of his or her **idea**; the stories themselves constitute the **evidence.** The exploratory essay can easily accommodate visual images and written texts. Written texts are included in the exploratory essay to call the reader to a deeper awareness of the idea that is being developed.

In the essay that follows, Claudia's work evolved primarily from an image, but she had read a number of essays about identity in her first college writing course. The image that haunted her was the painting *Ophelia,* by French artist Pascal Adolphe Jean Dagnan-Bouveret; for Claudia, it had a great deal to do with her own identity and the troubling transition from high school to college.

She had first seen the painting in a high school classroom where she had studied literature. Creating her essay, she then drew on a number of literary texts
she had read in other classes or for her own pleasure.

To see just how images can influence and shape good writing, we should begin where Claudia began, with the painting of *Ophelia*. This is the first in a series of exercises that led to her final essay:

> Select a painting, a photograph, or a sculpture that speaks to you in some im-
> portant way; re-create that art object in words so that others who have not seen
> it will be able to see what you see.

Here is Claudia's response to this *Preparing to Write* exercise:

Dagnan-Bouveret's rough brush strokes provide for a solid backdrop
to Ophelia's luminous yet insecure body. The forest, a vortex of black and
navy smudges, surrounds her from behind, suggesting her wasted and
short time spent alive. Ophelia stands in the limbo between her earthly
life and heaven, her back turned towards the river in which she died, her
left hand placed adamantly over her ear in an act of rebellion against her
former tormentors. The sleeping violets clutched by her milky right arm
starkly contrast with her heavily darkened eyes and nose. Her ghostly
pallor embalms her; the motion behind her glassy eyes is highlighted
only by the textured appearance of her strawberry-blonde hair and the
soft flounce of her virginal tunic. Wispy reeds surround the bottom of her
garment, some charging at her with their sharp green swords, others
surrendering their fight and greeting their deaths in the dirt.

This interesting response contains details from the painting itself, but it also
reveals interpretive gestures on Claudia's part. Claudia seems to have had the
character of Ophelia from Shakespeare's *Hamlet* working in her mind as she re-
created this image for her readers.

INTEGRATING A VISUAL TEXT

This particular writing exercise requires students to integrate a visual text into it. Such integration requires a deft touch. Too much detail overwhelms the reader; too little leaves him or her unable to visualize the object (painting, sculpture, photograph) itself. Describing the object is only part of the requirement; writers must use that descriptive work to clarify ideas. As the writer reflects on the object and the idea, readers become more aware of how the object (evidence) is being used to clarify and substantiate the idea.

- Begin with the re-creation of the art object in words.
- Add to the word picture what you can *see* because of that object.
- Construct a **scene** that will put you and the object into some kind of relationship.
- Determine what the object has to do with your idea.
- As you incorporate the object into your written text, be sure to name the artist and the painting so that your readers know what you are asking them to see.
- Make sure that your accompanying reflections clarify what the object has to do with your idea.

THE PRACTICE OF WRITING

1. While considering the painting *Ophelia* on page 12, see if you can detect the difference between factual detail from the painting and the ideas that those details evoke for Claudia. Make a list of the differences.

A subsequent *Moving toward Essay* exercise asked students to create a scene:

> **Put the painting in a scene that would show readers how the painting and the writer might be related in some interesting way.**

Claudia's scene captures a particular moment, re-created so that readers can actually be in the moment with Claudia as she experienced it. People speak within the scene, and readers can see and participate in the action.

I had frequently shirked her glance, spooked by her pallor, betrayed by the virginal garb that surrounded her seemingly stirring body. The soft nuances of her rounded face had been elusive to me, lost among our class discussions about the feminist overtones in Virginia Woolf's *To the Lighthouse* or the instances of absurdity in Tom Stoppard's *Rosencrantz and Guildenstern Are Dead.* I always thought of her as an enigmatically necessary observer to our classes, wise but unwilling to judge, much like her character in *Hamlet.*

"Okay, girls. Class is over now." A sluggish smile slowly clambered up Mrs. Springer's full cheeks, halting inches below her differently colored eyes. It was a dichotomous smile, emitting a glow that resulted from a successful and fulfilling school year while simultaneously piercing the heart of her sadness. "I hope this course has adequately prepared you all for college. Now before you girls move on to bigger and better English courses, I want you all to reflect upon what you have read. Think of the authors as your teachers. Ask yourself, 'What would James Joyce think of this essay?' or 'What argument might Sophocles make against my claim?'

And always remember that I believe in each of you." Behind her, Ophelia's sad eyes twinkled, reflecting the emotion that was swirling around the room and billowing against the walls and roof, like a school of fish thrashing wildly about in a net waiting to break free.

I looked around the room. Jordan, the girl voted "Most Likely to Sob at Graduation and Plan All High School Reunions," was squirming in her chair, actively fighting back tears. Emi and Kristina, my two best friends, gave me looks of mixed sentiments, peeping into the future but acquiescing to the present. Even Alina, the class clown, sat dumb in her seat, her eyes darting across the blackboard like a child choosing an ice cream flavor from the side of a musical truck. And then there was Ophelia, now more mysterious than ever, her hand perched decidedly over her ear, trouncing the past.

After the bell rang, I waited until most of my peers left the classroom before I approached the teacher. "Mrs. Springer," I exclaimed, "this has been the best and most mind-broadening class I've had in high school. Thank you so much for disproving my false notions and opening my eyes to good literature." Upon hearing this, Mrs. Springer's face flushed with the newfound fulfillment that comes from learning about making a difference. Her eyes quickly snapped into reality, as I focused more and more on *Ophelia*. I had never been so close to the painting. I had never noticed the oppressive coarseness of the background. I had never appreciated the gift of color so generously provided by the violets. I had never understood the pain of her nervous stare.

Mrs. Springer hugged me as Ophelia's gaze freed me. The emotions scattered and nested in my soul.

CREATING A SCENE

Scenes provide an effective way to incorporate a story of experience into an essay; scenes are particularly useful in **exploratory essays,** where experience is the primary form of **evidence.** Unlike a report or story about something that happened, a scene reveals the chosen moment. Think of a dramatic scene in a play. Such scenes usually cover a short interval of time; characters interact and often speak to one another; and the scene takes place in a clearly identifiable space or environment—we feel as if we are there.

· Show rather than tell.

· The scene itself should be bounded by place and time: a specific locale during a given time.

· Construct the scene so that your viewers or readers have a sense that they are there at the place itself, observing *inside* the scene.

· Allow characters into the scene. Let them speak.

· Include gestures and other informing details.

· Remember the difference between the person in the scene and the writer of the scene. The writer is controlling the construction of the scene and revealing meaning.

· Consider integrating reflection into the scene so that your readers will know how you intend for them to understand the scene.

THE PRACTICE OF WRITING

1. Identify places in the scene where Claudia makes explicit use of the painting. Characterize how these uses differ from one another.

2. Identify two places where Claudia effectively draws you into the scene. How does she do that?

3. Reread the scene, trying to grasp all that it tells you. In a brief paragraph speculate about what you think Claudia is trying to tell us—what the scene means.

Students worked together in class with these scenes, looking to see what ideas might have slipped into the scene without the writer actually knowing about them. In groups of three, they read one another's work and tried to puzzle out what the scene actually suggests to a reader. This work fed into the next *Moving toward Essay* exercise:

> Create another scene from your own experience that has something to do with the idea that has begun to crystallize in your mind from the previous scene. Create the scene, but do not feel responsible now for explaining the connection between the two scenes, or the idea. Formulating your complete idea is still tentative at this point.

Here is Claudia's response:

The bright lights of the mall shone, reflecting maliciously in our visual path as we walked out of the record store. The ubiquitous "Spring Sale" signs enticed shoppers young and old, who sashayed over the clear floor like unenthusiastic figure skaters performing their routines by rote. Overhead, the hazy sunlight wrestled its way through the rafters, contorting itself and eventually drowning into the electric fluorescence below. This was Judgment Day.

Kristin had driven home two hours earlier, leaving Lindsey, Emi, and me meandering around aimlessly and checking colorful kiosks for bargains. We all had explicitly yet silently understood anxieties about That Day, all of which pricked our conversations sporadically. Lindsey tried to lighten the mood, her eyes swelling hopefully as she described her new dog. "His fur is so silky; he's fabulous! But he's so small that my father sat on him yesterday!" She raised her head laughing in recalling the incident. But even her mirth was punctuated with nuances of uneasiness. The three of us walked silently for three minutes after that. The date, April 1st, swelled in our brains, wiping out all other thought and looming over us.

After picking up strawberry smoothies, we stopped in Bloomingdale's, where we each had the same unspoken intention to pass the time by pretending to admire the clothing. I absent-mindedly grabbed a gorgeous paletted Marc Jacobs cardigan and began admiring the stitching. I laid it against my body but noticed it fit better against Emi's. Her face crumpled, and her eyes bulged when she saw the price tag. "What piece of one-hundred percent cotton clothing is worth this much?!" she exclaimed. Before I could launch into my argument equating fashion to other art forms, I heard the familiar pull of my cell phone. The Verizon jingle danced on my nerves and created goosebumps on my skin. My tension only increased as I read those fateful words: Call From: Kristin Cell.

Answering, I knew things would only get worse after I heard Kristin's broken greeting. She managed to exclaim, "It didn't work out." My heart folded like a crumpled piece of origami. I knew nothing would be the same again. Judgment Day is irreversible. And that day not only decided the course of our lives, it also blurred their meanings.

We can consider all of this preliminary work as connecting work aimed at generating an idea while at the same time creating a substantial body of potential evidence for each student's essay. Recall that students were reading a common set of essays about identity as they worked on these exercises; they were permitted to choose among those essays and to add to them selections of their own, citing any text they might have read elsewhere. Recall too that each student had selected an image of his or her own choosing to set this whole process in motion. Claudia has moved in her scenes from a high school classroom to a shopping mall, and we cannot tell yet just what she is most concerned about. Yet we sense her anxiety in both scenes—first about leaving high school and second about getting into college.

One additional *Moving toward Essay* exercise contributed to this storehouse of potential evidence, and it too asked for further clarification (in the students' minds) of the evolving idea.

> Consider all that you have written so far. Make a brief outline in your head of the recurring concerns that appear in each of your previous exercises, and then select a written text from all of your readings (in the course, or elsewhere) that clarifies one or more of your concerns. Use this text in one of your previous scenes, or create a new scene or narrative to contain this written text.

Claudia chose two written texts, each of which gives us a clearer sense of the idea that she is beginning to focus on; we see her struggling still with moments of confusion as she tries to move from the comfort of the past into the uncertainty of her future life in college. We do not yet know what she will make of these concerns, but we can see clearly from the earlier scenes that it is on her mind.

"I felt very still and very empty, the way the eye of a tornado must feel, moving dully along in the middle of the surrounding hullabaloo." The words swirled around my brain, mixing with my thoughts, and funneling down to the center of my heart. My emotions were paralyzed by the stillness of the room. Lying there in my bed, I forfeited my whole body to my flannel sheets. The clock glared evilly against the dimness, its gaze markedly locked in my direction.

I put the novel face down upon my nightstand. A *New York Times* reviewer's praise jumped out at me from the glossy book cover, proclaiming Plath's sincere words as "true literature." I knew that *The Bell Jar* was considered good literature, but I never saw the truth in it until that very moment. Plath's description so accurately pinpointed my feelings that my own truth scared even me.

My worries jumbled, creating new confusions. I stood on the edge of chaos, there wrapped tightly in my bed, looking back on the past yet hearkening to the future. I thought about Mrs. Springer's inspiring lectures. I remembered the sadness I felt upon finishing James Joyce's *A Portrait of the Artist as a Young Man.* This sadness echoed my sadness now, as I found myself relating to Plath's narrator in *The Bell Jar. I can't go off to college,* I thought. *I'm just not ready. I love my life now too much.* I tried to imagine the next year, but I was so content in my present. My view of the future was pessimistic. I saw it as a gaping black hole, ready to suck me in and rid my memory of my happy past.

Then, I heard the creak of my door. The weak lights of my room spilled into the darkness of the hallway as my mother's tired face popped in. "Go to sleep, Claudia. It's almost three in the morning. Don't you want to be awake for your orientation?" It was too late for me; the future was already flooding in.

INTEGRATING A WRITTEN TEXT

Here you are asked to use written texts to enrich your ideas. You would not analyze these texts rigorously (as they might in a different kind of essay); instead, call on other writers briefly to clarify some aspect of the idea being developed, or to add a slightly different perspective. The title of the cited text and the writer's name are usually written into the essay so that this information becomes a natural, inherent part of the essay rather than a citation set off from the main text. Consider these guidelines for integrating the text.

· Begin with a thoughtful selection from a written text that has something to do with the idea or the point you are making.

· Select appropriate words from the written text that you want to include in a sentence of your own. When you write that sentence, name the text that you are citing and the author of that text. Within that same sentence include, in quotation marks, the selected words from the source text.

· Use the scene within your essay. Ensure that your reader can understand the relationship between the quoted material and the idea you are developing.

· Make sure that your accompanying reflections clarify what the object has to do with your idea.

THE PRACTICE OF WRITING

1. How does Claudia introduce her two writers? What does she want us to learn about her idea from them?

2. Consider Claudia's reflections (or thoughts) about these two writers' words. How do those reflections help you understand both Claudia's idea and the words she is quoting?

Students' responses provided the foundation for the *Writing Thoughtfully* exercises that followed. The next exercise constituted the first draft of the **exploratory essay** that students were to write; they were to use as much of this preliminary material in their final essays as their idea would permit them to use. They could also generate new material as important books and images and experiences occurred to them as they began drafting.

> Write a letter to the most interesting friend you have outside this class. Tell this friend what you have been thinking about in your various exercises. Let your idea emerge as you make use of the material from those exercises in any way that you can to help your friend better understand your idea. (Do not reveal in the letter that this is a classroom exercise.)

Here is Claudia's response:

Dear Lindsey,

I've been thinking about the last year a lot lately. I'm so glad that at least you came to New York City with me and Tessa, but I can't help but think nothing will be the same again. I realize that we have never really all sat down and talked about our future. We were always too busy goofing around, messing about in someone's business, or just laughing to avoid the inevitable separation. And even now when we see each other, it's as if nothing ever happened. We express the secret jealousies that we feel toward each other's new friends only to our own selves. Even though my lingering uncertainty is gone, it's amazing how different things will get.

I guess this random blurb of sadness/reflection has been brought on by my high state of stress. Keeping my scholarship is proving a difficult task, and I find myself missing your security and support. Classes are few but stress-inducing. And I'm suddenly surrounded by some pretentious people. But I love that I'm being challenged. I'm being challenged to change my news-consumption habits, and it's working well for me. The profound effect that music has played in my life since that concert is insane. Not just music, really. My poetry homework makes me cry sometimes. And those tears of mine are infused with love and joy. Even today my poetry professor broke down all barriers of awkwardness and aloofness and teared up while reading Wordsworth's "Tintern Abbey." It was an incredible moment for me.

Of course I don't mean that I'm unhappy where I stand right now. All the insecurities that uncertainty yields have been deflected, in my case at least, but I still know that things won't be like this summer ever again. After seeing Emi's photo album, I'm sure you agree with me! People change. It's not a bad thing. In fact, most people grow in their changed experiences. But I think that at these crossroads we have reached, our adjustment will develop into our inherent humanity. We have become adults not by accident, but through a series of caused experiences. I can't believe I'm being this deep with you, but I hope you understand.

I'm sorry I've thrown all this philosophy, reason, and even dreaded emotion in your face. But I think that at the age we are in, we should own up to our feelings. I gladly admit that the qualms that developed in my head throughout the past year were met with disappointment upon my happy reception at college. So far, everything has gone nearly perfect for me. Even the Shins concert, which I attended with a girl I'm almost afraid of because of her aloofness, opened my eyes. Now every time I hear "Saint Simon," I don't dwell on the past. I look happily toward the future, toward a time when my life could echo the jaunty melody. It's like I told you last week: I truly believe that song is the sonic representation of love.

Do you remember the afternoon we all went out to the bagel place and I played my scratched Beatles CD? I remember feeling so inconceivably happy at that time, laughing until it hurt, while driving through the rolling fields of Maryland. I suddenly saw a New York license plate and snapped back into reality. It's so difficult to adjust to the idea of new friends, and even harder to convince people who are older that it is a solid concern.

I haven't even been this crazy since my love affair with Mrs. Springer's English class. How amazing was that class? I can't believe I got so much from books. Did you read "Old School"? Incredible. I used to think I could do that, write. But I've met the competition in college, and it is not pretty. Tonight I went to a Music workshop at the Newspaper headquarters, and it just opened, or maybe I should say closed, my eyes to the world of journalism. I was humiliated by a SPIN editor who told me I don't know anything about punk. Whenever things like this happen, whenever I feel betrayed by what I thought I knew to do, I call to the past. I call my mom. I call you. I don't really know if people who I have known for three weeks will possibly understand the depth of my disappointment. It's sad to love something so much and be told you are not that great at it. I suppose I'll take a stab at the fashion section of the paper.

I never realized I could write this so outwardly and direct to you since, as you know, we always elude emotion whenever possible. It's funny how we could never show emotion in front of each other. We all even joked about it too! It's kind of pathetic. Your friends are the ones who are not supposed to judge you when you're crying and not supposed to disagree with your sadness. I guess if you were actually reading this we'd laugh about it and make some sarcastic joke. I hope I can see you this weekend.

Claudia

Claudia is still, at this point, better at revealing her concerns and anxieties about her changing life than she is in expressing a coherent, provocative idea. What she believes she is telling her readers, what she thinks is her idea, is more about the facts of her life than an idea.

Here is Claudia's own conception of her idea at the time she wrote the letter: "The process of building new friendships is both difficult and rewarding. Comfort can be found in the fact that the loss of old friends is met with the experience of growing up and seeing the growth that has occurred in others." This is a fine place for Claudia to have come to, but she hasn't yet figured out what all of the accumulated evidence means to her. That figuring-out work takes a long time, and it will be aided by the writing process itself, the drafting of her essay. Writing to a more general and less sympathetic audience than that of the letter, Claudia will have to think beyond her own personal concerns as she comes to terms with what her experiences actually might mean not only to her but also to all of us.

Claudia actually wrote three drafts of her essay before her professor read it; different students provided feedback for each of the drafts. They were concerned about the evolving idea and the relationship between that idea and the stories she presented as evidence to substantiate it. Her professor also provided feedback during a conference following the third draft, and then again after she turned in the completed essay. All of that drafting, feedback, conferencing, and revision led her to this completed version of her exploratory essay.

My Own Time Machine

Claudia Quiros

"Creativity requires the courage to let go of certainties."

- Erich Fromm

"Good morning, girls. Welcome to AP World Literature, a course that is designed to change your life." There I sat, squirming in my chair, nervously pulling down my plaid woolen skirt. I was terrified of starting a class with Mrs. Springer, who had been described by a former senior as "the devil incarnate." As she talked, her intimidating vocabulary escaped her mouth and loomed over my head menacingly. I caught pieces of important information here and there—"this course will challenge your way of thinking," "the AP is in May," "I will develop you all into real writers"—but it all added new depth to my uncertainty. How could I ever succeed in such an intensive class?

"Let's see . . . how about . . . Claudia Quiros. Identify yourself and tell me what you think." I snapped back into attention. My sweaty palms glided under my desk with uneasiness. I cleared my throat, looked around the room, and asked as nobly as possible, "Could you please repeat the question?"

Ever since I was young, I have had a chronic fear of the unknown. Whether it be the elusive answer to a difficult question or the state of my future, not having the knowledge to get myself through or out of a challenging situation has always incited my fear. I always signed up for the class I knew I would do well in or ate the same meal from my favorite restaurant because I could rely on the known to guide me along life. Delving headfirst into new prospects still proves a gradual and painful task for me, and unsurprisingly, I have never been known or acknowledged for my courage or spontaneity. But I have found a new perspective on anxiety that propels me into the future with assurance.

I walked into my first poetry class of the college year, rosy-cheeked and out of breath. As I wandered into the silent room, I felt the stinging eyes of my fellow classmates follow my path to the remaining empty desk. There we sat, alone together and in silence for fifteen minutes until Professor Liebman walked in. "Good afternoon. The purpose of this course is to change your life," he said assuredly. Several hours later, he launched into a heart-wrenching rendition of William Wordsworth's "Tintern Abbey." Each adjective, nuanced by the professor's delivery, burned a hole in my heart, and by the end of the poem, there we sat as a class in silence again, but this time not alone. We were joined by the harmonious emotion within our tears. All our anxieties had been lifted; we felt united in our glorious anonymity. Our emotions melted our cool barriers, our uncertainty, and exposed us to each other's beauty. Our collective honesty as a class, to ourselves and to each other, trounced our insecurity, and we were one for that long, satisfying moment.

In a famous letter to his brothers, John Keats wrote about his idea of "negative capability," or the state in which "a man is capable of being in uncertainties, mysteries, doubts, without any irritable reaching after fact and reason." Keats argues that the unknown should challenge us to think and move us to reflection. We only begin to swell into reality when we hunger for the unknown and take a proactive step to transform what is mysterious into an absolute truth. Only after the rawest emotions of sadness were expressed in my poetry class could we jump from our group uncertainty to an atmosphere of truth, a nurturing environment of learning and exploring. I had to accept my truths and feelings in order to break down preconceived notions and step into life. For it is when we crouch in the dark corner of denial, unable to embrace negative capability, that we lose sight of who we are and what we can be. Uncertainty, whether in a subjective or collective form, can hinder us from possibilities we never knew possible, but it can also move us forward.

I remember the first time I saw the painting of Ophelia in Mrs. Springer's room. The painter, Pascale Adolphe Jean Dagnan-Bouveret, used dark brush strokes to highlight Ophelia's insecurity. She stands in the limbo between her earthly life and heaven, her back turned towards the river in which she died, her left hand placed adamantly over her ear in an act of rebellion against her former tormentors. The bright violets she clutches under her right arm contrast with her darkened eyes and nose. Her ghostly pallor embalms her; the emotion behind her eyes is highlighted only by her textured hair and the soft flounce of her tunic. Wispy reeds surround the bottom of her garment, some charging at her with their sharp green swords, others surrendering their fight and greeting their deaths in the dirt.

I felt like I had been pierced by one of those reeds. I looked up to the painting, and I surrendered to the insecurity it represented, mostly because it closely resembled my own emotion. At the time, I too was at a crossroads; I was at the cusp between high school and college, the known and the unknown, and my emotions melded together in a combination of excitement and nervousness. My uncertainty was reflected in the painting. The painter had molded Ophelia into an artistic paradox: beautiful yet dark, alive yet desiring reality, adamant yet struggling with her own aching presence in the world. I saw my conflicting emotions literally drawn into every line in Ophelia's face. And though I tried to connect with my hope for the future, I was left wallowing in my insecurity about the present, unable to see the future as a harbinger of opportunity.

In *The Bell Jar,* Sylvia Plath describes herself as "very still and very empty, the way the eye of a tornado must feel, moving dully along in the middle of the surrounding hullabaloo." As I read them last summer, the words were powerful enough to swirl around my brain, mix with my thoughts, and funnel down to the center of my heart. At times I wonder about the inspiration behind these words. When we are poised at the edge of chaos, how are we to characterize our thoughts and actions? Sometimes, I feel as though I am oddly moved by the chaotic nature of things. Even though I suffered with my insecurity all through my summer before college, I know that it was necessary for me to realize how much smoother the transition would be than previously expected. I learned that through my insecurity, through my feelings that echoed Plath's words so closely, that there are few things as unbelievably human, raw, and emotive as expressing your anxieties. It is through our own self-analysis that we can confidently look to what lies ahead. But at the same time, if we dwell on the negative, if we dwell in the eye of the tornado, we will never know what true sunshine feels like. Even if the future seems hazy, jumping in and experiencing life as it is, in its fully blossomed glory, can lead to our own fulfillment.

The bright lights of the mall shone, reflecting maliciously in our visual path as we walked out of the record store. The ubiquitous "Spring Sale" signs enticed shoppers young and old. This was Judgment Day.

Kristin had driven home two hours earlier, leaving Lindsey, Emi, and me meandering around aimlessly and checking colorful kiosks for bargains. We all had silently understood anxieties about That Day, all of which pricked our conversations sporadically. Even our laughter was punctuated with nuances of uneasiness. The date, April 1st, swelled in our brains.

I heard the familiar digital beg of my cell phone. The Verizon jingle danced on my nerves as I answered to hear Kristin's broken admission. "I didn't get into Columbia." Those five words were all it took to inspire the feeling that had been denied by my hope that entire year. My heart crumpled up like a rejected piece of origami. I knew nothing would be the same again.

Judgment Day is irreversible. My anxieties were tainted by my immediate sadness, and the disappointment that overcame me would not allow hope into my heart. Over the past year, I had created happy images of my entire group of friends in New York City. Lindsey would be at Fordham, I would be at NYU, and Kristin would undoubtedly be at Columbia. But at that moment, it was as if someone had taken a photograph of the three of us and ripped her out of it, ripped her out of my future. I was so caught up with my own frustration that I didn't even pause to consider how she was handling the situation. Dwelling on my own uncertainties hindered me from searching for possibilities, meaning, even hope for the future, and I was drowning in my own self-pity. A few months later, after re-reading *The Bell Jar,* my worries solidified and jumbled, creating new confusions. I was hovering on the edge of disorder. Lying there in my bed, I forfeited my tired body to my sheets. The clock glared against the dimness, its gaze locked in my direction. Though wrapped comfortably in my bed, I found myself uneasily looking back on the past instead of to the future. I thought about Mrs. Springer's inspiring lectures. I remembered that day, the day when we found out Kristin didn't get into Columbia. *I can't go off to college,* I thought. *I'm just not ready. I love my life now too much.* I tried to imagine the next year, but I was so nervously content with my present. My view of the future was pessimistic. I saw it as a gaping black hole, ready to suck me in and rid my memory of my happy past.

Then, I heard the creak of my door. The weak lights of my room spilled into the darkness of the hallway as my mother's tired face popped in. "Go to sleep, Claudia; it's almost three in the morning. Don't you want to be awake for your orientation?" It was too late for me; my fate was already flooding in.

That night, I realized that the future would not be as static as I had thought. I reassured myself with the thought that most people grow in their changed experiences. When we arrive at a crossroads, our true test is our attempted adjustment in the face of that change. Our actions are, in a sense, a reflection of our confidence in a test of uncertainty. We grow into adults not by accident, but through a series of formative experiences. Our future is not set in stone by single instances. Our paths through life are processes of development rather than states of static existence. We are individually affected not only by our experience but also by every person and thing that moves us to a powerful emotion, whether negatively or positively. Uncertainty is one of these powerful emotions defined by our own experience, solidified by our own fears, and trounced upon by our own acquired courage. This uncertainty that may arise makes us stronger once we face up to it.

Several months later, there I sat in Mrs. Springer's room, sitting in the same desk that I had been humiliated in that crisp September day. This time my level of uneasiness was of a different breed. I looked around the room. Jordan, the girl voted "Most Likely to Sob at Graduation and Plan All High School Reunions," was squirming in her chair, actively fighting back tears. Emi and Kristina, my two best friends, gave me looks of mixed sentiments, peeping into the future but acquiescing to the present. Even Alina, the class clown, sat dumb in her seat, her eyes darting across the blackboard like those of a child choosing an ice cream flavor from the side of a musical truck. Ophelia appeared more mysterious and troubled than ever, her hand perched decidedly over her ear, trouncing the past.

"Okay, girls. Class is over now." A sluggish smile slowly clambered up Mrs. Springer's full cheeks, halting inches below her bright eyes. "I hope you always remember that I believe in each of you." Behind her, the painting looked at me. Ophelia's sad eyes twinkled, reflecting the emotion that was swirling around the room and billowing against the walls and roof, like a school of fish thrashing wildly about in a net waiting to break free.

Only much later did I realize that the worries that had arisen over those past few months had been unwarranted. On move-in day, as our car moved into 5th Avenue to my new dorm, I looked out my window and sat in awe of the city I had been in so many times before. This time it was different. It wasn't an aloof attraction or tourist haven. It was speaking to me, it was me. Sunshine poured into every lane, elevating my hope, alleviating my fears, symbolizing my future. I knew at that moment everything would be all right, that all my worries would amount to nothing, that I would still see my high school friends during breaks and visits. At that moment, I stood with one foot in the present and one foot firmly in the future. I realized that it is impossible to be content within our anxieties without taking a proactive step into the future. It is not until we are ready to accept the card life has dealt us that we recognize what it holds for us. And it is not unusual to find that our unfulfilled anxieties have been built up by false notions and prejudices. While stepping so directly into the future may create momentary anxiety, it is necessary for advancement in our lives. Only after arriving and moving into NYU did I finally have a view of my future and my potential, what I could be without influence of my friends. Only then could I see the truth in the future, and I am still striving to arrive at the heart of it.

We see that the process of drafting and revising, the process that moved from an initial image to stories of experience to written texts, took Claudia to a compelling idea about the benefits of anxiety and the necessity of dealing with it. Over the period of a month, she worked her way through the various exercises, creating scenes, combining them, enriching them with written texts and with images, until finally she knew what all of that evidence meant to her. The idea that she developed eventually helped reshape those initial scenes; her reflections about all of this evidence reveal just what it had come to mean to her. That meaning was the crux of her idea.

REFLECTING (ANALYSIS AND CONCEPTION)

Writers analyze as a way of understanding—breaking evidence down and putting it back together with a new understanding. Such understanding leads naturally to reflection. The writing that accompanies analysis, especially in the early stages, is a form of exploration, a joint effort of the mind and the pen (or the keyboard) to learn something about the evidence. Later writing preserves that analytical spirit, revealing to readers just how a writer's mind led him or her to an idea. The analytical act is almost always accompanied by an *interpretive* act. Interpretation amounts to figuring out what the evidence only *suggests*.

Finally, writers record the results of the analysis and the interpretation so that others can understand their reasoning and the idea that arises out of it. The written revelations constitute a writer's reflection.

- Begin with the evidence, taking up a story or scene at a particular time. Write as a way of figuring out what the evidence means. Be bold in your preliminary thinking; take risks.

- Begin at the outset to think about one piece of evidence in terms of other evidence. Relate two stories (or scenes) to see how one sheds light on the other, how one deepens or changes your understanding of the other.

- Then turn to yet another piece of evidence, seeing what it tells you about your idea that the other evidence did not reveal.

- As you are working, writing down your reflective thinking, allow the reading of the evidence to change your mind about your idea.

- As you write about the evidence and begin to link it together within your essay— interpreting it for your readers—show them, tell them, how it relates to your idea and to other evidence that has been or will be presented.

THE PRACTICE OF WRITING

1. Go through Claudia's essay and mark or highlight reflective passages. Pick two of them for comparison. What do you learn from them about interpreting evidence?

2. After you have read Claudia's essay, considered her evidence and reflections, and formulated your sense of what the essay means, write a short one-page reflection analyzing the effectiveness of Claudia's reflections.

3. Select two scenes from Claudia's final essay and determine how she enacts the principles for Creating a Scene. What is the effect on you of the two scenes? How do they differ in construction and in purpose?

4. Claudia makes use of the painting *Ophelia* in her final essay. How does she introduce the painting, and how effective is her use of it? Explain.

5. Locate in Claudia's final essay the reflection that most helps you understand her idea about the benefits of anxiety. Explain how that reflection works in terms of the evidence she is considering and the overall idea that she is developing in the essay.

RHETORICAL CONSIDERATIONS FOR EXPLORATORY ESSAYS

Writing an exploratory essay like the one that Claudia wrote depends on your knowing a few important rhetorical principles; each of these principles has been set forth within this chapter. Here are the steps that Claudia took to create her essay.

1. Select an art object that interests you. Create a word picture and then use that picture in a scene that reveals your relationship to the object. Follow the guidelines for *Integrating a Visual Text* and *Creating a Scene* (see pp. 15 and 18).

2. Let the idea from your initial scene draw you to another related experience. Re-create that moment for your readers. Pull them into the scene. Follow the guidelines for *Creating a Scene* (see p. 18).

3. Add a text, like Claudia's inclusion of Sylvia Plath's *The Bell Jar,* to the scene that you created for Exercise 1.

4. Looking back at your own scene and the written text that you have added to it, add a page of reflections about what you think the scene means. Follow the guidelines for *Reflecting* (see p. 34).

5. Exchange scenes with another writer and add reflections to that writer's scene. Compare the reflections and list what you learn about your own scene that you had not considered without the other writer's feedback.

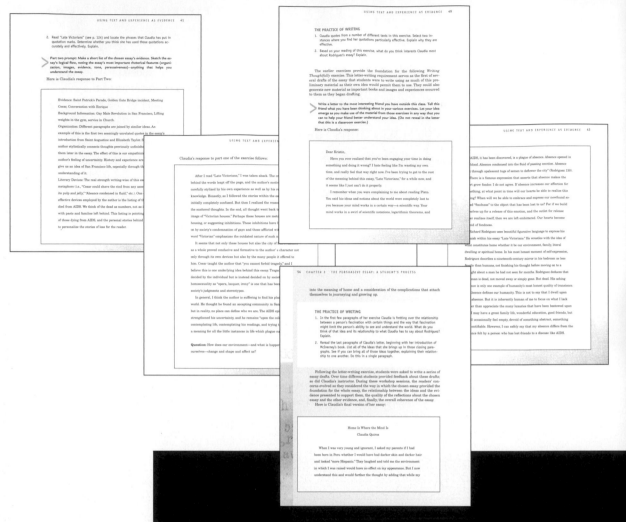

2. Read "Late Victorians" (see p. 124) and locate the phrases that Claudia has put in quotation marks. Determine whether you think she has used those quotations accurately and effectively. Explain.

Part two prompt: Make a short list of the chosen essay's evidence. Sketch the essay's logical flow, noting the essay's most important rhetorical features (organization, images, evidence, tone, persuasiveness)—anything that helps you understand the essay.

Here is Claudia's response to Part Two:

Evidence: Saint Patrick's Parade, Golden Gate Bridge incident, Meeting Cesar, Conversation with Enrique

Background Information: Gay Male Revolution in San Francisco, Lifting weights in the gym, service in Church.

Organization: Different paragraphs are joined by similar ideas. An example of this is the first two seemingly unrelated quotes in the essay's introduction from Saint Augustine and Elizabeth Taylor. The author stylistically connects thoughts previously unfinished, bringing them later in the essay. The effect of this is our empathizing with the author's feeling of uncertainty. History and experience are combined to give us an idea of San Francisco life, especially through the author's understanding of it.

Literary Devices: The real strength writing-wise of this essay is in the metaphors (i.e., "Cesar could shave the rind from any assertion and serve it up as the pulp and jelly," etc.). One of the most effective devices employed by the author is the listing of the various people he knew who died from AIDS. We think of the dead as numbers, not as individual people with pasts and families left behind. This listing is pointing out the stories of loss of those dying from AIDS, and the personal stories behind them. He wants to personalize the stories of loss for the reader.

THE PRACTICE OF WRITING

1. Claudia quotes from a number of different texts in this exercise. Select two instances where you find her quotations particularly effective. Explain why they are effective.

2. Based on your reading of this exercise, what do you think interests Claudia most about Rodriguez's essay? Explain.

The earlier exercises provide the foundation for the following *Writing Thoughtfully* exercise. This letter-writing requirement serves as the first of several drafts of the essay that students were to write using as much of this preliminary material as their own idea would permit them to see. They could also generate new material as important books and images and experiences occurred to them as they began drafting.

> Write a letter to the most interesting friend you have outside this class. Tell this friend what you have been thinking about in your various exercises. Let your idea emerge as you make use of the material from those exercises in any way that you can to help your friend better understand your idea. (Do not reveal in the letter that this is a classroom exercise.)

Here is Claudia's response:

Dear Kristin,

Have you ever realized that you've been engaging your time in doing something and doing it wrong? I hate feeling like I'm wasting my own time, and really feel that way right now. I've been trying to get to the root of the meaning behind this essay, "Late Victorians," for a while now, and it seems like I just can't do it properly.

I remember when you were complaining to me about reading Plato. You said his ideas and notions about the world were completely lost to you because your mind works in a certain way—a scientific way. Your mind works in a swirl of scientific notations, logarithmic theorems, and

---

Claudia's response to part one of the exercise follows:

After I read "Late Victorians," I was taken aback. The content behind the words leapt off the page, and the author's motives seemed carefully stylized by his own experience as well as by his religious knowledge. Honestly, as I followed the stories within the essay, I was initially completely confused. But then I realized the reason behind the scattered thoughts. In the end, all thought went back to one image of "Victorian houses." Perhaps these houses are metaphors for housing, or suggesting inhibitions. These inhibitions have built up on by society's condemnation of gays and those afflicted with AIDS. The word "Victorian" emphasizes the outdated nature of such notions.

It seems that not only these houses but also the city of San Francisco as a whole proved conducive and formative to the author's character not only through the own devices but also by the many people it offered to him. Cesar taught the author that "you cannot forbid tragedy," and I believe this is one underlying idea behind this essay. Tragedy is decided by the individual but is instead decided on by society. When homosexuality as "opera, lacquer, irony" is one that has been put up by society's judgments and stereotypes.

In general, I think the author is suffering to find his place in the world. He thought he found an accepting community in San Francisco, but in reality, no place can define who we are. The AIDS epidemic strengthened his uncertainty, and he remains "upon the solitary bench contemplating life, contemplating his readings, and trying to find a meaning for all the little instances in life which plague our minds."

Question: How does our environment—and what is happening around ourselves—change and shape and affect us?

AIDS, it has been discovered, is a plague of absence. Absence opened in blood. Absence condensed into the fluid of passing emotion. Absence . . . through opalescent tugs of semen to deflower the city" (Rodriguez 130).

There is a famous expression that asserts that absence makes the heart grow fonder. I do not agree. If absence increases our affection for something, at what point in time will our hearts be able to realize this feeling? When will we be able to embrace and express our newfound affection? "fondness" to the object that has been lost to us? For if we build ourselves up for a release of this emotion, and the outlet for release never realizes itself, then we are left embittered. Our hearts become void of fondness.

Richard Rodriguez uses beautiful figurative language to express his anguish within his essay "Late Victorians." He wrestles with the idea of what constitutes home whether it be our environment, family, literal dwelling or spiritual home. In his most honest moment of self-expression, Rodriguez describes a nineteenth-century mirror in his bedroom as less fragile than humans, not finishing his thought before moving on to a thought about a man he had not seen for months Rodriguez deduces that the man is dead, not moved away or simply gone. But dead. His aching absence is only one example of humanity's most honest quality of transience. Absence defines our humanity. This is not to say that I dwell upon my absence. But it is inherently human of me to focus on what I lack rather than appreciate the many luxuries that have been bestowed upon me. I may have a great family life, wonderful education, good friends, but I still occasionally feel empty, devoid of something abstract, something unidentifiable. However, I can safely say that my absence differs from the absence felt by a person who has lost friends to a disease like AIDS.

---

into the meaning of home and a consideration of the complications that attach themselves to journeying and growing up.

THE PRACTICE OF WRITING

1. In the first few paragraphs of her exercise Claudia is fretting over the relationship between a person's fascination with certain things and the way that fascination might limit the person's ability to see and understand the world. What do you think of that idea and its relationship to what Claudia has to say about Rodriguez? Explain.

2. Reread the last paragraphs of Claudia's letter, beginning with her introduction of McInerney's book. List all of the ideas that she brings up in those closing paragraphs. See if you can bring all of those ideas together, explaining their relationship to one another. Do this in a single paragraph.

Following the letter-writing exercise, students were asked to write a series of essay drafts. Over time different students provided feedback about these drafts; as did Claudia's instructor. During these workshop sessions, the readers' concerns evolved as they considered the way in which the chosen essay provided the foundation for the whole essay, the relationship between the ideas and the evidence presented to support them, the quality of the reflections about the chosen essay and the other evidence, and, finally, the overall coherence of the essay. Here is Claudia's final version of her essay:

Home Is Where the Mind Is
Claudia Quiroz

When I was very young and ignorant, I asked my parents if I had been born in Peru whether I would have had darker skin and darker hair and looked "more Hispanic." They laughed and told me the environment in which I was raised would have no effect on my appearance. But I now understand this and would further the thought by adding that while my

---

Writing about our text leads us to related texts.

Exploring these textual connections leads to ideas.

Ideas lead to essays.

3

THE PERSUASIVE ESSAY:
A STUDENT'S PROCESS

Using Text and Experience as Evidence

We will again follow one student writer, Claudia Quiros, as she moves from a consideration of **evidence** to the development of an **idea,** and then on to the presentation and substantiation of that idea in the form of an **essay**. Claudia's work in this chapter is different from her work in Chapter 2; here she is learning to work more effectively with written texts.

Claudia's essay will be set in motion by a written text: Richard Rodriguez's essay "Late Victorians" (see p. 124). She has to come to terms with Rodriguez's essay as she completes her preliminary writing exercises, but later in the sequence she will be putting that text in conversation with other texts and making important connections so that she can develop an idea and an essay of her own. The conversation among texts will evolve in Claudia's mind and on the pages of her own writing as she begins to see and develop important relationships among the various texts she is reading and studying. The beginning work for this essay will come primarily from those written texts, rather than from her own experiences as it did for the essay in Chapter 2. In the essay itself, Claudia's primary evidence will consist of written texts. She is, of course, always free to use experiential evidence to help her develop her idea, but this particular set of exercises is designed to help students learn to read and make use of complex written texts.

The pattern of development—the sequential and recursive steps that Claudia takes to create her essay—follows the same general pattern that informs the sequencing of exercises accompanying each of the *Occasions for Writing* in this reader. The exercises and the questions vary from Occasion to Occasion, but they always move back and forth along the journey from **evidence** to **idea** to **essay.**

As writers begin to read and analyze written texts, they discover immediately a host of ideas, both explicit and implicit. One text may confirm the ideas of another text, while a different text may call into question the ideas and methodologies of the initial text. Whereas images and experience merely suggest ideas to the writer, written texts are often more explicit. They put the reader immediately into the world of idea and controversy. That reader—who is, in fact, in the process of becoming a writer—must begin to pay close attention to the way the texts speak to one another. That conversation leads eventually to the reader/writer's own idea.

Although it is true that reading written texts puts the reader immediately into the world of ideas and controversy, it is unlikely that the reader will discover quickly just what his or her own idea will be. The time period for forming one's own ideas about written texts is often just as lengthy as it is when working with images and experience. However, with written texts, the reader's entry into the world of ideas is more direct, because the original author's ideas are written down. The ideas are in the text awaiting discovery, but the sorting out of those ideas, their analysis, and their use takes time. The process calls for an inquiry, requiring curiosity, rigorous analysis, and questioning of the written texts.

Text-based **persuasive** essays often seem to some readers more academic, more formal, than **exploratory** essays. Cited texts themselves lend a degree of formality to the writing. However, a writer can make serious use of textual evidence in combination with other forms of evidence (whether other written texts, visual images, or experience) and through a process of rigorous reasoning make a hard-earned claim that can become even more powerful. Any combination of compelling evidence lends authority to the argument. Experience can confirm and substantiate what might otherwise seem an empty, theoretical claim based solely on written texts. The rules are not hard and fast. What is crucial to this text-based essay, and to every good essay, is the spirit of exploration and inquiry that we also see manifested in the exploratory essay developed in Chapter 2.

Claudia's persuasive essay evolved primarily from the rigorous work she did with Rodriguez's "Late Victorians," but she was also asked to consider this essay in the context of several related written texts. The thematic emphasis for the work was identity, but students were free to let the essays suggest other thematic concerns.

The first four written exercises asked students to read and study their chosen essay, paying attention not only to what the essay says but also to how it works and how it creates meaning. Writing the essay itself would necessarily come later, after students worked with the chosen text. The initial writing exercises simply helped them better understand the chosen essay before they began in earnest to write their own essay.

Here is the first two-part *Preparing to Write* exercise in this sequence:

> **Part one prompt: After reading your chosen essay, determine what you consider to be the writer's motive for writing that essay. Also, formulate and write out the question that you believe the essay is trying to answer. Keep it for future reference.**

Claudia's response to part one of the exercise follows:

After I read "Late Victorians," I was taken aback. The crude honesty behind the words leapt off the page, and the author's motive was carefully stylized by his own experience as well as by his reading and knowledge. Honestly, as I followed the stories within the essay, I was initially completely confused. But then I realized the reasoning behind the scattered thoughts. In the end, all thought went back to the idea or image of "Victorian houses." Perhaps these houses are metaphorical for housing, or suggesting inhibitions. These inhibitions have been brought on by society's condemnation of gays and those afflicted with AIDS. The word "Victorian" emphasizes the outdated nature of such notions.

It seems that not only these houses but also the city of San Francisco as a whole proved conducive and formative to the author' s character not only through its own devices but also by the many people it offered to him. Cesar taught the author that "you cannot forbid tragedy," and I believe this is one underlying idea behind this essay. Tragedy is not decided by the individual but is instead decided on by society. The idea of homosexuality as "opera, lacquer, irony" is one that has been tainted by society's judgments and stereotypes.

In general, I think the author is suffering to find his place in the world. He thought he found an accepting community in San Francisco, but in reality, no place can define who we are. The AIDS epidemic only strengthened his uncertainty, and he remains "upon the cold hard pew" contemplating life, contemplating his readings, and trying to understand a meaning for all the little instances in life which plague our lives.

Question: How does our environment—and what is happening outside ourselves—change and shape and affect us?

READING AND RESPONDING TO WRITTEN TEXTS

Citing written texts or, more properly, borrowing ideas from them, lies at the heart of most academic writing. Written sources provide the primary material for most research and for evidence. Learning to read those texts critically and comprehensively leads to good ideas. Typically, reading and rigorous analysis will be followed by selection of evidence. But that selection of evidence most often comes after writers have begun to develop their own ideas about what the various texts mean, after they have begun to think about how to use those texts.

READING WRITTEN TEXTS

- Read to understand the whole text; annotate and highlight the text as you read.

- Look for connections within the text you are reading. Figure out how the parts of the text work together to create meaning.

- Keep track of your thoughts as you read and reread the text. Put your notes from the text itself on one page; put your reflections about the text on a facing page, and jot down connections between the text you are reading and other texts (written, visual, sonic).

- Pay attention to the writer's strategies and techniques used to express ideas and learn to adapt your own writing to specific purposes and audiences.

- Appreciate the rhythm of a well-constructed sentence, the value of a neatly turned phrase, the heft of a properly weighted word, the elegance of a properly placed punctuation mark, so that you can detect the organizational patterns that bind an essay.

RESPONDING TO WRITTEN TEXTS

- Summarize late in the reading process, after you understand what the whole text means.

- When you begin to select evidence from the text to support your own ideas, quote accurately in your notes or in your drafts.

- In your essay ensure that your readers know (1) when they are reading either quoted material or summary and (2) when they are reading your reflections about that material.

THE PRACTICE OF WRITING

1. Identify at least two ideas—two things about Rodriguez's thinking that seem to interest Claudia, things different from her expressed concern in her final question.

2. Read "Late Victorians" (see p. 124) and locate the phrases that Claudia has put in quotation marks. Determine whether you think she has used those quotations accurately and effectively. Explain.

> **Part two prompt: Make a short list of the chosen essay's evidence. Sketch the essay's logical flow, noting the essay's most important rhetorical features (organization, images, evidence, tone, persuasiveness)—anything that helps you understand the essay.**

Here is Claudia's response to Part Two:

Evidence: Saint Patrick's Parade, Golden Gate Bridge incident, Meeting Cesar, Conversation with Enrique

Background Information: Gay Male Revolution in San Francisco, Lifting weights in the gym, service in Church.

Organization: Different paragraphs are joined by similar ideas. An example of this is the first two seemingly unrelated quotes in the essay's introduction from Saint Augustine and Elizabeth Taylor. Sometimes, the author stylistically connects thoughts previously unfinished and finishes them later in the essay. The effect of this is our empathizing with the author's feeling of uncertainty. History and experience are intertwined to give us an idea of San Francisco life, especially through the author's understanding of it.

Literary Devices: The real strength writing-wise of this essay lies in its metaphors (i.e., "Cesar could shave the rind from any assertion to expose its pulp and jelly," "Absence condensed in fluid," etc.). One of the most effective devices employed by the author is the listing of those that have died from AIDS. We think of the dead as numbers, not as individuals with pasts and families left behind. This listing is pointing out our view of those dying from AIDS, and the personal stories behind them attempt to personalize the stories of loss for the reader.

More detailed questions about motive directed to the writer: How does our home and environment define and determine the people we become? Is home our refuge from the chaotic world? How do you think tragedy is formative to your character? How have your variety of environments affected you? What has each house you've lived in taught you?

In this initial exercise, Claudia is struggling to give voice to a complicated essay about the AIDS epidemic in San Francisco. In the essay Rodriguez reveals how he is especially affected by the loss of friends and by his own response to these deaths. But the essay has a larger idea at work in it. Rodriguez wants us to see how San Francisco was a kind of heavenly city, offering promise to those in need, but there turned out to be a difference between the dream and the reality. That difference informs much of what he tells us in this essay.

Claudia sees that San Francisco is in fact shaping the lives of those who have come to live there, and she is curious about what Rodriguez tells us about that shaping. She shows a basic understanding of how Rodriguez uses his evidence (much of it consisting of stories of experience) and how he weaves the various parts of his essay together through the construction of his sentences and through the use of literary devices.

But Claudia is not yet writing for an audience that hasn't read Rodriguez's essay. In future exercises, prompted by work done in class and by the exercises themselves, she will begin to be more aware of her readers' needs, and she will clarify these preliminary observations so that her readers will know more clearly what she means.

Here is the next *Preparing to Write* exercise, along with Claudia's response:

> Select the most fascinating moment in your chosen essay and reveal that moment to a reader who has never read the essay. Make sure that your reader can understand your fascination and can understand what that moment from your chosen essay has to do with the essay's larger concerns, its crucial ideas. Let your reader see you reflect about that moment and how it helps us understand the chosen essay.

"AIDS, it has been discovered, is a plague of absence. Absence opened in the blood. Absence condensed into the fluid of passing emotion. Absence shot through opalescent tugs of semen to deflower the city" (Rodriguez 130).

There is a famous expression that asserts that absence makes the heart grow fonder. I do not agree. If absence increases our affection for something, at what point in time will our hearts be able to realize this feeling? When will we be able to embrace and express our newfound so-called "fondness" to the object that has been lost to us? For if we build ourselves up for a release of this emotion, and the outlet for release never realizes itself, then we are left embittered. Our hearts become devoid of fondness.

Richard Rodriguez uses beautiful figurative language to express his anguish within his essay "Late Victorians." He wrestles with the idea of what constitutes home whether it be our environment, family, literal dwelling or spiritual home. In his most honest moment of self-expression, Rodriguez describes a nineteenth-century mirror in his bedroom as less fragile than humans, not finishing his thought before moving on to a thought about a man he had not seen for months. Rodriguez deduces that this man is dead, not moved away or simply gone. But dead. His aching absence is only one example of humanity's most honest quality of transience.

Absence defines our humanity. This is not to say that I dwell upon this absence. But it is inherently human of me to focus on what I lack rather than appreciate the many luxuries that have been bestowed upon me. I may have a great family life, wonderful education, good friends, but I still occasionally feel empty, devoid of something abstract, something unidentifiable. However, I can safely say that my absence differs from the absence felt by a person who has lost friends to a disease like AIDS.

"And then AIDS, it was discovered, is a non-metaphorical disease, a disease like any other. Absence sprang from substance—a virus, a hairy bubble perched upon a needle, a platter of no intention served round: fever, blisters, a death sentence" (Rodriguez 131).

What is the source of death? How can we really recognize all life has to offer if it is cut short by something so unnecessary and un-meaningful? While the answers to these questions are unanswerable by mere mortals, we realize that our time on earth is ephemeral. Youth and beauty corrode, exposing life's ultimate core, leaving us open to possibilities beyond the aesthetic. "We have become accustomed to figures disappearing from our landscape. Does this not lead us to interrogate the landscape?" (Rodriguez 130).

Comfort is the mother of blind acceptance. Once we become accustomed to and comfortable with the status of our lives, we unintentionally become slaves to our environment. We question nothing, and in this way, we become stuck in a circuitous route leading us nowhere; we become hamsters spinning on wheels, chasing our ends yet hindered by our ignorance. The absence of answers to our unrealized questions inhibits our growth.

Instead of choosing a single moment of fascination, Claudia selected three short quotations. She could just as well have chosen an image, or a character, or a fully developed scene from the essay. Claudia's reflections about the three short passages are becoming clearer than her reflections in the first exercise. She is more comfortable with what she is seeing in the essay, more confident that she is finding important things. From these small moments of connection, she should be able to go on and develop a more comprehensive sense of her chosen essay.

Her instructor has chosen not to have students summarize the essay before they have come to understand its details and how those details are connected. This initial work aims to ensure a more thorough reading of the chosen text.

INCORPORATING A WRITTEN TEXT

As writers begin to use a selected portion of a written text in their essays, that text should be incorporated so that it becomes a seamless part of their own writing. At the same time, readers must know when they are encountering quoted or summarized material and when they are encountering a writer's own thoughts and reflections about that material. Quoted material is always placed in quotation marks. Quotations that exceed four lines must be set off as a block of text, and the entire block must be indented five additional spaces. The blocked text is double-spaced. Summarized material is less easy to spot than quoted material, so writers must be careful to signal when they are summarizing. Follow these guidelines when citing a written text (see the appendix for more on documentation):

· Guidelines for incorporating a written source: Introduce the source by naming the writer and the source. Cite the source accurately. Reflect on the cited material.

· Incorporate quoted material into your sentences so that your own language and syntax match that of the quoted passage.

· Signal the beginning and end of your summaries so that readers can tell when you are using your source and when you are reflecting on it.

The next writing exercise begins the work of *Moving toward Essay*. It asks students to back away from the details of their close reading of the chosen essay and to begin to put the essay and its ideas into relation to other written texts that develop related thematic and ideological concerns. It urges students to begin to understand their chosen essays in larger contexts.

> **Direct a question to the writer of your chosen essay that will attempt to uncover something that you think is missing from that essay, something that might clarify things for you. Try to get at this question by putting the chosen essay up against (or in conversation with) other written texts that make you think more clearly about your chosen essay. Your sources, your other essays, can come from your syllabus; Internet research; the library; and/or readings from your other courses. You might also include in this search books you have already read. In a short written reflection, reveal what you have discovered.**

Here is Claudia's response:

How do we find our "home"? How do the seemingly random ideas of this essay contribute to this search for an environment that will affect us positively? I wonder what advice you, Richard Rodriguez, would offer to readers of your essay. You haven't gotten to the heart of life yet but then again, who has? It would be fascinating to hear how heterosexuals should search for acceptance or for a home of their own. I'm sure you would argue that straight people have an easier time navigating through the choppy waters of life, but we must take into account the fact that we all experience heartache, loss, dejection, deception, and sadness at one point or another. Tragedy is inevitable; even you argue "you cannot forbid [it]." But what role does the omnipresence of tragedy play in deciding our home?

The theme of a quest in life permeates throughout numerous texts. In "Late Victorians," you touch on the idea of a quest for a true home, what defines this home, and a longing for acceptance. In his acclaimed novel *Bright Lights, Big City,* Jay McInerney touches on the idea of the emptiness and superficiality that plague this search. His protagonist, who is technically himself as the novel is written in second person, is on a quest for ideas, knowledge, and meaning in his superficially glamorous but morally unsatisfying life. We trace his thoughts and follow his potholed road through life. Going back to another of Saint Augustine's teachings in *Confessions,* we find that he extols the value of human search for a meaning, a search for the good. Even Plato argues that we should journey out of the "cave" of ignorance and turn our souls to experience the larger world. While your essay deals less with such a journey, it elicits the same response from us. We become so emotionally attached to your actions and feelings and experiences that we experience your own uncertainty.

We see tragedy punctuating your own speech, from the beginning when you witnessed the young woman attempt suicide from the Golden Gate Bridge and then experienced the death of several close friends. Tragedy is embedded within humanity. You yourself state, "San Francisco toys with tragic conclusion." Your very home, though perfect for you, is not a utopia; it is not perfect. There is no perfection, even in our suitable surroundings. While your Victorian home hearkens back to a time when homosexuals lived in those homes and rebelled against the conformity of the time, it also recalls an age of moralistic importance, keeping up appearances, proper etiquette, and social standing. It takes a strong person to challenge these foundations of normalcy and established domesticity.

How can we as readers of your fine essay learn how to challenge our environments? What control do we have over our home's effect on us? In Voltaire's *Candide,* the protagonist, a young, impressionable and naive boy, travels around the globe, acquiring new experiences everywhere and forming his relationships and opinions based on his impressions of the world. However, we realize that at the end of it all, even though Candide has experienced life in so many different ways, witnessing different social classes, countries, and cultures, he still remains blind to his purpose. How will we know when we have found the environment most suited for us? You mention San Francisco's rejection of neighborhoods that inspire "idiosyncrasy." Why is this so, as the city itself is extolled for its acceptance of the nonconformists?

It is true that most of these questions are to be answered subjectively. And why should there only be one right answer to everything? Even if you, Richard Rodriguez, argue that "moralistic society has always judged emotion literally," what are you going to do about it?

Claudia is beginning to acquire a deeper understanding of the complexities associated with the need for a sheltering and nurturing environment and with the conflicting demands of culture, or the society in which one tries to live out one's life. Home, as Claudia thinks about it, is becoming a complicated concept rather than a particular place. She is beginning to see that home is not a simple dwelling place where one is safe from conflicting cultural and social forces. She has still not tried to come to terms with everything Rodriguez tells us in the essay, but she has begun to be reflective about the parts of the essay that have intrigued her from the outset. She has also begun to make interesting connections among a group of written texts.

CONNECTING TEXTS

When reading a complex written text such as Richard Rodriguez's "Late Victorians," writers should always read, as Claudia has done, with their minds open to connections with other things they have seen or read (essays, reports, images, movies, songs, books). Often when we read, we are reminded of a related idea by something in the text. For a second we see more clearly what we are reading. Often in such moments we tell ourselves a story or remind ourselves about something that we have read elsewhere that clarifies or intensifies the importance of what we are reading at any given moment. Keeping track of these connections as they occur can be important later when trying to come to terms with the meaning of a given text. Seeing how two different writers treat similar ideas or arguments can result in a more rounded perspective. Connections lead to clarification for writers, but when the writer uses those two texts together in her essay, she can give readers the same clarity.

- Read always with an open mind for connections.
- Keep track of the way your mind works as you read. Record connecting thoughts about other books, essays, images, and movies.
- Consider the way those connections can both clarify and complicate your understanding of the text you are reading.
- Be receptive to what those odd connections can tell you about what you are reading.
- Be prepared to change your mind about what you are reading in light of what you learn from some of the connections you make.
- When a connection seems particularly interesting, consult the other source; see how it clarifies or complicates the text you are reading. Follow up.

THE PRACTICE OF WRITING

1. Claudia quotes from a number of different texts in this exercise. Select two instances where you find her quotations particularly effective. Explain why they are effective.

2. Based on your reading of this exercise, what do you think interests Claudia most about Rodriguez's essay? Explain.

The earlier exercises provide the foundation for the following *Writing Thoughtfully* exercise. This letter-writing requirement serves as the first of several drafts of the essay that students were to write using as much of this preliminary material as their own idea would permit them to use. They could also generate new material as important books and images and experiences occurred to them as they began drafting.

> **Write a letter to the most interesting friend you have outside this class. Tell this friend what you have been thinking about in your various exercises. Let your idea emerge as you make use of the material from those exercises in any way that you can to help your friend better understand your idea. (Do not reveal in the letter that this is a classroom exercise.)**

Here is Claudia's response:

Dear Kristin,

Have you ever realized that you've been engaging your time in doing something and doing it wrong? I hate feeling like I'm wasting my own time, and really feel that way right now. I've been trying to get to the root of the meaning behind this essay, "Late Victorians," for a while now, and it seems like I just can't do it properly.

I remember when you were complaining to me about reading Plato. You said his ideas and notions about the world were completely lost to you because your mind works in a certain way—a scientific way. Your mind works in a swirl of scientific notations, logarithmic theorems, and biochemical vocabulary terms. I could never appreciate you more for having a mind like that. But should this prohibit you from understanding "The Republic"? I think you have the capability within you; you must simply draw this capability out through means of something you love.

I've been thinking a lot about useless facts about my friends lately. You're my only non-English major friend. In fact, you are the only person close to me who has been thinking of delving into the field of medicine. You probably think this isn't important or even worthy of note, but I feel that it reflects your character, personality, even how you think. Take, for example, my father. He looks at the world through the eyes of a doctor. Whenever he sees a homeless man, he observes his actions then mumbles to himself, "He must have AIDS." Upon moving me into my dorm, he noted that we should buy a hand-sanitizer because the hand-scanners we use to enter our rooms could spread infection. He is omnipresent in his scientific world, and while it limits some of his observations, it reflects his character, as you can tell that he is wholly devoted to and interested in what he's talking about.

I see you that way. I think you will grow like this; you will walk as a living celebration of science. And I know you are probably taking this lightly because I barely see you anymore since you are in Baltimore. But this essay—it underlined the shortness of life; it made me feel as if I were moving in no direction at all. I wasn't savoring each word for what it was, and this paralleled my lack of appreciation for the world, for life, for these happy days. It made me feel as though I were just existing rather than living.

I was listening to the new Interpol album, and I heard this lyric that had mentally escaped me each time I heard it: "You make me want to pick up my guitar/ And celebrate the myriad ways that I love you." This touched me, probably more than it should have. It deepened my need to connect with others and moved me to think about art's transformative quality. It made me want to actually act upon several desires I have had for a few months, since our existence on this earth is just an ephemeral state. So in this letter, I'm making up for lost time, and I'm appreciating you.

I hope you know that you were the first person I called when I discovered I was going to move. There I was that sweltering July day in a Barnard dorm room when I received a call from my mother. She asked me if I was doing my laundry, and how my classes were going, and how I liked New York so far, and all of those questions a concerned mother asks her little girl who has been gone for five weeks at a strange summer program in a strange college in a strange city. I was ready to say good-bye to her when she interrupted, "Oh, by the way, we've sold our house and bought one in D.C." My first reaction was excitement. This was so spontaneous! I was proud of my usually cautious parents. Then my confusion flooded in. I pondered about what was wrong with our house. After not being able to think of anything, I dialed your number.

We talked for about two hours. I barely knew you back then. We had become friends through Lindsey, so you didn't understand when I was spewing about all my newly revived memories in my old house. The incident in kindergarten when my brother conspired with my friend to throw basketballs at me in our backyard. Cleaning the giant windows with my dad while singing George Harrison songs, and making chocolate waffles. And even those solitary memories of my own like making up my own fantasy world out of old mattresses in the basement.

You understood these memories even though they held little substance to you. And you listened. And your interested silence meant more to me than any consolation or congratulation or anything.

I remember when I gave you a copy of *Bright Lights, Big City* last year. I told you to read it and get excited for college life in New York City. And I remember you told me it was horribly depressing and made you hate the city of "so-called opportunities." I guess it all worked out. I'm here, and you're there. But maybe that's how it's supposed to be. Maybe all our big city dreams were founded on fantasy. And just as the protagonist in Jay McInerney's novel, we should learn to transcend the illusions that life set up, for only within reality can we develop. Maybe we're living as he is, in a state of mass confusion, unable to differentiate our downfalls from our successes, running to and from ourselves, running into who we really are.

This makes me think back again on the essay I've been trying to comprehend. I've been failing. I've tried to elucidate the author's interpretation for myself and to grasp that notion and believe its truth. But I've realized this is not the way of going about it. I just ask for someone's direct opinion and take it at face value, especially when it's purposely not clearly expressed.

Take *Candide*. Sure, Voltaire wanted to write a satire about exploration and the Germans and whatever. But who was Candide supposed to represent? It's integral to understand that we are each Candides, walking through this world naively, making fun of those who do so, and in effect, being hypocrites. In *Candide,* the character Martin exclaims that people "live either in convulsions of misery or in the lethargy of boredom." I would agree, but add that this is true only without the presence of comfort. And how do we find this comfort? Comfort is a subjective matter, really. You would probably find comfort in a good presidential debate and an unlimited supply of carrot sticks. I would definitely find comfort in a lifetime supply of Nutella and being surrounded by music. But in the end, what we will mostly be comforted by is our idea of home. Candide wanders around the world and never really finds a place suited for him. At this age, we are meant to explore, to learn our options, take advantage of opportunities, travel, see what works for us. But we only do this through comparison. We can only recognize what is comfortable to us by comparing it to the known comfort of our homes. In this way only can we discover our true homes.

I find a home within your friendship. I want you to know that you are appreciated. I should express this more often, and you have given me the power to do so. Thank you.

Claudia

Claudia's letter is long and personal. We can begin to see why she has been so concerned about home and comfort. Her displacement to college and her parents' move have left her without the comfort of a particular place that she called home. By the end of this letter she has found a couple of interesting ideas, both near the end of her letter. She tells her friend, "I find a home within your friendship." That represents a conceptual shift in Claudia's thinking. She has moved from regret and confusion to a newfound clarity. In the preceding paragraph, she has also discovered that comfort is relative: "We can only recognize what is comfortable to us by comparing it to the known comfort of our homes. In this way only can we discover our true homes." She is moving into and playing in a world of ideas that draws its sustenance and clarity from her own experiences.

Claudia only touches on "Late Victorians" a couple of times in her letter, but it is clear that Rodriguez has set her on this intellectual journey—an inquiry into the meaning of home and a consideration of the complications that attach themselves to journeying and growing up.

THE PRACTICE OF WRITING

1. In the first few paragraphs of her exercise Claudia is fretting over the relationship between a person's fascination with certain things and the way that fascination might limit the person's ability to see and understand the world. What do you think of that idea and its relationship to what Claudia has to say about Rodriguez? Explain.

2. Reread the last paragraphs of Claudia's letter, beginning with her introduction of McInerney's book. List all of the ideas that she brings up in those closing paragraphs. See if you can bring all of those ideas together, explaining their relationship to one another. Do this in a single paragraph.

Following the letter-writing exercise, students were asked to write a series of essay drafts. Over time different students provided feedback about these drafts; so did Claudia's instructor. During these workshop sessions, the readers' concerns evolved as they considered the way in which the chosen essay provided the foundation for the whole essay, the relationship between the ideas and the evidence presented to support them, the quality of the reflections about the chosen essay and the other evidence, and, finally, the overall coherence of the essay.

Here is Claudia's final version of her essay:

Home Is Where the Mind Is

Claudia Quiros

When I was very young and ignorant, I asked my parents if I had been born in Peru whether I would have had darker skin and darker hair and looked "more Hispanic." They laughed and told me the environment in which I was raised would have no effect on my appearance. But I now understand this and would further the thought by adding that while my environment would have no direct effect on how I looked on the outside, it would affect how I looked *at* the outside. I learned from a young age to question my environment, to strive for an understanding of the good and especially of the bad. And in questioning this environment, I have discovered new environments which I never knew existed, like that of my own mind. In considering Richard Rodriguez's essay "Late Victorians," I have come to realize that only through experiencing tragedy and accounting for absence within our lives can we learn to accommodate a spiritual development within our mind's home.

In his essay "Late Victorians," Richard Rodriguez describes the literal and metaphorical ways in which San Francisco acts as home to the gay movement. The city acts as a "paradise" to "lonely teenagers aboard Greyhound buses" who have escaped their homophobic parents while maintaining its air of "tragic conclusion" (125). The same Victorian house in which Rodriguez now lives once served as home for the rebellious homosexuals who were "challenging the foundations of domesticity" (126). After several revolutions instigated by the gay movement, the city became a center for idiosyncrasy and nonconformity. This new city, a literal celebration of freedom, was impaired by homophobia and by the tragedy that soon affected many of its members: the disease of AIDS. Rodriguez uses his own home as a metaphor for the inconstancy of society, a quality reflected in the painting of the house itself, a faux "weathered look" attempting to reach an "illusion of permanence" (127). During this fragile time, many tragedies hit close to Rodriguez's home, especially in the case of the death of Rodriguez's friend Cesar. Rodriguez has difficulty in dealing with Cesar's absence, and he even calls out to him within the essay: "There were times, dear Cesar, when you tried to

[. . .] scorn American optimism" (125). In his essay, Rodriguez reflects on the formative role of the city as a center for expression and depression as well as learning to deal with the tragedy in his own life, like losing Cesar to AIDS.

I was sixteen when my grandfather died. Six years earlier, he told me that the world around me was waiting for me to make my mark. However big that mark would be would depend on the character of my soul. At the time of his death, I found myself thinking of this idea. What would form this so-called "character of my soul"? Only after heavy contemplation did I realize that my character derived from my reflection on little pieces of advice like this one. And these little tidbits of knowledge and wisdom and guidance came from the sources closest to me, from those around me, from those who knew me. My wisdom—and thus my character—is and always has been impressed upon me by those people who make up my environment.

Part of the soul of a human is shaped by the surroundings in which he or she is raised and taught to prosper. From our first homes we take away judgments, modes of thinking, ways of acting, and whether we agree with how we are conditioned or not, these formative qualities stay with us and gradually seep into our present. However, while this environment helps to shape us, it does not solely define who we are. Richard Rodriguez thought he had found an accepting community in San Francisco, but in reality, no place can define who we are if we do not consider our past experiences, particularly those of tragedy. Without tragedy, we would not recognize the goodness of happiness, and we would not appreciate the graces of luck. One question raised in "Late Victorians" is what role does the omnipresence of tragedy play in deciding our homes?

Tragedy personifies itself in Rodriguez's essay through insecurity, a feeling against which Rodriguez wrestles. Using brilliant judgment in the organization of his essay, Rodriguez begins with two quotes that showcase the nature of this insecurity. The first, from Saint Augustine, describes the nature of humanity and its connection with immortality. "Human unhappiness is evidence of our immortality. Intuition tells us we are meant for some other city" (124). The second quote is from Elizabeth Taylor who reflects on a past experience, recalling a moment of insecurity. She remembers "cerulean" days on her yacht, days which were marked by careful introspection. She recalls thinking "[t]his must end" (124). In using these quotes, Rodriguez begins expressing a sense of longing that transcends the generations, time periods, and social classes. What links the two quotes is the insecurity of each person, as shown by Augustine's uncertainty of what follows humanity's ephemeral earthly life and Elizabeth Taylor's longing to be somewhere else, anywhere else but in the seemingly glamorous environment which envelops her. Both of these individuals, different in more ways than not, partake in a quest for a world of comfort and seek solace within the context of their own mortality.

As previously mentioned, part of what helps us prosper as human beings is the inevitability of tragedy and its inevitable and unfortunate occurrence within our lives. Rodriguez himself is shaped by all sorts of little tragedies: his community experiences homophobia, and he wrestles with and attempts to defy stereotypes of gays. But most notably, the author reflects on his ability to cope with the ubiquitous presence of AIDS in his life. Cesar, one of the most developed characters in the essay, is described as experiencing "agony" throughout his experience with

AIDS. Only after Cesar's death does the author realize his own "unwillingness to embrace life" (132). In effect AIDS imposes itself upon Rodriguez's life. He not only reads about members of his community affected by the disease, they come into his home, they paint his home, they are his home. By the end of the essay, the AIDS epidemic only strengthens Rodriguez's uncertainty, and he remains "upon the cold, hard pew" (133) contemplating life, reflecting on his past, and trying to understand a meaning for all the little instances in life which plague our lives. Tragedy was an indelible shaper of Rodriguez's character, and as sad as its instances may have been, tragedy led him to reflection, led him to contemplation, and to a creation of his own, this very essay.

In his most honest moment of self-expression, Rodriguez describes a nineteenth century mirror in his bedroom as less fragile than humans. Not finishing his thought before moving on to a thought about a man he had not seen for months, Rodriguez deduces that this man is dead, instead of thinking that he has moved away or is simply gone. Dead. The very word hints at its somberness. This man is finally noticed, finally appreciated, finally thought about now that he is dead. It is characteristic of human nature to focus on what is absent rather than appreciate the many luxuries that have been bestowed upon us. Even with a great family life, wonderful education, good friends, one can still feel empty, devoid of something abstract, something unidentifiable. And sometimes this unknown entity hinders us from our own self-discovery.

Tragedy has the ability to shape our perception of the world. It is a subjective matter, marked by experience, marked by the moments we cherish and those we never had. Rodriguez aims to define his own tragedy through questioning his own environment and to a greater extent, the outside world when he describes the effects of Cesar's absence upon his life. "I stood aloof at Cesar's memorial, the kind of party he would enjoy, everyone said. And so for a time, Cesar lay [. . .] unconvincingly resurrected in the conditional: would enjoy. What else could they say? Cesar had no religion beyond aesthetic bravery." When Rodriguez views what is tragic as necessary, he recognizes its powerful reality because tragedy is never really real until it happens to you.

In Voltaire's famous satire *Candide,* the title protagonist, a naive and impressionable boy, traverses the globe, acquiring new experiences everywhere and forming his relationships and opinions based on his impressions of the world. At the end of the novel, we realize that even though Candide has experienced life in so many different ways, witnessing different social classes, countries, and cultures, he still remains blind to reality. Cunegonde, the girl he had loved at the beginning of the book, has aged, and he no longer accepts her because of her weathered looks. His mission throughout the entire novel is accomplished; he is united with her, but he rejects her solely based on her appearance. Moreover, he fails to recognize hypocrisy in his own life, most notably in the teachings of his childhood philosopher friend Pangloss, a hypocritical heretic. The only good person in his life, Jacques, a man who takes Candide into his home, dies. All of the formative elements of his early environment have been tainted by new discovery, and he ends up devoid of understanding his environment and essentially himself. While Candide experiences different forms of tragedy, including the death of his friends and family, the loss of love, and the experience of war, he doesn't learn from these misfortunes; rather, he remains easily molded by his environment, devoid of self-reflection and acceptance of tragedy. Candide later reflects, "Pangloss deceived me cruelly when he said that all is for the best in the world" (Voltaire 32). At first, Candide is shocked by the instances of hardship within his life. But as he comes to terms with his sadness, he leaves his optimism, and launches himself in reality. Candide's realization of tragedy at the end of the novel, his acceptance of bleak social conditions, is what liberates his mind and allows him finally to discover a world fit for him, a world without "theorizing," a world that, though simple, proves conducive to his development because he is finally able to accept his tragic past (149).

I remember reading Jay McInerney's novel *Bright Lights, Big City* my senior year of high school and looking forward to my life in New York, despite the novel's depressing portrayal of the faux opportunities that the city presents. Similarly, this gutting feeling reappeared in Rodriguez's essay, taking my understanding of how our environment shapes our ends to a new level. Our environment surrounds us, makes us recognize what is happening outside our immediate doors. McInerney's protagonist (who is technically the reader himself as the novel is written in the second person) is on a quest for ideas, knowledge, and meaning in his superficially glamorous but morally unsatisfying life. His supermodel wife leaves him, and he spirals downward in a flurry of cocaine and rejection within his job, love life, and, ultimately, society. He imagines escaping New York, escaping anywhere, even Kansas, the evil home state of his evil wife. He is so corrupted by his surroundings that he seeks solace within his own mind, within his thoughts, within his reflections on the past. It is in his introspection that he finds himself and his spiritual home, a home that houses happiness and hope for the future. But we mustn't forget that the creator of this introspection, the entity that nudged the protagonist into deeper thought was hardship. Only after his gorgeous wife leaves him does the protagonist recognize her faults and seek less shallow traits in future friends. Furthermore, the protagonist's recognition of past tragedies leads him to seek his original home at the end of the novel. We learn that the smell of fresh bread reminds him of home, and in the last few pages smelling this familiar scent leads him downtown to the mercy of a dockworker, with whom he trades his Ray-Bans for a bag of doughy rolls. "You get down on your knees and tear open the bag; the smell of the warm dough envelops you [. . .] You will have to learn everything all over again" (McInerney 182). He tears into the bread, into his past, into a warm, familiar environment, one of no worries, one of simpler times. An environment he could not appreciate until he was removed from its comfort.

This parallels one of Saint Augustine's teachings in *Confessions* in which he extols the value of our human search for a meaning, a search for the good. Saint Augustine was one of the first philosophers to emphasize the importance of such searching. Our searches through life include a quest for truth, a reflection on what we have done to achieve this truth, and a final discernment on all the knowledge we have acquired throughout the years. If we take all the tragedies of life only at face value, we lose sight of their deeper meaning. Without introspection, we fail to recognize the necessity of misfortune within our lives. And without reflection we cannot learn from our past environments or bring to the present all that we have been taught in our various homes.

I think that "Late Victorians" is Rodriguez's quest, his questioning, his attempt to get at truth. He questions his experience. He reflects upon not only the revolution that shaped his found home of San Francisco, but all those little revolutions that led to his clarification. But this quest for meaning is in fact a quest for home. Just as Elizabeth Taylor and Saint Augustine wish to be somewhere else, Rodriguez wishes for spiritual solace. He seeks his otherworldly environment, a place shaped and improved by the tragedy and absence that had plagued his life. And while he may not fulfill his quest any time soon, he has learned, perhaps what all of us must learn, to accommodate the environment of his past with the reality of his present. For it is within our internal acceptance of tragedy that we learn to see the beauty that lies beyond it.

Works Cited

McInerney, Jay. <u>Bright Lights, Big City</u>. New York: Random, 1981.

Rodriguez, Richard. "Late Victorians." <u>Occasions for Writing</u>. Ed. Pat C.
    Hoy II and Robert DiYanni. Boston: Wadsworth, 2008. 124-33.

St. Augustine. <u>Confessions</u>. Trans. Henry Chadwick. New York: Oxford
    UP, 1991.

Voltaire, Francois. <u>Candide</u>. New York: Penguin, 1990.

We see that the process of drafting and revising took Claudia to a compelling idea about the unexpected benefits of tragedy and the importance of a conception of home. Claudia worked her way through the various exercises, reading and writing first about Rodriguez's essay and then about other written texts, combining them, enriching them with relevant stories of experience, until finally she understood all of this evidence and what it meant to her. The idea that she developed in her essay eventually helped reshape her initial responses, and she showed us, finally, through her reflections about those texts just what they had to do with her idea about the beneficial relationship between tragedy and introspection that led her to see that home may be more in the mind than in a physical place.

REFLECTING (ANALYSIS AND CONCEPTION)

In a persuasive, text-based essay, writers bring together a group of written texts (primary evidence), their interpretation of those texts, and the reasoning that led them to the interpretation. Written revelations about those texts constitute their reflection. The meditative and thoughtful voice that accompanies those reflections makes sense of the evidence, presents an explanation and a revelation of something discovered, a new idea. For more on reflection, see the Reflecting (Analysis and Conception) box in Chapter 2 on page 34.

THE PRACTICE OF WRITING

1. Go through Claudia's final essay and mark or highlight her reflective passages. Pick two passages for comparison. Tell us what you learn from them about interpreting evidence.

2. After you have read Claudia's essay, considered her evidence and reflections, and formulated your sense of what the essay means, write a short one-page reflection analyzing the effectiveness of Claudia's reflections.

Think of your work with written texts as a recurring cycle: the initial reading and analysis of the texts leads you to an idea; that idea in turn leads you to the development of an essay; as you develop the essay, you will have to select evidence from those written texts to support and substantiate your idea; the cited evidence must be accompanied by your reflections so that your readers will understand the relationship between the cited evidence and the idea that you are developing in the essay. The work begins and ends with those written texts (and what you decide to do with them in your essay).

RHETORICAL CONSIDERATIONS FOR PERSUASIVE, TEXT-BASED ESSAYS

Writing a persuasive text-based essay like the one that Claudia wrote depends on your knowing a few important rhetorical principles; each of these principles has been set forth within this chapter. To review the principles, follow these questions to analyze the decisions Claudia made during the writing process.

1. Find three different moments in Claudia's essay when she either quotes a source or summarizes it. Which seems most effective to you, summary or quoting? Explain.

2. Consider the relationship between Claudia's reflection and the evidence she presents. Account for what makes the reflection effective.

3. Go to the sixth paragraph of Claudia's final essay on page 57. Refer as well to the first two paragraphs of Rodriguez's essay, "Late Victorians," on page 124. Revise Claudia's paragraph, keeping her argument within the paragraph intact. Try only to improve her selection of evidence from Rodriguez's essay and her reflections about that evidence. Clarity and persuasion are your goals.

4. Check the work that you did in the previous question to ensure that you retained Claudia's argument intact. Ensure that the paragraph you revised follows logically from the previous paragraph in her essay and flows logically into the subsequent paragraph.

5. How many connections with other texts does Claudia make in her essay? Which do you consider most meaningful and why?

6. How does Claudia make use of her own experiences in this essay? What would the essay lose if you deleted all of those pieces of evidence? Explain. Do you consider her use of experience effective? Explain.

7. Consider the last three sentences of the first paragraph as Claudia's formulation of her essay's idea. Find three other reflective passages in the essay that clarify for you what Claudia means by "our mind's home." Explain the relationship among these parts of the essay.

8. Consider Claudia's reflections in the final paragraph (conclusion) of her essay. How well do those reflections bring together the various aspects of her idea from the middle of the essay? Explain.

This picture by Thomas Roma is titled "Find the Dog."
It first appeared in Doubletake magazine.
Did the composition of the picture make it
difficult to see the dog before you knew the title?

AN INTRODUCTION TO VISUAL UNDERSTANDING

4

The poet William Carlos Williams often told a story about a woman who was preparing to buy a painting. As Williams tells it, the woman, an important customer, pointed to the lower part of the picture and asked the salesman, Alanson Hartpence, "What is all this down here in the corner?"

According to Williams, Hartpence inspected the area carefully and said to her, "That, Madam, I should say, is paint."

In telling this story, Williams was making a point about the painting as an object. When confronted with something visual, we can, like the woman, get bogged down in the details and lose sight of the whole. We can forget that we're looking at an object that calls for us to experience it in its entirety.

Take, for example, the picture at the right.

A quick glance, and you might not know exactly what you're looking at. Though you might recognize the rough bark of a tree, you might not see the moth that is resting on it. By choosing a tree with coloring and texture similar to its own, the moth blends in and camouflages itself. To see the moth, you must look carefully, noting its shadow and seeing the white spots behind its head and antennae.

At this point we can return to the terms **idea, evidence,** and **essay.** We can put together the Williams anecdote and the image of the tree bark and moth, and ask ourselves what idea begins to emerge from connecting them. It seems to be an idea about the complexity of seeing, of how seeing anything at all is not a simple or singular matter, and that we need to interpret what we are looking at, the evidence, to seek out our ideas. We need to find what to look for—to discover the idea—if we are to really see something, after all.

Williams's anecdote and the visual illustration of the tree bark and moth together serve as partial but not complete evidence for this evolving idea.

KEEPING YOUR EYES OPEN AND LEARNING TO SEE

In her essay "Seeing," Annie Dillard discusses this dilemma of looking but not seeing. She describes a moment when she was walking in late summer and came upon an Osage orange tree. Almost immediately, a hundred birds flew away, and then, when she walked closer, another hundred ascended, and then another. At first, these birds were "invisible." She wonders "how could so many hide in the tree" without her seeing them. Throughout the rest of her essay, she contemplates that question, concluding that there are different kinds of seeing. One can see like a lover, a seeing that involves a "letting go" and one can see like a specialist, a seeing that requires detailed knowledge. Both require keeping your eyes open.

Rudolf Arnheim, a famous art historian and professor of the psychology of art at Harvard University, explains that children develop the habit of using their eyes to learn early in their life. We learn to recognize our parents' faces early, and we learn quickly to sort out those items and people that matter to us. One of the key methods of learning involves categorizing, a process that led some German psychologists to develop a set of principles they called *gestalt*.

The German word *gestalt* is often translated as "whole" or "form," and the main idea is that in order to understand what we see, we find ways to categorize the parts or elements. In other words, "the whole is more than the sum of its parts." Simply put, the mind will try to find the simplest solution to a problem, looking for cues that help organize items into groups with characteristics in common. This method of looking at things helps to explain how people perceive and organize visual data to help them cope with the complex visual world.

In the process of continuing our reflection on the idea of seeing with Dillard and Arnheim as our guides, we begin to develop a more complex idea about seeing. This chapter, in fact, is just such an essay of understanding how to see. Putting Dillard's idea and evidence together with the idea and evidence from Arnheim's "gestalt," adding in our ideas about the Williams anecdote and the image of the tree bark with the moth, we continue to analyze *seeing*. Dillard encourages us to think about how differently lovers and specialists see, not only how they see different things when they look at anything, but also how the very act of seeing, the process of noticing and recording and responding to what they see, differs. Think, for example, of how a doctor looks at a child patient and how a parent looks at the child—one professionally, the other emotionally. And consider the language we use to describe the doctor's looking at a patient in comparison with the language we use to describe someone in love looking at that same patient. The doctor "examines" and "studies" the patient and looks specifically at a particular part of the patient's anatomy—a broken arm, for example, or a diseased breast, whereas the lover sees the beloved patient as a whole and embraces the beloved in a loving gaze rather than examining him or her in a clinical stare.

The lover sees the whole patient, the "gestalt" of the beloved; the doctor looks at only one particular part needing medical attention. Yet both the doctor's and the lover's ways of looking are important; their varied ways of seeing provide complementary perspectives. When we look at images, as we do throughout this book, we look at the image as a whole, as well as at its individual parts. This chapter looks at individual parts of an image in order to gain a sense of the whole, in order to better understand the image as a whole. We also reflect on the relationship of the parts to one another. This alternation of seeing and thinking we develop through our writing. Each of these activities—seeing, thinking, and writing—stimulates and reinforces the others.

Thinking about these and other complexities of "seeing" is the route we take to develop an essay that explores the topic and evidence and discovers the idea through the process of the essay rather than an essay that already knows exactly what it has to say at the outset of writing. You have seen examples of essays and the process by which they developed laid out in Chapters 1 through 3. We will show you another student essay at the end of this chapter, but first, let us explore some strategies for developing visual understanding.

A STRATEGY FOR VISUAL UNDERSTANDING

We will borrow from these theories to help you learn to make sense of what you see and then explain it to others. Communicating what you see and feel isn't always easy. For example, how often have you seen a sunset or a photo of a tragedy and felt something deeply but not been able to articulate exactly what you felt or why? The goal of this chapter, therefore, is twofold: to outline a process that will help you categorize and therefore understand what you see, and to provide a vocabulary that you can use to explain what you see and feel to others. In so doing, you will also begin to understand the rhetorical purposes and functions of visual images (or visual "texts" as they are sometimes called), recognizing that the artist or composer may be suggesting ideas through the design, often "spoken visually" through layout, form, shape, or color.

When you look at things, you most often have reactions first and the need to understand those reactions second. After understanding your reaction, you may explain or share what you have seen and felt with others. Thus, this process involves three activities: looking and responding, analyzing, and communicating.

In essence, these three activities are the essential elements of a strategy for visual understanding.

LOOKING AND RESPONDING

Although we begin in infancy to recognize, categorize, and make sense of what we see, learning to see is a lifelong process, and it involves different kinds of responses, both emotional and intellectual. Seeing is a physical and psychological process; you have a response to what you see, and the response is caused, in part, by the characteristics of the image. In "Seeing," Dillard describes the responses of blind patients who, after operations, are newly sighted: "to one patient, a human hand, unrecognized, is 'something bright and then holes.' Shown a bunch of grapes, a boy calls out, 'It is dark, blue, and shiny.'" These newly sighted people respond fully to the objects they see, articulating physical characteristics while experiencing emotions. They don't have a complete set of categories to use yet, but they try to verbalize what they experience using those categories they have begun to acquire (color and value, for instance).

Because we want you to see and respond to the thing itself, our strategy begins by asking you to look at images and respond to them holistically, focusing on the emotions you experience. Does the image convey peacefulness, abject misery, fear, solitude, or joy? Does it reflect a fleeting moment or one that was representative and lasting?

Look at two examples.

Kevin Carter's Pulitzer Prize-winning photograph above of a starving Sudanese child and a vulture in a drought-ridden field usually evokes an immediate emotional response in viewers. Photographs such as this one often are easy to talk about because the subject matter is so clear; people usually sense a story associated with the elements in the picture.

Other kinds of images require more effort. Take, for instance, the photograph of trees in Yosemite shown to the right. Here, there are no human actors, and thus no

drama. But there is a composition that evokes a response. The question, however, is why? What about the image evokes those feelings?

To answer this question, you need to consider a language of sensory descriptions. What did you notice about the picture of the trees? Their leaves or branches? The shape and size of their trunks? The angles at which they grow? How are they different from other trees? What about the season and the weather? What other elements are present in the picture?

Once you have a general impression of the image and what it means, the second step is to move beyond the sensory and emotional and talk about the composition and the visual cues present, many of which may have been intended by the artist or photographer. In the following sections you will find some ideas for analyzing and talking about images.

ANALYZING IMAGES: CATEGORIZING TO MAKE SENSE OF WHAT YOU SEE

Analyzing images is similar to reading a verbal text. Like written or spoken language, images have a structure, sometimes even a narrative quality. Whenever we attempt to make sense of what we see, we usually observe similarities and differences and establish relationships with other things that we know. In other words, we try to understand the language of visual texts—sometimes without even knowing it.

Talking about images requires that we be more observant, be willing to experience what we see, and then take time to analyze using a method and a language designed specifically for visual learning. The vocabulary of this language is based upon perception and includes terms such as *focal point, figure-ground contrast, similarity, proximity, orientation, texture, color,* and *shape*. These terms will give us a common language to use to talk, and ultimately to write, about images.

FOCAL POINT AND EMPHASIS

People tend to categorize the elements or figures in a composition depending on their visual properties. Usually there is at least one central figure, and that is often called the **focal point.** Officially defined as the point at which a concentrated light beam demonstrates its smallest diameter, a focal point is the spot where your eyes immediately go when viewing an image—the point on which your eyes focus. When an image has been composed by someone such as a photographer or designer, your attention is drawn to this point for a reason. Determining what you perceive to be the focal point will help guide your understanding of the image.

Look at the group of dots below. Your eye probably moves directly to the red dot near the center, almost as if drawn by a magnet. It does so because the red dot is the object of emphasis, the focal point. Look at the image again briefly and then turn away. How many red dots do you remember? How many black? You will likely remember that there is one red dot, but not that there are 48 black ones. The reason is that human beings tend to remember what is different, unusual, or unexpected.

Now look at the photograph of a scene that appears to be in a public square. In this picture, there are close to twenty people gathered, although they all do not seem to be together. Our eye is drawn to the white, circular object in the center, around which people seem to be congregating. Its position, which is very close to the center of the photograph as well as almost in the center of the octagon, makes it the focal point. So does the contrast created between the object and the darker, tiled floor beneath it.

Why would the artist focus on this white object so explicitly, and why from an angle above it? Perhaps he wants the viewer to see a natural symmetry between the octagon and the white object, which appears to be a fountain or some kind of washing station. Perhaps he wants us to feel the tension of being both drawn in and propelled outward—while it is clear that people are gathering around the white object, they also seem to radiate from it, almost in an octagonal pattern. In essence, the people in the photograph seem to be extensions of the points of the octagon. Perhaps the photographer is trying to say that shapes, like the octagon, the square, and the circle, have a powerful effect on us. Or perhaps the reason is even simpler: to show off the beauty of this intricately patterned floor that almost has the appearance of a flower surrounded by a number of buzzing bees. Usually a reader of a visual text cannot come to a conclusive analysis of an image based solely on the focal point. However, unless the reader takes the focal point into consideration, there will be no conclusive analysis.

FIGURE-GROUND CONTRAST

One of the most important elements of analysis is known as **figure-ground contrast,** which is the design principle that emphasizes the difference between what's in front (the **figure**) and what's in back (called the **ground,** as in *background*). The figure is usually the most important thing in the picture, and the composer often deliberately frames the image to display the most important thing in front. Often the figure is also the focal point.

Because people tend to organize what they see into figure and ground, considering the different relationships can help you understand the context. An easy way to imagine this principle is to think of a blank sheet of white writing paper on a smooth, highly polished mahogany desktop. The paper would be the figure, and the desk would be the ground.

There can be several levels in a discussion of figure-ground. For example, the desk is positioned on a cream-colored carpet, and as such, it is the figure and the carpet the ground. In the photograph to the left, the figure is the circular, white object, and the ground is the intricately tiled floor. You might argue, however, that the octagon (and everything contained within it) is also a figure, and the shapes surrounding it (the square formed by the tiles and the rectangle of the actual photograph) are the ground.

Figure-ground contrast plays an important role in all of our reading activities because contrast helps to establish importance. Take, for instance, a paragraph from a memo that was written very early on in the Space Shuttle *Challenger*'s performance testing, seven years before it blew up just 73 seconds after launch.

> The visit on February 1, 1979, to Precision Rubber Products Corporation by Mr.
> Eudy and Mr. Ray was very well received. Company officials, Mr. Howard Gillette,

Vice President for Technical Direction, Mr. John Hoover, Vice President for Engineering, and Mr. Gene Hale, Design Engineer attended the meeting and were presented with the SRM clevis joint seal test data by Mr. Eudy and Mr. Ray. After considerable discussion, company representatives declined to make immediate recommendations because of the need for more time to study the data. They did, however, voice concern for the design, stating that the SRM O-ring extrusion gap was larger than that covered by their experience. They also stated that more tests should be performed with the present design. Mr. Hoover promised to contact MSFC for further discussions within a few days. Mr. Gillette provided Mr. Eudy and Mr. Ray with the names of two consultants who may be able to help. We are indebted to the Precision Rubber Products Corporation for the time and effort being expended by their people in support of this problem, especially since they have no connection with the project.

The central idea of this paragraph, the fact that the "O-ring extrusion gap was larger than that covered by their experience," is buried in the center of the paragraph, and, as a result, had very little impact on the readers. If you were a busy NASA executive and were skimming this document, you might have disregarded it because the paragraph (and the memo itself) seems to be part of a trip report about the visit to Precision Rubber Company rather than a memo outlining potential problems with an essential component of the rocket motor booster.

The picture of the camouflaged moth we saw earlier and the figure to the left are, in essence, quite analogous to the NASA memo above. All are examples of what happens when the distinction between figure and ground is blurred.

Adding contrast can help the reader focus and separate the essential from the inessential. If the author of the paragraph had used italics or boldfaced text or had placed the sentence about the O-ring gap at the normal focal point of written text (first or last), he could have created the necessary figure-ground contrast that might have had more impact.

When there is no immediately recognizable contrast, as in the pictures of the moth and the dog, our eyes will keep searching, trying to find recognizable shapes or things we can use to create contrast and therefore meaning and understanding. If you look long enough at the picture of the dog, you'll see that the dog's head seems to be at a crossroads of two darker patches, which direct the eye toward the center of the picture. Once we "see" the dog, however, it is nearly impossible not to do so.

GROUPING: PROXIMITY & SIMILARITY

As psychologists have noted, we make sense of things by categorizing or grouping them together. We talk about "those books" on the shelf and use collective nouns like "a gaggle of geese" or "a parliament of owls," indicating that we are more comfortable representing items in groups rather than individually. Psychological studies in memory also show that we can remember more things in groups than we can individually.

Different relationships tend to give us further information we can use to analyze or read images. We tend to group things in two basic ways: by their relationship in space (**proximity**) or their relationship in size, color, shape, and so on (**similarity**). In the line of dots below, the dots all look alike because they are the same size and are evenly spaced. There is no easy way to differentiate among them.

● ●

However, by changing their physical location (below), we automatically group them by proximity. Now we have six groups of three and one group of six. Close objects, therefore, are perceived as grouped together. Grouping objects together shows a connection, a relationship. The nature of the relationship usually depends on other features of the image.

● ● ●   ● ● ●   ● ● ●   ● ● ●   ● ● ●   ● ● ●   ● ● ● ● ● ●

If, instead of changing their location, we change some of the black dots to red ones, we will begin to group by similarity—black dots and red dots. Elements that share similar features are often perceived as belonging together. Therefore, even though the dots are the same size and distance from one another, the fact that there are similar groupings (red and black) helps us to analyze the intent.

● ●

Similarity is a very effective grouping concept that often is used to create a sense of unity. In the photograph of the white object and the tiled floor, the figures are grouped by virtue of either their location or their color. The three figures in the lower right all wear some white clothing, and of the three figures in the lower left, two are very close to one another, and all three are wearing black. Overall, there are several pockets of interest caused by proximity and similarity. Some of the figures are moving toward the white object, and some seem to be moving away. The figures wearing very dark clothing seem to be turned away from the white object, while those wearing white seem drawn to it, almost like a magnet. Also, at the points of the octagon, there are what appear to be white, circular shapes, but within the octagon are black lines that tie or link these white shapes together.

We tend to order things by size, shape, and texture as well. Shapes work for different purposes: to convey meaning, to provide balance, or to represent the fundamental form of an object.

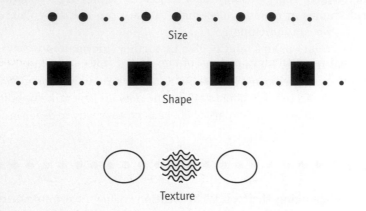

Size

Shape

Texture

COLOR

Most people respond immediately to color, often in an emotional way. Usually, the brighter the color, the more powerful its effects. These effects are often culturally based. In our culture, for instance, white is the color of purity and is worn by brides, but in China and Japan, it is the color of mourning. Within cultures and subcultures, the meaning of a color can change; for doctors, blue often is associated with death, but for corporate executives, it has a connotation of strength.

Color can focus our attention (as in the group of dots with the red one in the center), create contrast, appeal to emotions, and help to communicate nuances of meaning. According to Jan White, an award-winning designer and expert on color, it can "increase the velocity of comprehension [and] help to establish identity and character." Some colors remind us of warm things like fire and sun. Some colors remind us of cool things like water and forests. A red face might indicate embarrassment; a green face, envy; a blue face, cold or sickness; a purple face, rage; and a pink one, good health.

CONTINUATION

The principle of "good continuation" focuses on the belief that elements that suggest a continued visual line will be grouped together. This is a primary principle behind how we "see" images in the night sky, such as the zodiac signs and the Big Dipper. The following examples help illustrate how viewers will follow movement through an image and create connections.

In the figure on the left, instead of two dotted lines or four curves, we see a curvy letter X. In the figure on the right, we follow the smiley faces down and across the page and see what appears to be a backward check mark or a letter *L* leaning back.

LINE

Lines also help to provide a sense of motion or movement. Artists use lines to create edges and outline objects. The direction of a line can also convey mood. Consider the images below. Horizontal lines, such as those in the picture to the left, create a sense of calm and equilibrium, while vertical lines suggest movement, and diagonal lines can create stress. Finally, wavy lines (as on the right) often imply softness, grace, flow, or change.

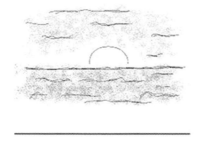

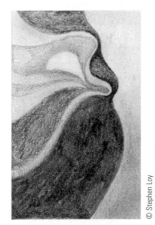

© Stephen Loy

CLOSURE

Human beings seem to have an innate need to complete pictures; according to psychologists, it may be part of our survival instinct. Thus, when we see incomplete figures such as the "F" in the word "Frames" on the next page, our minds create familiar patterns by filling in the missing information. In the group of images on the right, for instance, we continue to see a circle, even when only looking at the far right image. Nancy Brown, a commercial photographer, explains that artists will use closure to "encourage the viewer's eyes to move . . . in predictable and desirable ways" to complete forms. Leaving information out creates interest, generates a tension that contributes to the narrative quality of the image, and promotes viewer participation.

FRAMES

NARRATION OR STORY

Once we have a clear method that will help us visually distinguish objects, we can look at the image as a whole and consider whether the image tells a story. In a verbal story, the narrator's voice mediates between the reader and action. The story is shaped by the narrator's use of language to present a particular point of view. The themes that emerge can be implicit, as the author's beliefs affect the presentation of the characters, or explicit, as the author selects social concerns and conventions to which she wishes to draw the reader's attention. In an image, the elements are arranged so that the main focal point first attracts the viewer's attention. Each subsequent element, or minor point, creates relationships.

CONTEXT

Responding to images, noting what you see, and classifying and grouping elements will help you decode, explain, and understand the images you see. That said, keeping your eyes open isn't sufficient. Annie Dillard explains that sometimes one needs to be knowledgeable, claiming that "specialists can find the most incredibly well-hidden things." In order to explain your reaction, sometimes you have to think about the context of the image. Aldous Huxley once said, "the more you know, the more you see." Learning more about the world and applying what you learn will enable you, like the knowledgeable herpetologist in Dillard's essay, to find the three bags of snakes even when others claim there are none present. Like an experienced observer, it will enable you to understand that the little piles of cut stems you stumble across while walking in the field are the result of mice cutting down grass to reach the seeds at the head.

"The God Abandons Anthony," a poem by the Greek poet Cavafy, illustrates how contextual knowledge can assist in understanding. The poem begins with the lines, "When suddenly, at midnight, you hear / an invisible procession going by / with exquisite music, voices, / don't mourn your luck that's failing now." Most readers will see immediately that something is amiss; the narrator has as much said that Anthony's luck is "failing." What many readers will not know, unless they learn more about Anthony and his beliefs, is that Anthony believed he had the divine protection of the god Dionysius, but that protection is withdrawn, which leads to his demise. Edward Hirsch, an American poet and teacher who has written about this poem, offers this kind of background information and explains to his readers that unless they know more about Greek and Roman customs, they will not know that midnight is known as the "epiphanic hour of revelation," and this procession is indeed foreshadowing Anthony's downfall.

A similar principle works with our understanding of visual images. If you know that the photograph of the white object on page 72 was actually taken of a fountain in a courtyard outside of the tomb of Moulay Idriss II, a Moroccan ruler from the ninth century, you might reasonably conclude that the photographer wanted to make a point about the appeal of the white fountain and its water, or perhaps even about the intricate relationship of religion and daily life in Morocco. You might also guess that the people in the photograph have just come from or are going to a religious service. Even if we do not have the background or contextual information, the postures of the people, in particular the woman in pink who appears to be holding a child, and the fact that many of the figures appear to be covering their heads, help us to sense that there is some kind of ritual involved.

In many cases, an image will not provide all the background information necessary to fully understand the context, and it will be up to you to "read" the image's other elements to infer the context. As when reading written texts, your conclusions will often be limited by what is in the picture. Not knowing the social context of the photograph, you must rely on your own careful reading of what the other elements tell you.

THE WHOLE COMPOSITION

Learning to see and understand, then, is a process that involves both response and analysis. It also involves a recognition that the image you're seeing is composed, that it is put together or created by someone to communicate or create an effect in the viewer. This effect may be simply an attempt to recreate an emotional or intellectual response that the composer experienced, or it may be an attempt to persuade you to take action (for example, advertisements for products that hope to encourage you to buy). Knowing more about how to see will help you understand these images and their intended effects.

Take, for instance, a recent advertisement by DaimlerChrysler on page 80. Few readers of the *Time* magazine in which the ad appeared will doubt that the ad's purpose is to convince them to purchase a car, in this case the "redesigned Chrysler Concorde." However, readers don't necessarily see the many ways in which the designer used visual effects to create desire.

First, the designer uses the focal point, the car itself, which is seen through a closed set of venetian blinds. The person in the ad (in this case, the reader, since the reader occupies the same vantage point from behind the same desk) is peeking through the blinds at this car; it is an object of some attraction, and perhaps the obstructed view is meant to titillate. The color silver, a color of power and money, is repeated throughout the ad: in the clock (indicating that it is time to buy or time to drive), in the computer, the handheld PDA, the pen, the picture frame of the young child, and the logo at the far bottom right. All of these objects are objects of power, functionality, and also familiarity. The proximity of these items to the car highlights these connections.

Figure-ground contrast occurs throughout, with the two most visible instances being the figure of the car on the pavement and the figure of the notebook paper on the desk pad (or the pen on the notebook paper). The paper has no writing, indicating that there is no work left to do or that the car, pointed at by the pen—an example of continuation—has caused us to put our work down and think about buying/driving.

The designers use contrast and similarity/repetition as well—between the silver and the white of the blinds, the white of the document on the screen of the silver laptop, the white of the screen against the silver of the PDA, the reflected light off the car itself, the pad on which the silver pen rests, the white of the child's dress against the silver frame, and the white of the brand name compared to the silver of the logo. There is also the repetition of the sunglasses against the white of the desk and the dark windows of the car against the bright color of the car and the blinds.

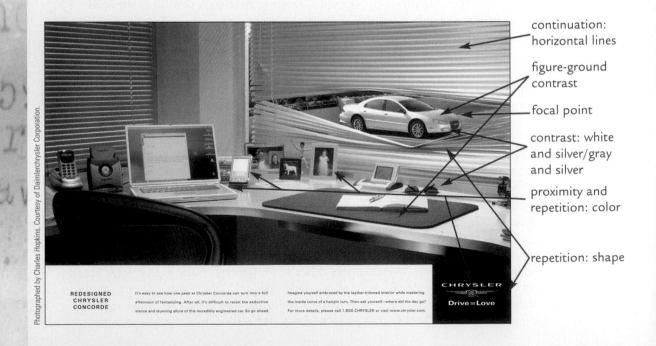

continuation: horizontal lines

figure-ground contrast

focal point

contrast: white and silver/gray and silver

proximity and repetition: color

repetition: shape

The proximity of the sunglasses and the car, amplified by the fact that the bottom of the opening in the blinds points toward the sunglasses (another use of continuation), highlights the connections between the car and the owner, who is presumably the person peeking and, by extension, the reader of the ad.

The horizontal lines of the blinds are soothing, and yet there is a break pointing toward the clock, the pad, and the sunglasses indicating that it is time to put work away and put on the sunglasses and go driving. The position, or lines, of the open book is echoed by both the open blinds and the Chrysler logo and words "Drive=Love," which is where the eye finally ends.

The reader is also asked to associate the family with the car; there are pictures of several children and a dog, and the car has four doors, so that even though it is somewhat sexy and inviting, it has a practical, safe association as well. The car is both "seductive" and "roomy"; the reader "can't take [his/her] eyes off of it." Somehow, the car will *complete* the picture. At the bottom of the ad, we are driven off the page, out of the office, toward the car and love.

Another, very different, example of a composition is the picture of President George W. Bush giving a speech at Mount Rushmore in August of 2002. In this picture, the focal point is the president, and he is the figure in contrast with the ground of the monument itself (which is the figure in contrast with the ground of the sky). By focusing on the president's head and looking up at him, the photographer has, through his angle and composition choices, positioned him as if to suggest that he were another figure in the monument (an example of effective uses of repetition and proximity), thus suggesting that President Bush is somehow similar to past presidents memorialized on the mountain. Notice also the president's deep-set, shadowed eyes that repeat or echo the eyes of the figures in the monument (uses of similarity). Notice also how President Bush's head juts into the sky as if it, too, were part of the figure of the monument.

figure-ground contrast

focal point

color contrast

repetition or similarity (shape & size)

continuation

© AP/Wide World Photos/Ken Lambert

The photographer has used continuation to direct our attention to the president. The microphones act as arrows pointing toward him, and Washington's eyes seem to be looking directly at him, as if he were his son or heir.

The use of contrast in terms of color highlights the living president. He is the most colorful figure, particularly when compared with the white granite of the monument. The president's blue tie echoes the blue sky, adding vitality to his figure.

Overall, the photographer or media consultant has done a wonderful job of *re*presenting President Bush. In essence, the photograph makes an argument that President Bush is a strong leader and an effective communicator. Under the approving eyes of some of our country's greatest leaders, the photograph argues, this president plans to continue in their tradition.

COMMUNICATING WHAT YOU SEE

Thus far, we've asked you to look at images, respond, and then analyze what you see, relying on terms that focus on perception. Now comes the more difficult part, which is to communicate what you see and feel to others so that they, too, can make sense of those same images. Because most art is beyond language—often more about experience, perception, and feeling than it is about words—it can be difficult to communicate what you see. You now have a strategy and a vocabulary that will enable you to offer perspectives and insight that, though colored by your own individual set of experiences, can still have relevance for others.

QUESTIONS FOR READING IMAGES

- What do you feel or experience as you view the image?

- Where does your eye go and why?

- What do you think are the key elements or features of the image? How do they contribute to what you see and feel?

- Look for elements in the image that are positioned close together. What connections do you see between/among those elements?

- Are there any elements in the image that seem similar (shape, texture, size, color, etc.)? Explain the effects of those elements on your response to the image.

- When you examine the image and your emotional response, how do the color(s) or degrees of shading contribute to that response?

- How do your own experiences or knowledge affect your reading of the image? Think about the image in terms of context: personal, historical, technical, or cultural.

- Is there a story or a narrative embedded in the image?

A SAMPLE STUDENT ESSAY

Ryan Pollack, a student at Virginia Polytechnic Institute and State University, wrote the paper below in response to the photograph of the vulture and the Sudanese child on page 70. As you will see in his paper, Ryan went through the three steps of looking and responding, analyzing, and communicating. His paper is the result. As you read it, pay particular attention to how he uses his analysis to make a larger point.

Make note, as well, of how Ryan Pollack develops his idea about seeing and feeling with evidence from the image itself. Be sure you can identify and explain his idea, along with the different kinds of evidence he provides in developing his essay.

Pollack 1

Ryan Pollack

Professor Weiss

English 101

April 18, 2006

Visible Feelings

When I first laid eyes on Kevin Carter's photograph of the vulture and the starving Sudanese child, I was immediately hit by several strong reactions. Taken in 1993 for *Life* magazine, the photograph first caused me to experience shock, then curiosity, then sadness. However, the strongest emotion I felt was guilt. I had never seen this picture before, and only vaguely knew what the subject matter was. I knew little to nothing about the situation surrounding the picture, who had taken it, or why, but I felt guilty that I am as privileged as I am, and that this child may not even be alive anymore. I found myself asking why I felt this way

Pollack 2

and began to analyze how the image produced these emotions. Though the photograph depicts what anyone would agree is a horrifying situation—an emaciated Sudanese girl being eyed by a lurking vulture—it is Kevin Carter's artistic choices in this photograph that ultimately shaped my reactions.

The child was the first part of the picture I saw. With her head bowed as if in acknowledgment of Sudan's terrible economic and political situation, the child serves as a starting point at which the viewer can begin to experience more feelings about the picture. By placing her so near the center, Carter decides to make the starving child one of the main focal points of this picture, immediately emphasizing the severity of Sudan's food crisis by personifying it. The child, with her skinny legs and distended belly, instantly produces a shocking and sympathetic reaction.

In my case, the sadness and despair I felt were heightened even more by the placement of the two figures (the child and the vulture) against the background. Almost the entire background is taken up by muddy-hued greens and browns, providing a stark contrast that causes the dark brown figures of the vulture and the child to stand out. By bringing his two main subjects to the forefront of the image, Carter creates a sense of immediacy that leaves no trace of doubt; I couldn't help but feel drawn in. Carter chose to narrow his image to include only the child and the vulture, leaving out any distracting element and using the muted background to his advantage. Since the two figures stand out so prominently, my

Pollack 3

emotions of shock and guilt about the image and the situation quickly rose to the forefront of my own mind.

In another instance, Carter's choice of emphasizing contrasts, whether incidental or not, in the image also drew my eye to different parts of the photograph—first, to the form of the white necklace around the child's dark brown neck. While white traditionally symbolizes relief or peace, the child's bowed head and neck—yielding to the gravity of her situation while her predator's head remains erect and alert—only highlights the vulture's arrogance. The bird seems almost to be celebrating a victory with its white, prominent beak pointing directly at its prey. The whiteness of the vulture's beak is emphasized much like the whiteness of the girl's necklace, yet contrasted in their shapes—the beak, a triangle; the necklace, circles.

The straight, downward-sloping line that can be drawn between the vulture and the child offers no obstructions should the vulture choose to strike, and though Carter could have taken this photograph from any angle, the shot that he chose illustrates the relationship of power and helplessness. The placement of the vulture above the child suggests power and dominance; the child's position, crouched and lower, suggests submission and even defeat. The image suggests that this child has no control over her situation, that she is at risk. The traditional roles of human as predator and animal as prey have been ironically reversed in this image.

Pollack 4

Perhaps even worse, the similarity of the vulture and the child seems to suggest that—for this child—life (represented by the strong, upright vulture) and death (represented by the weak, bent child) are two sides of the same coin. Both figures are dark brown. Both are about the same size. Again, Carter captures these similarities by the angle at which the photograph was shot. The vulture and the child, though at different heights, are parallel to one another, drawing a distinct connection of one to the other, child to death. Although one may briefly outshine the other, the existence of this Sudanese child is but a tiny part in a brutal cycle.

Beyond my reactions, and beyond the composition of the picture intended to produce those reactions, it is ultimately the story the picture tells that breaks the heart. But what is the story? Is the vulture ready to attack? Is it gloating in triumph over the weakened child? Is it hungrily eyeing a potential morsel of food? Is it resting for a moment on its way to a more pertinent destination? Will this child survive the encounter with the vulture? Will she admit defeat, lie down, and die? Will she rise from the ground and chase the vulture away? Or will she simply ignore the presence of this predatory bird and continue as she is—hunched, hungry, and beaten? The photograph will never tell us, as Carter has captured only this brief and stunning moment; yet his treatment of the subject will shock viewers for years.

FOR FURTHER READING ABOUT GESTALT, VISUAL DESIGN, AND COLOR

Arnheim, Rudolph. *Visual Thinking.* Berkeley: U of California P, 1969.

Berger, Arthur Asa. *Seeing Is Believing: An Introduction to Visual Communication.* Mountain View: Mayfield, 1997.

Berger, John. *Ways of Seeing.* London: BBC, 1972.

Dondis, Donis A. *A Primer of Visual Literacy.* Cambridge: MIT, 1973.

Eysenck, Michael, and Mark Keane. *Cognitive Psychology: A Student's Handbook.* London: Erlbaum, 1990.

Heller, Stephen. *Design Literacy (Continued): Understanding Graphic Design.* New York: Allworth, 1999.

McKim, Robert. *Experiences in Visual Thinking.* Monterey: Brooks/Cole, 1972.

Mason, Kathy. *Going Beyond Words.* Tucson: Zephyr, 1991.

Meggs, Phillip. *The Language of Graphic Design.* Indianapolis: Wiley, 1992.

Messaris, Paul. *Visual Literacy: Image, Mind, and Reality.* Boulder: Westview, 1994.

White, Jan V. *Color for the Electronic Age.* New York: Watson-Guptil, 1990.

Williams, Robin. *The Non-Designer's Design Book.* 2nd ed. Berkeley: Peachpit, 2003.

Images have the power to move us,
TO STIMULATE OUR MINDS.
*They almost always cause us to tell ourselves
(and perhaps others) a story. Is the story here
a story of destruction or preservation?*

5

STORIES

Joan Didion, in her essay "The White Album," says that she tells herself stories "in order to live," that stories impose "a narrative line on disparate images," on the "shifting phantasmagoria which is our actual experience." Think briefly about those disparate images that appear around us. We are bombarded by images. Some have been carefully designed and packaged by the retailers and merchants of the world to tell us how we ought to look, what we ought to eat, how we ought to respond to an event, how to rest, relax, travel, get along with others, entertain ourselves.

Other images are simply there, always have been: the grove of trees outside the window, the hidden lake, the haunting man or woman walking the beach late at night, the echoing sound of the owl out there just beyond the edge of the woods. Because the images are so pervasive in our culture, we can become insensitive to them and to other images that can tell us so much about who we are, what we are becoming, what we have become, what kind of world we actually live in. Perhaps our calling as writers is to learn to pay closer attention to these revealing images.

What Didion had in mind about telling stories in order to live is crucial to our understanding of the work we do as writers and to the lives we live. We reckon with and transform the chaos of our lives by paying attention to those disparate images and by imposing narrative order on those images, telling stories about what we see, what we experience, even what we read. Stories told, or committed to paper, lead to clarification, or understanding. They stop the chaos momentarily so that we can examine ourselves and what goes on around us.

E. M. Forster, a British novelist, clarifies the causal relationship between storytelling and understanding when he explains the difference between story and plot in fiction. "The king died and then the queen died is a story," according to Forster. One event merely follows another. "The king died and then the queen died of grief" establishes causality and a time sequence—it constitutes a plot. In other words, the story is told in such a way that listeners begin to understand the relationship among its parts; they begin to understand how one thing is related to another, how one thing follows from another.

Writers tell stories for a variety of reasons: to account for something that happened, to illustrate and clarify a complicated concept, to help create and develop an interesting idea for an essay, to enliven a piece of writing—or simply, as the Elizabethan poet Sydney might have suggested, to instruct and delight. The effectiveness of our storytelling depends, of course, on our effective use of language. We attempt to capture with words the disordered world outside our heads. That elusive and mysterious world—our experience of it—is there for the taking, but we have to try to pin it down with words so that others can see as we see. Such capturing is an act of ownership and translation.

British novelist Virginia Woolf says that if we look back on the events of our lives, even the most recent ones, we will not be able to recall much of what happened to us. She calls these stretches of lost time "non-being" and contrasts these periods with moments in time that embed themselves in our memory and last. Such moments need not be associated with big events—birth, death, war—but might well be what others, on first glance, would consider small and insignificant: the remembrance of a flower on a mother's dress, a snippet of conversation, a haunting smell. Underneath these moments, or within them, we can, if we look closely, discover something of the vastness of the universe. But we must begin always with the small particulars: the moment itself.

For the storyteller such moments and their particulars are full of potential. They carry significance that must be captured, and the scene must be re-created so that the reader can come to know what the storyteller knows, feel what the storyteller felt at the moment. Those compelling moments and images of experience carry within them the seeds of understanding. Didion may have gotten it just right; we tell those stories in order to live and to better understand our lives.

CONVERSING WITH IMAGES

Our work in this Cluster will focus on learning to see and read and collaborate with selected images from both the real world and the world of art. The underlying assumption behind this work is this: images, seriously considered, can tell us a great deal about ourselves and our culture. Images evoke stories—our own stories about what we see in them—which, in turn, lead us to ideas. Two of the writers we consider reveal how metaphorical language can lead us from the known (from the particular details of our experience) to an understanding of something larger than the details themselves, something about principles and ideas that govern our lives—sometimes without our knowing it. Another of the writers worries that in this electronic age we might be losing sight altogether of the visible, of that so-called real world that we encounter every day of our lives. Under the influence of these writers and the images selected for consideration, you will be investigating the revealing interplay between those images, the language you use to account for them, and the ideas you discover in them.

Mark Doty (b. 1953)

Mark Doty is the author of six books of poems and three nonfiction books, including the acclaimed *Still Life with Oysters and Lemons* (2001). He teaches in the graduate program at the University of Houston but divides his time between there and Provincetown, Massachusetts. His books have won the National Book Critics' Circle Award, Britain's T. S. Eliot Prize, the PEN/Martha Albrand Award for first book of nonfiction, and the *Los Angeles Times* Book Award for Poetry. He has also received fellowships from the National Endowment of the Arts, and the Guggenheim, Rockefeller, and Whiting Foundations. His nonfiction shows us how to bring lived experiences to bear on the rigorous but eloquent analysis of images.

SOULS ON ICE

In this short piece, Doty reveals how he converted an ordinary experience into an extraordinary poem. As he investigates his own process of composing, he reveals how image, metaphor, and idea work in his imagination to create a haunting poem about the value of the collective (a community, a group of friends, the larger culture) in times of loss and mourning.

1   In the Stop 'n Shop in Orleans, Massachusetts, I was struck by the elegance of the mackerel in the fresh-fish display. They were rowed and stacked, brilliant against the white of the crushed ice; I loved how black and glistening the bands of dark scales were, and the prismed sheen of the patches between, and their shining flat eyes. I stood and looked at them for a while, just paying attention while I leaned on my cart—before I remembered where I was and realized that I was standing in someone's way.

Our metaphors go on ahead of us, they know before we do. And thank goodness for that, for if I were dependent on other ways of coming to knowledge I think I'd be a very slow study. I need something to serve as a container for emotion and idea, a vessel that can hold what's too slippery or charged or difficult to touch. Will doesn't have much to do with this; I can't choose what's going to serve as a compelling image for me. But I've learned to trust that part of my imagination that gropes forward, feeling its way toward what it needs; to watch for the signs of fascination, the sense of compelled attention (*Look at me,* something seems to say, *closely*) that indicates that there's something I need to attend to. Sometimes it seems to me as if metaphor were the advance guard of the mind; something in us reaches out, into the landscape in front of us, looking for the right vessel, the right vehicle, for whatever will serve.

Driving home from the grocery, I found myself thinking again about the fish, and even scribbled some phrases on an envelope in the car, something about stained glass, soapbubbles, while I was driving. It wasn't long—that same day? the next?—before I was at my desk, trying simply to describe what I had seen. I almost always begin with description, as a way of focusing on that compelling image, the poem's "given." I know that what I can see is just the proverbial tip of the iceberg; if I do my work of study and examination, and if I am lucky, the image which I've been intrigued by will become a metaphor, will yield depth and meaning, will lead me to insight. The goal here is inquiry, the attempt to get at what it is that's so interesting about what's struck me. Because it isn't just beauty; the world is full of lovely things and that in itself wouldn't compel me to write. There's something else, some gravity or charge to this image that makes me need to investigate it.

Exploratory description, then; I'm a scientist trying to measure and record what's seen. The first two sentences of the poem attempt sheer observation, but by the second's list of tropes (abalone, soapbubble skin, oil on a puddle) it's clear to me that these descriptive terms aren't merely there to chronicle the physical reality of the object. Like all descriptions, they reflect the psychic state of the observer; they aren't "neutral," though they might pretend to be, but instead suggest a point of view, a stance toward what is being seen. In this case one of the things suggested by these tropes is interchangeability; if you've seen one abalone shell or prismy soapbubble or psychedelic puddle, you've seen them all.

5   And thus my image began to unfold for me, in the evidence these terms provided, and I had a clue toward the focus my poem would take. Another day, another time in my life, the mackerel might have been metaphor for something else; they might have served as the crux for an entirely different examination. But now I began to see why they mattered for *this* poem; and the sentence that follows commences the poem's investigative process:

> Splendor, and splendor,
> and not a one in any way
>
> distinguished from the other
> —nothing about them
> of individuality.

There's a terrific kind of exhilaration for me at this point in the unfolding of a poem, when a line of questioning has been launched, and the work has moved from evocation to meditation. A direction is coming clear, and it bears within it the energy that the image contained for me in the first pace. Now, I think, we're getting down to it. This élan carried me along through two more sentences, one that considers the fish as replications of the ideal, Platonic Mackerel, and one that likewise imagines them as the intricate creations of an obsessively repetitive jeweler.

Of course my process of unfolding the poem wasn't quite this neat. There were false starts, wrong turnings that I wound up throwing out when they didn't seem to lead anywhere. I can't remember now, because the poem has worked the charm of its craft on my memory; it convinces me that it is an artifact of a process of inquiry. The drama of the poem is its action of thinking through a question. Mimicking a sequence of perceptions and meditation, it tries to make us think that this feeling and thinking and knowing is taking place even as the poem is being written. Which, in a way, it *is*—just not this neatly or seamlessly! A poem is always a *made* version of experience.

Also, needless to say, my poem was full of repetitions, weak lines, unfinished phrases and extra descriptions, later trimmed. I like to work on a computer, because I can type quickly, put everything in, and still read the results later on, which isn't always true of my handwriting. I *did* feel early on that the poem seemed to want to be a short-lined one; I liked breaking the movement of these extended sentences over the clipped line, and the spotlight-bright focus the short line puts on individual terms felt right. "Iridescent, watery," for instance, pleased me as a line-unit, as did this stanza:

> prismatics: think abalone,
> the wildly rainbowed
> mirror of a soapbubble sphere,

Short lines underline sonic textures, heightening tension. The short a's of *prismatics* and *abalone* ring more firmly, as do the o's of *abalone, rainbowed* and *soapbubble*. The rhyme of mirror and sphere at beginning and end of line engages me, and I'm also pleased by the way in which these short lines slow the poem down, parceling it out as it were to the reader, with the frequent pauses introduced by the stanza breaks between tercets adding lots of white space, a meditative pacing.

10   And there, on the jeweler's bench, my poem seemed to come to rest, though it was clear there was more to be done. Some further pressure needed to be placed on the poem's material to force it to yield its depths. I waited a while, I read it over. Again, in what I had already written, the clues contained in image pushed the poem forward.

Soul, heaven . . . The poem had already moved into the realm of theology, but the question that arose ("Suppose we could iridesce . . .") startled me nonetheless, because the notion of losing oneself "entirely in the universe / of shimmer" referred both to these fish and to something quite other, something overwhelmingly close to home. The poem was written some six months after my partner of a dozen years had died of AIDS, and of course everything I wrote—everything I *saw*—was informed by that loss, by the overpowering emotional force of it. Epidemic was the central fact of the community in which I lived. Naively, I hadn't realized that my mackerel were already of a piece with the work I'd been writing for the previous couple of years—poems that wrestled, in one way or another, with the notion of limit, with the line between being someone and no one. What did it mean to be a self, when that self would be lost? To praise the collectivity of the fish, their common identity as "flashing participants," is to make a sort of anti-elegy, to suggest that what matters is perhaps not our individual selves but our brief soldiering in the broad streaming school of humanity—which is composed of us, yes, but also goes on without us.

> The one of a kind, the singular, like
> my dear lover, cannot last.
> And yet the collective life, which is
> also us, shimmers on.

Once I realized the poem's subject-beneath-the-subject, the final stanzas of the poem opened swiftly out from there. The collective momentum of the fish is such that even death doesn't seem to still rob its for-ward movement; the singularity of each fish more or less doesn't really exist, it's "all for all," like the Three Musketeers. I could not have considered these ideas "nakedly," without the vehicle of mackerel to help me think about human identity. Nor, I think, could I have addressed these things without a certain playfulness of tone, which appeared first in the archness of "oily fabulation" and the neologism of "iridesce." It's the blessed permission distance gives that allows me to speak of such things at all; a little comedy can also help to hold terrific anxiety at bay. Thus the "rainbowed school / and its acres of brilliant classrooms" is a joke, but one that's already collapsing on itself, since what is taught there—the limits of "me"—is our hardest lesson. No verb is singular because it is the school that acts, or the tribe, the group, the species; or every verb is singular because the only I there *is* is a we.

The poem held one more surprise for me, which was the final statement—it came as a bit of a shock, actually, and when I'd written it I knew I was done. It's a formulation of the theory that the poem has been moving toward all along: that our glory is not our individuality (much as we long for the Romantic self and its private golden heights) but our commonness. I do not like this idea. I would rather be one fish, sparkling in my own pond, but experience does not bear this out. And so I have tried to convince myself, here, that beauty lies in the whole and that therefore death, the loss of the part, is not so bad—is, in fact, almost nothing. What does our individual disappearance mean—or our love, or our desire—when, as the Marvelettes put it, "There's too many fish in the sea . . . ?"

I find this consoling, strangely, and maybe that's the best way to think of this poem—an attempt at cheering oneself up about the mystery of being both an individual and part of a group, an attempt on the part of the speaker in the poem (me) to convince himself that losing individuality, slipping into the life of the world, could be a good thing. All attempts to console ourselves, I believe, are doomed, because the world is more complicated than we are. Our explanations will fail, but it is our human work to make them. And my beautiful fish, limited though they may be as parable, do help me; they are an image I return to in order to remember, in the face of individual erasures, the burgeoning, good, common life. Even after my work of inquiry, my metaphor may still know more than I do; the bright eyes of those fish gleam on, in memory, brighter than what I've made of them.

A Display of Mackerel

They lie in parallel rows,
on ice, head to tail,
each a foot of luminosity

barred with black bands,
which divide the scales'
radiant sections

like seams of lead
in a Tiffany window.
Iridescent, watery

prismatics: think abalone,
the wildly rainbowed
mirror of a soapbubble sphere,

think sun on gasoline.
Splendor, and splendor,
and not a one in any way

distinguished from the other
—nothing about them
of individuality. Instead

they're *all* exact expressions
of one soul,
each a perfect fulfillment

of heaven's template,
mackerel essence. As if,
after a lifetime arriving

at this enameling, the jeweler's
made uncountable examples,
each as intricate

in its oily fabulation
as the one before.
Suppose we could iridesce,

like these, and lose ourselves
entirely in the universe
of shimmer—would you want

to be yourself only,
unduplicatable, doomed
to be lost? They'd prefer,

plainly, to be flashing participants,
multitudinous. Even now
they seem to be bolting

forward, heedless of stasis.
They don't care they're dead
and nearly frozen,

just as, presumably,
they didn't care that they were living:
all, all for all,

the rainbowed school
and its acres of brilliant classrooms,
in which no verb is singular,

or every one is. How happy they seem,
even on ice, to be together, selfless,
which is the price of gleaming.

READING AND THINKING

1. What does the first paragraph tell you about Doty himself, especially the last sentence?

2. The second paragraph takes us away from Doty and the mackerel. What is the overall purpose of that paragraph in terms of what Doty reveals in the rest of the essay?

3. What do you think Doty means when he tells us that, finally, his poem is just "an artifact of the process of inquiry"? Inquiry about what?

4. What does Doty mean when he says, "A poem is *always* a made version of experience"? Is that true also of an essay, or a short story or an academic article?

5. In his final paragraph Doty speaks of his "beautiful fish" as both an *image* and a *parable*. What is the difference between image and parable? As Doty sums up, what is he trying to make us see by calling our attention to those two concepts?

THINKING AND WRITING

1. In the second paragraph Doty talks about the importance of metaphor. Look *metaphor* up in a dictionary and then put in your own words what Doty and the dictionary tell you about the importance of metaphor in our everyday thinking.

2. Explain why description is so important to Doty as he goes about investigating the implications of his own metaphor.

3. Doty writes: "The one of a kind, the singular, like my dear lover, cannot last. And yet the collective life, which is also us, shimmers on." Explain in terms of your own experience the extent to which you agree or disagree.

4. How do you think death and loss inform the last lines of Doty's poem? Explain, using evidence from Doty's essay.

BRIDGE FISHING (FOR STORIES): AN OCCASION FOR WRITING

You have just studied Mark Doty's narrative account of making a poem. The story of his composing process reveals just how his poem "A Display of Mackerel" came into being as he moved from image to notes and drafting to a finished poem. You will now examine two images and think about those images in terms of Doty's story and your own experiences. The exercises that follow will lead you to create stories or an essay of your own.

© Free Agents Limited/Corbis

Seto Bridge and Okayama Skyline, Japan

© Matthias Weinrich

A school of mackerel

PREPARING TO WRITE: OCCASIONS TO THINK ABOUT WHAT YOU SEE

1. The bridges seen here connect multiple islands in Japan. How many islands can you identify that are being hopped?

2. How would you describe the composition of the photograph? How does the photograph's composition cause you to look at it? Do you follow the bridge or not? Make three other discoveries about the composition of this image and how it affects the story of this image.

3. Concentrate on how this photograph makes you feel and what you can thereby "see" that you may not be able to point to in the picture. In short, what does the image make you imagine?

4. Look at the image of a school of mackerel, the fish that sparks Doty's poem, but they are alive, unlike Doty's fish at the market. How many fish are there? Consider again. Might there be more? Explain.

5. Do these fish seem to form a collective, or do you see signs of independence in this school? What is the most pervasive pattern in this image, in your opinion?

6. Might this image be a painting rather than a photograph of a school of live fish? How would that fact change your reaction to the image? Why?

MOVING TOWARD ESSAY: OCCASIONS TO ANALYZE AND REFLECT

1. Reread what Mark Doty has to say about metaphor. Pay particular attention to the phrase "advance guard of the mind." How might the idea of a bridge help us understand what Doty means about the way metaphors function?

2. In World War II, American forces in the Far East engaged in a strategy they called "island-hopping" as a way of defeating Japan. Search the Internet for a deeper understanding of that strategic concept. How might that acquired knowledge change the way a viewer sees the Japanese Bridges? Explain.

3. Think about how the idea of a bridge might serve as a metaphor of a metaphor, a link from one identifiable (particular) thing to another thing (or concept) that is more difficult to see or to hold onto. Create a metaphor of your own that serves as such a bridge.

WRITING THOUGHTFULLY: OCCASIONS FOR IDEAS AND ESSAYS

1. Carl Jung, the psychologist, suggests that images are the equivalent of ideas, that we know what we know by way of images. Select a compelling image from American culture, or from your own local community. Re-create that image in words so that others might see it.

2. Tell a story that reveals your relationship to the image you selected in Question 1. Keep Doty's story in mind as an example of how you might proceed, and, as you tell your own story, be sure to let us see the image you're writing about (your word picture). Let your readers know why you selected the image, why it means so much to you.

3. Stay with that same image. What does the image tell us, either directly or indirectly, about American culture, the world we live in? What are its larger implications?

4. Consider your response to Question 3. To what extent did the image become metaphorical during that exercise? Tell a story that explains your discoveries about image and metaphor as you worked through these questions.

CREATING OCCASIONS

1. Select two or three images from popular culture that seem somehow to speak to each other. Tell the story of their relationship while also revealing what the images suggest to you about our culture.

2. Select one of your own best essays. Tell the story of how that essay came into being. Let Doty's essay be a guide.

3. Select a favorite family photograph and tell the story of what is not in the photograph. Then tell your readers why that missing information is so important to our understanding of the photograph itself.

Samuel Hubbard Scudder (1837–1911)

Samuel Scudder was the founder of American insect paleontology and was an authority on orthoptera and lepidoptera. He was educated at Williams College and Harvard. He served as assistant to Louis Agassiz (1862–1864), who, at the time, was the custodian of the Boston Society of Natural History (1864–1870). Scudder's works include *A Century of Orthoptera* (1879), *Butterflies: Their Structure, Changes, and Life-Histories* (1881), and *Fossil Insects of North America* (1890).

LOOK AT YOUR FISH

In this brief essay, Scudder recounts the story of how he learned a valuable lesson as a researcher while studying and working with Professor Louis Agassiz. On the surface this seems just to be an account of Scudder's learning to be a better observer, but as we look below the surface, paying closer attention, we can glean a few hidden secrets about scientific observation—and just plain looking.

1 It was more than fifteen years ago that I entered the laboratory of Professor Agassiz, and told him I had enrolled my name in the Scientific School as a student of natural history. He asked me a few questions about my object incoming, my antecedents generally, the mode in which I afterwards proposed to use the knowledge I might acquire, and, finally, whether I wished to study any special branch. To the latter I replied that, while I wished to be well grounded in all departments of zoology, I purposed to devote myself specially to insects. "When do you wish to begin?" he asked.

"Now," I replied.

This seemed to please him, and with an energetic "Very well!" he reached from a shelf a huge jar of specimens in yellow alcohol. "Take this fish," he said, "and look at it; we call it a haemulon; by and by I will ask what you have seen." With that he left me, but in a moment returned with explicit instructions as to the care of the object entrusted to me.

"No man is fit to be a naturalist," he said, "who does not know how to take care of specimens."

5 I was to keep the fish before me in a tin tray, and occasionally moisten the surface with alcohol from the jar, always taking care to replace the stopper tightly. These were not the days of ground-glass stoppers and elegantly shaped exhibition jars; all the old students will recall the huge neckless glass bottles with their leaky, wax-besmeared corks, half eaten by insects, and begrimed with cellar dust. Entomology was a cleaner science than ichthyology, but the example of the Professor, who had unhesitatingly plunged to the bottom of the jar to produce the fish, was infectious, and though this alcohol had a "very ancient and fishlike smell," I really dared not to show any aversion within these sacred precincts, and treated the alcohol as though it were pure water. Still I was conscious of a passing feeling of disappointment, for gazing at a fish did not commend itself to an ardent entomologist. My friends at home, too, were annoyed when they discovered that no amount of eau-de-Cologne would drown the perfume which haunted me like a shadow.

In ten minutes I had seen all that could be seen in that fish, and started in search of the Professor—who had, however, left the Museum; and when I returned, after lingering over some of the odd animals stored in the upper apartment, my specimen was dry all over. I dashed the fluid over the fish as if to resuscitate the beast from a fainting fit, and looked with anxiety for a return of the normal sloppy appearance. This little excitement over, nothing was to be done but to return to a steadfast gaze at my mute companion. Half an hour passed—an hour—another hour; the fish began to look loathsome. I turned it over and around; looked it in the face—ghastly; from behind, beneath, above, sideways, at a three-quarters' view—just as ghastly. I was in despair; at an early hour I concluded that lunch was necessary; so, with infinite relief, the fish was carefully replaced in the jar, and for an hour I was free.

On my return, I learned that Professor Agassiz had been at the Museum, but had gone, and would not return for several hours. My fellow students were too busy to be disturbed by continued conversation. Slowly I drew forth that hideous fish, and with a feeling of desperation again looked at it. I might not use a magnifying glass; instruments of all kinds were interdicted. My two hands, my two eyes, and the fish: it seemed a most limited field. I pushed my finger down its throat to feel how sharp the teeth were. I began to count the scales in the different rows, until I was convinced that that was nonsense. At last a happy thought struck me—I would draw the fish; and now with surprise I began to discover new features in the creature.

Just then the Professor returned.

"That is right," said he; "a pencil is one of the best of eyes. I am glad to notice, too, that you keep your specimen wet, and your bottle corked."

10   With these encouraging words, he added: "Well, what is it like?"

He listened attentively to my brief rehearsal of the structure of parts whose names were still unknown to me; the fringed gill-arches and movable operculum; the pores of the head, fleshy lips and lidless eyes; the lateral line, the spinous fins and forked tail; the compressed and arched body. When I finished, he waited as if expecting more, and then, with an air of disappointment: "You have not looked very carefully; why," he continued more earnestly, "you haven't even seen one of the most conspicuous features of the animal, which is as plainly before your eyes as the fish itself; look again, look again!" and he left me to my misery.

I was piqued; I was mortified. Still more of that wretched fish! But now I set myself to my task with a will, and discovered one new thing after another, until I saw how just the Professor's criticism had been. The afternoon passed quickly; and when, towards its close, the Professor inquired:

"Do you see it yet?"

"No," I replied, "I am certain I do not, but I see how little I saw before."

"That is next best," said he, earnestly, "but   15 I won't hear you now; put away your fish and go home; perhaps you will be ready with a better answer in the morning. I will examine you before you look at the fish."

This was disconcerting. Not only must I think of my fish all night, studying, without the object before me, what this unknown but most visible feature might be; but also, without reviewing my discoveries, I must give an exact account of them the next day. I had a bad memory; so I walked home by the Charles River in a distracted state, with my two perplexities.

The cordial greeting from the Professor the next morning was reassuring; here was a man who seemed to be quite as anxious as I that I should see for myself what he saw.

"Do you perhaps mean," I asked, "that the fish has symmetrical sides with paired organs?"

His thoroughly pleased "Of course! Of course!" repaid the wakeful hours of the previous night. After he had discoursed most happily and enthusiastically—as he always did— upon the importance of this point, I ventured to ask what I should do next.

"Oh, look at your fish!" he said, and left me   20 again to my own devices. In a little more than an hour he returned, and heard my new catalogue.

"That is good, that is good" he repeated; "but that is not all; go on;" and so for three long days he placed that fish before my eyes, forbidding me to look at anything else, or to use any artificial aid. "Look, look, look," was his repeated injunction.

This was the best entomological lesson I ever had—a lesson whose influence has extended to the details of every subsequent study; a legacy the Professor had left to me, as he has left it to many others, of inestimable value, which we could not buy, with which we cannot part.

The fourth day, a second fish of the same group was placed beside the first and I was bidden to point out the resemblances and differences between the two; another and another followed, until the entire family lay before me, and a whole legion of jars covered the table and surrounding shelves; the odor had become a pleasant perfume; and even now, the sight of an old, six-inch, worm-eaten cork brings fragrant memories.

The whole group of haemulons was thus brought in review; and whether engaged upon the dissection of the internal organs, the preparation and examination of the bony framework, or the description of the various parts, Agassiz's training in the method of observing facts and their orderly arrangement was ever accompanied by the urgent exhortation not to be content with them.

"Facts are stupid things," he would say, 25 "until brought into connection with some general law." At the end of eight months, it was almost with reluctance that I left these friends and turned to insects; but what I had gained by this outside experience has been of greater value than years of later investigation in my favorite groups.

A year afterward, some of us were amusing ourselves with chalking outlandish beasts on the Museum blackboard. We drew prancing starfishes; frogs in mortal combat; hydra-headed worms; stately crawfishes, standing on their tails, bearing aloft umbrellas; and grotesque fishes with gaping mouths and staring eyes. The Professor came in shortly after, and was as amused as any at our experiments. He looked at the fishes.

"Haemulons, every one of them," he said; "Mr. _____ drew them."

True; and to this day, if I attempt a fish, I can draw nothing but haemulons.

READING AND THINKING

1. Consider the first five paragraphs of the essay. What do they tell you about Scudder and his particular field of scientific inquiry? What is Scudder trying to convey through his scientific and descriptive language?

2. In terms of what Scudder has to learn as a young scientist, what do you consider the significance of this description: "My two hands, my two eyes, and the fish: it seemed a most limited field"?

3. Why was looking at the fish under Agassiz's guidance "the best entomological lesson" Scudder ever had?

THINKING AND WRITING

1. Explain the importance of Professor Agassiz's advice to Scudder that "a pencil is one of the best of eyes."

2. What is the significance of Scudder's having to leave the fish in the laboratory after his first day of observation and go home to continue his work "without the object before me"? Is there a lesson here? Explain.

3. Explain why Agassiz suggests, "Facts are stupid things." Do you agree?

4. Carefully reexamine Agassiz's "training in the method of observing facts and their orderly arrangement." Outline the methodology, laying out a general set of guidelines for conducting rigorous investigations.

MORE THAN MEETS THE EYE: AN OCCASION FOR WRITING

Samuel Scudder's interesting story about his first day of class tells us a great deal about the art of looking. The image here, *Fallen Frame,* is a photograph taken by a well-known artist who worked as a fashion photographer for *Vogue* magazine for more than 30 years, from 1955 to 1987. Guy Bourdin's photographs of stylish women are often provocative. On occasion he also makes violence seem beautiful and close at hand. But the photograph is provocative too because of what is not included in it. As we look, and look again at it, it elicits a story from us.

GUY
BOURDIN,
Fallen Frame

PREPARING TO WRITE: OCCASIONS TO THINK ABOUT WHAT YOU SEE

1. List details from this photograph suggesting that it might also be a fashion photograph.

2. List details that make you think it has nothing to do with fashion and sales. What do those details suggest to you about Bourdin's larger interests?

3. How important are the shadows?

MOVING TOWARD ESSAY: OCCASIONS TO REFLECT AND ANALYZE

1. What has happened to the woman in *Fallen Frame*? After a careful analysis of the facts depicted, tell a story about how you think she came to be there on the floor beneath the picture.

2. Recall how you formulated your story about the woman in *Fallen Frame*. Compare your analytical method with Scudder's method. Explain which method is more reliable for arriving at the truth.

3. Keep Samuel Scudder's investigative principles in mind and look at this sculpture by Duane Hanson. What is the most striking thing about this image? Give a detailed description of the man. Put him in a social class.

WRITING THOUGHTFULLY: OCCASIONS FOR IDEAS AND ESSAYS

1. Comparing Hanson's sculpture to Bourdin's photograph (which was also used as an advertisement for shoes), explore what they suggest about *class* in America or elsewhere. What do the artists seem to value? Write a brief essay that reveals your idea; use your own experience and the images by these two artists to clarify and substantiate that idea.

DUANE HANSON,
Janitor (1973)

2. Select three images of women's shoes from recent high-fashion magazines or from the Internet. Find two more Bourdin advertisements for Jourdan's shoes (available on the Internet). What story do these six images suggest about changes in taste and attitudes toward sexuality since the late 1960s and 1970s when Bourdin worked for Charles Jourdan?

3. Write a brief essay accounting for the difference in the way Doty and Scudder treat their evidence. One man is a poet; the other is a scientist. Are their methods at odds or complementary? Might each benefit from the other's methodology? Explain.

CREATING OCCASIONS

1. Select your own object (article of clothing, poem, prized possession, person), and tell a compelling story about your changing relationship with the object over time. Your story should teach your readers something about what you learned from that relationship, but the teaching must be done indirectly, the way Charles Scudder does in "Look at Your Fish."

2. Return to a complicated reading assignment from one of your most recent college courses. Take out the list of investigative principles that you derived from Scudder's essay and apply them to your reading of that assigned text. Tell the story of how your understanding of the text changed as you followed those principles over one or two days.

John Berger (b. 1926)

John Berger is an internationally acclaimed art critic, novelist, and playwright. His many books include the novels *G: A Novel* (1972, winner of the Booker Prize) and *A Fortunate Man: The Story of a Country Doctor* (1967); his most influential critical works include *About Looking* (1980) and *Ways of Seeing* (1973). His criticism focuses on how art embodies social and cultural values, and he asks us repeatedly to see how such values affect the way we see and look at the world. Because he became disenchanted with British culture, he has lived for years in voluntary exile in a small village in the French Alps.

STEPS TOWARD A SMALL THEORY OF THE VISIBLE

In this essay from his book *The Shape of a Pocket* (2001), Berger expresses his concern over a "system" that is causing us to lose touch with the real, with what is visible in the world around us. He encourages us to learn once again to listen to what our eyes tell us. And he specifies things that we might consider doing so that, like an accomplished painter, we too might be able to improve our listening and seeing.

1   When I say the first line of the Lord's Prayer: 'Our father who art in heaven . . .' I imagine this heaven as invisible, unenterable but intimately close. There is nothing baroque about it, no swirling infinite space or stunning foreshortening. To find it—if one had the grace—it would only be necessary to lift up something as small and as at hand as a pebble or a saltcellar on the table. Perhaps Cellini knew this.

'Thy kingdom come . . .' The difference is infinite between heaven and earth, yet the distance is minimal. Simone Weil wrote concerning this sentence: 'Here our desire pierces through time to find eternity behind it and this happens when we know how to turn whatever happens, no matter what it is, into an object of desire.'

Her words might also be a prescription for the art of painting.

Today images abound everywhere. Never has so much been depicted and watched. We have glimpses at any moment of what things look like on the other side of the planet, or the other side of the moon. Appearances registered, and transmitted with lightning speed.

Yet with this, something has innocently 5 changed. They used to be called *physical* appearances because they belonged to solid bodies. Now appearances are volatile. Technological innovation has made it easy to separate the apparent from the existent. And this is precisely what the present system's mythology continually needs to exploit. It turns appearances into refractions, like mirages: refractions not of light but of appetite, in fact a single appetite, the appetite for more.

Consequently—and oddly, considering the physical implications of the notion of *appetite*—the existent, the body, disappears. We live within a spectacle of empty clothes and unworn masks.

Consider any newsreader on any television channel in any country. These speakers are the mechanical epitome of the *disembodied*. It took the system many years to invent them and to teach them to talk as they do.

No bodies and no Necessity—for Necessity is the condition of the existent. It is what makes reality real. And the system's mythology requires only the not-yet-real, the virtual, the next purchase. This produces in the spectator, not, as claimed, a sense of freedom (the so-called freedom of choice) but a profound isolation.

Until recently, history, all the accounts people gave of their lives, all proverbs, fables, parables, confronted the same thing: the everlasting, fearsome, and occasionally beautiful, struggle of living with Necessity, which is the enigma of existence—that which followed from the Creation, and which subsequently has always continued to sharpen the human spirit. Necessity produces both tragedy and comedy. It is what you kiss or bang your head against.

10   Today, in the system's spectacle, it exists no more. Consequently no experience is communicated. All that is left to share is the spectacle, the game that nobody plays and everybody can watch. As has never happened before, people have to try to place their own existence and their own pains single-handed in the vast arena of time and the universe.

I had a dream in which I was a strange dealer: a dealer in looks or appearances. I collected and distributed them. In the dream I had just discovered a secret! I discovered it on my own, without help or advice.

The secret was to get inside whatever I was looking at—a bucket of water, a cow, a city (like Toledo) seen from above, an oak tree, and, once inside, to arrange its appearances for the better. *Better* did not mean making the thing seem more beautiful or more harmonious; nor did it mean making it more typical, so that the oak tree might represent all oak trees; it simply meant making it more itself so that the cow or the city or the bucket of water became more evidently unique!

The *doing* of this gave me pleasure and I had the impression that the small changes I made from the inside gave pleasure to others.

The secret of how to get inside the object so as to rearrange how it looked was as simple as opening the door of a wardrobe. Perhaps it was merely a question of being there

when the door swung open on its own. Yet when I woke up, I couldn't remember how it was done and I no longer knew how to get inside things.

The history of painting is often presented 15 as a history of succeeding styles. In our time art dealers and promoters have used this battle of styles to make brand-names for the market. Many collectors—and museums—buy names rather than works.

Maybe it's time to ask a naive question: what does all painting from the Palaeolithic period until our century have in common? Every painted image announces: *I have seen this,* or, when the making of the image was incorporated into a tribal ritual: *We have seen this.* The *this* refers to the sight represented. Non-figurative art is no exception. A late canvas by Rothko represents an illumination or a coloured glow which derived from the painter's experience of the visible. When he was working, he judged his canvas according to something else that he *saw.*

Painting is, first, an affirmation of the visible which surrounds us and which continually appears and disappears. Without the disappearing, there would perhaps be no impulse to paint, for then the visible itself would possess the surety (the permanence) which painting strives to find. More directly than any other art, painting is an affirmation of the existent, of the physical world into which mankind has been thrown.

Animals were the first subject in painting. And right from the beginning and then continuing through Sumerian, Assyrian, Egyptian and early Greek art, the depiction of these animals was extraordinarily true. Many millennia had to pass before an equivalent 'life-likeness' was achieved in the depiction of the human body. At the beginning, the existent was what confronted man.

The first painters were hunters whose lives, like everybody else's in the tribe, depended upon their close knowledge of animals. Yet the act of painting was not the same as the act of hunting: the relation between the two was magical.

20   In a number of early cave paintings there are stencil representations of the human hand beside the animals. We do not know what precise ritual this served. We do know that painting was used to confirm a magical 'companionship' between prey and hunter, or, to put it more abstractly, between the existent and human ingenuity. Painting was the means of making this companionship explicit and therefore (hopefully) permanent.

This may still be worth thinking about, long after painting has lost its herds of animals and its ritual function. I believe it tells us something about the nature of the act.

The impulse to paint comes neither from observation nor from the soul (which is probably blind) but from an encounter: the encounter between painter and model—even if the model is a mountain or a shelf of empty medicine bottles. Mont St Victoire as seen from Aix (seen from elsewhere it has a very different shape) was Cézanne's companion.

When a painting is lifeless it is the result of the painter not having the nerve to get close enough for a collaboration to start. He stays at a *copying* distance. Or, as in mannerist periods like today, he stays at an art-historical distance, playing stylistic tricks which the model knows nothing about.

To go in close means forgetting convention, reputation, reasoning, hierarchies and self. It also means risking incoherence, even madness. For it can happen that one gets too close and then the collaboration breaks down and the painter dissolves into the model. Or the animal devours or tramples the painter into the ground.

25   Every authentic painting demonstrates a collaboration. Look at Petrus Christus' portrait of a young girl in the Staatliche Museum of Berlin, or the stormy seascape in the Louvre by Courbet, or the mouse with an aubergine painted by Tchou-Ta in the seventeenth century, and it is impossible to deny the participation of the model. Indeed, the paintings are *not* first and foremost about a young woman, a rough sea or a mouse with a vegetable; they are about this participation. 'The brush,' wrote Shitao, the great seventeenth-century Chinese landscape painter, 'is for saving things from chaos.'

It is a strange area into which we are wandering and I'm using words strangely. A rough sea on the northern coast of France, one autumn day in 1870, *participating in being seen* by a man with a beard who, the following year, will be put in prison! Yet there is no other way of getting close to the actual practice of this silent art, which stops everything moving.

The *raison d'être* of the visible is the eye; the eye evolved and developed where there was enough light for the visible forms of life to become more and more complex and varied. Wild flowers, for example, are the colours they are in order to be seen. That an empty sky appears blue is due to the structure of our eyes and the nature of the solar system. There is a certain ontological basis for the collaboration between model and painter. Silesius, a seventeenth-century doctor of medicine in Wrocklau, wrote about the interdependence of the seen and the seeing in a mystical way.

La rose qui contemple ton oeil de chair
A fleuri de la sorte en Dieu dans l'éternel

How did you become what you visibly are? asks the painter.

I am as I am. I'm waiting, replies the mountain or the mouse or the child.

What for?   30

For you, if you abandon everything else.

For how long?

For as long as it takes.

There are other things in life.

Find them and be more normal.   35

And if I don't?

I'll give you what I've given nobody else, but it's worthless, it's simply the answer to your useless question.

Useless?

I am as I am.

40 No promise more than that?

None. I can wait for ever.

I'd like a normal life.

Live it and don't count on me.

And if I do count on you?

45 Forget everything and in me you'll find— me!

The collaboration which sometimes follows is seldom based on good will: more usually on desire, rage, fear, pity or longing. The modern illusion concerning painting (which post-modernism has done nothing to correct) is that the artist is a creator. Rather he is a receiver. What seems like creation is the act of giving form to what he has received.

Bogena and Robert and his brother Witek came to spend the evening because it was the Russian new year. Sitting at the table whilst they spoke Russian, I tried to draw Bogena. Not for the first time. I always fail because her face is very mobile and I can't forget her beauty. And to draw well you have to forget that. It was long past midnight when they left. As I was doing my last drawing Robert said: This is your last chance tonight, just draw her, John, draw her and be a man!

When they had gone, I took the least bad drawing and started working on it with colours—acrylic. Suddenly like a weather vane swinging round because the wind has changed, the portrait began to look like something. Her 'likeness' now was in my head— and all I had to do was to draw it out, not look for it. The paper tore. I rubbed on paint sometimes as thick as ointment. At four in the morning the face began to lend itself to, to smile at, its own representation.

The next day the frail piece of paper, heavy with paint, still looked good. In the daylight there were a few nuances of tone to change. Colours applied at night sometimes tend to be too desperate—like shoes pulled off without being untied. Now it was finished.

From time to time during the day I went 50 to look at it and I felt elated. Because I had done a small drawing I was pleased with? Scarcely. The elation came from something else. It came from the face's *appearing*—as if out of the dark. It came from the fact that Bogena's face had made a present of *what it could leave behind of itself.*

What is a likeness? When a person dies, they leave behind, for those who knew them, an emptiness, a space: the space has contours and is different for each person mourned. This space with its contours is the person's *likeness* and is what the artist searches for when making a living portrait. A likeness is something left behind invisibly.

Soutine was among the great painters of the twentieth century. It has taken fifty years for this to become clear, because his art was both traditional and uncouth, and this mixture offended all fashionable tastes. It was as if his painting had a heavy broken accent and so was considered inarticulate: at best exotic, and at worst barbarian. Now his devotion to the existent becomes more and more exemplary. Few other painters have revealed more graphically than he the collaboration, implicit in the act of painting, between model and painter. The poplars, the carcasses, the children's faces on Soutine's canvases clung to his brush.

Shitao—to quote him again—wrote:

> Painting is the result of the receptivity of ink: the ink is open to the brush: the brush is open to the hand: the hand is open to the heart: all this in the same way as the sky engenders what the earth produces: everything is the result of receptivity.

It is usually said about the late work of Titian or Rembrandt or Turner that their handling of paint became *freer*. Although, in a sense, true, this may give a false impression of *wilfulness*. In fact these painters in their old age simply became more receptive, more open to the appeal of the 'model' and its strange energy. It is as if their own bodies fall away.

55   When once the principle of collaboration has been understood, it becomes a criterion for judging works of any style, irrespective of their freedom of handling. Or rather (because *judgement* has little to do with art) it offers us an insight for seeing more clearly why painting moves us.

Rubens painted his beloved Hélène Fourment many times. Sometimes she collaborated, sometimes not. When she didn't, she remains a painted ideal; when she did, we too wait for her. There is a painting of roses in a vase by Morandi (1949) in which the flowers wait like cats to be let into his vision. (This is very rare for most flower paintings remain pure spectacle.) There is a portrait of a man painted on wood two millennia ago, whose participation we still feel. There are dwarfs painted by Velázquez, dogs by Titian, houses by Vermeer in which we recognise, as energy, the will-to-be-seen.

More and more people go to museums to look at paintings and do not come away disappointed. What fascinates them? To answer: Art, or the history of art, or art appreciation, misses, I believe, the essential.

In art museums we come upon the visible of other periods and it offers us company. We feel less alone in the face of what we ourselves see each day appearing and disappearing. So much continues to look the same: teeth, hands, the sun, women's legs, fish . . . in the realm of the visible all epochs coexist and are fraternal, whether separated by centuries or millennia. And when the painted image is not a copy but the result of a dialogue, the painted thing speaks if we listen.

In matters of seeing Joseph Beuys was the great prophet of the second half of our century, and his life's work was a demonstration of, and an appeal for, the kind of collaboration I'm talking about. Believing that everybody is potentially an artist, he took objects and arranged them in such a way that they beg the spectator to collaborate with them, not this time by painting, but by listening to what their eyes tell them and remembering.

I know of few things more sad (sad, not 60 tragic) than an animal who has lost its sight. Unlike humans, the animal has no supporting language left which can describe the world. If on a familiar terrain, the blind animal manages to find its way about with its nose. But it has been deprived of the existent and with this deprivation it begins to diminish until it does little but sleep, therein perhaps hunting for a dream of that which once existed.

The Marquise de Sorcy de Thélusson, painted in 1790 by David, looks at me. Who could have foreseen in her time the solitude in which people today live? A solitude confirmed daily by networks of bodiless and false images concerning the world. Yet their falseness is not an error. If the pursuit of profit is considered as the only means of salvation for mankind, turnover becomes the absolute priority, and, consequently, the existent has to be disregarded or ignored or suppressed.

Today, to try to paint the existent is an act of resistance instigating hope.

READING AND THINKING

1. The first ten paragraphs of this essay focus on change and loss. Identify as many aspects of loss as you can. Figure out what Berger means by "system." You will have to think inductively and imaginatively; he does not tell you straight out.

2. Berger begins with heaven, the "invisible," and suggests that the "difference is infinite between heaven and earth, yet the distance is minimal." How does he use Simone Weil to help us understand what he means about difference and distance?

3. According to Berger, the "system" (and its technology) gives us images that are disembodied. He tells us, "We live within a spectacle of empty clothes and unworn masks." We live without "Necessity," which "makes reality real." What does he mean?

4. Why are the early cave paintings of animals so important to Berger? Given what he says at the beginning about the disembodied images in our culture, what do you think is, for him, different about the cave paintings?

5. What happens when a painter stays at a "*copying* distance" from the objects that he or she is trying to paint? What happens when the painter gets too close to the object? What is the "right distance"? Why?

6. Why does Berger tell the story of drawing, or trying to draw, Bogena's face? What does he mean by *likeness?*

7. Berger does not use the word *synesthesia* in this essay. Look it up in an unabridged dictionary and determine its relationship to the last nine paragraphs of the essay.

THINKING AND WRITING

1. Berger relates a dream in which he discovered that he could get "inside" whatever he was looking at and "arrange its appearances for the better." Later, apart from the dream, he couldn't remember how to get inside, to rearrange appearances. To what extent is this essay an attempt to recover those abilities or to show his readers how to get inside the observed thing? Explain.

2. Explain what Berger means when he says, "Every authentic painting demonstrates a collaboration." How would Berger define *authentic* and *collaboration?* How are his definitions complicated or clarified by the words *creator* and *receiver?*

3. What does Berger mean when he tells us that if "the painted image is not a copy but the result of a dialogue, the painted thing speaks if we listen"?

HEARING AND SEEING, A BASIC MYSTERY: AN OCCASION FOR WRITING

This Occasion will give you an opportunity to see whether images can speak to us through our eyes. The images we will be considering suggest the results of such collaboration between the artist and his selected objects. Now consider your own relationship to what you are seeing. Will you be to able to figure out whether ordinary viewers like ourselves can enter into such collaborations? What is the language of such collaboration? Can we speak it by ourselves, or do we need the help of others, their words, explanations, hints? What are the conditions for our being able to collaborate?

The two cave painting photographs are from France and Argentina, where some of the world's oldest images were painted on the cave walls thousands of years ago. They almost certainly predated our use of human language. Many of these images were accompanied by a handprint on the wall of the caves, as if the artist left a signature of sorts, like the one seen here from Argentina.

The other two images are from the work of a German artist, Joseph Beuys (1921–1986), one of the most influential artists of the twentieth century. His widely influential experimental work concerned itself with breaking past traditional artistic boundaries. However, he was not simply interested in working with experimental forms; he was also deeply interested in making the world a more humane place in which to live.

© National Geographic/Getty Images

Paleolithic bulls and other animals on calcite walls at Lascaux Caves, France

Detail of 10,000-year-old pictographs from Cueva de los Manos, Argentina

© Hubert Stadler/CORBIS

PREPARING TO WRITE: OCCASIONS TO THINK ABOUT WHAT YOU SEE

1. How many animals do you see in the Lascaux Cave photograph? What seems to be their relationship one to the other? How would you characterize the two primary figures, the horse and the bull? Realistic, impressionistic, other?

2. What do the hands from the Argentinean cave signal to you?

3. What do you *hear* as you consider this image? Is there something going on around the images that you cannot literally point to, some mysterious quality?

4. How would you describe the overall effect of the cave paintings on you? Consider both your feeling and the work that your mind does while considering the image.

5. In Joseph Beuys sculptural installation *The Pack,* each sled carries a roll of felt, a lump of animal fat, and a torch. How many sleds do you see? What might those supplies be used for?

6. Where are these sleds coming from? Where do you suspect they are going?

7. What is the relationship between the sleds and the VW bus?

8. Why do you suppose Joseph Beuys titled this installation *The Pack*? How is he challenging us with this image?

© 1969 Joseph Beuys. Image used by permission of Staatliche Museen Kassel. Image © 2006 Artist Rights Society (ARS), New York/VG Bild-Kunst, Bonn.

JOSEPH BEUYS,
The Pack, 1969

MOVING TOWARD ESSAY: OCCASIONS TO REFLECT AND ANALYZE

1. Did Beuys manage to draw you into a collaborative relationship with his image? Explain how he did that or how he turned you away. Account for your relationship with the smaller images within the larger frame of *The Pack*.

2. How might we argue that both Berger and Beuys are trying to teach us something about survival? How do their methods differ?

3. Put Doty, Scudder, Berger, and Beuys in relationship with one another. How would you classify each man as a thinker? As an artist or a scientist? Explain.

WRITING THOUGHTFULLY: OCCASIONS FOR IDEAS AND ESSAYS

1. Return to Berger's assessment of Joseph Beuys's work (p. 110), where he proclaims Beuys "the great prophet of the second half of our century." Study that assessment and write Berger a short letter telling him how you feel about his claim. You might consider other pieces of Beuys's work on the Internet before writing to Berger.

2. Near the end of his essay Berger says that "once the principle of collaboration has been understood, it becomes a criterion for judging works of any style [. . .] or rather (because *judgement* has little to do with art) it offers us an insight for seeing more clearly why painting moves us." Write a brief essay—using these paintings and photographs (and others that interest you) as evidence—accounting for your assessment of Berger's claim. Your essay should necessarily assess the relative power of the selected paintings to entice you into your own collaboration with them.

3. Write an essay that addresses the general questions outlined in the introduction to this Occasion. Tell your readers something interesting about the language of feeling that art uses to speak to its viewers.

CREATING OCCASIONS

1. Midway through his essay, Berger has a painter pose a taunting question: "How did you become what you visibly are?" Someone answers: "I am as I am." Consider the dialogue that follows in that section of the essay and write a paragraph about what you think the exchange between these unnamed voices (a painter and a subject) might mean. What does Berger himself suggest that the artist *receives* from the object being painted? Explain by referring to one or two paintings that reveal something to you about this exchange.

2. Don Nice, a pop-realist painter, says regarding the subject of his painted objects: "The objects chose me because they had interesting aesthetic properties; they were interesting from a formal point of view." Consider recent paintings of Nice's that you find on the Internet and then, in a letter, tell him what you see that goes beyond (but does not ignore) those "subtle aesthetic properties" (the shapes, the reflections within the image of the horse, the isolation of the horse against a white background). Tell him why you think he might, as a painter, be interested in what Berger has to say about *collaboration* and *dialogue*.

3. Throughout this cluster of readings and images, we have been primarily concerned with the powerful and positive effect of images. Think now about the power that images have to *deceive* us, especially in this digital age when images can be manipulated and when what we are allowed to see is often controlled by government, the news media, or corporations. Write a brief essay titled "Image and the Power of Deception." Cite Berger and his concerns about the "system."

CREATING WORD PORTRAITS AND IDEAS

The work in this Cluster begins with a focus on the creation of word portraits. Our initial aim is to learn more about how to tell stories about people, how to re-create them in words so that our readers can begin to see and understand them. But we want readers to see at the same time how such individuals (in the hands of a good writer) can represent more than themselves. These portraits often reveal how our culture typecasts people, how clothing and friends and language suggest class distinctions and boundaries. Perhaps even more ironic, the portraits we create of others carry our own signature. There in our writing, no matter what its subject, our readers also find us.

Virginia Woolf (1882–1941)

Virginia Woolf, perhaps the most distinguished writer of the twentieth century, came from a family of prominent Victorians. She was self-educated. Her experimental novels have inspired movies, her essays have shown a whole generation how to think and how to write, and her views on women's rights have made her an exemplar for feminists seeking independence and, as she would say, a room of their own. Woolf has become the subject of numerous biographies and critical studies, and her novels—*To the Lighthouse, Mrs. Dalloway, Jacob's Room, The Waves*—stand against time, a class unto themselves.

PORTRAIT OF A LONDONER

In this short sketch, Woolf tells the story of an older woman whom she calls Mrs. Crowe. By the time we have finished reading this piece, Mrs. Crowe has come to stand for London; she has become a metaphor for something Woolf associates with the city itself. So it is important for us to pay close attention not only to what we hear about the old lady and her fireside chats with her stream of visitors but also to pay attention to the historical sketch of a city that Woolf creates around these social gatherings.

1 Nobody can be said to know London who does not know one true cockney—who cannot turn down a side street, away from the shops and the theatres, and knock at a private door in a street of private houses. Private houses in London are apt to be much of a muchness. The door opens on a dark hall; from the dark hall rises a narrow staircase; off the landing opens a double drawing-room, and in this double drawing-room are two sofas on each side of a blazing fire, six armchairs, and three long windows giving upon the street. What happens in the back half of the drawing-room which looks upon the gardens of other houses is often a matter of considerable conjecture. But it is with the front drawing-room that we are here concerned; for Mrs Crowe always sat there in an armchair by the fire; it was there that she had her being; it was there that she poured out tea.

That she was born in the country seems, though strange, to be a fact: that she sometimes left London, in those summer weeks when London ceases to be London, is also true. But where she went or what she did when she was out of London, when her chair was empty, her fire unlit and her table unlaid, nobody knew or could imagine. To figure Mrs Crowe in her black dress and her veil and her cap, walking in a field among turnips or climbing a hill where cows were grazing, is beyond the scope of the wildest imagination.

There by the fire in winter, by the window in summer, she had sat for 60 years—but not alone. There was always someone in the armchair opposite, paying a call. And before the first caller had been seated 10 minutes, the door always opened and the maid Maria, she of the prominent eyes and prominent teeth, who had opened the door for 60 years, opened it once more and announced a second visitor; and then a third, and then a fourth.

A tête-à-tête with Mrs Crowe was unknown. She disliked tête-à-têtes. It was part of a peculiarity that she shared with many hostesses that she was never specially intimate with anyone. For example, there was always an elderly man in the corner by the cabinet—who seemed, indeed, as much a part of that admirable piece of 18th-century furniture as its own brass claws. But he was always addressed as Mr Graham—never John, never William: though sometimes she would call him "dear Mr Graham" as if to mark the fact that she had known him for 60 years.

5   The truth was she did not want intimacy; she wanted conversation. Intimacy has a way of breeding silence, and silence she abhorred. There must be talk, and it must be general, and it must be about everything. It must not go too deep, and it must not be too clever, for if it went too far in either of these directions somebody was sure to feel out of it, and to sit balancing his tea cup, saying nothing.

Thus Mrs Crowe's drawing-room had little in common with the celebrated salons of the memoir writers. Clever people often came there—judges, doctors, members of parliament, writers, musicians, people who travelled, people who played polo, actors and complete nonentities, but if anyone said a brilliant thing it was felt to be rather a breach of etiquette—an accident that one ignored, like a fit of sneezing, or some catastrophe with a muffin. The talk that Mrs Crowe liked and inspired was a glorified version of village gossip. The village was London, and the gossip was about London life. But Mrs Crowe's great gift consisted in making the vast metropolis seem as small as a village with one church, one manor house and 25 cottages. She had first-hand information about every play, every picture show, every trial, every divorce case. She knew who was marrying, who was dying, who was in town and who was out. She would mention the fact that she had just seen Lady Umphleby's car go by, and hazard a guess that she was going to visit her daughter whose baby had been born last night, just as a village woman speaks of the squire's lady driving to the station to meet Mr John, who is expected down from town.

And as she had made these observations for the past 50 years or so, she had acquired an amazing store of information about the lives of other people. When Mr Smedley, for instance, said that his daughter was engaged to Arthur Beecham, Mrs Crowe at once remarked that in that case she would be a cousin twice removed to Mrs Firebrace, and in a sense niece to Mrs Burns, by her first marriage with Mr Minchin of Blackwater Grange. But Mrs Crowe was not in the least a snob. She was merely a collector of relationships; and her amazing skill in this direction served to give a family and domestic character to her gatherings, for it is surprising how many people are 20th cousins, if they did but know it.

To be admitted to Mrs Crowe's house was therefore to become the member of a club, and the subscription demanded was the payment of so many items of gossip every year. Many people's first thought when the house caught fire or the pipes burst or the housemaid decamped with the butler must have been, I will run round and tell that to Mrs Crowe. But here again, distinctions had to be observed. Certain people had the right to run round at lunchtime; others, and these were the most numerous, must go between the hours of five and seven. The class who had the privilege of dining with Mrs Crowe was a small one. Perhaps only Mr Graham and Mrs Burke actually dined with her, for she was not a rich woman. Her black dress was a trifle shabby; her diamond brooch was always the same diamond brooch. Her favourite meal was tea, because the tea table can be supplied economically, and there is an elasticity about tea which suited her gregarious temper. But whether it was lunch or tea, the meal had a distinct character, just as a dress and her jewellery suited her to perfection and had a fashion of their own. There would be a special cake, a special pudding—something peculiar to the house and as much part of the establishment as Maria the old servant, or Mr Graham the old friend, or the old chintz on the chair, or the old carpet on the floor.

That Mrs Crowe must sometimes have taken the air, that she did sometimes become a guest at other people's luncheons and teas, is true. But in society she seemed furtive and fragmentary and incomplete, as if she had merely looked in at the wedding or the evening party or the funeral to pick up some scraps of news that she needed to complete her own hoard. Thus she was seldom induced to take a seat; she was always on the wing. She looked out of place among other people's chairs and tables; she must have her own chintzes and her own cabinet and her own Mr Graham under it in order to be completely herself. As years went on these little raids into the outer world practically ceased. She had made her nest so compact and so complete that the outer world had not a feather or a twig to add to it. Her own cronies were so faithful, moreover, that she could trust them to convey any little piece of news that she ought to add to her collection. It was unnecessary that she should leave her own chair by the fire in winter, by the window in summer. And with the passage of years her knowledge became, not more profound—profundity was not her line—but more rounded, and more complete. Thus if a new play were a great success, Mrs Crowe was able next day not merely to record the fact with a sprinkle of amusing gossip from behind the scenes, but she could cast back to other first nights, in the 80s, in the 90s, and describe what Ellen Terry had worn, what Duse had done, how dear Mr Henry James had said—nothing very remarkable perhaps; but as she spoke it seemed as if all the pages of London life for 50 years past were being lightly shuffled for one's amusement. There were many; and the pictures on them were bright and brilliant and of famous people; but Mrs Crowe by no means dwelt on the past—she by no means exalted it above the present.

10 Indeed, it was always the last page, the present moment, that mattered most. The delightful thing about London was that it was always giving one something new to look at, something fresh to talk about. One only had to keep one's eyes open; to sit down in one's own chair from five to seven every day of the week. As she sat in her chair with her guests ranged round she would give from time to time a quick bird-like glance over her shoulder at the window, as if she had half an eye on the street, as if she had half an ear upon the cars and the omnibuses and the cries of the paper boys under the window. Why, something new might be happening this very moment. One could not spend too much time on the past: one must not give all one's attention to the present.

Nothing was more characteristic and perhaps a little disconcerting than the eagerness with which she would look up and break her sentence in the middle when the door opened and Maria, grown very portly and a little deaf, announced someone new. Who was about to enter? What had he or she got to add to the talk? But her deftness in extracting whatever might be their gift, her skill in throwing it into the common pool, were such that no harm was done; and it was part of her peculiar triumph that the door never opened too often; the circle never grew beyond her sway.

Thus, to know London not merely as a gorgeous spectacle, a mart, a court, a hive of industry, but as a place where people meet and talk, laugh, marry, and die, paint, write and act, rule and legislate, it was essential to know Mrs Crowe. It was in her drawing-room that the innumerable fragments of the vast metropolis seemed to come together into one lively, comprehensible, amusing and agreeable whole. Travellers absent for years, battered and sun-dried men just landed from India or Africa, from remote travels and adventures among savages and tigers, would come straight to the little house in the quiet street to be taken back into the heart of civilisation at one stride. But even London itself could not keep Mrs Crowe alive for ever. It is a fact that one day Mrs Crowe was not sitting in the armchair by the fire as the clock struck five; Maria did not open the door; Mr Graham had detached himself from the cabinet. Mrs Crowe is dead, and London—no, though London still exists, London will never be the same city again.

READING AND THINKING

1. What do you suppose Woolf means when she tells us that sitting there in the front drawing-room, Mrs Crowe "had her being"?

2. What is the difference between intimacy and conversation as Woolf describes it? Why is the distinction so important to Woolf's portrait?

3. How is it that Mrs Crowe's "village gossip" makes London a smaller, more interesting place?

4. Why does Woolf tell us about Mrs Crowe's visits to other houses?

THINKING AND WRITING

1. Trace the various ways Woolf turns Mrs Crowe into a metaphor for a historical moment in London's long history. In short, how does Woolf cause Mrs Crowe to become more than "one true cockney"?

2. Why was it, in Woolf's mind, "essential to know Mrs Crowe"?

3. To what extent does Woolf convince you that without Mrs Crowe "London will never be the same city again"? Explain.

4. How does Woolf's portrait of Mrs Crowe affect you? Account for the details of the "portrait" that either draw you to it or turn you away from it. What does Woolf make you *see*?

CREATING PORTRAITS: AN OCCASION FOR WRITING

In this Occasion your work will have its roots in what Virginia Woolf and Duane Hanson show us about creating human portraits. You will be learning to create word portraits that work in several dimensions at once. The portrait itself not only will tell us about its subject but will also locate the subject in a larger context, perhaps cultural, perhaps historical. Duane Hanson (1925–1996), born in Alexandria, Minnesota, received his BA from Macalester College and his MFA from the Cranbrook Academy of Art in Bloomfield Hills, Michigan. He taught art in Munich and Bremerhaven, Germany, from 1953 to 1960. After returning to the United States, he was an art professor at Oglethorpe University in Atlanta. While there he began to be recognized for his work with life-sized polyester resin and fiberglass sculpture. His work has been featured in exhibitions at the Whitney Museum of American Art, the Nelson-Atkins Museum, the Musée des Beaux Arts de Montréal, and the World Design Exposition in Nagoya, Japan.

PREPARING TO WRITE: OCCASIONS TO THINK ABOUT WHAT YOU SEE

1. Select one of these sculptures on this and the following page and list the details that make it seem real or lifelike.

2. In what ways does the sculpture you selected also seem representative of a particular kind of individual or a particular class of people? Explain.

3. Looking at these three sculptures and "Janitor" (p. 104), do you think that Hanson's characters have anything in common with Mrs. Crowe? Explain.

MOVING TOWARD ESSAY: OCCASIONS TO ANALYZE AND REFLECT

1. Do you think that Hanson's portraits of American life in the twentieth century pose important social and political questions about the human condition? Does Woolf's portrait of Mrs. Crowe pose such questions? Do they pose the same questions? Explain.

2. Woolf tells us that Mrs. Crowe was a "collector of relationships." Think back to John Berger's (p. 106) insistence that between every artist and her subject there should be a collaboration and that we can see that collaboration, that relationship, between artist and subject reflected in the finished painting. To what extent can you see such a reflection in Woolf's "portrait" of Mrs. Crowe or in one of Hanson's sculptures? Explain.

DUANE HANSON, *Cowboy (1995)*

DUANE HANSON,
Man on a Lawn Mower (1995)

WRITING THOUGHTFULLY: OCCASIONS FOR IDEAS AND ESSAYS

1. Paying particular attention to the way that Woolf and Hanson create their portraits of ordinary people, create a written portrait of an interesting person from your community who seems somehow representative of community values. Develop your portrait so that we can both see and know this person's routines and at the same time come to know what he or she represents.

2. Neil Pepe, the artistic director of New York's Atlantic Theatre Company, has spoken of our age as "an age when virtual reality and Internet relationships are becoming the norm, and also the fact that, ironically, in this time when communication seems so easy, real human contact seems more difficult." Write a short essay in which you develop your own idea about human communication in our time, using Hanson's images or other images from popular culture to help you develop and substantiate your idea.

DUANE HANSON, *Young Shopper (1973)*

CREATING OCCASIONS

1. In "Steps Towards a Small Theory of the Visible," John Berger (p. 107) argues that "Necessity" ("what makes reality real") no longer confronts us in our time. "All that is left to share is the spectacle, the game that nobody plays and everybody can watch." Using Woolf's and Hanson's work to guide you, create one portrait of your own that confirms Berger's idea and one that refutes it.

2. Making use of your own portraits, Hanson's and Woolf's portraits, and your experience, respond in a short essay to Berger's idea that we have become mere spectators in the game of life, living under the influence of a technology-induced "system" that causes us to "have to try to place [our] own existence and [our] own pains single-handed in the vast arena of time and the universe." Consider, for example, the differences between Mrs. Crowe (from the past) and any one of Hanson's characters (much closer to the present) as you work out your response.

Richard Rodriguez (b. 1944)

Richard Rodriguez, born in San Francisco, the son of Mexican immigrants, earned his BA from Stanford University and his PhD from the University of California at Berkeley. His essays and articles have appeared in *Harper's, Saturday Review, American Scholar,* the *New York Times,* the *Los Angeles Times,* and *New Republic.* He has written four books, including *Hunger of Memory: The Education of Richard Rodriguez* (1982) and *Days of Obligation: An Argument with My Mexican Father* (1992). His awards include the Frankel Medal from the National Endowment for the Humanities, a Fulbright fellowship, and the International Journalism Award from World Affairs Council of California. Rodriguez now works for the Pacific News Service.

LATE VICTORIANS

In this essay Rodriguez considers the importance of the city of San Francisco to the lives of gay men. His is a searching inquiry about the effect of the AIDS epidemic on his own life and on the community where he lived in San Francisco. The Victorian houses themselves come to speak metaphorically about the values and lifestyles of the gay men who inhabit them. From Rodriguez's close examination of this gay culture and his own foibles, we also learn something of our own, just as we learn from his examination of this lively and tightly bound community something of our own deep yearning for home—no matter what our sexual orientation.

1   St. Augustine writes from his cope of dust that we are restless hearts, for earth is not our true home. Human unhappiness is evidence of our immortality. Intuition tells us we are meant for some other city.

Elizabeth Taylor, quoted in a magazine article of twenty years ago, spoke of cerulean Richard Burton days on her yacht, days that were nevertheless undermined by the elemental private reflection: This must end.

On a Sunday in summer, ten years ago, I was walking home from the Latin Mass at St. Patrick's, the old Irish parish downtown, when I saw thousands of people on Market Street. It was San Francisco's Gay Freedom Day parade—not the first, but the first I ever saw. Private lives were becoming public. There were marching bands. There were floats. Banners blocked single lives thematically into a processional mass, not unlike the consortiums of the blessed in Renaissance paintings, each saint cherishing the apparatus of his martyrdom: GAY DENTISTS. BLACK AND WHITE LOVERS. GAYS FROM BAKERSFIELD.

LATINA LESBIANS. From the foot of Market Street they marched, east to west, following the mythic American path toward optimism.

I followed the parade to Civic Center Plaza, where flags of routine nations yielded sovereignty to a multitude. Pastel billows flowed over all.

Five years later, another parade. Politicians waved from white convertibles. Dykes on Bikes revved up, thumbs upped. But now banners bore the acronyms of death. AIDS. ARC. Drums were muffled as passing, plum-spotted young men slid by on motorized cable cars.

Though I am alive now, I do not believe that an old man's pessimism is truer than a young man's optimism simply because it comes after. There are things a young man knows that are true and are not yet in the old man's power to recollect. Spring has its sappy wisdom. Lonely teenagers still arrive in San Francisco aboard Greyhound buses. The city can still seem, I imagine, by comparison to where they came from, paradise.

Four years ago on a Sunday in winter—a brilliant spring afternoon—I was jogging near Fort Point while overhead a young woman was, with difficulty, climbing over the railing of the Golden Gate Bridge. Holding down her skirt with one hand, with the other she waved to a startled spectator (the newspaper next day quoted a workman who was painting the bridge) before she stepped onto the sky.

To land like a spilled purse at my feet.

Serendipity has an eschatological tang here. Always has. Few American cities have had the experience, as we have had, of watching the civic body burn even as we stood, out of body, on a hillside, in a movie theater. Jeanette MacDonald's loony scatting of "San Francisco" has become our go-to-hell anthem. San Francisco has taken some heightened pleasure from the circus of final things. To Atlantis, to Pompeii, to the Pillar of Salt, we add the Golden Gate Bridge, not golden at all but rust red. San Francisco toys with the tragic conclusion.

10   For most of its brief life, San Francisco has entertained an idea of itself as heaven on earth, whether as Gold Town or City Beautiful or Treasure Island or Haight-Ashbury.

San Francisco can support both comic and tragic conclusions because the city is geographically *in extremis,* a metaphor for the farthest-flung possibility, a metaphor for the end of the line. Land's end.

To speak of San Francisco as land's end is to read the map from one direction only—as Europeans would read or as the East Coast has always read it. In my lifetime, San Francisco has become an Asian city. To speak, therefore, of San Francisco as land's end is to betray parochialism. Before my parents came to California from Mexico, they saw San Francisco as the North. The West was not west for them.

I cannot claim for myself the memory of a skyline such as the one César saw. César came to San Francisco in middle age; César came here as to some final place. He was born in South America; he had grown up in Paris; he had been everywhere, done everything; he assumed the world. Yet César was not condescending toward San Francisco, not at all. Here César saw revolution, and he embraced it.

Whereas I live here because I was born here. I grew up ninety miles away, in Sacramento. San Francisco was the nearest, the easiest, the inevitable city, since I needed a city. And yet I live here surrounded by people for whom San Francisco is a quest.

I have never looked for utopia on a map.   15 Of course, I believe in human advancement. I believe in medicine, in astrophysics, in washing machines. But my compass takes its cardinal point from tragedy. If I respond to the metaphor of spring, I nevertheless learned, years ago, from my Mexican parents, from my Irish nuns, to count on winter. The point of Eden for me, for us, is not approach but expulsion.

After I met César in 1984, our friendly debate concerning the halcyon properties of San Francisco ranged from restaurant to restaurant. I spoke of limits. César boasted of freedoms.

It was César's conceit to add to the gates of Jerusalem, to add to the soccer fields of Tijuana, one other dreamscape hoped for the world over. It was the view from a hill, through a mesh of electrical tram wires, of an urban neighborhood in a valley. The vision took its name from the protruding wedge of a theater marquee. Here César raised his glass without discretion: To the Castro.

There were times, dear César, when you tried to switch sides if only to scorn American optimism, which, I remind you, had already become your own. At the high school where César taught, teachers and parents had organized a campaign to keep kids from driving themselves to the junior prom in an attempt to forestall liquor and death. Such a scheme momentarily reawakened César's Latin skepticism.

Didn't the Americans know? (His tone exaggerated incredulity.) Teenagers will crash into lampposts on their way home from proms, and there is nothing to be done about it. You cannot forbid tragedy.

20 By California standards I live in an old house. But not haunted. There are too many tall windows, there is too much salty light, especially in winter, though the windows rattle, rattle in summer when the fog flies overhead, and the house creaks and prowls at night. I feel myself immune to any confidence it seeks to tell.

To grow up homosexual is to live with secrets and within secrets. In no other place are those secrets more closely guarded than within the family home. The grammar of the gay city borrows metaphors from the nineteenth-century house. "Coming out of the closet" is predicated upon family laundry, dirty linen, skeletons.

I live in a tall Victorian house that has been converted to four apartments; four single men.

Neighborhood streets are named to honor nineteenth-century men of action, men of distant fame. Clay. Jackson. Scott. Pierce. Many Victorians in the neighborhood date from before the 1906 earthquake and fire.

Architectural historians credit the gay movement of the 1970s with the urban restoration of San Francisco. Twenty years ago this was a borderline neighborhood. This room, like all the rooms of the house, was painted headache green, apple green, boardinghouse green. In the 1970s homosexuals moved into black and working-class parts of the city, where they were perceived as pioneers or as blockbusters, depending.

25 Two decades ago some of the least expensive sections of San Francisco were wooden Victorian sections. It was thus a coincidence of the market that gay men found themselves living with the architectural metaphor for family. No other architecture in the American imagination is more evocative of family than the Victorian house. In those same years—the 1970s—and within those same Victorian houses, homosexuals were living rebellious lives to challenge the foundations of domesticity.

Was "queer-bashing" as much a manifestation of homophobia as a reaction against gentrification? One heard the complaint, often enough, that gay men were as promiscuous with their capital as otherwise, buying, fixing up, then selling and moving on. Two incomes, no children, described an unfair advantage. No sooner would flower boxes begin to appear than an anonymous reply was smeared on the sidewalk out front: kill faggots.

The three- or four-story Victorian house, like the Victorian novel, was built to contain several generations and several classes under one roof, behind a single oaken door. What strikes me is the confidence of Victorian architecture. Stairs, connecting one story with another, describe the confidence that bound generations together through time—confidence that the family would inherit the earth.

If Victorian houses exude a sturdy optimism by day, they are also associated in our imaginations with the Gothic—with shadows and cobwebby gimcrack, long corridors. The nineteenth century was remarkable for escalating optimism even as it excavated the backstairs, the descending architecture of nightmare—Freud's labor and Engels's.

I live on the second story, in rooms that have been rendered as empty as Yorick's skull—gutted, unrattled, in various ways unlocked, added skylights and new windows, new doors. The hallway remains the darkest part of the house.

30 This winter the hallway and lobby are being repainted to resemble an eighteenth-century French foyer. Of late we had walls and carpet of Sienese red; a baroque mirror hung in an alcove by the stairwell. Now we

are to have enlightened austerity of an expensive sort—black-and-white marble floors and faux masonry. A man comes in the afternoons to texture the walls with a sponge and a rag and to paint white mortar lines that create an illusion of permanence, of stone.

The renovation of Victorian San Francisco into dollhouses for libertines may have seemed, in the 1970s, an evasion of what the city was actually becoming. San Francisco's rows of storied houses proclaimed a multigenerational orthodoxy, all the while masking the city's unconventional soul. Elsewhere, meanwhile, domestic America was coming undone.

Suburban Los Angeles, the prototype for a new America, was characterized by a more apparently radical residential architecture. There was, for example, the work of Frank Gehry. In the 1970s Gehry exploded the nuclear-family house, turning it inside out intellectually and in fact. Though, in a way, Gehry merely completed the logic of the postwar suburban tract house—with its one story, its sliding glass doors, Formica kitchen, two-car garage. The tract house exchanged privacy for mobility. Heterosexuals opted for the one-lifetime house, the freeway, the birth-control pill, minimalist fiction.

The age-old description of homosexuality is of a sin against nature. Moralistic society has always judged emotion literally. The homosexual was sinful because he had no kosher place to stick it. In attempting to drape the architecture of sodomy with art, homosexuals have lived for thousands of years against the expectations of nature. Barren as Shakers and, interestingly, as concerned with the small effect, homosexuals have made a covenant against nature. Homosexual survival lay in artifice, in plumage, in lampshades, sonnets, musical comedy, couture, syntax, religious ceremony, opera, lacquer, irony.

I once asked Enrique, an interior decorator, if he had many homosexual clients. *"Mais non,"* said he, flexing his eyelids. "Queers don't need decorators. They were born knowing how. All this A.S.I.D. stuff—tests and regulations—as if you can confer a homosexuality diploma on a suburban housewife by granting her a discount card."

A knack? The genius, we are beginning to fear in an age of AIDS, is irreplaceable—but does it exist? The question is whether the darling affinities are innate to homosexuality or whether they are compensatory. Why have so many homosexuals retired into the small effect, the ineffectual career, the stereotype, the card shop, the florist? *Be gentle with me?* Or do homosexuals know things others do not?

This way power lay: Once upon a time the homosexual appropriated to himself a mystical province, that of taste. Taste, which is, after all, the insecurity of the middle class, became the homosexual's licentiate to challenge the rule of nature. (The fairy in his blood, he intimated.)

Deciding how best to stick it may be only an architectural problem or a question of physics or of engineering or of cabinetry. Nevertheless, society's condemnation forced the homosexual to find his redemption outside nature. *We'll put a little skirt here.* The impulse is not to create but to re-create, to sham, to convert, to sauce, to rouge, to fragrance, to prettify. No effect is too small or too ephemeral to be snatched away from nature, to be ushered toward the perfection of artificiality. *We'll bring out the highlights there.* The homosexual has marshaled the architecture of the straight world to the very gates of Versailles—that great Vatican of fairyland—beyond which power is converted to leisure.

In San Francisco in the 1980s the highest form of art became interior decoration. The glory hole was thus converted to an eighteenth-century French foyer.

I live away from the street, in a back apartment, in two rooms. I use my bedroom as a visitor's room—the sleigh bed tricked up with

35

shams into a sofa—whereas I rarely invite anyone into my library, the public room, where I write, the public gesture.

40   I read in my bedroom in the afternoon because the light is good there, especially now, in winter, when the sun recedes from the earth.

There is a door in the south wall that leads to a balcony. The door was once a window. Inside the door, inside my bedroom, are twin green shutters. They are false shutters, of no function beyond wit. The shutters open into the room; they have the effect of turning my apartment inside out.

A few months ago I hired a man to paint the shutters green. I wanted the green shutters of Manet—you know the ones I mean—I wanted a weathered look, as of verdigris. For several days the painter labored, rubbing his paints into the wood and then wiping them off again. In this way he rehearsed for me decades of the ravages of weather. Yellow enough? Black?

The painter left one afternoon, saying he would return the next day, leaving behind his tubes, his brushes, his sponges and rags. He never returned. Someone told me he has AIDS.

Repainted facades extend now from Jackson Street south into what was once the heart of the black "Mo"—black Fillmore Street. Today there are watercress sandwiches at three o'clock where recently there had been loudmouthed kids, hole-in-the-wall bars, pimps. Now there are tweeds and perambulators, matrons and nannies. Yuppies. And gays.

45   The gay male revolution had greater influence on San Francisco in the 1970s than did the feminist revolution. Feminists, with whom I include lesbians—such was the inclusiveness of the feminist movement—were preoccupied with career, with escape from the house in order to create a sexually democratic city. Homosexual men sought to reclaim the house, the house that traditionally had been the reward for heterosexuality, with all its selfless tasks and burdens.

Leisure defined the gay male revolution. The gay political movement began, by most accounts, in 1969, with the Stonewall riots in New York City, whereby gay men fought to defend the nonconformity of their leisure.

It was no coincidence that homosexuals migrated to San Francisco in the 1970s, for the city was famed as a playful place, more Catholic than Protestant in its eschatological intuition. In 1975 the state of California legalized consensual homosexuality, and about that same time Castro Street, southwest of downtown, began to eclipse Polk Street as the homosexual address in San Francisco. Polk Street was a string of bars. The Castro was an entire district. The Castro had Victorian houses and churches, bookstores and restaurants, gyms, dry cleaners, supermarkets, and an elected member of the Board of Supervisors. The Castro supported baths and bars, but there was nothing furtive about them. On Castro Street the light of day penetrated gay life through clear plate-glass windows. The light of day discovered a new confidence, a new politics. Also a new look—a noncosmopolitan, Burt Reynolds, butch-kid style: beer, ball games, Levi's, short hair, muscles.

Gay men who lived elsewhere in the city, in Pacific Heights or in the Richmond, often spoke with derision of "Castro Street clones," describing the look, or scorned what they called the ghettoization of homosexuality. To an older generation of homosexuals, the blatancy of sexuality on Castro Street threatened the discreet compromise they had negotiated with a tolerant city.

As the Castro district thrived, Folsom Street, south of Market, also began to thrive, as if in counterdistinction to the utopian Castro. The Folsom Street area was a warehouse district of puddled alleys and deserted streets. Folsom Street offered an assortment of leather bars, an evening's regress to the outlaw sexuality of the Fifties, the Forties, the nineteenth century, and so on—an eroticism of the dark, of the Reeperbahn, or of the guardsman's barracks.

50   The Castro district implied that sexuality was more crucial, that homosexuality was the central fact of identity. The Castro district, with its ice-cream parlors and hardware stores, was the revolutionary place.

Into which carloads of vacant-eyed teenagers from other districts or from middle-class suburbs would drive after dark, cruising the neighborhood for solitary victims.

The ultimate gay basher was a city supervisor named Dan White, ex-cop, ex-boxer, ex-fireman, ex-altar boy. Dan White had grown up in the Castro district; he recognized the Castro revolution for what it was. Gays had achieved power over him. He murdered the mayor and he murdered the homosexual member of the Board of Supervisors.

Katherine, a sophisticate if ever there was one, nevertheless dismisses the two men descending the aisle at the Opera House: "All so sleek and smooth-jowled and silver-haired— they don't seem real, poor darlings. It must be because they don't have children."

Lodged within Katherine's complaint is the perennial heterosexual annoyance with the homosexual's freedom from child-rearing, which places the homosexual not so much beyond the pale as it relegates the homosexual outside "responsible" life.

55   It was the glamour of gay life, after all, as much as it was the feminist call to career, that encouraged heterosexuals in the 1970s to excuse themselves from nature, to swallow the birth-control pill. Who needs children? The gay bar became the paradigm for the single's bar. The gay couple became the paradigm for the selfish couple—all dressed up and everywhere to go. And there was the example of the gay house in illustrated life-style magazines. At the same time that suburban housewives were looking outside the home for

fulfillment, gay men were reintroducing a new generation in the city—heterosexual men and women—to the complacencies of the barren house.

Puritanical America dismissed gay camp followers as Yuppies; the term means to suggest infantility. Yuppies were obsessive and awkward in their materialism. Whereas gays arranged a decorative life against a barren state, Yuppies sought early returns—lives that were not to be all toil and spin. Yuppies, trained to careerism from the cradle, wavered in their pursuit of the northern European ethic—indeed, we might now call it the pan-Pacific ethic—in favor of the Mediterranean, the Latin, the Catholic, the Castro, the Gay.

The international architectural idioms of Skidmore, Owings & Merrill, which defined the city's skyline in the 1970s, betrayed no awareness of any street-level debate concerning the primacy of play in San Francisco nor of any human dramas resulting from urban redevelopment. The repellent office tower was a fortress raised against the sky, against the street, against the idea of a city. Offices were hives where money was made, and damn all.

In the 1970s San Francisco was divided between the interests of downtown and the pleasures of the neighborhoods. Neighborhoods asserted idiosyncrasy, human scale, light. San Francisco neighborhoods perceived downtown as working against their influence in determining what the city should be. Thus neighborhoods seceded from the idea of a city.

The gay movement rejected downtown as representing "straight" conformity. But was it possible that heterosexual Union Street was related to Castro Street? Was it possible that either was related to the Latino Mission district? Or to the Sino-Russian Richmond? San Francisco, though complimented worldwide for holding its center, was in fact without a vision of itself entire.

60   In the 1980s, in deference to the neighborhoods, City Hall would attempt a counterreformation of downtown, forbidding

"Manhattanization." Shadows were legislated away from parks and playgrounds. Height restrictions were lowered beneath an existing skyline. Design, too, fell under the retrojurisdiction of the city planner's office. The Victorian house was presented to architects as a model of what the city wanted to uphold and to become. In heterosexual neighborhoods, one saw newly built Victorians. Downtown, postmodernist prescriptions for playfulness advised skyscrapers to wear party hats, buttons, comic mustaches. Philip Johnson yielded to the dollhouse impulse to perch angels atop one of his skyscrapers.

In the 1970s, like a lot of men and women in this city, I joined a gym. My club, I've even caught myself calling it.

In the gay city of the 1970s, bodybuilding became an architectural preoccupation of the upper middle class. Bodybuilding is a parody of labor, a useless accumulation of the laborer's bulk and strength. No useful task is accomplished. And yet there is something businesslike about the habitués, and the gym is filled with the punch-clock logic of the workplace. Machines clank and hum. Needles on gauges toll spent calories.

The gym is at once a closet of privacy and an exhibition gallery. All four walls are mirrored.

I study my body in the mirror. Physical revelation—nakedness—is no longer possible, cannot be desired, for the body is shrouded in meat and wears itself.

65 The intent is some merciless press of body against a standard, perfect mold. Bodies are "cut" or "pumped" or "buffed" as on an assembly line in Turin. A body becomes so many extrovert parts. Delts, pecs, lats.

I harness myself in a Nautilus cage.

Lats become wings. For the gym is nothing if not the occasion for transcendence. From homosexual to autosexual . . .

I lift weights over my head, baring my teeth like an animal with the strain.

. . . to nonsexual. The effect of the overdeveloped body is the miniaturization of the sexual organs—of no function beyond wit. Behold the ape become Blakean angel, revolving in an empyrean of mirrors.

70 The nineteenth-century mirror over the fireplace in my bedroom was purchased by a decorator from the estate of a man who died last year of AIDS. It is a top-heavy piece, confusing styles. Two ebony-painted columns support a frieze of painted glass above the mirror. The frieze depicts three bourgeois Graces and a couple of freerange cherubs. The lake of the mirror has formed a cataract, and at its edges it is beginning to corrode.

Thus the mirror that now draws upon my room owns some bright curse, maybe—some memory not mine.

As I regard this mirror, I imagine St. Augustine's meditation slowly hardening into syllogism, passing down through centuries to confound us: Evil is the absence of good.

We have become accustomed to figures disappearing from our landscape. Does this not lead us to interrogate the landscape?

With reason do we invest mirrors with the superstition of memory, for they, though glass, though liquid captured in a bay, are so often less fragile than we are. They— bright ovals or rectangles or rounds—bump down unscathed, unspilled through centuries, whereas we . . .

75 The man in the red baseball cap used to jog so religiously on Marina Green. By the time it occurs to me that I have not seen him for months, I realize he may be dead—not lapsed, not moved away. People come and go in the city, it's true. But in San Francisco in 1990, death has become as routine an explanation for disappearance as Allied Van Lines.

AIDS, it has been discovered, is a plague of absence. Absence opened in the blood. Absence condensed into the fluid of passing emotion. Absence shot through opalescent tugs of semen to deflower the city.

And then AIDS, it was discovered, is a non-metaphorical disease, a disease like any other. Absence sprang from substance—a virus, a hairy bubble perched upon a needle, a platter of no intention served round: fever, blisters, a death sentence.

At first I heard only a few names—names connected, perhaps, with the right faces, perhaps not. People vaguely remembered, as through the cataract of this mirror, from dinner parties or from intermissions. A few articles in the press. The rumored celebrities. But within months the slow beating of the blood had found its bay.

One of San Francisco's gay newspapers, the *Bay Area Reporter,* began to accept advertisements from funeral parlors and casket makers, inserting them between the randy ads for leather bars and tanning salons. The *Reporter* invited homemade obituaries—lovers writing of lovers, friends remembering friends and the blessings of unexceptional life.

80   *Peter. Carlos. Gary. Asel. Perry. Nikos.*

Healthy snapshots accompany each annal. At the Russian River. By the Christmas tree. Lifting a beer. In uniform. A dinner jacket. A satin gown.

He was born in Puerto La Libertad, El Salvador.

He attended Apple Valley High School, where he was their first male cheerleader.

From El Paso. From Medford. From Germany. From Long Island.

85   I moved back to San Francisco in 1979. Oh, I had had some salad days elsewhere, but by 1979 I was a wintry man. I came here in order not to be distracted by the ambitions or, for that matter, the pleasures of others but to pursue my own ambition. Once here, though, I found the company of men who pursued an earthly paradise charming. Skepticism became my demeanor toward them—I was the dinner-party skeptic, a firm believer in Original Sin and in the limits of possibility.

Which charmed them.

He was a dancer.

He settled into the interior-design department of Gump's, where he worked until his illness.

He was a teacher.

César, for example.   90

César could shave the rind from any assertion to expose its pulp and jelly. But César was otherwise ruled by pulp. César loved everything that ripened in time. Freshmen. Bordeaux. César could fashion liturgy from an artichoke. Yesterday it was not ready (cocking his head, rotating the artichoke in his hand over a pot of cold water). Tomorrow will be too late (Yorick's skull). Today it is perfect (as he lit the fire beneath the pot). We will eat it now.

If he's lucky, he's got a year, a doctor told me. If not, he's got two.

The phone rang. AIDS had tagged a friend. And then the phone rang again. And then the phone rang again. Michael had tested positive. Adrian, well, what he had assumed were shingles . . . Paul was back in the hospital. And César, dammit, César, even César, especially César.

That winter before his death César traveled back to South America. On his return to San Francisco he described to me how he had walked with his mother in her garden—his mother chafing her hands as if she were cold. But it was not cold, he said. They moved slowly. Her summer garden was prolonging itself this year, she said. The cicadas will not stop singing.

When he lay on his deathbed, César said   95 everyone else he knew might get AIDS and die. He said I would be the only one spared—"spared" was supposed to have been chased with irony, I knew, but his voice was too weak to do the job. "You are too circumspect," he said then, wagging his finger upon the coverlet.

So I was going to live to see that the garden of earthly delights was, after all, only wallpaper—was that it, César? Hadn't I always said so? It was then I saw that the greater sin against heaven was my unwillingness to embrace life.

It was not as in some Victorian novel—the curtains drawn, the pillows plumped, the streets strewn with sawdust. It was not to be a matter of custards in covered dishes, steaming possets, *Try a little of this, my dear.* Or gathering up the issues of *Architectural Digest* strewn about the bed. Closing the biography of Diana Cooper and marking its place. Or the unfolding of discretionary screens, morphine, parrots, pavilions.

César experienced agony.

Four of his high school students sawed through a Vivaldi quartet in the corridor outside his hospital room, prolonging the hideous garden.

100   *In the presence of his lover Gregory and friends, Scott passed from this life . . .*

He died peacefully at home in his lover Ron's arms.

Immediately after a friend led a prayer for him to be taken home and while his dear mother was reciting the Twenty-third Psalm, Bill peacefully took his last breath.

I stood aloof at César's memorial, the kind of party he would enjoy, everyone said. And so for a time César lay improperly buried, unconvincingly resurrected in the conditional: would enjoy. What else could they say? César had no religion beyond aesthetic bravery.

Sunlight remains. Traffic remains. Nocturnal chic attaches to some discovered restaurant. A new novel is reviewed in the *New York Times.* And the mirror rasps on its hook. The mirror is lifted down.

105   A priest friend, a good friend, who out of naiveté plays the cynic, tells me—this is on a bright, billowy day; we are standing outside— "It's not as sad as you may think. There is at least spectacle in the death of the young. Come to the funeral of an old lady sometime if you want to feel an empty church."

I will grant my priest friend this much: that it is easier, easier on me, to sit with gay men in hospitals than with the staring old. Young men talk as much as they are able.

But those who gather around the young man's bed do not see spectacle. This doll is Death. I have seen people caressing it, staring Death down. I have seen people wipe its tears, wipe its ass; I have seen people kiss Death on his lips, where once there were lips.

Chris was inspired after his own diagnosis in July 1987 with the truth and reality of how such a terrible disease could bring out the love, warmth, and support of so many friends and family.

Sometimes no family came. If there was family, it was usually mother. Mom. With her suitcase and with the torn flap of an envelope in her hand.

Brenda. Pat. Connie. Toni. Soledad.   110

Or parents came but then left without reconciliation, some preferring to say cancer.

But others came. Sissies were not, after all, afraid of Death. They walked his dog. They washed his dishes. They bought his groceries. They massaged his poor back. They changed his bandages. They emptied his bedpan.

Men who sought the aesthetic ordering of existence were recalled to nature. Men who aspired to the mock-angelic settled for the shirt of hair. The gay community of San Francisco, having found freedom, consented to necessity—to all that the proud world had for so long held up to them, withheld from them, as "real humanity."

And if gays took care of their own, they were not alone. AIDS was a disease of the entire city; its victims were as often black, Hispanic, straight. Neither were Charity and Mercy only white, only male, only gay. Others came. There were nurses and nuns and the couple from next door, co-workers, strangers, teenagers, corporations, pensioners. A community was forming over the city.

115 *Cary and Rick's friends and family wish to thank the many people who provided both small and great kindnesses.*

He was attended to and lovingly cared for by the staff at Coming Home Hospice.

And the saints of this city have names listed in the phone book, names I heard called through a microphone one cold Sunday in Advent as I sat in Most Holy Redeemer Church. It might have been any of the churches or community centers in the Castro district, but it happened at Most Holy Redeemer at a time in the history of the world when the Roman Catholic Church still pronounced the homosexual a sinner.

A woman at the microphone called upon volunteers from the AIDS Support Group to come forward. One by one, in twos and threes, throughout the church, people stood up, young men and women, and middle-aged and old, straight, gay, and all of them shy at being called. Yet they came forward and assembled in the sanctuary, facing the congregation, grinning self-consciously at one another, their hands hidden behind them.

I am preoccupied by the fussing of a man sitting in the pew directly in front of me—in his seventies, frail, his iodine-colored hair combed forward and pasted upon his forehead. Fingers of porcelain clutch the pearly beads of what must have been his mother's rosary. He is not the sort of man any gay man would have chosen to become in the 1970s. He is probably not what he himself expected to become. Something of the old dear about him, wizened butterfly, powdered old pouf. Certainly he is what I fear becoming. And then he rises, this old monkey, with the most beatific dignity, in answer to the microphone, and he strides into the sanctuary to take his place in the company of the Blessed.

So this is it—this, what looks like a 120 Christmas party in an insurance office and not as in Renaissance paintings, and not as we had always thought, not some flower-strewn, some sequined curtain call of grease-painted heroes gesturing to the stalls. A lady with a plastic candy cane pinned to her lapel. A Castro clone with a red bandanna exploding from his hip pocket. A perfume-counter lady with an Hermès scarf mantled upon her left shoulder. A black man in a checkered sports coat. The pink-haired punkess with a jewel in her nose. Here, too, is the gay couple in middle age, wearing interchangeable plaid shirts and corduroy pants. Blood and shit and Mr. Happy Face. These know the weight of bodies.

Bill died.

. . . Passed on to heaven.
. . . Turning over in his bed one night and then gone.

These learned to love what is corruptible, while I, barren skeptic, reader of St. Augustine, curator of the earthly paradise, inheritor of the empty mirror, I shift my tailbone upon the cold, hard pew.

READING AND THINKING

1. As you read "Late Victorians," highlight the religious allusions and images throughout the essay. How do they contribute to the essay's idea?

2. After reading the entire essay, consider why Rodriguez begins with Saint Augustine and a sense of "our true home"? What "other city" do you believe Rodriguez considers us "meant for"? Why does he think so?

3. What does Rodriguez make of the relationship between yuppies and homosexuals? Does he oversimplify? Explain.

4. What do you think Rodriguez learns, in the course of the essay, about himself and his own capacity for demonstrating compassion?

THINKING AND WRITING

1. Write a short account of what you think Rodriguez means by the "grammar of the gay city." Why are houses so important to that grammar? Why, especially, Victorian houses?

2. Write a paragraph about Rodriguez's implicit criticism of gay life in San Francisco. Focus not on those things he associates with "society's" criticism but on his own criticism. Cite specific examples where he suggests problems and shortcomings associated with gay life.

3. What are the most telling strengths of the homosexual community as Rodriguez reveals them? Cite specific evidence from the text as you develop a short, focused response paper.

4. How do both the *idea* and the *reality* of death inform this essay?

5. Interpret the final paragraph of the essay. Include evidence from the middle of the essay to support your interpretation.

CITIES ON THE HILL:
AN OCCASION FOR WRITING

Having read Rodriguez's account of that California city on the hill and having considered the far-reaching implications of that Mecca for gay men, you will now have an opportunity to consider how our human ideals—our deepest desires for a particular community, a way of life, or a meaningful human relationship—always come up against, always abut, the real. What to do in the face of that clash between idealized needs and desires and the reality that faces us, that is the prevailing question that will guide our inquiry. The following art objects (a photograph, a renaissance painting, and a fashion photograph) will give you a chance to ponder both the power of images and the clash between the real and the ideal in our culture and in our lives.

PREPARING TO WRITE: OCCASIONS TO THINK ABOUT WHAT YOU SEE

1. The first image appears to be a celebration. What might the rainbow colors tell us about the nature and purpose of the celebration? What can you tell from the people themselves?

2. Paysha Stockton, a correspondent for *The Boston Globe,* asked a pertinent question about a group of gay and lesbian men and women who paraded down main street in Plymouth, Massachusetts: "What would the pilgrims have thought?" Answering her own question, she replied, "Hard to say." What do you think? Another onlooker proclaimed: "That's why the Pilgrims came here, for religious freedom and to show individuality. . . . It's all very symbolic." What is the religious connection?

3. One participant from the Plymouth, Massachusetts, parade held a sign that admonished, "Please USA: Repent and Turn Back to Jesus." Which of these last two responses would more adequately represent your own community? Explain why.

© Tina Fineberg/AP Photo

Gay Pride Parade in New York City, 2003

PIERO DELLA FRANCESCA,
Saint Augustine (1454)

PIERO DELLA FRANCESCA, *Saint Michael the Archangel (1454)*

4. How would you characterize the paintings of the two saints (Augustine and Michael the Archangel) based on their costumes or clothing? Test your speculations by searching the Internet for a brief summary of what each saint represents to the Catholic church and to the mythology of saints in general.

5. Which saint appears the more likely to belong in an essay about the gay life in San Francisco as Rodriguez accounts for it? Why?

GUY BOURDIN, *Waiting*

6. Name five things that strike you about this photograph by Guy Bourdin. Which of the five things seems most important to you? Explain.

7. What is the relationship between the hanging clothes, the large clock, the two sets of beer cans on the floor, and the posture of the clothed man?

8. Why do you suppose the Bourdin photograph above appeared in the male version of *Vogue* magazine in France? What do you think it is selling?

MOVING TOWARD ESSAY: OCCASIONS TO ANALYZE AND REFLECT

1. Rodriguez begins his essay with a reference to Saint Augustine and then refers to him again in the final paragraph. Account for the different rhetorical use he makes of the saint in these two instances.

2. Consider the images of the Gay Pride Parade and Bourdin's *Waiting*. What do those images tell us about the needs and desires of gays and lesbians? How do these needs and desires differ from your own? Explain.

3. What has Rodriguez made visible in his essay about the value of community and the difficulty of maintaining one's identity within the collective? Explain.

WRITING THOUGHTFULLY: OCCASIONS FOR IDEAS AND ESSAYS

1. Tell a compelling story of your own about your experiences within a group that set out to pursue some ideal and then ran up against a wall of reality. Make visible in this essay, through your language and your re-creation of telling scenes of experience, just what your group gained and lost in the culture clash.

2. Consider a particular political or religious group's objection to something that is going on in America. Determine how effectively and logically the group uses word pictures, and perhaps other images, to make its case. Write a brief account of your analysis for the group itself, one that could either confirm or refute the objection.

CREATING OCCASIONS

1. Select a tightly-knit group that you have been excluded from or have simply chosen not to join. Reconsider that group from a new perspective. Observe the group in action, talk to those in it, perhaps even photograph members as they go about daily activities. Your task is to tell a revealing story about how your detailed investigation over a period of time shaped your final ideas about the group itself. Let Rodriguez show you how to use your own experiences to add a dimension to all else that you tell us about the group itself.

2. Select four or five images from magazines or newspapers that reveal something important about a peculiar aspect of America that seems most foreign to you. Write two assessments of those images: one that reveals what you believe that you can see in the images, and a second assessment that reveals what you believe has been left out of the pictures. Finally, reveal in a brief story what you learned from these assessments.

Jim W. Corder (1929–1998)

Jim Corder taught at Texas Christian University in Fort Worth, Texas, during his entire professional career. He was well known to his students and his colleagues as a classical rhetorician with a quirky bent toward the personal. He had an unending fascination with *ethos,* what Aristotle taught us about the character of the speaker. Against a host of countervailing scholarly views, Corder never abandoned his belief that the speaker (or writer) leaves discernable, important traces of himself or herself in written texts he or she creates. Two recent books have paid tribute to Corder's work, making his ideas and his texts available to all of us: *Beyond Postprocess and Postmodernism: Essays on the Spaciousness of Rhetoric* (2002) and *Selected Essays of Jim W. Corder: Pursuing the Personal in Scholarship, Teaching, and Writing* (2004). Corder's own books include *Chronicle of a Small Town* (1998), *Yonder: Life on the Far Side of Change* (1992), and *Hunting Lieutenant Chadbourne* (1993).

ACHING FOR A SELF

This essay was published posthumously in *Selected Essays of Jim W. Corder.* In it we hear Corder ruminating about whether we exist in the texts that we write. As Corder ponders this large question, he alternates between the scholarly and the ordinary, trying to figure out for himself and for us just how important we are as thinkers, writers, and storytellers. Two of the central questions that haunt Corder are, "Do we matter as individuals?" and "Can a reader find us in the texts we write?" His questioning is wide-ranging, his sources varied, but finally, he brings us to ourselves, asking us to see more clearly just how important we might be to history as we make a written record of our thoughts about our experiences.

1   Sometimes, late at night, I think that contemporary theorists have eradicated soul, selfhood, identity. Social constructionists declare that we don't exist, at least not as single, perceiving, autonomous, responsible souls. Intertextualists declare that our texts don't exist except as amalgamations of the culture's texts. Deconstructive theorists declare that if we exist, we don't exist as we thought we did, but in rhetorics holding diverse values and assumptions that we mistook for truths. Reader-response theorists declare that if we exist, we exist over yonder, not in our own creations, but in other people's perceptions of our creations. Those who advocate collaboration declare that we shouldn't exist; to claim autonomous selfhood is a sin, to be denounced as "radical individualism." I still sometimes think that I am real, but my existence is in doubt.

When you're facing bleakness, one thing to do is to go on into it, to see if you can come out on the other side.

We long to be absolutely present to the world, acknowledged, known, and cherished, and we long for the world to be absolutely present to us, there, real.

Words won't be things, and yet in words we long for the absolute presence of things. In *On Longing: Narratives of the Miniature, the Gigantic, the Souvenir, the Collection,* Susan Stewart remarks that nostalgia must face the gap between words and things. It is, she says, the "sadness without an object." We cannot catch lived experience, for it has already, as Stewart sees it, been processed into commodities, prized for exchange value, not for use value. Still, Samuel Johnson had thought that "domestic privacies," the "minute details of daily life," would show who we are, and Laurence Sterne judged that "the little occurrences of life" would exhibit the truth of character. Our hopes, of course, don't always eventuate as our announcements have predicted. What we write or show, Stewart says, is the "trace of the real."

5   Of course.

I had hoped to catch reminders of the world in words, sometimes in little pictures, small ink sketches that I entertain myself with. That may mean that I have tried, as Stewart puts it, to take "the world as still life." The still life, she suggests, "speaks to the cultural organization of the material world": it does so "by concealing history and temporality; it engages in an illusion of timelessness. The message of the still life is that nothing changes; the instant described will remain as it is in the eye of the beholder, the individual perceiving subject."

No, I think not.

Words and images are incomplete class notes from the world, a way of catching reminders. Of course they are only traces. They were never anything but traces. The still life does not conceal history and temporality; it dramatizes history and temporality. The still life invites because it is not still; it is always a trace, always fleeting, always only what a single soul beheld, as that could be rendered by errant perception, failed memory, and faltering hand, always only what somebody was able to see and to rearrange, calling from out there for us to see and to rearrange.

Nostalgia, I think, is not a "social disease," as Stewart calls it, or a neurosis. It is a predicament and a natural human condition. The possibility for nostalgia is always present, though some will always look away. During and after great change—and who has not lived during and after great change, and which moment does not occur during and after great change?—we sometimes need to know the name and look of things. The world is always coming unfixed, and we keep trying to know what it's like, what it was like in some before that we imagine.

10   Nostalgics—that is, most of us some of the time, some of us all of the time—can't have what they ache for. Neither can I. I have wanted to find sources, origins, forces, and track them all the way to here. I can't. There aren't enough words and pictures. I can't find the rest, or I'm unwilling to make the rest.

I can think about the words and pictures, think toward them, but probably not through them.

They are scraps. They are notes from the world. I finger them, as I finger the white rocks in my pocket, and wonder what the words and pictures, things, places, and people did to or for or with or against me, and you, and everyone.

I think there is no really real behind the pictures and words, no really real back or out or over there. My representations will not, as Ned Lukacher puts it in *Primal Scenes,* "provide access to the real." No "primal scene" waits that will alone show the truth all at once, once and for all.

And yet words and pictures are real. I am real. You are real. We are our time, already here, present, yet also ready to be found.

Scraps are what there is. Remnants.   15

Still we look for the world and for ourselves, yearning, calling out. We go on. We go on looking for the world and for ourselves in it. Some, perhaps, look for what Julia Kristeva calls the "lost thing," "that elusive pre-object," a memory of identity with the other before emotional severance. Some—including many commentators on education—look for a lost authority. Some search for the myths that, as Karsten Harries puts it, are "born of the human inability to accept that we and all we have created someday will be past, will have vanished without a trace, unremembered and unredeemed."

We have wanted to believe that we can be present to the world in what we say or write. Our identity now and our survival hereafter depended, we thought, on that possibility. We have been, whether knowingly or not, part of a two-thousand-year tradition that encouraged us to believe that our character could be in the text of what we say, that we do exist, that we can be in our words and own them even in the acts of giving them away. Character, we believed, can come through speech. If it is the real voice of a genuine personality, then presence will emerge in discourse. To that end, writing teachers have for generations urged students in composition classes to "find their voices," to show readers the directions of their thought and the particularities, anecdotes, and evidence of their lives.

Voluntary Exiles

We don't believe too easily now. We are not at the center. Our characters do not emerge in our discourses. The world is not present to us, and we are not present to the world. We miss ourselves. We dismiss ourselves. We are gone.

We decide against the individual. Where the soul is noticeable or insistent, we proclaim that "radical individualism" is at work and expect the troublesome soul to subside or to evolve.

20 No matter. I can learn not to be afraid of dismissal or extinction. I can learn what I have said myself: we are remnants, scraps, leftovers, already outside, at the edge. Where we were not exiles before, we have exiled ourselves.

When we fell into history—and sometimes we have to do that over and over, day after day—we tore ourselves loose from the past, and from our sacraments, from the contents and from the values we like to think once gave meaning to our lives. [. . .]

Still, if you are a soul in here, how do you become a self out there?

One answer: you don't. What goes on is what's taken, not what you give, traces of yourself, perhaps, but not yourself. Sometimes, people out there decide that we don't exist. In Pinkie Gordon Lane's "Poems to My Father," the speaker says

> I meant to tell you this, Papa,
> I've divorced myself
> from your memory.

Then later she goes on:

> You never happened,
> Papa.
> You were a shadow
> a low light
> a lost love
> folding into the oval
> of your night.

Sometimes we don't exist, regardless of 25 what people out there decide. Voice, Lukacher says, "has always been a mode of distortion and concealment, for along with its promise of presence, voice has also proclaimed [. . .] a haunting message of distance and absolute separation." We fade away from each other, and do not. We are not present to each other, and we are. There's less to me, and more, than meets the eye or ear.

If you are a soul in here, how do you become a self out there?

A second answer: you try.

If I set out and show myself to the other, what rhetoric do I use? Do I have any choice? Do I try to get into the other's rhetoric? That sounds friendly and companionable, but it would be pretty lonesome if I were still over here while trying to talk over yonder. Do I lose my rhetoric in the other's? When do I declare myself, if I know how, and will it matter all the way over yonder?

How do you compose yourself for another? Others, I think, might say that here and elsewhere I'm asking the wrong questions where none is right. Perhaps there is no composing yourself for another, no matter what you do: you're always left behind by your own text.

Reason enough to be a little doubtful. 30

Sometimes we speak or write tentatively and conditionally, trying to reconstruct ourselves jackleg style. We try to make do, try to tell soul to someone across the way. We try to get real only to learn that our own rhetorics won't let us: they go off and leave us behind, remnants.

Reason enough to be a little doubtful, to choose a tentative and provisional way. And I think I'd rather choose that way, even if, therefore, I cannot be real, even if I am perceived to have chosen altogether otherwise, than to fancy myself a completed, fully asserted person.

Were that possible, and were I to try to speak to the other across the way, my rhetoric would seek to expand, to take up space, to testify that I am real at the cost of the other's diminution. We are apart. I am here. You are there. Our rhetorics cannot occupy the same space at the same time. They compete. [. . .]

And yet, there's every reason to come together, not to merge ourselves in some new collective, but to save one another. We may seldom get things right in concert, but we never will if each of us remains alone.

35   The story I keep telling myself employs some images, whether they are accurate enough or not, but ignores or misses others. Memory is always a current record, encumbered, of another time that was also encumbered.

All the more reason, then, to hunt for versions of things, for images others saw. We might yet learn to tell our stories, slowly and painstakingly, to one another. I might yet catch what was, what transpires, myself. The daily domestic particulars of our lives give us texture, identity; they give local habitations to our histories. If you come toward me showing me the things of your life that gave you residence, perhaps I will see you. If you can see me in my local habitations, perhaps I existed there.

Blessed particulars always belong to someone. Can they be given to someone else, called back for someone else, given, offered? Offered, but not required of another? No one of us is a measure for mankind. The observation and rendition of particulars will not necessarily yield universal truth. One moment isn't all of time, or one look a whole view, or one sense of things a revelation about all things. To demand our particular experience of another is arrogance and dogma. May I offer particular experience? I have little else, if anything at all. The lives of particular persons "not distinguished," Samuel Johnson remarked, "by any striking or wonderful vicissitudes" can "lead the thoughts into domestic privacies, and display the details of daily life." Are there circumstances—present and visible, gone and invisible—that might matter as much as events of public moment? If we showed them to one another, fully, painstakingly, might we come to know one another? If we knew one another, might we let one another live? Other worlds always whisper beside this one, or pound against it. We are always in diverse, sometimes competing, rhetorics. The consequence is often sad and sometimes calamitous, but living among competing rhetorics also guarantees, if we will listen, that we stay resolutely multivocal against the ignorance, arrogance, and dogma of univocality.

Each of us, alone, must speak and write and go on speaking and writing, adding words, piling up words. Our conversation is not like sculpture, where you get what you're looking for by chipping and whittling away. Mostly, we have to add and pile on. Unless we're uncommonly lucky, the first words aren't enough. Oftener than not, John Kouwenhoven remarks, we use words as "general terms or names referring to things that are individual and particular. Even though we know, for example, that no two blades of grass are alike, the word 'grass' suggests an identity. This suggestion of identity encourages us to disregard the different looks, feels, tastes, and smells of the uncounted blades that constitute the actuality of grass as we experience it." But we don't have to disregard the differences. If we tell our stories carefully to one another, we might come to know what particular grass looks like and smells like and feels like and tastes like over here and over there and over yonder.

To make that possible, we have to save one another's views and words. And we have to remember that, however much we may have been socially constructed, however much we may be the creations of a discourse community, however much language may have written us, when a set of spoken or written words comes to us, some soul gathered them, whether under duress, through influence, or by choice. We ought to attend to that word-gathering soul.

40   As I suggested earlier, this is no longer a universally popular expectation. The individual speaker-writer blurs around the edges, fades from view.

Joel Haefner, for example, proposes that we convert the personal essay, which might have been a place to show our blades of grass, into a collaborative, collective enterprise. The personal essay, Haefner says, rests upon premises undergirded by "the shibboleth of individualism, and, concomitantly, the ideology of American democracy," and so was never free personal expression, though we have, he says, committed the genre to "radical individualism." The self is not unitary, Haefner says, but is created from and by groups, history, and social purposes; and language, he adds, is "not based on individual knowledge but on collective experience." This being so, he goes on, "then the referentiality of personal, expressive prose is called into question, and the accessibility of the personal essay to a universal readership that shares 'human experience' is also in doubt."

The linchpin for all these recent arguments for the revival of the essay remains the idea that the essay presents individualistic, "personal" knowledge. According to Good, "The essayist's personality is offered as a 'universal particular,' an example not of a particular virtue or vice, but of an 'actually existing' individual and the unorganized 'wholeness' of his experience." The problem raised here reflects what Terry Eagleton calls the "humanistic fallacy," "the naive notion that a literary text is just a kind of transcript of the living voice of a real man or woman addressing us."

Haefner argues further that, "if, as Robert Scholes suggests, 'the whole naive epistemology' that 'a complete self confronts a solid world, perceiving it directly and accurately, always capable of capturing it perfectly' is now 'lying in ruins around us,' then we need to find a new pedagogy that can still make use of the personal essay." This new essay, he proposes, will attempt "to balance the individualistic, expressive view of knowledge with a social, collective perspective," and the best approach is "to bring the personal essay into the collaborative writing project." Doing so, Haefner suggests, will, among other things, destabilize the personal essay further "by encouraging students not to create a unified, coherent first-person singular voice, but rather a mix of 'I' speakers."

Some essayists were always a mix of speakers. Some essayists were never complete selves, never confronted the world directly and accurately, never captured it perfectly, were never unified and coherent. Even Samuel Johnson sometimes changed direction in midessay.

But no matter. I think I'd rather we   45 emerged, not as a collective essay, but as an anthology of solitary shouts, remarks, grunts, and whispers.

I don't testify, by saying this, that together we'll get it all right. We more than likely wouldn't. I do mean that we can save one another, keep one another, hold one another, rather than lose one another in the collective, and I do mean that we will not, should not, escape the consequences of our selfhood. Instead of repudiating the self, let us own it by laying it bare.

That's not easy. It may not be possible. But it's what remnants have, and they may get there in the jackleg way, the remnant's itinerary. [. . .] I'm recommending texts that are open, owned, but also relinquished, given away. I'm recommending the given, shared jackleg text: "Well, there it is, by God—it ain't much, but it'll hold us until we can think of something better."

The ground for learning and writing and being is freedom. We don't achieve freedom; we are unreleased, always in some inventive world thinking the thoughts we can generate within it, always in some community thinking the thoughts we can generate in it. Nevertheless, freedom, the possibility of freedom, the hope of freedom makes the ground for learning and speaking and writing. And besides, there is a remarkable freedom that speakers and writers have: no one knows for sure the next word they'll say or inscribe.

Texts never were definitive unless we declared them so: Milton continues to emerge to us, unfinished; Johnson in the *Rambler* papers is as often exploring as proclaiming; "definitive" scholarly works require to be done again. The "definitive" text that we have sometimes imagined in the past is an owned and closed text. [. . .] When a text gets written, it becomes authority. When the words are said, the freedom seems to be over. In the classroom, for example, authority is always happening or about to happen; it can arise from diverse sources—from received notions about teaching, from the tyranny of the best student, from the tyranny of the most voluble student, from the arrangement of the room, from the personality of the teacher, from the general curriculum or the specific course plan, from textbooks.

50   This is not a notion that I'm easy with—the thought that authority (in texts, in classrooms, in life) is always happening or about to happen, that freedom, never wholly achieved, is always slipping away. Still, a little hope remains.

Over here is the *author,* who must be free, or have the hope of freedom, in order to learn and write. Over there is *authority,* the text become fixed, definitive. The *author* by making text makes *authority,* the definitive, the crafted, the finished. But in between is *authoring* or *authorship,* the process, the perpetual hunt for texts only to back off, to improvise, to try again, to search again for freedom in order to speak again in a continuous and provisional self-making. [. . .]

In *authorship,* we might begin to learn how to hold our own cyclings and dartings, dear though inept, to preserve them in order to change them, knowing that we invent in order to make structure in order to make styles in order to serve occasions in order to invent and make structures and styles and serve occasions, in order to be making ourselves.

I have sometimes despaired of jackleg carpentry, yearning for the well-crafted, the finished, the definitive. I should have known better.

Works Cited

Haefner, Joel. "Democracy, Pedagogy, and the Personal Essay." College English 54 (1992): 127–37.

Johnson, Samuel. Rambler No. 60. 1750. Samuel Johnson: Selected Poetry and Prose. Ed. Frank Brady and W. K. Wimsatt. Berkeley: U of California P, 1977. 181–85.

Lane, Pinkie Gordon. "Poems to My Father." Girl at the Window: Poems. Baton Rouge: Louisiana State UP, 1991. 1–5.

Lukacher, Ned. Primal Scenes: Literature, Philosophy, Psychoanalysis. Ithaca: Cornell UP, 1986.

Stewart, Susan. On Longing: Narratives of the Miniature, the Gigantic, the Souvenir, the Collection. Baltimore: Johns Hopkins UP, 1984.

READING AND THINKING

1. Corder's first paragraph is heady, scholarly, giving us a brief account of a number of "contemporary [composition] theorists." What, according to Corder, is the overall effect of these theories? How is the paragraph's final sentence a response to these theories?

2. In paragraph seventeen, Corder tells us, "We have been, whether knowingly or not, part of a two-thousand-year tradition that encouraged us to believe that our character could be in the text of what we say, that we do exist, that we can be in our words and own them even in the acts of giving them away"? How do you imagine that your own character might manifest itself in the words that you use, the texts that you create?

3. In the section of his essay titled "Voluntary Exiles" Corder worries over the relationship between our inside thoughts (the working of our souls) and the creation of thoughts in language for the outside world. Why is he so concerned about telling "our stories carefully to one another"? Why are such stories so important?

4. What, according to Corder, is the danger of the "collective"? What does the danger have to do with the soul, with our survival?

THINKING AND WRITING

1. Corder's seventh paragraph—"No, I think not."—is a response to a remark by Susan Stewart in the previous paragraph about the "still life." Consider the eighth paragraph and then explain in your own words why Corder rebuts Stewart's idea.

2. Consider again the first section of the essay, the first fourteen paragraphs. In a page or two explain the relationship between "words and images" and the concept of "nostalgia." What might that relationship have to do with the "aching" suggested in the essay's title?

3. In another essay Corder offers this definition of rhetoric: "Rhetoric, I think, can be taken to mean here the whole system by which a world is made, known, and made knowable in language." In "Aching for a Self," what does Corder suggest about the nature and importance of our own rhetorics? Why, despite the difficulty of making our rhetorics, must we go on to tell our stories? Cite crucial words from Corder's essay to substantiate your answer about why the stories that constitute our own rhetorics are so important.

4. What does Corder mean by "jackleg carpentry"? Why is the image so important to this essay? Cite evidence from the essay to substantiate your answer.

USING AND PRESERVING THE SELF: AN OCCASION FOR WRITING

Corder's concern about the power of the collective to stamp out aggressive individualism calls to mind Mark Doty's powerful tribute to the healing power of the collective during times of sorrow and loss. Rodriguez also alludes to such power in the final paragraphs of his essay when individuals come together to mourn and celebrate the lives of those they have lost, but we see struggling individuals form within the larger culture a smaller one as an act of preservation and survival. Virginia Woolf gives us yet another perspective on the individual, a perspective that aligns itself with Corder's as she reveals to us just how Mrs. Crowe, a single-minded individualist, comes to represent an entire city.

This Occasion will give you an opportunity to think about acts of individualism that seek to preserve the aching self that Corder writes about—a self that is always being remade as it attempts to make itself known to others. One of our chief concerns as we consider the images will be to think about the importance of writing as a way of preserving our own self.

Lancôme billboard, New York City

PREPARING TO WRITE: OCCASIONS TO THINK ABOUT WHAT YOU SEE

1. Characterize the woman on the billboard, whose maker proclaims her "BRONZED."
    Name specific details within the portrait.

2. Is bronzed woman a rugged individualist or an advertising pawn? Or both? Explain.
    What is she actually selling? Are you sure? What is her invitation to those who pass
    beneath her on Houston, one of New York City's busiest cross-streets?

3. Characterize the group of women in the Dove advertisement. What do you think they
    are proclaiming? Are they an advertising pawn for Dove soap? What in the advertise-
    ment informs you?

4. Compare these women to the bronzed woman in the Lancome advertisement. What
    does that comparison tell you about the women, the advertisers, and the targeted au-
    dience?

5. What does the comparison tell you about yourself and your values?

curvy thighs, bigger bums,
rounder stomachs.
What better way to
test our firming range?

There's not much point in testing
a new firming lotion on size-eight
supermodel thighs, is there?
That's why Dove's Firming range
was tested on ordinary women with
real lives to live – and real, curvy
thighs to firm. After using Dove's
nourishing and effective combination
of moisturisers and seaweed
extracts, we asked if they'd go in
front of the camera. What better
way to show how they felt about the
unretouched, unairbrushed results?

new Dove
Firming Range
Gel Cream · Body Wash · Lotion

MOVING TOWARD ESSAY: OCCASIONS TO ANALYZE AND REFLECT

1. Corder leans aggressively towards believing that we leave traces of ourselves in the texts we write. Select two or three sentences that give you a sense of Corder himself. Reveal what you see.

2. Select three more sentences that tell you something important about Corder based on the shape of the sentences and the way they work, something that characterizes his way of thinking. Explain what you see.

3. Select a telling sentence from Woolf, Rodriguez, and Corder. Compare these sentences in terms of style and content. Reveal what each tells you about the writer.

4. Corder suggests that we should come toward one another with our stories. Why does he believe that telling our stories is important?

WRITING THOUGHTFULLY: OCCASIONS FOR IDEAS AND ESSAYS

1. Woolf suggests in her essay "A Sketch of the Past" that certain moments from our lives embed themselves in memory; they seem to be accompanied, she says, by a sledge-hammer blow. They last. Such moments need not be about life, death, war, revolution. Instead they may involve a verbal exchange with another person, an overheard conversation, a smell, a telling gesture. Recover one of those moments from memory and re-create it so that others can enter it; make it scenic and dramatic as you capture it.

2. Reconsider the re-creation you did in Question 1 above. How might that story turn out to be a way of preserving your self? How might it also be historically significant? Explain in a short analysis of your own work.

3. The *New York Times,* in an editorial titled "Some Notes on Reality," tells us that the Dove women—"brightly lit, smiling broadly and unmodishly from the sides of buses—are not likely to put the tall, thin tribe of beauties out of work anytime soon. But they give heart to real women everywhere." They go on to ask us to imagine "what would happen if the world of television and magazine and billboard ads really represented the world we see around us." Write a letter to the editor of the *NYT* regarding what you think might happen.

4. Commenting on this same advertisement, in the same editorial, the *NYT* said, "You won't be seeing a 'real men' movement anytime soon, of course, but only because there is no need for it." Write a letter to the editor responding to this claim. Remember: such letters must be brief and to the point.

CREATING OCCASIONS

1. Create a conversation between Doty and Corder about the importance of the individual and the importance of the collective. Try to keep each speaker in character: use language the way they would; think and write under their influence.

2. Reconsider the Dove women. Why do you suppose it took a corporate-sponsored, collective act (four women instead of one rugged individualist) to present to the public the bodies of real women? We also know that Dove made its decision "to use real women after research showed 98% of British women think models used in beauty advertising are unrealistic." Write an essay about what you think it takes to overcome the power of the collective. (Do not forget what Berger taught you about the consequences of the "system.")

In thinking about identity, we consider,
among other aspects, our roles and
relationships. How would you describe the

ROLES AND RELATIONSHIPS

of some of the people depicted here?
For what occasion do you think this
mural was painted? What occasions
for writing does this image offer, or in
other words, what specific part about
this image would prompt you to write?

6

IDENTITY

How often, when you fill out an application for school or work or a questionnaire for a survey, are you asked to check a box designating your race or ethnicity? The answer, of course, is often, as race and ethnicity—as well as gender—are considered significant aspects of identity. Each of these forms of identity, unfortunately, has been used to typecast people to limit their opportunities for social advancement, jobs, promotions, and the like.

Our identity, however, is more than a matter of gender, race, or ethnicity. Beyond these categories, identity includes the myriad groups to which we belong—our identities as members of families, for example, and as members of formal and informal social groups. We may think of ourselves, for instance, as feminists (whatever our gender), as auto racing enthusiasts, as art lovers, as movie or history buffs. We may identify ourselves as students or teachers, as athletes or musicians, as avid readers or rap enthusiasts.

Identity is thus neither an absolute category nor a singular one. Nor is identity a static category. Our identities are multiple and changing, a blend of how we see ourselves and how others see us in our multiple roles, along with a shifting set of selves we present to the world—one face to our friends; another to our families; and still others to our classmates, coworkers, and acquaintances.

Taken together, the writers in this chapter make clear how identity is more than just a matter of race or gender or ethnicity, although they do so while focusing on one or more of those categories. Brent Staples, N. Scott Momaday, and James Baldwin emphasize issues of race in their essays; Zora Neale Hurston's "How It Feels to Be Colored Me" deals with issues of race and gender; Judith Ortiz Cofer's essay "The Myth of the Latin Woman" centers on issues about ethnicity; and Eva Hoffman deals with issues of social and cultural identity in her essay "Lost in Translation." Although one particular aspect of identity may be highlighted in a particular essay, it is highlighted against the backdrop of other aspects of identity.

151

THE RACIAL SELF

Racial identity can be a complicated matter. Things become far more complicated when we consider the question of whether race is a biological category based on genetic differences or a socially constructed category based on physical appearance or shared culture. If you are of mixed racial ancestry, which box do you check on surveys or forms, if you are inclined to check a racial category box at all? And why is there a box to check?

The question of racial identity, historically, has been more of an issue for nonwhites than for people of other races, at least in the United States. For whites, the identity question involves ethnicity—whether we are of Irish or Italian descent, for example. These ethnic categories, too, are fraught with complexity, because like racial categories they lump people of different backgrounds together without regard for their many differences. Not every person of Jewish heritage (or Chinese or Latino background) shares the same ethnic heritage. So how do we define a race without excluding anyone? Can we ever accurately define a race?

Socioeconomic inequality among whites, black Americans, and Hispanics continues to be a critical problem in the United States. Educational achievement gaps continue to exist among races. For instance, in 2004 in the state of Indiana, 39% of black high school children and 44% of Hispanic high school children passed their English language ability exit examination on the first try, whereas 75% of white high school children passed on the first try, according to the National Center for Education Statistics. The reasons for such achievement gaps are complex and involve many kinds of inequality, from those in educational opportunities and school funding to inequalities in health care, home life, and extracurricular support, but these problems should lead us to examine how race can affect various aspects of one's life. Racial antagonism remains and has been exacerbated by the increasing numbers of immigrant minorities of other races, including Asian and Hispanic populations, vying for their share of the American dream.

Race, however, is a personal as well as a social issue. Brent Staples's essay "Just Walk on By" deals with his feelings about how others perceive him. Judith Ortiz Cofer and Zora Neale Hurston confront their culture to identify how their identities have been shaped. Along with identity, culture and race are important categories of self-definition, significantly affecting how we define ourselves (and how others define us), even when that self-definition is assumed rather than announced, taken as self-evident rather than insisted upon as a social or political category. Whatever status we grant our race, it remains an inescapable aspect of who we are. The essays in this cluster make that point abundantly clear.

Brent Staples (b. 1951)

Brent Staples grew up in a poor neighborhood of Chester, Pennsylvania, and attended Widener University on scholarship, later receiving a doctorate in psychology from the University of Chicago. After a brief stint as a teacher, he took a job as a reporter with the *Chicago Sun-Times.* Later, he was hired to write for the *New York Times,* where he is now a member of the editorial board and a contributor of opinion columns under his own byline. His 1994 memoir, *Parallel Time: Growing Up in Black and White,* explores his experiences as a black youth trying to escape the poverty and violence that claimed the life of his younger brother.

JUST WALK ON BY

In "Just Walk on By," Staples tells a series of anecdotes that help us understand how race impinges on his experience. Through these interrelated stories, Staples makes clear how his race is inescapable in the way others perceive him. The fact that he is a big black man and not a small one further accentuates his race and contributes to the fear he engenders, irrespective of his behavior, his intentions, or his true self.

1   My first victim was a woman—white, well dressed, probably in her late twenties. I came upon her late one evening on a deserted street in Hyde Park, a relatively affluent neighborhood in an otherwise mean, impoverished section of Chicago. As I swung onto the avenue behind her, there seemed to be a discreet, uninflammatory distance between us. Not so. She cast back a worried glance. To her, the youngish black man—a broad six feet two inches with a beard and billowing hair, both hands shoved into the pockets of a bulky military jacket—seemed menacingly close. After a few more quick glimpses, she picked up her pace and was soon running in earnest. Within seconds she disappeared into a cross street.

That was more than a decade ago. I was twenty-two years old, a graduate student newly arrived at the University of Chicago. It was in the echo of that terrified woman's footfalls that I first began to know the unwieldy inheritance I'd come into—the ability to alter public space in ugly ways. It was clear that she thought herself the quarry of a mugger, a rapist, or worse. Suffering a bout of insomnia, however, I was stalking sleep, not defenseless wayfarers. As a softy who is scarcely able to take a knife to a raw chicken—let alone hold one to a person's throat—I was surprised, embarrassed, and dismayed all at once. Her flight made me feel like an accomplice in tyranny. It also made it clear that I was indistinguishable from the muggers who occasionally seeped into the area from the surrounding ghetto. That first encounter, and those that followed, signified that a vast, unnerving gulf lay between nighttime pedestrians—particularly women—and me. And I soon gathered that being perceived as dangerous is a hazard in itself. I only needed to turn a corner into a dicey situation, or crowd some frightened, armed person in a foyer somewhere, or make an errant move after being pulled over by a policeman. Where fear and weapons meet—and they often do in urban America—there is always the possibility of death.

In that first year, my first away from my hometown, I was to become thoroughly familiar with the language of fear. At dark, shadowy intersections, I could cross in front of a car stopped at a traffic light and elicit the *thunk, thunk, thunk, thunk* of the driver—black, white, male, or female—hammering down the door locks. On less traveled streets after dark, I grew accustomed to but never comfortable with people crossing to the other side of the street rather than pass me. Then there were the standard unpleasantries with policemen, doormen, bouncers, cab-drivers, and others whose business it is to screen out troublesome individuals *before* there is any nastiness.

I moved to New York nearly two years ago and I have remained an avid night walker. In central Manhattan, the near-constant crowd cover minimizes tense one-on-one street encounters. Elsewhere—in SoHo, for example, where sidewalks are narrow and tightly spaced buildings shut out the sky—things can get very taut indeed.

5   After dark, on the warrenlike streets of Brooklyn where I live, I often see women who fear the worst from me. They seem to have set their faces on neutral, and with their purse straps strung across their chests bandolier-style, they forge ahead as though bracing themselves against being tackled. I understand, of course, that the danger they perceive is not a hallucination. Women are particularly vulnerable to street violence, and young black males are drastically over-represented among the perpetrators of that violence. Yet these truths are no solace against the kind of alienation that comes of being ever the suspect, a fearsome entity with whom pedestrians avoid making eye contact.

It is not altogether clear to me how I reached the ripe old age of twenty-two without being conscious of the lethality night-time pedestrians attributed to me. Perhaps it was because in Chester, Pennsylvania, the small, angry industrial town where I came of age in the 1960s, I was scarcely noticeable against a backdrop of gang warfare, street knifings, and murders. I grew up one of the good boys, had perhaps a half-dozen fist-fights. In retrospect, my shyness of combat has clear sources.

As a boy, I saw countless tough guys locked away; I have since buried several,

too. They were babies, really—a teenage cousin, a brother of twenty-two, a childhood friend in his mid-twenties—all gone down in episodes of bravado played out in the streets. I came to doubt the virtues of intimidation early on. I chose, perhaps unconsciously, to remain a shadow—timid, but a survivor.

The fearsomeness mistakenly attributed to me in public places often has a perilous flavor. The most frightening of these confusions occurred in the late 1970s and early 1980s, when I worked as a journalist in Chicago. One day, rushing into the office of a magazine I was writing for with a deadline story in hand, I was mistaken for a burglar. The office manager called security and, with an ad hoc posse, pursued me through the labyrinthine halls, nearly to my editor's door. I had no way of proving who I was. I could only move briskly toward the company of someone who knew me.

Another time I was on assignment for a local paper and killing time before an interview. I entered a jewelry store on the city's affluent Near North Side. The proprietor excused herself and returned with an enormous red Doberman pinscher straining at the end of a leash. She stood, the dog extended toward me, silent to my questions, her eyes bulging nearly out of her head. I took a cursory look around, nodded, and bade her good night.

Relatively speaking, however, I never   10 fared as badly as another black male journalist. He went to nearby Waukegan, Illinois, a couple of summers ago to work on a story about a murderer who was born there. Mistaking the reporter for the killer, police officers hauled him from his car at gunpoint and but for his press credentials would probably have tried to book him. Such episodes are not uncommon. Black men trade tales like this all the time.

Over the years, I learned to smother the rage I felt at so often being taken for a criminal. Not to do so would surely have led to madness. I now take precautions to make myself less threatening. I move about with care, particularly late in the evening. I give a wide berth to nervous people on subway platforms during the wee hours, particularly when I have exchanged business clothes for jeans. If I happen to be entering a building behind some people who appear skittish, I may walk by, letting them clear the lobby before I return, so as not to seem to be following them. I have been calm and extremely congenial on those rare occasions when I've been pulled over by the police.

And on late-evening constitutionals I employ what has proved to be an excellent tension-reducing measure: I whistle melodies from Beethoven and Vivaldi and the more popular classical composers. Even steely New Yorkers hunching toward nighttime destinations seem to relax, and occasionally they even join in the tune. Virtually everybody seems to sense that a mugger wouldn't be warbling bright, sunny selections from Vivaldi's *Four Seasons*. It is my equivalent of the cowbell that hikers wear when they know they are in bear country.

READING AND THINKING

1. How does Staples begin his essay? Why do you think he begins this way? How effective is this opening? Explain.

2. What does Staples learn from his experience as a twenty-two-year-old walking the streets of Chicago at night? What other examples does Staples provide that are related to the experience he uses to begin his essay? Explain their relationship.

3. How does Staples conclude the essay? Why do you think he concludes the way he does? How effective is his ending? Explain.

4. Identify places where Staples makes a shift in point of view. What is the effect of these changes in perspective?

THINKING AND WRITING

1. What role do racial stereotypes play in Staples's essay? What is his response to being "profiled" as a mugger because of his race, size, and gender? What is your response to this problem? Explain.

2. How does Staples push his essay beyond mere personal anecdote? What social issues and problems does he refer to? What is his attitude toward the larger issues he raises?

3. Explain in a couple of paragraphs what Staples's essay suggests about being a "victim." Discuss the different kinds of victims he describes.

4. In a paragraph, explain the implications of the essay's subtitle: "A Black Man Ponders His Power to Alter Public Space."

PRE-JUDGING PUBLIC SPACE: AN OCCASION FOR WRITING

In "Just Walk On By," Brent Staples is aware that his presence in public often creates a certain impression—and therefore certain reactions—among others. Though in Staples's case the impression and reactions are based on racial prejudice, this Occasion will give you a chance to discuss a different kind of prejudice (in the sense of "pre-judging"): the kind that many businesses want you to do when they advertise their services. Included here are four hotel signs from different parts of the United States. As you look through the photographs and work toward your essay, think about how signs from all kinds of businesses advertise their products or services, and also consider the ways in which the signs interact with public space. Finally, think about how the ways businesses advertise relates to the different ways Staples describes being treated.

© Reinhard Eisele/CORBIS

© Alan Le Garsmeur/Alamy

PREPARING TO WRITE: OCCASIONS TO THINK ABOUT WHAT YOU SEE

1. Look carefully at the design elements of each sign: the lettering it uses, its size and shape, and so on. Refer to Chapter 4 to help you discuss the design of each sign. What does the design imply about the hotel it advertises?

2. Consider the context of each sign—the side of the road, for example. What is the purpose of each sign? Who is each sign talking to, and why?

3. What do the words on each sign seem to promise?

MOVING TOWARD ESSAY: OCCASIONS TO ANALYZE AND REFLECT

1. How many different kinds of hotels do you think these signs advertise? Make a list of different kinds and briefly describe what you might expect a room in each one to look like. What would you expect the surroundings to look like? Explain what in the sign makes you picture the interior and exterior the way you do.

2. Aside from being hotel signs, what ideas does each sign illustrate? What do they all have in common? You may want to consider more than the design elements of the signs. Who might be likely to stay in each hotel?

3. What kinds of hotel signs are left out of this collection? Think of particular hotel signs you have seen recently. How do those signs differ from the signs included here?

WRITING THOUGHTFULLY: OCCASIONS FOR IDEAS AND ESSAYS

1. List several examples of signs for other types of businesses that you see every day. In a few paragraphs, explain what a couple of those signs seem to promise by their design and location. What particular elements of the signs—their design elements, their wording, and so on—help to establish that implied promise?

2. Consider other forms of public advertising, such as billboards. Take note of a number of billboards and consider the same questions you have been considering: what promises does each sign seem to make? Who is the intended audience? How do the elements of the sign's design work together to create a certain impression?

3. Write an essay in which you explore the use of advertising in public space. As you write, carefully consider your thinking from the previous questions, but also consider the criteria on which people make judgments—about which restaurant to eat in, which hotel to stay in, and where to get their hair cut, for example. How do the signs in this Occasion—those included in this book, and those you have noticed on your own—relate to the product or service they advertise? How accurately do they depict the product or service? What decision-making process do they hope to engender in their audience? How does that process relate to the one Staples describes about his role in public space—in particular, how he is perceived by others? You may wish to use specific examples from Staples's essay in your own. In any case, be sure to use the examples of signs and their role in public spaces to illustrate your point.

CREATING OCCASIONS

1. Consider other times in which a kind of prejudice—pre-judging—plays a role in public spaces. Find several examples in public of particular things—objects or architecture, for example—that attempt to create an impression of something that may or may not live up to its impression. Take photographs or describe those elements that create the impression. Discuss in an essay how outward presentation can differ from the reality of a situation, place, person, or thing.

2. Work together with a few classmates to design a new sign for an existing hotel, motel, or restaurant chain. You should be familiar with the interior and exterior of whatever you choose. Try to make sure that the elements of your sign's design accurately depict what the potential consumer will encounter. Your job here will not be to advertise—that is, do not try to get your potential customers to patronize your establishment. Instead, try to give those customers an accurate way to judge what to expect. Sketch or describe the sign, and in a short essay, discuss how your approach compares with the approach you have seen in this Occasion.

Zora Neale Hurston (1891–1960)

Zora Neale Hurston was born in Notasulga, Alabama, where she spent her early years. After attending Howard University in Washington, DC, she went to New York City, where she became active in the Harlem cultural scene. She attended Barnard College from 1925 to 1928 and studied anthropology, which provided her with the background to do field research among African Americans in Harlem and in the rural southern United States. The results of this research informed her book of folklore *Mules and Men* (1935) and influenced her novel *Their Eyes Were Watching God* (1937) and her autobiographical *Dust Tracks on a Road* (1942).

HOW IT FEELS TO BE COLORED ME

In "How It Feels to Be Colored Me," Hurston explores multiple facets of her identity as a woman, as an African American, and as an artist. She focuses most on her racial self, noting how rather than considering her blackness a liability and a limitation, she envisions it as an opportunity and a reason for celebration.

1   I am colored but I offer nothing in the way of extenuating circumstances except the fact that I am the only Negro in the United States whose grandfather on the mother's side was *not* an Indian chief.

I remember the very day that I became colored. Up to my thirteenth year I lived in the little Negro town of Eatonville, Florida. It is exclusively a colored town. The only white people I knew passed through the town going to or coming from Orlando. The native whites rode dusty horses, the Northern tourists chugged down the sandy village road in automobiles. The town knew the Southerners and never stopped cane chewing when they passed. But the Northerners were something else again. They were peered at cautiously from behind curtains by the timid. The more venturesome would come out on the porch to watch them go past and got just as much pleasure out of the tourists as the tourists got out of the village.

The front porch might seem a daring place for the rest of the town, but it was a gallery seat for me. My favorite place was atop the gate-post. Proscenium box for a born first-nighter. Not only did I enjoy the show, but I didn't mind the actors knowing that I liked it. I usually spoke to them in passing. I'd wave at them and when they returned my salute, I would say something like this: "Howdy-do-well-I-thank-you-where-you-goin'?" Usually automobile or the horse paused at this, and after a queer exchange of compliments, I would probably "go a piece of the way" with them, as we say in farthest Florida. If one of my family happened to come to the front in time to see me, of course negotiations would be rudely broken off. But even so, it is clear that I was the first "welcome-to-our-state" Floridian, and I hope the Miami Chamber of Commerce will please take notice.

During this period, white people differed from colored to me only in that they rode through town and never lived there. They liked to hear me "speak pieces" and sing and wanted to see me dance the parse-me-la, and gave me generously of their small silver for doing these things, which seemed strange to me for I wanted to do them so much that I needed bribing to stop. Only they didn't know it. The colored people gave no dimes. They deplored any joyful tendencies in me, but I was their Zora nevertheless. I belonged to them, to the nearby hotels, to the county—everybody's Zora.

5   But changes came in the family when I was thirteen, and I was sent to school in Jacksonville. I left Eatonville, the town of the oleanders, as Zora. When I disembarked from the river-boat at Jacksonville, she was no more. It seemed that I had suffered a sea change. I was not Zora of Orange County any more, I was now a little colored girl. I found it out in certain ways. In my heart as well as in the mirror, I became a fast brown—warranted not to rub nor run.

II

But I am not tragically colored. There is no great sorrow dammed up in my soul, nor lurking behind my eyes. I do not mind at all. I do not belong to the sobbing school of Negrohood who hold that nature somehow has given them a lowdown dirty deal and whose feelings are all hurt about it. Even in the helter-skelter skirmish that is my life, I have seen that the world is to the strong regardless of a little pigmentation more or less. No, I do not weep at the world—I am too busy sharpening my oyster knife.

Someone is always at my elbow reminding me that I am that granddaughter of slaves. It fails to register depression with me. Slavery is sixty years in the past. The operation was successful and the patient is doing well, thank you. The terrible struggle that made me an American out of a potential slave said "On the line!" The Reconstruction said "Get set!"; and the generation before said "Go!" I am off to a flying start and I must not halt in the stretch to look behind and weep. Slavery is the price I paid for civilization, and the choice was not with me. It is a bully adventure and worth all that I have paid through my ancestors for it. No one on earth ever had a greater chance for glory. The world to be won and nothing to be lost. It is thrilling to think—to know that for any act of mine, I shall get twice as much praise or twice as much blame. It is quite exciting to hold the center of the national stage, with the spectators not knowing whether to laugh or to weep.

The position of my white neighbor is much more difficult. No brown specter pulls up a chair beside me when I sit down to eat. No dark ghost thrusts its leg against mine in bed. The game of keeping what one has is never so exciting as the game of getting.

I do not always feel colored. Even now I often achieve the unconscious Zora of Eatonville before the Hegira. I feel most colored when I am thrown against a sharp white background.

For instance at Barnard. "Beside the waters of the Hudson" I feel my race. Among the 10 thousand white persons, I am a dark rock surged upon, and overswept, but through it all, I remain myself. When covered by the waters, I am; and the ebb but reveals me again.

III

Sometimes it is the other way around. A white person is set down in our midst, but the contrast is just as sharp for me. For instance, when I sit in the drafty basement that is The New World Cabaret with a white person, my color comes. We enter chatting about any little nothing that we have in common and are seated by the jazz waiters. In the abrupt way that jazz orchestras have, this one plunges into a number. It loses no time in circumlocutions, but gets right down to business. It constricts the thorax and splits the heart with its tempo and narcotic harmonies. This orchestra grows rambunctious, rears on its hind legs and attacks the tonal veil with primitive fury, rending it, clawing it until it breaks through to the jungle beyond. I follow those heathen—follow them exultingly. I dance wildly inside myself; I yell within, I whoop; I shake my assegai above my head, I hurl it true to the mark *yeeeeooww!* I am in the jungle and living in the jungle way. My face is painted red and yellow and my body is painted blue. My pulse is throbbing like a war drum. I want to slaughter something—give pain, give death to what, I do not know. But the piece ends. The men of the orchestra wipe their lips and rest their fingers. I creep back slowly to the veneer we call civilization with the last tone and find the white friend sitting motionless in his seat, smoking calmly.

"Good music they have here," he remarks, drumming the table with his fingertips.

Music. The great blobs of purple and red emotion have not touched him. He has only heard what I felt. He is far away and I see him but dimly across the ocean and the continent that have fallen between us. He is so pale with his whiteness then and I am so colored.

IV

At certain times I have no race, I am *me*. When I set my hat at a certain angle and saunter down Seventh Avenue, Harlem City, feeling as snooty as the lions in front of the Forty-Second Street Library, for instance. So far as my feelings are concerned, Peggy Hopkins Joyce on the Bouie Mich with her gorgeous raiment, stately carriage, knees knocking together in a most aristocratic manner, has nothing on me. The cosmic Zora emerges. I belong to no race nor time. I am the eternal feminine with its string of beads.

I have no separate feeling about being an American citizen and colored. I am merely a fragment of the Great Soul that surges within the boundaries. My country, right or wrong. 15

Sometimes, I feel discriminated against, but it does not make me angry. It merely astonishes me. How *can* any deny themselves the pleasure of my company? It's beyond me.

But in the main, I feel like a brown bag of miscellany propped against a wall. Against a wall in company with other bags, white, red, and yellow. Pour out the contents, and there is discovered a jumble of small things priceless and worthless. A first-water diamond, an empty spool, bits of broken glass, lengths of string, a key to a door long since crumbled away, a rusty knife-blade, old shoes saved for a road that never was and never will be, a nail bent under the weight of things too heavy for any nail, a dried flower or two still a little fragrant. In your hand is the brown bag. On the ground before you is the jumble it held—so much like the jumble in the bags, could they be emptied, that all might be dumped in a single heap and the bags refilled without altering the content of any greatly. A bit of colored glass more or less would not matter. Perhaps that is how the Great Stuffer of Bags filled them in the first place—who knows?

READING AND THINKING

1. What do you make of Hurston's opening sentence? What are its tone and point?

2. How do the words "colored" and "Negro," which Hurston uses to refer to her race, compare with other such terms that became popular later, such as "Black" and "African American"?

3. What does Hurston mean when she says that she stopped being "Zora" and became instead "a little colored girl"? How does she respond to this change in others' perceptions of her?

4. How does Hurston characterize herself? How does she convey what it feels like to be Zora Neale Hurston?

THINKING AND WRITING

1. How does Hurston define "race"? To what extent is race a factor in her identity? What else is important to her sense of self? Explain in two or three paragraphs.

2. Hurston organizes her essay in four parts to emphasize different times and places. Identify the scenes and what you believe Hurston accomplishes with each. Then explain how the four parts are related.

3. In the third section of the essay, Hurston describes attending a jazz club in Harlem with a white acquaintance. Why does she include this scene? What point does she make through it? What details are most important in understanding this point?

4. Identify images Hurston includes of herself in sections 3 and 4. How does each image convey additional information about her identity and sense of self?

PRESENTING THE SELF: AN OCCASION FOR WRITING

In her essay "What It Feels Like to Be Colored Me," Zora Neale Hurston paints a portrait of herself in words. Other kinds of artists, such as painters and sculptors, sometimes present themselves in self-portraits. This Occasion for Writing gives you a chance to study some classic and contemporary self-portraits en route to creating a portrait of yourself. You will have a chance to study the self-portraits of modern painter Frida Kahlo. Kahlo (1907–1954) was a Mexican painter who married the prominent Mexican artist Diego Rivera. Her paintings were considered inferior to his during their lifetimes, but her artworks have eclipsed his in the eyes of many experts today. When Kahlo was 18 years old she was in a serious bus accident and was severely injured. Those injuries, which left her bedridden for some time (and spurred her into painting in her boredom), and the tempestuous relationship with her frequently unfaithful husband are recurring themes in her art.

PREPARING TO WRITE: OCCASIONS TO THINK ABOUT WHAT YOU SEE

1. Look closely at the pair of self-portraits of Frida Kahlo. Look first at *Self-Portrait with Diego*. Identify what you find unusual about this self-portrait. Speculate why she might have included the images of her husband and Maria. What further questions might you have about her life as you examine this image?

2. Examine Kahlo's self-portrait *The Little Hart*. What do you identify as the distinctive feature of this self-portrait? Why might Kahlo have painted herself as a wounded deer?

3. What do you see as common characteristics of these two self-portraits?

FRIDA KAHLO, *Self-Portrait with Diego on My Breast and Maria between My Eyebrows (1953–54)*

© Christie's Images/CORBIS

From the Collection of Dr. Carolyn Farb.

FRIDA KAHLO, *The Little Hart (1946)*

MOVING TOWARD ESSAY: OCCASIONS TO ANALYZE AND REFLECT

1. Not every artist paints his or her self-portrait. Consider why Kahlo painted portraits of herself and why she did so numerous times. Do some additional research on Kahlo. You might watch the movie *Frida* (2002), which is about Kahlo's life.

2. Consider why a writer would compose an essay self-portrait in the manner of Zora Neale Hurston, or a longer autobiography or memoir. If Kahlo had written her self-portraits, instead of painting them, what would you imagine them to be like? Draft a quick few paragraphs about Kahlo, letting Kahlo's self-portraits guide you.

3. Using Hurston's textual portrait as a guide, describe what you imagine her visual representation of herself might look like.

4. Look at the self-portrait by African American artist Adrian Piper. How does the additional dimension Piper adds—language—contribute to her self-portrait? What does her title suggest? Of what significance is the angle of her portrait and the expression on her face? How do you interpret Piper's self-portrait?

ADRIAN PIPER, *Self-Portrait as a Nice White Lady (1995)*

5. Examine this self-portrait in an-
    other media form, a sculptural self-
    portrait. Michael Chukes's
    self-portrait is meant to capture
    not his likeness but his inner self,
    as the title of his self-portrait indi-
    cates. How does his medium, sculp-
    ture, compare with the medium of
    paint used by Kahlo for her self-
    portraits? What does the color of
    Chukes's self-portrait convey about
    the painter and his "inner self?"

WRITING THOUGHTFULLY: OCCASIONS FOR IDEAS AND ESSAYS

1. Choose a portrait of one of the
    artists depicted here, and in a
    paragraph or two, try to capture
    the essence of the portrait, at-
    tempting to get at the artists'
    identity.

2. Select a few key scenes from differ-
    ent times in your life that, collec-
    tively, provide a sense of yourself.
    You may wish to use Hurston's es-
    say as a model and an inspiration.
    You may also wish to use more
    than one medium for your self-portrait.

© Michael Chukes, 2006

MICHAEL CHUKES, *Inner Self (2004)*

3. In an essay examine one, a few, or all of the portraits you have been working with
    here, including your own. How has identity emerged from the portrait(s)? Define
    "identity" as it has shown itself through the portrait(s) and the artist(s) you have
    been studying here. How has the definition of "self-portrait" changed for you
    throughout your experience of this Occasion for Writing?

CREATING OCCASIONS

1. Do some research in the library and on the Internet on the self-portraits of another artist, such as Rembrandt van Rijn (1609–1669) or Vincent Van Gogh (1853–1890). Describe what the pictures convey about the artist and the person. Consider what they reveal about the trajectory of the artist's life.

2. Consider other creative media for self-portraits, such as films or music. Find examples of self-portraits in these alternative media, and compare them with the more traditional self-portraits. Discuss how the artist's chosen medium conveys the sense of self portrayed in the work.

3. Compare a self-portrait that intrigues you with additional accounts of that person's life, such as documentaries, biographies, memoirs, interviews, and critiques, and examine how your understanding of that individual's identity has been shaped. Which story or stories seem most true to what you think of this person's identity? Use the self-portrait and the additional accounts as evidence in your writing.

Judith Ortiz Cofer (b. 1952)

Judith Ortiz Cofer is a novelist, poet, and essayist whose work has appeared in magazines and literary reviews such as *Glamour, The Georgia Review,* and *The Kenyon Review.* Cofer has won fellowships from the National Endowment for the Arts, the Georgia Council for the Arts, and the Fine Arts Council of Florida. Her work includes *The Line of the Sun* (1989), a novel; *Peregrina* (1986) and *Terms of Survival* (1987), poetry collections; *Silent Dancing : A Partial Remembrance of a Puerto Rican Childhood* (1990), essays and poems; and *The Latin Deli: Prose and Poetry* (1993), stories, essays, and poems, from which the following essay, "The Myth of the Latin Woman," has been taken.

THE MYTH OF THE LATIN WOMAN

In "The Myth of the Latin Woman," Judith Ortiz Cofer uses her Puerto Rican heritage to play off the stereotype of the Latina as a sexual "hot tamale," a young woman mature beyond her years and ready to provoke and satisfy male sexual desire. Cofer's subtitle, "I Just Met a Girl Named Maria," alludes to the Leonard Bernstein song from the Broadway musical *West Side Story.* Cofer's approach in the essay is to debunk and complicate the stereotypes of Latina women while promoting a more nuanced and complex idea of them.

1   On a bus trip to London from Oxford University where I was earning some graduate credits one summer, a young man, obviously fresh from a pub, spotted me and as if struck by inspiration went down on his knees in the aisle. With both hands over his heart he broke into an Irish tenor's rendition of "María" from *West Side Story.* My politely amused fellow passengers gave his lovely voice the round of gentle applause it deserved. Though I was not quite as amused, I managed my version of an English smile: no show of teeth, no extreme contortions of the facial muscles—I was at this time of my life practicing reserve and cool. Oh, that British control, how I coveted it. But María had followed me to London, reminding me of a prime fact of my life: you can leave the Island, master the English language, and travel as far as you can, but if you are a Latina, especially one like me who so obviously belongs to Rita Moreno's gene pool, the Island travels with you.

  This is sometimes a very good thing—it may win you that extra minute of someone's attention. But with some people, the same things can make *you* an island—not so much a tropical paradise as an Alcatraz, a place nobody wants to visit. As a Puerto Rican girl growing up in the United States and wanting like most children to "belong," I resented the stereotype that my Hispanic appearance called forth from many people I met.

  Our family lived in a large urban center in New Jersey during the sixties, where life was designed as a microcosm of my parents' casas on the island. We spoke in Spanish, we ate Puerto Rican food bought at the bodega, and we practiced strict Catholicism complete with Saturday confession and Sunday mass at a church where our parents were accommodated into a one-hour Spanish mass slot, performed by a Chinese priest trained as a missionary for Latin America.

  As a girl I was kept under strict surveillance, since virtue and modesty were, by cultural equation, the same as family honor. As a teenager I was instructed on how to behave as a proper señorita. But it was a conflicting message girls got, since the Puerto Rican mothers also encouraged their daughters to look and act like women and to dress in clothes our Anglo friends and their mothers found too "mature" for our age. It was, and is, cultural, yet I often felt humiliated when I appeared at an American friend's party wearing a dress more suitable to a semiformal than to a playroom birthday celebration. At Puerto Rican festivities, neither the music nor the colors we wore could be too loud. I still experience a vague sense of letdown when I'm invited to a "party" and it turns out to be a marathon conversation in hushed tones rather than a fiesta with salsa, laughter, and dancing—the kind of celebration I remember from my childhood.

5   I remember Career Day in our high school, when teachers told us to come dressed as if for a job interview. It quickly became obvious that to the barrio girls, "dressing up" sometimes meant wearing ornate jewelry and clothing that would be more appropriate (by mainstream standards) for the company Christmas party than as daily office attire. That morning I had agonized in front of my closet, trying to figure out what a "career girl" would wear because, essentially, except for Marlo Thomas on TV, I had no models on which to base my decision. I knew how to dress for school: at the Catholic school I attended we all wore uniforms; I knew how to dress for Sunday mass, and I knew what dresses to wear for parties at my relatives' homes. Though I do not recall the precise details of my Career Day outfit, it must have been a composite of the above choices. But I remember a comment my friend (an Italian-American) made in later years that coalesced my impressions of that day. She said that at the business school she was attending the Puerto Rican girls always stood out for wearing "everything at once." She meant, of course, too much jewelry, too many accessories. On that day at school, we were simply made the negative models by the nuns who were themselves not credible fashion experts to any of us. But it was painfully obvious to me that to the others, in their tailored skirts and silk blouses, we must have seemed "hopeless" and "vulgar." Though I now know that most adolescents feel out of step much of the time, I also know that for the Puerto Rican girls of my generation that sense was intensified. The way our teachers and classmates looked at us that day in school was just a taste of the culture clash that awaited us in the real world. where prospective employers and men on the street would often misinterpret our tight skirts and jingling bracelets as a come-on.

Mixed cultural signals have perpetuated certain stereotypes—for example, that of the Hispanic woman as the "Hot Tamale" or sexual firebrand. It is a one-dimensional view that the media have found easy to promote. In their special vocabulary, advertisers have designated "sizzling" and "smoldering" as the adjectives of choice for describing not only the foods but also the women of Latin America. From conversations in my house I recall hearing about the harassment that Puerto Rican women endured in factories where the "boss men" talked to them as if sexual innuendo was all they understood and, worse, often gave them the choice of submitting to advances or being fired.

It is custom, however, not chromosomes, that leads us to choose scarlet over pale pink. As young girls, we were influenced in our decisions about clothes and colors by the women—older sisters and mothers who had grown up on a tropical island where the natural environment was a riot of primary colors, where showing your skin was one way to keep cool as well as to look sexy. Most important of all, on the island, women perhaps felt freer to dress and move more provocatively, since, in most cases, they were protected by the traditions, mores, and laws of a Spanish/Catholic system of morality and machismo whose main rule was: *You may look at my sister, but if you touch her I will kill you.* The extended family and church structure could provide a young woman with a circle of safety in her small pueblo on the island; if a man "wronged" a girl, everyone would close in to save her family honor.

This is what I have gleaned from my discussions as an adult with older Puerto Rican women. They have told me about dressing in their best party clothes on Saturday nights and going to the town's plaza to promenade with their girlfriends in front of the boys they liked. The males were thus given an opportunity to admire the women and to express their admiration in the form of *piropos:* erotically charged street poems they composed on the spot. I have been subjected to a few piropos while visiting the Island, and they can be outrageous, although custom dictates that they must never cross into obscenity. This ritual, as I understand it, also entails a show of studied indifference on the woman's part; if she is "decent," she must not acknowledge the man's impassioned words. So I do understand how things can be lost in translation. When a Puerto Rican girl dressed in her idea of what is attractive meets a man from the mainstream culture who has been trained to react to certain types of clothing as a sexual signal, a clash is likely to take place. The line I first heard based on this aspect of the myth happened when the boy who took me to my first formal dance leaned over to plant a sloppy overeager kiss painfully on my mouth, and when I didn't respond with sufficient passion said in a resentful tone: "I thought you Latin girls were supposed to mature early"—my first instance of being thought of as a fruit or vegetable—I was supposed to *ripen*, not just grow into womanhood like other girls.

It is surprising to some of my professional friends that some people, including those who should know better, still put others "in their place." Though rarer, these incidents are still commonplace in my life. It happened to me most recently during a stay at a very classy metropolitan hotel favored by young professional couples for their weddings. Late one evening after the theater, as I walked toward my room with my new colleague (a woman with whom I was coordinating an arts program), a middle-aged man in a tuxedo, a young girl in satin and lace on his arm, stepped directly into our path. With his champagne glass extended toward me, he exclaimed, "Evita!"

Our way blocked, my companion and I listened as the man half-recited, half-bellowed "Don't Cry for Me, Argentina." When he finished, the young girl said: "How about a round of applause for my daddy?" We complied, hoping this would bring the silly spectacle to a close. I was becoming aware that our little group was attracting the attention of the other guests. "Daddy" must have perceived this too, and he once more barred the way as we tried to walk past him. He began to shout-sing a ditty to the tune of "La Bamba"—except the lyrics were about a girl named Maria whose exploits all rhymed with her name and gonorrhea. The girl kept saying "Oh, Daddy" and looking at me with pleading eyes. She wanted me to laugh along with the others. My companion and I stood silently waiting for the man to end his offensive song. When he finished, I looked not at him but at his daughter. I advised her calmly never to ask her father what he had done in the army. Then I walked between them and to my room. My friend complimented me on my cool handling of the situation. I confessed to her that I really had wanted to push the jerk into the swimming pool. I knew that this same man—probably a corporate executive, well educated, even worldly by most standards—would not have been likely to regale a white woman with a dirty song in public. He would perhaps have checked his impulse by assuming that she could be somebody's wife or mother, or at least *somebody* who might take offense. But to him, I was just an Evita or a Maria: merely a character in his cartoon-populated universe.

Because of my education and my proficiency with the English language, I have acquired many mechanisms for dealing with the anger I experience. This was not true for my parents, nor is it true for the many Latin women working at menial jobs who must put up with stereotypes about our ethnic group such as: "They make good domestics." This is another facet of the myth of the Latin woman in the United States. Its origin is simple to deduce. Work as domestics, waitressing, and factory jobs are all that's available to women with little English and few skills. The myth of the Hispanic menial has been sustained by the same media phenomenon that made "Mammy" from *Gone with the Wind* America's idea of the black woman for generations: Maria, the housemaid or counter girl, is now indelibly etched into the national psyche. The big and the little screens have presented us with the picture of the funny Hispanic maid, mispronouncing words and cooking up a spicy storm in a shiny California kitchen.

This media-engendered image of the Latina in the United States has been documented by feminist Hispanic scholars, who claim that such portrayals are partially responsible for the denial of opportunities for upward mobility among Latinas in the professions. I have a Chicana friend working on a Ph.D. in philosophy at a major university. She says her doctor still shakes his head in puzzled amazement at all the "big words" she uses. Since I do not wear my diplomas around my neck for all to see, I too have on occasion been sent to that "kitchen," where some think I obviously belong.

One such incident that has stayed with me, though I recognize it as a minor offense, happened on the day of my first public poetry reading. It took place in Miami in a boat-restaurant where we were having lunch before the event. I was nervous and excited as I walked in with my notebook in my hand. An older woman motioned me to her table. Thinking (foolish me) that she wanted me to autograph a copy of my brand new slender volume of verse, I went over. She ordered a cup of coffee from me, assuming that I was the waitress. Easy enough to mistake my poems for menus, I suppose. I know that it

wasn't an intentional act of cruelty, yet of all the good things that happened that day, I remember that scene most clearly, because it reminded me of what I had to overcome before anyone would take me seriously. In retrospect I understand that my anger gave my reading fire, that I have almost always taken doubts in my abilities as a challenge—and that the result is, most times, a feeling of satisfaction at having won a convert when I see the cold, appraising eyes warm to my words, the body language change, the smile that indicates that I have opened some avenue for communication. That day I read to that woman and her lowered eyes told me that she was embarrassed at her little faux pas, and when I willed her to look up at me, it was my victory, and she graciously allowed me to punish her with my full attention. We shook hands at the end of the reading, and I never saw her again. She has probably forgotten the whole thing but maybe not.

Yet I am one of the lucky ones. My parents made it possible for me to acquire a stronger footing in the mainstream culture by giving me the chance at an education. And books and art have saved me from the harsher forms of ethnic and racial prejudice that many of my Hispanic *compañeras* have had to endure. I travel a lot around the United States, reading from my books of poetry and my novel, and the reception I most often receive is one of positive interest by people who want to know more about my culture. There are, however, thousands of Latinas without the privilege of an education or the entrée into society that I have. For them life is a struggle against the misconceptions perpetuated by the myth of the Latina as whore, domestic or criminal. We cannot change this by legislating the way people look at us. The transformation, as I see it, has to occur at a much more individual level. My personal goal in my public life is to try to replace the old pervasive stereotypes and myths about Latinas with a much more interesting set of realities. Every time I give a reading, I hope the stories I tell, the dreams and fears I examine in my work, can achieve some universal truth which will get my audience past the particulars of my skin color, my accent, or my clothes.

15   I once wrote a poem in which I called us Latinas "God's brown daughters." This poem is really a prayer of sorts, offered upward, but also, through the human-to-human channel of art, outward. It is a prayer for communication, and for respect. In it, Latin women pray "in Spanish to an Anglo God / with a Jewish heritage," and they are "fervently hoping / that if not omnipotent, / at least He be bilingual."

READING AND THINKING

1. How does Cofer use her identity as a Latina woman to develop her idea in this essay? What, exactly, is her idea, and what is her purpose?

2. What cultural information does Cofer include, what cultural references does she mention, and what do they contribute to your understanding of her essay?

3. Cofer includes one foreign word in her essay—"piropos." What does this word mean, and why do you think Cofer includes it?

THINKING AND WRITING

1. Why does Cofer include the story of the bus trip from London to Oxford? Why do you think she begins with that story? How does she link it with other stories—and to what purpose?

2. What role does fashion, style of dress, play in Cofer's essay? Do you agree with what she says about how Puerto Rican girls dress? Write a few paragraphs in which you discuss the importance of dress as an index of a person's identity.

3. Write a paragraph in which you explain the title and subtitle of Cofer's essay. Include a few references to passages closely tied to her title and/or subtitle.

FACING RACES:
AN OCCASION FOR WRITING

Our faces—their size and shape, their color and markings, their proportions—provide clues to our racial and ethnic identities. Although Cofer's essay does refer specifically to her own facial details, to some extent the men who see her as a Latina derive the sense of her identity from her face, and perhaps her hair, from her look and her looks overall, irrespective of how she dresses. The following Occasion invites you to look at and into a series of faces to see what they reveal and conceal, how they reflect identity and personality and culture.

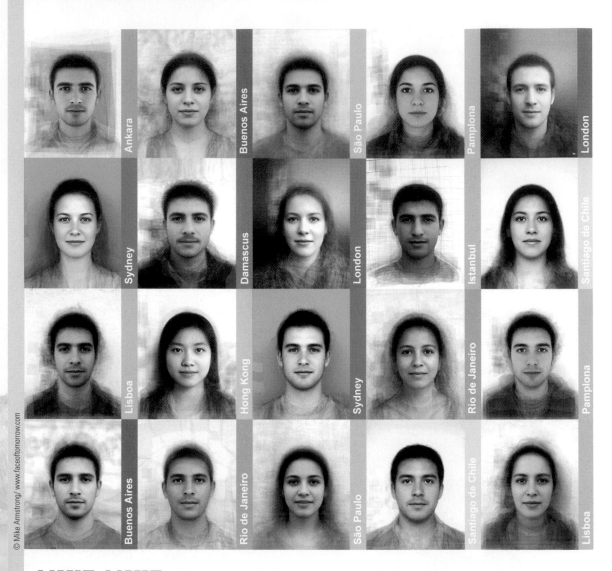

MIKE MIKE, *The Face of Tomorrow*

PREPARING TO WRITE: OCCASIONS TO THINK ABOUT WHAT YOU SEE

1. Look closely at the accompanying group of faces, *The Face of Tomorrow*. What do you notice about these faces? Which show the strongest contrast? The closest similarity? Why? Which faces stand out the most to you? Why?

2. Focus first on the male and then on the female faces. Which appear to vary more—the male or the female faces? Which aspects of the male and female faces seem to change most?

MOVING TOWARD ESSAY: OCCASIONS TO ANALYZE AND REFLECT

1. To what extent do the changing colors of the backgrounds in *The Face of Tomorrow* affect how we see and interpret the faces? To what extent are we predisposed to see the faces a particular way because of the country affiliation that has been provided with each?

2. Look at your own face in the mirror and at the faces of your family in photographs. Write a paragraph in which you attempt to trace your racial and ethnic identity from your physical features and those that run in your family. Consider which aspects of the faces convey that identity heritage most strongly. How do you see your racial and/or cultural identity changing over generations? (Think beyond mere physical changes.)

3. Consider how our faces not only reveal a sense of our identity, but also conceal aspects of our identity. Consider, for example, how actors playing various roles camouflage and conceal their actual identities to play roles on stage and screen. Costume, of course, has much to do with such role changes and with such role playing, but so too does facial expression, as well as camouflaging facial characteristics with facial hair, eyeglasses, and cosmetics.

4. Consider the significance of the following quotation from *The Face of Tomorrow*'s website as a commentary on the artist's goal in *The Face of Tomorrow*:

> On a personal level it is one artist's search for identity and belonging and the relationship of self to the larger world. On a deeper level it is an exploration of the systems behind globalizations. . . . The work is thus at the same time a document of a place at a moment in time and also an extrapolation of that place towards some utopian future where all differences of race or individuality are forgotten.

WRITING THOUGHTFULLY: OCCASIONS FOR IDEAS AND ESSAYS

1. Select three faces from a newspaper or magazine. Describe each face and then speculate about the identity of each individual, including racial and/or ethnic heritage as well as role and personality.

2. Write an essay in which you consider the extent to which faces reveal and/or conceal a person's true self. You can select examples from history, literature, art, sculpture, and contemporary life.

3. Write an essay in which you consider the relationship between identity and stereotyping. Consider the quotation about *The Face of Tomorrow* that emphasizes the elimination of individuality on the one hand and, on the other, the resistance to stereotyping found in Cofer's essay, "The Myth of the Latin Woman." Consider the extent to which individuality can be erased and the extent to which stereotypes will always remain with us. You may also, or instead, focus your essay on the relationship between identity and culture, particularly on the clashes between cultures as a person's identity is formed and developed.

CREATING OCCASIONS

1. Do some research about the French woman who had a face transplant. Interview some of your friends and family about her situation. Consider the extent to which she can remain the same person with a different face—with someone else's face.

2. Create your own panel of faces by collecting a series of faces from family photographs, print media, the Internet, cartoons, and other sources. Develop a few paragraphs in which you describe the logic or rationale of your panel of faces and what you learned from creating it.

THE HISTORIES OF SOCIAL IDENTITY

We define ourselves as individuals, and we define ourselves as members of social groups. Tension exists between our individual identities, our uniqueness, on the one hand, and, on the other, our social identity determined by our membership in various social groups, such as the schools we attend and graduate from, the clubs we belong to, and the companies we work for. These and other social markers of our identity rub against our unique selfhood—our habits and mannerisms, our peculiar gait and smile, our signature and smell, the highly individual ways we speak and move and exert our physical and mental selves in the world. Taken together, these social and personal markers constitute our identity.

Both of these complementary ways of viewing the self are necessary and are mutually supportive rather than mutually exclusive. On the one hand, we have the freedom to be the absolutely distinctive, one-of-a-kind person we aim to and are meant to be. On the other hand, we may define ourselves and be defined by the various social groups, however small, to which we belong. We are single or married—or perhaps widowed or divorced. We are conference attendees and churchgoers, concert goers and habitués of bars and clubs, bloggers and Internet sharers, linking up with friends and acquaintances in a rich panoply of criss-crossed mini-societies. Furthermore, however much we distinguish ourselves from others, we always exist in relation to others—both individual others and others as members of society.

In addition to its social dimension, identity also possesses a historical dimension. We are both similar to and different from the persons we were in the past. Analogously, we are both similar to and different from the selves we will become in the future. One way of thinking about identity is conservative: we are the unchanging essence that endures through the various and changing roles we assume in life over time. A complementary way of considering our identity is to see it as an ever shifting set of roles we play in a multitude of changing social circumstances, with an emphasis on the roles we play rather than on the continuity of the surviving self that exists above—or beneath—those changing social roles.

However we think of our essential selves—the essence that constitutes the who and what we are—we inevitably exist in relation to others—others who may differ from us in how they think, in how they look and act, in what they value, in why they interact with us at all. Thus we can never escape the social dimension of our identities. For as much as we control our identities, in equal measure, our multiple identities are a product of the many social interactions we assume. Eva Hoffman's essay reveals as much as she reinvents herself as an American immigrant from Poland. N. Scott Momaday's "The Way to Rainy Mountain" heralds the historical traditions of his Kiowa heritage, in the process revealing its unique characteristics against an alternative set of values. And James Baldwin translates himself into a foreign land and culture in "Stranger in the Village" to accentuate both his blackness and his Americanness, intertwined and indelible characteristics of his identity.

Eva Hoffman (b. 1945)

Eva Hoffman was born in Krakow, Poland, and emigrated to North America when she was thirteen, first to Canada and then to the United States. She has worked as an editor and writer for the *New York Times* and holds a PhD from Harvard. A recipient of a Guggenheim fellowship and a Whiting Award for writing, Hoffman splits her time between London and Cambridge, Massachusetts, where she is a visiting professor at the Massachusetts Institute of Technology. She is the author of *Exit into History: A Journey through the New Eastern Europe* (1993), *Shtetl: The Life and Death of a Small Town and the World of Polish Jews* (1997), *After Such Knowledge: Memory, History, and the Legacy of the Holocaust* (2004), and *Lost in Translation: A Life in a New Language* (1990), from which the following excerpt has been taken.

LOST IN TRANSLATION

In the following selection, Hoffman describes the traumatic yet exciting move her family made from Europe to North America. She captures what is gained and lost in such a "translation," with its shifts in culture and identity.

1   It is April 1959, I'm standing at the railing of the *Batory*'s upper deck, and I feel that my life is ending. I'm looking out at the crowd that has gathered on the shore to see the ship's departure from Gdynia—a crowd that, all of a sudden, is irrevocably on the other side—and I want to break out, run back, run toward the familiar excitement, the waving hands, the exclamations. We can't be leaving all this behind—but we are. I am thirteen years old, and we are emigrating. It's a notion of such crushing, definitive finality that to me it might as well mean the end of the world.

My sister, four years younger than I, is clutching my hand wordlessly; she hardly understands where we are, or what is happening to us. My parents are highly agitated; they had just been put through a body search by the customs police, probably as the farewell gesture of anti-Jewish harassment. Still, the officials weren't clever enough, or suspicious enough, to check my sister and me—lucky for us, since we are both carrying some silverware we were not allowed to take out of Poland in large pockets sewn onto our skirts especially for this purpose, and hidden under capacious sweaters.

When the brass band on the shore strikes up the jaunty mazurka rhythms of the Polish anthem, I am pierced by a youthful sorrow so powerful that I suddenly stop crying and try to hold still against the pain. I desperately want time to stop, to hold the ship still with the force of my will. I am suffering my first, severe attack of nostalgia, or *tesknota*—a word that adds to nostalgia the tonalities of sadness and longing. It is a feeling whose shades and degrees I'm destined to know intimately, but at this hovering moment, it comes upon me like a visitation from a whole new geography of emotions, an annunciation of how much an absence can hurt. Or a premonition of absence, because at this divide, I'm filled to the brim with what I'm about to lose—images of Cracow, which I loved as one loves a person, of the sun-baked villages where we had taken summer vacations, of the hours I spent poring over passages of music with my piano teacher, of conversations and escapades with friends. Looking ahead, I come across an enormous, cold blankness—a darkening, an erasure, of the imagination, as if a camera eye has snapped shut, or as if a heavy curtain has been pulled over the future. Of the place where we're going—Canada—I know nothing. There are vague outlines of half a continent, a sense of vast spaces and little habitation. When my parents were hiding in a branch-covered forest bunker during the war, my father had a book with him called *Canada Fragrant with Resin* which, in his horrible confinement, spoke to him of majestic wilderness, of animals roaming without being pursued, of freedom. That is partly why we are going there, rather than to Israel, where most of our Jewish friends have gone. But to me, the word "Canada" has ominous echoes of the "Sahara." No, my mind rejects the idea of being taken there, I don't want to be pried out of my childhood, my pleasures, my safety, my hopes for becoming a pianist. The *Batory* pulls away, the foghorn emits its lowing, shofar sounds, but my being is engaged in a stubborn refusal to move. My parents put their hands on my shoulders consolingly; for a moment, they allow themselves to acknowledge that there's pain in this departure, much as they wanted it.

Many years later, at a stylish party in New York, I met a woman who told me that she had had an enchanted childhood. Her father was a highly positioned diplomat in an Asian country, and she had lived surrounded by sumptuous elegance, the courtesy of servants, and the delicate advances of older men. No wonder, she said, that when this part of her life came to an end, at age thirteen, she felt she had been exiled from paradise, and had been searching for it ever since.

5   No wonder. But the wonder is what you can make a paradise out of. I told her that I grew up in a lumpen apartment in Cracow, squeezed into three rudimentary rooms with four other people, surrounded by squabbles, dark political rumblings, memories of wartime suffering, and daily struggle for existence. And yet, when it came time to leave, I, too, felt I was being pushed out of the happy, safe enclosures of Eden.

I am lying in bed, watching the slowly moving shadows on the ceiling made by the gently blowing curtains, and the lights of an occasional car moving by. I'm trying hard not to fall asleep. Being awake is so sweet that I want to delay the loss of consciousness. I'm snuggled under an enormous goose-feather quilt covered in hand-embroidered silk. Across the room from me is my sister's crib. From the next room, "the first room," I hear my parents' breathing. The maid—one of a succession of country girls who come to work for us—is sleeping in the kitchen. It is Cracow, 1949, I'm four years old, and I don't know that this happiness is taking place in a country recently destroyed by war, a place where my father has to hustle to get us a bit more than our meager ration of meat and sugar. I only know that I'm in my room, which to me is an everywhere, and that the patterns on the ceiling are enough to fill me with a feeling of sufficiency because . . . well, just because I'm conscious, because the world exists and it flows so gently into my head. Occasionally, a few blocks away, I hear the hum of the tramway, and I'm filled by a sense of utter contentment. I love riding the tramway, with its bracing but not overly fast swaying, and I love knowing, from my bed, the street over which it is moving; I repeat to myself that I'm in Cracow; Cracow, which to me is both home and the universe.

READING AND THINKING

1. What is the predominant feeling conveyed by Hoffman in this excerpt? Where is this feeling most clearly and forcefully expressed?

2. Why does Hoffman include a Polish word in this piece? What does this word, "tesknota," mean, and why is it important for Hoffman?

3. Why does she include the paragraph about the story of the woman Hoffman met at a New York party? How does this story help us understand Hoffman's experience and her idea?

4. What aspects of Hoffman's identity are under consideration here?

THINKING AND WRITING

1. What effects does Hoffman achieve with her shifts of verb tense in the passage? What would be gained and/or lost if Hoffman had used past tense verbs throughout? Explain.

2. Write a paragraph in which you explain the significance of the title *Lost in Translation*. Consider at least two meanings of the title.

3. Discuss your own ideas about being "translated" between cultures or perhaps between languages—if you speak more than one language. To what extent do you agree with what Hoffman says about such translations and what is lost in experiencing them?

4. Create a scene in which you recall a significant place in your life. Try to convey your experience—what the experience felt like for you then, and also what it means to you today, in retrospect.

GETTING LOST IN TRANSLATION: AN OCCASION FOR WRITING

"Poetry," as Robert Frost once said, "is what gets lost in translation." That is, in translating a poem from one language to another, there is an inevitable loss of the original poem's richness of linguistic resourcefulness, suggestion, and resonance. Hoffman talks about a lost world and culture—the country and culture she left behind when she emigrated. This Occasion invites you to think about what is gained and what is lost in a person's being "translated" from one country and culture to another.

Large grass hut on stilts in the Kaminabit Village near the Sepik River

Yurt tent on the Mongolian Steppe

PREPARING TO WRITE: OCCASIONS TO THINK ABOUT WHAT YOU SEE

1. Describe, in a few sentences each, the photographs of the Yurt tent and the grass hut house.

2. What is distinctive about each? How does each compare with the houses you are most familiar with?

MOVING TOWARD ESSAY: OCCASIONS TO ANALYZE AND REFLECT

1. Consider Hoffman's statement: "But the wonder is what you can make a paradise out of." What is implied here about how people adapt to their environment? What is implied about how people shape their environment? To what extent is our environment a part of our identity? To what extent do our roots, or lack of roots, in a particular place—or in a series of changing places—affect our various identities?

2. Make a list of what people lose or what they give up and leave behind when they emigrate from their home country to a foreign land. Make a similar list of what they gain.

3. In an essay about Ellis Island, Mary Gordon writes that "it is part of being an American to be engaged in a somewhat tiresome but always self-absorbing process of national definition." To what extent are you engaged in or have you and/or your family been engaged in such a discussion?

4. Reflect on your own sense of being an American and on your sense of heritage as an American, as well as your sense of possessing a legacy from another country, culture, and perhaps language. To what extent do you feel that you have "arrived" as an American; to what extent do you still have some distance to go toward defining yourself as an American? Explain.

WRITING THOUGHTFULLY: OCCASIONS FOR IDEAS AND ESSAYS

1. Write an essay in which you explore the issues raised in previous questions in earlier exercises. Consider the personal, social, cultural, religious, and other values that impelled your ancestors to come to America (or that influenced others to bring them here by force). Consider not only why they came but also how they lived once they arrived, and perhaps what kind of legacy they have left you.

2. Write an essay in which you consider the various ways environment impinges on identity. Some things to consider might be how leaving a comfort zone (your home and high school world, for example) affects your identity as you move to the new and different environments of college or the world of work. How much has your identity changed or adapted with the change of circumstances and environment? To what extent has your view of your previous world changed, and in what ways? How does a new environment effect a translation of self and identity? To what extent does a person translate or alter a place, and to what extent does a place translate or change a person?

3. If you speak two languages, write an essay about what is gained and what is lost when you communicate in each of those languages, including, perhaps, what is gained and lost in translating words and phrases across the language barrier. Or, write an essay about the experience of living in two cultures, being translated back and forth between the two cultures and their world views, habits of thinking, customs, and modes of behavior.

CREATING OCCASIONS

1. Do some research about the immigrant experience through reading and interviewing and Internet searching. Look for information about immigrants' expectations about leaving their homeland for a foreign country. To what extent were these expectations met and to what extent did the immigrants confront realities other than those they imagined? Try to get a perspective on what was gained and lost in the transition or translation. How is a cultural identity translated over time?

N. Scott Momaday (b. 1934)

N. Scott Momaday was born on a Kiowa Indian reservation in Oklahoma and grew up on a reservation in New Mexico. A graduate of the University of New Mexico and of Stanford University, he won a Pulitzer Prize for his first novel, *House Made of Dawn* (1968). Momaday has worked in many genres in addition to fiction; he has published volumes of poetry, including *The Gourd Dancer* (1976), and the memoirs *The Way to Rainy Mountain* (1969) and *The Names: A Memoir* (1976). He has also written essays, plays, and children's books. Momaday is an artist whose work has been widely exhibited. For many years a professor at the University of Arizona, Momaday often takes as his subject the history and culture of Native Americans, especially their relationship with the natural world.

THE WAY TO RAINY MOUNTAIN

In *The Way to Rainy Mountain,* Momaday memorializes his grandmother and the way of life of the Kiowa tribe to which she belonged. His vivid descriptions of her chanting prayers and his evocations of his ancestral tribal past highlight some ways culture and identity intersect.

1   A single knoll rises out of the plain in Oklahoma, north and west of the Wichita Range. For my people, the Kiowas, it is an old landmark, and they gave it the name Rainy Mountain. The hardest weather in the world is there. Winter brings blizzards, hot tornadic winds arise in the spring, and in summer the prairie is an anvil's edge. The grass turns brittle and brown, and it cracks beneath your feet. There are green belts along the rivers and creeks, linear groves of hickory and pecan, willow and witch hazel. At a distance in July or August the steaming foliage seems almost to writhe in fire. Great green-and-yellow grasshoppers are everywhere in the tall grass, popping up like corn to sting the flesh, and tortoises crawl about on the red earth, going nowhere in plenty of time. Loneliness is an aspect of the land. All things in the plain are isolate; there is no confusion of objects in the eye, but *one* hill or *one* tree or *one* man. To look upon that landscape in the early morning, with the sun at your back, is to lose the sense of proportion. Your imagination comes to life, and this, you think, is where Creation was begun.

I returned to Rainy Mountain in July. My grandmother had died in the spring, and I wanted to be at her grave. She had lived to be very old and at last infirm. Her only living daughter was with her when she died, and I was told that in death her face was that of a child.

I like to think of her as a child. When she was born, the Kiowas were living that last great moment of their history. For more than a hundred years they had controlled the open range from the Smoky Hill River to the Red, from the headwaters of the Canadian to the fork of the Arkansas and Cimarron. In alliance with the Comanches, they had ruled the whole of the southern Plains. War was their sacred business, and they were among the finest horsemen the world has ever known. But warfare for the Kiowas was preeminently a matter of disposition rather than of survival, and they never understood the grim, unrelenting advance of the U.S. Cavalry. When at last, divided and ill-provisioned, they were driven onto the Staked Plains in the cold rains of autumn, they fell into panic. In Palo Duro Canyon they abandoned their crucial stores to pillage and had nothing then but their lives. In order to save themselves, they surrendered to the soldiers at Fort Sill and were imprisoned in the old stone corral that now stands as a military museum. My grandmother was spared the humiliation of those high gray walls by eight or ten years, but she must have known from birth the affliction of defeat, the dark brooding of old warriors.

Her name was Aho, and she belonged to the last culture to evolve in North America. Her forebears came down from the high country in western Montana nearly three centuries ago. They were a mountain people, a mysterious tribe of hunters whose language has never been positively classified in any major group. In the late seventeenth century they began a long migration to the south and east. It was a long journey toward the dawn, and it led to a golden age. Along the way the Kiowas were befriended by the Crows, who gave them the culture and religion of the Plains. They acquired horses, and their ancient nomadic spirit was suddenly free of the ground. They acquired Tai-me, the sacred Sun Dance doll, from that moment the object and symbol of their worship, and so shared in the divinity of the sun. Not least, they acquired the sense of destiny, therefore courage and pride. When they entered upon the southern Plains, they had been transformed. No longer were they slaves to the simple necessity of survival; they were a lordly and dangerous society of fighters and thieves, hunters and priests of the sun. According to their origin myth, they entered the world through a hollow log. From one point of view, their migration was the fruit of an old prophecy, for indeed they emerged from a sunless world.

5   Although my grandmother lived out her long life in the shadow of Rainy Mountain, the immense landscape of the continental interior lay like memory in her blood. She could tell of the Crows, whom she had never seen, and of the Black Hills, where she had never been. I wanted to see in reality what she had seen more perfectly in the mind's eye, and traveled fifteen hundred miles to begin my pilgrimage.

Yellowstone, it seemed to me, was the top of the world, a region of deep lakes and dark timber, canyons and waterfalls. But, beautiful as it is, one might have the sense of confinement there. The skyline in all directions is close at hand, the high wall of the woods and deep cleavages of shade. There is a perfect freedom in the mountains, but it belongs to the eagle and the elk, the badger and the bear. The Kiowas reckoned their stature by the distance they could see, and they were bent and blind in the wilderness.

Descending eastward, the highland meadows are a stairway to the plain. In July the inland slope of the Rockies is luxuriant with flax and buckwheat, stonecrop and larkspur. The earth unfolds and the limit of the land recedes. Clusters of trees and animals grazing far in the distance cause the vision to reach away and wonder to build upon the mind. The sun follows a longer course in the day, and the sky is immense beyond all comparison. The great billowing clouds that sail upon it are shadows that move upon the grain like water, dividing light. Farther down, in the land of the Crows and Blackfeet, the plain is yellow. Sweet clover takes hold of the hills and bends upon itself to cover and seal the soil. There the Kiowas paused on their way; they had come to the place where they must change their lives. The sun is at home in the plains. Precisely there does it have the certain character of a god. When the Kiowas came to the land of the Crows, they could see the dark lees of the hills at dawn across the Bighorn River, the profusion of light on the grain shelves, the oldest deity ranging after the solstices. Not yet would they veer southward to the caldron of the land that lay below; they must wean their blood from the northern winter and hold the mountains a while longer in their view. They bore Tai-me in procession to the east.

A dark mist lay over the Black Hills, and the land was like iron. At the top of a ridge I caught sight of Devil's Tower upthrust against the gray sky as if in the birth of time the core of the earth had broken through its crust and the motion of the world was begun. There are things in nature that engender an awful quiet in the heart of man; Devil's Tower is one of them. Two centuries ago, because they could not do otherwise, the Kiowas made a legend at the base of the rock. My grandmother said:

> Eight children were there at play, seven sisters and their brother. Suddenly the boy was struck dumb; he trembled and began to run upon his hands and feet. His fingers became claws, and his body was covered with fur. Directly there was a bear where the boy had been. The sisters were terrified; they ran, and the bear after them. They came to the stump of a great tree, and the tree spoke to them. It bade them climb upon it, and as they did so, it began to rise into the air. The bear came to kill them, but they were just beyond its reach. It reared against the tree and scored the bark all around with its claws. The seven sisters were borne into the sky, and they became the stars of the Big Dipper.

From that moment, and so long as the legend lives, the Kiowas have kinsmen in the night sky. Whatever they were in the mountains, they could be no more. However tenuous their well-being, however much they had suffered and would suffer again, they had found a way out of the wilderness.

10   My grandmother had a reverence for the sun, a holy regard that now is all but gone out of mankind. There was a wariness in her, and an ancient awe. She was a Christian in her later years, but she had come a long way about, and she never forgot her birthright. As a child she had been to the Sun Dances; she had taken part in those annual rites, and by them she had learned the restoration of her people in the presence of Tai-me. She was about seven when the last Kiowa Sun Dance was held in 1887 on the Washita River above Rainy Mountain Creek. The buffalo were gone. In order to consummate the ancient sacrifice— to impale the head of a buffalo bull upon the medicine tree—a delegation of old men journeyed into Texas, there to beg and barter for an animal from the Goodnight herd. She was ten when the Kiowas came together for the last time as a living Sun Dance culture. They could find no buffalo; they had to hang an old hide from the sacred tree. Before the dance could begin, a company of soldiers rode out from Fort Sill under orders to disperse the tribe. Forbidden without cause the essential act of their faith, having seen the wild herds slaughtered and left to rot upon the ground, the Kiowas backed away forever from the medicine tree. That was July 20, 1890, at the great bend of the Washita. My grandmother was there. Without bitterness, and for as long as she lived, she bore a vision of deicide.

Now that I can have her only in memory, I see my grandmother in the several postures that were peculiar to her: standing at the wood stove on a winter morning and turning meat in a great iron skillet; sitting at the south window, bent above her beadwork, and afterwards, when her vision had failed, looking down for a long time into the fold of her hands; going out upon a cane, very slowly as she did when the weight of age came upon her; praying. I remember her most often at prayer. She made long, rambling prayers out of suffering and hope, having seen many things. I was never sure that I had the right to hear, so exclusive were they of all mere custom and company. The last time I saw her she prayed standing by the side of her bed at night, naked to the waist, the light of a kerosene lamp moving upon her dark skin. Her long, black hair, always drawn and braided in the day, lay upon her shoulders and against her breasts like a shawl. I do not speak Kiowa, and I never understood her prayers, but there was something inherently sad in the sound, some merest hesitation upon the syllables of sorrow. She began in a high and descending pitch, exhausting her breath to silence; then again and again—and always the same intensity of effort, of something that is, and is not, like urgency in the human voice. Transported so in the dancing light among the shadows of her room, she seemed beyond the reach of time. But that was illusion; I think I knew that I should not see her again.

Houses are like sentinels in the plain, old keepers of the weather watch. There, in a very little while, wood takes on the appearance of great age. All colors wear soon away in the wind and rain, and then the wood is burned gray and the grain appears and the nails turn red with rust. The windowpanes are black and opaque; you imagine there is nothing within, and indeed there are many ghosts, bones given up to the land. They stand here and there against the sky, and you approach them for a longer time than you expect. They belong in the distance; it is their domain.

Once there was a lot of sound in my grandmother's house, a lot of coming and going, feasting and talk. The summers there were full of excitement and reunion. The Kiowas are a summer people; they abide the cold and keep to themselves, but when the season turns and the land becomes warm and vital they cannot hold still; an old love of going returns upon them. The aged visitors who came to my grandmother's house when I was a child were made of lean and leather, and they bore themselves upright. They wore great black hats and bright ample shirts that shook in the wind. They rubbed fat upon their hair and wound their braids with strips of colored cloth. Some of them painted their faces and carried the scars of old and cherished enmities. They were an old council of warlords, come to remind and be reminded of who they were. Their wives and daughters served them well. The women might indulge themselves; gossip was at once the mark and compensation of their servitude. They made loud and elaborate talk among themselves, full of jest and gesture, fright and false alarm. They went abroad in fringed and flowered shawls, bright beadwork and German silver. They were at home in the kitchen, and they prepared meals that were banquets.

There were frequent prayer meetings, and great nocturnal feasts. When I was a child I played with my cousins outside, where the lamplight fell upon the ground and the singing of the old people rose up around us and carried away into the darkness. There were a lot of good things to eat, a lot of laughter and surprise. And afterwards, when the quiet returned, I lay down with my grandmother and could hear the frogs away by the river and feel the motion of the air.

Now there is a funeral silence in the rooms, the endless wake of some final word. The walls have closed in upon my grandmother's house. When I returned to it in mourning, I saw for the first time in my life how small it was. It was late at night, and there was a white moon, nearly full. I sat for a long time on the stone steps by the kitchen door. From there I could see out across the land; I could see the long row of trees by the creek, the low light upon the rolling plains, and the stars of the big dipper. Once I looked at the moon and caught sight of a strange thing. A cricket had perched upon the handrail, only a few inches away from me. My line of vision was such that the creature filled the moon like a fossil. It had gone there, I thought, to live and die, for there, of all places, was its small definition made whole and eternal. A warm wind rose up and purled like the longing within me.

The next morning I awoke at dawn and went out on the dirt road to Rainy Mountain. It was already hot, and the grasshoppers began to fill the air. Still, it was early in the morning, and the birds sang out of the shadows. The long yellow grass on the mountain shone in the bright light, and a scissortail hied above the land. There, where it ought to be, at the end of a long and legendary way, was my grandmother's grave. Here and there on the dark stones were ancestral names. Looking back once, I saw the mountain and came away.

READING AND THINKING

1. To what extent is this piece about Momaday the man and the writer? To what extent is it about his grandmother? About the Kiowa people and their culture? Explain.

2. How does Momaday use the image of the journey to help his readers understand the Kiowas' concepts of space and time?

3. What is the Kiowas' relationship with nature? How is nature described? Why does Momaday emphasize landscape so strongly?

4. What is the significance of Devil's Tower and the legend the Kiowas made there about the bear and the Big Dipper?

THINKING AND WRITING

1. Analyze and explain the images of his grandmother that Momaday presents. How does Momaday convey a sense of her character? What descriptive details do you find most effective? Why?

2. Explain the aspects of Kiowan culture Momaday highlights and celebrates.

3. Identify the various stories Momaday tells, and explain the purpose of each. Explain the relationship among the stories.

4. What kind of voice does Momaday employ in this reminiscence? Identify and explain the features of style Momaday employs to create this voice.

5. Compare the way one of your parents, grandparents, or older relatives ties you to your cultural heritage with the way Momaday's grandmother ties him to his.

NATIVE IDENTITY: AN OCCASION FOR WRITING

N. Scott Momaday presents a portrait of his grandmother and an introduction to the culture and values of the Kiowa people, his ancestors. The image of the particular Native American group presented here contains common and familiar elements of Native American Indian life. This Occasion for Writing presents you with two visual images of American Indians, first through the lens of photographer Edward S. Curtis, best known for his pictures of Native Americans, and then through a painting of the contemporary Minnesota Ojibway Indian artist, Lisa Fifield. From these images, you will be invited to think about how the American Indian has been portrayed in the past and why those images have such a powerful hold on the imagination.

© Christie's Images/CORBIS

EDWARD S. CURTIS, *Chief Joseph, Nez Perce (1903)*

PREPARING TO WRITE: OCCASIONS TO THINK ABOUT WHAT YOU SEE

1. What is distinctive about the photograph by Curtis? Why do you think Curtis took this particular photograph?

2. What impressions of Native Americans does Curtis's photograph convey? What details about the photograph influence your thinking?

3. How is Fifield's *Sisters of the Loon* related to the Curtis photograph? Explain.

4. What is suggested about Native American Indian life by this painting? How does Lisa Fifield convey her idea in this painting?

MOVING TOWARD ESSAY: OCCASIONS TO ANALYZE AND REFLECT

1. What cultural values do Curtis's photograph and Fifield's painting embody?

2. How do the Curtis photograph and Fifield painting relate to Momaday's reminiscence of Kiowa life? What aspects of Momaday's writing are evident in the images? Which aspects are missing?

© Lisa Fifield. Used with permission.

LISA FIFIELD, *Sisters of the Loon*

3. Consider the following information from an essay about Native Americans by Diana Hume George. What does this excerpt add to your understanding? Explain.

In 1890, the year of the final defeat of the Sioux at Wounded Knee, the Ghost Dance was sweeping the plains. Begun by a few leaders, especially the Paiute seer Wovoka, the Ghost Dance promised its practitioners among the warriors that the buffalo would return and the white man would be defeated. Ghost Dancers believed that their ceremonial dancing and the shirts they wore would make them proof against the white man's bullets. Among the Sioux warriors at Wounded Knee, the willing suspension of disbelief was complete. It made the warriors reckless and abandoned, throwing normal caution and survival strategy to the wind.

(Source: "Wounded Chevy at Wounded Knee," *Missouri Review,* 1989)

WRITING THOUGHTFULLY: OCCASIONS FOR ESSAYS AND IDEAS

1. Write a letter to Lisa Fifield in which you respond to her painting. Discuss how her painting portrays Native Americans to you.

2. The idea of the "Indian" as it came to inhabit the popular imagination was an invention of the Europeanized world. Discuss to what extent the following elements constitute the western European conception of Native American Indian life, and to what extent these elements are embodied in Curtis's photograph and Fifield's painting. You may wish to consult the book *The White Man's Indian,* which considers the following ideas about "Indians":

- Indians lived in an idealized landscape with a gentle climate.
- Indians lived in harmony with nature.
- Indians were strong, handsome, and sexually innocent.
- Indians lived in a world without work, war, or property.
- Indians lived simple and peaceful lives, unaffected by the complications of modern civilization.

3. In 2002, an intramural basketball team took the name the "Fightin' Whities" at the University of Northern Colorado. Read the following excerpt from Chryss Cada's March 2002 *Boston Globe* article and think about the team's motivations and the implications of their actions. What is your initial response to the team name? Drawing on other examples of Native American names, write an essay in which you examine the extent to which the cultural history of the Native American population informs its current social identity. How does race figure in that equation, as well? How does history, then, inform social identity?

> "It's interesting to sit around and think, what noise does a white person make?" said Solomon Little Owl, a member of the Fightin' Whities intramural basketball team at the University of Northern Colorado. "When you say that about a white person, you realize how ridiculous the whole idea of having people as mascots is. This is our way of making that point."

> Little Owl, director of Native American Student Services at the university, suggested adopting the mascot to draw attention to the use of American Indians as mascots for sports teams. All 10 team members—three Native Americans, two Hispanics, and five Anglos—supported the move.

CREATING OCCASIONS

1. Do some research in the library and on the Internet about Native American life and the battle at Wounded Knee. You might look into to *Black Elk Speaks* and Dee Brown's *Bury My Heart at Wounded Knee*.

2. Think about how images of people of different races create or feed ideas about those races. How do we come to an understanding of others—of strangers—who are different from us? How can we ensure that our understanding of the other is fair and accurate and not a simplification or a stereotype? How does this image complicate racial relations?

3. You may wish to consider some smaller-scale examples of social identity in cultural context, such as the importance of college fraternities and sororities historically or the significance of other social groups such as the Daughters of the American Revolution or the American Legion. (Some research may be in order for these latter topics.)

James Baldwin (1924–1987)

James Baldwin was born in Harlem, the son of fundamentalist religious parents. Baldwin followed his father's vocation and became, at fourteen, a preacher. At seventeen he abandoned the ministry and devoted himself to the craft of writing. He had been writing all along, from early childhood, but his writing had been discouraged by his family in favor of the religion that, at first, had overshadowed it. He used the proceeds of a fellowship to relocate to Paris, where he lived for much of his life. There he wrote his first two novels, *Go Tell It on the Mountain* (1953) and *Giovanni's Room* (1956), which like his third novel, *Another Country* (1962), dealt openly with themes of race and homosexuality. In addition to these and other works of fiction, Baldwin is also known for a number of books of essays, most notably *Notes of a Native Son* (1955) and *The Fire Next Time* (1963). In both his fiction and his essays Baldwin explored the question of what it means to be a black man in a world controlled by whites.

STRANGER IN THE VILLAGE

In "Stranger in the Village," Baldwin describes a time when he visited an isolated village in the Swiss Alps. The inhabitants of the village had never seen a black man before they encountered Baldwin and referred to him as "Neger" (black in their French-influenced Swiss dialect). Baldwin uses his experience of being a stranger among the Swiss to explore themes of race and identity and to reflect on culture and values, especially on the extent to which an American of African descent can share in the European cultural heritage.

1   From all available evidence no black man had ever set foot in this tiny Swiss village before I came. I was told before arriving that I would probably be a "sight" for the village; I took this to mean that people of my complexion were rarely seen in Switzerland, and also that city people are always something of a "sight" outside of the city. It did not occur to me—possibly because I am an American—that there could be people anywhere who had never seen a Negro.

It is a fact that cannot be explained on the basis of the inaccessibility of the village. The village is very high, but it is only four hours from Milan and three hours from Lausanne. It is true that it is virtually unknown. Few people making plans for a holiday would elect to come here. On the other hand, the villagers are able, presumably, to come and go as they please—which they do: to another town at the foot of the mountain, with a population of approximately five thousand, the nearest place to see a movie or go to the bank. In the village there is no movie house, no bank, no library, no theater; very few radios, one jeep, one station wagon; and, at the moment, one typewriter, mine, an invention which the woman next door to me here had never seen. There are about six hundred people living here, all Catholic—I conclude this from the fact that the Catholic church is open all year round, whereas the Protestant chapel, set off on a hill a little removed from the village, is open only in the summertime when the tourists arrive. There are four or five hotels, all closed now, and four or five *bistros,* of which, however, only two do any business during the winter. These two do not do a great deal, for life in the village seems to end around nine or ten o'clock. There are a few stores, butcher, baker, *épicerie,* a hardware store, and a money-changer—who cannot change travelers' checks, but must send them down to the bank, an operation which takes two or three days. There is something called the *Ballet Haus,* closed in the winter and used for God knows what, certainly not ballet, during the summer. There seems to be only one school-house in the village, and this for the quite young children; I suppose this to mean that their older brothers and sisters at some point descend from these mountains in order to complete their education—possibly, again, to the town just below. The landscape is absolutely forbidding, mountains towering on all four sides, ice and snow as far as the eye can reach. In this white wilderness, men and women and children move all day, carrying washing, wood, buckets of milk or water, sometimes skiing on Sunday afternoons. All week long boys and young men are to be seen shoveling snow off the rooftops, or dragging wood down from the forest in sleds.

The village's only real attraction, which explains the tourist season, is the hot spring water. A disquietingly high proportion of these tourists are cripples, or semicripples, who come year after year—from other parts of Switzerland, usually—to take the waters. This lends the village, at the height of the season, a rather terrifying air of sanctity, as though it were a lesser Lourdes. There is often something beautiful, there is always something awful, in the spectacle of a person who has lost one of his faculties, a faculty he never questioned until it was gone, and who struggles to recover it. Yet people remain people, on crutches or indeed on deathbeds; and whenever I passed, the first summer I was here, among the native villagers or among the lame, a wind passed with me—of astonishment, curiosity, amusement, and outrage. That first summer I stayed two weeks and never intended to return. But I did return in the winter, to work; the village offers, obviously, no distractions whatever and has the further advantage of being extremely cheap. Now it is winter again, a year later, and I am here again. Everyone in the village knows my name, though they scarcely ever use it, knows that I come from America—though, this, apparently, they will never really believe: black

men come from Africa—and everyone knows that I am the friend of the son of a woman who was born here, and that I am staying in their chalet. But I remain as much a stranger today as I was the first day I arrived, and the children shout *Neger! Neger!* as I walk along the streets.

It must be admitted that in the beginning I was far too shocked to have any real reaction. In so far as I reacted at all, I reacted by trying to be pleasant—it being a great part of the American Negro's education (long before he goes to school) that he must make people "like" him. This smile-and-the-world-smiles-with-you routine worked about as well in this situation as it had in the situation for which it was designed, which is to say that it did not work at all. No one, after all, can be liked whose human weight and complexity cannot be, or has not been, admitted. My smile was simply another unheard-of phenomenon which allowed them to see my teeth—they did not, really, see my smile and I began to think that, should I take to snarling, no one would notice any difference. All of the physical characteristics of the Negro which had caused me, in America, a very different and almost forgotten pain were nothing less than miraculous—or infernal—in the eyes of the village people. Some thought my hair was the color of tar, that it had the texture of wire, or the texture of cotton. It was jocularly suggested that I might let it all grow long and make myself a winter coat. If I sat in the sun for more than five minutes some daring creature was certain to come along and gingerly put his fingers on my hair, as though he were afraid of an electric shock, or put his hand on my hand, astonished that the color did not rub off. In all of this, in which it must be conceded there was the charm of genuine wonder and in which there was certainly no element of intentional unkindness, there was yet no suggestion that I was human: I was simply a living wonder.

I knew that they did not mean to be 5 unkind, and I know it now; it is necessary, nevertheless, for me to repeat this to myself each time that I walk out of the chalet. The children who shout *Neger!* have no way of knowing the echoes this sound raises in me. They are brimming with good humor and the more daring swell with pride when I stop to speak with them. Just the same, there are days when I cannot pause and smile, when I have no heart to play with them; when, indeed, I mutter sourly to myself, exactly as I muttered on the streets of a city these children have never seen, when I was no bigger than these children are now: *Your* mother *was a nigger*. Joyce is right about history being a nightmare—but it may be the nightmare from which no one *can* awaken. People are trapped in history and history is trapped in them.

There is a custom in the village—I am told it is repeated in many villages—of "buying" African natives for the purpose of converting them to Christianity. There stands in the church all year round a small box with a slot for money, decorated with a black figurine, and into this box the villagers drop their francs. During the *carnaval* which precedes Lent, two village children have their faces blackened—out of which bloodless darkness their blue eyes shine like ice—and fantastic horsehair wigs are placed on their blond heads; thus disguised, they solicit among the villagers for money for the missionaries in Africa. Between the box in the church and the blackened children, the village "bought" last year six or eight African natives. This was reported to me with pride by the wife of one of the *bistro* owners and I was careful to express astonishment and pleasure at the solicitude shown by the village for the souls of black folk. The *bistro* owner's wife beamed with a pleasure far more genuine than my own and seemed to feel that I might now breathe more easily concerning the souls of at least six of my kinsmen.

I tried not to think of these so lately baptized kinsmen, of the price paid for them, or the peculiar price they themselves would pay,

and said nothing about my father, who having taken his own conversion too literally never, at bottom, forgave the white world (which he described as heathen) for having saddled him with a Christ in whom, to judge at least from their treatment of him, they themselves no longer believed. I thought of white men arriving for the first time in an African village, strangers there, as I am a stranger here, and tried to imagine the astounded populace touching their hair and marveling at the color of their skin. But there is a great difference between being the first white man to be seen by Africans and being the first black man to be seen by whites. The white man takes the astonishment as tribute, for he arrives to conquer and to convert the natives, whose inferiority in relation to himself is not even to be questioned; whereas I, without a thought of conquest, find myself among a people whose culture controls me, has even, in a sense, created me, people who have cost me more in anguish and rage than they will ever know, who yet do not even know of my existence. The astonishment with which I might have greeted them, should they have stumbled into my African village a few hundred years ago, might have rejoiced their hearts. But the astonishment with which they greet me today can only poison mine.

And this is so despite everything I may do to feel differently, despite my friendly conversations with the *bistro* owner's wife, despite their three-year-old son who has at last become my friend, despite the *saluts* and *bonsoirs* which I exchange with people as I walk, despite the fact that I know that no individual can be taken to task for what history is doing, or has done. I say that the culture of these people controls me—but they can scarcely be held responsible for European culture. America comes out of Europe, but these people have never seen America, nor have most of them seen more of Europe than the hamlet at the foot of their mountain. Yet they move with an authority which I shall never have; and they regard me, quite rightly, not only as a stranger in their village but as a suspect latecomer, bearing no credentials, to everything they have—however unconsciously—inherited.

For this village, even were it incomparably more remote and incredibly more primitive, is the West, the West onto which I have been so strangely grafted. These people cannot be, from the point of view of power, strangers anywhere in the world; they have made the modern world, in effect, even if they do not know it. The most illiterate among them is related, in a way that I am not, to Dante, Shakespeare, Michelangelo, Aeschylus, Da Vinci, Rembrandt, and Racine; the cathedral at Chartres says something to them which it cannot say to me, as indeed would New York's Empire State Building, should anyone here ever see it. Out of their hymns and dances come Beethoven and Bach. Go back a few centuries and they are in their full glory—but I am in Africa, watching the conquerors arrive.

10   The rage of the disesteemed is personally fruitless, but it is also absolutely inevitable; this rage, so generally discounted, so little understood even among the people whose daily bread it is, is one of the things that makes history. Rage can only with difficulty, and never entirely, be brought under the domination of the intelligence and is therefore not susceptible to any arguments whatever. This is a fact which ordinary representatives of the *Herrenvolk*, having never felt this rage and being unable to imagine it, quite fail to understand. Also, rage cannot be hidden, it can only be dissembled. This dissembling deludes the thoughtless, and strengthens rage and adds, to rage, contempt. There are, no doubt, as many ways of coping with the resulting complex of tensions as there are black men in the world, but no black man can hope ever to be entirely liberated from this internal warfare—rage, dissembling, and contempt having inevitably accompanied his first realization of the power of white men. What is crucial here is that, since white men represent in the black man's world so heavy a weight, white men have for black men a reality which is far from being reciprocal; and hence all black men have toward all white men an attitude which is designed, really, either to rob the white man of the jewel of his naïveté, or else to make it cost him dear.

The black man insists, by whatever means he finds at his disposal, that the white man cease to regard him as an exotic rarity and recognize him as a human being. This is a very charged and difficult moment, for there is a great deal of will power involved in the white man's naïveté. Most people are not naturally reflective any more than they are naturally malicious, and the white man prefers to keep the black man at a certain human remove because it is easier for him thus to preserve his simplicity and avoid being called to account for crimes committed by his forefathers, or his neighbors. He is inescapably aware, nevertheless, that he is in a better position in the world than black men are, nor can he quite put to death the suspicion that he is hated by black men therefore. He does not wish to be hated, neither does he wish to change places, and at this point in his uneasiness he can scarcely avoid having recourse to those legends which white men have created about black men, the most usual effect of which is that the white man finds himself enmeshed, so to speak, in his own language which describes hell, as well as the attributes which lead one to hell, as being as black as night.

Every legend, moreover, contains its residuum of truth, and the root function of language is to control the universe by describing it. It is of quite considerable significance that black men remain, in the imagination, and in overwhelming numbers in fact, beyond the disciplines of salvation; and this despite the fact that the West has been "buying" African natives for centuries.

There is, I should hazard, an instantaneous necessity to be divorced from this so visibly unsaved stranger, in whose heart, moreover, one cannot guess what dreams of vengeance are being nourished; and, at the same time, there are few things on earth more attractive than the idea of the unspeakable liberty which is allowed the unredeemed. When, beneath the black mask, a human being begins to make himself felt one cannot escape a certain awful wonder as to what kind of human being it is. What one's imagination makes of other people is dictated, of course, by the laws of one's own personality and it is one of the ironies of black-white relations that, by means of what the white man imagines the black man to be, the black man is enabled to know who the white man is.

I have said, for example, that I am as much a stranger in this village today as I was the first summer I arrived, but this is not quite true. The villagers wonder less about the texture of my hair than they did then, and wonder rather more about me. And the fact that their wonder now exists on another level is reflected in their attitudes and in their eyes. There are the children who make those delightful, hilarious, sometimes astonishingly grave overtures of friendship in the unpredictable fashion of children; other children, having been taught that the devil is a black man, scream in genuine anguish as I approach. Some of the older women never pass without a friendly greeting, never pass, indeed, if it seems that they will be able to engage me in conversation; other women look down or look away or rather contemptuously smirk. Some of the men drink with me and suggest that I learn how to ski—partly, I gather, because they cannot imagine what I would look like on skis—and want to know if I am married, and ask questions about my *métier*. But some of the men have accused *le sale nègre*—behind my back—of stealing wood and there is already in the eyes of some of them that peculiar, intent, paranoiac

malevolence which one sometimes surprises in the eyes of American white men when, out walking with their Sunday girl, they see a Negro male approach.

There is a dreadful abyss between the streets of this village and the streets of the city in which I was born, between the children who shout *Neger!* today and those who shouted *Nigger!* yesterday—the abyss is experience, the American experience. The syllable hurled behind me today expresses, above all, wonder: I am a stranger here. But I am not a stranger in America and the same syllable riding on the American air expresses the war my presence has occasioned in the American soul.

For this village brings home to me this fact: that there was a day, and not really a very distant day, when Americans were scarcely Americans at all but discontented Europeans, facing a great unconquered continent and strolling, say, into a marketplace and seeing black men for the first time. The shock this spectacle afforded is suggested, surely, by the promptness with which they decided that these black men were not really men but cattle. It is true that the necessity on the part of the settlers of the New World of reconciling their moral assumptions with the fact—and the necessity—of slavery enhanced immensely the charm of this idea, and it is also true that this idea expresses, with a truly American bluntness, the attitude which to varying extents all masters have had toward all slaves.

But between all former slaves and slaveowners and the drama which begins for Americans over three hundred years ago at Jamestown, there are at least two differences to be observed. The American Negro slave could not suppose, for one thing, as slaves in past epochs had supposed and often done, that he would ever be able to wrest the power from his master's hands. This was a supposition which the modern era, which was to bring about such vast changes in the aims and dimensions of power, put to death; it only begins, in unprecedented fashion, and with dreadful implications, to be resurrected today. But even had this supposition persisted with undiminished force, the American Negro slave could not have used it to lend his condition dignity, for the reason that this supposition rests on another: that the slave in exile yet remains related to his past, has some means—if only in memory—of revering and sustaining the forms of his former life, is able, in short, to maintain his identity.

This was not the case with the American Negro slave. He is unique among the black men of the world in that his past was taken from him, almost literally, at one blow. One wonders what on earth the first slave found to say to the first dark child he bore. I am told that there are Haitians able to trace their ancestry back to African kings, but any American Negro wishing to go back so far will find his journey through time abruptly arrested by the signature on the bill of sale which served as the entrance paper for his ancestor. At the time—to say nothing of the circumstances—of the enslavement of the captive black man who was to become the American Negro, there was not the remotest possibility that he would ever take power from his master's hands. There was no reason to suppose that his situation would ever change, nor was there, shortly, anything to indicate that his situation had ever been different. It was his necessity, in the words of E. Franklin Frazier, to find a "motive for living under American culture or die." The identity of the American Negro comes out of this extreme situation, and the evolution of this identity was a source of the most intolerable anxiety in the minds and the lives of his masters.

For the history of the American Negro is unique also in this: that the question of his humanity, and of his rights therefore as a human being, became a burning one for several generations of Americans, so burning a question that it ultimately became one of those used to divide the nation. It is out of this argument that the venom of the epithet *Nigger!* is derived. It is an argument which Europe has never had, and hence Europe quite sincerely fails to understand how or why the argument arose in the first place, why its effects are so frequently disastrous and always so unpredictable, why it refuses until today to be entirely settled. Europe's black possessions remained—and do remain—in Europe's colonies, at which remove they represented no threat whatever to European identity. If they posed any problem at all for the European conscience, it was a problem which remained comfortingly abstract: in effect, the black man, *as a man*, did not exist for Europe. But in America, even as a slave, he was an inescapable part of the general social fabric and no American could escape having an attitude toward him. Americans attempt until today to make an abstraction of the Negro, but the very nature of these abstractions reveals the tremendous effects the presence of the Negro has had on the American character.

When one considers the history of the Negro in America it is of the greatest importance to recognize that the moral beliefs of a person, or a people, are never really as tenuous as life—which is not moral—very often causes them to appear; these create for them a frame of reference and a necessary hope, the hope being that when life has done its worst they will be enabled to rise above themselves and to triumph over life. Life would scarcely be bearable if this hope did not exist. Again, even when the worst has been said, to betray a belief is not by any means to have put oneself beyond its power; the betrayal of a belief is not the same thing as ceasing to believe. If this were not so there would be no moral standards in the world at all. Yet one must also recognize that morality is based on ideas and that all ideas are dangerous—dangerous because ideas can only lead to action and where the action leads no man can say. And dangerous in this respect: that confronted with the impossibility of remaining faithful to one's beliefs, and the equal impossibility of becoming free of them, one can be driven to the most inhuman excesses. The ideas on which American beliefs are based are not, though Americans often seem to think so, ideas which originated in America. They came out of Europe. And the establishment of democracy on the American continent was scarcely as radical a break with the past as was the necessity, which Americans faced, of broadening this concept to include black men.

20   This was, literally, a hard necessity. It was impossible, for one thing, for Americans to abandon their beliefs, not only because these beliefs alone seemed able to justify the sacrifices they had endured and the blood that they had spilled, but also because these beliefs afforded them their only bulwark against a moral chaos as absolute as the physical chaos of the continent it was their destiny to conquer. But in the situation in which Americans found themselves, these beliefs threatened an idea which, whether or not one likes to think so, is the very warp and woof of the heritage of the West, the idea of white supremacy.

Americans have made themselves notorious by the shrillness and the brutality with which they have insisted on this idea, but they did not invent it; and it has escaped the world's notice that those very excesses of which Americans have been guilty imply a certain, unprecedented uneasiness over the idea's life and power, if not, indeed, the idea's validity. The idea of white supremacy rests simply on the fact that white men are the creators of civilization (the present civilization, which is the only one that matters; all previous civilizations are simply "contributions" to our own) and are therefore civilization's guardians and defenders. Thus it was impossible for Americans to accept the black man as one of themselves, for to do so was to jeopardize their status as white men. But not so to accept him was to deny his human reality, his human weight and complexity, and the strain of denying the overwhelmingly undeniable forced Americans into rationalizations so fantastic that they approached the pathological.

At the root of the American Negro problem is the necessity of the American white man to find a way of living with the Negro in order to be able to live with himself. And the history of this problem can be reduced to the means used by Americans—lynch law and law, segregation and legal acceptance, terrorization and concession—either to come to terms with this necessity, or to find a way around it, or (most usually) to find a way of doing both these things at once. The resulting spectacle, at once foolish and dreadful, led someone to make the quite accurate observation that "the negro-in-America is a form of insanity which overtakes white men."

In this long battle, a battle by no means finished, the unforeseeable effects of which will be felt by many future generations, the white man's motive was the protection of his identity; the black man was motivated by the need to establish an identity. And despite the terrorization which the Negro in America endured and endures sporadically until today, despite the cruel and totally inescapable ambivalence of his status in his country, the battle for his identity has long ago been won. He is not a visitor to the West, but a citizen there, an American; as American as the Americans who despise him, the Americans who fear him, the Americans who love him—the Americans who became less than themselves, or rose to be greater than themselves by virtue of the fact that the challenge he represented was inescapable. He is perhaps the only black man in the world whose relationship to white men is more terrible, more subtle, and more meaningful than the relationship of bitter possessed to uncertain possessor. His survival depended, and his development depends, on his ability to turn his peculiar status in the Western world to his own advantage and, it may be, to the very great advantage of that world. It remains for him to fashion out of his experience that which will give him sustenance, and a voice.

The cathedral at Chartres, I have said, says something to the people of this village which it cannot say to me; but it is important to understand that this cathedral says something to me which it cannot say to them. Perhaps they are struck by the power of the spires, the glory of the windows; but they have known God, after all, longer than I have known him, and in a different way, and I am terrified by the slippery bottomless well to be found in the crypt, down which heretics were hurled to death, and by the obscene, inescapable gargoyles jutting out of the stone and seeming to say that God and the devil can never be divorced. I doubt that the villagers think of the devil when they face a cathedral because they have never been identified with the devil. But I must accept the status which myth, if nothing else, gives me in the West before I can hope to change the myth.

25   Yet, if the American Negro has arrived at his identity by virtue of the absoluteness of his estrangement from his past, American white men still nourish the illusion that there is some means of recovering the European innocence, of returning to a state in which black men do not exist. This is one of the greatest errors Americans can make. The identity they fought so hard to protect has, by virtue of that battle, undergone a change: Americans are as unlike any other white people in the world as it is possible to be. I do not think, for example, that it is too much to suggest that the American vision of the world—which allows so little reality, generally speaking, for any of the darker forces in human life, which tends un-

til today to paint moral issues in glaring black and white—owes a great deal to the battle waged by Americans to maintain between themselves and black men a human separation which could not be bridged. It is only now beginning to be borne in on us—very faintly, it must be admitted, very slowly, and very much against our will—that this vision of the world is dangerously inaccurate, and perfectly useless. For it protects our moral high-mindedness at the terrible expense of weakening our grasp of reality. People who shut their eyes to reality simply invite their own destruction, and anyone who insists on remaining in a state of innocence long after that innocence is dead turns himself into a monster.

The time has come to realize that the interracial drama acted out on the American continent has not only created a new black man, it has created a new white man, too. No road whatever will lead Americans back to the simplicity of this European village where white men still have the luxury of looking on me as a stranger. I am not, really, a stranger any longer for any American alive. One of the things that distinguishes Americans from other people is that no other people has ever been so deeply involved in the lives of black men, and vice versa. This fact faced, with all its implications, it can be seen that the history of the American Negro problem is not merely shameful, it is also something of an achievement. For even when the worst has been said, it must also be added that the perpetual challenge posed by this problem was always, somehow, perpetually met. It is precisely this black-white experience which may prove of indispensable value to us in the world we face today. This world is white no longer, and it will never be white again.

READING AND THINKING

1. How does Baldwin describe the Swiss village, and how does he characterize its inhabitants? What is their reaction to him? Explain.

2. How does Baldwin describe and characterize himself? What aspects of his appearance does he emphasize? Why? What aspects of his identity other than race are important to him?

3. How does Baldwin describe the difference between being called "Neger" (black) in the Swiss village and "Nigger" on the streets of an American city?

4. Why does Baldwin introduce slaves and slavery into the essay? What point does he make about the American Negro slave and his past?

5. What is the American Negro Problem as Baldwin sees and describes it? What is at the root of this problem, and what, according to Baldwin, are the prospects for its solution?

THINKING AND WRITING

1. What point does Baldwin make about history? What does he mean by saying that "people are trapped in history and history is trapped in them"? Write a paragraph to explain.

2. How does Baldwin introduce ideas about religion into the essay? What is his attitude toward the villagers "buying" African children to Christianize them?

3. Analyze the ideas about strangers and strangeness that Baldwin touches on. What is his purpose in connecting his own strangeness to the Swiss villagers with the strangeness of the first white visitors in Africa?

4. Explain why Baldwin feels disesteemed and disinherited with relation to European culture. To what extent is he, as an African American, shut out from the cultural world of Europe?

5. Analyze Baldwin's point about black rage in paragraphs 10 and 11. Why does he feel this rage, and what, if anything, can he and others do about it?

BEING WHITE: AN OCCASION FOR WRITING

In his essay "Stranger in the Village," James Baldwin discusses how whites are a privileged race and how he deals with his own "strangeness." In this Occasion for Writing, you'll explore whether "white" can be considered a race and how some artists understand or interpret the issue. The default for considerations of "race" as a category, typically, is a racial minority, such as Blacks or Native American Indians in America, but is whiteness overlooked as a racial characteristic and category?

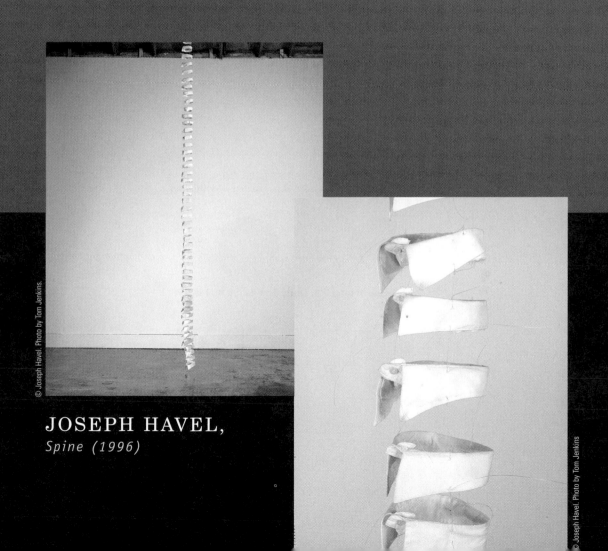

JOSEPH HAVEL,
Spine (1996)

PREPARING TO WRITE: OCCASIONS TO THINK ABOUT WHAT YOU SEE

1. *Spine* by Joseph Havel is what is known as installation art and consists of a stack of suspended collared white shirts. What is at stake from a racial standpoint in this artwork? What impression do you take from this image? What do you believe Havel's idea is in this piece?

2. Look closely at the two images here. Which one reveals more to you about Havel's goal? For what reasons?

MOVING TOWARD ESSAY: OCCASIONS TO ANALYZE AND REFLECT

1. In terms of race, what does Havel's artwork "say" or suggest about the significance of race and identity in America? Explain. What do you think the artist's opinions are about race and the term "whiteness"? Attempt to define race in terms of "white."

2. Consider the implications of the following graph, "A New Shade of White," which suggests that an increasing number of immigrants to the United States are identifying themselves as "white" on U.S. Census forms. Why do you think this trend is occurring? What does is suggest about race and people's beliefs about race?

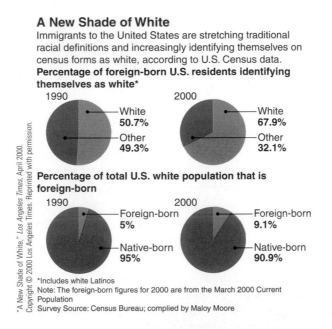

A New Shade of White
Immigrants to the United States are stretching traditional racial definitions and increasingly identifying themselves on census forms as white, according to U.S. Census data.
Percentage of foreign-born U.S. residents identifying themselves as white*

1990
White 50.7%
Other 49.3%

2000
White 67.9%
Other 32.1%

Percentage of total U.S. white population that is foreign-born

1990
Foreign-born 5%
Native-born 95%

2000
Foreign-born 9.1%
Native-born 90.9%

*Includes white Latinos
Note: The foreign-born figures for 2000 are from the March 2000 Current Population
Survey Source: Census Bureau; complied by Maloy Moore

"A New Shade of White," *Los Angeles Times*, April 2000. Copyright © 2000 Los Angeles Times. Reprinted with permission.

3. Nikki S. Lee, an Asian American artist, immerses herself in the life of minority groups by researching and adopting the group's dress code and identifying lifestyle accoutrements, body language, and behavior and she documents her transition and new lifestyle in photographs, usually without the group's knowledge of her artistic goal. What do you think of the idea behind Lee's image? What kind of comments does she make about race? How do you see Lee's photograph relating to Baldwin's experience as an outsider? Explain your thinking.

NIKKI S. LEE, *The Hip Hop Project (1) (2001)*

WRITING THOUGHTFULLY: OCCASIONS FOR IDEAS AND ESSAYS

1. Using all the text, photographs, artworks, and graphs you've examined thus far as evidence, define *race*. Can "white" be considered a race? Why or why not?

2. Write an essay on what it means to you to be a member of the majority "white" racial culture in the United States or what it means to be a member of a minority group with a different skin color and a different cultural perspective and tradition. Examine the differences between being an "insider" to a group (as Lee attempts in her photographs) and being an "outsider" to a group (as Baldwin journeys through in his essay).

CREATING OCCASIONS

1. Consider how "white" or "Caucasian" has been the default race category on census forms, school and work applications, and the like. Find other examples, in print and video ads, TV, radio, Internet, movies, sports, fashion, work, and other areas, in which whiteness is or is not considered the norm or default category. Do an Internet search for "white" and "whiteness" to see what other leads you find. Make a list of the varied connotations of the words "white" and "whiteness." Use these findings to create an Occasion for Writing about whiteness.

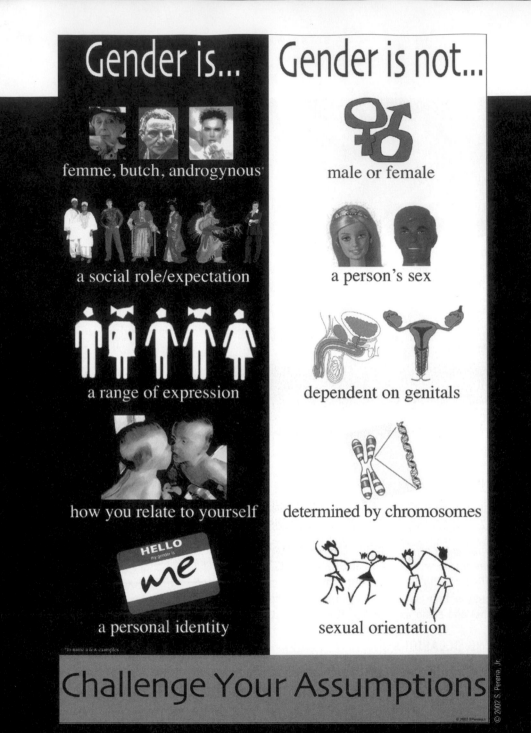

Gender is...

femme, butch, androgynous*

a social role/expectation

a range of expression

how you relate to yourself

a personal identity

*to name a few examples

Gender is not...

male or female

a person's sex

dependent on genitals

determined by chromosomes

sexual orientation

© 2002 S.Pereira

Challenge Your Assumptions

© 2002 S. Pereira, Jr.

Gender is a highly charged concept that is not easy to define. To what extent do this poster's comments about what gender is and is not challenge your CURRENT ASSUMPTIONS ABOUT GENDER? Which part of this poster would you consider your own Occasion for Writing?

7

GENDER

It is no accident that the first question asked about the birth of a baby concerns its sex. "Is it a boy or a girl?" people typically ask. From the color of the blanket the child sleeps under to the color of the tiny wardrobe, the child's sex is marked for difference. People's attitudes about the child's future activities, ambitions, and goals are linked inextricably with gender. Sexual differentiation, for better or worse, is a human universal, spanning societies worldwide. How we accommodate this reality, how we come to terms with sexual difference, informs the essays in this chapter.

Here you will find essays and Occasions for Writing that invite you to explore what it means to be a man or a woman. The essays and writing assignments provide opportunities for inquiry into the nature of femininity and masculinity and also into what the concept of beauty is for both men and women.

Not every writer in this chapter sees gender differences and their consequences the same way. Nor do all the writers agree on conceptions of masculinity and femininity. In addition, aspects of race and culture intrude into considerations of gender, as you will note in the images included in the Occasions for Writing, as well as in the essays gathered in this chapter's clusters.

All the writers have something interesting at least, and provocative at best, to say about being male or female. In the process they invite us to think about this critically distinctive aspect of our common humanity.

ENGENDERING IDENTITY

What does it mean to be a man? What does it mean to be a woman? How is gender defined in our society today? How was gender understood in the past? These are complex questions; the answers shift with changing social, political, and cultural attitudes. In the United States in the middle of the twentieth century, for example, a woman's place—middle-class women as well as upper-class women—was said to be in the home. Most lower-class women had fewer options, having to work to support families or themselves, and often at the least flattering and poorest paying jobs. Later in the century, with important shifts in the social and political climate, women flooded the workplace and began slowly earning rights and responsibilities outside the home that had once been considered out of bounds.

For many American women today what it means to be a woman includes more than being a homemaker and a mother. It now includes having an identity outside home and family. So, too, have definitions of manhood been in flux in the second half of the twentieth century and into the twenty-first century. While the traditional manly virtues have not lost their luster, they are now combined with other qualities—thoughtfulness, gentleness, compassion—that were long considered outside the male domain.

In her essay "About Men," originally published in *Time* magazine in 1985, Gretel Ehrlich writes about the western cowboy. In the process of deromanticizing the American cowboy, Ehrlich argues that it is the cowboy's softness, not his hardness, his compassion, and not his surliness, that matter, and that his gentleness is perhaps his greatest strength. If a cowboy is "gruff, handsome, and physically fit on the outside, he's androgynous at the core," she writes. And she notes that "what we've interpreted as toughness—weathered skin, calloused hands, a squint in the eye and a growl in the voice—only masks the tenderness inside."

In another essay, "Being a Man," Paul Theroux complains that the "whole idea of manhood in America is pitiful," and that the concept of "manliness [. . .] is a hideous and crippling lie [. . .] that connives at superiority." He further argues that the idea of manliness is both "emotionally damaging and socially harmful."

These comments of Ehrlich and Theroux take their point of departure from traditional concepts of masculinity but redefine the term explicitly (Ehrlich) and implicitly (Theroux). The essays in this group invite us to think about gender definition—what masculinity and femininity mean and what implications exist for each of us as we try to negotiate our way through life as women and as men.

Susan Brownmiller (b. 1935)

Susan Brownmiller was raised in Brooklyn, New York, and attended Cornell University and the Jefferson School of Social Sciences. During the 1960s she was active in feminist causes, helping to organize the New York Radical Feminists. After working as a newspaper reporter and network news writer, always with a strong interest in feminist issues, Brownmiller published her first book, *Against Our Will: Men, Women, and Rape* (1975), a book that was widely discussed. *Femininity* followed a decade later (1984), after which she published a novel, *Waverly Place* (1989), which centers on an abusive marriage.

FEMININITY

In "Femininity," an introductory essay that prefaces her book of that title, Brownmiller defines femininity by identifying its aspects and analyzing its qualities. She also considers the limitations that society has imposed upon females, invoking, in the process, her own experience as a woman and a writer.

1 We had a game in our house called "setting the table" and I was Mother's helper. Forks to the left of the plate, knives and spoons to the right. Placing the cutlery neatly, as I recall, was one of my first duties, and the event was alive with meaning. When a knife or a fork dropped on the floor, that meant a man was unexpectedly coming to dinner. A falling spoon announced the surprise arrival of a female guest. No matter that these visitors never arrived on cue, I had learned a rule of gender identification. Men were straight-edged, sharply pronged and formidable, women were softly curved and held the food in a rounded well. It made perfect sense, like the division of pink and blue that I saw in babies, an orderly way of viewing the world. Daddy, who was gone all day at work and who loved to putter at home with his pipe tobacco and tool chest, was knife and fork. Mommy and Grandma, with their ample proportions and pots and pans, were grownup soup spoons, large and capacious. And I was a teaspoon, small and slender, easy to hold and just right for pudding, my favorite dessert.

Being good at what was expected of me was one of my earliest projects, for not only was I rewarded, as most children are, for doing things right, but excellence gave pride and sta-bility to my childhood existence. Girls were different from boys, and the expression of that difference seemed mine to make clear. Did my loving, anxious mother, who dressed me in white organdy pinafores and Mary Janes and who cried hot tears when I got them dirty, give me my first instruction? Of course. Did my doting aunts and uncles with their gifts of pretty dolls and miniature tea sets add to my education? Of course. But even without the appropriate toys and clothes, lessons in the art of being feminine lay all around me and I absorbed them all: the fairy tales that were read to me at night, the brightly colored advertisements I pored over in magazines before I learned to decipher the words, the movies I saw, the comic books I hoarded, the radio soap operas I happily followed whenever I had to stay in bed with a cold. I loved being a little girl, or rather I loved being a fairy princess, for that was who I thought I was.

As I passed through a stormy adolescence to a stormy maturity, femininity increasingly became an exasperation, a brilliant, subtle esthetic that was bafflingly inconsistent at the same time that it was minutely, demandingly concrete, a rigid code of appearance and behavior defined by do's and don't-do's that went against my rebellious grain. Femininity was a challenge thrown down to the female sex, a challenge no proud, self-respecting young woman could afford to ignore, particularly one with enormous ambition that she nursed in secret, alternately feeding or starving its inchoate life in tremendous confusion.

"Don't lose your femininity" and "Isn't it remarkable how she manages to retain her femininity?" had terrifying implications. They spoke of a bottom-line failure so irreversible that nothing else mattered. The pinball machine has registered "tilt," the game had been called. Disqualification was marked on the forehead of a woman whose femininity was lost. No records would be entered in her name, for she had destroyed her birthright in her wretched, ungainly effort to imitate a man. She walked in limbo, this hapless creature, and it occurred to me that one day I might see her when I looked in the mirror. If the danger was so palpable that warning notices were freely posted, wasn't it possible that the small bundle of resentments I carried around in secret might spill out and place the mark on my own forehead? Whatever quarrels with femininity I had I kept to myself; whatever handicaps femininity imposed, they were mine to deal with alone, for there was no women's movement to ask the tough questions, or to brazenly disregard the rules.

5   Femininity, in essence, is a romantic sentiment, a nostalgic tradition of imposed limitations. Even as it hurries forward in the 1980s, putting on lipstick and high heels to appear well dressed, it trips on the ruffled petticoats and hoop-skirts of an era gone by. Invariably and necessarily, femininity is something that women had more of in the past, not only in the historic past of prior generations, but in each woman's personal past as well—in the virginal innocence that is replaced by knowledge, in the dewy cheek that is coarsened by age, in the "inherent nature" that a woman seems to misplace so forgetfully whenever she steps out of bounds. Why should this be so? The XX chromosomal mes-

sage has not been scrambled, the estrogen-dominated hormonal balance is generally as biology intended, the reproductive organs, whatever use one has made of them, are usually in place, the breasts of whatever size are most often where they should be. But clearly, biological femaleness is not enough.

Femininity always demands more. It must constantly reassure its audience by a willing demonstration of difference, even when one does not exist in nature, or it must seize and embrace a natural variation and compose a rhapsodic symphony upon the notes. Suppose one doesn't care to, has other things on her mind, is clumsy or tone-deaf despite the best instruction and training? To fall at the feminine difference is to appear not to care about men, and to risk the loss of their attention and approval. To be insufficiently feminine is viewed as a failure in core sexual identity, or as a failure to care sufficiently about oneself, for a woman found wanting will be appraised (and will appraise herself) as mannish or neutered or simply unattractive, as men have defined these terms.

We are talking, admittedly, about an exquisite esthetic. Enormous pleasure can be extracted from feminine pursuits as a creative outlet or purely as relaxation; indeed, indulgence for the sake of fun, or art, or attention, is among femininity's great joys. But the chief attraction (and the central paradox, as well) is the competitive edge that femininity seems to promise in the unending struggle to survive, and perhaps to triumph. The world smiles favorably on the feminine woman: it extends little courtesies and minor privilege. Yet the nature of this competitive edge is ironic, at best, for one works at femininity by accepting restrictions, by limiting one's sights, by choosing an indirect route, by scattering concentration and not giving one's all as a man would to his own, certifiably masculine, interests. It does not require a great leap of imagination for a woman to understand the feminine principle as a grand collection of compromises, large and small, that she simply must make in order to render herself a successful woman. If she has difficulty in satisfying femininity's demands, if its illusions go against her grain, or if she is criticized for her shortcomings and imperfections, the more she will see femininity as a desperate strategy of appeasement, a strategy she may not have the wish or the courage to abandon, for failure looms in either direction.

It is fashionable in some quarters to describe the feminine and masculine principles as polar ends of the human continuum and to sagely profess that both polarities exist in all people. Sun and moon, yin and yang, soft and hard, active and passive, etcetera, may indeed be opposites, but a linear continuum does not illuminate the problem. (Femininity, in all its contrivances, is a very active endeavor.) What, then, is the basic distinction? The masculine principle is better understood as a driving ethos of superiority designed to inspire straightforward, confident success, while the feminine principle is composed of vulnerability, the need for protection, the formalities of compliance and the avoidance of conflict—in short, an appeal of dependence and good will that gives the masculine principle its romantic validity and its admiring applause.

Femininity pleases men because it makes them appear more masculine by contrast; and, in truth, conferring an extra portion of un-earned gender distinction on men, an unchallenged space in which to breathe freely and feel stronger, wiser, more competent, is femininity's special gift. One could say that masculinity is often an effort to please women but masculinity is known to please by displays of mastery and competence while femininity pleases by suggesting that these concerns, except in small matters, are beyond its intent. Whimsy, unpredictability and patterns of thinking and behavior that are dominated by emotion, such as tearful expressions of sentiment and fear, are thought to be feminine precisely because they lie outside the established route to success.

If in the beginnings of history the feminine woman was defined by her physical dependency, her inability for reasons of reproductive biology to triumph over the forces of nature that were the tests of masculine strength and power, today she reflects both an economic and emotional dependency that is still considered "natural," romantic and attractive. After an unsettling fifteen years in which many basic assumptions about the sexes were challenged, the economic disparity did not disappear. Large numbers of women—those with small children, those left high and dry after a mid-life divorce—need financial support. But even those who earn their own living share a universal need for connectedness (call it love, if you wish). As unprecedented numbers of men abandon their sexual interest in women, others, sensing opportunity, choose to demonstrate their interest through variety and a change in partners. A sociological fact of the 1980s is that female competition for two scarce resources—men and jobs—is especially fierce.

So it is not surprising that we are currently witnessing a renewed interest in femininity and an unabashed indulgence in feminine pursuits. Femininity serves to reassure men that women need them and care about them enormously. By incorporating the decorative and the frivolous into its definition of style, femininity functions as an effective antidote to the unrelieved seriousness, the pressure of making one's way in a harsh, difficult world. In its mandate to avoid direct confrontation and to smooth over the fissures of conflict, femininity operates as a value system of niceness, a code of thoughtfulness and sensitivity that in modern society is sadly in short supply.

There is no reason to deny that indulgence in the art of feminine illusion can be reassuring to a woman, if she happens to be good at it. As sexuality undergoes some dizzying revisions, evidence that one is a woman "at heart" (the inquisitor's question) is not without worth. Since an answer of sorts may be furnished by piling on additional documentation, affirmation can arise from such identifiable but trivial feminine activities as buying a new eyeliner, experimenting with the latest shade of nail color, or bursting into tears at the outcome of a popular romance novel. Is there anything destructive in this? Time and cost factors, a deflection of energy and an absorption in fakery spring quickly to mind, and they need to be balanced, as in a ledger book, against the affirming advantage.

READING AND THINKING

1. What is Brownmiller's definition of femininity? How does she go about developing this definition? Do you think it an adequate definition? Why or why not?

2. How does Brownmiller organize her piece? How does she begin? How does she end? To what extent are this beginning and ending successful? Explain.

3. Brownmiller claims that femininity gives women a "competitive edge," in acquiring "minor privileges," which, ironically, restrict a woman's options in many ways, especially in how she relates to men. To what extent do you agree with this assessment? Explain.

4. Brownmiller wrote this piece just over twenty years ago. To what extent are her definition of femininity and the ideas she advances still current? What adjustments do you think Brownmiller would make if she were to revise the piece today?

THINKING AND WRITING

1. Compare what Brownmiller says about femininity here with what Zora Neale Hurston says about it in her essay about being a black woman, "How It Feels to Be Colored Me" (see p. 159), or compare Brownmiller's assessment of gender with that of Bernard Cooper in his essay "Burl's" (p. 692), about growing up gay.

2. Consider the extent to which the following paragraph from Paul Theroux's essay "Being a Man" (see the full essay on p. 772) is relevant to a discussion of Brownmiller's "Femininity."

> I have always disliked being a man. The whole idea of manhood in America is pitiful, in my opinion. [. . .] Even the expression "Be a man!" strikes me as insulting and abusive. It means: Be stupid, be unfeeling, obedient, soldierly, and stop thinking. Man means "manly"—how can one think about men without considering the terrible ambition of manliness? And yet it is part of every man's life. It's a hideous and crippling lie; it not only insists on difference and connives at superiority, it is also by its very nature destructive—emotionally damaging and socially harmful.

3. Make a list of the aspects and qualities of femininity as Brownmiller describes them. Then, write a one-paragraph summary of Brownmiller's introduction to her book, *Femininity*.

SEX AND PACKAGES:
AN OCCASION FOR WRITING

Susan Brownmiller's essay describes how women can be and speak and act "feminine," how they can convey in their appearance, gestures, and verbal and social behavior a feminine ideal. In the following Occasion you will have a chance to think about how packages in which everyday products are boxed and bottled and wrapped can be viewed as "masculine" or "feminine" or neutral. Although we can consider many aspects of packaging, such as size and color and materials, we will concentrate on the shape of packages, and how those shapes resonate with gender implications.

©SSPL / The Image Works

© Steven Lunetta Photography, 2006

© Steven Lunetta Photography, 2006

PREPARING TO WRITE: OCCASIONS TO THINK ABOUT WHAT YOU SEE

1. Look at the packaging of the Coca-Cola can and bottle, Mr. Clean cleaner, and Mrs. Butterworth's syrup. Group them into packages that would be more likely to appeal to men and packages that would probably appeal more to women. Provide rationale in a couple of sentences for why you put each package in its masculine or feminine group.

2. How do the shape, size, and color of the product containers convey suggestions of masculinity and femininity? Write a paragraph or two explaining your thinking about the sexual connotations of the products from a visual standpoint. Write an additional paragraph or two about the way the words on the packages contribute to the products' sexual allure.

MOVING TOWARD ESSAY: OCCASIONS TO ANALYZE AND REFLECT

1. Analyze the visual images in the pair of advertisements for male and female beauty products here and on the next page. Use the work you did in *Preparing to Write* to consider how the advertisements' images of the products resonate with sexual innuendo. Focus your attention on the packaging for each product—its size, shape, and color. Consider as well other visual details in the advertisement—how the people depicted are posed, how they are dressed, the expressions on their faces, their gestures, how words and fonts are used. Look for connections among the sex and gender implications of each advertisement's visual details.

2. Analyze the language of each advertisement. Consider the headlines for explicit and implied messages, particularly for the sexual dimensions of the headlines' suggestiveness. Read the body text of the ad carefully. Look for any words or phrases that have explicit or implied sexual appeal. Finally, examine the concluding words of the ads—their tag lines at the end. Consider what these words convey, and whether they would appeal more to men or to women, and why.

© Colgate Palmolive

WRITING THOUGHTFULLY: OCCASIONS FOR IDEAS AND ESSAYS

1. Write an essay in which you explore how the packaging of products uses sexual elements to appeal to prospective purchasers. Use your work from the previous sections as a starting point, but do some additional observing of ads in newspapers and magazines; of packages on supermarket and corner grocery store shelves; and of products sold in pharmacies, hair salons, beauty parlors, health clubs, and so on. Consider such questions as why packaging includes obvious or subtle sexual implications; whether and how such sexual appeal (especially the subtle ones) operates on buyers' subconscious minds; and the extent to which such packaging should be regulated, if at all.

in the eye
of the storm
i am

still
jennifer lopez

still
jennifer lopez

a new fragrance premiere by jennifer lopez

ROBINSONS-MAY HECHT'S FILENE'S FOLEY'S

www.jenniferlopez.com/fragrances

Image provided courtesy of The Advertising Archives

2. Think about daily products you have bought and how you have or have not been targeted by your gender. What about those products made you purchase them? Have you bought products targeted at another gender? Why or why not? Examine the consumer choices you have made and analyze in an essay how gender and commercialism do or do not have a relationship with one another.

3. Write a short essay modeled on Brownmiller's, focusing on masculinity rather than femininity. Identify the aspects and qualities of masculinity you consider essential. Be sure to provide examples and reasons to support your definition. Explore whether the media has influenced the way you understand masculinity and, if so, how.

CREATING OCCASIONS

1. Locate several newspaper, magazine, or Internet advertisements or billboards that use similar techniques to seduce viewers into buying their products. Show how each uses language and images to portray sexual implications and gender references.

2. Identify two television programs that do not have "sex" or a gender-specific word in their titles (that is, not *Sex and the City* or *Desperate Housewives*). Consider how the shows use language and images in the form of dialogue, dress, setting, action sequences, and so on that have sexual and gender implications. Define how gender is represented by television shows and your views on their accuracy. Recall (or view if possible) shows you watched as a child and examine how those shows contributed to your gender views. What do you think children today are learning about gender roles from television, movies, or even celebrities themselves?

Deborah Tannen (b. 1945)

Deborah Tannen grew up in Brooklyn, New York, and attended the State University of New York at Binghamton, followed by doctoral work at the University of California, Berkeley, where she earned a PhD In addition to her specialist scholarship in intercultural communication, she has published popular studies of communication that have focused on gender, social, and ethnic aspects. A professor of linguistics at Georgetown University, Tannen's books include *That's Not What I Meant!: How Conversational Style Makes or Breaks Relationships* (1986), *You Just Don't Understand: Women and Men in Conversation* (1990), *Talking from 9 to 5: How Women's and Men's Conversational Styles Affect Who Gets Heard, Who Gets Credit, and What Gets Done at Work* (1994), and *I Only Say This Because I Love You: How the Way We Talk Can Make or Break Family Relationships throughout Our Lives* (2001).

ASYMMETRIES: MEN AND WOMEN TALKING AT CROSS-PURPOSES

In "Asymmetries: Men and Women Talking at Cross-Purposes," a section from her book *You Just Don't Understand,* Tannen analyzes the different ways that men and women use language. Tannen argues that while men and women often use the same words and phrases, they mean very different things by them, even going so far as to suggest that it is sometimes as if men and women are speaking different languages.

1   Many years ago I was married to a man who shouted at me, "I do not give you the right to raise your voice to me, because you are a woman and I am a man." This was frustrating, because I knew it was unfair. But I also knew just what was going on. I ascribed his unfairness to his having grown up in a country where few people thought women and men might have equal rights.

Now I am married to a man who is a partner and friend. We come from similar backgrounds and share values and interests. It is a continual source of pleasure to talk to him. It is wonderful to have someone I can tell everything to, someone who understands. But he doesn't always see things as I do, doesn't always react to things as I expect him to. And I often don't understand why he says what he does.

At the time I began working on this book, we had jobs in different cities. People frequently expressed sympathy by making comments like "That must be rough," and "How do you stand it?" I was inclined to accept their sympathy and say things like "We fly a lot." Sometimes I would reinforce their concern: "The worst part is having to pack and unpack all the time." But my husband reacted differently, often with irritation. He might respond by de-emphasizing the inconvenience: As academics, we had four-day weekends together, as well as long vacations throughout the year and four months in the summer. We even benefited from the intervening days of uninterrupted time for work. I once overheard him telling a dubious man that we were lucky, since studies have shown that married couples who live together spend less than half an hour a week talking to each other; he was implying that our situation had advantages.

I didn't object to the way my husband responded—everything he said was true—but I was surprised by it. I didn't understand why he reacted as he did. He explained that he sensed condescension in some expressions of concern, as if the questioner were implying,

"Yours is not a real marriage; your ill-chosen profession has resulted in an unfortunate arrangement. I pity you, and look down at you from the height of complacence, since my wife and I have avoided your misfortune." It had not occurred to me that there might be an element of one-upmanship in these expressions of concern, though I could recognize it when it was pointed out. Even after I saw the point, though, I was inclined to regard my husband's response as slightly odd, a personal quirk. He frequently seemed to see others as adversaries when I didn't.

5   Having done the research that led to this book, I now see that my husband was simply engaging the world in a way that many men do: as an individual in a hierarchical social order in which he was either one-up or one-down. In this world, conversations are negotiations in which people try to achieve and maintain the upper hand if they can, and protect themselves from others' attempts to put them down and push them around. Life, then, is a contest, a struggle to preserve independence and avoid failure.

I, on the other hand, was approaching the world as many women do: as an individual in a network of connections. In this world, conversations are negotiations for closeness in which people try to seek and give confirmation and support, and to reach consensus. They try to protect themselves from others' attempts to push them away. Life, then, is a community, a struggle to preserve intimacy and avoid isolation. Though there are hierarchies in this world too, they are hierarchies more of friendship than of power and accomplishment.

Women are also concerned with achieving status and avoiding failure, but these are not the goals they are *focused* on all the time, and they tend to pursue them in the guise of connection. And men are also concerned with achieving involvement and avoiding isolation, but they are not *focused* on these goals, and they tend to pursue them in the guise of opposition.

Discussing our differences from this point of view, my husband pointed out to me a distinction I had missed: He reacted the way I just described only if expressions of concern came from men in whom he sensed an awareness of hierarchy. And there were times when I too disliked people's expressing sympathy about our commuting marriage. I recall being offended by one man who seemed to have a leering look in his eye when he asked, "How do you manage this long-distance romance?" Another time I was annoyed when a woman who knew me only by reputation approached us during the intermission of a play, discovered our situation by asking my husband where he worked, and kept the conversation going by asking us all about it. In these cases, I didn't feel put down; I felt intruded upon. If my husband was offended by what he perceived as claims to superior status, I felt these sympathizers were claiming inappropriate intimacy.

Intimacy and Independence

Intimacy is key in a world of connection where individuals negotiate complex networks of friendship, minimize differences, try to reach consensus, and avoid the appearance of superiority, which would highlight differences. In a world of status, *independence* is key, because a primary means of establishing status is to tell others what to do, and taking orders is a marker of low status. Though all humans need both intimacy and independence, women tend to focus on the first and men on the second. It is as if their lifeblood ran in different directions.

10   These differences can give women and men differing views of the same situation, as they did in the case of a couple I will call Linda and Josh. When Josh's old high-school chum called him at work and announced he'd be in town on business the following month, Josh invited him to stay for the weekend. That evening he informed Linda that they were going to have a houseguest, and that he

and his chum would go out together the first night to shoot the breeze like old times. Linda was upset. She was going to be away on business the week before, and the Friday night when Josh would be out with his chum would be her first night home. But what upset her the most was that Josh had made these plans on his own and informed her of them, rather than discussing them with her before extending the invitation.

Linda would never make plans, for a weekend or an evening, without first checking with Josh. She can't understand why he doesn't show her the same courtesy and consideration that she shows him. But when she protests, Josh says, "I can't say to my friend, 'I have to ask my wife for permission'!"

To Josh, checking with his wife means seeking permission, which implies that he is not independent, not free to act on his own. It would make him feel like a child or an underling. To Linda, checking with her husband has nothing to do with permission. She assumes that spouses discuss their plans with each other because their lives are intertwined, so the actions of one have consequences for the other. Not only does Linda not mind telling someone, "I have to check with Josh"; quite the contrary—she likes it. It makes her feel good to know and show that she is involved with someone, that her life is bound up with someone else's.

Linda and Josh both felt more upset by this incident, and others like it, than seemed warranted, because it cut to the core of their primary concerns. Linda was hurt because she sensed a failure of closeness in their relationship: He didn't care about her as much as she cared about him. And he was hurt because he felt she was trying to control him and limit his freedom.

A similar conflict exists between Louise and Howie, another couple, about spending money. Louise would never buy anything costing more than a hundred dollars without discussing it with Howie, but he goes out and buys whatever he wants and feels they can afford, like a table saw or a new power mower. Louise is disturbed, not because she disapproves of the purchases, but because she feels he is acting as if she were not in the picture.

Many women feel it is natural to consult with their partners at every turn, while many men automatically make more decisions without consulting their partners. This may reflect a broad difference in conceptions of decision making. Women expect decisions to be discussed first and made in consensus. They appreciate the discussion itself as evidence of involvement and communication. But many men feel oppressed by lengthy discussions about what they see as minor decisions, and they feel hemmed in if they can't just act without talking first. When women try to initiate a freewheeling discussion by asking, "What do you think?" men often think they are being asked to decide.

Communication is a continual balancing act, juggling the conflicting needs for intimacy and independence. To survive in the world, we have to act in concert with others, but to survive as ourselves, rather than simply as cogs in a wheel, we have to act alone. In some ways, all people are the same: We all eat and sleep and drink and laugh and cough, and often we eat, and laugh at, the same things. But in some ways, each person is different, and individuals' differing wants and preferences may conflict with each other. Offered the same menu, people make different choices. And if there is cake for dessert, there is a chance one person may get a larger piece than another—and an even greater chance that one will *think* the other's piece is larger, whether it is or not.

Asymmetries

If intimacy says, "We're close and the same," and independence says, "We're separate and different," it is easy to see that intimacy and independence dovetail with connection and status. The essential element of connection is symmetry: People are the same, feeling equally close to each other. The essential element of status is asymmetry: People are not the same; they are differently placed in a hierarchy.

This duality is particularly clear in expressions of sympathy or concern, which are all potentially ambiguous. They can be interpreted either symmetrically, as evidence of fellow feeling among equals, or asymmetrically, offered by someone one-up to someone one-down. Asking if an unemployed person has found a job, if a couple have succeeded in conceiving the child they crave, or whether an untenured professor expects to get tenure can be meant—and interpreted, regardless of how it is meant—as an expression of human connection by a person who understands and cares, or as a reminder of weakness from someone who is better off and knows it, and hence as condescending. The latter view of sympathy seems self-evident to many men. For example, a handicapped mountain climber named Tom Whittaker, who leads groups of disabled people on outdoor expeditions, remarked, "You can't feel sympathetic for someone you admire"—a statement that struck me as not true at all.

The symmetry of connection is what creates community: If two people are struggling for closeness, they are both struggling for the same thing. And the asymmetry of status is what creates contest: Two people can't both have the upper hand, so negotiation for status is inherently adversarial. In my earlier work, I explored in detail the dynamics of intimacy (which I referred to as involvement) and independence, but I tended to ignore the force of status and its adversarial nature. Once I identified these dynamics, however, I saw them all around me. The puzzling behavior of friends and co-workers finally became comprehensible.

20   Differences in how my husband and I approached the same situation, which previously would have been mystifying, suddenly made sense. For example, in a jazz club the waitress recommended the crab cakes to me, and they turned out to be terrible. I was uncertain about whether or not to send them back. When the waitress came by and asked how the food was, I said that I didn't really like the crab cakes. She asked, "What's wrong with them?" While staring at the table, my husband answered. "They don't taste fresh." The waitress snapped. "They're frozen! What do you expect?" I looked directly up at her and said. "We just don't like them." She said, "Well, if you don't like them, I could take them back and bring you something else."

After she left with the crab cakes, my husband and I laughed because we realized we had just automatically played out the scripts I had been writing about. He had heard her question "What's wrong with them?" as a challenge that he had to match. He doesn't like to fight, so he looked away, to soften what he felt was an obligatory counterchallenge: He felt instinctively that he had to come up with something wrong with the crab cakes to justify my complaint. (He was fighting for me.) I had taken the question "What's wrong with them?" as a request for information. I instinctively sought a way to be right without making her wrong. Perhaps it was because she was a woman that she responded more favorably to my approach.

When I have spoken to friends and to groups about these differences, they too say that now they can make sense of previously perplexing behavior. For example, a woman said she finally understood why her husband refused to talk to his boss about whether or not he stood a chance of getting promoted. He wanted to know because if the answer was no, he would start looking for another job. But instead of just asking, he stewed and fretted, lost sleep, and worried. Having no others at her disposal, this wife had fallen back on psychological explanations: Her husband must be insecure, afraid of rejection. But then, everyone is insecure, to an extent. Her husband was actually quite a confident person. And she, who believed herself to be at least as insecure as he, had not hesitated to go to her boss to ask whether he intended to make her temporary job permanent.

Understanding the key role played by status in men's relations made it all come clear. Asking a boss about chances for promotion highlights the hierarchy in the relationship, reminding them both that the employee's future is in the boss's hands. Taking the low-status position made this man intensely uncomfortable. Although his wife didn't especially relish taking the role of supplicant with respect to her boss, it didn't set off alarms in her head, as it did in his.

In a similar flash of insight, a woman who works in sales exclaimed that now she understood the puzzling transformation that the leader of her sales team had undergone when he was promoted to district manager. She had been sure he would make a perfect boss because he had a healthy disregard for authority. As team leader, he had rarely bothered to go to meetings called by management and had encouraged team members to exercise their own judgment, eagerly using his power to waive regulations on their behalf. But after he became district manager, this man was unrecognizable. He instituted more regulations than anyone had dreamed of, and insisted that exceptions could be made only on the basis of written requests to him.

25 This man behaved differently because he was now differently placed in the hierarchy. When he had been subject to the authority of management, he'd done all he could to limit it. But when the authority of management was vested in him, he did all he could to enlarge it. By avoiding meetings and flouting regulations, he had evidenced not disregard for hierarchy but rather discomfort at being in the subordinate position within it.

Yet another woman said she finally understood why her fiancé, who very much believes in equality, once whispered to her that she should keep her voice down. "My friends are downstairs," he said. "I don't want them to get the impression that you order me around."

That women have been labeled "nags" may result from the interplay of men's and women's styles, whereby many women are inclined to do what is asked of them and many men are inclined to resist even the slightest hint that anyone, especially a woman, is telling them what to do. A woman will be inclined to repeat a request that doesn't get a response because she is convinced that her husband would do what she asks, if he only understood that she *really* wants him to do it. But a man who wants to avoid feeling that he is following orders may instinctively wait before doing what she asked, in order to imagine that he is doing it of his own free will. Nagging is the result, because each time she repeats the request, he again puts off fulfilling it.

Mixed Judgments and Misjudgments

Because men and women are regarding the landscape from contrasting vantage points, the same scene can appear very different to them, and they often have opposite interpretations of the same action.

A colleague mentioned that he got a letter from a production editor working on his new book, instructing him to let her know if he planned to be away from his permanent address at any time in the next six months, when his book would be in production. He commented that he hadn't realized how like a parole officer a production editor could be. His response to this letter surprised me, because I have received similar letters from publishers, and my response is totally different: I like them, because it makes me feel important to know that my whereabouts matter. When I mentioned this difference to my colleague, he was puzzled and amused, as I was by his reaction. Though he could understand my point of view intellectually, emotionally he could not imagine how one could not feel framed as both controlled and inferior in rank by being told to report one's movements to someone. And though I could understand his perspective intellectually, it simply held no emotional resonance for me.

30   In a similar spirit, my colleague remarked that he had read a journal article written by a woman who thanked her husband in the acknowledgments section of her paper for helpful discussion of the topic. When my colleague first read this acknowledgment, he thought the author must be incompetent, or at least insecure: Why did she have to consult her husband about her own work? Why couldn't she stand on her own two feet? After hearing my explanation that women value evidence of connection, he refrained the acknowledgment and concluded that the author probably valued her husband's involvement in her work and made reference to it with the pride that comes of believing one has evidence of a balanced relationship.

If my colleague's reaction is typical, imagine how often women who think they are displaying a positive quality—connection—are misjudged by men who perceive them as revealing a lack of independence, which the men regard as synonymous with incompetence and insecurity.

In Pursuit of Freedom

A woman was telling me why a long-term relationship had ended. She recounted a recurrent and pivotal conversation. She and the man she lived with had agreed that they would both be free, but they would not do anything to hurt each other. When the man began to sleep with other women, she protested, and he was incensed at her protest. Their conversation went like this:

> *SHE:* How can you do this when you know it's hurting me?
> *HE:* How can you try to limit my freedom?
> *SHE:* But it makes me feel awful.
> *HE:* You are trying to manipulate me.

On one level, this is simply an example of a clash of wills: What he wanted conflicted with what she wanted. But in a fundamental way, it reflects the difference in focus I have been describing. In arguing for his point of view, the key issue for this man was his independence, his freedom of action. The key issue for the woman was their interdependence—how what he did made her feel. He interpreted her insistence on their interdependence as "manipulation": She was using her feelings to control his behavior.

The point is not that women do not value freedom or that men do not value their connection to others. It is rather that the desire for freedom and independence becomes more of an issue for many men in relationships, whereas interdependence and connection become more of an issue for many women. The difference is one of focus and degree.

In a study of how women and men talk about their divorces, Catherine Kohler Riessman found that both men and women mentioned increased freedom as a benefit of divorce. But the word *freedom* meant different things to them. When women told her they had gained freedom by divorce, they meant that they had gained "independence and autonomy." It was a relief for them not to have to worry about how their husbands would react to what they did, and not have to be "responsive to a disgruntled spouse." When men mentioned freedom as a benefit of divorce, they meant freedom from obligation—the relief of feeling "less confined," "less claustrophobic," and having "fewer responsibilities."

35   Riessman's findings illuminate the differing burdens that are placed on women and men by their characteristic approaches to relationships. The burden from which divorce delivered the women was perceived as internally motivated: the continual preoccupation with how their husbands would respond to them and how they should respond to their husbands. The burden from which it delivered

the men was perceived as externally imposed: the obligations of the provider role and a feeling of confinement from having their behavior constrained by others. Independence was not a gift of divorce for the men Riessman interviewed, because, as one man put it, "I always felt independent and I guess it's just more so now."

The Chronicle of Higher Education conducted a small survey, asking six university professors why they had chosen the teaching profession. Among the six were four men and two women. In answering the question, the two women referred to teaching. One said, "I've always wanted to teach." The other said, "I knew as an undergraduate that I wanted to join a faculty. . . . I realized that teaching was the thing I wanted to do." The four men's answers had much in common with each other and little in common with the women's. All four men referred to independence as their main motive. Here are excerpts from each of their responses:

> I decided it was academe over industry because I would have my choice of research. There's more independence.

> I wanted to teach, and I like the freedom to set your own research goals.

> I chose an academic job because the freedoms of academia outweighed the money disadvantages—and to pursue the research interest I'd like to, as opposed to having it dictated.

> I have a problem that interests me. . . . I'd rather make $30,000 for the rest of my life and be allowed to do basic research than to make $100,000 and work in computer graphics.

Though one man also mentioned teaching, neither of the women mentioned freedom to pursue their own research interests as a main consideration. I do not believe this means that women are not interested in research, but rather that independence, freedom from being told what to do, is not as significant a preoccupation for them.

In describing what appealed to them about teaching, these two women focused on the ability to influence students in a positive way. Of course, influencing students reflects a kind of power over them, and teaching entails an asymmetrical relationship, with the teacher in the higher-status position. But in talking about their profession, the women focused on connection to students, whereas the men focused on their freedom from others' control.

Male-Female Conversation Is Cross-Cultural Communication

If women speak and hear a language of connection and intimacy, while men speak and hear a language of status and independence, then communication between men and women can be like cross-cultural communication, prey to a clash of conversational styles. Instead of different dialects, it has been said they speak different genderlects.

The claim that men and women grow up   40 in different worlds may at first seem patently absurd. Brothers and sisters grow up in the same families, children to parents of both genders. Where, then, do women and men learn different ways of speaking and hearing?

It Begins at the Beginning

Even if they grow up in the same neighborhood, on the same block, or in the same house, girls and boys grow up in different worlds of words. Others talk to them differently and expect and accept different ways of talking from them. Most important, children learn how to talk, how to have conversations, not only from their parents but from their peers. After all, if their parents have a foreign or regional accent, children do not emulate it: they learn to speak with the pronunciation of the region where they grow up. Anthropologists Daniel Maltz and Ruth Borker summarize research showing that boys and girls have very different ways of talking to their friends. Although they often play together, boys and girls spend most of their time playing in same-sex groups. And, although some of the activities they play at are similar, their favorite games are different, and their ways of using language in their games are separated by a world of difference.

Boys tend to play outside, in large groups that are hierarchically structured. Their groups have a leader who tells others what to do and how to do it, and resists doing what other boys propose. It is by giving orders and making them stick that high status is negotiated. Another way boys achieve status is to take center stage by telling stories and jokes, and by sidetracking or challenging the stories and jokes of others. Boys' games have winners and losers and elaborate systems of rules that are frequently the subjects of arguments. Finally, boys are frequently heard to boast of their skill and argue about who is best at what.

Girls, on the other hand, play in small groups or in pairs; the center of a girl's social life is a best friend. Within the group, intimacy is key: Differentiation is measured by relative closeness, in their most frequent games, such as jump rope and hopscotch, everyone gets a turn. Many of their activities (such as playing house) do not have winners or losers. Though some girls are certainly more skilled than others, girls are expected not to boast about it, or show that they think they are better than the others. Girls don't give orders; they express their preferences as suggestions, and suggestions are likely to be accepted. Whereas boys say, "Gimme that!" and "Get outta here!" girls say, "Let's do this," and "How about doing that?" Anything else is put down as "bossy." They don't grab center stage—they don't want it—so they don't challenge each other directly. And much of the time, they simply sit together and talk. Girls are not accustomed to jockeying for status in an obvious way; they are more concerned that they be liked.

Gender differences in ways of talking have been described by researchers observing children as young as three. Amy Sheldon videotaped three- to four-year-old boys and girls playing in threesomes at a day-care center. She compared two groups of three—one of boys, one of girls—that got into fights about the same play item: a plastic pickle. Though both groups fought over the same thing, the dynamics by which they negotiated their conflicts were different. In addition to illustrating some of the patterns I have just described, Sheldon's study also demonstrates the complexity of these dynamics.

While playing in the kitchen area of the day-care center, a little girl named Sue wanted the pickle that Mary had, so she argued that Mary should give it up because Lisa, the third girl, wanted it. This led to a conflict about how to satisfy Lisa's (invented) need. Mary proposed a compromise, but Sue protested:

> MARY: I cut it in half. One for Lisa, one for me, one for me.
> SUE: But, Lisa wants a *whole* pickle!

Mary comes up with another creative compromise, which Sue also rejects:

> MARY: Well, it's a whole *half* pickle.
> SUE: No, it isn't.
> MARY: Yes, it is, a whole *half* pickle.
> SUE: *I'll* give her a whole half. I'll give her a *whole whole*. I gave her a whole one.

At this point. Lisa withdraws from the alliance with Sue, who satisfies herself by saying, "I'm pretending I gave you one."

On another occasion, Sheldon videotaped three boys playing in the same kitchen play area, and they too got into a fight about the plastic pickle. When Nick saw that Kevin had the pickle, he demanded it for himself:

> NICK: [Screams] Kevin, but the, oh, I *have* to cut! I want to cut it! It's mine!

Like Sue, Nick involved the third child in his effort to get the pickle:

> NICK: [Whining to Joe] Kevin is not letting me cut the pickle:

45

JOE: Oh, I know! I can pull it away from him and give it back to you. That's an idea!

The boys' conflict, which lasted two and a half times longer than the girls', then proceeded as a struggle between Nick and Joe on the one hand and Kevin on the other.

In comparing the boys' and girls' pickle fights, Sheldon points out that, for the most part, the girls mitigated the conflict and preserved harmony by compromise and evasion. Conflict was more prolonged among the boys, who used more insistence, appeals to rules, and threats of physical violence. However, to say that these little girls and boys used *more* of one strategy or another is not to say that they didn't use the other strategies at all. For example, the boys did attempt compromise, and the girls did attempt physical force. The girls, like the boys, were struggling for control of their play. When Sue says by mistake, "*I'll* give her a whole half," then quickly corrects herself to say, "I'll give her a *whole whole*," she reveals that it is not really the size of the portion that is important to her, but who gets to serve it.

50   While reading Sheldon's study, I noticed that whereas both Nick and Sue tried to get what they wanted by involving a third child, the alignments they created with the third child, and the dynamics they set in motion, were fundamentally different. Sue appealed to Mary to fulfill someone else's desire; rather than saying that *she* wanted the pickle, she claimed that Lisa wanted it. Nick asserted his own desire for the pickle, and when he couldn't get it on his own, he appealed to Joe to get it for him. Joe then tried to get the pickle by force. In both these scenarios, the children were enacting complex lines of affiliation.

Joe's strong-arm tactics were undertaken not on his own behalf but, chivalrously, on behalf of Nick. By making an appeal in a whining voice, Nick positioned himself as one-down in a hierarchical structure, framing himself as someone in need of protection.

When Sue appealed to Mary to relinquish her pickle, she wanted to take the one-up position of serving food. She was fighting not for the right to *have* the pickle, but for the right to *serve* it. (This reminded me of the women who said they'd become professors in order to teach.) But to accomplish her goal. Sue was depending on Mary's desire to fulfill others' needs.

This study suggests that boys and girls both want to get their way, but they tend to do so differently. Though social norms encourage boys to be openly competitive and girls to be openly cooperative, different situations and activities can result in different ways of behaving. Marjorie Harness Goodwin compared boys and girls engaged in two task-oriented activities: The boys were making slingshots in preparation for a fight, and the girls were making rings. She found that the boys' group was hierarchical: The leader told the others what to do and how to do it. The girls' group was egalitarian: Everyone made suggestions and tended to accept the suggestions of others. But observing the girls in a different activity—playing house—Goodwin found that they too adopted hierarchical structures: The girls who played mothers issued orders to the girls playing children, who in turn sought permission from their play-mothers. Moreover, a girl who was a play-mother was also a kind of manager of the game. This study shows that girls know how to issue orders and operate in a hierarchical structure, but they don't find that mode of behavior appropriate when they engage in task activities with their peers. They do find it appropriate in parent-child relationships, which they enjoy practicing in the form of play.

These worlds of play shed light on the world views of women and men in relationships. The boys' play illuminates why men would be on the lookout for signs they are being put down or told what to do. The chief commodity that is bartered in the boys' hierarchical world is status, and the way to achieve and maintain status is to give orders and get others to follow them. A boy in a low-status position finds himself being pushed around. So boys monitor their relations for subtle shifts in status by keeping track of who's giving orders and who's taking them.

55   These dynamics are not the ones that drive girls' play. The chief commodity that is bartered in the girls' community is intimacy. Girls monitor their friendships for subtle shifts in alliance, and they seek to be friends with popular girls. Popularity is a kind of status, but it is founded on connection. It also places popular girls in a bind. By doing field work in a junior high school, Donna Eder found that popular girls were paradoxically—and inevitably—disliked. Many girls want to befriend popular girls, but girls' friendships must necessarily be limited, since they entail intimacy rather than large group activities. So a popular girl must reject the overtures of most of the girls who seek her out—with the result that she is branded "stuck up."

The Key Is Understanding

If adults learn their ways of speaking as children growing up in separate social worlds of peers, then conversation between women and men is cross-cultural communication. Although each style is valid on its own terms, misunderstandings arise because the styles are different. Taking a cross-cultural ap-proach to male-female conversations makes it possible to explain why dissatisfactions are justified without accusing anyone of being wrong or crazy.

Learning about style differences won't make them go away, but it can banish mutual mystification and blame. Being able to understand why our partners, friends, and even strangers behave the way they do is a comfort, even if we still don't see things the same way. It makes the world into more familiar territory. And having others understand why we talk and act as we do protects us from the pain of their puzzlement and criticism.

In discussing her novel *The Temple of My Familiar*, Alice Walker explained that a woman in the novel falls in love with a man because she sees in him "a giant ear." Walker went on to remark that although people may think they are falling in love because of sexual attraction or some other force, "really what we're looking for is someone to be able to hear us."

We all want, above all, to be heard—but not merely to be heard. We want to be under-stood—heard for what we think we are saying, for what we know we meant. With increased understanding of the ways women and men use language should come a de-crease in frequency of the complaint "You just don't understand."

READING AND THINKING

1. What distinctions does Tannen make between how men see the world and how women see it? What effect does this differing perception of the world have on how men and women communicate?

2. How does Tannen organize her piece—a chapter from her book *You Just Don't Under-stand*? How does the title of the book relate to the title of this selection from it?

3. What strategies does Tannen employ to make her ideas clear and understandable? To what extent do you find these strategies helpful? Explain.

4. Tannen describes "communication as a continual balancing act." What elements need to be balanced in any successful communication?

THINKING AND WRITING

1. Write a letter to Tannen in which you support, modify, or refute the claims about the different ways men and women communicate. Provide examples as evidence for your views.

2. Do you agree with Tannen that communication between men and women is a form of "cross-cultural" communication? Provide examples to support your views.

3. Identify Tannen's central argument in this selection in one sentence, and then provide half a dozen additional sentences to flesh out, clarify, and provide evidence of this idea.

DON'T YOU UNDERSTAND ME?
AN OCCASION FOR WRITING

At one point in her essay on the different ways men and women communicate with spoken language, Deborah Tannen considers their differences comparable to differences in the ways members of different cultures communicate. In the following Occasion for Writing, you are invited to consider some aspects of intercultural communication, analyzing a set of visual images of objects that mean different things in different cultures. You will also be encouraged to think about how concepts of space and time mean quite different things across cultures.

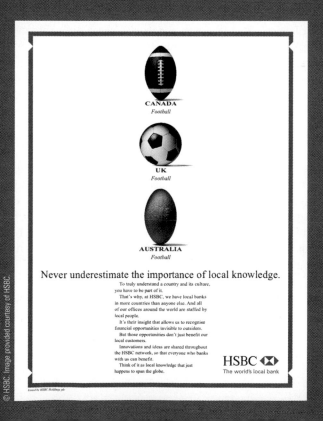

© HSBC. Image provided courtesy of HSBC.

PREPARING TO WRITE: OCCASIONS TO THINK ABOUT WHAT YOU SEE

1. What is this image showing? Was this something you were surprised about? What can you learn from viewing the images in this advertisement with its corresponding place and explanatory information?

MOVING TOWARD ESSAY: OCCASIONS TO ANALYZE AND REFLECT

1. Explore how communication across cultures is more than a matter of learning a foreign language, such as Spanish, Chinese, English, German, or French, particularly in relation to a second language you speak or have studied. Consider the ways in which misunderstandings can occur when you try to communicate in a language other than your native language. You can include situations where you yourself may be using your native language and the person or people you are communicating with in speech or writing are using your language, but which for them is a foreign language.

2. Consider the extent to which cultural differences are related to aspects of language differences. You may know, for example, that Chinese culture traditionally puts great emphasis on respect for age and for elaborate forms of protocol regarding family relationships. Although English has words to indicate some of those relationships—elder brother, second oldest brother, mother's brother, father's brother, for example—the English words do not convey the full significance and meaning attached to the concepts in Chinese culture. Try to identify one or two other examples of how different languages reflect cultural differences even when you can translate words and phrases easily between the languages.

3. Follow up on Tannen's idea that men and women speak different languages, that even when they may be using the same words, they understand and mean different things when using those words and phrases. Identify two additional examples besides those she provides in her essay. Consider the extent to which your examples cause serious misunderstandings between men and women, and what consequences can occur because of those misunderstandings.

WRITING THOUGHTFULLY: OCCASIONS FOR IDEAS AND ESSAYS

1. Write an essay in which you explore the topic of intercultural communication. You may choose to focus on intercultural understanding across two languages—English and Spanish, or English and Chinese, for example. Or you may wish to consider how different images or actions mean very different things in a variety of cultures. Use the work you did in the *Preparing to Write* and *Moving Toward Essay* sections as a starting point for your thinking, but provide other examples from your experience, your observation, or your reading.

2. Write an essay in which you explore Deborah Tannen's notion of men's and women's use of language as a form of cross-cultural communication—with all its pitfalls. You may include some of Tannen's examples in your essay, but you can also use the examples you identified in the *Moving Toward Essay* section, as well as others that occur to you based on your reading, observation, and experience. You might also consider interviewing some of your friends to get further ideas on this topic.

3. Just as men and women understand language differently, cultures understand time and space differently. Explore how these concepts of time and of space vary across cultures. You might consider how words like "morning," "afternoon," and "evening" refer to different hours of the day in different places—in the United States and Spain, for example. You can consider the importance of time—of being on time and what that means in Germany or the United States as compared with Mexico or Egypt, for example (or another Latin, Middle Eastern, or European country). You might consider writing about private and public space, and how differences in what is considered intimate distance, personal distance, social distance, and other forms of "distance" between people affect people's comfort levels across cultures. Think about what, for you, is a comfortable distance when talking with a friend as opposed to when talking with an acquaintance, a teacher, or a stranger and how gender might affect your actions. How might your comfort zones for each of these distances compare with the comfort level of someone from another country and culture in the same situations? How do such distance differences affect communication? Write an essay examining all the different aspects of understanding these differences.

CREATING OCCASIONS

1. Pick up a copy of Edward T. Hall's *The Silent Language* (1959), a classic popular study of intercultural communication. Read one chapter in the book, isolate three examples Hall provides there, and relate what he says in the examples to your personal experience and to the answers you provided and the writing you did for the previous exercises.

2. Do gender research by listening carefully to a number of conversations during the course of the next few days. Select two or three conversations between males, two or three between females, and two or three mixed gender conversations. Select some of these examples from school, others from work, and still others from social conversations. After making notes about the conversations, write up a short paper about your findings.

Judy Ruiz (b. 1944)

Judy Ruiz earned a Master of Fine Arts in poetry from the University of Arkansas in 1988, and she won an Arkansas Arts Fellowship shortly afterward. Ruiz has published poems in a wide variety of journals, with her first books of poems, *Talking Razzmatazz: Poems,* published in 1991. In addition to poetry, Ruiz has published nonfiction, which has been included in *Surviving Crisis* (1997) and *Connecting* (1998). "Oranges and Sweet Sister Boy" originally appeared in *Iowa Woman* magazine in 1988. It was included in *The Best American Essays 1989.*

ORANGES AND SWEET SISTER BOY

In "Oranges and Sweet Sister Boy," Judy Ruiz describes the sexual transformation of her brother. Ruiz explains her brother's emotional and psychological reasons for the sex change operation he undergoes, and she includes the impact the transformation had on her and other members of her family.

1 I am sleeping, hard, when the telephone rings. It's my brother, and he's calling to say that he is now my sister. I feel something fry a little, deep behind my eyes. Knowing how sometimes dreams get mixed up with not-dreams, I decide to do a reality test at once. "Let me get a cigarette," I say, knowing that if I reach for a Marlboro and it turns into a trombone or a snake or anything else on the way to my lips that I'm still out in the large world of dreams.

The cigarette stays a cigarette. I light it. I ask my brother to run that stuff by me again.

It is the Texas Zephyr at midnight—the woman in a white suit, the man in a blue uniform; she carries flowers—I know they are flowers. The petals spill and spill into the aisle, and a child goes past this couple who have just come from their own wedding—goes past them and past them, going always to the toilet but really just going past them; and the child could be a horse or she could be the police and they'd not notice her any more than they do, which is not at all—the man's hands high up on the woman's legs, her skirt up, her stockings and garters, the petals and finally all the flowers spilling out into the aisle and his mouth open on her. My mother. My father. I am conceived near Dallas in the dark while a child passes, a young girl who knows and doesn't know, who witnesses, in glimpses, the creation of the universe, who feels an odd hurt as her own mother, fat and empty, snores with her mouth open, her false teeth slipping down, snores and snores just two seats behind the Creators.

News can make a person stupid. It can make you think you can do something. So I ask The Blade question, thinking that if he hasn't had the operation yet that I can fly to him, rent a cabin out on Puget Sound. That we can talk. That I can get him to touch base with reality.

"Begin with an orange," I would tell him. "Because oranges are mildly intrusive by nature, put the orange somewhere so that it will not bother you—in the cupboard, in a drawer, even a pocket or a handbag will do. The orange, being a patient fruit, will wait for you much longer than say a banana or a peach."

I would hold an orange out to him. I would 5 say, "This is the one that will save your life." And I would tell him about the woman I saw in a bus station who bit right into her orange like it was an apple. She was wild looking, as if she'd been outside for too long in a wind that blew the same way all the time. One of the dregs of humanity, our mother would have called her, the same mother who never brought fruit into the house except in cans. My children used to ask me to "start" their oranges for them. That meant to make a hole in the orange so they could peel the rind away, and their small hands weren't equipped with fingernails that were long enough or strong enough to do the job. Sometimes they would suck the juice out of the hole my thumbnail had made, leaving the orange flat and sad.

The earrings are as big as dessert plates, fil-igree gold-plated with thin dangles hanging down that touch her bare shoulders. She stands in front of the Alamo while a bald man takes her picture. The sun is absorbed by the earrings so quickly that by the time she feels the heat, it is too late. The hanging dangles make small blisters on her shoulders, as if a centipede had traveled there. She takes the famous river walk in spiked heels, rides in a boat, eats some Italian noodles, returns to the motel room, soaks her feet, and applies small band-aids to her toes. She is briefly concerned about the gun on the nightstand. The toilet flushes. She pretends to be sleeping. The gun is just large and heavy. A .45? A .357 magnum? She's never been good with names. She hopes he doesn't try to. Or that if he does, that it's not loaded. But he'll say it's loaded just for fun. Or he'll pull the trigger and the bullet will lodge in her medulla oblongata, ripping through her womb first, taking everything else vital on the way.

In the magazine articles, you don't see this: "Well, yes. The testicles have to come out. And yes. The penis is cut off." What you get is tonsils. So-and-so has had a "sex change" operation. A sex change operation. How precious. How benign. Doctor, just what do you people do with those penises?

News can make a person a little crazy also. News like, "We regret to inform you that you have failed your sanity hearing."

The bracelet on my wrist bears the necessary information about me, but there is one small error. The receptionist typing the infor-mation asked me my religious preference. I said, "None." She typed, "Neon."

Pearl doesn't have any teeth and her tongue looks weird. She says "Pumpkin pie." That's all she says. Sometimes she runs her hands over my bed sheets and says pumpkin pie. Sometimes I am under the sheets. Marsha got stabbed in the chest, but she tells everyone she fell on a knife. Elizabeth—she's the one who thinks her shoe is a baby—hit me in the back with a tray right after one of the cooks gave me extra toast. There's a note on the bulletin board about a class for the nurses: "How Putting A Towel On Someone's Face Makes Them Stop Banging Their Spoon/OR Reduction of Disruptive Mealtime Behavior By Facial Screening—7 P.M.—Conference Room." Another note announces the topic for remotivation class: "COWS." All the paranoid schizophrenics will be there.

Here, in the place for the permanently bewildered, I fit right in. Not because I stood at the window that first night and listened to the trains. Not because I imagined those trains were bracelets, the jewelry of earth. Not even because I imagined that one of those bracelets was on my own arm and was the Texas Zephyr where a young couple made love and conceived me. I am eighteen and beautiful and committed to the state hospital by a district court judge for a period of one day to life. Because I am a paranoid schizophrenic.

I will learn about cows.

So I'm being very quiet in the back of the classroom, and I'm peeling an orange. It's the smell that makes the others begin to turn around, that mildly intrusive nature. The course is called "Women and Modern Literature," and the diaries of Virginia Woolf are up for discussion except nobody has anything to say. I, of course, am making a mess with the orange; and I'm wanting to say that my brother is now my sister.

Later, with my hands still orangey, I wander in to leave something on a desk in a pro- 10 fessor's office, and he's reading so I'm being very quiet, and then he says, sort of out of nowhere, "Emily Dickinson up there in her room making poems while her brother was making love to her best friend right downstairs on the dining room table. A regular thing. Think of it. And Walt Whitman out sniffing around the boys. Our two great American poets." And I want to grab this professor's arm and say, "Listen. My brother called me and now he's my sister, and I'm having trouble making sense out of my life right now, so would you mind not telling me any more stuff about sex." And I want my knuckles to turn white while the pressure of my fingers leaves imprints right through his jacket, little indentations he can interpret as urgent. But I don't say anything. And I don't grab his arm. I go read a magazine. I find this:

"I've never found an explanation for why the human race has so many languages. When the brain became a language brain, it obviously needed to develop an intense degree of plasticity. Such plasticity allows languages to be logical, coherent systems and yet be extremely variable. The same brain that thinks in words and symbols is also a brain that has to be freed up with regard to sexual turn-on and partnering. God knows why sex attitudes have not been subject to the corresponding degrees of modification and variety as language. I suspect there's a close parallel between the two. The brain doesn't seem incredibly efficient with regard to sex."

John Money said that. The same John Money who, with surgeon Howard W. Jones, performed the first sex change operation in the United States in 1965 at Johns Hopkins University and Hospital in Baltimore.

Money also tells about the *hijra* of India who disgrace their families because they are too effeminate: "The ultimate stage of the *hijra* is to get up the courage to go through the amputation of penis and testicles. They had no anesthetic." Money also answers anyone who might think that "heartless members of the medical

profession are forcing these poor darlings to go and get themselves cut up and mutilated," or who think the medical profession should leave them alone. "You'd have lots of patients willing to get a gun and blow off their own genitals if you don't do it. I've had several who got knives and cut themselves trying to get rid of their sex organs. That's their obsession!"

Perhaps better than all else, I understand obsession. It is of the mind. And it is language-bound. Sex is of the body. It has no words. I am stunned to learn that someone with an obsession of the mind can have parts of the body surgically removed. This is my brother I speak of. This is not some lunatic named Carl who becomes Carlene. This is my brother.

So while we're out in that cabin on Puget Sound, I'll tell him about LuAnn. She is the sort of woman who orders the in-season fruit and a little cottage cheese. I am the sort of woman who orders a double cheeseburger and fries. LuAnn and I are sitting in her car. She has a huge orange, and she peels it so the peel falls off in one neat strip. I have a sack of oranges, the small ones. The peel of my orange comes off in hunks about the size of a baby's nail. "Oh, you bought the *juice* oranges," LuAnn says to me. Her emphasis on the word "juice" makes me want to die or something. I lack the courage to admit my ignorance, so I smile and breathe "yes," as if I know some secret, when I'm wanting to scream at her about how my mother didn't teach me about fruit and my own blood pounds in my head wanting out, out.

There is a pattern to this thought as there is a pattern for a jumpsuit. Sew the sleeve to the leg, sew the leg to the collar. Put the garment on. Sew the mouth shut. This is how I tell about being quiet because I am bad, and because I cannot stand it when he beats me or my brother.

"The first time I got caught in your clothes was when I was four years old and you were 15 over at Sarah what's-her-name's babysitting. Dad beat me so hard I thought I was going to die. I really thought I was going to die. That was the day I made up my mind I would *never* get caught again. And I never got caught again." My brother goes on to say he continued to go through my things until I was hospitalized. A mystery is solved.

He wore my clothes. He played in my makeup. I kept saying, back then, that someone was going through my stuff. I kept saying it and saying it. I told the counselor at school. "Someone goes in my room when I'm not there, and I *know* it—goes in there and wears my clothes and goes through my stuff." I was assured by the counselor that this was not so. I was assured by my mother that this was not so. I thought my mother was doing it, snooping around for clues like mothers do. It made me a little crazy, so I started deliberately leaving things in a certain order so that I would be able to prove to myself that someone, indeed, was going through my belongings. No one, not one person, ever believed that my room was being ransacked; I was accused of just making it up. A paranoid fixation.

And all the time it was old Goldilocks.

So I tell my brother to promise me he'll see someone who counsels adult children from dysfunctional families. I tell him he needs to deal with the fact that he was physically abused on a daily basis. He tells me he doesn't remember being beaten except on three occasions. He wants me to get into a support group for families of people who are having a sex change. Support groups are people who are in the same boat. Except no one has any oars in the water.

I tell him I know how it feels to think you are in the wrong body. I tell him how I wanted my boyfriend to put a gun up inside me and blow the woman out, how I thought wearing spiked heels and low-cut dresses would somehow help my crisis, that putting on an ultra-feminine outside would mask the maleness I

felt needed hiding. I tell him it's the rule, rather than the exception, that people from families like ours have very spooky sexual identity problems. He tells me that his sexuality is a birth defect. I recognize the lingo. It's support-group-for-transsexuals lingo. He tells me he sits down to pee. He told his therapist that he used to wet all over the floor. His therapist said, "You can't aim the bullets if you don't touch the gun." Lingo. My brother is hell-bent for castration, the castration that started before he had language: the castration of abuse. He will simply finish what was set in motion long ago.

I will tell my brother about the time I took ten sacks of oranges into a school so that I could teach metaphor. The school was for special students—those who were socially or intellectually impaired. I had planned to have them peel the oranges as I spoke about how much the world is like the orange. I handed out the oranges. The students refused to peel them, not because they wanted to make life difficult for me—they were enchanted with the gift. One child asked if he could have an orange to take home to his little brother. Another said he would bring me ten dollars the next day if I would give him a sack of oranges. And I knew I was at home, that these children and I shared something that *makes* the leap of mind the metaphor attempts. And something in me healed.

A neighbor of mine takes pantyhose and cuts them up and sews them up after stuffing them. Then she puts these things into Mason jars and sells them, you know, to put out on the mantel for conversation. They are little penises and little scrotums, complete with hair. She calls them "Pickled Peters."

A friend of mine had a sister who had a sex change operation. This young woman had her breasts removed and ran around the house with no shirt on before the stitches were taken out. She answered the door one evening. A young man had come to call on my friend. The sex-changed sister invited him in and offered him some black bean soup as if she were perfectly normal with her red surgical wounds and her black stitches. The young man left and never went back. A couple years later, my friend's sister/brother died when s/he ran a car into a concrete bridge railing. I hope for a happier ending. For my brother, for myself, for all of us.

My brother calls. He's done his toenails: Shimmering Cinnamon. And he's left his wife and children and purchased some nightgowns at a yard sale. His hair is getting longer. He wears a special bra. Most of the people he works with know about the changes in his life. His voice is not the same voice I've heard for years; he sounds happy.

My brother calls. He's always envied me, my woman's body. The same body I live in and have cursed for its softness. He asks me how I feel about myself. He says, "You know, you are really our father's first-born son." He tells me he used to want to be me because I was the only person our father almost loved.

25   The drama of life. After I saw that woman in the bus station eat an orange as if it were an apple, I went out into the street and smoked a joint with some guy I'd met on the bus. Then I hailed a cab and went to a tattoo parlor. The tattoo artist tried to talk me into getting a nice bird or butterfly design; I had chosen a design on his wall that appealed to me—a symbol I didn't know the meaning of. It is the Yin-Yang, and it's tattooed above my right ankle bone. I supposed my drugged, crazed consciousness knew more than I knew: that yin combines with yang to produce all that comes to be. I am drawn to androgyny.

Of course there is the nagging possibility that my brother's dilemma is genetic. Our father used to dress in drag on Halloween, and he made a beautiful woman. One year, the year my mother cut my brother's blond curls off, my father taped those curls to his own head and tied a silk scarf over the tape. Even his close friends didn't know it was him. And my youngest daughter was a body builder for

a while, her lean body as muscular as a man's. And my sons are beautiful, not handsome: they look androgynous.

Then there's my grandson. I saw him when he was less than an hour old. He was naked and had hiccups. I watched as he had his first bath, and I heard him cry. He had not been named yet, but his little crib had a blue card affixed to it with tape. And on the card were the words "Baby Boy." There was no doubt in me that the words were true.

When my brother was born, my father was off flying jets in Korea. I went to the hospital with my grandfather to get my mother and this new brother. I remember how I wanted a sister, and I remember looking at him as my mother held him in the front seat of the car. I was certain he was a sister, certain that my mother was joking. She removed his diaper to show me that he was a boy. I still didn't believe her. Considering what has happened lately, I wonder if my child-skewed consciousness knew more than the anatomical proof suggested.

I try to make peace with myself. I try to understand his decision to alter himself. I try to think of him as her. I write his woman name, and I feel like I'm betraying myself. I try to be open-minded, but something in me shuts down. I think we humans are in big trouble, that many of us don't really have a clue as to what acceptable human behavior is. Something in me says no to all this, that this surgery business is the ultimate betrayal of the self. And yet, I want my brother to be happy.

It was in the city of San Antonio that my   30 father had his surgery. I rode the bus from Kansas to Texas, and arrived at the hospital two days after the operation to find my father sitting in the solarium playing solitaire. He had a type of cancer that particularly thrived on testosterone. And so he was castrated in order to ease his pain and to stop the growth of tumors. He died six months later.

Back in the sleep of the large world of dreams, I have done surgeries under water in which I float my father's testicles back into him, and he—the brutal man he was—emerges from the pool a tan and smiling man, parting the surface of the water with his perfect head. He loves all the grief away.

I will tell my brother all I know of oranges, that if you squeeze the orange peel into a flame, small fires happen because of the volatile oil in the peel. Also, if you squeeze the peel and it gets into your cat's eyes, the cat will blink and blink. I will tell him there is no perfect rhyme for the word "orange," and that if we can just make up a good word we can be immortal. We will become obsessed with finding the right word, and I will be joyous at our legitimate pursuit.

I have purchased a black camisole with lace to send to my new sister. And a card. On the outside of the card there's a drawing of a woman sitting by a pond and a zebra is off to the left. Inside are these words: "The past is ended. Be happy." And I have asked my companions to hold me and I have cried. My self is wet and small. But it is not dark. Sometimes, if no one touches me, I will die.

Sister, you are the best craziness of the family. Brother, love what you love.

READING AND THINKING

1. How would you characterize the experience of reading this essay? How did you respond to the first two sentences? The first two paragraphs? Why do you think the author includes descriptions of dreams? How do those dream descriptions link up with the reality of her brother's sex-change operation as she describes it?

2. Why do you think Ruiz includes the passages about oranges? How are those passages connected to the central concerns of her essay? How would the essay differ if all the passages about oranges were instead about another fruit—pears, apples, or bananas, for example?

3. What do the sections describing the Texas Zephyr train contribute to the essay? What about the section on the hijra of India? The section about the author's hospitalization for paranoid schizophrenia? Why do you think she included mention of the poets Walt Whitman and Emily Dickinson? The sections about her father?

4. Why do you think Judy Ruiz wrote this essay? What family issues, besides the specific case of her brother's sexual identity, does she allude to? To what extent are those issues resolved for her family?

5. How does Ruiz conclude her essay? Do you find this conclusion effective? Explain.

THINKING AND WRITING

1. Write a letter to Ruiz responding to her essay. Single out three or four sections that interest you, puzzle you, appall you, or otherwise engage you to comment on or question.

2. Write a paragraph or two in which you explain what Ruiz is communicating in "Oranges and Sweet Sister Boy."

3. Read Bernard Cooper's essay, "Burl's," in Part Three of this text, and discuss some ways that Burl's experience in coming to terms with his identity as a gay man connects with what you can ascertain of the experience of Ruiz's brother, as he comes to terms with his sexual identity.

TRANSFORMATIONS: AN OCCASION FOR WRITING

In her essay, Judy Ruiz writes about her response to her brother's sex change operation, so that she ends her essay with two sentences, one of which addresses her sibling as "brother" and the other as "sister." Clearly, her sibling has undergone a transformation. So, too, has Judy Ruiz, as she tries to come to terms with such a dramatic change. In the following Occasion for Writing, you will be invited to read a short selection about another transgender change, one set in another time and place, paired with an image of a modern-day transformation.

Paris, France.
L'Alcazar (1982)

Maxine Hong Kingston

ON DISCOVERY

In the following reading selection from her book *China Men*, Maxine Hong Kingston tells a strange and fascinating story of Tang Ao, a man who became transformed into a woman. After reading the piece, follow up with the reading, thinking, and writing assignments based on it.

1 Once upon a time, a man, named Tang Ao, looking for the Gold Mountain, crossed an ocean, and came upon the Land of Women. The women immediately captured him, not on guard against ladies. When they asked Tang Ao to come along, he followed; if he had had male companions, he would've winked over his shoulder.

"We have to prepare you to meet the queen," the women said. They locked him in a canopied apartment equipped with pots of makeup, mirrors, and a woman's clothes. "Let us help you off with your armor and boots," said the women. They slipped his coat off his shoulders, pulled it down his arms, and shackled his wrists behind him. The women who kneeled to take off his shoes chained his ankles together.

A door opened, and he expected to meet his match, but it was only two old women with sewing boxes in their hands. "The less you struggle, the less it'll hurt," one said, squinting a bright eye as she threaded her needle. Two captors sat on him while another held his head. He felt an old woman's dry fingers trace his ear; the long nail on her little finger scraped his neck. "What are you doing?" he asked. "Sewing your lips together," she joked, blackening needles in a candle flame. The ones who sat on him bounced with laughter. But the old woman did not sew his lips together. They pulled his earlobes taut and jabbed a needle through each of them. They had to poke and probe before puncturing the layers of skin correctly, the hole in the front of the lobe in line with the one in back, the layers of skin sliding about so. They worked the needle through—a last jerk for the needle's wide eye ("needle's nose" in Chinese). They strung his raw flesh with silk threads; he could feel the fibers.

The women who sat on him turned to direct their attention to his feet. They bent his toes so far backward that his arched foot cracked. The old ladies squeezed each foot and broke many tiny bones along the sides. They gathered his toes, toes over and under one another like a knot of ginger root. Tang Ao wept with pain. As they wound the bandages tight and tighter around his feet, the women sang foot-binding songs to distract him: "Use aloe for binding feet and not for scholars."

5 During the months of a season, they fed him on women's food: the tea was thick with white chrysanthemums and stirred the cool female winds inside his body; chicken wings made his hair shine; vinegar soup improved his womb. They drew the loops of thread through the scabs that grew daily over the holes in his earlobes. One day they inserted gold hoops. Every night they unbound his feet, but his veins had shrunk, and the blood pumping through them hurt so much, he begged to have his feet rewrapped tight. They forced him to wash his used bandages, which were embroidered with flowers and smelled of rot and cheese. He hung the bandages up to dry, streamers that drooped and draped wall to wall. He felt embarrassed; the wrappings were like underwear, and they were his.

One day his attendants changed his gold hoops to jade studs and strapped his feet to shoes that curved like bridges. They plucked out each hair on his face, powdered him white, painted his eyebrows like a moth's wings, painted his cheeks and lips red. He served a meal at the queen's court. His hips swayed and his shoulders swiveled because of his shaped feet. "She's pretty, don't you agree?" the diners said, smacking their lips at his dainty feet as he bent to put dishes before them.

In the Women's Land there are no taxes and no wars. Some scholars say that that country was discovered during the reign of Empress Wu (A.D. 694–705), and some say earlier than that, A.D. 441, and it was in North America.

PREPARING TO WRITE: OCCASIONS TO THINK ABOUT WHAT YOU SEE

1. To what extent do you think "On Discovery" is about gender roles, gender switching, and power? Do you think the title fits the piece? Why or why not? What two alternative titles can you provide? Explain your rationale for each.

2. "On Discovery" is a kind of parable, and as such it contains an implied lesson or teaching. What do you consider its central point or idea? Why?

3. Martina Franck's photograph depicts a man preparing himself for a drag appearance as a woman in a Paris drag show. What evidence of male and female identity is evident in the picture?

4. What seems to be highlighted in Franck's photograph, both in the foreground and the background? Why do you think the photographer decided to use a black and white photograph rather than a color one?

5. Look carefully at the image of the actress Marlene Dietrich, who was nicknamed "the best dressed man in Hollywood." Identify details that highlight gender in Franck's photograph. To what extent do you agree with writer Kenneth Tynan, who said of Dietrich "she has sex—but no particular gender"? What do you make of this statement?

© Paramount/The Kobal Collection

Marlene Dietrich (1930)

MOVING TOWARD ESSAY: OCCASIONS TO ANALYZE AND REFLECT

1. Reread the final paragraph of "On Discovery." Why do you think Kingston included it? What would be gained and what lost if it were omitted? Explain.

2. What ironies does Kingston play up here? Consider verbal irony, in which words actually mean the opposite of what they appear to mean, and situational irony, in which an expected outcome does not occur, but rather its opposite does instead.

3. To what extent do you think "On Discovery" transcends its specifically Chinese cultural and historical context? How might the story told in Kingston's piece be enacted today in the United States or another western country, for example?

WRITING THOUGHTFULLY: OCCASIONS FOR IDEAS AND ESSAYS

1. Write a short essay in which you analyze and interpret "On Discovery." Use the notes and comments you made in the previous exercises as a starting point for developing your essay. You can also read Kingston's essay "No-Name Woman" in Chapter 8 (p. 308), from her book *The Woman Warrior: Memoirs of a Girlhood among Ghosts* (1976), for additional ideas regarding how sex and gender are considered from a traditional Chinese cultural perspective.

2. The French feminist philosopher Simone de Beauvoir writes: "One is not born a woman; one becomes a woman." Use this quote as a point of departure for your own essay about how one is and/or becomes a woman. If you wish, you can include references to "On Discovery" as well in developing your essay. You may also wish to consider your reading and thinking about Susan Brownmiller's essay "Femininity" (see p. 205) or any of the other essays in this chapter, especially those by Tannen and Sontag.

CREATING OCCASIONS

1. Find examples from books and magazines, Internet, television, Broadway, and movies of transvestite behavior and other forms of gender switching, including gender transformation. The recent films of Pedro Almadovar provide one example, as does the Broadway show *Hairspray* and the popular films *Tootsie* (1982) and *Mrs. Doubtfire* (1993). Do some research in these various media through reading and viewing; in addition talk with those who have encountered transvestites and transsexuals in these media or in their everyday lives. How is gender defined in these media versions? Based on your own experiences, how do you explain gender bending or transformations?

THE BEAUTY OF THE GENDERS

Beauty is a perennial subject of interest. What constitutes beauty in women and in men? What passes today for an ideal image of the male body, of the female form? If you look at magazine ads for clothing for both men and women, if you look at ads for beauty products for women (although these are also beginning to be advertised to men), you find very specific images of male and female beauty. What is the standard for female beauty? What male body types are favored? What are the implications of these images of beauty, male and female? Why do they seem to matter so much in our society?

To answer these questions is to begin an inquiry into not only what kinds of bodies and faces we tend to favor, but also why these particular body forms and facial features are so favored. We can also ask to what extent current images of male and female beauty have been popular in the past, or whether different images of male and female beauty were favored in different times and places.

As you can readily see from images of women on television, in film, and in print ads for all kinds of products, thin is in. But this was not always the case. In the seventeenth century, for example, paintings of women by the Flemish artist Peter Paul Rubens feature amply proportioned women. Such women appear also in the work of the twentieth-century Spanish artist Fernando Botero.

Most contemporary images of the female figure vary dramatically from those of Rubens and Botero. Not only is the fashion model much thinner, but her figure is firmer and stronger as well. While contemporary models don't boast visible muscles, their bodies exhibit good muscle tone, with no flabby or sagging flesh showing.

If images of women's beauty have changed over the centuries, images of male beauty have remained remarkably consistent, particularly the image of the male body. During the Renaissance, for example, especially in Italy, the male figure was portrayed as strong, solid, and muscular. Among the most "pumped–up" male figures are those depicted in paintings by Michelangelo. His famous depiction of the creation of Adam on the ceiling of the Sistine Chapel in Rome reveals a muscular Adam coming to consciousness as his index finger is touched by the index finger of an equally powerfully built God. Michelangelo's well-built males also populate his sculptures, most famously, his *David,* sculpted from a massive hunk of Carrara marble into a statue that stands more than fourteen feet high and that displays a powerfully built youth with bulging veins and enormous hands.

Today's muscular bodybuilders illustrate one aspect of the ideal of masculine strength. With chests bulging and abdomens and backs rippling with muscles, bodybuilders oil their torsos till they shine. They display their impressive physiques on beaches and in gyms as well as on stage in bodybuilding contests and in films.

However, bulging muscularity is not the only contemporary male physical ideal. Advertisements for contemporary men's fashions reveal well-toned male bodies, but not necessarily with bodybuilder physiques. The male figures displayed feature less monumental physiques in favor of bodies that are finely toned and strong with a broad chest and narrow waist, without the muscular definition of the bodybuilder.

Paul Fussell (b. 1924)

Paul Fussell was born in 1924 in Pasadena, California. A Professor Emeritus of English Literature at the University of Pennsylvania, Fussell is a cultural historian who has written books on English literature, social class, and the First and Second World Wars. After earning a doctorate in English at Harvard University, Fussell taught at a number of colleges and universities in the United States and abroad, including Rutgers, University of Pennsylvania, University of Heidelberg, and King's College London. Wounded in France in 1944 during the Second World War, Fussell later recounted his military experience in an autobiography, *Doing Battle: The Making of a Skeptic* (1996), and he brought his knowledge and experience of warfare to bear on a number of future studies of literature and culture. He is perhaps best known for *The Great War and Modern Memory* (1975), which won the National Book Award, the National Book Critics Circle Award, and the Ralph Waldo Emerson Award from Phi Beta Kappa. Other notable books by Fussell include *Thank God for the Atom Bomb and Other Essays* (1988), and *Uniforms: Why We Are What We Wear* (2002), from which the following piece has been excerpted.

UNIFORMS

In "Uniforms," Paul Fussell examines the fascination both men and women have for different types of uniforms, but especially for military uniforms. In the essay, Fussell makes observations and raises questions about the sexual connotations of male dress. The subtitle of the book from which this essay is drawn, *Uniforms: Why We Are What We Wear,* suggests a close connection between clothes and identity. Throughout the essay included here and throughout the book overall, Fussell considers how gender and class are reflected and manifested in the clothes we choose to wear as emblems of how we see ourselves.

1 Attention to the shoulders as a theater of honorific male display is standard in military uniforms the world over. As everyone knows, male shoulders, together with chest hair, constitute precious secondary sexual characteristics. It follows that broad and well-developed shoulders are important for male self-respect and pride. Unlike women, whose hips tend to be broader than their shoulders, men's shoulders, ideally, at least, are supposed to be broader than their hips. An infant may ride on a woman's hips, but men like to carry their issue neck-high, spread-eagled on their shoulders. Military emphasis on shoulders thus accentuates the masculinity and presumed bellicosity of uniform wearers. During the Second World War, fashion designers had to go along with the prevailing military imagery and widen the shoulders on women's attire. But, the war over, couturiers quickly reverted to the former "more natural" style.

Christian Dior was one who lamented the perversions war had forced upon his garments. It was, he noted, "a period of uniforms, of soldier-women with shoulders like boxers."

Just before the D-day invasion, General Eisenhower was bolstering the morale of the paratroops of the 101st Airborne Division, destined to drop into Normandy before anyone else. Mixing among these anxious troops, Eisenhower started some informal conversations. As was his habit, he asked the men where they were from.

"Pennsylvania," answered one.

Eisenhower noticed the man's broad and rugged shoulders and asked him if he'd got them working in the coal mines.

"Yes, sir!"   5

Eisenhower, apparently satisfied that this soldier was going to do all right, wished him luck and passed on.

Adolf Hitler was another who regarded conspicuous shoulders as a special index of male strength—and virtue. The perfect physiques of the early SS men accorded with the model for male physical perfection established by the classical scholar and archeologist Johann Joachim Winckelmann in the eighteenth century. Anti-Semitic theory in the German twentieth century came forward to invoke a disgusting antitype, the alleged Jewish male body—unathletic, bookish, ruined by excessive study and attention to the affairs of the countinghouse and the clothing trade. So highly regarded was Winckelmann's model for the ideal male body that his birthday was celebrated in all-male German universities.

Hitler's enthusiasm for this male ideal, available in ancient Greek sculpture, echoed throughout German society as patriotic young men rushed to measure their bodies against the Winckelmann model and the demands of the SS. The object was to assist in generating a "New Man" for the Reich, one strong and brave enough to forward the ultimate transformation of all Europe into something like an immense health farm. The success of the Nazi ideal would manifest itself in shoulder width.

The historian George Mosse, in his book *Images of Man: The Creation of Modern Masculinity*, reprints a patriotic newspaper cartoon of 1933. It depicts Hitler, functioning as a sculptor, in the act of creating this new, physically perfect German. The four panels of this cartoon depict, first, Hitler, together with a bespectacled Jew, viewing a tabletop scene of social disorder, especially street fighting. In the next panel, Hitler smashes this mess with his fist as the Jew looks on in horror. In the third panel, Hitler shapes up a large mass of clay. And in the climactic last scene, he has sculpted a nude statuette of the new male ideal, legs apart, fists clenched, ready for noble action. As the reader leaves this happy sequence he beholds Hitler at his final chore, shaping not the biceps, chest, or stomach muscles but the broad shoulders of the ideal New Man.

In the American Army from 1918 on, the 10 enlisted men had a grievance not often articulated but deeply felt. While officers could indicate their rank by faux gold or silver pin-on insignia on shoulders, as well as on collar, cap, and lapels, soldiers had to make do with sewed-on cloth chevrons positioned not on the place of honor, the shoulders, but merely halfway down the upper sleeve. One of the revolutionary post–World War II Army uniform changes allows enlisted men to wear their own little brass badges of rank, in the form of chevrons, on collars and shoulders. The effect has been to narrow the visual gap separating officers from men.

Previously, an element of uniform reminding the men that they were in no way like officers was the officer's special shirt, which they were forbidden to wear. It bore shoulder straps, thus calling attention to those sites of honor available only to people of commissioned rank. James Jones, in his novel *Whistle*, expressed the enlisted man's desires as well as anyone ever has. He wanted to depict First Sergeant Mart Winch as thoroughly angry and outraged upon his return to the United States after severe combat in the Pacific. To indicate the nature of his fury, Jones has him locate a tailoring shop in San Francisco that sells him an unauthorized officer's shirt with the significant shoulder straps. Milder versions of this sort of semi-revolutionary behavior were the wearing of forbidden flashy belt buckles and the flaunting of nonregulation jewelry. By the time of the Vietnam War, officers were to be seen wearing shirts without shoulder straps. Now, ironically, such straps performed on only enlisted men's shoulders their original utilitarian function, keeping in place other straps attached to heavy weights carried by the shoulders. And it's worth noticing that in the world of visual fiction—theater, film, and advertising—the locus of the soldier's fictional wound (heroic but not fatal) is most likely to be a shoulder. Today, the popular trench coat is the one with the ostentatious shoulder straps sold by Burberry's. They are quite useless, reduced to the status of a trademark. Without the straps, the garment is merely a raincoat, all romantic suggestion gone.

Those who have worn military uniform know how it feels when contrasted to civilian clothes. I'm not talking about the glory of full-dress uniform, white gloves and all, but about what is sometimes called "walking-out kit," the way you'd dress leaving the post for the evening or going home on furlough. This uniform usually requires jacket and tie, and it is crucial that the jacket fit snugly, with shoulders emphasized by straps or epaulets and with a crimped-in waist. The trousers must fit closely, with, of course, no pleats, it being a precious military myth that no soldier is even slightly obese and thus in need of such waist camouflage. The shape delineated by the uniform is that of an ideal combatant—athletic, obedient, wonderfully self-controlled, tightly focused, with no looseness or indication of comfort about him. One reason the "lounge suit" was so named on its first appearance is that its looseness promoted lounging, an action unthinkable for a military man. The uniform was made to stand up straight in, and its full meaning is not available when the wearer is sitting down.

The Austrian novelist Hermann Broch meditated on military uniforms as well as on their civilian analogs and arrived at a principle true of both:

> A uniform provides its wearer with a definitive line of demarcation between his person and the world. . . . It is the uniform's true function to manifest and ordain order in the world, to arrest the confusion and flux of life, just as it conceals whatever in the human body is soft and flowing, covering up the soldier's underclothes and skin. . . . Closed up in his hard casing, braced in with straps and belts, he begins to forget his own undergarments and the uncertainty of life.

This military trim-fit look has a history, dating back at least to the eighteenth century, when, as George Mosse pointed out, the image of the man aimed at by the military uniform arose, betraying its origin in the Greek sculptures admired by Winckelmann. The ideal for the contemporary wearer of military uniform was "a smooth body, tight and firm like marble." For the eighteenth century, the opposite image was available in the figure of the effeminate dancing master. If today any item of menswear could be posited as the opposite of the military uniform, it might be the sloppy bathrobe of terry cloth, worn unfastened and in need of laundering.

Thus it was archeological excavation in 15 the eighteenth century that uncovered a masculine form successive ages have taken for granted and allowed to stand as "representative." That is, the new focus on ancient sculpture instructed people in what the male body should look like, or be made by clothing to look like. The ideal male look, wrote Anne Hollander, historian and theorist of clothing, was the one most suggestive of perfect male strength, perfect virtue, and perfect honesty, with overtones of independence and rationality. By the beginning of the nineteenth century, "however a man was really built, his tailor replaced his old short-legged pear-shaped body with a lean well-muscled and very sexy body with long legs."

If it can be said that soldiers are created by their uniforms, what man could contain his vanity when garbed in a suit suggesting a perfect torso as well as immense physical efficiency and ample supplies of courage? Every national defense department all over the world must engage itself in the mental operation of mistaking soldiers for what they have been made to look like.

It is, of course, possible to go too far in the trim-fit direction, as did some Victorian British cavalry units where swank, earned by tightening the uniform, prevented troops from raising their arms to use their sabers.

READING AND THINKING

1. What connection does Fussell identify between military and athletic uniforms? What are some of the associations each kind of uniform conveys? Why?

2. What differentiates military and athletic uniforms? How, for example, does the treatment of the shoulder in each type of uniform compare and contrast, and with what effects?

3. To what extent has the evolution of the football uniform followed the increased violence of the sport? To what extent might the uniform contribute to, or allow for, the increased violent nature of the game?

THINKING AND WRITING

1. Have you ever worn a uniform—for school, a sports team, or a club? If so, write a few paragraphs about the uniform you wore and what it revealed about the group it represented. If not, explain in a few paragraphs why you would or would not like to wear some type of uniform.

2. To what extent do you agree with Professor Jirousek that the padded shoulders of football uniforms reflect "the exaggerated ideal of male musculature dominating the body-building culture"? Do you agree that the image of the outfitted football player "has contributed to a national obsession with physical fitness and sport"? Explain.

3. Compare two different uniforms. Explain the implications of each uniform for what it suggests about images of men, images of women, or both. You might consider a "uniform" in the broad sense, for example, the dark business suit as a type of uniform.

THE WELL-DRESSED MAN: AN OCCASION FOR WRITING

We have all heard the saying "The clothes make the man." And particular kinds of clothes—military, athletic, and western "uniforms"—have traditionally been associated with manly qualities such as discipline, physical prowess, and courage. Paul Fussell's essay on uniforms invites us to consider how manliness can be related to such types of clothing as well as to masculine body images. The following Occasion encourages you to consider the extent to which clothes, especially uniforms, confirm the thesis of the adage that clothes do "make the man." The Occasion also invites you to consider the extent to which clothes conceal as well as reveal, the extent to which uniforms suppress individuality while promoting uniformity.

PREPARING TO WRITE: OCCASIONS TO THINK ABOUT WHAT YOU SEE

1. Look at the advertisement for Marks and Spencer, a British department store. Which aspects of the advertisement draw your attention? What do you notice about the way the model is posed? About the physique of the man depicted? About his facial expression? What is your reaction to this advertisement? Think about the text included in the advertisement and how it relates to the photo of the male model. Do you find the advertisement appealing or appalling or something else? Explain.

© Bill Grove

© Royalty-Free/Corbis

2. Now, turn your attention to the man depicted in the clothing advertisement for Ralph Lauren. How is this man posed? What do you notice about his body posture and facial expression? What kind of background is included in the image? What is suggested about the product being advertised? To what extent, if any, do you think the male model in this advertisement is being "used"? Consider this ad in relation to the Marks and Spencer advertisement. Explain.

3. Look at the image of the football player in his padded protective uniform. What impression does the picture of this player convey? Why?

4. Focus now on the picture of the military man in uniform. What is suggested about the man in this picture? To what extent, if any, does the race of the men depicted affect your response?

5. How does the picture of cowboys play off of western clichés? What do you notice about their clothing, stance, and facial expressions? To what extent is the setting important?

© Lee Carmichael, 2006

MOVING TOWARD ESSAY: OCCASIONS TO ANALYZE AND REFLECT

1. Consider the images of maleness depicted in all these pictures. Identify three qualities or characteristics of the human male that these images collectively represent. Why are these qualities significant? To what extent are the images and the qualities they reflect culture-bound—that is, limited to certain cultures and geographical locations? How do you imagine students in an Asian culture might respond to these images of men? Why?

2. Choose one of the sets of images—the uniformed figures or the men of advertising—to focus on more closely. Make a list of at least five observations about each image in that group. Then write a couple of paragraphs in which you reflect on the significance of the details you noticed about each image. You might focus on their faces, for example, or on their torsos, or on the ways their clothing emphasizes particular bodily features.

WRITING THOUGHTFULLY: OCCASIONS FOR IDEAS AND ESSAYS

1. Write an essay in which you explore what it means to be a man, based on the images of masculinity you have been looking at along with the essays and questions in this chapter. You may include analysis of any of the images, and you may also include personal experience.

2. Read "Bodybuilders Contest" by Wislawa Szymborska. Her poem pokes fun at the muscularly distorted men who compete against one another for titles such as "Mr. America," "Mr. World," and "Mr. Universe." Use the following questions as a way to begin your analysis:

   What is the speaker's attitude toward bodybuilders and their contests?

   Does the speaker admire bodybuilders?

   Does the speaker find them a bit silly?

   What words and phrases convey the speaker's attitude?

   How does the poet convey the physiques of the bodybuilders?

   What words and phrases best help you to "see" them?

   What is the importance of the poses the bodybuilders assume?

   What is the speaker's attitude toward those poses?

Wislawa Szymborska
Bodybuilders' Contest
translated by Stanlislaw Baranzcak and Clare Cavanagh

From scalp to sole, all muscles in slow motion.
The ocean of his torso drips with lotion.
The king of all is he who preens and wrestles
with sinews twisted into monstrous pretzels.

Onstage, he grapples with a grizzly bear
the deadlier for not really being there.
Three unseen panthers are in turn laid low,
each with one smoothly choreographed blow.

He grunts while showing his poses and paces.
His back alone has twenty different faces.
The mammoth fist he raises as he wins
is tribute to the force of vitamins.

CREATING OCCASIONS

1. Identify at least two other contexts besides sports and fashion where men's strength and physical attractiveness are considered important. For each of these contexts select two specific characteristics that illustrate these qualities; find a few images that show them off visually. Consider these examples in relation to the images in the previous exercises and in relation to the male characteristics discussed in Fussell's essay on uniforms.

2. Examining other media outlets, such as film, television, magazines, and music, how do you see male beauty being defined? How is it different from female beauty? Give specific evidence from the sources you've examined to support your opinions.

3. Consider examining how men's bodies have been depicted in art, such as Michelangelo's *David,* or other famous statues. How do those artworks complicate the notion of how man's body is perceived by society?

Susan Sontag (1933–2004)

One of America's leading intellectuals, Susan Sontag studied at the University of California, Berkeley before earning a BA in philosophy from the University of Chicago at the age of eighteen. Following her study of religion at Union Theological Seminary in New York, she studied philosophy and literature at Oxford University and the Sorbonne. Sontag taught and lectured extensively at many universities, especially at Rutgers and Columbia. Her books include *On Photography* (1977), *Under the Sign of Saturn* (1980), and *AIDS and Its Metaphors* (1989)—all essay collections—and the novels *The Volcano Lover: A Romance* (1992) and *In America: A Novel* (2000). Her work is characterized by erudition and incisive analysis. The following essay originally appeared in *Vogue* magazine.

WOMAN'S BEAUTY: PUT-DOWN OR POWER SOURCE

In "Woman's Beauty: Put-Down or Power Source," Susan Sontag analyzes the social pressures on women to be beautiful. She contrasts women's need for beauty with the lack of that need for men. Along the way she examines historical trends and causes for what has become in modern times a near obsession with female beauty.

1   For the Greeks, beauty was a virtue: a kind of excellence. Persons then were assumed to be what we now have to call—lamely, enviously—*whole* persons. If it did occur to the Greeks to distinguish between a person's "inside" and "outside," they still expected that inner beauty would be matched by beauty of the other kind. The well-born young Athenians who gathered around Socrates found it quite paradoxical that their hero was so intelligent, so brave, so honorable, so seductive—and so ugly. One of Socrates' main pedagogical acts was to be ugly—and teach those innocent, no doubt splendid-looking disciples of his how full of paradoxes life really was.

They may have resisted Socrates' lesson. We do not. Several thousand years later, we are more wary of the enchantments of beauty. We not only split off—with the greatest facility—the "inside" (character, intellect) from the "outside" (looks); but we are actually surprised when someone who is beautiful is also intelligent, talented, good.

It was principally the influence of Christianity that deprived beauty of the central place it had in classical ideals of human excellence. By limiting excellence (*virtus* in Latin) to *moral* virtue only, Christianity set beauty adrift—as an alienated, arbitrary, superficial enchantment. And beauty has continued to lose prestige. For close to two centuries it has become a convention to attribute beauty to only one of the two sexes: the sex which, however Fair, is always Second. Associating beauty with women has put beauty even further on the defensive, morally.

A beautiful woman, we say in English. But a handsome man. "Handsome" is the masculine equivalent of—and refusal of—a compliment which has accumulated certain demeaning overtones, by being reserved for women only. That one can call a man "beautiful" in French and in Italian suggests that Catholic countries—unlike those countries shaped by the Protestant version of Christianity—still retain some vestiges of the pagan admiration for beauty. But the difference, if one exists, is of degree only. In every modern country that is Christian or post-Christian, women *are* the beautiful sex—to the detriment of the notion of beauty as well as of women.

5   To be called beautiful is thought to name something essential to women's character and concerns. (In contrast to men—whose essence is to be strong, or effective, or competent.) It does not take someone in the throes of advanced feminist awareness to perceive that the way women are taught to be involved with beauty encourages narcissism, reinforces dependence and immaturity. Everybody (women and men) knows that. For it is "everybody," a whole society, that has identified being feminine with caring about how one *looks*. (In contrast to being masculine—which is identified with caring about what one *is* and *does* and only secondarily, if at all, about how one looks.) Given these stereotypes, it is no wonder that beauty enjoys, at best, a rather mixed reputation.

It is not, of course, the desire to be beautiful that is wrong but the obligation to be—or to try. What is accepted by most women as a flattering idealization of their sex is a way of making women feel inferior to what they actually are—or normally grow to be. For the ideal of beauty is administered as a form of self-oppression. Women are taught to see their bodies in *parts*, and to evaluate each part separately. Breasts, feet, hips, waistline, neck, eyes, nose, complexion, hair, and so on— each in turn is submitted to an anxious, fretful, often despairing scrutiny. Even if some pass muster, some will always be found wanting. Nothing less than perfection will do.

In men, good looks is a whole, something taken in at a glance. It does not need to be confirmed by giving measurements of different regions of the body, nobody encourages a man to dissect his appearance, feature by feature. As for perfection, that is considered trivial— almost unmanly. Indeed, in the ideally good-looking man a small imperfection or blemish is considered positively desirable. According to one movie critic (a woman) who is a declared Robert Redford fan, it is having that cluster of skin-colored moles on one cheek that saves Redford from being merely a "pretty face." Think of the depreciation of women—as well as of beauty—that is implied in that judgment.

"The privileges of beauty are immense," said Cocteau. To be sure, beauty is a form of power. And deservedly so. What is lamentable is that it is the only form of power that most women are encouraged to seek. This power is always conceived in relation to men; it is not the power to do but the power to attract. It is a power that negates itself. For this power is not one that can be chosen freely—at least, not by women—or renounced without social censure.

To preen, for a woman, can never be just a pleasure. It is also a duty. It is her work. If a woman does real work—and even if she has clambered up to a leading position in politics, law, medicine, business, or whatever—she is always under pressure to confess that she still works at being attractive. But in so far as she is keeping up as one of the Fair Sex, she brings under suspicion her very capacity to be objective, professional, authoritative, thoughtful. Damned if they do—women are. And damned if they don't.

One could hardly ask for more important   10 evidence of the dangers of considering persons as split between what is "inside" and what is "outside" than that interminable half-comic half-tragic tale, the oppression of women. How easy it is to start off by defining women as caretakers of their surfaces, and then to disparage them (or find them adorable) for being "superficial." It is a crude trap, and it has worked for too long. But to get out of the trap requires that women get some critical distance from that excellence and privilege which is beauty, enough distance to see how much beauty itself has been abridged in order to prop up the mythology of the "feminine." There should be a way of saving beauty *from* women—and *for* them.

READING AND THINKING

1. What point does Sontag make about the distinction between a person's inner and outer beauty? Why do you think she introduces this distinction? What is the effect of her mentioning the Greeks, specifically, Socrates?

2. What does Christianity add to the subject of beauty, and, specifically, to notions about women's beauty? What effects, according to Sontag, derive from the influence of Christianity regarding women's beauty? What is Sontag's attitude about these effects?

3. What differences does Sontag draw between the way men are viewed and considered compared with the ways women are perceived and described? How effective is her presentation of these differences? Why?

THINKING AND WRITING

1. Write a paragraph in which you agree with, qualify, or dissent from the ideas Sontag advances about women's beauty. Explain your thinking.

2. Write a paragraph or two in which you attempt to define your understanding of beauty. You may wish to write about male beauty, female beauty, natural beauty, or some combination of these. You may also take your point of departure from Sontag's essay or from another essay in this chapter.

3. Write a one-sentence summary of each paragraph of Sontag's essay. Use those sentences as the basis for a one-paragraph summary of the essay. Be sure to provide a beginning, middle, and end to your paragraph rather than simply copying your 10 sentences for the individual paragraphs.

BEAUTEOUS AND BOUNTIFUL LADIES: AN OCCASION FOR WRITING

Susan Sontag's essay focuses on the need for women to appear beautiful. In the following Occasion, you are provided with two images of women that question and toy with the idea of what is beautiful. Consider how these artists have portrayed a woman's beauty and how these images compare with others you have seen in the media. Does beauty change with time or does beauty have multiple definitions?

© Edimédia/CORBIS

EDGAR DEGAS,
Dancer with a Tambourine (1882)

PREPARING TO WRITE: OCCASIONS TO THINK ABOUT WHAT YOU SEE

1. How does Degas's painting compare with images of women depicted in contemporary film and fashion? How does the image of the woman portrayed in Degas's painting compare with Paton's painting? Why do you think Paton depicted women as she did?

2. To what extent do the following lines from Wislawa Szymborska's poem "Rubens' Women," which follows, describe the woman in the Paton painting? What is the speaker's attitude toward this woman?

> O pumpkin plump! O pumped up corpulence
>   inflated double by disrobing
> and tripled by your tumultuous poses!
> O fatty dishes of love!

© Kristine Paton, 2006. "Big Beautiful Ballet." www.bigbeautifuls.com.

KRISTINE PATON, *Big Beautiful Ballet (2003)*

MOVING TOWARD ESSAY: OCCASIONS TO ANALYZE AND REFLECT

1. Consider the images of femaleness depicted in these images. Identify three qualities or characteristics of the human female that these images collectively represent. Why are these qualities significant?

2. To what extent are the images and the qualities they reflect bound by the cultures in which they were produced? To what extent is that significant? Explain.

WRITING THOUGHTFULLY: OCCASIONS FOR IDEAS AND ESSAYS

1. Write an essay about what it means to be a woman, based on the images of women you have been looking at along with any of the readings in this chapter. You may include as part of your essay your analysis of one or more of the images; you may also include personal experience.

2. Read Lucille Clifton's "Homage to My Hips." In the following brief poem, Clifton's speaker celebrates her ample size. Unashamed of her big hips, she sees them as powerful and beautiful in a strong contrast to more conventional images of female bodily beauty. Use the following questions to begin your analysis:

   What image of her hips does Clifton's speaker provide?

   What is her attitude toward her hips—and thus toward her heft and size and weight?

   What other characteristics of her hips does the speaker highlight?

   What does each of these qualities imply or suggest about the speaker?

Lucille Clifton
homage to my hips

these hips are big hips.
they need space to
move around in.
they don't fit into little
petty places. these hips
are free hips.
they don't like to be held back.
these hips have never been enslaved,
they go where they want to go
they do what they want to do.
these hips are mighty hips.
these hips are magic hips.
i have known them
to put a spell on a man and
spin him like a top

CREATING OCCASIONS

1. Do some research on the Internet and in your school library on images of male and female beauty, or on aspects of masculinity or femininity. Be sure to look for examples that cross cultures and that transcend time. Find your own examples of what you consider beautiful women and beautiful (or handsome) men.

Alice Walker (b. 1944)

Alice Walker was born in Eatonton, Georgia and attended Spelman College in Atlanta, Georgia, before graduating in 1965 from Sarah Lawrence College in Yonkers, New York. Walker has worked as a political activist, advocating for civil, environmental, feminist, and animal rights. She has also been an editor of *Ms.* Magazine, stimulating a renewed interest in the works of Zora Neale Hurston with an article Walker published in *Ms.* Walker has written more than thirty books, including poetry, fiction, and essays. Her novel *The Color Purple* (1982), which won both a Pulitzer Prize and an American Book Award, was made into a feature film. Her essays and speeches have been collected in a number of volumes, the best known and perhaps best written of which is *In Search of Our Mothers' Gardens: Womanist Prose* (1983), from which the following essay has been taken.

BEAUTY: WHEN THE OTHER DANCER IS THE SELF

In "Beauty: When the Other Dancer Is the Self," Walker describes a childhood incident that left her blind in one eye. The injury left a psychological scar as well as a physical one, because it affected Walker's self-esteem, largely because she believed that it made her less beautiful. The essay traces Walker's response to her injury from initial self-pity to a form of self-acceptance. In the process Walker explores, through a series of interrelated incidents, just what is beautiful in her life.

1   It is a bright summer day in 1947. My father, a fat, funny man with beautiful eyes and a subversive wit, is trying to decide which of his eight children he will take with him to the county fair. My mother, of course, will not go. She is knocked out from getting most of us ready: I hold my neck stiff against the pressure of her knuckles as she hastily completes the braiding and the beribboning of my hair.

My father is the driver for the rich old white lady up the road. Her name is Miss Mey. She owns all the land for miles around, as well as the house in which we live. All I remember about her is that she once offered to pay my mother thirty-five cents for cleaning her house, raking up piles of her magnolia leaves, and washing her family's clothes, and that my mother—she of no money, eight children, and a chronic earache—refused it. But I do not think of this in 1947. I am two-and-a-half years old. I want to go everywhere my daddy goes. I am excited at the prospect of riding in a car. Someone has told me fairs are fun. That there is room in the car for only three of us doesn't faze me at all. Whirling happily in my starchy frock, showing off my biscuit-polished patent-leather shoes and lavender socks, tossing my head in a way that makes my ribbons bounce, I stand, hands on hips, before my father. "Take me, Daddy," I say with assurance; "I'm the prettiest!"

Later, it does not surprise me to find myself in Miss Mey's shiny black car, sharing the back seat with the other lucky ones. Does not surprise me that I thoroughly enjoy the fair. At home that night I tell the unlucky ones all I can remember about the merry-go-round, the man who eats live chickens, and the teddy bears, until they say: that's enough, baby Alice. Shut up now, and go to sleep.

It is Easter Sunday, 1950. I am dressed in a green, flocked, scalloped-hem dress (handmade by my adoring sister, Ruth) that has its own smooth satin petticoat and tiny hot-pink roses tucked into each scallop. My shoes, new T-strap patent leather, again highly biscuit-polished. I am six years old and have learned one of the longest Easter speeches to be heard that day, totally unlike the speech I said when I was two: "Easter lilies/pure and white/blossom in/the morning light." When I rise to give my speech I do so on a great wave of love and pride and expectation. People in the church stop rustling their new crinolines. They seem to hold their breath. I can tell they admire my dress, but it is my spirit, bordering on sassiness (womanishness), they secretly applaud.

5   "That girl's a little *mess*," they whisper to each other, pleased.

Naturally I say my speech without stammer or pause, unlike those who stutter, stammer, or, worst of all, forget. This is before the word "beautiful" exists in people's vocabulary, but "Oh, isn't she the *cutest* thing!" frequently floats my way. "And got so much sense!" they gratefully add . . . for which thoughtful addition I thank them to this day.

It was great fun being cute. But then, one day, it ended.

I am eight years old and a tomboy. I have a cowboy hat, cowboy boots, checkered shirt and pants, all red. My playmates are my brothers, two and four years older than I. Their colors are black and green, the only difference in the way we are dressed. On Saturday nights we all go to the picture show, even my mother; Westerns are her favorite kind of movie. Back home, "on the ranch," we pretend we are Tom Mix, Hopalong Cassidy, Lash LaRue (we've even named one of our dogs Lash LaRue); we chase each other for hours rustling cattle, being outlaws, delivering damsels from distress. Then my parents decide to buy my brothers guns. These are not "real" guns. They shoot BBs, copper pellets my brothers say will kill birds. Because I am a girl, I do not get a gun. Instantly I am relegated to the position of Indian. Now there appears a great distance between us. They shoot and shoot at everything with their new guns. I try to keep up with my bow and arrows.

One day while I am standing on top of our makeshift "garage"—pieces of tin nailed across some poles—holding my bow and arrow and looking out toward the fields, I feel an incredible blow in my right eye. I look down just in time to see my brother lower his gun.

Both brothers rush to my side. My eye   10 stings, and I cover it with my hand. "If you tell," they say, "we will get a whipping. You don't want that to happen, do you?" I do not. "Here is a piece of wire," says the older brother, picking it up from the roof; "say you stepped on one end of it and the other flew up and hit you." The pain is beginning to start. "Yes," I say. "Yes, I will say that is what happened." If I do not say this is what happened, I know my brothers will find ways to make me wish I had. But now I will say anything that gets me to my mother.

Confronted by our parents we stick to the lie agreed upon. They place me on a bench on the porch and I close my left eye while they examine the right. There is a tree growing from underneath the porch that climbs past the railing to the roof. It is the last thing my right eye sees. I watch as its trunk, its branches, and then its leaves are blotted out by the rising blood.

I am in shock. First there is intense fever, which my father tries to break using lily leaves bound around my head. Then there are chills: my mother tries to get me to eat soup. Eventually, I do not know how, my parents learn what has happened. A week after the "accident" they take me to see a doctor. "Why did you wait so long to come?" he asks, looking into my eye and shaking his head. "Eyes are sympathetic," he says. "If one is blind, the other will likely become blind too."

This comment of the doctor's terrifies me. But it is really how I look that bothers me most. Where the BB pellet struck there is a glob of whitish scar tissue, a hideous cataract, on my eye. Now when I stare at people—a favorite pastime, up to now—they will stare back. Not at the "cute" little girl, but at her scar. For six years I do not stare at anyone, because I do not raise my head.

Years later, in the throes of a mid-life crisis, I ask my mother and sister whether I changed after the "accident." "No," they say, puzzled. "What do you mean?"

15 *What do I mean?*

I am eight, and, for the first time, doing poorly in school, where I have been something of a whiz since I was four. We have just moved to the place where the "accident" occurred. We do not know any of the people around us because this is a different county. The only time I see the friends I knew is when we go back to our old church. The new school is the former state penitentiary. It is a large stone building, cold and drafty, crammed to overflowing with boisterous, ill-disciplined children. On the third floor there is a huge circular imprint of some partition that has been torn out.

"What used to be here?" I ask a sullen girl next to me on our way past it to lunch.

"The electric chair," says she.

At night I have nightmares about the electric chair, and about all the people reputedly "fried" in it. I am afraid of the school, where all the students seem to be budding criminals.

20 "What's the matter with your eye?" they ask, critically.

When I don't answer (I cannot decide whether it was an "accident" or not), they shove me, insist on a fight.

My brother, the one who created the story about the wire, comes to my rescue. But then brags so much about "protecting" me, I become sick.

After months of torture at school, my parents decide to send me back to our old community, to my old school. I live with my grandparents and the teacher they board. But there is no room for Phoebe, my cat. By the time my grandparents decide there is room, and I ask for my cat, she cannot be found. Miss Yarborough, the boarding teacher, takes me under her wing, and begins to teach me to play the piano. But soon she marries an African—a "prince," she says—and is whisked away to his continent.

At my old school there is at least one teacher who loves me. She is the teacher who "knew me before I was born" and bought my first baby clothes. It is she who makes life bearable. It is her presence that finally helps me turn on the one child at the school who continually calls me "one-eyed bitch." One day I simply grab him by his coat and beat him until I am satisfied. It is my teacher who tells me my mother is ill.

My mother is lying in bed in the middle of 25 the day, something I have never seen. She is in too much pain to speak. She has an abscess in her ear. I stand looking down on her, knowing that if she dies, I cannot live. She is being treated with warm oils and hot bricks held against her cheek. Finally a doctor comes. But I must go back to my grandparents' house. The weeks pass but I am hardly aware of it. All I know is that my mother might die, my father is not so jolly, my brothers still have their guns, and I am the one sent away from home.

"You did not change," they say.

Did I imagine the anguish of never looking up?

I am twelve. When relatives come to visit I hide in my room. My cousin Brenda, just my age, whose father works in the post office and whose mother is a nurse, comes to find me. "Hello," she says. And then she asks, looking at my recent school picture, which I did not want taken, and on which the "glob," as I think of it, is clearly visible, "You still can't see out of that eye?"

"No," I say, and flop back on the bed over my book.

30   That night, as I do almost every night, I abuse my eye. I rant and rave at it, in front of the mirror. I plead with it to clear up before morning. I tell it I hate and despise it. I do not pray for sight. I pray for beauty.

"You did not change," they say.

I am fourteen and baby-sitting for my brother Bill, who lives in Boston. He is my favorite brother and there is a strong bond between us. Understanding my feelings of shame and ugliness he and his wife take me to a local hospital, where the "glob" is removed by a doctor named O. Henry. There is still a small bluish crater where the scar tissue was, but the ugly white stuff is gone. Almost immediately I become a different person from the girl who does not raise her head. Or so I think. Now that I've raised my head I win the boyfriend of my dreams. Now that I've raised my head I have plenty of friends. Now that I've raised my head classwork comes from my lips as faultlessly as Easter speeches did, and I leave high school as valedictorian, most popular student, and *queen,* hardly believing my luck. Ironically, the girl who was voted most beautiful in our class (and was) was later shot twice through the chest by a male companion, using a "real" gun, while she was pregnant. But that's another story in itself. Or is it?

"You did not change," they say.

It is now thirty years since the "accident." A beautiful journalist comes to visit and to interview me. She is going to write a cover story for her magazine that focuses on my latest book. "Decide how you want to look on the cover," she says. "Glamorous, or whatever."

35   Never mind "glamorous," it is the "whatever" that I hear. Suddenly all I can think of is whether I will get enough sleep the night before the photography session: If I don't, my eye will be tired and wander, as blind eyes will.

At night in bed with my lover I think up reasons why I should not appear on the cover of a magazine. "My meanest critics will say I've sold out," I say. "My family will now realize I write scandalous books."

"But what's the real reason you don't want to do this?" he asks.

"Because in all probability," I say in a rush, "my eye won't be straight."

"It will be straight enough," he says. Then, "Besides, I thought you'd made your peace with that."

And I suddenly remember that I have.   40

I remember:

I am talking to my brother Jimmy, asking if he remembers anything unusual about the day I was shot. He does not know I consider that day the last time my father, with his sweet home remedy of cool lily leaves, chose me, and that I suffered and raged inside because of this. "Well," he says, "all I remember is standing by the side of the highway with Daddy, trying to flag down a car. A white man stopped, but when Daddy said he needed somebody to take his little girl to the doctor, he drove off."

I remember:

I am in the desert for the first time. I fall totally in love with it. I am so overwhelmed by its beauty, I confront for the first time, consciously, the meaning of the doctor's words years ago: "Eyes are sympathetic. If one is blind, the other will likely become blind too." I realize I have dashed about the world madly, looking at this, looking at that, storing up images against the fading of the light. *But I might have missed seeing the desert!* The shock of that possibility—and gratitude for over twenty-five years of sight—sends me literally to my knees. Poem after poem comes—which is perhaps how poets pray.

On Sight

I am so thankful I have seen
The Desert
And the creatures in the desert
And the desert Itself.

The desert has its own moon
Which I have seen
With my own eye.
There is no flag on it.

Trees of the desert have arms
All of which are always up
That is because the moon is up
The sun is up
Also the sky
The Stars
Clouds
None with flags.

If there were flags, I doubt
the trees would point.
Would you?

45   *But mostly, I remember this:*

I am twenty-seven, and my baby daughter is almost three. Since her birth I have worried about her discovery that her mother's eyes are different from other people's. Will she be embarrassed? I think. What will she say? Every day she watches a television program called *Big Blue Marble*. It begins with a picture of the earth as it appears from the moon. It is bluish, a little battered-looking, but full of light, with whitish clouds swirling around it. Every time I see it I weep with love, as if it is a picture of Grandma's house. One day when I am putting Rebecca down for her nap, she suddenly focuses on my eye. Something inside me cringes, gets ready to try to protect myself. All children are cruel about physical differences, I know from experience, and that they don't always mean to be is another matter. I assume Rebecca will be the same.

But no-o-o-o. She studies my face intently as we stand, her inside and me outside her crib. She even holds my face maternally between her dimpled little hands. Then, looking every bit as serious and lawyerlike as her father, she says, as if it may just possibly have slipped my attention: "Mommy, there's a *world* in your eye." (As in, "Don't be alarmed, or do anything crazy.") And then gently, but with great interest: "Mommy, where did you *get* that world in your eye?"

For the most part, the pain left then. (So what, if my brothers grew up to buy even more powerful pellet guns for their sons and to carry real guns themselves. So what, if a young "Morehouse man" once nearly fell off the steps of Trevor Arnett Library because he thought my eyes were blue.) Crying and laughing I ran to the bathroom, while Rebecca mumbled and sang herself to sleep. Yes indeed, I realized, looking into the mirror. There *was* a world in my eye. And I saw that it was possible to love it: that in fact, for all it had taught me of shame and anger and inner vision, I *did* love it. Even to see it drifting out of orbit in boredom, or rolling up out of fatigue, not to mention floating back at attention in excitement (bearing witness, a friend has called it), deeply suitable to my personality, and even characteristic of me.

That night I dream I am dancing to Stevie Wonder's song "Always" (the name of the song is really "As," but I hear it as "Always"). As I dance, whirling and joyous, happier than I've ever been in my life, another bright-faced dancer joins me. We dance and kiss each other and hold each other through the night. The other dancer has obviously come through all right, as I have done. She is beautiful, whole, and free. And she is also me.

READING AND THINKING

1. To what extent did Walker's injury affect her self-image? How important is it that her injury was facial?

2. Why does Walker change her attitude toward her injury and its consequences? What does she learn from her trip to the desert and from her daughter's observation about a world in Walker's eye?

3. What is the significance of the image of the dancer and the dance?

THINKING AND WRITING

1. To what extent do you share Walker's concern with self-image? Describe a time when an accident or another turn of events may have damaged your self-image, or made you feel insecure or unhappy with yourself. Explain how you came to terms with your situation and what the consequences for your later life have been, or might yet be.

2. Analyze Walker's use of imagery to convey her experience and meaning. Pay special attention to all her descriptions of her injury.

3. Consider Walker's essay in light of Sontag's essay on women's beauty or in relation to the images of women pictured in one of the Occasions for Writing in this chapter.

WHAT IS BEAUTY?
AN OCCASION FOR WRITING

In her essay, Alice Walker stresses the importance of beauty for herself—that she be considered pretty as a child and, later, beautiful as a woman. The following Occasion invites you to think about beauty in some quite different cultural contexts, a number of which may appear strange or exotic upon first viewing. For each image, you are provided with information that partly explains why the woman depicted is considered beautiful in the context of her culture.

Among the Padung people of Myanmar (formerly Burma), girls begin wearing rings around their necks at age 6 and add a ring every 2 years. The neck rings represent status, wealth, and beauty. Although the practice does not technically elongate the girl's neck, it slowly crushes her collarbone so that its seems as if her neck has been lengthened.

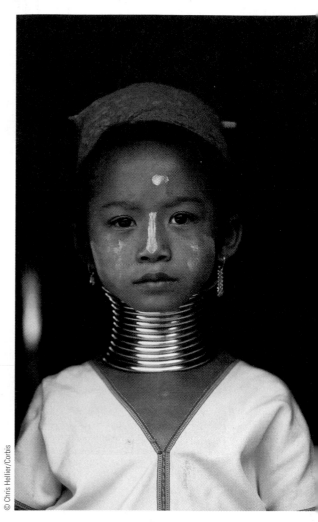

© Chris Hellier/Corbis

PREPARING TO WRITE: OCCASIONS TO THINK ABOUT WHAT YOU SEE

1. After examining each picture carefully, describe what you notice about the ways in which beauty is contextualized in the photos.

2. What is depicted in each picture? Which picture/image is most beautiful and least beautiful to you? Why?

MOVING TOWARD ESSAY: OCCASIONS TO ANALYZE AND REFLECT

1. What cultural values are suggested by or embodied in each image?

2. How do those cultural values influence and affect our perceptions of what is beautiful or attractive?

In Ethiopia, a Surma woman, when she accepts a man as her husband, pierces her lip and inserts a plate into the hole to stretch it. The size of the plate symbolizes the size of her dowry and just how valuable she is.

In some Islamic religions a woman's beauty is "interiorized"; women are required to veil themselves and to guard their beauty, which is associated with danger, sin, and the devil.

WRITING THOUGHTFULLY: IDEA AND ESSAY

1. Choose one of the images in this Occasion to focus on. Using the previous questions as a guide, develop a short essay explaining, first, your personal response to the picture, and second, its cultural significance. That is, discuss what aspects of beauty the image conveys and what social and cultural values are associated with that perception of beauty.

2. Write an essay in which you identify three or four qualities or characteristics of male or female beauty. Explain why each of these characteristics or qualities is important in its cultural and historical context. Consider, that is, the extent to which the qualities or characteristics you select for discussion were different ten or twenty years ago.

3. Write an essay in which your primary aim is to define the concept of beauty. You may focus on male or female beauty, but you should not limit your discussion and definition to a single culture. Rather, strive for a definition that transcends any individual culture.

CREATING OCCASIONS

1. Using your library, the Internet, or popular magazines to which you have easy access, make a portfolio of images you find beautiful. Provide for each a title and brief description. Then, write a 500- to 1000-word analysis of what your portfolio of images suggests about male and/or female beauty.

Mealtimes have traditionally been an occasion for families
TO CONNECT AND COMMUNICATE.
What strikes you as an Occasion for Writing in this image?
What in this busy image do you connect with? Why?

8

FAMILIES

Intact nuclear families—consisting of father, mother, and children—have long been the standard by which family life is measured, at least in the West. In other countries and cultures, however, such as those of Africa, the extended family, which includes the generation of grandparents and the addition of aunts and uncles and cousins, has been the norm. Even in some western European countries, such as Italy, Greece, and Spain, extended families are fairly common.

In the early twenty-first century, however, the idea of a family has become more complicated. With a soaring divorce rate and with single parents and gay couples adopting children, the traditional nuclear family continues to undergo changes. A further complicating factor has been the remarriage of divorced couples so that children often find themselves with stepfathers, stepmothers, half-brothers and sisters, and a myriad of other relatives.

Family life is frequently the subject of literature—ancient, modern, and contemporary. For example, take the genre of drama, in particular Greek plays, such as those about Oedipus and Agamemnon. These plays revolve around generations of families, usually with tragic stories. Shakespeare's plays, too, are rich in family dynamics, from the husband–wife relationship of Macbeth to the father–son and mother–son relationships in Hamlet, to the shifting relationships of King Lear and his daughters. The same is true with more modern plays, including Eugene O'Neill's *Long Day's Journey into Night,* Lorraine Hansberry's *A Raisin in the Sun,* and August Wilson's *Fences;* each chronicles the tribulations of a family.

Family life offers a rich field for social scientists, who analyze its intricacies from social, political, and economic perspectives. The dynamics of living in families also provides a rich topic for autobiographers and essayists to mine, as Lee's "Coming Home Again," Ehrenreich's "Family Values," Sedaris's "Cyclops," and hooks's "Inspired Eccentricity" illustrate. As you read these selections, along with Kingsolver's "Stone Soup" and Kingston's "No Name Woman," and as you work through the writing assignments for each of the essays, consider how families differ and why families remain of such interest not just to scholars and writers, but to so many others as well.

DEFINING FAMILY

What do we mean when we say of someone "he (or she) is family?" We mean, usually, that a particular person is special, holds the same place of affection in our hearts, and merits the special protection, sympathy, and love that family members often but not always have for one another. Only the most extraordinary circumstances permit a close friend to assume such a place in a family.

The closeness of family members leads to the most intense of emotions between and among them. Most of us know of deep emotional attachments, of powerful ties of feeling to parents and siblings, often ties of love and care but sometimes equally compelling feelings of anger, resentment, and even of hatred. One of the reasons that a country's civil wars are often fiercer and more ferocious than wars with external enemies is the intense passion that proximity breeds, in this case among a nation's "brothers," that echoes the intensity of a family's emotional bonds. And we know, too, of the intensity of feeling men and women have for their comrades, their "brothers" and "sisters" in arms, as well as for their sports teammates.

"Blood is thicker than water," writes the Greek tragic dramatist Euripides in an oft quoted line. This truth reflects the special place we accord family members and relatives, of how we stand by and with them against outsiders, whatever the circumstances. But the thickness of that blood is also evident when it flows within a "family" in circumstances inviting competition, coercion, and conflict.

"Happy families are all alike; every unhappy family is unhappy in its own way," writes Tolstoy at the opening of his novel *Anna Karenina*. But we could also argue the converse—that unhappy families are all alike and that happy families find their happiness in different ways. Pretty much anything we say about families is true, even when one thing we might say appears to contradict another. The reason of course is that families are complicated and often conflicted. This is certainly the case with Chang-rae Lee's Korean American family as he describes it in "Coming Home Again." The complexity has to do with family feelings, with conflicting cultural values, and is complicated by the death of one of the family members. Kingsolver's "Stone Soup" reveals a different kind of family complexity, one resulting from divorce and remarriage, with the conflicts divorce often involves, and the proliferation of relatives that remarriage entails. The conflict and complexity appear as well in Barbara Ehrenreich's "Family Values," in which politics is the central concern and the animating energy in the lives of her family members.

Chang-rae Lee (b. 1965)

Chang-rae Lee was born in Seoul, South Korea, and immigrated with his family to the United States when he was three years old. Lee grew up in a Westchester County suburb north of New York City. Following his graduation from Yale University, he worked for a year as an analyst on Wall Street before earning a Master of Fine Arts at the University of Oregon. A creative writing teacher at Hunter College of the City University of New York, Lee writes novels that focus on the lives of contemporary Asian Americans, including *Native Speaker* (1995) and *A Gesture Life* (1999). His most recent book is *Aloft* (2004).

COMING HOME AGAIN

In "Coming Home Again," Lee describes his Korean American family, especially his mother and his relationship with her. Lee's essay is by turns funny and poignant, as he recounts stories of his mother cooking, her little son by her side, absorbing not just the aromas of the foods she prepared, but also lessons in how to wield a knife to chop and mince and slice and dice. Lee highlights the conflicts that develop within the family when he goes off to boarding school to experience a culture and set of values that differ from those of his Korean family.

1 When my mother began using the electronic pump that fed her liquids and medication, we moved her to the family room. The bedroom she shared with my father was upstairs, and it was impossible to carry the machine up and down all day and night. The pump itself was attached to a metal stand on casters, and she pulled it along wherever she went. From anywhere in the house, you could hear the sound of the wheels clicking out a steady time over the grout lines of the slate-tiled foyer, her main thoroughfare to the bathroom and the kitchen. Sometimes you would hear her halt after only a few steps, to catch her breath or steady her balance, and whatever you were doing was instantly suspended by a pall of silence.

I was usually in the kitchen, preparing lunch or dinner, poised over the butcher block with her favorite chef's knife in my hand and her old yellow apron slung around my neck. I'd be breathless in the sudden quiet, and, having ceased my mincing and chopping, would stare blankly at the brushed sheen of the blade. Eventually, she would clear her throat or call out to say she was fine, then begin to move again, starting her rhythmic *ka-jug;* and only then could I go on with my cooking, the world of our house turning once more, wheeling through the black.

I wasn't cooking for my mother but for the rest of us. When she first moved downstairs she was still eating, though scantily, more just to taste what we were having than from any genuine desire for food. The point was simply to sit together at the kitchen table and array ourselves like a family again. My mother would gently set herself down in her customary chair near the stove. I sat across from her, my father and sister to my left and right, and crammed in the center was all the food I had made—a spicy codfish stew, say, or a casserole of gingery beef, dishes that in my youth she had prepared for us a hundred times.

It had been ten years since we'd all lived together in the house, which at fifteen I had left to attend boarding school in New Hampshire. My mother would sometimes point this out, by speaking of our present time as being "just like before Exeter," which surprised me, given how proud she always was that I was a graduate of the school.

My going to such a place was part of my 5 mother's not so secret plan to change my character, which she worried was becoming too much like hers. I was clever and able enough, but without outside pressure I was readily given to sloth and vanity. The famous school—which none of us knew the first thing about—would prove my mettle. She was right, of course, and while I was there I would falter more than a few times, academically and otherwise. But I never thought that my leaving home then would ever be a problem for her, a private quarrel she would have even as her life waned.

Now her house was full again. My sister had just resigned from her job in New York City, and my father, who typically saw his psychiatric patients until eight or nine in the evening, was appearing in the driveway at four-thirty. I had been living at home for nearly a year and was in the final push of work on what would prove a dismal failure of a novel. When I wasn't struggling over my prose, I kept occupied with the things she usually did—the daily errands, the grocery shopping, the vacuuming and the cleaning, and, of course, all the cooking.

When I was six or seven years old, I used to watch my mother as she prepared our favorite meals. It was one of my daily pleasures. She shooed me away in the beginning, telling me that the kitchen wasn't my place, and adding, in her half-proud, half-deprecating way, that her kind of work would only serve to weaken me. "Go out and play with your friends," she'd snap in Korean, "or better yet, do your reading and homework." She knew that I had already done both, and that as the evening approached there was no place to go save her small and tidy kitchen, from which the clatter of her mixing bowls and pans would ring through the house.

I would enter the kitchen quietly and stand beside her, my chin lodging upon the point of her hip. Peering through the crook of her arm, I beheld the movements of her hands. For *kalbi*, she would take up a butchered short rib in her narrow hand, the flinty bone shaped like a section of an airplane wing and deeply embedded in gristle and flesh, and with the point of her knife cut so that the bone fell away, though not completely, leaving it connected to the meat by the barest opaque layer of tendon. Then she methodically butterflied the flesh, cutting and unfolding, repeating the action until the meat lay out on her board, glistening and ready for seasoning. She scored it diagonally, then sifted sugar into the crevices with her pinched fingers, gently rubbing in the crystals. The sugar would tenderize as well as sweeten the meat. She did this with each rib, and then set them all aside in a large shallow bowl. She minced a half-dozen cloves of garlic, a stub of ginger-root, sliced up a few scallions, and spread it all over the meat. She wiped her hands and took out a bottle of sesame oil, and, after pausing for a moment, streamed the dark oil in two swift circles around the bowl. After adding a few splashes of soy sauce, she thrust her hands in and kneaded the flesh, careful not to dislodge the bones. I asked her why it mattered that they remain connected. "The meat needs the bone nearby," she said, "to borrow its richness." She wiped her hands clean of the marinade, except for her little finger, which she would flick with her tongue from time to time, because she knew that the flavor of a good dish developed not at once but in stages.

Whenever I cook, I find myself working just as she would, readying the ingredients— a mash of garlic, a julienne of red peppers, fantails of shrimp—and piling them in little mounds about the cutting surface. My mother never left me any recipes, but this is how I learned to make her food, each dish coming not from a list or a card but from the aromatic spread of a board.

I've always thought it was particularly cruel that the cancer was in her stomach, and that for a long time at the end she couldn't eat. The last meal I made for her was on New Year's Eve, 1990. My sister suggested that in-

10

stead of a rib roast or a bird, or the usual overflow of Korean food, we make all sorts of finger dishes that our mother might fancy and pick at.

We set the meal out on the glass coffee table in the family room. I prepared a tray of smoked-salmon canapés, fried some Korean bean cakes, and made a few other dishes I thought she might enjoy. My sister supervised me, arranging the platters, and then with some pomp carried each dish in to our parents. Finally, I brought out a bottle of champagne in a bucket of ice. My mother had moved to the sofa and was sitting up, surveying the low table. "It looks pretty nice," she said. "I think I'm feeling hungry."

This made us all feel good, especially me, for I couldn't remember the last time she had felt any hunger or had eaten something I cooked. We began to eat. My mother picked up a piece of salmon toast and took a tiny corner in her mouth. She rolled it around for a moment and then pushed it out with the tip of her tongue, letting it fall back onto her plate. She swallowed hard, as if to quell a gag, then glanced up to see if we had noticed. Of course we all had. She attempted a bean cake, some cheese, and then a slice of fruit, but nothing was any use.

She nodded at me anyway, and said, "Oh, it's very good." But I was already feeling lost and I put down my plate abruptly, nearly shattering it on the thick glass. There was an ugly pause before my father asked me in a weary, gentle voice if anything was wrong, and I answered that it was nothing, it was the last night of a long year, and we were together, and I was simply relieved. At midnight, I poured out glasses of champagne, even one for my mother, who took a deep sip. Her manner grew playful and light, and I helped her shuffle to her mattress, and she lay down in the place where in a brief week she was dead.

My mother could whip up most anything, but during our first years of living in this coun-

try we ate only Korean foods. At my harangue-like behest, my mother set herself to learning how to cook exotic American dishes. Luckily, a kind neighbor, Mrs. Churchill, a tall, florid young woman with flaxen hair, taught my mother her most trusted recipes. Mrs. Churchill's two young sons, palish, weepy boys with identical crew cuts, always accompanied her, and though I liked them well enough, I would slip away from them after a few minutes, for I knew that the real action would be in the kitchen, where their mother was playing guide. Mrs. Churchill hailed from the state of Maine, where the finest Swedish meatballs and tuna casserole and angel food cake in America are made. She readily demonstrated certain techniques—how to layer wet sheets of pasta for a lasagna or whisk up a simple roux, for example. She often brought gift shoeboxes containing curious ingredients like dried oregano, instant yeast, and cream of mushroom soup. The two women, though at ease and jolly with each other, had difficulty communicating, and this was made worse by the often confusing terminology of Western cuisine ("corned beef," "deviled eggs"). Although I was just learning the language myself, I'd gladly play the interlocutor, jumping back and forth between their places at the counter, dipping my fingers into whatever sauce lay about.

I was an insistent child, and, being my mother's firstborn, much too prized. My mother could say no to me, and did often enough, but anyone who knew us—particularly my father and sister—could tell how much the denying pained her. And if I was overconscious of her indulgence even then, and suffered the rushing pangs of guilt that she could inflict upon me with the slightest wounded turn of her lip, I was too happily obtuse and venal to let her cease. She reminded me daily that I was her sole son, her reason for living, and that if she were to lose me, in either body or spirit, she wished that God would mercifully smite her, strike her down like a weak branch.

In the traditional fashion, she was the house accountant, the maid, the launderer, the disciplinarian, the driver, the secretary, and, of course, the cook. She was also my first basketball coach. In South Korea, where girls' high school basketball is a popular spectator sport, she had been a star, the point guard for the national high school team that once won the all-Asia championships. I learned this one Saturday during the summer, when I asked my father if he would go down to the school-yard and shoot some baskets with me. I had just finished the fifth grade, and wanted desperately to make the middle school team the coming fall. He called for my mother and sister to come along. When we arrived, my sister immediately ran off to the swings, and I recall being annoyed that my mother wasn't follow-ing her. I dribbled clumsily around the key, on the verge of losing control of the ball, and flung a flat shot that caromed wildly off the rim. The ball bounced to my father, who took a few not so graceful dribbles and made an easy layup. He dribbled out and then drove to the hoop for a layup on the other side. He re-bounded his shot and passed the ball to my mother, who had been watching us from the foul line. She turned from the basket and be-gan heading the other way.

"*Um-mah*," I cried at her, my exasperation already bubbling over, "the basket's over *here!*"

After a few steps she turned around, and from where the professional three-point line must be now, she effortlessly flipped the ball up in a two-handed set shot, its flight truer and higher than I'd witnessed from any boy or man. The ball arced cleanly into the hoop, stiffly popping the chain-link net. All after-noon, she rained in shot after shot, as my fa-ther and I scrambled after her.

When we got home from the playground, my mother showed me the photograph album of her team's championship run. For years I kept it in my room, on the same shelf that housed the scrapbooks I made of basketball stars, with magazine clippings of slick players like Bubbles Hawkins and Pistol Pete and George (the Iceman) Gervin.

It puzzled me how much she considered her own history to be immaterial, and if she never patently diminished herself, she was able to finesse a kind of self-removal by speaking of my father whenever she could. She zealously recounted his excellence as a student in medical school and reminded me, each night before I started my homework, of how hard he drove himself in his work to make a life for us. She said that because of his Asian face and imperfect English, he was "working two times the American doctors." I knew that she was building him up, buttress-ing him with both genuine admiration and her own brand of anxious braggadocio, and that her overarching concern was that I might fail to see him as she wished me to—in the most dawning light, his pose steadfast and solitary.

In the year before I left for Exeter, I be-came weary of her oft-repeated accounts of my father's success. I was a teenager, and so ever inclined to be dismissive and bitter to-ward anything that had to do with family and home. Often enough, my mother was the ob-ject of my derision. Suddenly, her life seemed so small to me. She was there, and sometimes, I thought, *always* there, as if she were con-fined to the four walls of our house. I would even complain about her cooking. Mostly, though, I was getting more and more impa-tient with the difficulty she encountered in doing everyday things. I was afraid for her. One day, we got into a terrible argument when she asked me to call the bank, to ques-tion a discrepancy she had discovered in the monthly statement. I asked her why she couldn't call herself. I was stupid and brutal, and I knew exactly how to wound her.

"Whom do I talk to?" she said. She would mostly speak to me in Korean, and I would answer in English.

"The bank manager, who else?"

"What do I say?"

25 "Whatever you want to say."

"Don't speak to me like that!" she cried.

"It's just that you should be able to do it yourself," I said.

"You know how I feel about this!"

"Well, maybe then you should consider it *practice*," I answered lightly, using the Korean word to make sure she understood.

30 Her face blanched, and her neck suddenly became rigid, as if I were throttling her. She nearly struck me right then, but instead she bit her lip and ran upstairs. I followed her, pleading for forgiveness at her door. But it was the one time in our life that I couldn't convince her, melt her resolve with the blandishments of a spoiled son.

When my mother was feeling strong enough, or was in particularly good spirits, she would roll her machine into the kitchen and sit at the table and watch me work. She wore pajamas day and night, mostly old pairs of mine.

She said, "I can't tell, what are you making?"

"*Mahn-doo* filling."

"You didn't salt the cabbage and squash."

35 "Was I supposed to?"

"Of course. Look, it's too wet. Now the skins will get soggy before you can fry them."

"What should I do?"

"It's too late. Maybe it'll be OK if you work quickly. Why didn't you ask me?"

"You were finally sleeping."

40 "You should have woken me."

"No way."

She sighed, as deeply as her weary lungs would allow.

"I don't know how you were going to make it without me."

"I don't know, either. I'll remember the salt next time."

45 "You better. And not too much."

We often talked like this, our tone decidedly matter-of-fact, chin up, just this side of being able to bear it. Once, while inspecting a potato fritter batter I was making, she asked me if she had ever done anything that I wished she hadn't done. I thought for a moment, and told her no. In the next breath, she wondered aloud if it was right of her to have let me go to Exeter, to live away from the house while I was so young. She tested the batter's thickness with her finger and called for more flour. Then she asked if, given a choice, I would go to Exeter again.

I wasn't sure what she was getting at, and I told her that I couldn't be certain, but probably yes, I would. She snorted at this and said it was my leaving home that had once so troubled our relationship. "Remember how I had so much difficulty talking to you? Remember?"

She believed back then that I had found her more and more ignorant each time I came home. She said she never blamed me, for this was the way she knew it would be with my wonderful new education. Nothing I could say seemed to quell the notion. But I knew that the problem wasn't simply the *education;* the first time I saw her again after starting school, barely six weeks later, when she and my father visited me on Parents Day, she had already grown nervous and distant. After the usual campus events, we had gone to the motel where they were staying in a nearby town and sat on the beds in our room. She seemed to sneak looks at me, as though I might discover a horrible new truth if our eyes should meet.

My own secret feeling was that I had missed my parents greatly, my mother especially, and much more than I had anticipated. I couldn't tell them that these first weeks were a mere blur to me, that I felt completely overwhelmed by all the studies and my much brighter friends and the thousand irritating details of living alone, and that I had really learned nothing, save perhaps how to put on a necktie while sprinting to class. I felt as if I had plunged too deep into the world, which, to my great horror, was much larger than I had ever imagined.

50   I welcomed the lull of the motel room. My father and I had nearly dozed off when my mother jumped up excitedly, murmured how stupid she was, and hurried to the closet by the door. She pulled out our old metal cooler and dragged it between the beds. She lifted the top and began unpacking plastic containers, and I thought she would never stop. One after the other they came out, each with a dish that traveled well—a salted stewed meat, rolls of Korean-style sushi. I opened a container of radish kimchi and suddenly the room bloomed with its odor, and I reveled in the very peculiar sensation (which perhaps only true kimchi lovers know) of simultaneously drooling and gagging as I breathed it all in. For the next few minutes, they watched me eat. I'm not certain that I was even hungry. But after weeks of pork parmigiana and chicken patties and wax beans, I suddenly realized that I had lost all the savor in my life. And it seemed I couldn't get enough of it back. I ate and I ate, so much and so fast that I actually went to the bathroom and vomited. I came out dizzy and sated with the phantom warmth of my binge.

And beneath the face of her worry, I thought, my mother was smiling.

From that day, my mother prepared a certain meal to welcome me home. It was always the same. Even as I rode the school's shuttle bus from Exeter to Logan Airport, I could already see the exact arrangement of my mother's table.

I knew that we would eat in the kitchen, the table brimming with plates. There was the *kalbi* of course, broiled or grilled depending on the season. Leaf lettuce, to wrap the meat with. Bowls of garlicky clam broth with miso and tofu and fresh spinach. Shavings of cod dusted in flour and then dipped in egg wash and fried. Glass noodles with onions and shiitake. Scallion-and-hot-pepper pancakes. Chilled steamed shrimp. Seasoned salads of bean sprouts, spinach, and white radish. Crispy squares of seaweed. Steamed rice with barley and red beans. Homemade kimchi. It was all there—the old flavors I knew, the beautiful salt, the sweet, the excellent taste.

After the meal, my father and I talked about school, but I could never say enough for it to make any sense. My father would often recall his high school principal, who had gone to England to study the methods and traditions of the public schools, and regaled students with stories of the great Eton man. My mother sat with us, paring fruit, not saying a word but taking everything in. When it was time to go to bed, my father said good night first. I usually watched television until the early morning. My mother would sit with me for an hour or two, perhaps until she was accustomed to me again, and only then would she kiss me and head upstairs to sleep.

During the following days, it was always 55 the cooking that started our conversations. She'd hold an inquest over the cold leftovers we ate at lunch, discussing each dish in terms of its balance of flavors or what might have been prepared differently. But mostly I begged her to leave the dishes alone. I wish I had paid more attention. After her death, when my father and I were the only ones left in the house, drifting through the rooms like ghosts, I sometimes tried to make that meal for him. Though it was too much for two, I made each dish anyway, taking as much care as I could. But nothing turned out quite right—not the color, not the smell. At the table, neither of us said much of anything. And we had to eat the food for days.

I remember washing rice in the kitchen one day and my mother's saying in English, from her usual seat, "I made a big mistake."

"About Exeter?"

"Yes. I made a big mistake. You should be with us for that time. I should never let you go there."

"So why did you?" I said.

60 "Because I didn't know I was going to die."

I let her words pass. For the first time in her life, she was letting herself speak her full mind, so what else could I do?

"But you know what?" she spoke up. "It was better for you. If you stayed home, you would not like me so much now."

I suggested that maybe I would like her even more.

She shook her head. "Impossible."

65 Sometimes I still think about what she said, about having made a mistake. I would have left home for college, that was never in doubt, but those years I was away at boarding school grew more precious to her as her illness progressed. After many months of exhaustion and pain and the haze of the drugs, I thought that her mind was beginning to fade, for more and more it seemed that she was seeing me again as her fifteen-year-old boy, the one she had dropped off in New Hampshire on a cloudy September afternoon.

I remember the first person I met, another new student, named Zack, who walked to the welcome picnic with me. I had planned to eat with my parents—my mother had brought a cooler full of food even that first day—but I learned of the cookout and told her that I should probably go. I wanted to go, of course. I was excited, and no doubt fearful and nervous, and I must have thought I was only thinking ahead. She agreed wholeheartedly, saying I certainly should. I walked them to the car, and perhaps I hugged them, before saying goodbye. One day, after she died, my father told me what happened on the long drive home to Syracuse.

He was driving the car, looking straight ahead. Traffic was light on the Massachusetts Turnpike, and the sky was nearly dark. They had driven for more than two hours and had not yet spoken a word. He then heard a strange sound from her, a kind of muffled chewing noise, as if something inside her were grinding its way out.

"So, what's the matter?" he said, trying to keep an edge to his voice.

She looked at him with her ashen face and she burst into tears. He began to cry himself, and pulled the car over onto the narrow shoulder of the turnpike, where they stayed for the next half hour or so, the blank-faced cars droning by them in the cold, onrushing night.

Every once in a while, when I think of her, 70 I'm driving alone somewhere on the highway. In the twilight, I see their car off to the side, a blue Olds coupe with a landau top, and as I pass them by I look back in the mirror and I see them again, the two figures huddling together in the front seat. Are they sleeping? Or kissing? Are they all right?

READING AND THINKING

1. What is your response to Lee's mother as he presents her in this essay? To Lee's behavior towards his mother?

2. How does Lee use food as a means of describing character and family relationships? Identify specific examples that reveal his family's character.

3. What role does Lee's father play in this piece? How are other family members characterized?

4. What conflicts are at the heart of this essay? What ironies can you identify?

THINKING AND WRITING

1. Select one scene from the essay and analyze how Lee gets it going, develops, and then concludes it, paying attention to his language. How does that scene contribute to Lee's larger point?

2. Continue to analyze each of Lee's scenes and track how and why each scene is important to the larger story and the developing idea of Lee's essay.

3. Compare Lee's characterization of his mother and father with the characterization of her parents in bell hooks's "Inspired Eccentricity" (p. 299).

4. Describe a central conflict in the life of your family. Try to show how the conflict develops through a series of three or four short scenes, as Lee does in "Coming Home Again."

5. How do traditions play a role in Lee's essay? Use examples from his essay to discuss how traditions play a role in family relationships.

THE FAMILY CIRCLE: AN OCCASION FOR WRITING

Lee describes how certain traditions have been continued in his family from one generation to the next; how, for example, he has inherited the love and lore of cooking Korean dishes from his mother. In the following Occasion for Writing, you will view another example of a family cycle—how a family's tradition of working as circus performers binds the generations together in E. B. White's essay "The Ring of Time."

E.B. White (1899–1985)

from THE RING OF TIME

1   After the lions had returned to their cages, creeping angrily through the chutes, a little bunch of us drifted away and into an open doorway nearby, where we stood for a while in semidarkness, watching a big brown circus horse go harumphing around the practice ring. His trainer was a woman of about forty, and the two of them, horse and woman, seemed caught up in one of those desultory treadmills of afternoon from which there is no apparent escape. The day was hot, and we kibitzers were grateful to be briefly out of the

sun's glare. The long rein, or tape, by which the woman guided her charge counterclockwise in his dull career formed the radius of their private circle, of which she was the revolving center; and she, too, stepped a tiny circumference of her own, in order to accommodate the horse and allow him his maximum scope. She had on a short-skirted costume and a conical straw hat. Her legs were bare and she wore high heels, which probed deep into the loose tanbark and kept her ankles in a state of constant turmoil. The great size and meekness of the horse, the repetitious exercise, the heat of the afternoon, all exerted a hypnotic charm that invited boredom; we spectators were experiencing a languor—we neither expected relief nor felt entitled to any. We had paid a dollar to get into the grounds, to be sure, but we had got our dollar's worth a few minutes before, when the lion trainer's whiplash had got caught around a toe of one of the lions. What more did we want for a dollar?

Behind me I heard someone say, "Excuse me, please," in a low voice. She was halfway into the building when I turned and saw her—a girl of sixteen or seventeen, politely threading her way through us onlookers who blocked the entrance. As she emerged in front of us, I saw that she was barefoot, her dirty little feet fighting the uneven ground. In most respects she was like any of two or three dozen showgirls you encounter if you wander about the winter quarters of Mr. John Ringling North's circus, in Sarasota—cleverly proportioned, deeply browned by the sun, dusty, eager, and almost naked. But her grave face and the naturalness of her manner gave her a sort of quick distinction and brought a new note into the gloomy octagonal building where we had all cast our lot for a few moments. As soon as she had squeezed through the crowd, she spoke a word or two to the older woman, whom I took to be her mother, stepped to the ring, and waited while the horse coasted to a stop in front of her. She gave the animal a couple of affectionate swipes on his enormous neck and then swung herself aboard. The horse immediately resumed his rocking canter, the woman goading him on, chanting something that sounded like "Hop! Hop!" . . .

The ten-minute ride the girl took achieved—as far as I was concerned who wasn't looking for it, and quite unbeknownst to her, who wasn't even striving for it—the thing that is sought by performers everywhere, on whatever stage, whether struggling in the tidal currents of Shakespeare or bucking the difficult motion of a horse. I somehow got the idea she was just cadging a ride, improving a shining ten minutes in the diligent way all serious artists seize free moments to hone the blade of their talent and keep themselves in trim. Her brief tour included only elementary postures and tricks, perhaps because they were all she was capable of, perhaps because her warmup at this hour was unscheduled and the ring was not rigged for a real practice session. She swung herself off and on the horse several times, gripping his mane. She did a few knee-stands—or whatever they are called—dropping to her knees and quickly bouncing back up on her feet again. Most of the time she simply rode in a standing position, well aft on the beast, her hands hanging easily at her sides, her head erect, her straw-colored ponytail lightly brushing her shoulders, the blood of exertion showing faintly through the tan of her skin. Twice she managed a one-foot stance—a sort of ballet pose, with arms outstretched. At one point the neck strap of her bathing suit broke and she went twice around the ring in the classic attitude of a woman making minor repairs to a garment. The fact that she was standing on the back of a moving horse while doing this invested the matter with a clownish significance that perfectly fitted the spirit of the circus—jocund, yet charming. She just rolled the strap into a neat ball and stowed it inside her bodice while the horse rocked and rolled beneath her in dutiful innocence. The bathing suit proved as self-reliant as its owner and stood up well enough without benefit of strap. . . .

As I watched with the others, our jaws adroop, our eyes alight, I became painfully conscious of the element of time. Everything in the hideous old building seemed to take the shape of a circle, conforming to the course of the horse. The rider's gaze, as she peered straight ahead, seemed to be circular, as though bent by force of circumstance; then time itself began running in circles, and so the beginning was where the end was, and the two were the same, and one thing ran into the next and time went round and around and got nowhere. The girl wasn't so young that she did not know the delicious satisfaction of having a perfectly behaved body and the fun of using it to do a trick most people can't do, but she was too young to know that time does not really move in a circle at all. I thought: "She will never be as beautiful as this again"—a thought that made me acutely unhappy—and in a flash my mind (which is too much of a busybody to suit me) had projected her twenty-five years ahead, and she was now in the center of the ring, on foot, wearing a conical hat and high-heeled shoes, the image of the older woman, holding the long rein, caught in the treadmill of an afternoon long in the future. "She is at that enviable moment in life [I thought] when she believes she can go once around the ring, make one complete circuit, and at the end be exactly the same age as at the start." Everything in her movements, her expression, told you that for her the ring of time was perfectly formed, changeless, predictable, without beginning or end, like the ring in which she was traveling at this moment with the horse that wallowed under her. And then I slipped back into my trance, and time was circular again—time, pausing quietly with the rest of us, so as not to disturb the balance of a performer.

Her ride ended as casually as it had begun. The older woman stopped the horse, and the girl slid to the ground. As she walked toward us to leave, there was a quick, small burst of applause. She smiled broadly, in surprise and pleasure; then her face suddenly regained its gravity and she disappeared through the door. 5

PREPARING TO WRITE: OCCASIONS TO THINK ABOUT WHAT YOU SEE

1. After reading the excerpt from E. B. White's essay "The Ring of Time," identify ways in which the girl riding horseback and the woman holding the horse's reins in the center of the ring are related.

2. What do you think White means by the "ring of time"? In what ways is time a "ring"?

MOVING TOWARD ESSAY: OCCASIONS TO ANALYZE AND REFLECT

1. Consider the implications of the ring of time for the girl riding horseback and for the woman at center ring (the girl's mother). What do you imagine the woman did when she was a girl? What about the woman's mother?

2. Consider the significance of Lee's and his mother's cooking. How does their shared interest in special Korean foods and their preparation connect mother with son and son with mother?

3. To what extent are Lee's essay and White's "Ring of Time" about family traditions and the cycle of time? Explain.

WRITING THOUGHTFULLY: OCCASIONS FOR IDEAS AND ESSAYS

1. Describe a scene from your memory in which you were being taught how to do something by one of your parents.

2. Revisit your scene and write a follow-up to it in which you recount a story where you are teaching your parents something. Compare the two scenes to find similarities and differences in each experience. What stands out to you in both scenes? Write an essay based on these two scenes that examines your relationship with one or both of your parents, possibly using Lee's and White's essays as additional evidence of your findings.

3. Read and then write a two-paragraph summary of E. B. White's "Once More to the Lake." In your first paragraph, describe what happens in the essay. In your second paragraph, explain the significance—the main idea of the essay and how the author illustrates and supports that idea. In a longer analysis discuss how all these essays support the cyclical nature of parental relationships. Do you agree with what the writers say? If so use your own experiences as a piece of evidence (possibly reusing scenes you have created above). If not, how would you challenge the writers?

CREATING OCCASIONS

1. Think about other aspects of family life that get "passed down," such as family heirlooms, or even characteristics. Think about why families feel they need to "keep it in the family." Consider in an essay how possession and family might be interwoven.

2. Examine a family tree or genealogical chart and see what the shape or pattern of the chart reveals about the family. Does the tree or chart support or refute the cyclical nature of families, as Lee and White suggest?

Barbara Kingsolver (b. 1955)

Barbara Kingsolver was born in Maryland and grew up in rural Kentucky. She was educated at Depauw University and the University of Arizona, where she studied biology and became interested in both nature and writing. Kingsolver has written poetry and fiction as well as essays. Her novels include *The Bean Trees* (1988), *Animal Dreams* (1990), *Pigs in Heaven* (1993), and *The Poisonwood Bible: A Novel* (1998). Her books of essays include *High Tide in Tucson: Essays from Now or Never* (1995) and *Small Wonder* (2002).

STONE SOUP

In "Stone Soup," Kingsolver uses her personal experience as an entry point for discussing various kinds of families. In the course of a marital breakup, Kingsolver was confronted with issues and messy problems that many families face every day. Her essay challenges common assumptions about just what form of family is best.

1   In the catalog of family values, where do we rank an occasion like this? A curly-haired boy who wanted to run before he walked, age seven now, a soccer player scoring a winning goal. He turns to the bleachers with his fists in the air and a smile wide as a gap-toothed galaxy. His own cheering section of grown-ups and kids all leap to their feet and hug each other, delirious with love for this boy. He's Andy, my best friend's son. The cheering section includes his mother and her friends, his brother, his father and stepmother, a stepbrother and stepsister, and a grandparent. Lucky is the child with this many relatives on hand to hail a proud accomplishment. I'm there too, witnessing a family fortune. But in spite of myself, defensive words take shape in my head. I am thinking: I dare *anybody* to call this a broken home.

Families change, and remain the same. Why are our names for home so slow to catch up to the truth of where we live?

When I was a child, I had two parents who loved me without cease. One of them attended every excuse for attention I ever contrived, and the other made it to the ones with higher production values, like piano recitals and appendicitis. So I was a lucky child too. I played with a set of paper dolls called "The Family of Dolls," four in number, who came with the factory-assigned names of Dad, Mom, Sis, and Junior. I think you know what they looked like, at least before I loved them to death and their heads fell off.

Now I've replaced the dolls with a life. I knit my days around my daughter's survival and happiness, and am proud to say her head is still on. But we aren't the Family of Dolls. Maybe you're not, either. And if not, even though you are statistically no oddity, it's probably been suggested to you in a hundred ways that yours isn't exactly a real family, but an impostor family, a harbinger of cultural ruin, a slapdash substitute—something like counterfeit money. Here at the tail end of our century, most of us are up to our ears in the noisy business of trying to support and love a thing called family. But there's a current in the air with ferocious moral force that finds its way even into political campaigns, claiming there is only one right way to do it, the Way It Has Always Been.

In the face of a thriving, particolored 5 world, this narrow view is so pickled and absurd I'm astonished that it gets airplay. And I'm astonished that it still stings.

Every parent has endured the arrogance of a child-unfriendly grump sitting in judgment, explaining what those kids of ours really need (for example, "a good licking"). If we're polite, we move our crew to another bench in the park. If we're forthright (as I am in my mind, only, for the rest of the day), we fix them with a sweet imperious stare and say, "Come back and let's talk about it after you've changed a thousand diapers."

But it's harder somehow to shrug off the Family-of-Dolls Family Values crew when they judge (from their safe distance) that divorced people, blended families, gay families, and single parents are failures. That our children are at risk, and the whole arrangement is messy and embarrassing. A marriage that ends is not called "finished," it's called *failed*. The children of this family may have been born to a happy union, but now they are called *the children of divorce*.

I had no idea how thoroughly these assumptions overlaid my culture until I went through divorce myself. I wrote to a friend: "This might be worse than being widowed. Overnight I've suffered the same losses—companionship, financial and practical support, my identity as a wife and partner, the future I'd taken for granted. I am lonely, grieving, and hard-pressed to take care of my household alone. But instead of bringing casseroles, people are acting like I had a fit and broke up the family china."

Once upon a time I held these beliefs about divorce: that everyone who does it could have chosen not to do it. That it's a lazy way out of marital problems. That it selfishly puts personal happiness ahead of family integrity. Now I tremble for my ignorance. It's easy, in fortunate times, to forget about the ambush that could leave your head reeling: serious mental or physical illness, death in the family, abandonment, financial calamity, humiliation, violence, despair.

10 I started out like any child, intent on being the Family of Dolls. I set upon young womanhood believing in most of the doctrines of my generation: I wore my skirts four inches above the knee. I had that Barbie with her zebra-striped swimsuit and a figure unlike anything found in nature. And I understood the Prince Charming Theory of Marriage, a quest for Mr. Right that ends smack dab where you find him. I did not completely understand that another whole story *begins* there, and no fairy tale prepared me for the combination of bad luck and persistent hope that would interrupt my dream and lead me to other arrangements. Like a cancer diagnosis, a dying marriage is a thing to fight, to deny, and finally, when there's no choice left, to dig in and survive. Casseroles would help. Likewise, I imagine it must be a painful reckoning in adolescence (or later on) to realize one's own true love will never look like the soft-focus fragrance ads because Prince Charming (surprise!) is a princess. Or vice versa. Or has skin the color your parents didn't want you messing with, except in the Crayola box.

It's awfully easy to hold in contempt the straw broken home, and that mythical category of persons who toss away nuclear family for the sheer fun of it. Even the legal terms we use have a suggestion of caprice. I resent the phrase "irreconcilable differences," which suggests a stubborn refusal to accept a spouse's little quirks. This is specious. Every happily married couple I know has loads of irreconcilable differences. Negotiating where to set the thermostat is not the point. A nonfunctioning marriage is a slow asphyxiation. It is waking up despised each morning, listening to the pulse of your own loneliness before the radio begins to blare its raucous gospel that you're nothing if you aren't loved. It is sharing your airless house with the threat of suicide or other kinds of violence, while the ghost that whispers, "Leave here and destroy your children," has passed over every door and nailed it shut. Disassembling a marriage in these circumstances is as much *fun* as amputating your own gangrenous leg. You do it, if you can, to save a life—or two, or more.

I know of no one who really went looking to hoe the harder row, especially the daunting one of single parenthood. Yet it seems to be the most American of customs to blame the burdened for their destiny. We'd like so desperately to believe in freedom and justice for all, we can hardly name that rogue bad luck, even when he's a close enough snake to bite us. In the wake of my divorce, some friends (even a few close ones) chose to vanish, rather than linger within striking distance of misfortune.

But most stuck around, bless their hearts, and if I'm any the wiser for my trials, it's from having learned the worth of steadfast friendship. And also, what not to say. The least helpful question is: "Did you want the divorce, or didn't you?" Did I want to keep that gangrenous leg, or not? How to explain, in a culture that venerates choice: two terrifying options are much worse than none at all. Give me any day the quick hand of cruel fate that will leave me scarred but blameless. As it was, I kept thinking of that wicked third-grade joke in which some boy comes up behind you and grabs your ear, starts in with a prolonged tug, and asks, "Do you want this ear any longer?"

Still, the friend who holds your hand and says the wrong thing is made of dearer stuff than the one who stays away. And generally, through all of it, you live. My favorite fictional character, Kate Vaiden (in the novel by Reynolds Price), advises: "Strength just comes in one brand—you stand up at sunrise and meet what they send you and keep your hair combed."

15   Once you've weathered the straits, you get to cross the tricky juncture from casualty to survivor. If you're on your feet at the end of a year or two, and have begun putting together a happy new existence, those friends who were kind enough to feel sorry for you when you needed it must now accept you back to the ranks of the living. If you're truly blessed, they will dance at your second wedding. Everybody else, for heavens sake, should stop throwing stones.

Arguing about whether nontraditional families deserve pity or tolerance is a little like the medieval debate about left-handedness as a mark of the devil. Divorce, remarriage, single parenthood, gay parents, and blended families simply are. They're facts of our time. Some of the reasons listed by sociologists for these family reconstructions are: the idea of marriage as a romantic partnership rather than a pragmatic one; a shift in women's expectations, from servility to self-respect and independence; and longevity (prior to antibiotics no marriage was expected to last many decades—in Colonial days the average couple lived to be married less than twelve years). Add to all this, our growing sense of entitlement to happiness and safety from abuse. Most would agree these are all good things. Yet their result—a culture in which serial monogamy and the consequent reshaping of families are the norm—gets diagnosed as "failing."

For many of us, once we have put ourselves Humpty-Dumpty-wise back together again, the main problem with our reorganized family is that other people think we have a problem. My daughter tells me the only time she's uncomfortable about being the child of divorced parents is when her friends say they feel sorry for her. It's a bizarre sympathy, given that half the kids in her school and nation are in the same boat, pursuing childish happiness with the same energy as their married-parent peers. When anyone asks how she feels about it, she spontaneously lists the benefits: our house is in the country and we have a dog, but she can go to her dad's neighborhood for the urban thrills of a pool and sidewalks for roller-skating. What's more, she has three sets of grandparents!

Why is it surprising that a child would revel in a widened family and the right to feel at home in more than one house? Isn't it the opposite that should worry us—a child with no home at all, or too few resources to feel safe? The child at risk is the one whose parents are too immature themselves to guide wisely; too diminished by poverty to nurture; too far from opportunity to offer hope. The number of children in the U.S. living in poverty at this moment is almost unfathomably large: twenty percent. There are families among us that need help all right, and by no means are they new on the landscape. The rate at which teenage girls had babies in 1957 (ninety-six per thousand) was twice what it is now. That remarkable statistic is ignored by the religious right—probably because the teen birth rate was cut in half mainly by legalized abortion. In fact, the policy gatekeepers who coined the phrase "family values" have steadfastly ignored the desperation of too-small families, and since 1979 have steadily reduced the amount of financial support available to a single parent. But, this camp's most outspoken attacks seem aimed at the notion of families getting too complex, with add-ons and extras such as a gay parent's partner, or a remarried mother's new husband and his children.

To judge a family's value by its tidy symmetry is to purchase a book for its cover. There's no moral authority there. The famous family comprised by Dad, Mom, Sis, and Junior living as an isolated economic unit is not built on historical bedrock. In *The Way We Never Were*, Stephanie Coontz writes, "Whenever people propose that we go back to the traditional family, I always suggest that they pick a ballpark date for the family they have in mind." Colonial families were tidily disciplined, but their members (meaning everyone but infante) labored incessantly and died young. Then the Victorian family adopted a new division of labor, in which women's role was domestic and children were allowed time for study and play, but this was an upper-class construct supported by myriad slaves. Coontz writes, "For every nineteenth-century middle-class family that protected its wife and child within the family circle, there was an Irish or German girl scrubbing floors . . . A Welsh boy mining coal to keep the homebaked goodies warm, a black girl doing the family laundry, a black mother and child picking cotton to be made into clothes for the family, and a Jewish or an Italian daughter in a sweat-shop making 'ladies' dresses or artificial flowers for the family to purchase."

The abolition of slavery brought slightly more democratic arrangements, in which extended families were harnessed together in cottage industries; at the turn of the century came a steep rise in child labor in mines and sweat-shops. Twenty percent of American children lived in orphanages at the time; their parents were not necessarily dead, but couldn't afford to keep them.

During the Depression and up to the end of World War II, many millions of U.S. households were more multigenerational than nuclear. Women my grandmother's age were likely to live with a fluid assortment of elderly relatives, in-laws, siblings, and children. In many cases they spent virtually every waking hour working in the company of other women—a companionable scenario in which it would be easier, I imagine, to tolerate an estranged or difficult spouse. I'm reluctant to idealize a life of so much hard work and so little spousal intimacy, but its advantage may have been resilience. A family so large and varied would not easily be brought down by a single blow: it could absorb a death, long illness, an abandonment here or there, and any number of irreconcilable differences.

The Family of Dolls came along midcentury as a great American experiment. A booming economy required a mobile labor force and demanded that women surrender jobs to returning soldiers. Families came to be defined by a single breadwinner. They struck out for single-family homes at an earlier age than ever before, and in unprecedented numbers they raised children in suburban isolation. The nuclear family was launched to sink or swim.

More than a few sank. Social historians corroborate that the suburban family of the postwar economic boom, which we have recently selected as our definition of "traditional," was no panacea. Twenty-five percent of Americans were poor in the mid-1950s, and as yet there were no food stamps. Sixty percent of the elderly lived on less than $1,000 a year, and most had no medical insurance. In the sequestered suburbs, alcoholism and sexual abuse of children were far more widespread than anyone imagined.

Expectations soared, and the economy sagged. It's hard to depend on one other adult for everything, come what may. In the last three decades, that amorphous, adaptable structure we call "family" has been reshaped once more by economic tides. Compared with fifties families, mothers are far more likely now to be employed. We are statistically more likely to divorce, and to live in blended families or other extranuclear arrangements. We are also more likely to plan and space our children, and to rate our marriages as "happy." We are less likely to suffer abuse without recourse, or to stare out at our lives through a glaze of prescription tranquilizers. Our aged parents are less likely to be destitute, and we're half as likely to have a teenage daughter turn up a mother herself. All in all, I would say that if "intact" in modern family-values jargon means living quietly desperate in the bell jar, then hip-hip-hooray for "broken." A neat family model constructed to service the Baby Boom economy seems to be returning gradually to a grand, lumpy shape that human families apparently have tended toward since they first took root in the Olduvai Gorge. We're social animals, deeply fond of companionship, and children love best to run in packs. If there is a *normal* for humans, at all, I expect it looks like two or three Families of Dolls, connected variously by kinship and passion, shuffled like cards and strewn over several shoeboxes.

25   The sooner we can let go the fairy tale of families functioning perfectly in isolation, the better we might embrace the relief of community. Even the admirable parents who've stayed married through thick and thin are very likely, at present, to incorporate other adults into their families—household help and baby-sitters if they can afford them or neighbors and grandparents if they can't. For single parents, this support is the rock-bottom definition of family. And most parents who have split apart, however painfully, still manage to maintain family continuity for their children, creating in many cases a boisterous phenomenon that Constance Ahrons in her book *The Good Divorce* calls the "binuclear family." Call it what you will—when ex-spouses beat swords into plowshares and jump up and down at a soccer game together, it makes for happy kids.

Cinderella, look, who needs her? All those evil stepsisters? That story always seemed like too much cotton-picking fuss over clothes. A childhood tale that fascinated me more was the one called "Stone Soup," and the gist of it is this: Once upon a time, a pair of beleaguered soldiers straggled home to a village empty-handed, in a land ruined by war. They were famished, but the villagers had so little they shouted evil words and slammed their doors. So the soldiers dragged out a big kettle, filled it with water, and put it on a fire to boil. They rolled a clean round stone into the pot, while the villagers peered through their curtains in amazement.

"What kind of soup is that?" they hooted.

"Stone soup," the soldiers replied. "Everybody can have some when it's done."

"Well, thanks," one matron grumbled, coming out with a shriveled carrot. "But it'd be better if you threw this in."

30   And so on, of course, a vegetable at a time, until the whole suspicious village managed to feed itself grandly.

Any family is a big empty pot, save for what gets thrown in. Each stew turns out different. Generosity, a resolve to turn bad luck into good, and respect for variety—these things will nourish a nation of children. Name-calling and suspicion will not. My soup contains a rock or two of hard times, and maybe yours does too. I expect it's a heck of a bouillabaisse.

READING AND THINKING

1. Kingsolver uses personal experience as evidence to make her argument about families. To what extent do you find this use of personal experience as evidence effective? Explain.

2. What are Kingsolver's views about divorce? Why did she change her point of view about divorce?

3. Explain the significance of the title—and the fairy tale Kingsolver tells at the end of her essay.

4. Of what significance are the historical allusions and references Kingsolver makes? Why do you think she includes references to earlier historical decades?

THINKING AND WRITING

1. Select two of the family types that Kingsolver describes and discuss the merits and drawbacks of each type of family.

2. How does Kingsolver use personal experience and anecdotes? Identify at least three instances of the personal that Kingsolver brings to bear as evidence to support her ideas about divorce and about families.

3. Document your own experience of family. You may wish to describe not only the type of family you are presently part of, but also various other family patterns you may have experienced. Consider the advantages and disadvantages of the different forms of family life you have experienced.

DEFINING THE FAMILY: AN OCCASION FOR WRITING

In "Stone Soup," Barbara Kingsolver argues for the need to extend the conventional definition of the family to include other family structures besides that of mother, father, and children. In the following brief essay, written when she was a student, Ariane Harracksingh describes an unconventional family.

Ariane Harracksingh

FAMILY PORTRAITS

Pray God you can cope
I stand outside this woman's work
this woman's world…
— Kate Bush, "This Woman's Work"

i

My mother sits with her hands folded in her lap. I stand behind her with my hand on her shoulder. I stand close, smiling, trying to convey feelings of warmth and unity I know aren't there. Next to me stands my brother, his left hand slightly raised near his belt and his right hand at his side. My mother turns slightly towards him.

ii

The empty space in our family portrait is the space for my father. Posed, he would have hidden my brother's moving hands.

My brother never did learn to keep still, one of the symptoms of his no-male-role-model disease, an epidemic that infects countless innocent sufferers. The disease's symptoms are more generally visible in its male victims. The females, more often than not, suffer internal injuries. Fatherless, they face the world without the protection of being Daddy's Little Girls. They suffer silently with their mothers; the more visible victims, the young boys, are incapable of concealing its effects.

The disease was particularly hard on my brother.

iii

I have always regarded my home life as unusual. I have long been aware of the pressure my relatives (my grandparents especially) exerted on my mother in urging her to remarry. This type of blatant pressure, however, was at least confrontable, unlike the pressure exerted by strangers. Unsolicited disapproving looks came from the elderly, along with inquisitive stares from men, the awkwardness of my father's absence doubly apparent in their unspoken, unwarranted judgments. In their opinion, as in that of my grandparents, remarrying was the one thing my mother should have done—immediately after my father divorced her. With their accusatory glances, they intimated that my mother had driven our father away, when instead she should have given in to his abuse. She should have given up her pursuit of a medical career. She should have given us a father.

iv

Symptoms of our affliction showed even in school, especially when there was a father-son picnic on an afternoon Mom couldn't get off from work. My brother, discreetly grateful, would take me instead. We sat on the bleachers and watched the activities, content to be regarded as orphans or latchkey kids, as long as we just didn't seem fatherless. But no matter what we did that fact was obvious. There was clearly no man around the house. There was only my brother, a boy trying to emulate what he thought was a man. A man he never knew.

Fortunately, the ideal of a happy family is not unattainable. A breath of life remains in this social structure, its cohesion directly linked with responsibilities once shirked and now fulfilled in other roles, as grandparents and relatives lend their support to the double-duty mothers. The units they form create strength upon which new family structures will be built.

v

My friend Molly's family portrait depicts such strength. In it stand three women, dressed casually. Behind them are trees, suggestive of life and growth. But it is the foreground that is extraordinary. The three women are of equal height, and, with lens angled, their faces form the picture's only horizontal line. Looking out from the same level, they all appear genuinely happy to be standing beside each other. Molly stands in the middle with her daughter Merle to her left, while to her right stands her lover, Laura.

From talking with Merle, you would never know how different her family is. The reaction to Merle's family situation, however, is typically a disguised, unconfrontable attack against her parents' sexual orientation. But, as with my family picture, in time that of Merle, Molly, and Laura will also be seen as a representation of what it is: a family portrait.

Gay couple Stacey Kargman-Kaye, left, and Jodi Kelber-Kaye, plaintiffs in the case against the city of Baltimore, walking to their car with their 1-year-old son after a news conference held to announce that the American Civil Liberties Union is suing Baltimore and four Maryland counties for the right of same-sex couples to marry (2004).

© Matt Houston/AP Photo

PREPARING TO WRITE: OCCASIONS TO THINK ABOUT WHAT YOU SEE

1. Make a list of three things you notice about the picture that Harracksingh paints in her essay, "Family Portraits." Describe what you imagine her family portrait looks like.

2. Write up an inventory of what is included in each of the essay's separate sections.

3. How does the photograph here relate to Harracksingh's essay? What about both the photograph and the essay stand out the most to you?

MOVING TOWARD ESSAY: OCCASIONS TO ANALYZE AND REFLECT

1. Using your inventory from Question 2 in the previous exercise, explain how each part of the essay relates to one adjacent part. Explain how the essay is structured or organized.

2. To what extent does the essay create expectations about the unconventionality of Harracksingh's family? To what extent were your expectations either frustrated or satisfied?

3. Explain the overall idea of Harracksingh's essay. What do the parts, cumulatively, add up to?

4. How does the image further complicate or resolve the notion of families for you? What exactly in the image has made you feel the way you do about families?

WRITING THOUGHTFULLY: OCCASIONS FOR IDEAS AND ESSAYS

1. Create a scene in which you isolate a single event that you believe describes your own family—nuclear or extended. Try to highlight what is distinctive, special, idiosyncratic, or otherwise unique about your family.

2. Attempt to define the term "family" for the twenty-first century. You may wish to classify different types of families, to compare different family structures, to consider the benefits and drawbacks of different types of families, and so on.

3. Revise your scene to create a larger essay that brings together your scene of your family with your definition of family. How do you see your family as a model for that definition or as veering away from that definition?

CREATING OCCASIONS

1. Using the images and texts in this Occasion for Writing, as well as anything else you think would be appropriate, explore whether you believe a family is ever "unconventional" or "conventional." Do you think that a perfect definition for families exists? Explain.

Barbara Ehrenreich (b. 1941)

Barbara Ehrenreich is a journalist and historian, a regular contributor to *The Nation* magazine, and an occasional contributor to the *New York Times*. Ehrenreich is the author of numerous essays and books, including *Fear of Falling: The Inner Life of the Middle Class* (1989); *The Snarling Citizen* (1995); *Nickel and Dimed: On (Not) Getting By in America* (2001); and, most recently, *Bait and Switch: The (Futile) Pursuit of the American Dream* (2005). She has received many awards, including a Guggenheim fellowship and the National Magazine Award for Excellence in Reporting.

FAMILY VALUES

In "Family Values," Ehrenreich highlights the ways her parents lived their values and passed those values on to her. She relishes the stories she tells about her parents' political lives, and she celebrates what they stood for, which is, in significant ways, what Ehrenreich herself now stands for.

1   Sometime in the eighties, Americans had a new set of "traditional values" installed. It was part of what may someday be known as the "Reagan renovation," that finely balanced mix of cosmetic refinement and moral coarseness which brought $200,000 china to the White House dinner table and mayhem to the beleaguered peasantry of Central America. All of the new traditions had venerable sources. In economics, we borrowed from the Bourbons; in foreign policy, we drew on themes fashioned by the nomad warriors of the Eurasian steppes. In spiritual matters, we emulated the braying intolerance of our archenemies and esteemed customers, the Shi'ite fundamentalists.

A case could be made, of course, for the genuine American provenance of all these new "traditions." We've had our own robber barons, military adventures, and certainly more than our share of enterprising evangelists promoting ignorance and parochialism as a state of grace. From the vantage point of the continent's original residents, or, for example, the captive African laborers who made America a great agricultural power, our "traditional values" have always been bigotry, greed, and belligerence, buttressed by wanton appeals to a God of love.

The kindest—though from some angles most perverse—of the era's new values was "family." I could have lived with "flag" and "faith" as neotraditional values—not happily, but I could have managed—until "family" was press-ganged into joining them. Throughout the eighties, the winning political faction has been aggressively "profamily." They have invoked "the family" when they trample on the rights of those who hold actual families together, that is, women. They have used it to justify racial segregation and the formation of white-only, "Christian" schools. And they have brought it out, along with flag and faith, to silence any voices they found obscene, offensive, disturbing, or merely different.

Now, I come from a family—was raised in one, in fact—and one salubrious effect of right-wing righteousness has been to make me hew ever more firmly to the traditional values of my own progenitors. These were not people who could be accused of questionable politics or ethnicity. Nor were they members of the "liberal elite" so hated by our current conservative elite. They were blue-eyed, Scotch-Irish Democrats. They were small farmers, railroad workers, miners, shopkeepers, and migrant farm workers. In short, they fit the stereotype of "real" Americans; and their values, no matter how unpopular among today's opinion-shapers, are part of America's tradition, too. To my mind, of course, the finest part.

5   But let me introduce some of my family, beginning with my father, who was, along with my mother, the ultimate source of much of my radicalism, feminism, and, by the standards of the eighties, all-around bad attitude.

One of the first questions in a test of mental competency is "Who is the president of the United States?" Even deep into the indignities of Alzheimer's disease, my father always did well on that one. His blue eyes would widen incredulously, surprised at the neurologist's ignorance, then he would snort in majestic indignation, "Reagan, that dumb son of a bitch." It seemed to me a good deal—two people tested for the price of one.

Like so many of the Alzheimer's patients he came to know, my father enjoyed watching the president on television. Most programming left him impassive, but when the old codger came on, his little eyes twinkling piggishly above the disciplined sincerity of his lower face, my father would lean forward and commence a wickedly delighted cackle. I think he was prepared, more than the rest of us, to get the joke.

But the funniest thing was Ollie North. For an ailing man, my father did a fine parody. He would slap his hand over his heart, stare rigidly at attention, and pronounce, in his deepest bass rumble, "God Bless Am-ar-ica!" I'm sure he couldn't follow North's testimony—who can honestly say that they did?—but the main themes were clear enough in pantomime: the watery-eyed patriotism, the extravagant self-pity, the touching servility toward higher-ranking males. When I told my father that many people considered North a hero, a representative of the finest American traditions, he scowled and swatted at the air. Ollie North was the kind of man my father had warned me about, many years ago, when my father was the smartest man on earth.

My father had started out as a copper miner in Butte, Montana, a tiny mountain city famed for its bars, its brawls, and its distinctly unservile work force. In his view,

which remained eagle-sharp even after a stint of higher education, there were only a few major categories of human beings. There were "phonies" and "decent" people, the latter group having hardly any well-known representative outside of Franklin Delano Roosevelt and John L. Lewis, the militant and brilliantly eloquent leader of the miners' union. "Phonies," however, were rampant, and, for reasons I would not understand until later in life, could be found clustered especially thick in the vicinity of money or power.

Well before he taught me other useful   10
things, like how to distinguish fool's gold, or iron pyrite, from the real thing, he gave me some tips on the detection of phonies. For one thing, they broadened the *e* in "America" to a reverent *ahh*. They were the first to leap from their seats at the playing of "The Star Spangled Banner," the most visibly moved participants in any prayer. They espoused clean living and admired war. They preached hard work and paid for it with nickels and dimes. They loved their country above all, but despised the low-paid and usually invisible men and women who built it, fed it, and kept it running.

Two other important categories figured in my father's scheme of things. There were dumb people and smart ones: a distinction which had nothing to do with class or formal education, the dumb being simply all those who were taken in by the phonies. In his view, dumbness was rampant, and seemed to increase in proportion to the distance from Butte, where at least a certain hard-bodied irreverence leavened the atmosphere. The best prophylactic was to study and learn all you could, however you could, and, as he adjured me over and over: always ask *why*.

Finally, there were the rich and the poor. While poverty was not seen as an automatic virtue—my parents struggled mightily to escape it—wealth always carried a presumption of malfeasance. I was instructed that, in the presence of the rich, it was wise to keep one's hand on one's wallet. "Well," my father fairly growled, "how do you think they got their money in the first place?"

It was my mother who translated these lessons into practical politics. A miner's daughter herself, she offered two overarching rules for comportment: never vote Republican and never cross a union picket line. The pinnacle of her activist career came in 1964, when she attended the Democratic Convention as an alternate delegate and joined the sit-in staged by civil rights leaders and the Mississippi Freedom Democratic Party. This was not the action of a "guilt-ridden" white liberal. She classified racial prejudice along with superstition and other manifestations of backward thinking, like organized religion and overcooked vegetables. The worst thing she could find to say about a certain in-law was that he was a Republican and a church-goer, though when I investigated these charges later in life, I was relieved to find them baseless.

My mother and father, it should be explained, were hardly rebels. The values they imparted to me had been "traditional" for at least a generation before my parents came along. According to my father, the first great steps out of mental passivity had been taken by his maternal grandparents, John Howes and Mamie O'Laughlin Howes, sometime late in the last century. You might think their rebellions small stuff, but they provided our family with its "myth of origins" and a certain standard to uphold.

15   I knew little about Mamie O'Laughlin except that she was raised as a Catholic and ended up in western Montana sometime in the 1880s. Her father, very likely, was one of those itinerant breadwinners who went west to prospect and settled for mining. At any rate, the story begins when her father lay dying, and Mamie dutifully sent to the next town for a priest. The message came back that the priest would come only if twenty-five dollars was sent in advance. This being the

West at its wildest, he may have been justified in avoiding house calls. But not in the price, which was probably more cash than my great-grandmother had ever had at one time. It was on account of its greed that the church lost the souls of Mamie O'Laughlin and all of her descendents, right down to the present time. Futhermore, whether out of filial deference or natural intelligence, most of us have continued to avoid organized religion, secret societies, astrology, and New Age adventures in spiritualism.

As the story continues, Mamie O'Laughlin herself lay dying a few years later. She was only thirty-one, the mother of three small children, one of them an infant whose birth, apparently, led to a mortal attack of pneumonia. This time, a priest appeared unsummoned. Because she was too weak to hold the crucifix, he placed it on her chest and proceeded to administer the last rites. But Mamie was not dead yet. She pulled herself together at the last moment, flung the crucifix across the room, fell back, and died.

This was my great-grandmother. Her husband, John Howes, is a figure of folkloric proportions in my memory, well known in Butte many decades ago as a powerful miner and a lethal fighter. There are many stories about John Howes, all of which point to a profound inability to accept authority in any of its manifestations, earthly or divine. As a young miner, for example, he caught the eye of the mine owner for his skill at handling horses. The boss promoted him to an aboveground driving job, which was a great career leap for the time. Then the boss committed a foolish and arrogant error. He asked John to break in a team of horses for his wife's carriage. Most people would probably be flattered by such a request, but not in Butte, and certainly not John Howes. He declared that he was no man's servant, and quit on the spot.

Like his own wife, John Howes was an atheist or, as they more likely put it at the time, a freethinker. He, too, had been raised as a Catholic—on a farm in Ontario—and he, too, had had a dramatic, though somehow less glorious, falling out with the local clergy. According to legend, he once abused his position as an altar boy by urinating, covertly of course, in the holy water. This so enhanced his enjoyment of the Easter communion service that he could not resist letting a few friends in on the secret. Soon the priest found out and young John was defrocked as an altar boy and condemned to eternal damnation.

The full weight of this transgression hit a few years later, when he became engaged to a local woman. The priest refused to marry them and forbade the young woman to marry John anywhere, on pain of excommunication. There was nothing to do but head west for the Rockies, but not before settling his score with the church. According to legend, John's last act in Ontario was to drag the priest down from his pulpit and slug him, with his brother, presumably, holding the scandalized congregation at bay.

20   I have often wondered whether my great-grandfather was caught up in the radicalism of Butte in its heyday: whether he was an admirer of Joe Hill, Big Bill Haywood, or Mary "Mother" Jones, all of whom passed through Butte to agitate, and generally left with the Pinkertons on their tails. But the record is silent on this point. All I know is one last story about him, which was told often enough to have the ring of another "traditional value."

According to my father, John Howes worked on and off in the mines after his children were grown, eventually saving enough to buy a small plot of land and retire to farming. This was his dream, anyway, and a powerful one it must have been for a man who had spent so much of his life underground in the dark. So he loaded up a horse-drawn cart with all his money and belongings and headed downhill, toward Montana's eastern plains. But along the way he came to an Indian woman walking with a baby in her arms. He offered her a lift and ascertained, pretty

easily, that she was destitute. So he gave her his money, all of it, turned the horse around, and went back to the mines.

Far be it from me to interpret this gesture for my great-grandfather, whom I knew only as a whiskery, sweat-smelling, but straight-backed old man in his eighties. Perhaps he was enacting his own uncompromising version of Christian virtue, even atoning a little for his youthful offenses to the faithful. But at another level I like to think that this was one more gesture of defiance of the mine owners who doled out their own dollars so grudgingly—a way of saying, perhaps, that whatever they had to offer, he didn't really need all that much.

So these were the values, sanctified by tradition and family loyalty, that I brought with me to adulthood. Through much of my growing-up, I thought of them as some mutant strain of Americanism, an idiosyncracy which seemed to grow rarer as we clambered into the middle class. Only in the sixties did I begin to learn that my family's militant skepticism and oddball rebelliousness were part of a much larger stream of American dissent. I discovered feminism, the antiwar movement, the civil rights movement. I learned that millions of Americans, before me and around me, were "smart" enough, in my father's terms, to have asked "Why?"—and, beyond that, the far more radical question, "Why not?"

These are also the values I brought into the Reagan-Bush era, when all the dangers I had been alerted to as a child were suddenly realized. The "phonies" came to power on the strength, aptly enough, of a professional actor's finest performance. The "dumb" were being led and abetted by low-life preachers and intellectuals with expensively squandered educations. And the rich, as my father predicted, used the occasion to dip deep into the wallets of the desperate and the distracted.

It's been hard times for a traditionalist 25 of my persuasion. Long-standing moral values—usually claimed as "Judeo-Christian" but actually of much broader lineage—were summarily tossed, along with most familiar forms of logic. We were told, at one time or another, by the president or his henchpersons, that trees cause pollution, that welfare causes poverty, and that a bomber designed for mass destruction may be aptly named the *Peacemaker*. "Terrorism" replaced missing children to become our national bugaboo and—simultaneously—one of our most potent instruments of foreign policy. At home, the poor and the middle class were shaken down, and their loose change funneled blithely upwards to the already overfed.

Greed, the ancient lubricant of commerce, was declared a wholesome stimulant. Nancy Reagan observed the deep recession of '82 and '83 by redecorating the White House, and continued with this Marie Antoinette theme while advising the underprivileged, the alienated, and the addicted to "say no." Young people, mindful of their elders' Wall Street capers, abandoned the study of useful things for finance banking and other occupations derived, ultimately, from three-card monte. While the poor donned plastic outerware and cardboard coverings, the affluent ran nearly naked through the streets, working off power meals of goat cheese, walnut oil, and crème fraîche.

Religion, which even I had hoped would provide a calming influence and reminder of mortal folly, decided to join the fun. In an upsurge of piety, millions of Americans threw their souls and their savings into evangelical empires designed on the principle of pyramid scams. Even the sleazy downfall of our telemessiahs—caught masturbating in the company of ten-dollar prostitutes or fornicating in their Christian theme parks—did not discourage the faithful. The unhappily pregnant were mobbed as "baby-killers"; sexual nonconformists—gay and lesbian—were denounced as "child molesters"; atheists found themselves lumped with "Satanists," Communists, and consumers of human flesh.

Yet somehow, despite it all, a trickle of dissent continued. There were homeless people who refused to be shelved in mental hospitals for the crime of poverty, strikers who refused to join the celebration of unions in faraway countries and scabs at home, women who insisted that their lives be valued above those of accidental embryos, parents who packed up their babies and marched for peace, students who protested the ongoing inversion of normal, nursery-school-level values in the name of a more habitable world.

I am proud to add my voice to all these. For dissent is also a "traditional value," and in a republic founded by revolution, a more deeply native one than smug-faced conservatism can ever be. Feminism was practically invented here, and ought to be regarded as one of our proudest exports to the world. Likewise, it tickles my sense of patriotism that Third World insurgents have often borrowed the ideas of our own African-American movement. And in what ought to be a source of shame to some and pride to others, our history of labor struggle is one of the hardest-fought and bloodiest in the world.

No matter that patriotism is too often the 30 refuge of scoundrels. Dissent, rebellion, and all-around hell-raising remain the true duty of patriots.

READING AND THINKING

1. How would you characterize the tone of the first three paragraphs of Ehrenreich's essay? Why does she use quotation marks around certain words, such as "traditions," "traditional values," "flag," and "family"? What is the effect of those quotation marks?

2. Why does Ehrenreich introduce her parents into her essay? How does she characterize them? What has she learned from them? Why does she describe her great-grandparents? What is her attitude toward them?

3. What is the main idea of Ehrenreich's essay? Where is it most visible?

4. Which "family values" does Ehrenreich celebrate? Which does she condemn? Why?

THINKING AND WRITING

1. Write a letter to Ehrenreich in which you support or refute her argument, siding with the values she celebrates, dissenting from her views, or perhaps doing a little of both.

2. Define, illustrate, and provide reasons for your set of "family values."

3. What specifically has Ehrenreich learned from her parents and her grandparents?

IT'S ALL POLITICS:
AN OCCASION FOR WRITING

Barbara Ehrenreich writes about the importance of political activism in her family. Her family is nothing if not political. The following Occasion invites you to examine the politics of your own family as well as to consider the way politics has been central in the lives of other families.

PREPARING TO WRITE: OCCASIONS TO THINK ABOUT WHAT YOU SEE

1. Examine each of these cartoons and describe the politics implied in each. How are the parents portrayed in each cartoon?

2. What political parties are mentioned in each cartoon? How are the political parties portrayed in each cartoon?

MOVING TOWARD ESSAY: OCCASIONS TO ANALYZE AND REFLECT

1. Describe the political leanings, if any, of your family, including, if possible, the political inclinations of your parents, grandparents, and siblings captured in a single scene or story you retell. Go on to explain to what extent your family has influenced your political choices and your political leanings.

2. What do you think of husbands and wives who have opposite political beliefs? Consider, for example, the political couple James Carville and Mary Matalin, he a Democrat and she a Republican. In your opinion, to what extent are such differences a significant issue in a marriage or a serious relationship?

"THEY WERE IDENTICAL TWINS UNTIL JIM JOINED THE ARMY AND JOHN JOINED THE PEACE CORPS."

"Someday, son, all this and more will be yours if you remember to always support the Republican party."

WRITING THOUGHTFULLY: OCCASIONS FOR IDEAS AND ESSAYS

1. How else is the word *politics* used among families or groups of people? Does it always involve government or power? In an essay, attempt to define *politics* in terms of your own family in whatever way seems the most appropriate to your experiences. Use the scene you crafted in the previous exercises as part of your essay, or add others that make your definition stronger.

© JIM YOUNG/Reuters/Corbis

2. Consider how politicians use family values and the value of family life to define and portray themselves. What does this image of 2004 Democratic Vice-Presidential nominee John Edwards and his family say about his views on family? Consider the details of the image and what each contributes to the larger message of the image. What other examples from current or recent political campaigns reveal this aspect of the family/politics connection? Write an essay in which you discuss the "political family" using Ehrenreich, anything presented to you in this Occasion, or material you find as evidence.

CREATING OCCASIONS

1. Examine other instances in which "politics" emerge—for example, in the workplace or at school. Don't limit your thinking to politics in the governmental sense. How have these issues come about? How might they be resolved? How have they affected relationships? In your analysis, think about how what you have found could benefit a family dealing with politics.

FAMILY STORIES

Every family has its share of stories. Often, at family holiday gatherings, stories claim center stage, both new stories of recent events happening throughout a family and older, familiar, classic stories remembered and repeated almost ritualistically at family gatherings.

Family stories center on people, places, and events of special interest to the family. Each family has its central characters who play their roles in the family drama—the eccentric aunt or uncle, the rich relation, the accomplished youngster, the promising or troubled adolescent, the successful or struggling young married couple, to name a few. And though every family's drama and dynamics bear their own peculiar stamp and style, common themes and situations recur.

Family stories that focus on relationships between parents and children are paramount both in frequency and in importance. We find stories of conflict and continuity, of the struggle by the young to assert their independence while their parents try to delay that independence and maintain authority and control. We find stories of the young leaving home to create their own new and independent lives, while negotiating a balancing act of breaking free of old patterns and traditions and maintaining family ties to those same patterns and traditions.

We not only recall our family stories, but we also embellish them, adding to and shaping them to better remember them and highlight their drama and their meaning. David Sedaris does this in his essay "Cyclops," exaggerating some of his father's traits to better convey an impression of the man. We remember actual events we ourselves experienced and we remember having heard of events from other family members. Some of our family stories we receive second or third hand. Others we experience directly. All, however, undergo the shaping hand of memory and form. This is certainly the case with bell hooks's essay, "Inspired Eccentricity," in which she hears stories of her grandparents from her parents, and then links stories about both generations in her essay. It is also the case with Maxine Hong Kingston's "No Name Woman," a story about a rebellious aunt who comes to grief and whose story was kept secret because of its unsavory details.

David Sedaris (b. 1956)

David Sedaris is a humorist, essayist, and radio commentator who has written plays as well as prose. He was born and grew up in Raleigh, North Carolina; he has also lived in France and in London. Sedaris was named "Humorist of the Year" by *Time* magazine in 2001 and received the Thurber Prize for American Humor. A contributor to *This American Life* of National Public Radio, Sedaris is the author of a number of books, including *Barrel Fever: Stories and Essays* (1994); *The SantaLand Diaries and Season's Greetings: Two Plays* (1998); *Me Talk Pretty One Day* (2000); and *Naked* (1997), an autobiographical/fictional work from which "Cyclops" has been taken. His most recent book is *Dress Your Family in Corduroy and Denim* (2004).

CYCLOPS

In "Cyclops," a quasi-autobiographical essay about Sedaris's family, in particular his father, the author conveys something of his father's excessive fear that catastrophes are ready and waiting to happen to his family. Sedaris creates a humorous portrait of his father by using hyperbole, or exaggeration, as a rhetorical strategy.

1   When he was young my father shot out his best friend's eye with a BB gun. That is what he told us. "One foolish moment and, Jesus, if I could take it back, I would." He winced, shaking his fist as if it held a rattle. "It eats me alive," he said. "I mean to tell you that it absolutely tears me apart."

On one of our summer visits to his hometown, my father took us to meet this guy, a shoe salesman whose milky pupil hugged the corner of his mangled socket. I watched the two men shake hands and turned away, sickened and ashamed by what my father had done.

Our next-door neighbor received a BB gun for his twelfth birthday and accepted it as a personal challenge to stalk and maim any living creature: sunbathing cats, sparrows, slugs, and squirrels—if it moved, he shot it. I thought this was an excellent idea, but every time I raised the gun to my shoulder, I saw my father's half-blind friend stumbling forth with an armload of Capezios. What would it be like to live with that sort of guilt? How could my father look himself in the mirror without throwing up?

While watching television one afternoon my sister Tiffany stabbed me in the eye with a freshly sharpened pencil. The blood was copious, and I rode to the hospital knowing that if I was blinded, my sister would be my slave for the rest of her life. Never for one moment would I let her forget what she'd done to me. There would be no swinging cocktail parties in her future, no poolside barbeques or episodes of carefree laughter, not one moment of joy—I would make sure of that. I'd planned my vengeance so thoroughly that I was almost disappointed when the doctor announced that this was nothing but a minor puncture wound, located not on but beneath the eye.

5   "Take a look at your brother's face," my father said, pointing to my Band-Aid. "You could have blinded him for life! Your own brother, a. Cyclops, is that what you want?" Tiffany's suffering eased my pain for an hour or two, but then I began to feel sorry for her. "Every time you reach for a pencil, I want you to think about what you've done to your brother," my father said. "I want you to get on your knees and beg him to forgive you."

There are only so many times a person can apologize before it becomes annoying. I lost interest long before the bandage was removed, but not my father. By the time he was finished, Tiffany couldn't lift a dull crayon without breaking into tears. Her pretty, sun-tanned face assumed the characteristics of a wrinkled, grease-stained bag. Six years old and the girl was broken.

Danger was everywhere and it was our father's lifelong duty to warn us; attending the country club's Fourth of July celebration, we were told how one of his Navy buddies had been disfigured for life when a cherry bomb exploded in his lap. "Blew his balls right off the map," he said. "Take a second and imagine what that must have felt like!" Racing to the farthest edge of the golf course, I watched the remainder of the display with my hands be-tween my legs.

Fireworks were hazardous, but thunder-storms were even worse. "I had a friend, used to be a very bright, good-looking guy. He was on top of the world until the day he got struck by lightning. It caught him right between the eyes while he was trout fishing and cooked his brain just like you'd roast a chicken. Now he's got a metal plate in his forehead and can't even chew his own food; everything has to be put in a blender and taken through a straw."

If the lightning was going to get me, it would have to penetrate walls. At the first hint of a storm I ran to the basement, crouch-ing beneath a table and covering my head with a blanket. Those who watched from their front porches were fools. "The lightning can be attracted by a wedding ring, even the fill-ings in your teeth," my father said. "The mo-ment you let down your guard is guaranteed to be the day it strikes."

10   In junior high I signed up for shop class, and our first assignment was to build a nap-kin holder. "You're not going to be using a table saw, are you?" my father asked. "I knew a guy, a kid about your size, who was using a table saw when the blade came loose, flew out of the machine, and sliced his face right in half." Using his index finger, my father drew an imaginary line from his forehead to his chin. "The guy survived, but nobody wanted anything to do with him. He turned into an alcoholic and wound up marrying a Chinese woman he'd ordered through a catalog. Think about it." I did.

My napkin holder was made from found boards and, once finished, weighed in at close to seven pounds. My bookshelves were even worse. "The problem with a hammer," I was told, "is that the head can fly off at any mo-ment and, boy, let me tell you, you've never imagined pain like that."

After a while we began to wonder if my fa-ther had any friends who could still tie their own shoes or breathe without the aid of a res-pirator. With the exception of the shoe sales-man, we'd never seen any of these people, only heard about them whenever one of us at-tempted to deep-fry chicken or operate the garbage disposal. "I've got a friend who buys a set of gloves and throws one of them away. He lost his right hand doing the exact same thing you're doing. He had his arm down the drain when the cat rubbed against the switch to the garbage disposal. Now he's wearing clip-on ties and having the restaurant waiters cut up his steak. Is that the kind of life you want for yourself?"

He allowed me to mow the lawn only be-cause he was too cheap to pay a landscaper and didn't want to do it himself. "What hap-pened," he said, "is that the guy slipped, prob-ably on a pile of crap, and his leg got caught up in the blade. He found his foot, carried it to the hospital, but it was too late to sew it back on. Can you imagine that? The guy drove fif-teen, twenty miles with his foot in his lap."

Regardless of the heat, I mowed the lawn wearing long pants, knee-high boots, a football helmet, and a pair of goggles. Before starting, I scouted the lawn for rocks and dog feces, slowly combing the area as if it were mined. Even then I pushed the mower haltingly, aways fear-ing that this next step might be my last.

Nothing bad ever happened, and within   15 a few years I was mowing in shorts and sneakers, thinking of the supposed friend my father had used to illustrate his warning. I imagined this man jumping into his car and pressing on the accelerator with his bloody stump, a warm foot settled in his lap like a sleeping puppy. Why hadn't he just called an ambulance to come pick him up? How, in his shock, had he thought to search the weeds for his missing foot? It didn't add up.

I waited until my junior year of high school to sign up for driver's education. Before taking to the road, we sat in the darkened classroom, watching films that might have been written and directed by my father. *Don't do it,* I thought, watching the prom couple attempt to pass a lumbering dump truck. Every excursion ended with the young driver wrapped around a telephone pole or burned beyond recognition, the camera focusing in on a bloody corsage littering the side of the highway.

I drove a car no faster than I pushed the lawn mower, and the instructor soon lost patience.

"That license is going to be your death warrant," my father said on the day I received my learner's permit. "You're going to get out there and kill someone, and the guilt is going to tear your heart out."

The thought of killing myself had slowed me down to five miles per hour. The thought of killing someone else stopped me completely.

20 My mother had picked me up from a play rehearsal one rainy night when, cresting a hill, the car ran over something it shouldn't have. This was not a brick or a misplaced boot but some living creature that cried out when caught beneath the tire. "Shit," my mother whispered, tapping her forehead against the steering wheel. "Shit, shit shit." We covered our heads against the rain and searched the darkened street until we found an orange cat coughing up blood into the gutter.

"You killed me," the cat said, pointing at my mother with its flattened paw. "Here I had

so much to live for, but now it's over, my whole life wiped out just like that." The cat wheezed rhythmically before closing its eyes and dying.

"Shit," my mother repeated. We walked door to door until finding the cat's owner, a kind and understanding woman whose young daughter shared none of her qualities. "You killed my cat," she screamed, sobbing into her mother's skirt. "You're mean and you're ugly and you killed my cat."

"She's at that age," the woman said, stroking the child's hair.

My mother felt bad enough without the lecture that awaited her at home. "That could have been a child!" my father shouted. "Think about that the next time you're tearing down the street searching for kicks." He made it sound as if my mother ran down cats for sport. "You think this is funny," he said, "but we'll see who's laughing when you're behind bars awaiting trial for manslaughter." I received a variation on the same speech after sideswiping a mailbox. Despite my mother's encouragement, I surrendered my permit and never drove again. My nerves just couldn't take it. It seemed much safer to hitchhike.

My father objected when I moved to 25 Chicago, and waged a full-fledged campaign of terror when I announced I would be moving to New York. "New York! Are you out of your mind? You might as well take a razor to your throat because, let me tell you something, those New Yorkers are going to eat you alive." He spoke of friends who had been robbed and bludgeoned by packs of roving gangs and sent me newspaper clippings detailing the tragic slayings of joggers and vacationing tourists. "This could be you!" he wrote in the margins.

I'd lived in New York for several years when, traveling upstate to attend a wedding, I stopped in my father's hometown. We hadn't visited since our grandmother moved in with us, and I felt my way around with a creepy familiarity. I found my father's old apartment, but his friend's shoe store had been converted into a pool hall. When I called to tell him about it, my father said, "What shoe store? What are you talking about?"

"The place where your friend worked," I said. "You remember, the guy whose eye you shot out."

"Frank?" he said. "I didn't shoot his eye out; the guy was born that way."

My father visits me now in New York. We'll walk through Washington Square, where he'll yell, "Get a look at the ugly mug on that one!" referring to a three-hundred-pound biker with grinning skulls tattooed like a choker around his neck. A young man in Central Park is photographing his girlfriend, and my father races to throw himself into the picture. "All right, sweetheart," he says, placing his arm around the startled victim, "it's time to get comfortable." I cower as he marches into posh grocery stores, demanding to speak to the manager. "Back home I can get this exact same cantaloupe for less than half this price," he says. The managers invariably suggest that he do just that. He screams at waiters and cuts in line at tony restaurants. "I have a friend," I tell him, "who lost his right arm snapping his fingers at a waiter."

"Oh, you kids," he says. "Not a one of you 30 has got so much as a teaspoon of gumption. I don't know where you got it from, but in the end, it's going to kill you."

READING AND THINKING

1. How does Sedaris open this autobiographical essay? What impression of Sedaris's father does this opening story create? How does Sedaris himself react to his father's accidental shooting of a friend?

2. Why do you think Sedaris includes the story of his sister's stabbing him in the eye with a pencil? What comic effects does he draw from this family story?

3. Where does Sedaris begin to draw out a generalization about his father's horror stories? What do those stories have in common? To what use does Sedaris's father put them? With what effects?

4. To what extent do you find "Cyclops" funny? How do you think Sedaris wants us to respond to his father's stories—and to the essay as a whole?

THINKING AND WRITING

1. Identify places in the essay where you think Sedaris is stretching the truth—where he exaggerates, or perhaps invents details to embellish his father's stories.

2. Write a paragraph in which you describe and characterize Sedaris's father. Use examples from the essay to illustrate and support your characterization.

3. Write a short piece in which you reflect on the reasons writers use humor. Consider the example of Sedaris in "Cyclops." Explain the effects he achieves through humor.

4. Write an essay in which you tell three or four brief connected stories about a member of your family. The little stories—or anecdotes—should cumulatively paint a portrait of this family member. You may wish to use humor.

FAMOUS FAMILIES:
AN OCCASION FOR WRITING

David Sedaris tells humorous stories about his father—an ordinary man in an ordinary family. Sedaris makes his father interesting and comical by exaggerating his tendency to see catastrophe around every corner. The following Occasion invites you to consider how exaggeration enables writers and visual artists to highlight ideas and clarify truths about their subjects. It also invites you to consider why we exaggerate characteristics of our family members and what the humor contributes to the exaggerated characterizations.

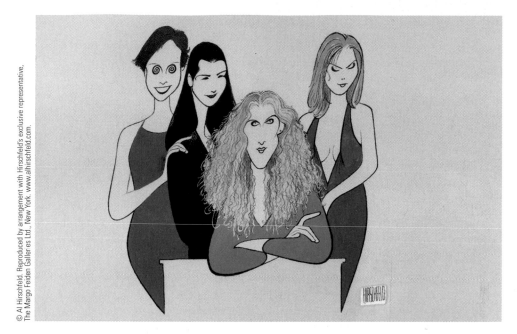

AL HIRSCHFELD, *Sex and the City*

PREPARING TO WRITE: OCCASIONS TO THINK ABOUT WHAT YOU SEE

1. Look carefully at the caricatures of television's *Seinfeld* and *Sex and the City* "families." Describe the details the artist uses to capture each of the characters he portrays. In what ways do the two groups appear like "families"?

2. Al Hirschfeld (1903–2003) was a famed caricature artist of Broadway stars and celebrities for the *New York Times* and other publications and created these two caricatures. What qualities of the television characters and personalities has Hirschfeld captured and conveyed in these images? How did he do it?

MOVING TOWARD ESSAY: OCCASIONS TO ANALYZE AND REFLECT

1. What are the benefits and what are the drawbacks of such exaggerated caricature? To what extent is such caricature a distortion of the character being portrayed? To what extent does caricature get at the essence of a character?

2. What writers do you know of who use caricature or other forms of exaggeration? Consider how comic writers who also have a serious purpose, such as Charles Dickens and Mark Twain, use humor and exaggeration in their work to convey attitudes, perspectives, and ideas. Select a story or a chapter from a novel that uses humor or exaggeration to portray characters. Identify ways that the author uses humor, caricature, or other forms of exaggeration to convey character and describe incidents.

WRITING THOUGHTFULLY: IDEA AND ESSAY

1. Write an essay in which you analyze the techniques used by Al Hirschfeld (or another caricaturist) to reveal character. Compare Hirschfeld's use of caricature with that of David Levine or another caricature artist.

2. Think about a time when you've talked about your family with others and you have intentionally exaggerated a family member's personality or physical trait. Analyze the effects of your exaggeration and why you used it in your description. In an essay, describe this moment and use what you've discovered through Sedaris's essay and Hirschfeld's caricatures as evidence to explore the function of exaggeration in families.

3. Write a character sketch—a description of a character "type"—in which you exaggerate the characteristics of the character type you are describing. Possible topics include the weight lifter, the beauty pageant contestant, the librarian, the company man, the dentist, the disco habitué, or the desperate housewife.

4. Bill Cosby is a well-known celebrity and comedian who frequently uses exaggeration in his comedy, especially when discussing children and families. Consider viewing some of Cosby's comedy sketches to see how he employs exaggeration and compare that with Sedaris's and other authors', like Dickens or Twain, techniques. Connect your analysis with the following quote by Bill Cosby:

   > Through humor, you can soften some of the worst blows that life delivers. And once you find laughter, no matter how painful your situation might be, you can survive it.

CREATING OCCASIONS

1. Films and television shows also use exaggeration that we as viewers outright recognize as fantastical (*The Simpsons* or *The Family Guy* scenes frequently do this). Examine the effects on the viewer of such exaggeration from any film or television show of your choice.

bell hooks (b. 1952)

bell hooks was born Gloria Jean Watkins but took the name of her great-grandmother, who was known for saying what was on her mind. hooks is a professor and a writer, largely on social and feminist issues, with a focus on race, class, and gender. Her books include *Ain't I a Woman: Black Women and Feminism* (1981); *Talking Back: Thinking Feminist, Thinking Black* (1989); *Yearning: Race, Gender and Cultural Politics* (1990); and *Remembered Rapture: The Writer at Work* (1999). She has taught women's studies and African American studies at Yale, Oberlin, and the City College of New York.

INSPIRED ECCENTRICITY

In "Inspired Eccentricity," first published in 1996, hooks focuses on her grandparents but includes anecdotes about her parents as well. hooks focuses on what she learned from her ancestors and how she is living the lessons she learned from them.

1 There are family members you try to forget and ones that you always remember, that you can't stop talking about. They may be dead— long gone—but their presence lingers and you have to share who they were and who they still are with the world. You want everyone to know them as you did, to love them as you did.

All my life I have remained enchanted by the presence of my mother's parents, Sarah and Gus Oldham. When I was a child they were already old. I did not see that then, though. They were Baba and Daddy Gus, together for more than seventy years at the time of his death. Their marriage fascinated me. They were strangers and lovers – two eccentrics who created their own world.

More than any other family members, together they gave me a worldview that sustained me during a difficult and painful childhood. Reflecting on the eclectic writer I have become, I see in myself a mixture of these two very different but equally powerful figures from my childhood. Baba was tall, her skin so white and her hair so jet black and straight that she could have easily "passed" denying all traces of blackness. Yet the man she married was short and dark, and sometimes his skin looked like the color of soot from burning coal. In our childhood the fireplaces burned coal. It was bright heat, luminous and fierce. If you got too close it could burn you.

Together Baba and Daddy Gus generated a hot heat. He was a man of few words, deeply committed to silence – so much so that it was like a religion to him. When he spoke you could hardly hear what he said. Baba was just the opposite. Smoking an abundance of cigarettes a day, she talked endlessly. She preached. She yelled. She fussed. Often her vitriolic rage would heap itself on Daddy Gus, who would sit calmly in his chair by the stove, as calm and still as the Buddha sits. And when he had enough of her words, he would reach for his hat and walk.

5 Neither Baba nor Daddy Gus drove cars. Rarely did they ride in them. They preferred walking. And even then their styles were different. He moved slow, as though carrying a great weight; she with her tall, lean, boyish frame moved swiftly, as though there was never time to waste. Their one agreed-upon passion was fishing. Though they did not do even that together. They lived close but they created separate worlds.

In a big two-story wood frame house with lots of rooms they constructed a world that could contain their separate and distinct personalities. As children one of the first things we noticed about our grandparents was that they did not sleep in the same room. This arrangement was contrary to everything we understood about marriage. While Mama never wanted to talk about their separate worlds, Baba would tell you in a minute that Daddy Gus was nasty, that he smelled like tobacco juice, that he did not wash enough, that there was no way she would want him in her bed. And while he would say nothing nasty about her, he would merely say why would he want to share somebody else's bed when he could have his own bed to himself, with no one to complain about anything.

I loved my granddaddy's smells. Always, they filled my nostrils with the scent of happiness. It was sheer ecstasy for me to be allowed into his inner sanctum. His room was a small Van Gogh–like space off from the living room. There was no door. Old-fashioned curtains were the only attempt at privacy. Usually the curtains were closed. His room reeked of tobacco. There were treasures everywhere in that small room. As a younger man Daddy Gus did odd jobs, and sometimes even in his old age he would do a chore for some needy lady. As he went about his work, he would pick up found objects, scraps. All these objects would lie about his room, on the dresser, on the table near his bed. Unlike all other grownups he never cared about children looking through his things. Anything we wanted he gave to us.

Daddy Gus collected beautiful wooden cigar boxes. They held lots of the important stuff—the treasures. He had tons of little diaries that he made notes in. He gave me my first wallet, my first teeny little book to write in, my first beautiful pen, which did not write for long, but it was still a found and shared treasure. When I would lie on his bed or sit close to him, sometimes just standing near, I would feel all the pain and anxiety of my troubled childhood leave me. His spirit was calm. He gave me the unconditional love I longed for.

"Too calm," his grown-up children thought. That's why he had let this old woman rule him, my cousin BoBo would say. Even as children we knew that grown-ups felt sorry for Daddy Gus. At times his sons seemed to look upon him as not a "real man." His refusal to fight in wars was another sign to them of weakness. It was my grandfather who taught me to oppose war. They saw him as a man controlled by the whims of others, by this tall, strident, demanding woman he had married. I saw him as a man of profound beliefs, a man of integrity. When he heard their put-downs—for they talked on and on about his laziness—he merely muttered that he had no use for them. He was not gonna let anybody tell him what to do with his life.

Daddy Gus was a devout believer, a deacon at his church; he was one of the right-hand men of God. At church, everyone admired his calmness. Baba had no use for church. She liked nothing better than to tell us all the ways it was one big hypocritical place: "Why, I can find God anywhere I want to—I do not need a church." Indeed, when my grandmother died, her funeral could not take place in a church, for she had never belonged. Her refusal to attend church bothered some of her daughters, for they thought she was sinning against God, setting a bad example for the children. We were not supposed to listen when she began to damn the church and everybody in it.

Baba loved to "cuss." There was no bad word she was not willing to say. The improvisational manner in which she would string those words together was awesome. It was the goddamn sons of bitches who thought that they could fuck with her when they could just kiss her black ass. A woman of strong words and powerful metaphors, she could not read or write. She lived in the power of language. Her favorite sayings were a prelude for storytelling. It was she who told me, "Play with a puppy, he'll lick you in the mouth." When I heard this saying, I knew what was coming— a long polemic about not letting folks get too close, 'cause they will mess with you.

10

Baba loved to tell her stories. And I loved to hear them. She called me Glory. And in the midst of her storytelling she would pause to say, "Glory, are ya listenin'. Do you understand what I'm telling ya." Sometimes I would have to repeat the lessons I had learned. Sometimes I was not able to get it right and she would start again. When Mama felt I was learning too much craziness "over home" (that is what we called Baba's house), my visits were curtailed. As I moved into my teens I learned to keep to myself all the wisdom of the old ways I picked up over home.

Baba was an incredible quilt maker, but by the time I was old enough to really understand her work, to see its beauty; she was already having difficulty with her eyesight. She could not sew as much as in the old days, when her work was on everybody's bed. Unwilling to throw anything away, she loved to make crazy quilts, 'cause they allowed every scrap to be used. Although she would one day order patterns and make perfect quilts with colors that went together, she always collected scraps.

Long before I read Virginia Woolf's *A Room of One's Own* I learned from Baba that a woman needed her own space to work. She had a huge room for her quilting. Like every other space in the private world she created upstairs, it had her treasures, an endless array of hatboxes, feathers, and trunks filled with old clothes she had held on to. In room after room there were feather tick mattresses; when they were pulled back, the wooden slats of the bed were revealed, lined with exquisite hand-sewn quilts.

15   In all these trunks, in crevices and drawers were braided tobacco leaves to keep away moths and other insects. A really hot summer could make cloth sweat, and stains from tobacco juice would end up on quilts no one had ever used. When I was a young child, a quilt my grandmother had made kept me warm, was my solace and comfort. Even though Mama protested when I dragged that old

raggedy quilt from Kentucky to Stanford, I knew I needed that bit of the South, of Baba's world, to sustain me.

Like Daddy Gus, she was a woman of her word. She liked to declare with pride, "I mean what I say and I say what I mean." "Glory," she would tell me, "nobody is better than their word—if you can't keep ya word you ain't worth nothin' in this world." She would stop speaking to folk over the breaking of their word, over lies. Our mama was not given to loud speech or confrontation. I learned all those things from Baba—"to stand up and speak up" and not to "give a good goddamn" what folk who "ain't got a pot to pee in" think. My parents were concerned with their image in the world. It was pure blasphemy for Baba to teach that it did not matter what other folks thought—"Ya have to be right with yaself in ya own heart—that's all that matters." Baba taught me to listen to my heart—to follow it. From her we learned as small children to remember our dreams in the night and to share them when we awakened. They would be interpreted by her. She taught us to listen to the knowledge in dreams. Mama would say this was all nonsense, but she too was known to ask the meaning of a dream.

In their own way my grandparents were rebels, deeply committed to radical individualism. I learned how to be myself from them. Mama hated this. She thought it was important to be liked, to conform. She had hated growing up in such an eccentric, otherworldly household. This world where folks made their own wine, their own butter, their own soap; where chickens were raised, and huge gardens were grown for canning everything. This was the world Mama wanted to leave behind. She wanted store-bought things.

Baba lived in another time, a time when all things were produced in the individual household. Everything the family needed was made at home. She loved to tell me stories about learning to trap animals, to skin, to soak possum and coon in brine, to fry up a

fresh rabbit. Though a total woman of the outdoors who could shoot and trap as good as any
man, she still believed every woman should
sew—she made her first quilt as a girl. In her
world, women were as strong as men because
they had to be. She had grown up in the country and knew that country ways were the best
ways to live. Boasting about being able to do
anything that a man could do and better, this
woman who could not read or write was confident about her place in the universe.

My sense of aesthetics came from her. She
taught me to really look at things, to see underneath the surface, to see the different
shades of red in the peppers she had dried
and hung in the kitchen sunlight. The beauty
of the ordinary, the everyday, was her feast of
light. While she had no use for the treasures
in my granddaddy's world, he too taught me
to look for the living spirit in things—the
things that are cast away but still need to be
touched and cared for. Picking up a found object he would tell me its story or tell me how
he was planning to give it life again.

20   Connected in spirit but so far apart in the
life of everydayness, Baba and Daddy Gus
were rarely civil to each other. Every shared
talk begun with goodwill ended in disagreement and contestation. Everyone knew Baba
just loved to fuss. She liked a good war of
words. And she was comfortable using words
to sting and hurt, to punish. When words
would not do the job, she could reach for the
strap, a long piece of black leather that would
leave tiny imprints on the flesh.

There was no violence in Daddy Gus.
Mama shared that he had always been that
way, a calm and gentle man, full of tenderness. I remember clinging to his tenderness
when nothing I did was right in my mother's
eyes, when I was constantly punished. Baba
was not an ally. She advocated harsh punishment. She had no use for children who would
not obey. She was never ever affectionate.
When we entered her house, we gave her a
kiss in greeting and that was it. With Daddy

Gus we could cuddle, linger in his arms, give
as many kisses as desired. His arms and
heart were always open.

In the back of their house were fruit trees,
chicken coops, and gardens, and in the front
were flowers. Baba could make anything
grow. And she knew all about herbs and roots.
Her home remedies healed our childhood
sicknesses. Of course she thought it crazy for
anyone to go to a doctor when she could tell
them just what they needed. All these things
she had learned from her mother, Bell Blair
Hooks, whose name I would choose as my pen
name. Everyone agreed that I had the temperament of this great-grandmother I would
not remember. She was a sharp-tongued
woman. Or so they said. And it was believed I
had inherited my way with words from her.

Families do that. They chart psychic ge-
nealogies that often overlook what is right before our eyes. I may have inherited my great-
grandmother bell hooks's way with words, but
I learned to use those words listening to my
grandmother. I learned to be courageous by
seeing her act without fear. I learned to risk
because she was daring. Home and family
were her world. While my grandfather journeyed downtown, visited at other folks'
houses, went to church, and conducted affairs
in the world, Baba rarely left home. There
was nothing in the world she needed. Things
out there violated her spirit.

As a child I had no sense of what it would
mean to live a life, spanning so many generations, unable to read or write. To me Baba was
a woman of power. That she would have been
extraordinarily powerless in a world beyond
1200 Broad Street was a thought that never
entered my mind. I believed that she stayed
home because it was the place she liked best.
Just as Daddy Gus seemed to need to walk—
to roam.

After his death it was easier to see the 25
ways that they complemented and completed
each other. For suddenly, without him as a
silent backdrop, Baba's spirit was diminished.

Something in her was forever lonely and could not find solace. When she died, tulips, her favorite flower, surrounded her. The preacher told us that her death was not an occasion for grief, for "it is hard to live in a world where your choicest friends are gone." Daddy Gus was the companion she missed most. His presence had always been the mirror of memory. Without it there was so much that could not be shared. There was no witness.

Seeing their life together, I learned that it was possible for women and men to fashion households arranged around their own needs. Power was shared. When there was an imbalance, Baba ruled the day. It seemed utterly alien to me to learn about black women and men not making families and homes together. I had not been raised in a world of absent men. One day I knew I would fashion a life using the patterns I inherited from Baba and Daddy Gus. I keep treasures in my cigar box, which still smells after all these years. The quilt that covered me as a child remains, full of ink stains and faded colors. In my trunks are braided tobacco leaves, taken from over home. They keep evil away—keep bad spirits from crossing the threshold, like the ancestors they guard and protect.

READING AND THINKING

1. What is the purpose of the essay's opening paragraph? What would be lost if the essay had begun with the second paragraph?

2. How does hooks characterize her grandparents, Sarah, and Gus Oldham? What is special about them? How do you respond to their eccentricities?

3. Why are Sarah and Gus Oldham important to hooks? What does she learn from them? What does she draw from each of them?

4. Why does hooks also write about her mother in this piece? What is her mother's perspective on the lives of hooks's grandparents?

THINKING AND WRITING

1. Write a paragraph about each of her grandparents that sums up what hooks shows us about each of them.

2. Write a paragraph about your response to one of hooks's grandparents. Explain why you respond to Sarah or to Gus as you do.

3. Create a scene in which you characterize one or two of your grandparents, or any of your other relatives. Try in your description to convey a sense of your relative's character and personality—what made or makes that person distinctive.

4. Write a few paragraphs in which you explain what you have learned from one or more members of your family, pulling, if possible, from the scene you created in the previous exercise. You may wish to write about "negative lessons"—things to avoid—as well as positive ones.

TREASURING FAMILY: AN OCCASION FOR WRITING

In her essay, bell hooks presents a portrait of her grandparents. In the following Occasion for Writing, you are invited to consider the way two poets and one artist depict their parents. You are also invited to think about how you might portray your own parents.

Photo by Eduardo Calderone. Image provided courtesy of the Paula Cooper Gallery, New York

SOPHIE CALLE
The Birthday Ceremony (1983), 1997, gifts, text, and display case dimensions of case: 67h × 33 1/2 w × 18 3/4 d

Robert Mezey
My Mother

My mother writes from Trenton,
a comedian to the bone
but underneath, serious
and all heart. "Honey," she says,
"be a mensch and Mary too,
it's no good to worry, you
are doing the best you can
your Dad and everyone
thinks you turned out very well
as long as you pay your bills
nobody can say a word
you can tell them to drop dead
so save a dollar it can't
hurt—remember Frank you went
to highschool with? he still lives
with his wife's mother, his wife
works while he writes his books and
did he ever sell a one
the four kids run around naked
36 and he's never had,
you'll forgive my expression
even a pot to piss in

or a window to throw it,
such a smart boy he couldn't
read the footprints on the wall
honey you think you know all
the answers you don't, please try
to put some money away
believe me it wouldn't hurt
artist shmartist life's too short
for that kind of, forgive me,
horseshit, I know what you want
better than you, all that counts
is to make a good living
and the best of everything,
as Sholem Aleichem said
he was a great writer did
you ever read his books dear,
you should make what he makes a year
anyway he says some place
Poverty is no disgrace
but it's no honor either
    that's what I say,
        love,
            Mother"   *1970*

Robert Hayden
Those Winter Sundays

Sundays too my father got up early
and put his clothes on in the blueblack cold,
then with cracked hands that ached
from labor in the weekday weather made
banked fires blaze. No one ever thanked him.

I'd wake and hear the cold splintering, breaking.
When the rooms were warm, he'd call,
and slowly I would rise and dress,
fearing the chronic angers of that house,

Speaking indifferently to him,
who had driven out the cold
and polished my good shoes as well.
What did I know, what did I know
of love's austere and lonely offices?

PREPARING TO WRITE: OCCASIONS TO THINK ABOUT WHAT YOU SEE

1. Make a list of the items you find in Sophie Calle's *The Birthday Ceremony*. Describe how each item is portrayed.

2. Explain the meaning of each of the items in Calle's artwork. How do you understand the image overall? What does it say to you?

3. Identify three words or phrases in each poem that characterize the parent. How is the speaker's attitude toward the parent described? What can you infer about the relationship between the speaker and parent in each poem?

4. What do you notice about the language of each poem? What is noteworthy about its sentences?

MOVING TOWARD ESSAY: OCCASIONS TO ANALYZE AND REFLECT

1. Artist Sophie Calle created *The Birthday Ceremony;* frequently in her artwork Calle examines personal treasures to display in a public fashion. Imagine your own personal "treasures" and how to anyone else the special meaning is lost or not evident. Describe a sentimental object's importance to you—draw a verbal picture of it and then explain in a few sentences exactly why this object is important to you.

2. How are Calle's *The Birthday Ceremony* and Mezey's and Hayden's poems related? Do you think anything personal can accurately be portrayed publicly?

3. How does hooks comment on the nature of personal versus private treasures or memories in her essay? How do her views build or comment on what you have seen in the poems and Calle's artwork?

WRITING THOUGHTFULLY: OCCASIONS FOR IDEAS AND ESSAYS

1. Write an interpretation of Mezey's or Hayden's poem, with an emphasis on how the parent is portrayed and how the poet conveys the type of relationship the speaker has or has had with the parent. Provide evidence in the form of textual details to support your interpretation. In what ways do you think the memory has been, or could have been, altered?

2. Do some role playing by writing a letter in response to the mother in Mezey's poem or to the father in Hayden's poem.

3. Write an interpretation of Calle's *The Birthday Ceremony.* Consider the extent to which it triggers memories of your own family. What items remind you of your family and why? Consider the larger question of the extent to which personal treasures can be translated into memories and how treasures can transcend the family that originated them. Use hooks's essay as evidence in your own essay.

4. Find a picture of one of your parents or grandparents that reveals something essential about that person. Explain in a paragraph what the picture reveals and how it reveals what it does. Consider the extent to which this picture and what it represents for you can speak to others and become a meaningful trigger for their own family pictures, stories, and memories.

CREATING OCCASIONS

1. Find two additional poems about mothers and/or fathers (or a mother and a father). Write a set of questions for the poems that invites comparison between them and that includes some comparisons with Mezey's and Hayden's poems. Research the relationship the poet had with his or her parent and compare that with how the poet has chosen to portray the relationship or the memory of that relationship.

Maxine Hong Kingston (b. 1940)

Maxine Hong Kingston grew up in Stockton, California, the daughter of Chinese immigrants in a close-knit Asian community. Her first language was Chinese. After graduating from the University of California, Berkeley, she taught high school English in California and Hawaii. Kingston's first two books, *The Woman Warrior: Memoirs of a Girlhood among Ghosts* (1976) and *China Men* (1980), focused, respectively, on stories of real and legendary women and men in Chinese culture. Kingston has also published a novel, *Tripmaster Monkey: His Fake Book* (1988) and *Hawai'i One Summer* (1987), essays on life in Hawai'i. In 1997 she was awarded a National Humanities Medal by President Clinton.

NO NAME WOMAN

In "No Name Woman," Kingston describes an aunt who broke a number of taboos, the most important of which was having sex and conceiving and bearing a child out of wedlock. In the course of describing her aunt's tragic life, Kingston dramatizes the cultural conflicts that exist between Chinese and Chinese-American societies.

1   "You must not tell anyone," my mother said, "what I am about to tell you. In China your father had a sister who killed herself. She jumped into the family well. We say that your father has all brothers because it is as if she had never been born.

"In 1924 just a few days after our village celebrated seventeen hurry-up weddings—to make sure that every young man who went 'out on the road' would responsibly come home—your father and his brothers and your grandfather and his brothers and your aunt's new husband sailed for America, the Gold Mountain. It was your grandfather's last trip. Those lucky enough to get contracts waved good-bye from the decks. They fed and guarded the stowaways and helped them off in Cuba, New York, Bali, Hawaii. 'We'll meet in California next year,' they said. All of them sent money home.

"I remember looking at your aunt one day when she and I were dressing; I had not noticed before that she had such a protruding melon of a stomach. But I did not think, 'She's pregnant,' until she began to look like other pregnant women, her shirt pulling and the white tops of her black pants showing. She could not have been pregnant, you see, because her husband had been gone for years.

No one said anything. We did not discuss it. In early summer she was ready to have the child, long after the time when it could have been possible.

"The village had also been counting. On the night the baby was to be born the villagers raided our house. Some were crying. Like a great saw, teeth strung with lights, files of people walked zigzag across our land, tearing the rice. Their lanterns doubled in the disturbed black water, which drained away through the broken bunds. As the villagers closed in, we could see that some of them, probably men and women we knew well, wore white masks. The people with long hair hung it over their faces. Women with short hair made it stand up on end. Some had tied white bands around their foreheads, arms, and legs.

"At first they threw mud and rocks at the   5 house. Then they threw eggs and began slaughtering our stock. We could hear the animals scream their deaths—the roosters, the pigs, a last great roar from the ox. Familiar wild heads flared in our night windows; the villagers encircled us. Some of the faces stopped to peer at us, their eyes rushing like searchlights. The hands flattened against the panes, framed heads, and left red prints.

"The villagers broke in the front and the back doors at the same time, even though we had not locked the doors against them. Their knives dripped with the blood of our animals. They smeared blood on the doors and walls. One woman swung a chicken, whose throat she had slit, splattering blood in red arcs about her. We stood together in the middle of our house, in the family hall with the pictures and tables of the ancestors around us, and looked straight ahead.

"At that time the house had only two wings. When the men came back we would build two more to enclose our courtyard and a third one to begin a second courtyard. The villagers pushed through both wings, even your grandparents' rooms, to find your aunt's, which was also mine until the men returned. From this room a new wing for one of the younger families would grow. They ripped up her clothes and shoes and broke her combs, grinding them underfoot. They tore her work from the loom. They scattered the cooking fire and rolled the new weaving in it. We could hear them in the kitchen breaking our bowls and banging the pots. They overturned the great waist-high earthenware jugs; duck eggs, pickled fruits, vegetables burst out and mixed in acrid torrents. The old woman from the next field swept a broom through the air and loosed the spirits-of-the-broom over our heads. 'Pig.' 'Ghost.' 'Pig,' they sobbed and scolded while they ruined our house.

"When they left, they took sugar and oranges to bless themselves. They cut pieces from the dead animals. Some of them took bowls that were not broken and clothes that were not torn. Afterward we swept up the rice and sewed it back up into sacks. But the smells from the spilled preserves lasted. Your aunt gave birth in the pigsty that night. The next morning when I went up for the water, I found her and the baby plugging up the family well.

"Don't let your father know that I told you. He denies her. Now that you have started to menstruate, what happened to her could happen to you. Don't humiliate us. You wouldn't like to be forgotten as if you had never been born. The villagers are watchful."

Whenever she had to warn us about life, my mother told stories that ran like this one, a story to grow up on. She tested our strength to establish realities. Those in the emigrant generations who could not reassert brute survival died young and far from home. Those of us in the first American generations have had to figure out how the invisible world the emigrants built around our childhoods fit in solid America.

The emigrants confused the gods by diverting their curses, misleading them with crooked streets and false names. They must try to confuse their offspring as well, who, I suppose, threaten them in similar ways—always trying to get things straight, always trying to name the unspeakable. The Chinese I know hide their names; sojourners take new names when their lives change and guard their real names with silence.

Chinese-Americans, when you try to understand what things in you are Chinese, how do you separate what is peculiar to childhood, to poverty, insanities, one family, your mother who marked your growing with stories, from what is Chinese? What is Chinese tradition and what is the movies?

If I want to learn what clothes my aunt wore, whether flashy or ordinary, I would have to begin, "Remember Father's drowned-in-the-well sister?" I cannot ask that. My mother has told me once and for all the useful parts. She will add nothing unless powered by Necessity, a riverbank that guides her life. She plants vegetable gardens rather than lawns; she carries the odd-shaped tomatoes home from the fields and eats food left for the gods.

Whenever we did frivolous things, we used up energy; we flew high kites. We children came up off the ground over the melting cones our parents brought home from work and the American movie on New Year's Day—*Oh, You Beautiful Doll* with Betty Grable one year, and *She Wore a Yellow Ribbon* with John Wayne another year. After the one carnival ride each, we paid in guilt; our tired father counted his change on the dark walk home.

15   Adultery is extravagance. Could people who hatch their own chicks and eat the embryos and the heads for delicacies and boil the feet in vinegar for party food, leaving only the gravel, eating even the gizzard lining—could such people engender a prodigal aunt? To be a woman, to have a daughter in starvation time was a waste enough. My aunt could not have been the lone romantic who gave up everything for sex. Women in the old China did not choose. Some man had commanded her to lie with him and be his secret evil. I wonder whether he masked himself when he joined the raid on her family.

Perhaps she encountered him in the fields or on the mountain where the daughters-in-law collected fuel. Or perhaps he first noticed her in the marketplace. He was not a stranger because the village housed no strangers. She had to have dealings with him other than sex. Perhaps he worked an adjoining field, or he sold her the cloth for the dress she sewed and wore. His demand must have surprised, then terrified her. She obeyed him; she always did as she was told.

When the family found a young man in the next village to be her husband, she stood tractably beside the best rooster, his proxy, and promised before they met that she would be his forever. She was lucky that he was her age and she would be the first wife, an advantage secure now. The night she first saw him, he had sex with her. Then he left for America. She had almost forgotten what he looked like. When she tried to envision him, she only saw the black and white face in the group photograph the men had had taken before leaving.

The other man was not, after all, much different from her husband. They both gave orders: she followed. "If you tell your family, I'll beat you. I'll kill you. Be here again next week." No one talked sex, ever. And she might have separated the rapes from the rest of living if only she did not have to buy her oil from him or gather wood in the same forest. I want her fear to have lasted just as long as rape lasted so that the fear could have been contained. No drawn-out fear. But women at sex hazarded birth and hence lifetimes. The fear did not stop but permeated everywhere. She told the man, "I think I'm pregnant." He organized the raid against her.

On nights when my mother and father talked about their life back home, sometimes they mentioned an "outcast table" whose business they still seemed to be settling, their voices tight. In a commensal tradition, where food is precious, the powerful older people made wrongdoers eat alone. Instead of letting them start separate new lives like the Japanese, who could become samurais and geishas, the Chinese family, faces averted but eyes glowering sideways, hung on to the offenders and fed them leftovers. My aunt must have lived in the same house as my parents and eaten at an outcast table. My mother spoke about the raid as if she had seen it, when she and my aunt, a daughter-in-law to a different household, should not have been living together at all. Daughters-in-law lived with their husbands' parents, not their own; a synonym for marriage in Chinese is "taking a daughter-in-law." Her husband's parents could have sold her, mortgaged her, stoned her. But they had sent her back to her own mother and father, a mysterious act hinting at disgraces not told me. Perhaps they had thrown her out to deflect the avengers.

20   She was the only daughter; her four brothers went with her father, husband, and uncles "out on the road" and for some years became western men. When the goods were divided among the family, three of the brothers took land, and the youngest, my father, chose an education. After my grandparents gave their

daughter away to her husband's family, they had dispensed all the adventure and all the property. They expected her alone to keep the traditional ways, which her brothers, now among the barbarians, could fumble without detection. The heavy, deep-rooted women were to maintain the past against the flood, safe for returning. But the rare urge west had fixed upon our family, and so my aunt crossed boundaries not delineated in space.

The work of preservation demands that the feelings playing about in one's guts not be turned into action. Just watch their passing like cherry blossoms. But perhaps my aunt, my forerunner, caught in a slow life, let dreams grow and fade and after some months or years went toward what persisted. Fear at the enormities of the forbidden kept her desires delicate, wire and bone. She looked at a man because she liked the way the hair was tucked behind his ears, or she liked the question-mark line of a long torso curving at the shoulder and straight at the hip. For warm eyes or a soft voice or a slow walk—that's all—a few hairs, a line, a brightness, a sound, a pace, she gave up family. She offered us up for a charm that vanished with tiredness, a pigtail that didn't toss when the wind died. Why, the wrong lighting could erase the dearest thing about him.

It could very well have been, however, that my aunt did not take subtle enjoyment of her friend, but, a wild woman, kept rollicking company. Imagining her free with sex doesn't fit, though. I don't know any women like that, or men either. Unless I see her life branching into mine, she gives me no ancestral help.

To sustain her being in love, she often worked at herself in the mirror, guessing at the colors and shapes that would interest him, changing them frequently in order to hit on the right combination. She wanted to look back.

On a farm near the sea, a woman who tended her appearance reaped a reputation for eccentricity. All the married women blunt-cut their hair in flaps about their ears or pulled it back in tight buns. No nonsense. Neither style blew easily into heart-catching tangles. And at their weddings they displayed themselves in their long hair for the last time. "It brushed the backs of my knees," my mother tells me. "It was braided, and even so, it brushed the backs of my knees."

At the mirror my aunt combed individuality into her bob. A bun could have been contrived to escape into black streamers blowing in the wind or in quiet wisps about her face, but only the older women in our picture album wear buns. She brushed her hair back from her forehead, tucking the flaps behind her ears. She looped a piece of thread, knotted into a circle between her index fingers and thumbs, and ran the double strand across her forehead. When she closed her fingers as if she were making a pair of shadow geese bite, the string twisted together catching the little hairs. Then she pulled the thread away from her skin, ripping the hairs out neatly, her eyes watering from the needles of pain. Opening her fingers, she cleaned the thread, then rolled it along her hairline and the tops of the eyebrows. My mother did the same to me and my sisters and herself. I used to believe that the expression "caught by the short hairs" meant a captive held with a depilatory string. It especially hurt at the temples, but my mother said we were lucky we didn't have to have our feet bound when we were seven. Sisters used to sit on their beds and cry together, she said, as their mothers or their slave removed the bandages for a few minutes each night and let the blood gush back into their veins. I hope that the man my aunt loved appreciated a smooth brow, that he wasn't just a tits-and-ass man.

Once my aunt found a freckle on her chin, at a spot that the almanac said predestined her for unhappiness. She dug it out with a hot needle and washed the wound with peroxide.

More attention to her looks than these pullings of hairs and pickings at spots would

25

have caused gossip among the villagers. They owned work clothes and good clothes, and they wore good clothes for feasting the new seasons. But since a woman combing her hair hexes beginnings, my aunt rarely found an occasion to look her best. Women looked like great sea snails—the corded wood, babies, and laundry they carried were the whorls on their backs. The Chinese did not admire a bent back; goddesses and warriors stood straight. Still there must have been a marvelous freeing of beauty when a worker laid down her burden and stretched and arched.

Such commonplace loveliness, however, was not enough for my aunt. She dreamed of a lover for the fifteen days of New Year's the time for families to exchange visits, money, and food. She plied her secret comb. And sure enough she cursed the year, the family, the village, and herself.

Even as her hair lured her imminent lover, many other men looked at her. Uncles, cousins, nephews, brothers would have looked, too, had they been home between journeys. Perhaps they had already been restraining their curiosity, and they left, fearful that their glances, like a field of nesting birds, might be startled and caught. Poverty hurt, and that was their first reason for leaving. But another, final reason for leaving the crowded house was the never-said.

30   She may have been unusually beloved, the precious only daughter, spoiled and mirror-gazing because of the affection the family lavished on her. When her husband left, they welcomed the chance to take her back from the in-laws; she could live like the little daughter for just a while longer. There are stories that my grandfather was different from other people, "crazy ever since the little Jap bayoneted him in the head." He used to put his naked penis on the dinner table, laughing. And one day he brought home a baby girl, wrapped up inside his brown western-style greatcoat. He had traded one of his sons, probably my father, the youngest, for

her. My grandmother made him trade back. When he finally got a daughter of his own, he doted on her. They must have all loved her, except perhaps my father, the only brother who never went back to China, having once been traded for a girl.

Brothers and sisters, newly men and women, had to efface their sexual color and present plain miens. Disturbing hair and eyes, a smile like no other, threatened the ideal of five generations living under one roof. To focus blurs, people shouted face to face and yelled from room to room. The immigrants I know have loud voices, unmodulated to American tones even after years away from the village where they called their friendships out across the fields. I have not been able to stop my mother's screams in public libraries or over telephones. Walking erect (knees straight, toes pointed forward, not pigeon-toed, which is Chinese-feminine) and speaking in an inaudible voice, I have tried to turn myself American-feminine. Chinese communication was loud, public. Only sick people had to whisper. But at the dinner table, where the family members came nearest one another, no one could talk, not the outcasts nor any eaters. Every word that falls from the mouth is a coin lost. Silently they gave and accepted food with both hands. A preoccupied child who took his bowl with one hand got a sideways glare. A complete moment of total attention is due everyone alike. Children and lovers have no singularity here, but my aunt used a secret voice, a separate attentiveness.

She kept the man's name to herself throughout her labor and dying; she did not accuse him that he be punished with her. To save her inseminator's name she gave silent birth.

He may have been somebody in her own household, but intercourse with a man outside the family would have been no less abhorrent. All the village were kinsmen, and the titles shouted in loud country voices never let kinship be forgotten. Any man within visiting distance would have been neutralized as a lover—"brother," "younger brother," "older brother"—115 relationship titles. Parents researched birth charts probably not so much to assure good fortune as to circumvent incest in a population that has but one hundred surnames. Everybody has eight million relatives. How useless then sexual mannerisms, how dangerous.

As if it came from an atavism deeper than fear, I used to add "brother" silently to boys' names. It hexed the boys, who would or would not ask me to dance, and made them less scary and as familiar and deserving of benevolence as girls.

35   But, of course, I hexed myself also—no dates. I should have stood up, both arms waving, and shouted out across libraries, "Hey, you! Love me back." I had no idea, though, how to make attraction selective, how to control its direction and magnitude. If I made myself American-pretty so that the five or six Chinese boys in the class fell in love with me, everyone else—the Caucasian, Negro, and Japanese boys—would too. Sisterliness, dignified and honorable, made much more sense.

Attraction eludes control so stubbornly that whole societies designed to organize relationships among people cannot keep order, not even when they bind people to one another from childhood and raise them together. Among the very poor and the wealthy, brothers married their adopted sisters, like doves. Our family allowed some romance, paying adult brides' prices and providing dowries so that their sons and daughters could marry strangers. Marriage promises to turn strangers into friendly relatives—a nation of siblings.

In the village structure, spirits shimmered among the live creatures, balanced and held in equilibrium by time and land. But one human being flaring up into violence could open up a black hole, a maelstrom that pulled in the sky. The frightened villagers, who depended on one another to maintain the

real, went to my aunt to show her a personal, physical representation of the break she made in the "roundness." Misallying couples snapped off the future, which was to be embodied in true offspring. The villagers punished her for acting as if she could have a private life, secret and apart from them.

If my aunt had betrayed the family at a time of large grain yields and peace, when many boys were born, and wings were being built on many houses, perhaps she might have escaped such severe punishment. But the men—hungry, greedy, tired of planting in dry soil, cuckolded—had been forced to leave the village in order to send food-money home. There were ghost plagues, bandit plagues, wars with the Japanese, floods. My Chinese brother and sister had died of an unknown sickness. Adultery, perhaps only a mistake during good times, became a crime when the village needed food.

The round moon cakes and round doorways, the round tables of graduated size that fit one roundness inside another, round windows and rice bowls—these talismans had lost their power to warn this family of the law: A family must be whole, faithfully keeping the descent line by having sons to feed the old and the dead who in turn look after the family. The villagers came to show my aunt and lover-in-hiding a broken house. The villagers were speeding up the circling of events because she was too shortsighted to see that her infidelity had already harmed the village, that waves of consequences would return unpredictably, sometimes in disguise, as now, to hurt her. This roundness had to be made coin-sized so that she would see its circumference: Punish her at the birth of her baby. Awaken her to the inexorable. People who refused fatalism because they could invent small resources insisted on culpability. Deny accidents and wrest fault from the stars.

40   After the villagers left, their lanterns now scattering in various directions toward home, the family broke their silence and cursed her.

"Aiaa, we're going to die. Death is coming. Death is coming. Look what you've done. You've killed us. Ghost! Dead Ghost! Ghost! You've never been born." She ran out into the fields, far enough from the house so that she could no longer hear their voices, and pressed herself against the earth, her own land no more. When she felt the birth coming, she thought that she had been hurt. Her body seized together. "They've hurt me too much," she thought. "This is gall, and it will kill me." With forehead and knees against the earth, her body convulsed and then relaxed. She turned on her back, lay on the ground. The black well of sky and stars went out and out forever; her body and her complexity seemed to disappear. She was one of the stars, a bright dot in blackness, without home, without a companion, in eternal cold and silence. An agoraphobia rose in her, speeding higher and higher, bigger and bigger; she would not be able to contain it; there would be no end to fear.

Flayed, unprotected against space, she felt pain return, focusing her body. This pain chilled her—a cold, steady kind of surface pain. Inside, spasmodically, the other pain, the pain of the child, heated her. For hours she lay on the ground, alternately body and space. Sometimes a vision of normal comfort obliterated reality: She saw the family in the evening gambling at the dinner table, the young people massaging their elders' backs. She saw them congratulating one another, high joy on the mornings the rice shoots came up. When these pictures burst, the stars drew yet further apart. Black space opened.

She got to her feet to fight better and remembered that old-fashioned women gave birth in their pigsties to fool the jealous, pain-dealing gods, who do not snatch piglets. Before the next spasms could stop her, she ran to the pigsty, each step a rushing out into emptiness. She climbed over the fence and knelt in the dirt. It was good to have a fence enclosing her, a tribal person alone.

Laboring, this woman who had carried her child as a foreign growth that sickened her everyday, expelled it at last. She reached down to touch the hot, wet, moving mass, surely smaller than anything human, and could feel that it was human after all—fingers, toes, nails, nose. She pulled it up on to her belly, and it lay curled there, butt in the air, feet precisely tucked one under the other. She opened her loose shirt and buttoned the child inside. After resting, it squirmed and thrashed and she pushed it up to her breast. It turned its head this way and that until it found her nipple. There, it made little snuffling noises. She clenched her teeth at its preciousness, lovely as a young calf, a piglet, a little dog.

She may have gone to the pigsty as a last act of responsibility: She would protect this child as she had protected its father. It would look after her soul, leaving supplies on her grave. But how would this tiny child without family find her grave when there would be no marker for her anywhere, neither in the earth nor the family hall? No one would give her a family hall name. She had taken the child with her into the wastes. At its birth the two of them had felt the same raw pain of separation, a wound that only the family pressing tight could close. A child with no descent line would not soften her life but only trail after her, ghostlike, begging her to give it purpose. At dawn the villagers on their way to the fields would stand around the fence and look.

Full of milk, the little ghost slept. When it awoke, she hardened her breasts against the milk that crying loosens. Toward morning she picked up the baby and walked to the well.

Carrying the baby to the well shows loving. Otherwise abandon it. Turn its face into the mud. Mothers who love their children take them along. It was probably a girl; there is some hope of forgiveness for boys.

"Don't tell anyone you had an aunt. Your father does not want to hear her name. She has

45

never been born." I have believed that sex was unspeakable and words so strong and fathers so frail that "aunt" would do my father mysterious harm. I have thought that my family, having settled among immigrants who had also been their neighbors in the ancestral land, needed to clean their name, and a wrong word would incite the kinspeople even here. But there is more to this silence: They want me to participate in her punishment. And I have.

In the twenty years since I heard this story I have not asked for details nor said my aunt's name; I do not know it. People who comfort the dead can also chase after them to hurt them further—a reverse ancestor worship. The real punishment was not the raid swiftly inflicted by the villagers, but the family's deliberately forgetting her. Her betrayal so maddened them, they saw to it that she would suffer forever, even after death. Always hungry, always needing, she would have to beg food from other ghosts, snatch and steal it from those whose living descendants give them gifts. She would have to fight the ghosts massed at crossroads for the buns a few thoughtful citizens leave to decoy her away from village and home so that the ancestral spirits could feast unharassed. At peace, they could act like gods, not ghosts, their descent lines providing them with paper suits and dresses, spirit money, paper houses, paper automobiles, chicken, meat, and rice into eternity—essences delivered up in smoke and flames, steam and incense rising from each rice bowl. In an attempt to make the Chinese care for people outside the family, Chairman Mao encourages us now to give our paper replicas to the spirits of outstanding soldiers and workers, no matter whose ancestors they may be. My aunt remains forever hungry. Goods are not distributed evenly among the dead.

My aunt haunts me—her ghost drawn to me because now, after fifty years of neglect, I alone devote pages of paper to her, though not origamied into houses and clothes. I do not think she always means me well. I am telling on her, and she was a spite suicide, drowning herself in the drinking water. The Chinese are always very frightened of the drowned one, whose weeping ghost, wet hair hanging and skin bloated, waits silently by the water to pull down a substitute.

READING AND THINKING

1. Kingston begins this piece with a shocking family story. What is the effect of opening with this story rather than working it in later? What is the point of this story, and how does Kingston reveal its significance?

2. What ideas about cultural origins appear in "No Name Woman?" Which cultural attitudes does Kingston feature most prominently? Why?

3. How are women portrayed? What details does Kingston select to represent relations between men and women?

4. What significance does Kingston give to the Chinese family "circle" and the "roundness" of family life? In what ways are secrecy and silence determining factors in the cultural experience Kingston describes?

THINKING AND WRITING

1. Tell a story that has been part of your family lore. Be sure to account for the story's significance—for what it reveals (or conceals) about family attitudes and values.

2. Tell a series of interrelated family stories that reveal significant ideals of the race, culture, or ethnicity to which your family belongs.

3. Write an essay in which you compare the cultural conflicts between American and Chinese values and ideals in Kingston's essay.

FAMILY SECRETS:
AN OCCASION FOR WRITING

In Kingston's essay, we are presented with a woman who stepped outside the boundaries of the permissible. In transgressing against the conventions of behavior for Chinese women of a particular time, Kingston's aunt exhibited a defiant independence that led, ultimately, to her death. In the following Occasion you are asked to consider the roles the unspoken plays in families. You are invited both to consider how the anonymous postcards submitted to the Web log PostSecret is a kind of confessional in which those who contribute unburden themselves of their own secrets and to compare the nature of the family secrets with Kingston's.

PREPARING TO WRITE: OCCASIONS TO THINK ABOUT WHAT YOU SEE

1. Of these "secrets," which one (or ones) stands out the most to you? What specifically draws you to that image?

2. What do you note about the anonymous artists' styles? How do they use images and text to reveal their secrets? Do some reveal more details about their secrets than others? Why do you suppose that is, if they are revealing themselves anonymously?

MOVING TOWARD ESSAY: OCCASIONS TO ANALYZE AND REFLECT

1. Discuss in a few paragraphs the kind of bond a secret creates between those who share it. How important is the bond of secrecy? What kind of bond do you think the PostSecret Project creates?

2. What makes a secret a secret? If you know something that someone else knows, is that a secret, or must a secret be some knowledge or information that only one person has? Explain.

3. Highlight two passages from Kingston's essay in which the importance of family secrets is paramount. Explain the implications of the passages regarding keeping or not keeping family secrets.

4. Do different kinds of secrets require stricter or less strict obligations to maintain secrecy? Are medical secrets different from political or military secrets? Under what circumstances might the lawyer-client bond of secrecy or the secrets of the religious confession be relaxed?

5. Explain the extent to which you agree or disagree with the following quote from Gilbert Parker about secrecy:

> In all secrets there is a kind of guilt, however beautiful or joyful they may be, or for what good end they may be set to serve. Secrecy means evasion, and evasion means a problem to the moral mind.

WRITING THOUGHTFULLY: OCCASIONS FOR IDEAS AND ESSAYS

1. Using as much as you wish from any or all of the previous exercises, write an essay about family secrets. Consider the extent to which family secrets should or should not be kept. Consider different kinds of family secrets, perhaps making distinctions among them that would result in differences in their degree of strictness of secrecy.

2. Create your own anonymous postcard that reveals a family secret. In an essay, discuss your experience in thinking about and creating the postcard (you may either reveal your secret in your essay or keep it secret). Compare your experience with Kingston's experience in learning her family secret. When was the first time the secret you chose was revealed to you? If it's a secret you keep, discuss why you think you keep it.

3. Write a response to the following essay excerpt in which the philosopher Sissela Bok identifies some issues involved in the keeping of certain kinds of secrets.

Sissela Bok

THE DANGERS OF SECRECY

Against every claim to secrecy stands, however, the awareness of its dangers. It is the experience of these dangers that has led so many to view secrecy negatively, and that underlies statements such as that by Lord Acton, that "every thing secret degenerates." Such categorical dismissals are too sweeping, but they do point to the harm that secrets can do both to those who keep them and to those from whom they are kept—harm that often thwarts and debilitates the very needs for which I have argued that control over secrecy is indispensable.

Secrecy can harm those who make use of it in several ways. It can debilitate judgment, first of all, whenever it shuts out criticism and feedback, leading people to become mired down in stereotyped, unexamined, often erroneous beliefs and ways of thinking. Neither their perception of a problem nor their reasoning about it then receives the benefit of challenge and exposure. Scientists working under conditions of intense secrecy have testified to its stifling effect on their judgment and creativity. And those who have written about their undercover work as journalists, police agents, and spies, or about living incognito for political reasons, have described similar effects of prolonged concealment on their capacity to plan and to choose, at times on their sense of identity.

Secrecy can affect character and moral choice in similar ways. It allows people to maintain facades that conceal traits such as callousness or vindictiveness—traits which can, in the absence of criticism or challenge from without, prove debilitating. And guilty or deeply embarrassing secrets can corrode from within before outsiders have a chance to respond or to be of help. This deterioration from within is the danger Acton referred to in his statement, and is at the root of the common view that secrecy, like other exercises of power, can corrupt.

These risks of secrecy multiply because of its tendency to spread. Aware of the importance of exercising control over secrecy and openness, people seek more control whenever they can, and rarely give up portions of it voluntarily. In imitation and in self-protection, others then seek more as well. The control shifts in the direction of secrecy whenever there is negligence or abuse to cover up; as a result, as Weber pointed out, bureaucracies and other organizations surround themselves with ever greater secrecy to the extent that circumstances permit.

As secrecy debilitates character and judgment, it can also lower resistance to the irrational and the pathological. It then poses great difficulties for individuals whose controls go awry. We know all the stifling rigidity that hampers those who become obsessed with secrecy. For them, secrecy no longer serves sanity and free choice. It shuts off the safety valve between the inner and the shared worlds. We know, too, the pathologies of prying into the private spheres of others, and of losing all protection for one's own: voyeurism and the corresponding hunger for self-exposure that destroy the capacity to discriminate and to choose.

The danger of secrecy, however, obviously goes far beyond risks to those who *keep* secrets. If they alone were at risk, we would have fewer reasons to try to learn about, and sometimes interfere with, their secret practices. Our attitude changes radically as soon as we suspect that these practices also hurt others. And because secrecy can debilitate judgment and choice, spread, and become obsessive, it often affects others even when it is not intended to. This helps explain why, in the absence of clear criteria for when secrecy is and is not injurious, many people have chosen to regard all secrecy as potentially harmful.

When the freedom of choice that secrecy gives one person limits or destroys that of others, it affects not only his own claims to respect for identity, plans, action, and property, but theirs. The power of such secrecy can be immense. Because it bypasses inspection and eludes interference, secrecy is central to the planning of every form of injury to human beings. It cloaks the execution of these plans and wipes out all traces afterward. It enters into all prying and intrusion that cannot be carried out openly. While not all that is secret is meant to deceive—as jury deliberations, for instance, are not—all deceit does rely on keeping something secret. And while not all secrets are discreditable, all that is discreditable and all wrongdoing seek out secrecy (unless they can be carried out openly without interference, as when they are pursued by coercive means).

Such secrecy can hamper the exercise of rational choice at every step: by preventing people from adequately understanding a threatening situation, from seeing the relevant alternatives clearly, from assessing the consequences of each, and from arriving at preferences with respect to them. Those who have been hurt in such a way by the secrecy of others may in turn seek greater control over secrecy, and thus in turn experience its impairment of choice, its tendency to spread, its capacity to corrupt and to invite abuse.

Moral Considerations

Given both the legitimacy of some control over secrecy and openness, and the dangers this control carries for all involved, there can be no presumption either for or against secrecy in general. Secrecy differs in this respect from lying, promise-breaking, violence, and other practices for which the burden of proof rests on those who would defend them. Conversely, secrecy differs from truthfulness, friendship, and other practices carrying a favorable presumption.

The resulting challenge for ethical inquiry into the aims and methods of secrecy is great. Not only must we reject definitions of secrecy that invite approval or disapproval; we cannot even begin with a moral presumption in either direction. This is not to say, however, that there can be none for particular practices, nor that these practices are usually morally neutral. But it means that it is especially important to look at them separately, and to examine the moral arguments made for and against each one.

In studying these moral arguments, I shall rely on two presumptions that flow from the needs and dangers of secrecy that I have set forth. The first is one of *equality*. Whatever control over secrecy and openness we conclude is legitimate for some individuals should, in the absence of special considerations, be legitimate for all. If we look back at the four imaginary societies as illustrations, I can see no reason why some individuals should lack all such control, as in the first and

second societies, and not others: no reason why, as in the first society, only you and I should be unable to keep anything secret or, as in the second, be able to penetrate all secrets. No just society would, if it had the choice, allocate controls so unequally. This is not to say that some people might not be granted limited powers for certain of those purposes under constraints that minimize the risks—in journalism, for instance, or government; but they would have to advance reasons sufficient to overcome the initial presumption favoring equality. On the basis of this presumption, I reject both the first and the second of the imaginary societies, and any others that come close to them even in part.

My second presumption is in favor of *partial individual control* over the degree of secrecy or openness about personal matters—those most indisputably in the private realm. (I shall leave for later consideration the question of large-scale collective control over secrecy and openness regarding personal matters, as well as individual *or* collective control over less personal matters, such as professional, business, or government secrets.) Without a premise supporting a measure of individual control over personal matters, it would be impossible to preserve the indispensable respect for identity, plans, action, and belongings that all of us need and should legitimately be able to claim.

Such individual control should extend, moreover, to what people choose to share with one another about themselves—in families, for example, or with friends and colleagues. Without the intimacy that such sharing makes possible, human relationships would be impossible, and identity and plans would themselves suffer. For these reasons, I reject also the third imaginary society, in which all is openness, and where people have no choice between such openness and secrecy, even in personal and intimate matters.

At the same time, however, it is important to avoid any presumption in favor of *full* control over such matters for individuals. Such full control is not necessary for the needs that I have discussed, and would aggravate the dangers. It would force us to disregard the legitimate claims of those persons who might be injured, betrayed, or ignored as a result of secrets inappropriately kept or revealed. I must therefore also reject the fourth imaginary society, in which all have such control and can exercise it at will.

Given these two presumptions, in favor of equal control over secrecy and openness among all individuals, and in favor of partial individual control over personal matters, exercised singly or shared with other individuals, I shall go on to ask: *What considerations override these presumptions?* This will require us to look at the reasons advanced in favor of unusual secrecy, probing, or revelation by some, and to ask when even the partial control exercised by an individual in personal matters must be overridden. It will also require us to examine the role of loyalty and promises in counteracting such reasons to override personal control; and the crucial difference it makes if it is one's own secret or that of another that one wonders whether to reveal.

In approaching such questions about the ethics of secrecy, I hope to show how they mirror and shed light on aspects of ethics more generally. But these questions also create special difficulties; for no matter what moral principles one takes to be important in moral reasoning, they have a near paradoxical relationship with secrecy. Thus, secrecy both promotes and endangers what we think beneficial, even necessary, for survival. It may prevent harm, but it follows maleficence like a shadow. Every misdeed cloaks itself in secrecy unless accompanied by such power that it can be performed openly. And while secrecy may heighten a sense of equality and brotherhood among persons sharing the secret, it can fuel gross intolerance and hatred toward outsiders. At the heart of secrecy lies discrimination of some form, since its essence is sifting, setting apart, drawing lines. Secrecy, moreover, preserves liberty, yet this very liberty allows the invasion of that of others.

CREATING OCCASIONS

1. Write an essay on secrecy in which you consider the secrets kept by one or more famous families, such as the Kennedy family or the family of Thomas Jefferson, for example. Consider how those secrets affected history.

2. Popular movies and books tend to weave stories around a secret to be revealed at the end to the viewer or reader. Discuss the secrets included in a classic or contemporary book or film, such as *Jane Eyre, Star Wars, Psycho, The DaVinci Code,* and *Harry Potter and the Chamber of Secrets*. Do you think the secret found within has contributed to the book's or film's popularity? What makes secrets so appealing to society?

THERE'S NOT ENOUGH ART IN OUR SCHOOLS.

NO WONDER PEOPLE THINK

LOUIS ARMSTRONG

WAS THE FIRST MAN TO WALK ON THE MOON.

It's a long way from the Apollo Theatre to the Apollo program. And while his playing may have been "as lofty as a moon flight," as *Time* magazine once suggested, that would be as close as Louis Daniel Armstrong would ever get to taking "one small step for man." But as the jazz musician of the 20th century, giant leaps were simply a matter of course for Satchmo. For no one has ever embodied the art form the way he did. It was he who helped make virtuoso solos a part of the vocabulary. It was he who was honored with the title "American goodwill ambassador" by the State Department. It was he who was the last jazz musician to hit #1 on the Billboard pop chart.

Not bad for a kid whose first experience with

Instead of a giant leap, Louis Armstrong delivered one giant free-form crazy jazz groove for mankind.

Armstrong left his footprints on the jazz world, wearing lace-up oxfords.

the trumpet was as a guest in a correctional home for wayward boys. If only today's schools were as enlightened and informed as that reformatory was.

Alas, the arts are dismissed as extravagant in today's schools. This, despite all the studies that show parents believe music and dance and art and drama make their children much better students and better people. If you feel like your kids aren't getting their fair share, make some noise. To find out how, or for more information about the benefits of arts education, please visit us on the web at AmericansForTheArts.org. Just like the great Louis Armstrong, all you need is a little brass.

READIN'
'RITING
ART
'RITHMETIC

There's plenty of brain to go around. Give more to art.

ART. ASK FOR MORE.

For more information about the importance of arts education, contact www.AmericansForTheArts.org.

Photo used with permission, Louis Armstrong Educational Foundation.

Ad Council

AMERICANS for the ARTS

DORIS DUKE CHARITABLE FOUNDATION

The arts are sometimes considered an

EDUCATIONAL FRILL OR LUXURY

that can be dispensed with when budgets are tight. Are there ever occasions to dispense with any kind of education? What do you think are some benefits of participating in the arts—in music, art, theatre, and dance?

EDUCATION

9

Most people would agree that education is the key to success in life. But what kind of education is needed for what kind of success? Acquiring a sound education involves developing fundamental academic skills—reading, writing, and basic math. Being literate and numerate are considered the foundation for any further education, and certainly for the kind of education acquired in schools.

In the twenty-first century it remains clear that for the majority of those aspiring to even a modicum of prosperity, for those hoping to achieve and maintain middle-class socioeconomic status, being able to read, write, and compute are necessities. These fundamental skills remain critical, but possessing only a rudimentary knowledge of them—a mere basic reading, writing, and numerical literacy—will not suffice for anything but entry level positions.

Higher levels of literacy, like computer literacy and visual literacy are becoming increasingly essential. Beyond these literacies are other important learning skills, such as being able to learn and work in groups and teams, being able to organize and synthesize information, and being able to communicate ideas clearly and cogently. All these kinds of learning and more are necessary for what is typically considered a decent life in most industrialized nations in the twenty-first century.

Certainly as important as any of these kinds of learning is the development of critical and creative thinking skills. As life becomes increasingly complex, becoming a competent and confident thinker assumes ever-greater importance. Because rapid change is a fact of contemporary life worldwide, an equally critical skill, perhaps the most important of all, is learning how to learn.

Frederick Douglass's "Learning to Read and Write" demonstrates the centrality and importance of these critical skills. Maya Angelou's "Graduation" speaks to social issues in education, including teachers' expectations for their students. Bernard Cooper's "Labyrinthine" deals less with formal education than with learning in everyday life. Eudora Welty's "Clamorous to Learn" highlights the young Welty's love of learning and the inspiration she derived from her first teachers. Adrienne Rich's "Taking Women Students Seriously" urges teachers to consider their female students equal to and as capable as their male students. Paolo Freire contrasts two diametrically opposed concepts of teaching and learning in his "Banking Concept of Education."

EDUCATION AND EXPECTATIONS

Among the many reasons any of us learns anything is that we are expected to learn—by parents and teachers, by classmates and friends, by coaches and mentors and employers. When expectations for learning are high, and when opportunities to learn are frequent and enticing, we learn best and most. Conversely, when expectations for learning are low, when opportunities are restricted and uninteresting, we learn least and worst.

We tend to learn those things we love. We learn what interests us, what excites and stimulates our imagination, what inspires us. For those things—learning to ski or swim, for example, or to play the guitar, dance, draw, or read history—we learn because we want to, not because we have to. Motivation is the key. The rewards of this kind of learning are intrinsic, embedded in the act of learning itself.

For what we have less interest in and inclination for—and these are often the very things that others enjoy and excel at—we struggle, learning listlessly, grudgingly, forgetfully. We remember what we care most about; we forget what matters little to us.

As with individual learning, so with group learning—school learning. Classes and subjects made intellectually exciting by teachers passionate about their subjects lead us to study harder and learn more. Classes where we are held to high performance expectations tend to bring out the best in us.

Stories of teaching and learning often touch on these themes, whether what is learned is practical or theoretical, and whether it is learned in school or out. The impulse to learn is what counts. Expectations from within and outside the self both matter.

Frederick Douglass sets his own goals for learning to read and write. His piece shows the great lengths Douglass went to and how resourceful he was in acquiring these essential skills. Maya Angelou highlights the culminating celebration of educational accomplishment, the expectations that she and her classmates have about their prospects for the future. She contrasts their expectations with the lesser expectations some of their teachers have, especially for their Black students. And Bernard Cooper explores the way learning is not a simple, linear process, but instead one that becomes increasingly complex, even convoluted—like life itself.

Frederick Douglass (1818–1895)

Frederick Douglass was born a slave in rural Maryland. As a boy, he worked as a house servant. Once he learned the rudiments of reading from a slaveholder's wife, Douglass educated himself and escaped to the north when he was twenty-one. He became an eloquent orator and an ardent abolitionist. He also edited the *North Star,* also called *Frederick Douglass' Paper.* Later he served as United States marshal and consul general to the Republic of Haiti. He is best known, however, for his autobiography, *Narrative of the Life of Frederick Douglass, An American Slave,* first published in 1845.

LEARNING TO READ AND WRITE

In "Learning to Read and Write," taken from Douglass's autobiography, he movingly describes the strategies and stratagems he employed to teach himself these critical basic skills. In the passage, Douglass both celebrates and laments his accomplishment as his ability to read and write exacerbate the agony of his remaining a slave. Moreover, Douglass transcends his personal story in explaining why slaveholders kept their slaves illiterate.

1   I lived in Master Hugh's family about seven years. During this time, I succeeded in learning to read and write. In accomplishing this, I was compelled to resort to various stratagems. I had no regular teacher. My mistress, who had kindly commenced to instruct me, had, in compliance with the advice and direction of her husband, not only ceased to instruct, but had set her face against my being instructed by any one else. It is due, however, to my mistress to say of her, that she did not adopt this course of treatment immediately. She at first lacked the depravity indispensable to shutting me up in mental darkness. It was at least necessary for her to have some training in the exercise of irresponsible power, to make her equal to the task of treating me as though I were a brute.

My mistress was, as I have said, a kind and tender-hearted woman; and in the simplicity of her soul she commenced, when I first went to live with her, to treat me as she supposed one human being ought to treat another. In entering upon the duties of a slaveholder, she did not seem to perceive that I sustained to her the relation of a mere chattel, and that for her to treat me as a human being was not only wrong, but dangerously so.

Slavery proved as injurious to her as it did to me. When I went there, she was a pious, warm, and tender-hearted woman. There was no sorrow or suffering for which she had not a tear. She had bread for the hungry, clothes for the naked, and comfort for every mourner that came within her reach. Slavery soon proved its ability to divest her of these heavenly qualities. Under its influence, the tender heart became stone, and the lamblike disposition gave way to one of tiger-like fierceness. The first step in her downward course was in her ceasing to instruct me. She now commenced to practise her husband's precepts. She finally became even more violent in her opposition than her husband himself. She was not satisfied with simply doing as well as he had commanded; she seemed anxious to do better. Nothing seemed to make her more angry than to see me with a newspaper. She seemed to think that here lay the danger. I have had her rush at me with a face made all up of fury, and snatch from me a newspaper, in a manner that fully revealed her apprehension. She was an apt woman; and a little experience soon demonstrated, to her satisfaction, that education and slavery were incompatible with each other.

From this time I was most narrowly watched. If I was in a separate room any considerable length of time, I was sure to be suspected of having a book, and was at once called to give an account of myself. All this, however, was too late. The first step had been taken. Mistress, in teaching me the alphabet, had given me the *inch*, and no precaution could prevent me from taking the *ell*.

The plan which I adopted, and the one by which I was most successful, was that of making friends of all the little white boys whom I met in the street. As many of these as I could, I converted into teachers. With their kindly aid, obtained at different times and in different places, I finally succeeded in learning to read. When I was sent on errands, I always took my book with me, and by doing one part of my errand quickly, I found time to get a lesson before my return. I used also to carry bread with me, enough of which was always in the house, and to which I was always welcome; for I was much better off in this regard than many of the poor white children in our neighborhood. This bread I used to bestow upon the hungry little urchins, who, in return, would give me that more valuable bread of knowledge. I am strongly tempted to give the names of two or three of those little boys, as a testimonial of the gratitude and affection I bear them; but prudence forbids:—not that it would injure me, but it might embarrass them; for it is almost an unpardonable offence to teach slaves to read in this Christian country. It is enough to say of the dear little fellows, that they lived on Philpot Street, very near Durgin and Bailey's ship-yard. I used to talk this matter of slavery over with them. I would sometimes say to them, I wished I could be as free as they would be when they got to be men. "You will be free as soon as you are twenty-one, *but I am a slave for life!* Have not I as good a right to be free as you have?" These words used to trouble them; they would express for me the liveliest sympathy, and console me with the hope that something would occur by which I might be free.

I was now about twelve years old, and the thought of being a *slave for life* began to bear heavily upon my heart. Just about this time, I got hold of a book entitled "The Columbian Orator." Every opportunity I got, I used to read this book. Among much of other interesting matter, I found in it a dialogue between a master and his slave. The slave was represented as having run away from his master three times. The dialogue represented the conversation which took place between them, when the slave was retaken the third time. In this dialogue, the whole argument in behalf of slavery was brought forward by the master, all of which was disposed of by the slave. The slave was made to say some very smart as well as impressive things in reply to his master—things which had the desired though unexpected effect; for the conversation resulted in the voluntary emancipation of the slave on the part of the master.

In the same book, I met with one of Sheridan's mighty speeches on and in behalf of Catholic emancipation. These were choice documents to me. I read them over and over again with unabated interest. They gave tongue to interesting thoughts of my own soul, which had frequently flashed through my mind, and died away for want of utterance. The moral which I gained from the dialogue was the power of truth over the conscience of even a slaveholder. What I got from Sheridan was a bold denunciation of slavery, and a powerful vindication of human rights. The reading of these documents enabled me to utter my thoughts, and to meet the arguments brought forward to sustain slavery; but while they relieved me of one difficulty, they brought on another even more painful than the one of which I was relieved. The more I read, the more I was led to abhor and detest my enslavers. I could regard them in no other light than a band of successful

5

robbers, who had left their homes, and gone to Africa, and stolen us from our homes, and in a strange land reduced us to slavery. I loathed them as being the meanest as well as the most wicked of men. As I read and contemplated the subject, behold! that very discontentment which Master Hugh had predicted would follow my learning to read had already come, to torment and sting my soul to unutterable anguish. As I writhed under it, I would at times feel that learning to read had been a curse rather than a blessing. It had given me a view of my wretched condition, without the remedy. It opened my eyes to the horrible pit, but to no ladder upon which to get out. In moments of agony, I envied my fellow-slaves for their stupidity. I have often wished myself a beast. I preferred the condition of the meanest reptile to my own. Any thing, no matter what, to get rid of thinking! It was this everlasting thinking of my condition that tormented me. There was no getting rid of it. It was pressed upon me by every object within sight or hearing, animate or inanimate. The silver trump of freedom had roused my soul to eternal wakefulness. Freedom now appeared, to disappear no more forever. It was heard in every sound, and seen in every thing. It was ever present to torment me with a sense of my wretched condition. I saw nothing without seeing it, I heard nothing without hearing it, and felt nothing without feeling it. It looked from every star, it smiled in every calm, breathed in every wind, and moved in every storm.

I often found myself regretting my own existence, and wishing myself dead; and but for the hope of being free, I have no doubt but that I should have killed myself, or done something for which I should have been killed. While in this state of mind, I was eager to hear any one speak of slavery. I was a ready listener. Every little while, I could hear something about the abolitionists. It was some time before I found what the word meant. It was always used in such connec-

tions as to make it an interesting word to me. If a slave ran away and succeeded in getting clear, or if a slave killed his master, set fire to a barn, or did any thing very wrong in the mind of a slaveholder, it was spoken of as the fruit of *abolition*. Hearing the word in this connection very often, I set about learning what it meant. The dictionary afforded me little or no help. I found it was "the act of abolishing;" but then I did not know what was to be abolished. Here I was perplexed. I did not dare to ask any one about its meaning, for I was satisfied that it was something they wanted me to know very little about. After a patient waiting, I got one of our city papers, containing an account of the number of petitions from the north, praying for the abolition of slavery in the District of Columbia, and of the slave trade between the States. From this time I understood the words *abolition* and *abolitionist*, and always drew near when that word was spoken, expecting to hear something of importance to myself and fellow-slaves. The light broke in upon me by degrees. I went one day down on the wharf of Mr. Waters; and seeing two Irishmen unloading a scow of stone, I went, unasked, and helped them. When we had finished, one of them came to me and asked me if I were a slave. I told him I was. He asked, "Are ye a slave for life?" I told him that I was. The good Irishman seemed to be deeply affected by the statement. He said to the other that it was a pity so fine a little fellow as myself should be a slave for life. He said it was a shame to hold me. They both advised me to run away to the north; that I should find friends there, and that I should be free. I pretended not to be interested in what they said, and treated them as if I did not understand them; for I feared they might be treacherous. White men have been known to encourage slaves to escape, and then, to get the reward, catch them and return them to their masters. I was afraid that these seemingly good men might use me so; but I nevertheless remembered their advice, and from that time I resolved to run away. I looked forward to a time at which it would be safe for me to escape. I was too young to think of doing so immediately; besides, I wished to learn how to write, as I might have occasion to write my own pass. I consoled myself with the hope that I should one day find a good chance. Meanwhile, I would learn to write.

The idea as to how I might learn to write was suggested to me by being in Durgin and Bailey's shipyard, and frequently seeing the ship carpenters, after hewing, and getting a piece of timber ready for use, write on the timber the name of that part of the ship for which it was intended. When a piece of timber was intended for the larboard side, it would be marked thus—"L." When a piece was for the starboard side, it would be marked thus—"S." A piece for the larboard side forward, would be marked thus—"L. F." When a piece was for starboard side forward, it would be marked thus—"S. F." For larboard aft, it would be marked thus—"L. A." For starboard aft, it would be marked thus—"S. A." I soon learned the names of these letters, and for what they were intended when placed upon a piece of timber in the shipyard. I immediately commenced copying them, and in a short time was able to make the four letters named. After that, when I met with any boy who I knew could write, I would tell him I could write as well as he. The next word would be, "I don't believe you. Let me see you try it." I would then make the letters which I had been so fortunate as to learn, and ask him to beat that. In this way I got a good many lessons in writing, which it is quite possible I should never have gotten in any other way. During this time, my copy-book was the board fence, brick wall, and pavement; my pen and ink was a lump of chalk. With these, I learned mainly how to write. I then commenced and continued copying the Italics in Webster's Spelling Book, until I could make them all without looking on the book. By this time, my little Master Thomas had gone to school, and learned how to write, and had written over a number of copy-books. These had been brought home, and shown to some of our near neighbors, and then laid aside. My mistress used to go to class meeting at the Wilk Street meetinghouse every Monday afternoon, and leave me to take care of the house. When left thus, I used to spend the time in writing in the spaces left in Master Thomas's copy-book, copying what he had written. I continued to do this until I could write a hand very similar to that of Master Thomas. Thus, after a long, tedious effort for years, I finally succeeded in learning how to write.

READING AND THINKING

1. What is Douglass's main reason for wanting to learn how to read? For learning how to write? What motivates him?

2. What does Douglass mean by suggesting that literacy—learning to read and write—and slavery are incompatible?

3. To what extent is Douglass's essay an argument against slavery? What details suggest such an antislavery argument?

4. What strategies and tricks does Douglass use to advance his knowledge of reading and writing?

THINKING AND WRITING

1. To what extent can you relate to the experience Douglass describes of learning to read and to write? To what extent can you apply his experience to your own advancing literacy?

2. Explain the significance for Douglass of Sheridan's speeches on behalf of Catholic emancipation. Why was the book *The Columbian Orator* so important for Douglass?

3. Identify one passage in the essay that you find especially compelling or moving. Analyze Douglass's words, phrases, and sentences in that passage to see what makes it so effective.

4. Describe one of your own experiences learning to read or write.

PURSUING A PASSION: AN OCCASION FOR WRITING

Douglass describes his hunger for learning, his obsessive drive to learn how to read and write. Evident on every page, in every sentence are his passion for learning and his determination to succeed. However, as we learn from Douglass's experience, knowledge can be simultaneously liberating, frustrating or difficult, and rewarding. Having learned to read, Douglass now had to face the reality of his circumstance in life. This Occasion invites you to consider how learning has been viewed as a challenge and yet rewarding in ways that are sometimes not obvious.

TITIAN, *Adam and Eve (16th century)*

PREPARING TO WRITE: OCCASIONS TO THINK ABOUT WHAT YOU SEE

1. Explain how the image of Adam and Eve ties in with the theme of knowledge and learning. What do Adam and Eve learn from their experience and what is the cost of that learning? (For the story of Adam and Eve, see the book of Genesis in the Bible, Chapters 1–3.) What elements of this image have to do with knowledge and help interpret the story of the fall of man?

2. This image of the Buddha is thought to be from Tibet. Before attaining Enlightenment, the Buddha endured demons and evil sent by Mara, the head of all demons, to question and break his concentration. How does this image signify the difficulty of learning?

TIBETAN SCHOOL, *Life of Buddha Sakymuni, the Armies of Mara Attacking the Blessed (18th century)*

© Réunion des Musées Nationaux / Art Resource, NY

MOVING TOWARD ESSAY: OCCASIONS TO ANALYZE AND REFLECT

1. Describe a time when you were challenged to learn something. Create a scene for your reader in which you show your feelings toward the task. At what points were you motivated, dejected, excited, or annoyed? What was the final outcome, and how do you look at learning that task now that it's behind you? What effects has this pursuit had on your learning in the particular area of your passionate interest? What effects has this pursuit had on your learning more generally?

2. With your knowledge of the story of the fall of Adam and Eve, what do you think was the challenge and the reward of their experience? What knowledge was gained? Were they liberated in any way? How can their experience be likened to Douglass's experience?

3. If you are unfamiliar with the Buddhist story of Enlightenment, do some quick research on the topic. How can you relate your own story of a learning challenge to the representation of the Buddha's attack by demons? What type of concentration would be necessary to sustain the obstacles the Buddha faced and those that you faced?

WRITING THOUGHTFULLY: OCCASIONS FOR IDEAS AND ESSAYS

1. Consider how all the stories presented in this Occasion, including your own, help to define knowledge. Is knowledge punishing or liberating? Can it be both? Using the sources provided in this Occasion, write an essay in which you explore how you perceive the ultimate goals of knowledge.

2. Identify what the motivation behind acquiring knowledge is in the stories provided in this Occasion. How does your motivation for knowledge compare with the famous parables of Adam and Eve and of Buddha? Douglass emphasizes in his essay his passion and desire to succeed. In an essay, identify what you believe are the elements of motivation and passion for learning. What defines success? Use evidence from this Occasion or any other evidence you think will help clarify and broaden your thoughts.

CREATING OCCASIONS

1. Do some research about a person who has pursued a passion. You may want to follow the lives and fortunes of the founders of a company such as Microsoft, Google, Federal Express, or Martha Stewart Multimedia, for example; or of an athlete, such as Lance Armstrong or Venus and Serena Williams; or a historical figure like Socrates, Leonardo da Vinci, or Madame Curie. Pick some images of one of these individuals that you find engaging. Find an interview or something the individual has written. Read an article or book about the person. Then write an essay about this person's pursuit of passion and what others can learn from that passionate pursuit. How does this person complicate or add to your previous thoughts on motivation and success in attaining knowledge?

Maya Angelou (b. 1928)

Maya Angelou grew up in St. Louis, Missouri, and in the rural community of Stamps, Arkansas. After studying dance, she had an early career as an actress and later worked as a journalist while living in Africa. She was active in the civil rights movement, serving as northern coordinator for the Southern Christian Leadership Conference. Her first volume of memoirs, *I Know Why the Caged Bird Sings,* appeared in 1970. It was followed by several more autobiographical volumes, as well as numerous collections of poems and books for children. Angelou has also written for television and film and directed the feature-length film *Down in the Delta,* released in 1998. Her poem "On the Pulse of Morning" was commissioned for the 1993 presidential inauguration, and her recording of it won a Grammy award. She is on the faculty of Wake Forest University.

GRADUATION

In "Graduation," an excerpt from *I Know Why the Caged Bird Sings,* Angelou describes her grade-school graduation in Stamps, Arkansas. She describes the excitement of preparing for the big event and then her disappointment at the words spoken by the school principal before concluding with the spiritual uplift in response to the valedictory speech of her friend, Bailey, and the words of the African American poet James Weldon Johnson that Bailey quotes in his speech. Angelou not only describes her graduation experience, but also, in the process, conveys an idea about race and education.

1 The children in Stamps trembled visibly with anticipation. Some adults were exited too, but to be certain the whole young population had come down with graduation epidemic. Large classes were graduating from both the grammar school and the high school. Even those who were years removed from their own day of glorious release were anxious to help with preparations as a kind of dry run. The junior students who were moving into the vacating classes' chairs were tradition-bound to show their talents for leadership and management. They strutted through the school and around the campus exerting pressure on the lower grades. Their authority was so new that occasionally if they pressed a little too hard it had to be overlooked. After all, next term was coming, and it never hurt a sixth grader to have a play sister in the eighth grade, or a tenth-year student to be able to call a twelfth grader Bubba. So all was endured in a spirit of shared understanding. But the graduating classes themselves were the nobility. Like travelers with exotic destinations on their minds, the graduates were remarkably forgetful. They came to school without their books, or tablets or even pencils. Volunteers fell over themselves to secure replacements for the missing equipment. When accepted, the willing workers might or might not be thanked, and it was of no importance to the pregraduation rites. Even teachers were respectful of the now quiet and aging seniors, and tended to speak to them, if not as equals, as beings only slightly lower than themselves. After tests were returned and grades given, the student body, which acted like an extended family, knew who did well, who excelled, and what piteous ones had failed.

Unlike the white high school, Lafayette County Training School distinguished itself by having neither lawn, nor hedges, nor tennis court, nor climbing ivy. Its two buildings (main classrooms, the grade school and home economics) were set on a dirt hill with no fence to limit either its boundaries or those of bordering farms. There was a large expanse to the left of the school which was used alternately as a baseball diamond or basketball court. Rusty hoops on swaying poles represented the permanent recreational equipment, although bats and balls could be borrowed from the P.E. teacher if the borrower was qualified and if the diamond wasn't occupied.

Over this rocky area relieved by a few shady tall persimmon trees the graduating class walked. The girls often held hands and no longer bothered to speak to the lower students. There was a sadness about them, as if this old world was not their home and they were bound for higher ground. The boys, on the other hand, had become more friendly, more outgoing. A decided change from the closed attitude they projected while studying for finals. Now they seemed not ready to give up the old school, the familiar paths and classrooms. Only a small percentage would be continuing on to college—one of the South's A & M (agricultural and mechanical) schools, which trained Negro youths to be carpenters, farmers, handymen, masons, maids, cooks and baby nurses. Their future rode heavily on their shoulders, and blinded them to the collective joy that had pervaded the lives of the boys and girls in the grammar school graduating class.

Parents who could afford it had ordered new shoes and readymade clothes for themselves from Sears and Roebuck or Montgomery Ward. They also engaged the best seamstresses to make the floating graduating dresses and to cut down secondhand pants which would be pressed to a military slickness for the important event.

5   Oh, it was important, all right. Whitefolks would attend the ceremony, and two or three would speak of God and home, and the Southern way of life, and Mrs. Parsons, the principal's wife, would play the graduation march while the lower-grade graduates paraded down the aisles and took their seats below the platform. The high school seniors would wait in empty classrooms to make their dramatic entrance.

In the Store I was the person of the moment. The birthday girl. The center. Bailey had graduated the year before, although to do so he had had to forfeit all pleasures to make up for his time lost in Baton Rouge.

My class was wearing butter-yellow piqué dresses, and Momma launched out on mine. She smocked the yoke into tiny crisscrossing puckers, then shirred the rest of the bodice. Her dark fingers ducked in and out of the lemony cloth as she embroidered raised daisies around the hem. Before she considered herself finished she had added a crocheted cuff on the puff sleeves, and a pointy crocheted collar.

I was going to be lovely. A walking model of all the various styles of fine hand sewing and it didn't worry me that I was only twelve years old and merely graduating from the eighth grade. Besides, many teachers in Arkansas Negro schools had only that diploma and were licensed to impart wisdom.

The days had become longer and more noticeable. The faded beige of former times had been replaced with strong and sure colors. I began to see my classmates' clothes, their skin tones, and the dust that waved off pussy willows. Clouds that lazed across the sky were objects of great concern to me. Their shiftier shapes might have held a message that in my new happiness and with a little bit of time I'd soon decipher. During that period I looked at the arch of heaven so religiously my neck kept a steady ache. I had taken to smiling more often, and my jaws hurt from the unaccustomed activity. Between the two physical sore spots, I suppose I could have been uncomfortable, but that was not the case. As a member of the winning team (the graduating class of 1940) I had outdistanced unpleasant sensations by miles. I was headed for the freedom of open fields.

10   Youth and social approval allied themselves with me and we trammeled memories of slights and insults. The wind of our swift passage remodeled my features. Lost tears

were pounded to mud and then to dust. Years of withdrawal were brushed aside and left behind, as hanging ropes of parasitic moss.

My work alone had awarded me a top place and I was going to be one of the first called in the graduating ceremonies. On the classroom blackboard, as well as on the bulletin board in the auditorium, there were blue stars and white stars and red stars. No absences, no tardinesses, and my academic work was among the best of the year. I could say the preamble to the Constitution even faster than Bailey. We timed ourselves often: "We the people of the United States in order to form a more perfect union . . ." I had memorized the Presidents of the United States from Washington to Roosevelt in chronological as well as alphabetical order.

My hair pleased me too. Gradually the black mass had lengthened and thickened, so that it kept at last to its braided pattern, and I didn't have to yank my scalp off when I tried to comb it.

Louise and I had rehearsed the exercises until we tired ourselves out. Henry Reed was class valedictorian. He was a small, very black boy with hooded eyes, a long, broad nose and an oddly shaped head. I had admired him for years because each term he and I vied for the best grades in our class. Most often he bested me, but instead of being disappointed I was pleased that we shared top places between us. Like many Southern Black children, he lived with his grandmother, who was as strict as Momma and as kind as she knew how to be. He was courteous, respectful and soft-spoken to elders, but on the playground he chose to play the roughest games. I admired him. Anyone, I reckoned, sufficiently afraid or sufficiently dull could be polite. But to be able to operate at a top level with both adults and children was admirable.

His valedictory speech was entitled "To Be or Not to Be." The rigid tenth-grade teacher had helped him write it. He'd been working on the dramatic stresses for months.

The weeks until graduation were filled with heady activities. A group of small children were to be presented in a play about buttercups and daisies and bunny rabbits. They could be heard throughout the building practicing their hops and their little songs that sounded like silver bells. The older girls (nongraduates, of course) were assigned the task of making refreshments for the night's festivities. A tangy scent of ginger, cinnamon, nutmeg and chocolate wafted around the home economics building as the budding cooks made samples for themselves and their teachers.

In every corner of the workshop, axes and saws split fresh timber as the woodshop boys made sets and stage scenery. Only the graduates were left out of the general bustle. We were free to sit in the library at the back of the building or look in quite detachedly, naturally, on the measures being taken for our event.

Even the minister preached on graduation the Sunday before. His subject was, "Let your light so shine that men will see your good works and praise your Father, Who is in Heaven." Although the sermon was purported to be addressed to us, he used the occasion to speak to backsliders, gamblers and general ne'er-do-wells. But since he had called our names at the beginning of the service we were mollified.

Among Negroes the tradition was to give presents to children going only from one grade to another. How much more important this was when the person was graduating at the top of the class. Uncle Willie and Momma had sent away for a Mickey Mouse watch like Bailey's. Louise gave me four embroidered handkerchiefs. (I gave her crocheted doilies.) Mrs. Sneed, the minister's wife, made me an undershirt to wear for graduation, and nearly every customer gave me a nickel or maybe even a dime with the instruction "Keep on moving to higher ground," or some such encouragement.

Amazingly the great day finally dawned and I was out of bed before I knew it. I threw open the back door to see it more clearly, but Momma said, "Sister, come away from that door and put your robe on."

20 I hoped the memory of that morning would never leave me. Sunlight was itself young, and the day had none of the insistence maturity would bring it in a few hours. In my robe and barefoot in the backyard, under cover of going to see about my new beans, I gave myself up to the gentle warmth and thanked God that no matter what evil I had done in my life He had allowed me to live to see this day. Somewhere in my fatalism I had expected to die, accidentally, and never have the chance to walk up the stairs in the auditorium and gracefully receive my hard-earned diploma. Out of God's merciful bosom I had won reprieve.

Bailey came out in his robe and gave me a box wrapped in Christmas paper. He said he had saved his money for months to pay for it. It felt like a box of chocolates, but I knew Bailey wouldn't save money to buy candy when we had all we could want under our noses.

He was as proud of the gift as I. It was a soft-leather-bound copy of a collection of poems by Edgar Allan Poe, or, as Bailey and I called him, "Eap." I turned to "Annabel Lee" and we walked up and down the garden rows, the cool dirt between our toes, reciting the beautifully sad lines.

Momma made a Sunday breakfast although it was only Friday. After we finished the blessing, I opened my eyes to find the watch on my plate. It was a dream of a day. Everything went smoothly and to my credit, I didn't have to be reminded or scolded for anything. Near evening I was too jittery to attend to chores, so Bailey volunteered to do all before his bath.

Days before, we had made a sign for the Store, and as we turned out the lights Momma hung the cardboard over the doorknob. It read clearly: CLOSED. GRADUATION.

25 My dress fitted perfectly and everyone said that I looked like a sunbeam in it. On the hill, going toward the school, Bailey walked behind with Uncle Willie, who muttered, "Go on, Ju." He wanted him to walk ahead with us because it embarrassed him to have to walk so slowly. Bailey said he'd let the ladies walk together, and the men would bring up the rear. We all laughed, nicely.

Little children dashed by out of the dark like fireflies. Their crepe-paper dresses and butterfly wings were not made for running and we heard more than one rip, dryly, and the regretful "uh uh" that followed.

The school blazed without gaiety. The windows seemed cold and unfriendly from the lower hill. A sense of ill-fated timing crept over me, and if Momma hadn't reached for my hand I would have drifted back to Bailey and Uncle Willie, and possibly beyond. She made a few slow jokes about my feet getting cold, and tugged me along to the now-strange building.

Around the front steps, assurance came back. There were my fellow "greats," the graduating class. Hair brushed back, legs oiled, new dresses and pressed pleats, fresh pocket handkerchiefs and little handbags, all home-sewn. Oh, we were up to snuff, all right. I joined my comrades and didn't even see my family go in to find seats in the crowded auditorium.

The school band struck up a march and all classes filed in as had been rehearsed. We stood in front of our seats, as assigned, and on a signal from the choir director, we sat. No sooner had this been accomplished than the band started to play the national anthem. We rose again and sang the song, after which we recited the pledge of allegiance. We remained standing for a brief minute before the choir director and the principal signaled to us, rather desperately I thought, to take our seats. The command was so unusual that our carefully rehearsed and smooth-running machine was thrown off. For a full minute we fumbled for our chairs and bumped into each other awkwardly. Habits change or solidify under pressure, so in our state of nervous tension we had been ready to follow our usual assembly pattern: the American national anthem, then the pledge of allegiance, then the song every Black person I knew called the Negro national anthem. All done in the same key, with the same passion and most often standing on the same foot.

30   Finding my seat at last, I was overcome with a presentiment of worse things to come. Something unrehearsed, unplanned, was going to happen, and we were going to be made to look bad. I distinctly remember being explicit in the choice of pronoun. It was "we," the graduating class, the unit, that concerned me then.

The principal welcomed "parents and friends" and asked the Baptist minister to lead us in prayer. His invocation was brief and punchy, and for a second I thought we were getting on the high road to right action. When the principal came back to the dais, however, his voice had changed. Sounds always affected me profoundly and the principal's voice was one of my favorites. During assembly it melted and lowed weakly into the audience. It had not been in my plan to listen to him, but my curiosity was piqued and I straightened up to give him my attention.

He was talking about Booker T. Washington, our "late great leader," who said we can be as close as the fingers on the hand, etc. . . . Then he said a few vague things about friendship and the friendship of kindly people to those less fortunate than themselves. With that his voice nearly faded, thin, away. Like a river diminishing to a stream and then to a trickle. But he cleared his throat and said, "Our speaker tonight, who is also our friend, came from Texarkana to deliver the commencement address, but due to the irregularity of the train schedule, he's going to, as they say, 'speak and run.'" He said that we understood and wanted the man to know that we were most grateful for the time he was able to give us and then something about how we were willing always to adjust to another's program, and without more ado—"I give you Mr. Edward Donleavy."

Not one but two white men came through the door off-stage. The shorter one walked to the speaker's platform, and the tall one moved to the center seat and sat down. But that was our principal's seat, and already occupied. The dislodged gentleman bounced around for a long breath or two before the Baptist minister gave him his chair, then with more dignity than the situation deserved, the minister walked off the stage.

Donleavy looked at the audience once (on reflection, I'm sure that he wanted only to reassure himself that we were really there), adjusted his glasses and began to read from a sheaf of papers.

He was glad "to be here and to see the work   35 going on just as it was in the other schools."

At the first "Amen" from the audience I willed the offender to immediate death by choking on the word. But Amens and Yes, sir's began to fall around the room like rain through a ragged umbrella.

He told us of the wonderful changes we children in Stamps had in store. The Central School (naturally, the white school was Central) had already been granted improvements that would be in use in the fall. A well-known artist was coming from Little Rock to teach art to them. They were going to have the newest microscopes and chemistry equipment for their laboratory. Mr. Donleavy didn't leave us long in the dark over who made these improvements available to Central High. Nor were we to be ignored in the general betterment scheme he had in mind.

He said that he had pointed out to people at a very high level that one of the first-line football tacklers at Arkansas Agricultural and Mechanical College had graduated from good old Lafayette County Training School. Here fewer Amen's were heard. Those few that did break through lay dully in the air with the heaviness of habit.

He went on to praise us. He went on to say how he had bragged that "one of the best basketball players at Fisk sank his first ball right here at Lafayette County Training School."

40 The white kids were going to have a chance to become Galileos and Madame Curies and Edisons and Gauguins, and our boys (the girls weren't even in on it) would try to be Jesse Owenses and Joe Louises.

Owens and the Brown Bomber were great heroes in our world, but what school official in the white-goddom of Little Rock had the right to decide that those two men must be our only heroes? Who decided that for Henry Reed to become a scientist he had to work like George Washington Carver, as a bootblack, to buy a lousy microscope? Bailey was obviously always going to be too small to be an athlete, so which concrete angel glued to what country seat had decided that if my brother wanted to become a lawyer he had to first pay penance for his skin by picking cotton and hoeing corn and studying correspondence books at night for twenty years?

The man's dead words fell like bricks around the auditorium and too many settled in my belly. Constrained by hard-learned manners I couldn't look behind me, but to my left and right the proud graduating class of 1940 had dropped their heads. Every girl in my row had found something new to do with her handkerchief. Some folded the tiny squares into love knots, some into triangles, but most were wadding them, then pressing them flat on their yellow laps.

On the dais, the ancient tragedy was being replayed. Professor Parsons sat, a sculptor's reject, rigid. His large, heavy body seemed devoid of will or willingness, and his eyes said he was no longer with us. The other teachers examined the flag (which was draped stage right) or their notes, or the windows which opened on our now-famous playing diamond.

Graduation, the hush-hush magic time of frills and gifts and congratulations and diplomas, was finished for me before my name was called. The accomplishment was nothing. The meticulous maps, drawn in three colors of ink, learning and spelling decasyllabic words, memorizing the whole of *The Rape of Lucrece*—it was for nothing. Donleavy had exposed us.

We were maids and farmers, handymen 45 and washerwomen, and anything higher that we aspired to was farcical and presumptuous.

Then I wished that Gabriel Prosser and Nat Turner had killed all whitefolks in their beds and that Abraham Lincoln had been assassinated before the signing of the Emancipation Proclamation, and that Harriet Tubman had been killed by that blow on her head and Christopher Columbus had drowned in the *Santa Maria*.

It was awful to be a Negro and have no control over my life. It was brutal to be young and already trained to sit quietly and listen to charges brought against my color with no chance of defense. We should all be dead. I thought I should like to see us all dead, one on top of the other. A pyramid of flesh with the whitefolks on the bottom, as the broad base, then the Indians with their silly tomahawks and teepees and wigwams and treaties, the Negroes with their mops and recipes and cotton sacks and spirituals sticking out of their mouths. The Dutch children should all stumble in their wooden shoes and break their necks. The French should choke to death on the Louisiana Purchase (1803) while silkworms ate all the Chinese with their stupid pigtails. As a species, we were an abomination. All of us.

Donleavy was running for election, and assured our parents that if he won we could count on having the only colored paved playing field in that part of Arkansas. Also—he never looked up to acknowledge the grunts of acceptance—also, we were bound to get some new equipment for the home economics building and the workshop.

He finished, and since there was no need to give any more than the most perfunctory thank-you's, he nodded to the men on the stage, and the tall white man who was never introduced joined him at the door. They left with the attitude that now they were off to something really important. (The graduation ceremonies at Lafayette County Training School had been a mere preliminary.)

50   The ugliness they left was palpable. An uninvited guest who wouldn't leave. The choir was summoned and sang a modern arrangement of "Onward, Christian Soldiers," with new words pertaining to graduates seeking their place in the world. But it didn't work. Elouise, the daughter of the Baptist minister, recited "Invictus," and I could have cried at the impertinence of "I am the master of my fate, I am the captain of my soul."

My name had lost its ring of familiarity and I had to be nudged to go and receive my diploma. All my preparations had fled. I neither marched up to the stage like a conquering Amazon, nor did I look in the audience for Bailey's nod of approval. Marguerite Johnson, I heard the name again, my honors were read, there were noises in the audience of appreciation, and I took my place on the stage as rehearsed.

I thought about colors I hated: ecru, puce, lavender, beige and black.

There was shuffling and rustling around me, then Henry Reed was giving his valedictory address, "To Be or Not to Be." Hadn't he heard the whitefolks? We couldn't *be,* so the question was a waste of time. Henry's voice came out clear and strong. I feared to look at him. Hadn't he got the message? There was no "nobler in the mind" for Negroes because the world didn't think we had minds, and they let us know it. "Outrageous fortune"? Now, that was a joke. When the ceremony was over I had to tell Henry Reed some things. That is, if I still cared. Not "rub," Henry, "erase." "Ah, there's the erase." Us.

Henry had been a good student in elocution. His voice rose on tides of promise and fell on waves of warnings. The English teacher had helped him to create a sermon winging through Hamlet's soliloquy. To be a man, a doer, a builder, a leader, or to be a tool, an unfunny joke, a crusher of funky toadstools. I marveled that Henry could go through with the speech as if we had a choice.

I had been listening and silently rebutting 55 each sentence with my eyes closed; then there was a hush, which in an audience warns that something unplanned is happening. I looked up and saw Henry Reed, the conservative, the proper, the A student, turn his back to the audience and turn to us (the proud graduating class of 1940) and sing, nearly speaking,

> "Lift ev'ry voice and sing
> Till earth and heaven ring
> Ring with the harmonies of Liberty . . ."

It was the poem written by James Weldon Johnson. It was the music composed by J. Rosamond Johnson. It was the Negro national anthem. Out of habit we were singing it.

Our mothers and fathers stood in the dark hall and joined the hymn of encouragement. A kindergarten teacher led the small children onto the stage and the buttercups and daisies and bunny rabbits marked time and tried to follow:

> "Stony the road we trod
> Bitter the chastening rod
> Felt in the days when hope, unborn, had died.
> Yet with a steady beat
> Have not our weary feet
> Come to the place for which our fathers sighed?"

Each child I knew had learned that song with his ABC's and along with "Jesus Loves Me This I Know." But I personally had never heard it before. Never heard the words, despite the thousands of times I had sung them. Never thought they had anything to do with me.

On the other hand, the words of Patrick Henry had made such an impression on me that I had been able to stretch myself tall and trembling and say, "I know not what course others may take, but as for me, give me liberty or give me death."

60   And now I heard, really for the first time:

> "We have come over a way that with tears has been watered,
> We have come, treading our path through the blood of the slaughtered."

While echoes of the song shivered in the air, Henry Reed bowed his head, said "Thank you," and returned to his place in the line. The tears that slipped down many faces were not wiped away in shame.

We were on top again. As always, again. We survived. The depths had been icy and dark, but now a bright sun spoke to our souls.

I was no longer simply a member of the proud graduating class of 1940; I was a proud member of the wonderful, beautiful Negro race.

Oh, Black known and unknown poets, how often have your auctioned pains sustained us? Who will compute the lonely nights made less lonely by your songs, or the empty pots made less tragic by your tales?

If we were a people much given to revealing secrets, we might raise monuments and sacrifice to the memories of our poets, but slavery cured us of that weakness. It may be enough, however, to have it said that we survive in exact relationship to the dedication of our poets (include preachers, musicians and blues singers).

READING AND THINKING

1. What is the main idea of Angelou's "Graduation"? What idea about race and education does she convey, and where is it most visibly evident?

2. What details of Angelou's description do you find most interesting and engaging? Why?

3. Trace the shifting moods that Angelou describes her young self as experiencing. What accounts for her shifts of mood and feeling?

4. Explain the significance of the allusions to the following historical figures: Booker T. Washington, Gabriel Prosser, Nat Turner, Harriet Tubman, Christopher Columbus. If you are unfamiliar with any of these people, research their lives to better understand why Angelou includes them here.

THINKING AND WRITING

1. Analyze the structure of "Graduation." Where does the introduction end? Where does the conclusion begin? How does Angelou accommodate her changing moods in the overall structure of her essay?

2. Identify a key moment in the essay, one that you find especially interesting or engaging. Explain what Angelou has done in that passage stylistically by analyzing her language, sentences, and imagery there.

3. What implications for the segregation and tracking of students do you find in "Graduation"? What does Angelou seem to suggest about such educational differentiation for black and white students? What do you think about educational tracking?

4. Describe a scene or tell a story based on your graduation from grade school or from high school. Provide specific details to make the scene or story come alive for your readers. Decide on an idea you want your piece to convey.

EDUCATIONAL EXPECTATIONS: AN OCCASION FOR WRITING

In "Graduation," Maya Angelou describes a school graduation, including the speeches traditionally presented on such occasions. In this Occasion for Writing, you are invited to reflect on the "expectations" of education—what people expect of certain classes and races in terms of their educational promise and progress. Consider the "expectations" of education. What do people expect of different social and racial groups when it comes to education? Why?

School segregation protest, St. Louis, Missouri (1963)

First day of desegregation, Fort Myer, Virginia (1954)

PREPARING TO WRITE: OCCASIONS TO THINK ABOUT WHAT YOU SEE

1. Examine each of the preceding photographs. Describe what you see in each. Focus first on the human figures and then on background figures and props.

2. To what extent do these two images "talk" to one another? What do they "say" individually and together? Explain.

MOVING TOWARD ESSAY: OCCASIONS TO ANALYZE AND REFLECT

1. What are the educational expectations of the people depicted in the segregation protest picture? What do you think stimulated their protest? Why?

2. What do you surmise are the expectations of the two young students highlighted in the classroom picture? What elements in the photograph help you make those assumptions? What of your prior knowledge helps you make your assumptions? What might be the expectations of the teacher for these students? Explain.

WRITING THOUGHTFULLY: OCCASIONS FOR IDEAS AND ESSAYS

1. Describe a scene or tell a story from your experience about education and the expectations others had of you.

2. Tell a second story or describe a second scene from a different educational moment you experienced or witnessed. What expectations did you have for yourself in this learning situation?

3. Identify at least two connections or links between the stories or scenes from the memories you described and from the educational situations you described earlier.

4. Using the work you did in any or all of the previous exercises, write an essay in which you explore the significance of educational expectations that parents have for their children, those that teachers have for their students, and those that students have for themselves.

CREATING OCCASIONS

1. Consider other expectations of learning, like standardized testing, President Bush's educational initiative No Child Left Behind, or even grades given out in schools. How do these types of expectations affect our learning? Select another expectation of learning and discuss it in terms of Angelou's essay and the images presented in this Occasion.

Bernard Cooper (b. 1951)

Bernard Cooper grew up in Hollywood, California, and received a Bachelor of Fine Arts and Master of Fine Arts from California Institute of the Arts. Cooper is the author of the short story collections *Maps to Anywhere* (1990), for which he won an Ernest Hemingway Foundation/PEN Award, and *Guess Again: Short Stories* (2000), his first novel *A Year of Rhymes* (1993), and the memoir *Truth Serum: Memoirs* (1997). Cooper's essays have appeared in *Harper's,* the *Los Angeles Times Magazine,* and the *Paris Review,* among other periodicals.

LABYRINTHINE

In "Labyrinthine," Cooper uses the image of the maze to explore aspects of aging and of learning. His childhood story of doing mazes in coloring books initiates a series of reflections about the labyrinthine complexities of learning and facing truths about our lives.

1   When I discovered my first maze among the pages of a coloring book, I dutifully guided the mouse in the margins toward his wedge of cheese at the center. I dragged my crayon through narrow alleys and around corners, backing out of dead ends, trying this direction instead of that. Often I had to stop and re-think my strategy, squinting until some unobstructed path became clear and I could start to move the crayon again.

I kept my sights on the small chamber in the middle of the page and knew that being lost would not be in vain; wrong turns only improved my chances, showed me that one true path toward my reward. Even when trapped in the hallways of the maze, I felt an embracing safety, as if I'd been zipped in a sleeping bag.

Reaching the cheese had about it a triumph and finality I'd never experienced after coloring a picture or connecting the dots. If only I'd known a word like "inevitable," since that's how it felt to finally slip into the innermost room. I gripped the crayon, savored the place.

The lines on the next maze in the coloring book curved and rippled like waves on water. The object of this maze was to lead a hungry dog to his bone. Mouse to cheese, dog to bone—the premise quickly ceased to matter. It was the tricky, halting travel I was after, forging a passage, finding my way.

5   Later that day, as I walked through our living room, a maze revealed itself to me in the mahogany coffee table. I sat on the floor, fingered the wood grain, and found a winding avenue through it. The fabric of my parents' blanket was a pattern of climbing ivy and, from one end of the bed to the other, I traced the air between the tendrils. Soon I didn't need to use a finger, mapping my path by sight. I moved through the veins of the marble heart, through the space between the paisleys on my mother's blouse. At the age of seven I changed forever, like the faithful who see Christ on the side of a barn or peering up from a corn tortilla. Everywhere I looked, a labyrinth meandered.

Soon the mazes in the coloring books, in the comic-strip section of the Sunday paper, or on the placemats of coffee shops that served "children's meals" became too easy. And so I began to make my own. I drew them on the cardboard rectangles that my father's dress shirts were folded around when they came back from the cleaner's. My frugal mother, hoarder of jelly jars and rubber bands, had saved a stack of them. She was happy to put the cardboard to use, if a bit mystified by my new obsession.

The best method was to start from the center and work outward with a sharpened pencil, creating layers of complication. I left a few gaps in every line, and after I'd gotten a feel for the architecture of the whole, I'd close off openings, reinforce walls, a slave sealing the pharaoh's tomb. My blind alleys were especially treacherous; I constructed them so that, by the time one realized he'd gotten stuck, turning back would be an exquisite ordeal.

My hobby required a twofold concentration: carefully planning a maze while allowing myself the fresh pleasure of moving through it. Alone in my bedroom, sitting at my desk, I sometimes spent the better part of an afternoon on a single maze. I worked with the patience of a redwood growing rings. Drawing myself into corners, erasing a wall if all else failed, I fooled and baffled and freed myself.

Eventually I used shelf paper, tearing off larger and larger sheets to accommodate my burgeoning ambition. Once I brought a huge maze to my mother, who was drinking a cup of coffee in the kitchen. It wafted behind me like an ostentatious cape. I draped it over the table and challenged her to try it. She hadn't looked at it for more than a second before she refused. "You've got to be kidding," she said, blotting her lips with a paper napkin. "I'm lost enough as it is." When my father returned from work that night, he hefted his briefcase into the closet, his hat wet and drooping from the rain. "Later," he said (his code word for "never") when I waved the banner of my labyrinth before him.

10   It was inconceivable to me that someone wouldn't want to enter a maze, wouldn't lapse into the trance it required, wouldn't sacrifice the time to find a solution. But mazes had a strange effect on my parents: they took one look at those tangled paths and seemed to wilt.

I was a late child, a "big surprise" as my mother liked to say; by the time I'd turned seven, my parents were trying to cut a swath through the forest of middle age. Their mortgage ballooned. The plumbing rusted. Old friends grew sick or moved away. The creases in their skin deepened, so complex a network of lines, my mazes paled by comparison. Father's hair receded, Mother's grayed. "When you've lived as long as we have . . . ," they'd say, which meant no surprises loomed in their future; it was repetition from here on out. The endless succession of burdens and concerns was enough to make anyone forgetful. Eggs were boiled until they turned brown, sprinklers left on till the lawn grew soggy, keys and glasses and watches misplaced. When I asked my parents about their past, they cocked their heads, stared into the distance, and often couldn't recall the details.

Thirty years later, I understand my parents' refusal. Why would anyone choose to get mired in a maze when the days encase us, loopy and confusing? Remembered events merge together or fade away. Places and dates grow dubious, a jumble of guesswork and speculation. *What's-his-name* and *thingamajig* replace the bright particular. Recollecting the past becomes as unreliable as forecasting the future; you consult yourself with a certain trepidation and take your answer with a grain of salt. The friends you turn to for confirmation are just as muddled; they furrow their brows and look at you blankly. Of course, once in a while you find the tiny, pungent details poised on your tongue like caviar. But more often than not, you settle for sloppy approximations—"I was visiting Texas or Colorado, in 1971 or '72"—and the anecdote rambles on regardless. When the face of a friend from childhood suddenly comes back to me, it's sad to think that if a certain synapse hadn't fired just then, I may never have recalled that friend again. Sometimes I'm not sure if I've overheard a story in conversation, read it in a book, or if I'm the person to whom it happened; whose adventures, besides my own, are wedged in my memory? Then there are the things I've dreamed and mistaken as fact. When you've lived as long as I have, uncertainty is virtually indistinguishable from the truth, which as far as I know is never naked, but always wearing some disguise.

Mother, Father: I'm growing middle-aged, lost in the folds and bones of my body. It gets harder to remember the days when you were here. I suppose it was inevitable that, gazing down at this piece of paper, I'd feel your weary expressions on my face. What have things been like since you've been gone? Labyrinthine. The very sound of that word sums it up—as slippery as thought, as perplexing as the truth, as long and convoluted as a life.

READING AND THINKING

1. What does Cooper learn as a child about mazes, especially about finding his way to the goal? What does he mean by saying that wrong turns actually improved his chances of solving the maze?

2. Why did Cooper, as a child, prefer solving mazes to connecting dots and coloring pictures? What other examples of mazes does Cooper identify? Why do they cease to satisfy him?

3. Why does Cooper begin constructing his own mazes? How does he do it? What method does he adopt in building his mazes? Why does he do it the way he does? How does he fool and baffle and free himself?

THINKING AND WRITING

1. What does Cooper convey about his parents by describing their response to his mazes? Through his description of their aging faces? Through his mention of eggs and sprinklers and keys and watches? What idea is he developing by means of these examples?

2. Explain what Cooper means by saying that "uncertainty is virtually indistinguishable from truth" and that truth is "never naked" but always "wearing some disguise"?

3. What is the effect of Cooper's addressing his parents in his final paragraph? What does he say to them? Why? What is the significance for Cooper of the word "labyrinthine" and of the final sentence of the essay?

LABYRINTHS AND LEARNING: AN OCCASION FOR WRITING

In his essay "Labyrinthine," Bernard Cooper uses the image of the labyrinth to convey his experience and perspective on coming to an understanding of truths. In the following Occasion for Writing you will have an opportunity to learn about and to think about various kinds of mazes and labyrinths and their connections with learning.

PREPARING TO WRITE: OCCASIONS TO THINK ABOUT WHAT YOU SEE

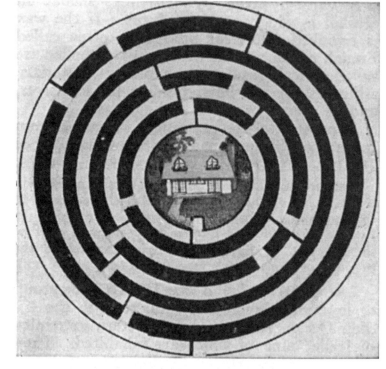

1. Describe one of the mazes seen here. Put yourself in it and try to find your way out.

2. Identify a time when you played with or in a maze as a child, or later in your life when you found yourself in a maze-like situation.

MOVING TOWARD ESSAY: OCCASIONS TO ANALYZE AND REFLECT

1. Explain how you solved the maze figure above. What did you do first, second, third? What did you do when you became stuck?

2. Describe how you solved a maze-like problem in your young adult life, something bureaucratic perhaps. Discuss your feelings at the time of being involved in the maze-like or labyrinthine situation and explain your solution to it.

WRITING THOUGHTFULLY: OCCASIONS FOR IDEAS AND ESSAYS

1. Summarize Cooper's essay "Labyrinthine." Identify its main idea and explain how Cooper conveys, illustrates, and supports it. How do the mazes you've just examined complement or complicate Cooper's essay?

2. Read the following parable about labyrinths and then write a three-sentence interpretation of it. How does the parable build on the work you've done previously in this Occasion?

Jorge Luis Borges
The Two Kings and the Two Labyrinths

It is said by men worthy of belief (though Allah's knowledge is greater) that in the first days there was a king of the isles of Babylonia who called together his architects and his priests and bade them build him a labyrinth so confused and so subtle that the most prudent men would not venture to enter it, and those who did would lose their way. Most unseemly was the edifice that resulted, for it is the prerogative of God, not man, to strike confusion and inspire wonder. In time there came to the court a king of the Arabs, and the king of Babylonia (to mock the simplicity of his guest) bade him enter the labyrinth, where the king of the Arabs wandered, humiliated and confused, until the coming of the evening, when he implored God's aid and found the door. His lips offered no complaint, though he said to the king of Babylonia that in his land he had another labyrinth, and Allah willing, he would see that someday the king of Babylonia made its acquaintance. Then he returned to Arabia with his captains and his wardens and he wreaked such havoc upon the kingdoms of Babylonia, and with such great blessing by fortune, that he brought low its castles, crushed its people and took the king of Babylonia himself captive. He tied him atop a swift-footed camel and led him into the desert. Three days they rode, and then he said to him, "O king of time and substance and cipher of the century! In Babylonia didst thou attempt to make me lose my way in a labyrinth of brass with many stairways, doors, and walls; now the Powerful One has seen fit to allow me to show thee mine, which has no stairways to climb, nor doors to force, nor wearying galleries to wander through, nor walls to impede thy passage."

Then he untied the bonds of the king of Babylonia and abandoned him in the middle of the desert, where he died of hunger and thirst. Glory to Him who does not die.

3. Using the work you did in the previous exercises, and in conjunction with Cooper's essay, write your own essay about mazes and labyrinths and the connection you feel they have to education. How can education and learning be like a maze?

CREATING OCCASIONS

1. In Greek mythology the labyrinth refers to the maze in which the mythological Minotaur, half-bull and half-man, was confined. Each year Greek youths were led into the labyrinth and devoured by the Minotaur. The labyrinth's designer, Daedalus, got himself and his son, Icarus, out of the maze by making wax wings, attaching them to their arms and feet, and flying out. Do some research about what happened to Daedalus and Icarus when they flew out of the labyrinth. Research images, artwork, or texts about them. Find out, also, how the Minotaur was finally slain by Theseus, a Greek hero, and how Theseus was able to get out of the labyrinth after slaying the Minotaur. What do these myths contribute to the discussion of mazes and education?

THE RIGHT AND PRIVILEGE OF EDUCATION

Education has not always been a right, but rather for a long time was the preserve of the wealthy and the privileged. What Americans and Europeans have come to perceive as a right remains for many people around the world a near impossibility due to poverty or to politics. Women are denied educations in some cultures; the poor often lack opportunities to become educated beyond basic literacy.

Even when opportunities for being educated exist, they always exist at different levels of quality. All schools are not the same: they differ in the facilities and services they provide; they differ according to the administrators who run them and the teachers who teach in them; they differ in the students attending them. They differ economically and socially, and those differences spell greater opportunities for the few and much lesser opportunities for the many.

Yet even with unequal opportunities, with the deck stacked against them, some individuals become well educated against the odds. They read and they observe; they listen and learn. They seize every chance to learn, and they invent occasions for their own learning. Abraham Lincoln reading by firelight; Malcolm X studying the dictionary in prison; Richard Wright taking advantage of the public library; Frederick Douglass coaxing education out of his playmates—these are just a few of the celebrated self-motivated learners who educated themselves.

As with inequalities in learning, there exist inequalities in teaching. All teachers are not equal: they are not equally well prepared; they are not equally talented or dedicated. One inspiring teacher, however, can light the spark that ignites the fire of learning. Moreover, not all educational institutions provide the same opportunities—the amount of funding differs among schools, and budgets for schooling can change every year. But these inequalities do not necessarily mar the educational standard of the school.

In her essay "Clamorous to Learn," Eudora Welty describes her first teachers and how they influenced her early learning. In "Taking Women Students Seriously," Adrienne Rich urges college teachers to accord their women students the same respect they give to their men and to present students of both sexes with equal challenges and expectations. In a strong political critique of the education of the poor in his "Banking Concept of Education," Paolo Freire argues for more relevant and engaging kinds of teaching and learning.

Eudora Welty (1909–2001)

Eudora Welty was born in Jackson, Mississippi; she attended Mississippi State College for Women and the University of Wisconsin. During World War II, Welty was on staff at the *New York Times Book Review,* where she indulged her prodigious appetite for reading. She began publishing short stories in 1941 with *The Curtain of Green and Other Stories.* Over thirty years later, in 1973, she was awarded a Pulitzer Prize in fiction for *The Optimist's Daughter.* Welty has also published novels, as well as criticism, some of which has been collected in *The Eye of the Story* (1978).

CLAMOROUS TO LEARN

Welty's 1984 memoir, *One Writer's Beginnings,* describes her early experience with language, learning, literature, and life. The following excerpt, "Clamorous to Learn," is taken from a chapter entitled "Listening." In it, Welty characterizes her first-grade teacher, Miss Duling, who is as much dedicated to the moral and social improvement of her young pupils as she is to their intellectual development. What comes through Welty's recounting of early school memories is a clear love of books along with a deep passion for learning.

1   From the first I was clamorous to learn—I wanted to know and begged to be told not so much what, or how, or why, or where, as when. How soon?

> Pear tree by the garden gate,
> How much longer must I wait?

This rhyme from one of my nursery books was the one that spoke for me. But I lived not at all unhappily in this craving, for my wild curiosity was in large part suspense, which carries its own secret pleasure. And so one of the godmothers of fiction was already bending over me.

When I was five years old, I knew the alphabet, I'd been vaccinated (for smallpox), and I could read. So my mother walked across the street to Jefferson Davis Grammar School and asked the principal if she would allow me to enter the first grade after Christmas.

"Oh, all right," said Miss Duling. "Probably the best thing you could do with her."

5   Miss Duling, a lifelong subscriber to perfection, was a figure of authority, the most whole-souled I have ever come to know. She was a dedicated schoolteacher who denied herself all she might have done or whatever other way she might have lived (this possibility was the last that could have occurred to us, her subjects in school). I believe she came of well-off people, well-educated, in Kentucky, and certainly old photographs show she was a beautiful, high-spirited-looking young lady—and came down to Jackson to its new grammar school that was going begging for a principal. She must have earned next to nothing; Mississippi then as now was the nation's lowest-ranking state economically, and our legislature has always shown a painfully loud reluctance to give money to public education. That challenge *brought* her.

In the long run she came into touch, as teacher or principal, with three generations of Jacksonians. My parents had not, but everybody else's parents had gone to school to her. She'd taught most of our leaders somewhere along the line. When she wanted something done—some civic oversight corrected, some injustice made right overnight, or even a tree spared that the fool telephone people were about to cut down—she telephoned the mayor, or the chief of police, or the president of the power company, or the head doctor at the hospital, or the judge in charge of a case, or whoever, and calling them by their first names, *told* them. It is impossible to imagine her meeting with anything less than compliance. The ringing of her brass bell from their days at Davis School would still be in their ears. She also proposed a spelling match between the fourth grade at Davis School and the Mississippi Legislature, who went through with it; and that told the Legislature.

Her standards were very high and of course inflexible, her authority was total; why *wouldn't* this carry with it a brass bell that could be heard ringing for a block in all directions? That bell belonged to the figure of Miss Duling as though it grew directly out of her right arm, as wings grew out of an angel or a tail out of the devil. When we entered, marching, into her school, by strictest teaching, surveillance, and order we learned grammar, arithmetic, spelling, reading, writing, and geography; and she, not the teachers, I believe, wrote out the examinations: need I tell you, they were "hard."

She's not the only teacher who has influenced me, but Miss Duling, in some fictional shape or form, has stridden into a larger part of my work than I'd realized until now. She emerges in my perhaps inordinate number of schoolteacher characters. I loved those characters in the writing. But I did not, in life, love Miss Duling. I was afraid of her higharched bony nose, her eyebrows lifted in half-circles above her hooded, brilliant eyes, and of the Kentucky R's in her speech, and the long steps she took in her hightop shoes. I did nothing but bear her bearing-down authority, and did not connect this (as of course we were meant to) with our own need or desire to learn, perhaps because I already had this wish, and did not need to be driven.

She was impervious to lies or foolish excuses or the insufferable plea of not knowing any better. She wasn't going to have any frills, either, at Davis School. When a new governor moved into the mansion, he sent his daughter to Davis School; her name was Lady Rachel Conner. Miss Duling at once called the governor to the telephone and told him, "She'll be plain Rachel here."

Miss Duling dressed as plainly as a Pilgrim on a Thanksgiving poster we made in the schoolroom, in a longish black-and-white checked gingham dress, a bright thick wool sweater the red of a railroad lantern—she'd knitted it herself—black stockings and her narrow elegant feet in black hightop shoes with heels you could hear coming, rhythmical as a parade drum down the hall. Her silky black curly hair was drawn back out of curl, fastened by high combs, and knotted behind. She carried her spectacles on a gold chain hung around her neck. Her gaze was in general sweeping, then suddenly at the point of concentration upon you. With a swing of her bell that took her whole right arm and shoulder, she rang it, militant and impartial, from the head of the front steps of Davis School when it was time for us all to line up, girls on one side, boys on the other. We were to march past her and the school building, while the fourth-grader she nabbed played time on the piano, mostly to a tune we could have skipped to, but we didn't skip into Davis School.

Little recess (open-air exercises) and big recess (lunch-boxes from home opened and eaten on the grass, on the girls' side and the boys' side of the yard) and dismissal were also regulated by Miss Duling's bell. The bell was also used to catch us off guard with fire drill.

It was examinations that drove my wits away, as all emergencies do. Being expected to measure up was paralyzing. I failed to make 100 on my spelling exam because I missed one word and that word was "uncle." Mother, as I knew she would, took it personally. "You couldn't spell *uncle?* When you've got those five perfectly splendid uncles in West Virginia? What would *they* say to that?"

It was never that Mother wanted me to beat my classmates in grades; what she wanted was for me to have my answers right. It was unclouded perfection I was up against.

10

My father was much more tolerant of possible error. He only said, as he steeply and impeccably sharpened my pencils on examination morning, "Now just keep remembering: the examinations were made out for the *average* student to pass. That's the majority. And if the majority can pass, think how much better *you* can do."

15   I looked to my mother, who had her own opinions about the majority. My father wished to treat it with respect, she didn't. I'd been born left-handed, but the habit was broken when I entered the first grade in Davis School. My father had insisted. He pointed out that everything in life had been made for the convenience of right-handed people, because they were the majority, and he often used "what the majority wants" as a criterion for what was for the best. My mother said she could not promise him, could not promise him at all, that I wouldn't stutter as a consequence. Mother had been born left-handed too; her family consisted of five left-handed brothers, a left-handed mother, and a father who could write with both hands at the same time, also backwards and forwards and upside down, different words with each hand. She had been broken of it when she was young, and she said she used to stutter.

"But you still stutter," I'd remind her, only to hear her say loftily, "You should have heard me when I was your age."

In my childhood days, a great deal of stock was put, in general, in the value of doing well in school. Both daily newspapers in Jackson saw the honor roll as news and published the lists, and the grades, of all the honor students. The city fathers gave the children who made the honor roll free season tickets to the baseball games down at the grandstand. We all attended and all worshiped some player on the Jackson Senators: I offered up my 100's in arithmetic and spelling, reading and writing, attendance and, yes, deportment—I must have been a prig!—to Red McDermott, the third baseman. And our happiness matched that of knowing Miss Duling was on her summer vacation, far, far away in Kentucky.

Every school week, visiting teachers came on their days for special lessons. On Mondays, the singing teacher blew into the room fresh from the early outdoors, singing in her high soprano "How do you do?" to do-mi-sol-do, and we responded in chorus from our desks, "I'm ve-ry well" to do-sol-mi-do. Miss Johnson taught us rounds—"Row row row your boat gently down the stream"—and "Little Sir Echo," with half the room singing the words and the other half being the echo, a competition. She was from the North, and she was the one who wanted us all to stop the Christmas carols and see snow. The snow falling that morning outside the window was the first most of us had ever seen, and Miss Johnson threw up the window and held out wide her own black cape and caught flakes on it and ran, as fast as she could go, up and down the aisles to show us the real thing before it melted.

Thursday was Miss Eyrich and Miss Eyrich was Thursday. She came to give us physical training. She wasted no time on nonsense. Without greeting, we were marched straight outside and summarily divided into teams (no choosing sides), put on the mark, and ordered to get set for a relay race. Miss Eyrich cracked out "Go!" Dread rose in my throat. My head swam. Here was my turn, nearly upon me. (Wait, have I been touched—was that slap the touch? Go on! Do I go on without our passing a word? What word? Now am I racing too fast to turn around? Now I'm nearly home, but where is the hand waiting for mine to touch? Am I too late? Have I lost the whole race for our side?) I lost the relay race for our side before I started, through living ahead of myself, dreading to make my start, feeling too late prematurely, and standing transfixed by emergency, trying to think of a password. Thursdays will make me hear Miss Eyrich's voice, "On your mark–get set–GO!"

20   Very composedly and very slowly, the art teacher, who visited each room on Fridays, paced the aisle and looked down over your shoulder at what you were drawing for her. This was Miss Ascher. Coming from behind you, her deep, resonant voice reached you without being a word at all, but a sort of purr. It was much the sound given out by our family doctor when he read the thermometer and found you were running a slight fever: "Um-hm. Um-hm." Both alike, they let you go right ahead with it.

The school toilets were in the boys' and girls' respective basements. After Miss Duling had rung to dismiss school, a friend and I were making our plans for Saturday from adjoining cubicles. "Can you come spend the day with me?" I called out, and she called back, "I might could."

"Who—said—MIGHT—COULD?" It sounded like "Fe Fi Fo Fum!"

We both were petrified, for we knew whose deep measured words these were that came from just outside our doors. That was the voice of Mrs. McWillie, who taught the other fourth grade across the hall from ours. She was not even our teacher, but a very heavy, stern lady who dressed entirely in widow's weeds with a pleated black shirtwaist with a high net collar and velvet ribbon, and a black skirt to her ankles, with black circles under her eyes and a mournful, Presbyterian expression. We children took her to be a hundred years old. We held still.

"You might as well tell me," continued Ms. McWillie. "I'm going to plant myself right here and wait till you come out. Then I'll see who it was I heard saying 'MIGHT-COULD.'"

25   If Elizabeth wouldn't go out, of course I wouldn't either. We knew her to be a teacher who would not flinch from standing there in the basement all afternoon, perhaps even all day Saturday. So we surrendered and came out. I priggishly hoped Elizabeth would clear it up which child it was—it wasn't me.

"So it's you." She regarded us as a brace, made no distinction: whoever didn't say it was guilty by association. "If I ever catch you down here one more time saying 'MIGHT-COULD,' I'm going to carry it to Miss Duling. You'll be kept in every day for a week! I hope you're both sufficiently ashamed of yourselves?" Saying "might-could" was bad, but saying it in the basement made bad grammar a sin. I knew Presbyterians believed that you could go to Hell.

Mrs. McWillie never scared us into grammar, of course. It was my first-year Latin teacher in high school who made me discover I'd fallen in love with it. It took Latin to thrust me into bona fide alliance with words in their true meaning. Learning Latin (once I was free of Caesar) fed my love for words upon words, words in continuation and modification, and the beautiful, sober accretion of a sentence. I could see the achieved sentence finally standing there, as real, intact, and built to stay as the Mississippi State Capital at the top of my street, where I could walk through it on my way to school and hear underfoot the echo of its marble floor, and over me the bell of its rotunda.

On winter's rainy days, the schoolrooms would grow so dark that sometimes you couldn't see the figures on the blackboard. At that point, Mrs. McWillie, that stern fourth-grade teacher, would let her children close their books, and she would move, broad in widow's weeds like darkness itself, to the window and by what light there was she would stand and read aloud "The King of the Golden River." But I was excluded—in the other fourth grade, across the hall. Miss Louella Varnado, my teacher, didn't copy Mrs. McWillie; we had a spelling match: you could spell in the dark. I did not then suspect that there was any other way I could learn the story of "The King of the Golden River" than to have been assigned in the beginning to Mrs. McWillie's cowering fourth grade, then wait for her to treat you to it on the rainy day of her choice. I only now realize how much the treat depended, too, on there not having been money enough to put electric lights in Davis School. John Ruskin had to come in through courtesy of darkness. When in time I found the story in a book and read it to myself, it didn't seem to live up to my longings for a story with that name; as indeed, how could it?

READING AND THINKING

1. What do you think Welty means when she writes that she was "clamorous to learn"? What effect does Welty create by beginning this piece with a nursery rhyme?

2. How does Welty characterize Miss Duling? What does Welty emphasize most about her? What has she learned from Miss Duling?

3. How does Welty characterize the other teachers she mentions? What do you think Welty wants us to make of them?

4. Why was the study of Latin important to Welty as a child? How does the young Welty's love of Latin tie in with her love of stories read aloud to her?

THINKING AND WRITING

1. What is your view of Welty's grammar school teachers? To what extent are these teachers effective? Do they do anything that could be considered educationally harmful, or at least ineffective? Explain.

2. Write a paragraph in which you summarize what Welty says about one of her elementary school teachers.

3. Describe a short scene you remember from elementary school. Try to describe the scene in such a way that your readers can visualize it as they read.

4. Describe a teacher from your past. It need not be an elementary school teacher—and it need not be a favorable portrait.

SPACE TO LEARN:
AN OCCASION FOR WRITING

In "Clamorous to Learn," Eudora Welty describes her passion for learning. An eager and ever-ready student, Welty was both intimidated and inspired by her elementary school teachers. Welty also examines the environment in which she was learning. In this Occasion you will have a chance to reflect on your own educational experience by focusing on key places of learning—how setting can and cannot affect the standards and effectiveness of learning.

Georgia, USA (1941)

© Bettmann/Corbis

© Ed Kashi/Corbis

Cairo, Egypt (1993)

© Rick Friedman/Corbis

Cambridge, MA (2004)

PREPARING TO WRITE: OCCASIONS TO THINK ABOUT WHAT YOU SEE

1. What stands out most about each learning space you see here? How do you identify (or not) with any of these learning environments?

2. Imagine under what circumstances such learning spaces come to be. Make a list of your ideas for each image. Which do you think, if any, is the most effective learning space?

MOVING TOWARD ESSAY: OCCASIONS TO ANALYZE AND REFLECT

1. Consider the implications of the educational settings depicted in the photographs. Explain the differing expectations of teachers and students in those settings. Which setting most closely resembles your own educational experiences? How do these images relate to Welty's essay and her learning environment?

2. One type of learning environment is the vocational shop, or place in which a trade or skill is learned. In learning a trade, a student serves an apprenticeship under a master of that trade. To learn the craft of making violins, for example, you would apprentice yourself to a maker with his or her own shop. To what extent does the master/apprentice educational model appear in schools today? Can any aspects of this vocational model of education be adapted to other forms of teaching and learning? Explain.

3. Another kind of learning place is the home rather than the school setting. Some parents have opted to educate their children at home rather than send them to neighborhood schools. What are some of the advantages and drawbacks for children of such an approach to teaching and learning?

WRITING THOUGHTFULLY: OCCASIONS FOR IDEAS AND ESSAYS

1. Create a scene about one of the best educational experiences in a school setting that you ever had. How did your environment, both inside school and outside, impact your experience? Explain what was special and what was valuable about this experience.

2. Attempt to define what an effective learning experience is to you. Must learning experiences always be in the classroom? Describe the ultimate "classroom" as you believe it should be and use the evidence presented here along with your own to support your views. In choosing your college, how did the environment, setting, campus, buildings, and such affect your decision?

3. Research the educational budgets set out by your hometown and see what types of relationships exist between the economics of your town to the school buildings, classrooms, resources, etc. Write an essay in which you explore the role of money in educational settings. Consider your own college and where money is being spent; how does this reflect on the quality of the education you are receiving?

CREATING OCCASIONS

1. Using the images of educational settings, develop an Occasion for Writing that considers the relationships between students and teachers, the settings for teaching and learning, and the expected outcomes. Link the images you select with something from Welty's essay—or from one of the other essays in this chapter. Develop your own essay about teaching and learning from viewing the images and reading the essay(s).

Adrienne Rich (b. 1929)

Adrienne Rich was born in Baltimore, Maryland. She graduated from Radcliffe College, Harvard University. In 1951, Rich published her first book of poems, *A Change of World,* which won the Yale Younger Poets Award. She went on to publish numerous books, including more than a dozen volumes of poetry, one of which, *Diving into the Wreck* (1973), won the National Book award for Poetry that year. Rich has also published four volumes of essays on literary and political subjects, including *Arts of the Possible* (2001).

CLAIMING AN EDUCATION

"Claiming an Education" was originally given as a lecture in 1978 to an audience of women. In it, Rich makes connections between the education of disadvantaged students and the education of women. She calls for a reconsideration of how women students should be taught and what they need to learn.

1   For this convocation, I planned to separate my remarks into two parts: some thoughts about you, the women students here, and some thoughts about us who teach in a women's college. But ultimately, those two parts are indivisible. If university education means anything beyond the processing of human beings into expected roles, through credit hours, tests, and grades (and I believe that in a women's college especially it *might* mean much more), it implies an ethical and intellectual contract between teacher and student. This contract must remain intuitive, dynamic, unwritten, but we must turn to it again and again if learning is to be reclaimed from the depersonalizing and cheapening pressures of the present-day academic scene.

The first thing I want to say to you who are students is that you cannot afford to think of being here to *receive* an education, you will do much better to think of yourselves as being here to *claim* one. One of the dictionary definitions of the verb "to claim" is: *to take as the rightful owner, to assert in the face of possible contradiction.* "To receive" is *to come into possession of; to act as receptacle or container for; to accept as authoritative or true.* The difference is that between acting and being acted-upon, and for women it can literally mean the difference between life and death.

One of the devastating weaknesses of university learning, of the store of knowledge and opinion that has been handed down through academic training, has been its almost total erasure of women's experience and thought from the curriculum, and its exclusion of women as members of the academic community. Today, with increasing numbers of women students in nearly every branch of higher learning, we still see very few women in the upper levels of faculty and administration in most institutions. Douglass College itself is a women's college in a university administered overwhelmingly by men, who in turn are answerable to the state legislature, again composed predominantly of men. But the most significant fact for you is that what you learn here, the very texts you read, the lectures you hear, the way your studies are divided into categories and fragmented one from the other—all this reflects, to a very large degree, neither objective reality, nor an accurate picture of the past, nor a group of rigorously tested observations about human behavior. What you can learn here (and I mean not only at Douglass but any college in any university) is how *men* have perceived and organized their experience, their history, their ideas of social relationships, good and evil, sickness and health, etc. When you read or hear about "great issues," "major texts," "the mainstream of Western thought," you are hearing about what men, above all white men, in their male subjectivity, have decided is important.

Black and other minority peoples have for some time recognized that their racial and ethnic experience was not accounted for in the studies broadly labeled human; and that even the sciences can be racist. For many reasons, it has been more difficult for women to comprehend our exclusion, and to realize that even the sciences can be sexist. For one thing, it is only within the last hundred years that higher education has grudgingly been opened up to women at all, even to white, middle-class women. And many of us have found ourselves poring eagerly over books with titles like: *The Descent of Man; Man and His Symbols; Irrational Man; The Phenomenon of Man; The Future of Man; Man and the Machine; From Man to Man; May Man Prevail?; Man, Science and Society;* or *One-Dimensional Man*—books pretending to describe a "human" reality that does not include over one-half the human species.

5   Less than a decade ago, with the rebirth of a feminist movement in this country, women students and teachers in a number of universities began to demand and set up women's studies courses—to *claim* a woman-directed education. And, despite the inevitable accusations of "unscholarly," "group therapy," "faddism," etc., despite backlash and budget cuts, women's studies are still growing, offering to more and more women a new intellectual grasp on their lives, new understanding of our history, a fresh vision of the human experience, and also a critical basis for evaluating what they hear and read in other courses, and in the society at large.

But my talk is not really about women's studies, much as I believe in their scholarly, scientific, and human necessity. While I think that any Douglass student has everything to gain by investigating and enrolling in women's studies courses, I want to suggest that there is a more essential experience that you owe yourselves, one which courses in women's studies can greatly enrich, but which finally depends on you, in all your interactions with yourself and your world. This is the experience of *taking responsibility toward yourselves*. Our upbringing as women has so often told us that this should come second to our relationships and responsibilities to other people. We have been offered ethical models of the self-denying wife and mother; intellectual models of the brilliant but slapdash dilettante who never commits herself to anything the whole way, or the intelligent woman who denies her intelligence in order to seem more "feminine," or who sits in passive silence even when she disagrees inwardly with everything that is being said around her.

Responsibility to yourself means refusing to let others do your thinking, talking, and naming for you; it means learning to respect and use your own brains and instincts; hence, grappling with hard work. It means that you do not treat your body as a commodity with which to purchase superficial intimacy or economic security; for our bodies and minds are inseparable in this life, and when we allow our bodies to be treated as objects, our minds are in mortal danger. It means insisting that those to whom you give your friendship and love are able to respect your mind. It means being able to say, with Charlotte Brontë's *Jane Eyre:* "I have an inward treasure born with me, which can keep me alive if all the extraneous delights should be withheld or offered only at a price I cannot afford to give."

Responsibility to yourself means that you don't fall for shallow and easy solutions—predigested books and ideas, weekend encounters guaranteed to change your life, taking "gut" courses instead of ones you know will challenge you, bluffing at school and life instead of doing solid work, marrying early as an escape from real decisions, getting pregnant as an evasion of already existing problems. It means that you refuse to sell your talents and aspirations short, simply to avoid conflict and confrontation. And this, in turn, means resisting the forces in society which say that women should be nice, play safe, have low professional expectations, drown in love and forget about work, live through others, and stay in the places assigned to us. It means that we insist on a life of meaningful work, insist that work be as meaningful as love and friendship in our lives. It means, therefore, the courage to be "different"; not to be continuously available to others when we need time for ourselves and our work; to be able to demand of others—parents, friends, roommates, teachers, lovers, husbands, children—that they respect our sense of purpose and our integrity as persons. Women everywhere are finding the courage to do this, more and more, and we are finding that courage both in our study of women in the past who possessed it, and in each other as we look to other women for comradeship, community, and challenge. The difference between a life lived actively, and a life of passive drifting and dispersal of energies, is an immense difference. Once we begin to feel committed to our lives, responsible to ourselves, we can never again be satisfied with the old, passive way.

Now comes the second part of the contract. I believe that in a women's college you have the right to expect your faculty to take you seriously. The education of women has been a matter of debate for centuries, and old, negative attitudes about women's role, women's ability to think and take leadership, are still rife both in and outside the university. Many male professors (and I don't mean only at Douglass) still feel that teaching in a women's college is a second-rate career. Many tend to eroticize their women students—to treat them as sexual objects—instead of demanding the best of their minds. (At Yale a legal suit [*Alexander v. Yale*] has been brought against the university by a group of women students demanding a stated policy against sexual advances toward female students by male professors.) Many teachers, both men and women, trained in the male-centered tradition, are still handing the ideas and texts of that tradition on to students without teaching them to criticize its antiwoman attitudes, its omission of women as part of the species. Too often, all of us fail to teach the most important thing, which is that clear thinking, active discussion, and excellent writing are all necessary for intellectual freedom, and that these require *hard work*. Sometimes, perhaps in discouragement with a culture which is both anti-intellectual and antiwoman, we may resign ourselves to low expectations for our students before we have given them half a chance to become more thoughtful, expressive human beings. We need to take to heart the words of Elizabeth Barrett Browning, a poet, a thinking woman, and a feminist, who wrote in 1845 of her impatience with studies which cultivate a "passive recipiency" in the mind, and asserted that "women want to be made to *think actively:* their apprehension is quicker than that of men, but their defect lies for the most part in the logical faculty and in the higher mental activities." Note that she implies a defect which can be remedied by intellectual training; *not* an inborn lack of ability.

I have said that the contract on the student's part involves that you demand to be taken seriously so that you can also go on taking yourself seriously. This means seeking out criticism, recognizing that the most affirming thing anyone can do for you is demand that you push yourself further, show you the range of what you *can* do. It means rejecting attitudes of "take-it-easy," "why-be-so-serious," "why-worry-you'll-probably-get-married-anyway." It means assuming your share of responsibility for what happens in the classroom, because that affects the quality of your daily life here. It means that the student sees herself engaged *with* her teachers in an active, 10 ongoing struggle for a real education. But for her to do this, her teachers must be committed to the belief that women's minds and experience are intrinsically valuable and indispensable to any civilization worthy of the name; that there is no more exhilarating and intellectually fertile place in the academic world today than a women's college—*if* both students and teachers in large enough numbers are trying to fulfill this contract. The contract is really a pledge of mutual seriousness about women, about language, ideas, methods, and values. It is our shared commitment toward a world in which the inborn potentialities of so many women's minds will no longer be wasted, raveled-away, paralyzed, or denied.

READING AND THINKING

1. What prompted Rich to present her lecture and essay on women students? What deficiencies in the education of women does Rich identify?

2. What role does Rich's own educational experience as a student and teacher play in the development of her thinking about this topic?

3. What connections does Rich identify between the education of the disadvantaged urban students she taught in New York City and the education of women?

4. What does Rich advocate as a corrective to the inadequate approach to the education of women?

5. What, according to Rich, does a woman need to know? Explain.

THINKING AND WRITING

1. Summarize in a paragraph Rich's central argument in the essay.

2. To what extent do you agree—or not—with Rich's claim that women do not receive an education equal to that of men "because outside the classroom women are perceived [. . .] as prey"?

3. To what extent do you agree—or not—with Rich's claim that the voices of women in classrooms differ in important ways from the voices of men. Consider your experience of the way male and female students speak out in class discussions.

4. How important and of what significance are the various social and cultural contexts Rich mentions as influences on the education of women? To what extent have those contexts changed in the quarter century since Rich wrote this essay? In what ways and to what extent are any of those contexts similar today? Explain.

PROTESTING FOR AND AGAINST EDUCATION: AN OCCASION FOR WRITING

Adrienne Rich's essay constitutes a form of protest against the way women have been treated in various educational settings. In this Occasion for Writing you will have a chance to consider how different groups protest for and against various educational ideas, values, and circumstances.

Female students demonstrate for freedom, Tehran University, Iran (2000).

University of Anglia students protesting the university's adjustment of their grades, Norwich, England (1995).

© Bryn Colton/Assignments Photographers/CORBIS

© Bruce Davidson / Magnum Photos

A woman sits to protest racial discrimination in schools, Birmingham, Alabama (1963.).

© MITCHELL SMITH/CORBIS SYGMA

Cadets at The Citadel celebrate the resignation of Shannon Faulkner, the first woman to be admitted to the all-male military academy (1995).

PREPARING TO WRITE: OCCASIONS TO THINK ABOUT WHAT YOU SEE

1. Describe what you see in each of the accompanying pictures. What dominant impression does each picture convey?

2. Which picture do you find most engaging? Why?

MOVING TOWARD ESSAY: OCCASIONS TO ANALYZE AND REFLECT

1. What have been the historical and cultural reasons for having schools just for boys or girls, men or women? Do you think the move toward admitting women to men's colleges and, later, admitting men to women's colleges was a good one? Why or why not?

2. Do you believe that education is discriminatory against certain groups currently or that it has been in the past? Discuss the political implications of the accompanying images for this Occasion for Writing, and explain how they relate to the message of Rich's speech.

WRITING THOUGHTFULLY: OCCASIONS FOR IDEAS AND ESSAYS

1. Adrienne Rich attended Radcliffe and taught at Douglass, the women's colleges of Harvard and Rutgers universities, respectively. In an essay, examine to what extent the ideas about women's education that Rich advocates are important for women in same-sex schools and for women in coeducational settings. How do the images presented in this Occasion for Writing either support or undermine Rich's argument? To what extent can the issues that Rich raises in her essay be applied to groups other than women?

2. Are educational issues always worth a "fight"? Protests over education have been happening over centuries and on numerous topics like right to education to educational budgets to who should and should not teach. Why do you suppose education creates such tension among groups? Write an essay in which you examine these issues using the evidence from this Occasion or from any current events surrounding education you think are valuable to your essay.

3. Write a letter to Adrienne Rich in which you respond to the ideas she advances in "Claiming an Education." Raise the issue of how her ideas about women can be applied to other groups that have experienced educational discrimination. Do you support same-sex education or coeducation? Why or why not?

CREATING OCCASIONS

1. Examine how the government views education. What bills have been passed recently or are waiting to be passed that influence education? What kinds of protests do you imagine could stem from these reforms?

Paolo Freire (1921–1997)

Born in Brazil, Paulo Freire is best known for his work among the Brazilian peasants, particularly for his approach to pedagogy designed to heighten the critical consciousness of the oppressed. Freire's creative efforts on behalf of adult literacy in Brazil resulted in his exile. His method of education was intensely social and ineradicably political. His ideas, which have become widely known well beyond Brazil, are amply explained in two books, *Pedagogy of the Oppressed* (1964) and *Education for Critical Consciousness* (1973).

THE BANKING CONCEPT OF EDUCATION

In "The Banking Concept of Education," taken from *Education for Critical Consciousness,* Freire contrasts two dramatically different approaches to education. One is a teacher-centered approach in which the teacher is the supreme authority, the dominant figure who speaks, acts, and makes all decisions for his students. The other is a student-centered approach, which reverses the lines of authority and activity, empowering students, energizing them, and making them active centers of their own learning.

1   A careful analysis of the teacher-student relationship at any level, inside or outside the school, reveals its fundamentally narrative character. This relationship involves a *narrating* subject (the teacher) and patient, listening objects (the students). The contents, whether values or empirical dimensions of reality, tend in the process of being narrated to become lifeless and petrified. Education is suffering from narration sickness.

The teacher talks about reality as if it were motionless, static, compartmentalized, and predictable. Or else he expounds on a topic completely alien to the existential experience of the students. His task is to "fill" the students with the contents of his narration—contents which are detached from reality, disconnected from the totality that engendered them and could give them significance. Words are emptied of their concreteness and become a hollow, alienated, and alienating verbosity.

The outstanding characteristic of this narrative education, then, is the sonority of words, not their transforming power. "Four times four is sixteen; the capital of Pará is Belém." The student records, memorizes, and repeats these phrases without perceiving what four times four really means, or realizing the true significance of "capital" in the affirmation "the capital of Pará is Belém," that is, what Belém means for Pará and what Pará means for Brazil.

Narration (with the teacher as narrator) leads the students to memorize mechanically the narrated content. Worse yet, it turns them into "containers," into "receptacles" to be "filled" by the teacher. The more completely she fills the receptacles, the better a teacher she is. The more meekly the receptacles permit themselves to be filled, the better students they are.

Education thus becomes an act of depositing, in which the students are the depositories and the teacher is the depositor. Instead of communicating, the teacher issues communiqués and makes deposits which the students patiently receive, memorize, and repeat. This is the "banking" concept of education, in which the scope of action allowed to the students extends only as far as receiving, filing, and storing the deposits. They do, it is true, have the opportunity to become collectors or cataloguers of the things they store. But in the last analysis, it is the people themselves who are filed away through the lack of creativity, transformation, and knowledge in this (at best) misguided system. For apart from inquiry, apart from the praxis, individuals cannot be truly human. Knowledge emerges only through invention and re-invention, through the restless, impatient, continuing, hopeful inquiry human beings pursue in the world, with the world, and with each other.

In the banking concept of education, knowledge is a gift bestowed by those who consider themselves knowledgeable upon those whom they consider to know nothing. Projecting an absolute ignorance onto others, a characteristic of the ideology of oppression, negates education and knowledge as processes of inquiry. The teacher presents himself to his students as their necessary opposite; by considering their ignorance absolute, he justifies his own existence. The students, alienated like the slave in the Hegelian dialectic, accept their ignorance as justifying the teacher's existence—but, unlike the slave, they never discover that they educate the teacher.

The *raison d'être* of libertarian education, on the other hand, lies in its drive towards reconciliation. Education must begin with the solution of the teacher-student contradiction, by reconciling the poles of the contradiction so that both are simultaneously teachers *and* students.

This solution is not (nor can it be) found in the banking concept. On the contrary, banking education maintains and even stimulates the contradiction through the following attitudes and practices, which mirror oppressive society as a whole:

a. the teacher teaches and the students are taught;
b. the teacher knows everything and the students know nothing;
c. the teacher thinks and the students are thought about;
d. the teacher talks and the students listen—meekly;
e. the teacher disciplines and the students are disciplined;
f. the teacher chooses and enforces his choice, and the students comply;
g. the teacher acts and the students have the illusion of acting through the action of the teacher;
h. the teacher chooses the program content, and the students (who were not consulted) adapt to it;
i. the teacher confuses the authority of knowledge with his or her own professional authority, which she and he sets in opposition to the freedom of the students;
j. the teacher is the subject of the learning process, while the pupils are mere objects.

It is not surprising that the banking concept of education regards men as adaptable, manageable beings. The more students work at storing the deposits entrusted to them, the less they develop the critical consciousness which would result from their intervention in the world as transformers of that world. The more completely they accept the passive role imposed on them, the more they tend simply to adapt to the world as it is and to the fragmented view of reality deposited in them.

The capability of banking education to minimize or annul the students' creative power and to stimulate their credulity serves the interests of the oppressors, who care neither to have the world revealed nor to see it transformed. The oppressors use their "humanitarianism" to preserve a profitable situation. Thus they react almost instinctively against any experiment in education which stimulates the critical faculties and is not content with a partial view of reality but always seeks out the ties which link one point to another and one problem to another.

Indeed, the interests of the oppressors lie in "changing the consciousness of the oppressed, not the situation which oppresses them";[1] for the more the oppressed can be led to adapt to that situation, the more easily they can be dominated. To achieve this end, the oppressors use the banking concept of education in conjunction with a paternalistic social action apparatus, within which the oppressed receive the euphemistic title of "welfare recipients." They are treated as individual cases, as marginal persons who deviate from the general configuration of a "good, organized, and just" society. The oppressed are regarded as the pathology of the healthy society, which must therefore adjust these "incompetent and lazy" folk to its own patterns by changing their mentality. These marginals need to be "integrated," "incorporated" into the healthy society that they have "forsaken."

The truth is, however, that the oppressed are not "marginals," are not people living "outside" society. They have always been "inside"—inside the structure which made them "beings for others." The solution is not to "integrate" them into the structure of oppression, but to transform that structure so that they can become "beings for themselves." Such transformation, of course, would undermine the oppressors' purposes; hence their utilization of the banking concept of education to avoid the threat of student *conscientização*.

The banking approach to adult education, for example, will never propose to students that they critically consider reality. It will deal instead with such vital questions as whether Roger gave green grass to the goat, and insist upon the importance of learning that, on the contrary, *R*oger gave green grass to the *r*abbit. The "humanism" of the banking approach masks the effort to turn women and men into automatons—the very negation of their ontological vocation to be more fully human.

Those who use the banking approach, knowingly or unknowingly (for there are innumerable well-intentioned bank-clerk teachers who do not realize that they are serving only to dehumanize), fail to perceive that the deposits themselves contain contradictions about reality. But, sooner or later, these contradictions may lead formerly passive students to turn against their domestication and the attempt to domesticate reality. They may discover through existential experience that their present way of life is irreconcilable with their vocation to become fully human. They may perceive through their relations with reality that reality is really a *process,* undergoing constant transformation. If men and women are searchers and their ontological vocation is humanization, sooner or later they may perceive the contradiction in which banking education seeks to maintain them, and then engage themselves in the struggle for their liberation.

But the humanist, revolutionary educator 15 cannot wait for this possibility to materialize. From the outset, her efforts must coincide with those of the students to engage in critical thinking and the quest for mutual humanization. His efforts must be imbued with a profound trust in people and their creative power. To achieve this, they must be partners of the students in their relations with them.

The banking concept does not admit to such partnership—and necessarily so. To resolve the teacher-student contradiction, to exchange the role of depositor, prescriber, domesticator, for the role of student among students would be to undermine the power of oppression and serve the cause of liberation.

Implicit in the banking concept is the assumption of a dichotomy between human beings and the world: a person is merely *in* the world, not *with* the world or with others; the individual is spectator, not re-creator. In this view, the person is not a conscious being *(corpo consciente);* he or she is rather the possessor of *a* consciousness: an empty "mind" passively open to the reception of deposits of reality from the world outside. For example, my desk, my books, my coffee cup, all the objects before me—as bits of the world which surrounds me—would be "inside" me, exactly as I am inside my study right now. This view makes no distinction between being accessible to consciousness and entering consciousness. The distinction, however, is essential: the objects which surround me are simply accessible to my consciousness, not located within it. I am aware of them, but they are not inside me.

It follows logically from the banking notion of consciousness that the educator's role is to regulate the way the world "enters into" the students. The teacher's task is to organize a process which already occurs spontaneously, to "fill" the students by making deposits of information which he or she considers to constitute true knowledge.[2] And since people "receive" the world as passive entities, education should make them more passive still, and adapt them to the world. The educated individual is the adapted person, because she or he is better "fit" for the world. Translated into practice, this concept is well suited to the purposes of the oppressors, whose tranquility rests on how well people fit the world the oppressors have created, and how little they question it.

The more completely the majority adapt to the purposes which the dominant minority prescribe for them (thereby depriving them of the right to their own purposes), the more easily the minority can continue to prescribe. The theory and practice of banking education serve this end quite efficiently. Verbalistic lessons, reading requirements,[3] the methods for evaluating "knowledge," the distance between the teacher and the taught, the criteria for promotion: everything in this ready-to-wear approach serves to obviate thinking.

20   The bank-clerk educator does not realize that there is no true security in his hypertrophied role, that one must seek to live *with* others in solidarity. One cannot impose oneself, nor even merely co-exist with one's students. Solidarity requires true communication, and the concept by which such an educator is guided fears and proscribes communication.

Yet only through communication can human life hold meaning. The teacher's thinking is authenticated only by the authenticity of the students' thinking. The teacher cannot think for her students, nor can she impose her thought on them. Authentic thinking, thinking that is concerned about *reality,* does not take place in ivory tower isolation, but only in communication. If it is true that thought has meaning only when generated by action upon the world, the subordination of students to teachers becomes impossible.

Because banking education begins with a false understanding of men and women as objects, it cannot promote the development of what Fromm calls "biophily," but instead produces its opposite: "necrophily."

> While life is characterized by growth in a structured, functional manner, the necrophilous person loves all that does not grow, all that is mechanical. The necrophilous person is driven by the desire to transform the organic into the inorganic, to approach life mechanically, as if all living persons were things. . . . Memory, rather than experience; having, rather than being, is what counts. The necrophilous person can relate to an object—a flower or a person—only if he possesses it; hence a threat to his possession is a threat to himself; if he loses possession he loses contact with the world. . . . He loves control, and in the act of controlling he kills life.[4]

Oppression—overwhelming control—is necrophilic; it is nourished by love of death, not life. The banking concept of education, which serves the interests of oppression, is also necrophilic. Based on a mechanistic, static, naturalistic, spatialized view of consciousness, it transforms students into receiving objects. It attempts to control thinking and action, leads women and men to adjust to the world, and inhibits their creative power.

When their efforts to act responsibly are frustrated, when they find themselves unable to use their faculties, people suffer. "This suffering due to impotence is rooted in the very fact that the human equilibrium has been disturbed."[5] But the inability to act which causes people's anguish also causes them to reject their impotence, by attempting

> . . . to restore [their] capacity to act. But can [they], and how? One way is to submit to and identify with a person or group having power. By this symbolic participation in another person's life, [men have] the illusion of acting, when in reality [they] only submit to and become part of those who act.[6]

25   Populist manifestations perhaps best exemplify this type of behavior by the oppressed, who, by identifying with charismatic leaders, come to feel that they themselves are active and effective. The rebellion they express as they emerge in the historical process is motivated by that desire to act effectively. The dominant elites consider the remedy to be more domination and repression, carried out in the name of freedom, order, and social peace (that is, the peace of the elites). Thus they can condemn—logically, from their point of view—"the violence of a strike by workers and [can] call upon the state in the same breath to use violence in putting down the strike."[7]

Education as the exercise of domination stimulates the credulity of students, with the ideological intent (often not perceived by educators) of indoctrinating them to adapt to the world of oppression. This accusation is not made in the naïve hope that the dominant elites will thereby simply abandon the practice. Its objective is to call the attention of true humanists to the fact that they cannot use banking educational methods in the pursuit of liberation, for they would only negate that very pursuit. Nor may a revolutionary society inherit these methods from an oppressor society. The revolutionary society which practices banking education is either misguided or mistrusting of people. In either event, it is threatened by the specter of reaction.

Unfortunately, those who espouse the cause of liberation are themselves surrounded and influenced by the climate which generates the banking concept, and often do not perceive its true significance or its dehumanizing power. Paradoxically, then, they utilize this same instrument of alienation in what they consider an effort to liberate. Indeed, some "revolutionaries" brand as "innocents," "dreamers," or even "reactionaries" those who would challenge this educational practice. But one does not liberate people by alienating them. Authentic liberation—the process of humanization—is not another deposit to be made in men. Liberation is a praxis: the action and reflection of men and women upon their world in order to transform it. Those truly committed to the cause of liberation can accept neither the mechanistic concept of consciousness as an empty vessel to be filled, nor the use of banking methods of domination (propaganda, slogans—deposits) in the name of liberation.

Those truly committed to liberation must reject the banking concept in its entirety, adopting instead a concept of women and men as conscious beings, and consciousness as consciousness intent upon the world. They must abandon the educational goal of deposit-making and replace it with the posing of the problems of human beings in their relations with the world. "Problem-posing" education, responding to the essence of consciousness—intentionality—rejects communiqués and embodies communications. It epitomizes the special characteristic of consciousness: being conscious of, not only as intent on objects but as turned in upon itself in a Jasperian "split"—consciousness as consciousness of consciousness.

Liberating education consists in acts of cognition, not transferrals of information. It is a learning situation in which the cognizable object (far from being the end of the cognitive act) intermediates the cognitive actors—teacher on the one hand and students on the other. Accordingly, the practice of problem-posing education entails at the outset that the teacher-student contradiction be resolved. Dialogical relations—indispensable to the capacity of cognitive actors to cooperate in perceiving the same cognizable object—are otherwise impossible.

30   Indeed, problem-posing education, which breaks with the vertical patterns characteristic of banking education, can fulfill its function as the practice of freedom only if it can overcome the above contradiction. Through dialogue, the teacher-of-the-students and the students-of-the-teacher cease to exist and a new term emerges: teacher-student with students-teachers. The teacher is no longer merely the-one-who-teaches, but one who is himself taught in dialogue with the students, who in turn while being taught also teach. They become jointly responsible for a process in which all grow. In this process, arguments based on "authority" are no longer valid; in order to function, authority must be *on the side of* freedom, not *against* it. Here, no one teaches another, nor is anyone self-taught. People teach each other, mediated by the world, by the cognizable objects which in banking education are "owned" by the teacher.

The banking concept (with its tendency to dichotomize everything) distinguishes two stages in the action of the educator. During the first, he cognizes a cognizable object while he prepares his lessons in his study or his laboratory; during the second, he expounds to his students about that object. The students are not called upon to know, but to memorize the contents narrated by the teacher. Nor do the students practice any act of cognition, since the object towards which that act should be directed is the property of the teacher rather than a medium evoking the critical reflection of both teacher and students. Hence in the name of the "preservation of culture and knowledge" we have a system which achieves neither true knowledge nor true culture.

The problem-posing method does not dichotomize the activity of the teacher-student: she is not "cognitive" at one point and "narrative" at another. She is always "cognitive," whether preparing a project or engaging in dialogue with the students. He does not regard cognizable objects as his private property, but as the object of reflection by himself and the students. In this way, the problem-posing educator constantly re-forms his reflections in the reflection of the students. The students—no longer docile listeners—are now critical co-investigators in dialogue with the teacher. The teacher presents the material to the students for their consideration, and re-considers her earlier considerations as the students express their own. The role of the problem-posing educator is to create, together with the students, the conditions under which knowledge at the level of the *doxa* is superseded by true knowledge, at the level of the *logos*.

Whereas banking education anesthetizes and inhibits creative power, problem-posing education involves a constant unveiling of reality. The former attempts to maintain the *submersion* of consciousness; the latter strives for the *emergence* of consciousness and *critical intervention* in reality.

Students, as they are increasingly posed with problems relating to themselves in the world and with the world, will feel increasingly challenged and obliged to respond to that challenge. Because they apprehend the challenge as interrelated to other problems within a total context, not as a theoretical question, the resulting comprehension tends to be increasingly critical and thus constantly less alienated. Their response to the challenge evokes new challenges, followed by new understandings; and gradually the students come to regard themselves as committed.

35   Education as the practice of freedom—as opposed to education as the practice of domination—denies that man is abstract, isolated, independent, and unattached to the world; it also denies that the world exists as a reality apart from people. Authentic reflection considers neither abstract man nor the world without people, but people in their relations

with the world. In these relations consciousness and world are simultaneous: consciousness neither precedes the world nor follows it.

> La conscience et le monde sont dormés d'un même coup: extérieur par essence à la conscience, le monde est, par essence relatif à elle.[8]

In one of our culture circles in Chile, the group was discussing (based on a codification) the anthropological concept of culture. In the midst of the discussion, a peasant who by banking standards was completely ignorant said: "Now I see that without man there is no world." When the educator responded: "Let's say, for the sake of argument, that all the men on earth were to die, but that the earth itself remained, together with trees, birds, animals, rivers, seas, the stars . . . wouldn't all this be a world?" "Oh no," the peasant replied emphatically. "There would be no one to say: 'This is a world.'"

The peasant wished to express the idea that there would be lacking the consciousness of the world which necessarily implies the world of consciousness. *I* cannot exist without a *non-I*. In turn, the *not-I* depends on that existence. The world which brings consciousness into existence becomes the world *of* that consciousness. Hence, the previously cited affirmation of Sartre: *"La conscience et le monde sont dormés d'un même coup."*

As women and men, simultaneously reflecting on themselves and on the world, increase the scope of their perception, they begin to direct their observations towards previously inconspicuous phenomena:

> In perception properly so-called, as an explicit awareness [*Gewahren*], I am turned towards the object, to the paper, for instance. I apprehend it as being this here and now. The apprehension is a singling out, every object having a background in experience. Around and about the paper lie books, pencils, ink-well, and so forth, and these in a certain sense are also "perceived," perceptually there, in the "field of intuition"; but whilst I was turned towards the paper there was no turning in their direction, nor any apprehending of them, not even in a secondary sense. They appeared and yet were not singled out, were not posited on their own account. Every perception of a thing has such a zone of background intuitions or background awareness, if "intuiting" already includes the state of being turned towards, and this also is a "conscious experience," or more briefly a "consciousness of" all indeed that in point of fact lies in the co-perceived objective background.[9]

That which had existed objectively but had not been perceived in its deeper implications (if indeed it was perceived at all) begins to "stand out," assuming the character of a problem and therefore of challenge. Thus, men and women begin to single out elements from their "background awarenesses" and to reflect upon them. These elements are now objects of their consideration, and, as such, objects of their action and cognition.

In problem-posing education, people develop their power to perceive critically *the way they exist* in the world *with which* and *in which* they find themselves; they come to see the world not as a static reality, but as a reality in process, in transformation. Although the dialectical relations of women and men with the world exist independently of how these relations are perceived (or whether or not they are perceived at all), it is also true that the form of action they adopt is to a large extent a function of how they perceive themselves in the world. Hence, the teacher-student and the students-teachers reflect simultaneously on themselves and the world without dichotomizing this reflection from action, and thus establish an authentic form of thought and action.

Once again, the two educational concepts and practices under analysis come into conflict. Banking education (for obvious reasons) attempts, by mythicizing reality, to conceal certain facts which explain the way human beings exist in the world; problem-posing education sets itself the task of demythologizing. Banking education resists dialogue; problem-posing education regards dialogue as indispensable to the act of cognition which unveils reality. Banking education treats students as objects of assistance; problem-posing education makes them critical thinkers. Banking education inhibits creativity and domesticates (although it cannot completely destroy) the *intentionality* of consciousness by isolating consciousness from the world, thereby denying people their ontological and historical vocation of becoming more fully human. Problem-posing education bases itself on creativity and stimulates true reflection and action upon reality; thereby responding to the vocation of persons as beings who are authentic only when engaged in inquiry and creative transformation. In sum: banking theory and practice, as immobilizing and fixating forces, fail to acknowledge men and women as historical beings; problem-posing theory and practice take the people's historicity as their starting point.

Problem-posing education affirms men and women as beings in the process of *becoming*—as unfinished, uncompleted beings in and with a likewise unfinished reality. Indeed, in contrast to other animals who are unfinished, but not historical, people know themselves to be unfinished; they are aware of their incompletion. In this incompletion and this awareness lie the very roots of education as an exclusively human manifestation. The unfinished character of human beings and the transformational character of reality necessitate that education be an ongoing activity.

Education is thus constantly remade in the praxis. In order to *be,* it must *become.* Its "duration" (in the Bergsonian meaning of the word) is found in the interplay of the opposites *permanence* and *change.* The banking method emphasizes permanence and becomes reactionary; problem-posing education which

accepts neither a "well-behaved" present nor a predetermined future—roots itself in the dynamic present and becomes revolutionary.

Problem-posing education is revolutionary futurity. Hence, it is prophetic (and, as such, hopeful). Hence, it corresponds to the historical nature of humankind. Hence, it affirms women and men as beings who transcend themselves, who move forward and look ahead, for whom immobility represents a fatal threat, for whom looking at the past must only be a means of understanding more clearly what and who they are so that they can more wisely build the future. Hence, it identifies with the movement which engages people as beings aware of their incompletion—an historical movement which has its point of departure, its subjects and its objective.

The point of departure of the movement lies in the people themselves. But since people do not exist apart from the world, apart from reality, the movement must begin with the human-world relationship. Accordingly, the point of departure must always be with men and women in the "here and now," which constitutes the situation within which they are submerged, from which they emerge, and in which they intervene. Only by starting from this situation—which determines their perception of it—can they begin to move. To do this authentically they must perceive their state not as fated and unalterable, but merely as limiting—and therefore challenging.

Whereas the banking method directly or indirectly reinforces men's fatalistic perception of their situation, the problem-posing method presents this very situation to them as a problem. As the situation becomes the object of their cognition, the naïve or magical perception which produced their fatalism gives way to perception which is able to perceive itself even as it perceives reality, and can thus be critically objective about that reality.

A deepened consciousness of their situation leads people to apprehend that situation as an historical reality susceptible of transformation. Resignation gives way to the drive for transformation and inquiry, over which men feel themselves to be in control. If people, as historical beings necessarily engaged with other people in a movement of inquiry, did not control that movement, it would be (and is) a violation of their humanity. Any situation in which some individuals prevent others from engaging in the process of inquiry is one of violence. The means used are not important; to alienate human beings from their own decision-making is to change them into objects.

This movement of inquiry must be directed towards humanization—the people's historical vocation. The pursuit of full humanity, however, cannot be carried out in isolation or individualism, but only in fellowship and solidarity; therefore it cannot unfold in the antagonistic relations between oppressors and oppressed. No one can be authentically human while he prevents others from being so. Attempting *to be more* human, individualistically, leads to *having more,* egotistically, a form of dehumanization. Not that it is not fundamental *to have* in order *to be* human. Precisely because it *is* necessary, some men's *having* must not be allowed to constitute an obstacle to others' *having,* must not consolidate the power of the former to crush the latter.

Problem-posing education, as a humanist and liberating praxis, posits as fundamental that the people subjected to domination must fight for their emancipation. To that end, it enables teachers and students to become Subjects of the educational process by overcoming authoritarianism and an alienating intellectualism; it also enables people to overcome their false perception of reality. The world—no longer something to be described with deceptive words—becomes the object of that transforming action by men and women which results in their humanization.

Problem-posing education does not and cannot serve the interests of the oppressor. No oppressive order could permit the oppressed to begin to question: Why? While only a revolutionary society can carry out this education in systematic terms, the revolutionary leaders need not take full power before they can employ the method. In the revolutionary process, the leaders cannot utilize the banking method as an interim measure, justified on grounds of expediency, with the intention of *later* behaving in a genuinely revolutionary fashion. They must be revolutionary—that is to say, dialogical—from the outset.

NOTES

[1]Simone de Beauvoir, *La pensée de droite, aujourd'hui* (Paris); ST, *El pensamiento politico de la derecha* (Buenos Aires, 1963), p. 34.

[2]This concept corresponds to what Sartre calls the "digestive" or "nutritive" concept of education, in which knowledge is "fed" by the teacher to the students to "fill them out." See Jean-Paul Sartre, "Une idée fundamentale de la phénomenologie de Husserl: L'intentionalité," *Situations* I (Paris, 1947).

[3]For example, some professors specify in their reading lists that a book should be read from pages 10 to 15—and do this to "help" their students!

[4]Eric Fromm, *The Heart of Man* (New York, 1966), p. 41.

[5]Ibid., p. 31.

[6]Ibid.

[7]Reinhold Niebuhr, *Moral Man and Immoral Society* (New York, 1960), p. 130.

[8]Sartre, op. cit., p. 32. [The passage is obscure but could be read as "Consciousness and the world are given at one and the same time: the exterior world as it enters consciousness is relative to our ways of seeing and understanding that world."—Editors' note]

[9]Edmund Husserl, *Ideas—General Introduction to Pure Phenomenology* (London, 1969), pp. 105–06.

READING AND THINKING

1. Explain what Freire means when he says that the relationship between students and teachers is essentially narrative in character. Do you agree? Why or why not?

2. Explain the banking analogy that informs Freire's picture of the classroom. What aspects of this analogy seem most convincing? Least convincing? Why?

3. What do you think was Freire's purpose in writing this piece? What is its central idea, and where is it most forcibly evident?

4. What does Freire propose as an alternative to the banking concept of and approach to education? What are the virtues, the strengths, and the attractions of Freire's more libertarian educational model?

THINKING AND WRITING

1. Draw up a counter-list to the one Freire provides (p. 369) that lists the features of the banking concept of education.

2. Write a one-paragraph summary of Freire's central argument in this essay.

3. Tell a story about your own education that illustrates or modifies the banking approach to education that Freire describes here.

4. Discuss in a few paragraphs the advantages and attractions of Freire's libertarian education model; you may also wish to highlight what you consider might be some disadvantages of the educational model that Freire proposes.

ALTERNATIVE LEARNING: AN OCCASION FOR WRITING

In "The Banking Concept of Education," Paolo Freire condemns the traditional style of teaching in which the teacher lectures and the students listen. He proposes a more active and dynamic educational style in which students have power over their learning, and in which the teacher is a guide, coach, and mentor. In the following Occasion you will have a chance to develop your own thinking about teaching and learning, especially by considering schools and settings that offer "alternative learning."

Purpose of the Organization: Deep Springs College Mission Statement

The purpose of Deep Springs College is to prepare its students for a life of service. As students of Deep Springs College we dedicate ourselves to this responsibility through our three pillars. We engage in academics not merely to learn, but to learn how to learn, to hone our intellects, to learn intellectual humility from each other. We undertake labor not merely to accomplish specific tasks, but to learn how to work, to instill in ourselves dedication and self-discipline, to be reminded that lofty ideals can only be realized through concrete efforts. We participate in self-governance not merely to rule ourselves, but to learn how to govern both ourselves and others, to understand democracy and compromise, to become more responsible by taking on more responsibility. Furthermore, we fulfill these pillars in order to find the innate beauty in learning, in laboring and in leading. Each year, we come together to redefine our ideals anew, and to begin the process of merging them with practical necessities. During our time here, we draw from one another an abundance of heart, an optimistic enthusiasm in undertaking our responsibility of service and we draw from the desert a profound tranquility of spirit. Finally, at the end of our time here, we turn outwards from Deep Springs towards to world at large, prepared to take our places in it.

Drafted by the Student Body, Term 2, 2002

The Grind

Students often rise before the sun. At 6:00 the dairy boys are already milking cows half asleep when the feedman gets up to do his first feed run. A farm teamer may have been in the tractor baling hay since 4:30. All of these people are especially thankful for the breakfast cook, who's up early preparing the morning's fixin's.

But they're not the only ones up. Some people pull all-nighters to get their work done. Others sleep first and wake up excruciatingly early to do classwork. At every hour of the day there are at least a couple people up, discussing Heidegger, playing chess, or strumming guitars.

Classes are usually held on weekday mornings between breakfast and lunch. The class schedule is put together by the chair of CurCom at the beginning of each term to accomodate the needs of all students. Typically a student has one or two classes each day.

After classes the community saunters to the Boarding House (BH), summoned by five clangs of the big bell. Conversation at the lunch table varies widely. Some students just out of Epic Literature may be continuing their class discussion over lunch. Others argue about the worth of *People* magazine. And many work out the plan for afternoon labor. The General Labor crew meets to work out today's projects, the Farm Teamers discuss their irrigation schedule, and the cooks plan their dinner.

Soon after lunch the BH crew is hard at work scrubbing pots, the feedman is back on another run, and the rest of the students are scattered about, each with special projects for the afternoon.

Most labor positions entail working from lunch until dinner. This could mean spending an entire day alone in an alfalfa field fixing leaks in irrigation lines, repairing fences and gates with a partner, or working as a group to dig up frozen pipes that need to be repaired and insulated. There are less romantic jobs that could mean spending the day in the office or scrubbing toilets in the main building.

By the time the dinner bell rings outside the BH, most people are well worn and ready for a warm meal. Students here become very aware of how much the meals really provide them with energy and sustenance for the day. Over dinner people also talk about classes, committee work, and labor, but in general most conversations are frivolous and relaxing. We have to shoot the breeze every once in a while. What are the new movies out? Most of us have no idea. Do we have the latest *New York Times?* Yeah, it's two days late. So it goes.

After dinner the BH crew is at it again scrubbing pots and mopping floors. The dinner crowd thins out as some go to play soccer or ultimate frisbee and others get started with their committee and class work. Sometimes a group will go out for a labor emergency. If the cows break out of a grazing area, we need to gather them and fix the fence as soon as possible or they could bloat from eating fresh alfalfa and die. Labor emergencies can happen at any time of the day.

On Tuesday nights the community gathers for Public Speaking. Public Speaking consists of several short (10 min.) speeches, or sometimes lengthy presentations by only one or two students. Other special activities happen at night, too. A poetry reading group meets, committees convene, a bible study group gathers, and other cool things go on. But for the most part, students are hard at work with the next few hundred pages of Proust or Derrida.

It's the grind, and it develops a very noticeable rhythm.

PREPARING TO WRITE: OCCASIONS TO THINK ABOUT WHAT YOU SEE

1. Read through the mission statement and student life description of Deep Springs College. What specifically is unique about this mission statement? What words strike you as unusual to be paired with an educational institution? What words or phrases are expected?

2. Visit the websites of any of the following schools or any of your choosing: Deep Springs College; Harvey Mudd College; or St. John's College, Annapolis. Compare their mission statements. What is emphasized most at each? Why? What elements of the design of their websites emphasize their mission statement?

3. Read Walt Whitman's poem "When I Heard the Learn'd Astronomer" reprinted here. Why do you think the speaker in Whitman's poem gets up and walks out of the astronomy lecture?

Walt Whitman
When I Heard The Learn'd Astronomer (1865)

When I heard the learn'd astronomer,
When the proofs, the figures, were ranged in columns before me,
When I was shown the charts and diagrams, to add, divide, and measure them,
When I sitting heard the astronomer where he lectured with much applause in the
      lecture-room,
How soon unaccountable I became tired and sick,
Till rising; and gliding out I wander'd off by myself,
In the mystical moist night-air, and from time to time,
Look'd up in perfect silence at the stars.

4. What kind of language does the poet use in the first four lines to describe the
    lecture?

5. How does that language compare with the kind of language used in the second four
    lines, after the speaker has left the lecture hall?

MOVING TOWARD ESSAY: OCCASIONS TO ANALYZE AND REFLECT

1. How do you respond to the mission statement for Deep Springs College (p. 378) and
    those you researched? How do you think Paolo Freire would respond to those mission
    statements? Explain.

2. What do you think that the poet, Walt Whitman, is suggesting about learning in his
    poem? Explain the rationale for your thinking. Take into account the kinds of lan-
    guage emphasized in the first and second halves of the poem.

3. After reading the following excerpt from Charles Dickens's novel *Hard Times,* describe
    the view of education proposed by Mr. Gradgrind. How does Gradgrind's perspective on
    education compare with the "banking" concept of education described by Paolo Freire
    (p. 368)? What do you think Whitman's poem's speaker would say to Mr. Gradgrind re-
    garding his emphasis on "facts"? Explain.

Charles Dickens

From Hard Times

"Now, what I want is, Facts, Teach these boys and girls nothing but Facts. Facts alone are wanted in life. Plant nothing else, and root out everything else. You can only form the minds of reasoning animals upon Facts: nothing else will ever be of any service to them. This is the principle on which I bring up my own children, and this is the principle on which I bring up these children. Stick to Facts, sir!" . . .

"In this life, we want nothing but Facts, sir; nothing but Facts!"

The speaker, and the schoolmaster, and the third grown person present, all backed a little, and swept with their eyes the inclined plane of little vessels then, and there arranged in order, ready to have imperial gallons of facts poured into them until they were full to the brim.

WRITING THOUGHTFULLY: OCCASIONS FOR IDEAS AND ESSAYS

1. Using all the evidence given to you in this Occasion as support, write an essay in which you explore the current state of education as you see it. Consider including Samuel Scudder's essay "Look at Your Fish" (p. 100) in your discussion as well. How has your experience with education thus far compared with what each of these writers has examined? Isolate a single moment in one of these writings that speaks to you the most and use it as the centerpiece for your essay.

2. Write a one-paragraph summary of the "banking" concept of education. Then write a one-paragraph summary of an alternative approach to teaching and learning. In an essay using these summaries, describe an experience you have had that could be considered an "alternative approach" to learning. How was this experience better or worse than the more traditional classroom setting of education?

3. Think about the choices you made when deciding where to go to college. Write an essay in which you explore what educational benefits you saw in each of your choices and why you eventually made the choice you did. Use any of the evidence presented in this Occasion to help support you and your choices.

CREATING OCCASIONS

1. Think about alternative ways to learning other things, not just academic material. Think up new ways to teach driving, cooking, photography, or any activity you enjoy. Suppose that you could not use traditional methods of teaching; how would you engage a student of yours in these activities?

Is this photograph a question of
ownership or just a still life? Imagine
what occasioned this scene:

HOW DOES SOMETHING LIKE THIS HAPPEN?

10

NATURE AND THE ENVIRONMENT

The environment is politically charged, linked unavoidably as it is with global warming, hurricanes, endangered species, the destruction of dwindling natural resources, and other so-called natural disasters. There is, of course, no simple solution to any of these problems, but one thing is certain. They will not go away of their own accord. We have used and misused the natural world to serve our own ends, and now there is nothing left to do but take stock of where we are and to move collectively and in earnest to discover a greater harmony between our human world and the nonhuman world that abuts it. At various times the human world seeks to enclose the other world; occasionally, to make unrestricted use of it; and more often than not, simply to take it for granted—while also trying to preserve it in ways that are sometimes at odds with the laws of nature.

The work in this chapter will call on you to think about that nonhuman world in ways that should increase your awareness of what it offers; what it has offered; and how, in the years to come, we can reconceive what we mean by wilderness and reimagine what to do with the larger world that surrounds all of us—the human and the nonhuman.

The work of the first Cluster will acquaint you with a small group of writers who draw inspiration from the natural world. They tend to see in that natural world parallels and correspondences between it and our own smaller world; they see similar correspondences between the creatures who inhabit the larger world and ourselves. The work of the second Cluster calls on all of us to reconceive the natural world and our relationship to it. There is something both political and philosophical in the appeals made by the writers in this Cluster, something that calls on us to contemplate deeply the meaning of wilderness and to take our minds and bodies out into the world as actors and preservationists. But the call is not to be narrow in our views but rather to be more circumspect and more aware of our relationship to the actual world in which we all live. The essential appeal is to become more aware that we inhabit one world, not two worlds, and that we humans bear the responsibility for what we do to and with that world.

MEDITATIONS ON NATURE
AND THE HUMAN CONDITION

Writers often turn to nature for inspiration. What they find there surprises them and leads to new thoughts and ideas about the human condition. Their work reminds us that the division we sense between life in nature and life in community is misleading, even false. It is not simply that we can learn about ourselves by looking more closely into nature but that we can learn to not see ourselves as different, living apart, special. Closer to the earth, we begin to understand that we are bound together—people, communities, creatures large and small—in ways that are at once revealing and mysterious. We see too that nature's lessons reveal themselves nonstop, whether we notice or not. Only our busyness and our failure to observe keep us from seeing what is there—independent of our limitations or our desires.

The writers that we consider in this Cluster call to our attention the natural relationship between life and death, and their meditations on death serve to heighten our sense of life. Virginia Woolf not only meditates on the death of a moth, she also causes us to sense the presence of the life force pulsing through the universe just outside her window. Roy Reed, looking at a fascinating character named Ira Solenberger, asks us to pause and consider the force that pushes the older Solenberger outside each spring to plant yet another garden. With Reed's help we see how inextricably we are bound to the seasons that govern Solenberger's life and our own. Annie Dillard's vision is darker but no less illuminating as she makes us see how the transformation of a moth into an incandescent flame approximates the condition of a writer as she transforms and is transformed by her work.

These writers call us into awareness, ask us to see more clearly our relationships with creatures large and small, and they teach us how to write about what we notice. Our own writing, under their guidance, calls us into compelling relationships.

Virginia Woolf (1882–1941)

For a full biographical note on Virginia Woolf, see p. 117.

THE DEATH OF THE MOTH

"The Death of the Moth" asks you to consider just how closely intertwined are life and death. In this brief essay, Woolf sheds light on the intermingling of those two powerful forces. We see the tiniest of creatures struggling with a force that both energizes it and defeats it. But Woolf asks us to think twice about the defeat as she gives us, finally, a stunning yet calming image of the moth's repose in death.

1   Moths that fly by day are not properly to be called moths; they do not excite that pleasant sense of dark autumn nights and ivy-blossom which the commonest yellow-underwing asleep in the shadow of the curtain never fails to rouse in us. They are hybrid creatures, neither gay like butterflies nor somber like their own species. Nevertheless the present specimen, with his narrow hay-colored wings, fringed with a tassel of the same color, seemed to be content with life. It was a pleasant morning, mid-September, mild, benignant, yet with a keener breath than that of the summer months. The plough was already scoring the field opposite of the window, and where the share had been, the earth was pressed flat and gleamed with moisture. Such vigor came rolling in from the fields and the down beyond that it was difficult to keep the eyes strictly turned upon the book. The rooks too were keeping one of their annual festivities; soaring round the tree tops until it looked as if a vast net with thousands of black knots in it had been cast up into the air; which, after a few moments sank slowly down upon the trees until every twig seemed to have a knot at the end of it. Then, suddenly, the net would be thrown into the air again in a wider circle this time, with the utmost clamor and vociferation, as though to be thrown into the air and settle slowly down upon the tree tops were a tremendously exciting experience.

The same energy which inspired the rooks, the ploughmen, the horse, and even, it seemed the lean bare-backed downs, sent the moth fluttering from side to side of his square of the windowpane. One could not help watching him. One was, indeed, conscious of a queer feeling of pity for him. The possibilities of pleasure seemed that morning so enormous and so various that to have only a moth's part in life, and a day moth's at that, appeared a hard fate, and his zest in enjoying his meager opportunities to the full, pathetic. He flew vigorously to one corner of his compartment, and after waiting there a second, flew across to the other. What remained for him but to fly to a third corner and then to a fourth? That was all he could do, in spite of the size of the downs, the width of the sky, the far-off smoke of houses, and the romantic voice, now and then, of a steamer out at sea. What he would do he did. Watching him, it seemed as if a fiber, very thin but pure, of the enormous energy of the world had been thrust into his frail and diminutive body. As often as he crossed the pane, I could fancy that a thread of vital light became visible. He was little or nothing but life.

Yet, because he was so small, and so simple a form of the energy that was rolling in at the open window and driving its way through so many narrow and intricate corridors in my own brain and in those of other human beings, there was something marvelous as well as pathetic about him. It was as if someone had taken a tiny bead of pure life and decking it as lightly as possible with down and feathers, had set it dancing and zigzagging to show us the true nature of life. Thus displayed one could not get over the strangeness of it. One is apt to forget all about life, seeing it humped and bossed and garnished and cumbered so that it has to move with the greatest circumspection and dignity. Again, the thought of all that life might have been had he been born in any other shape caused one to view his simple activities with a kind of pity.

After a time, tired by his dancing apparently, he settled on the window ledge in the sun, and, the queer spectacle being at an end, I forgot about him. Then, looking up, my eye was caught by him. He was trying to resume his dancing, but seemed either so stiff or so awkward that he could only flutter to the bottom of the windowpane; and when he tried to fly across it he failed. Being intent on other matters I watched these futile attempts for a time without thinking, unconsciously waiting for him to resume his flight, as one waits for a machine, that has stopped momentarily, to start again without considering the reason of its failure. After perhaps a seventh attempt he slipped from the wooden ledge and fell, fluttering his wings, on to his back on the windowsill. The helplessness of his attitude roused me. It flashed upon me that he was in difficulties; he could no longer raise himself; his legs struggled vainly. But, as I stretched out a pencil, meaning to help him to right himself, it came over me that the failure and awkwardness were the approach of death. I laid the pencil down again.

5   The legs agitated themselves once more. I looked as if for the enemy against which he struggled. I looked out of doors. What had happened there? Presumably it was midday, and work in the fields had stopped. Stillness and quiet had replaced the previous animation. The birds had taken themselves off to feed in the brooks. The horse stood still. Yet the power was there all the same, massed outside, indifferent, impersonal, not attending to anything in particular. Somehow it was opposed to the little hay-colored moth. It was useless to try to do anything. One could only watch the extraordinary efforts made by those tiny legs against an oncoming doom which would, had it chosen, have submerged an entire city, not merely a city, but masses of human beings; nothing, I knew, had any chance against death. Nevertheless after a pause of exhaustion the legs fluttered again. It was superb this last protest, and so frantic that he succeeded at last in righting himself. One's sympathies, of course, were all on the side of life. Also, when there was nobody to care or to know, this gigantic effort on the part of an insignificant little moth, against a power of such magnitude, to retain what no one else valued or desired to keep, moved one strangely. Again, somehow, one saw life, a pure bead. I lifted the pencil again, useless though I knew it to be. But even as I did so, the unmistakable tokens of death showed themselves. The body relaxed, and instantly grew stiff. The struggle was over. The insignificant little creature now knew death. As I looked over at the dead moth, this minute wayside triumph of so great a force over so mean an antagonist filled me with wonder. Just as life had been strange a few minutes before, so death was now as strange. The moth having righted himself now lay most decently and uncomplainingly composed. O yes, he seemed to say, death is stronger than I am.

READING AND THINKING

1. What does Woolf reveal about the natural world she's looking at through her window by way of the extended image of the "rooks" (black birds)? Explain the "vast net with thousands of black knots."

2. Explain what it is that sets the moth "fluttering."

3. When the moth nears the end of its life, Woolf is "roused" by its helplessness. Why does she extend her pencil to the moth and then put it down again?

4. What do you think is most surprising for Woolf—most "strange"—about the moth's final response to death?

THINKING AND WRITING

1. Why do you suppose Woolf was "conscious of a queer feeling of pity" for the moth? Cite evidence from the essay.

2. Woolf tells us there was "something marvelous" about the moth. Explain how Woolf's explanation of the "marvelous" moves her essay beyond herself and the moth to us, to all of humanity.

3. As the moth is dying, Woolf looks outside again for the "enemy against which he struggled." Account for what she finds.

4. How does Woolf make use of the pencil she lifts a final time to assist the moth? Why has she bothered with this pencil throughout the essay?

STRANGE BEAUTIES: AN OCCASION FOR WRITING

This Occasion gives you a chance to heighten your powers of observation as you practice looking for strange beauties in nature. Your aim will be to see something small that catches your eye and then, after looking closely, as if through a magnifying glass, to imagine far-reaching implications. You will be learning to let your mind move out from the object under observation, to move from the thing under your microscopic lens out into the larger world. These acts of extension will stretch your mind and sharpen your powers of perception.

PREPARING TO WRITE: OCCASIONS TO THINK ABOUT WHAT YOU SEE

1. Make a list of the things you see in the photograph of the moth. How would you compare this observer with Woolf? With yourself? What has been discovered through the looking glass?

2. The painting of the wing of a roller (a variety of tumbler pigeon) by Albrecht Durer seems to speak to us beyond death. What do you think the painting suggests?

3. Compare *Dying flower* and *Wing of a Roller*. Make a brief list of the details you see in each image. What do the two images say to one another? To you?

4. How does O'Keeffe's title, *Summer Days,* influence the way you see the painting? Explain. List four things that O'Keeffe is causing you to see—two things that you can point to in the painting and two things that you see only in your mind's eye because of the painting.

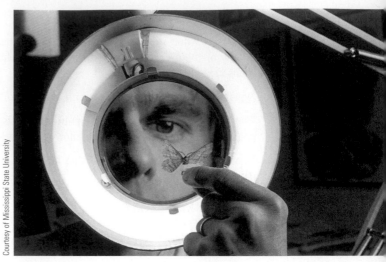

Courtesy of Mississippi State University

Moth

© Art Resource, NY

ALBRECHT DURER, *Wing of a Roller (1512)*

Dying flower

Georgia O'Keeffe 1887–1986; *Summer Days*, 1936. Oil on canvas, 36 × 30 in. (91.44 × 76.2 cm).
Whitney Museum of American Art, New York; Gift of Calvin Klein 94.171. Photograph by Steven Sloman.

GEORGIA O'KEEFFE,
Summer Days (1936)

MOVING TOWARD ESSAY: OCCASIONS TO ANALYZE AND REFLECT

1. Consider yourself the human eye looking at the moth photograph, looking through some kind of optical device that improves your vision. Your object of concern is *Wing of a Roller*. What do you see now, looking closer, that you did not see before?

2. How do you think your closer look at *Wing of a Roller* differed from Woolf's look at the moth in her essay? What is the relationship between a broader view and the close-up view for a writer?

3. Try not to look at the content (skull, flowers, sky, landscape) in *Summer Days* so that you can see only the shape and the colors. What do you see? Make a mental list in your head.

4. Repeat Exercise 3 for *Dying flower*.

WRITING THOUGHTFULLY: OCCASIONS FOR IDEAS AND ESSAYS

1. Tell a brief story about the way your mind moves across these four images, from *Moth* to *Summer Days*. Try to make the story reveal a coherent vision about either life and death or about seeing and knowing.

2. How close do you think O'Keeffe's vision about the relationship between life and death is to Woolf's vision about that same intriguing subject? Write a brief essay in response to this question, citing evidence from both the painting and the essay to help you develop your idea about these two artists.

3. Reconsider that notion about the close-up view and the broader view. How might a good writer use both to give us a better sense of an idea? Frame your answer within an essay titled "Seeing and Knowing from Two Vantage Points."

CREATING OCCASIONS

1. Woolf seems to find a comforting kind of beauty as she writes about and considers the moth's fate. She seems to find both beauty and consolation in that particular death. Consider two or three odd occasions when you have found beauty in strange places. Re-create two of those moments and then use your experiences as evidence in an essay that reveals the significance of your discoveries.

2. Go away from your normal habitat into a more natural setting—a park, the woods, a river basin, a yard, a garden. Spend enough time there to observe the "workings" of the space. Keep track of what you see and the associations you make as you sit quietly observing and thinking. Select the most fascinating thing you saw and, using Woolf as a guide, write a brief essay that gives us both a close-up view of what you saw and a longer-range view of what it meant.

Roy Reed (b. 1930)

Roy Reed was born in Hot Springs, Arkansas, was educated at the University of Missouri School of Journalism, and was a Nieman fellow at Harvard (1963–1964). After serving on the staff of the *Arkansas Gazette* (1956–1964), he joined the staff of the *New York Times,* reporting on the civil rights movement. He later reported for the *Times* from Washington, New Orleans, and London. He taught journalism at the University of Arkansas in Fayetteville from 1979 to 1995 and now lives in Hogeye, Arkansas. His books include *Looking for Hogeye* (1986) and *Faubus: The Life and Times of an American Prodigal* (1997).

SPRING COMES TO HOGEYE

"Spring Comes to Hogeye" introduces us to an Arkansas character, Ira Solenberger, who clearly amuses and delights Reed. Mr. Solenberger's legendary gardens and his theories about gardening provide the focus for this essay that looks beneath the surface of life to highlight a general pattern of ebb and flow that governs not only our natural lives but the ever-recurring seasons. Reed's powers of observation call us to reconsider our own individual lives against the "terrible force" that flowers the Ozarks each spring and brings Mr. Solenberger out of doors in early spring to plant one last garden.

1   Spring was late in the Ozark Mountains. The first week of April had passed, and the oaks and maples were only then risking a few pale green shoots, tentative little leaves that would not constitute much of a loss if another frost stole in at night on the villainous northwest air.

Ira Solenberger was also late. Practically everybody else in Hogeye had braved the hazard of frost and had planted corn, onions, English peas and Irish potatoes. A few, emulating the bold dogwood and redbud trees, which for more than a week had been blooming bright white and purple against the dark hills, had gone so far as to put out beans, squash and even tender tomato plants.

But Mr. Solenberger, who was regarded as the best gardener in Washington County, had not plowed a furrow or planted a seed. Like the craggy maple in front of his house (itself one of the oldest things in Hogeye, a relic of the Butterfield Stage era), he found that his sap was slow to rise that spring. It had not occurred to him to blame it on his eighty-six years.

"It's that old flu," he said. "Got it back in the winter and can't get rid of it. First time I've had it since 19 and 18."

He opened the door of his heating stove and threw another chunk of wood on the fire. He closed it a little sharply and glanced out the window toward his empty garden.

Every April, the main thing going on in the rural South is vegetable gardening. A farmer might take an hour to talk politics or help a cow give birth, but the really urgent business for him, his wife and all of the children who are old enough to keep their feet off the onion sets is getting seeds and plants in the ground to take advantage of the warming days. With a little luck, the sweet corn planted in early April will have roasting ears ("roashnears," they are called) by the middle of June.

This is a pursuit that seeks every year to outwit the awful force that pushes the shoots from the oak's branches, and that turns Seth Timmons's meadow from brown to green, and impels swallows to build nests in weathered barns.

It was the same force, that spring, that pushed Ira Solenberger out the door in a hat and coat, hunched against the biting bright air blowing up from the Illinois River, to kick the dirt and study the sky, and then retreat to the house to throw another chunk of wood on the fire.

There is still a poet up the road at Fayetteville who, in those days, drove into the hills every April to study the hills and watch for Robert Frost's signs—the gold that is nature's first evidence, "her hardest hue to hold"—and for private signs of his own that stirred his spirit.

10   Ira Solenberger's mind ran less to poetry than to science. He was an amateur magician, and he performed magic with plants as well as cards.

"Summer before last, I grafted some tomatoes on some poke stalks."

Why?

"Just to see if they would grow."

But when he talked of nature and growth, he used words that Frost might have used, or Thoreau.

15   "Plow deep. There's one acre right under another acre. I plow both of them."

"Phosphorous makes things grow roots. If you get roots, you're going to get something else."

"I farm with a tractor. But when it gets rowed up and a-growing, I use a roan horse."

He was now in the April sun, away from the stove. His eye scanned the three and a half acres where, just a year earlier—unencumbered by the flu—he had planted rhubarb, corn, tomatoes, squash, sweet potatoes, Irish potatoes, okra, green beans, cantaloupes, radishes, onions, cucumbers and strawberries. He had harvested a bumper crop of everything. He had eaten what he wanted and sold the rest at the farmers' market on the square at Fayetteville.

He pointed to a fallow patch and said, "That's where I had my watermelons last year." He spoke in a loud, professorial voice, as if addressing the cows at the top of the hill.

20   "They told me I raised the biggest watermelons in Northwest Arkansas. One of them weighed eighty-three pounds.

"I've had people ask me, 'What's your secret for raising watermelons?' I tell them, 'I ain't got no secret.'"

Then, still addressing the cows, he proceeded to tell the secret. Plow the ground deep. Watermelons need more air than water, and deep plowing lets in air.

"I plow turrible deep. Eight or ten inches." He grinned with private satisfaction and moved on to a strawberry patch.

Mr. Solenberger believed in humus. He produced it by placing mulch between the rows. I once knew a Mississippi liberal who enjoyed a minor reputation as a gardener by mulching old copies of *The New York Times.* Mr. Solenberger did not take the *Times.* He used dead crab grass.

25   "Make sure it's rotten," he said, jabbing the air with an open pocket knife. "If you plow under something that ain't rotten, it's a detriment to you for the first season."

Many of his neighbors planted by the moon, and still do. Mr. Solenberger did not.

"I don't pay any attention to the moon, and I'll tell you why. I've got a neighbor that plants by the moon, and I asked him a question one day that he couldn't answer. I said, 'You plant a seed in dry ground, when the moon is right, and it won't come up. Then ten days later it comes a rain and that seed sprouts and comes up. But by then the sign of the moon is wrong. How do you account for that?' He couldn't answer that. I don't plant by the moon. I plant by the ground."

He was troubled, though, by another phenomenon, and he was a little reluctant to talk about it. He said the frosts seemed to come later each spring, just as the force that drove him to the plow seemed to have arrived late that year.

"The timber's awful slow a-leafing out." He cast a blue eye toward the hill across the road. "When I was a boy, we weren't bothered with frost. When spring come, it come. Our spring's almost a month later than it used to be."

30   I asked him what he thought the reason was. He glanced at my face to see whether I was ready to accept what he had to say. He decided to risk it.

"Well, sir, I believe the world twists a little bit. You know, everything that grows twists around to the right. Follows the sun. Even our storms that come out of the Gulf, they twist to the right. It's just nature."

Why was a man of eighty-six still involved every April with the earth's greening, as if it were his own? He passed the question off quickly. He indicated that it was merely the same motive that led him to do card tricks and tell jokes and graft tomatoes to poke weed.

"I just like to be doing things."

He returned to the question later, however, sidling up to it so as not to sound too serious. He began by confessing that spring was his favorite season. I asked him why, and he said, "Life is at a high ebb in the spring."

He leaned his chair back against the porch wall and hooked his shoe heels over the lower rung. He studied the trees on the hill across the road, and then he said, "People who are getting up in years, more of them die in the winter when the days are short, and in the hours after midnight. Life is at a low ebb after midnight and in the short days. Did you know that? And the shorter the days, the lower the ebb."

Thus it was the lengthening days that sent Ira Solenberger to the garden, and he could no more resist than the hapless oak bud could resist becoming a leaf.

He was also right about the other. He thrived for one more season of the high ebb. He made one more garden. Then he died in the winter, during the short days.

READING AND THINKING

1. What do the first sentences of the first two paragraphs foreshadow about the essay's main idea?

2. What is the "awful force" that Ira Solenberger and others are trying to "outwit" every spring? Why does Reed call the force "awful"?

3. How do you account for Mr. Solenberger's impatience? What are the signs in Reed's language that point to that impatience?

4. Why do you suppose Reed permits Mr. Solenberger to do most of the talking in this essay?

THINKING AND WRITING

1. Reed tells us that Mr. Solenberger's mind tended toward science rather than poetry. Write a short account of Mr. Solenberger's science, then determine whether it has any poetry in it.

2. Explain in a paragraph why you believe Mr. Solenberger is troubled by the "lateness of spring." What does it have to do with his statement, "Life is at a high ebb in the spring"?

3. What is Reed's attitude towards Mr. Solenberger? Explain in a paragraph how you know, citing evidence from the essay.

4. Explain why this is not just an essay about an aging man from Hogeye. What does the essay's main idea have to do with the rest of us?

BRINGING NATURE INSIDE: AN OCCASION FOR WRITING

This Occasion will ask you to consider how a life lived close to nature distinguishes itself from the lives of those who spend most of their days inside buildings, inside cities and towns, closed off from the outside. You will be looking at architecture that aims to bring nature inside, and you will be considering Reed and Solenberger, two men who have a deep attachment to their rural origins, one who seems never to have left his farm, the other, an expatriate of sorts, who returned to rural Arkansas for the final phase of his life. The work of the Occasion intends to draw you out of interior spaces into the open air, or, better yet, to bring nature inside.

Image provided courtesy of Thorncrown Chapel. www.thorncrown.com.

Thorncrown Chapel, Eureka Springs, Arkansas

Image provided courtesy of Thorncrown Chapel. www.thorncrown.com

PREPARING TO WRITE: OCCASIONS TO THINK ABOUT WHAT YOU SEE

1. Thorncrown Chapel depicted to the left was designed by award-winning architect Fay Jones, who lived in the Ozarks and taught at the University of Arkansas. He was once a pupil of Frank Lloyd Wright. Characterize the relationship between the chapel and the world outside it, the natural world.

2. How does this image of the interior of Thorncrown Chapel change your sense of Jones's architectural concepts?

3. The photograph of a heating stove on the following page is similar, perhaps, to the one Mr. Solenberger kept returning to, to throw another "chunk of wood on the fire." Do you see beauty in the stove itself? Explain.

Interior of Thorncrown Chapel

4. Examine the photograph of the flower on the following page. This is a Yellow Trout Lily, also called a "Yellow Dog-Tooth Violet," a name taken from the shape of the bulb from which this flower sprouts each spring. Large colonies of this flower can be found along shaded streams and wooded slopes. The bloom period is about two weeks. How might Reed have made thematic use of this particular flower in his essay?

5. What are the similarities between the Hogeye, Arkansas, home and the Thorncrown Chapel?

Hogeye, Arkansas home

© Timothy Hursley, 2006

© Gary Cooley

© Johann Helgason

MOVING TOWARD ESSAY: OCCASIONS TO ANALYZE AND REFLECT

1. The Hogeye, Arkansas, home is Roy Reed's house; it was designed by Fay Jones. Imagine what it feels like inside that house as Reed looks out onto nature. He tells us, "Pestering my rural origins, I deliberately built a house that could be heated only by wood." He also tells us, "I yearn to entwine myself in nature, but the simplest feat—one my cat performs without effort—is beyond me." What draws Reed and Solenberger into such close contact with nature? What are the rewards and the tribulations? Might the two be connected?

2. Reed cites a Robert Frost poem, "Nothing Gold Can Stay," in his essay. Here is the full poem:

> Nature's first green is gold,
> Her hardest hue to hold.
> Her early leaf's a flower;
> But only so an hour.
> Then leaf subsides to leaf.
> So Eden sank to grief,
> So dawn goes down to day.
> Nothing gold can stay.

What does the poem help you understand about the essay?

3. What do you think Frost means by the line "So Eden sank to grief"? What is Eden? What causes "grief"? How do you think Reed's attitude about nature differs from Frost's?

4. How do you suppose the yellow-gold that you see in the Yellow Trout Lily differs from the gold that Reed and Frost are talking about?

WRITING THOUGHTFULLY: OCCASIONS FOR IDEAS AND ESSAYS

1. Reed draws us into a rural way of life in "Spring," making Mr. Solenberger carry the weight of his own ideas about nature and a life lived close to the earth. Select a character from your own life and use that character to create an essay about some hidden aspect of nature that you care a great deal about.

2. Write a brief meditation on the final line of Frost's poem: "Nothing gold can stay." You need not agree with Frost.

3. Write an essay that considers whether Mr. Solenberger's "mind ran less to poetry than to science," as Reed claims in his essay. Analyze the evidence presented in Reed's essay to substantiate your claim.

4. Write a short essay in which you consider whether Reed has something spiritual (not necessarily religious) in mind that informs this essay, or whether he is only concerned with the difference between poetry and science.

CREATING OCCASIONS

1. Let Reed's essay draw you toward a consideration of the differences between city life and county life. Consider telling aspects of country life (heating stoves, water wells, coal oil lamps, smokehouses, firewood, churns, animals, flowers, gardens), and use one or two of those aspects in an essay to reveal something significant about life apart from the city.

2. In a brief essay, compare Reed's view of death with the view expressed by Virginia Woolf in "Death of a Moth." How does nature itself inform their views?

3. Research Fay Jones and account for his architectural vision. What part does nature play in shaping that vision?

Annie Dillard (b. 1945)

The work of Annie Dillard covers a range of literary genres: memoir, fiction, poetry, and essay. *Pilgrim at Tinker Creek* (1974), a collection of meditations on nature, won the Pulitzer Prize when Dillard was only twenty-eight years old. Her other works include *Living by Fiction* (1982), a critical study; *Holy the Firm* (1977), the source for "Transfiguration"; *Teaching a Stone to Talk: Expeditions and Encounters* (1982), a collection of essays; *An American Childhood* (1987), a memoir; and *The Writing Life* (1989). Her prose is often lush and exuberant, and her questions about life's mysteries are always challenging and evocative.

TRANSFIGURATION

"Transfiguration," which we could call an extended meditation on moths, echoes Woolf's "Death of a Moth" but leads us to consider, finally, not moths and death but transformation. Dillard focuses on the act of writing, drawing our attention to a writer caught in a moment of productivity during which she sacrifices herself to the act of creating. Dillard's focus is on the transfiguring experience of writing itself, where that experience takes the writer—where her essay might take students in a writing class.

1   I live on northern Puget Sound, in Washington State, alone. I have a gold cat, who sleeps on my legs, named Small. In the morning I joke to her blank face, Do you remember last night? Do you remember? I throw her out before breakfast, so I can eat.

There is a spider, too, in the bathroom, with whom I keep a sort of company. Her little outfit always reminds me of a certain moth I helped to kill. The spider herself is of uncertain lineage, bulbous at the abdomen and drab. Her six-inch mess of a web works, works somehow, works miraculously, to keep her alive and me amazed. The web itself is in a corner behind the toilet, connecting tile wall to tile wall and floor, in a place where there is, I would have thought, scant traffic. Yet under the web are sixteen or so corpses she has tossed to the floor.

The corpses appear to be mostly sow bugs, those little armadillo creatures who live to travel flat out in houses, and die round. There is also a new shred of earwig, three old spider skins crinkled and clenched, and two moth bodies, wingless and huge and empty, moth bodies I drop to my knees to see.

Today the earwig shines darkly and gleams, what there is of him: a dorsal curve of thorax and abdomen, and a smooth pair of cerci by which I knew his name. Next week, if the other bodies are any indication, he will be shrunken and gray, webbed to the floor with dust. The sow bugs beside him are hollow and empty of color, fragile, a breath away from brittle fluff. The spider skins lie on their sides, translucent and ragged, their legs drying in knots. And the moths, the empty moths, stagger against each other, headless, in a confusion of arching strips of chitin like peeling varnish, like a jumble of buttresses for cathedral domes, like nothing resembling moths, so that I should hesitate to call them moths, except that I have had some experience with the figure Moth reduced to a nub.

5   Two summers ago I was camping alone in the Blue Ridge Mountains in Virginia. I had hauled myself and gear up there to read, among other things, James Ramsey Ullman's *The Day on Fire*, a novel about Rimbaud that had made me want to be a writer when I was sixteen; I was hoping it would do it again. So I read, lost, every day sitting under a tree by my tent, while warblers swung in the leaves overhead and bristle worms trailed their

inches over the twiggy dirt at my feet; and I read every night by candlelight, while barred owls called in the forest and pale moths massed round my head in the clearing, where my light made a ring.

Moths kept flying into the candle. They would hiss and recoil, lost upside down in the shadows among my cooking pans. Or they would singe their wings and fall, and their hot wings, as if melted, would stick to the first thing they touched—a pan, a lid, a spoon—so that the snagged moths could flutter only in tiny arcs, unable to struggle free. These I could release by a quick flip with a stick; in the morning I would find my cooking stuff gilded with torn flecks of moth wings, triangles of shiny dust here and there on the aluminum. So I read, and boiled water, and replenished candles, and read on.

One night a month flew into the candle, was caught, burnt dry, and held. I must have been staring at the candle, or maybe I looked up when a shadow crossed my page; at any rate, I saw it all. A golden female moth, a biggish one with a two-inch wing-span, flapped into the fire, dropped her abdomen into the wet wax, stuck, flamed, frazzled and fried in a second. Her moving wings ignited like tissue paper, enlarging the circle of light in the clearing and creating out of the darkness the sudden blue sleeves of my sweater, the green leaves of jewelweed by my side, the ragged red trunk of a pine. At once the light contracted again and the moth's wings vanished in a fine, foul smoke. At the same time her six legs clawed, curled, blackened, and ceased, disappearing utterly. And her head jerked in spasms, making a spattering noise; her antennae crisped and burned away and her heaving mouth parts crackled like pistol fire. When it was all over, her head was, so far as I could determine, gone, gone the long way of her wings and legs. Had she been new, or old? Had she mated and laid her eggs, had she done her work? All that was left was the glowing horn shell of her abdomen and thorax—a

fraying, partially collapsed gold tube jammed upright in the candle's round pool.

And then this moth-essence, this spectacular skeleton, began to act as a wick. She kept burning. The wax rose in the moth's body from her soaking abdomen to her thorax to the jagged hole where her head should be, and widened into flame, a saffron-yellow flame that robed her to the ground like any immolating monk. That candle had two wicks, two flames of identical height, side by side. The moth's head was fire. She burned for two hours, until I blew her out.

She burned for two hours without changing, without bending or leaning—only glowing within, like a building fire glimpsed through silhouetted walls, like a hollow saint, like a flame-faced virgin gone to God, while I read by her light, kindled, while Rimbaud in Paris burnt out his brains in a thousand poems, while night pooled wetly at my feet.

And that is why I believe those hollow 10 crisps on the bathroom floor are moths. I think I know moths, and fragments of moths, and chips and tatters of utterly empty moths, in any state. How many of you, I asked the people in my class, which of you want to give your lives and be writers? I was trembling from coffee, or cigarettes, or the closeness of faces all around me. (Is this what we live for? I thought; is this the only final beauty: the color of any skin in any light, and living, human eyes?) All hands rose to the question. (You, Nick? Will you? Margaret? Randy? Why do I want them to mean it?) And then I tried to tell them what the choice must mean: you can't be anything else. You must go at your life with a broadax. . . . They had no idea what I was saying. (I have two hands, don't I? And all this energy, for as long as I can remember. I'll do it in the evenings, after skiing, or on the way home from the bank; or after the children are asleep. . . .) They thought I was raving again. It's just as well.

I have three candles here on the table which I disentangle from the plants and light when visitors come. Small usually avoids them, although once she came too close and her tail caught fire; I rubbed it out before she noticed. The flames move light over every-one's skin, draw light to the surface of the faces of my friends. When the people leave I never blow the candles out, and after I'm asleep they flame and burn.

READING AND THINKING

1. In the first sentence, Dillard claims to be alone on Puget Sound. Do you think that is true? Why or why not?

2. An image need not be pictorial—something we can stand back from and *see*. An image can also be sonic, sensual, suggestive, haunting. Even a concept can take on the quality of image. Trace one of Dillard's images from beginning to end and think about what it tells you.

3. Why does Dillard bring the poet Rimbaud into this essay?

4. Why does Dillard tell the story of her students near the end of the essay? What would happen to the essay if we took that section out?

5. How does Dillard use her cat to highlight an important thing about humans? How does that information allow us to believe that Dillard might be "alone" on Puget Sound?

THINKING AND WRITING

1. From the outset, Dillard repeats words. Find three occasions of repetition, and account for why she repeats the word. What is the effect on the reader? Does this repetition slow down or speed up your reading? Clarify or confuse?

2. Underline or highlight all of the words in this essay that you do not know. Consult an unabridged dictionary and consider all their meanings. How do those meanings complicate or clarify the essay?

3. Make a list of all the references to things religious and spiritual. Are these allusions just for decoration or do they have something to do with Dillard's idea?

4. What is the nature of death in this essay? How are death and transfiguration related in Dillard's mind? Explain how you know, citing evidence from the essay.

CONSIDERING THE NATURE OF TRANSFIGURATION: AN OCCASION FOR WRITING

Perception is again the focus in this Occasion, but instead of looking at some small object as you did in the first Occasion, your primary business will be to look at a selected space (outside in nature) over time. You will be trying to improve your eyesight without the aid of a microscope, without anything to help you except your attention to the changes that take place from day to day in that selected space. Some of those changes will be real changes brought on by weather or people, but other changes will be more perceived than real. Nothing will have changed except your ability to see more. You will have become a more skillful observer—because you know more, because you look harder, because you grow to love or hate the place in ways that affect what you are able to see.

JOHANNES VERMEER, *A lady at the virginal with a gentleman (c. 1662–1665)*

HIROSHI SUGIMOTO,
The Piano Lesson
(1999)

PREPARING TO WRITE: OCCASIONS TO THINK ABOUT WHAT YOU SEE

1. In painting by Johannes Vermeer, the lady is taking a keyboard lesson. Name all the objects that you see in the painting.

2. What do you imagine is most important to Vermeer about this painting: the keyboard lesson, the colors, the light, the objects, their relationships? Explain.

3. What is the relationship between *The Piano Lesson,* by photographer Hiroshi Sugimoto, and Vermeer's painting? How are the two images alike and how do they differ?

4. Sugimoto calls his work conceptual art. He tells us that "usually a photographer sees something and tries to capture it, but in my case I just see it in my head and then the technical process is how to make it happen in the real world. The image, then, is a kind of decoration of the concept. Concept is concept, it's not solid so I need an image to make it solid and visual." How do you imagine he made this photograph (the technical process), and what is he trying to allow us to see?

MOVING TOWARD ESSAY: OCCASIONS TO ANALYZE AND REFLECT

1. The *Oxford English Dictionary* (*OED*) offers this definition of the verb *transfigure:* "To alter the figure or appearance of; to change in outward appearance; to transform." Account for the precise way you believe Sugimoto transfigured Vermeer's painting.

2. *The Piano Lesson* is actually a photograph of a wax replica of Vermeer's painting. How does that fact change your own conception of what you see? Can you now *see* the conception that Sugimoto has attached to this image? Other than the objects in the photograph, what do you think Sugimoto is trying to get us to see? Explain in a paragraph.

3. The *OED* offers another definition of the verb *transfigure:* "To elevate, glorify, idealize, spiritualize." Which image, Vermeer's or Sugimoto's, best makes "solid or visual" this definition? Explain in a paragraph.

WRITING THOUGHTFULLY: OCCASIONS FOR IDEAS AND ESSAYS

1. In her essay Dillard has transfigured her own experience in nature so that we can, in turn, learn something about the nature of transfiguration. By so doing, she reveals something powerful about the act of writing. Write a brief essay in which you account for that *something.* Use Sugimoto, the *OED,* and your own experience as you develop your interpretation of Dillard's essay.

2. Recall two or three of your own transfiguring experiences with nature and re-create each of those moments in writing. Make your re-creations scenic (dramatic) so that we can actually see them, enter them as if we were there with you. Bring those moments to life and use them as evidence to help you develop an essay of your own. Let the evidence lead you to your idea. It need not be about transfiguration.

3. Compare Dillard's sense of death with Woolf's in a short essay. Cite evidence from both "Transfiguration" and "Death of a Moth" to clarify your idea.

CREATING OCCASIONS

1. Sugimoto says, "My eye has become so well trained that I can see the same things in different ways, more detailed ways. You are powering up the ability of your eyes and it is simply an endless process." Select a favorite place somewhere outdoors, or from inside looking out onto nature, and spend time in that place a number of times over two weeks. Make it your business to notice and record differences—to see more than you were able to see on previous occasions. Based on what you learn, write a brief essay titled "Powering Up the Eyes."

2. Sugimoto did a series of photographs titled "Portraits." Study those portraits by accessing the images on the Internet. Read what you can about the series, and then write an essay that responds to one of the critic's assessments of Sugimoto's work in the series.

TENDING THE ENVIRONMENT

The work of this Cluster challenges us in quiet ways to pay attention to what is worth preserving in that space *out there* variously called *the wilderness; our natural world; the wild;* or simply, *nature.* In America we tend to associate wilderness with the westward expansion that led to opportunities and riches for those brave enough to make that arduous journey. That expansion led as well to notions about our national character. Our romance with rugged individualism, the exploration and acquisition of open spaces, the necessity of facing and overcoming danger—that essentially masculine romance still plays in our minds. Sometimes we fail to consider the darker side of that romance: the violence and destructiveness, the unfairness to those not strong enough to prevail, the presumption of ownership.

Barry Lopez draws our attention to those who peopled that world long before our arrival, and he shows us that they left traces on the wild world that are worth preserving, artifacts that speak directly to us of a spiritual world we may have lost touch with over time. Ann Zwinger gives us a meditative moment that both names the gifts of the desert and seeks, albeit indirectly, a political response—a desire to motivate politicians to preserve the Utah wilderness. Finally, William Cronon asks us to reconceive wilderness as we have come to understand it, to cut it loose from its nineteenth-century moorings that make too much of its peculiarly American associations with masculinity and character and to extend it directly into our backyards, wherever they may be, inside the city or out. What each of these writers reminds us is this: that nonhuman world, whatever we may choose to call it, is ours, and only ours, to use and to tend. Being human carries with it an obligation to use and preserve wisely what has been left to us. We are the stewards of the land and the environment.

Barry Lopez (b. 1945)

Barry Lopez was educated at the University of Notre Dame and has taught at the University of Iowa and Carlton College. He has served as an editor at *Harper's* and the *North American Review*. Lopez is best known as a writer whose passionate commitment to history and preservation has brought him into touch with knowledge often hidden from those who fail to see that the world reveals its secrets only when we have the patience, interest, and experience to discern them. His books include *Of Wolves and Men* (1978), *Crossing Open Ground* (1988), *The Rediscovery of North America* (1991), and *About This Life: Journeys on the Threshold of Memory* (1998). He has received the John Burroughs Medal and an Award in Literature from the American Academy and Institute of Arts and Letters. Lopez has also been a Guggenheim and a National Science Foundation fellow.

STONE HORSE

"Stone Horse" is the tale of an encounter with history in the form of a huge horse outlined on the desert floor in Southern California, created long ago (perhaps 400 years), most probably by the Quechan people. Fascinated by the horse and troubled by vandals who desecrate such historical artifacts, Lopez tries to transfer his excitement and his concern as he comes upon the horse for the first time.

I

1   The deserts of southern California, the high, relatively cooler and wetter Mojave and the hotter, dryer Sonoran to the south of it, carry the signatures of many cultures. Prehistoric rock drawings in the Mojave's Coso Range, probably the greatest concentration of petroglyphs in North America, are at least three thousand years old. Big-game-hunting cultures that flourished six or seven thousand years before that are known from broken spear tips, choppers, and burins left scattered along the shores of great Pleistocene lakes, long since evaporated. Weapons and tools discovered at China Lake may be thirty thousand years old; and worked stone from a quarry in the Calico Mountains is, some argue, evidence that human beings were here more than 200,000 years ago.

Because of the long-term stability of such arid environments, much of this prehistoric stone evidence still lies exposed on the ground, accessible to anyone who passes by— the studious, the acquisitive, the indifferent, the merely curious. Archaeologists do not agree on the sequence of cultural history be-

yond about twelve thousand years ago, but it is clear that these broken bits of chalcedony, chert, and obsidian, like the animal drawings and geometric designs etched on walls of basalt throughout the desert, anchor the earliest threads of human history, the first record of human endeavor here.

Western man did not enter the California desert until the end of the eighteenth century, 250 years after Coronado brought his soldiers into the Zuni pueblos in a bewildered search for the cities of Cibola. The earliest appraisals of the land were cursory, hurried. People traveled *through* it, en route to Santa Fe or the California coastal settlements. Only miners tarried. In 1823 what had been Spain's became Mexico's, and in 1848 what had been Mexico's became America's; but the bare, jagged mountains and dry lake beds, the vast and uniform plains of creosote bush and yucca plants, remained as obscure as the northern Sudan until the end of the nineteenth century.

Before 1940 the tangible evidence of twentieth-century man's passage here consisted of very little—the hard tracery of travel corridors; the widely scattered, relatively insignificant evidence of mining operations; and the fair expanse of irrigated fields at the desert's periphery. In the space of a hundred years or so the wagon roads were paved, railroads were laid down, and canals and high-tension lines were built to bring water and electricity across the desert to Los Angeles from the Colorado River. The dark mouths of gold, talc, and tin mines yawned from the bony flanks of desert ranges. Dust-encrusted chemical plants stood at work on the lonely edges of dry lake beds. And crops of grapes, lettuce, dates, alfalfa, and cotton covered the Coachella and Imperial valleys, north and south of the Salton Sea, and the Palo Verde Valley along the Colorado.

5   These developments proceeded with little or no awareness of earlier human occupations by cultures that preceded those of the historic Indians—the Mohave, the Chemehuevi, the Quechan. (Extensive irrigation began actually to change the climate of the Sonoran Desert, and human settlements, the railroads, and farming introduced many new, successful plants into the region.)

During World War II, the American military moved into the desert in great force, to train troops and to test equipment. They found the clear weather conducive to year-round flying, the dry air and isolation very attractive. After the war, a complex of training grounds, storage facilities, and gunnery and test ranges was permanently settled on more than three million acres of military reservations. Few perceived the extent or significance of the destruction of the aboriginal sites that took place during tank maneuvers and bombing runs or in the laying out of highways, railroads, mining districts, and irrigated fields. The few who intuited that something like an American Dordogne Valley lay exposed here were (only) amateur archaeologists; even they reasoned that the desert was too vast for any of this to matter.

After World War II, people began moving out of the crowded Los Angeles basin into homes in Lucerne, Apple, and Antelope val-leys in the western Mojave. They emigrated as well to a stretch of resort land at the foot of the San Jacinto Mountains that included Palm Springs, and farther out to old railroad and military towns like Twentynine Palms and Barstow. People also began exploring the desert, at first in military-surplus jeeps and then with a variety of all-terrain and off-road vehicles that became available in the 1960s. By the mid-1970s, the number of people using such vehicles for desert recreation had increased exponentially. Most came and went in innocent curiosity; the few who didn't wreaked a havoc all out of proportion to their numbers. The disturbance of previously isolated archaeological sites increased by an order of magnitude. Many sites were vandalized before archaeologists, themselves late to the desert, had any firm grasp of the bounds of human history in the desert. It was as though in the same moment an Aztec library had been discovered intact various lacunae had begun to appear.

The vandalism was of three sorts: the general disturbance usually caused by souvenir hunters and by the curious and the oblivious; the wholesale stripping of a place by professional thieves for black-market sale and trade; and outright destruction, in which vehicles were actually used to ram and trench an area. By 1980, the Bureau of Land Management estimated that probably 35 percent of the archaeological sites in the desert had been vandalized. The destruction at some places by rifles and shotguns, or by power winches mounted on vehicles, was, if one cared for history, demoralizing to behold.

In spite of public education, land closures, and stricter law enforcement in recent years, the BLM estimates that, annually, about 1 percent of the archaeological record in the desert continues to be destroyed or stolen.

II

10   A BLM archaeologist told me, with understandable reluctance, where to find the in-

taglio. I spread my Automobile Club of Southern California map of Imperial County out on his desk, and he traced the route with a pink felt-tip pen. The line crossed Interstate 8 and then turned west along the Mexican border.

"You can't drive any farther than about here," he said, marking a small X. "There's boulders in the wash. You walk up past them."

On a separate piece of paper he drew a route in a smaller scale that would take me up the arroyo to a certain point where I was to cross back east, to another arroyo. At its head, on higher ground just to the north, I would find the horse.

"It's tough to spot unless you know it's there. Once you pick it up . . ." He shook his head slowly, in a gesture of wonder at its existence.

I waited until I held his eye. I assured him I would not tell anyone else how to get there. He looked at me with stoical despair, like a man who had been robbed twice, whose belief in human beings was offered without conviction.

15   I did not go until the following day because I wanted to see it at dawn. I ate breakfast at four A.M. in El Centro and then drove south. The route was easy to follow, though the last section of road proved difficult, broken and drifted over with sand in some spots. I came to the barricade of boulders and parked. It was light enough by then to find my way over the ground with little trouble. The contours of the landscape were stark, without any masking vegetation. I worried only about rattlesnakes.

I traversed the stone plain as directed, but, in spite of the frankness of the land, I came on the horse unawares. In the first moment of recognition I was without feeling. I recalled later being startled, and that I held my breath. It was laid out on the ground with its head to the east, three times life size. As I took in its outline I felt a growing concentration of all my senses, as though my attentiveness to the pale rose color of the morning sky and other peripheral images had now ceased to be important. I was aware that I was straining for sound in the windless air, and I felt the uneven pressure of the earth hard against my feet. The horse, outlined in a standing profile on the dark ground, was as vivid before me as a bed of tulips.

I've come upon animals suddenly before, and felt a similar tension, a precipitate heightening of the senses. And I have felt the inexplicable but sharply boosted intensity of a wild moment in the bush, where it is not until some minutes later that you discover the source of electricity—the warm remains of a grizzly bear kill, or the still moist tracks of a wolverine.

But this was slightly different. I felt I had stepped into an unoccupied corridor. I had no familiar sense of history, the temporal structure in which to think: This horse was made by Quechan people three hundred years ago. I felt instead a headlong rush of images: people hunting wild horses with spears on the Pleistocene veld of southern California; Cortés riding across the causeway into Montezuma's Tenochtitlán; a short-legged Comanche, astride his horse like some sort of ferret, slashing through cavalry lines of young men who rode like farmers; a hood exploding past my face one morning in a corral in Wyoming. These images had the weight and silence of stone.

When I released my breath, the images softened. My initial feeling, of facing a wild animal in a remote region, was replaced with a calm sense of antiquity. It was then that I became conscious, like an ordinary tourist, of what was before me, and thought: this horse was probably laid out by Quechan people. But when? I wondered. The first horses they saw, I knew, might have been those that came north from Mexico in 1692 with Father Eusebio Kino. But Cocopa people, I recalled, also came this far north on occasion, to fight with their neighbors, the Quechan. And *they* could have seen horses with Melchior Diaz, at the mouth of the Colorado River in the fall of

1540. So, it could be four hundred years old. (No one in fact knows.)

20   I still had not moved. I took my eyes off the horse for a moment to look south over the desert plain into Mexico, to look east past its head at the brightening sunrise, to situate myself. Then, finally, I brought my trailing foot slowly forward and stood erect. Sunlight was running like a thin sheet of water over the stony ground and it threw the horse into relief. It looked as though no hand had ever disturbed the stones that gave it its form.

The horse had been brought to life on ground called desert pavement, a tight, flat matrix of small cobbles blasted smooth by sand-laden winds. The uniform, monochromatic blackness of the stones, a patina of iron and magnesium oxides called desert varnish, is caused by long-term exposure to the sun. To make this type of low-relief ground glyph, or intaglio, the artist either selectively turns individual stones over to their lighter side or removes areas of stone to expose the lighter soil underneath, creating a negative image. This horse, about eighteen feet from brow to rump and eight feet from withers to hoof, had been made in the latter way, and its outline was bermed at certain points with low ridges of stone a few inches high to enhance its three-dimensional qualities. (The left side of the horse was in full profile; each leg was extended at 90 degrees to the body and fully visible, as though seen in three-quarter profile.)

I was not eager to move. The moment I did I would be back in the flow of time, the horse no longer quivering in the same way before me. I did not want to feel again the sequence of quotidian events—to be drawn off into deliberation and analysis. A human being, a four-footed animal, the open land. That was all that was present—and a "thoughtless" understanding of the very old desires bearing on this particular animal: to hunt it, to render it, to fathom it, to subjugate it, to honor it, to take it as a companion.

What finally made me move was the light. The sun now filled the shallow basin of the horse's body. The weighted line of the stone berm created the illusion of a mane and the distinctive roundness of an equine belly. The change in definition impelled me. I moved to the left, circling past its rump, to see how the light might flesh the horse out from various points of view. I circled it completely before squatting on my haunches. Ten or fifteen minutes later I chose another view. The third time I moved, to a point near the rear hooves, I spotted a stone tool at my feet. I stared at it a long while, more in awe than disbelief, before reaching out to pick it up. I turned it over in my left palm and took it between my fingers to feel its cutting edge. It is always difficult, especially with something so portable, to rechannel the desire to steal.

I spent several hours with the horse. As I changed positions and as the angle of the light continued to change I noticed a number of things. The angle at which the pastern carried the hoof away from the ankle was perfect. Also, stones had been placed within the image to suggest at precisely the right spot the left shoulder above the foreleg. The line that joined thigh and hock was similarly accurate. The muzzle alone seemed distorted—but perhaps these stones had been moved by a later hand. It was an admirably accurate representation, but not what a breeder would call perfect conformation. There was the suggestion of a bowed neck and an undershot jaw, and the tail, as full as a winter coyote's, did not appear to be precisely to scale.

The more I thought about it, the more I   25 felt I was looking at an individual horse, a unique combination of generic and specific detail. It was easy to imagine one of Kino's horses as a model, or a horse that ran off from one of Coronado's columns. What kind of horses would these have been? I wondered. In the sixteenth century the most sought-after horses in Europe were Spanish, the offspring of Arabian stock and Barbary horses that the Moors brought to Iberia and bred to the older, eastern European strains brought in by the

Romans. The model for this horse, I speculated, could easily have been a palomino, or a descendant of horses trained for lion hunting in North Africa.

A few generations ago, cowboys, cavalry quartermasters, and draymen would have taken this horse before me under consideration and not let up their scrutiny until they had its heritage fixed to their satisfaction. Today, the distinction between draft and harness horses is arcane knowledge, and no image may come to mind for a blue roan or a claybank horse. The loss of such refinement in everyday conversation leaves me unsettled. People praise the Eskimo's ability to distinguish among forty types of snow but forget the skill of others who routinely differentiate between overo and tobiano pintos. Such distinctions are made for the same reason. You have to do it to be able to talk clearly about the world.

For parts of two years I worked as a horse wrangler and packer in Wyoming. It is dim knowledge now; I would have to think to remember if a buckskin was a kind of dun horse. And I couldn't throw a double-diamond hitch over a set of panniers—the packer's basic tie-down—without guidance. As I squatted there in the desert, however, these more personal memories seemed tenuous in comparison with the sweep of this animal in human time. My memories had no depth. I thought of the Hittite cavalry riding against the Syrians 3,500 years ago. And the first of the Chinese emperors, Ch'in Shih Huang, buried in Shensi Province in 210 B.C. with thousands of life-size horses and soldiers, a terra-cotta guardian army. What could I know of what was in the mind of whoever made this horse? Was there some racial memory of it as an animal that had once fed the artist's ancestors and then disappeared from North America? And then returned in this strange alliance with another race of men?

Certainly, whoever it was, the artist had observed the animal very closely. Certainly the animal's speed had impressed him. Among the first things the Quechan would have learned from an encounter with Kino's horses was that their own long-distance runners—men who could run down mule deer—were no match for this animal.

From where I squatted I could look far out over the Mexican plain. Juan Bautista de Anza passed this way in 1774, extending El Camino Real into Alta California from Sinaloa. He was followed by others, all of them astride the magical horse; *gente de razon*, the people of reason, coming into the country of *los primitivos*. The horse, like the stone animals of Egypt, urged these memories upon me. And as I drew them up from some forgotten corner of my mind—huge horses carved in the white chalk downs of southern England by an Iron Age people; Spanish horses rearing and wheeling in fear before alligators in Florida—the images seemed tethered before me. With this sense of proportion, a memory of my own—the morning I almost lost my face to a horse's hoof—now had somewhere to fit.

I rose up and began to walk slowly around 30 the horse again. I had taken the first long measure of it and was now looking for a way to depart, a new angle of light, a fading of the image itself before the rising sun, that would break its hold on me. As I circled, feeling both heady and serene at the encounter, I realized again how strangely vivid it was. It had been created on a barren bajada between two arroyos, as nondescript a place as one could imagine. The only plant life here was a few wands of ocotillo cactus. The ground beneath my shoes was so hard it wouldn't take the print of a heavy animal even after a rain. The only sounds I heard here were the voices of quail.

The archaeologist had been correct. For all its forcefulness, the horse is inconspicuous. If you don't care to see it you can walk right past it. That pleases him, I think. Unmarked on the bleak shoulder of the plain, the site signals to no one; so he wants no protective fences here, no informative plaque, to act as beacons. He would rather take a chance that no motorcyclist, no aimless wanderer with a flair for violence and a depth of ignorance, will ever find his way here.

The archaeologist had given me something before I left his office that now seemed peculiar—an aerial photograph of the horse. It is widely believed that an aerial view of an intaglio provides a fair and accurate depiction. It does not. In the photograph the horse looks somewhat crudely constructed; from the ground it appears far more deftly rendered. The photograph is of a single moment, and in that split second the horse seems vaguely impotent. I watched light pool in the intaglio at dawn; I imagine you could watch it withdraw at dusk and sense the same animation I did. In those prolonged moments its shape and so, too, its general character changed—noticeably. The living quality of the image, its immediacy to the eye, was brought out by the light-in-time, not, at least here, in the camera's frozen instant.

Intaglios, I thought, were never meant to be seen by gods in the sky above. They were meant to be seen by people on the ground, over a long period of shifting light. This could even be true of the huge figures on the Plain of Nazca in Peru, where people could walk for the length of a day beside them. It is our own impatience that leads us to think otherwise.

This process of abstraction, almost unintentional, drew me gradually away from the horse. I came to a position of attention at the edge of the sphere of its influence. With a slight bow I paid my respects to the horse, its maker, and the history of us all, and departed.

III

35   A short distance away I stopped the car in the middle of the road to make a few notes. I could not write down what I was thinking when I was with the horse. It would have seemed disrespectful, and it would have re-

quired another kind of attention. So now I patiently drained my memory of the details it had fastened itself upon. The road I'd stopped on was adjacent to the All American Canal, the major source of water for the Imperial and Coachella valleys. The water flowed west placidly. A disjointed flock of coots, small, dark birds with white bills, was paddling against the current, foraging in the rushes.

I was peripherally aware of the birds as I wrote, the only movement in the desert, and of a series of sounds from a village a half-mile away. The first sounds from this collection of ramshackle houses in a grove of cottonwoods were the distracted dawn voices of dogs. I heard them intermingled with the cries of a rooster. Later, the high-pitched voices of children calling out to each other came disembodied through the dry desert air. Now, a little after seven, I could hear someone practicing on the trumpet, the same rough phrases played over and over. I suddenly remembered how as children we had tried to get the rhythm of a galloping horse with hands against our thighs, or by fluttering our tongues against the roofs of our mouths.

After the trumpet, the impatient calls of adults summoning children. Sunday morning. Wood smoke hung like a lens in the trees. The first car starts—a cold eight-cylinder engine, of Chrysler extraction perhaps, goosed to life, then throttled back to murmur through dual mufflers, the obbligato music of a shade-tree mechanic. The rote bark of mongrel dogs at dawn, the jagged outcries of men and women, an engine coming to life. Like a thousand villages from West Virginia to Guadalajara.

I finished my notes—where was I going to find a description of the horses that came north with the conquistadors? Did their manes come forward prominently over the brow, like this one's, like the forelocks of Blackfeet and Assiniboin men in nineteenth-century paintings? I set the notes on the seat beside me.

The road followed the canal for a while and then arced north, toward Interstate 8. It was slow driving and I fell to thinking how the desert had changed since Anza had come through. New plants and animals—the MacDougall cottonwood, the English house sparrow, the chukar from India—have about them now the air of the native born. Of the native species, some—no one knows how many—are extinct. The populations of many others, especially the animals, have been sharply reduced. The idea of a desert impoverished by agricultural poisons and varmint hunters, by off-road vehicles and military operations, did not seem as disturbing to me, however, as this other horror, now that I had been those hours with the horse. The vandals, the few who crowbar rock art off the desert's walls, who dig up graves, who punish the ground that holds intaglios, are people who devour history. Their self-centered scorn, their disrespect for ideas and images beyond their ken, create the awful atmosphere of loose ends in which totalitarianism thrives, in which the past is merely curious or wrong.

40   I thought about the horse sitting out there on the unprotected plain. I enumerated its qualities in my mind until a sense of its vulnerability receded and it became an anchor for something else. I remembered that history, a history like this one, which ran deeper than Mexico, deeper than the Spanish, was a kind of medicine. It permitted the great breadth of human expression to reverberate, and it did not urge you to locate its apotheosis in the present.

Each of us, individuals and civilizations, has been held upside down like Achilles in the River Styx. The artist mixing his colors in the dim light of Altamira; an Egyptian ruler lying still now, wrapped in his byssus, stored against time in a pyramid; the faded Dorset culture of the Arctic; the Hmong and Samburu and Walbiri of historic time; the modern nations. This great, imperfect stretch of human expression is the clarification and encouragement, the urging and the reminder, we call history. And it is inscribed everywhere in the face of the land, from the mountain passes of the Himalayas to a nameless bajada in the California desert.

Small birds rose up in the road ahead, startled, and flew off. I prayed no infidel would ever find that horse.

READING AND THINKING

1. This essay is divided into three sections. Title each section with one or two words, trying to capture the essence of what Lopez presents in each section.

2. What do you think Lopez means by a "low-relief ground glyph, or intaglio"? Try to visualize what the horse on the ground actually looks like. Is it above the ground or etched into the ground? Study Lopez's various descriptions.

3. Why is the aerial photograph of the horse unsatisfactory to Lopez?

4. In the final section of the essay why do you think Lopez emphasizes sounds (birds, people, cars) and "the great breadth of human expression"?

THINKING AND WRITING

1. Make a chart that traces the various stages of Lopez's encounter with the horse; characterize in a few words what happens at each stage.

2. Refer to the chart in Question 1 and account for how the writing task itself changes from stage to stage; think in terms of factual, descriptive, emotive, scientific, and historical language. Write a paragraph about your favorite stage, accounting for how Lopez captures your attention.

3. Besides the actual loss of the horse through vandalism, what other loss is Lopez most concerned about? Explain in a brief paragraph.

4. Explain in a paragraph why you think Lopez offers a "slight bow" as he leaves the horse.

5. Convince someone in a brief email why the horse really is "a kind of medicine" for Lopez. Assume your reader knows nothing about the essay itself.

PRESERVATION AND DESTRUCTION: AN OCCASION FOR WRITING

This Occasion will give you an opportunity to think about the human urge to be mischievous (and sometimes destructive), played out against a countervailing, perhaps deeper, urge to preserve. We see all around us signs of environmental destruction: defaced advertisements, pervasive graffiti, broken windows, abandoned junk, dropped cigarette butts, snapped-off car antennas, marked-up library books, trash. Isolated instances often appear to be mere pranks or thoughtless acts committed randomly, but when we stop to consider the larger patterns of destruction that result from such negligence, the effects are sobering. Your work during this Occasion will ask you to consider ways of reversing vandalism and minimizing the effects on our threatened environment.

PREPARING TO WRITE: OCCASIONS TO THINK ABOUT WHAT YOU SEE

1. What does the image of vandalism itself tell you about the nature of vandalism?

2. Given what you actually see in the photograph of the vandalism sign, what do you imagine you are seeing, vandalism or art?

3. Look closely at *For Duf* and make a mental list of all the things that you can actually see. Write out the words that make sense to you.

4. *For Duf* was part of an exhibit called "Reversing Vandalism" that was installed at the San Francisco Public Library. Based only on what you see in the image, what do you imagine the show was about?

MOVING TOWARD ESSAY: OCCASIONS TO ANALYZE AND REFLECT

1. For nearly a year, a vandal mutilated almost 600 books related to gay and lesbian themes in the San Francisco Public Library. The library sent these damaged books to artists across the country, and more than 200 of them fashioned art objects from them, creating the exhibit "Reversing Vandalism." What do you see in *For Duf,* now that you know this information?

Royalty Free/Alamy

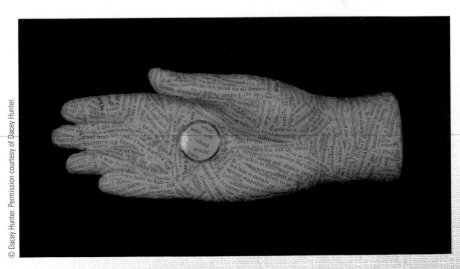

© Dacey Hunter. Permission courtesy of Dacey Hunter.

DACEY HUNTER,
For Duf (2003)

2. Over the years, some artistic activity has tended to support vandalism (Dada during WWI, Gustave Courbet's attempt to dismantle the Palace Vendome's column during the 1871 Paris Commune). Consider other politically motivated vandalism during your lifetime. Find an image to represent it.

3. Consider acts of vandalism in your community or on your campus (graffiti, defacement of public monuments or billboards, trashing abandoned property). Are any of these acts harmless, justified?

4. Reconsider the photograph of vandalism in terms of Lopez's essay. What would be the collateral consequences if such signs were posted on the perimeter of that Southern California desert, or any of our outdoor parks and wildlife preserves?

WRITING THOUGHTFULLY: OCCASIONS FOR IDEAS AND ESSAYS

1. Write two short argumentative essays (500 words each) about some controversy that has to do with the preservation of our natural world or our national heritage. The arguments should adopt opposing points of view.

2. Now re-examine the work you did for Question 1 and put your two essays together to create a more reasonable essay about the controversy.

3. Consider now the most ubiquitous act of vandalism that you know about based on your own personal observation. Write a brief but persuasive essay to those responsible for such acts that will convince them to reconsider their behavior. Use Lopez and anything else you have considered during this Occasion to help you develop your essay.

4. Write an essay of your own about a powerful experience you have had with one of our country's national or local treasures. Taking your cue from Lopez, put that experience in some larger context as you write about it.

CREATING OCCASIONS

1. Find an act of vandalism much closer to home, one that you want to help solve. Your project will be entitled "Reversing Vandalism 2." Organize a response to the vandalism and then write an epistolary essay (a brief letter) to those who will help you achieve your goal. The essay's purpose will be to reveal the nature of your project and to enlist their support.

2. Search the Internet for information about "Reversing Vandalism," the exhibit at the San Francisco Public Library. Consider two additional art objects from that show and write a brief essay about the effectiveness of what you see. Consider the extent to which you think art might be able to reverse vandalism.

Ann Zwinger (b. 1925)

Ann Zwinger , who graduated from Wellesley College, is an artist and historian who teaches at Colorado College. Her books include *Run River Run: A Naturalist's Journey Down One of the Great Rivers of the West* (1975, winner of the John Burroughs Medal), *Wind in the Rock: The Canyonlands of Southeastern Utah* (1978), and *Downcanyon: A Naturalist Explores the Colorado River through the Grand Canyon* (1995, winner Western States Book Award). Her writing has also appeared in *Audubon, Smithsonian,* and *National History.* She is the recipient of the John Hay Medal of The Orion Society and the 2006 Frank Waters Award for lifetime achievements as a writer, teacher, and naturalist.

A DESERT WORLD

"A Desert World" (editors' title for this unnamed piece) gives us a rare opportunity to "sit" inside a woman's head as she looks out from a prehistoric cave on the Utah desert and meditates on its strange, haunting beauty. She outlines the gifts that the land has given her and suggests to us the larger implications of the lessons she has learned from the desert. Implicit in all she says is a plea to preserve what is there in front of her—the beauty, the astonishing array of life, the lessons about adaptability, the secrets of the desert's night life. This short meditation was one of 21 contributions made by writers in 1996 to help preserve the wilderness in Utah; the collection, *Testimony,* was presented to members of the United States Congress. Senator Bill Bradley had this to say about the book: "If writing itself can be an act of public service, then this collection is it."

1   The clamshell opening of the cave sits a couple of hundred feet above the floor of the Great Basin Desert, where once the waters of the Great Salt Lake sparkled and flickered, where once a prehistoric people made a living and shared in the bounty of a wetter climate. This cave was not a permanent residence but a temporary one, utilized by archaic peoples on their never-ending rounds of hunting and gathering and fishing. I sit cross-legged, gazing out upon a vast landscape, reflecting on a lifestyle so different from mine.

During good growing years, when Indian populations were small, archaic life was good, for there was enough to eat. When times were bad and populations high, resources sparser and harder to find, life became poor to desperate. But out of these periods of stress came innovation, invention, and change. I, twentieth-century woman, rest here, settled in the silt of centuries, rolling the toothpick thigh bone of a mouse in my fingers, find this thought incredibly reassuring and ponder what I have come to understand about people who tracked these threadbare desert lands and my own necessity for clear horizons and long vistas. Out here there is an order, a cause and effect that is logical and persistent. The sun always rises in the east.

Insights into this beautifully attuned world to which I am not adapted make the fine-tuning of those small creatures that hop and stalk, scurry and slither in the deserts objects of respect from which humans can extract survival skills and medical miracles: a kangaroo rat and a black-throated sparrow that survive well without free water; specialized toads that dream away the cold times burrowed far underground, metabolism slowed almost to zero; cactus wrens that preadjust their clutch size to the soon-to-be-available food. I tally the physiological adjustments of blood and urine, hearing and seeing, of adaptations in behavior that make life in the desert not only possible but possible with verve, qualities seen and unseen that spell not only survival, but survival with zest. I contemplate plants that can withstand salt-laden soils and those that cannot and their different modes of photosynthesis. I number the ingenious seeds that germinate under precise regimes and their measured sequences: time to remain dormant, time to sprout, time to flower and set seed, time to dazzle the desert. Utah's Great Basin Desert brims with good health and good spirits and a vibrating heat that locks in the marrow against a cold and lightless winter.

Scanning this irreplaceable desert below me, which has exacted its own tributes of this slow-boned human, memories come crowding to my mind of the gifts these desert years have laid on my doorstep, a mosaic of experiences made up of sprigs of creosote bush and sagebrush, an owl feather and a grasshopper wing, and a chip of obsidian tied up with the song of a spadefoot toad, my own medicine bundle for my own ceremonies of passage. The desert grants each of us our own understandings, charges us with the preservation of its messages.

To the west a single thin cloud hangs over 5 the evening mountains, a vasa murrhina cloud illuminated from beneath. Alone in the sky, it incandesces as I watch, then fades. The ends still glow while the middle darkens to absorb the mountains beneath.

The sky behind the mountains segues to a pale steely blue, without warmth, bending upward to dusk. Where the sun has departed, the sky bleaches. Dust spirits sleep. A Cyclops moon rises to the east. The wind abides. Silence streams from the mountains. Black feathers of darkness drift downward, and the desert comes alive.

READING AND THINKING

1. What is Ann Zwinger's post of observation? How many times does she tell us, and why is it important to *locate* her physically?

2. What is most important about the desert for this "twentieth-century woman"?

3. Why do you imagine Zwinger tells us that the desert is "irreplaceable"? Does she mean to herself? Or to all of us?

4. How would you characterize the "gifts" that the desert has given Zwinger? Do they seem like gifts to you?

THINKING AND WRITING

1. Write a brief explanation about what you think Zwinger means when she reminds us that in the desert "there is an order, a cause and effect that is logical and persistent"? Do you imagine that this order is universal or just in the desert? Is it just more possible to discern it in the desert? Explain.

2. While considering and making use of Zwinger's evidence, explain why she thinks the desert is a "beautifully attuned world." What natural process informs her claim? Explain.

3. Make a list of the four most striking images in Zwinger's short meditation. Write out what you consider her idea and explain the relationship between it and the four images.

4. Explain why you think the desert comes alive at night.

THE WAY WE PERCEIVE WILDERNESS: AN OCCASION FOR WRITING

In this Occasion you will consider three different perspectives on wilderness, in addition to your own. You will be thinking about the way wilderness presents itself according to our particular vantage point—whether that vantage point be a physical location on the ground, or a space, or a sensibility inside ourselves. Wilderness changes, takes on other dimensions, when we learn to see it the way others see it; we need but trade places with another to see it differently. Time too will change our conception of wilderness—time and need. What we decide to preserve during one historical period may become the object of our need or greed in another. To see what is out there (and to preserve it) requires our vigilance and our collaboration.

Courtesy Frederic Remington Art Museum, Ogdensburg, New York

FREDERICK REMINGTON,
The Buffalo Runners (1914)

GEORGIA O'KEEFFE,
Ram's Head, White Hollyhock-Hills (1935)

© The Georgia O'Keeffe Foundation/Artists Rights Society (ARS), New York. Image courtesy of The Brooklyn Museum.

PREPARING TO WRITE: OCCASIONS TO THINK ABOUT WHAT YOU SEE

1. List all of the things that you actually see in the Frederick Remington print, *The Buffalo Runners*. What else can you discern about Remington's sense of wilderness that you cannot actually point to in the image?

2. What does Georgia O'Keeffe's title, *Ram's Head, White Hollyhock-Hills,* suggest to you about her perspective on just the objects within this painting—their relationship, their relative importance, their overall significance?

3. Compare the objects within these two images. Consider changing one or two of the objects from one image to the other. Is it possible? Explain.

MOVING TOWARD ESSAY: OCCASIONS TO ANALYZE AND REFLECT

1. What does *The Buffalo Runners* suggest to you about Remington's sense of the wilderness? Find one or two other Remington images on the Internet to test your "reading" of this image and write a brief reflection about Remington's ideas.

2. What does *Ram's Head* suggest to you about O'Keeffe's sense of wilderness? Check your assessment against at least two other O'Keeffe images that you find on the Internet, one that focuses on desert life and one that focuses on the city (Manhattan, perhaps).

3. Return to Zwinger's "A Desert World"; consider her meditation a *word picture*. Characterize her view of wilderness in your own words.

4. What is your first impression about the relationship between Zwinger's perspective and that of the other two artists? Is hers more akin to one or the other, or is hers quite different from either? Explain briefly.

WRITING THOUGHTFULLY: OCCASIONS FOR IDEAS AND ESSAYS

1. Write an essay in which you compare and contrast the views of nature represented by the images you have been working with. Use this comparative work to help you provide your own view of wilderness. If you need them, use other sources to clarify your ideas.

2. Consider the images again. Write an essay that reveals the extent to which you believe gender informs these artists' differing views of wilderness. Cite compelling evidence to substantiate and clarify your ideas.

3. Focus on one of the artists you have been considering here and write an essay about his or her work that accounts for the relationship between that body of work (the vision of wilderness reflected therein) and the artist's life and times.

CREATING OCCASIONS

1. Zwinger's "A Desert World" appears in *Testimony: Writers of the West Speak on Behalf of Utah Wilderness* (1996). Research the development of this book, and write an essay that accounts for the extent to which the book influenced the preservation of wilderness.

2. Write an essay that advances your views about whether we should attempt to preserve wilderness. Focus on one particular wilderness area.

William J. Cronon (b. 1954)

William J. Cronon is the Frederick Jackson Turner and Vilas Research Professor of History, Geography, and Environmental Studies at the University of Wisconsin, Madison. He specializes in environmental history, the history of the American West and Frontier, and the writing and rhetoric of history and geography. His books include *Nature's Metropolis: Chicago and the Great West* (1991, awarded the Bancroft Prize and nominated for the Pulitzer) and *Changes in the Land: Colonists, and the Ecology of New England* (1983). He is the editor of *Uncommon Ground: Toward Reinventing Nature*. Cronon is a Rhodes scholar and has been a Danforth, Guggenheim, and MacArthur fellow.

THE TROUBLE WITH WILDERNESS

"The Trouble with Wilderness" is a far-ranging appeal to reconceive the way we think about wilderness. Cronon allows us to see historically how our inherited myth of wilderness emerged. He also reveals our susceptibility to skewed conceptions of who we think we are as creatures of history and of what we think of as the untamed parts of our world. He seems especially interested in the relationship between the American character and the land that many believe helped form that character.

1   The time has come to rethink wilderness.

This will seem a heretical claim to many environmentalists, since the idea of wilderness has for decades been a fundamental tenet—indeed, a passion—of the environmental movement, especially in the United States. For many Americans wilderness stands as the last remaining place where civilization, that all too human disease, has not fully infected the earth. It is an island in the polluted sea of urban-industrial modernity, the one place we can turn for escape from our own too-muchness. Seen in this way, wilderness presents itself as the best antidote to our human selves, a refuge we must somehow recover if we hope to save the planet. As Henry David Thoreau once famously declared, "In Wildness is the preservation of the World."

But is it? The more one knows of its peculiar history, the more one realizes that wilderness is not quite what it seems. Far from being the one place on earth that stands apart from humanity, it is quite profoundly a human creation—indeed the creation of very particular human cultures at very particular moments in human history. It is not a pristine sanctuary where the last remnant of an untouched, endangered, but still transcendent nature can for at least a little while longer be encountered without the contaminating taint of civilization. Instead, it is a product of that civilization, and could hardly be contaminated by the very stuff of which it is made. Wilderness hides its unnaturalness behind a mask that is all the more beguiling because it seems so natural. As we gaze into the mirror it holds up for us, we too easily imagine that what we behold is Nature when in fact we see the reflection of our own unexamined longings and desires. For this reason, we mistake ourselves when we suppose that wilderness can be the solution to our culture's problematic relationships with the nonhuman world, for wilderness is itself no small part of the problem.

To assert the unnaturalness of so natural a place will no doubt seem absurd or even perverse to many readers, so let me hasten to add that the nonhuman world we encounter in wilderness is far from being merely our own invention. I celebrate with others who love wilderness and the beauty and power it contains. Each of us who has spent time there can conjure images and sensations that seem all the more hauntingly real for having engraved themselves so indelibly on our memories. Such memories may be uniquely our own, but they are also familiar enough to be instantly recognizable to others. Remember this? The torrents of mist shooting out from the base of a great waterfall in the depths of a Sierra canyon, the tiny droplets cooling your face as you listen to the roar of the water and gaze up toward the sky through a rainbow that hovers just out of reach. Remember this too: looking out across a desert canyon in the evening air, the only sound a lone raven calling in the distance, the rock walls dropping away into a chasm so deep that its bottom all but vanishes as you squint into the amber light of the setting sun. And this: the moment beside the trail as you sit on a sandstone ledge, your boots damp with the morning dew while you take in the rich smell of the pines, and the small red fox—or maybe for you it was a raccoon or a coyote or a deer—that suddenly ambles across your path, stopping for a long moment to gaze in your direction with cautious indifference before continuing on its way. Remember the feelings of such moments, and you will know as well as I do that you were in the presence of something irreducibly nonhuman, something profoundly Other than yourself. Wilderness is made of that, too.

5   And yet: what brought each of us to the places where such memories became possible is entirely a cultural invention. Go back 250 years in American and European history, and you do not find nearly so many people wandering around remote corners of the planet looking for what today we would call "the wilderness experience." As late as the eighteenth century, the most common usage of the word "wilderness" in the English language referred to landscapes that generally carried adjectives far different from the ones they attract today. To be a wilderness then was to be "deserted," "savage," "desolate," "barren"—in short, a "waste," the word's nearest synonym. Its connotations were anything but positive, and the emotion one was most likely to feel in its presence was "bewilderment"—or terror.

Many of the word's strongest associations then were biblical, for it is used over and over again in the King James Version to refer to places on the margins of civilization where it is all too easy to lose oneself in moral confusion and despair. The wilderness was where Moses had wandered with his people for forty years, and where they had nearly abandoned their God to worship a golden idol. "For Pharaoh will say of the Children of Israel," we read in Exodus, "They are entangled in the land, the wilderness hath shut them in." The wilderness was where Christ had struggled with the Devil and endured his temptations: "And immediately the Spirit driveth him into the wilderness. And he was there in the wilderness for forty days tempted of Satan; and was with the wild beasts; and the angels ministered unto him." The "delicious Paradise" of John Milton's Eden was surrounded by "a steep wilderness, whose hairy sides / Access denied" to all who sought entry. When Adam and Eve were driven from that garden, the world they entered was a wilderness that only their labor could redeem. Wilderness, in short, was a place to which one came against one's will, and always in fear and trembling. Whatever value it might have arose solely from the possibility that it might be "reclaimed" and turned toward human ends—plants, say, or a city upon a hill. In its raw state, it had little or nothing to offer civilized men and women.

But by the end of the nineteenth century all this had changed. The wastelands that had once seemed worthless had for some people come to seem almost beyond price. That Thoreau in 1862 could declare wildness to be the preservation of the world suggests the sea change that was going on. Wilderness had once been the antithesis of all that was orderly and good—it had been the darkness, one might say, on the far side of the garden wall—and yet now it was frequently likened to Eden itself. When John Muir arrived in the Sierra Nevada in 1869, he would declare, "No description of Heaven that I have ever heard or read of seems half so fine." He was hardly alone in expressing such emotions. One by one, various corners of the American map came to be designated as sites whose wild beauty was so spectacular that a growing number of citizens had to visit and see them for themselves. Niagara Falls was the first to undergo this transformation, but it was soon followed by the Catskills, the Adirondacks, Yosemite, Yellowstone, and others. Yosemite was deeded by the U.S. government to the State of California in 1864 as the nation's first wildland park, and Yellowstone became the first true national park in 1872.

By the first decade of the twentieth century, in the single most famous episode in American conservation history, a national debate had exploded over whether the city of San Francisco should be permitted to augment its water supply by damming the Tuolumne River in Hetch Hetchy valley, well within the boundaries of Yosemite National Park. The dam was eventually built, but what today seems no less significant is that so many people fought to prevent its completion. Even as the fight was being lost, Hetch Hetchy became the battle cry of an emerging movement to preserve wilderness. Fifty years earlier, such opposition would have been unthinkable. Few would have questioned the merits of "reclaiming" a wasteland like this in order to put it to human use. Now the defenders of Hetch Hetchy attracted widespread national attention by portraying such an act not as improvement or progress but as desecration and vandalism. Lest one doubt that the old biblical metaphors had been turned completely on their heads, listen to John Muir attack the dam's defenders. "Their arguments," he wrote, "are curiously like those of the devil, devised for the destruction of the first garden—so much of the very best Eden fruit going to waste; so much of the best Tuolumne water and Tuolumne scenery going to waste." For Muir and the growing number of Americans who shared his views, Satan's home had become God's own temple.

The sources of this rather astonishing transformation were many but for the purposes of this essay they can be gathered under two broad headings: the sublime and the frontier. Of the two, sublime is the older and more pervasive cultural construct, being one of the most important expressions of that broad transatlantic movement we today label as romanticism; the frontier is more peculiarly American, though it too had its European antecedents and parallels. The two converged to remake wilderness in their own image, freighting it with moral values and cultural symbols that it carries to this day. Indeed, it is not too much to say that the modern environmental movement is itself a grandchild of romanticism and postfrontier ideology, which is why it is no accident that so much environmentalist discourse takes its bearings from the wilderness these intellectual movements helped create. Although wilderness may today seem to be just one environmental concern among many, it in fact serves as the foundation for a long list of other such concerns that on their face seem quite remote from it. That is why its influence is so pervasive and, potentially, so insidious.

To gain such remarkable influence, the concept of wilderness had to become loaded with some of the deepest core values of the culture that created and idealized it: it had to become sacred. This possibility had been present in wilderness even in the days when it had been a place of spiritual danger and moral temptation. If Satan was there, then so was Christ, who had found angels as well as wild beasts during his sojourn in the desert. In the wilderness the boundaries between human and nonhuman, between natural and supernatural, had always seemed less certain than elsewhere. This was why the early Christian saints and mystics had often emulated Christ's desert retreat as they sought to experience for themselves the visions and spiritual testing he had endured. One might meet devils and run the risk of losing one's soul in such a place, but one might also meet God. For some that possibility was worth almost any price.

By the eighteenth century this sense of the wilderness as a landscape where the supernatural lay just beneath the surface was expressed in the doctrine of the *sublime,* a word whose modern usage has been so watered down by commercial hype and tourist advertising that it retains only a dim echo of its former power. In the theories of Edmund Burke, Immanuel Kant, William Gilpin, and others, sublime landscapes were those rare places on earth where one had more chance than elsewhere to glimpse the face of God. Romantics had a clear notion of where one could be most sure of having this experience. Although God might, of course, choose to show himself anywhere, he would most often be found in those vast, powerful landscapes where one could not help feeling insignificant and being reminded of one's own mortality. Where were these sublime places? The eighteenth-century catalogue of their locations feels very familiar, for we still see and value landscapes as it taught us to do. God was on the mountaintop, in the chasm, in the waterfall, in the thundercloud, in the rainbow, in the sunset. One has only to think of the sites that Americans chose for their first national parks—Yellowstone, Yosemite, Grand Canyon, Rainier, Zion—to realize that virtually all of them fit one or more of these categories. Less sublime landscapes simply did not appear worthy of such protection; not until the 1940s, for instance, would the first swamp be honored, in Everglades National Park, and to this day there is no national park in the grasslands.

Among the best proofs that one had entered a sublime landscape was the emotion it evoked. For the early romantic writers and artists who first began to celebrate it, the sublime was far from being a pleasurable experience. The classic description is that of William Wordsworth as he recounted climbing the Alps and crossing the Simplon Pass in his autobiographical poem *The Prelude.* There, surrounded by crags and waterfalls, the poet felt himself literally to be in the presence of the divine—and experienced an emotion remarkably close to terror:

> The immeasurable height
> Of woods decaying, never to be decayed,
> The stationary blasts of waterfalls,
> And in the narrow rent at every turn
> Winds thwarting winds, bewildered and forlorn,
> The torrents shooting from the clear blue sky,
> The rocks that muttered close upon our ears,
> Black drizzling crags that spake by the way-side
> As if a voice were in them, the sick sight
> And giddy prospect of the raving stream,
> The unfettered clouds and region of the
>   Heavens,
> Tumult and peace, the darkness and the light —
> Were all like workings of one mind, the features
> Of the same face, blossoms upon one tree;
> Characters of the great Apocalypse,
> The types and symbols of Eternity,
> Of first, and last, and midst, and without end.

This was no casual stroll in the mountains, no simple sojourn in the gentle lap of non-human nature. What Wordsworth described was nothing less than a religious experience, akin to that of the Old Testament prophets as they conversed with their wrathful God. The symbols he detected in this wilderness landscape were more supernatural than natural, and they inspired more awe and dismay than joy or pleasure. No mere mortal was meant to linger long in such a place, so it was with considerable relief that Wordsworth and his companion made their way back down from the peaks to the sheltering valleys.

Lest you suspect that this view of the sublime was limited to timid Europeans who lacked the American know-how for feeling at home in the wilderness, remember Henry David Thoreau's 1846 climb of Mount Katahdin, in Maine. Although Thoreau is regarded by many today as one of the great American celebrators of wilderness, his emotions about Katahdin were no less ambivalent than Wordsworth's about the Alps.

> It was vast, Titanic, and such as man never inhabits. Some part of the beholder, even some vital part, seems to escape through the loose grating of his ribs as he ascends. He is more lone than you can imagine. . . . Vast, Titanic, inhuman Nature has got him at disadvantage, caught him alone, and pilfers him of some of his divine faculty. She does not smile on him as in the plains. She seems to say sternly, why came ye here before your time? This ground is not prepared for you. Is it not enough that I smile in the valleys? I have never made this soil for thy feet, this air for thy breathing, these rocks for thy neighbors. I cannot pity nor fondle thee here, but forever relentlessly drive thee hence to where I *am* kind. Why seek me where I have not called thee, and then complain because you find me but a stepmother?

15 This is surely not the way a modern backpacker or nature lover would describe Maine's most famous mountain, but that is because Thoreau's description owes as much to Wordsworth and other romantic contemporaries as to the rocks and clouds of Katahdin itself. His words took the physical mountain on which he stood and transmuted it into an icon of the sublime: a symbol of God's presence on earth. The power and the glory of that icon were such that only a prophet might gaze on it for long. In effect, romantics like Thoreau joined Moses and the children of Israel in Exodus when "they looked toward the wilderness, and behold, the glory of the Lord appeared in the cloud."

But even as it came to embody the awesome power of the sublime, wilderness was also being tamed—not just by those who were building settlements in its midst but also by those who most celebrated its inhuman beauty. By the second half of the nineteenth century, the terrible awe that Wordsworth and Thoreau regarded as the appropriately pious stance to adopt in the presence of their mountaintop God was giving way to a much more comfortable, almost sentimental demeanor. As more and more tourists sought out the wilderness as a spectacle to be looked at and enjoyed for its great beauty, the sublime in effect became domesticated. The wilderness was still sacred, but the religious sentiments it evoked were more those of a pleasant parish church than those of a grand cathedral or a harsh desert retreat. The writer who best captures this late romantic sense of a domesticated sublime is undoubtedly John Muir whose descriptions of Yosemite and the Sierra Nevada reflect none of the anxiety or terror one finds in earlier writers. Here he is, for instance, sketching on North Dome in Yosemite Valley:

> No pain here, no dull empty hours, no fear of the past, no fear of the future. These blessed mountains are so compactly filled with God's beauty, no petty personal hope or experience has room to be. Drinking this champagne water is pure pleasure, so is breathing the living air, and every movement of limbs is pleasure, while the body seems to feel beauty when exposed to it as it feels the campfire or sunshine, entering not by the eyes alone, but equally through all one's flesh like radiant heat, making a passionate ecstatic pleasure glow not explainable.

The emotions Muir describes in Yosemite could hardly be more different from Thoreau's on Katahdin or Wordsworth's on the Simplon Pass. Yet all three men are participating in the same cultural tradition and contributing to the same myth: the mountain as cathedral. The three may differ in the way they choose to express their piety—Wordsworth favoring an awe-filled bewilderment, Thoreau a stern loneliness, Muir a welcome ecstasy—but they agree completely about the church in which they prefer to worship. Muir's closing words on North Dome diverge from his older contemporaries only in mood, not in their ultimate content:

> Perched like a fly on this Yosemite dome, I gaze and sketch and bask, oftentimes settling down into dumb admiration without definite hope of ever learning much, yet with the longing, unresting effort that lies at the door of hope, humbly prostrate before the vast display of God's power, and eager to offer self-denial and renunciation with eternal toil to learn any lesson in the divine manuscript.

Muir's "divine manuscript" and Wordsworth's "Characters of the great Apocalypse" were in fact pages from the same holy book. The sublime wilderness had ceased to be a place of satanic temptation and become instead a sacred temple, much as it continues to be for those who love it today.

But the Romantic sublime was not the only cultural movement that helped transform wilderness into a sacred American icon during the nineteenth century. No less important was the powerful romantic attraction of primitivism, dating back at least to Rousseau—the belief that the best antidote to the ills of an overly refined and civilized modern world was a return to simpler, more primitive living. In the United States, this was embodied most strikingly in the national myth of the frontier. The historian Frederick Jackson Turner wrote in 1893 the classic academic statement of this myth, but it had been part of American cultural traditions for well over a century. As Turner described the process, easterners and European immigrants, in moving to the wild unsettled lands of the frontier, shed the trappings of civilization, rediscovered their primitive racial energies, reinvented direct democratic institutions, and thereby reinfused themselves with a vigor, an independence, and a creativity that were the source of American democracy and national character. Seen in this way, wild country be-

came a place not just of religious redemption but of national renewal, the quintessential location for experiencing what it meant to be an American.

One of Turner's most provocative claims 20 was that by the 1890s the frontier was passing away. Never again would "such gifts of free land offer themselves" to the American people. "The frontier has gone," he declared, "and with its going has closed the first period of American history." Built into the frontier myth from its very beginning was the notion that this crucible of American identity was temporary and would pass away. Those who have celebrated the frontier have almost always looked backward as they did so, mourning an older, simpler, truer world that is about to disappear forever. That world and all of its attractions, Turner said, depended on free land—on wilderness. Thus, in the myth of the vanishing frontier lay the seeds of wilderness preservation in the United States, for if wild land had been so crucial in the making of the nation, then surely one must save its last remnants as monuments to the American past—and as an insurance policy to protect its future. It is no accident that the movement to set aside national parks and wilderness areas began to gain real momentum at precisely the time that laments about the passing frontier reached their peak. To protect wilderness was in a very real sense to protect the nation's most sacred myth of origin.

Among the core elements of the frontier myth was the powerful sense among certain groups of Americans that wilderness was the last bastion of rugged individualism. Turner tended to stress communitarian themes when writing frontier history, asserting that Americans in primitive conditions had been forced to band together with their neighbors to form communities and democratic institutions. For other writers, however, frontier democracy for communities was less compelling than frontier freedom for individuals. By fleeing to the outer margins of settled land and society—so the story ran—an individual could escape the confining strictures of civilized life. The mood among writers who celebrated frontier individualism was almost always nostalgic; they lamented not just a lost way of life but the passing of the heroic men who had embodied that life. Thus Owen Wister in the introduction to his classic 1902 novel *The Virginian* could write of "a vanished world" in which "the horseman, the cow-puncher, the last romantic figure upon our soil" rode only "in his historic yesterday" and would "never come again." For Wister, the cowboy was a man who gave his word and kept it ("Wall Street would have found him behind the times"), who did not talk lewdly to women ("Newport would have thought him old-fashioned"), who worked and played hard, and whose "ungoverned hours did not unman him." Theodore Roosevelt wrote with much the same nostalgic fervor about the "fine, manly qualities" of the "wild rough-rider of the plains." No one could be more heroically masculine, thought Roosevelt, or more at home in the western wilderness:

> There he passes his days, there he does his life-work, there, when he meets death, he faces it as he has faced many other evils, with quiet, uncomplaining fortitude. Brave, hospitable, hardy, and adventurous, he is the grim pioneer of our race; he prepares the way for the civilization from before whose face he must himself disappear. Hard and dangerous though his existence is, it has yet a wild attraction that strongly draws to it his bold, free spirit.

This nostalgia for a passing frontier way of life inevitably implied ambivalence, if not downright hostility, toward modernity and all that it represented. If one saw the wild lands of the frontier as freer, truer, and more natural than other, more modern places, then one was also inclined to see the cities and factories of urban-industrial civilization as confining, false, and artificial. Owen Wister looked at the post-frontier "transition" that had followed "the horseman of the plains," and did not like what he saw: "a shapeless state, a condition of men and manners as unlovely as is that moment in the year when winter is gone and spring not come, and the face of Nature is ugly." In the eyes of writers who shared Wister's distaste for modernity, civilization contaminated its inhabitants and absorbed them into the faceless, collective, contemptible life of the crowd. For all of its troubles and dangers, and despite the fact that it must pass away, the frontier had been a better place. If civilization was to be redeemed, it would be by men like the Virginian who could retain their frontier virtues even as they made the transition to post-frontier life.

The mythic frontier individualist was almost always masculine in gender: here, in the wilderness, a man could be a real man, the rugged individual he was meant to be before civilization sapped his energy and threatened his masculinity. Wister's contemptuous remarks about Wall Street and Newport suggest what he and many others of his generation believed—that the comforts and seductions of civilized life were especially insidious for men, who all too easily became emasculated by the feminizing tendencies of civilization. More often than not, men who felt this way came, like Wister and Roosevelt, from elite class backgrounds. The curious result was that frontier nostalgia became an important vehicle for expressing a peculiarly bourgeois form of anti-modernism. The very men who most benefited from urban-industrial capitalism were among those who believed they must escape its debilitating effects. If the frontier was passing, then men who had the means to do so should preserve for themselves some remnant of its wild landscape so that they might enjoy the regeneration and renewal that came from sleeping under the stars, participating in blood sports, and living off the land. The frontier might be gone, but the frontier experience could still be had if only wilderness were preserved.

Thus the decades following the Civil War saw more and more of the nation's wealthiest citizens seeking out wilderness for themselves. The elite passion for wild land took many forms: enormous estates in the Adirondacks and elsewhere (disingenuously called "camps" despite their many servants and amenities), cattle ranches for would-be rough riders on the Great Plains, guided big-game hunting trips in the Rockies, and luxurious resort hotels whereby railroads pushed their way into sublime landscapes. Wilderness suddenly emerged as the landscape of choice for elite tourists, who brought with them strikingly urban ideas of the countryside through which they traveled. For them, wild land was not a site for productive labor and not a permanent home; rather, it was a place of recreation. One went to the wilderness not as a producer but as a consumer, hiring guides and other backcountry residents who could serve as romantic surrogates for the rough riders and hunters of the frontier, if one was willing to overlook their new status as employees and servants of the rich.

25   In just this way, wilderness came to embody the national frontier myth, standing for the wild freedom of America's past and seeming to represent a highly attractive natural alternative to the ugly artificiality of modern civilization. The irony, of course, was that in the process wilderness came to reflect the very civilization its devotees sought to escape. Ever since the nineteenth century, celebrating wilderness has been an activity mainly for well-to-do city folks. Country people generally know far too much about working the land to regard *un*worked land as their ideal. In contrast, elite urban tourists and wealthy sportsmen projected their leisure-time frontier fantasies onto the American landscape and so created wilderness in their own image.

There were other ironies as well. The movement to set aside national parks and wilderness areas followed hard on the heels of the final Indian wars, in which the prior human inhabitants of these areas were rounded up and moved onto reservations. The myth of the wilderness as "virgin," uninhabited land had always been especially cruel when seen from the perspective of the Indians who had once called that land home. Now they were forced to move elsewhere, with the result that tourists could safely enjoy the illusion that they were seeing their nation in its pristine, original state, in the new morning of God's own creation. Among the things that most marked the new national parks as reflecting a post-frontier consciousness was the relative absence of human violence within their boundaries. The actual frontier had often been a place of conflict, in which invaders and invaded fought for control of land and resources. Once set aside within the fixed and carefully policed boundaries of the modern bureaucratic state, the wilderness lost its savage image and became safe: a place more of reverie than of revulsion or fear. Meanwhile, its original inhabitants were kept out by dint of force, their earlier uses of the land redefined as inappropriate or even illegal. To this day, for instance, the Blackfeet continue to be accused of "poaching" on the lands of Glacier National Park that originally belonged to them and that were ceded by treaty only with the proviso that they be permitted to hunt there.

The removal of Indians to create an "uninhabited wilderness"—uninhabited as never before in the human history of the place—reminds us just how invented, just how constructed, the American wilderness really is. To return to my opening argument: there is nothing natural about the concept of wilderness. It is entirely a creation of the culture that holds it dear, a product of the very history it seeks to deny. Indeed, one of the most striking proofs of the cultural invention of wilderness is its thoroughgoing erasure of the history from which it sprang. In virtually all of its manifestations, wilderness represents a flight from history. Seen as the original garden, it is a place outside of time from which human beings had to be ejected before the fallen world of history could properly begin. Seen as the frontier, it is a savage world at the dawn of civilization, whose transformation represents the very beginning of the national historical epic. Seen as the bold landscape of frontier heroism, it is the place of youth and childhood, into which men escape by abandoning their pasts and entering a world of freedom where the constraints of civilization fade into memory. Seen as the sacred sublime, it is the home of a God who transcends history by standing as the One who remains untouched and unchanged by time's arrow. No matter what the angle from which we regard it, wilderness offers us the illusion that we can escape the cares and troubles of the world in which our past has ensnared us.

This escape from history is one reason why the language we use to talk about wilderness is often permeated with spiritual and religious values that reflect human ideals far more than the material world of physical nature. Wilderness fulfills the old romantic project of secularizing Judeo-Christian values so as to make a new cathedral not in some petty human building but in God's own creation, Nature itself. Many environmentalists who reject traditional notions of the godhead and who regard themselves as agnostics or even atheists nonetheless express feelings tantamount to religious awe when in the presence of wilderness—a fact that testifies to the success of the romantic project. Those who have no difficulty seeing God as the expression of our human dreams and desires nonetheless have trouble recognizing that in a secular age Nature can offer precisely the same sort of mirror.

Thus it is that wilderness serves as the unexamined foundation on which so many of the quasi-religious values of modern environmentalism rest. The critique of modernity that is one of environmentalism's most important contributions to the moral and political discourse of our time more often than not appeals, explicitly or implicitly, to wilderness as the standard against which to measure the failings of our human world. Wilderness is the natural unfallen antithesis of an unnatural civilization that has lost its soul. It is a place of freedom in which we can recover the true selves we have lost to the corrupting influences of our artificial lives. Most of all, it is the ultimate landscape of authenticity. Combining the sacred grandeur of the sublime with the primitive simplicity of the frontier, it is the place where we can see the world as it really is, and so know ourselves as we really are—or ought to be.

But the trouble with wilderness is that it 30 quietly expresses and reproduces the very values its devotees seek to reject. The flight from history that is very nearly the core of wilderness represents the false hope of an escape from responsibility, the illusion that we can somehow wipe clean the slate of our past and return to the tabula rasa that supposedly existed before we began to leave our marks on the world. The dream of an unworked natural landscape is very much the fantasy of people who have never themselves had to work the land to make a living—urban folk for whom food comes from a supermarket or a restaurant instead of a field, and for whom the wooden houses in which they live and work apparently have no meaningful connection to the forests in which trees grow and die. Only people whose relation to the land was already alienated could hold up wilderness as a model for human life in nature, for the romantic ideology of wilderness leaves precisely nowhere for human beings actually to make their living from the land.

This, then, is the central paradox: wilderness embodies a dualistic vision in which the human is entirely outside the natural. If we allow ourselves to believe that nature, to be true, must also be wild, then our very presence in nature represents its fall. The place where we are is the place where nature is not.

If this is so—if by definition wilderness leaves no place for human beings, save perhaps as contemplative sojourners enjoying their leisurely reverie in God's natural cathedral—then also by definition it can offer no solution to the environmental and other problems that confront us. To the extent that we celebrate wilderness as the measure with which we judge civilization, we reproduce the dualism that sets humanity and nature at opposite poles. We thereby leave ourselves little hope of discovering what an ethical, sustainable, *honorable* human place in nature might actually look like.

Worse: to the extent that we live in an urban-industrial civilization but at the same time pretend to ourselves that our *real* home is in the wilderness, to just that extent we give ourselves permission to evade responsibility for the lives we actually lead. We inhabit civilization while holding some part of ourselves—what we imagine to be the most precious part—aloof from its entanglements. We work our nine-to-five jobs in its institutions, we eat its food, we drive its cars (not least to reach the wilderness), we benefit from the intricate and all too invisible networks with which it shelters us, all the while pretending that these things are not an essential part of who we are. By imagining that our true home is in the wilderness, we forgive ourselves the homes we actually inhabit. In its flight from history, in its siren song of escape, in its reproduction of the dangerous dualism that sets human beings outside of nature—in all of these ways, wilderness poses a serious threat to responsible environmentalism at the end of the twentieth century.

By now I hope it is clear that my criticism in this essay is not directed at wild nature per se, or even at efforts to set aside large tracts of wild land, but rather at the specific habits of thinking that flow from this complex cultural construction called wilderness. It is not the things we label as wilderness that are the problem—for nonhuman nature and large tracts of the natural world *do* deserve protection—but rather what we ourselves mean when we use that label. Lest one doubt how pervasive these habits of thought really are in contemporary environmentalism, let me list some of the places where wilderness serves as the ideological underpinning for environmental concerns that might otherwise seem quite remote from it. Defenders of biological diversity, for instance, although sometimes appealing to more utilitarian concerns, often point to "untouched" ecosystems as the best and richest repositories of the undiscovered species we must certainly try to protect. Although at first blush an apparently more "scientific" concept than wilderness, biological diversity in fact invokes many of the same sacred values, which is why organizations like the Nature Conservancy have been so quick to employ it as an alternative to the seemingly fuzzier and more problematic concept of wilderness. There is a paradox here, of course. To the extent that biological diversity (indeed, even wilderness itself) is likely to survive in the future only by the most vigilant and self-conscious management of the ecosystems that sustain it, the ideology of wilderness is potentially in direct conflict with the very thing it encourages us to protect.

The most striking instances of this have revolved around "endangered species," which serve as vulnerable symbols of biological diversity while at the same time standing as surrogates for wilderness itself. The terms of the Endangered Species Act in the United States have often meant that those hoping to defend pristine wilderness have had to rely on a single endangered species like the spotted owl to gain legal standing for their case—thereby making the full power of sacred land inhere in a single numinous organism whose habitat then becomes the object of intense debate about appropriate management and use. The ease with which anti-environmental forces like the wise-use movement have attacked such single-species preservation efforts suggests the vulnerability of strategies like these.

35   Perhaps partly because our own conflicts over such places and organisms have become so messy, the convergence of wilderness values with concerns about biological diversity and endangered species has helped produce a deep fascination for remote ecosystems, where it is easier to imagine that nature might somehow be "left alone" to flourish by its own pristine devices. The classic example is the tropical rain forest, which since the 1970s has become the most powerful modern icon of unfallen, sacred land—a veritable Garden of Eden—for many Americans and Europeans. And yet protecting the rain forest in the eyes of First World environmentalists all too often means protecting it from the people who live there. Those who seek to preserve such "wilderness" from the activities of native peoples run the risk of reproducing the same tragedy—being forcibly removed from an ancient home—that befell American Indians. Third World countries face massive environmental problems and deep social conflicts, but these are not likely to be solved by a cultural myth that encourages us to "preserve" peopleless landscapes that have not existed in such places for millennia. At its worst, as environmentalists are beginning to realize, exporting American notions of wilderness in this way can become an unthinking and self-defeating form of cultural imperialism.

Perhaps the most suggestive example of the way that wilderness thinking can underpin other environmental concerns has emerged in the recent debate about "global change." In 1989 the journalist Bill McKibben published a book entitled *The End of Nature,* in which he argued that the prospect of global climate change as a result of unintentional human manipulation of the atmosphere means that nature as we once knew it no longer exists. Whereas earlier generations inhabited a natural world that remained more or less unaffected by their actions, our own generation is uniquely different. We and our children will henceforth live in a biosphere completely altered by our own activity, a planet in which the human and the natural can no longer be distinguished because the one has overwhelmed the other. In McKibben's view, nature has died, and we are responsible for killing it. "The planet," he declares, "is utterly different now."

But such a perspective is possible only if we accept the wilderness premise that nature, to be natural, must also be pristine—remote from humanity and untouched by our common past. In fact, everything we know about environmental history suggests that people have been manipulating the natural world on various scales for as long as we have a record of their passing. Moreover, we have unassailable evidence that many of the environmental changes we now face also occurred quite apart from human intervention at one time or another in the earth's past. The point is not that our current problems are trivial, or that our devastating effects on the earth's ecosystems should be accepted as inevitable or "natural." It is rather that we seem unlikely to make much progress in solving these problems if we hold up to ourselves as the mirror of nature a wilderness we ourselves cannot inhabit.

To do so is merely to take to a logical extreme the paradox that was built into wilderness from the beginning: if nature dies because we enter it, then the only way to save nature is to kill ourselves. The absurdity of this proposition flows from the underlying dualism it expresses. Not only does it ascribe greater power to humanity than we in fact possess—physical and biological nature will surely survive in some form or another long after we ourselves have gone the way of all flesh—but in the end it offers us little more than a self-defeating counsel of despair. The tautology gives us no way out: if wild nature is the only thing worth saving, and if our mere presence destroys it, then the sole solution to our own unnaturalness, the only way to protect sacred wilderness from profane humanity, would seem to be suicide. It is not a proposition that seems likely to produce very positive or practical results.

And yet radical environmentalists and deep ecologists all too frequently come close to accepting this premise as a first principle. When they express, for instance, the popular notion that our environmental problems began with the invention of agriculture, they push the human fall from natural grace so far back into the past that all of civilized history becomes a tale of ecological declension. Earth First! founder Dave Foreman captures the familiar parable succinctly when he writes:

> Before agriculture was midwifed in the Middle East, humans were in the wilderness. We had no concept of "wilderness" because everything was wilderness and *we were a part of it*. But with irrigation ditches, crop surpluses, and permanent villages, we became *apart from* the natural world. . . . Between the wilderness that created us and the civilization created by us grew an ever-widening rift.

40   In this view, the farm becomes the first and most important battlefield in the long war against wild nature, and all else follows in its wake. From such a starting place, it is hard not to reach the conclusion that the only way human beings can hope to live naturally on earth is to follow the hunter-gatherers back into a wilderness Eden and abandon virtually everything that civilization has given us. It may indeed turn out that civilization will end in ecological collapse or nuclear disaster, whereupon one might expect to find any human survivors returning to a way of life closer to that celebrated by Foreman and his followers. For most of us, though, such a debacle would be cause for regret, a sign that humanity had failed to fulfill its own promise and failed to honor its own highest values—including those of the deep ecologists.

In offering wilderness as the ultimate hunter-gatherer alternative to civilization, Foreman reproduces an extreme but still easily recognizable version of the myth of frontier primitivism. When he writes of his fellow Earth Firsters that "we believe we must return to being animal, to glorying in our sweat, hormones, tears, and blood" and that "we struggle against the modern compulsion to become dull, passionless androids," he is following in the footsteps of Owen Wister. Although his arguments give primacy to defending biodiversity and the autonomy of wild nature, his prose becomes most passionate when he speaks of preserving "the wilderness experience." His own ideal "Big Outside" bears an uncanny resemblance to that of the frontier myth: wide open spaces and virgin land with no trails, no signs, no facilities, no maps, no guides, no rescues, no modern equipment. Tellingly, it is a land where hardy travelers can support themselves by hunting with "primitive weapons (bow and arrow, atlatl, knife, sharp rock)." Foreman claims that "the primary value of wilderness is not as a proving ground for young Huck Finns and Annie Oakleys," but his heart is with Huck and Annie all the same. He admits that "preserving a quality wilderness experience for the human visitor, letting her or him flex Paleolithic muscles or seek visions, remains a tremendously important secondary purpose." Just so does Teddy Roosevelt's Rough Rider live on in the greener garb of a new age.

However much one may be attracted to such a vision, it entails problematic consequences. For one, it makes wilderness the locus for an epic struggle between malign civilization and benign nature, compared with which all other social, political, and moral concerns seem trivial. Foreman writes, "The preservation of wildness and native diversity is *the* most important issue. Issues directly affecting only humans pale in comparison." Presumably so do any environmental problems whose victims are mainly people, for such problems usually surface in landscapes that have already "fallen" and are no longer wild. This would seem to exclude from the radical environmentalist agenda problems of occupational health and safety in industrial settings, problems of toxic waste exposure on "unnatural" urban and agricultural sites, problems of poor children poisoned by lead exposure in the inner city, problems of famine and poverty and human suffering in the "overpopulated" places of the earth—problems, in short, of environmental justice. If we set too high a stock on wilderness, too many other corners of the earth become less than natural and too many other people become less than human, thereby giving us permission not to care much about their suffering or their fate.

It is no accident that these supposedly inconsequential environmental problems affect mainly poor people, for the long affiliation between wilderness and wealth means that the only poor people who count when wilderness is *the* issue are hunter-gatherers, who presumably do not consider themselves to be poor in the first place. The dualism at the heart of wilderness encourages its advocates to conceive of its protection as a crude conflict between the "human" and the "nonhuman"— or, more often, between those who value the nonhuman and those who do not. This in turn tempts one to ignore crucial differences *among* humans and the complex cultural and historical reasons why different peoples may feel very differently about the meaning of wilderness.

Why, for instance, is the "wilderness experience" so often conceived as a form of recreation best enjoyed by those whose class privileges give them the time and resources to leave their jobs behind and "get away from it all"? Why does the protection of wilderness so often seem to pit urban recreationists against rural people who actually earn their living from the land (excepting those who sell goods and services to the tourists themselves)? Why

in the debates about pristine natural areas are "primitive" peoples idealized, even sentimentalized, until the moment they do something unprimitive, modern, and unnatural, and thereby fall from environmental grace? What are the consequences of a wilderness ideology that devalues productive labor and the very concrete knowledge that comes from working the land with one's own hands? All of these questions imply conflicts among different groups of people, conflicts that are obscured behind the deceptive clarity of "human" versus "nonhuman." If in answering these knotty questions we resort to so simplistic an opposition, we are almost certain to ignore the very subtleties and complexities we need to understand.

But the most troubling cultural baggage that accompanies the celebration of wilderness has less to do with remote rain forests and peoples than with the ways we think about ourselves—we American environmentalists who quite rightly worry about the future of the earth and the threats we pose to the natural world. Idealizing a distant wilderness too often means not idealizing the environment in which we live, the landscape that for better or worse we call home. Most of our most serious environmental problems start right here, at home, and if we are to solve those problems, we need an environmental ethic that will tell us as much about using nature as about not using it. The wilderness dualism tends to cast any use as abuse, and thereby denies us a middle ground in which responsible use and non-use might attain some kinship. My own belief is that only by exploring this middle ground will we learn ways of imagining a better world for all of us: humans and nonhumans, rich people and poor, women and men, First Worlders and Third Worlders, white folks and people of color, consumers and producers—a world better for humanity in all of its diversity and for all the rest of nature too. The middle ground is where we actually live. It is where we—all of us, in our different places and ways—make our homes.

That is why, when I think of the times I myself have come closest to experiencing what I might call the sacred in nature, I often find myself remembering wild places much closer to home. I think, for instance, of a small pond near my house where water bubbles up from limestone springs to feed a series of pools that rarely freeze in winter and so play home to waterfowl that stay here for the protective warmth even on the coldest of winter days, gliding silently through steaming mists as the snow falls from gray February skies. I think of a November evening long ago when I found myself on a Wisconsin hilltop in rain and dense fog, only to have the setting sun break through the clouds to cast an otherworldly golden light on the misty farms and woodlands below, a scene so unexpected and joyous that I lingered past dusk so as not to miss any part of the gift that had come my way. And I think perhaps most especially of the blown-out, bankrupt farm in the sand country of central Wisconsin where Aldo Leopold and his family tried one of the first American experiments in ecological restoration, turning ravaged and infertile soil into carefully tended ground where the human and the nonhuman could exist side by side in relative harmony. What I celebrate about such places is not *just* their wildness, though that certainly is among their most important qualities; what I celebrate even more is that they remind us of the wildness in our own backyards, of the nature that is all around us if only we have eyes to see it.

Indeed, my principal objection to wilderness is that it may teach us to be submissive or even contemptuous of such humble places and experiences. Without our quite realizing it, wilderness tends to privilege some parts of nature at the expense of others. Most of us, I suspect, still follow the conventions of the romantic sublime in finding the mountaintop more glorious than the plains, the ancient for-

est nobler than the grasslands, the mighty canyon more inspiring than the humble marsh. Even John Muir, in arguing against those who sought to dam his beloved Hetch Hetchy valley in the Sierra Nevada, argued for alternative dam sites in the gentler valleys of the foothills—a preference that had nothing to do with nature and everything with the cultural traditions of the sublime. Just as problematically, our frontier traditions have encouraged Americans to define "true" wilderness as requiring very large tracts of roadless land—what Dave Foreman calls the Big Outside. Leaving aside the legitimate empirical question in conservation biology of how large a tract of land must be before a given species can reproduce on it, the emphasis on big wilderness reflects a romantic frontier belief that one hasn't really gotten away from civilization unless one can go for days at a time without encountering another human being. By teaching us to fetishize sublime places and wide open country, these peculiarly American ways of thinking about wilderness encourage us to adopt too high a standard for what counts as "natural." If it isn't hundreds of square miles big, if it doesn't give us God's-eye views or grand vistas, if it doesn't permit us the illusion that we are alone on the planet, then it really isn't natural. It's too small, too plain, or too crowded to be *authentically* wild.

In critiquing wilderness as I have done in this essay, I'm forced to confront my own deep ambivalence about its meaning for modern environmentalism. On the one hand, one of my own most important environmental ethics is that people should always be conscious that they are part of the nature world, inextricably tied to the ecological systems that sustain their lives. Any way of looking at nature that encourages us to believe we are separate from nature—as wilderness tends to do—is likely to reinforce environmentally irresponsible behavior. On the other hand, I also think it no less crucial for us to recognize and honor nonhuman nature as a world we did not create, a world with its own independent, nonhuman reasons for being as it is. The autonomy of nonhuman nature seems to me an indispensable corrective to human arrogance. Any way of looking at nature that helps us remember—as wilderness also tends to do—that the interests of people are not necessarily identical to those of every other creature or of the earth itself is likely to foster *responsible* behavior. To the extent that wilderness has served as an important vehicle for articulating deep moral values regarding our obligations and responsibilities to the nonhuman world, I would not want to jettison the contributions it has made to our culture's ways of thinking about nature.

If the core problem of wilderness is that it distances us too much from the very things it teaches us to value, then the question we must ask is what it can tell us about home, the place where we live. How can we take the positive values we associate with wilderness and bring them closer to home? I think the answer to this question will come by broadening our sense of the otherness that wilderness seeks to define and protect. In reminding us of the world we did not make, wilderness can teach profound feelings of humility and respect as we confront our fellow beings and the earth itself. Feelings like these argue for the importance of self-awareness and self-criticism as we exercise our own ability to transform the world around us, helping us set responsible limits to human mastery—which without such limits too easily becomes human hubris. Wilderness is the place where, symbolically at least, we try to withhold our power to dominate.

50   Wallace Stegner once wrote of

> the special human mark, the special record of human passage, that distinguishes man from all other species. It is rare enough among men, impossible to any other form of life. *It is simply the deliberate and chosen refusal to make any marks at all. . . .* We are the most dangerous

species of life on the planet, and every other species, even the earth itself, has cause to fear our power to exterminate. But we are also the only species which, when it chooses to do so, will go to great effort to save what it might destroy.

The myth of wilderness, which Stegner knowingly reproduces in these remarks, is that we can somehow leave nature untouched by our passage. By now it should be clear that this for the most part is an illusion. But Stegner's deeper message then becomes all the more compelling. If living in history means that we cannot help leaving marks on a fallen world, then the dilemma we face is to decide what kinds of marks we wish to leave. It is just here that our cultural traditions of wilderness remain so important. In the broadest sense, wilderness teaches us to ask whether the Other must always bend to our will, and, if not, under what circumstances it should be allowed to flourish without our intervention. This is surely a question worth asking about everything we do, and not just about the natural world.

When we visit a wilderness area, we find ourselves surrounded by plants and animals and physical landscapes whose otherness compels our attention. In forcing us to acknowledge that they are not of our making, that they have little or no need of our continued existence, they recall for us a creation far greater than our own. In the wilderness, we need no reminder that a tree has its own reasons for being, quite apart from us. The same is less true in the gardens we plant and tend ourselves: there it is far easier to forget the otherness of the tree. Indeed, one could almost measure wilderness by the extent to which our recognition of its otherness requires a conscious, willed act on our part. The romantic legacy means that wilderness is more a state of mind than a fact of nature, and the state of mind that today most defines wilderness is *wonder*. The striking power of the wild is that wonder in the face of it requires no act of will, but forces itself upon us—as an expression of the nonhuman world experienced through the lens of our cultural history—as proof that ours is not the only presence in the universe.

Wilderness gets us into trouble only if we imagine that this experience of wonder and otherness is limited to the remote corners of the planet, or that it somehow depends on pristine landscapes we ourselves do not inhabit. Nothing could be more misleading. The tree in the garden is in reality no less other, no less worthy of our wonder and respect, than the tree in an ancient forest that has never known an ax or a saw—even though the tree in the forest reflects a more intricate web of ecological relationships. The tree in the garden could easily have sprung from the same seed as the tree in the forest, and we can claim only its location and perhaps its form as our own. Both trees stand apart from us; both share our common world. The special power of the tree in the wilderness is to remind us of this fact. It can teach us to recognize the wildness we did not see in the tree we planted in our own back yard. By seeing the otherness in that which is most unfamiliar, we can learn to see it too in that which at first seemed merely ordinary. If wilderness can do this—if it can help us perceive and respect a nature we had forgotten to recognize as natural—then it will become part of the solution to our environmental dilemmas rather than part of the problem.

This will happen, however, only if we abandon the dualism that sees the tree in the Eden as artificial—completely fallen and unnatural—and the tree in the wilderness as natural—completely pristine and wild. Both trees in some ultimate sense are wild; both in a practical sense now depend on our management and care. We are responsible for both, even though we can claim credit for neither. Our challenge is to stop thinking of such things according to a set of bipolar moral scales in which the human and the nonhu-

man, the unnatural and the natural, the fallen and the unfallen, serve as our conceptual map for understanding and valuing the world. Instead, we need to embrace the full continuum of a natural landscape that is also cultural, in which the city, the suburb, the pastoral, and the wild each has its proper place, which we permit ourselves to celebrate without needlessly denigrating the others. We need to honor the Other within and the Other next door as much as we do the exotic Other that lives far away—a lesson that applies as much to people as it does to (other) natural things. In particular, we need to discover a common middle ground in which all of these things, from the city to the wilderness, can somehow be encompassed in the word "home." Home, after all, is the place where finally we make our living. It is the place for which we take responsibility, the place we try to sustain so we can pass on what is best in it (and in ourselves) to our children.

The task of making a home in nature is what Wendell Berry has called "the forever unfinished lifework of our species." "The only thing we have to preserve nature with," he writes, "is culture; the only thing we have to preserve wildness with is domesticity." Calling a place home inevitably means that we will use the nature we find in it, for there can be no escape from manipulating and working and even killing some parts of nature to make our home. But if we acknowledge the autonomy and otherness of the things and creatures around us—an autonomy our culture has taught us to label with the word "wild"—then we will at least think carefully about the uses to which we put them, and even ask if we should use them at all. Just so can we still join Thoreau in declaring that "in Wildness is the preservation of the World," for *wild*ness (as opposed to wilderness) can be found anywhere: in the seemingly tame fields and woodlots of Massachusetts, in the cracks of a Manhattan sidewalk, even in the cells of our own bodies. As

55

Gary Snyder has wisely said, "A person with a clear heart and open mind can experience the wilderness anywhere on earth. It is a quality of one's own consciousness. The planet is a wild place and always will be." To think ourselves capable of causing "the end of nature" is an act of great hubris, for it means forgetting the wildness that dwells everywhere within and around us.

Learning to honor the wild—learning to remember and acknowledge the autonomy of the Other—means striving for critical self-consciousness in all of our actions. It means that deep reflection and respect must accompany each act of use, and means too that we must always consider the possibility of non-use. It means looking at the part of nature we intend to turn toward our own ends and asking whether we can use it again and again and again—sustainably—without its being diminished in the process. It means never imagining that we can flee into a mythical wilderness to escape history and the obligation to take responsibility for our own actions that history inescapably entails. Most of all, it means practicing remembrance and gratitude, for thanksgiving is the simplest and most basic of ways for us to recollect the nature, the culture, and the history that have come together to make the world as we know it. If wildness can stop being (just) out there and start being (also) in here, if it can start being as humane as it is natural, then perhaps we can get on with the unending task of struggling to live rightly in the world—not just in the garden, not just in the wilderness, but in the home that encompasses them both.

READING AND THINKING

1. Cronon relates contemporary ideas about wilderness to ideas from the historical past. Why does he quote Wordsworth, Thoreau, and others?

2. What, historically, has wilderness meant to Americans? What does Cronon mean when he says that "wilderness is not quite what it seems"? How does he define wilderness?

3. When, in America, did wilderness first become "sublime" and special, a place of almost sacred importance worth preserving?

4. What does Cronon suggest about the relationship between nature and culture?

5. What does Cronon mean when he says that "we need an environmental ethic that will tell us as much about using nature as about not using it"?

THINKING AND WRITING

1. Trace Cronon's emphasis on two of these aspects of wilderness: *religious* (*sacred*), *wild, Other, natural, uncivilized*. Highlight his emphasis, and, in a paragraph about each of the aspects, explain why the aspect is important to our understanding of what Cronon is saying.

2. Write a revealing paragraph about the relationship between American character and the land, as Cronon sees it. Write a second paragraph calling into question Cronon's beliefs.

3. Write a paragraph that explains why Cronon celebrates and wants us to celebrate "the wildness in our own backyards"?

4. Cronon closes his essay with a telling trio of metaphors: "If wildness can stop being (just) out there and start being (also) in here, if it can start being as humane as it is natural, then perhaps we can get on with the unending task of struggling to live rightly in the world—not just in the garden, not just in the wilderness, but in the home that encompasses them both." Write a brief paragraph in which you capture the essence and importance of those three metaphors: *garden, wilderness, home.*

CALLING OURSELVES TO QUESTION: AN OCCASION FOR WRITING

This Occasion calls on you to conceive or reconceive wilderness on your own terms, doing so against William Cronon's challenges, aided by artists and other thinkers who highlight various aspects of our natural environment. Of particular interest will be Cronon's notion that wilderness can be in our own backyards, whether those yards be in the city, away from large tracts of land, or out in the country. What are we to do, wherever we may be, with the natural resources we have at our disposal? How do we learn to use and not misuse what is available to us, and how does our own conception of wilderness help us answer these questions?

PREPARING TO WRITE: OCCASIONS TO THINK ABOUT WHAT YOU SEE

1. Name the various contrasts that you see in the English garden between order and wildness, civilization and nature. Be specific.

2. What is the relationship between the pathways and the garden? Between what you imagine as British culture and the natural world?

3. Describe what you see besides trees in *Wrapped Trees*. Why do you imagine the artist wrapped these trees? What is the effect on you of the wrapping?

4. Consider as artists those who created the English garden and those who designed the tree-wrapping. What have they made of nature?

English Garden

CHRISTO AND JEANNE-CLAUDE,
Wrapped Trees (1998)

MOVING TOWARD ESSAY: OCCASIONS TO ANALYZE AND REFLECT

1. How do these images help you see, perhaps more clearly, what Cronon calls the "unnaturalness of so natural a place as nature"? What is natural and what is unnatural in these two images?

2. Select at least two of the key terms (concepts) that Cronon uses to develop his ideas about wilderness—*religious* (*sacred*), *wild, Other, natural, uncivilized*. How are those concepts reflected in these images?

3. The wrapping of the trees was done in November 1998 in a park around the Fondation Beyeler (Riehen, Switzerland) and in an adjacent meadow, along a creek. The artists Christo and Jeanne-Claude designed the project and supervised the wrapping of 178 trees with 592,034 feet of woven polyester fabric and 14.35 miles of rope. Does this monumental effort reveal nature to us or hide it from us? Explain.

4. Imagine that Christo and Jeanne-Claude had chosen some part of the American wilderness in the West for their tree-wrapping project. Would that project have complemented or called into question Frederick Jackson Turner's "frontier myth," described by Cronon in his essay?

WRITING THOUGHTFULLY: OCCASIONS FOR IDEAS AND ESSAYS

1. Cronon calls on us to see the "wildness" in our own backyards, whether we live inside or outside the city. Write an essay in which you consider your own relationship to such wildness; do so as a response to Cronon's appeal for us to learn how to "use nature."

2. Write an essay in response to either Thoreau's claim that "In Wildness is the preservation of the World" or Gary Snyder's claim that wilderness is simply "a quality of one's own consciousness."

3. Using Cronon's ideas about wilderness and the wild in conjunction with your own reading of two other essays in this chapter (Woolf, Reed, Dillard, Lopez, Zwinger), write an essay about the natural world that reveals your own most important idea about it. In your essay consider the relationship among the ideas expressed in all of your sources.

CREATING OCCASIONS

1. Visit a store dedicated to nature (such as the Nature Company) and write an essay that investigates the idea of nature that is on sale there.

2. Research *The Gates,* another project conceived and executed by Christo and Jeanne-Claude in New York City's Central Park in 2005, or another of Christo's public art installations. Write an essay that assesses the effectiveness of this installation and its comment on nature.

3. Working under the influence of Christo and Jeanne-Claude, design and explain an artistic project that will call to the public's attention an important idea about wilderness. Design this project for a space of your own that calls into question the importance of either preservation or the use of the natural world.

In the context of this photograph, what is the

NATURE OF REALITY?

Who decides? On what occasions would this

scene be "real"?

11

SCIENCE
AND TECHNOLOGY

We live, unmistakably, in an extended era of scientific discovery, the benefits of which we reap on a daily basis. The last half of the twentieth century yielded organ transplants, nuclear power, color television, polio vaccine, the discovery of DNA, lasers, space travel, space stations, floppy disks, VCRs, pocket calculators, and the Internet. But along with those advances came complications: nuclear war, ozone depletion, oil spills, nuclear accidents, space disasters, and various epidemics. The beneficial and the catastrophic seem entwined, the causal relationships between them not always clear. Because there is something powerfully seductive about cell phones, iPods, plasma television screens, faster and faster computers, the Internet, life-saving vaccines, alternative sources of electrical power, and faster cars and airplanes, we often fail to notice the spin-offs—the complications and consequences. We've grown accustomed to living in a bigger-bang-for-the-buck kind of culture, and we naturally enjoy conveniences and efficiency.

Science, creativity, and discovery lie behind these sweeping scientific and cultural changes. A century ago, when the breakthroughs started to occur, it seemed as if science might bring us everything we ever dreamed of. Some thought of science as a new religion. At that moment of change, we could sit back in wonder and amazement, dazzled by the events and the products that materialized before us. The first moon walk was a momentous occasion—celebrated across the world. Now we hardly notice the liftoffs in Florida, and when we remember, we remember most profoundly the moments when things went awry and lives were lost. We tend to forget that behind all of these momentous occasions, there is a long trail of scientific discovery, a group of dedicated, creative men and women finding secrets, discovering hidden natural laws that actually govern our lives, often without our knowing it.

In this chapter we will focus on the nature of scientific discovery, looking carefully at how science and imagination work together to give us more interesting and more complicated lives. We will be especially focused on how passion and imagination working together lead to discoveries far more significant and longer lasting than the men and women who make them. We will also consider just how one aspect of the scientific revolution—what writer Sven Birkerts calls "the electronic millennium"—might be affecting our lives in ways that we have not yet considered. Our aim is to better understand just how science and the humanities complement one another and to see more clearly how our lives are being affected by the work of things we rarely see and understand. We will foster a more serious consideration of just what it means to be scientific and just what it costs us to reap the benefits of science.

THE SCIENTIFIC IMAGINATION

Much of our formal education tends to reinforce the notion that science and the humanities belong on opposite sides of the proverbial street, that science is hard, the humanities soft—the one rigidly logical, certain; the other notoriously free-wheeling, loose, uncertain. When colleges and universities offer a core curriculum, the core often tries to ensure that students diversify their interests, round out their education by taking a prescribed number of science courses and a prescribed number of courses in the humanities. Even so, students rarely study how scientific thinking and imaginative thinking work together to lead toward new discoveries.

This cluster of readings and exercises takes up that task; it introduces you to three eminent scientists who have a deep interest in dispelling the division between what C. P. Snow once called the "the two cultures"—the sciences and the humanities. Our three writers—Jacob Bronowski, Alan Lightman, and E. O. Wilson—reveal just how wrong-headed such a division is, and they lead us to recognize how important our own passionate commitment is to the investigative work that we do in all of our studies, just how important it is to move beyond the facts to our own new ideas.

Jacob Bronowski (1908–1974)

Jacob Bronowski is perhaps best known for his work and commentary on the BBC television series, *The Ascent of Man*. He was both a scientist and a poet whose distinguished career led him from university teaching positions into Operations Research during WWII. He was an official observer of the aftermath of the Nagasaki and Hiroshima bombings, and he later directed research for the National Coal Board (UK) before becoming the Associate Director of the Salk Institute. His many books include *The Face of Violence: An Essay with a Play* (1950), *Science and Human Values* (1964), *The Identity of Man* (1965), *The Sense of the Future: Essays in Natural Philosophy* (1977), and *The Origins of Knowledge and Imagination* (1978).

THE NATURE OF SCIENTIFIC REASONING

Bronowski challenges us to think about the imaginative and conceptual processes that lead scientists from mere facts and observations to a theory about the facts (ideas). He wants us to understand that reasoning and imagination are deeply connected in these processes of discovery and that the scientist's primary business is to find "likenesses" in nature and, in those likenesses, to discover order. The hidden laws of nature lie in that discovered order.

1   What is the insight in which the scientist tries to see into nature? Can it indeed be called either imaginative or creative? To the literary man the question may seem merely silly. He has been taught that science is a large collection of facts; and if this is true, then the only seeing which scientists need to do is, he supposes, seeing the facts. He pictures them, the colorless professionals of science, going off to work in the morning into the universe in a neutral, unexposed state. They then expose themselves like a photographic plate. And then in the darkroom or laboratory they develop the image, so that suddenly and startlingly it appears, printed in capital letters, as a new formula for atomic energy.

Men who have read Balzac and Zola are not deceived by the claims of these writers that they do no more than record the facts. The readers of Christopher Isherwood do not take him literally when he writes "I am a camera." Yet the same readers solemnly carry with them from their school days this foolish picture of the scientist fixing by some mechanical process the facts of nature. I have had of all people a historian tell me that science is a collection of facts, and his voice had not even the ironic rasp of one filing cabinet reproving another.

It seems impossible that this historian had ever studied the beginnings of a scientific discovery. The Scientific Revolution can be held to begin in the year 1543 when there was brought to Copernicus, perhaps on his deathbed, the first printed copy of the book he had finished about a dozen years earlier. The thesis of this book is that the earth moves around the sun. When did Copernicus go out and record this fact with his camera? What appearance in nature prompted his outrageous guess? And in what odd sense is this guess to be called a neutral record of fact?

Less than a hundred years after Copernicus, Kepler published (between 1609 and 1619) the three laws which describe the paths of the planets. The work of Newton and with it most of our mechanics spring from these laws. They have a solid, matter-of-fact sound. For example, Kepler says that if one squares the year of a planet, one gets a number which is proportional to the cube of its average distance from the sun. Does anyone think that such a law is found by taking enough readings and then squaring and cubing everything in sight? If he does, then, as a scientist, he is doomed to a wasted life; he has as little prospect of making a scientific discovery as an electronic brain has.

5   It was not this way that Copernicus and Kepler thought, or that scientists think today. Copernicus found that the orbits of the planets would look simpler if they were looked at from the sun and not from the earth. But he did not in the first place find this by routine calculation. His first step was a leap of imagination—to lift himself from the earth, and put himself wildly, speculatively into the sun. "The earth conceives from the sun," he wrote; and "the sun rules the family of stars." We catch in his mind an image, the gesture of the virile man standing in the sun, with arms outstretched, overlooking the planets. Perhaps Copernicus took the picture from the drawings of the youth with outstretched arms which the Renaissance teachers put into their books on the proportions of the body. Perhaps he had seen Leonardo's drawings of his loved pupil Salai. I do not know. To me, the gesture of Copernicus, the shining youth looking outward from the sun, is still vivid in a drawing which William Blake in 1780 based on all these: the drawing which is usually called *Glad Day*.

Kepler's mind, we know, was filled with just such fanciful analogies; and we know what they were. Kepler wanted to relate the speeds of the planets to the musical intervals. He tried to fit the five regular solids into their orbits. None of these likenesses worked, and they have been forgotten; yet they have been and they remain the stepping stones of every creative mind. Kepler felt for his laws by way of metaphors, he searched mystically for likenesses with what he knew in every strange corner of nature. And when among these guesses he hit upon his laws, he did not think of their numbers as the balancing of a cosmic bank account, but as a revelation of the unity in all nature. To us, the analogies by which

Kepler listened for the movement of the planets in the music of the spheres are farfetched. Yet are they more so than the wild leap by which Rutherford and Bohr in our own century found a model for the atom in, of all places, the planetary system?

No scientific theory is a collection of facts. It will not even do to call a theory true or false in the simple sense in which every fact is either so or not so. The Epicureans held that matter is made of atoms 2000 years ago and we are now tempted to say that their theory was true. But if we do so we confuse their notion of matter with our own. John Dalton in 1808 first saw the structure of matter as we do today, and what he took from the ancients was not their theory but something richer, their image: the atom. Much of what was in Dalton's mind was as vague as the Greek notion, and quite as mistaken. But he suddenly gave life to the new facts of chemistry and the ancient theory together, by fusing them to give what neither had: a coherent picture of how matter is linked and built up from different kinds of atoms. The act of fusion is the creative act.

All science is the search for unity in hidden likenesses. The search may be on a grand scale, as in the modern theories which try to link the fields of gravitation and electromagnetism. But we do not need to be browbeaten by the scale of science. There are discoveries to be made by snatching a small likeness from the air too, if it is bold enough. In 1935 the Japanese physicist Hideki Yukawa wrote a paper which can still give heart to a young scientist. He took as his starting point the known fact that waves of light can sometimes behave as if they were separate pellets. From this he reasoned that the forces which hold the nucleus of an atom together might sometimes also be observed as if they were solid pellets. A schoolboy can see how thin Yukawa's analogy is, and his teacher would be severe with it. Yet Yukawa without a blush calculated the mass of the pellet he expected to see, and waited. He was right; his meson was found, and a range of other mesons, neither the existence nor the nature of which had been suspected before. The likeness had borne fruit.

The scientist looks for order in the appearances of nature by exploring such likenesses. For order does not display itself of itself; if it can be said to be there at all, it is not there for the mere looking. There is no way of pointing a finger or camera at it; order must be discovered and, in a deep sense, it must be created. What we see, as we see it, is mere disorder.

10   This point has been put trenchantly in a fable by Karl Popper. Suppose that someone wishes to give his whole life to science. Suppose that he therefore sat down, pencil in hand, and for the next twenty, thirty, forty years recorded in notebook after notebook everything that he could observe. He may be supposed to leave out nothing: today's humidity, the racing results, the level of cosmic radiation and the stockmarket prices and the look of Mars, all would be there. He would have compiled the most careful record of nature that has ever been made; and, dying in the calm certainty of a life well spent, he would of course leave his notebooks to the Royal Society. Would the Royal Society thank him for the treasure of a lifetime of observation? It would not. The Royal Society would treat his notebooks exactly as the English bishops have treated Joanna Southcott's box. It would refuse to open them at all, because it would know without looking that the notebooks contain only a jumble of disorderly and meaningless items.

Science finds order and meaning in our experience, and sets about this in quite a different way. It sets about it as Newton did in the story which he himself told in his old age, and of which the schoolbooks give only a carica-

ture. In the year 1665, when Newton was 22, the plague broke out in southern England, and the University of Cambridge was closed. Newton therefore spent the next 18 months at home, removed from traditional learning, at a time when he was impatient for knowledge and, in his own phrase, "I was in the prime of my age for invention." In this eager, boyish mood, sitting one day in the garden of his widowed mother, he saw an apple fall. So far the books have the story right; we think we even know the kind of apple; tradition has it that it was a Flower of Kent. But now they miss the crux of the story. For what struck the young Newton at the sight was not the thought that the apple must be drawn to the earth by gravity; that conception was older than Newton. What struck him was the conjecture that the same force of gravity, which reaches to the top of the tree, might go on reaching out beyond the earth and its air, endlessly into space. Gravity might reach the moon: this was Newton's new thought; and it might be gravity which holds the moon in her orbit. There and then he calculated what force from the earth (falling off as the square of the distance) would hold the moon, and compared it with the known force of gravity at tree height. The forces agreed; Newton says laconically, "I found the answer pretty nearly." Yet they agreed only nearly; the likeness and the approximation go together, for no likeness is exact. In Newton's science modern sciences is full grown.

It grows from a comparison. It has seized a likeness between two unlike appearances; for the apple in the summer garden and the grave moon overhead are surely as unlike in their movements as two things can be. Newton traced in them two expressions of a single concept, gravitation; and the concept (and the unity) are in that sense his free creation. The progress of science is the discovery at each step of a new order which gives unity to what had long seemed unlike.

READING AND THINKING

1. Consider the first six paragraphs of the essay. Why does Bronowski devote so much time to Balzac, Zola, Isherwood, and the unnamed historian? Why end the beginning with Kepler's "fanciful analogies"?

2. What do you think Bronowski would have thought of Mark Doty's idea that metaphors are the advance guards of the mind (p. 92)? Explain.

3. What is the difficulty of *seeing* likenesses, or *seeing* order in nature? Why can't a scientist point a camera at these likenesses or the detected order and take a picture of them?

4. What do we learn from Bronowski's version of the Newton story that other versions tend to overlook? Why is the difference so important and what does that difference have to do with metaphor?

THINKING AND WRITING

1. Write a paragraph about the importance of the imagination to scientific reasoning. What might Bronowski say about Einstein's idea that imagination is more important than knowledge? Explain.

2. Find at least two instances in which Bronowski refers to the importance of images. Account for why an image seems more important to him than a fact, or a set of facts.

3. Outline or otherwise account for how science finds "order and meaning in our experience," according to Bronowski.

4. Why is the discovery of hidden likenesses more important than a compilation of facts and observations? Think especially about why Bronowski tells us about Karl Popper's fable.

5. Explain how the act of *reading* a complicated novel or a complex essay, or even nature, might be analogous to Bronowski's notion of scientific reasoning? Think especially in terms of "hidden likenesses" or hidden structures of meaning.

REASONING AND IMAGINING: AN OCCASION FOR WRITING

You will have additional opportunities to consider the way imagination and reason work together, helping us make important discoveries about ourselves and the world in which we live. We will consider how scientific thinkers confront the fact that nature tends to hide many of her most interesting secrets from us. Our task then is to learn how to investigate such secrets and how to capture and examine what often seems fleeting, or ephemeral—how to work against the scientific odds. Bronowski urges us to use images not only to help us represent the thought processes that have led to important discoveries but also to allow ourselves to indulge in "fanciful analogies" as a way of making discoveries of our own. This Occasion prompts you to respond to Bronowski's encouragement.

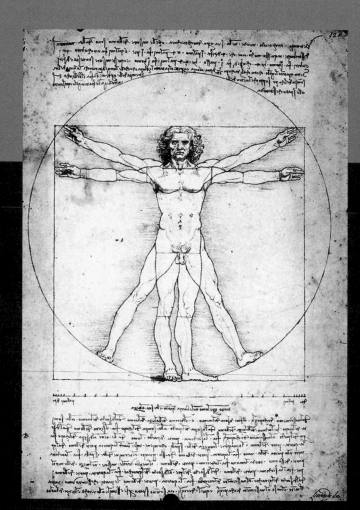

LEONARDO DA VINCI,
Vitruvian Man
(c. 1490)

© British Museum, London, UK/The Bridgeman Art Library

WILLIAM BLAKE, *Glad Day (1794–1795)*

PREPARING TO WRITE: OCCASIONS TO THINK ABOUT WHAT YOU SEE

1. Imagine what *Vitruvian Man* might have illustrated to Leonardo da Vinci and his audience about man and his place in the world. Does this sketch seem scientific? Explain.

2. Who is Vitruvius? Consult Wikipedia, the free encyclopedia on the Internet.

3. *Vitruvian Man* is said by one critic to contain "many layers of geometry and symbolism that concord in one single image delineating the proportions of the human body." Search the Internet for evidence of this claim. Explore the geometry.

4. What obvious likenesses do you see between *Glad Day* by William Blake, the English poet, painter, and engraver (1757–1827), and *Vitruvian Man*? What differences?

5. What hidden likenesses can you see with a more scientific application of mind? Hint: Pay particular attention to circles and squares.

6. What are your initial impressions of the two images titled *Ghost* and *Play of Lights*? Which do you consider the more scientific? Explain.

7. In *Play of Lights* what effect do lights on the water have on your imagination? How many sets of lights do you see in this image? Explain.

8. What besides the natural landscape in these two images seems most *real* to you? What most unreal?

9. Search the Internet for "northern lights" or "aurora borealis." How do your findings change the way you see and understand these images that won photo contests for capturing the northern lights?

MOVING TOWARD ESSAY: OCCASIONS TO ANALYZE AND REFLECT

1. Bronowski tells us in his essay that he associates "the gesture of Copernicus" with Blake's drawing. He seems to favor it over the Renaissance drawings that came before and influenced it. Why do you suppose he favors Blake?

2. What do you find most "hidden" in these four images? What most obvious? Where is the science? The art?

3. What do you make of the "ghost"? Scientists call such shapes *coronas*. To capture them, a photographer must have skill, the right equipment, and luck. Speculate about how you think the corona of the ghost was formed, or created.

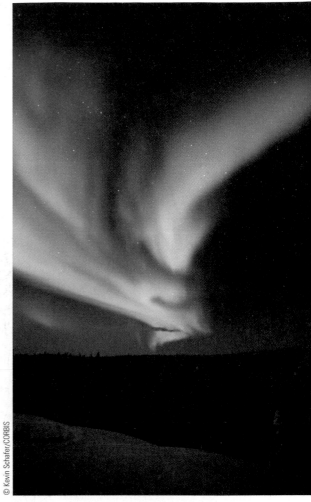

© Kevin Schafer/CORBIS

Ghost

© Hinrich Bäsemann/dpa/Corbis

Play of Lights

WRITING THOUGHTFULLY: OCCASIONS FOR IDEAS AND ESSAYS

1. In the two images of the auroras, we find that nature may be stingy with her secrets, that there is something ephemeral and elusive about her mysteries. How do you imagine that Bronowski would deal with this challenge since he seems averse to a picture-taking approach to scientific discovery? Alternatively, would he be averse to these photographs of fact? How *is* science dealing with the hidden mysteries?

2. Consider scientists' equipment. Research the earliest pieces of equipment and compare them with their modern-day equivalents. What trend is represented by this change in scientific instruments? Toward sophistication and increasing complexity? Away from imagination and simplicity? Investigate any recent scientific breakthrough that interests you (in medicine, art, environment, recording, and reproduction) and write an essay about your sense of how technology and imagination worked together to foster the breakthrough.

3. An ephemeris, according to the *Oxford English Dictionary* (*OED*), is "a table showing the predicted (rarely the observed) positions of a heavenly body for every day during a given period." Determine the usefulness of such tables of prediction. On the basis of your limited research, write a short reflective (and speculative) essay about the importance of relying in our daily lives on scientific predictions about the unseen.

4. Investigate the aurora borealis. Find a scientific explanation for this aesthetically beautiful phenomenon. After you have done so, write an essay that reveals how such scientific explanations affect our perception of the beautiful.

CREATING OCCASIONS

1. Select a recent invention (MP3, PDA, data projector, digital camera, portable printer, or an item of your choice) and inquire about the science behind the invention. Select an image or create one that accounts for the major scientific breakthrough that led to the invention (recall Bronowski's selection of *Glad Day* to represent Copernicus's sun-centric universe).

2. Write an explanation that relates your selected or created image (from Exercise 1) to the process or act of thinking that led to the recent invention.

3. Recall a moment when you figured out the answer to an important question in your life or in your studies. Explain to a neutral (scientifically objective) observer how you managed to solve the problem, paying particular attention to the interplay between imagination and reason.

Alan Lightman (b. 1948)

Alan Lightman is a novelist, essayist, physicist, and educator whose many awards include the 1996 American Institute of Physics Andrew Gemant Award for linking science to the humanities and the 2006 John P. McGovern Science and Society Award from the Scientific Research Society. Lightman's scientific research has focused on gravitational theory, the structure and behavior of accretion disks, stellar dynamics, radioactive processes, and relativistic plasmas. In recognition of his contributions to physics, he was elected a fellow of the American Physical Society and the American Association for the Advancement of Science in 1989. He has taught at Cornell, Harvard, and MIT, where he now serves as an adjunct professor, having resigned his chair as the John E. Burchard Professor of Humanities to allow more time for his writing. His many books include *Ancient Light: Our Changing View of the Universe* (1991); *Einstein's Dreams* (1993); and *The Discoveries: Great Breakthroughs in 20th Century Science* (2005).

THE ART OF SCIENCE

In "The Art of Science" Lightman asks us to understand that laboratory or scientific research can be as creative as literature. Lightman believes that we know too little about the creative aspects of scientific research because of a mistaken assumption that personal information distorts objectivity. But Lightman agrees with chemist Michael Polanyi that "personal passions are probably essential for the success of science." He also believes that acknowledging "the passions and struggles and creative moments of individual scientists [. . .] will help strengthen the understanding between scientists and others." Examining these moments can take us to the heart of the creative process.

1 I vividly remember the occasion, years ago, when I look my two-year-old daughter to the ocean the first time. It was a mild, hazy day in June. We parked our car a half-mile from the water and walked the rest of the way. A speckled pink crab shell lying on the sand caught her attention. Then, a few hundred yards farther on, we heard the long roll of the waves. And I could tell that my daughter was curious about what made that sound she had never heard before.

Holding her up with one arm, I pointed to the sea. Her eyes followed along my arm, across the sand and then out to the vast, blue-green of the sea. For a moment she hesitated. I wasn't sure whether she would be puzzled or frightened by that first sight of infinity. Then she broke out into a radiant smile and giggled with pleasure. It was as if she already understood something about the sea, as if the sea were both unexpected and expected at the same time. I knew how she felt. This seemingly contradictory combination of qualities is exactly what I have experienced in my most creative moments: a stunning surprise joined with a feeling of rightness and inevitability.

It has been my good fortune to have worked both as a physicist and as a novelist. And I have found that the "creative moment" feels the same in both professions. Indeed this particular sensation, one of the deepest and most beautiful of human experiences, provides the basis for a powerful understanding between the scientist and the artist—an understanding that Charles Percy Snow (also a physicist and a novelist) overlooked in his grim differentiation between "the two cultures."

Creativity, of course, eludes easy grasp. Like a timid forest animal, it quickly darts behind a tree when you stare at it. How does one articulate that sense of the expected and unexpected at once? Where does it come from? How does one prepare for discovery? Most difficult of all to describe is the creative moment, that luscious instant when an idea, or an insight, or an unorthodox understanding, suddenly gels. I say "instant," but whenever I experience the creative moment, in science or in art, I lose all sense of time. I also lose all sense of my body, my ego, my surroundings. I forget who I am and where I am. I dissolve into the imagined world. I become pure spirit. Perhaps it is part of the essence of this delicate and mysterious experience that it cannot be understood. Certainly, the sensations cannot be trapped and defined while in motion.

5   Despite these difficulties, writers, musicians, actors and other artists often attempt to describe their creative process. Scientists, however, rarely do. In a paper written for *Nature* in 1920 but never published, Einstein mentions the "happiest thought of my life," when he suddenly realised that the force of gravity disappears for a person falling freely through space. That simple but profound insight became the foundation of his general theory of relativity.

Max von Laue, in his Nobel Prize Lecture of 1915, briefly describes a meeting with another scientist one evening in February 1912 when they discussed the behaviour of long-wavelength electromagnetic waves in crystals. During that conversation, von Laue was "suddenly struck" by the image of short-wavelength waves traversing an atomic lattice, producing telltale interference patterns. And so was crested the new field of X-ray diffraction. In *The Double Helix,* exceptional for its detailed and personal story of discovery, Jim Watson writes that "my mouth fell open and my pulse began to race" the instant he saw Rosalind Franklin's new X-ray diffraction picture of DNA, realising that the patterns could arise only from a double-helical structure.

But accounts like these are few. Such comments by scientists often amount to only a sentence or two, and they hardly ever describe the emotional and psychological sensations of creating.

My own first experience with the creative moment in science occurred when I was a graduate student in physics in the early 1970s. After waffling around with course work for a year, I had finally settled into some genuine research. My first couple of research problems were tidy and brief. Then I fastened onto a more open-ended investigation, something that held the distinct possibility of leading me off a cliff. My project, inconsequential in the grand sweep of science, was to prove or disprove the conjecture that known experiments required all theories of gravity to be geometrical in form.

After an initial period of study and work, I had succeeded in writing down all the equations I thought relevant. Then I hit a wall. I knew something was amiss, because a simple result at an early stage of the calculation was not coming out right. But I could not find my error. And I didn't even know what kind of error it was. Perhaps one of the equations was wrong. Or maybe the equations were right and I was making a silly arithmetic mistake. Or perhaps the conjecture was false, but would require an especially devious counterexample to disprove it. Or maybe I had misconceived the investigation from the beginning. Day after day I checked each equation, paced back and forth in my little, windowless office, but I didn't know what I was doing wrong—what I had missed. This confusion and failure went on for months. I began keeping cans of tuna in my desk drawer and eating my meals in the office.

Then one morning, I remember that it was   10
a Sunday, I woke at about five o'clock and couldn't get back to sleep. I felt terribly excited. Something strange was happening in my mind. I was thinking about my research problem, and I was seeing deeply into it. I was seeing it in ways I never had before. I felt that my head was lifting off my shoulders. I felt weightless. And I had absolutely no sense of

self. It was an experience completely without ego, without any thought about consequences or approval or fame.

The ego, so important to our sense of consciousness and identity, is in some ways a kind of friction, a drag, and it magically slips away when we're creating. For me, the best analogy is what sometimes happens when I'm sailing a round-bottomed boat in strong wind. Normally the hull stays down in the water and the drag greatly limits the speed of the boat. But in high wind, every once in a while the hull lifts out of the water and the drag disappears. It feels like a great hand has suddenly grabbed hold and flung me across the surface like a skimming stone. It's called planing.

So I woke up at five in the morning to find myself planing. Although I had no sense of my ego, I did have a feeling of rightness. I had a strong sensation of seeing deeply into this problem and understanding it and knowing that I was right—a certain kind of inevitability. With these sensations surging through me, I tiptoed out of my bedroom, almost reverently, afraid to disturb whatever strange magic was going on in my head, and went to the kitchen. There I sat down at my ramshackle, faux-wood kitchen table. I got out the pages of my calculations, by now curling and stained. A tiny bit of daylight was starting to seep through the window.

I was oblivious to myself, my body and everything around me, though I was completely alone. I don't think any other person in the world would have been able to help me at that moment, and I didn't want any help. I had all these sensations and revelations in my head, and being alone with all that was an essential part of it.

I sat down at the table and began working. Somehow I had reconceptualised the project. I immediately spotted the error in my thinking and began anew. I'm not sure how this rethinking happened, but it didn't occur by going from one equation to the next. After a while at the kitchen table, I solved my research problem. I had proved that the conjecture was true. Feeling stunned and powerful, I strode out of the room. Suddenly I heard a noise and looked up at a clock on the wall and saw that it was two o'clock in the afternoon.

The experience I've just described is quite similar to the creative moments I've had as a novelist. I write in two places. One is an island in Maine. From my writing desk, I can see spruce trees and cedars and a pine needle path that goes down a hill from my house to the ocean. The other place I write is a small storage room, without windows, attached to the garage of my house in Massachusetts. There, my view is a rough plaster wall. Both places have served me equally well in my writing, because after twenty minutes I disappear into the imaginary world I am creating.

I had an extraordinary moment with my last novel, *The Diagnosis*. I was stuck on a character called Melissa, the wife of my protagonist. Just as I had been stuck on my equations in the physics problem. Being desperately stuck is apparently one of the best goads to creativity. After several drafts of the novel, the character was still wrong. In one draft, she was too mechanical and hard, in another she was a stereotypic alcoholic, in another her affection for her husband seemed false. When she spoke, her words didn't sound real. I could never hear her speaking with her own voice. She always spoke with my voice, or said what I wanted her to say, or what I thought she should be saying. She wasn't alive, even though I had been trying to breathe life into her for more than two years. Then one day, when I was discussing her with a friend, I suddenly felt myself inside of her. Unconsciously, I stopped talking because the universe had lifted. I was no longer myself. I was her. And I was suffering. I began to cry. I sat there numb, for how long I don't know. After that moment I was able to write her.

Similar accounts of the creative process have appeared in dozens of interviews with writers in *The Paris Review* over the past two or three decades. In Janet Sonenberg's book *The Actor Speaks* (Crown Trade Paperbacks, 1996), two dozen leading actors describe their acting techniques. From John Turturro: "Once the scene's dynamic is starting to occur, I'll go with it and then try to shift it, too, just like you would in life. The shifting is important. Then, if I can get to the point when that's happening and I don't know what I'm doing, that's inspiration. I've done all my work and then I try to achieve this other, living dimension, the human dimension. It ceases being my work and it becomes living."

The research and hard work. The prepared mind. The being stuck. The sudden shift. The letting go of control. The letting go of self. The pattern seems almost universal.

20 I am not sure why scientists have been more reluctant than artists to write about their creative moments. But I believe that a major factor must be the understanding of objectivity in science. What is most important in science is the final, dispassionate, impersonal result: the law of nature that would be known by smart Martians, or the experiment that can be duplicated in any laboratory in the world. Max Delbruck, in his Nobel Prize Lecture of 1969, put it well: "A scientist's message is not devoid of universality, but its universality is disembodied and anonymous. While the artist's communication is linked forever with its original form, that of the scientist is modified, amplified, fused with the ideas and results of others and melts into the stream of knowledge and ideas which forms our culture."

Somehow, this understanding of science, which I share in most ways, has spawned the more dubious notion that any sign of personal struggle or emotionality in the individual scientist will compromise the whole enterprise. Thus, scientists are trained to write in the passive voice, humour in journal articles is usually frowned upon, and until recent years there has been a substantial stigma against scientists "popularising" their work for the public. (In the 19th century, Carl Friedrich Gauss—one of the greatest mathematicians of all time—took pains to destroy all written traces of his heuristic methods and winding paths, so that his theorems and proofs appear to have been born fully formed and perfect, like Athena from the head of Zeus.) All these admonitions, in subtle and not subtle ways, reflect the deep-seated idea that the scientist must wear sterile gloves at all times.

By now it is well known that this notion is false. It is certainly true that scientists, with the exception of behavioural scientists, study objects that reside outside the emotions while for artists the emotional life lies at the centre. But the process of doing science is human. Individual scientists have all the passions, the prejudices and biases, the psychological hills and valleys of other creative people. Indeed, as chemist Michael Polanyi so forcefully describes in his book *Personal Knowledge* (University of Chicago Press, 1974), these personal passions are probably essential for the success of science. The objectivity and method of science come not so much from the individual scientist as from the community of scientists, who are always eager to criticise and test each other's work.

Acknowledging the passions and struggles and creative moments of individual scientists will not diminish the discipline at all. Instead, it will help strengthen the understanding between scientists and others.

READING AND THINKING

1. Lightman's two-paragraph beginning comes down to this: a "seemingly contradictory combination of qualities." What exactly is contradictory about those qualities, and why use the adverb "seemingly"?

2. Why do you suppose Lightman resorts to *simile* ("like a timid forest animal") to help us understand creativity?

3. Why do you think scientists are so reluctant to describe the "emotional and psychological sensations of creating," and artists are not?

4. Lightman gives a long account of one of his own creative moments as a scientist. Why, in that account, does he not tell us precisely what he discovered? Where is his emphasis?

THINKING AND WRITING

1. Recall your most "creative moment" and capture it in words for your readers. Let them know what happened to you and how it struck you.

2. Compare Lightman's two creative moments, one as a scientist and one as a novelist. Explain what they have in common.

3. Explain why you think Lightman works so hard to bring the methods of science and the methods of literature together in this essay.

4. How well does this short series of sentence fragments sum up what Lightman has to say to us about the "universal pattern" of creativity?

> The research and hard work. The prepared mind. The being stuck. The sudden shift. The letting go of control. The letting go of self.

Explain the relationship, from your own point of view, among these aspects of creativity.

UNDERSTANDING CREATIVITY: AN OCCASION FOR WRITING

This Occasion will allow you to practice the art of investigation and to pay particular attention to the way you and others go about solving interesting problems. Lightman challenges us to think about our deepest personal connections to these investigative, problem-solving processes whether they are focused on scientific or literary matters. Sometime during that process, the mind moves beyond the facts to a new understanding of them. Our focus will be on those creative moments, even though Lightman warns us that creativity "eludes easy grasp. Like a timid forest animal, it quickly darts behind a tree when you stare at it."

Andy Goldsworthy. Pebbles around a hole, 1987. Kiinagashima-cho, Japan. © Andy Goldsworthy. Courtesy Galerie Lelong, New York

PREPARING TO WRITE: OCCASIONS TO THINK ABOUT WHAT YOU SEE

1. Make a chart with two columns labeled Image 1 and Image 2. Under each column, name *what* you see in the image. Then name the medium (photograph, painting, frozen animation, microscope picture, etc.) in which you think each image is created. Finally, title each image, trying to account for its essence.

2. Compare your answers from Exercise 1 with those of at least two other people. How varied are your answers?

3. What can you, as an individual investigator, conclude about a reasonable answer to the initial questions: what is the object/image, the medium, a reasonable title?

4. Outline the creative process that led to your conclusion and try to account for what was most personal about it.

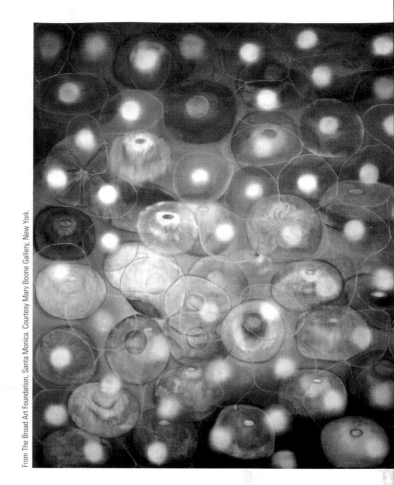

From The Broad Art Foundation, Santa Monica. Courtesy Mary Boone Gallery, New York.

MOVING TOWARD ESSAY: OCCASIONS TO ANALYZE AND REFLECT

1. Stay with the images and record how your mind processes the following factual information as it reconsiders the images: Image 1 is a photograph. Image 2 is a painting.

2. How does your thinking change when you know that the objects in Image 1 are sculpted from natural materials? That Image 2 is imagined? Does knowing more enhance what you see, or limit it? Explain.

3. The titles of the images, in order, are *Pebbles around a Hole* and *In Sickness and in Health*. How does language affect your previous hypotheses?

4. Finally, turn to biography and critical commentary. Search the Internet for information about Andy Goldsworthy (creator of *Pebbles around a Hole*) and Ross Bleckner (creator of *In Sickness and in Health*). Make working notes about what you consider to be the general characteristics of their work.

WRITING THOUGHTFULLY: OCCASIONS FOR IDEAS AND ESSAYS

1. Select either Bleckner or Goldsworthy as an artist for further investigation. Choose at least three new images by your chosen artist and bring four of his images together in one essay. Your task will be to give your reader a sense of either Bleckner's or Goldsworthy's vision, how you believe he responds as an artist to the world around him. You will necessarily consider the artist's values, preoccupations, and ideas *as they are reflected in the works of art*.

2. Consider your own mind's work part of your investigative material for an essay that responds to Lightman's claims about the nature of the creative process. Pay particular attention to your own passionate moments during your investigation of either Bleckner or Goldsworthy. Your essay will reveal your sense of the creative process, how it works, and what characterizes it.

CREATING OCCASIONS

1. Keep track of your mind's work in one of your science or math courses, paying particular attention to the way you learn and the way you go about solving problems. Select two occasions during the course when you managed to make some kind of interpretive breakthrough while solving a troubling problem. Write a short analysis of your problem-solving technique. Compare it with that outlined in Lightman's essay.

2. Compare your scientific problem-solving methodology in the science or math course with the methodology you used to reach your conclusions about the work of Bleckner or Goldsworthy. Are there two different kinds of thinking (one scientific and one artistic) leading to your conclusions or are they quite similar? Explain.

E. O. Wilson (b. 1929)

E. O. Wilson was born in Birmingham, Alabama, and was educated at the University of Alabama and Harvard University. He has been a Harvard professor for more than forty years and is a fellow of the American Academy of Arts and Sciences. Wilson is the winner of the National Medal of Science. He has also won two Pulitzer prizes for *On Human Nature* (1978), and *The Ants* (1990). His more than twenty books include *Sociobiology: The New Synthesis* (1975), *The Diversity of Life* (1992), *In Search of Nature* (1996), and *Consilience: The Unity of Knowledge* (1998).

THE BIRD OF PARADISE:
THE HUNTER AND THE POET

Science and art, according to Wilson, play the same role. Scientists, like artists, work to see and understand larger patterns; "they struggle to make order out of the infinitely varying patterns of nature." Wilson's more immediate focus in this essay is on the bird of paradise. Revealing what we do know about this bird through the beautiful images of its mating ritual, Wilson turns our minds, finally, to what we do not know, what we still do not understand about all that is "encoded within its chromosomes." What we do not know about the bird of paradise takes us back to Wilson's opening remarks concerning "more distant meaning." The promise of science and art working together (the hunter and the poet of the chapter's subtitle) is that technological advances coupled with intuition permit us to look back into the deeper structures of the bird's genetic origins and understand more fully the bird's behavior. Only the "combined idiom of science and the humanities" can lead us back to that answer about the bird, and about ourselves.

1   The role of science, like that of art, is to blend proximate imagery with more distant meaning, the parts we already understand with those given as new into larger patterns that are coherent enough to be acceptable as truth. Biologists know this relation by intuition during the course of fieldwork, as they struggle to make order out of the infinitely varying patterns of nature.

Picture the Huon Peninsula of New Guinea, about the size and shape of Rhode Island, a weathered horn projecting from the northeastern coast of the main island. When I was twenty-five, with a fresh Ph.D. from Harvard and dreams of physical adventure in far-off places with unpronounceable names, I gathered all the courage I had and made a difficult and uncertain trek directly across the peninsular base. My aim was to collect a sample of ants and a few other kinds of small animals up from the lowlands to the highest part of the mountains. To the best of my knowledge I was the first biologist to take this particular route. I knew that almost everything I found would be worth recording, and all the specimens collected would be welcomed into museums.

Three days' walk from a mission station near the southern Lae coast brought me to the spine of the Sarawaget range, 12,000 feet above sea level. I was above treeline, in a grassland sprinkled with cycads, squat gymnospermous plants that resemble stunted palm trees and date from the Mesozoic era; closely similar ancestral forms might have been browsed by dinosaurs 80 million years before. On a chill morning when the clouds lifted and the sun shone brightly, my Papuan guides stopped hunting alpine wallabies with dogs and arrows, I stopped putting beetles and frogs into bottles of alcohol, and together we scanned the rare panoramic view. To the north we could make out the Bismarck Sea, to the south the Markham Valley and the more distant Herzog Mountains. The primary forest covering most of this mountainous country was broken into bands of different vegetation according to elevation. The zone just below us was the cloud forest, a labyrinth of interlocking trunks and branches blanketed by a thick layer of moss, orchids, and other epiphytes that ran unbroken off the tree trunks and across the ground. To follow game trails across this high country was like crawling through a dimly illuminated cave lined with a spongy green carpet.

A thousand feet below, the vegetation opened up a bit and assumed the appearance of typical lowland rain forest, except that the trees were denser and smaller and only a few flared out into a circle of blade-thin buttresses at the base. This is the zone botanists call the mid-mountain forest. It is an enchanted world of thousands of species of birds, frogs, insects, flowering plants, and other organisms, many found nowhere else. Together they form one of the richest and most nearly pure segments of the Papuan flora and fauna. To visit the mid-mountain forest is to see life as it existed before the coming of man thousands of years ago.

5   The jewel of the setting is the male Emperor of Germany bird of paradise (*Paradisaea guilielmi*), arguably the most beautiful bird in the world, certainly one of the twenty or so most striking in appearance. By moving quietly along secondary trails you might glimpse one on a lichen-encrusted branch near the treetops. Its head is shaped like that of a crow—no surprise, since the birds of paradise and crows have a close common lineage—but there the outward resemblance to any ordinary bird ends. The crown and upper breast of the bird are metallic oil-green and shine in the sunlight. The back is glossy yellow, the wings and tail deep maroon. Tufts of ivory-white plumes sprout from the flanks and sides of the breast, turning lacy in texture

toward the tips. The plume rectrices continue on as wirelike appendages past the breast and tail for a distance equal to the full length of the bird. The bill is blue-gray, the eyes clear amber, the claws brown and black.

In the mating season the male joins others in leks, common courtship arenas in the upper tree branches, where they display their dazzling ornaments to the more somberly caparisoned females. The male spreads his wings and vibrates them while lifting the gossamer flank plumes. He calls loudly with bubbling and flutelike notes and turns upside down on the perch, spreading wings and tail and pointing his rectrices skyward. The dance reaches a climax as he fluffs up the green breast feathers and opens out the flank plumes until they form a brilliant white circle around his body, with only the head, tail, and wings projecting beyond. The male sways gently from side to side, causing the plumes to wave gracefully as if caught in an errant breeze. Seen from a distance, his body now resembles a spinning and slightly out-of-focus white disk.

This improbable spectacle in the Huon forest has been fashioned by thousands of generations of natural selection in which males competed and females made choices, and the accouterments of display were driven to a visual extreme. But this is only one trait, seen in physiological time and thought about at a single level of causation. Beneath its plumed surface, the Emperor of Germany bird of paradise possesses an architecture marking the culmination of an equally ancient history, with details exceeding those that can be imagined from the elaborate visible display of color and dance.

Consider one such bird analytically, as an object of biological research. Encoded within its chromosomes is the developmental program that has led to a male *Paradisaea guilielmi*. Its nervous system is a structure of fiber tracts more complex than that of any existing computer, and as challenging as all the rain forests of New Guinea surveyed on foot.

Someday microscopic studies will permit us to trace the events culminating in the electric commands carried by the efferent neurons to the skeletal-muscular system and to reproduce, in part, the dance of the courting male. We will be able to dissect and understand this machinery at the level of the cell through enzymatic catalysis, microfilament configuration, and active sodium transport during electric discharge. Because biology sweeps the full range of space and time, more and more discoveries will renew our sense of wonder at each step of research. Altering the scale of perception to the micrometer and millisecond, the cellular biologist's trek parallels that of the naturalist across the land. He looks out from his own version of the mountain crest. His spirit of adventure, as well as personal history of hardship, misdirection, and triumph, is fundamentally the same.

Described this way, the bird of paradise may seem to have been turned into a metaphor of what humanists dislike most about science: that it reduces nature and is insensitive to art, that scientists are conquistadors who melt down the Inca gold. But science is not just analytic; it is also synthetic. It uses artlike intuition and imagery. True, in the early analytic stages, individual behavior can be mechanically reduced to the level of genes and neurosensory cells. But in the synthetic phase even the most elementary activity of these biological units is seen to create rich and subtle patterns at the levels of organism and society. The outer qualities of *Paradisaea guilielmi*, its plumes, dance, and daily life, are functional traits open to a deeper understanding through the exact description of their constituent parts. They can be redefined as holistic properties that alter our perception and emotion in surprising ways.

There will come a time when the bird of paradise is reconstituted through a synthesis of all the hard-won analytic information. The mind, exercising a newfound power, will journey back to the familiar world of seconds and centimeters, where once again the glittering plumage takes form and is viewed at a distance through a network of leaves and mist. Once again we see the bright eye open, the head swivel, the wings extend. But the familiar motions are now viewed across a far greater range of cause and effect. The species is understood more completely; misleading illusions have given way to more comprehensive light and wisdom. With the completion of one full cycle of intellect, the scientist's search for the true material nature of the species is partially replaced by the more enduring responses of the hunter and poet.

What are these ancient responses? The full answer is available only through a combined idiom of science and the humanities, whereby the investigation turns back into itself. The human being, like the bird of paradise, awaits our examination in the analytic-synthetic manner. Feeling and myth can be viewed at a distance through physiological time, idiosyncratically, in the manner of traditional art. But they can also be penetrated more deeply than was ever possible in the prescientific age, to their physical basis in the processes of mental development, the brain structure, and indeed the genes themselves. It may even be possible to trace them back beyond the formation of cultures to the evolutionary origins of human nature. As each new phase of synthesis emerges from biological inquiry, the humanities will expand their reach and capability. In symmetric fashion, with each redirection of the humanities, science will add dimensions to human biology.

READING AND THINKING

1. Identify the key terms in Wilson's first sentence. Look them up if you do not understand them. In the first paragraph, what idea does Wilson promise to develop in his essay?

2. Consider the next three paragraphs (2–4). Why do you imagine Wilson has chosen to focus on the Huon Peninsula of New Guinea? Why does he pause during his trek to give us the distant, panoramic view?

3. Now focus on paragraphs 5–6. What is the relationship between those two descriptive paragraphs and the previous three paragraphs about his trek across the peninsula?

4. Finally, consider paragraphs 7–11. How does Wilson create his argument in those paragraphs? Can you detect a further organizational division within these last five paragraphs that points to the changing nature of scientific analysis? Explain.

THINKING AND WRITING

1. Why do you suppose Wilson singles out the bird of paradise to convey his argument? Is his explanation about going back into the origin of things adequate, or do you suppose there is more to it?

2. Consider paragraphs 5–6 again. Are Wilson's seemingly pure descriptions colored by his relationship to the creature being observed? Explain.

3. Look at Wilson's title again. What do the hunter and the poet have to do with one another? What can hunter and poet (analyst and synthesizer) achieve working together that they might miss working in only one frame of mind or the other?

POETIC MOMENTS: AN OCCASION FOR WRITING

E. O. Wilson raises some ideas about the scientific process and how the scientist and the poet must somehow combine their ways of seeing and knowing to arrive at a deeper understanding about nature. For Wilson, going back is a way of going forward into deeper understanding. This Occasion asks you initially to respond to the beauty and mystery of a photograph by Yann Arthus-Bertrand.

Yann Arthus-Bertrand (b. 1946) is a French photographer and naturalist who is known the world over for his aerial photographs. He was once a game reserve director in France, and he studied lions in Kenya. He founded the Earth from Above project in 1995 and has been awarded the Legion D'Honneur for his environmental work. His photos have appeared in numerous books, including *Earth from Above* (2002) and *Turkey from the Air* (2004).

PREPARING TO WRITE: OCCASIONS TO THINK ABOUT WHAT YOU SEE

1. Record your initial impression of Arthus-Bertrand's photograph, trying to capture the poetic essence of what you see. Be imaginative. Create a brief word-picture that will allow others to see what you are seeing.

2. Reconsider the photograph. Look carefully at the details. Be aware that you are looking *down* from *above*. What is the object with shadow near the very center? What might the bare spot around object and shadow be? What about the web of lines that seems to converge (or diverge) on that bare area? What can you see now that you did not see when you formed your initial impression of the photographic image?

© Altitude/Yann Arthus-Bertrand

YANN ARTHUS-BERTRAND, *Tree of Life, Tsavo East National Park, Kenya*

MOVING TOWARD ESSAY: OCCASIONS TO ANALYZE AND REFLECT

1. Here is the written text that accompanies Arthus-Bertrand's photograph in his book *Earth from Above:*

   > The acacia in Tsavo East National park is a symbol of life in vast desolate expanses, where wild animals come to take advantage of its leaves or its shade. Crossed by the Nairobi-Mobasa road and railway axis, the western region of the park is open to the public, whereas two-thirds of its more arid eastern segment is reserved to scientists. Tsavo was already famous for its many elephants when, in the 1970s, more pachyderms fleeing drought or poachers entered the park. Crowded into the limited space of the park, the elephants seriously damaged the vegetation. Controversy surrounded the question of whether selective slaughter was necessary, but poachers put a clear-cut end to the debate by exterminating more than 80 percent of the 36,000 elephants in the park. Today, Tsavo National Park receives 100,000 visitors a day.

   How does this written text influence your thinking about the photograph? Do you consider this the final word about what you see? Explain.

2. The title of this photograph—*Tree of Life*—is a reference as much to the function of the tree in the park as to the biblical Tree of Life in the Garden of Eden, also sometimes called "The Tree of Knowledge." In the biblical story, God has forbidden Adam and Eve to eat the fruit of the tree. However, a serpent tempts Eve to eat the fruit, and she, in turn, tempts Adam. By eating the fruit, they have disobeyed God's order, and they are banished from the garden's paradise forever. What does the biblical reference in the title suggest about the tree in the photograph? Would you consider what you see in the photograph a kind of paradise lost (as in the biblical story), or an unspoiled paradise? Explain.

3. Think about E. O. Wilson's discussion of the poet and the hunter, and consider this poem by Aron Keesbury about the biblical story.

Aron Keesbury
And Eve

And Eve,
she didn't know
who to believe

so she chose

the most reasonable
argument.

How do Wilson's ideas about the poet and the hunter relate to Eve's experience as it is portrayed in this poem? Considering that the Tree of Life is also called the Tree of Knowledge, what choice does Eve face? What is she choosing between? In this poem, which is she, poet or hunter? Explain. As you experience the photograph, which are you? Make notes toward a short paragraph, providing details from the photograph and elsewhere that you will use to convince your readers to see what you see, to experience what you experience.

WRITING THOUGHTFULLY: OCCASIONS FOR IDEAS AND ESSAYS

1. Revisit the question of whether this is an image of Paradise Lost or an image of beauty. Before you formulate your response, consider Daphne Sheldrick's argument that the "destruction" the elephants do to the landscape is actually crucial to the Park and its eco-structure. Her article entitled "The Impact of Elephants in Tsavo," can be found on the Sheldrick Wildlife Trust website. Consider her argument before you construct your argument about what the photograph reveals. Make your argument in the form of a short essay, using appropriate evidence from your analysis.

© Altitude/Yann Arthus-Bertrand

YANN ARTHUS-BERTRAND,
Thunderstorm

Life Cycle of a Thunderstorm

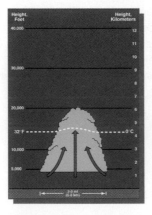 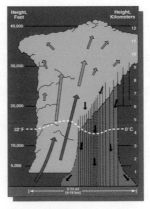 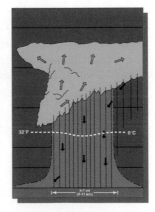

Developing Stage

✔ Towering cumulus cloud indicates rising air.
✔ Usually little if any rain during this stage.
✔ Lasts about 10 minutes.
✔ Occasional lightning during this stage.

Mature Stage

✔ Most likely time for hail, heavy rain, frequent lightning, strong winds, and tornadoes.
✔ Storm occasionally has a black or dark green appearance.
✔ Lasts an average of 10 to 20 minutes but may last much longer in some storms.

Dissipating Stage

✔ Rainfall decreases in intensity.
✔ Some thunderstorms produce a burst of strong winds during this stage.
✔ Lightning remains a danger during this stage.

2. Write a brief account of how your seeing was affected by your knowing. How do reason and beauty interact in your experience of the photograph? Consider whether at some point in your analysis, "knowing" began to limit what you could see in the photograph, or whether knowing more was always beneficial to your deeper understanding of the photograph. Think again of Wilson. Did you find yourself shifting between being a poet and being a hunter, being a synthesizer and being an analyst? Explain in your account.

CREATING OCCASIONS

1. Consider another of Arthus-Bertrand's photographs. Begin this time with both his image and his title. Record your poetic impression of what you see. Does the title restrict what you are able to see? Explain.

2. Consider the scientific representation of a thunderstorm. Think carefully about the relationship between the photograph and the illustration. Identify what each leaves out. What is the effect of putting the two images together? Explain.

3. Considering the photograph, the illustration, and your experience, use your poetic mind to create for readers your own sense of a thunderstorm. Make your account as scientifically accurate as possible.

THE WAGES OF SCIENTIFIC DISCOVERY

There is something powerfully seductive about the life-enhancing by-products of scientific discovery. Even before the most recent wave of discoveries were the telephones, radios, black-and-white televisions, automobiles, machinery of all kinds, airplanes, submarines, and satellites. Yet there is another side to scientific discovery that has also developed over a long period of time. Science has led us to weapons: bombs, cluster bombs, laser-guided missiles, weapons of mass destruction. The troubling aspects of war (along with its instruments of destruction) are easy to spot, but we often see less clearly the underlying consequences of those by-products of science that make our lives exciting and our work easier and sometimes more meaningful. In this cluster we will consider the less-obvious effects of science on our lives, on the lives of our fellow creatures (bugs, insects, animals), and on planet earth itself. Our guides—a humanist (Sven Birkerts), a natural scientist (Terry Tempest Williams), and a doctor and medical researcher (Lewis Thomas)—will help us see as we move into this new millennium not only our successes but also some of the complications underlying those successes.

Birkerts and Williams ask us to think long and hard about ideas. Birkerts wants us to pause for a moment and think about the consequences of our electronic bounty—the Internet, the gadgets, the pleasures. Are we being drawn into closer relationships as we become "connected," or are we being nudged into isolation, losing touch with ourselves and the world? What reality is the real one? Williams calls us indirectly to consider how we might reconceive wilderness as a work of art so that we become more aware of it and our destructive tendencies. She makes us wonder about our indifference, what we really care about. Thomas takes us into the fascinating world of chaos and reminds us that order and even our own thinking are more complicated than we might have imagined. Under his influence we are led to think about the very nature of thinking.

Sven Birkerts (b. 1951)

Sven Birkerts is the editor of *Agni,* a literary journal. He has taught at Harvard, Emerson College, Amherst, and Mount Holyoke College. He is a member of the core faculty of the Bennington Writing Seminars. Birkerts has written extensively about the effects of the electronic age on literacy. His books include *An Artificial Wilderness: Essays on 20th Century Literature* (1987), *The Gutenberg Elegies: The Fate of Reading in an Electronic Age* (1994), and *My Sky Blue Trades: Growing Up Counter in a Contrary Time* (2002). He has received grants from the *Reader's Digest*–Lila Wallace Foundation and the Guggenheim Foundation. His awards include the Citation for Excellence in Reviewing from the National Book Critics Circle in 1985 and the Spielvogel-Diamonstein Citation, PEN for the best book of essays in 1990.

INTO THE ELECTRONIC MILLENNIUM

In "Into the Electronic Millennium" Birkerts asks us to think about the immediate and long-range consequences of the ubiquitous electronic products that are now a staple in our everyday lives. His aim is to push us to the level of idea, to ask us to think past our fascination with computers, Blackberries, iPods, text-messaging, and cell-phones to the consequences of this "electronic millennium" that we find ourselves living in. What does our use of the Internet, with its connective devices, tell us about ourselves and our needs? Does the electronic revolution lead to closer ties among world-wide communities or to the increasing isolation of the individual? Under the influence of electronics, are we likely to abandon the solidity of books while turning inadvertently to the language of vanishing images? If so, does it matter?

1   Some years ago, a friend and I comanaged a used and rare book shop in Ann Arbor, Michigan. We were often asked to appraise and purchase libraries—by retiring academics, widows, and disgruntled graduate students. One day we took a call from a professor of English at one of the community colleges outside Detroit. When he answered the buzzer I did a double take—he looked to be only a year or two older than we were. "I'm selling everything," he said, leading the way through a large apartment. As he opened the door of his study I felt a nudge from my partner. The room was wall-to-wall books and as neat as a chapel.

The professor had a remarkable collection. It reflected not only the needs of his vocation— he taught nineteenth- and twentieth-century literature—but a book lover's sensibility as well. The shelves were strictly arranged, and the books themselves were in superb condition. When he left the room we set to work in-specting, counting, and estimating. This is always a delicate procedure, for the buyer is at once anxious to avoid insult to the seller and eager to get the goods for the best price. We adopted our usual strategy, working out a lower offer and a more generous fallback price. But there was no need to worry. The professor took our first offer without batting an eye.

As we boxed up the books, we chatted. My partner asked the man if he was moving. "No," he said, "but I am getting out." We both looked up. "Out of the teaching business, I mean. Out of books." He then said that he wanted to show us something. And indeed, as soon as the books were packed and loaded, he led us back through the apartment and down a set of stairs. When we reached the basement, he flicked on the light. There, on a long table, displayed like an exhibit in the Space Museum, was a computer. I didn't know what kind it was then, nor could I tell you now, fifteen years later.

But the professor was keen to explain and demonstrate.

While he and my partner hunched over the terminal, I roamed to and fro, inspecting the shelves. It was purely a reflex gesture, for they held nothing but thick binders and paperbound manuals. "I'm changing my life," the ex-professor was saying. "This is definitely where it's all going to happen." He told us that he already had several good job offers. And the books? I asked. Why was he selling them all? He paused for a few beats. "The whole profession represents a lot of pain to me," he said. "I don't want to see any of these books again."

5   The scene has stuck with me. It is now a kind of marker in my mental life. That afternoon I got my first serious inkling that all was not well in the world of print and letters. All sorts of corroborations followed. Our professor was by no means an isolated case. Over a period of two years we met with several others like him. New men and new women who had glimpsed the future and had decided to get out while the getting was good. The selling off of books was sometimes done for financial reasons, but the need to burn bridges was usually there as well. It was as if heading to the future also required the destruction of tokens from the past.

A change is upon us—nothing could be clearer. The printed word is part of a vestigial order that we are moving away from—by choice and by societal compulsion. I'm not just talking about disaffected academics, either. This shift is happening throughout our culture, away from the patterns and habits of the printed page and toward a new world distinguished by its reliance on electronic communications.

This is not, of course, the first such shift in our long history. In Greece, in the time of Socrates, several centuries after Homer, the dominant oral culture was overtaken by the writing technology. And in Europe another epochal transition was effected in the late fif-teenth century after Gutenberg invented movable type. In both cases the long-term societal effects were overwhelming, as they will be for us in the years to come.

The evidence of the change is all around us, though possibly in the manner of the forest that we cannot see for the trees. The electronic media, while conspicuous in gadgetry, are very nearly invisible in their functioning. They have slipped deeply and irrevocably into our midst, creating sluices and circulating through them. I'm not referring to any one product or function in isolation, such as television or fax machines or the networks that make them possible. I mean the interdependent totality that has arisen from the conjoining of parts—the disk drives hooked to modems, transmissions linked to technologies of reception, recording, duplication, and storage. Numbers and codes and frequencies. Buttons and signals. And this is no longer "the future," except for the poor or the self-consciously atavistic—it is now. . . .

To get a sense of the enormity of the change, you must force yourself to imagine—deeply and in nontelevisual terms—what the world was like a hundred, even fifty, years ago. If the feat is too difficult, spend some time with a novel from the period. Read between the lines and reconstruct. Move through the sequence of a character's day and then juxtapose the images and sensations you find with those in the life of the average urban or suburban dweller today.

Inevitably, one of the first realizations is 10 that a communications net, a soft and pliable mesh woven from invisible threads, has fallen over everything. The so-called natural world, the place we used to live, which served us so long as the yardstick for all measurements, can now only be perceived through a scrim. Nature was then; this is now. Trees and rocks have receded. And the great geographical Other, the faraway rest of the world, has been transformed by the pure possibility of access. The numbers of distance and time no longer mean what they used to. Every place, once unique, itself, is strangely shot through with radiations from every other place. "There" was then; "here" is now. . . .

To underscore my point, I have been making it sound as if we were all abruptly walking out of one room and into another, leaving our books to the moths while we settle ourselves in front of our state-of-the-art terminals. The truth is that we are living through a period of overlap; one way of being is pushed athwart another. Antonio Gramsci's often-cited sentence comes inevitably to mind: "The crisis consists precisely in the fact that the old is dying and the new cannot be born; in this interregnum a great variety of morbid symptoms appears." The old surely is dying but I'm not so sure that the new is having any great difficulty being born. As for the morbid symptoms, these we have in abundance.

The overlap in communications modes, and the ways of living that they are associated with, invites comparison with the transitional epoch in ancient Greek society, certainly in terms of the relative degree of disturbance. Historian Eric Havelock designated that period as one of "protoliteracy," of which his fellow scholar Oswyn Murray has written:

> To him [Havelock] the basic shift from oral to literate culture was a slow process; for centuries, despite the existence of writing, Greece remained essentially an oral culture. This culture was one which depended heavily on the encoding of information in poetic texts, to be learned by rote and to provide a cultural encyclopedia of conduct. It was not until the age of Plato in the fourth century that the dominance of poetry in an oral culture was challenged in the final triumph of literacy.

That challenge came in the form of philosophy, among other things, and poetry has never recovered its cultural primacy. What oral poetry was for the Greeks, printed books in general are for us. But our historical moment, which we might call "proto-electronic,"

will not require a transition period of two centuries. The very essence of electronic transmissions is to surmount impedances and to hasten transitions. Fifty years, I'm sure, will suffice. As for what the conversion will bring—and *mean*—to us, we might glean a few clues by looking to some of the "morbid symptoms" of the change. But to understand what these portend, we need to remark a few of the more obvious ways in which our various technologies condition our senses and sensibilities.

I won't tire my reader with an extended rehash of the differences between the print orientation and that of electronic systems. Media theorists from Marshall McLuhan to Walter Ong to Neil Postman have discoursed upon these at length. What's more, they are reasonably commonsensical. I therefore will abbreviate.

The order of print is linear, and is bound to logic by the imperatives of syntax. Syntax is the substructure of discourse, a mapping of the ways that the mind makes sense through language. Print communication requires the active engagement of the reader's attention, for reading is fundamentally an act of translation. Symbols are turned into their verbal referents and these are in turn interpreted. The print engagement is essentially private. While it does represent an act of communication, the contents pass from the privacy of the sender to the privacy of the receiver. Print also posits a time axis; the turning of pages, not to mention the vertical descent down the page, is a forward-moving succession, with earlier contents at every point serving as a ground for what follows. Moreover, the printed material is static—it is the reader, not the book, that moves forward. The physical arrangements of print are in accord with our traditional sense of history. Materials are layered; they lend themselves to rereading and to sustained attention. The pace of reading is variable, with progress determined by the reader's focus and comprehension.

The electronic order is in most ways opposite. Information and contents do not simply move from one private space to another, but they travel along a network. Engagement is intrinsically public, taking place within a circuit of larger connectedness. The vast resources of the network are always there, potential, even if they do not impinge on the immediate communication. Electronic communication can be passive, as with television watching, or interactive, as with computers. Contents, unless they are printed out (at which point they become part of the static order of print) are felt to be evanescent. They can be changed or deleted with the stroke of a key. With visual media (television, projected graphs, highlighted "bullets") impression and image take precedence over logic and concept, and detail and linear sequentiality are sacrificed. The pace is rapid, driven by jump-cut increments, and the basic movement is laterally associative rather than vertically cumulative. The presentation structures the reception and, in time, the expectation about how information is organized.

Further, the visual and nonvisual technology in every way encourages in the user a heightened and ever-changing awareness of the present. It works against historical perception, which must depend on the inimical notions of logic and sequential succession. If the print medium exalts the word, fixing it into permanence, the electronic counterpart reduces it to a signal, a means to an end.

Transitions like the one from print to electronic media do not take place without rippling or, more likely, *reweaving* the entire social and cultural web. The tendencies outlined above are already at work. We don't need to look far to find their effects. We can begin with the newspaper headlines and the millennial lamentations sounded in the op-ed pages: that our educational systems are in decline; that our students are less and less able to read and comprehend their required texts, and that their aptitude scores have leveled off well below those of previous generations. Tagline communication, called "bite-speak" by some, is destroying the last remnants of political discourse; spin doctors and media consultants are our new shamans. As communications empires fight for control of all information outlets, including publishers, the latter have succumbed to the tyranny of the bottom line; they are less and less willing to publish work, however worthy, that will not make a tidy profit. And, on every front, funding for the arts is being cut while the arts themselves appear to be suffering a deep crisis of relevance. And so on.

Every one of these developments is, of course, overdetermined, but there can be no doubt that they are connected, perhaps profoundly, to the transition that is underway.

Certain other trends bear watching. One [20] could argue, for instance, that the entire movement of postmodernism in the arts is a consequence of this same macroscopic shift. For what is postmodernism at root but an aesthetic that rebukes the idea of an historical time line, as well as previously uncontested assumptions of cultural hierarchy. The postmodern artifact manipulates its stylistic signatures like Lego blocks and makes free with combinations from the formerly sequestered spheres of high and popular art. Its combinatory momentum and relentless referencing of the surrounding culture mirror perfectly the associative dynamics of electronic media.

One might argue likewise, that the virulent debate within academia over the canon and multiculturalism may not be a simple struggle between the entrenched ideologies of white male elites and the forces of formerly disenfranchised gender, racial, and cultural groups. Many of those who would revise the canon (or end it altogether) are trying to outflank the assumption of historical tradition itself. The underlying question, avoided by many, may be not only whether the tradition is relevant, but whether it might not be too taxing a system for students to comprehend. Both the traditionalists and the progressives have valid arguments, and we must certainly have sympathy for those who would try to expose and eradicate the hidden assumptions of bias in the Western tradition. But it also seems clear that this debate could only have taken the form it has in a society that has begun to come loose from its textual moorings. To challenge repression is salutary. To challenge history itself, proclaiming it to be simply an archive of repressions and justifications, is idiotic.* . . .

A collective change of sensibility may already be upon us. We need to take seriously the possibility that the young truly "know no other way," that they are not made of the same stuff that their elders are. In her *Harper's* magazine debate with Neil Postman, Camille Paglia observed:

> Some people have more developed sensoriums than others. I've found that most people born before World War II are turned off by the modern media. They can't understand how we who were born after the war can read and watch TV at the same time. But we *can*. When I wrote my book, I had earphones on, blasting rock music or Puccini and Brahms. The soap operas—with the sound turned down—flickered on my TV. I'd be talking on the phone at the same time. Baby boomers have a multilayered multitrack ability to deal with the world.

I don't know whether to be impressed or depressed by Paglia's ability to disperse her focus in so many directions. Nor can I say, not having read her book, in what ways her multitrack sensibility has informed her prose. But I'm baffled by what she means when she talks about an ability to "deal with the world." From the context, "dealing" sounds more like a matter of incessantly repositioning the self within a barrage of on-rushing stimuli. . . .

My final exhibit—I don't know if it qualifies as a morbid symptom as such—is drawn from a *Washington Post Magazine* essay on the future of the Library of Congress, our national shrine to the printed word. One of the individuals interviewed in the piece is Robert Zich, so-called "special projects czar" of the institution. Zich, too, has seen the future, and he is surprisingly candid with his interlocutor. Before long, Zich maintains, people will be able to get what information they want directly off their terminals. The function of the Library of Congress (and perhaps libraries in general) will change. He envisions his library becoming more like a museum: "Just as you go to the National Gallery to see its Leonardo or go to the Smithsonian to see the *Spirit of St. Louis* and so on, you will want to go to libraries to see the Gutenberg or the original printing of Shakespeare's plays or to see Lincoln's hand-written version of the Gettysburg Address."

Zich is outspoken, voicing what other administrators must be thinking privately. The big research libraries, he says, "and the great national libraries and their buildings will go the way of the railroad stations and the movie palaces of an earlier era which were really vital institutions in their time. . . . Somehow folks moved away from that when the technology changed."

And books? Zich expresses excitement about Sony's hand-held electronic book, and a miniature encyclopedia coming from Franklin Electronic Publishers. "Slip it in your pocket," he says. "Little keyboard, punch in your

25

---

* The outcry against the modification of the canon can be seen as a plea for old reflexes and routines. And the cry for multicultural representation may be a last-ditch bid for connection to the fading legacy of print. The logic is simple. When a resource is threatened—made scarce—people fight over it. In this case the struggle is over textual power in an increasingly nontextual age. The future of books and reading is what is at stake, and a dim intuition of this drives the contending factions.

As Katha Pollitt argued so shrewdly in her much-cited article in *The Nation:* If we were a nation of readers, there would be no issue. No one would be arguing about whether to put Toni Morrison on the syllabus because her work would be a staple of the reader's regular diet anyway. These lists are suddenly so important because they represent, very often, the only serious works that the student is ever likely to be exposed to. Whoever controls the lists comes out ahead in the struggle for the hearts and minds of the young.

words and it will do the full text searching and all the rest of it. Its limitation, of course, is that it's devoted just to that one book." Zich is likewise interested in the possibility of memory cards. What he likes about the Sony product is the portability: one machine, a screen that will display the contents of whatever electronic card you feed it.

I cite Zich's views at some length here because he is not some Silicon Valley research and development visionary, but a highly placed executive at what might be called, in a very literal sense, our most conservative public institution. When men like Zich embrace the electronic future, we can be sure it's well on its way.

Others might argue that the technologies cited by Zich merely represent a modification in the "form" of reading, and that reading itself will be unaffected, as there is little difference between following words on a pocket screen or a printed page. Here I have to hold my line. The context cannot but condition the process. Screen and book may exhibit the same string of words, but the assumptions that underlie their significance are entirely different depending on whether we are staring at a book or a circuit-generated text. As the nature of looking—at the natural world, at paintings—changed with the arrival of photography and mechanical reproduction, so will the collective relation to language alter as new modes of dissemination prevail.

Whether all of this sounds dire or merely "different" will depend upon the reader's own values and priorities. I find these portents of change depressing, but also exhilarating—at least to speculate about. On the one hand, I have a great feeling of loss and a fear about what habitations will exist for self and soul in the future. But there is also a quickening, a sense that important things are on the line. As Heraclitus once observed, "The mixture that is not shaken soon stagnates." Well, the mixture is being shaken, no doubt about it. And here are some of the kinds of develop-

ments we might watch for as our "proto-electronic" era yields to an all-electronic future:

1. *Language erosion.* There is no question 30 but that the transition from the culture of the book to the culture of electronic communication will radically alter the ways in which we use language on every societal level. The complexity and distinctiveness of spoken and written expression, which are deeply bound to traditions of print literacy, will gradually be replaced by a more telegraphic sort of "plainspeak." Syntactic masonry is already a dying art. Neil Postman and others have already suggested what losses have been incurred by the advent of telegraphy and television—how the complex discourse patterns of the nineteenth century were flattened by the requirements of communication over distances. That tendency runs riot as the layers of mediation thicken. Simple linguistic prefab is now the norm, while ambiguity, paradox, irony, subtlety, and wit are fast disappearing. In their place, the simple "vision thing" and myriad other "things." Verbal intelligence, which has long been viewed as suspect as the act of reading, will come to seem positively conspiratorial. The greater part of any articulate person's energy will be deployed in dumbing-down her discourse.

Language will grow increasingly impoverished through a series of vicious cycles. For, of course, the usages of literature and scholarship are connected in fundamental ways to the general speech of the tribe. We can expect that curricula will be further streamlined, and difficult texts in the humanities will be pruned and glossed. One need only compare a college textbook from twenty years ago to its contemporary version. A poem by Milton, a play by Shakespeare—one can hardly find the text among the explanatory notes nowadays. Fewer and fewer people will be able to contend with the so-called masterworks of literature or ideas. Joyce, Woolf, Soyinka, not to mention the masters who preceded them, will go unread, and the civilizing energies of their prose will circulate aimlessly between closed covers.

2. *Flattening of historical perspectives.* As the circuit supplants the printed page, and as more and more of our communications involve us in network processes—which of their nature plant us in a perpetual present—our perception of history will inevitably alter. Changes in information storage and access are bound to impinge on our historical memory. The depth of field that is our sense of the past is not only a linguistic construct, but is in some essential way represented by the book and the physical accumulation of books in library spaces. In the contemplation of the single volume, or mass of volumes, we form a picture of time past as a growing deposit of sediment; we capture a sense of its depth and dimensionality. Moreover, we meet the past as much in the presentation of words in books of specific vintage as we do in any isolated fact or statistic. The database, useful as it is, expunges this context, this sense of chronology, and admits us to a weightless order in which all information is equally accessible. . . .

3. *The waning of the private self.* We may even now be in the first stages of a process of social collectivization that will over time all but vanquish the ideal of the isolated individual. For some decades now we have been edging away from the perception of private life as something opaque, closed off to the world; we increasingly accept the transparency of a life lived within a set of systems, electronic or otherwise. Our technologies are not bound by season or light—it's always the same time in the circuit. And so long as time is money and money matters, those circuits will keep humming. The doors and walls of our habitations matter less and less—the world sweeps through the wires as it needs to, or as we need it to. The monitor light is always blinking; we are always potentially on-line.

I am not suggesting that we are all about to become mindless, soulless robots, or that personality will disappear altogether into an oceanic homogeneity. But certainly the idea of what it means to be a person living a life will be much changed. The figure-ground model, which has always featured a solitary self before a background that is the society of other selves, is romantic in the extreme. It is ever less tenable in the world as it is becoming. There are no more wildernesses, no more lonely homesteads, and, outside of cinema, no more emblems of the exalted individual.

The self must change as the nature of subjective space changes. And one of the many incremental transformations of our age has been the slow but steady destruction of subjective space. The physical and psychological distance between individuals has been shrinking for at least a century. In the process, the figure-ground image has begun to blur its boundary distinctions. One day we will conduct our public and private lives within networks so dense, among so many channels of instantaneous information, that it will make almost no sense to speak of the differentiations of subjective individualism.

We are already captive in our webs. Our slight solitudes are transected by codes, wires, and pulsations. We punch a number to check in with the answering machine, another to tape a show that we are too busy to watch. The strands of the web grow finer and finer—this is obvious. What is no less obvious is the fact that they will continue to proliferate, gaining in sophistication, merging functions so that one can bank by phone, shop via television, and so on. The natural tendency is toward streamlining: The smart dollar keeps finding ways to shorten the path, double-up the function. We might think in terms of a circuit-board model, picturing ourselves as the contact points. The expansion of electronic options is always at the cost of contractions in the private sphere. We will soon be navigating with ease among cataracts of organized pulsations, putting out and taking in signals. We will bring our terminals, our modems, and menus further and further into our former privacies; we will implicate ourselves by degrees in the unitary life, and there may come a day when we no longer remember that there was any other life. . . .

Trafficking with tendencies—extrapolating and projecting as I have been doing—must finally remain a kind of gambling. One bets high on the validity of a notion and low on the human capacity for resistance and for unpredictable initiatives. No one can really predict how we will adapt to the transformations taking place all around us. We may discover, too, that language is a hardier thing than I have allowed. It may flourish among the beep and the click and the monitor as readily as it ever did on the printed page. I hope so, for language is the soul's ozone layer and we thin it at our peril.

READING AND THINKING

1. Why does Birkerts begin his essay with the story about the professor who sells his books? What does that story suggest about the future of literature?

2. Pinpoint the moment in the essay when Birkerts begins his serious reflections about the opening story. What does he mean when he tells us that the "printed word is part of a vestigial order"?

3. How large is the "communications net" that Birkerts talks about? Why is its size important to him?

4. What do you think of Birkerts's comparison of the "print orientation" of earlier cultures and the "electronic systems" of our own culture? Is it accurate? Balanced or biased?

THINKING AND WRITING

1. Find Birkerts's various references to ancient cultures and account for their importance to the essay. Explain their historical significance to the idea Birkerts is developing.

2. According to Birkerts, what are the most serious consequences of the "electronic systems" he describes? Provide your own thoughtful reflections about three of those consequences.

3. Is Birkerts's speculation right, that the very young know no other way than that of the "electronic systems"? Has there in fact, from your point of view, been a "change of sensibility" between your generation and your parents' generation? How do you know? Explain.

4. Write Birkerts a short letter about what you consider to be the future of books.

CONSEQUENCES OF SCIENTIFIC ADVANCEMENT: AN OCCASION FOR WRITING

You will now experience an Occasion for Writing to consider the interplay between literacy and technology. The spectrum of images that follow suggests a story that will allow you to consider for yourself how various electronic inventions are shaping the world in which you live and to think about both the immediate and long-range consequences of such inventions on our future.

JEAN-BAPTISTE-SIMÉON CHARDIN, *Le Philosophe lisant (1734)*

PREPARING TO WRITE: OCCASIONS TO THINK ABOUT WHAT YOU SEE

1. George Steiner, a literary critic, tells us that Chardin's painting points to a "revolution of values" in our time. In his essay "The Common Reader," Steiner argues that the reader's formal costume in this painting, the quality of the light, the beauty of the book itself, the instruments that accompany the act of reading (the quill and the ink), the reader's medallions, and the silence of his vocation suggest that to Chardin's viewers reading was a highly respected and vested ceremony, a ritual. Can you see what Steiner asks you to see, or is this just a painting of a man too dressed up for the reading he is doing? Explain.

2. What does Chardin's painting suggest to you about eighteenth-century culture? How does it differ from your own?

3. The *Newsweek* cover is full of suggestions. Name five of them, paying particular attention to images, words, and their interplay. Does this cover of *Newsweek* accurately portray our national priorities?

MOVING TOWARD ESSAY: OCCASIONS TO ANALYZE AND REFLECT

1. Consider the *Newsweek* cover. What does it suggest to you about the importance of what Birkerts calls "the print orientation" in our culture? Has Steve Jobs, CEO of Apple, become the developer and the carrier of our values? How does he differ from *Le Philosophe lisant*?

2. What do you think about *Newsweek*'s allusion to René Descarte's "I think, therefore I am"? Does "iPod therefore iAm" bode ill or well for our future?

3. Leonard Shlain, a polymath—doctor and intellectual historian, suggests in his book *The Alphabet versus the Goddess: The Conflict between Word and Image* (1999) that in cultures where the printed word is most important, men dominate, and that in cultures where image is the language of literacy, women rule. How would you characterize our culture now in terms of Shlain's suggestions?

WRITING THOUGHTFULLY: OCCASIONS FOR IDEAS AND ESSAYS

1. Write a short essay that reckons with the speed of technological advancement in the last 50 years. Focus on visual technology (computers, video devices, sound and image production, and mechanical reproduction) using Birkerts's essay and the images provided in this Occasion, plus anything from your other classes or the Internet.

2. Write a short essay in which you consider technological life in twenty-first-century America. Think about your own experiences, what they reveal to you and to us about our lives. As you work out your idea think about what this evidence tells you about our collective psychology, the way we think and live. To what extent do you think our wants and our own fascination with ourselves are driving innovation? Is there something dark and sinister at work or are we acting responsibly with our new gadgets?

CREATING OCCASIONS

1. Choose what you consider the most beneficial discovery of the last half century. Write an illustrated essay that accounts for your judgment. Do not leave out of consideration the harmful spin-offs of this beneficial discovery.

2. Write an essay that explores the intriguing relationship between scientific discoveries and the application of such discoveries to the art and science of war. Select appropriate images to support your findings.

3. Write an essay that attempts to reveal the relationship between scientific breakthrough and marketing. How do science and marketing conspire to alter our lives? How complicated is this relationship in our so-called consumer-driven society?

Terry Tempest Williams (b. 1955)

Terry Tempest Williams is an environmentalist whose writing lyrically captures the landscape of the western United States. Hers is often a passionate voice that explores the hidden beauties of what some would consider desolate territory. Yet she has another voice as well, one that speaks out in innovative ways against the dangers of destruction and forgetting. Her books include *Coyote's Canyon* (1989); *Refuge: An Unnatural History of Family and Place* (1992); *Desert Quartet: An Erotic Landscape* (1995); and, most recently, *The Open Space of Democracy* (2004). She has served on the Governing Council of the Wilderness Society; on the President's Council for Sustainable Development; and on the advisory boards of the National Parks and Conservation Association, The Nature Conservancy, and the Southern Utah Wilderness Alliance. She has also been inducted to the Rachel Carson Honor Roll and has received the National Wildlife Federation's conservation award for special achievement.

A SHARK IN THE MIND
OF ONE CONTEMPLATING WILDERNESS

In "A Shark in the Mind of One Contemplating Wilderness" we find Williams poetic, seriously playful, and intriguingly persuasive as she affords us a new way of conceiving wilderness. She focuses on various pieces of museum art ranging from a preserved tiger shark in the American Museum of Natural History to the alternately disturbing and fascinating work of Damien Hirst. Williams ponders Hirst's work, trying to capture it for us: "Art. Artifact. Art by designation." Working with various museum pieces, with Hirst's installation pieces, and the criticism of those pieces by other writers, she shows us how we might re-conceptualize wilderness as a work of art. The consequence of doing so, she believes, might cause us to preserve rather than destroy our natural world. Science and history silently inform Williams's conservationist musings in this challenging essay whose form—the particular way Williams shapes and presents her thinking—is as intriguing as its ideas. This essay was selected for publication in *Best American Essays 2000*.

1   A shark swims past me in a kelp forest that sways back and forth with the current. It is deliberate and focused. I watch the shark's sleek body dart left and right as its caudal fin propels it forward. Its eyes seem to slice through the water in a blood gaze as the gills open and close, open and close. Around and around, I watch the shark maneuver through schools of fish. It must not be hungry. The only thing separating me from the shark is a tall glass pane at the Monterey Sea Aquarium. Everything is in motion. I press my hands on the glass, waiting for the shark to pass by again, and when it does I feel my own heart beating against the mind of this creature that kills.

In the enormous blue room of the American Museum of Natural History, I stare at the tiger shark mounted on the wall of the second floor. Its surface shines with the light of taxidermy, creating the illusion of having just left the sea, now our own natural-history trophy. I see how out of proportion its mouth is to the rest of its body and wonder how many teeth hung from its gums during its lifetime, the rows of teeth, five to twenty of them, biting and tearing, thrashing and chomping on flesh, the teeth constantly being replaced by something akin to a conveyor-belt system. Somewhere in my mind I hold the fact that a shark may go through 20,000 teeth in a life span of ten years. I imagine the shark sensing the electrical field of a seal, swimming toward the diving black body now rising to the surface, delivering with great speed its deadly blow, the jaws that dislocate and protrude out of its mouth, the strong muscles that open, then close, the razor teeth that clamp down on the prey with such force that skin, cartilage, and bone are reduced to one clean round bite, sustained over and over again. The blue water now bloody screams to the surface. Even in death, I see this shark in motion.

Sensation. I enter the Brooklyn Museum of Art to confront another tiger shark, this the most harrowing of all the requiem sharks I have encountered in a week-long period. Requiem sharks. They say the name is derived from the observation that once these large sharks of the family Carcharhinidae attack a victim, the only task remaining is to hold a requiem, a mass for the dead. *Galeocerdo cuvieri.* It is neither dead nor alive, but rather a body floating in space, a shark suspended in solution. Formaldehyde. To preserve. What do we choose to preserve? I note the worn, used sense of its mouth, shriveled and receding, looking more manly than fish. The side view creates a triptych of head, dorsal fin, and tail through the three panels of glass in the frame of white painted steel. I walk around the shark and feel the charge of the front view, a turquoise nightmare of terror that spills into daylight. Sensation. Damien Hirst is the creator of *The Physical Impossibility of Death in the Mind of Someone Living* (1991).

I do not think about the shark.

> *I like the idea of a thing to describe a feeling. A shark is frightening, bigger than you are in an environment unknown to you. It looks alive when it's dead and dead when it's alive. . . . I like ideas of trying to understand the world by taking things out of the world. . . . You expect [the shark] to look back at you.* — Damien Hirst.

5   As a naturalist who has worked in a museum of natural history for more than fifteen years, how am I to think about a shark in the context of art, not science? How is my imagination so quickly rearranged to see the suspension of a shark, pickled in formaldehyde, as the stopped power of motion in the jaws of death, an image of my own mortality?

My mind becomes wild in the presence of creation, the artist's creation. I learn that the box in which the shark floats was built by the same company that constructs the aquariums of Brighton Sea World. I think about the killer whales kept in tanks for the amusement of humans, the killer whales that jump through hoops, carry humans on their backs as they circle and circle and circle the tank, day after day after week after month, how they go mad, the sea of insanity churning inside them, inside me as I feel my own captivity within a culture—any culture—that would thwart creativity: we are stopped cold, our spirits suspended, controlled, controlled sensation.

Tiger shark, glass, steel, 5 percent formaldehyde solution.

Damien Hirst calls the shark suspended in formaldehyde a sculpture. If it were in a museum of natural history, it would be called an exhibit, an exhibit in which the organism is featured as the animal it is. Call it art or call it biology, what is the true essence of shark?

How is the focus of our perceptions decided?

Art. Artifact. Art by designation.   10

Thomas McEvilley, art critic and author of *Art & Otherness*, states:

> The fact that we designate something as art means that it is art for us, but says nothing about what it is in itself or for other people. Once we realize that the quest for essences is an archaic religious quest, there is no reason why something should not be art for one person or culture and non-art for another.

Wild. Wilderness. Wilderness by designation. What is the solution to preserving that which is wild?

I remember standing next to an old rancher in Escalante, Utah, during a contentious political debate over wilderness in the canyon country of southern Utah. He kicked the front tire of his pickup truck with his cowboy boot.

"What's this?" he asked me.

15   "A Chevy truck," I responded.

"Right, and everybody knows it."

He then took his hand and swept the horizon. "And what's all that?" he asked with the same matter-of-fact tone.

"Wilderness," he answered before I could speak. "And everybody knows it, so why the hell do you have to go have Congress tell us what it is?"

Damien Hirst's conceptual art, be it his shark or his installation called *A Thousand Years* (1990)—where the eye of a severed cow's head looks upward as black flies crawl over it and lay eggs in the flesh that metamorphose into maggots that mature into flies that gather in the pool of blood to drink, leaving tiny red footprints on the glass installation, while some flies are destined to die as a life-stopping buzz in the electric fly-killing machine—all his conceptual pieces of art, his installations, make me think about the concept and designation of wilderness.

20   Why not designate wilderness as an installation of art? Conceptual art? A true sensation that moves and breathes and changes over time with a myriad of creatures that formulate an instinctual framework of interspecies dialogues; call them predator-prey relations, or symbolic relations, niches and ecotones, never before seen as art, as dance, as a painting in motion, but imagined only through the calculations of biologists, their facts now metamorphosed into designs, spontaneously choreographed moment to moment among the living. Can we not watch the habits of animals, the adaptations of plants, and call them performance art within the conceptual framework of wilderness?

To those who offer the critique that wilderness is merely a received idea, one that might be "conceptually incoherent" and entranced by "the myth of the pristine," why not answer with a resounding yes, yes, wilderness is our received idea as artists, as human beings, a grand piece of performance art that can embody and inspire *The Physical Impossibility of Death in the Mind of Someone Living* or *Isolated Elements Swimming in the Same Direction for the Purpose of Understanding* (1991).

Call it a cabinet of fish preserved in salt solution to honor the diversity of species, where nothing is random. Or call it a piece of art to celebrate color and form found in the bodies of fishes. Squint your eyes: *imagine a world of spots*. Colored dots in the wilderness. *They're all connected*. Damien Hirst paints spots.

"Art's about life and it can't really be about anything else. There isn't anything else." Tell us again, Damien Hirst, with your cabinet of wonders; we are addicted to wonders, bottles of drugs lined up, shelf after shelf, waiting to be opened, minds opened, veins opened, nerves opened. Wilderness is a cabinet of pharmaceuticals waiting to be discovered.

Just as we designate art, we designate wilderness, large and small, as much as we can, hoping it begins a dialogue with our highest and basest selves. We are animals, in search of a home, in relationship to Other, an expanding community with a mosaic of habitats, domestic and wild; there is nothing precious or nostalgic about it. We designate wilderness as an instillation of essences, open for individual interpretation, full of controversy and conversation.

25   "*I always believe in contradiction, compromise . . . it's unavoidable. In life it can be positive or negative, like saying, 'I can't live without you.'*" Damien Hirst speaks again.

I cannot live without art. I cannot live without wilderness. Call it *Brilliant Love* (1994–95). Thank the imagination that some people are brave enough, sanely crazy enough, to designate both.

"Art is dangerous because it doesn't have a definable function. I think that is what people are afraid of."

Yes, Damien, exactly, you bad boy of British art who dares to slice up the bodies of cows, from the head to the anus, and mix them all up to where nothing makes sense and who allows us to walk through with no order in mind, twelve cross-sections of cow, so we have to take note of the meat that we eat without thinking about the photography of the body, the cow's body, our body, we confront the wonder of the organism as is, not as a continuum but as a design, the sheer beauty and texture of functional design. We see the black-and-white hide; there is no place to hide inside the guts of a cow sliced and stretched through space like an accordion between your very large hands. You ask us to find *Some Comfort Gained from the Acceptance of the Inherent Lies in Everything* (1996).

We have been trying to explain, justify, codify, give biological and ecological credence as to why we want to preserve what is wild, like art, much more than a specimen behind glass. But what if we were to say, Sorry, you are right, wilderness has no definable function. Can we let it be, designate it as art, *art of the wild,* just in case one such definition should arise in the mind of one standing in the tallgrass prairies of middle America or the sliding slope of sandstone in the erosional landscape of Utah?

30   Wilderness as an aesthetic.

Freeze. Damien Hirst brought together a community of artists and displayed their work in a warehouse in England, these neo-conceptualists who set out to explore the big things like death and sex and the meaning of life. Wilderness designation is not so dissimilar. In your tracks, *freeze,* and watch the performance art of a grizzly walking through the gold meadows of the Hayden Valley in Yellowstone. In your tracks, *freeze,* a constellation of monarch butterflies has gathered in the mountains of Mexico. No definable function except to say, wilderness exists like art, look for an idea with four legs, with six legs and wings that resemble fire, and recognize this feeling called survival, in this received idea of wilderness, our twentieth-century installation as neo-conservationists.

A shark in a box.

Wilderness as a box.

Wilderness as *A Thousand Years* with flies and maggots celebrating inside the corpse of things.

Q: What is in the boxes?
A: Maggots.
Q: So you're going to put maggots in the white boxes, and then they hatch and then they fly around . . .
A: And then they get killed by the fly-killer, and maybe lay eggs in the cow heads.
Q: It's a bit disgusting.
A: A bit. I don't think it is. I like it.
Q: Do you think anyone will buy it?
A: I hope so!
    — Damien Hirst interview with Liam Gillick, *Modern Medicine,* 1990

Do I think anyone will buy the concept of   35 wilderness as conceptual art? It is easier to create a sensation over art than a sensation over the bald, greed-faced sale and development of open lands, wild lands, in the United States of America.

I would like to bring Damien Hirst out to the American West, let him bring along his chain saw, *Cutting Ahead* (1994), only to find out somebody has beat him to it, creating clear-cut sculptures out of negative space, eroding space, topsoil running like blood down the mountainsides as mud. Mud as material. He would have plenty of material.

The art of the wild is flourishing.

How are we to see through the lens of our own creative destruction?

A shark in a box.
Wilderness as an installation.
A human being suspended in
formaldehyde.

My body floats between contrary equilibriums.
—Federico García Lorca

When I leaned over the balcony of the great blue room in the American Museum of Natural History, I looked up at the body of the blue whale, the largest living mammal on earth, suspended from the ceiling. I recalled being a docent, how we brought the schoolchildren to this room to lie on their backs, thrilled beyond words as they looked up at this magnificent leviathan, who, if alive, with one quick swoosh of its tall would be halfway across Central Park.

40   I only then noticed that the open space below where the children used to lie on their backs in awe was now a food court filled with plastic tables and chairs. The tables were crowded with visitors chatting away, eating, drinking, oblivious to the creatures surrounding them. How had I missed the theater lights, newly installed on the balcony, pointing down to illuminate the refrigerators humming inside the showcases with a loud display of fast foods advertising yogurt, roast beef sandwiches, apples and oranges?

The blue whale, the tiger shark, sunfish, tunas, eels and manta rays, the walrus, the elephant seals, the orca with its head poking through the diorama of ice in Antarctica, are no longer the natural histories of creatures associated with the sea but simply decoration.

Everything feels upside-down these days, created for our entertainment. Requiem days. The natural world is becoming invisible, appearing only as a backdrop for our own human dramas and catastrophes: hurricanes, tornadoes, earthquakes, and floods. Perhaps if we bring art to the discussion of the wild we can create a sensation where people will pay attention to the shock of what has always been here *Away from the Flock* (1994).

Wild Beauty in the Minds of the Living.

READING AND THINKING

1. Consider the first two paragraphs of the essay. Why does Williams put side-by-side her first two exhibits, one a live shark, the other a dead one? Compare her responses to the two specimens. What do her responses suggest to you about her and her biases as an observer of what we might call scientific artifacts?

2. Why do you suppose Williams turns to Damien Hirst ("bad boy of British art") to help her develop her ideas about wilderness and art? Is the key in the first Hirst quotation, in this sentence: "I like the ideas of trying to understand the world by taking things out of the world"? Or is her rhetorical use of Hirst more complicated? Explain.

3. Why is "sensation" so important to Williams and her ideas? Might the explanation lie in her reflective paragraph about being trapped, being captive? In that paragraph she and the shark temporarily occupy the same space.

4. Compare the beginning and ending of Williams's essay. What does that comparison tell you about her ideas? Explain.

THINKING AND WRITING

1. Trace (and make notes about) Williams's references to death. Taken together, what do they suggest to you about her idea of preservation?

2. Look at the way Williams repeats words or groups of words throughout the essay. Trace at least two of those series of repetitions. Explain the effect on your mind and on her idea of the repeated words. Notice especially how so many of her key words reappear in the final paragraphs of her essay.

3. Mid-essay, Williams asks her most pertinent question: "Why not designate wilderness as an installation of art?" What is her answer? What are the implications of that answer? Explain.

4. What is your answer to Williams's question, "How are we to see through the lens of our own creative destruction?"

ACT OF CONCEPTUALIZING: AN OCCASION FOR WRITING

Perhaps the most interesting moment in our writing lives occurs when we begin to see the meaning of the evidence we are considering. It is the moment when an idea clarifies itself to us. We hope that eventually others will be able to see what we see, but we hope even more fervently that the evidence will show us something that no one else has ever seen. That moment of meaning-making is difficult to pin down, because even though we may be able to mark it with an "Ah ha!" at the precise moment of clarity, the exact origins of a particular act of conceptualizing are almost impossible to identify. As Alan Lightman has told us, the moments of clarity are always preceded by hard work, study, and analysis, and almost always, there is a movement away from the work itself, a moment of disengagement, that allows the thinker both to distance herself from the work and to gain a different perspective on it. This conceptualizing work lies at the heart of science and at the heart of essay writing.

Conceptualize: To form a concept or idea of.

Oxford English Dictionary

The conceptualising process [. . .] lands us in the Aristotelian distinction of *genus, differentia,* and *species,* which may be [. . .] called the logical categories. These categories are not found ready made in thought, but are products of the process of conceptualising the chains of perceptual reintegration.

S. H. Hodgson, 1878

© Damien Hirst. Photographer: Stephen White. Courtesy Jay Jopling/White Cube (London)

DAMIEN HIRST, *Virgin Mother, New York City*

PREPARING TO WRITE: OCCASIONS TO THINK ABOUT WHAT YOU SEE

1. In his 35-foot sculpture *Virgin Mother,* Damien Hirst depicts a pregnant mother and declares her The Virgin. Why do you suppose he does that? Is he simply being a bad boy, as Williams calls him, or is there a more serious conception at work in this sculpture? Explain.

2. *Virgin Mother* is placed against the backdrop of Lever House, a groundbreaking New York City building completed in 1952. The architects broke with tradition and rested the horizontal slab of the building on pillars, leaving a large pavilion under most of the structure. The building's clean, blue-green, mirrored façade brought color and space to the city's theretofore closed and drab corporate landscape. How do *Virgin Mother* and Lever House complement or detract from one another?

3. In Hirst's pieces he reveals the insides of bodies, giving us a sense of what's behind the facade. What do Hirst's pieces have in common with Picasso's cubist methods (the fracturing of the image into planes) reflected in *Weeping Woman*? Explain.

LEVER HOUSE,
New York City

PABLO PICASSO,
Weeping Woman (1937)

MOVING TOWARD ESSAY: OCCASIONS TO ANALYZE AND REFLECT

1. Recall Williams's methodology, or strategy, in her essay. She introduces a number of images as a way of leading us into a consideration of her idea about the relationship between art and wilderness. That movement from evidence (images and reflection in this case) to idea required a conceptualizing leap of imagination on Williams's part. We do not know how her mind made that leap, but we do know that she had to discover the idea in the evidence. Try now, on a small scale, to practice such leaping. Work with any two of the images from this Occasion to discover something fresh and meaningful about the relationships that you see depicted in them.

2. Leaping from evidence to conception may require a change of perspective—moving away from the details of what you see in the evidence so that you can see it from a different angle. That distancing may be actual, or simply mental. Consider how these two different perspectives on *Virgin Mother* alter (1) your sense of the sculpture and (2) her spatial relation to Lever House.

   Make extensive notes about the way your mind processes how these images cause you to reevaluate the sculpture and its relationship to the space it occupies.

3. Scientific investigation requires that you look deeply into the evidence—the facts of the matter at hand. But such investigation eventually requires that you step back from your work to make of the facts something that no one else may see without your help. Investigate two or three pieces from Hirst's "Natural History" series and then step back to figure out what Hirst (and your work with his images) can teach all of us about being better investigators.

WRITING THOUGHTFULLY: OCCASIONS FOR IDEAS AND ESSAYS

1. Write an essay titled "The Scientific Leap," revealing to your readers what you have learned about the important moment when a thinker actually creates meaning from the evidence under consideration. Include in your essay accounts of your own moments of creation (when you have conceptualized something new) as well as evidence from any of the essays that you have read in this chapter or elsewhere.

2. Consider again Williams's central question: "Can we not watch the habits of animals, the adaptations of plants, and call them performance art within the conceptual framework of wilderness?" Think about her example of the performing grizzly bear, and think about Hirst's conceptual pieces in "Natural History" that are conceived to make us rethink art, ourselves, and the world. Respond to Williams's question in a letter; be sure to clarify your own conception of performance art and your own conceptual framework of wilderness. Use the Internet and your school's library for additional research.

CREATING OCCASIONS

1. Focus on your favorite movie or television series. Pay attention to what is implied by the action in the film or the series—how people talk and behave, what they seem to care about, how they value their lives and their decisions, what the show's outcomes reveal about the importance of the depicted lives. Consider too how the show advertises itself. Finally, assess the overall value of the show and then write an essay that reveals and substantiates your conceptual appraisal.

2. Focus on one of your most pressing concerns about the world around you, something close enough at hand that it affects you and others. Investigate this concern thoroughly, trying to put your personal biases aside. Read about the problem. Listen to others. Make notes as you investigate and learn. Finally, follow Williams's lead and figure out a new way to conceive the problem, one that will make those around you both share your concern and share your way of *seeing* and *understanding* the problem. Use art or images, if you can, to help you conceptualize and reveal your findings in an innovative, persuasive essay. Title your essay "A _____ in the Mind of One Contemplating _____." Fill in the blanks appropriately.

Lewis Thomas (1913–1993)

Lewis Thomas served as president of Memorial Sloan-Kettering Cancer Center from 1973 to 1980. Earlier, he had worked as a research pathologist and as a medical administrator in the South Pacific during WWII, and at the Rockefeller Institute, Tulane University, the University of Minnesota, New York University, and the Yale University School of Medicine. His essay collections include *The Lives of a Cell: Notes of a Biology Watcher* (1974, National Book Award in Arts and Letters and in Science winner), *The Medusa and the Snail: More Notes of a Biology Watcher* (1979), and *The Youngest Science: Notes of a Medicine-Watcher* (1983). Thomas wrote regularly in the *New England Journal of Medicine*. He was elected to the Academy of Arts and Sciences and to the National Academy of Science.

CRICKETS, BATS, CATS & CHAOS

In "Crickets, Bats, Cats & Chaos" Thomas asks us to think about the relationship between ourselves and the other inhabitants of the earth, namely cats, crickets, and bats. He challenges us to think about the complex mechanisms within these other creatures that govern their behavior and their survival. He plays with the idea of mind, wondering just what the difference between humans and nonhumans might be. In the most general sense, Thomas challenges us to think hard about what we can learn about ourselves and the planet earth by being more aware of our fellow inhabitants.

1   I am not sure where to classify the mind of my cat Jeoffry. He is a small Abyssinian cat, a creature of elegance, grace, and poise, a piece of moving sculpture, and a total mystery. We named him Jeoffry after the eighteenth-century cat celebrated by the unpredictable poet Christopher Smart in a poem titled "Jubilate Agno," one section of which begins, "For I will consider my cat Jeoffry." The following lines are selected more or less at random:

> For he counteracts the powers of darkness by his electrical skin and glaring eyes.
> For he counteracts the Devil, who is death, by brisking about the life . . .
> For he is of the tribe of Tiger . . .
> For he purrs in thankfulness, when God tells him he's a good Cat . . .
> For he is an instrument for the children to learn benevolence upon . . .
> For he is a mixture of gravity and waggery . . .
> For there is nothing sweeter than his peace when at rest.
> For there is nothing brisker than his life when in motion.

I have not the slightest notion what goes on in the mind of my cat Jeoffry, beyond the conviction that it is a genuine mind, with genuine thoughts and a strong tendency to chaos, but in all other respects a mind totally unlike mine. I have a hunch, based on long moments of observing him stretched on the rug in sunlight, that his mind has more periods of geometric order, and a better facility for switching itself almost, but not quite, entirely off, and accordingly an easier access to pure pleasure. Just as he is able to hear sounds that I cannot hear, and smell important things of which I am unaware, and suddenly leap like a crazed gymnast from chair to chair, upstairs and downstairs through the house, flawless in every movement and searching for something he never finds, he has periods of meditation on matters I know nothing about.

While thinking about what nonhumans think is, in most biological quarters, an outlandish question, even an impermissible one, to which the quick and easy answer is nothing, or almost nothing, or certainly nothing like *thought* as we use the word, I still think about it. For while none of them may have real thoughts, foresee the future, regret the past, or be self-aware, most of us up here at the peak of evolution cannot manage the awareness of our own awareness, a state of mind only achieved when the mind succeeds in emptying itself of all other information and switches off all messages, interior and exterior. This is the state of mind for which the Chinese Taoists long ago used a term meaning, literally, no-knowledge. With no-knowledge, it is said, you get a different look at the world, an illumination.

Falling short of this, as I do, and dispossessed of anything I could call illumination, it has become my lesser satisfaction to learn secondhand whatever I can, and then to think, firsthand, about the behavior of other kinds of animals.

5   I think of crickets, for instance, and the thought of their unique, very small thoughts—principally about mating and bats—but also about the state of cricket society. The cricket seems to me an eminently suitable animal for sorting out some of the emotional issues bound to arise in any consideration of animal awareness. Nobody, so far as I know, not even an eighteenth-century minor poet, could imagine any connection between events in the mind of a cricket and those in the mind of a human. If there was ever a creature in nature meriting the dismissive description of a living machine, mindless and thoughtless, the cricket qualifies. So in talking about what crickets are up to when they communicate with each other, as they unmistakably do, by species-unique runs and rhythms of chirps and trills, there can be no question of *anthropomorphization,* that most awful of all terms for the deepest error a modern biologist can fall into.

If you reduce the temperature of a male cricket, the rate of his emission of chirping signals is correspondingly reduced. Indeed, some of the earlier naturalists used the technical term "thermometer crickets" because of the observation that you can make a close guess at the air temperature in a field by counting the rate of chirps of familiar crickets.

This is curious, but there is a much more curious thing going on when the weather changes. The female crickets in the same field, genetically coded to respond specifically to the chirp rhythm of their species, adjust their recognition mechanism to the same temperature change and the same new, slower rate of chirps. That is, as John Doherty and Ronald Hoy wrote on observing the phenomenon, "warm females responded best to the songs of warm males, and cold females responded best to the songs of cold males." The same phenomenon, known as temperature coupling, has been encountered in grasshoppers and tree frogs, and also in fireflies, with their flash communication system. The receiving mind of the female cricket, if you are willing to call it that, adjusts itself immediately to match the sending mind of the male. This has always struck me as one of the neatest examples of animals adjusting to a change in their environment.

But I started thinking about crickets with something quite different in mind, namely bats. It has long been known that bats feed voraciously on the nocturnal flights of crickets and moths, which they detect on the wing by their fantastically accurate ultrasound mechanism. What should have been guessed at, considering the ingenuity of nature, is that certain cricket species, green lacewings, and certain moths have ears that can detect the ultrasound emissions of a bat, and can analyze the distance and direction from which the ultrasound is coming. These insects can employ two separate and quite distinct defensive maneuvers for evading the bat's keen sonar.

The first is simply swerving away. This is useful behavior when the bat signal is coming from a safe distance, twenty to thirty meters away. At this range the insect can detect the bat, but the bat is too far off to receive the bounced ultrasound back to its state of being is rather like the concept of chaos that has emerged in higher mathematical circles in recent years.

10   As I understand it, and I am quick to say that I understand it only quite superficially, chaos occurs when any complex, dynamic system is perturbed by a small uncertainty in one or another of its subunits. The inevitable result is an amplification of the disturbance and then the spread of unpredictable, random behavior throughout the whole system. It is the total unpredictability and randomness that makes the word "chaos" applicable as a technical term, but it is not true that the behavior of the system becomes disorderly. Indeed, as James P. Crutchfield and his associates have written, "There is order in chaos: underlying chaotic behavior there are elegant geometric forms that create randomness in the same way as a card dealer shuffles a deck of cards or a blender mixes cake batter." The random behavior of a turbulent stream of water, or of the weather, or of Brownian movement, or of the central nervous system of a cricket in flight from a bat, are all determined by the same mathematical rules. Behavior of this sort has been encountered in computer models of large cities: When a small change was made in one small part of the city model, the amplification of the change resulted in enormous upheavals, none of them predictable, in the municipal behavior at remote sites in the models.

A moth or a cricket has a small enough nervous system to *seem* predictable and orderly most of the time. There are not all that many neurons, and the circuitry contains what seem to be mostly simple reflex pathways. Laboratory experiments suggest that in a normal day, one thing—the sound of a bat at a safe distance, say—leads to another, predictable thing—a swerving off to one side in flight. It is only when something immensely new and important happens—the bat sound at three meters away—that the system is thrown into chaos.

I suggest that the difference with us is that chaos is the norm. Predictable, small-scale, orderly, cause-and-effect sequences are hard to come by and don't last long when they do turn up. Something else almost always turns up at the same time, and then another sequential thought intervenes alongside, and there come turbulence and chaos again. When we are lucky, and the system operates at its random best, something astonishing may suddenly turn up, beyond predicting or imagining. Events like these we recognize as good ideas.

My cat Jeoffry's brain is vastly larger and more commodious than that of a cricket, but I wonder if it is qualitatively all that different. The cricket lives with his two great ideas in mind, mating and predators, and his world is a world of particular, specified sounds. He is a tiny machine, I suppose, depending on what you mean by "machine," but it is his occasional moments of randomness and unpredictability that entitle him to be called aware. In order to achieve that feat of wild chaotic flight, and thus escape, he has to make use, literally, of his brain. When Int-1, an auditory interneuron, is activated by the sound of a bat closing in, the message is transmitted by an axon connected straight to the insect's brain, and it is here, and only here, that the swerving is generated. This I consider to be a thought, a very small thought, but still a thought. Without knowing what to count as a thought, I figure that Jeoffry, with his kind of brain, has a trillion thoughts of about the same size in any waking moment. As for me, and my sort of brain, I can't think where to begin.

We like to think of our minds as containing trains of thought, or streams of consciousness, as though they were orderly arrangements of linear events, one notion leading in a cause-and-effect way to the next notion. Logic is the way to go; we set a high price on logic, unlike

E. M. Forster's elderly lady in *Aspects of the Novel,* who, when accused of being illogical, replied, "Logic? Good gracious! What rubbish! How can I tell what I think till I see what I say?"

15 But with regard to our own awareness of nature, I believe we've lost sight of, lost track of, lost touch with, and to some measurable degree lost respect for, the chaotic and natural in recent years—and during the very period of history when we humans have been learning more about the detailed workings of nature than in all our previous millennia. The more we learn, the more we seem to distance ourselves from the rest of life, as though we were separate creatures, so different from other occupants of the biosphere as to have arrived from another galaxy. We seek too much to explain, we assert a duty to run the place, to dominate the planet, to govern its life, but at the same time we ourselves seem to be less a part of it than ever before.

We leave it whenever we can, we crowd ourselves from open green countrysides onto the concrete surfaces of massive cities, as far removed from the earth as we can get, staring at it from behind insulated glass, or by way of half-hour television clips.

At the same time, we talk a great game of concern. We shout at each other in high virtue, now more than ever before, about the befoulment of our nest and about whom to blame. We have mechanized our lives so extensively that most of us live with the illusion that our only connection with nature is the nagging fear that it may one day turn on us and do us in. Polluting our farmlands and streams, even the seas, worries us because of what it may be doing to the food and water supplies necessary for human beings. Raising the level of CO_2, methane, and hydro-fluoro-carbons in the atmosphere troubles us because of the projected effects of climate upheaval on human habitats. These anxieties do not extend, really, to nature at large. They are not the result of any new awareness.

Nature itself, that vast incomprehensible meditative being, has come to mean for most of us nothing much more than odd walks in the nearby woods, or flowers in the rooftop garden, or the soap opera stories of the last giant panda or whooping crane, or curiosities like the northward approach, from Florida, of the Asiatic flying cockroach.

I will begin to feel better about us, and about our future, when we finally start learning about some of the things that are still mystifications. Start with the events in the mind of a cricket, I'd say, and then go on from there. Comprehend my cat Jeoffry and we'll be on our way. Nowhere near home, but off and dancing, getting within a few millennia of understanding why the music of Bach is what it is, ready at last for open outer space. Give us time, I'd say, the kind of endless time we mean when we talk about the real world.

READING AND THINKING

1. Explain how the first sentence of the essay foreshadows all that follows.

2. What does the first sentence following the quotation from "Jubilate Agno" add to your understanding of the idea that governs this essay?

3. What does the word "anthropomorphization" mean and why is it the "most awful of all terms" for a modern biologist?

4. How does Thomas sidestep and play with the notion of mind as he reveals his scientific evidence about crickets?

5. Why do you suppose Thomas decides to tell his readers about bats, instead of, say, butterflies? What does the evidence about bats allow him to introduce into his essay?

THINKING AND WRITING

1. Outline the various ways in which Thomas's cat's mind differs from his own mind.

2. Why do you suppose Thomas tells us of the Chinese Taoists and their sense of the importance of "no-knowledge"? Cite evidence from the essay to support your explanation.

3. What is the difference between learning "secondhand" and thinking "firsthand"? What are the values of firsthand thinking and how does Thomas demonstrate such thinking?

4. One of the things that crickets and bats share is their inherent or instinctive or mindful use of chaos, according to Thomas. Explain how chaos helps us understand crickets and bats.

5. Why does Thomas believe that "with us [humans] chaos is the norm"? What are the implications of such a belief? Explain.

OUR NEIGHBORS ON PLANET EARTH: AN OCCASION FOR WRITING

This Occasion gives you an opportunity to think about two seemingly unrelated subjects: chaos and the life of insects and animals. These exercises encourage you to think about rather large concepts: how is the universe ordered; how much of that order can we actually see; how are the inhabitants of planet earth related; if insects and bugs and animals do not think the way we humans think, how do they think, or is *thinking* the wrong term; what is the nature of mind and how do human minds differ from those of our fellow creatures? Our aim is not to answer these large questions in a definitive way but to think, as Lewis Thomas might say, "firsthand" about the evidence available to us for consideration.

Lorenz Attractor

L. P. BROWER,
Butterfly Movement

ERWIN OLAF, *Pig*

PREPARING TO WRITE: OCCASIONS TO THINK ABOUT WHAT YOU SEE

1. What do you see in the image of the Lorenz Attractor? Name it. Be imaginative. Compare your answers with those of others in your class. Does it resemble any other image in this group? Explain.

2. What are the flying objects in Brower's photograph? Can you see or imagine order in this chaotic array? Explain.

3. What does Erwin Olaf's *Pig* suggest to you about humans and their fellow creatures?

MOVING TOWARD ESSAY: OCCASIONS TO ANALYZE AND REFLECT

1. What you see depicted in the Lorenz Attractor image is called a "strange attractor," a computer generated image of chaos; this picture stops the movement of the attractor, so you see only a frozen moment—a glimpse of the order inherent in chaos. Compare this image with a moving screen saver on a computer. How does the moving attractor on the computer screen illustrate what Thomas tells us about the nature of chaos?

2. Brower's photograph actually depicts a frozen moment during the migration of Monarch butterflies from a colder to a warmer climate. How does that information about migration affect your ability to see or imagine order in the chaotic array of the butterflies in flight? How do you suppose butterflies know where they are going?

3. How do you think Lewis Thomas would react to Olaf's *Pig*? Would he see beyond the humor of the images to something scientific? Explain.

4. Consider what you have learned from your own experiences with animals or insects. What can you tell us about how these nonhumans "think"?

Read this brain teaser. . . . bet you CAN!

The phaonmneel pweor of the hmuan mnid: I cdnuolt blveiee taht
I cluod aulaclty uesdnatnrd waht I was rdanieg. Aoccdrnig to a
rseheearcr at Cmagbride Uinervtisy, it deosn't mttaer in waht
oredr the ltteers of a wrod are, the olny iprmoatnt tihng is taht
the frist and lsat ltteer be in the rghit pclae. The rset can be a
taotl mses and you can sitll raed it wouthit a porbelm. Tihs is
bcuseae the huamn mnid deos not raed ervey lteter by istlef, but
the wrod as a wlohe. Amzanig huh?

How difficult was it for you to read this brainteaser?
What point does it make about how our
BRAINS PROCESS LETTERS AND WORDS?
When would an occasion arise to use language and
thought skills like these?

WRITING THOUGHTFULLY: OCCASIONS FOR IDEAS AND ESSAYS

1. Write a thoughtful essay about the effects of chaos in your everyday life. Focus on one or two moments when things were so chaotic that you seemed overwhelmed, only to discover that within those turbulent experiences some ordering principle was at work. As you write your essay reveal what you think about Thomas's claim that chaos is actually our "norm."

2. Select an animal or an insect that fascinates you. Investigate this creature's way of surviving, keeping in mind Thomas's research into secondhand information (that provided by other researchers). Finally write an essay in which you do some "firsthand" thinking about whether the evidence suggests that the creature has a "mind." You can also use your firsthand observations of the creature's behavior if you have been able to observe it.

3. A new field of research known as "animal personality" has emerged in the last decade or so. In a *New York Times* article entitled "The Animal Self" (January 22, 2006), Charles Siebert reports that as scientists track animal traits and behaviors, "they are also beginning to unravel such core mysteries as the bioevolutionary underpinnings of personality, both animal and human, the dynamic interplay between genes and environment in the expression of various personality traits, and why it is that nature invented such a thing as personality in the first place." Investigate some aspect of this personality research and determine whether you believe scientists are veering into what Thomas calls the "deepest error a modern biologist can fall into" (anthropomorphization); if so do the results warrant the risk? Write an essay about your discoveries and your idea about them.

CREATING OCCASIONS

1. Margaret Wheatley, an organizational behavior specialist, in *Leadership and the New Science* (2001), poses a lively question about the broader application of chaos: "Scientists of chaos study shapes in motion; if we were to approach organizations in a similar way, what would constitute the shape and motion of an organization?" Consider any organization that you know well (anything from a corporation to a classroom) and write an essay that responds to Wheatley's question.

2. Take the same organization from the first question and do some different "firsthand" thinking about it with Thomas in mind. Write an essay in which you explore the notion of a collective or governing intelligence at work, something that binds the organization together. Consider how freedom and constraints play against one another in the organization.

12

{ LANGUAGE
AND THOUGHT

The connections between language and thought are deep and pervasive. Language, at least human language, is thought. It involves thinking by means of concepts and abstractions in the form of words, which stand in for or represent objects or things. When we talk about shoes, for example, we do not need to have any particular shoe in mind—although we could, if we like. Rather we use the word "shoes," itself an abstraction, to refer to the concept of things we wear on our feet, from sandals to snowshoes to stiletto heels.

If language involves thought, so too does thought involve language. We think in our native language, the language we know best. And though we do not always think in words, we often do. For those times we think wordlessly, we often think with images. Images themselves are concepts that need not be pictorial.

To use language effectively, we have to practice thinking in, with, and through language. Reading the words and ideas of others helps us to develop and formulate our own thinking. Putting our ideas into words—in writing—helps us clarify our thinking. Together, reading and writing stimulate and reinforce one another in an intricate web of language and thought. We cannot read and write without doing at least some thinking. Conversely, we often do our best thinking when we use reading as a spur to thought and writing as a means of refining and clarifying our thinking. Language and thought, then, are inextricably intertwined.

The essays in this chapter touch on various aspects of language and their relationship to thinking. Richard Rodriguez's "Aria: A Memoir of a Bilingual Childhood" considers the double perspective we experience when learning in two languages, a perspective that is both enabling and conflicted. In his classic essay "Politics and the English Language," George Orwell presents a critical perspective on language use in academic writing. In "Signs and Symbols," Suzanne K. Langer explains the difference between human and animal communication and the implications for differences in human and animal thinking. Ursula K. Le Guin considers how thinking and writing connect her creative writing of fantasy and science fiction in "Where Do You Get Your Ideas From?" In "On Lateral Thinking," Edward de Bono explains the differences between logical thinking and lateral thinking, and why both kinds of thinking are necessary. Finally, Matthew Goulish, in "Criticism," connects language and thinking through metaphor.

LANGUAGE AND CONSCIOUSNESS

We tend to take language for granted. We use language all day long, mostly without paying much attention to how we say things, sometimes without attending carefully to what we say. Using language is something we do, almost, we might say, without thinking.

It is helpful to be mindful not only of what we say but how we say it, and even how well we say it, for the precision of the *saying* affects the meaning of what we say. The form of our speech and writing affects the content, in some cases making what we say fuzzy and unclear, and in the worst cases, perhaps even incomprehensible.

Verbal and nonverbal, words and images, reading and writing, speaking and listening—these interrelated pairs of terms refer to how we use and absorb language, day in and day out. We hear the languages of radio and television broadcasts—news, sports, sitcoms, police dramas, soap operas, MTV. We see the language of these broadcasts as well in the images they deploy. We read the verbal and visual languages of magazines, newspapers, books, and the Internet, as well, focusing our attention typically more on what is said than on how it is said.

By attending to the language of words and images, by asking questions about why certain words, phrases, and images are being used, we raise our consciousness of language, and with some effort, we can improve our ability to understand language and use it more effectively. The three essays here can aid in that process. Richard Rodriguez's "Aria" raises our consciousness about the ways different languages filter and shape our thought and experience. George Orwell's "Politics and the English Language" illustrates how careless language can reflect sloppy thinking. In "Signs and Symbols," the philosopher Suzanne K. Langer helps us understand the differences between the simple, single meaning of signs and the more abstract, complex, and multiple meanings of symbols.

Richard Rodriguez (b. 1944)

Richard Rodriguez is a native of San Francisco, the son of Mexican American immigrants. A self-described "scholarship boy," Rodriguez attended Catholic schools as a child and later Stanford and Columbia Universities. He received undergraduate and graduate degrees in English from the University of California at Berkeley. Rodriguez works primarily as a journalist: he is an editor for the Pacific News Service, and he contributes to such periodicals as *Harper's* and *US News and World Report,* as well as writing columns for the *Los Angeles Times.* His commentary about American life and Hispanic culture on PBS's *MacNeil-Lehrer NewsHour* won him the prestigious Peabody Award in 1997. His best known publication, however, is *Hunger of Memory: The Education of Richard Rodriguez* (1982), his collection of autobiographical essays that explore his growing up as the son of immigrant parents.

ARIA: A MEMOIR OF A BILINGUAL CHILDHOOD

In "Aria: A Memoir of a Bilingual Childhood," originally published in *The American Scholar* (1980/1981), and which later served as the opening chapter of *Hunger of Memory,* Rodriguez describes growing up in a bilingual and a bicultural world. Rodriguez reflects on the tensions he experienced at home at school. He describes what he has gained and what he has lost as he makes the transition from the Spanish-speaking world of his parents and native culture to the English-speaking world of his education.

1 I remember to start with that day in Sacramento—a California now nearly thirty years past—when I first entered a classroom, able to understand some fifty stray English words.

The third of four children, I had been preceded to a neighborhood Roman Catholic school by an older brother and sister. But neither of them had revealed very much about their classroom experiences. They left each morning and returned each afternoon, always together, speaking Spanish as they climbed the five steps to the porch. And their mysterious books, wrapped in brown shopping-bag paper, remained on the table next to the door, closed firmly behind them.

An accident of geography sent me to a school where all my classmates were white and many were the children of doctors and lawyers and business executives. On that first day of school, my classmates must certainly have been uneasy to find themselves apart from their families, in the first institution of their lives. But I was astonished. I was fated to be the "problem student" in class.

The nun said, in a friendly but oddly impersonal voice: "Boys and girls, this is Richard Rodriguez." (I heard her sound *it* out: *Rich-heard Road-ree-guess.*) It was the first time I had heard anyone say my name in English. "Richard," the nun repeated more slowly, writing my name down in her book. Quickly I turned to see my mother's face dissolve in a watery blur behind the pebbled-glass door.

Now, many years later, I hear of something 5 called "bilingual education"—a scheme proposed in the late 1960s by Hispanic American social activists, later endorsed by a congressional vote. It is a program that seeks to permit non-English-speaking children (many from lower class homes) to use their "family language" as the language of school. Such, at least, is the aim its supporters announce. I hear them, and am forced to say no: It is not possible for a child, any child, ever to use his family's language in school. Not to understand this is to misunderstand the public uses of schooling and to trivialize the nature of intimate life.

Memory teaches me what I know of these matters. The boy reminds the adult. I was a bilingual child, but of a certain kind: "socially disadvantaged," the son of working-class parents, both Mexican immigrants.

In the early years of my boyhood, my parents coped very well in America. My father had steady work. My mother managed at home. They were nobody's victims. When we moved to a house many blocks from the Mexican American section of town, they were not intimidated by those two or three neighbors who initially tried to make us unwelcome. ("Keep your brats away from my sidewalk!") But despite all they achieved, or perhaps because they had so much to achieve, they lacked any deep feeling of ease, of belonging in public. They regarded the people at work or in crowds as being very distant from us. Those were the others, *los gringos*. That term was interchangeable in their speech with another, even more telling, *los americanos*.

I grew up in a house where the only regular guests were my relations. On a certain day, enormous families of relatives would visit us, and there would be so many people that the noise and the bodies would spill out to the backyard and onto the front porch. Then for weeks no one would come. (If the doorbell rang, it was usually a salesman.) Our house stood apart—gaudy yellow in a row of white bungalows. We were the people with the noisy dog, the people who raised chickens. We were the foreigners on the block. A few neighbors would smile and wave at us. We waved back. But until I was seven years old, I did not know the name of the old couple living next door or the names of the kids living across the street.

In public, my father and mother spoke a hesitant, accented, and not always grammatical English. And then they would have to strain, their bodies tense, to catch the sense of what was rapidly said by *los gringos*. At home, they returned to Spanish. The language of their Mexican past sounded in counterpoint to the English spoken in public. The words would come quickly, with ease. Conveyed through those sounds was the pleasing, soothing, consoling reminder that one was at home.

During those years when I was first learning to speak, my mother and father addressed me only in Spanish; in Spanish I learned to reply. By contrast, English *(inglés)* was the language I came to associate with *gringos*, rarely heard in the house. I learned my first words of English overhearing my parents speaking to strangers. At six years of age, I knew just enough words for my mother to trust me on errands to stores one block away—but no more. 10

I was then a listening child, careful to hear the very different sounds of Spanish and English. Wide-eyed with hearing, I'd listen to sounds more than to words. First, there were English *(gringo)* sounds. So many words still were unknown to me that when the butcher or the lady at the drugstore said something, exotic polysyllabic sounds would bloom in the midst of their sentences. Often the speech of people in public seemed to me very loud, booming with confidence. The man behind the counter would literally ask, "What can I do for you?" But by being so firm and clear, the sound of his voice said that he was a *gringo;* he belonged in public society. There were also the high, nasal notes of middle-class American speech—which I rarely am conscious of hearing today because I hear them so often, but could not stop hearing when I was a boy. Crowds at Safeway or at bus stops were noisy with the birdlike sounds of *los gringos*. I'd move away from them all—all the chirping chatter above me.

My own sounds I was unable to hear, but I knew that I spoke English poorly. My words could not extend to form complete thoughts. And the words I did speak I didn't know well enough to make distinct sounds. (Listeners would usually lower their heads to hear better what I was trying to say.) But it was one thing for *me* to speak English with difficulty; it was more troubling to hear my parents speaking in public: their high-whining vowels and guttural consonants; their sentences that got stuck with "eh" and "ah" sounds; the confused syntax; the hesitant rhythm of sounds so different from the way *gringos* spoke. I'd notice, moreover, that my parents' voices were softer than those of *gringos* we would meet.

I am tempted to say now that none of this mattered. (In adulthood I am embarrassed by childhood fears.) And, in a way, it didn't matter very much that my parents could not speak English with ease. Their linguistic difficulties had no serious consequences. My mother and father made themselves understood at the county hospital clinic and at government offices. And yet, in another way, it mattered very much. It was unsettling to hear my parents struggle with English. Hearing them, I'd grow nervous, and my clutching trust in their protection and power would be weakened.

There were many times like the night at a brightly lit gasoline station (a blaring white memory) when I stood uneasily hearing my father talk to a teenage attendant. I do not recall what they were saying, but I cannot forget the sounds my father made as he spoke. At one point his words slid together to form one long word—sounds as confused as the threads of blue and green oil in the puddle next to my shoes. His voice rushed through what he had left to say. Toward the end, he reached falsetto notes, appealing to his listener's understanding. I looked away at the lights of passing automobiles. I tried not to hear anymore. But I heard only too well the attendant's reply, his calm, easy tones. Shortly afterward, headed for home, I shivered when my father put his hand on my shoulder. The very first chance that I got, I evaded his grasp and ran on ahead into the dark, skipping with feigned boyish exuberance.

But then there was Spanish: *español,* the language rarely heard away from the house; *español,* the language which seemed to me therefore a private language, my family's language. To hear its sounds was to feel myself specially recognized as one of the family, apart from *los otros.* A simple remark, an inconsequential comment could convey that assurance. My parents would say something to me and I would feel embraced by the sounds of their words. Those sounds said: *I am speaking with ease in Spanish. I am addressing you in words I never use with* los gringos. *I recognize you as someone special, close, like no one outside. You belong with us. In the family. Ricardo.*

At the age of six, well past the time when most middle-class children no longer notice the difference between sounds uttered at home and words spoken in public, I had a different experience. I lived in a world compounded of sounds. I was a child longer than most. I lived in a magical world, surrounded by sounds both pleasing and fearful. I shared with my family a language enchantingly private— different from that used in the city around us.

Just opening or closing the screen door behind me was an important experience. I'd rarely leave home all alone or without feeling reluctance. Walking down the sidewalk, under the canopy of tall trees, I'd warily notice the (suddenly) silent neighborhood kids who stood warily watching me. Nervously, I'd arrive at the grocery store to hear there the sounds of the *gringos,* reminding me that in this so-big world I was a foreigner. But if leaving home was never routine, neither was coming back. Walking toward our house, climbing the steps from the sidewalk, in summer when the front door was open, I'd hear voices beyond the screen door talking in Spanish. For a second or two I'd stay, linger there listening. Smiling, I'd hear my mother call out, saying in Spanish, "Is that you, Richard?" Those were her words, but all the while her sounds would assure me: *You are home now. Come close inside. With us.*

"*Sí,*" I'd reply.

Once more inside the house, I would resume my place in the family. The sounds would grow harder to hear. Once more at home, I would grow less conscious of them. It required, however, no more than the blurt of the doorbell to alert me all over again to listen to sounds. The house would turn instantly quiet while my mother went to the door. I'd hear her hard English sounds. I'd wait to hear her voice turn to soft-sounding Spanish, which assured me, as surely as did the clicking tongue of the lock on the door, that the stranger was gone.

20   Plainly, it is not healthy to hear such sounds so often. It is not healthy to distinguish public from private sounds so easily. I remained cloistered by sounds, timid and shy in public, too dependent on the voices at home. I remember many nights when my father would come back from work, and I'd hear him call out to my mother in Spanish, sounding relieved. In Spanish, his voice would sound the light and free notes that he never could manage in English. Some nights I'd jump up just hearing his voice. My brother and I would come running into the room where he was with our mother. Our laughing (so deep was the pleasure!) became screaming. Like others who feel the pain of public alienation, we transformed the knowledge of our public separateness into a consoling reminder of our intimacy. Excited, our voices joined in a celebration of sounds. *We are speaking now the way we never speak out in public—we are together,* the sounds told me. Some nights no one seemed willing to loosen the hold that sounds had on us. At dinner we invented new words that sounded Spanish, but made sense only to us. We pieced together new words by taking, say, an English verb and giving it Spanish endings. My mother's instructions at bedtime would be lacquered with mock-urgent tones. Or a word like *sí,* sounded in several notes, would convey added measures of feeling. Tongues lingered around the edges of words, especially fat vowels, and we happily sounded that military drum roll, the twirling roar of the Spanish *r.* Family language, my family's sounds: the voices of my parents and sisters and brother. Their voices insisting: *You belong here. We are family members. Related. Special to one another. Listen!* Voices singing and sighing, rising and straining, then surging, teeming with pleasure which burst syllables into fragments of laughter. At times it seemed there was steady quiet only when, from another room, the rustling whispers of my parents faded and I edged closer to sleep.

Supporters of bilingual education imply today that students like me miss a great deal by not being taught in their family's language. What they seem not to recognize is that, as a socially disadvantaged child, I regarded Spanish as a private language. It was a ghetto language that deepened and strengthened my feeling of separateness. What I needed to learn in school was that I had the right, and the obligation, to speak the public language. The odd truth is that my first-grade classmates could have become bilingual, in the conventional sense of the word, more easily than I. Had they been taught early (as upper-middle-class children often are taught) a "second language" like Spanish or French, they could have regarded it simply as another public language. In my case, such bilingualism could not have been so quickly achieved. What I did not believe was that I could speak a single public language.

Without question, it would have pleased me to have heard my teachers address me in Spanish when I entered the classroom. I would have felt much less afraid. I would have imagined that my instructors were somehow "related" to me; I would indeed have heard their Spanish as my family's language. I would have trusted them and responded with ease. But I would have delayed—postponed for how long?—having to learn the language of public society. I would have evaded—and for how long?—learning the great lesson of school: that I had a public identity.

Fortunately, my teachers were unsentimental about their responsibility. What they understood was that I needed to speak public English. So their voices would search me out, asking me questions. Each time I heard them I'd look up in surprise to see a nun's face frowning at me. I'd mumble, not really meaning to answer. The nun would persist. "Richard, stand up. Don't look at the floor. Speak up. Speak to the entire class, not just to me!" But I couldn't believe English could be my language to use. (In part, I did not want to believe it.) I continued to mumble. I resisted the teacher's demands. (Did I somehow suspect that once I learned this public language my family life would be changed?) Silent, waiting for the bell to sound, I remained dazed, diffident, afraid.

Because I wrongly imagined that English was intrinsically a public language and Spanish was intrinsically private, I easily noted the difference between classroom language and the language at home. At school, words were directed to a general audience of listeners. ("Boys and girls . . .") Words were meaningfully ordered. And the point was not self-expression alone, but to make oneself understood by many others. The teacher quizzed: "Boys and girls, why do we use that word in this sentence? Could we think of a better word to use there? Would the sentence change its meaning if the words were differently arranged? Isn't there a better way of saying much the same thing?" (I couldn't say. I wouldn't try to say.)

25   Three months passed. Five. A half year. Unsmiling, ever watchful, my teachers noted my silence. They began to connect my behavior with the slow progress my brother and sisters were making. Until, one Saturday morning, three nuns arrived at the house to talk to our parents. Stiffly they sat on the blue living-room sofa. From the doorway of another room, spying on the visitors, I noted the incongruity, the clash of two worlds, the faces and voices of school intruding upon the familiar setting of home. I overheard one voice gently wondering, "Do your children speak only Spanish at home, Mrs. Rodriguez?" While another voice added, "That Richard especially seems so timid and shy."

That Rich-heard!

With great tact, the visitors continued, "Is it possible for you and your husband to encourage your children to practice their English when they are home?" Of course my parents complied. What would they not do for their children's well-being? And how could they question the Church's authority which those women represented? In an instant they agreed to give up the language (the sounds) which had revealed and accentuated our family's closeness. The moment after the visitors left, the change was observed. "*Ahora*, speak to us only *en inglés*," my father and mother told us.

At first, it seemed a kind of game. After dinner each night, the family gathered together to practice "our" English. It was still then *inglés*, a language foreign to us, so we felt drawn to it as strangers. Laughing, we would try to define words we could not pronounce. We played with strange English sounds, often overanglicizing our pronunciations. And we filled the smiling gaps of our sentences with familiar Spanish sounds. But that was cheating, somebody shouted, and everyone laughed.

In school, meanwhile, like my brother and sisters, I was required to attend a daily tutoring session. I needed a full year of this special work. I also needed my teachers to keep my attention from straying in class by calling out, "*Rich-heard*"—their English voices slowly loosening the ties to my other name, with its three notes, *Ri-car-do.* Most of all, I needed to hear my mother and father speak to me in a moment of seriousness in "broken"—suddenly heartbreaking—English. This scene was inevitable. One Saturday morning I entered the kitchen where my parents were talking, but I did not realize that they were talking in

Spanish until, the moment they saw me, their voices changed and they began speaking English. The *gringo* sounds they uttered startled me. Pushed me away. In that moment of trivial misunderstanding and profound insight, I felt my throat twisted by unsounded grief. I simply turned and left the room. But I had no place to escape to where I could grieve in Spanish. My brother and sisters were speaking English in another part of the house.

30   Again and again in the days following, as I grew increasingly angry, I was obliged to hear my mother and father encouraging me: "Speak to us *en inglés.*" Only then did I determine to learn classroom English. Thus, sometime afterward it happened: One day in school, I raised my hand to volunteer an answer to a question. I spoke out in a loud voice and I did not think it remarkable when the entire class understood. That day I moved very far from being the disadvantaged child I had been only days earlier. Taken hold at last was the belief, the calming assurance, that I belonged in public.

Shortly after, I stopped hearing the high, troubling sounds of *los gringos.* A more and more confident speaker of English, I didn't listen to *how* strangers sounded when they talked to me. With so many English-speaking people around me, I no longer heard American accents. Conversations quickened. Listening to persons whose voices sounded eccentrically pitched, I might note their sounds for a few seconds, but then I'd concentrate on what they were saying. Now when I heard someone's tone of voice—angry or questioning or sarcastic or happy or sad—I didn't distinguish it from the words it expressed. Sound and word were thus tightly wedded. At the end of each day I was often bemused, and always relieved, to realize how "soundless," though crowded with words, my day in public had been. An eight-year-old boy, I finally came to accept what had been technically true since my birth: I was an American citizen.

But diminished by then was the special feeling of closeness at home. Gone was the desperate, urgent, intense feeling of being at home among those with whom I felt intimate. Our family remained a loving family, but one greatly changed. We were no longer so close, no longer bound tightly together by the knowledge of our separateness from *los gringos.* Neither my older brother nor my sisters rushed home after school anymore. Nor did I. When I arrived home, often there would be neighborhood kids in the house. Or the house would be empty of sounds.

Following the dramatic Americanization of their children, even my parents grew more publicly confident—especially my mother. First she learned the names of all the people on the block. Then she decided we needed to have a telephone in our house. My father, for his part, continued to use the word gringo, but it was no longer charged with bitterness or distrust. Stripped of any emotional content, the word simply became a name for those Americans not of Hispanic descent. Hearing him, sometimes, I wasn't sure if he was pronouncing the Spanish word *gringo,* or saying gringo in English.

There was a new silence at home. As we children learned more and more English, we shared fewer and fewer words with our parents. Sentences needed to be spoken slowly when one of us addressed our mother or father. Often the parent wouldn't understand. The child would need to repeat himself. Still the parent misunderstood. The young voice, frustrated, would end up saying, "Never mind"—the subject was closed. Dinners would be noisy with the clinking of knives and forks against dishes. My mother would smile softly between her remarks; my father, at the other end of the table, would chew and chew his food while he stared over the heads of his children.

My *mother!* My *father!* After English be-   35 came my primary language, I no longer knew what words to use in addressing my parents.

The old Spanish words (those tender accents of sound) I had earlier used—*mamá* and *papá*—I couldn't use anymore. They would have been all-too-painful reminders of how much had changed in my life. On the other hand, the words I heard neighborhood kids call *their* parents seemed equally unsatisfactory. *Mother* and *father,* "ma," "pa," "dad," "pop" (how I hated the all-American sound of that last word)—all these I felt were unsuitable terms of address for *my* parents. As a result, I never used them at home. Whenever I'd speak to my parents, I would try to get their attention by looking at them. In public conversations, I'd refer to them as my "parents" or my "mother" and "father."

My mother and father, for their part, responded differently, as their children spoke to them less. My mother grew restless, seemed troubled and anxious at the scarceness of words exchanged in the house. She would question me about my day when I came home from school. She smiled at my small talk. She pried at the edges of my sentences to get me to say something more. ("What . . . ?") She'd join conversations she overheard, but her intrusions often stopped her children's talking. By contrast, my father seemed to grow reconciled to the new quiet. Though his English somewhat improved, he tended more and more to retire into silence. At dinner he spoke very little. One night his children and even his wife helplessly giggled at his garbled English pronunciation of the Catholic "Grace Before Meals." Thereafter he made his wife recite the prayer at the start of each meal, even on formal occasions when there were guests in the house.

Hers became the public voice of the family. On official business it was she, not my father, who would usually talk to strangers on the phone or in stores. We children grew so accustomed to his silence that, years later, we would routinely refer to his "shyness." (My mother often tried to explain: Both of his parents died when he was eight. He was raised by an uncle who treated him as little more than a menial servant. He was never encouraged to speak. He grew up alone. A man of few words.) But I realized my father was not shy, I realized whenever I'd watch him speaking Spanish with relatives. Using Spanish, he was quickly effusive. Especially when talking with other men, his voice would spark, flicker, flare alive with varied sounds. In Spanish, he expressed ideas and feelings he rarely revealed when speaking English. With firm Spanish sounds, he conveyed a confidence and authority that English would never allow him.

The silence at home, however, was not simply the result of fewer words, passing between parents and children. More profound for me was the silence created by my inattention to sounds. At about the time I no longer bothered to listen with care to the sounds of English in public, I grew careless about listening to the sounds made by the family when they spoke. Most of the time I would hear someone speaking at home and didn't distinguish his sounds from the words people uttered in public. I didn't even pay much attention to my parents' accented and ungrammatical speech. At least not at home. Only when I was with them in public would I become alert to their accents. But even then their sounds caused me less and less concern. For I was growing increasingly confident of my own public identity.

I would have been happier about my public success had I not recalled sometimes, what it had been like earlier, when my family conveyed its intimacy through a set of conveniently private sounds. Sometimes in public, hearing a stranger, I'd hark back to my lost past. A Mexican farm worker approached me one day downtown. He wanted directions to some place. "*Hijito,* . . . ?" he said. And his voice stirred old longings. Another time, I was standing beside my mother in the visiting room of a Carmelite convent, before the dense screen which rendered the nuns shadowy figures. I heard several of them speaking Spanish in their busy, singsong, overlapping voices, assuring my mother that, yes, yes, we were remembered, all our family was remembered, in their prayers. Those voices echoed faraway family sounds. Another day, a dark-faced old woman touched my shoulder lightly to steady herself as she boarded a bus. She murmured something to me I couldn't quite comprehend. Her Spanish voice came near, like the face of a never-before-seen relative in the instant before I was kissed. That voice, like so many of the Spanish voices I'd hear in public, recalled the golden age of my childhood.

40   Bilingual educators say today that children lose a degree of "individuality" by becoming assimilated into public society. (Bilingual schooling is a program popularized in the seventies, that decade when middle-class "ethnics" began to resist the process of assimilation—the "American melting pot.") But the bilingualists oversimplify when they scorn the value and necessity of assimilation. They do not seem to realize that a person is individualized in two ways. So they do not realize that, while one suffers a diminished sense of *private* individuality by being assimilated into public society, such assimilation makes possible the achievement of *public* individuality.

Simplistically again, the bilingualists insist that a student should he reminded of his difference from others in mass society, of his "heritage." But they equate mere separateness with individuality. The fact is that only in private—with intimates—is separateness from the crowd a prerequisite for individuality; an intimate "tells" me that I am unique, unlike all others, apart from the crowd. In public, by contrast, full individuality is achieved, paradoxically, by those who are able to consider themselves members of the crowd. Thus it happened for me. Only when I was able to think of myself as an American, no longer an alien in *gringo* society, could I seek the rights and opportunities necessary for full public individuality. The social and political advantages I enjoy as a man began on the day I came to believe that my name is indeed *Rich-heard Road-ree-guess*. It is true that my public society today is often impersonal; in fact, my public society is usually mass society. But despite the anonymity of the crowd, and despite the fact that the individuality I achieve in public is often tenuous—because it depends on my being one in a crowd—I celebrate the day I acquired my new name. Those middle-class ethnics who scorn assimilation seem to me filled with decadent self-pity, obsessed by the burden of public life. Dangerously, they romanticize public separateness and trivialize the dilemma of those who are truly socially disadvantaged.

If I rehearse here the changes in my private life after my Americanization, it is finally to emphasize a public gain. The loss implies the gain. The house I returned to each afternoon was quiet. Intimate sounds no longer greeted me at the door. Inside there were other noises. The telephone rang. Neighborhood kids ran past the door of the bedroom where I was reading my schoolbooks—covered with brown shopping-bag paper. Once I learned the public language, it would never again be easy for me to hear intimate family voices. More and more of my day was spent hearing words, not sounds. But that may only be a way of saying that on the day I raised my hand in class and spoke loudly to an entire roomful of faces, my childhood started to end.

READING AND THINKING

1. How do you respond to the educational experiences that Rodriguez describes? What connections can you make with your own educational experience?

2. What are the drawbacks and what are the benefits for Rodriguez and his family as he makes the transition from the Spanish-speaking world of his parents to the English-speaking world of his teachers?

3. How does Rodriguez characterize each of the languages and cultures he describes? Does he seem to favor one over the other? Explain.

4. Single out one passage that resonates particularly strongly for you. Explain why.

THINKING AND WRITING

1. Discuss Rodriguez's arguments against bilingual education—or at least against some forms of bilingual education. Explain his reasons for not allowing students to be educated in their native language and recommending instead that they be immersed, in school, in English. What are your own views on this issue?

2. Analyze the strategies Rodriguez uses to make his argument. What is his main method of persuasion? Provide evidence from his essay to support your views.

3. Discuss the importance of language and culture in Rodriguez's essay. Consider the places where Rodriguez highlights linguistic difference.

4. Write a short essay about your own experience with language and learning. Use a single moment that sticks out in your memory to create a piece that reflects on an experience you had at home, in school, or at work, in which your use of language had important ramifications for your education.

THE BILINGUAL DEBATE: AN OCCASION FOR WRITING

In "Aria: A Memoir of a Bilingual Childhood," Richard Rodriguez uses his own experience on which to base an argument against bilingual education, the approach to teaching immigrant children with little English in their native language while they simultaneously learn English. In this Occasion you will have an opportunity to hear both sides of the argument over bilingual education and to develop your own position on the matter.

© Lisa McDonald

Photo courtesy of Roger Lerud

PREPARING TO WRITE: OCCASIONS TO THINK ABOUT WHAT YOU SEE

1. Do you think signs such as the one shown here should appear in Spanish as well as English? Do you think signs should include other languages? Why or why not?

2. How is language used (or misused) in the signs seen here? What do you think Rodriguez would have thought of these signs?

MOVING TOWARD ESSAY: OCCASIONS TO ANALYZE AND REFLECT

1. What newspapers, radio stations, televisions stations, and websites do you know of that are published or presented in a language other than English? What languages are used? To what extent are these foreign language media read, listened to, and watched in your community? What purpose do they serve?

2. Consider the perspective on bilingual education offered in the following passage. Explain what the writer says and the arguments and evidence used to support his position. Consider whether the editorial writer shares any aspect of Rodriguez's position on the issue.

New York Times
Ending the Bilingual Double-Talk

The new guidelines on bilingual education just proposed by the Department of Education should end much confusion and political double-talk. They require that non-English-speaking pupils be taught English as quickly as possible; but also that they be protected, in the interim, from falling behind in their other work with instruction in their native language.

That such self-evident goals need to be spelled out in the first place is a measure of the messiness of bilingual education. Deliberate abuses have combined with pedagogical ineptitude to turn much bilingual education into permanent detention for children, segregated and dependent, and into a boondoggle for those who keep them there. Such disregard of the children's interests has occasionally been given an air of legitimacy by the mistaken idea that this country should become bilingual, with Spanish as the second official language.

The new guidelines set matters straight. They reaffirm English as the language of school and country. They recommend bilingual education as the way to make the transition to English least painful and most efficient. As they should, the guidelines leave open the use of other routes to the same goal. For example, "English as a Second Language" stresses separate instruction in English for foreign youngsters while letting them attend regular classes in all other subjects. The most suitable method of learning English and getting the most out of their education is best left to local pedagogical discretion.

What cannot be left to discretion is the children's right to equal opportunity. Those who glorify the days when immigrant children were thrown into the educational pool to sink or swim do not realize how callous that approach could sometimes be. Many sank.

Not to use new pedagogical devices to help non-English-speaking youngsters violates those children's rights. That is what the Supreme Court said in 1974, in *Lau v. Nichols*. It left the nature of the remedies to responsible educational authorities. What makes the new guidelines necessary is that these authorities often have lacked pedagogical responsibility, or abdicated to political pressures. Federal bilingual funds are intended to help Hispanic children, not to make Spanish an official language or to make jobs for Hispanic teachers unqualified to teach in English.

Sound as the guidelines are, they cannot do the job alone. Unless local school districts and state authorities insure that bilingual teachers are also fluent in English, the transition process will fail. Each pupil's progress should be monitored, to insure that transitional attendance in bilingual classes is as brief as possible. In fact, our only quarrel with the guidelines is that they would let children stay segregated in these classes for five years—at least two years too long.

The guidelines will be debated in hearings next month. They are certain to be attacked both by those who want to scuttle bilingual education, and those who want to scuttle English as the nation's single official language. There will be diversionary calls for maintaining children's personal heritage. The Department of Education, having embarked on the right course, should not be deflected from leading every youngster, as quickly as possible, toward fluency in English. It is one of the few indisputable tools for success in school, and in American society.

3. What additional perspective is offered by Paul Zweig in the following excerpt from his 1982 review of Rodriguez's book, *Hunger of Memory*? Explain how Zweig's view is related to the views of those expressed by the *New York Times* editorial writer, by Richard Hoggart, and by Rodriguez himself in "Aria."

Paul Zweig

The Child of Two Cultures

These chapters are remarkably moving and vividly detailed. At the beginning of the book it is noted that versions of several chapters were published in magazines as long ago as 1973. The exquisite clarity of Mr. Rodriguez's writing is the product of long care, an attention to nuance that, one senses, is not only esthetic but moral. These chapters are, in the best sense, an elegy, an act of love and farewell. They are moving, too, because their subject, rendered with such care, is quite simply growing up. This book will be a source of controversy among educators committed to the recent idea of bilingual education, and to other forms of special treatment, in schools, for "minorities." For Mr. Rodriguez believes the nuns were right to insist that he learn English.

The wedge driven into his family's intimate life was not English, he now believes, but education, the emotionally charged evolution every family must experience as its children go to school and grow partly away, become amphibians living in and out of the house, speaking with two voices, living two lives. When the change doesn't center on different languages, as it does in immigrant families, it may be less noticeable, a matter of voice, intonation. It is nonetheless real and crucial. Mr. Rodriguez's success in *Hunger of Memory* lies in his ability to identify this universal labor of growing up in his own particular experience.

Advocates of bilingual education are wrong, he insists, in supposing that the values of home life are embodied in language, not per-

sons. If students at school can learn in their home language, it is claimed, they will be less disoriented, better able to attend to the business of schooling. But the business of schooling is to take children out of the home and thrust upon them a new set of demands. Education, to work, must change children. That is its function, according to Richard Rodriguez. It must teach them a new voice, indeed a new language, less charged with ultimate feelings than the old language, less comfortable, but appropriate to the impersonal world in which self-respect, success, money, culture are won. To win is also to lose, yes; but this can't be avoided, shouldn't be avoided.

Here is the political point Mr. Rodriguez wants to drive home. The struggle for social justice begun 20 years ago with the civil rights movement in the South and expanded since to include all "minority" groups—Hispanics, Chicanos, Haitians, but also gays and women— has taken a wrong turn in the matter of education. Affirmative action and bilingual school programs; the demand for ethnic studies in the university, for relevance; the attempt to legitimize black ghetto English—all ignore the essential function of education, which is to change the student, extract him from his intimate circumstance—family, ghetto, minority community—and give him access to the public world, which in the United States is negotiated in standard English, embodied by a set of attitudes, a voice which is everywhere recognized as a passport to all the larger ambitions the public world makes possible.

WRITING THOUGHTFULLY: OCCASIONS FOR IDEAS AND ESSAYS

1. Write a letter in response to the *New York Times* editorial "Ending the Bilingual Double Talk." In your response, make clear your own position on bilingual education. Use Rodriguez, the bilingual signs, any of the excerpts included in this Occasion, or any other evidence you think would strengthen your response.

2. Write an essay about the central issues at stake in the bilingual education debate. Create a powerful argument about whether you believe immigrant students should be "immersed" in English in all their classes or whether they should be taught in their native language while learning English. Use any of the evidence presented in this Occasion, or whatever you feel would help prove your point. If you have a firsthand experience, include that in your essay.

3. If you have experience in a bilingual program, either directly or indirectly, describe what the program was like or what you know about it. How was language treated? Was one language more important than another? Were students treated differently because of their languages? Alternatively, think of situations in which you have heard many languages spoken in public. Consider how that made you and others feel. Write an essay in which you explore how different languages affect how people are treated; don't feel limited to discuss only educational situations.

CREATING OCCASIONS

1. Find two or three signs that appear in two (or more than two) languages. Take a look at one foreign language newspaper to note the kinds of articles and advertisements it includes. Spend a few minutes watching one foreign language television show, as well. On the basis of what you observe, develop an Occasion for Writing that invites consideration of the need for and uses of bilingualism in American culture.

2. If you have traveled abroad to a country where a foreign language was spoken, reminisce about your experience with language there. Make a list of all the things you didn't understand and a list of all the things you did understand, giving a reason for each item. How did the language barrier affect your trip? If you have not traveled abroad, imagine being immersed in a foreign language and what kind of excitement or fear that brings out in you. Why do you think you feel the way you do?

George Orwell (1903–1950)

George Orwell was born Eric Blair in Bengal, India, where his father was a minor functionary in the British colonial government. Educated in England, Orwell chose not to attend university, instead opting to join the Indian Imperial Police in Burma. After five years, however, he became disillusioned with the whole notion of colonial rule and returned to England to pursue a career as a writer. His first book, *Down and Out in Paris and London* (1933), chronicled his experiences living a self-imposed hand-to-mouth existence among the poor of the two cities. In addition to the many works of nonfiction that followed, Orwell is best known for his satirical political novels *Animal Farm* (1945) and *Nineteen Eighty-Four* (1949).

POLITICS AND THE ENGLISH LANGUAGE

In "Politics and the English Language," Orwell makes a plea for using language with clarity and honesty. He argues that far too much published writing suffers from vagueness, obscurity, and downright ugliness. Orwell insists that confused writing reflects confused thinking, and that the way to think more clearly is to write more clearly.

1 Most people who bother with the matter at all would admit that the English language is in a bad way, but it is generally assumed that we cannot by conscious action do anything about it. Our civilization is decadent and our languages—so the argument runs—must inevitably share in the general collapse. It follows that any struggle against the abuse of language is a sentimental archaism, like preferring candles to electric light or hansom cabs to aeroplanes. Underneath this lies the half-conscious belief that language is a natural growth and not an instrument which we shape for our own purposes.

Now, it is clear that the decline of a language must ultimately have political and economic causes: it is not due simply to the bad influence of this or that individual writer. But an effect can become a cause, reinforcing the original cause and producing the same effect in an intensified form, and so on indefinitely. A man may take to drink because he feels himself to be a failure, and then fail all the more completely because he drinks. It is rather the same thing that is happening to the English language. It becomes ugly and inaccurate because our thoughts are foolish, but the slovenliness of our language makes it easier for us to have foolish thoughts. The point is that the process is reversible. Modern English, especially written English, is full of bad habits which spread by imitation and which can be avoided if one is willing to take the necessary trouble. If one gets rid of these habits one can think more clearly, and to think clearly is a necessary first step towards political regeneration: so that the fight against bad English is not frivolous and is not the exclusive concern of professional writers. I will come back to this presently, and I hope that by that time the meaning of what I have said here will have become clearer. Meanwhile, here are five specimens of the English language as it is now habitually written.

These five passages have not been picked out because they are especially bad—I could have quoted far worse if I had chosen—but because they illustrate various of the mental vices from which we now suffer. They are a little below the average, but are fairly representative samples. I number them so that I can refer back to them when necessary:

"(1) I am not, indeed, sure whether it is not true to say that the Milton who once seemed not unlike a seventeenth-century Shelley had not become, out of an experience ever more bitter in each year, more alien [*sic*] to the founder of that Jesuit sect which nothing could induce him to tolerate."

Professor Harold Laski (Essay
in Freedom of Expression)

"(2) Above all, we cannot play ducks and drakes with a native battery of idioms which prescribes such egregious collocations of vocables as the Basic *put up with* for *tolerate* or *put at a loss* for *bewilder*."

Professor Lancelot Hogben (Interglossa)

"(3) On the one side we have the free personality: by definition it is not neurotic, for it has neither conflict nor dream. Its desires, such as they are, are transparent, for they are just what institutional approval keeps in the forefront of consciousness; another institutional pattern would alter their number and intensity; there is little in them that is natural, irreducible, or culturally dangerous. But *on the other side,* the social bond itself is nothing but the mutual reflection of these self-secure integrities. Recall the definition of love. Is not this the very picture of a small academic? Where is there a place in this hall of mirrors for either personality or fraternity?"

Essay on psychology in Politics (New York)

"(4) All the 'best people' from the gentlemen's clubs, and all the frantic fascist captains, united in common hatred of Socialism and bestial horror of the rising tide of the mass revolutionary movement, have turned to acts of provocation, to foul incendiarism, to medieval legends of poisoned wells, to legalize their own destruction of proletarian organizations, and rouse the agitated petty-bourgeoisie to chauvinistic fervour on behalf of the fight against the revolutionary way out of the crisis."

Communist Pamphlet

"(5) If a new spirit *is* to be refused into this old country, there is one thorny and contentious reform which must be tackled, and that is the humanization and galvanization of the B.B.C. Timidity here will bespeak cancer and atrophy of the soul. The heart of Britain may be sound and of strong beat, for instance, but the British lion's roar at present is like that of Bottom in Shakespeare's *Midsummer Night's Dream*—as gentle as any sucking dove. A virile new Britain cannot continue indefinitely to be traduced in the eyes or rather ears, of the world by the effete languors of Langham Place, brazenly masquerading as 'standard English'. When the Voice of Britain is heard at nine o'-clock, better far and infinitely less ludicrous to hear aitches honestly dropped than the present priggish, inflated, inhibited, schoolma'amish arch braying of blameless bashful mewing maidens!"

Letter in Tribune

Each of these passages has faults of its own, but, quite apart from avoidable ugliness, two qualities are common to all of them. The first is staleness of imagery: the other is lack of precision. The writer either has a meaning and cannot express it, or he inadvertently says something else, or he is almost indifferent as to whether his words mean anything or not. This mixture of vagueness and sheer incompetence is the most marked characteristic of modern English prose, and especially of any kind of political writing. As soon as certain topics are raised, the concrete melts into the abstract and no one seems able to think of turns of speech that are not hackneyed: prose consists less and less of *words* chosen for the sake of their meaning, and more and more of *phrases* tacked together like the sections of a prefabricated henhouse. I list below, with notes and examples, various of the tricks by means of which the work of prose-construction is habitually dodged:

Dying Metaphors

A newly invented metaphor assists thought 5 by evoking a visual image, while on the other hand a metaphor which is technically "dead" (e.g. *iron resolution*) has in effect reverted to being an ordinary word and can generally be used without loss of vividness. But in between these two classes there is a huge dump of worn-out metaphors which have lost all evocative power and are merely used because they save people the trouble of inventing phrases for themselves. Examples are: *Ring the changes on, take up the cudgels for, to the line, ride roughshod over, stand shoulder to shoulder with, play into the hands of, no axe to grind, grist to the mill, fishing in troubled waters, on the order of the day, Achilles heel, swan song, hotbed.* Many of these are used without knowledge of their meaning (what is a "rift," for instance?), and incompatible metaphors are frequently mixed, a sure sign that the writer is not interested in what he is saying. Some metaphors now current have been twisted out of their original meaning without those who use them even being aware of the fact. For example, *toe the line* is sometimes written *tow the line.* Another example is *the hammer and the anvil,* now always used with the implication that the anvil gets the worst of it. In real life it is always the anvil that breaks the hammer, never the other way about: a writer who stopped to think what he was saying would be aware of this, and would avoid perverting the original phrase.

Operators or Verbal False Limbs

These save the trouble of picking out appropriate verbs and nouns, and at the same time pad each sentence with extra syllables which give it an appearance of symmetry. Characteristic phrases are: *render inoperative, militate against, make contact with, be subjected to, give rise to, give grounds for, have the effect of, play a leading part (role) in, make itself felt, take effect, exhibit a tendency to, serve the purpose of, etc., etc.* The keynote is the elimination of simple verbs. Instead of being a single word, such as *break, stop, spoil, mend, kill,* a verb becomes a *phrase,* made up of a noun or adjective tacked on to some general-purposes verb such as *prove, serve, form, play, render.* In addition, the passive voice is wherever possible used in preference to the active, and noun constructions are used instead of

gerunds *(by examination of* instead of *by examining).* The range of verbs is further cut down by means of the *-ize* and *de-* formation, and the banal statements are given an appearance of profundity by means of the *not un-* formation. Simple conjunctions and prepositions are replaced by such phrases as *with respect to, having regard to, the fact that, by dint of, in view of, in the interest of, on the hypothesis that;* and the ends of sentences are saved from anticlimax by such resounding commonplaces as *greatly to be desired, cannot be left out of account, a development to be expected in the near future, deserving of serious consideration, brought to a satisfactory conclusion,* and so on and so forth.

Pretentious Diction

Words like *phenomenon, element, individual* (as noun), *objective, categorical, effective, virtual, basic, primary, promote, constitute, exhibit, exploit, utilize, eliminate, liquidate,* are used to dress up simple statements and give an air of scientific impartiality to biased judgments. Adjectives like *epoch-making, epic, historic, unforgettable, triumphant, age-old, inevitable, inexorable, veritable,* are used to dignify the sordid processes of international politics, while writing that aims at glorifying war usually takes on an archaic colour, its characteristic words being: *realm, throne, chariot, mailed fist, trident, sword, shield, buckler, banner, jackboot, clarion.* Foreign words and expressions such as *cul de sac, ancien régime, deus ex machina, mutatis mutandis, status quo, Gleichschaltung, Weltanschauung,* are used to give an air of culture and elegance. Except for the useful abbreviations *i.e., e.g.,* and *etc.,* there is no real need for any of the hundreds of foreign phrases now current in English. Bad writers, and especially scientific, political and sociological writers, are nearly aways haunted by the notion that Latin or Greek words are grander than Saxon ones, and unnecessary words like *expedite, ameliorate, predict, extraneous, deracinated, clandestine, subaqueous* and hundreds of others constantly gain ground from their Anglo-Saxon opposite numbers.[1] The jargon peculiar to Marxist writing (*hyena, hangman, cannibal, petty bourgeois, these gentry, lacquey, flunkey, mad dog, White Guard*, etc., consists largely of words and phrases translated from Russian, German or French; but the normal way of coining a new word is to use a Latin or Greek root with the appropriate affix and, where necessary, the *-ize* formation. It is often easier to make up words of this kind (*deregionalize, impermissible, extramarital, nonfragmentatory* and so forth) than to think up the English words that will cover one's meaning. The result, in general, is an increase in slovenliness and vagueness.

Meaningless Words

In certain kinds of writing, particularly in art criticism and literary criticism, it is normal to come across long passages which are almost completely lacking in meaning.[2] Words like *romantic, plastic, values, human, dead, sentimental, natural, vitality*, as used in art criticism, are strictly meaningless in the sense that they not only do not point to any discoverable object, but are hardly ever expected to do so by the reader. When one critic writes, "The outstanding feature of Mr. X's work is its living quality," while another writes, "The immediately striking thing about Mr. X's work is its peculiar deadness," the reader accepts this as a simple difference of opinion. If words like *black* and *white* were involved instead of the jargon words *dead* and *living*, he would see at once that language was being used in an improper way. Many political words are similarly abused. The word *Fascism* has now no meaning except in so far as it signifies "something not desirable." The words *democracy, socialism, freedom, patriotic, realistic, justice*, have each of them several different meanings which cannot be reconciled with one another. In the case of a word like *democracy*, not only is there no agreed definition, but the attempt to make one is resisted from all sides. It is almost universally felt that when we call a country democratic we are praising it: consequently the defenders of every kind of régime claim that it is a democracy, and fear that they might have to stop using the word if it were tied down to any one meaning. Words of this kind are often used in a consciously dishonest way. That is, the person who uses them has his own private definition, but allows his hearer to think he means something quite different. Statements like *Marshal Pétain was a true patriot, The Soviet Press is the freest in the world, The Catholic Church is opposed to persecution*, are almost always made with intent to deceive. Other words used in variable meanings, in most cases more or less dishonestly, are: *class, totalitarian, science, progressive, reactionary, bourgeois, equality*.

Now that I have made this catalogue of swindles and perversions, let me give another example of the kind of writing that they lead to. This time it must of its nature be an imaginary one. I am going to translate a passage of good English into modern English of the worst sort. Here is a well-known verse from *Ecclesiastes*:

> "I returned and saw under the sun, that the race is not to the swift, nor the battle to the strong, neither yet bread to the wise, nor yet riches to men of understanding, nor yet favour to men of skill; but time and chance happeneth to them all."

---

[1] An interesting illustration of this is the way in which the English flower names which were in use till very recently are being ousted by Greek ones, *snapdragon* becoming *antirrhinum, forget-me-not* becoming *myosotis*, etc. It is hard to see any practical reason for this change of fashion: it is probably due to an instinctive turning-away from the more homely word and a vague feeling that the Greek word is scientific [Orwell's note].

[2] Example: "Comfort's catholicity of perception and image, strangely Whitmanesque in range, almost the exact opposite in aesthetic compulsion, continues to evoke that trembling atmospheric accumulative hinting at a cruel, an inexorably serene timelessness. . . . Wrey Gardiner scores by aiming at simple bull's-eyes with precision. Only they are not so simple, and through this contented sadness runs more than the surface bittersweet of resignation" (*Poetry Quarterly*) [Orwell's note].

Here it is in modern English:

"Objective consideration of contemporary phenomena compels the conclusion that success or failure in competitive activities exhibits no tendency to be commensurate with innate capacity, but that a considerable element of the unpredictable must invariably be taken into account."

10   This is a parody, but not a very gross one. Exhibit (3), above, for instance, contains several patches of the same kind of English. It will be seen that I have not made a full translation. The beginning and ending of the sentence follow the original meaning fairly closely, but in the middle the concrete illustrations—race, battle, bread—dissolve into the vague phrase "success or failure in competitive activities." This had to be so, because no modern writer of the kind I am discussing—no one capable of using phrases like "objective consideration of contemporary phenomena"—would ever tabulate his thoughts in that precise and detailed way. The whole tendency of modern prose is away from concreteness. Now analyse these two sentences a little more closely. The first contains forty-nine words but only sixty syllables, and all its words are those of everyday life. The second contains thirty-eight words of ninety syllables: eighteen of its words are from Latin roots, and one from Greek. The first sentence contains six vivid images, and only one phrase ("time and chance") that could be called vague. The second contains not a single arresting phrase, and in spite of its ninety syllables it gives only a shortened version of the meaning contained in the first. Yet without a doubt it is the second kind of sentence that is gaining ground in modern English. I do not want to exaggerate. This kind of writing is not yet universal, and outcrops of simplicity will occur here and there in the worst-written page. Still, if you or I were told to write a few lines on the uncertainty of human fortunes, we should probably come much nearer to my imaginary sentence than to the one from *Ecclesiastes*.

As I have tried to show, modern writing at its worst does not consist in picking out words for the sake of their meaning and inventing images in order to make the meaning clearer. It consists in gumming together long strips of words which have already been set in order by someone else, and making the results presentable by sheer humbug. The attraction of this way of writing is that it is easy. It is easier—even quicker, once you to have the habit—to say *In my opinion it is a not unjustifiable assumption that* than to say *I think*. If you use ready-made phrases, you not only don't have to hunt about for words; you also don't have to bother with the rhythms of your sentences, since these phrases are generally so arranged as to be more or less euphonious. When you are composing in a hurry—when you are dictating to a stenographer, for instance, or making a public speech—it is natural to fall into a pretentious, Latinized style. Tags like *a consideration which we should do well to bear in mind* or *a conclusion to which all of us would readily assent* will save many a sentence from coming down with a bump. By using stale metaphors, similes and idioms, you save much mental effort, at the cost of leaving your meaning vague, not only for your reader but for yourself. This is the significance of mixed metaphors. The sole aim of a metaphor is to call up a visual image. When these images clash—as in *The Fascist octopus has sung its swan song, the jackboot is thrown into the melting pot*—it can be taken as certain that the writer is not seeing a mental image of the objects he is naming; in other words he is not really thinking. Look again at the examples I gave at the beginning of this essay. Professor Laski (1) uses five negatives in fifty-three words. One of these is superfluous, making nonsense of the whole passage, and in addition there is the slip *alien* for akin, making further nonsense, and several avoidable pieces of clumsiness which increase the general vagueness. Professor Hogben (2) plays ducks and drakes with a battery which is able to write prescriptions, and, while disapproving of the everyday phrase *put up with,* is unwilling to look *egregious* up in the dictionary and see what it means. (3), if one takes an uncharitable attitude towards it, is simply meaningless: probably one could work out its intended meaning by reading the whole of the article in which it occurs. In (4), the writer knows more or less what he wants to say, but an accumulation of stale phrases chokes him like tea leaves blocking a sink. In (5), words and meaning have almost parted company. People who write in this manner usually have a general emotional meaning—they dislike one thing and want to express solidarity with another—but they are not interested in the detail of what they are saying. A scrupulous writer, in every sentence that he writes, will ask himself at least four questions, thus: What am I trying to say? What words will express it? What image or idiom will make it clearer? Is this image fresh enough to have an effect? And he will probably ask himself two more: Could I put it more shortly? Have I said anything that is avoidably ugly? But you are not obliged to go to all this trouble. You can shirk it by simply throwing your mind open and letting the ready-made phrases come crowding in. They will construct your sentences for you—even think your thoughts for you, to a certain extent—and at need they will perform the important service of partially concealing your meaning even from yourself. It is at this point that the special connection between politics and the debasement of language becomes clear.

In our time it is broadly true that political writing is bad writing. Where it is not true, it will generally be found that the writer is some kind of rebel, expressing his private opinions and not a "party line." Orthodoxy, of whatever colour, seems to demand a lifeless, imitative style. The political dialects to be found in pamphlets, leading articles, manifestos, White Papers and the speeches of under-secretaries do, of course, vary from party to party, but they are all alike in that one almost never finds in them a fresh, vivid, homemade turn of speech. When one watches some tired hack on the platform mechanically repeating the familiar phrases—*bestial atrocities, iron heel, bloodstained tyranny, free peoples of the world, stand shoulder to shoulder*—one often has a curious feeling that one is not watching a live human being but some kind of dummy: a feeling which suddenly becomes stronger at moments when the light catches the speaker's spectacles and turns them into blank discs which seem to have no eyes behind them. And this is not altogether fanciful. A speaker who uses that kind of phraseology has gone some distance towards turning himself into a machine. The appropriate noises are coming out of his larynx, but his brain is not involved as it would be if he were choosing his words for himself. If the speech he is making is one that he is accustomed to make over and over again, he may be almost unconscious of what he is saying, as one is when one utters the responses in church. And this reduced state of consciousness, if not indispensable, is at any rate favourable to political conformity.

In our time, political speech and writing are largely the defence of the indefensible. Things like the continuance of British rule in India, the Russian purges and deportations, the dropping of the atom bombs on Japan, can indeed be defended, but only by arguments which are too brutal for most people to face, and which do not square with the professed aims of political parties. Thus political language has to consist largely of euphemism, question-begging and sheer cloudy vagueness. Defenceless villages are bombarded from the air, the inhabitants driven out into the countryside, the cattle machine-gunned, the huts set on fire with incendiary bullets: this is called *pacification.* Millions of peasants are robbed of their farms and sent trudging along the roads with no more than they can carry: this is called *transfer of population* or *rectification of frontiers*. People are imprisoned for years without trial, or shot in the back of the neck or sent to die of scurvy in Arctic lumber camps: this is called *elimination of unreliable elements*. Such phraseology is needed if one wants to name things without calling up mental pictures of them. Consider for instance some comfortable English professor defending Russian totalitarianism. He cannot say outright, "I believe in killing off your opponents when you can get good results by doing so." Probably, therefore, he will say something like this:

"While freely conceding that the Soviet régime exhibits certain features which the humanitarian may be inclined to deplore, we must, I think, agree that a certain curtailment of the right to political opposition is an unavoidable concomitant of transitional periods, and that the rigors which the Russian people have been called upon to undergo have been amply justified in the sphere of concrete achievement."

15   The inflated style is itself a kind of euphemism. A mass of Latin words falls upon the facts like soft snow, blurring the outlines and covering up all the details. The great enemy of clear language is insincerity. When there is a gap between one's real and one's declared aims, one turns as it were instinctively to long words and exhausted idioms, like a cuttlefish squirting out ink. In our age there is no such thing as "keeping out of politics." All issues are political issues, and politics itself is a mass of lies, evasions, folly, hatred and schizophrenia. When the general atmosphere is bad, language must suffer. I should expect to find—this is a guess which I have not sufficient knowledge to verify—that the German, Russian and Italian languages have all deteriorated in the last ten or fifteen years, as a result of dictatorship.

But if thought corrupts language, language can also corrupt thought. A bad usage can spread by tradition and imitation, even among people who should and do know better. The debased language that I have been discussing is in some ways very convenient. Phrases like *a not unjustifiable assumption, leaves much to be desired, would serve no good purpose, a consideration which we should do well to bear in mind,* are a continuous temptation, a packet of aspirins always at one's elbow. Look back through this essay, and for certain you will find that I have again and again committed the very faults I am protesting against. By this morning's post I have received a pamphlet dealing with conditions in Germany. The author tells me that he "felt impelled" to write it. I open it at random, and here is almost the first sentence that I see: "(The Allies) have an opportunity not only of achieving a radical transformation of Germany's social and political structure in such a way as to avoid a nationalistic reaction in Germany itself, but at the same time of laying the foundations of a co-operative and unified Europe." You see, he "feels impelled" to write—feels, presumably, that he has something new to say—and yet his words, like cavalry horses answering the bugle, group themselves automatically into the familiar dreary pattern. This invasion of one's mind by ready-made phrases *(lay the foundations, achieve a radical transformation)* can only be prevented if one is constantly on guard against them, and every such phrase anaesthetizes a portion of one's brain.

I said earlier that the decadence of our language is probably curable. Those who deny this would argue, if they produced an argument at all, that language merely reflects existing social conditions, and that we cannot influence its development by any direct tinkering with words and constructions. So far as the general tone or spirit of a language goes, this may be true, but it is not true in detail. Silly words and expressions have often disappeared, not through any evolutionary process but owing to the conscious action of a minority. Two recent examples were *explore every avenue* and *leave no stone unturned,* which were killed by the jeers of a few journalists. There is a long list of fly-blown metaphors which could similarly be got rid of if enough people would interest themselves in the job; and it should also be possible to laugh the *not un-* formation out of existence,[3] to reduce the amount of Latin and Greek in the average sentence, to drive out foreign phrases and strayed scientific words, and, in general, to make pretentiousness unfashionable. But all these are minor points. The defence of the English language implies more than this, and perhaps it is best to start by saying what it does *not* imply.

To begin with it has nothing to do with archaism, with the salvaging of obsolete words and turns of speech, or with the setting up of a "standard English" which must never be departed from. On the contrary, it is especially concerned with the scrapping of every word or idiom which has outworn its usefulness. It has nothing to do with correct grammar and syntax, which are of no importance so long as one makes one's meaning clear, or with the avoidance of Americanisms, or with having what is called a "good prose style." On the other hand it is not concerned with fake simplicity and the attempt to make written English colloquial. Nor does it even imply in every case preferring the Saxon word to the Latin one, though it does imply using the fewest and shortest words that will cover one's meaning. What is above all needed is to let the meaning choose the word, and not the other way about. In prose, the worst thing one can do with words is to surrender to them. When you think of a concrete object, you think wordlessly, and then, if you want to describe the thing you have been visualizing you probably hunt about till you find the exact words that seem to fit. When you think of something abstract you are more inclined to use words from the start, and unless you make a conscious effort to prevent it, the existing dialect will come rushing in and do the job for you, at the expense of blurring or even changing your meaning. Probably it is better to put off using words as long as possible and get one's meaning as clear as one can through pictures or sensations. Afterwards one can choose—not simply *accept*—the phrases that will best cover the meaning, and then switch round and decide what impression one's words are likely to make on another person. This last effort of the mind cuts out all stale or mixed images, all prefabricated phrases, needless repetitions, and humbug and vagueness generally. But one can often be in doubt about the effect of a word or a phrase, and one needs rules that one can rely on when instinct fails. I think the following rules will cover most cases:

(i)   Never use a metaphor, simile or other figure of speech which you are used to seeing in print.

(ii)   Never use a long word where a short one will do.

(iii)   If it is possible to cut a word out, always cut it out.

(iv)   Never use the passive where you can use the active.

(v)   Never use a foreign phrase, a scientific word or a jargon word if you can think of an everyday English equivalent;

(vi)   Break any of these rules sooner than say anything outright barbarous.

These rules sound elementary, and so they are, but they demand a deep change of attitude in anyone who has grown used to writing in the style now fashionable. One could keep all of them and still write bad English, but one could not write the kind of stuff that I quoted in those five specimens at the beginning of this article.

I have not here been considering the literary use of language, but merely language as

---

[3] One can cure oneself of the *not un-*formation by memorizing this sentence: *A not unblack dog was chasing a not unsmall rabbit across a not ungreen field* [Orwell's note].

an instrument for expressing and not for concealing or preventing thought. Stuart Chase and others have come near to claiming that all abstract words are meaningless, and have used this as a pretext for advocating a kind of political quietism. Since you don't know what Fascism is, how can you struggle against Fascism? One need not swallow such absurdities as this, but one ought to recognize that the present political chaos is connected with the decay of language, and that one can probably bring about some improvement by starting at the verbal end. If you simplify your English, you are freed from the worst follies of orthodoxy. You cannot speak any of the necessary dialects, and when you make a stupid remark its stupidity will be obvious, even to yourself. Political language—and with variations this is true of all political parties, from Conservatives to Anarchists—is designed to make lies sound truthful and murder respectable, and to give an appearance of solidity to pure wind. One cannot change this all in a moment, but one can at least change one's own habits, and from time to time one can even, if one jeers loudly enough, send some worn-out and useless phrase—some *jackboot, Achilles' heel, hotbed, melting pot, acid test, veritable inferno* or other lump of verbal refuse—into the dustbin where it belongs.

READING AND THINKING

1. Explain what Orwell means by each of the terms he uses as heads: "dying metaphors," "verbal false limbs," "pretentious diction," and "meaningless words." Which do you think causes the most serious kinds of writing problems?

2. Why do you think Orwell is so concerned with the state of the English language in his day? What differences does he believe his suggestions for reforming English will make? Why?

3. What common problems do the five passages exemplifying bad writing share? What is wrong with the writing in each of these quoted passages?

4. Who is Orwell addressing in this essay? What is his general point, and how does the example of the man who drinks in paragraph 2 clarify and illustrate it?

THINKING AND WRITING

1. Explain Orwell's objections to clichés. Comment on the examples he provides, and offer some contemporary clichés of your own that you have seen in print or heard on television or in the movies.

2. Keep a journal for a week noting violations of Orwell's standards in the speech and writing of public figures.

3. Discuss how you can apply Orwell's list of guidelines for good writing to your own writing.

4. In a brief essay support, contest, or qualify Orwell's argument that thought can corrupt language and that language can corrupt thought.

LANGUAGE AND CULTURE: AN OCCASION FOR WRITING

In "Politics and the English Language," George Orwell situates language in a political context, arguing for the close connection between language and thought. In the following Occasion you will consider how language bears a range of cultural implications and values. You will also have a chance to see how verbal and visual clichés bear cultural implications.

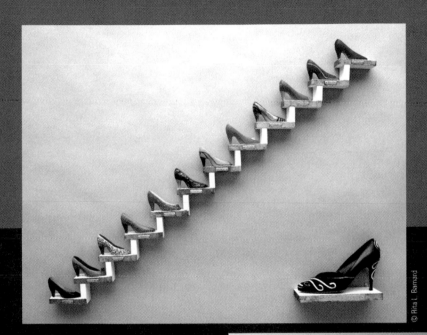

RITA BARNARD,
Put Your Best Foot Forward (2002)

ANITA HORTON,
Target Audience (2002)

PREPARING TO WRITE: OCCASIONS TO THINK ABOUT WHAT YOU SEE

1. Describe what you see in each of the images.

2. Explain how text and image are related in each image. How are the clichés, made of words, given visual form? Explain the logic of the artists' choices.

3. Find another image/text that plays off of a familiar saying or popular cultural cliché, perhaps from the world of fashion, or sports, or work. Describe the image and explain its link with the text that accompanies it.

4. Make a list of the visual details you observe in this advertisement for Genuine Madras Curry Powder. Consider the colors used in the ad.

Image courtesy of The Advertising Archives

5. List the words you find used throughout the ad.

MOVING TOWARD ESSAY: OCCASIONS TO ANALYZE AND REFLECT

1. What inferences can you draw about each of the clichéd images? Explain the idea behind each of the clichés. What does it mean to "put your best foot forward," and what is a "target audience"? Who "targets" audiences, and why?

2. To what extent are these clichés about feet and targets culture bound—limited, for example, to an American context? To what extent do you think either or both of the concepts behind the clichés are relevant for other cultures?

3. What implications do the words and the pictures in the curry advertisement, cumulatively, suggest? What do they suggest about the nature and quality of the product advertised? What cultural implications does the advertisement convey? How is Indian culture communicated? Why would conveying the product as authentically Indian be of value for the advertiser?

WRITING THOUGHTFULLY: OCCASIONS FOR IDEAS AND ESSAYS

1. Using the work you did in the previous exercises, write an essay in which you explain how images and actions convey more than what appears on the surface. Consider the cultural implications of the images and the words, using these images, and any other you think appropriate, as evidence for your position. How do you think Orwell would respond?

2. Write an analysis of the curry advertisement. Include some discussion of both words and images and how the language and the pictures reinforce one another to convey the advertisement's meaning. Consider how other advertisements use words and images to create a particular mood or situation for its viewers.

CREATING OCCASIONS

1. Find images that represent and/or advertise a particular type of popular phenomenon—Barbie dolls, for example, or a popular video game, or the Harry Potter books/films. Look especially at how the phenomenon is advertised or how it appears in television, movies, and print advertising. Analyze the images and the words used for their gender, social, cultural, political, religious, or other implied values. Compare what you found with what is said in one of the essays in this chapter or in Chapter 7, "Gender." Explain the popularity of the phenomenon you selected.

Suzanne K. Langer (1895–1985)

Suzanne K. Langer was born and raised in New York City. She earned her Bachelor's, Master's, and Doctorate degrees from Radcliffe College, Harvard University. She also studied at the University of Vienna, and she taught philosophy at a number of colleges and universities, including Radcliffe, Columbia, and Connecticut College, where she chaired the philosophy department. In 1960 she was elected to the American Academy of Arts and Sciences. Among her influential works are *Philosophy in a New Key: A Study in the Symbolism of Reason, Rite, and Art* (1942), *Feeling and Form: A Theory of Art* (1953), and *Mind: An Essay on Human Feeling* (1967).

SIGNS AND SYMBOLS

In "Signs and Symbols," which appeared as an essay in *Fortune Magazine* (1944), Langer identifies the use of symbols as a distinctively human trait and the use of language as the supreme example of symbolic thinking. She makes an important distinction between human and animal thinking, emphasizing the transformative and creative power of human thought compared with the more limited transmittal capacity of some animals.

1 The trait that sets human mentality apart from every other is its preoccupation with symbols, with images and names that *mean* things, rather than with things themselves. This trait may have been a mere sport of nature once upon a time. Certain creatures do develop tricks and interests that seem biologically unimportant. Pack rats, for instance, and some birds of the crow family take a capricious pleasure in bright objects and carry away such things for which they have, presumably, no earthly use. Perhaps man's tendency to see certain forms as *images,* to hear certain sounds not only as signals but as expressive tones, and to be excited by sunset colors or starlight, was originally just a peculiar sensitivity in a rather highly developed brain. But whatever its cause, the ultimate destiny of this trait was momentous; for all human activity is based on the appreciation and use of symbols. Language, religion, mathematics, all learning, all science and superstition, even right and wrong, are products of symbolic expression rather than direct experience. Our commonest words, such as "house" and "red" and "walking," are symbols; the pyramids of Egypt and the mysterious circles of Stonehenge are symbols; so are dominions and empires and astronomical universes. We live in a mind-made world, where the things of prime importance are images or words that embody ideas and feelings and attitudes.

The animal mind is like a telephone exchange; it receives stimuli from outside through the sense organs and sends out appropriate responses through the nerves that govern muscles, glands, and other parts of the body. The organism is constantly interacting with its surroundings, receiving messages and acting on the new state of affairs that the messages signify.

But the human mind is not a simple transmitter like a telephone exchange. It is more like a great projector, for instead of merely mediating between an event in the outer world and a creature's responsive action, it transforms or, if you will, distorts the event into an image to be looked at, retained, and contemplated. For the images of things that we remember are not exact and faithful transcriptions even of our actual sense impressions. They are made as much by what we think as by what we see. It is a well-known fact that if you ask several people the size of the moon's disk as they look at it, their estimates will vary from the area of a dime to that of a barrel top. Like a magic lantern, the mind projects its ideas of things on the screen of what we call "memory"; but like all projections, these ideas are transformations of actual things. They are, in fact, *symbols* of reality, not pieces of it.

A symbol is not the same thing as a sign; that is a fact that psychologists and philosophers often overlook. All intelligent animals use signs; so do we. To them as well as to us sounds and smells and motions are signs of food, danger, the presence of other beings, or of rain or storm. Furthermore, some animals not only attend to signs but produce them for the benefit of others. Dogs bark at the door to be let in; rabbits thump to call each other; the cooing of doves and the growl of a wolf defending his kill are unequivocal signs of feelings and intentions to be reckoned with by other creatures.

5   We use signs just as animals do, though with considerably more elaboration. We stop at red lights and go on green; we answer calls and bells, watch the sky for coming storms, read trouble or promise or anger in each other's eyes. That is animal intelligence raised to the human level. Those of us who are dog lovers can probably all tell wonderful stories of how high our dogs have sometimes risen in the scale of clever sign interpretation and sign using.

A sign is anything that announces the existence or the imminence of some event, the presence of a thing or a person, or a change in a state of affairs. There are signs of the weather, signs of danger, signs of future good or evil, signs of what the past has been. In every case a sign is closely bound up with something to be noted or expected in experience. It is always a part of the situation to which it refers, though the reference may be remote in space and time. In so far as we are led to note or expect the signified event we are making correct use of a sign. This is the essence of rational behavior, which animals show in varying degrees. It is entirely realistic, being closely bound up with the actual objective course of history—learned by experience, and cashed in or voided by further experience.

If man had kept to the straight and narrow path of sign using, he would be like the other animals, though perhaps a little brighter. He would not talk, but grunt and gesticulate and point. He would make his wishes known, give warnings, perhaps develop a social system like that of bees and ants, with such a wonderful efficiency of communal enterprise that all men would have plenty to eat, warm apartments—all exactly alike and perfectly convenient—to live in, and everybody could and would sit in the sun or by the fire, as the climate demanded, not talking but just basking, with every want satisfied, most of his life. The young would romp and make love, the old would sleep, the middle-aged would do the routine work almost unconsciously and eat a great deal. But that would be the life of a social, superintelligent, purely sign-using animal.

To us who are human, it does not sound very glorious. We want to go places and do things, own all sorts of gadgets that we do not absolutely need, and when we sit down to take it easy we want to talk. Rights and property, social position, special talents and virtues, and above all our ideas, are what we live for. We have gone off on a tangent that takes us far away from the mere biological cycle that animal generations accomplish; and that is because we can use not only signs but symbols.

A symbol differs from a sign in that it does not announce the presence of the object, the being, condition, or whatnot, which is its meaning, but merely *brings this thing to mind*. It is not a mere "substitute sign" to which we react as though it were the object itself. The fact is that our reaction to hearing a person's name is quite different from our reaction to the person himself. There are certain rare cases where a symbol stands directly for its meaning: in religious experience, for instance, the Host is not only a symbol but a Presence. But symbols in the ordinary sense are not mystic. They are the same sort of thing that ordinary signs are; only they do not call our attention to something necessarily present or to be physically dealt with—they call up merely a conception of the thing they "mean."

10   The difference between a sign and a symbol is, in brief, that a sign causes us to think or act *in face of* the thing signified, whereas a symbol causes us to think *about* the thing symbolized. Therein lies the great importance of symbolism for human life, its power to make this life so different from any other animal biography that generations of men have found it incredible to suppose that they were of purely zoological origin. A sign is always embedded in reality, in a present that emerges from the actual past and stretches to the future; but a symbol may be divorced from reality altogether. It may refer to what is not the case, to a mere idea, a figment, a dream. It serves, therefore, to liberate thought from the immediate stimuli of a physically present world; and that liberation marks the essential difference between human and nonhuman mentality. Animals think, but they think *of* and *at* things; men think primarily *about* things. Words, pictures, and memory images are symbols that may be combined and varied in a thousand ways. The result is a symbolic structure whose meaning is a complex of all their respective meanings, and this kaleidoscope of *ideas* is the typical product of the human brain that we call the "stream of thought."

The process of transforming all direct experience into imagery or into that supreme mode of symbolic expression, language, has so completely taken possession of the human mind that it is not only a special talent but a dominant, organic need. All our sense impressions leave their traces in our memory not only as signs disposing our practical reactions in the future but also as symbols, images representing our *ideas* of things; and the tendency to manipulate ideas, to combine and abstract, mix and extend them by playing with symbols, is man's outstanding characteristic. It seems to be what his brain most naturally and spontaneously does. Therefore his primitive mental function is not judging reality, but *dreaming his desires.*

Dreaming is apparently a basic function of human brains, for it is free and unexhausting like our metabolism, heartbeat, and breath. It is easier to dream than not to dream, as it is easier to breathe than to refrain from breathing. The symbolic character of dreams is fairly well established. Symbol mongering, on this ineffectual, uncritical level, seems to be instinctive, the fulfillment of an elementary need rather than the purposeful exercise of a high and difficult talent.

The special power of man's mind rests on the evolution of this special activity, not on any transcendently high development of animal intelligence. We are not immeasurably higher than other animals; we are different. We have a biological need and with it a biological gift that they do not share.

Because man has not only the ability but the constant need of *conceiving* what has happened to him, what surrounds him, what is demanded of him—in short, of symbolizing nature, himself, and his hopes and fears—he has a constant and crying need of *expression.* What he cannot express, he cannot conceive; what he cannot conceive is chaos, and fills him with terror.

If we bear in mind this all-important craving   15 for expression we get a new picture of man's behavior; for from this trait spring his powers and his weaknesses. The process of symbolic transformation that all our experiences undergo is nothing more nor less than the process of *conception,* which underlies the human faculties of abstraction and imagination.

When we are faced with a strange or difficult situation, we cannot react directly, as other creatures do, with flight, aggression, or any such simple instinctive pattern. Our whole reaction depends on how we manage to conceive the situation—whether we cast it in a definite dramatic form, whether we see it as a disaster, a challenge, a fulfillment of doom, or a fiat of the Divine Will. In words or dreamlike images, in artistic or religious or even in cynical form, we must *construe* the events of life. There is great virtue in the figure of speech, "I can *make* nothing of it," to express a failure to understand something. Thought and memory are processes of *making* the thought content and the memory image; the pattern of our ideas is given by the symbols through which we express them. And in the course of manipulating those symbols we inevitably distort the original experience, as we abstract certain features of it, embroider and reinforce those features with other ideas, until the conception we project on the screen of memory is quite different from anything in our real history.

Conception is a necessary and elementary process; what we do with our conceptions is another story. That is the entire history of human culture—of intelligence and mortality, folly and superstition, ritual, language, and the arts—all the phenomena that set man apart from, and above, the rest of the animal kingdom. As the religious mind has to make all human history a drama of sin and salvation in order to define its own moral attitudes, so a scientist wrestles with the mere presentation of "the facts" before he can reason about them. The process of *envisaging* facts, values, hopes, and fears underlies our whole behavior pattern; and this process is reflected in the evolution of an extraordinary phenomenon found always, and only, in human societies—the phenomenon of language.

Language is the highest and most amazing achievement of the symbolistic human mind. The power it bestows is almost inestimable, for without it anything properly called "thought" is impossible. The birth of language is the dawn of humanity. The line between man and beast—between the highest ape and the lowest savage—is the language line. Whether the primitive Neanderthal man was anthropoid or human depends less on his cranial capacity, his upright posture, or even his use of tools and fire, than on one issue we shall probably never be able to settle—whether or not he spoke.

In all physical traits and practical responses, such as skills and visual judgments, we can find certain continuity between animal and human mentality. Sign using is an ever evolving, ever improving function throughout the whole animal kingdom, from the lowly worm that shrinks into his hole at the sound of an approaching foot, to the dog obeying his master's command, and even to the learned scientist who watches the movements of an index needle.

This continuity of the sign-using talent [20] has led psychologists to the belief that language is evolved from the vocal expressions, grunts and coos and cries, whereby animals vent their feelings or signal their fellows; that man has elaborated this sort of communication to the point where it makes a perfect exchange of ideas possible.

I do not believe that this doctrine of the origin of language is correct. The essence of language is symbolic, not signific; we use it first and most vitally to formulate and hold ideas in our own minds. Conception, not social control, is its first and foremost benefit.

Watch a young child that is just learning to speak play with a toy; he says the name of the object, e.g.: "Horsey! horsey! horsey!" over and over again, looks at the object, moves it, always saying the name to himself or to the world at large. It is quite a time before he talks to anyone in particular; he talks first of all to himself. This is his way of forming and fixing the *conception* of the object in his mind, and around this conception all his knowledge of it grows. *Names* are the essence of language; for the *name* is what abstracts the conception of the horse from the horse itself, and lets the mere idea recur at the speaking of the name. This permits the conception gathered from one horse experience to be exemplified again by another instance of a horse, so that the notion embodied in the name is a general notion.

To this end, the baby uses a word long before he *asks for* the object; when he wants his horsey he is likely to cry and fret, because he is reacting to an actual environment, not forming ideas. He uses the animal language of *signs* for his wants; talking is still a purely symbolic process—its practical value has not really impressed him yet.

Language need not be vocal; it may be purely visual, like written language, or even tactual, like the deaf-mute system of speech; but it *must be denotative*. The sounds, intended or unintended, whereby animals communicate do not constitute a language, because they are signs, not names. They never fall into an organic pattern, a meaningful syntax of even the most rudimentary sort, as all language seems to do with a sort of driving necessity. That is because signs refer to actual situations, in which things have obvious reactions to each other that require only to be noted; but symbols refer to ideas, which are not physically there for inspection, so their connections and features have to be represented. This gives all true language a natural tendency toward growth and development, which seems almost like a life of its own. Languages are not invented; they grow with our need for expression.

In contrast, animal "speech" never has a structure. It is merely an emotional response. Apes may greet their ration of yams with a shout of "Nga!" But they do not say "Nga" between meals. If they could *talk about* their yams instead of just saluting them they would be the most primitive men instead of the most anthropoid of beasts. They would have ideas, and tell each other things, true or false, rational or irrational; they would make plans and invent laws and sing their own praises, as men do.

READING AND THINKING

1. What does Langer consider as the supremely distinctive and important faculty of human thought? What do pyramids and mathematical equations and words, such as "house" and "red," all have in common?

2. What distinction does Langer make between a "symbol" and a "sign"? What do a dog's bark, a wolf's growl, a red stoplight, and a wind-driven cloudy sky have in common? How do these examples differ from those cited in Question 1?

3. What does Langer mean by saying that, unlike a sign, a symbol "does not announce the presence of the object, the being, condition, or whatnot, which is its meaning, but merely *brings this thing to mind*"? Why is symbolism so important for human life, according to Langer?

4. Why is the difference between the direct experience of an event and the abstract conception of it as an image or a concept so important to humans?

THINKING AND WRITING

1. To what extent do you agree with Langer's contention that "Language is the highest and most amazing achievement of the symbolistic human mind [. . .] for without it anything properly called 'thought' is impossible"? Explain.

2. To what extent do you agree with Langer's assertion that "the essence of language is symbolic, not signific; we use it first and most vitally to formulate and hold ideas in our own minds. Conception, not social control, is its first and foremost benefit"?

3. Langer mentions but does not discuss in detail other symbol systems besides language. Identify one other such symbolic system and explain in a paragraph or two how it works. (You may wish to consider, for example, mathematics, computers, instant text messaging, etc.)

BRANDED FOR LIFE: AN OCCASION FOR WRITING

Suzanne K. Langer argues that language is a symbolic system that allows people to conceptualize, to abstract, to think about thinking. In the following Occasion you will have an opportunity to explore how some companies, organizations, and countries use letters, logos, and flags to symbolize, represent, and "brand" themselves.

HEIDI CODY, *American Alphabet (2000)*

Kingdom of Italy flag

United Nations flag

Cyprus flag

PREPARING TO WRITE: OCCASIONS TO THINK ABOUT WHAT YOU SEE

1. Look at the individual letters in *American Alphabet*. How many products can you identify on the basis of one letter? (Each letter is taken from the logo or lettering associated with a product.)

2. Look carefully at each of the three flags pictured here. Describe each flag in detail.
   Which flag strikes you as most unusual? Why?

MOVING TOWARD ESSAY: OCCASIONS TO ANALYZE AND REFLECT

1. Choose three of the alphabet letters from *American Alphabet* that you linked with particular products and explain how the shape, color, size, and style of lettering "fits"
   the product that uses it.

2. For each of the flags, analyze what the various elements/components (and colors) of
   the flag might represent.

WRITING THOUGHTFULLY: OCCASIONS FOR IDEAS AND ESSAYS

1. Write an essay in which you consider the concept of branding. Identify and explain the aspects of identity a company or other organization needs to consider in an attempt to "brand" itself—that is, to convey an impression of itself to those outside the company or organization. How do you think Langer would have weighed in on the issue of branding?

2. Think of yourself as a "brand"—a unique individual with a particular skill set and array of interests and talents. How would you "brand" yourself, or identify yourself to others whom you wanted to serve or work for? Design a logo that conveys the branding impression of yourself you would like to suggest. Explain in words the significance of your logo and the importance of your "brand."

3. Write an essay about the significance of national or cultural monuments. How do these buildings or places act as logos or signs or symbols of the place? Or have the monuments defined the place itself? Provide at least two examples as evidence in your essay. Explore why such cultural and national monuments exist at all—why they were originally created and what purpose they continue to serve.

CREATING OCCASIONS

1. Find examples of what Langer would call signs—road signs are one prominent type. But think of others that you see everyday. Think of signs used in sports like baseball or soccer, for example. Then identify some examples of images that have come to symbolize or stand for something larger than themselves—the Parthenon, for example, or the *Mona Lisa,* or the bald eagle, and so on. Consider how signs and symbols differ. What makes a sign a sign and a symbol a symbol? Consider also different kinds of signs and different kinds of symbols. Try to create a taxonomy or set of categories for different kinds of signs and symbols. You might wish to think about natural symbols, such as the sun and moon, or light and darkness, along with conventional symbols, such as the Eiffel Tower or red, green, and yellow street lights.

2. Find examples of the ways companies and organizations use letters, logos, signs, and symbols to represent themselves. Consider how groups of similar or related companies or organizations find ways to represent their commonalities—for example, educational institutions or athletic leagues, such as the National Football League, the National Hockey League, the National Basketball Association, the Major League of American Baseball, the Olympic Games, and so on. Develop an occasion for writing based on the ways in which one such group identifies itself and the ways in which individual members within the larger group brand themselves.

CRITICAL AND CREATIVE THINKING

The term "critical thinking" is much bandied about. It is a term that is used and abused, one that is little defined, and one that means different things to different people. We all think we know what "thinking" is because we do it every day. Most people, when asked, would probably say that they are good thinkers; some would even describe themselves as critical thinkers.

But just what is critical thinking? Why does thinking critically matter? Why should we care about it, and why might we want to become better thinkers, both critical and creative, ourselves?

One way to begin thinking about these questions is to ask ourselves who we consider to be exemplars of critical/creative thinking. Many of us would begin our lists with great philosophers—Socrates, Plato, Aristotle, and Confucius, for example. Many of us would include famous artists—painters and sculptors, like Michelangelo and Rodin, Van Gogh and Picasso. We would, very likely, include inventors like Thomas Edison and Eli Whitney; political leaders, including Winston Churchill and Indira Gandhi; scientists, such as Albert Einstein and Marie Curie; and so on.

The key question remains: what makes such individuals good thinkers? What are the attributes or elements of critical/creative thinking? How are critical and creative thinking, however conceptualized, related? And how can we develop our own powers to become better critical and creative thinkers ourselves?

The essays in this cluster attend in various ways to these issues. Ursula K. Le Guin's "Where Do You Get Your Ideas From?" argues against the notion that ideas come magically to writers, who don't begin working until inspiration strikes. Edward de Bono, in "Lateral Thinking," explains what lateral thinking is, how it aids in generating ideas, and why it is a necessary complement to logical thinking. Finally, Matthew Goulish, in "Criticism," demonstrates critical and creative thinking by using metaphor to explain and analyze the analytical process of thinking critically.

Ursula K. Le Guin (b. 1929)

Ursula K. Le Guin was born in Berkeley, California, and educated at Radcliffe College and Columbia University. She is best known as a writer of fantasy and science fiction. Among her more than twenty novels are *The Earthsea Trilogy* (1968–1972), *The Left Hand of Darkness* (1969), and *The Other Wind* (2001). Le Guin has also published children's books, short stories, and collections of poems and essays.

WHERE DO YOU GET YOUR IDEAS FROM?

In this essay, Le Guin discusses the act of writing and the sources of her own creativity. In the process she offers advice about both reading and writing, as well as about creative thinking. The key point she makes is that there is no mystery and no magic about writing creatively and writing well. Using her own experience as evidence, Le Guin explains, argues, and demonstrates how the work of writing gets done. One of her nicer points concerns the importance of reading for writers. As she suggests, no writer who wishes to be taken seriously is not also a serious reader.

1   Whenever I talk with an audience after a reading or lecture, somebody asks me, "Where do you get your ideas from?" A fiction writer can avoid being asked that question only by practicing the dourest naturalism and forswearing all acts of the imagination. Science-fiction writers can't escape it, and develop habitual answers to it: "Schenectady," says Harlan Ellison. Vonda N. McIntyre takes this further, explaining that there is a mail order house for ideas in Schenectady, to which writers can subscribe for five or ten or (bargain rate) twenty-five ideas a month; then she hits herself on the head to signify remorse, and tries to answer the question seriously. Even in its most patronizing form—"Where do you get all those crazy ideas from?"—it is almost always asked seriously: the asker really wants to know.

The reason why it is unanswerable is, I think, that it involves at least two false notions, myths, about how fiction is written.

First myth: There is a secret to being a writer. If you can just learn the secret, you will instantly be a writer, and the secret might be where the ideas come from.

Second myth: Stories start from ideas; the origin of a story is an idea.

I will dispose of the first myth as quickly as   5
possible. The "secret" is skill. If you haven't learned how to do something, the people who have may seem to be magicians, possessors of mysterious secrets. In a fairly simple art, such as making pie crust, there are certain teachable "secrets" of method that lead almost infallibly to good results; but in any complex art, such as housekeeping, piano-playing, clothes-making, or story-writing, there are so many techniques, skills, choices of method, so many variables, so many "secrets," some teachable and some not, that you can learn them only by methodical, repeated, long-continued practice—in other words, by work.

Who can blame the secret-seekers for hoping to find a shortcut and avoid all the work?

Certainly the work of learning any art is hard enough that it is unwise (so long as you have any choice in the matter) to spend much time and energy on an art you don't have a decided talent for. Some of the secretiveness of many artists about their techniques, recipes, etc., may be taken as a warning to the unskilled: What works for me isn't going to work for you unless you've worked for it.

My talent and inclination for writing stories and keeping house were strong from the start, and my gift for and interest in music and sewing were weak; so that I doubt that I would ever have been a good seamstress or pianist, no matter how hard I worked. But nothing I know about how I learned to do the things I am good at doing leads me to believe that there are "secrets" to the piano or the sewing machine or any art I'm no good at. There is just the obstinate, continuous cultivation of a disposition, leading to skill in performance.

So much for secrets. How about ideas?

10 The more I think about the word "idea," the less idea I have what it means. Writers do say things like "That gives me an idea" or "I got the idea for that story when I had food poisoning in a motel in New Jersey." I think this is a kind of shorthand use of "idea" to stand for the complicated, obscure, un-understood process of the conception and formation of what is going to be a story when it gets written down. The process may not involve ideas in the sense of intelligible thoughts; it may well not even involve words. It may be a matter of mood, resonances, mental glimpses, voices, emotions, visions, dreams, anything. It is different in every writer, and in many of us it is different every time. It is extremely difficult to talk about, because we have very little terminology for such processes.

I would say that as a general rule, though an external event may trigger it, this inceptive state or story-beginning phase does not come from anywhere outside the mind that can be pointed to; it arises in the mind, from psychic contents that have become unavailable to the conscious mind, inner or outer experience that has been, in Gary Snyder's lovely phrase, composted. I don't believe that a writer "gets" (takes into the head) an "idea" (some sort of mental object) "from" somewhere, and then turns it into words and writes them on paper. At least in my experience, it doesn't work that way. The stuff has to be transformed into oneself, it has to be composted, before it can grow a story.

The rest of this paper will be an attempt to analyze what I feel I am actually working with when I write, and where the "idea" fits into the whole process.

There seem to be five principal elements to the process:

1. The patterns of the language—the sounds of words.
2. The patterns of syntax and grammar; the ways the words and sentences connect themselves together; the ways their connections interconnect to form the larger units (paragraphs, sections, chapters); hence, the movement of the work, its tempo, pace, gait, and shape in time.

   (Note: In poetry, especially lyric poetry, these first two kinds of patterning are salient, obvious elements of the beauty of the work—word sounds, rhymes, echoes, cadences, the "music" of poetry. In prose the sound patterns are far subtler and looser and must indeed avoid rhyme, chime, assonance, etc., and the patterns of sentencing, paragraphing, movement and shape in time, may be on such a large, slow scale as to escape conscious notice; the "music" of fiction, particularly the novel, is often not perceived as beautiful at all.)

3. The patterns of the images: what the words make us or let us see with the mind's eye or sense imaginatively.
4. The patterns of the ideas: what the words and the narration of events make us understand, or use our understanding upon.
5. The patterns of the feelings: what the words and the narration, by using all the above means, make us experience emotionally or spiritually, in areas of our being not directly accessible to or expressible in words.

All these kinds of patterning—sound, syntax, images, ideas, feelings—have to work together; and they all have to be there in some degree. The inception of the work, that mysterious stage, is perhaps their coming together: when in the author's mind a feeling begins to connect itself to an image that will express it, and that image leads to an idea, until now half-formed, that begins to find words for itself, and the words lead to other words that make new images, perhaps of people, characters of a story, who are doing things that express the underlying feelings and ideas that are now resonating with each other. . . .

15   If any of the processes get scanted badly or left out, in the conception stage, in the writing stage, or in the revising stage, the result will be a weak or failed story. Failure often allows us to analyze what success triumphantly hides from us. I do not recommend going through a story by Chekhov or Woolf trying to analyze out my five elements of the writing process; the point is that in any successful piece of fiction, they work in one insoluble unitary movement. But in certain familiar forms of feeble writing or failed writing, the absence of one element or another may be a guide to what went wrong.

For example: Having an interesting idea, working it up into a plot enacted by stock characters, and relying upon violence to replace feeling, may produce the trash-level mystery, thriller, or science-fiction story; but not a good mystery, thriller, or science-fiction story.

Contrariwise, strong feelings, even if strong characters enact them, aren't enough to carry a story if the ideas connected with those feelings haven't been thought through. If the mind isn't working along with the emotions, the emotions will slosh around in a bathtub of wish fulfillment (as in most mass-market romances) or anger (as in much of the "mainstream" genre) or hormones (as in porn).

Beginners' failures are often the result of trying to work with strong feelings and ideas without having found the images to embody them, or without even knowing how to find the words and string them together. Ignorance of English vocabulary and grammar is a considerable liability to a writer of English. The best cure for it is, I believe, reading. People who learned to talk at two or so and have been practicing talking ever since feel with some justification that they know their language; but what they know is their spoken language, and if they read little, or read schlock, and haven't written much, their writing is going to be pretty much what their talking was when they were two. It's going to require considerable practice. The attempt to play complicated music on an instrument which one hasn't even learned the fingering of is probably the commonest weakness of beginning writers.

A rarer kind of failure is the story in which the words go careering around bellowing and plunging and kicking up a lot of dust, and when the dust settles you find they never got out of the corral. They got nowhere, because they didn't know where they were going. Feeling, idea, image, just got dragged into the stampede, and no story happened. All the same, this kind of failure sometimes strikes me as promising, because it reveals a writer reveling in pure language—letting the words take over. You can't go on that way, but it's not a bad place to start from.

The novelist-poet Boris Pasternak said 20 that poetry makes itself from "the relationship between the sounds and the meanings of words." I think that prose makes itself the same way, if you will allow "sounds" to include syntax and the large motions, connections, and shapes of narrative. There is a relationship, a reciprocity, between the words and the images, ideas, and emotions evoked by those words: the stronger that relationship, the stronger the work. To believe that you can achieve meaning or feeling without coherent, integrated patterning of the sounds, the rhythms, the sentence structures, the images, is like believing you can go for a walk without bones.

Of the five kinds of patterning that I have invented or analyzed here, I think the central one, the one through which all the others connect, is the imagery. Verbal imagery (such as a simile or a description of a place or an event) is more physical, more bodily, than thinking or feeling, but less physical, more internal, than the actual sounds of the words. Imagery takes place in "the imagination," which I take to be the meeting place of the thinking mind with the sensing body. What is imagined isn't physically real, but it *feels as if it were:* the reader sees or hears or feels what goes on in the story, is drawn into it, exists in it, among its images, in the imagination (the reader's? the writer's?) while reading.

This illusion is a special gift of narrative, including the drama. Narration gives us entry to a shared world of imagination. The sounds and movement and connections of the words work to make the images vivid and authentic; the ideas and emotions are embodied in and grow out of those images of places, of people, of events, deeds, conversations, relationships; and the power and authenticity of the images may surpass that of most actual experience, since in the imagination we can share a capacity for experience and an understanding of truth far greater than our own. The great writers share their souls with us— "literally."

This brings me to the relationship of the writer to the reader: a matter I again find easiest to approach through explainable failure. The shared imaginative world of fiction cannot be taken for granted, even by a writer telling a story set right here and now in the suburbs among people supposed to be familiar to everybody. The fictional world has to be created by the author, whether by the slightest hints and suggestions, which will do for the suburbs, or by very careful guidance and telling detail, if the reader is being taken to the planet Gzorx. When the writer fails to imagine, to *image,* the world of the narrative, the work fails. The usual result is abstract, didactic fiction. Plots that make points. Charac-

ters who don't talk or act like people, and who are in fact not imaginary people at all but mere bits of the writer's ego got loose, glibly emitting messages. The intellect cannot do the work of the imagination; the emotions cannot do the work of the imagination; and neither of them can do anything much in fiction without the imagination.

Where the writer and the reader collaborate to make the work of fiction is perhaps, above all, in the imagination. In the joint creation of the fictive world.

Now, writers are egoists. All artists are. 25 They can't be altruists and get their work done. And writers love to whine about the Solitude of the Author's Life, and lock themselves into cork-lined rooms or droop around in bars in order to whine better. But although most writing is done in solitude, I believe that it is done, like all the arts, for an audience. That is to say, with an audience. All the arts are performance arts, only some of them are sneakier about it than others.

I beg you please to attend carefully now to what I am not saying. I am not saying that you should think about your audience when you write. I am not saying that the writing writer should have in mind, "Who will read this? Who will buy it? Who am I aiming this at?"—as if it were a gun. No.

While *planning* a work, the writer may and often must think about readers; particularly if it's something like a story for children, where you need to know whether your reader is likely to be a five-year-old or a ten-year-old. Considerations of who will or might read the piece are appropriate and sometimes actively useful in planning it, thinking about it, thinking it out, inviting images. But once you start writing, it is fatal to think about anything but the writing. True work is done for the sake of doing it. What is to be done with it afterwards is another matter, another job. A story rises from the springs of creation, from the pure will to be; it tells itself; it takes its own course, finds its own way, its own words; and the writer's job is to be its medium. What a teacher or editor or market or critic or Alice will think of it has to be as far from the writing writer's mind as what breakfast was last Tuesday. Farther. The breakfast might be useful to the story.

Once the story is written, however, the writer must forgo that divine privacy and accept the fact that the whole thing has been a performance, and it had better be a good one.

When I, the writer, reread my work and settle down to reconsider it, reshape it, revise it, then my consciousness of the reader, of collaborating with the reader, is appropriate and, I think, necessary. Indeed I may have to make an act of faith and declare that they will exist, those unknown, perhaps unborn people, my dear readers. The blind, beautiful arrogance of the creative moment must grow subtle, self-conscious, clear-sighted. It must ask questions, such as: Does this say what I thought it said? Does it say all I thought it did? It is at this stage that I, the writer, may have to question the nature of my relationship to my readers, as manifested in my work. Am I shoving them around, manipulating them, patronizing them, showing off to them? Am I punishing them? Am I using them as a dump site for my accumulated psychic toxins? Am I telling them what they better damn well believe or else? Am I running circles around them, and will they enjoy it? Am I scaring them, and did I intend to? Am I interesting them, and if not, hadn't I better see to it that I am? Am I amusing, teasing, alluring them? Flirting with them? Hypnotizing them? Am I giving to them, tempting them, inviting them, drawing them into the work *to work with me*—to be the one, the Reader, who completes my vision?

30   Because the writer cannot do it alone. The unread story is not a story; it is little black marks on wood pulp. The reader, reading it, makes it live: a live thing, a story.

A special note to the above: If the writer is a socially privileged person—particularly a White or a male or both—his imagination may have to make an intense and conscious effort to realize that people who don't share his privileged status may read his work and will not share with him many attitudes and opinions that he has been allowed to believe or to pretend are shared by "everybody." Since the belief in a privileged view of reality is no longer tenable outside privileged circles, and often not even within them, fiction written from such an assumption will make sense only to a decreasing, and increasingly reactionary, audience. Many women writing today, however, still choose the male viewpoint, finding it easier to do so than to write from the knowledge that feminine experience of reality is flatly denied by many potential readers, including the majority of critics and professors of literature, and may rouse defensive hostility and contempt. The choice, then, would seem to be between collusion and subversion; but there's no use pretending that you can get away without making the choice. Not to choose, these days, is a choice made. All fiction has ethical, political, and social weight, and sometimes the works that weigh the heaviest are those apparently fluffy or escapist fictions whose authors declare themselves "above politics," "just entertainers," and so on.

The writer writing, then, is trying to get all the patterns of sounds, syntax, imagery, ideas, emotions, working together in one process, in which the reader will be drawn to participate. This implies that writers do one hell of a lot of controlling. They control all their material as closely as they can, and in doing so they are trying to control the reader, too. They are trying to get the reader to go along helplessly, putty in their hands, seeing, hearing, feeling, believing the story, laughing at it, crying at it. They are trying to make innocent little children cry.

But though control is a risky business, it need not be conceived in confrontational terms as a battle with and a victory over the material or the reader. Again, I think it comes down to collaboration, or sharing the gift: the writer tries to get the reader working with the text in the effort to keep the whole story all going along in one piece in the right direction (which is my general notion of a good piece of fiction).

In this effort, writers need all the help they can get. Even under the most skilled control, the words will never fully embody the vision. Even with the most sympathetic reader, the truth will falter and grow partial. Writers have to get used to launching something beautiful and watching it crash and burn. They also have to learn when to let go control, when the work takes off on its own and flies, farther than they ever planned or imagined, to places they didn't know they knew. All makers must leave room for the acts of the spirit. But they have to work hard and carefully, and wait patiently, to deserve them.

READING AND THINKING

1. What myths about writing does Le Guin identify? How does she dispose of them?

2. How does Le Guin define "idea"? How does she answer the question about the origin of her own ideas?

3. What kinds of patterns does Le Guin identify as essential for her own creativity?

4. Why does Le Guin recommend that novice writers read? What kinds of books do you think she believes writers should read? Why?

THINKING AND WRITING

1. Explain how patterns are important to Le Guin as a writer and why she recommends that writers (and readers) pay attention to these patterns.

2. Explain Le Guin's view of the relationship between readers and writers. Consider what she says about how, when, and why a writer should think about her readers. How can you apply this to your own writing?

3. Identify and discuss three things you learned about the process of writing or thinking from reading Le Guin's essay.

4. Explain where your own ideas come from. What strategies do you use to generate ideas when you need them?

THE STRANGE AND THE FAMILIAR:
AN OCCASION FOR WRITING

In her essay about her own ideas and writing, Ursula K. Le Guin discusses the importance of imagination and the ordinariness of her own thinking and writing process. She attempts to demystify the interesting and intricate linkages between thinking and writing. In the following Occasion, you will have a chance to do some of your own thinking about imagining and writing.

MAX ERNST,
Bryce Canyon Translation

PREPARING TO WRITE: OCCASIONS TO THINK ABOUT WHAT YOU SEE

1. Describe what is strange about the Max Ernst painting; describe what is familiar about the picture of the stairs.

2. Provide a title for each picture. Explain in one sentence the meaning of your title.

3. Find a passage in Le Guin's essay that relates to either the Ernst painting or the photograph of the stairs. Explain the connection you see between her text and the image you chose.

MOVING TOWARD ESSAY: OCCASIONS TO ANALYZE AND REFLECT

1. Analyze the Ernst image. Consider color, line, volume—the size and shape of the image. Imagine the same image in two other colors. Imagine the same image in black and white. What differences in the effect of the image in another color and in black and white would you identify? Why?

2. Analyze in detail the photograph of the stairs. Explain the overall effect the image conveys. Consider the perspective from which the photograph has been taken. Imagine two different perspectives—one photograph of the scene taken from an angle above the stairs and another from a head-on perspective. How would the impression created by the image change with those shifts in perspective?

WRITING THOUGHTFULLY: OCCASIONS FOR IDEAS AND ESSAYS

1. Write an essay about where and how you get your own ideas. Refer back to Le Guin's essay during the course of your own to quote her in support of your own thinking or to take issue with something she says.

2. Write a response to Le Guin's argument about the importance of reading for writers. You may wish to agree or disagree with her argument, or you may wish to qualify it.

3. Write an interpretation of either the Ernst image or of the photograph of the stairs.

CREATING OCCASIONS

1. Among the many ideas about creativity advocated by writers and consultants is the notion that creative thinking occurs when we break away from habitual ways of thinking and doing things. Introducing change is one way to jolt people out of their expected and conventional ways of thinking. Create an occasion for writing in which you consider how some of the following spurs to creativity can help you generate ideas: (a) Break the rules. (b) Be illogical. (c) Be foolish. (d) Be impractical. (e) Make mistakes. Consider how this unconventional advice can help stimulate fresh thinking. Provide examples from your own life and thinking. And do some research on the Internet by checking into the creative ideas of Thomas Edison, Steve Jobs, Walt Disney, Benjamin Franklin, the Beatles, or some other individual or group you think of as creative.

Edward de Bono (b. 1933)

Edward de Bono is an internationally recognized expert in critical and creative thinking and the teaching of thinking as a skill. He derived the formal tools for lateral thinking, a term he coined, from an understanding of the human brain as a self-organizing system. He has published more than sixty books that have been translated into more than three dozen world languages. Among them are *New Think: The Use of Lateral Thinking in the Generation of New Ideas* (1968), *Lateral Thinking: Creativity Step by Step* (1973), *Six Thinking Hats* (1985), and *How to Have a Beautiful Mind* (2004). Edward de Bono holds a Doctor of Medicine from Malta; a Master of Arts and Doctor of Philosophy from Oxford, where he was a Rhodes Scholar; and a Doctor of Philosophy from Cambridge University. He has had faculty appointments at Oxford, Cambridge, London, and Harvard Universities.

ON LATERAL THINKING

The following piece is excerpted from his book *Lateral Thinking*. In it de Bono explains the differences between lateral and logical (or vertical) thinking, the need for lateral thinking, and its value and benefits. Basic strategies and techniques of lateral thinking are illustrated and exemplified.

1   Lateral thinking is closely related to insight, creativity and humour. All four processes have the same basis. But whereas insight, creativity and humour can only be prayed for, lateral thinking is a more deliberate process. It is as definite a way of using the mind as logical thinking—but a very different way.

Culture is concerned with establishing ideas. Education is concerned with communicating those established ideas. Both are concerned with improving ideas by bringing them up to date. The only available method for changing ideas is conflict which works in two ways. In the first way there is a head on confrontation between opposing ideas. One or other of the ideas achieves a practical dominance over the other idea which is suppressed but not changed. In the second way there is a conflict between new information and the old idea. As a result of this conflict the old idea is supposed to be changed. This is the method of science which is always seeking to generate new information to upset the old ideas and bring about new ones. It is more than the method of science—it is the method of human knowledge.

Education is based on the safe assumption that one only has to go on collecting more and more information for it to sort itself into useful ideas. We have developed tools for handling the information: mathematics for extending it, logical thinking for refining it.

The conflict method for changing ideas works well where the information can be evaluated in some objective manner. But the method does not work at all when the new information can only be evaluated through the old idea. Instead of being changed the old idea is strengthened and made ever more rigid.

The most effective way of changing ideas 5 is not from outside by conflict but from within by the insight rearrangement of available information. Insight is the only effective way of changing ideas in a myth situation—when information cannot be evaluated objectively. Even when information can be evaluated objectively, as in science, an insight rearrangement of information leads to huge leaps forward. Education is not only concerned with collecting information but also with the best ways of using information that has been collected.

When ideas lead information rather than lag behind progress is rapid. Yet we have developed no practical tools for handling insight. We can only go on collecting information and hope that at some stage it will come about. Lateral thinking is an insight tool.

Insight, creativity and humour are so elusive because the mind is so efficient. The mind functions to create patterns out of its surroundings. Once the patterns are formed it becomes possible to recognize them, to react to them, to use them. As the patterns are used they become ever more firmly established.

The pattern using system is a very efficient way of handling information. Once established the patterns form a sort of code. The advantage of a code system is that instead of having to collect all the information one collects just enough to identify the code pattern which is then called forth even as library books on a particular subject are called forth by a catalogue code number.

It is convenient to talk of the mind as if it were some information handling machine—perhaps like a computer. The mind is not a machine however, but a special environment which allows information to organize itself into patterns. This self-organizing, self-maximizing, memory system is very good at creating patterns and that is the effectiveness of mind.

10   But inseparable from the great usefulness of a patterning system are certain limitations. In such a system it is easy to combine patterns or to add to them but it is extremely difficult to restructure them for the patterns control attention. Insight and humour both involve the restructuring of patterns. Creativity also involves restructuring but with more emphasis on the escape from restricting patterns. Lateral thinking involves restructuring, escape and the provocation of new patterns.

Lateral thinking is closely related to creativity. But whereas creativity is too often only the description of a result lateral thinking is the description of a process. One can only admire a result but one can learn to use a process. There is about creativity a mystique of talent and intangibles. This may be justified in the art world where creativity involves aesthetic sensibility, emotional resonance and a gift for expression. But it is not justified outside that world. More and more creativity is coming to be valued as the essential ingredient in change and in progress. It is coming to be valued above knowledge and above technique since both these are becoming so accessible. In order to be able to use creativity one must rid it of this aura of mystique and regard it as a way of using the mind—a way of handling information. This is what lateral thinking is about.

Lateral thinking is concerned with the generation of new ideas. There is a curious notion that new ideas have to do with technical invention. This is a very minor aspect of the matter. New ideas are the stuff of change and progress in every field from science to art, from politics to personal happiness.

Lateral thinking is also concerned with breaking out of the concept prisons of old ideas. This leads to changes in attitude and approach; to looking in a different way at things which have always been looked at in the same way. Liberation from old ideas and the stimulation of new ones are twin aspects of lateral thinking.

Lateral thinking is quite distinct from vertical thinking which is the traditional type of thinking. In vertical thinking one moves forward by sequential steps each of which must be justified. The distinction between the two sorts of thinking is sharp. For instance in lateral thinking one uses information not for its own sake but for its effect. In lateral thinking one may have to be wrong at some stage in order to achieve a correct solution; in vertical thinking (logic or mathematics) this would be impossible. In lateral thinking one may deliberately seek out irrelevant information; in vertical thinking one selects out only what is relevant.

Lateral thinking is not a substitute for   15 vertical thinking. Both are required. They are complementary. Lateral thinking is generative. Vertical thinking is selective.

With vertical thinking one may reach a conclusion by a valid series of steps. Because of the soundness of the steps one is arrogantly certain of the correctness of the conclusion. But no matter how correct the path may be the starting point was a matter of perceptual choice which fashioned the basic concepts used. For instance perceptual choice tends to create sharp divisions and use extreme polarization. Vertical thinking would then work on the concepts produced in this manner. Lateral thinking is needed to handle the perceptual choice which is itself beyond the reach of vertical thinking. Lateral thinking would also temper the arrogance of any rigid conclusion no matter how soundly it appeared to have been worked out.

Lateral thinking enhances the effectiveness of vertical thinking. Vertical thinking develops the ideas generated by lateral thinking. You cannot dig a hole in a different place by digging the same hole deeper. Vertical thinking is used to dig the same hole deeper. Lateral thinking is used to dig a hole in a different place.

The exclusive emphasis on vertical thinking in the past makes it all the more necessary to teach lateral thinking. It is not just that vertical thinking alone is insufficient for progress but that by itself it can be dangerous.

Like logical thinking lateral thinking is a way of using the mind. It is a habit of mind and an attitude of mind. There are specific techniques that can be used just as there are specific techniques in logical thinking. There is some emphasis on techniques in this book not because they are an important part of lateral thinking but because they are practical. Goodwill and exhortation are not enough to develop skill in lateral thinking. One needs an actual setting in which to practise and some tangible techniques with which to practise. From an understanding of the techniques, and from fluency in their use, lateral thinking develops as an attitude of mind. One can also make practical use of the techniques.

Lateral thinking is not some magic new system. There have always been instances where people have used lateral thinking to produce some result. There have always been people who tended naturally toward lateral thinking. The purpose of this book is to show that lateral thinking is a very basic part of thinking and that one can develop some skill in it. Instead of just hoping for insight and creativity one can use lateral thinking in a deliberate and practical manner.

Difference between Lateral and Vertical Thinking

Since most people believe that traditional vertical thinking is the only possible form of effective thinking it is useful to indicate the nature of lateral thinking by showing how it differs from vertical thinking. Some of the most outstanding points of difference are indicated below. So used are we to the habits of vertical thinking that some of these points of difference may seem sacrilegious. It may also seem that in some cases there is contradiction for the sake of contradiction. And yet in the context of the behaviour of a self-maximizing memory system lateral thinking not only makes good sense but is also necessary.

Vertical thinking is selective, lateral thinking is generative

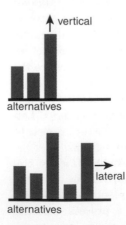

Rightness is what matters in vertical thinking. Richness is what matters in lateral thinking. Vertical thinking selects a pathway by excluding other pathways. Lateral thinking does not select but seeks to open up other pathways. With vertical thinking one selects the most promising approach to a problem, the best way of looking at a situation. With lateral thinking one generates as many alternative approaches as one can. With vertical thinking one may look for different approaches until one finds a promising one. With lateral thinking one goes on generating as many approaches as one can even *after* one has found a promising one. With vertical thinking one is trying to select the best approach but with lateral thinking one is generating different approaches for the sake of generating them.

Vertical thinking moves only if there is a direction in which to move, lateral thinking moves in order to generate a direction

25 With vertical thinking one moves in a clearly defined direction towards the solution of a problem. One uses some definite approach or some definite technique. With lateral thinking one moves for the sake of moving.

One does not have to be moving towards something, one may be moving away from something. It is the movement or change that matters. With lateral thinking one does not move in order to follow a direction but in order to generate one. With vertical thinking one designs an experiment to show some effect. With lateral thinking one designs an experiment in order to provide an opportunity to change one's ideas. With vertical thinking one must always be moving usefully in some direction. With lateral thinking one may play around without any purpose or direction. One may play around with experiments, with models, with notation, with ideas.

The movement and change of lateral thinking is not an end in itself but a way of bringing about repatterning. Once there is movement and change then the maximizing properties of the mind will see to it that something useful happens. The vertical thinker says: 'I know what I am looking for.' The lateral thinker says: 'I am looking but I won't know what I am looking for until I have found it.'

Vertical thinking is analytical, lateral thinking is provocative.

One may consider three different attitudes to the remark of a student who had come to the conclusion: 'Ulysses was a hypocrite.'
1. 'You are wrong, Ulysses was not a hypocrite.'
2. 'How very interesting, tell me how you reached that conclusion.'
3. 'Very well. What happens next. How are you going to go forward from that idea.'

In order to be able to use the provocative   30 qualities of lateral thinking one must also be able to follow up with the selective qualities of vertical thinking.

Vertical thinking is sequential, lateral thinking can make jumps

With vertical thinking one moves forward one step at a time. Each step arises directly from the preceding step to which it is firmly connected. Once one has reached a conclusion the soundness of that conclusion is proved by the soundness of the steps by which it has been reached.

With lateral thinking the steps do not have to be sequential. One may jump ahead to a new point and then fill in the gap afterwards. In the diagram opposite vertical 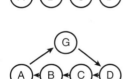 thinking proceeds steadily from A to B to C to D. With lateral thinking one may reach D via G and then having got there may work back to A.

When one jumps right to the solution then the soundness of that solution obviously cannot depend on the soundness of the path by which it was reached. Nevertheless the solution may still make sense in its own right without having to depend on the pathway by which it was reached. As with trial-and-error a successful trial is still successful even if there was no good reason for trying it. It may also happen that once one has reached a particular point it becomes possible to construct a sound logical pathway back to the starting point. Once such a pathway has been constructed then it cannot possibly matter from which end it was constructed—and yet it may only have been possible to construct it from the wrong end. It may be necessary to be on the top of a mountain in order to find the best way up.

35 *With vertical thinking one has to be correct at every step, with lateral thinking one does not have to be*

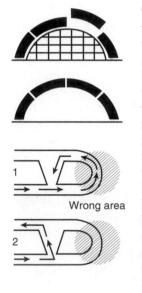

Wrong area

The very essence of vertical thinking is that one must be right at each step. This is absolutely fundamental to the nature of vertical thinking. Logical thinking and mathematics would not function at all without this necessity. In lateral thinking however one does not have to be right at each step provided the conclusion is right. It is like building a bridge. The parts do not have to be self-supporting at every stage but when the last part is fitted into place the bridge suddenly becomes self-supporting.

With vertical thinking one uses the negative in order to block off certain pathways. With lateral thinking there is no negative

There are times when it may be necessary to be wrong in order to be right at the end. This can happen when one is judged wrong according to the current frame of reference and

then is found to be right when the frame of reference itself gets changed. Even if the frame of reference is not changed it may still be useful to go through a wrong area in order to reach a position from which the right pathway can be seen. This is shown diagrammatically opposite. The final pathway cannot of course pass through the wrong area but having gone through this area one may more easily discover the correct pathway.

With vertical thinking one concentrates and excludes what is irrelevant, with lateral thinking one welcomes chance intrusions

Vertical thinking is selection by exclusion. 40 One works within a frame of reference and throws out what is not relevant. With lateral thinking one realizes that a pattern cannot be restructured from within itself but only as the result of some outside influence. So one welcomes outside influences for their provocative action. The more irrelevant such influences are the more chance there is of altering the established pattern. To look only for things that are relevant means perpetuating the current pattern.

With vertical thinking categories, classifications and labels are fixed, with lateral thinking they are not

With vertical thinking categories, classifications and labels are useful only if they are consistent, for vertical thinking depends on identifying something as a member of some class or excluding it from that class. If

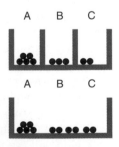

something is given a label or put into a class it is supposed to stay there. With lateral thinking labels may change as something is looked at now in one way and now in another.

Classifications and categories are not fixed pigeonholes to aid identification but signposts to help movement. With lateral thinking the labels are not permanently attached but are used for temporary convenience.

Vertical thinking depends heavily on the rigidity of definitions just as mathematics does on the unalterable meaning of a symbol once this has been allocated. Just as a sudden change of meaning is the basis of humour so an equal fluidity of meaning is useful for the stimulation of lateral thinking.

Vertical thinking follows the most likely paths, lateral thinking explores the least likely

45 Lateral thinking can be deliberately perverse. With lateral thinking one tries to look at the least obvious approaches rather than the most likely ones. It is the willingness to explore the least likely pathways that is important for often there can be no other reason for exploring such pathways. At the entrance to an unlikely pathway there is nothing to indicate that it is worth exploring and yet it may lead to something useful. With vertical thinking one moves ahead along the widest pathway which is pointing in the right direction.

Vertical thinking is a finite process, lateral thinking is a probabilistic one

With vertical thinking one expects to come up with an answer. If one uses a mathematical technique an answer is guaranteed. With lateral thinking there may not be any answer at all. Lateral thinking increases the chances for a restructuring of the patterns, for an insight solution. But this may not come about. Vertical thinking promises at least a minimum solution. Lateral thinking increases the chances of a maximum solution but makes no promises.

If there were some black balls in a bag and just one white ball the chances of picking out that white ball would be low. If you went on adding white balls to the bag your chances

of picking out a white ball would increase all the time. Yet at no time could you be absolutely certain of picking out a white ball. Lateral thinking increases the chances of bringing about insight restructuring and the better one is at lateral thinking the better are the chances. Lateral thinking is as definite a procedure as putting more white balls into the bag but the outcome is still probabilistic. Yet the pay off from a new idea or an insight restructuring of an old idea can be so huge that it is worth trying lateral thinking for there is nothing to be lost. Where vertical thinking has come up against a blank wall one would have to use lateral thinking even if the chances of success were very low.

Summary

The differences between lateral and vertical thinking are very fundamental. The processes are quite distinct. It is not a matter of one process being more effective than the other for both are necessary. It is a matter of realizing the differences in order to be able to use both effectively.

With vertical thinking one uses informa- 50 tion for its own sake in order to move forward to a solution.

With lateral thinking one uses information not for its own sake but provocatively in order to bring about repatterning.

Basic Nature of Lateral Thinking

In Chapter Two the nature of lateral thinking was indicated by contrasting it with vertical thinking. In this chapter the basic nature of lateral thinking is indicated in its own right.

Lateral thinking is concerned with changing patterns

By pattern is meant the arrangement of information on the memory surface that is mind. A pattern is a repeatable sequence of neural activity. There is no need to define it any more rigidly. In practice a pattern is any repeatable concept, idea, thought, image. A pattern may also refer to a repeatable sequence in time of such concepts or ideas. A pattern may also refer to an arrangement of other patterns which together make up an approach to a problem, a point of view, a way of looking at things. There is no limit to the size of a pattern. The only requirements are that a pattern should be repeatable, recognizable, usable.

55   Lateral thinking is concerned with changing patterns. Instead of taking a pattern and then developing it as is done in vertical thinking, lateral thinking tries to restructure the pattern by putting things together in a different way. Because the sequence of arrival of information in a self-maximizing system has so powerful an influence on the way it is arranged some sort of restructuring of patterns is necessary in order to make the best use of the information imprisoned within them.

In a self-maximizing system with a memory the arrangement of information must always be less than the best possible arrangement.

The rearrangement of information into another pattern is insight restructuring. The purpose of the rearrangement is to find a better and more effective pattern.

A particular way of looking at things may have developed gradually. An idea that was very useful at one time may no longer be so useful today and yet the current idea has developed directly from that old and outmoded idea. A pattern may develop in a particular way because it was derived from the combination of two other patterns but had all the information been available at one time the pattern would have been quite different. A pattern may persist because it is useful and adequate and yet a restructuring of the pattern could give rise to something very much better.

In the diagram opposite two pieces come together to give a pattern. This pattern then combines with another similar pattern in a straightforward manner. Without the addition of any new pieces the pattern can suddenly be restructured to give a much better pattern. Had all four pieces been presented at once this final pattern is the one that would have resulted but owing to the *sequence of arrival* of the pieces it was the other pattern that developed.

Lateral thinking is both an attitude and a 60 *method of using information*

The lateral thinking attitude regards any particular way of looking at things as useful but not unique or absolute. That is to say one acknowledges the usefulness of a pattern but instead of regarding it as inevitable one regards it as only one way of putting things together. This attitude challenges the assumption that what is a convenient pattern at the moment is the only possible pattern. This attitude tempers the arrogance of rigidity and dogma. The lateral thinking attitude involves firstly a refusal to accept rigid patterns and secondly an attempt to put things together in different ways. With lateral thinking one is always trying to generate alternatives, to restructure patterns. It is not a matter of declaring the current pattern wrong or inadequate.

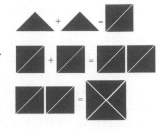

Lateral thinking is never a judgment.

One may be quite satisfied with the current pattern and yet try to generate alternative patterns. As far as lateral thinking is concerned the only thing that can be wrong with a pattern is the arrogant rigidity with which it is held.

In addition to being an attitude, lateral thinking is also a particular way of using information in order to bring about pattern restructuring. There are specific techniques which can be used deliberately and these will be discussed later. Underlying them all are certain general principles. In lateral thinking information is used not for its own sake but for its effect. This way of using information involves looking forward not backward: one is not interested in the reasons which lead up to and justify the use of a piece of information but in the effects that might follow such a use. In vertical thinking one assembles information into some structure, bridge or pathway. The information becomes part of the line of development. In lateral thinking information is used to alter the structure but not to become part of it.

65   One might use a pin to hold two pieces of paper together or one might use a pin to jab into someone and make him jump. Lateral thinking is not stabilizing but provocative. It has to be in order to bring about repatterning. Because it is not possible to restructure a pattern by following the line of development of that pattern lateral thinking may be deliberately perverse. For the same reason lateral thinking may use irrelevant information or it may involve suspending judgment and allowing an idea to develop instead of shutting it off by pronouncing it wrong.

Lateral thinking is directly related to the information handling behaviour of mind

The need for lateral thinking arises from the limitations of a self-maximizing memory system. Such a system functions to create patterns and then to perpetuate them. The system contains no adequate mechanism for changing patterns and bringing them up to date. Lateral thinking is an attempt to bring about this restructuring or insight function.

Not only does the need for lateral thinking arise from the information handling of mind but the effectiveness of lateral thinking also depends on this behaviour. Lateral thinking uses information provocatively. Lateral thinking breaks down old patterns in order to liberate information. Lateral thinking

stimulates new pattern formation by juxtaposing unlikely information. All these manoeuvres will only produce a useful effect in a self-maximizing memory system which snaps the information together again into a new pattern. Without this behaviour of the system lateral thinking would be purely disruptive and useless.

The Use of Lateral Thinking

Once one has acquired the lateral thinking attitude one does not need to be told on what occasions to use lateral thinking.

Throughout this book lateral thinking is   70 kept quite distinct from vertical thinking in order to avoid confusion. This is also done so that one can acquire some skill in lateral thinking without impairing one's skill in vertical thinking. When one is thoroughly familiar with lateral thinking one no longer has to keep it separate. One no longer has to be conscious whether one is using lateral or vertical thinking. The two blend together so that at one moment vertical thinking is being used and the next moment lateral thinking is being used. Nevertheless there are certain occasions which call for the deliberate use of lateral thinking.

New Ideas

Most of the time one is not conscious of the need for new ideas even though one is grateful enough when they turn up. One does not try and generate new ideas because one suspects that new ideas can not be generated by trying. Though new ideas are always useful there are times when one is very much aware of the need for a new idea. There are also jobs which demand a continual flow of new ideas (research, design, architecture, engineering, advertising etc).

The deliberate generation of new ideas is always difficult. Vertical thinking is not much help otherwise new ideas would be far easier to come by, indeed one would be able to programme a computer to churn them out. One can wait for chance or inspiration or one can pray for the gift of creativity. Lateral thinking is a rather more deliberate way of setting about it.

Many people suppose that new ideas mean new inventions in the form of mechanical contrivances. This is perhaps the most obvious form a new idea can take but new ideas include new ways of doing things, new ways of looking at things, new ways of organizing things, new ways of presenting things, new ideas about ideas. From advertising to engineering, from art to mathematics, from cooking to sport, new ideas are always in demand. This demand need not be just a general inclination but can be as specific as one likes. One can actually set out to generate new ideas.

Problem Solving

Even if one has no incentive to generate new ideas, problems are thrust upon one. There is little choice but to try and solve them. A problem does not have to be presented in a formal manner, nor is it a matter for pencil and paper working out. *A problem is simply the difference between what one has and what one wants*. It may be a matter of avoiding something, of getting something, of getting rid of something, of getting to know what one wants.

75   There are three types of problem:

- The first type of problem requires for its solution more information or better techniques for handling information
- The second type of problem requires no new information but a rearrangement of information already available: an insight restructuring.
- The third type of problem is the problem of no problem. One is blocked by the adequacy of the present arrangement from moving to a much better one. There is no point at which one can focus one's efforts to reach the better arrangement because one is not even aware that there is a better arrangement. The problem is to realize that there is a problem—to realize that things can be improved and to define this realization as a problem.

The first type of problem can be solved by vertical thinking. The second and third type of problem require lateral thinking for their solution.

Processing Perceptual Choice

Logical thinking and mathematics are both second stage information processing techniques. They can only be used at the end of the first stage. In this first stage information is parcelled up by perceptual choice into the packages that are so efficiently handled by the second stage techniques. It is perceptual choice which determines what goes into each package. *Perceptual choice is the natural patterning behaviour of mind.* Instead of accepting the packages provided by perceptual choice and going ahead with logical or mathematical processing one might want to process the packages themselves. To do this one would have to use lateral thinking.

Periodic Reassessment

Periodic reassessment means looking again at things which are taken for granted, things which seem beyond doubt. Periodic reassessment means challenging all assumptions. It is not a matter of reassessing something because there is a need to reassess it; there may be no need at all. It is a matter of reassessing something simply because it is there and has not been assessed for a long time. It is a deliberate *and quite unjustified* attempt to look at things in a new way.

Prevention of Sharp Divisions and Polarizations

Perhaps the most necessary use of lateral thinking is when it is not used deliberately at all but acts as an attitude. As an attitude lateral thinking should prevent the emergence of those problems which are only created by those sharp divisions and polarizations which the mind imposes on what it studies. While acknowledging the usefulness of the patterns created by mind one uses lateral thinking to counter arrogance and rigidity.

READING AND THINKING

1. What is lateral thinking and how does it differ from logical or vertical thinking?

2. Why is lateral thinking necessary, according to Edward de Bono? To what extent do you agree with his arguments? Explain.

3. Identify three strategies of lateral thinking and an example of each. How effective do you find these examples and strategies?

4. How effective are the diagrams that de Bono includes to illustrate his ideas about lateral thinking?

THINKING AND WRITING

1. Make a list or a chart of the differences between lateral and logical thinking. How would you characterize the relationship between these two kinds of thinking?

2. Discuss the reasons de Bono articulates for why people favor logical thinking over lateral thinking and why they are sometimes suspicious of lateral thinking.

3. Identify and explain the primary uses of lateral thinking. What, in short, is lateral thinking good for? To what extent do you agree with de Bono about the utility of lateral thinking?

4. Describe a situation at home, at school, or at work in which you think lateral thinking could be of use to you. Explain.

THINK HOW: AN OCCASION FOR WRITING

In his piece on lateral thinking, Edward de Bono defines and exemplifies a kind of thinking that he argues is a necessary analogue to logic. In the following Occasion for Writing, you will have a chance to exercise and develop your own capacity to think in different ways. You will be looking at a series of letters—o-u-l-i-p-o—arranged in a variety of uncommon ways, which push you to look closely and to think about how each of the designs creates a different effect.

PREPARING TO WRITE: OCCASIONS TO THINK ABOUT WHAT YOU SEE

1. Describe what you see in each of the accompanying images.

2. Which image do you find most interesting? Which least interesting? Why?

3. Explain how each of the images contains the letters for the word "Oulipo." Which image represents this rearrangement most creatively? What do you find so creative about that image?

ANDY
WARHOL,
*Fragile Handle with
Care (1962)*

© Andy Warhol Foundation/CORBIS

MOVING TOWARD ESSAY: OCCASIONS TO ANALYZE AND REFLECT

1. Provide two additional rearrangements of the letters for "OuLiPo." Explain the basis for your rearrangement of letters or your new image of "OuLiPo."

2. The OuLiPo, as known as Workshop for Potential Literature, is a group of writers and artists who mix creativity with rules. Founded in 1960 by François Le Lionnais and Raymond Queneau, these artists use mathematical algorithms, formulas, or arbitrary constraints to create their art. How do you think OuLiPo and Edward de Bono would react to Andy Warhol's silkscreen shown here? Why do you think each would respond that way? What do you make of Warhol's piece? What is the effect of the repetition?

3. Describe what each of the following have in common.

Black	Man	Knee	Wear	Stand
___	___	___	___	___
Coat	Board	Light	Long	I

Explain the "meaning" of these paired words. Explain how you came to understand the challenge. How would you describe the thinking you did for the previous exercises? Explain how the exercises illustrate what de Bono means by lateral thinking.

(Hint: Eggs = "eggs over easy")
        Easy

WRITING THOUGHTFULLY: OCCASIONS FOR IDEAS AND ESSAYS

1. Explain how OuLiPo illustrates what Edward de Bono says about lateral thinking. Are there any ways in which OuLiPo contradicts or at least complicates what de Bono says there? Explain.

2. Explain how the following poem by Emily Dickinson reverses relationships—turns things around from the normally expected.

> Much Madness is divinest Sense—
> To a discerning Eye—
> Much Sense—the starkest Madness—
> 'Tis the Majority
> In this, as All—prevail—
> Assent—and you are sane
> Demur—you're straightway dangerous—
> And handled with a Chain—

How does Dickinson's poem interact with what you know about OuLiPo and de Bono's essay? Write an essay in which you consider all the text and images presented to you about critical and creative thinking. What have you been made more aware of in your own thinking? Do you utilize lateral thinking? Do we all? Do you think artists use creative thought more than critical thought?

3. Write an essay in which you define and illustrate lateral thinking and why, according to de Bono, it is necessary. Agree or disagree with what he says about lateral thinking—or qualify it in some way in your essay. If you support what he says, exemplify one or another aspect of lateral thinking in your essay itself, or choose an example from your experience that illustrates some aspect of lateral thinking.

CREATING OCCASIONS

1. Consider where we learn how to think critically and creatively. What experiences have you had that stand out as moments of clarity about thinking? Think as far back as grade school. If you were an educator, how would you encourage your students to think in the ways de Bono sets forth? What have your teachers done for you in the past to broaden your ways of thinking? Do some outside research about how teachers go about teaching creative and critical thinking. What kind of lesson would you create if you were an educator?

Matthew Goulish

Matthew Goulish, who graduated from Kalamazoo College, is a performer and a writer. He has collaborated on the creation of seven performances with the group Goat Island. A founding member of that group, Goulish also teaches at the School of the Art Institute of Chicago. His book *39 Microlectures in Proximity of Performance* is a compendium of small stories, essays, musings on the nature of writing, reading, performing, criticizing, collaborating . . . "everything," the advertising copy says. Goulish pushes against and crosses all kinds of boundaries. He seems to delight in such trespassings, asking us to see and experience fluidity where we are inclined to certainty or fixity.

CRITICISM

Goulish's essay "Criticism" is an act of extended definition enriched through the auspices of three intriguing metaphors: glass, windows, and rain. You will look into the way these metaphors extend the meaning of criticism as Goulish understands it, how glass, windows, and rain add a tactile, visual, and auditory dimension to the act of defining.

2. Criticism

2.1 The example of glass
2.2 The example of windows
2.3 The example of rain

2.1 The Example of Glass

1 Each time we experience a work of performance, we start over almost from nothing. Despite recognizable trends, we face infinite differences—individual or cultural details, opposing traditions, idiosyncratic forms and settings, all kinds of aesthetic extremes.

Where do we begin, how do we begin, to engage a critical mind?

This question does not limit itself to performance. It relates to all art forms. In fact, it applies to all human endeavors and perceptions, from the humanities to the sciences to the practice of everyday life. Irreducible complexity seems to characterize the late twentieth century itself.

As a result, each field structures itself by propagating its own specialized vocabulary so that its practitioners might share some basic concepts. Yet each field necessarily interfaces and intersects any number of other fields, sometimes even spawning hybrid fields. Even the purist, in order to reach any depth of understanding on any given subject, must confront conflicting discourses. A serious student of performance thus might encounter the terminology of theatre, literature, music, psychology, architecture, anthropology, and biology, among other disciplines.

5 One might say that we face a landscape of vistas opening only onto more vistas. On the threshold of this landscape we might pause to recall the writer Isaac Babel who described his grandmother's sobering admonition when, as a child, he told her he wanted to grow up to be writer, and she replied, "To be a writer, you must know everything."

Faced with the impossibility of the task of knowing everything, we sometimes feel the desire to reject intellectuality altogether in favor of passionate expression. Such expression may take the form of the urgently political, the assertion of a solidified identity, or the following of individual inspiration wherever it may lead. And yet even these roads, if sincerely followed lead back to the discourse of complexity.

We have no choice but to accept this terrain, with the hope of discovering its exhilarating creative possibilities. Such acceptance requires a softening of the dividing lines between traditional differences: artist and critic, passion and intellect, accessible and hermetic, success and failure.

The softening of dividing lines does not however imply the disintegration of difference. Take for example the problem of glass. What is glass? Until recently, glass was considered a mostly transparent solid. It behaved like a solid; if struck, it shattered. But then, in the ancient cathedrals of Europe, it was observed that the tops of windows let in more light than the bottoms. A simple measurement proved that a window of once uniform thickness had grown thicker at the bottom and thinner at the top. Only one explanation exists for this phenomenon. Glass flows in the direction of the pull of gravity, exhibiting the behavior of a liquid. Thus one cannot conclusively define glass without the inclusion of time. At any given moment, glass is a solid, but over a period of one thousand years, it is a liquid. The problem of glass forces us to accept the inaccuracy of the traditional distinctions of solid or liquid. While the qualities of solidity and liquidity retain their difference, glass in fact is both, depending on the duration of observation, thus proving that these two states inextricably coexist.

We must ask not only how to engage the critical mind, but also why. Any act of critical thought finds its value through fulfilling one or both of two interrelated purposes:

1) to cause a change;
2) to understand how to understand.

10   As creative and critical thinkers, we may find it rewarding to attempt works of criticism, which, over time, reveal themselves as works of art, thus following the example of glass.

2.2 The Example of Windows

Most critics would not contest the idea that criticism exists to cause a change. But to cause a change in what?

Rarely has a work of critical thought successfully caused a change in the artwork it addresses. If a critic sees a film one day, and writes a review the next excoriating the weakness of the lead actor's performance, that same critic could return to the theater on the third day, and, despite the conviction of his argument, encounter the actor's performance unchanged. The same holds true for countless examples: condemned paintings, ridiculed concertos, buildings of reviled design, all survive, oblivious. Yet critics continue to offer their views. What are they trying to change?

Perhaps they attempt to change the future by effecting audience perceptions. If they can convince enough people, they believe they will achieve critical mass, causing an elimination of the despised, and an encouragement of the admired. But is this an accurate assessment of events? A critique may influence the thoughts of many audience members, but in the end they will make up their own minds. And those few powerful individuals who function in a producing capacity have the option of following the will of the majority, the minority, whatever sells the most tickets, or the advice of the critic. In this equation, the critic's power seems slight. If a critic believes in his or her own power to cause a change in audience thinking, that critic lives in delusion. Any changes of this kind are peripheral effects of a more central event.

Criticism only consistently changes the critic—whether further narrowing the views of the art policeman, or incrementally expanding the horizons of the open-minded thinker. If we accept this severe limitation—that in fact the first function of criticism is to cause a change in the critic—then we may begin to act accordingly.

We may agree on the premise that each 15 work of art is at least in part perfect, while each critic is at least in part imperfect. We may then look to each work of art not for its faults and shortcomings, but for its moments of exhilaration, in an effort to bring our own imperfections into sympathetic vibration with these moments, and thus effect a creative change in ourselves. These moments will of course be somewhat subjective, and if we don't see one immediately, we will out of respect look again, because each work contains at least one, even if it occurs by accident. We may look at the totality of the work in the light of this moment—whether it be a moment of humor or sadness, an overarching structural element, a mood, a personal association, a distraction, an honest error, anything at all that speaks to us. In this way we will treat the work of art, in the words of South African composer Kevin Volans, not as an object in this world but as a window into another world. If we can articulate one window's particular exhilaration, we may open a way to inspire a change in ourselves, so that we may value and work from these recognitions.

What I advocate is not so unusual, because if we have been trained at all, we have probably been trained to spot the negatives, and to try to improve the work by eliminating them. Given, as we have established, that criticism always changes the critic, this approach means trouble. Whatever we fix our attention on seems to multiply before our eyes. If we look for problems, we will find them everywhere. Out of concern for ourselves and our psychic well-being, let us look instead for the aspects of wonder.

If others choose to change their own thinking as an inspired result of our critical articulations, or if they decide to dismiss us as idealists, that is their business, and we will leave it to them.

But can we recognize windows to other worlds without some formal, historical, or theoretical understanding of what we are looking at? If we deepen our understanding, might we increase our chances of locating these moments? How do we deepen our understanding?

We may think of critical thought itself as a process through which we deepen our understanding. This brings us to the second proposed function of criticism, to understand how to understand.

2.3 The Example of Rain

How do we understand something? We understand something by approaching it. How do we approach something? We approach it from any direction. We approach it using our eyes, our ears, our noses, our intellects, our imaginations. We approach it with silence. We approach it with childhood. We use pain or embarrassment. We use history. We take a safe route or a dangerous one. We discover our approach and we follow it.

In his 1968 essay "Rain and the Rhinoceros," the American Trappist monk Thomas Merton attempted to understand Eugene Ionesco's play *Rhinoceros* by comparing it to the rain. Trappist monks take vows of silence. They almost never speak. In keeping with their silent life, they live in a silent place. The sound of the rain on the tin roof of his isolated monastic cabin in the Kentucky woods must have given Merton the only inspiration he needed to approach Ionesco's rhinoceros. And when the rain stopped, he heard the sound of the military airplane overhead, leaving the nearby base, on its way to Vietnam. When the airplane passed, he heard the hiss of his lantern burning. The rain provided the window to the rhinoceros, and the rhinoceros the window to the rain. The essay's analysis balances the work of art, with the work of nature, with the work of war. Merton understood critical thought as an act of contemplation, not an act of production. At the same time, he understood it to be, like all human activity, absurd. And thus he liberated his critical mind to follow whatever might cross its path. As the zen saying goes, no matter where we go, we are never far from enlightenment.

How then can we understand the rain? We can understand it as a scientist might, by studying climatic conditions and learning the Latin names for clouds. Or we may

20

understand the rain by looking at it and how it falls—straight down, or at an angle, or lashed by the wind. Is it a light drizzly rain, or is it only a mist and hardly rain at all? Is it the kind that falls when the sun is shining just down the street? We could understand rain by examining its effects—on plants, on people, on cities. Or we may catalogue the sounds it makes on glass, on water, on stone, on metal. We could even study the moods it evokes before it has started and after it has stopped. We could not look at it directly, but rather at what it reminds us of—childhood, violence, love, tears. Who could tell us that any of these approaches to rain is not valid? And yet we would be the first to admit their absurdity.

The modernists believed that each work of art somehow outstretches interpretation, that each criticism reduces the infinite possibilities of the work, that no critique is exhaustive. I agree to the extent that the opposite is also true—each artwork reduces its critique. Only when criticism can step a little away from the artwork that fostered it will it achieve a life of its own as a way of understanding. The way a critique discovers and explores becomes as personal, intellectual, and creative as any artwork; not to offer a comprehensive analysis of the rain, but instead one singular approach to it. Thus it might return us to our first purpose, that of causing a change. If our critique of rain allows us a different rain experience, then it has caused a change, if not in the rain, at least in the critic. And as our approaches to the rain increase, so too increases our understanding of the fleeting and fragile qualities of human life. And as our ways of understanding the rain multiply, so too will we begin to see the presence of rain in even the driest of subjects. We will realize at last that our objective all along was to understand that it is always raining.

READING AND THINKING

1. In the first section, "The Example of Glass," Goulish focuses on various kinds of performances, leading the reader to consider the intersections between performance and "theatre, literature, music, psychology, architecture, anthropology, and biology, among other disciplines." Goulish suggests that the critic's work comes down to a single phrase: the discourse of complexity. What does he mean by this term? What are its implications for the critic and for "readers" of performance or other art forms? How does the example of glass help clarify what Goulish means?

2. In the second section, "The Example of Windows," Goulish focuses on what we might call the function of criticism. He says that criticism should "cause a change." What does he mean by "cause a change"? Who or what undergoes change? What does the phrase "windows to other worlds" suggest about the function of criticism?

3. "The Example of Rain" has to do with how critics go about trying to understand whatever it is that they are criticizing. To understand what Goulish himself is doing with rain, we have to understand what he says the rain did for Thomas Merton. Study paragraph 21 to figure out what Goulish suggests that the rain did for Merton as he wrote about Eugene Ionesco's play *Rhinoceros*.

THINKING AND WRITING

1. Define glass in your own words, then expand your definition to include Goulish's suggestions about the nature of glass.

2. Define window in your own words. Provide at least two definitions of the word: 1) one that accounts for the physical object itself, and 2) one that points to its function. Modify one of those definitions to include Goulish's sense of the word in "windows to other worlds."

3. Define rain in your own words. Account for the way rain can come to the aid of a critic, according to Goulish. Does Goulish change your sense of the word itself? Does the word as he uses it change your understanding of criticism? Explain.

BOUNDARY CROSSING: AN OCCASION FOR WRITING

This Occasion will be as challenging as reading Goulish's playful piece "Criticism." You will consider two photographs that are so unusual they take on the characteristics of paintings. In the face of such polished realism, you may be compelled to blink, to rethink, or "doublethink." These two photographs call into question the definitions of things: *trees, houses, inside, outside, windows, glass,* and *perspective* itself.

Jerry N. Uelsmann

Jerry N. Uelsmann (b. 1934) is an influential experimental photographer, fascinated with the work of the darkroom, where he combines images, superimposes them, and recreates them to produce a series of interesting effects. Uelsmann seems to challenge the very meaning of limitation. The accompanying two photographs were taken from *Uelsmann: Process and Perception.* The epigraph suggests that the book appeals "to the spirit of play in all of us."

PREPARING TO WRITE: OCCASIONS TO THINK ABOUT WHAT YOU SEE

1. Imagine that the image on page 562 is called Tree-house. Write a simple, comprehensive definition for treehouse, and then explain how you would have to change that definition to accommodate Uelsmann's photograph.

2. Imagine that the name of the photograph on page 563 is Inside/Outside. Explain how you would have to modify your sense of the meaning of inside and outside after looking at this photograph. Is the table inside or outside? Where is the person—outside the door or inside the house? Explain.

MOVING TOWARD ESSAY: OCCASIONS TO ANALYZE AND REFLECT

1. Compare the windows in the two photographs. What do they tell you about windows that you are not likely to find in a standard dictionary definition?

2. If you begin at the bottom of Tree-house and move up, what does that movement suggest about the connection between roots and sky?

3. What do these two photographs suggest about the nature of glass and the nature of nature? What about the scale of nature and the scale of human-made objects? How does Uelsmann define that scale with his photography?

WRITING THOUGHTFULLY: OCCASIONS FOR IDEAS AND ESSAYS

1. Compare Goulish's metaphor and Uelsmann's Tree-house. Write a short paper explaining how the tranformation in that photograph might help a reader better understand Goulish's sense of complexity.

2. Consider the windows in the two photographs and use them to help an interested reader understand how an act of criticism can open windows onto a larger world. Pay attention to the light and the dark in both photographs, and to the fuzziness of the windows in Inside/Outside. How do those characteristics of particular windows suggest something more complicated about Goulish's metaphor?

3. Using Goulish's critical method outlined in "Criticism," write your own critical essay about the two Uelsmann photographs. You can find other photographs of his to include in the essay.

CREATING OCCASIONS

1. Select a movie that both fascinates and puzzles you. Write a short essay about that movie under the influence of Goulish. In the essay be sure that you clearly develop your own critical vocabulary. If you borrow terms from Goulish, be sure that you let your readers know the meaning of those terms.

2. Select one of the essays from Part 3 of this book that you have not read but that seems, on first glance, to interest you. Approach that essay under the influence of Goulish. Find within that essay one or two "moments of exhilaration" and explain to someone else why one of those moments is exhilarating and what the moment has to do with your understanding of the overall essay.

To what extent do you think greed is a
SERIOUS MORAL ISSUE
in contemporary society? Are there
ever occasions when greed would
be acceptable?

ETHICS AND VALUES

13

Ethics involves the "good"—what societies and civilizations throughout history have considered to be right as opposed to what is wrong. Every society has established norms of acceptable behavior, what is permissible and what is not, what is considered moral and what immoral. Typically right and wrong behavior is codified in law.

In addition to legal codes mandating acceptable or unacceptable behavior, religions establish standards regarding ethical and unethical behavior. One example of a set of religious laws is the Judaeo-Christian Decalogue, or the Ten Commandments, which forbid adultery and idolatry, along with murder, lying, theft, and more.

Values involve what we consider important, significant, and meaningful in our lives. We live by a series of values, including social values, such as justice and fairness for all; political values, such as every person being afforded the right to vote; religious values, such as the golden rule of treating others as you would have them treat you; and cultural values, such as respect for the elderly in East Asian cultures and the adulation of youth in some western countries.

Cultural values concern all manner of things, including attitudes toward food and fashion; work and play; modes of transportation and communication; ways of celebrating holidays and holy days; and approaches to ceremonies involving birth, death, marriage, and other significant demarcations in people's lives. Customs are inextricably linked with culture, and what appears normal and necessary to one social and cultural group may appear strange and needless to others. Cultural values are a general constant worldwide, but they vary specifically from one locality to another.

The essays in this chapter invite your consideration about what is and is not ethical, as well as why certain kinds of values are held in esteem and others not. Joan Didion invites your consideration of "self-respect," including what it means and why it matters. Henry David Thoreau explains why he retreats from society to find solitude and the purpose of his life. Sissela Bok raises serious questions about lying and truth-telling and examines the consequences of lying for liars and those to whom they lie. Langston Hughes tells a personal story about social pressure and religious faith—and its loss. Nancy Wilson Ross invites us into the world of Zen Buddhism as she provides an overview of its principles and practices. Finally, Martin Luther King, Jr., in his "Letter from Birmingham Jail," urges his original readers (and all later readers, including us) to think rightly about and act morally upon a critical issue of social justice—the equality of all people regardless of the color of their skin.

ETHICAL QUESTIONS AND ISSUES

Because ethics is a branch of philosophy rather than of science, it deals in approximations, in beliefs and assertions that are not measurable or quantifiable. Ethics is about "being good" and making moral choices, but what constitutes "good" and "moral" depends upon the belief system and the cultural values of various social, religious, and cultural groups.

Right and wrong, moreover, good and bad, are subject to historical influence, so that, for example, slavery was considered acceptable in eighteenth-century America, and throughout much of the nineteenth century. Similarly, it was considered perfectly acceptable to disallow women the right to vote in America until the early twentieth century.

Beyond such socially and culturally influenced beliefs and attitudes, additional factors complicate ethical considerations. In cultures that honor truth telling and discourage lying as a breach of ethics, what constitutes "lying" and what may justify it in some circumstances make all-or-nothing, black-or-white ethical judgments suspect. Should you lie, for example, to a man with a loaded gun looking for someone he intends to murder? Is lying permissible to dying patients in hospitals? Is it okay to lie when a friend asks how you are or how he or she looks?

We make ethical decisions every day, as we decide whether to shirk responsibility or shoulder it, to tell the truth or avoid telling it, to live and act according to ethical principles or not. In addition to the ethical decisions we make normally as part of our everyday living, we may also be confronted from time to time by larger, more complex issues, such as decisions about and arguments over abortion, euthanasia, capital punishment, and cloning.

The essays in this cluster touch on personal values as well as ethical questions. Joan Didion's essay "On Self-Respect" encourages us to think about the qualities that self-respect involves and how we measure up against them. Henry David Thoreau invites us to consider what is important to us, what matters most, what is truly essential in life, as he describes how he sought solitude and freedom at Walden Pond. Finally, Sissela Bok provides a number of provocative questions about the ethics of lying and telling the truth.

Joan Didion (b. 1934)

Joan Didion grew up in central California, where her family had lived for many generations. After graduating from the University of California at Berkeley in 1956, Didion joined the staff of *Vogue* magazine, where she worked until the publication of her first novel, *Run River,* in 1963. Other novels followed, including *Play It As It Lays* (1970), *A Book of Common Prayer* (1977), and *The Last Thing He Wanted* (1996), among others. However, it is her essays, especially those collected in *Slouching toward Bethlehem* (1968), *The White Album* (1979), and, most recently, *The Year of Magical Thinking* (2005), that best reveal her skillful blending of personal and impersonal reportorial analysis.

ON SELF-RESPECT

In "On Self-Respect," Didion defines the concept of self-respect, at first by saying what it is not, and then by identifying its essential characteristics. In Didion's view, self-respect is primarily about honesty and about character, about confronting one's limitations, facing up forthrightly to failings, and assessing one's essential self. Using herself as an example, Didion anatomizes self-respect and enriches our understanding of the concept.

1   Once, in a dry season, I wrote in large letters across two pages of a notebook that innocence ends when one is stripped of the delusion that one likes oneself. Although now, some years later, I marvel that a mind on the outs with itself should have nonetheless made painstaking record of its every tremor, I recall with embarrassing clarity the flavor of those particular ashes. It was a matter of misplaced self-respect.

I had not been elected to Phi Beta Kappa. This failure could scarcely have been more predictable or less ambiguous (I simply did not have the grades), but I was unnerved by it; I had somehow thought myself a kind of academic Raskolnikov, curiously exempt from the cause-effect relationships which hampered others. Although even the humorless nineteen-year-old that I was must have recognized that the situation lacked real tragic stature, the day that I did not make Phi Beta Kappa nonetheless marked the end of something, and innocence may well be the word for it. I lost the conviction that lights would always turn green for me, the pleasant certainty that those rather passive virtues which had won me approval as a child automatically guaranteed me not only Phi Beta Kappa keys but happiness, honor, and the love of a good man; lost a certain touching faith in the totem power of good manners, clean hair, and proven competence on the Stanford-Binet scale. To such doubtful amulets had my self-respect been pinned, and I faced myself that day with the nonplused apprehension of someone who has come across a vampire and has no crucifix at hand.

Although to be driven back upon oneself is an uneasy affair at best, rather like trying to cross a border with borrowed credentials, it seems to me now the one condition necessary to the beginnings of real self-respect. Most of our platitudes notwithstanding, self-deception remains the most difficult deception. The tricks that work on others count for nothing in that very well-lit back alley where one keeps assignations with oneself: no winning smiles will do here, no prettily drawn lists of good intentions. One shuffles flashily but in vain through one's marked cards—the kindness done for the wrong reason, the apparent triumph which involved no real effort, the seemingly heroic act into which one had been shamed. The dismal fact is that self-respect has nothing to do with the approval of others—who are, after all, deceived easily enough; has nothing to do with reputation, which, as Rhett Butler told Scarlett O'Hara, is something people with courage can do without.

To do without self-respect, on the other hand, is to be an unwilling audience of one to an interminable documentary that details one's failings, both real and imagined, with fresh footage spliced in for every screening. *There's the glass you broke in anger, there's the hurt on X's face: watch now, this next scene, the night Y came back from Houston, see how you muff this one.* To live without self-respect is to lie awake some night, beyond the reach of warm milk, phenobarbital, and the sleeping hand on the coverlet, counting up the sins of commission and omission, the trusts betrayed, the promises subtly broken, the gifts irrevocably wasted through sloth or cowardice or carelessness. However long we postpone it, we eventually lie down alone in that notoriously uncomfortable bed, the one we make ourselves. Whether or not we sleep in it depends, of course, on whether or not we respect ourselves.

5   To protest that some fairly improbable people, some people who *could not possibly respect themselves* seem to sleep easily enough is to miss the point entirely, as surely as those people miss it who think that self-respect has necessarily to do with not having safety pins in one's underwear. There is a common superstition that "self-respect" is a kind of charm against snakes, something that keeps those who have it locked in some unblighted Eden, out of strange beds, ambivalent conversations, and trouble in general. It does not at all. It has nothing to do with the face of things, but concerns instead a separate peace, a private reconciliation. Although the careless, suicidal Julian English in *Appointment in Samarra* and the careless, incurably dishonest Jordan Baker in *The Great Gatsby* seem equally improbable candidates for self-respect, Jordan Baker had it, Julian English did not. With that genius for accommodation more often seen in women than in men, Jordan took her own measure, made her own peace, avoided threats to that peace. "I hate careless people." she told Nick Carraway. "It takes two to make an accident."

Like Jordan Baker, people with self-respect have the courage of their mistakes. They know the price of things. If they choose to commit adultery, they do not then go running, in an access of bad conscience, to receive absolution from the wronged parties; nor do they complain unduly of the unfairness, the undeserved embarrassment, of being named co-respondent. In brief, people with self-respect exhibit a certain toughness, a kind of moral nerve; they display what was once called *character,* a quality which, although approved in the abstract, sometimes loses ground to other, more instantly negotiable virtues. The measure of its slipping prestige is that one tends to think of it only in connection with homely children and United States senators who have been defeated, preferably in the primary, for reelection. Nonetheless, character—the willingness to accept responsibility for one's own life—is the source from which self-respect springs.

Self-respect is something that our grandparents, whether or not they had it, knew all about. They had instilled in them, young, a certain discipline, the sense that one lives by doing things one does not particularly want to do, by putting fears and doubts to one side, by weighing immediate comforts against the possibility of larger, even intangible, comforts. It seemed to the nineteenth century admirable, but not remarkable, that Chinese Gordon put on a clean white suit and held Khartoum against the Mahdi; it did not seem unjust that the way to free land in California involved death and difficulty and dirt. In a diary kept during the winter of 1846, an emigrating twelve-year-old named Narcissa Cornwall noted coolly: "Father was busy reading and did not notice that the house was being filled with strange Indians until Mother spoke about it." Even lacking any clue as to what Mother said, one can scarcely fail to be impressed by the entire incident: the father reading, the Indians filing in, the mother choosing the words that would not alarm, the child duly recording the event and noting further that those particular Indians were not, "fortunately for us," hostile. Indians were simply part of the *donnée*.

In one guise or another, Indians always are. Again, it is a question of recognizing that anything worth having has its price. People who respect themselves are willing to accept the risk that the Indians will be hostile, that the venture will go bankrupt, that the liaison may not turn out to be one in which *every day is a holiday because you're married to me*. They are willing to invest something of themselves; they may not play at all, but when they do play, they know the odds.

That kind of self-respect is a discipline, a habit of mind that can never be faked but can be developed, trained, coaxed forth. It was once suggested to me that, as an antidote to crying, I put my head in a paper bag. As it happens, there is a sound physiological reason, something to do with oxygen, for doing exactly that, but the psychological effect alone is incalculable: it is difficult in the extreme to continue fancying oneself Cathy in *Wuthering Heights* with one's head in a Food Fair bag. There is a similar case for all the small disciplines, unimportant in themselves; imagine maintaining any kind of swoon, commiserative or carnal, in a cold shower.

10 But those small disciplines are valuable only insofar as they represent larger ones. To say that Waterloo was won on the playing fields of Eton is not to say that Napoleon might have been saved by a crash program in cricket; to give formal dinners in the rain forest would be pointless did not the candlelight flickering on the liana call forth deeper, stronger disciplines, values instilled long before. It is a kind of ritual, helping us to remember who and what we are. In order to remember it, one must have known it.

To have that sense of one's intrinsic worth which constitutes self-respect is potentially to have everything: the ability to discriminate, to love and to remain indifferent. To lack it is to be locked within oneself, paradoxically incapable of either love or indifference. If we do not respect ourselves, we are on the one hand forced to despise those who have so few resources as to consort with us, so little perception as to remain blind to our fatal weaknesses. On the other, we are peculiarly in thrall to everyone we see, curiously determined to live out—since our self-image is untenable—their false notions of us. We flatter ourselves by thinking this compulsion to please others an attractive trait: a gist for imaginative empathy, evidence of our willingness to give. *Of course* I will play Francesca to your Paolo, Helen Keller to anyone's Annie Sullivan: no expectation is too misplaced, no role too ludicrous. At the mercy of those we cannot but hold in contempt, we play roles doomed to failure before they are begun, each defeat generating fresh despair at the urgency of divining and meeting the next demand made upon us.

It is the phenomenon sometimes called "alienation from self." In its advanced stages, we no longer answer the telephone, because someone might want something; that we could say *no* without drowning in self-reproach is an idea alien to this game. Every encounter demands too much, tears the nerves, drains the will, and the specter of something as small as an unanswered letter arouses such disproportionate guilt that answering it becomes out of the question. To assign unanswered letters their proper weight, to free us from the expectations of others, to give us back to ourselves—there lies the great, the singular power of self-respect. Without it, one eventually discovers the final turn of the screw: one runs away to find oneself, and finds no one at home.

READING AND THINKING

1. Why do you think Didion begins by discussing what she calls "misplaced self-respect"? What does Didion say self-respect is not?

2. What are the characteristic qualities or features of self-respect? What other qualities, if any, would you add to those Didion includes?

3. To what extent do you agree with Didion that self-respect is "a kind of ritual"? What does she mean by that assertion?

4. How do you measure up against Didion's ideas about self-respect? Who do you know who measures up well? Explain.

THINKING AND WRITING

1. Write a letter to Didion responding to her discussion of self-respect.

2. Discuss the examples Didion uses to illustrate the aspects of her definition of self-respect.

3. Describe the differences among the following terms: "character," "courage," "discipline," and "private reconciliation."

4. Define "self-respect" from your own perspective, offering examples to suggest people you believe do and do not possess it.

RESPECT TO THE BODY: AN OCCASION FOR WRITING

In "On Self-Respect," Joan Didion identifies qualities of character that she considers essential for self-acceptance. One aspect of self-respect, self-acceptance begins with an acceptance of our own bodies—and especially how we treat our bodies. In this Occasion for Writing you will have the opportunity to consider the ways people perceive themselves, the respect one holds for oneself, and what that respect conveys to others.

©2005 China Photos/Getty Images

ZHANG JING,
Shanghai, China (2005)

PREPARING TO WRITE: OCCASIONS TO THINK ABOUT WHAT YOU SEE

1. Describe what you see in each of the accompanying images. What is your initial reaction to each image?

2. Why do you imagine these people treat their bodies in this way—and with what effects?

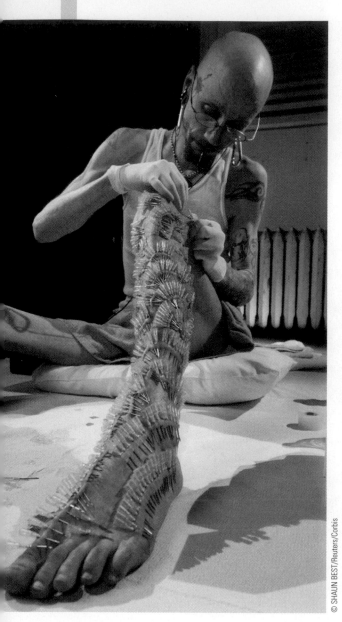

© SHAUN BEST/Reuters/Corbis

BRENT MOFFATT,
Winnipeg, Canada (2003)

MOVING TOWARD ESSAY: OCCASIONS TO ANALYZE AND REFLECT

1. Plastic surgery has become more popular in recent years. In the first image, the woman, Zhang Jing, was known as "Ugly Girl" during her childhood in China and left her school because of her classmates' jeers. The photograph in her lap is what she looked like before four plastic surgeries, which were offered to her free of charge when the media ran her "ugly duckling story," reporting that she had applied to more than one thousand jobs but had been denied because of her physical appearance. Knowing this, how has your opinion changed of this image? Do you think she needed the surgeries based on the photo of her former self? Explain how self-respect plays a role in Jing's story, as well as how gaining the respect of others is connected to acceptance in society.

2. In the second image, in 2003 Brent Moffatt went for the Guinness world record for most body piercings, inserting 900 needles in himself. What type of self-respect do you think Moffatt holds for himself—and how does competition enter into play here? Is there any art to his trade? Consider also the relationship to acupuncture techniques. Research Eastern thoughts on respecting the body and soul.

3. What is most striking about the image of the anorexic girl in the doctor's office? Analyze Evan Boland's poem "Anorexic." Explain what the poem reveals about anorexia and relate it to this image.

Wilkins Center for Eating Disorders,
Greenwich, Connecticut (1993)

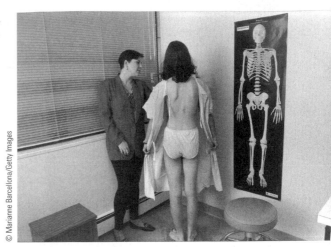

Eavan Boland (b. 1944)
Anorexic

Flesh is heretic.
My body is a witch.
I am burning it.

Yes I am torching
her curves and paps and wiles.
They scorch in my self denials.

How she meshed my head
in the half-truths
of her fevers

till I renounced
milk and honey
and the taste of lunch.

I vomited
her hungers.
Now the bitch is burning.

I am starved and curveless.
I am skin and bone.
She has learned her lesson.

Thin as a rib
I turn in sleep.
My dreams probe

a claustrophobia
a sensuous enclosure.
How warm it was and wide

once by a warm drum,
once by the song of his breath
and in his sleeping side.

Only a little more,
only a few more days
sinless, foodless,

I will slip
back into him again
as if I had never been away.

Caged so
I will grow
angular and holy

past pain,
keeping his heart
such company

as will make me forget
in a small space
the fall

into forked dark,
into python needs
heaving to hips and breasts
and lips and heat
and sweat and fat and greed.

4. Considering all the images, what do you think motivates their attention, even obsession, with their appearance? Is there a healthy and unhealthy self-respect? What other personal qualities do you think are important for maintaining one's self-respect and for developing personal character? Why are personal appearance and self-respect often paired together?

WRITING THOUGHTFULLY: OCCASIONS FOR IDEAS AND ESSAYS

1. Write an analysis and interpretation of Didion's "On Self-Respect." Explain what Didion means by the concept, and explain how she goes about defining the term. Use the images in this Occasion as evidence to support or refute Didion's main points.

2. Write an assessment of your own character. How do you personally relate to the images provided in this Occasion? Consider your own piercings, tattoos, or other ways you treat your body. How do these relate, if at all, to your strengths and weaknesses of character? Consider the extent to which you possess self-respect and the source of your self-respect.

3. In an essay consider the various ways that people treat their bodies. In the process, explain which of these bodily interventions you consider positive, which negative, and why. Consider the extent to which Didion's concept of self-respect plays a role in how people treat their bodies.

CREATING OCCASIONS

1. People usually get tattoos to pay tribute to something important in their lives. Interview your friends with tattoos. Ask them why they chose their particular tattoo and try to understand more fully what the tattoo says about their character and what they value. Then, create short, but powerful, character sketches based on the tattoos your friends have.

Henry David Thoreau

Henry David Thoreau (1817-1862) was born in Concord, Massachusetts, where he spent most of his life. A graduate of Harvard, he was an early follower of Ralph Waldo Emerson, whose ideas about nature Thoreau exemplified in his life and his writings. For two years Thoreau retreated from society to live alone at Walden Pond, where he built himself a simple wooden cabin, grew much of his own food, and spent his time reading, thinking, and observing nature. Out of this experience came his book *Walden,* a classic of American nonfiction. Aside from *Walden,* Thoreau is best known for his essay "On Civil Disobedience," which had a profound influence on subsequent political movements, particularly those of Mahatma Ghandi in India and the Reverend Dr. Martin Luther King, Jr., in the United States.

WHY I WENT TO THE WOODS

In this excerpt from the second chapter of Walden, Thoreau explains why he "went to the woods," that is, why he took a sabbatical from civilization to get away from it all for a while. Essentially, Thoreau wanted time to read, write, and think. He wanted to make time for nature. And he wanted to test himself, to see just how much he could simplify his life, to determine how much time he could save to do what he really wanted to do every minute of every day.

The appeal of Thoreau's central idea and fundamental ideal is especially acute for twenty-first-century America, where people strive to accomplish as much as they can as fast as they can so as to accumulate everything they think they need. Thoreau postulates an opposite alternative idea: to see how little we really require to live our lives, with an appreciation for what is truly essential and a respect for the rhythms of the natural world.

1 I went to the woods because I wished to live deliberately, to front only the essential facts of life, and see if I could not learn what it had to teach, and not, when I came to die, discover that I had not lived. I did not wish to live what was not life, living is so dear; nor did I wish to practice resignation, unless it was necessary. I wanted to live deep and suck out all the marrow of life to live so sturdily and Spartan-like as to put out all that was not life, to cut a broad swath and shave close, to drive life into a corner, and reduce it to its lowest terms, and, if it proved to be mean, why then to get the whole and genuine meanness of it, and publish its meanness to the world; or if it were sublime, to know it by experience, and be able to give a true account of it in my next excursion. For most men, it appears to me, are in a strange uncertainty about it, whether it is of the devil or of God, and have *somewhat hastily* concluded that it is the chief end of man here to "glorify God and enjoy him forever."

Still we live meanly, like ants; though the fable tells us that we were long ago changed into men; like pygmies we fight with cranes; it is error upon error, and clout upon clout, and our best virtue has for its occasion a superfluous and evitable wretchedness. Our life is frittered away by detail. An honest man has hardly need to count more than his ten fingers, or in extreme cases he may add his ten toes, and lump the rest. Simplicity, simplicity, simplicity! I say, let your affairs be as two or three, and not a hundred or a thousand; instead of a million count half a dozen, and keep your accounts on your thumb-nail. In the midst of this chopping sea of civilized life, such are the clouds and storms and quicksands and thousand-and-one items to be allowed for, that a man had to live, if he would not founder and go to the bottom and not make his port at all, by dead reckoning and he must be a great calculator indeed who succeeds. Simplify, simplify. Instead of three meals a day, if it be necessary to eat but one; instead of a hundred dishes, five; and reduce other things in proportion. Our life is like a German Confederacy, made up of petty states, with its boundary forever fluctuating, so that even a German cannot tell you how it is bounded at any moment. The nation itself, with all its so-called internal improvements, which by the way are all external and superficial, is just such an unwieldy and overgrown establishment, cluttered with furniture and tripped up by its own traps, ruined by luxury and heedless expense, by want of calculation and a worthy aim, as the million households in the lands; and the only cure for it, as for them, is in a rigid economy, a stern and more than Spartan simplicity of life and elevation of purpose. It lives too fast. Men think that it is essential that the *Nation* have commerce, and export ice, and talk through a telegraph, and ride thirty miles an hour, without a doubt, whether *they* do or not; but whether we should live like baboons or like men, is a little uncertain. If we do not get our sleepers, and forge rails, and devote days and nights to the work, but go to tinkering upon our *lives* to improve *them,* who will build railroads? And if railroads are not built, how shall we get to heaven in season? But if we stay at home and mind our business, who will want railroads? We do not ride on the railroad; it rides upon us. Did you ever think what those sleepers are that underlie the railroad? Each one is a man, an Irishman, or a Yankee man. The rails are laid on them, and they are covered with sand, and the cars run smoothly over them. They are sound sleepers, I assure you. And every few years a new lot is laid down and run over; so that, if some have the pleasure of riding on a rail, others have the misfortune to be ridden upon. And when they run over a man that is walking in his sleep, a supernumerary sleeper in the wrong position, and wake him up, they suddenly stop the cars, and make a

hue and cry about it, as if this were an exception. I am glad to know that it takes a gang of men for every five miles to keep the sleepers down and level in their beds as it is, for this is a sign that they may sometimes get up again.

Why should we live with such hurry and waste of life? We are determined to be starved before we are hungry. Men say that a stitch in time saves nine, and so they take a thousand stitches to-day to save nine to-morrow. As for *work,* we haven't any of any consequence. We have the Saint Vitus' dance, and cannot possibly keep our heads still. If I should only give a few pulls at the parish bell-rope, as for a fire, that is, without setting the bell, there is hardly a man on his farm in the outskirts of Concord, notwithstanding that press of engagements which was his excuse so many times this morning, nor a boy, nor a woman, I might almost say, but would forsake all and follow that sound, not mainly to save property from the flames, but if we will confess the truth, much more to see it burn, since burn it must, and we, be it known, did not set it on fire—or to see it put out, and have a hand in it, if that is done as handsomely; yes, even if it were the parish church itself. Hardly a man takes a half-hour's nap after dinner, but when he wakes he holds up his head and asks, "What's the news?" as if the rest of mankind had stood his sentinels. Some give directions to be waked every half-hour, doubtless for no other purpose; and then, to pay for it, they tell what they have dreamed. After a night's sleep the news is as indispensable as the breakfast. "Pray tell me anything new that has happened to a man anywhere on this globe"—and he reads it over his coffee and rolls, that a man has had his eyes gouged out this morning on the Wachito River; never dreaming the while that he lives in the dark unfathomed mammoth cave of this world, and has but the rudiment of an eye himself.

For my part, I could easily do without the post-office. I think that there are very few important communications made through it. To speak critically, I never received more than one or two letters in my life—I wrote this some years ago—that were worth the postage. The penny-post is, commonly, an institution through which you seriously offer a man that penny for his thoughts which is so often safely offered in jest. And I am sure that I never read any memorable news in a newspaper. If we read of one man robbed, or murdered, or killed by accident, or one house burned, or one vessel wrecked, or one steamboat blown up, or one cow run over on the Western Railroad, or one mad dog killed, or one lot of grasshoppers in the winter—we never need read of another. One is enough. If you are acquainted with the principle, what do you care for a myriad instances and applications? To a philosopher all *news,* as it is called, is gossip, and they who edit and read it are old women over their tea. Yet not a few are greedy after this gossip. There was such a rush, as I hear, the other day at one of the offices to learn the foreign news by the last arrival, that several large squares of plate glass belonging to the establishment were broken by the pressure—news which I seriously think a ready wit might write a twelvemonth, or twelve years, beforehand with sufficient accuracy. As for Spain, for instance, if you know how to throw in Don Carlos and the Infanta, and Don Pedro and Seville and Granada, from time to time in the right proportions—they may have changed the names a little since I saw the papers—and serve up a bullfight when other entertainments fail, it will be true to the letter, and give us as good an idea of the exact state or ruin of things in Spain as the most succinct and lucid reports under this head in the newspapers; and as for England, almost the last significant scrap of news from that quarter was the revolution of 1649; and if you have learned the history of her crops for an average year, you never need attend to that thing again, unless your speculations are of a merely pecuniary character. If one may judge who rarely looks into the newspapers, nothing new does ever

happen in foreign parts, a French revolution not excepted.

What news! how much more important to know what that is which was never old! "Kieou-he-yu (great dignitary of the state of Wei) sent a man to Khoung-tseu to know his news. Khoung-tseu caused the messenger to be seated near him, and questioned him in these terms: What is your master doing? The messenger answered with respect: My master desires to diminish the number of his faults, but he cannot come to the end of them. The messenger being gone, the philosopher remarked: What a worthy messenger! What a worthy messenger!" The preacher, instead of vexing the ears of drowsy farmers on their day of rest at the end of the week—for Sunday is the fit conclusion of an ill-spent week, and not the fresh and brave beginning of a new one—with this one other draggle-tail of a sermon, should shout with thundering voice, "Pause! Avast! Why so seeming fast, but deadly slow?"

Shams and delusions are esteemed for soundless truths, while reality is fabulous. If men would steadily observe realities only, and not allow themselves to be deluded, life, to compare it with such things as we know, would be like a fairy tale and the Arabian Nights' Entertainments. If we respected only what is inevitable and has a right to be, music and poetry would resound along the streets. When we are unhurried and wise, we perceive that only great and worthy things have any permanent and absolute existence, that petty fears and petty pleasures are but the shadow of the reality. This is always exhilarating and sublime. By closing the eyes and slumbering, and consenting to be deceived by shows, men establish and confirm their daily life of routine and habit everywhere, which still is built on purely illusory foundations. Children, who play life, discern its true law and relations more clearly than men, who fail to live it worthily, but who think that they are wiser by experience, that is, by failure. I have read in a Hindoo book, that "there was a king's son, who, being expelled in infancy from his native city, was brought up by a forester, and, growing up to maturity in that state, imagined himself to belong to the barbarous race with which he lived. One of his father's ministers having discovered him, revealed to him what he was, and the misconception of his character was removed, and he knew himself to be a prince. So soul," continues the Hindoo philosopher, "from the circumstances in which it is placed, mistakes its own character, until the truth is revealed to it by some holy teacher and then it knows itself to be *Brahme."* I perceive that we inhabitants of New England live this mean life that we do because our vision does not penetrate the surface of things. We think that that *is* which *appears* to be. If a man should walk through this town and see only the reality, where, think you, would the "Milldam" go to? If he should give us an account of the realities he beheld there, we should not recognize the place in his description. Look at the meetinghouse, or a courthouse, or a jail, or a shop, or a dwelling-house, and say what that thing really is before a true gaze, and they would all go to pieces in your account of them. Men esteem truth remote, in the outskirts of the system, behind the farthest star, before Adam and after the last man. In eternity there is indeed something true and sublime. But all these times and places and occasions are now and here. God himself culminates in the present moment, and will never be more divine in the lapse of all the ages. And we are enabled to apprehend at all what is sublime and noble only by the perpetual instilling and drenching of the reality that surrounds us. The universe constantly and obediently answers to our conceptions; whether we travel fast or slow, the track is laid for us. Let us spend our lives in conceiving then. The poet or the artist never yet had so fair and noble a design but some of his posterity at least could accomplish it.

Let us spend one day as deliberately as Nature, and not be thrown off the track by every nutshell and mosquito's wing that falls on the rails. Let us rise early and fast, or breakfast, gently, and without perturbation; let company come and let company go, let the bells ring and the children cry—determined to make a day of it. Why should we knock under and go with the stream? Let us not be upset and overwhelmed in that terrible rapid and whirlpool called a dinner, situated in the meridian shallows. Weather this danger and you are safe, for the rest of the way is downhill. With unrelaxed nerves, with morning vigor, sail by it, looking another way, tied to the mast like Ulysses. If the engine whistles, let it whistle till it is hoarse for its pains. If the bell rings, why should we run? We will consider what kind of music they are like. Let us settle ourselves and work and wedge our feet downward through the mud and slush of opinion, and prejudice, and tradition, and delusion, and appearance, that alluvion which covers the globe, through Paris and London, through New York and Boston and Concord, through Church and State, through poetry and philosophy and religion, till we come to a hard bottom and rocks in place, which we can call *reality,* and say, This is, and no mistake; and then begin, having a *point d'appui,* below freshet and frost and fire, a place where you might found a wall or a state, or set a lamppost safely, or perhaps a gauge, not a Nilometer, but a Realometer, that future ages might know how deep a freshet of shams and appearances had gathered from time to time. If you stand right fronting and face to face to a fact, you will see the sun glimmer on both its surfaces, as if it were a cimeter, and feel its sweet edge dividing you through the heart and marrow, and so you will happily conclude your mortal career. Be it life or death, we crave only reality. If we are really dying, let us hear the rattle in our throats and feel cold in the extremities; if we are alive, let us go about our business.

Time is but the stream I go afishing in. I drink at it; but while I drink I see the sandy bottom and detect how shallow it is. Its thin current slides away but eternity remains. I would drink deeper; fish in the sky, whose bottom is pebbly with stars. I cannot count one. I know not the first letter of the alphabet. I have always been regretting that I was not as wise as the day I was born. The intellect is a cleaver; it discerns and rifts its way into the secret of things. I do not wish to be any more busy with my hands than is necessary. My head is hands and feet. I feel all my best faculties concentrated in it. My instinct tells me that my head is an organ for burrowing, as some creatures use their snout and fore paws, and with it I would mine and burrow my way through these hills. I think that the richest vein is somewhere hereabouts; so by the divining-rod and thin rising vapors, I judge; and here I will begin to mine.

READING AND THINKING

1. What do you think was Thoreau's purpose in this essay? Where is this purpose clearest and most explicit? What is Thoreau's central idea, and where is it expressed most strongly?

2. Identify three key images and/or metaphors Thoreau uses to explain his thinking here. How do those metaphors work to convey his meaning and his feeling?

3. Analyze Thoreau's tone in this piece. How would you characterize his tone? Does the tone change at any point? If so, where and to what effect?

THINKING AND WRITING

1. Use the notes you made for the first three questions to write an analysis of "Why I Went to the Woods." Be sure to explain not only what Thoreau says in the piece, but his manner of saying it—his rhetorical strategies—as well.

2. Write a response to Thoreau's ideas about how we should live our lives. Consider the extent to which his ideas can be adapted to life in the twenty-first century.

3. Select a few advertisements that use nature as part of their selling strategy. Identify the selling pitch and the way nature is used to help make that pitch either directly or indirectly.

THE NATURE OF CONSCIOUSNESS: AN OCCASION FOR WRITING

The photographs in this Occasion will give you an opportunity to think and write about some of the ideas Henry David Thoreau has raised regarding human nature, wilderness, and the relationship between our needs and our wants.

Bruce Davidson

Bruce Davidson (b. 1933) was born in Oak Park, Illinois. He studied photography at Rochester Institute of Technology and also attended Yale University. After military service, he worked for a year as a freelance photographer for *Life* magazine. In 1958 he became a member of the international photography agency Magnum Photos. His widely acclaimed work can be seen in the permanent collections of the Metropolitan Museum and Museum of Modern Art in New York, and in Museum Ludwig in Köln, Germany.

The images included here appeared in Central Park, a series of photographs Davidson worked on for four years in the early 1990s. His photographs are known for their depth of feeling and poetic mood. Davidson has a fascination for people not in the limelight—celebrities are not his subjects.

© Bruce Davidson/Magnum Photos

Young Interracial Couple, New York City, (1992)

Central Park, New York City (1992)

© Bruce Davidson/Magnum Photos

PREPARING TO WRITE: OCCASIONS TO THINK ABOUT WHAT YOU SEE

1. Divide the photograph of the young interracial couple into two parts, one on each side of the couple. List what you see to the right and then list what you see to the left. What do the lists suggest about what might be Davidson's concerns and values? Explain.

2. Start at the intersection of the two faces. Follow the line along the curve of the girl's face and extend the line up toward the top of the photograph. What do you notice with this extension? Look for other lines and movement. How do those lines break up the photograph? What do you see in the various sections created by these lines?

3. Focus on the expression of each face. How would you describe each expression?

4. Divide the photograph of the boys in Central Park into two parts. List what you see to the right and then list what you see to the left. Attend to details, making the lists as complete as you can. What do the lists suggest about what might be Davidson's concerns and values? Explain.

5. How does the photograph divide itself into parts? Are the divisions predominantly vertical or horizontal? Identify and describe them.

6. What dominates this image? Is it one thing, or might there be tension between two forces? Explain.

7. Characterize the play between light and shadow throughout the entire photograph. Does it suggest meaning, or is it simply aesthetic?

MOVING TOWARD ESSAY: OCCASIONS TO ANALYZE AND REFLECT

1. Anna Norris, when she was studying photography at the Tisch School of the Arts in New York, wrote that "pictures are fashioned to serve a particular purpose." In the first image, do you imagine Davidson's purpose was to give us the couple or to give us something more? Explain.

2. Make a list of the qualities of life Thoreau seemed to be searching for in his explanation of why he went to the woods. What values animate Thoreau in his search? How do his values relate to Davidson's images?

3. Thoreau writes at one point that he went to the woods because he "wished to live deliberately." Consider the various meanings of the words "deliberate," "deliberately," and "deliberation." What denotations and connotations do these words share? What does it mean to live your life "deliberately"?

4. In the second image, the boys dominate the foreground of this photograph and tall buildings dominate the background. Between them, we see the reflective serenity of nature. What does Davidson's photograph suggest about the movement from foreground to background, or from background to foreground? More specifically, what do you think happens to the boys when they move back into the background, back into the city?

WRITING THOUGHTFULLY: OCCASIONS FOR IDEAS AND ESSAYS

1. People are central in these photographs. Use Davidson's photographs as a starting point and develop your own essay about the relationship between nature and civilization. Consider what Thoreau does value and how his views do or do not align with your own. Think too about this comment by the noted naturalist Terry Tempest Williams:

    > Everything feels upside-down these days, created for our entertainment. . . . The natural world is becoming invisible, appearing only as a backdrop for our own human dramas and catastrophes: hurricanes, tornadoes, earthquakes, and floods. Perhaps if we bring art to the discussion of the wild we can create a sensation where people will pay attention to the shock of what has always been here.
    >
    > *Away from the Flock* (1994)

    Develop your essay as a general response to Davidson, Thoreau, and Williams. Use those three artists to help you analyze the ever-changing relationship between nature and civilization and to formulate your own interpretation of this complex issue.

2. Write an essay about what path in life you are taking, regardless of how far along that path you have come. What values have animated your major decisions in your life so far? What constraints and realities have you bumped up against in trying to live out some of your ideals? Use the evidence presented in this Occasion along with whatever you feel is appropriate to support your views.

CREATING OCCASIONS

1. William Cronon, a professor of history, geography, and environmental studies at the University of Wisconsin, Madison, offers this rebuttal to those who make of wilderness an unspoiled paradise:

    > The removal of Indians to create an "uninhabited wilderness"—uninhabited as never before in the human history of the place—reminds us just how invented, just how constructed, the American wilderness really is. . . . there is nothing natural about the concept of wilderness. It is entirely a creation of the culture that holds it dear, a product of the very history it seeks to deny. Indeed, one of the most striking proofs of the cultural invention of wilderness is its thoroughgoing erasure of the history from which it sprang. In virtually all of its manifestations, wilderness represents a flight from history. . . . No matter what the angle from which we regard it, wilderness offers us the illusion that we can escape the cares and troubles of the world in which our past has ensnared us.

    Consider you own view of wilderness. Write it down. Then analyze how your views about wilderness have evolved. Figure out, to the extent possible, where those views originated, how they took shape. Write a short account of that analysis, including your interpretation of just what you believe about wilderness and why you hold your views.

Sissela Bok (b. 1934)

Sissela Bok, a writer and philosopher, was born in Sweden and educated in Switzerland and France before coming to the United States. She earned her Bachelor of Arts and Master of Arts degrees from George Washington University, concentrating in clinical psychology; she then went on to earn a Doctor of Philosophy at Harvard University in philosophy in 1970. She has been a Professor of Philosophy at Brandeis University and a Distinguished Fellow at the Harvard Center for Population and Development Studies. She has written and edited numerous books, including *Secrets: On the Ethics of Concealment and Revelation* (1983) and *Lying: Moral Choice in Public and Private Life* (1978). Bok is a former member of the Pulitzer Prize Board, and she has served on the editorial boards of a number of professional journals. Among her many prizes and awards are Barnard College Medal of Distinction and the Harvard Graduate School of Arts and Sciences Centennial Award.

ON LYING

In "On Lying," excerpted from her book *Lying: Moral Choice in Public and Private Life,* Sissela Bok raises questions about the morality and immorality of lying. Bok describes lying as a kind of "assault" on people, examining the consequences of lies on those lied to and on the liars themselves. Throughout the section of her book excerpted here Bok follows through analyzing the implications of her definition of a lie as "an intentionally deceptive message in the form of a 'statement.'" Her analysis employs a careful analysis of language, subtle use of distinctions, and a critical cast of mind.

1   Deceit and violence—these are the two forms of deliberate assault on human beings. Both can coerce people into acting against their will. Most harm that can befall victims through violence can come to them also through deceit. But deceit controls more subtly, for it works on belief as well as action. Even Othello, whom few would have dared to try to subdue by force, could be brought to destroy himself and Desdemona through falsehood.

The knowledge of this coercive element in deception, and of our vulnerability to it, underlies our sense of the *centrality* of truthfulness. Of course, deception—again like violence—can be used also in self-defense, even for sheer survival. Its use can also be quite trivial, as in white lies. Yet its potential for coercion and for destruction is such that society could scarcely function without some degree of truthfulness in speech and action.*

Imagine a society, no matter how ideal in other respects, where word and gesture could never be counted upon. Questions asked, answers given, information exchanged—all would be worthless. Were all statements randomly truthful or deceptive, action and choice would be undermined from the outset. There must be a minimal degree of trust in communication for language and action to be more than stabs in the dark. This is why some level of truthfulness has always been seen as essential to human society, no matter how deficient the observance of other moral principles. Even the devils themselves, as Samuel Johnson said, do not lie to one another, since the society of Hell could not subsist without truth any more than others.

A society, then, whose members were unable to distinguish truthful messages from deceptive ones, would collapse. But even before such a general collapse, individual choice and survival would be imperiled. The search for food and shelter could depend on no ex-

---

* But truthful statements, if they are not meant to deceive, can, of course, themselves be coercive and destructive; they can be used as weapons, to wound and do violence.

pectations from others. A warning that a well was poisoned or a plea for help in an accident would come to be ignored unless independent confirmation could be found.

5   All our choices depend on our estimates of what is the case; these estimates must in turn often rely on information from others. Lies distort this information and therefore our situation as we perceive it, as well as our choices. A lie, in Hartmann's words, "injures the deceived person in his life; it leads him astray."

To the extent that knowledge gives power, to that extent do lies affect the distribution of power; they add to that of the liar, and diminish that of the deceived, altering his choices at different levels. A lie, first, may misinform, so as to obscure some *objective,* something the deceived person wanted to do or obtain. It may make the objective seem unattainable or no longer desirable. It may even create a new one, as when Iago deceived Othello into wanting to kill Desdemona.

Lies may also eliminate or obscure relevant *alternatives,* as when a traveler is falsely told a bridge has collapsed. At times, lies foster the belief that there are more alternatives than is really the case; at other times, a lie may lead to the unnecessary loss of confidence in the best alternative. Similarly, the estimates of *costs and benefits* of any action can be endlessly varied through successful deception. The immense toll of life and human welfare from the United States' intervention in Vietnam came at least in part from the deception (mingled with self-deception) by those who channeled overly optimistic information to the decision-makers.

Finally, the degree of *uncertainty* in how we look at our choices can be manipulated through deception. Deception can make a situation falsely uncertain as well as falsely certain. It can affect the objectives seen, the alternatives believed possible, the estimates made of risks and benefits. Such a manipulation of the dimension of certainty is one of the

main ways to gain power over the choices of those deceived. And just as deception can initiate actions a person would otherwise never have chosen, so it can prevent action by obscuring the necessity for choice. This is the essence of camouflage and of the cover-up—the creation of apparent normality to avert suspicion.

Everyone depends on deception to get out of a scrape, to save face, to avoid hurting the feelings of others. Some use it much more consciously to manipulate and gain ascendancy. Yet all are intimately aware of the threat lies can pose, the suffering they can bring. This two-sided experience which we all share makes the singleness with which either side is advocated in action all the more puzzling. Why are such radically different evaluations given to the effects of deception, depending on whether the point of view is that of the liar or the one lied to?

The Perspective of the Deceived

Those who learn that they have been lied to in   10 an important matter—say, the identity of their parents, the affection of their spouse, or the integrity of their government—are resentful, disappointed, and suspicious. They feel wronged; they are wary of new overtures. And they look back on their past beliefs and actions in the new light of the discovered lies. They see that they were manipulated, that the deceit made them unable to make choices for themselves according to the most adequate information available, unable to act as they would have wanted to act had they known all along.

It is true, of course, that personal, informed choice is not the only kind available to them. They may *decide* to abandon choosing for themselves and let others decide for them—as guardians, financial advisors, or political representatives. They may even decide to abandon choice based upon information of a conventional nature altogether and trust instead to the stars or to throws of the dice or to soothsayers.

But such alternatives ought to be personally chosen and not surreptitiously imposed by lies or other forms of manipulation. Most of us would resist loss of control over which choices we want to delegate to others and which ones we want to make ourselves, aided by the best information we can obtain. We resist because experience has taught us the consequences when others choose to deceive us, even "for our own good." Of course, we know that many lies are trivial. But since we, when lied to, have no way to judge which lies are the trivial ones, and since we have no confidence that liars will restrict themselves to just such trivial lies, the perspective of the deceived leads us to be wary of *all* deception.

Nor is this perspective restricted to those who are actually deceived in any given situation. Though only a single person may be deceived, many others may be harmed as a result. If a mayor is deceived about the need for new taxes, the entire city will bear the consequences. Accordingly, the perspective of the deceived is shared by all those who feel the consequences of a lie, whether or not they are themselves lied to. When, for instance, the American public and world opinion were falsely led to believe that bombing in Cambodia had not begun, the Cambodians themselves bore the heaviest consequences, though they can hardly be said to have been deceived about the bombing itself.

An interesting parallel between skepticism and determinism exists here. Just as skepticism denies the possibility of *knowledge,* so determinism denies the possibility of *freedom.* Yet both knowledge and freedom to act on it are required for reasonable choice. Such choice would be denied to someone genuinely convinced—to the very core of his being—of both skepticism and determinism. He would be cast about like a dry leaf in the wind. Few go so far. But more may adopt such views selectively, as when they need convenient excuses for lying. Lies, they may then claim, do not add to or subtract from the general misinformation or "unfreedom" of those lied to. Yet were they to adopt the perspective of the deceived, such excuses for lying to them would seem hollow indeed. Both skepticism and determinism have to be bracketed—set aside—if moral choice is to retain the significance for liars that we, as deceived, know it has in our lives.

Deception, then, can be coercive. When it succeeds, it can give power to the deceiver—power that all who suffer the consequences of lies would not wish to abdicate. From this perspective, it is clearly unreasonable to assert that people should be able to lie with impunity whenever they want to do so. It would be unreasonable, as well, to assert such a right even in the more restricted circumstances where the liars claim a good reason for lying. This is especially true because lying so often accompanies every *other* form of wrongdoing, from murder and bribery to tax fraud and theft. In refusing to condone such a right to decide when to lie and when not to, we are therefore trying to protect ourselves against lies which help to execute or cover up all other wrongful acts.

For this reason, the perspective of the deceived supports the statement by Aristotle:

> Falsehood is in itself mean and culpable, and truth noble and full of praise.

There is an initial imbalance in the evaluation of truth-telling and lying. Lying requires a *reason,* while truth-telling does not. It must be excused; reasons must be produced, in any one case, to show why a particular lie is not "mean and culpable."

The Perspective of the Liar

Those who adopt the perspective of would-be liars, on the other hand, have different concerns. For them, the choice is often a difficult one. They may believe, with Machiavelli, that "great things" have been done by those who have "little regard for good faith." They may trust that they can make wise use of the power that lies bring. And they may have confidence in their own ability to distinguish the times when good reasons support their decision to lie.

Liars share with those they deceive the desire not to *be* deceived. As a result, their choice to lie is one which they would like to reserve for themselves while insisting that others be honest. They would prefer, in other words, a "free-rider" status, giving them the benefits of lying without the risks of being lied to. Some think of this free-rider status as for them alone. Others extend it to their friends, social group, or profession. This category of persons can be narrow or broad; but it does require as a necessary backdrop the ordinary assumptions about the honesty of most persons. The free rider trades upon being an exception, and could not exist in a world where everybody chose to exercise the same prerogatives.

20   At times, liars operate as if they believed that such a free-rider status is theirs and that it excuses them. At other times, on the contrary, it is the very fact that others *do* lie that excuses their deceptive stance in their own eyes. It is crucial to see the distinction between the free-loading liar and the liar whose deception is a strategy for survival in a corrupt society.*

All want to avoid being deceived by *others* as much as possible. But many would like to be able to weigh the advantages and disadvantages in a more nuanced way whenever they are themselves in the position of choosing whether or not to deceive. They may invoke special reasons to lie—such as the need to protect confidentiality or to spare someone's feelings. They are then much more willing, in particular, to exonerate a well-intentioned lie on their own part; dupes tend to be less sanguine about the good intentions of those who deceive them.

But in this benevolent self-evaluation by the liar of the lies he might tell, certain kinds of disadvantage and harm are almost always overlooked. Liars usually weigh only the immediate harm to others from the lie against the benefits they want to achieve. The flaw in such an outlook is that it ignores or underestimates two additional kinds of harm—the harm that lying does to the liars themselves and the harm done to the general level of trust and social cooperation. Both are cumulative; both are hard to reverse.

How is the liar affected by his own lies? The very fact that he *knows* he has lied, first of all, affects him. He may regard the lie as an inroad on his integrity; he certainly looks at those he has lied to with a new caution. And if they find out that he has lied, he knows that his credibility and the respect for his word have been damaged. When Adlai Stevenson had to go before the United Nations in 1961 to tell falsehoods about the United States' role in the Bay of Pigs invasion, he changed the course of his life. He may not have known beforehand that the message he was asked to convey was untrue; but merely to carry the burden of being the means of such deceit must have been difficult. To lose the confidence of his peers in such a public way was harder still.

Granted that a public lie on an important matter, once revealed, hurts the speaker, must we therefore conclude that *every* lie has this effect? What of those who tell a few white lies once in a while? Does lying hurt them in the same way? It is hard to defend such a notion. No one trivial lie undermines the liar's integrity. But the problem for liars is that they tend to see *most* of their lies in this benevolent light and thus vastly underestimate the risks they run. While no one lie always carries harm for the liar, then, there is *risk* of such harm in most.

These risks are increased by the fact that 25 so few lies are solitary ones. It is easy, a wit observed, to tell a lie, but hard to tell only one.

* While different, the two are closely linked. If enough persons adopt the free-rider strategy for lying, the time will come when all will feel pressed to lie to survive.

The first lie "must be thatched with another or it will rain through." More and more lies may come to be needed; the liar always has more mending to do. And the strains on him become greater each time—many have noted that it takes an excellent memory to keep one's untruths in good repair and disentangled. The sheer energy the liar has to devote to shoring them up is energy that honest people can dispose of freely.

After the first lies, moreover, others can come more easily. Psychological barriers wear down; lies seem more necessary, less reprehensible; the ability to make moral distinctions can coarsen; the liar's perception of his chances of being caught may warp. These changes can affect his behavior in subtle ways; even if he is not found out he will then be less trusted than those of unquestioned honesty. And it is inevitable that more frequent lies *do* increase the chance that some will be discovered. At that time, even if the liar has no personal sense of loss of integrity* from his deceitful practices, he will surely regret the damage to his credibility which their discovery brings about. Paradoxically, once his word is no longer trusted, he will be left with greatly *decreased* power—even though a lie often does bring at least a short-term gain in power over those deceived.

Even if the liar cares little about the risks to others from his deception, therefore, all these risks to himself argue in favor of at least weighing any decision to lie quite seriously. Yet such risks rarely enter his calculations. Bias skews all judgment, but never

*The word "integrity" comes from the same roots which have formed "intact" and "untouched." It is used especially often in relation to truthfulness and fair dealing and reflects, I believe, the view that by lying one hurts oneself. The notion of the self-destructive aspects of doing wrong is part of many traditions. See, for example, the *Book of Mencius:* "Every man has within himself these four beginnings [of humanity, righteousness, decorum, wisdom.] The man who considers himself incapable of exercising them is destroying himself." See Merle Severy, ed., *Great Religions of the World* (Washington, D.C.: National Geographic Society, 1971), p. 167; and W.A.C.H. Dobson trans., *Mencius* (Toronto: University of Toronto Press, 1963), p. 132.

more so than in the search for good reasons to deceive. Not only does it combine with ignorance and uncertainty so that liars are apt to overestimate their own good will, high motives, and chances to escape detection; it leads also to overconfidence in their own imperviousness to the personal entanglements, worries, and loss of integrity which might so easily beset them.

The liar's self-bestowed free-rider status, then, can be as corrupting as all other unchecked exercises of power. There are, in fact, very few "free rides" to be had through lying. I hope to examine, in this book, those exceptional circumstances where harm to self and others from lying is less likely, and procedures which can isolate and contain them. But the chance of harm to liars can rarely be ruled out altogether.

Bias causes liars often to ignore the second type of harm as well. For even if they make the effort to estimate the consequences to *individuals*—themselves and others—of their lies, they often fail to consider the many ways in which deception can spread and give rise to practices very damaging to human communities. These practices clearly do not affect only isolated individuals. The veneer of social trust is often thin. As lies spread—by imitation, or in retaliation, or to forestall suspected deception—trust is damaged. Yet trust is a social good to be protected just as much as the air we breathe or the water we drink. When it is damaged, the community as a whole suffers; and when it is destroyed, societies falter and collapse.

We live at a time when the harm done to 30 trust can be seen first-hand. Confidence in public officials and in professionals has been seriously eroded. This, in turn, is a most natural response to the uncovering of practices of deceit for high-sounding aims such as "national security" or the "adversary system of justice." It will take time to rebuild confidence in government pronouncements that the CIA did not participate in a Latin American coup, or that new figures show an economic upturn around the corner. The practices engendering such distrust were entered upon, not just by the officials now so familiar to us, but by countless others, high and low, in the government and outside it, each time for a reason that seemed overriding.

Take the example of a government official hoping to see Congress enact a crucial piece of antipoverty legislation. Should he lie to a Congressman he believes unable to understand the importance and urgency of the legislation, yet powerful enough to block its passage? Should he tell him that, unless the proposed bill is enacted, the government will push for a much more extensive measure?

In answering, shift the focus from this case taken in isolation to the vast practices of which it forms a part. What is the effect on colleagues and subordinates who witness the deception so often resulting from such a choice? What is the effect on the members of Congress as they inevitably learn of a proportion of these lies? And what is the effect on the electorate as it learns of these and similar practices? Then shift back to the narrower world of the official troubled about the legislation he believes in, and hoping by a small deception to change a crucial vote.

It is the fear of the harm lies bring that explains statements such as the following from Revelations (22.15), which might otherwise seem strangely out of proportion:

> These others must stay outside [the Heavenly City]: dogs, medicine-men, and fornicators, and murderers, and idolaters, and everyone of false life and false speech.[8]

It is the deep-seated concern of the multitude which speaks here; there could be few contrasts greater than that between this statement and the self-confident, individualistic view by Machiavelli:

> Men are so simple and so ready to obey present necessities, that one who deceives will always find those who allow themselves to be deceived.

READING AND THINKING

1. Why do people lie? What are some of their reasons for lying that Bok mentions? What other reasons can you add?

2. What consequences of lying does Bok describe for a society in which truth and falsehood are indistinguishable?

3. Why does Bok claim that deception "can be coercive" and that it "can give power to the deceiver"?

4. What rationale do liars sometimes offer for their lies? How do liars feel about being lied to themselves? Why?

5. Bok mentions in passing that some lies are "trivial." Give an example of such a trivial lie and explain why it is trivial and not serious.

THINKING AND WRITING

1. Write a one-paragraph summary of the section "The Perspective of the Deceived."

2. Write a one-paragraph summary of the section "The Perspective of the Liar."

3. Identify and explain the purpose and significance of the quotations that Bok includes from Niccolo Machiavelli.

4. Describe a time in your life when you lied—or when you were tempted to lie, and didn't. Explain what was at stake and why you did or did not tell the truth.

5. Describe one scenario in which you think it would be acceptable either to withhold the truth or to falsify the truth.

DILEMMAS OF TRUTH-TELLING: AN OCCASION FOR WRITING

In "On Lying," Sissela Bok raises some questions about the effects of lying on those who lie and on those who are lied to. In other sections of her book, Bok identifies a series of professional scenarios that pose problems with revealing the truth. In this Occasion for Writing you will have a chance to consider how lies and lying play out in the political arena.

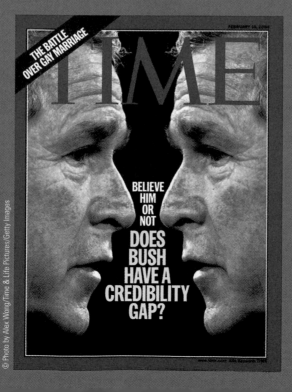

© Photo by Alex Wong/Time & Life Pictures/Getty Images

© New York Daily News, 1999

PREPARING TO WRITE: OCCASIONS TO THINK ABOUT WHAT YOU SEE

1. Describe what you see in the pictures of Presidents Clinton and Bush.

2. How do the words that accompany each image convey a message linked with the picture?

MOVING TOWARD ESSAY: OCCASIONS TO ANALYZE AND REFLECT

1. To what extent do the photographs of the presidents make a claim about the deceitfulness of Clinton and Bush?

2. Do you think there should be a code of ethics governing the ethics of truth-telling among political leaders? Why or why not? Explain.

3. To what extent do you think journalists and police investigators are justified in using lies to gain knowledge to help them solve crimes? To what extent do you think psychiatrists are justified in distorting information about their patients to preserve confidentiality or to keep them out of military service? What kind of ethics or values are in place in these situations?

WRITING THOUGHTFULLY: OCCASIONS FOR IDEAS AND ESSAYS

1. Write an essay in which you consider the subject of lying by focusing on one or more stories of lying and truth-telling. You may wish to use your own experience or the experiences of others—or both.

2. Consider the subject of lying from a social, psychological, or philosophical (ethical) perspective. You might wish to consider, for example, the social effects of lies, the psychological reasons for lies, or ethical standards regarding truth-telling or lying in one of the professions. Use Bok's essay in conjunction with the media's portrayal of (or participation in) lying to bring your discovery to light.

3. Write an essay in which you consider the following comments about truth and art:

    Pablo Picasso: "Art is a lie that makes us realize the truth."
    Richard Selzer: "Truth is stranger than fiction."

CREATING OCCASIONS

1. Consider how deceit is portrayed in movies and television. Choose a specific movie, a television series, or an individual episode of a show. What values do you see emerging? How are lies and truths presented? After analyzing your movie or show, imagine yourself a parent; would you want your children being exposed to the behaviors and values you've just witnessed? Explain.

VALUES AND EVALUATION

When we "evaluate" something, we assess it, judge it, measuring it against some norm or standard of value. Sometimes we acknowledge our standards of judgment; often we do not.

Whether or not our standards are evident, we frequently make judgments about the quality of things—about their worth or excellence, about how good they are compared with others of their kind, in short about their value.

We also use the word *value* in connection with what is important to us, what matters, what we value. In this sense we refer to our "values," the principles that guide our choices and decisions. We might value social justice, for example, and decide to work for causes that advance social justice. We might value education, and thus, save money and invest time, money, and energy to educate ourselves and our children. We might value travel or fitness or music or any number of things and therefore expend our energies and our resources on them.

Our values both in the sense of the principles we live by and the things that matter to us can change. Just as social and cultural values of societies change over time, so too can personal values. What was important to us a decade ago may be more or less valuable to us today or ten years from now.

The essays in this cluster invite us to consider large-scale issues of faith, values, and morals. Langston Hughes raises questions about the power of religion to coerce belief and pressure conforming behavior. Nancy Wilson Ross's "Introduction to Zen" explains key Zen beliefs while considering why many Americans became interested in Zen during the mid-twentieth century. Martin Luther King, Jr., urges Americans to respect the equality of all people, including especially African Americans, whose rights were so long denied.

Langston Hughes

Langston Hughes (1902–1967) was born in Missouri to a prominent African American family. He attended Columbia University as an engineering major but dropped out after his first year to pursue his literary aspirations, later graduating from Lincoln University. Spurred by the flourishing of black artists during the Harlem Renaissance, Hughes found a distinctive voice in the culture of African American experience. Best known for his poetry, Hughes also wrote fiction, essays, plays, children's books, and several volumes of autobiography.

SALVATION

In "Salvation," Hughes describes an incident from his youth that had a decisive impact on his view of the world. In the span of just a few paragraphs, Hughes tells a story of faith and doubt, of belief and disbelief. The essay's paradoxical opening establishes a tension that culminates in an ironic reversal of expectations for the reader and a life-altering realization for Hughes.

1 I was saved from sin when I was going on thirteen. But not really saved. It happened like this. There was a big revival at my Auntie Reed's church. Every night for weeks there had been much preaching, singing, praying, and shouting, and some very hardened sinners had been brought to Christ, and the membership of the church had grown by leaps and bounds. Then just before the revival ended, they held a special meeting for children, "to bring the young lambs to the fold." My aunt spoke of it for days ahead. That night I was escorted to the front row and placed on the mourners' bench with all the other young sinners, who had not yet been brought to Jesus.

My aunt told me that when you were saved you saw a light, and something happened to you inside! And Jesus came into your life! And God was with you from then on! She said you could see and hear and feel Jesus in your soul. I believed her. I had heard a great many old people say the same thing and it seemed to me they ought to know. So I sat there calmly in the hot, crowded church, waiting for Jesus to come to me.

The preacher preached a wonderful rhythmical sermon, all moans and shouts and lonely cries and dire pictures of hell, and then he sang a song about the ninety and nine safe in the fold, but one little lamb was left out in the cold. Then he said: "Won't you come? Won't you come to Jesus? Young lambs, won't you come?" And he held out his arms to all us young sinners there on the mourners' bench. And the little girls cried. And some of them jumped up and went to Jesus right away. But most of us just sat there.

A great many old people came and knelt around us and prayed, old women with jet-black faces and braided hair, old men with work-gnarled hands. And the church sang a song about the lower lights are burning, some poor sinners to be saved. And the whole building rocked with prayer and song.

Still I kept waiting to *see* Jesus.

5 Finally all the young people had gone to the altar and were saved, but one boy and me. He was a rounder's son named Westley. Westley and I were surrounded by sisters and deacons praying. It was very hot in the church, and getting late now. Finally Westley said to me in a whisper: "God damn! I'm tired o' sitting here. Let's get up and be saved." So he got up and was saved.

Then I was left all alone on the mourners' bench. My aunt came and knelt at my knees and cried, while prayers and songs swirled all around me in the little church. The whole congregation prayed for me alone, in a mighty wail of moans and voices. And I kept waiting serenely for Jesus, waiting, waiting—but he didn't come. I wanted to see him, but nothing happened to me. Nothing! I wanted something to happen to me, but nothing happened.

I heard the songs and the minister saying: "Why don't you come? My dear child, why don't you come to Jesus? Jesus is waiting for you. He wants you. Why don't you come? Sister Reed, what is this child's name?"

"Langston," my aunt sobbed.

10   "Langston, why don't you come? Why don't you come and be saved? Oh, Lamb of God! Why don't you come?"

Now it was really getting late. I began to be ashamed of myself, holding everything up so long. I began to wonder what God thought about Westley, who certainly hadn't seen Jesus either, but who was now sitting proudly on the platform, swinging his knickerbockered legs and grinning down at me, surrounded by deacons and old women on their knees praying. God had not struck Westley dead for taking his name in vain or for lying in the temple. So I decided that maybe to save further trouble, I'd better lie, too, and say that Jesus had come, and get up and be saved.

So I got up.

Suddenly the whole room broke into a sea of shouting, as they saw me rise. Waves of rejoicing swept the place. Women leaped in the air. My aunt threw her arms around me. The minister took me by the hand and led me to the platform.

When things quieted down, in a hushed silence, punctuated by a few ecstatic "Amens," all the new young lambs were blessed in the name of God. Then joyous singing filled the room.

That night, for the last time in my life but   15 one—for I was a big boy twelve years old—I cried. I cried, in bed alone, and couldn't stop. I buried my head under the quilts, but my aunt heard me. She woke up and told my uncle I was crying because the Holy Ghost had come into my life, and because I had seen Jesus. But I was really crying because I couldn't bear to tell her that I had lied, that I had deceived everybody in the church, and I hadn't seen Jesus, and that now I didn't believe there was a Jesus any more, since he didn't come to help me.

READING AND THINKING

1. Why do you think Hughes entitles his essay "Salvation"? In what sense is the essay about and not about salvation—and salvation from what?

2. Why do you think Hughes begins the piece as he does, with three very short sentences? Explain the point and the effect of each of these sentences.

3. What do you think is Hughes's main idea in "Salvation"? Where is this idea conveyed most clearly and forcefully? Explain.

4. Besides narration, what other patterns does Hughes employ? Where, and to what effect?

THINKING AND WRITING

1. Write an analysis of Hughes's essay, focusing on how he uses descriptive details, including dialogue, to convey the feeling, flavor, and force of southern religious Protestant fundamentalism.

2. To what extent does Hughes's essay deal with issues of conformity and deception? How does Hughes link conformity and deception with religious belief? Explain.

3. Think about your own experience (or lack of experience) with religion. Write an essay that explores your religious background. You may wish to tell a story or two to convey an idea about this experience, or you may choose to explain why you are or are not religious.

CONFORMING TO FASHION: AN OCCASION FOR WRITING

In "Salvation," Langston Hughes tells a story about how he lost his religious faith. Along the way, Hughes shows how powerful are the pressures of conformity and how difficult it is to go against what everyone else is doing, to disappoint those who expect something from you that you do not feel and cannot give. In the following Occasion for Writing, you will have a chance to consider these issues in more detail.

Tokyo, Japan (1984)

© Burt Glinn/Magnum Photos

Tokyo, Japan (1997)

© Harry Gruyaert/Magnum Photos

PREPARING TO WRITE: OCCASIONS TO THINK ABOUT WHAT YOU SEE

1. Describe what you see in each of the pictures of men and women dressed alike—or differently. Does the first image remind you of anything in particular?

2. Take note of what appears in the background of the second image. What logos do you recognize? To what extent do background details in each picture speak to the issue of conformity?

MOVING TOWARD ESSAY: OCCASIONS TO ANALYZE AND REFLECT

1. These two images were taken in Tokyo, Japan, exhibiting Harajuku fashion—a subculture of fashion born out of imitating other cultures, but adding one's own flair, named after a trendy, artists' neighborhood in Tokyo. To what extent are the boys and girls depicted in each picture doing what is expected of them? To what extent are they doing something unexpected? What role does culture play in what you see represented in these pictures? To what extent is gender a factor? Explain.

2. Consider the image that follows. What message do school uniforms send about conformity? What about this image, if anything, signals nonconformity? Why do you think we sometimes feel great pressure to conform to what others expect of us or to conform our behavior to the behavior of others?

Schoolchildren at their desks, Moscow, Russia (1986)

3. To what extent is the young Langston Hughes's behavior as he describes it in "Salvation" influenced by the behavior of his classmates, by the expectations of the congregation, by the hopes and dreams of his aunt? Explain.

WRITING THOUGHTFULLY: OCCASIONS FOR IDEAS AND ESSAYS

1. Write an analysis and interpretation of "Salvation" in which you consider why Langston Hughes behaved as he did, how he felt about it afterward, and how the experience affected his life in the future.

2. Write an essay about changing fashions in clothing, music, consumer electronics, or another aspect of popular culture. Discuss the role of conformity and of creativity or originality in your essay.

3. In an essay explain what conformity is, why many people are drawn to conform, and why some are inclined to rebel against conformity. You can use examples from your experience, your observation, and your reading to illustrate, support, and develop your ideas.

CREATING OCCASIONS

1. Do some research on conformity, looking for the causes and the consequences of conforming behaviors. You may want to consider researching the rise of Nazism during World War II or even the rise of cults. Write up your research notes as a short essay interspersed with references to Hughes, the images in this chapter, and your own personal experience of conformity and nonconformity.

Nancy Wilson Ross (1901–1986)

Nancy Wilson Ross was born and raised in the Pacific Northwest, graduating from the University of Oregon in 1924. She made her first trip to Asia in 1939 when she visited China, Japan, and Korea. She traveled extensively in Asia and wrote on Asian topics for many periodicals, including the *Atlantic Monthly, Harper's Bazaar, Horizon, Mademoiselle, The New Yorker,* and *Vogue.* Her article "What Is Zen?" was widely distributed by the Japan Society to schools, libraries, and universities throughout the United States. Among her many books are the novels *The Left Hand Is The Dreamer* (1947) and *Times Corner* (1952), as well as historical works about the Pacific Northwest, including *Westward the Women* (1944), a biography, *Joan of Arc* (1953), and a study of Asian religions, *Three Ways of Asian Wisdom: Hinduism, Buddhism, Zen, and Their Significance for the West* (1966). Ross served on the board of the Asia Society from its founding by John Rockefeller III in 1956 until 1985. For the last decade of her life, she was extremely involved in Buddhism, sharing her house with a member of the San Francisco Zen Center and writing *Buddhism, A Way of Life and Thought* (1980).

AN INTRODUCTION TO ZEN

In "An Introduction to Zen," excerpted from *The World of Zen,* readers are provided with an overview of Zen's basic principles and practices. In the essay, Ross touches on the origins of Zen and describes its unique perspective on how to live a life. The essay serves offers a clear overview of Zen for readers unfamiliar with its unique spiritual aspects. The book it introduces includes a wide range of essays and images describing and portraying Zen as a way of living. Ross's introductory essay captures the spirit of that endeavor.

1   During the past few years in America a small Japanese word, with a not inappropriate buzzing sound, has begun to be heard in unlikely places: on academic platforms, at cocktail parties and ladies' luncheons, and in campus hangouts. This word is "Zen." Sometimes called a religion, sometimes "the religion of no-religion," sometimes identified simply as a "way of life," Zen is ancient and alien in origin, its philosophy paradoxical and complex. Its sudden Western blooming is therefore something of a phenomenon.

The applied tenets of Zen—formulations and adaptations of original Buddhist principles—lie at the root of the most unique elements in Japanese life. Zen's influence, implicit or explicit, can be traced through almost every aspect of Japan's culture from garden planning to architecture, ceremonial swordsmanship to Judo, flower arrangement to archery, poetry composition to the formal tea ceremony, painting techniques to the conventions of the theater. So complete has been Zen's infiltration for centuries that it is by now quite impossible to understand the contradictory and long-enduring civilization of this small island country without some understanding of Zen itself.

Traveling a long distance in space and time from its origins in India in the sixth century B.C., to reach Japan via China and Korea in the twelfth and thirteenth centuries A.D. (although other forms of Buddhism reached Japan as early as the sixth century A.D.), Zen Buddhism first touched American shores about 1900. After some fifty years of incubation—and ironically enough, since the war in the Pacific—it has suddenly begun to attract a growing number of enthusiastic supporters in this country, among them distinguished scientists, artists, and psychoanalysts.

Although Zen in America has become generally associated in the public mind with the "beat" generation, it may not finally matter that the present advance of this philosophy in the Western world has such unorthodox associations. Trained Zennists are notably tolerant people. The West Coast's beloved *roshi* (venerable teacher), Nyogen Senzaki, who died in 1958, liked to quote an old saying: "There are three kinds of disciples: those who impart Zen to others, those who maintain the temples and shrines, and then there are the rice bags and the clothes hangers."

5 From Japan some pertinent remarks on the fad side of Zen were recently offered by Chicago-born Ruth Fuller Sasaki, who has been ordained a Zen priest and is now in full charge of a Kyoto subtemple—a quite extraordinary honor for a Westerner and a woman. In an interview given at the time of her ordination in 1958 she commented: "In the Western world Zen seems to be going through the cult phase. Zen is not a cult. The problem with Western people is that they want to believe in something and at the same time they want something easy. Zen is a lifetime work of self-discipline and study." Mrs. Sasaki went on to describe how, during her period of training, she learned to spend seven days at a time in a monks' hall sleeping only one hour a night, and sitting in meditation or contemplation for as long as eighteen hours without a break.

Disciplines similar, though by no means as rigorous, are not altogether unknown among Zen followers in this country. Members of New York's First Zen Institute have been meeting to practice meditative exercises for almost three decades. Each summer for a number of years Los Angeles Zennists have held a week of strict training in group meditation. A recent session was led by a Zen *roshi* from an old and noted Japanese monastery. The printed invitation to the *sesshin* (a Zen word for a special period devoted to meditation and study) read, "Bring your sleeping bag and toothbrush. There is no charge." Alongside the week's Spartan schedule appeared a sketch of fierce-eyed Bodhidharma, the legendary First Patriarch who brought the Great Teaching from India to the Sino-Japanese world, and the notice: "Let us keep the promise of complete SILENCE during our *sesshin*." This meant silence for seven full days—a rule faithfully adhered to by a mixed group of disciples: social figures, teachers, college students, artisans and artists, housewives and businessmen.

Now what is it that these people from diverse backgrounds are seeking so earnestly outside the bounds of their own religious, philosophical, and aesthetic orientation, and that has led the more serious among them to submit to difficult and puzzling disciplines? The answer would seem to lie in the basic qualities that distinguish Zen as a way of life, and these may be very loosely summed up as follows: Zen, although considered a religion by its followers, has no sacred scriptures whose words are law; no fixed canon; no rigid dogma; no Savior or Divine Being through whose favor or intercession one's eventual salvation is assured. The absence of attributes common to all other religious systems lends Zen a certain air of freedom to which many modern people respond. Furthermore, Zen's stated aim of bringing about—through the employment of its special methods—a high degree of self-knowledge with a resultant gain of peace of mind has caught the attention of certain Western psychologists, among them Carl Jung, Erich Fromm and the late Karen Horney. Other Western names included in modern discussions of Zen range from Korzybski to Kierkegaard, Sartre to Jaspers, Kerouac to Kafka, Heisenberg to Martin Buber. When the existentialist German philosopher Martin Heidegger encountered Zen writings he professed to discover in them the very ideas he had been independently developing.

The gravest obstacle in discussing Zen's possible meaning for the West is the difficulty of explaining "How it works." In its own four statements, Zen emphasizes particularly that its teaching lies beyond and outside words:

> A special transmission outside the Scriptures;
> No dependence upon words and letters;
> Direct pointing to the soul of man;
> Seeing into one's nature and the attainment of Buddhahood.

To know Zen—even to begin to understand it—it is necessary to practice it. And here Westerners come to a dilemma. Ruth Sasaki believes it is not possible to get at Zen's deepest roots or to rightly utilize its unique method without the aid of a master, a *guru,* to use the Indian term.

10   To reach the state of illumination—*satori*—and the "spiritual equilibrium" that follows, certain definite techniques are used by the Zen master and pupil. There is a form of question and answer known as the *mondo* by which ordinary thought processes are speeded up to the point of the hoped-for abrupt breakthrough into "awareness." And then there is the *koan,* a formulation in words not soluble by the intellect alone—indeed, often quite senseless to the rational mind, a veritable "riddle." But the *koan* contains the possible seeds of the shock that may also break open the sealed door of ordinary consciousness, which is forever caught in the contradictory bonds of dualism, forever balancing this with that, unable to take hold of "reality" because always immersed in a series of distinctions, discriminations, and differences.

To work on a *koan* necessitates a sincere and enduring eagerness to solve it, but also— and here comes the twist, and one of the many paradoxes in which Zen abounds—you must *face it without thinking about it.* This point is stressed in the unbending effort to force the student beyond the eternally dualistic and dialectic pattern of ordinary thinking. Again and again it is emphasized that one cannot take hold of the true merely by abandoning the false, nor can one reach peace of mind or any final "answer" by argument or logic. Science might be cited as a prime example of the failure to bring solace or release through "facts." Scientists reduce matter to molecules, molecules to atoms; they present the theory of the infinite divisibility of matter. They also assert that all life is merely force or energy. The sum total of their brilliant findings remains almost totally incomprehensible to the average mind, even to the exceptional mind that happens to be unscientific. How, then, in the modern world, ruled by conflicting theories, with global problems and personal problems forever presenting themselves for solution, can the individual ever "come to rest," struggling as he still is—but in an ever more complex environment—with the very same basic questions of individual meaning, of the riddle of life and death, that Siddartha Gautama, the historic Buddha, faced in the sixth century B.C.?

Once you have taken up this ancient basic question of "meaning," you are on your way to an impasse which your so-called "rational" mind cannot solve for you. And it is at this point that the Zen *koan* is presented as a sort of spiritual dynamite. But one cannot, alas, "explain" a *koan. Koans* are meant to be directly experienced. They are formulations on which to practice that famous "law of reversed effort" by which results are often mysteriously obtained in the hidden, unconscious depths of one's being.

A subject for meditation might be these lines from an old Japanese poem: "The cherry tree blooms each year in the Yoshino Mountains. But split the tree and tell me where the flowers are." Or the last line from another famous Japanese poem: "Now I know my true being has nothing to do with birth and death."

An instructor giving this line as a *koan* might question: "How can you free yourself from birth and death? What is your true being? *No! No! Do not think about it! Just gaze at it closely.*" Perhaps a few hints would be offered: "Zen, it is asserted, has the aim of enabling you to see directly into your own nature. Very well. Where *is* your true nature? Can you locate it? If you can locate it you are then said to be free of birth and death. All right, you have become a corpse. Are you free of birth and death? Now do you know where you are? . . . Now your body has separated into its four basic elements. Where are you now?"

15   Doshin asked Sosan: "What is the method of liberation?" The master replied: "Who binds you?" "No one binds me." "Why then," said the master, "should you seek liberation?" Replies of this type, says Alan Watts, "seem to throw attention back upon the state of mind from which the question arises, as if to say: If your feelings are troubling you, find out who or what it is that is being troubled. The psychological response is therefore to try to feel what feels and to know what knows—to make an object of the subject." Yet this is not easy. It is indeed "much like looking for an ox when you are riding on it" or "like an eye that sees, but cannot see itself."

Carl Jung has been at some pains to point out that the master-pupil relationship is not easy for the average Occidental to accept. In his introduction to one of Dr. Suzuki's books, Dr. Jung wrote: "Who among us would produce such implicit trust in a superior master and his incomprehensible ways? This respect for the greater human personality exists only in the East." Even were it not for the ordinary Westerner's psychological resistance to the notion of a personal master, other difficulties arise in the passing on of strict Zen training. There are, for instance, far from enough English-speaking *roshis* to go around. Most people who take on a partial—or total—dedication to Zen's "heterodoxical transformation process" must perforce seek the way for themselves.

Just how far the ordinary, unaided seeker can penetrate toward the core of Zen is difficult to assess, but whichever way he seeks it—either under direct personal guidance or alone—the key to realization lies in the words "direct immediate perception," or "direct seeing into." The condition of enlightenment itself, and not words *about* that condition, are what matter in Zen. Zen masters sternly reject all the speculation, ratiocination, and verbalism so dear to the intellectual Westerner. Overemphasis on the brain, at the expense of other parts of the total consciousness, can seem both amusing and amazing to Asian teachers. A Zen abbot once set before an American aspirant two sets of small legless Japanese dolls, one pair weighted in the bottom part, the other in the head part. When the pair weighted in the head were pushed over, they remained on their sides; the ones weighted in the bottom bounced back at once. The abbot roared with laughter over this illustration of the plight of Western man, forever stressing the thinking function at the expense of his totality.

Some extremely useful hints on this point in particular and Zen training methods in general, as well as the possible rewards for a Westerner who submits to them, may be found in Eugen Herrigel's *Zen in the Art of Archery* [. . .]. This little book describes in detail the agonizing, bewildering five-year trials of a European pupil—a college professor and a crack marksman with pistol and rifle—who attempted to learn archery, Zen style, while in Japan. The mastery of this ancient sacred sport turned out to be much more than the mere acquiring of new techniques. In the mind of the Zen master who acted as Herrigel's instructor it was nothing less than "a profound and far-reaching contest of the archer with himself." The contest had little to do with learning to hit the target in successful, professional style—a paltry goal held to be "sheer devilry," leading to the unfortunate state in which a man could "get stuck in his own achievement." Instead, day after day for five years, with few words yet unswerving intention, the master's emphasis was placed on acquiring a condition called "waiting without

purpose but in a state of highest tension"—
not physical tension, but with a body at once
aware yet *relaxed*. The pupil was not to be
braced for "failure"—the natural result of a
competitive viewpoint—but to think in terms
of "fulfillment." When at long last the patient
but puzzled Westerner had learned how "not
to shoot," but simply to "let the shot fall from
him" with the ease and naturalness of ripe
fruit from a tree or snow from a slowly bending bamboo, he felt that he was finally in possession of a great secret of enlightened
human behavior.

To get at the underpinnings of the
Zen way of life, it is helpful—perhaps even
essential—to go behind the Taoistic Chinese
influence which flavors it, back to Buddhism's
beginnings in India more than two thousand
years ago, for Zen considers itself to be nearer
the original doctrines of Siddartha Gautama,
the Great Teacher, than any other of the
many sects belonging to the two main Buddhist branches, Mahayana and Hinayana.
Zen's emphasis on self-reliance, on effort towards discovery of "the 'light' man can find in
himself," recalls the Buddha's revolutionary
challenge to his first disciples, "Look within,
thou art the Buddha"—a tacit denial of any
special divinity in his own person not also
shared by all men.

20   The birth of the Indian founder of Buddhism, around 560 B.C., occurred in a period
not unlike our own, a time when the minds of
thinking men were torn with warring philosophies and conflicting theories on the origin,
meaning, and purpose of life. Siddartha Gautama, destined to become the Buddha—which
which simply means the Enlightened One—
was the son and heir of a wealthy rajah of the
military caste in what is present-day Nepal.
From birth—so legend says—the young
prince was zealously protected by an overde-
voted father who hoped to prevent the eyes of
his adored son from ever falling on any
gloomy or tragic scene. But after Gautama
reached young manhood he made a series of
forbidden and secret journeys outside the
gates of the family palace and there saw three
unhappy sights which forever altered his destiny: an abject beggar, a corpse surrounded by
weeping mourners, a hopelessly diseased
cripple.

His peace of mind shattered, Gautama began to ask himself certain serious questions.
What was the possible meaning or value of
human life when suffering lay at its root,
when poverty and sickness were not exceptional but universal—as he had just learned
from the palace servant who accompanied
him on his forbidden journeys? What purpose
had individual human existence since it must
be terminated inevitably in the mysterious
oblivion of death?

Unable, in the face of these racking questions, to endure any longer his protected and
luxurious life, Gautama finally stole away in
the middle of the night, leaving behind a
beautiful wife and first-born son, to undertake seven years of wandering from teacher
to teacher in search of answers to his inescapable Why's. He at last attained illumination while sitting alone in deep meditation
under a sacred fig tree. This figure of the contemplative man seated cross-legged, hands in
lap, eyes directed within—so often seen in
Asian sculpture and paintings—is to the
Eastern world what the figure of Christ on
the crucifix is to the Western.

Having attained enlightenment, Gautama—
now become "The Buddha"—went forth to
preach up and down the Indian roads for forty-
nine fruitful years. His aim was not to save others but to help them to save themselves: this
is the differentiating crux of Mahayana Buddhism from which Zen stems. Buddha
preached a doctrine of a Middle Way between
the Opposites. The teaching was essentially
psychological, a training in discipline of mind
and body aiming at self-mastery and nonat-
tachment. Its principles were embodied in an
Eight Fold Path of Right Thought and Right
Behavior that would, if earnestly followed,

enable a man to rid himself of his greed, his desire for possessions, his "clinging" to objects and persons (claimed as the chief cause of suffering). Finally it would bring him to complete freedom from the restrictive and—to the Buddhists—totally false sense of a separate "self," or individual ego, walling him off from the rest of life. When he had reached this state of being, all fear of inadequacy, of deprivation, and also of death would inevitably be conquered.

Although the direct, pragmatic, and at the same time serene and immensely tolerant teaching of the Buddha lost out in the land of its birth to the more sensual Hinduism, it has flourished for centuries throughout the rest of Asia taking on coloring from the various cultures through which it passed much as a moving river reflects different scenes from its ever changing banks. Zen—or Ch'an, as the Chinese called it—is, then, the Sino-Japanese expression of this ancient teaching, and it was the Chinese with their Taoistic outlook who developed Zen's peculiar form of dynamic meditation, that "stilling of the self," that condition of full awareness, neither passive nor aggressive. When the young and eager country of Japan took over China's already highly developed civilization—not by war or conquest, but voluntarily and with the fullest enthusiasm—it also acquired Chinese Buddhism. Then, true to their practical yet basically aesthetic and mystical natures, the Japanese applied Ch'an's (Zen's) subtle dynamic laws in many original ways to their own indigenous culture.

25   The question inevitably arises whether the present American response to things Japanese—and specifically to the paradoxical subtleties of Zen—may have its root in our recent occupation of Japan. Although it is unlikely that more than a handful of GI's ever heard the word "Zen," it is certainly plain that many were affected by a milieu so completely unlike anything they had ever known. An initial interest in Zen might have come to them

through quite indirect stimuli. Old Chinese and Japanese landscape paintings, whose values and virtues differ so markedly from our own, have been the entrance into the Zen world for many people. In the Chinese and Japanese aesthetic, emphasis falls on asymmetry rather than on symmetry, on space seen not merely as something to be "filled in" but as something *positive in itself.* These deceptively simple works of art, often rendered only in ink strokes of varied styles and weights, manage to suggest, with incomparable nuance, both life's mystery and its reassuring homely quality: the bird resting on the bough; the tree bent with snow; the distant mountains, half-veiled, half-revealed by mist; man always presented small, not set forth as the "master" of all he surveys but instead as a *related part of the whole.*

The experience of the Japanese tea ceremony has also been known to rouse sensitive Westerners to an awareness of something truly unique in the spirit of this contradictory people. The tea ceremony, stressing as it does the virtues of silence, a quiet exchange between friends, the contemplation of one or two simple but beautiful objects, takes place in a small garden structure whose interior is meant to be seen as "the abode of vacancy." The traditional Japanese garden—exemplifying laws of abstract composition unpracticed in the West until the work of some modern painters—has its most famous expression in the raked sand–and–rock garden of Ryoanji [. . .]. The sense of timelessness implicit in the tea ceremony may be caught again at a performance of the stylized ancient drama called the No. Even the more spectacular and popular Kabuki affords fleeting glimpses of Zen's way for those prepared to catch them. A stage silence prolonged past Western limits of pleasure or comfort, when not impatiently resisted but simply "gone with," can finally register with the force of a great sound; the slight movement of an actor's fan, a barely perceptible shift of an arm or a foot, other unstressed gestures that produce from a Japanese audience mysterious cries of approbation—these delicately sustained moments could conceivably lead a puzzled Occidental into new avenues of insight. And finally, a first step into Zen's paradoxical pleasures can lie through poetry, for in the stripped, evocative brevity of a *haiku* or a *tanka* there often lurks the very essence of Zen.

> The wild geese do not intend to cast their reflections,
> The water has no mind to receive their image.

To account fully for the present enthusiasm for Zen may not be possible, but there is no denying its growing American and European popularity. Zen seems to be serving as one of a number of fresh elements in a more dynamic exchange between East and West. This long-desired rapprochement, quietly developing despite appearances to the contrary, may contribute in time to the realization of that old-new vision—a general World Culture, a Civilization of Man. A minor aspect of the new and properly paradoxical Japanese-American exchange was touched on by Sabro Hasegawa, a gifted Japanese painter and Zen disciple, in a piece written not long before his recent death:" "'Old' Japan was newer than the new Occident, while new Japan is apparently more old-fashioned than either the new Occident or old Japan itself." He went on to describe the contemporary Japanese painters' growing concern with photographic realism in art, while at the same time so many Western artists are turning to abstraction.

Perhaps also it is not too far-fetched to assume that some of the same disillusionment, the same disturbing sense of things gone awry in a familiar world, that has affected the intellectual climate of Japan is turning many Westerners toward less familiar philosophies, attracting them to un-Western, non-Aristotelian ways of regarding life and the meaning of personal existence.

When Aldous Huxley wrote his little book *The Doors of Perception,* a description of the effects of a scientific experiment with carefully controlled dosages of the drug mescaline, he referred specifically to one of the famed bits of classic Zen dialogue with which aspirants to enlightenment are sometimes confronted. This passage, which had puzzled Huxley very much when he read it in one of D. T. Suzuki's books, tells of a young novice who asks his master, "What is the Dharma-Body of the Buddha?" (in our Western terminology, "What is Universal Mind or the Godhead?"). The master replies, "with the prompt irrelevance," says Huxley, "of one of the Marx Brothers, 'The hedge at the bottom of the garden.'" When the bewildered novice pursues the problem further, he may get for his second answer a real Groucho whack on the shoulder with the master's ever ready staff, and a second seemingly nonsensical reply: "A golden-haired lion."

Huxley reported that under the effect of the drug—which had thoroughly relaxed the grip of the rational top brain and the insistent habitual separativeness of his own personal ego—he saw, with delighted amusement, just what these fantastic Zen replies really meant. They now appeared not in the least nonsensical, for in this moment of freedom and illumination, all life stood revealed to him as a totality, a great "One-ness." Thus any answer made to a question about Universal Mind would, of necessity, be as true as any other.

A passage of this nature serves to recall the dadaists and surrealists of Europe who, after World War I, attempted to bring about a "general and emphatic crisis in Western consciousness." This they tried to do by a number of unusual devices. In painting they played the game of *trompe l'oeil;* on their canvases one frequently finds two or more objects presented as one. Dali's early painting of his old nurse is a familiar example, with her spine shown as a crutch-propped aperture through which one gets a view of sea and sand. In writing as well as painting the dadaists delighted in unlikely juxtapositions of images and ideas: "the cave bear and the lout his companion, the *vol-au-vent* and the wind his valet, the cannibal and his brother the carnival, the Mississippi and its little dog . . ." or "beautiful as the chance meeting on a dissecting table of a sewing machine and an umbrella." It was thus, acting as Breton's "modest registering machines," that surrealists expressed themselves—to the pleasure of their compeers and the bewilderment of outsiders. At dadaist gatherings speakers would sometimes sit in silence or ring bells or "make poetry" by poking holes through bits of paper. (Zen behavior, not entirely dissimilar though differently motivated, is described in other parts of this volume.) Lines from Eluard, Breton, and Rimbaud often have a Zen ring. Among Eluard's *Proverbs* one reads, "Make two o'clock with one o'clock," "I came, I sat, I departed," "A crab by any other name would not forget the sea," "Who hears but me hears all." Among Zen sayings one finds: "When Tom drinks, Dick gets tipsy," "Last night a wooden horse neighed and a stone man cut capers," "Lo, a cloud of dust is rising from the ocean, and the roaring of waves is heard over the land," "Who is the teacher of all the Buddhas, past, present and future? John the cook."

Zen enlightenment, which carries with it a deep and lasting comprehension of one's place in the totality of the universe, is not easily gained—contrary to the impression of "immediacy" that many people have taken away from their cursory reading of Zen literature. Although illumination may come in a sudden flash, during which one perceives one's "self" and the rest of the world as they really are, this galvanic charge is unlikely to occur short of an extended period of disciplined personal effort. The seeker, as one Zen master asserts, must pursue for a very long time the problem of final "knowing" with a single-purposed ferocity and all the attendant frustrations of a "mosquito trying to bite on a bar of iron."

Those who, to begin with, find Zen not only paradoxical and puzzling but annoying, even enraging, might profit from an old story of a certain learned man who came to a Zen master to inquire about this rare philosophy. The master politely invited his visitor to share a cup of ceremonial tea while they discoursed together. When the master had brewed the tea by the strict procedures of the tea ceremony, he began to pour the whisked green liquid into the visitor's cup and continued pouring until the cup had overflowed. Even then he went on pouring until the discomfited guest, unable longer to restrain himself, cried out in agitation, "Sir, my cup is already full. No more will go in." At once the master put down the teapot and remarked, "Like this cup, you are full of your own opinions and speculations. How can I show you Zen unless you first empty your cup?"

READING AND THINKING

1. What point does Wilson Ross make about the relationship of Zen and Japanese culture?

2. Why do you think Wilson Ross mentions the origins of Zen and tells the story of Siddhartha Gautama?

3. What is the basic goal of Zen? What are its basic tenets or principles?

4. Why do you think Zen became popular in America in the middle of the twentieth century?

THINKING AND WRITING

1. Explain what a *koan* is and how *koans* are used by Zen teachers.

2. Discuss the possible significance of the *koan* question: "What is the sound of one hand clapping?" What kind of question is this, and what kinds of answers might be offered to it?

3. Identify two or three aspects of Zen teaching or practice that can be compared with the beliefs or practices of another philosophy or religion with which you are familiar.

4. Write a brief personal response to one or two aspects of Ross's essay that struck you most forcefully.

ZEN: AN OCCASION FOR WRITING

Nancy Wilson Ross's essay on Zen identifies a number of aspects of a Zen approach to living. In the following Occasion for Writing, you are invited to explore a number of images and texts to consider your own way of thinking about them from a Zen perspective.

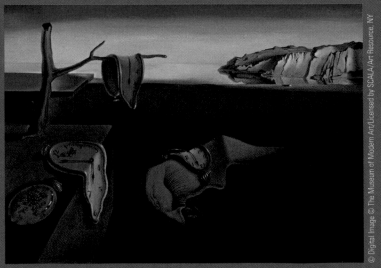

SALVADOR DALI, *The Persistence of Memory (1931)*

© Digital Image © The Museum of Modern Art/Licensed by SCALA/Art Resource, NY

HENRI ROUSSEAU,
The Dream (1910)

PREPARING TO WRITE: OCCASIONS TO THINK ABOUT WHAT YOU SEE

1. Try to look at these images from a Zen perspective. What Zen principle(s) can be inferred from Dali's *The Persistence of Memory*? What connections can you make between Dali's painting and Rousseau's *The Dream*? To what extent does Rousseau's painting echo Zen ideas?

2. How do Kono's picture of the tree and hills and *Ryoanji Rock and Sand Garden* illustrate important aspects of Zen?

MOVING TOWARD ESSAY: OCCASIONS TO ANALYZE AND REFLECT

1. Explain how you decided on the aspects of Zen perspective to highlight for the two western paintings, the ones by Dali and Rousseau.

2. Explain how you arrived at the Zen elements reflected in the Kono and Ryoanji pictures.

ASAHACHI KONO,
Untitled (c. 1920)

Ryoanji Rock and Sand Garden, Kyoto, Japan

3. Identify the Zen principles at stake in the following parable:

Learning to Be Silent

The pupils of the Tendai school used to study meditation before Zen entered Japan. Four of them who were intimate friends promised one another to observe seven days of silence.

On the first day all were silent. Their meditation had begun auspiciously, but when night came and the oil lamps were growing dim one of the pupils could not help exclaiming to a servant: "Fix those lamps."

The second pupil was surprised to hear the first one talk. "We are not supposed to say a word," he remarked.

"You two are stupid. Why did you talk?" asked the third.

"I am the only one who has not talked," concluded the fourth pupil.

4. Explain the significance of each of the following details in "Learning to Be Silent": (1) the promise; (2) the oil lamps; (3) the first spoken words: "Fix those lamps." What inferences can you make about the four friends—their ages, for example, or their gender? On what basis do you make those inferences?

WRITING THOUGHTFULLY: OCCASIONS FOR IDEAS AND ESSAYS

1. Select one of the images from this Occasion and write a paragraph explaining what you see in it and how you think about it when you look at it from the perspective of Zen.

2. Write an analysis of "Learning to Be Silent." Explain the meaning or significance of the parable, providing evidence from the parable's details to support your interpretation.

3. Write two or three paragraphs about the value of silence. Why would Zen novices—or novices of other religious groups—want to spend days in silence?

CREATING OCCASIONS

1. Do some research on Zen in everyday life by consulting one of the following: *Zen in the Art of Archery* by Eugene Herrigel, *Zen and the Art of Motorcycle Maintenance* by Robert Pirsig, or *Zen and Japanese Culture* by D. T. Suzuki. Consider how the principles of Zen can be applied to athletic competition (including not only Japanese forms of competition such as Judo and Sumo wrestling, but also to American sports such as baseball and football). Consider how Zen principles might be used in musical performance, in dance, in painting, in taking examinations, and in other areas of life. Develop an Occasion for Writing based on your research and your thinking.

Martin Luther King, Jr.

Martin Luther King, Jr. (1929–1968), who earned a PhD from Boston University, was an ordained minister who worked tirelessly on behalf of civil rights. He rose up against unjust laws and encouraged other Americans to do the same. His tactic was nonviolent resistance, what he called civil disobedience; he staged and led protests all over the South. Many consider him the most influential civil rights leader in American history. The nation now honors Dr. King's efforts with a national holiday. By the time of his assassination in Memphis, Tennessee, many of King's dreams had been realized, but the struggle for civil rights had obviously not ended, nor had the hatred against minority groups.

LETTER FROM BIRMINGHAM JAIL

"Letter from Birmingham Jail" was written to a group of clergyman who had criticized Dr. King for leading sit-ins at lunch counters in and around Birmingham, Alabama. He and his followers had been subjected to violence and arrests for demonstrating against practices that violated their civil rights. During those days in the South, African Americans were not allowed to use the same restrooms as whites, could sit only in designated sections of some restaurants, were required to ride in the back of public busses, were unable to live in the best neighborhoods, could not rent rooms in most motels and hotels, and could not attend the best public schools. Segregation was the enforced practice across much of the country.

April 16, 1963

1 My Dear Fellow Clergymen:

While confined here in the Birmingham city jail, I came across your recent statement calling my present activities "unwise and untimely." Seldom do I pause to answer criticism of my work and ideas. If I sought to answer all the criticisms that cross my desk, my secretaries would have little time for anything other than such correspondence in the course of the day, and I would have no time for constructive work. But since I feel that you are men of genuine good will and that your criticisms are sincerely set forth, I want to try to answer your statement in what I hope will be patient and reasonable terms.

I think I should indicate why I am here in Birmingham, since you have been influenced by the view which argues against "outsiders coming in." I have the honor of serving as president of the Southern Christian Leadership Conference, an organization operating in every southern state, with headquarters in Atlanta, Georgia. We have some eighty-five affiliated organizations across the South, and one of them is the Alabama Christian Movement for Human Rights. Frequently we share staff, educational, and financial resources with our affiliates. Several months ago the affiliate here in Birmingham asked us to be on call to engage in a nonviolent direct-action program if such were deemed necessary. We readily consented, and when the hour came we lived up to our promise. So I, along with several members of my staff, am here because I was invited here. I am here because I have organizational ties here.

But more basically, I am in Birmingham because injustice is here. Just as the prophets of the eighth century B.C. left their villages and carried their "thus saith the Lord" far beyond the boundaries of their home towns, and just as the Apostle Paul left his village of Tarsus and carried the gospel of Jesus Christ to the far corners of the GrecoRoman world, so am I compelled to carry the gospel of freedom beyond my own home town. Like Paul, I must constantly respond to the Macedonian call for aid.

5   Moreover, I am cognizant of the interrelatedness of all communities and states. I cannot sit idly by in Atlanta and not be concerned about what happens in Birmingham. Injustice anywhere is a threat to justice everywhere. We are caught in an inescapable network of mutuality, tied in a single garment of destiny. Whatever affects one directly, affects all indirectly. Never again can we afford to live with the narrow, provincial, "outside agitator" idea. Anyone who lives inside the United States can never be considered an outsider anywhere within its bounds.

You deplore the demonstrations taking place in Birmingham. But your statement, I am sorry to say, fails to express a similar concern for the conditions that brought about the demonstrations. I am sure that none of you would want to rest content with the superficial kind of social analysis that deals merely with effects and does not grapple with underlying causes. It is unfortunate that demonstrations are taking place in Birmingham, but it is even more unfortunate that the city's white power structure left the Negro community with no alternative.

In any nonviolent campaign there are four basic steps: collection of the facts to determine whether injustices exist; negotiation; self-purification; and direct action. We have gone through all these steps in Birmingham. There can be no gainsaying the fact that racial injustice engulfs this community. Birmingham is probably the most thoroughly segregated city in the United States. Its ugly record of brutality is widely known. Negroes have experienced grossly unjust treatment in courts. There have been more unsolved bombings of Negro homes and churches in Birmingham than in any other city in the nation. These are the hard, brutal facts of the case. On the basis of these conditions, Negro leaders sought to negotiate with the city fathers. But the latter consistently refused to engage in good-faith negotiation.

Then, last September, came the opportunity to talk with leaders of Birmingham's economic community. In the course of the negotiations, certain promises were made by the merchants—for example, to remove the stores' humiliating racial signs. On the basis of these promises, the Reverend Fred Shuttlesworth and the leaders of the Alabama Christian Movement for Human Rights agreed to a moratorium on all demonstrations. As the weeks and months went by, we realized that we were the victims of a broken promise. A few signs, briefly removed, returned; the others remained.

As in so many past experiences, our hopes had been blasted, and the shadow of deep disappointment settled upon us. We had no alternative except to prepare for direct action, whereby we would present our very bodies as means of laying our case before the conscience of the local and the national community. Mindful of the difficulties involved, we decided to undertake a process of self-purification. We began a series of workshops on nonviolence, and we repeatedly asked ourselves: "Are you able to accept blows without retaliating?" "Are you able to endure the ordeal of jail?" We decided to schedule our direct-action program for the Easter season, realizing that except for Christmas, this is the main shopping period of the year. Knowing that a strong economic-withdrawal program would be the by-product of direct action, we felt that this would be the best time to bring pressure to bear on the merchants for the needed change.

Then it occurred to us that Birmingham's 10 mayoral election was coming up in March, and we speedily decided to postpone action until after election day. When we discovered that the Commissioner of Public Safety, Eugene "Bull" Connor, had piled up enough votes to be in the run-off, we decided again to postpone action until the day after the run-off so that the demonstrations could not be used to cloud the issues. Like many others, we waited to see Mr. Connor defeated, and to this end we endured postponement after postponement. Having aided in this community need, we felt that our direct-action program could be delayed no longer.

You may well ask, "Why direct action? Why sit-ins, marches, and so forth? Isn't negotiation a better path?" You are quite right in calling for negotiation. Indeed, this is the very purpose of direct action. Nonviolent direct action seeks to create such a crisis and foster such a tension that a community which has constantly refused to negotiate is forced to confront the issue. It seeks so to dramatize the issue that it can no longer be ignored. My citing the creation of tension as part of the work of the nonviolent-resistor may sound rather shocking. But I must confess that I am not afraid of the word "tension." I have earnestly opposed violent tension, but there is a type of constructive, nonviolent tension which is necessary for growth. Just as Socrates felt that it was necessary to create a tension in the mind so that individuals could rise from the bondage of myths and half-truths to the unfettered realm of creative analysis and objective appraisal, so must we see the need for nonviolent gadflies to create the kind of tension in society that will help men rise from the dark depths of prejudice and racism to the majestic heights of understanding and brotherhood.

The purpose of our direct-action program is to create a situation so crisis-packed that it will inevitably open the door to negotiation. I therefore concur with you in your call for negotiation. Too long has our beloved Southland been bogged down in a tragic effort to live in monologue rather than dialogue.

One of the basic points in your statement is that the action that I and my associates have taken in Birmingham is untimely. Some have asked: "Why didn't you give the new city administration time to act?" The only answer that I can give to this query is that the new Birmingham administration must be prodded about as much as the outgoing one, before it will act. We are sadly mistaken if we feel that the election of Albert Boutwell as mayor will bring the millennium to Birmingham. While Mr. Boutwell is a much more gentle person than Mr. Connor, they are both segregationists, dedicated to maintenance of the status quo. I have hoped that Mr. Boutwell will be reasonable enough to see the futility of massive resistance to desegregation. But he will not see this without pressure from devotees of civil rights. My friends, I must say to you that we have not made a single gain in civil rights without determined legal and nonviolent pressure. Lamentably, it is an historical fact that privileged groups seldom give up their privileges voluntarily. Individuals may see the moral light and voluntarily give up their unjust posture; but, as Reinhold Niebuhr has reminded us, groups tend to be more immoral than individuals.

We know through painful experience that freedom is never voluntarily given by the oppressor; it must be demanded by the oppressed. Frankly, I have yet to engage in a direct-action campaign that was "well-timed" in the view of those who have not suffered unduly from the disease of segregation. For years now I have heard the word "Wait!" It rings in the ear of every Negro with piercing familiarity. This "Wait" has almost always meant "Never." We must come to see, with one of our distinguished jurists, that "justice too long delayed is justice denied."

We have waited for more than 340 years 15 for our constitutional and God-given rights. The nations of Asia and Africa are moving with jetlike speed toward gaining political independence, but we still creep at horse-and-buggy pace toward gaining a cup of coffee at a lunch counter. Perhaps it is easy for those who have never felt the stinging darts of segregation to say, "Wait." But when you have seen vicious mobs lynch your mothers and fathers at will and drown your sisters and brothers at whim; when you have seen hate-filled policemen curse, kick, and even kill your black brothers and sisters; when you see the vast majority of your twenty million Negro brothers smothering in an airtight cage of poverty in the midst of an affluent society; when you suddenly find your tongue twisted and your speech stammering as you seek to explain to your six-year-old daughter why she can't go to the public amusement park that has just been advertised on television, and see tears welling up in her eyes when she is told that Funtown is closed to colored children, and see ominous clouds of inferiority beginning to form in her little mental sky, and see her beginning to distort her personality by developing an unconscious bitterness toward white people; when you have to concoct an answer for a five-year-old son who is asking, "Daddy, why do white people treat colored people so mean?"; when you take a cross-country drive and find it necessary to sleep night after night in the uncomfortable corners of your automobile because no motel will accept you; when you are humiliated day in and day out by nagging signs reading "white" and "colored"; when your first name becomes "nigger," your middle name becomes "boy" (however old you are) and your last name becomes "John," and your wife and mother are never given the respected title "Mrs."; when you are harried by day and haunted by night by the fact that you are a Negro, living constantly at tiptoe stance, never quite knowing what to expect next, and are plagued with inner fears and outer resentments; when you are forever fighting a degenerating sense of "nobodiness"—then you will understand why we find it difficult to wait. There comes a time when the cup of endurance runs over, and men are no longer willing to be plunged into the abyss of despair. I hope, sirs, you can understand our legitimate and unavoidable impatience.

You express a great deal of anxiety over our willingness to break laws. This is certainly a legitimate concern. Since we so diligently urge people to obey the Supreme Court's decision of 1954 outlawing segregation in the public schools, at first glance it may seem rather paradoxical for us consciously to break laws. One may well ask: "How can you advocate breaking some laws and obeying others?" The answer lies in the fact that there are two types of laws: just and unjust. I would be the first to advocate obeying just laws. One has not only a legal but a moral responsibility to obey just laws. Conversely, one has a moral responsibility to disobey unjust laws. I would agree with St. Augustine that "an unjust law is no law at all."

Now, what is the difference between the two? How does one determine whether a law is just or unjust? A just law is a man-made code that squares with the moral law or the law of God. An unjust law is a code that is out of harmony with the moral law. To put it in the terms of St. Thomas Aquinas: An unjust law is a human law that is not rooted in eternal law and natural law. Any law that uplifts human personality is just. Any law that degrades human personality is unjust. All segregation statutes are unjust because segregation distorts the soul and damages the personality. It gives the segregator a false sense of superiority and the segregated a false sense of inferiority. Segregation, to use the terminology of the Jewish philosopher Martin Buber, substitutes an "I-it" relationship for an "I-thou" relationship and ends up relegating persons to the status of things. Hence segregation is not only politically, economically, and sociologically unsound, it is morally wrong and sinful. Paul Tillich has said that sin is separation. Is not segregation an existential expression of man's tragic separation, his awful estrangement, his terrible sinfulness? Thus it is that I can urge men to obey the 1954 decision of the Supreme Court, for it is morally right; and I can urge them to disobey segregation ordinances, for they are morally wrong.

Let us consider a more concrete example of just and unjust laws. An unjust law is a code that a numerical or power majority group compels a minority group to obey but does not make binding on itself. This is *difference* made legal. By the same token, a just law is a code that a majority compels a minority to follow and that it is willing to follow itself. This is *sameness* made legal.

Let me give another explanation. A law is unjust if it is inflicted on a minority that, as a result of being denied the right to vote, had no part in enacting or devising the law. Who can say that the legislature of Alabama which set up that state's segregation laws was democratically elected? Throughout Alabama all sorts of devious methods are used to prevent Negroes from becoming registered voters, and there are some counties in which, even though Negroes constitute a majority of the population, not a single Negro is registered. Can any law enacted under such circumstances be considered democratically structured?

20   Sometimes a law is just on its face and unjust in its application. For instance, I have been arrested on a charge of parading without a permit. Now, there is nothing wrong in having an ordinance which requires a permit for a parade. But such an ordinance becomes unjust when it is used to maintain segregation and to deny citizens the First-Amendment privilege of peaceful assembly and protest.

I hope you are able to see the distinction I am trying to point out. In no sense do I advocate evading or defying the law, as would the rabid segregationist. That would lead to anarchy. One who breaks an unjust law must do so openly, lovingly, and with a willingness to accept the penalty. I submit that an individual who breaks a law that conscience tells him is unjust, and who willingly accepts the penalty of imprisonment in order to arouse the conscience of the community over its injustice, is in reality expressing the highest respect for law.

Of course, there is nothing new about this kind of civil disobedience. It was evidenced sublimely in the refusal of Shadrach, Meshach, and Abednego to obey the laws of Nebuchadnezzar, on the ground that a higher moral law was at stake. It was practiced superbly by the early Christians, who were willing to face hungry lions and the excruciating pain of chopping blocks rather than submit to certain unjust laws of the Roman Empire. To a degree, academic freedom is a reality today because Socrates practiced civil disobedience. In our own nation, the Boston Tea Party represented a massive act of civil disobedience.

We should never forget that everything Adolph Hitler did in Germany was "legal" and everything the Hungarian freedom fighters did in Hungary was "illegal." It was "illegal" to aid and comfort a Jew in Hitler's Germany. Even so, I am sure that, had I lived in Germany at the time, I would have aided and comforted my Jewish brothers. If today I lived in a Communist country where certain principles dear to the Christian faith are suppressed, I would openly advocate disobeying that country's anti-religious laws.

I must make two honest confessions to you, my Christian and Jewish brothers. First, I must confess that over the past few years I have been gravely disappointed with the white moderate. I have almost reached the regrettable conclusion that the Negro's great stumbling block in his stride toward freedom is not the White Citizens Counciler or the Ku Klux Klanner, but the white moderate, who is more devoted to "order" than to justice; who prefers a negative peace which is the absence of tension to a positive peace which is the presence of justice; who constantly says, "I agree with you in the goal you seek, but I cannot agree with your methods of direct action"; who paternalistically believes he can set the timetable for another man's freedom; who lives by a mythical concept of time and who constantly advises the Negro to wait for a "more convenient season." Shallow understanding from people of good will is more frustrating than absolute misunderstanding from people of ill will. Lukewarm acceptance is much more bewildering than outright rejection.

25   I had hoped that the white moderate would understand that law and order exist for the purpose of establishing justice and that when they fail in this purpose they become the dangerously structured dams that block the flow of social progress. I had hoped that the white moderate would understand that the present tension in the South is a necessary phase of the transition from an obnoxious negative peace, in which the Negro passively accepted his unjust plight, to a substantive and positive peace, in which all men will respect the dignity and worth of human personality. Actually, we who engage in nonviolent direct action are not the creators of tension. We merely bring to the surface the hidden tension that is already alive. We bring it out in the open, where it can be seen and dealt with. Like a boil that can never be cured so long as it is covered up but must be opened with all its ugliness to the natural medicines of air and light, injustice must be exposed, with all the tension its exposure creates, to the light of human conscience and the air of national opinion, before it can be cured.

In your statement you assert that our actions, even though peaceful, must be condemned because they precipitate violence. But is this a logical assertion? Isn't this like condemning a robbed man because his possession of money precipitated the evil act of robbery? Isn't this like condemning Socrates because his unswerving commitment to truth and his philosophical inquiries precipitated the act by the misguided populace in which they made him drink hemlock? Isn't this like condemning Jesus because his unique God-consciousness and never-ceasing devotion to God's will precipitated the evil act of crucifixion? We must come to see that, as the federal courts have consistently affirmed, it is wrong to urge an individual to cease his efforts to gain his basic constitutional rights because the quest may precipitate violence. Society must protect the robbed and punish the robber.

I had also hoped that the white moderate would reject the myth concerning time in relation to the struggle for freedom. I have just received a letter from a white brother in Texas. He writes: "All Christians know that the colored people will receive equal rights eventually, but it is possible that you are in too great a religious hurry. It has taken Christianity almost two thousand years to accomplish what it has. The teachings of Christ take time to come to earth." Such an attitude stems from a tragic misconception of time, from the strangely irrational notion that there is something in the very flow of time that will inevitably cure all ills. Actually, time itself is neutral; it can be used either destructively or constructively. More and more I feel that the people of ill will have used time much more effectively than have the people of good will. We will have to repent in this generation not merely for the hateful words and actions of the bad people, but for the appalling silence of the good people. Human progress never rolls in on wheels of inevitability; it comes through the tireless efforts of men willing to be coworkers with God, and without his hard work, time itself becomes an ally of the forces of social stagnation. We must use time creatively, in the knowledge that the time is always ripe to do right. Now is the time to make real the promise of democracy and transform our pending national elegy into a creative psalm of brotherhood. Now is the time to lift our national policy from the quicksand of racial injustice to the solid rock of human dignity.

You speak of our activity in Birmingham as extreme. At first I was rather disappointed that fellow clergymen would see my nonviolent efforts as those of an extremist. I began thinking about the fact that I stand in the middle of two opposing forces in the Negro community. One is a force of complacency, made up in part of Negroes who, as a result of long years of oppression, are so drained of self-respect and a sense of "somebodiness" that they have adjusted to segregation; and in part of a few middle-class Negroes who, because of a degree of academic and economic security and because in some ways they profit by segregation, have become insensitive to the problems of the masses. The other force is one of bitterness and hatred, and it comes perilously close to advocating violence. It is expressed in the various black nationalist groups that are springing up across the nation, the largest and best-known being Elijah Muhammad's Muslim movement. Nourished by the Negro's frustration over the continued existence of racial discrimination, this movement is made up of people who have lost faith in America, who have absolutely repudiated Christianity, and who have concluded that the white man is an incorrigible "devil."

I have tried to stand between these two forces, saying that we need emulate neither the "do-nothingism" of the complacent nor the hatred and despair of the black nationalist. For there is the more excellent way of love and nonviolent protest. I am grateful to God that, through the influence of the Negro church, the way of nonviolence became an integral part of our struggle.

30   If this philosophy had not emerged, by now many streets of the South would, I am convinced, be flowing with blood. And I am further convinced that if our white brothers dismiss as "rabble-rousers" and "outside agitators" those of us who employ nonviolent direct action, and if they refuse to support our nonviolent efforts, millions of Negroes will, out of frustration and despair, seek solace and security in black-nationalist ideologies—a development that would inevitably lead to a frightening racial nightmare.

Oppressed people cannot remain oppressed forever. The yearning for freedom eventually manifests itself, and that is what has happened to the American Negro. Something within has reminded him of his birthright of freedom, and something without has reminded him that it can be gained. Consciously or unconsciously, he has been caught up by the *Zeitgeist,* and with his black brothers of Africa and his brown and yellow brothers of Asia, South America, and the Caribbean, the United States Negro is moving with a sense of great urgency toward the promised land of racial justice. If one recognizes this vital urge that has engulfed the Negro community, one should readily understand why public demonstrations are taking place. The Negro has many pent-up resentments and latent frustrations, and he must release them. So let him march; let him make prayer pilgrimages to the city hall; let him go on freedom rides—and try to understand why he must do so. If his repressed emotions are not released in nonviolent ways, they will seek expression through violence; this is not a threat but a fact of history. So I have not said to my people, "Get rid of your discontent." Rather, I have tried to say that this normal and healthy discontent can be channeled into the creative outlet of nonviolent direct action. And now this approach is being termed extremist.

But though I was initially disappointed at being categorized as an extremist, as I continued to think about the matter I gradually gained a measure of satisfaction from the label. Was not Jesus an extremist for love: "Love your enemies, bless them that curse you, do good to them that hate you, and pray for them which despitefully use you, and persecute you." Was not Amos an extremist for justice: "Let justice roll down like waters and righteousness like an ever-flowing stream." Was not Paul an extremist for the Christian gospel: "I bear in my body the marks of the Lord Jesus." Was not Martin Luther an extremist: "Here I stand; I cannot do otherwise, so help me God." And John Bunyan: "I will stay in jail to the end of my days before I make a butchery of my conscience." And

Abraham Lincoln: "This nation cannot survive half slave and half free." And Thomas Jefferson: "We hold these truths to be self-evident, that all men are created equal. . . ." So the question is not whether we will be extremists, but what kind of extremists we will be. Will we be extremists for hate or for love? Will we be extremists for the preservation of injustice or for the extension of justice? In that dramatic scene on Calvary's hill three men were crucified. We must never forget that all three were crucified for the same crime—the crime of extremism. Two were extremists for immorality, and thus fell below their environment. The other, Jesus Christ, was an extremist for love, truth, and goodness, and thereby rose above his environment. Perhaps the South, the nation, and the world are in dire need of creative extremists.

I had hoped that the white moderate would see this need. Perhaps I was too optimistic; perhaps I expected too much. I suppose I should have realized that few members of the oppressor race can understand the deep groans and passionate yearnings of the oppressed race, and still fewer have the vision to see that injustice must be rooted out by strong, persistent, and determined action. I am thankful, however, that some of our white brothers in the South have grasped the meaning of this social revolution and committed themselves to it. They are still all too few in quantity, but they are big in quality. Some—such as Ralph McGill, Lillian Smith, Harry Golden, James McBride Dabbs, Ann Braden, and Sarah Patton Boyle—have written about our struggle in eloquent and prophetic terms. Others have marched with us down nameless streets of the South. They have languished in filthy, roach-infested jails, suffering the abuse and brutality of policemen who view them as "dirty nigger-lovers." Unlike so many of their moderate brothers and sisters, they have recognized the urgency of the moment and sensed the need for powerful "action" antidotes to combat the disease of segregation.

Let me take note of my other major disappointment. I have been so greatly disappointed with the white church and its leadership. Of course, there are some notable exceptions. I am not unmindful of the fact that each of you has taken some significant stands on this issue. I commend you, Reverend Stallings, for your Christian stand on this past Sunday, in welcoming Negroes to your worship service on a nonsegregated basis. I commend the Catholic leaders of this state for integrating Spring Hill College several years ago.

But despite these notable exceptions, I must honestly reiterate that I have been disappointed with the church. I do not say this as one of those negative critics who can always find something wrong with the church. I say this as a minister of the gospel, who loves the church; who was nurtured in its bosom; who has been sustained by its spiritual blessings and who will remain true to it as long as the cord of life shall lengthen.

When I was suddenly catapulted into the leadership of the bus protest in Montgomery, Alabama, a few years ago, I felt we would be supported by the white church. I felt that the white ministers, priests, and rabbis of the South would be among our strongest allies. Instead, some have been outright opponents, refusing to understand the freedom movement and misrepresenting its leaders; all too many others have been more cautious than courageous and have remained silent behind the anesthetizing security of stained-glass windows.

In spite of my shattered dreams, I came to Birmingham with the hope that the white religious leadership of this community would see the justice of our cause and, with deep moral concern, would serve as the channel through which our just grievances could reach the power structure. I had hoped that each of you would understand. But again I have been disappointed.

There was a time when the church was very powerful—in the time when the early

Christians rejoiced at being deemed worthy to suffer for what they believed. In those days the church was not merely a thermometer that recorded the ideas and principles of popular opinion; it was a thermostat that transformed the mores of society. Whenever the early Christians entered a town, the people in power became disturbed and immediately sought to convict the Christians for being "disturbers of the peace" and "outside agitators." But the Christians pressed on, in the conviction that they were "a colony of heaven," called to obey God rather than man. Small in number, they were big in commitment. They were too God-intoxicated to be "astronomically intimidated." By their effort and example they brought an end to such ancient evils as infanticide and gladiatorial contests.

Things are different now. So often the contemporary church is a weak, ineffectual voice with an uncertain sound. So often it is an archdefender of the status quo. Far from being disturbed by the presence of the church, the power structure of the average community is consoled by the church's silent—and often even vocal—sanction of things as they are.

40   But the judgment of God is upon the church as never before. If today's church does not recapture the sacrificial spirit of the early church, it will lose its authenticity, forfeit the loyalty of millions, and be dismissed as an irrelevant social club with no meaning for the twentieth century. Every day I meet young people whose disappointment with the church has turned into outright disgust.

Perhaps I have once again been too optimistic. Is organized religion too inextricably bound to the status quo to save our nation and the world? Perhaps I must turn my faith to the inner spiritual church, the church within the church, as the true *ekklesia* and the hope of the world. But again I am thankful to God that some noble souls from the ranks of organized religion have broken loose from the paralyzing chains of conformity and joined us as active partners in the struggle for freedom. They have left their secure congregations and walked the streets of Albany, Georgia, with us. They have gone down the highways of the South on torturous rides for freedom. Yes, they have gone to jail with us. Some have been dismissed from their churches, have lost the support of their bishops and fellow ministers. But they have acted in the faith that right defeated is stronger than evil triumphant. Their witness has been the spiritual salt that has preserved the true meaning of the gospel in these troubled times. They have carved a tunnel of hope through the dark mountain of disappointment.

I hope the church as a whole will meet the challenge of this decisive hour. But even if the church does not come to the aid of justice, I have no despair about the future. I have no fear about the outcome of our struggle in Birmingham, even if our motives are at present misunderstood. We will reach the goal of freedom in Birmingham and all over the nation, because the goal of America is freedom. Abused and scorned though we may be, our destiny is tied up with America's destiny. Before the pilgrims landed at Plymouth, we were here. Before the pen of Jefferson etched the majestic words of the Declaration of Independence across the pages of history, we were here. For more than two centuries our forebears labored in this country without wages; they made cotton king; they built the homes of their masters while suffering gross injustice and shameful humiliation—and yet out of a bottomless vitality they continued to thrive and develop. If the inexpressible cruelties of slavery could not stop us, the opposition we now face will surely fail. We will win our freedom because the sacred heritage of our nation and the eternal will of God are embodied in our echoing demands.

Before closing I feel impelled to mention one other point in your statement that has troubled me profoundly. You warmly commended the Birmingham police for keeping "order" and "preventing violence." I doubt that you would have so warmly commended the police force if you had seen its dogs sinking their teeth into unarmed, nonviolent Negroes. I doubt that you would so quickly commend the policemen if you were to observe their ugly and inhumane treatment of Negroes here in the city jail; if you were to watch them push and curse old Negro women and young Negro girls; if you were to see them slap and kick old Negro men and young boys; if you were to observe them, as they did on two occasions, refuse to give us food because we wanted to sing our grace together. I cannot join you in your praise of the Birmingham police department.

It is true that the police have exercised a degree of discipline handling the demonstrators. In this sense they have conducted themselves rather "nonviolently" in public. But for what purpose? To preserve the evil system of segregation. Over the past few years I have consistently preached that nonviolence demands that the means we use must be as pure as the ends we seek. I have tried to make clear that it is wrong to use immoral means to attain moral ends. But now I must affirm that it is just as wrong, or perhaps even more so, to use moral means to preserve immoral ends. Perhaps Mr. Connor and his policemen have been rather nonviolent in public, as was Chief Pritchett in Albany, Georgia, but they have used the moral means of nonviolence to maintain the immoral end of racial injustice. As T. S. Eliot has said, "The last temptation is the greatest treason: To do the right deed for the wrong reason."

45   I wish you had commended the Negro sit-inners and demonstrators of Birmingham for their sublime courage, their willingness to suffer, and their amazing discipline in the midst of great provocation. One day the South will recognize its real heroes. They will be the James Merediths, with the noble sense of purpose that enables them to face jeering and hostile mobs, and with the agonizing loneliness that characterizes the life of the pioneer. They will be old, oppressed, battered Negro women, symbolized in a seventy-two-year-old woman in Montgomery, Alabama, who rose up with a sense of dignity and with her people decided not to ride segregated buses, and who responded with ungrammatical profundity to one who inquired about her weariness: "My feets is tired, but my soul is at rest." They will be the young high school and college students, the young ministers of the gospel and a host of their elders, courageously and nonviolently sitting in at lunch counters and willingly going to jail for conscience' sake. One day the South will know that when these disinherited children of God sat down at lunch counters, they were in reality standing up for what is best in the American dream and for the most sacred values in our Judaeo-Christian heritage, thereby bringing our nation back to those great wells of democracy which were dug deeply by the founding fathers in their formulation of the Constitution and the Declaration of Independence.

Never before have I written so long a letter. I'm afraid it is much too long to take your precious time. I can assure you that it would have been much shorter if I had been writing from a comfortable desk, but what else can one do when he is alone in a narrow jail cell, other than write long letters, think long thoughts, and pray long prayers?

If I have said anything in this letter that overstates the truth and indicates an unreasonable impatience, I beg you to forgive me. If I have said anything that understates the truth and indicates my having a patience that allows me to settle for anything less than brotherhood, I beg God to forgive me.

I hope this letter finds you strong in the faith. I also hope that circumstances will soon make it possible for me to meet each of you, not as an integrationist or a civil-rights leader but as a fellow clergyman and a Christian brother. Let us all hope that the dark clouds of racial prejudice will soon pass away and the deep fog of misunderstanding will be lifted from our fear-drenched communities, and in some not too distant tomorrow the radiant stars of love and brotherhood will shine over our great nation with all their scintillating beauty.

Yours for the cause of Peace and Brotherhood,
Martin Luther King, Jr.

READING AND THINKING

1. Consider the ethos of "Letter from Birmingham Jail." What does the first paragraph of the letter suggest about Dr. King's character? How can you tell from his language?

2. What does King gain or lose by comparing himself to the apostle Paul?

3. Notice how King's language in paragraph 4 becomes figurative: "an inescapable network of mutuality, tied in a single garment of destiny." What is the effect of this language? Why do you think King uses it in that particular paragraph and later in the letter?

4. In paragraph 5, King finally challenges the clergymen. How effective is that challenge? Consider its position in the letter—what came before and what comes after. Consider too the logic of his comparisons.

5. What does King mean by creative tension and how does he answer the criticism that his campaign based on nonviolent action is "untimely"?

6. Read paragraph 15 aloud so that you can experience the rhythm of King's language. How does that rhythm—set in motion by the repetition of the single word *when*—affect you emotionally (pathos)?

7. Find at least one other place in the letter where King uses parallel structure and repetition to create a rhythm of involvement. Does that rhetorical tactic, in his hands, ever appeal to logos or ethos, that is, to logic or emotion? Explain.

8. What paradox does King have in mind when he responds to the clergymen's complaint that the nonviolent protestors are breaking the law?

THINKING AND WRITING

1. Consider King's argument about just and unjust laws. Prepare a two-page analysis of that argument in which you assess his effectiveness in terms of logos. Consider his evidence and the way he uses it, and then respond to King's argument with an argument of your own about such laws.

2. Consider King's closing paragraphs (45–47). How would you characterize them? Sarcastic, conciliatory, reproachful, apologetic? Provide your answer in a short paragraph, justifying your classification with evidence from the letter itself.

3. King refers explicitly to Jefferson at least twice in the letter. Make a list of other places in the letter where King seems to be under Jefferson's rhetorical influence, and then write a paragraph defending your selections.

CONSIDERING LIBERTY: AN OCCASION FOR WRITING

In "Letter from Birmingham Jail," Martin Luther King, Jr., argues that African Americans in the 1960s had a right to engage in civil disobedience so that they could gain access to the civil liberties they had long been denied. This Occasion allows you to discuss and consider a different threat to our national and individual freedoms.

We live in an interesting time when the so-called free world lives under the threat of a pervasive terrorism. But no one is quite sure where the terrorists are or just exactly how they are all connected. Since September 11, 2001, the United States has faced heightened security, fluctuating alerts, activation of the reserves and the national guard, a fear about homeland security, and a protracted war with Iraq, a country whose terrorist connections remain unclear. The insecurity that follows terrorism continues to threaten us, our freedoms, and our very way of life.

The following image by American photographer Keith Carter allows you to think about the longterm effects of terrorism and to consider how America's interests and values seem to have shifted in the last few decades from matters of civil disobedience on the national front to matters of threatened civil liberty and national security on both the local and international scene.

KEITH CARTER, *George Washington (1990)*

© Keith Carter

PREPARING TO WRITE: OCCASIONS TO THINK ABOUT WHAT YOU SEE

1. What do you see in the child's eyes in Carter's photograph? In Washington's eyes?

2. Everyone knows that George Washington is considered the "Father of our Country." What else does he stand for in the nation's folklore?

3. Carter's photograph looks posed. Does that pose appeal to logos or pathos? Would the appeal have been different if the child had been photographed against a different backdrop, say an American flag?

4. What do you suppose this child's relationship is to the picture he is holding? Why do you imagine Carter deprives us of specific knowledge about that relationship by photographing the child and Washington in a relatively neutral context?

5. Consider the text in the cartoon. What do you suppose the security guard means by "civil liberties"? How can civil liberties be "removed" from our person?

6. What can you tell about Uncle Sam by his expression and his dress? Explain.

7. Who is Uncle Sam anyway? Conduct an Internet search to discover what he has stood for in America's history.

8. What does the cartoonist suggest that America has lost (other than some of its civil liberties) by depicting Uncle Sam under scrutiny by airport security?

9. Where do you suppose Uncle Sam is going?

MOVING TOWARD ESSAY: OCCASIONS TO ANALYZE AND REFLECT

1. With your eye on Carter's photograph, imagine another child in need within America, a child you know more about. Whose portrait would he or she hold? What would that pair of faces tell us about the state of civil rights in America today? Defend your analysis in a 2-page response.

2. Consider the child in Carter's photograph along with Dr. King's comments about children in "Letter from Birmingham Jail." In a paragraph, explain how the child in the photograph seems either to underscore or contradict King's hopes for the future.

3. Considering the cartoon and the photograph together, speculate about the relationship that now exists in America between these two iconic figures: Uncle Sam (representative of the federal government's power) and George Washington ("Father of our Country," whose leadership led to the ratification of the Constitution and the Bill of Rights and also paved the way for the modern federal judiciary). Write a 2-page essay presenting your ideas.

WRITING THOUGHTFULLY: OCCASIONS FOR IDEAS AND ESSAYS

1. Consider the cartoon again, especially the way it depicts Uncle Sam. Compare that depiction with this World War I poster—one of the most popular posters ever printed in the United States. Using these two images of Uncle Sam as your primary evidence, write a 4- to 5-page essay in which you reveal the extent to which the country's collective mindset has changed in less than a century. You can also use evidence that you find on the Internet or that your own experience calls to mind.

© Swim Ink/CORBIS

2. Return to "Letter from Birmingham Jail" and reconsider King's case against the "white moderate" and the "white church" (paras. 23–32, 33–41). Make a three-column list with the headings logos, ethos, and pathos. As you read through the appropriate sections of the letter, put a checkmark under one heading or the other for each of King's paragraphs. At the end of your analysis, characterize King's argument in terms of those three aspects of persuasion. Defend your characterization with evidence from your analysis and from the text itself.

CREATING OCCASIONS

1. Go to Keith Carter's website at http://keithcarterphotographs.com and find another photograph to replace the one that appears in this section. Justify your selection in a 3-page letter to the editors of this book. Attach the photograph to your letter.

2. Select a Carter photograph that helps you understand something crucial about "Letter from Birmingham Jail." The photograph need not suggest anything about race or civil disobedience. It might very well highlight other features of Dr. King's argument. Justify your selection in a 3-page letter to the editors of this book. Attach the photograph to your letter.

On what occasions might an individual do this kind of work?

What details of the image lead you to this conclusion?

WHAT ARE THE DANGERS OF JOBS?

WORK AND WORKING

14

Work is something we have to do; it's what we do to support ourselves. If we are lucky it may also engage and interest us. Furthermore, it may enable us to develop our skills, talents, and proficiencies.

Work can be enjoyable and challenging, but most people would recognize that even the best of work requires at least some kinds of tedium or drudgery. Work tends to be tedious for the uneducated, for the underprepared, for those without choices about how to make a living or support themselves. Work tends to be more likely to provide pleasures of mind and spirit, to offer interesting opportunities for personal growth, and to yield private satisfactions for those prepared by education, money, and luck to make their living doing things they find engaging, even fulfilling.

For many people, finding enjoyable work—a kind of work that provides the rewards of both pleasure and profit, the satisfactions of successful achievement—is a chief aim of life.

In today's economy, finding work, any kind of work, is becoming increasingly competitive. With U.S. businesses outsourcing jobs and off-shoring work, an ever-larger number of Americans will be vying for jobs and careers with competitors from faraway places, including India and China.

Because work is inescapable for most people, because many people define themselves, at least in part, by the kind of work they do, and because the kinds of jobs we hold and the people we work with are matters of great importance, the essays in this chapter are of special relevance. George Orwell's description of his exhausting and tedious work as a hotel dishwasher contrasts sharply with Donald Hall's essay about finding fulfilling "lifework" as a writer. Christopher Clausen's arguments against work, arguments for why we should work less rather than more, dovetails with Ellen Gilchrist's essay about finding a

627

balance between work and family, between work and life. Ellen Goodman's "Company Man" presents a case-study of someone who did not achieve Gilchrist's balancing act, instead making his work his life and his life his work. Finally, Thomas L. Friedman assesses the ways many kinds of jobs are going global.

THE WORKING LIFE

Some people work to live, others live to work. Work, at least the right kinds of work in the right amounts at the right time, can be enjoyable, fulfilling, and rewarding. That is one reason some people can be said to live to work. Their rewards might be financial; they want to make so much money that they can retire early or live a life of luxury. For others the rewards might be those of social prestige or psychological fulfillment for doing work that society values and that they strongly believe in.

Another reason some people fill their lives with work is that they have no real interests, no intensive and alluring leisure pursuits outside their work, and so they work to fill their time and their days. Perhaps, too, some people work to escape problems at home—bad marriages, unhappy relationships, or other unpleasantness in their personal lives.

Regardless of our reasons for working, whether out of love for our careers; out of necessity to make ends meet; for social, political, economic, religious, or other reasons, work is something that most of us will always do. Even when many of us retire from active, full-time work, we will work at hobbies, we will do volunteer work, and we may also work part-time. For all these reasons, work is worth thinking about.

The essays in this cluster help us think about what our work accomplishes and what we gain from doing it. What types of priorities do our work lives signal to others? How do our work lives mesh with our personal lives? Why do we define ourselves, and sometimes our lives, in terms of our work? The essays presented here not only vary in focus and perspective, but also in the kinds of work the writers discuss and how their work rewards their expectations. Ellen Goodman provides a character sketch of a man who lives for his work, devoting his life to his work as a "company man." George Orwell offers an inside look at the grueling and exhausting work that goes on behind the doors of hotel kitchens, offering an implied critique of those who exploit low-wage earners. Donald Hall, in excerpts from his book *Life Work,* looks at work from a more positive angle as he describes what work means for him and why and how he performs the kind of work he does.

Ellen Goodman (b. 1941)

Ellen Goodman is a native of Newton, Massachusetts and a graduate of Radcliffe College, Harvard University. After working as a reporter for several news organizations, she joined the *Boston Globe* in 1967 and has been on the staff there ever since. She writes an editorial column titled "At Large" that blends the personal with the political. Her column has been syndicated in more than 250 newspapers nationwide. A winner of the Pulitzer Prize for commentary in 1980, Goodman has collected her columns in a number of books, including *Close to Home* (1979). She also coauthored *I Know Just What You Mean: The Power of Friendship in Women's Lives* (2000).

THE COMPANY MAN

In "The Company Man," Goodman presents a character sketch of a man who sacrifices everything for his job. He gives up his social life and his family life, keeping his focus instead completely on his work as a corporate vice president. Goodman's parable invites us to consider the kinds of trade-offs the company man has made.

1   He worked himself to death, finally and precisely, at 3:00 A.M. Sunday morning.

The obituary didn't say that, of course. It said that he died of a coronary thrombosis—I think that was it—but everyone among his friends and acquaintances knew it instantly. He was a perfect Type A, a workaholic, a classic, they said to each other and shook their heads—and thought for five or ten minutes about the way they lived.

This man who worked himself to death finally and precisely at 3:00 A.M. Sunday morning—on his day off—was fifty-one years old and a vice-president. He was, however, one of six vice-presidents, and one of three who might conceivably—if the president died or retired soon enough—have moved to the top spot. Phil knew that.

He worked six days a week, five of them until eight or nine at night, during a time when his own company had begun the four-day week for everyone but the executives. He worked like the Important People. He had no outside "extracurricular interests," unless, of course, you think about a monthly golf game that way. To Phil, it was work. He always ate egg salad sandwiches at his desk. He was, of course, overweight, by 20 or 25 pounds. He thought it was okay, though, because he didn't smoke.

On Saturdays, Phil wore a sports jacket to   5 the office instead of a suit, because it was the weekend.

He had a lot of people working for him, maybe sixty, and most of them liked him most of the time. Three of them will be seriously considered for his job. The obituary didn't mention that.

But it did list his "survivors" quite accurately. He is survived by his wife, Helen, forty-eight years old, a good woman of no particular marketable skills, who worked in an office before marrying and mothering. She had, according to her daughter, given up trying to compete with his work years ago, when the children were small. A company friend said, "I know how much you will miss him." And she answered, "I already have."

"Missing him all these years," she must have given up part of herself which had cared too much for the man. She would be "well taken care of."

His "dearly beloved" eldest of the "dearly beloved" children is a hard-working executive in a manufacturing firm down South. In the day and a half before the funeral, he went around the neighborhood researching his father, asking the neighbors what he was like. They were embarrassed.

10   His second child is a girl, who is twenty-four and newly married. She lives near her mother and they are close, but whenever she was alone with her father, in a car driving somewhere, they had nothing to say to each other.

The youngest is twenty, a boy, a high-school graduate who has spent the last couple of years, like a lot of his friends, doing enough odd jobs to stay in grass and food. He was the one who tried to grab at his father, and tried to mean enough to him to keep the man at home. He was his father's favorite. Over the last two years, Phil stayed up nights worrying about the boy.

The boy once said, "My father and I only board here."

At the funeral, the sixty-year-old company president told the forty-eight-year-old widow that the fifty-one-year-old deceased had meant much to the company and would be missed and would be hard to replace. The widow didn't look him in the eye. She was afraid he would read her bitterness and, after all, she would need him to straighten out the finances—the stock options and all that.

Phil was overweight and nervous and worked too hard. If he wasn't at the office, he was worried about it. Phil was a Type A, a heart-attack natural. You could have picked him out in a minute from a lineup.

So when he finally worked himself to   15 death, at precisely 3:00 A.M. Sunday morning, no one was really surprised.

By 5:00 P.M. the afternoon of the funeral, the company president had begun, discreetly of course, with care and taste, to make inquiries about his replacement. One of the three men. He asked around: "Who's been working the hardest?"

READING AND THINKING

1. Do you agree with Goodman's description of Phil as a "workaholic"? Why or why not?

2. What is Goodman's attitude toward Phil and toward the general type he represents? What words and phrases led you to your understanding of her tone?

3. Why do you think Goodman includes details about the time of his death? What effect does she achieve by repeating those details?

4. What is the effect of Goodman's use of generic terms, such as "the widow," "the son," "the daughter," "the company president," and "the company man"?

5. What is implied by the question the boss asks at the end of the essay?

THINKING AND WRITING

1. How does Goodman organize her essay? Where would you mark off the following parts: introduction, body, and conclusion? How are paragraphs 1 and 16 related? How about paragraphs 2 and 3 and paragraph 15?

2. Why do you think Goodman puts so many words in quotation marks? What is the effect of those quotation marks?

3. Imagine that you are the president of the company for which Phil worked. Write a letter to Phil's wife. Decide what you want to say in the letter and what tone you will take. Do the same letter-writing exercise, imagining you are Phil's wife writing to the company president.

4. Write a defense of Phil as a "company man." Try to imagine what Phil himself would say about why he made the decisions about his work that he did.

CONFORMITY AND THE COMPANY MAN: AN OCCASION FOR WRITING

In "The Company Man," Ellen Goodman portrays Phil as a man so devoted to (or at least caught up in) his work that he leaves little if any time for living. By designating Phil a "company man," she emphasizes how he takes his identity from his employer, making his job define his life. To the extent that he does this, Phil conforms to a set of American cultural norms that elevate work above all other aspects of life. In this Occasion for Writing, you will have a chance to think about the power and dangers of conformity.

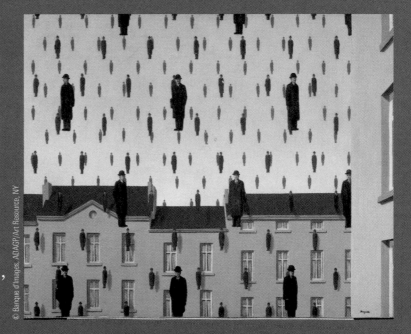

RENÉ MAGRITTE, *Golconde (1953)*

© Banque d'images, ADAGP/Art Resource, NY

© Photothèque R. Magritte-ADAGP/Art Resource, NY

RENÉ MAGRITTE,
The Son of Man (1964)

PREPARING TO WRITE: OCCASIONS TO THINK ABOUT WHAT YOU SEE

1. Describe what you see in each of Magritte's paintings. What does the repeating image in *Golconde* seem to suggest? What is the effect of the facial detail in *The Son of Man*? Explain.

2. Make a list of qualities or characteristics in these two paintings that, taken together, define—or at least identify—"the company man" as Goodman explains it.

MOVING TOWARD ESSAY: OCCASIONS TO ANALYZE AND REFLECT

1. Compare the way René Magritte's paintings use repetition with the way Ellen Goodman uses repetition in "The Company Man."

2. What do you think prompted Magritte to paint these images? Based on the images alone, what do you think are his opinions on the "company man"? Do some research on Magritte to find out more about his views and his artworks.

3. From the list of qualities or characteristics of the company man you created earlier, write a couple of paragraphs in which you explain the importance of each trait to the "company." What traits emphasize conformity?

4. Tell a story about a company man or a company woman you have known. Rather than generalize, provide a specific scene that shows the individual demonstrating "company"-like behavior.

WRITING THOUGHTFULLY: OCCASIONS FOR IDEAS AND ESSAYS

1. Write an essay about the kind of work you envision yourself doing when you complete your studies. To what extent do you see yourself as a future "company" man or woman? Why? Consider the extent to which your work and career will or may put you into the situation of having to be a "company man" or a "company woman." Does conformity ever play a role in work? What are your opinions of conformity in the workplace? In what instances would or would you not conform for your career?

2. Write an essay in which you identify the writer's and artist's attitude toward the figures depicted in the essay and paintings. Analyze the rhetorical techniques Ellen Goodman uses to convey her attitude toward Phil, and analyze the artistic techniques and details used by René Magritte to convey an attitude toward the figures depicted in the paintings. What kind of commentary are both these artists making on society and work? How do you agree and disagree with them?

CREATING OCCASIONS

1. Find three or four visual images that convey a sense of conformity and a couple of images that convey a sense of nonconformity. Consider how the conforming images are alike and how the images of nonconformity differ from them. Next, select two individuals who can be considered as nonconformists and explain how their beliefs, behavior, or both are nonconformist. Possibilities include Socrates, Jesus, Gandhi, Thoreau, and Florence Nightingale. How did your chosen individuals' nonconformity advance their careers?

George Orwell (1903–1950)

For a full biographical note on George Orwell, please see page 514.

HOTEL KITCHENS

In "Hotel Kitchens," Orwell describes various jobs he did in the kitchens of Parisian hotels. Orwell shares his experience not only of the work but of the lives of his fellow workers who struggle to make a living performing exhausting work with little time off. Throughout the piece, Orwell uses imagery and metaphor to convey vividly what this particular work experience was like.

1   The Hôtel X. was a vast, grandiose place with a classical façade, and at one side a little, dark doorway like a rat-hole, which was the service entrance. I arrived at a quarter to seven in the morning. A stream of men with greasy trousers were hurrying in and being checked by a doorkeeper who sat in a tiny office. I waited, and presently the *chef du personnel,* a sort of assistant manager, arrived and began to question me. He was an Italian, with a round, pale face, haggard from overwork. He asked whether I was an experienced dishwasher, and I said that I was; he glanced at my hands and saw that I was lying, but on hearing that I was an Englishman he changed his tone and engaged me.

"We have been looking for someone to practice our English on," he said. "Our clients are all Americans, and the only English we know is—" He repeated something that little boys write on the walls in London. "You may be useful. Come downstairs."

He led me down a winding staircase into a narrow passage, deep underground, and so low that I had to stoop in places. It was stiflingly hot and very dark, with only dim, yellow bulbs several yards apart. There seemed to be miles of dark labyrinthine passages—actually, I suppose, a few hundred yards in all—that reminded one queerly of the lower decks of a liner; there were the same heat and cramped space and warm reek of food, and a humming, whirring noise (it came from the kitchen furnaces) just like the whir of engines. We passed doorways which let out sometimes a shouting of oaths, sometimes the red glare of a fire, once a shuddering draught from an ice chamber. As we went along, something struck me violently in the back. It was a hundred-pound block of ice, carried by a blue-aproned porter. After him came a boy with a great slab of veal on his shoulder, his cheek pressed into the damp, spongy flesh. They shoved me aside with a cry of *"Sauve-toi, idiot!"* and rushed on. On the wall, under one of the lights, someone had written in a very neat hand: "Sooner will you find a cloudless sky in winter, than a woman at the Hôtel X. who has her maidenhead." It seemed a queer sort of place.

One of the passages branched off into a laundry, where an old, skullfaced woman gave me a blue apron and a pile of dishcloths. Then the *chef du personnel* took me to a tiny underground den—a cellar below a cellar, as it were—where there were a sink and some gas-ovens. It was too low for me to stand quite upright, and the temperature was perhaps 110 degrees Fahrenheit. The *chef du personnel* explained that my job was to fetch meals for the higher hotel employees, who fed in a small dining room above, clean their room and wash their crockery. When he had gone, a waiter, another Italian, thrust a fierce, fuzzy head into the doorway and looked down at me.

"English, eh?" he said. "Well, I'm in charge 5 here. If you work well"—he made the motion of up-ending a bottle and sucked noisily. "If you don't"—he he gave the doorpost several vigorous kicks. "To me, twisting your neck would be no more than spitting on the floor. And if there's any trouble, they'll believe me, not you. So be careful."

After this I set to work rather hurriedly. Except for about an hour, I was at work from seven in the morning till a quarter-past nine at night; first at washing crockery, then at scrubbing the tables and floors of the employees' dining room, then at polishing glasses and knives, then at fetching meals, then at washing crockery again, then at fetching more meals and washing more crockery. It was easy work, and I got on well with it except when I went to the kitchen to fetch meals. The kitchen was like nothing I had ever seen or imagined—a stifling, low-ceilinged inferno of a cellar, red-lit from the fires, and deafening with oaths and the clanging of pots and pans. It was so hot that all the metal work except the stoves had to be covered with cloth. In the middle were furnaces, where twelve cooks skipped to and fro, their faces dripping sweat in spite of their white caps. Round that were counters where a mob of waiters and *plongeurs* clamored with trays. Scullions, naked to the waist, were stoking the fires and scouring huge copper saucepans with sand. Everyone seemed to be in a hurry and a rage. The head cook, a fine, scarlet man with big moustachios, stood in the middle booming continuously, *"Ça marche deux oeufs brouillés! Ça marche un Château-briand aux pommes sautées!"* except when he broke off to curse at a *plongeur*. There were three counters, and the first time I went to the kitchen I took my tray unknowingly to the wrong one. The head cook walked up to me, twisted his moustaches, and looked me up and down. Then he beckoned to the breakfast cook and pointed at me.

"Do you see *that?* That is the type of *plongeur* they send us nowadays. Where do you come from, idiot? From Charenton, I suppose?" (There was a large lunatic asylum at Charenton.)

"From England," I said.

"I might have known it. Well, *mon cher monsieur l'Anglais,* may I inform you that you are the son of a whore? And now——the camp to the other counter, where you belong."

I got this kind of reception every time I went to the kitchen, for I always made some mistake; I was expected to know the work, and was cursed accordingly. From curiosity I counted the number of times I was called *maquereau* during the day, and it was thirty-nine.

At half-past four the Italian told me that I could stop working, but that it was not worth going out, as we began again at five. I went to the lavatory for a smoke; smoking was strictly forbidden, and Boris had warned me that the lavatory was the only safe place. After that I worked again till a quarter-past nine, when the waiter put his head into the doorway and told me to leave the rest of the crockery. To my astonishment, after calling me pig, mackerel, etc., all day, he had suddenly grown quite friendly. I realized that the curses I had met with were only a kind of probation.

"That'll do, *mon p'tit,*" said the waiter. "*Tu n'es pas débrouillard,* but you work all right. Come up and have your dinner. The hotel allows us two liters of wine each, and I've stolen another bottle. We'll have a fine booze."

We had an excellent dinner from the leavings of the higher employees. The waiter, grown mellow, told me stories about his love affairs, and about two men whom he had stabbed in Italy, and about how he had dodged his military service. He was a good fellow when one got to know him; he reminded me of Benvenuto Cellini, somehow. I was tired and drenched with sweat, but I felt a new man after a day's solid food. The work did not seem difficult, and I felt that this job would suit me. It was not certain, however, that it would continue, for I had been engaged as an "extra" for the day only, at twenty-five francs. The sour-faced doorkeeper counted out the money, less fifty centimes which he said was for insurance (a lie, I discovered afterward).

Then he stepped out into the passage, made me take off my coat, and carefully prodded me all over, searching for stolen food. After this the *chef du personnel* appeared and spoke to me. Like the waiter, he had grown more genial on seeing that I was willing to work.

"We will give you a permanent job if you like," he said. "The head waiter says he would enjoy calling an Englishman names . . ."

15   . . . I worked . . . four days a week in the cafeterie, one day helping the waiter on the fourth floor, and one day replacing the woman who washed up for the dining room. My day off, luckily, was Sunday, but sometimes another man was ill and I had to work that day as well. The hours were from seven in the morning till two in the afternoon, and from five in the evening till nine—eleven hours; but it was a fourteen-hour day when I washed up for the dining room. By the ordinary standards of a Paris *plongeur*, these are exceptionally short hours. The only hardship of life was the fearful heat and stuffiness of these labyrinthine cellars. Apart from this the hotel, which was large and well organized, was considered a comfortable one.

Our cafeterie was a murky cellar measuring twenty feet by seven by eight high, and so crowded with coffee-urns, bread-cutters and the like that one could hardly move without banging against something. It was lighted by one dim electric bulb, and four or five gas fires that sent out a fierce red breath. There was a thermometer there, and the temperature never fell below 110 degrees Fahrenheit—it neared 130 at some times of the day. At one end were five service lifts, and at the other an ice cupboard where we stored milk and butter. When you went into the ice cupboard you dropped a hundred degrees of temperature at a single step; it used to remind me of the hymn about Greenland's icy mountains and India's coral strand. Two men worked in the cafeterie besides Boris and myself. One was Mario, a huge, excitable Italian—he was like

a city policeman with operatic gestures—and the other, a hairy, uncouth animal whom we called the Magyar; I think he was a Transylvanian, or something even more remote. Except the Magyar we were all big men, and at the rush hours we collided incessantly.

The work in the cafeterie was spasmodic. We were never idle, but the real work only came in bursts of two hours at a time—we called each burst *"un coup de feu."* The first *coup de feu* came at eight, when the guests upstairs began to wake up and demand breakfast. At eight a sudden banging and yelling would break out all through the basement; bells rang on all sides, blue-aproned men rushed through the passages, our service lifts came down with a simultaneous crash, and the waiters on all five floors began shouting Italian oaths down the shafts. I don't remember all our duties, but they included making tea, coffee, and chocolate, fetching meals from the kitchen, wines from the cellar, and fruit and so forth from the dining room, slicing bread, making toast, rolling pats of butter, measuring jam, opening milk cans, counting lumps of sugar, boiling eggs, cooking porridge, pounding ice, grinding coffee—all this for from a hundred to two hundred customers. The kitchen was thirty yards away, and the dining room sixty or seventy yards. Everything we sent up in the service lifts had to be covered by a voucher, and the vouchers had to be carefully filed, and there was trouble if even a lump of sugar was lost. Besides this, we had to supply the staff with bread and coffee, and fetch the meals for the waiters upstairs. All in all, it was a complicated job.

I calculated that one had to walk and run about fifteen miles during the day, and yet the strain of the work was more mental than physical. Nothing could be easier, on the face of it, than this stupid scullion work, but it is astonishingly hard when one is in a hurry. One has to leap to and fro between a multitude of jobs—it is like sorting a pack of cards against the clock. You are, for example, making toast, when bang! down comes a service lift with an order for tea, rolls, and three different kinds of jams, and simultaneously bang! down comes another demanding scrambled eggs, coffee, and grapefruit; you run to the kitchen for the eggs and to the dining room for the fruit, going like lightning so as to be back before your toast burns, and having to remember about the tea and coffee, besides half a dozen other orders that are still pending; and at the same time some waiter is following you and making trouble about a lost bottle of soda water, and you are arguing with him. It needs more brains than one might think. Mario said, no doubt truly, that it took a year to make a reliable cafetier.

The time between eight and half-past ten was a sort of delirium. Sometimes we were going as though we had only five minutes to live; sometimes there were sudden lulls when the orders stopped and everything seemed quiet for a moment. Then we swept up the litter from the floor, threw down fresh sawdust, and swallowed gallipots of wine or coffee or water—anything, so long as it was wet. Very often we used to break off chunks of ice and suck them while we worked. The heat among the gas fires was nauseating; we swallowed quarts of drink during the day, and after a few hours even our aprons were drenched with sweat. At times we were hopelessly behind with the work, and some of the customers would have gone without their breakfast, but Mario always pulled us through. He had worked fourteen years in the cafeterie, and he had the skill that never wastes a second between jobs. The Magyar was very stupid and I was inexperienced, and Boris was inclined to shirk, partly because of his lame leg, partly because he was ashamed of working in the cafeterie after being a waiter; but Mario was wonderful. The way he would stretch his great arms right across the cafeterie to fill a coffee-pot with one hand and boil an egg with the other, at the same time watching toast and shouting directions to the Magyar, and between whiles singing snatches from *Rigoletto,* was beyond all praise. The *patron* knew his value, and he was paid a thousand francs a month, instead of five hundred like the rest of us.

The breakfast pandemonium stopped at half-past ten. Then we scrubbed the cafeterie tables, swept the floor and polished the brasswork, and, on good mornings, went one at a time to the lavatory for a smoke. This was our slack time—only relatively slack, however, for we had only ten minutes for lunch, and we never got through it uninterrupted. The customers' luncheon hour, between twelve and two, was another period of turmoil like the breakfast hour. Most of our work was fetching meals from the kitchen, which meant constant *engueulades* from the cooks. By this time the cooks had sweated in front of their furnaces for four or five hours, and their tempers were all warmed up.

At two we were suddenly free men. We threw off our aprons and put on our coats, hurried out of doors, and, when we had money, dived into the nearest *bistro*. It was strange, coming up into the street from those firelit cellars. The air seemed blindingly clear and cold, like arctic summer; and how sweet the petrol did smell, after the stenches of sweat and food! Sometimes we met some of our cooks and waiters in the *bistros,* and they were friendly and stood us drinks. Indoors we were their slaves, but it is an etiquette in hotel life that between hours everyone is equal, and the *engueulades* do not count.

At a quarter to five we went back to the hotel. Till half-past six there were no orders, and we used this time to polish silver, clean out the coffee-urns, and do other odd jobs. Then the grand turmoil of the day started—the dinner hour. I wish I could be Zola for a little while, just to describe that dinner hour. The essence of the situation was that a hundred or two hundred people were demanding individually different meals of five or six courses, and that fifty or sixty people had to cook and serve them and clean up the mess afterward; anyone with experience of catering will know what that means. And at this time when the work was doubled, the whole staff was tired out, and a number of them were drunk. I could write pages about the scene without giving a true idea of it. The chargings to and fro in the narrow passages, the collisions, the yells, the struggling with crates and trays and blocks of ice, the heat, the darkness, the furious festering quarrels which there was no time to fight out—they pass description. Anyone coming into the basement for the first time would have thought himself in a den of maniacs. It was only later, when I understood the working of a hotel, that I saw order in all this chaos.

At half-past eight the work stopped very suddenly. We were not free till nine, but we used to throw ourselves full length on the floor, and lie there resting our legs, too lazy even to go to the ice cupboard for a drink. Sometimes the *chef du personnel* would come in with bottles of beer, for the hotel stood us an extra beer when we had had a hard day. The food we were given was no more than eatable, but the *patron* was not mean about drink; he allowed us two liters of wine a day each, knowing that if a *plongeur* is not given two liters he will steal three. We had the heeltaps of bottles as well, so that we often drank too much—a good thing, for one seemed to work faster when partially drunk.

Four days of the week passed like this; of the other two working days, one was better and one worse. After a week of this life I felt in need of a holiday. It was Saturday night, so the people in our *bistro* were busy getting drunk, and with a free day ahead of me I was ready to join them. We all went to bed, drunk, at two in the morning, meaning to sleep till noon. At half-past five I was suddenly awakened. A night watchman, sent from the hotel, was standing at my bedside. He stripped the clothes back and shook me roughly.

25 "Get up!" he said. *"Tu t'es bien saoulé la gueule, eh?* Well, never mind that, the hotel's a man short. You've got to work today."

"Why should I work?" I protested. "This is my day off."

"Day off, nothing! The work's got to be done. Get up!"

I got up and went out, feeling as though my back were broken and my skull filled with hot cinders. I did not think that I could possibly do a day's work. And yet, after only an hour in the basement, I found that I was perfectly well. It seemed that in the heat of those cellars, as in a Turkish bath, one could sweat out almost any quantity of drink. *Plongeurs* know this, and count on it. The power of swallowing quarts of wine, and then sweating it out before it can do much damage, is one of the compensations of their life.

By far my best time at the hotel was when I went to help the waiter on the fourth floor. We worked in a small pantry which communicated with the cafeterie by service lifts. It was delightfully cool after the cellars, and the work was chiefly polishing silver and glasses, which is a humane job. Valenti, the waiter, was a decent sort, and treated me almost as an equal when we were alone, though he had to speak roughly when there was anyone else present, for it does not do for a waiter to be friendly with *plongeurs*. He used sometimes to tip me five francs when he had had a good day. He was a comely youth, aged twenty-four but looking eighteen, and, like most waiters, he carried himself well and knew how to wear his clothes. With his black tail coat and white tie, fresh face and sleek brown hair, he looked just like an Eton boy; yet he had earned his living since he was twelve, and worked his way up literally from the gutter. Crossing the Italian frontier without a passport, and selling chestnuts from a barrow on the northern boulevards, and being given fifty days' imprisonment in London for working without a permit, and being made love to by a rich old woman in a hotel, who gave him a diamond ring and afterward accused him of stealing it, were among his experiences. I used to enjoy talking to him, at slack times when we sat smoking down the lift shaft.

30   My bad day was when I washed up for the dining room. I had not to wash the plates, which were done in the kitchen, but only the other crockery, silver, knives and glasses; yet, even so, it meant thirteen hours' work, and I used between thirty and forty dishcloths during the day. The antiquated methods used in France double the work of washing up. Plate racks are unheard of, and there are no soap flakes, only the treacly soft soap, which refuses to lather in the hard, Paris water. I worked in a dirty, crowded little den, a pantry and scullery combined, which gave straight on the dining room. Besides washing up, I had to fetch the waiters' food and serve them at table; most of them were intolerably insolent, and I had to use my fists more than once to get common civility. The person who normally washed up was a woman, and they made her life a misery.

It was amusing to look round the filthy little scullery and think that only a double door was between us and the dining room. There sat the customers in all their splendor—spotless table-cloths, bowls of flowers, mirrors and gilt cornices and painted cherubim; and here, just a few feet away, we in our disgusting filth. For it really was disgusting filth. There was no time to sweep the floor till evening, and we slithered about in a compound of soapy water, lettuce-leaves, torn paper, and trampled food. A dozen waiters with their coats off, showing their sweaty armpits, sat at the table mixing salads and sticking their thumbs into the cream pots. The room had a dirty, mixed smell of food and sweat. Everywhere in the cupboards, behind the piles of crockery, were squalid stores of food that the waiters had stolen. There were only two sinks, and no washing basin, and it was nothing unusual for a waiter to wash his face in the water in which clean crockery was rinsing. But the customers saw nothing of this. There were a coconut mat and a mirror outside the dining-room door, and the waiters

used to preen themselves up and go in looking the picture of cleanliness.

It is an instructive sight to see a waiter going into a hotel dining-room. As he passes the door a sudden change comes over him. The set of his shoulders alters; all the dirt and hurry and irritation have dropped off in an instant. He glides over the carpet, with a solemn priest-like air. I remember our assistant *maître d'hôtel,* a fiery Italian, pausing at the dining-room door to address an apprentice who had broken a bottle of wine. Shaking his fist above his head he yelled (luckily the door was more or less soundproof):

"Tu me fais——Do you call yourself a waiter, you young bastard? You a waiter! You're not fit to scrub floors in the brothel your mother came from. *Maquereau!"*

Words failing him, he turned to the door; and as he opened it he delivered a final insult in the same manner as Squire Western in *Tom Jones.*

35   Then he entered the dining room and sailed across it dish in hand, graceful as a swan. Ten seconds later he was bowing reverently to a customer. And you could not help thinking, as you saw him bow and smile, with that benign smile of the trained waiter, that the customer was put to shame by having such an aristocrat to serve him.

This washing up was a thoroughly odious job—not hard, but boring and silly beyond words. It is dreadful to think that some people spend their whole decades at such occupations. The woman whom I replaced was quite sixty years old, and she stood at the sink thirteen hours a day, six days a week, the year round; she was, in addition, horribly bullied by the waiters. She gave out that she had once been an actress—actually, I imagine, a prostitute; most prostitutes end as charwomen. It was strange to see that in spite of her age and her life she still wore a bright blonde wig, and darkened her eyes and painted her face like a girl of twenty. So apparently even a seventy-eight-hour week can leave one with some vitality.

READING AND THINKING

1. What is your reaction to the world and the work that Orwell describes in "Hotel Kitchens"? Explain.

2. What details best convey for you what it was like to work in a Parisian hotel kitchen in the early part of the twentieth century? What overall impression do the accumulated details convey?

3. Why do you think Orwell describes the dining room as well as the kitchen? What is implied by his comparison of dining room and kitchen?

4. What is the effect of Orwell's inclusion of French words and phrases, such as "mon cher monsieur," "chef du personnel," "maquereau," and "coup de feu"? To what extent could you understand these foreign words and phrases from context?

THINKING AND WRITING

1. What do you think of the people with whom Orwell works in the kitchen of Hôtel X? How does he characterize each of them?

2. Explain why you think Orwell wrote this piece. What do you think he wants his readers to take away from a reading of it?

3. Describe a time when you had to perform hard physical labor. Try to convey what the work was like. Include specific details and some comparisons.

4. Describe a scene from a job you once had in which you characterize two or three of your coworkers as you provide a sense of the shared work you performed with them.

ON THE JOB: AN OCCASION FOR WRITING

Orwell's description of his work not only provides a vivid look at the working conditions in a particular type of big-city hotel kitchen, but also provides character sketches of his fellow workers. In the following Occasion for Writing you will be invited to consider how others have portrayed work and workers, and you will have a chance to consider your own work experience.

Studs Terkel was born in New York City and moved as a child to Chicago, where he spent most of his life. Terkel, who has published more than a dozen volumes, is best known for his books of oral history, which include *Hard Times: An Oral History of the Great Depression* and *Working* (1970), from which the following excerpt was taken.

BRUCE GILDEN,
Mercedes Benz marketing show, Washington, D.C. (2005)

© Bruce Gilden/Magnum Photos

THOMAS HOEPKER, SILVIA WOODS,
"The Queen of Soul Food," New York City (1986)

© Thomas Hoepker/Magnum Photos

Studs Terkel
from Working

Carl Murray Bates, Mason

1   With stone we build just about anything. Stone is the oldest and best building material that ever was. Stone was being used even by the cavemen that put it together with mud. They built out of stone before they even used logs. He got him a cave, he built stone across the front. And he learned to use dirt, mud, to make the stones lay there without sliding around—which was the beginnings of mortar, which we still call mud. The Romans used mortar that's almost as good as we have today.

Everyone hears these things, they just don't remember 'em. But me being in the profession, when I hear something in that line, I remember it. Stone's my business. I, oh, sometimes talk to architects and engineers that have made a study and I pick up the stuff here and there.

Every piece of stone you pick up is different, the grain's a little different and this and that. It'll split one way and break the other. You pick up your stone and look at it and make an educated guess. It's a pretty good day layin' stone or brick. Not tiring. Anything you like to do isn't tiresome. It's hard work; stone is heavy. At the same time, you get interested in what you're doing and you usually fight the clock the other way. You're not lookin' for quittin'. You're wondering you haven't got enough done and it's almost quittin' time. (Laughs.) I ask the hod carrier what time it is and he says two thirty. I say, "Oh, my Lord, I was gonna get a whole lot more than this."

One of my sons is an accountant and the other two are bankers. They're mathematicians, I suppose you'd call 'em that. Air-conditioned offices and all that. They always look at the house I build. They stop by and see me when I'm aworkin'. Always want me to come down and fix somethin' on their house,

too. (Laughs.) They don't buy a house that I don't have to look at it first. Oh, sure, I've got to crawl under it and look on the roof, you know. . . .

5   I can't seem to think of any young masons. So many of 'em before, the man lays stone and his son follows his footsteps. Right now the only one of these sons I can think of is about forty, fifty years old.

I started back in the Depression times when there wasn't any apprenticeships. You just go out and if you could hold your job, that's it. I was just a kid then. Now I worked real hard and carried all the blocks I could. Then I'd get my trowel and I'd lay one or two. The second day the boss told me: I think you could lay enough blocks to earn your wages. So I guess I had only one day of apprenticeship. Usually it takes about three years of being a hod carrier to start. And it takes another ten or fifteen years to learn the skill.

I admired the men that we had at that time that were stonemasons. They knew their trade. So naturally I tried to pattern after them. There's been very little change in the work. Stone is still stone, mortar is still the same as it was fifty years ago. The style of stone has changed a little. We use a lot more, we call it golf. A stone as big as a baseball up to as big as a basketball. Just round balls and whatnot. We just fit 'em in the wall that way.

Automation has tried to get in the bricklayer. Set 'em with a crane. I've seen several put up that way. But you've always got in-between the windows and this and that. It just doesn't seem to pan out. We do have a power saw. We do have an electric power mix to mix the mortar, but the rest of it's done by hand as it always was.

In the old days they all seemed to want it cut out and smoothed. It's harder now because you have no way to use your tools. You have no way to use a string, you have no way to use a level or a plumb. You just have to look at it because it's so rough and many irregularities. You have to just back up and look at it.

10   Stone's my life. I daydream all the time, most time it's on stone. Oh, I'm gonna build me a stone cabin down on the Green River. I'm gonna build stone cabinets in the kitchen. That stone door's gonna be awful heavy and I don't know how to attach the hinges. I've got to figure out how to make a stone roof. That's the kind of thing. All my dreams, it seems like it's got to have a piece of rock mixed in it.

I can't imagine a job where you go home and maybe go by a year later and you don't know what you've done. My work, I can see what I did the first day I started. All my work is set right out there in the open and I can look at it as I go by. It's something I can see the rest of my life. Forty years ago, the first blocks I ever laid in my life, when I was seventeen years old. I never go through Eureka—a little town down there on the river—that I don't look thataway. It's always there.

Immortality as far as we're concerned. Nothin' in this world lasts forever, but did you know that stone—Bedford limestone, they claim—deteriorates one-sixteenth of an inch every hundred years? And it's around four or five inches for a house. So that's gettin' awful close. (Laughs.)

PREPARING TO WRITE: OCCASIONS TO THINK ABOUT WHAT YOU SEE

1. Describe what you see in each picture. How would you characterize each of the people you see?

2. What do the two photographs have in common? How do they differ? Why do you think Halpern took an interest in these people?

3. Read the excerpted interview passages from Studs Terkel's book, *Working*. Identify two key points made by Carl Murray Bates, a stone mason, that reveal his attitude toward his work.

4. To what extent can you relate Bates's comments about his work with the photographs of workers? To the passage about Parisian hotel kitchen workers by George Orwell?

MOVING TOWARD ESSAY: OCCASIONS TO ANALYZE AND REFLECT

1. How does the following stanza from Robert Frost's poem "Two Tramps in Mud Time" relate to either Orwell's description of his job or to Terkel's stonemason? Use specific details from both the poem and the selections to support the relationship.

> Good blocks of oak it was I split,
> As large around as the chopping block;
> And every piece I squarely hit
> Fell splinterless as a cloven rock.
> The blows that a life of self-control
> Spares to strike for the common good,
> That day, giving a loose my soul,
> I spent on the unimportant wood.

2. How do the photographs of workers relate to the work Orwell describes in "Hotel Kitchens" or the Frost excerpt? To what extent do workers, such as those shown in the accompanying photographs, typically go unnoticed? Why are they sometimes "invisible" and to whom?

WRITING THOUGHTFULLY: OCCASIONS FOR IDEAS AND ESSAYS

1. Write an essay in which you consider what kind of work you would like to do—and why. What specific details about the evidence you've seen in this Occasion has made you come to this decision or reinforced any previous decisions you've made?

2. Write an editorial or opinion piece about the status and working conditions of service workers, such as those described in words and images in this chapter. What sort of stereotypes, if any, did you find yourself making? In your opinion, can all work be viewed as equally important in our society? Should all work be viewed as equal? What role does respect play in the workplace and how we view workers?

CREATING OCCASIONS

1. Do some research on what it is like to work in the service sector—at a restaurant or a hotel, for example—by interviewing friends and acquaintances who may have done such work or those currently working at hotel and/or restaurant jobs. Look also for the ways hotel and restaurant workers are characterized in movies, television, and print advertising. Consider consulting Barbara Ehrenreich's *Nickel and Dimed: On (Not) Getting by in America* (2001), Studs Terkel's *Working: People Talk about What They Do All Day and How They Feel about What They Do* (1974), and John Royston Coleman's *Blue-Collar Journal: A College President's Sabbatical* (1974).

Donald Hall (b. 1928)

Donald Hall was born in New Haven, Connecticut, and educated at Harvard University. He taught English until 1975 at the University of Michigan, when he retired from teaching to live on his family's farm in New Hampshire, where he devoted himself full-time to writing. Hall has published numerous books, including college textbooks, children's books, memoirs, plays, fiction, and many books of poetry, including *Old and New Poems* (1990) and *The Painted Bed* (2002). In 1993, while writing *Life Work,* Hall was diagnosed with cancer. His treatment was successful, but a short time later, his wife, the poet Jane Kenyon, died of breast cancer at the age of 47. Hall edited a book of her poems, *Otherwise* (1997), and wrote a book of poignant poems about his loss, *Without* (1998).

LIFE WORK

The following selection is a set of excerpted passages from Hall's memoir *Life Work,* a book structured as a series of meditations on work that ranges widely and includes anecdotes about Hall's ancestors and the worlds of work they inhabited. In the following selection, Hall raises questions about the meanings of "work," why we work, what we give to it, and what we gain from it.

I

1 I've never worked A day in my life. With the trivial exceptions of some teenage summers, I've never worked with my hands or shoulders or legs. I never stood on the line in Flint among the clangor and stench of embryonic Buicks for ten hours of small operations repeated on a large machine. Oh, I've watched this work, visiting a plant; I've watched *Modern Times* also. When I taught at the University of Michigan, many of my students worked summers installing gas tanks at River Rouge or building generators in Ypsilanti. Some of them came from families of line-workers; the university was a way out of Flint and Toledo. These children of line-parents moved to desks in offices, nine-to-five, which was my own father's work, and which I escaped. Doubtless my grandfather Hall, my father, and I made a stereotypical three generations: My father's father grew up without much school, doing muscle-work, and built a successful business; so he sent my father to college who worked out his life at a desk adding columns of figures among blonde-wood cubicles where properly dressed men and women worked with numbers five days a week and half a day on Saturday. Then there's me: I stay home and write poems—and essays, stories, textbooks, children's books, biography . . . Work?

Work. I make my living at it. Almost twenty years ago I quit teaching—giving up tenure, health insurance, and annual raises—as one of my children began college and the other was about to. I worked like crazy to pay tuitions and mortgages—but because I loved my work it was as if I did not work at all.

There are jobs, there are chores, and there is work. Reading proof is a chore; checking facts is a chore. When I edit for a magazine or a publisher, I do a job. When I taught school, the classroom fit none of these categories. I enjoyed teaching James Joyce and Thomas Wyatt too much to call it a job. The classroom was a lark because I got to show off, to read poems aloud, to help the young, and to praise authors or books that I loved. But teaching was not entirely larkish: Correcting piles of papers is tedious, even discouraging, because it tends to correct one's sanguine notions about having altered the young minds arranged in the classroom's rows. Reading papers was a chore—and after every ten papers, I might tell myself that I could take a break and read a Flannery O'Connor short story. But when I completed the whole pile, then I could reward myself with a real break: When I finished reading and correcting and grading and commenting on seventy-five essay-questions about a Ben Jonson or a Tom Clark poem, *then*—as a reward—I could get to work.

II

When the *Britannica* takes on Work, it qualifies the noun and addresses "Work, Organization of," but it supplies a definition when you're not looking: Work is "activities necessary to society's survival." (The *Britannica* does not think of work as something people *do;* everything is passive.) How boring it sounds, like most discussions of work. When Adam Smith talks about the eighteen divisions of labor in making a pin, or when Emile Durkheim does something similar, I fall asleep. Slaveowner Cicero writes more to my taste.

5   It is the family farm—which historians of work's structure derive from utter antiquity—that provides a model for my own work; one task after another, all day all year, and every task different. Of course: It was precisely the Connecticut family business of the Brock-Hall Dairy—milk pasteurizing and bottling and delivering; every-day-the-same, temporarily efficient subdivision of the industrial world; my father's curse—that I grew up determined to avoid or evade. And did.

In the "Day-Timer" beside my blue chair I keep a daily list. It is a pleasure, sleepy at night watching the Red Sox one-run behind in the seventh inning, to pick up the "Day-Timer," tear off today's corner, flip to tomorrow's page and list the next day's work. Recent pages read "Mertens at 2" (an interview about the National Endowment for the Arts); "5 o'clock Jerry" (my appointment with the dentist who is my son-in-law); and "Ct" (driv-ing to Connecticut for a visit with my mother.) Most days begin with laconic single words in a semantic order:

> poems
> prose

but today I write "proses" to suggest multiplicity: the tenth or eighteenth version of a periodical piece as well as a letter of recommendation and a proposal to the New Hampshire Arts Council. Underneath "proses" I place another pair of syllables:

> *Life Work*

Doubtless italic permits me to distinguish general from particular, and late in the day I will draw a straight line through:

> ~~poems~~
> ~~prose~~
> ~~*Life Work*~~

and a wavery line, to indicate failure, through the projects I didn't get to, as it were:

> ~~shovel snow~~
> ~~spade garden~~
> ~~rake leaves~~

III

My Connecticut great-grandfather Charlie Hall worked with his hands. After the reservoir job and the war, as an older man with a grown family, he worked for Farmer Webb in a part of Hamden now called, after a 1920 developer's dainty device of onomastic invention, Spring Glen. Charlie was a farmhand when my grandfather Henry (1875–1966) was born in a worker's cottage belonging to Farmer Webb. One of Charlie's tasks, in middle age, was to milk Webb's cattle and deliver raw milk from the pail into the receptacles of Webb's cowless neighbors. When Charlie quarreled with his boss, as the family story records, he started his own business by buying milk from another farmer to sell to Webb's customers. From hired hand he became middleman, founding the Hall Dairy—that would grow, expand, combine with Charlie Brock's to become Brock-Hall Dairy, wax over southern Connecticut, acquire moribund family dairies, metamorphose stables of workhorses into fleets of delivery trucks . . . and finally fail, *fail,* as supermarkets with loss-leader half-gallon milk cartons knocked out home delivery in the 1950s and 1960s.

My grandfather Henry Hall labored for Farmer Webb as a boy, odd jobs a boy could do, especially in harvest. When he was ninety years old, he lived on Norris Street in a suburban block of Spring Glen built over Farmer Webb's strawberry fields, where as a boy he had picked strawberries for ten cents an hour. At ninety, he told such stories in a deep slow voice, shaking his head over the changes he had lived to see—bewildered by progress, still commanding, never judging the effects of change.

10   Henry quit school about 1885, after the fifth grade, and worked beside his father. When Charlie Hall quarreled with Webb and went off on his own, Henry worked with his father. They built up two routes for the home delivery of milk, invested in glass to deliver milk in bottles—O luxury of innovation!—which they washed by hand every day in the kitchen of a rented house. People moved out to Hamden from New Haven, especially to Whitneyville, two miles closer to the city than Spring Glen. Maybe the trolley came as far out as Whitneyville, allowing workers to commute. Before Charlie died, he and Henry disputed over expansion. Charlie believed in keeping small, his son in expanding.

Henry Hall expanded. When I first remember the Brock-Hall Dairy, in the early 1930s, we (I relished the pronoun) built a big milk processing plant on Whitney Avenue in Whitneyville. (Eli Whitney had built workers' housing in the nineteenth century—Whitney's Village—when he raised a gun factory beside the dam at the end of the lake.) Who built a plant in 1934? Home delivery of good milk prospered—the cream line on *our* Grade A was deeper than any other dairy's—and route added to route, and behind the new brick building stretched long low wooden stables for the fifty great shaggy workhorses that pulled the red wagons of Brock-Hall.

Henry expanded, Henry prospered, and Henry knew exactly how he did it. He was a man of few words but, like E. B. White's William Strunk, he said his words three times: "Woik-woik-woik," I heard him say in his eighties—retired from management, working long days in his garden and as volunteer caretaker in the Whitneyville Cemetery where Augusta lay. The southern New Englander's old-fashioned accent pronounced vowels as Brooklyn did. (Walt Whitman's accent, who said "pome" not "poem," must have resembled Henry Hall's.) "Keep your health," he said in one of his longer sentences, "keep your health—and woik-woik-woik."

Henry passed to his grandson, as he approached and passed ninety, the secret of life.

IV

Absorbedness is the paradise of work, but what is its provenance or etiology? Surely it is an ecstasy of transport, of loss of ego; but it is also something less transcendent: To work is to please the powerful masters who are parents—who are family, who are church, who are custom or culture. Not to work is to violate the contract or to disobey the injunction, and to displease the dispensers of supper and love, of praise's reward. Not working becomes conviction of unworthiness. We prove ourselves worthy by the numbers of work.

15   When I sold lightbulbs door-to-door for the Andover Lions Club, every October a woman in Danbury told me about how much she had canned that year. She lived in a small rickety cottage, almost a shack, with an old propane cooker. Each year her prodigies increased in

prodigiousness. She told me: "This year I did 347 peas, 414 string beans, 77 peaches, 402 corn, 150 strawberry jams . . ." She talked plain, the New Hampshire way without affect, but I felt pride surging in every century of Ball jars, self-worth assembled in dense rows of vegetable love packed into her root cellar. And as I listened I thrilled with her, felt pride with her and for her. Four hundred cans of corn! Did her family *eat* four cans of corn each day all winter? Heavens, no. Every time I visited, I took home several examples of her canning.

Once when I was a teacher I took part in a television panel on English composition in California with two other college professors and a high school teacher. We talked about what each of us wanted from our students and how each of us went about the task; we talked about getting through to students by individual conferences and by comments on their papers. After a while the high school teacher—she was a large vigorous forthright forty-year-old—asked some questions: How many students were we speaking of? How many papers did we correct and hand back every week? One of the professors said eighteen, another twenty-two; I handled about twenty papers a week, teaching one section of comp at the University of Michigan. We had an inkling of the point she was making, and one of us asked the question we were asked to ask. "Three hundred and twenty," she answered.

How I admired her, as she sat with the three pampered males and assured us that she *read* every one and *wrote a comment* on every one and *what's more spoke with each student* at least once a term. I could tell—talking with her before she produced her numbers on camera—that she had the energy and compassion of a wonderful teacher. She must have foregone sleep and stayed up late with high school prose seven nights a week the whole school year. She must have been born with that energy, and she took suitably

massive pride in what she did—but what terrible sins and shortcomings did her labors expiate?

As I like to say: I average four books a year—counting revised editions of old books; counting everything I can damned well count. Counting books, book reviews, notes, poems, and essays, I reckon I publish about one item a week, year-in year-out. Were I fifteen years old, this would be the moment when I would pretend to blow on the backs of my fingernails, then rub them against my chest.

Work, work, work.

V

When I hear talk about "the work ethic" I puke. CEOs talk about it, whose annual salaries average one hundred and thirty times their workers' wages. Whatever the phrase purports to describe, it is not an ethic; it is not an idea of work's value or a moral dictate but a feeling or tone connected to work, and it is temperamental and cultural. Studs Terkel's stonemason has it, and his line-worker does not; instead, the line-worker has a work anger, or a work malevolence, which is entirely appropriate. Mind you, the stonemason works alone with his hands solving problems that change with every stone. He does something that he can look at and put his name to. He can measure what he has done in walls and buildings not in units of the same thing, like so many Chevrolet Impalas or so many distributor cap linings. Shades of John Ruskin. I no more have a work ethic than I have self-discipline. I have so many pages a day, so many books and essays.

Visiting my mother in Connecticut, I sit beside her recliner and she asks what I am up to. I tell her about *Life Work*. "I think your book will be *inspirational* to people," she responds; she has been building me up since I was born; but she has her own ego: "When I look around this house," she goes on, "I see so much that I have made. Drapes, curtains, bedspreads, most of the quilts. Not the blankets of course. Lace for the pillowcases." She points to the drapes in the sunroom where she lives waking and sleeping. "I made those drapes in 1938 and the edges are all worn. I hope they live longer than I do." After a moment she says, "I *know* the upstairs drapes need washing but I *can't.*" In fact she cannot mount the stairs to see that they are dirty but she knows it well enough. Then she goes back to thinking of a life's work, shaped into objects throughout this house. "They are *mine,*" she says.

All winter I find Jane standing by the dining-room windows looking into the secluded garden she has made behind the house; all winter she plans next summer's back garden. On mild days in March she begins cleaning the garden patch for the better days coming; when we hear that the temperature will drop below freezing again—March, April, even May—she covers or recovers bulbs and emerging snowdrops with mulch from last year's leaves. Snowdrops, daffodils, tulips, roses, peonies, hollyhocks, lilies. All summer she works every day that it does not rain, and sometimes she works in rain. She works on poems early at her desk, when the garden is wet with dew, or she might not write at all in summer. By nine-thirty or ten she is outside armed with spoons and spades, trimming and feeding, helping and preparing. On late warm evenings of June and July, only darkness forces her inside. She gardens twelve hours a day, some days.

And her flowers reward her work by their magnificence: peonies whiter than the idea of white and as big as basketballs; hollyhocks seven feet tall with a blossom delicately peach-pink. People swerve and slow down driving by, if they are flower people; we fear accidents.

I call it work and so does Jane although it is voluntary and produces no revenue—except when, in bare cold November or a rainy stretch of June, Jane writes a poem or an essay out of her gardening. Her garden is work because it is a devotion undertaken with passion and conviction; because it absorbs her; because it is a task or unrelenting quest which cannot be satisfied. True gardening is atavistic and represents or embodies or fulfills the centuries or millennia that her ancestors (all of our ancestors) spent working in dirt. Our forefathers and foremothers farmed not for pleasure but to stay alive or to satisfy the Squire, to survive on leavings from milord's table or to lay up sheepswool and turnips to sustain themselves through the snows of winter. Whatever the source or motive for their work, the hymns of dirt-work continue their chorus below the level of our consciousness.

As we look back across millennia, we see a social structure that is largely agricultural. Although many males from fourteen to fifty fight in the emperor's army or climb the rigging of the emperor's ships, the remaining males together with children and women plough, dig, plant seed, carry water, weed, and harvest. Thus in the suburbs we rake leaves together; thus we trim the forsythia; thus we arrange a sprinkler on the suburban lawn, edge the grass neatly against the sidewalk, mow, and mulch. If we could look from outer space down on North America on an August Saturday, we would watch a suburban nation of farmers tending tiny plots. Canceling time, or standing at a telescope further out in space, we would watch multitudes in 1000 B.C. growing wheat in Mesopotamia. In the city apartment when we raise African violets in the window we plant wheat beside the Nile. In Connecticut the millionaire in his modern house with a swimming pool spends one day a week driving his tractor—he could hire it done a thousand times over—to mow the smooth acres of his estate. He is never so happy—not playing bridge that night drinking Chivas, not reading the *Journal* over coffee or estimating his net worth at the market's close—as he is while he bumps over lawn on his Farmall, master of his lands gathering his weekly harvest.

VI

Who is worst-off, for work, in human history? When I read Studs Terkel's *Working* I choose our nomadic Mexican farm laborers, laboring in the fields from early childhood until death, days sometimes elongated to seventeen hours. When I read Richard Henry Dana's *Two Years Before the Mast* I switch to sailors in nineteenth century merchant fleets: They never spent more than four hours in bed and usually worked a sixteen-hour day (longer in danger; and don't forget the danger) often seven days a week, away from land for months and from home for years at a time. Then I think of the soldier, legionary or hoplite marching all night to fight at dawn, hardtack and salt beef and what you can loot. I have not mentioned slavery, and the history of humanity is the history of slavery. Mind you, in some cultures or historical eras slaves were better off than gentleman soldiers. But the chattel slavery of the Americans, perpetuated until late in the Christian era, I propose as the nineteenth century's equivalent to Hitler's and Stalin's exterminations. Or read *Das Kapital*—or any objective history of the same period—and compare the labors of miners or factory workers in England—often women and children—with labors of the felaheen in the Old Kingdom.

Work is what we do to feed ourselves and keep ourselves warm. Some hunter-gatherers, in a fortunate climate with fortunate vegetation, can work twelve hours a week—leaving the rest of their time for lovemaking, magic, religion, gossip, games, and drinking the local brew. Watching television ads during sports events, I note that we aspire to the condition of this hunter-gatherer. D. H. Lawrence wrote that "for some mysterious or obvious reason, the modern woman and the modern man hate physical work," and "The dream of every man

is that in the end he shall have to work no more." When there is work in the TV advertisement, it is something done quickly—and the reward is drinking beer. Do we want a house? A house goes up in twenty seconds in a crafted sequence of thirty shots; we watch the house rise as we watch a flower open when the camera takes a frame every four hours over two days. These work-ads remind me of my dreams of gardening, which never included a sore back, in which I never dropped a hoe or misplaced a trowel; in television ads no one is tired, and no one is old. The hunting-gathering TV young, all slim and beautiful and energetic, gather to drink and dance and flirt at the Silver Bullet, aka the Earthly Paradise. We understand that centuries of off-stage labor, not to mention evolution and history and civilization and the opposable thumb, have brought us to this time and moment of sexual leisure. We also understand the hunting-gathering young must have a life-expectancy like a slave's in a Hittite galley, because nobody here is as old as twenty-seven.

Lawrence writing seventy years ago foresaw the Silver Bullet. "It means, apart from the few necessary hours of highly paid and congenial labor, that men and women shall have nothing to do except enjoy themselves. No beastly housework for the women, no beastly homework for the men. Free! free to enjoy themselves. More films, more motorcars, more dances, more golf, more tennis and more getting completely away from yourself. And the goal of life is enjoyment."

Baudelaire on the other hand claimed that work was less boring than amusing yourself. Surely I agree, but not everyone does: Enjoyment in the shape of golf absorbed my father as his work did not; work and its anxiety *engaged* him—but worry and dread do not characterize the absorbedness that Gurchuran Das described. Golf was an engaging pastime, and the atavistic sources of sport are as clear as the origins of lawncare: not agriculture but warfare.

30   Pastimes are always atavistic and they will not do for a life's structure. When work is utterly disagreeable, and week awaits weekend, our delight in recreation reveals our misery. The Silver Bullet, like the touch football game that precedes it, is the house of wretchedness. The goal of life is enjoyment? It depends on the quality of the joy; elsewhere Lawrence wrote, "It seems as if the great aim and purpose in human life were to bring all life into the human consciousness. And this is the final meaning of work: the extension of human consciousness." We understand: Not everyone can work to extend the consciousness of others. For most of us, the exercise of freedom—doing what we like doing—may best extend our own.

But the goal is worthy: As Swami Vivekananda says: "work like a *master* and not as a *slave;* work incessantly, but do not do slave's work. Do you not see how everybody works? Nobody can be altogether at rest; ninety-nine percent of mankind work like slaves, and the result is misery; it is all selfish work. Work through freedom! Work through love!"

READING AND THINKING

1. What effect does Hall achieve with his opening sentence (which is the first sentence of his book *Life Work*)? What distinction does Hall imply when he says that he has never worked a day in his life?

2. What does Hall relish most about his own work? Why do you think he gave up the security of a tenured faculty position at a prestigious university?

3. Why do you think Hall writes about his grandfather Henry Hall? What attitudes toward and ideas about work are conveyed in section III?

4. Why do you think Hall tells the stories of the woman who canned vegetables and the high school teacher? How does he link their stories of work with his own?

5. What point does Hall make about people who work with their hands in the dirt—in their gardens and on their lawns, for example?

THINKING AND WRITING

1. To what extent do you share Hall's attitude toward the term and the concept "the work ethic" (section V)? Explain.

2. In section VI Hall considers some of the worst kinds of work and the worst-off kinds of workers. Do you agree with his assessments there? What else would you add to what he says about the worst kinds of work and the worst-off workers? Explain.

3. Choose a specific phrase, detail, story, or part of Hall's essay that strikes you as important or has had some kind of effect on you. Explain why, and, if possible, link it to your own personal experience with work. You can choose to agree or disagree with Hall.

4. Write up a short sketch of what you imagine your "lifework" might be, similar to how Hall does in his essay.

DEFINING WORK: AN OCCASION FOR WRITING

In the excerpts from *Life Work*, Donald Hall defines work a number of ways. He situates himself in relation to his ancestors, considering the kinds of work they did and the kinds of lives they lived in relation to his own. In thinking about his lifework, writing, Hall invites us to consider the value of work and the values we associate with it. In the following Occasion you will have a chance to develop your own definition(s) of work and, in the process, consider its value for your life.

Modern Times (1936)

© Chaplin/United Artists/the Kobal Collection

© 20th Century-Fox/the Kobal Collection/Joppe, Alan

Office Space (1999)

The Matrix (1999) © Warner Bros/the Kobal Collection

PREPARING TO WRITE: OCCASIONS TO THINK ABOUT WHAT YOU SEE

1. What image of work is suggested by the still film shot of Charlie Chaplin in *Modern Times* (1936)? Consider that this was a silent movie (with sound effects) made during a time when "talkies" were first released and gaining popularity.

2. What is suggested in the still shot of the three workers in the film still from *Office Space*? Even if you are not familiar with the film, what do you imagine is taking place in this scene?

3. What does this still from *The Matrix* suggest about our place in life and how our paths might already be determined?

MOVING TOWARD ESSAY: OCCASIONS TO ANALYZE AND REFLECT

1. In *Modern Times,* Charlie Chaplin is set to work on a production line and an automated feeding machine. Due to comical mishaps, his boss suspects insanity and sends him to a mental hospital. What is Charlie Chaplin suggesting about the industry of his day? To what extent is this point of view still relevant today? Explain.

2. *Office Space* depicts a comedic and satirical view in the day of a life of office employees who decide to rebel against their boss. With your work experience, how do you view office life? If you have seen the movie, how do you relate to this film? What parts are funny and which are not? How might *The Matrix* fit into this same discussion? How much are we part of a "matrix" when at work?

3. Consider the following comments on work and labor by W. H. Auden. To what extent do you agree with Auden's distinction between work and labor? To what extent can Auden's remarks be linked with what Hall says about work and chores?

W. H. Auden

Work and Labor

In a society where slavery in the strict sense has been abolished, the sign that what a man does is of social value is that he is paid money to do it, but a laborer today can rightly be called a wage slave. A man is a laborer if the job society offers him is of no interest to himself but he is compelled to take it by the necessity of earning a living and supporting his family. . . .

A man is a worker if he is personally interested in the job which society pays him to do; what from the point of view of society is necessary labor is from his own point of view voluntary play. Whether a job is to be classified as labor or work depends, not on the job itself, but on the tastes of the individual who undertakes it. The difference does not, for example, coincide with the difference between a manual and a mental job; a gardener or a cobbler may be a worker, a bank clerk a laborer. Which a man is can be seen from his attitude toward leisure. To a worker, leisure means simply the hours he needs to relax and rest in order to work efficiently. He is therefore more likely to take too little leisure than too much; workers die of coronaries and forget their wives' birthdays. To the laborer, on the other hand, leisure means freedom from compulsion, so that it is natural for him to imagine that the fewer hours he has to spend laboring, and the more hours he is free to play, the better.

WRITING THOUGHTFULLY: OCCASIONS FOR IDEAS AND ESSAYS

1. Using the thinking and writing you did in the previous exercises, write an essay in which you define the concept of "work." You may wish to make distinctions among different types of work and different types of workers—agricultural and industrial, for example, or manual and intellectual work, or work in different types of service industries, such as food and hotel service on the one hand and financial or social services on the other. In your essay, make reference to at least two of the essays in this chapter and to at least one of the images or texts included in the Occasions.

2. Write an essay in which you define work by focusing on the structure of work—how work is organized and divided, how it is structured by time and space—by the seasons of the year or hours of the day in which it is performed and by the spaces and places in which it is done. Consider the extent to which technology, especially computer technologies and including email and voicemail, have altered the structure of work.

CREATING OCCASIONS

1. Research how other cultures view and value work. How do their views differ from how work is portrayed in America? Consider watching some foreign films that deal with the topic of work to see how they differ from the films presented here.

ASPECTS OF WORK

Working every weekday year after year may cause many workers to wish they could work less. However, not working for a while prompts those out of work to wish they could get into or back into the work force. Not working to take a vacation to change your routine, to break out of the rut and ritual of habit, can be a boon, proving restorative to a tired mind and body. But not working when you want to work, not working because you can't find work is another matter entirely.

One of the difficulties many people encounter with their work is finding a good balance between their work and their leisure or between devotion to their work and devotion to their families. People's happiness often hinges on their ability to find the right balance for these and other conflicting life factors involving work. Questions involving the balance between work and family are raised and answered by Ellen Gilchrist in her essay "The Middle Way: Learning to Balance Family and Work."

What happens in a world where more and more kinds of work are becoming increasingly competitive? Thomas L. Friedman provides a picture of a seismic shift in how companies get work done with increasing efficiency, resulting in sending some kinds of work to other countries via outsourcing and off-shoring strategies. Friedman describes the implications of this significant change in the world of work today.

Why should we work at all? Why not look for ways to limit and reduce the amount of work we do? Why not work shorter weeks and take longer annual vacations, as the French and Germans do? Christopher Clausen raises such questions in his essay "Against Work," in which he describes some of his own work experience, while inviting readers to consider views that counter work-ethic values he finds embedded in American culture.

Ellen Gilchrist (b. 1935)

Ellen Gilchrist was born in Vicksburg, Mississippi, and attended Vanderbilt University, where she received a Bachelor's degree in philosophy. Later, after her marriage and divorce, she took a creative writing course at Millsaps College in Jackson, Mississippi, where she studied fiction writing with the prize-winning novelist and short story writer Eudora Welty. Gilchrist also studied creative writing at the University of Arkansas. Gilchrist has published nineteen books of fiction, both novels and short story collections, including *Victory Over Japan: A Book of Stories* (1984), for which she received a National Book Award. She has also published two books of poetry and a book of essays.

THE MIDDLE WAY: LEARNING
TO BALANCE FAMILY AND WORK

In "The Middle Way: Learning to Balance Family and Work," Ellen Gilchrist explains how she solved the problem that so many people confront. In achieving a balance between competing duties and interests, Gilchrist comes to terms with what matters most in her life and why. Although the particulars of her story may vary from the specific competing claims of any particular reader, Gilchrist's way of finding equilibrium between her family life and her working life provide one solution to this pervasive problem.

1   Maybe you have to wait for happiness. Maybe the rest is only words.

When I was a child I had a book about a small boy in Scotland whose father was a Highlander and whose mother was a Lowlander. All his life they argued in his presence about whether he was a Lowlander or a Highlander and each tried to persuade him of their case.

In the winters they lived with his mother's people and farmed and cared for domestic animals. In the summers they stayed in the Highlands with his father's people and he hunted the high hills with his father and his uncles. He was a strong boy and the altitude caused him to grow powerful lungs. When he called the goats and cattle on his mother's farm, his voice rose above the rest. In the hills he sometimes stood and called out across great distances to the other hunters. So he grew until he was almost tall as a man.

The year he was sixteen, as they were making their way from the Highlands to the Lowlands, they came upon a man sitting on a rock playing bagpipes. The boy had never heard such heavenly music. He begged his parents to let him stay and learn to play bagpipes. Finally, when the man agreed to teach him, his parents left him there. And there he stayed the rest of his life, halfway between the Lowlands and the Highlands, playing beautiful music and looking up and down at the worlds he had left behind. Because his lungs were strong from working on the farm and climbing in the hills, he was able to make music so fine it could be heard from miles away.

I loved that story the most of anything I 5 had ever read. I can still see each page of the book in my mind's eye, and I think I have finally found a place between the worlds where I can live in peace and do what I was meant to do. The middle way, the Zen masters call it. Ever since I first heard of that I have known that is what I was seeking.

Family and work. Family and work. I can let them be at war, with guilt as their nuclear weapon and mutually assured destruction as their aim, or I can let them nourish each other. In my life, as I have finally arranged it, the loneliness of being a writer and living alone in the Ozark Mountains is balanced against the worry and control issues of being a mother and a grandmother. I move back and forth between these two worlds. Somewhere in the middle I play my bagpipes and am at peace.

Of course, it wasn't always this easy. I have written two books of poetry and eighteen books of fiction about the struggle to free myself from my family and my conditioning so I could write and/or live as an artist with a mind that was free to roam, discriminate, and choose. I will leave the details of that struggle, which included four marriages, three cesarean sections, an abortion, twenty-four years of psychotherapy, and lots of lovely men, to your imaginations and go on with the story of where I landed, on this holy middle ground that I don't feel the need to fortify or protect, only to be grateful for having, as long as my destiny allows. I tell myself I am satisfied to be here now, but, of course, I would fight to keep my life if I had to, with sharp number two lead pencils and legal pads, my weapons of choice for all battles.

Still, I don't remember the events of my life as a struggle. I think of myself as a thinking, planning, terribly energetic competitor in games I believed I could win. It's all perception. If I cried I thought of the tears as some sort of mistake. Later, I knew that tears are unexpressed rage. But my father was a professional baseball player until I was born. At our house we had no respect for crybabies. We believed in Channel swimmers and home run kings and people who learned to walk after they had polio. My daddy set the bar high. He taught me it didn't matter if you won or lost, it was how you played the game.

Practically speaking, I have worked it out this way. Part of the time I live on the Gulf Coast near my family and participate in their lives

as hard as I can. I don't change my personality to do that. I am a bossy, highly opinionated person and I say what I think. On the other hand, I love them deeply and help them in every way I can. They don't have to ask for help. I see what is needed and I act.

Then, when I have had enough of trying to control the lives of people just as willful and opinionated as I am, I drive back up to the Ozark Mountains and write books and run around with writers, artists, photographers, fitness experts, professors, and politicians. Sometimes I stay away from the coast for months and don't even think about my family unless they call me. If they need me I am here.

Because I don't like to fly on airplanes or stay in hotels, I have to make the life I live in Arkansas as rich as I can figure out how to make it. If I have a good life here I can leave my children alone to live their lives without interference. I want to help them but I don't want to need them.

Two years ago I decided I was getting stagnant, so I asked the university here to give me a job teaching writing. I had never taught but I thought I would be good at it. I wanted to be with younger people who were not related to me. Also, it was the year my oldest grandson went to college, a rite of passage for both of us. I think subconsciously I wanted to be with other young people who were experiencing what he was. I have always participated very deeply in his life. Perhaps teaching at a university was one more way of staying near him. So, now, to add to my happiness, I am teaching. What I do aside from that is get up at dawn every day and run or walk or work out at the health club. I love endorphins and I love to write and I love to read. I read and read and read. I live like a nun. I eat only fresh vegetables and high-protein foods. I drink only water and coffee. On Sunday afternoons I have a group of friends who come over and read the plays of William Shakespeare out loud. We've been doing that for fifteen years. Talk about bagpipes, this is the World Series of intellectual endorphins.

I think I am happy because I have quit trying to find happiness through other people. No one else can give you happiness after you become an adult. Happiness is self-derived and self-created. I derive happiness from the fact that my children and grandchildren are alive and breathing and that I am here to watch their lives unfold. Aside from that it's up to me. "To be alive becomes the fundamental luck each ordinary, compromising day manages to bury," it says on a piece of paper I have tacked up in the room where my children stay when they come to visit. I have internalized that knowledge. I want them to begin to learn it, too.

What else? I have learned to wait. I no longer have to *always* be the one who makes things happen. Sometimes I write every day for months on end. Sometimes I immerse myself in teaching. Sometimes I go to the coast and try to control my progeny's lives. Sometimes I don't do a thing but watch tennis on television and exercise obsessively and read books and go shopping at the mall. I have written and published twenty-two books. I have been the best mother I knew how to be and a better grandmother. In the light of that I refuse to feel guilty about a thing, past, present, or forevermore.

15   Who knows how long my happiness will last? It won't last forever. That's for sure, but I have a plan for when it ends. When I can no longer call the shots about my life or if I become ill with a disease that would make me an invalid, I will, I hope, cheerfully kill myself. I will find a fast, chemical way to do it and go somewhere where I won't leave a mess and get it over with. Whatever I was will rejoin the dazzling, star-filled carbon mass from which it came. I'll leave my DNA in three sons and twelve grandchildren and that's enough for me. I have told my family for twenty years that is how I intend to die and they all know

it's true. No one will be surprised and the ones who loved me will know better than to be sad.

I believe with all my heart and soul that happiness begins with great good health and is nurtured in solitude. Perhaps the reason so many young mothers are stressed and unhappy is that they never get to be alone long enough to calm down and play the bagpipes. When I am taking care of small children I can't find time *to take a bath.*

Also, women in my generation had children when they were very young. A nineteen- or twenty-year-old girl is a much different mother than a highly educated, thirty-year-old woman who has had a responsible job or a career and interrupts it to have children. I was a child myself when I had my first two children and I played with them as if I were a child. I'm still pretty childish, which is why small children like to be with me. I lapse back into a childhood state quite easily, as I have a wonderful, inventive mother who taught me to believe that fairies played at night in my sandpile and left footprints on my castles. She would go out after I was asleep and walk around the castles with her fingers. Also, she told me that beautiful fairies hid behind the leaves of trees to watch over me. She is ninety-three and still a lovely, ethereal creature.

It may be easier to be a mother when you have never had any real achievements until you produce a baby. Here it is, the reason for existence, and you created it! I think older women probably make better mothers in many ways. But young women are more selfish and you have to be selfish to demand time for yourself when you have children. Young women are closer to the time when they were manipulative and childish and they don't let their babies manipulate them as much as older mothers do. These are only my conclusions from watching children in grocery stores. I love to watch them work on their mothers to get what they want, and because I am always a child, I'm pulling for them to get the candy and get it NOW. The other day I watched a little blond beauty pull her mother's face to her and lay her hands on her mother's cheeks and kiss her nose. Needless to say, they opened the bag of cookies then and there.

One of the reasons I am happy now is that I did the work I had always dreamed of doing. But I didn't start doing it seriously and professionally until I was forty years old. I have always loved books and always thought of myself as a writer but didn't have an overwhelming desire to write and publish things until my children were almost grown. I had published things off and on during my life and I enjoyed the process but I had no sustained desire to be a writer. It was just something I knew I could do if I wanted to. I was busy falling in love and getting married to three different men (I married the father of my children twice), and having babies and buying clothes and getting my hair fixed and running in the park and playing tennis. During those years my desire for literature was satisfied by reading. If there was something that needed writing, like the minutes for a PTA meeting or a play for my husband's law firm's dinner party, I wrote it and everyone liked it but I didn't want to keep on writing. To tell the truth, I was forty years old before I had enough experience to be a writer. I barely knew what I thought, much less what anything meant.

20 I wouldn't be happy now if I had no progeny. The reason I don't fear death is that every chromosome of me is already in younger people, spread around in all my lovely grandchildren. Some of them have my red hair. Others have my temperament. A few have my verbal skills. One has my cynicism. Several have my vanity and pride.

The years I spent raising my sons are as important to my happiness as the books I have written. If some of that time was frustrating, if occasionally I wondered if I was wasting my talents, then that was the price I had to pay for being happy now. There are always dues to pay.

The month my first book of fiction was published was also the month my first grandchild was born. "I don't know which thing makes me happier," I told Eudora Welty in July of that year, just weeks before the two events occurred.

"They aren't in competition, Ellen," she answered.

When I think of that conversation I remember running into her once on the Millsaps College campus, years before, when she was my teacher there. I had my three little redheaded boys with me. They were four and five and two, gorgeous, funny little creatures, fat and powerful, with beautiful faces. I had never mentioned to Eudora that I had children. I suppose it took her by surprise to see me coming down the path with my sons. I think they were wearing white summer outfits. When they were young I loved to dress them in white sailor suits or buttoned-up shirts with ruffles down the front.

"Oh, my," Eudora said. "Are they yours? Do   25 they belong to you?"

"They're mine," I answered. "Aren't they funny?"

"Why would you need anything else?" she said. "Why would you need to be a writer?"

I did not understand what she was saying to me but I do now. Eudora had no children of her own and that year she had lost her father and her brother. Her mother was in a nursing home. Think how my riches must have looked to her.

In the end happiness is always a balance. I hope the young women of our fortunate world find ways to balance their young lives. I hope they learn to rejoice and wait.

READING AND THINKING

1. What purpose does Gilchrist's opening anecdote about the Scottish boy serve? What contrasts does that anecdote illustrate, and what is their significance?

2. What does Gilchrist mean by "the middle way between the worlds," and why is it important to her to have found it?

3. How does Gilchrist negotiate the "middle way" between the contrasting and competing claims of her life?

4. What personal details does Gilchrist reveal about herself? To what extent do these personal details affect your perception and judgment of her? Explain.

THINKING AND WRITING

1. What do you think of Gilchrist's prescription for happiness? To what extent is her "middle way" suitable for you—or for others? Explain.

2. What do you think of Gilchrist's ideas about happiness? Where has she found it? How does she expect to retain it?

3. Why do you think Gilchrist mentions dying, especially her own death? What do you think of her views about death?

4. What is the significance of Eudora Welty's comment to Gilchrist? Why do you think the author included it in her essay?

FINDING THE RIGHT BALANCE: AN OCCASION FOR WRITING

In her essay on finding the right balance between her family life and her work, Ellen Gilchrist raises a number of questions about how important finding such a balance is, and how difficult it can be. Gilchrist explains how she balances her work as a writer with her obligations as a mother and wife. In this Occasion for Writing, you will have the opportunity to reflect on balancing the competing pressures and obligations of your own life.

PREPARING TO WRITE: OCCASIONS TO THINK ABOUT WHAT YOU SEE

1. Describe the balancing act depicted in this cartoon.

2. Notice how the cartoon makes its statement without the use of any words. What exactly is effective about the cartoonist's choices in this illustration? What words would you add to this cartoon, either in the form of a caption or dialogue box? Does it diminish the strength of the cartoon?

3. How might this cartoon be transformed for a male worker? What might be portrayed on his computer screen?

© Best of Latin America, Cagle Cartoons, El Universal, Mexico City

caglecartoons.com

MOVING TOWARD ESSAY: OCCASIONS TO ANALYZE AND REFLECT

1. Explain what you do when you lose the balance between competing obligations in your life. How do you go about restoring that balance? Create a scene that helps to describe all the different ways you might be pulled in a given day.

2. How does the cartoon speak to Gilchrist's essay? Do you think the cartoon portrayal is accurate, generally?

3. Try to interpret the cartoon in another way—must it be so negative or bleak? Make a list of pros and cons that could be depicted in the cartoon.

4. When you sit at your computer to complete a task, do you find yourself wandering around your computer—playing a game, chatting with friends, or surfing the Web? Write a brief paragraph in which you discuss your thoughts about doing personal tasks while on the job, or during any task, like writing a paper for a class.

WRITING THOUGHTFULLY: OCCASIONS FOR IDEAS AND ESSAYS

1. Write an essay about a time when your life got out of balance. Explain the causes of the imbalance and what you did to address them and get your life back in balance. Consider the extent to which your competing obligations and interests were unavoidable and the extent to which they were self-created. How did it affect your personal relationships? Your health? Your success? Use Gilchrist's essay and the cartoon as starting points for your essay.

2. Write a letter to Ellen Gilchrist responding to her ideas about balancing work and family life. Include some comments about how her solution might or might not be something you could use yourself.

3. In an essay, consider how living an unbalanced life might have some advantages. You may wish to write a humorous essay, a kind of "Modest Proposal" (see p. 766) for living an unbalanced life.

CREATING OCCASIONS

1. Do some research on finding balance in one's life. You can use your school library and also the Internet. A few Internet leads you might follow are advancingwomen.com, fastcompany.com, and llamagraphics.com. You may also interview friends or family members about how they do or don't achieve a balanced life. Write up your research findings in a short essay.

Thomas L. Friedman (b. 1953)

Thomas L. Friedman has won the Pulitzer Prize three times for his work at the *New York Times*, where he serves as the foreign affairs columnist. He is the author of four bestselling books: *From Beirut to Jerusalem* (1989), *The Lexus and the Olive Tree: Understanding Globalization* (1999), *Longitudes and Attitudes: Exploring the World after September 11* (2002), and *The World Is Flat: A Brief History of the Twenty-First Century* (2005). He lives in Bethesda, Maryland, with his family.

THE WORLD IS FLAT

In "The World Is Flat," an excerpt from the opening chapter of his recent book of that title, Friedman explains how the world has entered a new era of globalization, one that offers unparalleled opportunities to workers from all over the world. Friedman introduces his thesis about the "flat" world and the reasons why he thinks the globalization of today differs from that of earlier times.

> Your Highnesses, as Catholic Christians, and princes who love and promote the holy Christian faith, and are enemies of the doctrine of Mahomet, and of all idolatry and heresy, determined to send me, Christopher Columbus, to the above-mentioned countries of India, to see the said princes, people, and territories, and to learn their disposition and the proper method of converting them to our holy faith; and furthermore directed that I should not proceed by land to the East, as is customary, but by a Westerly route, in which direction we have hitherto no certain evidence that anyone has gone.
>
> —Entry from the journal of Christopher Columbus on his voyage of 1492

1   No one ever gave me directions like this on a golf course before: "Aim at either Microsoft or IBM." I was standing on the first tee at the KGA Golf Club in downtown Bangalore, in southern India, when my playing partner pointed at two shiny glass-and-steel buildings off in the distance, just behind the first green. The Goldman Sachs building wasn't done yet; otherwise he could have pointed that out as well and made it a threesome. HP and Texas Instruments had their offices on the back nine, along the tenth hole. That wasn't all. The tee markers were from Epson, the printer company, and one of our caddies was wearing a hat from 3M. Outside, some of the traffic signs were also sponsored by Texas Instruments, and the Pizza Hut billboard on the way over showed a steaming pizza, under the headline "Gigabites of Taste!"

No, this definitely wasn't Kansas. It didn't even seem like India. Was this the New World, the Old World, or the Next World?

I had come to Bangalore, India's Silicon Valley, on my own Columbus-like journey of exploration. Columbus sailed with the *Niña,* the *Pinta,* and the *Santa María* in an effort to discover a shorter, more direct route to India by heading west, across the Atlantic, on what he presumed to be an open sea route to the East Indies—rather than going south and east around Africa, as Portuguese explorers of his day were trying to do. India and the magical Spice Islands of the East were famed at the time for their gold, pearls, gems, and silk—a source of untold riches. Finding this shortcut by sea to India, at a time when the Muslim powers of the day had blocked the overland routes from Europe, was a way for both Columbus and the Spanish monarchy to become wealthy and powerful. When Columbus set sail, he apparently assumed the Earth was round, which was why he was convinced that he could get to India by going west. He miscalculated the distance, though. He thought the Earth was a smaller sphere than it is. He also did not anticipate running into a landmass before he reached the East Indies. Nevertheless, he called the aboriginal peoples he encountered in the new world "Indians." Returning home, though, Columbus was able to tell his patrons, King Ferdinand and Queen Isabella, that although he never did find India, he could confirm that the world was indeed round.

I set out for India by going due east, via Frankfurt. I had Lufthansa business class. I knew exactly which direction I was going thanks to the GPS map displayed on the screen that popped out of the armrest of my airline seat. I landed safely and on schedule. I too encountered people called Indians. I too was searching for the source of India's riches. Columbus was searching for hardware—precious metals, silk, and spices—the source of wealth in his day. I was searching for software, brainpower, complex algorithms, knowledge workers, call centers, transmission protocols, breakthroughs in optical engineering—the sources of wealth in our day. Columbus was happy to make the Indians he met his slaves, a pool of free manual labor.

5   I just wanted to understand why the Indians I met were taking our work, why they had become such an important pool for the outsourcing of service and information technology work from America and other industrialized countries. Columbus had more than one hundred men on his three ships; I had a small crew from the Discovery Times channel that fit comfortably into two banged-up vans, with Indian drivers who drove barefoot. When I set sail, so to speak, I too assumed that the world was round, but what I encountered in the real India profoundly shook my faith in that notion. Columbus accidentally ran into America but thought he had discovered part of India. I actually found India and thought many of the people I met there were Americans. Some had actually taken American names, and others were doing great imitations of American accents at call centers and American business techniques at software labs.

Columbus reported to his king and queen that the world was round, and he went down in history as the man who first made this discovery. I returned home and shared my discovery only with my wife, and only in a whisper.

"Honey," I confided, "I think the world is flat."

How did I come to this conclusion? I guess you could say it all started in Nandan Nilekani's conference room at Infosys Technologies Limited. Infosys is one of the jewels of the Indian information technology world, and Nilekani, the company's CEO, is one of the most thoughtful and respected captains of Indian industry. I drove with the Discovery Times crew out to the Infosys campus, about forty minutes from the heart of Bangalore, to tour the facility and interview Nilekani. The Infosys campus is reached by a pockmarked road, with sacred cows, horse-drawn carts, and motorized rickshaws all jostling alongside our vans. Once you enter the gates of Infosys, though, you are in a different world. A massive resort-size swimming pool nestles amid boulders and manicured lawns, adjacent to a huge putting green. There are multiple restaurants and a fabulous health club. Glass-and-steel buildings seem to sprout up like weeds each week. In some of those buildings, Infosys employees are writing specific software programs for American or European companies; in others, they are running the back rooms of major American- and European-based multinationals—everything from computer maintenance to specific research projects to answering customer calls routed there from all over the world. Security is tight, cameras monitor the doors, and if you are working for American Express, you cannot get into the building that is managing services and research for General Electric. Young Indian engineers, men and women, walk briskly from building to building, dangling ID badges. One looked like he could do my taxes. Another looked like she could take my computer apart. And a third looked like she designed it!

After sitting for an interview, Nilekani gave our TV crew a tour of Infosys's global conferencing center—ground zero of the Indian outsourcing industry. It was a cavernous wood-paneled room that looked like a tiered classroom from an Ivy League law school. On one end was a massive wall-size screen and overhead there were cameras in the ceiling for teleconferencing. "So this is our conference room, probably the largest screen in Asia—this is forty digital screens [put together]," Nilekani explained proudly, pointing to the biggest flat-screen TV I had ever seen. Infosys, he said, can hold a virtual meeting of the key players from its entire global supply chain for any project at any time on that supersize screen. So their American designers could be on the screen speaking with their Indian software writers and their Asian manufacturers all at once. "We could be sitting here, somebody from New York, London, Boston, San Francisco, all live. And maybe the implementation is in Singapore, so the Singapore person could also be live here. . . . That's globalization," said Nilekani. Above the screen there were eight clocks that pretty well summed up the Infosys workday: 24/7/365. The clocks were labeled US West, US East, GMT, India, Singapore, Hong Kong, Japan, Australia.

10   "Outsourcing is just one dimension of a much more fundamental thing happening today in the world," Nilekani explained. "What happened over the last [few] years is that there was a massive investment in technology, especially in the bubble era, when hundreds of millions of dollars were invested in putting broadband connectivity around the world, undersea cables, all those things." At the same time, he added, computers became cheaper and dispersed all over the world, and there was an explosion of software—e-mail, search engines like Google, and proprietary software that can chop up any piece of work and send one part to Boston, one part to Bangalore, and one part to Beijing, making it easy for anyone to do remote development. When all of these things suddenly came together around 2000, added Nilekani, they "created a platform where intellectual work, intellectual capital, could be delivered from anywhere. It could be disaggregated, delivered, distributed, produced, and put back together again—and this gave a whole new degree of freedom to the way we do work, especially work of an intellectual nature . . . And what you are seeing in Bangalore today is really the culmination of all these things coming together."

We were sitting on the couch outside of Nilekani's office, waiting for the TV crew to set up its cameras. At one point, summing up the implications of all this, Nilekani uttered a phrase that rang in my ear. He said to me, "Tom, the playing field is being leveled." He meant that countries like India are now able to compete for global knowledge work as never before—and that America had better get ready for this. America was going to be challenged, but, he insisted, the challenge would be good for America because we are always at our best when we are being challenged. As I left the Infosys campus that evening and bounced along the road back to Bangalore, I kept chewing on that phrase: "The playing field is being leveled."

What Nandan is saying, I thought, is that the playing field is being flattened. . . . Flattened? Flattened? My God, he's telling me the world is flat!

Here I was in Bangalore—more than five hundred years after Columbus sailed over the horizon, using the rudimentary navigational technologies of his day, and returned safely to prove definitively that the world was round—and one of India's smartest engineers, trained at his country's top technical institute and backed by the most modern technologies of his day, was essentially telling me that the world was *flat*—as flat as that screen on which he can host a meeting of his whole global supply chain. Even more interesting, he was citing this development as a good thing, as a new milestone in human progress and a great opportunity for India and the world—the fact that we had made our world flat!

In the back of that van, I scribbled down four words in my notebook: "The world is flat." As soon as I wrote them, I realized that this was the underlying message of everything that I had seen and heard in Bangalore in two weeks of filming. The global competitive playing field was being leveled. The world was being flattened.

15   As I came to this realization, I was filled with both excitement and dread. The journalist in me was excited at having found a framework to better understand the morning headlines and to explain what was happening in the world today. Clearly, it is now possible for more people than ever to collaborate and compete in real time with more other people on more different kinds of work from more different corners of the planet and on a more equal footing than at any previous time in the history of the world—using computers, e-mail, networks, teleconferencing, and dynamic new software. That is what Nandan was telling me. That was what I discovered on my journey to India and beyond. And that is what this book is about. When you start to think of the world as flat, a lot of things make sense in ways they did not before. But I was also excited personally, because what the flattening of the world means is that we are now connecting all the knowledge centers on the planet together into a single global network, which—if politics and terrorism do not get in the way—could usher in an amazing era of prosperity and innovation.

But contemplating the flat world also left me filled with dread, professional and personal. My personal dread derived from the obvious fact that it's not only the software writers and computer geeks who get empowered to collaborate on work in a flat world. It's also al-Qaeda and other terrorist networks. The playing field is not being leveled only in ways that draw in and superempower a whole new group of innovators. It's being leveled in a way that draws in and superempowers a whole new group of angry, frustrated, and humiliated men and women.

Professionally, the recognition that the world was flat was unnerving because I realized that this flattening had been taking place while I was sleeping, and I had missed it. I wasn't really sleeping, but I was otherwise engaged. Before 9/11, I was focused on tracking globalization and exploring the tension between the "Lexus" forces of economic integration and the "Olive Tree" forces of identity and nationalism—hence my 1999 book, *The Lexus and the Olive Tree*. But after 9/11, the olive tree wars became all-consuming for me. I spent almost all my time traveling in the Arab and Muslim worlds. During those years I lost the trail of globalization.

I found that trail again on my journey to Bangalore in February 2004. Once I did, I realized that something really important had happened while I was fixated on the olive groves of Kabul and Baghdad. Globalization had gone to a whole new level. If you put *The Lexus and the Olive Tree* and this book together, the broad historical argument you end up with is that there have been three great eras of globalization. The first lasted from 1492—when Columbus set sail, opening trade between the Old World and the New World—until around 1800. I would call this era Globalization 1.0. It shrank the world from a size large to a size medium. Globalization 1.0 was about countries and muscles. That is, in Globalization 1.0 the key agent of change, the dynamic force driving the process of global integration was how much brawn—how much muscle, how much horsepower, wind power, or, later, steam power—your country had and how creatively you could deploy it. In this era, countries and governments (often inspired by religion or imperialism or a combination of both) led the way in breaking down walls and knitting the world together, driving global integration. In Globalization 1.0, the primary questions were: Where does my country fit into global competition and opportunities? How can I go global and collaborate with others through my country?

The second great era, Globalization 2.0, lasted roughly from 1800 to 2000, interrupted by the Great Depression and World Wars I and II. This era shrank the world from a size medium to a size small. In Globalization 2.0, the key agent of change, the dynamic force driving global integration, was multinational companies. These multinationals went global for markets and labor, spearheaded first by the expansion of the Dutch and English joint-stock companies and the Industrial Revolution. In the first half of this era, global integration was powered by falling transportation costs, thanks to the steam engine and the railroad, and in the second half by falling telecommunication costs—thanks to the diffusion of the telegraph, telephones, the PC, satellites, fiber-optic cable, and the early version of the World Wide Web. It was during this era that we really saw the birth and maturation of a global economy, in the sense that there was enough movement of goods and information from continent to continent for there to be a global market, with global arbitrage in products and labor. The dynamic forces behind this era of globalization were breakthroughs in hardware—from steamships and railroads in the beginning to telephones and mainframe computers toward the end. And the big questions in this era were: Where does my company fit into the global economy? How does it take advantage of the opportunities? How can I go global and collaborate with others through my company? *The Lexus and the Olive Tree* was primarily about the climax of this era, an era when the walls started falling all around the world, and integration, and the backlash to it, went to a whole new level. But

even as the walls fell, there were still a lot of barriers to seamless global integration. Remember, when Bill Clinton was elected president in 1992, virtually no one outside of government and the academy had e-mail, and when I was writing *The Lexus and the Olive Tree* in 1998, the Internet and e-commerce were just taking off.

Well, they took off—along with a lot of other things that came together while I was sleeping. And that is why I argue in this book that around the year 2000 we entered a whole new era: Globalization 3.0. Globalization 3.0 is shrinking the world from a size small to a size tiny and flattening the playing field at the same time. And while the dynamic force in Globalization 1.0 was countries globalizing and the dynamic force in Globalization 2.0 was companies globalizing, the dynamic force in Globalization 3.0—the thing that gives it its unique character—is the newfound power for *individuals* to collaborate and compete globally. And the lever that is enabling individuals and groups to go global so easily and so seamlessly is not horsepower, and not hardware, but software—all sorts of new applications—in conjunction with the creation of a global fiber-optic network that has made us all next-door neighbors. Individuals must, and can, now ask, Where do *I* fit into the global competition and opportunities of the day, and how can *I,* on my own, collaborate with others globally?

But Globalization 3.0 not only differs from the previous eras in how it is shrinking and flattening the world and in how it is empowering individuals. It is different in that Globalization 1.0 and 2.0 were driven primarily by European and American individuals and businesses. Even though China actually had the biggest economy in the world in the eighteenth century, it was Western countries, companies, and explorers who were doing most of the globalizing and shaping of the system. But going forward, this will be less and less true. Because it is flattening and shrinking the world, Globalization 3.0 is going to be more and more driven not only by individuals but also by a much more diverse—non-Western, non-white—group of individuals. Individuals from every corner of the flat world are being empowered. Globalization 3.0 makes it possible for so many more people to plug and play, and you are going to see every color of the human rainbow take part.

(While this empowerment of individuals to act globally is the most important new feature of Globalization 3.0, companies—large and small—have been newly empowered in this era as well. I discuss both in detail later in the book.)

Needless to say, I had only the vaguest appreciation of all this as I left Nandan's office that day in Bangalore. But as I sat contemplating these changes on the balcony of my hotel room that evening, I did know one thing: I wanted to drop everything and write a book that would enable me to understand how this flattening process happened and what its implications might be for countries, companies, and individuals. So I picked up the phone and called my wife, Ann, and told her, "I am going to write a book called *The World Is Flat.*" She was both amused and curious—well, maybe *more* amused than curious! Eventually, I was able to bring her around, and I hope I will be able to do the same with you, dear reader. Let me start by taking you back to the beginning of my journey to India, and other points east, and share with you some of the encounters that led me to conclude the world was no longer round—but flat.

READING AND THINKING

1. Where does Friedman state his thesis, or main idea, most directly and most clearly? Explain his idea.

2. Why do you think Friedman begins with an epigraph from Christopher Columbus? How does Columbus's journal entry tie in with Friedman's ideas?

3. What is Friedman's reaction to his growing realization of the "flattening" of the global business playing field? To what extent is his response professional? To what extent is it personal? Explain.

4. Who is Nandan Nilekani, and why does Friedman include extensive quotations from him? What point does Nilekani make about the globalization of business?

THINKING AND WRITING

1. Explain your thoughts regarding Friedman's idea about the flattening of the world and his reactions, both personal and professional, to that flattening.

2. Identify the two sides in the debate over outsourcing of jobs that Friedman refers to in this selection. Explain why Friedman believes that outsourcing is a good idea from the standpoint of business.

3. Identify and explain the three historical eras or steps of globalization and what makes each of these globalization steps different.

4. Summarize, in one paragraph, Friedman's argument in "The World Is Flat." Then write a second paragraph in which you explain why you agree or disagree with Friedman's argument.

THE FUTURE OF WORK: AN OCCASION FOR WRITING

In "The World Is Flat," Thomas Friedman identifies how the globalization of business has affected employment throughout the world, how it is currently affecting American workers, and what it portends for Americans' jobs in the future. In the following Occasion for Writing, you are asked to consider the consequences of globalization for the future of work, including your own future working prospects.

PREPARING TO WRITE: OCCASIONS TO THINK ABOUT WHAT YOU SEE

1. Describe the scenes depicted in the accompanying pictures. How do these two images relate to one another in terms of Friedman's essay?

2. Describe what happens in a globalized world of work. What does a globalized work force look like? What part does outsourcing play? What part does moving people play? What part does politics play?

© Sherwin Crasto/Reuters/Corbis

© Najlah Feanny/CORBIS SABA

MOVING TOWARD ESSAY: OCCASIONS TO ANALYZE AND REFLECT

1. Make a list that considers how each of the following would react to the pictures you described earlier: (1) the workers themselves; (2) their families and friends; (3) their employers, both locally and internationally; (4) people in the company's home country; (5) workers in the home country who lost their jobs.

2. Identify and explain at least two causes of globalization and at least two consequences of globalization—beyond the gaining and losing of jobs by different groups.

WRITING THOUGHTFULLY: OCCASIONS FOR IDEAS AND ESSAYS

1. One thing noticeable in Thomas L. Friedman's description of the three stages of globalization is the increasing acceleration of change. Write an essay in which you explain how people (and companies) typically respond to change, particularly to the kinds of changes that a globalized economy has brought and continues to bring.

2. Write an essay in which you discuss the causes and consequences, the pros and cons, of globalization. Be sure to define what you mean by "globalization"; you may wish to restrict your discussion to global business, global travel, global education, or global political or social problems. How do Friedman's essay and the images provided in this Occasion help prove or disprove your response?

3. Write a response to Thomas L. Friedman's essay "The World Is Flat," in which you agree or disagree with Friedman, or in which you modify his claims. Provide additional evidence to support what he says, evidence to counter his argument, or both.

Courtesy www.adbusters.org

CREATING OCCASIONS

1. Consider how the above advertisement satirizes or spoofs Nike. Find conventional ads published by each company that promote Nike footwear and explain what image of the company the conventional ads suggest. Identify the issues at stake in the spoof ads, and consider how the companies criticized are responding to or ignoring the criticisms.

Christopher Clausen (b. 1942)

Christopher Clausen is a professor of English at Pennsylvania State University. Dr. Clausen has a Bachelor of Arts from Earlham College, a Master of Arts from the University of Chicago, and a doctorate from Queen's University in Canada. His books include *The Place of Poetry: Two Centuries of an Art in Crisis* (1981), *The Moral Imagination: Essays on Literature and Ethics* (1986), *My Life with President Kennedy* (1994), and *Faded Mosaic: The Emergence of Post-Cultural America* (2000).

AGAINST WORK

In "Against Work," Christopher Clausen makes a case for not working, for becoming one of the leisured class. Clausen identifies and analyzes the reasons people work and decides that many would be better off not working. He both locates and enlarges his discussion of not working by contrasting American attitudes toward work with those of French and German workers. In the process he addresses fundamental questions about the nature of work and our reasons for spending so much of our lives working.

1   A history of my suburban early ambitions would sound utterly conventional. At the age of six I wanted to be a cowboy. At twelve I decided instead to become a professional football player, which, for someone who would never weigh more than a hundred and thirty pounds, was even more hopeless. In high school I made up my mind to be a writer. As in most such cases, it wasn't the work of writing that appealed to me. It was that, secretly, I never wanted to do any work at all. But teenagers are rarely of one mind, and their inconsistent wishes seldom come true in a recognizable way.

"What is the use of having money if you have to work for it?" Violet Malone disdainfully asks her father-in-law, a self-made Irish-American billionaire, in George Bernard Shaw's play *Man and Superman*. A century ago, when Shaw was writing, the different valuation that Americans and Europeans set on work as an abstract ideal was already evident to anyone who had a chance to compare them. By that time the "gospel of work" preached by Thomas Carlyle, who repeated endlessly that "work is alone noble," was a mid-Victorian relic.

To her perfectly reasonable question, the Englishwoman Violet receives no answer. She would be just as baffled a hundred years later.

If humans are the only animal that doesn't think the purpose of life is to enjoy it, Americans are an especially hard case. Today those of us with full-time employment typically put in several hundred more hours per year than western Europeans—the equivalent of seven additional weeks, according to some surveys. Even the proverbially hardworking Germans spend only about three-quarters as many hours on the job and retire younger. Our disposable income is correspondingly higher, though when asked whether we would prefer more leisure to greater wealth, most of us opt for leisure. Statistics on voluntary overtime, however, suggest that we may not be telling the truth. A long American tradition leads people to define themselves not just by their occupations but also by the amount of labor they put in.

Captain John Smith's declaration that those who do not work shall not eat is the real national motto, ratified by subsequent authorities from Benjamin Franklin to Donald Trump. Rockefellers and Kennedys, whose international counterparts would spend all their time collecting works of art, instead work conspicuously hard at finance or politics. The American way is to prove one's worth by long hours, almost regardless of what one actually accomplishes. The fact that many people appear to work hard while actually coasting through the week merely confirms the gap between what they think they should be doing and their actual preferences.

5   Consider the fate of the word *workaholism,* coined by W. E. Oates in 1968 to identify a disturbing psychological obsession—an "addiction," a "compulsion"—that Oates had noticed around him. Others took up the new term enthusiastically. "The workaholic, as an addict is called, neglects his family, withdraws from social life, and loses interest in sex," the *Sydney Bulletin* explained ominously in 1973. But within a decade the term lost all connotation of pathology and became a compliment. "Unlike their workaholic American cousins," *Time* reported in 1981, "Europeans tend to see lengthy vacations as somehow part of the natural order of things." Today the word is most often heard in the proud boast. "I'm a workaholic," recited ad nauseam by type A personalities in corporations, politics, and the professions. Carlyle lives, if only in America.

Why on earth do we do it? Do most of us really prefer to work—to spend our lives in labor as an end rather than as an unavoidable means to our own or others' happiness? Of course not. Most jobs are boring at best, with few psychic rewards. Nobody works on an assembly line or at Wal-Mart, or recites the weather on Channel 9, simply for lack of a pleasanter way to spend two thousand hours every year. It's true that the most energetic and gregarious of us, the kind who have been claiming since high school that they "want to work with people," often find even jobs like these a relief from loneliness. One suspects, though, that if they suddenly didn't need the money or respect, they would quickly turn to playing games instead, or traveling the world, or finding innovative new ways to cope. The upper-middle-class professions are supposed to be a different story. Doctors, lawyers, and college professors usu-

ally think of themselves as "committed," with the implication that there is nothing they would rather be doing.

Speaking from experience, I can attest that being a senior academic is one of the more privileged assignments in life, although anyone who thinks universities are relaxed, humane centers for the free play of intellect hasn't spent much time in one lately. Plenty of hard work goes into getting a Ph.D., achieving tenure, and practicing a profession that despite its flattering self-image involves as much stress, conformity, and tedium as other occupations. In response to charges made a few years ago that professors are slackers, the Department of Education released a survey concluding that the average full-time university faculty member puts in between forty-five and fifty-five hours a week. Some of what I do for a living is fun—though I discovered early that writing anything meant to be read by others involves a good deal of labor—and the rest is pleasanter than what many people have to do. But still. Most of your waking hours for forty years?

There is something deeply conflicted about the devotion to work, vocation, career as an ideal in any society, but especially in one that has zealously cast off so many of its other repressions. Americans at the beginning of the twenty-first century pursue pleasure with the same avid desperation as upscale high school students pursue getting into the right college—that is, with a hell of a lot of work. We have all been so oversocialized that unnatural devotion to toil leaves its mark on every area of life. It could even be argued that the most highly prized pleasures have themselves become a form of work, complete with their own uniforms, disciplines, and special lingo.

My own conflicted attitude probably owes something to the fact that during the summer between high school and college, I worked as an information clerk for the National Heart

Institute in a suburb of the capital. As a temporary, I spent my days keeping track of offprints from medical journals, answering requests for the Heart Institute's own publications, and cleaning out the primitive photocopier. Much of the time there was not enough work to keep me busy, and like other low-level civil servants, I soon discovered that the Washington summer in a building with no air conditioning called for a relaxed approach to the public's business.

10   Most mornings I stayed in my office filling orders from schoolteachers for our most popular publication, a garish poster titled "The Living Pump." Having answered the mail as best I could, I generally retreated in the heat of the afternoon to the comfortable underground vault where our own materials and hundreds of articles on heart disease were stored. This fastness lay beneath a building that had been constructed with nuclear attack in mind. In addition to a normal basement, it had four subbasements reached by a freight elevator that no one else seemed to use. Once I got to the bottom, I made my way through nearly half a mile of corridors filled with abandoned office furniture. I never encountered another human being down there, just thousands of desks and chairs and filing cabinets that nobody wanted anymore. After several hours in this environment, it was easy to believe the world had ended, and all that was left of the United States government was one GS-2 surrounded by acres of junk five levels below ground zero. It seemed odd to me that reams of Living Pumps would survive Armageddon while the doctors who ran the National Institutes of Health turned into dust, but eighteen-year-olds have a high tolerance for irrationality. That's one reason they make good soldiers. I catalogued the contents of my bunker, restocked as necessary, composed juvenile light verse, and read a lot of novels in the cool silence. Some July afternoons I thought seriously about canceling my college plans and staying underground in the government forever.

The Department of Health, Education, and Welfare, as it was then called, had its headquarters on Independence Avenue in downtown Washington. Olive, a Southern widow who must have been in her fifties, presided over the Heart Institute's offices there. She had worked in similar offices since the New Deal and had seen bosses come and go. A slim woman of vast charm and presence, she liked young men who would spend Friday afternoons in her office drinking coffee and conversing. I retain only the general impression of an elegant lady from a different world where manners and human contact counted for nearly everything and bureaucratic procedures for nothing. Without ever saying so, she conveyed through her demeanor that the government was too absurd to worry about. My guess, although I really have no idea, is that Olive did her job very well, if in an unconventional fashion. Whoever was nominally her superior must have had a difficult time until he tacitly agreed that everything she did would be done her way.

As I look back, it's hard for me to believe what her way meant to my weekly routine. Every Thursday I would receive a slip entitling me to take a pickup truck out of the motor pool on Friday and drive it downtown to HEW. On alternate Friday mornings I would load the truck with publications from the bunker. Then I would have lunch, drive to Olive's office, unload the truck, and spend the afternoon listening, like a young man out of a Faulkner novel. The next Friday I would drive an empty truck to HEW, load it up with the same publications I had delivered the previous week, and return them to Bethesda. It sounds worse than it seemed at the time. Perhaps I'm forgetting some deliveries that served a real purpose beyond bringing me into Olive's presence. The possibility that my cheerful, un-ambitious colleagues would object to these excursions did not occur to me, and nobody ever did.

Everyone has met people who boast (sometimes repetitively) of loving their work so much that they rarely take vacations and can't bear the thought of retirement. Star athletes, successful artists, and research scientists are sometimes credible when they make these assertions. Occasionally an obstetrician goes on delivering babies into his nineties, and the local newspaper praises his enthusiasm for life. But who believes middle managers when they claim to spend the weekend looking forward to Monday? Who takes teachers seriously in June when they say they can't wait for September? If hypocrisy is the tribute vice pays to virtue, the oddity here is that so many people believe work as such, work divorced from any particular achievement, is especially virtuous. Working to earn one's bread is something few people can escape. Working out of moral vanity is sheer self-deception.

Of course Americans didn't invent the idea. As with so many things, we merely perfected it. To get people to do their best over a long period of time, it has always been necessary to make what they do seem both a duty and a pleasure, something like rearing children. Seneca assured affluent Roman parents, "Nothing is so certain as that the evils of idleness can be shaken off by hard work." In a similar vein, Voltaire wrote, "Work keeps us from three great evils, boredom, vice, and need." These are the homilies of the fortunate. Those who have been forced to work hard are often more realistic about what is at stake. "I don't like work—no man does," Joseph Conrad's alter ego Marlow announces in *Heart of Darkness,* and then adds, "—but I like what is in work—the chance to find yourself. Your own reality—for yourself, not for others—what no other man can ever know." The self-respect that comes from being financially self-supporting, as well as capable of some useful accomplishment for oneself or others, is a worthy goal for anyone. Fetishizing the labor itself is merely a form of bondage, workaholism in the true, perverse sense.

Because it serves so many different practical and psychic purposes, it's no wonder that, in the celebrated words of C. Northcote Parkinson, "work expands so as to fill the time available for its completion." Still, much can be said not just for the strenuous, cultivated leisure that hardworking professionals sometimes allow themselves to imagine as an alternative to virtuous toil, but for bone-idleness. There is in fact no indication that those who work are happier than those who choose not to. After surveying a mass of research on what it takes to make people happy, the psychologist David Watson declares, "With the notable exception of involuntary unemployment, we see little evidence that occupational and employment status have a major impact on well-being. Generally speaking, people in seemingly uninteresting, low-status jobs report levels of happiness and life satisfaction that are quite comparable to those of individuals in high-status occupations. Moreover, the employed and voluntarily unemployed report extremely similar levels of affect and well-being." He concludes, "One particularly interesting implication of this literature is that people apparently devote much of their lives to striving after things—education, marriage, money, and so on—that ultimately have little effect on their happiness." Although having some goals in life seems to work better than having none, "happiness is primarily a subjective phenomenon . . . not highly constrained by objective circumstances."

If your work won't make you or anyone else happier, why do more of it than you have to? Believers in the gospel of work typically consider happiness irrelevant. Deep down, they think we have a duty to be miserable. As usual, the bullying Carlyle put it most brutally: "'Happy,' my brother? First of all, what difference is it whether thou art happy or not! . . . The only happiness a brave man ever troubled himself with asking much about was, happiness enough to get his work done. Not 'I can't eat!' but 'I can't work!' that was the burden of all wise complaining among men." Men must work, and women must weep, as Carlyle's friend Charles Kingsley decreed. Work itself, work as a sacred abstraction, had become a substitute for the God that Carlyle and many of his readers no longer believed in.

In America this grim pseudo-religion continues to draw worshippers on a scale no longer seen elsewhere in the Western world. The only major change is that women are now expected to work like men. We speak in reverent tones of the "work ethic"; politicians praise "working families" and, even in times of relatively low unemployment, make job creation an issue in every campaign. A few years ago, cutting the work week was a central promise in a French election, and the government actually passed laws on the subject. In the United States, by contrast, legislation has been introduced to make overtime easier for companies to afford. We abolished mandatory retirement in the 1980s. Despite the growth in productivity and affluence over the past decades, all the social pressures are for working longer hours and later in life rather than cashing in on the promise of greater leisure—partly to take some of the pressure off Social Security and Medicare, but mostly because work is such an ingrained American value.

I don't know about the civil service, but not many Olives are left in major universities. Sometimes I dream of my vault full of Living Pumps. A colleague and I recently passed the time by talking speculatively of retirement. "You wouldn't actually retire at sixty-five, would you?" this proud workaholic asked with incredulity.

"Of course," I gulped, suddenly and unexpectedly defensive about my secret plan to quit at sixty-two. "Why not?"

He shrugged disdainfully and went back 20 to writing his next book on Chaucer. Truly, we are the last Puritans.

READING AND THINKING

1. Why do you think Clausen begins his essay with a reference to his teenage ideas of careers? What did you think your future work would be when you were twelve years old? What do you think are more likely possibilities now? Why?

2. What do you think Thomas Carlyle means by the "gospel of work"? Why might Carlyle have believed that "work is alone noble"? What does Clausen mean by writing that "Carlyle lives, if only in America"?

3. Why do you think Clausen compares American work hours and habits with those of French and German workers? What are the major differences between American workers and their European counterparts? Who do you think is making a better choice? Why?

4. What point does Clausen make about the words "workaholic" and "workaholism"?

5. What is the effect of the many questions that Clausen asks, such as "Why on earth do we do it?" and "Most of your working hours for forty years"?

THINKING AND WRITING

1. Summarize the reasons Clausen mentions for why people work. Explain what he thinks of those reasons.

2. Identify the conflicts between work and leisure pleasures Clausen identifies. Explain why he, himself, possesses a conflicted attitude toward work.

3. Describe your own attitude toward work and leisure. What, for you, is the ideal balance between work and leisure? Explain.

4. Explain Clausen's attitude toward those who boast that they love their work so much they hardly ever take a vacation and can't bear the thought of retirement. To what extent do you agree with his statement that "Working out of moral vanity is sheer self-deception"?

MAXIMIZING LEISURE: AN OCCASION FOR WRITING

Christopher Clausen reminds us that there is more to life than work. Even if we are lucky enough to have interesting work to do, we still need time off from that work, time for leisure, for relaxing, and for pursuing other of life's interests and pleasures. This Occasion invites you to consider the purposes and pleasures of leisure for your own life.

© Scott Leigh

PREPARING TO WRITE: OCCASIONS TO THINK ABOUT WHAT YOU SEE

1. What is your initial reaction to this image? How do you relate to this image? What personal experiences does it remind you of?

2. Imagine this image as an image in an advertisement for a vacation resort. Why might a company use an image like this? In your opinion, what is appealing about the image? What might be seen as unappealing?

MOVING TOWARD ESSAY: OCCASIONS TO ANALYZE AND REFLECT

1. How does the image pair with Clausen's essay? Do you agree or disagree with the message that both the essay and the image are sending?

2. Do you think people should use their leisure time to improve themselves, to develop their work skills or their life skills? Do you think leisure should be used primarily for relaxation, for doing nothing "productive"? Explain.

3. People with a lot of money don't have to work, yet some do so out of choice. People with little or no money typically have to work to make a living. Many of them wish they had much more leisure time, like the wealthy who don't work. Explain what would happen if the two groups could change places and circumstances.

4. Consider how people in two different countries typically spend their leisure time. Explain the extent to which those differences are cultural, and the extent to which they might be economic, social, political, or religious.

WRITING THOUGHTFULLY: OCCASIONS FOR IDEAS AND ESSAYS

1. Write an essay in which you argue that American workers should have more (or less) leisure time. You may wish to increase (or decrease) the work day or work week, or to increase or decrease holiday and vacation time. Provide reasons for each of the recommendations you make.

2. Read the following excerpt from Thorstein Veblen's *Theory of the Leisure Class*. Then write an essay in which you support, qualify, or contest Veblen's ideas using all the evidence provided to you in this Occasion.

Thorstein Veblen

Theory of the Leisure Class

The quasi-peaceable gentleman of leisure, then, not only consumes of the staff of life beyond the minimum required for subsistence and physical efficiency, but his consumption also undergoes a specialisation as regards the quality of the goods consumed. He consumes freely and of the best, in food, drink, narcotics, shelter, services, ornaments, apparel, weapons and accoutrements, amusements, amulets, and idols or divinities. In the process of gradual amelioration which takes place in the articles of his consumption, the motive principle and the proximate aim of innovation is no doubt the higher efficiency of the improved and more elaborate products for personal comfort and well-being. But that does not remain the sole purpose of their consumption. The canon of reputability is at hand and seizes upon such innovations as are, according to its standard, fit to survive. Since the consumption of these more excellent goods is an evidence of wealth, it becomes honorific; and conversely, the failure to consume in due quantity and quality becomes a mark of inferiority and demerit.

This growth of punctilious discrimination as to qualitative excellence in eating, drinking, etc., presently affects not only the manner of life, but also the training and intellectual activity of the gentleman of leisure. He is no longer simply the successful, aggressive male—the man of strength, resource, and intrepidity. In order to avoid stultification he must also cultivate his tastes, for it now becomes incumbent on him to discriminate with some nicety between the noble and the ignoble in consumable goods. He becomes a connoisseur in creditable viands of various degrees of merit, in manly beverages and trinkets, in seemly apparel and architecture, in weapons, games, dancers, and the narcotics. This cultivation of the aesthetic faculty requires time and application, and the demands made upon the gentleman in this direction therefore tend to change his life of leisure into a more or less arduous application to the business of learning how to live a life of ostensible leisure in a becoming way. Closely related to the requirement that the gentleman must consume freely and of the right kind of goods, there is the requirement that he must know how to consume them in a seemly manner. His life of leisure must be conducted in due form. Hence arise good manners in the way pointed out in an earlier chapter. High-bred manners and ways of living are items of conformity to the norm of conspicuous leisure and conspicuous consumption.

CREATING OCCASIONS

1. Do some research on leisure. Did leisure always exist? Did it exist in some places and times but not others? For some groups but not for others? To what extent is leisure a modern invention? To what extent has it become a human right?

2. Read some excerpts from the work of Thorstein Veblen, particularly from his book *Theory of the Leisure Class*. Find two additional passages from Veblen that you find interesting and engaging. Discuss what you find of interest in these passages, summarize what Veblen says in them, and explain whether you agree with what he says there and why.

Diane Ackerman (b. 1948)

Diane Ackerman writes poetically and rigorously about science, nature, creativity, and the sensual life. She received a Master of Arts, Master of Fine Arts, and Doctor of Philosophy from Cornell University. A poet, she also writes prize-winning nonfiction. Her books include the *A Natural History of the Senses* (1990), *Cultivating Delight: A Natural History of My Garden* (2001), *An Alchemy of the Mind: The Marvel and Mystery of the Brain* (2004). Her essays have appeared in the *New York Times, The New Yorker,* and *National Geographic,* and she has received a Guggenheim Fellowship, the John Burroughs Nature Award, and the Peter I. B. Lavan Younger Poet Award.

IN THE MEMORY MINES

"In the Memory Mines" first appeared in the *Michigan Quarterly Review* and was later republished in *Best American Essays 2001*. This essay is built on partial reconstructions of Ackerman's childhood, moments recovered under hypnosis. We are told that she was instructed at the end of each hypnotic session that she would remember only what she "felt comfortable with." But the writing down of those comfortable things seems to have made room for wondering about moments of a different kind, moments associated with discomfort, perhaps trauma.

1 I don't remember being born, but opening my eyes for the first time, yes. Under hypnosis many years later, I wandered through knotted jungles of memory to the lost kingdoms of my childhood, which for some reason I had forgotten, the way one casually misplaces a hat or a glove. Suddenly I could remember waking in a white room, with white walls, and white sheets, and a round white basin on a square white table, and looking up into the face of my mother, whose brown hair, flushed complexion, and dark eyes were the only contrast to the white room and daylight that stung her with its brightness. Lying on my mother's chest, I watched the flesh-colored apparition change its features, as if triangles were being randomly shuffled. Then a row of white teeth flashed out of nowhere, dark eyes widened, and I, unaware there was such a thing as motion, or that I was powerless even to roll over, watched the barrage of colors and shapes, appearing, disappearing, like magic scarves out of hats, and was completely enthralled.

What I couldn't know was how yellow I had been, and covered with a film of silky black hair, which made me look even more monkey-like than newborns usually do, and sent my pediatrician into a well-concealed tizzy. He placed the cud-textured being on its mother's chest, smiled as he said, "You have a baby girl," and, forgetting to remove his gloves or even thank the anesthesiologist as was his habit, he left the hospital room to find a colleague fast. Once he had delivered a deformed baby, which came out rolled up like a volleyball, its organs outside its body, and its brain, mercifully, dead. Once he had delivered premature twins, only one of which survived the benign sham of an incubator, and now was a confused, growing teenager he sometimes saw concealing a cigarette outside the high school. Stillborns he had delivered so many times he no longer could remember how many there were, or whose. But never had he delivered a baby so near normal yet brutally different before. He knew that I was jaundiced (which he could treat easily enough), and presumed the hairy coat was due to a hormonal imbalance of some sort, though he understood neither its cause nor its degree. When he found the staff endocrinologist equally puzzled, he decided the best course was not to worry the mother, who was herself not much more than a young girl, and one with a volatile marriage, from what he'd heard from a mutual friend at the country club. He decided he would tell her that the condition was normal—something the baby would outgrow ("like life," he thought cynically)—and prescribed a drug for the jaundice, lifting the clipboard in the maternity office with one hand and writing the prescription carefully, in an unnecessarily ornate script, which was his only affectation. As he did so, New York State seemed to him suddenly shabby and outmoded, like the hospital on whose cracked linoleum he stood; like the poor practice he conducted on the first floor of his old, street-front, brick house, whose porch slats creaked at the footstep of each patient so that, at table or in his study, or even lying down on the sofa in the den wallpapered with small tea roses, he would hear that indelible creaking and be halfway across the room before his wife knew he hadn't merely taken a yen for a dish of ice cream or gone to fetch a magazine from the waiting room; like the apple-cheeked woman he had married almost twenty-five years ago, when she was slender and prankish and such a willing chum; like the best clothes of most of his patients, who had made it through the Depression by doing with less until less was all they wanted; like the shabby future of this hairy little baby, on whom fate had played an as yet unspecified trick. It was that compound malaise that my mother saw on Dr. Petersen's face as she glanced over the clean, well-used crib at her bedside and out of the hospital window just as Dr. Petersen was walking to his car to drive home for lunch and a short nap before his afternoon hours.

My mother let her eyes drowse over the crib, where her baby, a summoned life, was lying on its stomach, knees out like a tiny gymnast, still faintly yellow, and still covered with a delicate down. If anything, she found me more vulnerable, a plaintive little soul whose face looked rumpled as an unmade bed when it cried, and whose eyes could be more eloquent than a burst of sudden speech. She sang softly as she held my tiny life in her arms, my every whim and need encapsulated in a body small as a trinket, something she could carry in the crook of her arm. How could there be a grownup in so frail and pupal a creature, one so easily frightened, so easily animated, so utterly dependent on her for everything but breath? If only her husband could be there to see her, she thought as she watched my hand move like a wayward crab across the sheet, if only he could have gotten leave to be with her. There was no telling how long it would take the Red Cross to get word to him that he had a baby girl. And what would he make of such news, anyway, in a foxhole somewhere in the middle of France, with civilians and soldiers dying all around him, at his hands even, what would he make of bringing this new civilian into the world? Though nearly over, the war seemed endless. The radio had run out of see-you-when-the-war-is-over songs. His letters were infrequent and jaggedly expressed, not that they'd talked much or even politely before he'd left. Marrying him had been like walking into a typhoon. But once in it, her pride had prevented her from returning to her parents' house in Detroit. They had warned her about marrying a man as "difficult" as he was, and, anyway, they still had so many children at home to feed and clothe on her dad's poor salary. She had always been a trouble to them, wanting to go to the fairyland of "college" when there were six other children to give minimum schooling, then running off with him when life on the South Side became suffocating. If she couldn't be a good daughter, or a good wife it would seem (no matter how pliable she tried to be), she could at least be a good mother to this odd little being. When would he return? In shameful moments, she almost wished he wouldn't; it would mean a reprieve, a chance to start life over with someone who shared more of her interests and barked at her less over trivial matters like his fried potatoes not being as crisp as he wished when he walked in the door at 7 P.M. and wanted nothing from the world but a perfect, ready dinner. His mother had always managed it for the menfolk in her family, for whom she'd baked and cooked and tended all afternoon, until they walked in hungry and demanding at nightfall, and he demanded it from his wife, period. It was the least she could do while he was out working hard to earn money for the bread she ate, etc. etc. No, he would probably return from war, and life would go on, though perhaps the experience would mellow him. If not . . . well, she could always have another baby. She looked at me. Just imagine, the baby was alive and didn't even know that. What a helpless, lovable bundle she had created! She spent the rest of the afternoon watching me and fantasizing about my limitless future.

My infant years might have happened in an aquarium, so silent and full of mixing shapes were they. How strange that a time filled with my own endless wailings, gurglings, and the soothing coos and baby talk of my mother should remain in my memory as a thick, silent dream in which clearer than any sound was the blond varnish on my crib, whose pale streaky gloss I knew like a birthmark, as it was for so many months of my life. At one, six months is half of a lifetime, and for half my lifetime I'd lain in my crib watching how the blond wood bars seemed to stretch from floor to ceiling, my mother's hands coming over them, though it seemed nothing could be higher. My mother's hands always appeared with a smile on her face, which I knew only as a semicircle that amazed me with its calm delight which each day renewed. It would rise over my crib like one of those devastating moons you can't take your eyes off of. I would knit my forehead, perplexed for a moment, and then smile without thinking about it, and my mother's soft hand would stretch over the bars to touch me, though the touch I couldn't remember in later years, nor any sound. It was a time of shapes and colors, and the puzzling changes in the air as the day moved and I could see the sunlight on a thousand flecks of milling dust, watch the sky turn blue as a bead, then strange, vapory colors ghost through the dark and frighten me before night fell. It was a time of complete passivity and ignorance. Odd things happened to me which I could neither explain nor predict. Life was like that, full of caretakers appearing over my crib wall, sometimes carrying things with shapes and colors so vibrant they startled me, things that would ring or chatter or huff. Long, ribboned, shiny things I found especially monstrous, and sometimes a shocking blue or yellow would be so intense it made my ribs shiver and my eyes scrunch closed. When that happened, the caretaker's face would change like a Kabuki mask, and through my wet, twitching eyes I would see the moon-mask waiting, watching, filled with delight. The moon shone on me daily. Often, in the black ether I sometimes woke in, when the blond crib varnish was nowhere to be found, I could sense the moon's presence standing nearby and watching me, feel its warm breath and know it was close, transfixed by my every stirring. Sometimes the moon would vanish for long spells and my ribs would shake. Sometimes the moon would appear, all angles like a piece of broken glass, though usually that happened only when another face, shattery and florid, was there, too. To see their faces shuffle and twist scared me, though I didn't know what "scared" was exactly, only that my bones felt too large for my body, my eyes seemed to draw closer together, and I forgot everything but the grating noise, the awful, scraping barks. My thoughts, such as they were, were like a dog's or an ape's. Things happened, but what a thing was I didn't know, nor could I fathom the idea of happen. Not thoughts but images paraded through my days, and feelings I couldn't associate with anything special like a part of my body or a soft blanket. I was like a plastic doll, except that I was, and, if death had taken me, I would not have known it. There was no confusion, no thought, no sentiment, no want. But, for some reason, the blond crib wood pleased me. I touched it with my eyes, I drank it, I smelled its glossy shimmer. When I watched it, I was not with my body but with the wood. I explored its details for long, blond hours; then I explored the sunlight catching dust in the air. Each time I explored them, or a fluffy being put next to me, or a twirling color-flock above me, it was as if I had stepped onto another planet where nothing was but that sight, nothing mattered, nothing gave me deeper pleasure, nothing came to mind.

5   At two, most of my excess body hair had fallen off like scales, except for a triangular swath above my fanny, and a single silky stripe from my ribs to my pudendum. My skin softened to the buttery translucence of a two-year-old's, and my black hair made me look like an Inca. Things had names. All animals were "dog," all people were "mommy" or "daddy," but my voice could follow my pointing finger, and when it did it was almost like touching. I was enchanted equally by oddly shaped animals and kitchen utensils, and the maple jungle of recoiling legs below the dining room table. My world stopped at the shadowy heights of the closet, but some things were close to me that were lost to my mother—the clawed plastic brackets holding the bottom of the long mirror in my parents' bedroom, the heavy ruffles along the sofa that tickled my knees when I climbed up to straddle the armrest and play horsey, the sheet of glass on top of the low coffee table, into whose edge I would peer each day for long, dizzying spells, transfixed by the bright, rippling green waves I saw there.

Some parts of the house had no mystery, and consequently I never visited them. For example, the two closets facing each other in the tiny foyer. Long ago, I'd discovered nothing of any interest was in them, just over-coats, scarves, boots, and drab clothes in cellophane cleaning bags. Toys for Christmas or birthdays were hidden in the bathroom closet upstairs, the one I could just reach at three years old by standing on the toilet, leaning forward until I could brace one foot on the windowsill, and then leaping onto the lowest plywood shelf while grabbing hold of an upper bracket with one hand. I could swiftly explore with the other before I fell onto the bathmat. Only once had I actually touched a box, but I could see them up high, brightly colored and covered with unfamiliar words that soon enough I would know by heart. Games I had tired of were kept there as well, forgotten so completely I thought they were brand new. Sometimes, while I was banging down the long flight of carpeted stairs on my fanny, as I loved to do and always did when my mother wasn't around to scold me for it, it would occur to me that I had played with such and such a toy before, long ago, almost beyond remembering. Early one morning, I walked into my parents' bedroom and stood by my mother's side of the bed. Slowly my mother opened her eyes and, seeing me standing so close to her, smiled a spontaneous full-hearted smile. She held my tiny hand for a moment, enraptured by her child's presence. Then, reassured by the rightness of all things, I scampered out of the room, walked down the hallway whose boards creaked even when my slight weight strained them, jumped into the carpeted stairwell as if it were a lifeboat, and gleefully bumped down the stairs on my fanny.

It was a lonely world for me, my mother knew, what with my father on the road selling until late at night, and my mother herself making ends meet by canvassing for long hours on the telephone. Half the money she made she put in an account my father didn't know about, just in case she one day had the courage to bundle me up and leave him. I had turtles and fish and dolls to play with, but no children who lived close enough to be casual with. And, often, I would come to her mopey in the middle of the day, complaining pathetically that I was "bored." How could a three-year-old be bored, she wondered, and where could I even have learned such a word? Then she would feel sorry for me and devise some games with empty egg cartons or paper bags and crayons I could play at her feet while she continued telephoning anonymous users of unnecessary products to ask them intrusive questions about their laundry or eating habits or television viewing. Oddest of all was my father's response to me. Perhaps it was because he was away when I was born, or because he feared being vulnerable and weak, or because he had not been raised in a demonstrative home himself, but whatever tenderness I sought upset him. He recoiled at the thought of brushing my hair or bathing me. My lidless appetite for love and attention suffocated him. My zest made him nervous, perhaps because it seemed faintly erotic, and that aroused in him feelings that disgusted and frightened him. And whenever I ran to him, as I did mainly on Sundays, since I rarely saw him during the week, he would always find ways and reasons for not holding me, turning his head when I tried to kiss him, keeping me just out of reach when I wanted to snuggle. My mother wondered how such a revulsion could be, and, if she dared to broach the subject with him, he would yell and storm out of the room, muttering "Women! Always some nagging, pea-brained nonsense!" and other irate things, until, finally, she thought the scenes worse for me than the withheld affection.

At four, I had a tower of gaily colored plastic records, and I knew how to make them sing on the toy record player. But for long hours I would listen to a slow, plaintive song, "Farewell to the Mountains," which I played over and over as I sat on the living room rug and grew more and more withdrawn. What would a four-year-old dream about? My mother often wondered when she saw me like

that, and wondered too if it was normal for a child to be so subdued. But to find out she would have had to have spoken to someone—a friend, a doctor, or, most horrifying of all, perhaps even a psychiatrist, which was a shame only whispered about in nice families. In fact, it was no longer possible for such a family to be "nice" at all if one of its members admitted to insanity by seeking a psychiatrist. My mother shuddered at the thought, as she fed stray wisps of hair back into her pageboy, and checked her list for the next household to call about their consumption of presweetened cereal. She could hear "Farewell to the Mountains" softly wailing in the next room, and knew I would be sitting inertly by the speaker, dreaming of whatever things a four-year-old dreamt of. A new doll, perhaps, or a dog . . . my experience was so limited, thank goodness; how could the daydreams hurt me? She lifted a pencil with which to dial the next number, so as not to callus her index finger. In less than a year, I would be going to kindergarten, with playmates and things to do, and life would be smoother.

In the living room, while my lugubrious record repeated, I dreamt of escape, of life beyond the windowpanes, of gigantic trees that led into magic kingdoms, of strange, cacophonous animals, and endless kisses and hugs, and a giant dollhouse in which I could live, and flowers so big and perfumed I could crawl into them to sleep, and, most of all, I dreamt of a sleek black horse which I had seen on television and had been utterly thrilled by. How it had reared and flailed when people tried to get near it. How it arched its tail and shone in the dazzling sunlight when it ran up the side of a mountain. How it lathered and whinnied and looked ready to explode. I dreamt of playing with the frantic black horse which would scare and excite me and, sometimes, if I were very good, let me get close enough to stroke and ride. Together we would run out to those flat, funny-bushed prairies that stretched forever and we would make the sound of rain falling as we galloped. On her way to bed, my mother would peek in on me, and most days she would find me wide awake at midnight, lying quietly in my bed like a tiny Prince of Darkness, my brain raw as henna, just pacing, pacing. If insomnia was unusual for a child, it was normal for me. There was a switch in my cells that wouldn't turn off at night, which is not to say that I was one of those rare few who could get by with little sleep and wake to conquer the world. If I slept badly, I was tired the next day, and, since most days I slept badly, I was mostly tired. Dark circles formed under my eyes, and I looked oddly debauched for a four-year-old girl. Once, my mother gave me a quarter of one of her sleeping pills, and out of that cruel prankishness of which children seem the liveliest masters, I had pretended not to be able to wake up the next morning, even though my mother shook and shook me. When I finally deigned to open my eyes and fake a spontaneous yawn, I found my mother in a cold sweat and the most attentive and adoring spirit, which lasted all day. After that, she just let me grope for sleep by myself, but insisted on a ritual "going to bed" at 8 P. M., since at the very least I would then get some rest from lying still.

10   It was hard to say who looked forward most to my going to school. Six times my mother practiced the route with me, holding my hand as we walked through the vest-pocket-sized plum orchard that separated my street from Victory Park Elementary School. There was a more conventional way of getting there, of course, full of sidewalks and rigid corners and car-infested streets, but it was twice as long and meant crossing three intersections. My mother preferred to lead me across the street my house sat on and watch me as I walked down the well-worn shortcut leading almost unswervingly through the orchard. Only one part of the path, twenty yards or so, dipped behind a stand of bushes

and out of view. But at that point I would be able to see the crosswalk guard clearly, since she was always there, to-ing and fro-ing in her yellow jacket and bright red sash. Perhaps another mother in another city would have been frightened to let her five-year-old walk into an orchard alone each day, but in my hometown crime was not a problem. As I had discovered, boredom was. And the orchard was full of such extravagant smells and sights: low, scuffly hunchbacked things with long tails, Chaplinesque squirrels that looked like gray mittens when they climbed trees, mump-cheeked chipmunks, insects that looked like tiny buttons or tanks, feathered shudders in high nests, chattery seedpods, and tall, silky flowers with long red tongues hanging out. Best of all I liked to see the ripe plums, huddled like bats high above me. With my Roy Rogers tablet in one hand and a brown bag lunch in the other, I would go to school each day in a fine mood because I knew I had the orchard to look forward to. Then, too, I liked this new business of dressing up: purple corduroy pinafore, gray check with a lace collar, red and white jumper striped like a candy cane. White ankle socks, black patent leather shoes, matching ribbon. I would take my seat in the classroom and do the lessons and play the games and sing the songs, and in the afternoon I would come home again, through the orchard alive with buzzing and twittering, at the other side of which would be my mother, dependable as sunlight, waiting in a pale shirtwaist dress, her hair curled into a long pageboy roll.

The novelty of school lasted only a few months. The lessons were dull, the games were always the same, the other children were so distant and alien. They seemed to share a secret I alone didn't know. What they said was different, what they laughed at was different, what they saw was different. When I drew the plum bats curled high in the trees, or used six crayons to draw a rock, which everybody knows is gray, *airhead,* they teased me mercilessly, or, worse, ignored me for hours. Most of all, I liked running games in which I ran until I dropped in an exhausted heap, or spun around in circles until I got dizzy. Next to that, I liked looking at the butterfly and rock collections in the science locker, and sometimes I would spend all of recess playing with the kaleidoscope. The other children played jacks, or marbles, or house, or cowboys. I liked cowboys, but wanted to be the horse, not a man shooting nonstop and pretending to die. In time, I discovered the knack of talking like the others, but it was hard to sustain, and though I dearly wanted the friendship of the other children, nothing I could do seemed to endear me to them. I was different; it was as if I had spots or a tail. I hovered on the edge of elementary social life, making a friend here, a friend there, mainly among the boys, who didn't mind including me in their running and jumping games, where more bodies made little difference. At home, my father had begun taking photographs with a Kodak box camera he had bought at a flea market, snapshots of the family and neighbors on special days like Fourth of July or Christmas. The first time I saw a photograph it was as if a bucketful of light had been poured over me. In the picture people were always smiling, frozen happy forever. I pestered my father to take more and more pictures, and pleaded until he let me keep a few from each roll, to line up on my pink, Humpty-Dumpty decaled dresser next to the bed. With my dolls sitting rigid in a semicircle on the bed, and all the smiling faces in the photographs, I had quite a large gathering for mock tea parties and classrooms and cowboys and family fights, in one of which a doll's pudgy plastic arm snapped off.

Though I knew the orchard well, and loved to play in its chin-high weeds, bopping the teasel heads with a bat, or hunting for "British soldiers," red-capped fungi, among the blankets of green moss, my sense of geography was very poor. Getting anywhere was a blur. The world seemed without boundary, unimaginable and infinite. Even though, on most days, I had no desire to go farther than my neighborhood, I sensed the world dropped off at a perilous angle just beyond it. I was frightened at the literal perimeter of what I knew. Had I been a grownup, I might have been reminded of the Duke Ellington song "There's Nothing on the Brink of What You Think." What did I fear? I didn't know. It was not a rational fear. Just as wailing for my mother if we became separated in a supermarket was not a rational act. I just feared. But the fear fled when I was with a gang of children strolling the neighborhood, as we did each Halloween when, often, we would go as far afield as three or four streets away, bags laden, ready to perform the simple acrobatics it took to con strangers out of sweet booty. Spreading my loot on the living room floor afterward, I would go through it with my mother, who adored sifting the haul and always got all of the Mary Janes, which I loathed the taste of.

One day, as if a typhoon had just ended, my father died of an ailment that sounded to me like "pullman throbs," and thus disappeared from my life the same stranger he had always been, a lodger who directed my life with his shouts, who had absolute control over my fate, and could not be appealed to by tears or reason. He had been an omnipotent, mysterious stranger who left the house before I got up each morning and came home after I went to sleep each night, and on weekends was sullen and tired. He only ever seemed to read the paper or watch television or sleep or yell at my mother or slam the door to their bedroom, after which I would sometimes hear my mother crying. For some reason he never had time for me. In my heart, I knew it must be my fault, that I must be somehow unworthy of his love, his attention even, the way the newspaper or television at least had his attention. I understood deep down in my soul that something serious must be wrong with me, that I lacked something—I wasn't pretty enough, or smart enough, or funny enough . . . I didn't know what quality exactly—whatever that alchemical thing was, I lacked it. Otherwise he would surely have loved me. I had tried in prismatically different ways to delight him, to please him, ultimately to win him. Some mornings I would spend fifteen minutes choosing the right ribbon—checked versus striped, plain edged or lace, flat cotton or broad glossy satin—and then tug on my embroidered ankle socks, and deliberate over the dresses in my closet as if I were a floozy primping for the man who brought me chocolates and cheap jewelry on Sundays. I was like a war bride with a shellshocked husband at home, attentive to his every whim, trying hard to reconstruct their tender armistices. After so many silent, private years, I seemed suddenly to be an extrovert, and my mother delighted in the long-awaited change toward what she saw as a normal, if hyperactive, childhood. Without understanding why exactly, I would play the clown whenever my father was around, dancing little jigs, doing impressions of TV characters, pretending to be a dog by fetching his slippers in my mouth and then sitting up in front of him as he read the newspaper in the enormous, rose-colored armchair by the picture window, my tiny hands lifted and loosely flapping like paws. Sometimes I would bake him ginger cookies, his favorite, which my mother would let me cut with bright red plastic cookie cutters shaped like men and women, clowns, and Christmas trees, into which I would press candy buttons and eyes. When he was around, I would follow him like a tropic flower the sun, needy, riveted, always open for warmth. Sometimes he would take me on his knees, or pat my head lightly, and, when he did, I would feel happy and even-hearted all day. But most days he simply ignored me, or yelled at me for pestering him, and, when he did, I would try extra hard to please him. I would eat my food

without playing with it first, though I loved taking dollops of mashed potatoes in my hands and rolling them into balls for a snowman, which I would stand on the rim of my plate while I ate. Once, for Sunday lunch, mother and I concocted a "Happy Jack" out of a tomato, tunafish salad, and a hard-boiled egg, scooping out the tomato, filling it with tunafish, and toothpicking the egg upright in the middle. I painted paprika eyes and mouth onto the egg with a wet finger, stuck in a whole clove for a nose, and then attached the cutaway tomato lid with a toothpick to make a beret. Then I dressed up in my Halloween clown suit, and presented it to my father on a dinner plate. He laughed out loud, and hugged my shoulders by wrapping one of his enormous arms around them, and that pleased me so much I was contented for days. But nothing less extreme seemed to waylay his thoughts, which were always galloping away from me. Then he died, and it was as if a door had slammed shut. There was no warning, no reassurance; he just left. Though I had not gone to the funeral, I understood that dead meant being broken beyond repair, as my mother had explained it, and could see that, when it happened, grownups cried torrentially and then walked around gloomy and snuffling for days, as if they shared a secret cold. I understood that he was gone now on weekends, too, and that he had left without saying goodbye to me, though perhaps, surely, he had said goodbye to my mother. While he lived, he would at least wave when he left. Now there was not even that. Now I could no longer even try to please him. Without meaning to, I reverted to my sullen, dreamy ways. My mother shook her head and, without going into details, told friends that his death had come "at the worst possible time for everyone."

The last instruction I received as each hypnotic session came to a close was that I would remember only what I felt comfortable with.

It was a relative fiat, and it worked, letting just enough of my subterranean past seep through to give me a sense of origin, of development, without reminding me of any war crimes that might alarm me. And so it was no surprise that in my waking life I remembered little of my recaptured childhood: its sensory delights, a few events, and its tense, poignant moods. Whether or not a crucial drama lay salted away in my memory, I never knew. Once, coming out of the well of a trance, I noticed my eyes were sore and my nose blocked from crying. Where had I gone? Toward a sexual event? A violent one? I didn't know. At first, the childhood I began discovering mystified me, its iceberg fragments were so high-focus and yet remote. And what was there between the fragments I didn't wish to remember? But gradually, as slants of my past surfaced, I felt as if I had adopted a child on the installment plan, a child that was myself, and it felt good suddenly to be part of a community, even if it was only a community of previous selves.

READING AND THINKING

1. After you have read through this piece to the end, go back to the beginning. To what extent does the ending influence your understanding of the first paragraph, of the essay as a whole?

2. Consider the second (long) paragraph. How do you suppose Ackerman knows the many things she tells us? What do you imagine that her sources were? Why should we care?

3. In the essay's final paragraph, Ackerman refers to "war crimes," "a crucial drama," "sore eyes and a blocked nose," and experiences that might be there between the "iceberg fragments," things she "didn't wish to remember." Does the rest of the essay tell us what she might be referring to? Does the title hint at that same thing?

THINKING AND WRITING

1. Create two lists with these two headings: Baby Thoughts/Other Thoughts. Select any paragraph associated with the first few years of Ackerman's life and list her thinking in that paragraph under the appropriate heading. Explain what you discover.

2. Characterize Ackerman's relationship with her parents: one paragraph for each parent, citing evidence from the essay.

3. Write a brief analysis of the essay's title. Determine the extent to which you think the title is appropriate.

4. To what extent do you believe the essay is simply an attempt by Ackerman to reveal what it's like to be a "different" kind of child? Draw on the evidence of the text to support your analysis of the question.

Roland Barthes (1915–1980)

Roland Barthes was born in France and earned a license in classical letters at the Sorbonne. He taught at various institutes in France, Romania, and Egypt while continuing to study and write about philology, semiology, sociology, and structuralism. One of France's most distinguished New Critics, Barthes's unorthodox thinking kept him in the cultural and academic limelight. His most influential works include *Mythologies* (1972), *A Lover's Discourse: Fragments* (1978), and *Camera Lucida: Reflections on Photography* (1981).

TOYS

"Toys" is terse and concise; its implications are broad and critical. Barthes suggests that children, brought up with toys, are unwittingly learning cultural values as they play. So in a very real sense children are little adults, moving around absorbing values without realizing what is happening to them. Barthes trusts that *creativity* could serve as an antidote to such cultural poisoning.

1   French toys: One could not find a better illustration of the fact that the adult Frenchman sees the child as another self. All the toys one commonly sees are essentially a microcosm of the adult world; they are all reduced copies of human objects, as if in the eyes of the public the child was, all told, nothing but a smaller man, a homunculus to whom must be supplied objects of his own size.

Invented forms are very rare: a few sets of blocks, which appeal to the spirit of do-it-yourself, are the only ones which offer dynamic forms. As for the others, French toys *always mean something,* and this something is always entirely socialized, constituted by the myths or the techniques of modern adult life: the army, broadcasting, the post office, medicine (miniature instrument cases, operating theaters for dolls), school, hair styling (driers for permanent-waving), the air force (parachutists), transport (trains, Citroëns, Vedettes, Vespas, petrol stations), science (Martian toys).

The fact that French toys *literally* prefigure the world of adult functions obviously cannot but prepare the child to accept them all, by constituting for him, even before he can think about it, the alibi of a Nature which has at all times created soldiers, postmen and Vespas. Toys here reveal the list of all the things the adult does not find unusual: war, bureaucracy, ugliness, Martians, etc. It is not so much, in fact, the imitation which is a sign of an abdication, as its literalness. French toys are like a Jivaro head, in which one recognizes, shrunken to the size of an apple, the wrinkles and hair of an adult. There exist, for instance, dolls which urinate; they have an esophagus, one gives them a bottle, they wet their nappies; soon, no doubt, milk will turn to water in their stomachs. This is meant to prepare the little girl for the causality of housekeeping, to "condition" her to her future role as mother. However, faced with this world of faithful and complicated objects, the child can only identify himself as owner, as user, never as creator; he does not invent the world, he uses it: There are, prepared for him, actions without adventure, without wonder, without joy. He is turned into a little stay-at-home householder who does not even have to invent the mainsprings of adult causality; they are supplied to him ready-made: He has only to help himself, he is never allowed to discover anything from start to finish. The merest set of blocks, provided it is not too refined, implies a very different learning of the world: Then, the child does not in any way create meaningful objects, it matters little to him whether they have an adult name; the actions he performs are not those of a user but those of a demiurge. He creates forms which walk, which roll, he creates life, not property: Objects now act by themselves, they are no longer an inert and complicated material in the palm of his hand. But such toys are rather rare: French toys are usually based on imitation, they are meant to produce children who are users, not creators.

The bourgeois status of toys can be recognized not only in their forms, which are all functional, but also in their substances. Current toys are made of a graceless material, the product of chemistry, not of nature. Many are now molded from complicated mixtures; the plastic material of which they are made has an appearance at once gross and hygienic, it destroys all the pleasure, the sweetness, the humanity of touch. A sign which fills one with consternation is the gradual disappearance of wood, in spite of its being an ideal material because of its firmness and its softness, and the natural warmth of its touch. Wood removes, from all the forms which it supports, the wounding quality of angles which are too sharp, the chemical coldness of metal. When the child handles it and knocks it, it neither vibrates nor grates, it has a sound at once muffled and sharp. It is a familiar and poetic substance, which does not sever the child from close contact with the tree, the table, the floor. Wood does not wound or break down; it does not shatter, it wears out, it can last a long time, live with the child, alter little by little the relations between the object and the hand. If it dies, it is in dwindling, not in swelling out like those mechanical toys which disappear behind the hernia of a broken spring. Wood makes essential objects, objects for all time. Yet there hardly remain any of these wooden toys from the Vosges, these fretwork farms with their animals, which were only possible, it is true, in the days of the craftsman. Henceforth, toys are chemical in substance and color; their very material introduces one to a coenaesthesis of use, not pleasure. These toys die in fact very quickly, and once dead, they have no posthumous life for the child.

READING AND THINKING

1. What does Barthes suggest when he says that a child is "nothing but a smaller man, a homunculus"?

2. Why do blocks constitute for Barthes the ultimate of good toys?

3. Why does wood itself give Barthes so much pleasure?

4. What do you think Barthes means by "form"? He speaks of two aspects of form. What are they?

5. What *should* toys do, according to Barthes?

THINKING AND WRITING

1. Consider Barthes's claim in the second paragraph of the essay that "French toys *always mean something* and this something is entirely socialized." Make a list of American toys and test his claim against the ingrained, or socialized, values of American culture.

2. Explain in a few paragraphs whether you believe that as a child, the toys of your culture caused you to think of yourself only "as owner, as user, never as creator."

3. What about adult "toys" (MP3 players, plasma TVs, digital cameras)? Do they turn users into creators, or do they simply attest to a capitulation to advertising and consumerism? Explain.

4. Assess Barthes's third paragraph. How convincing is the evidence and the analysis of it in that paragraph? Explain in a tightly reasoned paragraph of your own.

Bernard Cooper (b. 1951)

Bernard Cooper grew up in Hollywood, California, and received a Bachelor of Fine Arts and a Master of Fine Arts from the California Institute of the Arts. Cooper has been a recipient of the O. Henry Prize and the PEN/Ernest Hemingway Award. He has published collections of short stories, including *Guess Again* (2000), as well as collections of essays, including *Maps to Anywhere* (1990) and *Truth Serum* (1997). He has taught writing at Antioch College in Los Angeles and writes for the *Los Angeles Times* as their art critic.

BURL'S

In "Burl's," Cooper explores the theme of sexual identity through a series of interrelated boyhood stories about his growing awareness of his gay sexuality. Cooper presents a young boy's understanding through the lens and from the perspective of his adult self.

I

1 I loved the restaurant's name, a compact curve of a word. Its sign, five big letters rimmed in neon, hovered above the roof. I almost never saw the sign with its neon lit; my parents took me there for early summer dinners, and even by the time we left—father cleaning his teeth with a toothpick, mother carrying steak bones in a doggie bag—the sky was still bright. Heat rippled off the cars parked along Hollywood Boulevard, the asphalt gummy from hours of sun.

With its sleek architecture, chrome appliances, and arctic temperature, Burl's offered a refuge from the street. We usually sat at one of the booths in front of the plate-glass windows. During our dinner, people came to a halt before the news-vending machine on the corner and burrowed in their pockets and purses for change.

The waitresses at Burl's wore brown uniforms edged in checked gingham. From their breast pockets frothed white lace handkerchiefs. In between reconnaissance missions to the table, they busied themselves behind the counter and shouted "Tuna to travel" or "Scorch that patty" to a harried short-order cook who manned the grill. Miniature pitchers of cream and individual pats of butter were extracted from an industrial refrigerator. Coca-Cola shot from a glinting spigot. Waitresses dodged and bumped one another, frantic as atoms.

My parents usually lingered after the meal, nursing cups of coffee while I played with the beads of condensation on my glass of ice water, tasted Tabasco sauce, or twisted pieces of my paper napkin into mangled animals. One evening, annoyed with my restlessness, my father gave me a dime and asked me to buy him a *Herald Examiner* from the vending machine in front of the restaurant.

Shouldering open the heavy glass door, I 5 was seared by a sudden gust of heat. Traffic roared past me and stirred the air. Walking toward the newspaper machine, I held the dime so tightly it seemed to melt in my palm. Duty made me feel large and important. I inserted the dime and opened the box, yanking a *Herald* from the spring contraption that held it as tight as a mousetrap. When I turned around, paper in hand, I saw two women walking toward me.

Their high heels clicked on the sun-baked pavement. They were tall, broad-shouldered women who moved with a mixture of haste and defiance. They'd teased their hair into nearly identical black beehives. Dangling earrings flashed in the sun, brilliant as prisms. Each of them wore the kind of clinging, strapless outfit my mother referred to as a cocktail dress. The silky fabric—one dress was purple, the other pink—accentuated their breasts and hips and rippled with insolent highlights. The dresses exposed their bare arms, the slope of their shoulders and the smooth, powdered plane of flesh where their cleavage began.

I owned at the time a book called *Things for Boys and Girls to Do*. There were pages to color, intricate mazes, and connect-the-dots. But another type of puzzle came to mind as I watched those women walking toward me: What's Wrong with This Picture? Say the drawing of a dining room looked normal at first glance; on closer inspection, a chair was missing its leg and the man who sat atop it wore half a pair of glasses.

The women had Adam's apples.

The closer they came, the shallower my breathing was. I blocked the sidewalk, an in-credulous child stalled in their path. When they saw me staring, they shifted their purses and linked their arms. There was something sisterly and conspiratorial about their sudden closeness. Though their mouths didn't move, I thought they might have been communicat-ing without moving their lips, so telepathic did they seem as they joined arms and pressed together, synchronizing their heavy steps. The pages of the *Herald* fluttered in the wind. I felt them against my arm, light as bat-ted lashes.

10   The woman in pink shot me a haughty glance and yet she seemed pleased that I'd taken notice, hungry to be admired by a man, or even an awestruck eight-year-old boy. She tried to stifle a grin, her red lipstick more voluptuous than the lips it painted. Rouge deepened her cheekbones. Eye shadow dusted her lids, a clumsy abundance of blue. Her face was like a page in *Things for Boys and Girls to Do,* colored by a kid who went outside the lines.

At close range, I saw that her wig was slightly askew. I was certain it was a wig be-cause my mother owned several; three Styro-foam heads lined a shelf in my mother's closet; upon them were perched a Page-Boy, an Empress, and a Baby-Doll, all in shades of auburn. The woman in the pink dress wore her wig like a crown of glory.

But it was the woman in the purple dress who passed nearest me, and I saw that her jaw was heavily powdered, a half-successful attempt to disguise the telltale shadow of a beard. Just as I noticed this, her heel caught on a crack in the pavement and she reeled on her stilettos. It was then that I witnessed a rift in her composure, a window through which I could glimpse the shades of maleness that her dress and wig and makeup obscured. She shifted her shoulders and threw out her hands like a surfer riding a curl. The instant she regained her balance, she smoothed her dress, patted her hair, and sauntered onward.

Any woman might be a man. The fact of it clanged through the chambers of my brain. In broad day, in the midst of traffic, with my par-ents drinking coffee a few feet away, I felt as if everything I understood, everything I had taken for granted up to that moment—the curve of the earth, the heat of the sun, the re-liability of my own eyes—had been squeezed out of me. Who were those men? Did they help each other get inside those dresses? How many other people and things were not what they seemed? From the back, the impostors looked like women once again, slinky and cur-vaceous, purple and pink. I watched them dis-appear into the distance, their disguises so convincing that other people on the street seemed to take no notice, and for a moment I wondered if I had imagined the whole en-counter, a visitation by two unlikely muses.

Frozen in the middle of the sidewalk, I caught my reflection in the window of Burl's, a silhouette floating between his parents. They faced one another across a table. Once the solid embodiments of woman and man, pedestrians and traffic appeared to pass through them.

II

There were some mornings, seconds before 15 my eyes opened and my senses gathered into consciousness, that the child I was seemed to hover above the bed, and I couldn't tell what form my waking would take—the body of a boy or the body of a girl. Finally stirring, I'd blink against the early light and greet each incarnation as a male with mild surprise. My sex, in other words, didn't seem to be an absolute fact so much as a pleasant, recurring accident.

By the age of eight, I'd experienced this groggy phenomenon several times. Those ethereal moments above my bed made waking up in the tangled blankets, a boy steeped in body heat, all the more astonishing. That this might be an unusual experience never occurred to me; it was one among a flood of sensations I could neither name nor ignore.

And so, shocked as I was when those transvestites passed me in front of Burl's, they confirmed something about which I already had an inkling: the hazy border between the sexes. My father, after all, raised his pinky when he drank from a teacup, and my mother looked as faded and plain as my father until she fixed her hair and painted her face.

Like most children, I once thought it possible to divide the world into male and female columns. Blue/Pink. Rooster/Hens. Trousers/Skirts. Such divisions were easy, not to mention comforting, for they simplified matter into compatible pairs. But there also existed a vast range of things that didn't fit neatly into either camp: clocks, milk, telephones, grass. There were nights I fell into a fitful sleep while trying to sex the world correctly.

Nothing typified the realms of male and female as clearly as my parents' walk-in closets. Home alone for any length of time, I always found my way inside them. I could stare at my parents' clothes for hours, grateful for the stillness and silence, haunting the very heart of their privacy.

20   The overhead light in my father's closet was a bare bulb. Whenever I groped for the chain in the dark, it wagged back and forth

and resisted my grasp. Once the light clicked on, I saw dozens of ties hanging like stalactites. A monogrammed silk bathrobe sagged from a hook, a gift my father had received on a long-ago birthday and, thinking it fussy, rarely wore. Shirts were cramped together along the length of an aluminum pole, their starched sleeves sticking out as if in a half-hearted gesture of greeting. The medicinal odor of mothballs permeated the boxer shorts that were folded and stacked in a built-in drawer. Immaculate underwear was proof of a tenderness my mother couldn't otherwise express; she may not have touched my father often, but she laundered his boxers with infinite care. Even back then, I suspected that a sense of duty was the final erotic link between them.

Sitting in a neat row on the closet floor were my father's boots and slippers and dress shoes. I'd try on his wingtips and clomp around, slipping out of them, with every step. My wary, unnatural stride made me all the more desperate to effect some authority. I'd whisper orders to imagined lackeys and take my invisible wife in my arms. But no matter how much I wanted them to fit, those shoes were as cold and hard as marble.

My mother's shoes were just as uncomfortable, but a lot more fun. From a brightly colored array of pumps and slingbacks, I'd pick a pair with the glee and deliberation of someone choosing a chocolate. Whatever embarrassment I felt was overwhelmed by the exhilaration of being taller in a pair of high heels. Things will look like this someday, I said to myself, gazing out from my new and improved vantage point as if from a crow's nest. Calves elongated, arms akimbo, I gauged each step so that I didn't fall over and moved with what might have passed for grace had someone seen me, a possibility I scrupulously avoided by locking the door.

Back and forth I went. The longer I wore a pair of heels, the better my balance. In the periphery of my vision, the shelf of wigs looked like a throng of kindly bystanders. Light streamed down from a high window, causing crystal bottles to glitter, the air ripe with perfume. A makeup mirror above the dressing table invited my self-absorption. Sound was muffled. Time slowed. It seemed as if nothing bad could happen as long as I stayed within those walls.

Though I'd never been discovered in my mother's closet, my parents knew that I was drawn toward girlish things—dolls and jump rope and jewelry—as well as to the games and preoccupations that were expected of a boy. I'm not sure now if it was my effeminacy itself that bothered them as much as my ability to slide back and forth, without the slightest warning, between male and female mannerisms. After I'd finished building the model of an F-17 bomber, say, I'd sit back to examine my handiwork, pursing my lips in concentration and crossing my legs at the knee.

III

25 One day my mother caught me standing in the middle of my bedroom doing an imitation of Mary Injijikian, a dark, overeager Armenian girl with whom I believed myself to be in love, not only because she was pretty but because I wanted to be like her. Collector of effortless A's, Mary seemed to know all the answers in class. Before the teacher had even finished asking a question, Mary would let out a little grunt and practically levitate out of her seat, as if her hand were filled with helium. "Could we please hear from someone else today besides Miss Injijikian," the teacher would say. *Miss Injijikian.* Those were the words I was repeating over and over to myself when my mother caught me. To utter them was rhythmic, delicious, and under their spell I raised my hand and wiggled like Mary. I heard a cough and spun around. My mother froze in the doorway. She clutched the folded sheets to her stomach and turned without saying a word. My sudden flush of shame confused me. Weren't boys supposed to swoon

over girls? Hadn't I seen babbling, heartsick men in a dozen movies?

Shortly after the Injijikian incident, my parents decided to send me to gymnastics class at the Los Angeles Athletic Club, a brick relic of a building on Olive Street. One of the oldest establishments of its kind in Los Angeles, the club prohibited women from the premises. My parents didn't have to say it aloud: they hoped a fraternal atmosphere would toughen me up and tilt me toward the male side of my nature.

My father drove me downtown so I could sign up for the class, meet the instructor, and get a tour of the place. On the way there, he reminisced about sports. Since he'd grown up in a rough Philadelphia neighborhood, sports consisted of kick-the-can or rolling a hoop down the street with a stick. The more he talked about his physical prowess, the more convinced I became that my daydreams and shyness were a disappointment to him.

The hushed lobby of the athletic club was paneled in dark wood. A few solitary figures were hidden in wing chairs. My father and I introduced ourselves to a man at the front desk who seemed unimpressed by our presence. His aloofness unnerved me, which wasn't hard considering that no matter how my parents put it, I knew their sending me here was a form of disapproval, a way of banishing the part of me they didn't care to know.

A call went out over the intercom for someone to show us around. While we waited, I noticed that the sand in the standing ashtrays had been raked into perfect furrows. The glossy leaves of the potted plants looked as if they'd been polished by hand. The place seemed more like a well-tended hotel than an athletic club. Finally, a stoop-shouldered old man hobbled toward us, his head shrouded in a cloud of white hair. He wore a T-shirt that said "Instructor"; his arms were so wrinkled and anemic, I thought I might have misread it. While we followed him to the elevator, I readjusted my expectations, which had involved fantasies of a hulking drill sergeant barking orders at a flock of scrawny boys.

30   The instructor, mumbling to himself and never turning around to see if we were behind him, showed us where the gymnastics class took place. I'm certain the building was big, but the size of the room must be exaggerated by a trick of memory, because when I envision it, I picture a vast and windowless warehouse. Mats covered the wooden floor. Here and there, in remote and lonely pools of light, stood a pommel horse, a balance beam, and parallel bars. Tiers of bleachers rose into darkness. Unlike the cloistered air of a closet, the room seemed incomplete without a crowd.

Next we visited the dressing room, empty except for a naked middle-aged man. He sat on a narrow bench and clipped his formidable toenails. Moles dotted his back. He glistened like a fish.

We continued to follow the instructor down an aisle lined with numbered lockers. At the far end, steam billowed from the doorway that led to the showers. Fresh towels stacked on a nearby table made me think of my mother; I knew she liked to have me at home with her— I was often her only companion—and I resented her complicity in the plan to send me here.

The tour ended when the instructor gave me a sign-up sheet. Only a few names preceded mine. They were signatures, or so I imagined, of other soft and wayward sons.

IV

When the day of the first gymnastics class arrived, my mother gave me money and a gym bag and sent me to the corner of Hollywood and Western to wait for a bus. The sun was bright, the traffic heavy. While I sat there, an argument raged inside my head, the familiar, battering debate between the wish to be like other boys and the wish to be like myself. Why shouldn't I simply get up and go back home, where I'd be left alone to read and think? On the other hand, wouldn't life be easier if I liked athletics, or learned to like them?

35   No sooner did I steel my resolve to get on the bus than I thought of something better: I could spend the morning wandering through Woolworth's, then tell my parents I'd gone to the class. But would my lie stand up to scrutiny? As I practiced describing phantom gymnastics, I became aware of a car circling the block. It was a large car in whose shaded interior I could barely make out the driver, but I thought it might be the man who owned the local pet store. I'd often gone there on the pretext of looking at the cocker spaniel puppies huddled together in their pen, but I really went to gawk at the owner, whose tan chest, in the V of his shirt, was the place I most wanted to rest my head. Every time the man moved, counting stock or writing a receipt, his shirt parted, my mouth went dry, and I smelled the musk of sawdust and dogs.

I found myself hoping that the driver was the man who ran the pet store. I was thrilled by the unlikely possibility that the sight of me, slumped on a bus bench in my T-shirt and shorts, had caused such a man to circle the block. Up to that point in my life, lovemaking hovered somewhere in the future, an impulse a boy might aspire to but didn't indulge. And there I was, sitting on a bus bench in the middle of the city, dreaming I could seduce an adult. I showered the owner of the pet store with kisses and, as aquariums bubbled, birds sang, and mice raced in a wire wheel, slipped my hand beneath his shirt. The roar of traffic brought me to my senses. I breathed deeply and blinked against the sun. I crossed my legs at the knee in order to hide an erection. My fantasy left me both drained and changed. The continent of sex had drifted closer.

The car made another round. This time the driver leaned across the passenger seat and peered at me through the window. He was a complete stranger, whose gaze filled me with fear. It wasn't the surprise of not recognizing him that frightened me, it was what I did recognize—the unmistakable shame in his expression, and the weary temptation that drove him in circles. Before the car behind him honked, he mouthed "hello" and cocked his head. What now, he seemed to be asking. A bold, unbearable question.

I bolted to my feet, slung the gym bag over my shoulder, and hurried toward home. Now and then I turned around to make sure he wasn't trailing me, both relieved and disappointed when I didn't see his car. Even after I became convinced that he wasn't at my back—my sudden flight had scared him off—I kept turning around to see what was making me so nervous, as if I might spot the source of my discomfort somewhere on the street. I walked faster and faster, trying to outrace myself. Eventually, the bus I was supposed to have taken roared past. Turning the corner, I watched it bob eastward.

Closing the kitchen door behind me, I vowed never to leave home again. I was resolute in this decision without fully understanding why, or what it was I hoped to avoid; I was only aware of the need to hide and a vague notion, fading fast, that my trouble had something to do with sex. Already the mechanism of self-deception was at work. By the time my mother rushed into the kitchen to see why I'd returned so early, the thrill I'd felt while waiting for the bus had given way to indignation.

40   I poured out the story of the man circling the block and protested, with perhaps too great a passion, my own innocence. "I was just sitting there," I said again and again. I was so determined to deflect suspicion away from myself, and to justify my missing the class, that I portrayed the man as a grizzled pervert who drunkenly veered from lane to lane as he followed me halfway home.

My mother cinched her housecoat. She seemed moved and shocked by what I told her, if a bit incredulous, which prompted me to be more dramatic. "It wouldn't be safe," I insisted, "for me to wait at the bus stop again."

No matter how overwrought my story, I knew my mother wouldn't question it, wouldn't bring the subject up again; sex of any kind, especially sex between a man and a boy, was simply not discussed in our house. The gymnastics class, my parents agreed, was something I could do another time.

And so I spent the remainder of that summer at home with my mother, stirring cake batter, holding the dustpan, helping her fold the sheets. For a while I was proud of myself for engineering a reprieve from the athletic club. But as the days wore on, I began to see that my mother had wanted me with her all along, and forcing that to happen wasn't such a feat. Soon a sense of compromise set in; by expressing disgust for the man in the car, I'd expressed disgust for an aspect of myself. Now I had all the time in the world to sit around and contemplate my desire for men. The days grew long and stifling and hot, an endless sentence of self-examination.

Only trips to the pet store offered any respite. Every time I went there, I was too electrified with longing to think about longing in the abstract. The bell tinkled above the door, animals stirred within their cages, and the handsome owner glanced up from his work.

V

I handed my father the *Herald*. He opened   45 the paper and disappeared behind it. My mother stirred her coffee and sighed. She gazed at the sweltering passersby and probably thought herself lucky. I slid into the vinyl booth and took my place beside my parents.

For a moment, I considered asking them about what had happened on the street, but they would have reacted with censure and alarm, and I sensed there was more to the story than they'd ever be willing to tell me. Men in dresses were only the tip of the iceberg. Who knew what other wonders existed—a boy, for example, who wanted to kiss a man— exceptions the world did its best to keep hidden.

It would be years before I heard the word "transvestite," so I struggled to find a word for what I'd seen. "He-she" came to mind, as lilting as "Injijikian." "Burl's" would have been perfect, like "boys" and "girls" spliced together, but I can't claim to have thought of this back then.

I must have looked stricken as I tried to figure it all out, because my mother put down her coffee cup and asked if I was O.K. She stopped just short of feeling my forehead. I assured her I was fine, but something within me had shifted, had given way to a heady doubt. When the waitress came and slapped down our check—"Thank You," it read, "Dine out more often"—I wondered if her lofty hairdo or the breasts on which her nametag quaked were real. Wax carnations bloomed at every table. Phony wood paneled the walls. Plastic food sat in a display case: fried eggs, a hamburger sandwich, a sundae topped with a garish cherry.

READING AND THINKING

1. What makes "Burl's" an essay and not just a series of anecdotes?

2. How do the details in the paragraphs about Cooper's parents in Part I connect with the details about the transvestites, also in Part I?

3. What connections link the scenes Cooper describes? What links Mary Injijikian, the gymnastics class, the driver of the circling car, and the owner of the pet store?

4. Where do you first sense that "Burl's" describes Cooper's growing boyhood awareness of his homosexuality?

THINKING AND WRITING

1. Describe a scene from your life in which you first became interested in your own sexuality.

2. Discuss Cooper's sexing of the world, dividing it into male/female, pink/blue, roosters/hens, trousers/skirts, and how and the extent to which his theory is subverted.

3. Analyze Cooper's essay, explaining what happens in each scene and how the essay builds its idea through its scenes and images.

4. Consider how as a child you came to understand the larger world of adults and the mysteries of growing up. Select one experience in which you found yourself understanding something for the first time, something that had always mystified or confused you.

Brian Doyle

Brian Doyle is the editor of *Portland Magazine* at the University of Portland (Oregon). His wit, his elegant prose, and his penchant for exploring life's mysteries distinguish his essays, which have appeared in *The American Scholar, The Atlantic Monthly, Harper's, Orion, Commonweal,* and *The Georgia Review.* Three of his essays have also appeared in *The Best American Essays* (1998, 1999, 2003). The most recent of his four collections of essays is *Leaping: Revelations & Epiphanies.* He is also the editor of *God is Love,* a collection of the best spiritual essays from *Portland Magazine.*

YES

"Yes" was reprinted in *The Best American Essays of 2003.* As you read through it, consider the title and the organization together. Doyle's meditation ranges from subject to subject, and as it does—at least in your first reading—what the title means may shift along with the particular subjects he discusses. When you've finished the essay, ask yourself how your idea of "Yes" has changed from the beginning to the end. How does Doyle tie up all the subjects he discusses? Or does he?

1   Lately I have been delving early Irish literature and language, and so have been raiding cattle in Cuailnge, and pondering the visions of Oenghus, and feasting at Bricriu, and wooing Etain, which last has led me to some tension with my wife, who is of Belgian extraction and does not like to hear me tell of the beautiful Etain, the loveliest woman in all Ireland, although Etain was changed to an insect and banished for a thousand years, until she was reborn as the wife of Eochaid Airem, king of the green lands.

I try to explain to my wife that I am only wooing by proxy, as it were, and that Eochaid has the inside track, he being in the story and me only reading it. This line of talk leads me inevitably to Flan O'Brien and Myles na gCopaleen and Brian O'Nolan, all of whom I wheel into the conversation, the three men standing all in the same spot, as if they were the same man, which they were, except when O'Nolan was writing, which is when he became one of the others, depending on what he was writing—novels as O'Brien, journalism as na gCopaleen ("of the little horses") or sometimes Count O'Blather, or James Doe, or Brother Barrabus, or George Knowall.

My wife is unmoved; she will not have Etain in the house.

After a while I realize that the problem is the word *woo. It is a word that may be applied to your wife and your wife only, if you have a wife,* she is saying without saying. She is a subtle woman, which is part of the reason I wooed her some years ago, and won her from various rivals, who did not woo so well, and went away, one may say, full of rue.

5   I spent some time after that saying *woo,* which is a very fine word, rife with meaning, and emitted with a lift from the lips, like *whee* or *who,* or *no.* By chance I happened to be saying *woo* in the presence of my new son Joseph, a curious young man three months of age. Like his father he is intrigued by sounds, and soon enough he too was saying *woo,* and then my other new son, Liam, also three months old, picked it up, and the three of us were wooing to beat the band, although then Liam burst into tears, and had to be carried away to another room for milk.

Joe and I kept it up, though; he is an indefatigable fellow. After a while he switched to *who,* and I went with him, to see where this would go, and it went back and forth between us for a while, and then it went to *whee,* and then back to *woo,* and then my wife came back in the room and found us wooing like crazy men. By then it was Joe's turn for a suckle and off he went, and I went downstairs to raid cattle in Cuailnge, and ponder Oenghus, and feast at Bricriu, and woo Etain, of whom the less said the better.

The wooing of Etain demands a certain familiarity with the Gaelic tongue, which has fascinated me since I was a boy in my grandmother's lap listening to the swell and swing of Irish from her lips, which more often than you might expect has Gaelic oaths on them, as she was a shy woman with a sharp temper, though gentle as the night is long, and much mourned by many to this day. I still hear her voice on windy nights, banshee nights, saying to me, gently, *bi I do bhuachaill mhaith,* be a good boy, or *go mbeannai Dia thu,* God bless you. So partly in memory of my grandmother, a McCluskey before she was a Clancey giving her daughter to a Doyle, I have been marching through the thickets of the Irish tongue, the second oldest in Europe behind Basque, and the cold hard fact is that the Gaelic language is a most confusing creature, and although I don't understand very much of it, I read about it at every opportunity, and have been able to note several interesting observations on small scraps of paper, which are then distributed willy-nilly in various pants pockets, emerging here and there like crumpled fish, and reminding me that I had meant to write an essay on the topic at, or more accurately in, hand.

Thus this essay, which was supposed to be about the fact that there is no way to say the words *yes* and *no* in Gaelic, but which has swerved unaccountably into a disquisition about sounds, of which some are exuberant, like Joe's *woo,* and some affirmative, like *sa,* which is Gaelic for *it is,* and *yes* and *sí* and *ja* and *oui,* which are English and Spanish and German and French for *yes,* which there is no way to say in Gaelic, try as you might.

Is it sayable in the Irish?

Nil—it is not.   10

Nil is as fascinating as *sa* to me, especially lately because my daughter, Lily, a rebellious angel, age three, is fixated on *no,* which she says often, in different accents, with various degrees of vehemence. She says it morning, noon, and night, particularly at night, when she wakes up screaming *no no no no no,* and answers *nooooo* when I ask what is the matter. Sometimes she says *neuwh,* which is a sort of no, which is said usually after she has been watching *Mary Poppins* and is afflicted with a sort of stiffening of the upper lip which prevents the proper pronunciation of simple words like *no.* It is interesting that she is riveted by *no* because her brother Liam is riveted by *ho,* which is the only word he owns at the moment. Like a geyser he emits *ho!* regularly and then subsides. I expect him to pick up *no* pretty soon, his sister being a whiz at it and the boys certain to learn at her knee, and then Joe will get *no* too, and then my children will be saying *no* to beat the band, not to mention the thin stretched rubber of their father's patience, which they hammer upon like a bodhran, the wee drum of my Wicklow ancestors.

But their father is in the basement at the moment musing over the fact that Gaelic is the only language on the Continent that always uses *tu,* or thou, when speaking to one person, or *sibh,* you, for more than one, which habit, he thinks, reflects a certain native friendliness in the tongue and in its speakers; and he further puzzles over the fact that Irish counts in twenties, not tens; and further he muses that Gaelic, at least in Ireland, has no terms for the *Mister* and *Señor* and *Herr* in English and Spanish and German used as terms of bourgeois respect, which makes him wonder about Irish independence as well as rural isolation. Also he spends a good deal of time pondering ogham, the alphabet used in Ireland for writing on wood and stone before the year 500 or so, when

Christianity and the Latin alphabet rose into Ireland together on strong winds, and the fact that Gaelic has perhaps sixty phonemes, which are sounds that convey meaning, and of which there are perhaps forty-four in English, which comparative fact makes me wonder about the width of the respective languages, so to speak, which width is also reflected in the simple spelling and pronunciation of terms in each tongue: I might say of Liam that he is *an buachaill,* the boy, for example, and roll the former off my tongue and pop the latter out rather like ho!, which is what Liam is saying as I am calling him *an buachaill.*

Further, I am fascinated by the fact that Gaelic is a language in love with nouns, as can be seen with a phrase that often occurs to me when I think about my daughter's and my sons' futures, *to eagla orm,* which in English would be I fear, but in Gaelic is fear upon me, which it is, like a demon between my shoulders. To exorcise it I sometimes whistle; in English I whistle, just so, but in Gaelic *ligim fead,* I let a whistle, or *taim ag feadail,* I am at whistling.

I am at whistling a great deal these days, it turns out, trying to get the fear off me. For I am terrified of the fates that may befall my children—fates over which I have no power at all, not the slightest, other than keeping my little children close to me in the presence of cars and dogs and such. So there are times now, I can honestly say—for I am sometimes an honest man, and admiring always of honesty—that I am exhausted by, and frightened for, my raft of children, and in the wee hours of the night when up with one or another of the little people, I sometimes, to be honest, find myself wondering what it might have been like not to have so many.

It would have been lonely.   15

I know this.

I know it in my heart, my bones, in the chalky exhausted shiver of my soul. For there were many nights before my children came to me on magic wooden boats from seas unknown that I wished desperately for them, that I cried because they had not yet come; and now that they are here I know I pray for them every minute with fear for their safety and horror at the prospect of losing them to disease and accidents and the harsh fingers of the Lord, who taketh whomever He wishes, at which time He alone appoints, and leaves huddled and broken the father and the mother, who begged for the joy of these round faces groping for milk in the dark. So as I trudge upstairs to hold Lily in my lap, and rub my old chapped hands across the thin sharp blades of her shoulders, and shuffle with sons on shoulders in the blue hours of the night, waiting patiently from them to belch like river barges, or hear Joe happily blowing bubbles of spit in his crib simply because he can do it and is pretty proud of himself about the whole thing, or hear Liam suddenly say ho! for no reason other than Liamly joy at the sound of his own voice like a bell in his head, I say yes to them, yes yes yes, and to exhaustion I say yes, and to the puzzling wonder of my wife's love I say O yes, and to horror and fear and jangled joys I say yes, to rich cheerful chaos that leads me sooner to the grave and happier along that muddy grave road I say yes, to my absolute surprise and with unbidden tears I say yes yes O yes.

Is this a mystery and a joy beyond my wisdom?

Sa—it is.

READING AND THINKING

1. This relatively short essay has a rather long two-part beginning, ten paragraphs in all, three of them only one sentence long. Try not to be put off by the odd-sounding Irish and Gaelic names in the first two paragraphs. Instead identify what you think are the inherent conflicts that Doyle highlights in those two paragraphs. Find at least two.

2. Based on what he says in the first two paragraphs, what is it like for Doyle to read fiction? What is he trying to explain to his wife?

3. Select at least three odd English words that Doyle uses. Look them up in a good unabridged dictionary.

4. Trace Doyle's use of the word *woo* from the beginning through the essay. How does he make use of both the meaning of the word and its sounds?

5. In the seventh paragraph, what is the relationship between Gaelic and Doyle's grandmother? What do you find most interesting about that paragraph? What are "banshee nights"?

6. Follow Doyle's emphasis on things Gaelic throughout the rest of the essay. List three reasons why you think he tells and shows us so much about his interest in the language.

THINKING AND WRITING

1. List all of the women (and girls) who appear in the essay, along with brief notes about Doyle's characterization of them and their foibles. Do the same for the men (and boys). Then write two paragraphs, one focusing on the females and one on the males, revealing what you believe to be Doyle's sense of gender. Don't forget to include Doyle in your list of males.

2. In a full paragraph, characterize Doyle's family.

3. In a paragraph, account for the role that superstition and fate play in this essay.

4. Pick out the most fascinating moment in the essay and defend your choice in a page or two of analysis about that moment; reveal both its fascination and its importance to you and to the essay.

5. Doyle seems to be playing with translations throughout this essay. If it is not possible to say yes and no in Gaelic, has Doyle perhaps given us the Gaelic equivalent in English of yes in the final three paragraphs? Write out your sense of his definition.

Gretel Ehrlich (b. 1946)

Gretel Ehrlich is a native Californian who attended Bennington College and the film school at New York University. Her work as a documentary filmmaker took her to Wyoming in 1979, where she was drawn to the dramatic countryside and the local people. During the seventeen years she worked as a rancher, Ehrlich wrote a number of books, including *The Solace of Open Spaces* (1985) and *A Match to the Heart: One Woman's Story of Being Struck by Lightning* (1995). She has also written a novel and other works, including *Questions from Heaven: The Chinese Journeys of an American Buddhist* (1997), an account of a pilgrimage to Buddhist shrines in China, and *John Muir: Nature's Visionary* (2000), a biography of the American naturalist and conservationist.

ABOUT MEN

In "About Men," first published in *Time* magazine and included in her first essay collection, Ehrlich considers some stereotypes about men, in particular, cowboys. Through a series of carefully selected examples and sharply etched dialogue and details, Ehrlich reveals the complex and challenging lives led by western cowboys.

1 When I'm in New York but feeling lonely for Wyoming. I look for the Marlboro ads in the subway. What I'm aching to see is horseflesh, the glint of a spur, a line of distant mountains, brimming creeks, and a reminder of the ranchers and cowboys I've ridden with for the last eight years. But the men I see in those posters with their stern, humorless looks remind me of no one I know here. In our hell-bent earnestness to romanticize the cowboy we've ironically disesteemed his true character. If he's "strong and silent" it's because there's probably no one to talk to. If he "rides away into the sunset" it's because he's been on horseback since four in the morning moving cattle and he's trying, fifteen hours later, to get home to his family. If he's "a rugged individualist" he's also part of a team: Ranch work is teamwork and even the glorified open-range cowboys of the 1880s rode up and down the Chisholm Trail in the company of twenty or thirty other riders. Instead of the macho, trigger-happy man our culture has perversely wanted him to be, the cowboy is more apt to be convivial, quirky, and soft-hearted. To be "tough" on a ranch has nothing to do with conquests and displays of power. More often than not, circumstances—like the colt he's riding or an unexpected blizzard—are overpowering him. It's not toughness but "toughing it out" that counts. In other words, this macho cultural artifact the cowboy has become is simply a man who possesses resilience, patience, and an instinct for survival. "Cowboys are just like a pile of rocks—everything happens to them. They get climbed on, kicked, rained and snowed on, scuffed up by wind. Their job is 'just to take it,'" one old-timer told me.

A cowboy is someone who loves his work. Since the hours are long—ten to fifteen hours a day—and the pay is $30 he has to. What's required of him is an odd mixture of physical vigor and maternalism. His part of the beef-raising industry is to birth and nurture calves and take care of their mothers. For the most part his work is done on horseback and in a lifetime he sees and comes to know more animals than people. The iconic myth surrounding him is built on American notions of heroism: the index of a man's value as measured in physical courage. Such ideas have perverted manliness into a self-absorbed race for cheap thrills. In a rancher's world, courage has less to do with facing danger than with acting spontaneously—usually on behalf of an animal or another rider. If a cow is stuck in a boghole he throws a loop around her neck, takes his dally (a half hitch around the saddle horn), and pulls her out with horsepower. If a calf is born sick, he may take her home, warm her in front of the kitchen fire, and massage her legs until dawn. One friend, whose favorite horse was trying to swim a lake with hobbles on, dove under water and cut her legs loose with a knife, then swam her to shore, his arm around her neck lifeguard-style, and saved her from drowning. Because these incidents are usually linked to someone or something outside himself, the westerner's courage is selfless, a form of compassion.

The physical punishment that goes with cowboying is greatly underplayed. Once fear is dispensed with, the threshold of pain rises to meet the demands of the job. When Jane Fonda asked Robert Redford (in the film *Electric Horseman*) if he was sick as he struggled to his feet one morning, he replied. "No, just bent." For once the movies had it right. The cowboys I was sitting with laughed in agreement. Cowboys are rarely complainers; they show their stoicism by laughing at themselves.

If a rancher or cowboy has been thought of as a "man's man"—laconic, hard-drinking, inscrutable—there's almost no place in which the balancing act between male and female, manliness and femininity, can be more natural. If he's gruff, handsome, and physically fit on the outside, he's androgynous at the core. Ranchers are midwives, hunters, nurturers, providers, and conservationists all at once. What we've interpreted as toughness—weathered skin, calloused hands, a squint in the eye and a growl in the voice—only masks the tenderness inside. "Now don't go telling me these lambs are cute," one rancher warned me the first day I walked into the football-field-sized lambing sheds. The next thing I knew he was holding a black lamb. "Ain't this little rat good-lookin'?"

5   So many of the men who came to the West were southerners—men looking for work and a new life after the Civil War—that chivalrousness and strict codes of honor were soon thought of as western traits. There were very few women in Wyoming during territorial days, so when they did arrive (some as mail-order brides from places like Philadelphia) there was a standoffishness between the sexes and a formality that persists now. Ranchers still tip their hats and say, "Howdy, ma'am" instead of shaking hands with me.

Even young cowboys are often evasive with women. It's not that they're Jekyll and Hyde creatures—gentle with animals and rough on women—but rather, that they don't know how to bring their tenderness into the house and lack the vocabulary to express the complexity of what they feel. Dancing wildly all night becomes a metaphor for the explosive emotions pent up inside, and when these are, on occasion, released, they're so battery-charged and potent that one caress of the face or one "I love you" will peal for a long while.

The geographical vastness and the social isolation here make emotional evolution seem impossible. Those contradictions of the heart between respectability, logic, and convention on the one hand, and impulse, passion, and intuition on the other, played out wordlessly against the paradisical beauty of the West, give cowboys a wide-eyed but drawn look. Their lips pucker up, not with kisses but with immutability. They may want to break out, staying up all night with a lover just to talk, but they don't know how and can't imagine what the consequences will be. Those rare occasions when they do bare themselves result in confusion. "I feel as if I'd sprained my heart," one friend told me a month after such a meeting.

My friend Ted Hoagland wrote, "No one is as fragile as a woman but no one is as fragile as a man." For all the women here who use "fragileness" to avoid work or as a sexual ploy, there are men who try to hide theirs, all the while clinging to an adolescent dependency on women to cook their meals, wash their clothes, and keep the ranch house warm in winter. But there is true vulnerability in evidence here. Because these men work with animals, not machines or numbers, because they live outside in landscapes of torrential beauty, because they are confined to a place and a routine embellished with awesome variables, because calves die in the arms that pulled others into life, because they go to the mountains as if on a pilgrimage to find out what makes a herd of elk tick, their strength is also a softness, their toughness, a rare delicacy.

READING AND THINKING

1. What is the common stereotype of the western man, the cowboy? How does Ehrlich undermine that stereotype?

2. What does Ehrlich find admirable and appealing about cowboys and ranchers?

3. What role does landscape and nature generally play in this essay?

4. What cultural values does Ehrlich touch on in describing her cowboys? What other cultural values are mentioned or alluded to in the essay?

5. To what extent do you find Ehrlich's argument persuasive? To what extent do you credit her testimony?

THINKING AND WRITING

1. Write a note to Ehrlich in which you respond to her celebration of the androgynous nature of the men she describes.

2. Analyze "About Men." Identify Ehrlich's purpose, and explain how she goes about achieving it. Comment on her use of dialogue and on her references to popular media and to history.

3. Discuss Ehrlich's description of how cowboys relate to women.

4. Explain what other qualities, besides those mentioned by Ehrlich, that you think are significant characteristics of men.

E. M. Forster (1879–1970)

E. M. Forster is known to us today through his novels and the movies that have been based on them, especially *A Room with a View* and *Howards End*. But Forster was also a fine essayist with a wry, self-deprecating sense of humor. His style is brisk, clear, and often playful as he sets out with us to explore difficult, far-reaching topics. Always, we sense that we are in the company of someone who cares about decency, meaningful human relationships, and a world free of cant and the misuse of power. People and art matter more to him than conquest, so reading him, we begin to know that we can trust his judgments, whether they be about looking at art, the strong, the sensual pull of Italy and the Mediterranean, or the foibles of the English at home and abroad.

ON NOT LOOKING AT PICTURES

In "On Not Looking at Pictures," Forster takes us into an art gallery with his friends Roger Fry and Charles Mauron. Each friend teaches Forster and the reader (as eavesdropper) something about art that Forster himself claims not to know much about—its structure or form. When Forster tries to look at art, his mind darts off to other places; the images set his imagination to work. Fry and Mauron insist that we look not only at the image itself but at the way it is made. They focus our attention on diagonals, paint, composition, texture, foreground, background, and movement. The reader is asked to see the paintings and to not see the paintings, to learn and to play under Forster's guidance.

1   Pictures are not easy to look at. They generate private fantasies, they furnish material for jokes, they recall scraps of historical knowledge, they show landscapes where one would like to wander and human beings whom one would like to resemble or adore, but looking at them is another matter, yet they must have been painted to be looked at. They were intended to appeal to the eye, but almost as if it were gazing at the sun itself the eye often reacts by closing as soon as it catches sight of them. The mind takes charge instead and goes off on some alien vision. The mind has such a congenial time that it forgets what set it going. Van Gogh and Corot and Michelangelo are three different painters, but if the mind is indisciplined and uncontrolled by the eye, they may all three induce the same mood, we may take just the same course through dreamland or funland from them, each time, and never experience anything new.

I am bad at looking at pictures myself, and the late Roger Fry enjoyed going to a gallery with me now and then, for this very reason. He found it an amusing change to be with someone who scarcely ever saw what the painter had painted. "Tell me, why do you like this, why do you prefer it to that?" he would ask, and listen agape for the ridiculous answer. One day we looked at a fifteenth-century Italian predella, where a St. George was engaged in spearing a dragon of the plesiosaurus type. I laughed. "Now, *what* is there funny in this?" pounced Fry. I readily explained. The fun was to be found in the expression upon the dragon's face. The spear had gone through its hooped-up neck once, and now startled it by arriving at a second thickness. "Oh dear, here it comes again, I hoped that was all" it was thinking. Fry laughed too, but not at the misfortunes of the dragon. He was amazed that anyone could go so completely off the lines. There was no harm in it—but really, really! He was even more amazed when our enthusiasms coincided: "I fancy we are talking about different things," he would say, and we always were; I liked the mountain-back because it reminded me of a peacock, he because it had some structural significance, though not as much as the sack of potatoes in the foreground.

Long years of wandering down miles of galleries have convinced me that there must be something rare in those coloured slabs called "pictures," something which I am incapable of detecting for myself, though glimpses of it are to be had through the eyes of others. How much am I missing? And what? And are other modern sight-seers in the same fix? Ours is an aural rather than a visual age, we do not get so lost in the concert hall, we seem able to hear music for ourselves, and to hear it as music, but in galleries so many of us go off at once into a laugh or a sigh or an amorous day-dream. In vain does the picture recall us. "What have your obsessions got to do with me?" it complains. "I am neither a theatre of varieties nor a spring-mattress, but paint. Look at my paint." Back we go—the picture kindly standing still meanwhile, and being to that extent more obliging than music—and resume the looking-business. But something is sure to intervene—a tress of hair, the half-open door of a summer-house, a Crivelli dessert, a Bosch fish-and-fiend salad—and to draw us away.

One of the things that helps us to keep looking is composition. For many years now I have associated composition with a diagonal line, and when I find such a line I imagine I have gutted the picture's secret. Giorgione's Castelfranco Madonna has such a line in the lance of the warrior-saint, and Titian's Entombment at Venice has a very good one indeed. Five figures contribute to make up the diagonal; beginning high on the left with the statue of Moses, it passes through the heads of the Magdalene, Mary, and the dead Christ, and plunges through the body of Joseph of Arimathea into the ground. Making a right angle to it, flits the winged Genius of Burial. And to the right, apart from it, and perpendi-

cular, balancing the Moses, towers the statue of Faith. Titian's Entombment is one of my easiest pictures. I look at photographs of it intelligently, and encourage the diagonal and the pathos to reinforce one another. I see, with more than usual vividness, the grim alcove at the back and the sinister tusked pedestals upon which the two statues stand. Stone shuts in flesh; the whole picture is a tomb. I hear sounds of lamentation, though not to the extent of shattering the general scheme; that is held together by the emphatic diagonal, which no emotion breaks. Titian was a very old man when he achieved this masterpiece; that too I realise, but not immoderately. Composition here really has been a help, and it is a composition which no one can miss; the diagonal slopes as obviously as the band on a threshing-machine, and vibrates with power.

Unfortunately, having no natural esthetic aptitude, I look for diagonals everywhere, and if I cannot find one think the composition must be at fault. It is a word which I have learnt—a solitary word in a foreign language. For instance, I was completely baffled by Velásquez's Las Meninas. Wherever was the diagonal? Then the friend I was with—Charles Mauron, the friend who, after Roger Fry, has helped me with pictures most—set to work on my behalf, and cautiously underlined the themes. There is a wave. There is a half-wave. The wave starts up on the left, with the head of the painter, and curves down and up through the heads of the three girls. The half-wave starts with the head of Isabel de Velasco, and sinks out of the canvas through the dwarfs. Responding to these great curves, or inverting them, are smaller ones on the women's dresses or elsewhere. All these waves are not merely pattern; they are doing other work too—e.g., helping to bring out the effect of depth in the room, and the effect of air. Important too is the pushing forward of objects in the extreme left and right foregrounds, the easel of the painter in the one case, the paws of a placid dog in the other. From these, the composition curves back to the central figure, the lovely child-princess. I put it more crudely than did Charles Mauron, nor do I suppose that his account would have been Velásquez's, or that Velásquez would have given any account at all. But it is an example of the way in which pictures should be tackled for the benefit of us outsiders: coolly and patiently, as if they were designs, so that we are helped at last to the appreciation of something non-mathematical. Here again, as in the case of the Entombment, the composition and the action reinforced one another. I viewed with increasing joy that adorable party, which had been surprised not only by myself but by the King and Queen of Spain. There they were in the looking-glass! Las Meninas has snap-shot quality. The party might have been taken by Philip IV, if Philip IV had had a Kodak. It is all so casual—and yet it is all so elaborate and sophisticated, and I suppose those curves and the rest of it help to bring this out, and to evoke a vanished civilisation.

Besides composition there is colour. I look for that, too, but with even less success. Colour is visible when thrown in my face—like the two cherries in the great grey Michael Sweertz group in the National Gallery. But as a rule it is only material for dream.

On the whole, I am improving, and after all these years, I am learning to get myself out of the way a little, and to be more receptive, and my appreciation of pictures does increase. If I can make any progress at all, the average outsider should do better still. A combination of courage and modesty is what he wants. It is so unenterprising to annihilate everything that's made to a green thought, even when the thought is an exquisite one. Not looking at art leads to one goal only. Looking at it leads to so many.

READING AND THINKING

1. What do you think of Forster's claim that when looking at pictures, the "mind takes charge . . . and goes off on some alien vision"? Is that true of your own experience?

2. Roger Fry was a distinguished art critic during the last century. Why do you think that Forster puts him in this essay along with Charles Mauron?

3. Besides describing the paintings that he and Fry see in the gallery, Forster describes other things. Select the description that most interests you, and characterize how Forster uses descriptive language and how he organizes his description. Account for his larger purpose.

THINKING AND WRITING

1. Describe Forster's way of approaching a painting. Describe Roger Fry's way.

2. Look up the word *esthetic* (or *aesthetic*). Forster uses the phrase "esthetic aptitude" and claims that he doesn't have any. Based on what he tells you about his way of seeing and Fry's way of seeing, do you believe Forster's claim about himself? Explain.

3. Write a short essay in response to Forster's final pair of claims: "Not looking at art leads to one goal only. Looking at it leads to so many." Select your own art objects to help you support your idea. Be sure to recreate those objects so that the reader can see them through your words.

Malcolm Gladwell (b. 1963)

Malcolm Gladwell was born in England and graduated with a degree in history from the University of Toronto. A former business and science writer at the *Washington Post,* he was named the newspaper's New York City bureau chief. Gladwell is currently a staff writer for *The New Yorker* magazine.

THE TIPPING POINT

In "The Tipping Point," excerpted from his book of the same title, Gladwell describes the phenomenon of "tipping," the process by which a sequence of events proceeds to the point of becoming an epidemic. In his essay, Gladwell identifies three factors that lead up to the tipping point of a physical or social epidemic. As you read his essay, try to identify each of these different causes.

1   In the mid-1990s, the city of Baltimore was attacked by an epidemic of syphilis. In the space of a year, from 1995 to 1996, the number of children born with the disease increased by 500 percent. If you look at Baltimore's syphilis rates on a graph, the line runs straight for years and then, when it hits 1995, rises almost at a right angle.

What caused Baltimore's syphilis problem to tip? According to the Centers for Disease Control [CDC], the problem was crack cocaine. Crack is known to cause a dramatic increase in the kind of risky sexual behavior that leads to the spread of things like HIV and syphilis. It brings far more people into poor areas to buy drugs, which then increases the likelihood that they will take an infection home with them to their own neighborhood. It changes the patterns of social connections between neighborhoods. Crack, the CDC said, was the little push that the syphilis problem needed to turn into a raging epidemic.

John Zenilman of Johns Hopkins University in Baltimore, an expert on sexually transmitted diseases, has another explanation: the breakdown of medical services in the city's poorest neighborhoods. "In 1990–91, we had thirty-six thousand patient visits at the city's sexually transmitted disease clinics," Zenilman says. "Then the city decided to gradually cut back because of budgetary problems.

The number of clinicians [medical personnel] went from seventeen to ten. The number of physicians went from three to essentially nobody. Patient visits dropped to twenty-one thousand. There also was a similar drop in the amount of field outreach staff. There was a lot of politics—things that used to happen, like computer upgrades, didn't happen. It was a worst-case scenario of city bureaucracy not functioning. They would run out of drugs."

When there were 36,000 patient visits a year in the STD clinics of Baltimore's inner city, in other words, the disease was kept in equilibrium. At some point between 36,000 and 21,000 patient visits a year, according to Zenilman, the disease erupted. It began spilling out of the inner city, up the streets and highways that connect those neighborhoods to the rest of the city. Suddenly, people who might have been infectious for a week before getting treated were now going around infecting others for two or three or four weeks before they got cured. The breakdown in treatment made syphilis a much bigger issue than it had been before.

There is a third theory, which belongs to   5 John Potterat, one of the country's leading epidemiologists. His culprits are the physical changes in those years affecting East and West Baltimore, the heavily depressed neighborhoods on either side of Baltimore's downtown, where the syphilis problem was centered. In the mid-1990s, he points out, the city of Baltimore embarked on a highly publicized policy of dynamiting the old 1960s-style public housing high-rises in East and West Baltimore. Two of the most publicized demolitions—Lexington Terrace in West Baltimore and Lafayette Courts in East Baltimore—were huge projects, housing hundreds of families, that served as centers for crime and infectious disease. At the same time, people began to move out of the old row houses in East and West Baltimore, as those began to deteriorate as well.

"It was absolutely striking," Potterat says, of the first time he toured East and West Baltimore. "Fifty percent of the row houses were boarded up, and there was also a process where they destroyed the projects. What happened was a kind of hollowing out. This fueled the diaspora. For years syphilis had been confined to a specific region of Baltimore, within highly confined sociosexual networks. The housing dislocation process served to move these people to other parts of Baltimore, and they took their syphilis and other behaviors with them."

What is interesting about these three explanations is that none of them is at all dramatic. The CDC thought that crack was the problem. But it wasn't as if crack came to Baltimore for the first time in 1995. It had been there for years. What they were saying is that there was a subtle increase in the severity of the crack problem in the mid-1990s, and that change was enough to set off the syphilis epidemic. Zenilman, likewise, wasn't saying that the STD clinics in Baltimore were shut down. They were simply scaled back, the number of clinicians cut from seventeen to ten. Nor was Potterat saying that all Baltimore was hollowed out. All it took, he said, was the demolition of a handful of housing projects and the abandonment of homes in key downtown neighborhoods to send syphilis over the top. It takes only the smallest of changes to shatter an epidemic's equilibrium.

The second, and perhaps more interesting, fact about these explanations is that all of them are describing a very different way of tipping an epidemic. The CDC is talking about the overall context for the disease—how the introduction and growth of an addictive drug can so change the environment of a city that it can cause a disease to tip. Zenilman is talking about the disease itself. When the clinics were cut back, syphilis was given a second life. It had been an acute infection. It was now a chronic infection. It had become a lingering problem that stayed around for weeks. Potterat, for his part, was focused on the people who were carrying syphilis. Syphilis, he was saying, was a disease carried by a certain kind of person in Baltimore—a very poor, probably drug-using, sexually active individual. If that kind of person was suddenly transported from his or her old neighborhood to a new one—to a new part of town, where syphilis had never been a problem before—the disease would have an opportunity to tip.

There is more than one way to tip an epidemic, in other words. Epidemics are a function of the people who transmit infectious agents, the infectious agent itself, and the environment in which the infectious agent is operating. And when an epidemic tips, when it is jolted out of equilibrium, it tips because something has happened, some change has occurred in one (or two or three) of those areas. These three agents of change I call the Law of the Few, the Stickiness Factor, and the Power of Context.

1.

When we say that a handful of East Village kids started the Hush Puppies epidemic, or that the scattering of the residents of a few housing projects was sufficient to start Baltimore's syphilis epidemic, what we are really saying is that in a given process or system some people matter more than others. This is not, on the face of it, a particularly radical notion. Economists often talk about the 80/20

10

Principle, which is the idea that in any situation roughly 80 percent of the "work" will be done by 20 percent of the participants. In most societies, 20 percent of criminals commit 80 percent of crimes. Twenty percent of motorists cause 80 percent of all accidents. Twenty percent of beer drinkers drink 80 percent of all beer. When it comes to epidemics, though, this disproportionality becomes even more extreme: a tiny percentage of people do the majority of the work.

Potterat, for example, once did an analysis of a gonorrhea epidemic in Colorado Springs, Colorado, looking at everyone who came to a public health clinic for treatment of the disease over the space of six months. He found that about half of all the cases came, essentially, from four neighborhoods representing about 6 percent of the geographic area of the city. Half of those in that 6 percent, in turn, were socializing in the same six bars. Potterat then interviewed 768 people in that tiny subgroup and found that 600 of them either didn't give gonorrhea to anyone else or gave it to only one other person. These people he called nontransmitters. The ones causing the epidemic to grow—the ones who were infecting two and three and four and five others with their disease—were the remaining 168. In other words, in all of the city of Colorado Springs—a town of well in excess of 100,000 people—the epidemic of gonorrhea tipped because of the activities of 168 people living in four small neighborhoods and basically frequenting the same six bars.

Who were those 168 people? They aren't like you or me. They are people who go out every night, people who have vastly more sexual partners than the norm, people whose lives and behavior are well outside of the ordinary. In the mid-1990s, for example, in the pool halls and rollerskating rinks of East St. Louis, Missouri, there was a man named Darnell "Boss Man" McGee. He was big—over six feet—and charming, a talented skater, who wowed young girls with his exploits on the rink. His spe-

cialty was thirteen- and fourteen-year-olds. He bought them jewelry, took them for rides in his Cadillac, got them high on crack, and had sex with them. Between 1995 and 1997, when he was shot dead by an unknown assailant, he slept with at least 100 women and—it turned out later—infected at least 30 of them with HIV.

In the same two-year period, fifteen hundred miles away, near Buffalo, New York, another man—a kind of Boss Man clone—worked the distressed downtown streets of Jamestown. His name was Nushawn Williams, although he also went by the names "Face," "Sly," and "Shyteek." Williams juggled dozens of girls, maintaining three or four different apartments around the city, and all the while supporting himself by smuggling drugs up from the Bronx. (As one epidemiologist familiar with the case told me flatly, "The man was a genius. If I could get away with what Williams did, I'd never have to work a day again in my life.") Williams, like Boss Man, was a charmer. He would buy his girlfriends roses, let them braid his long hair, and host all-night marijuana and malt liquor–fueled orgies at his apartments. "I slept with him three or four times in one night," one of his partners remembered. "Me and him, we used to party together all the time. . . . After Face had sex, his friends would do it too. One would walk out, the other would walk in." Williams is now in jail. He is known to have infected at least sixteen of his former girlfriends with the AIDS virus. And most famously, in the book *And the Band Played On* Randy Shilts discusses at length the so-called Patient Zero of AIDS, the French-Canadian flight attendant Gaetan Dugas, who claimed to have 2,500 sexual partners all over North America, and who was linked to at least 40 of the earliest cases of AIDS in California and New York. These are the kinds of people who make epidemics of disease tip.

Social epidemics work in exactly the same way. They are also driven by the efforts of a handful of exceptional people. In this case, it's not sexual appetites that set them apart. It's things like how sociable they are, or how energetic or knowledgeable or influential among their peers. In the case of Hush Puppies, the great mystery is how those shoes went from something worn by a few fashion-forward downtown Manhattan hipsters to being sold in malls across the country. What was the connection between the East Village and Middle America? The Law of the Few says the answer is that one of these exceptional people found out about the trend, and through social connections and energy and enthusiasm and personality spread the word about Hush Puppies just as people like Gaetan Dugas and Nushawn Williams were able to spread HIV.

2.

15   In Baltimore, when the city's public clinics suffered cutbacks, the nature of the syphilis affecting the city's poor neighborhoods changed. It used to be an acute infection, something that most people could get treated fairly quickly before they had a chance to infect many others. But with the cutbacks, syphilis increasingly became a chronic disease, and the disease's carriers had three or four or five times longer to pass on their infection. Epidemics tip because of the extraordinary efforts of a few select carriers. But they also sometimes tip when something happens to transform the epidemic agent itself.

This is a well-known principle in virology. The strains of flu that circulate at the beginning of each winter's flu epidemic are quite different from the strains of flu that circulate at the end. The most famous flu epidemic of all—the pandemic of 1918—was first spotted in the spring of that year and was, relatively speaking, quite tame. But over the summer the virus underwent some strange transformation and over the next six months ended up killing between 20 and 40 million people worldwide. Nothing had changed in the way in which the virus was being spread. But the virus had suddenly become much more deadly.

The Dutch AIDS researcher Jaap Goudsmit argues that this same kind of dramatic transformation happened with HIV. Goudsmit's work focuses on what is known as *Pneumocystis carinii* pneumonia, or PCP. All of us carry the bacterium in our bodies, probably since birth or immediately thereafter. In most of us it is harmless. Our immune systems keep it in check easily. But if something, such as HIV, wipes out our immune system, it becomes so uncontrollable that it can cause a deadly form of pneumonia. PCP is so common among AIDS patients, in fact, that it has come to be seen as an almost certain indication of the presence of the virus. What Goudsmit did was go back in the medical literature and look for cases of PCP, and what he found is quite chilling. Just after World War II, beginning in the Baltic port city of Danzig and spreading through central Europe, there was an epidemic of PCP that claimed the lives of thousands of small children.

Goudsmit has analyzed one of the towns hit hardest by the PCP epidemic, the mining town of Heerlen in the Dutch province of Limburg. Heerlen had a training hospital for midwives called the Kweekschool voor Vroedvrouwen, a single unit of which—the so-called Swedish barrack—was used in the 1950s as a special ward for underweight or premature infants. Between June 1955 and July 1958, 81 infants in the Swedish barrack came down with PCP and 24 died. Goudsmit thinks that this was an early HIV epidemic, and that somehow the virus got into the hospital, and was spread from child to child by the then, apparently common, practice of using the same needles over and over again for blood transfusions or injections of antibiotics. He writes:

> Most likely at least one adult—probably a coal miner from Poland, Czechoslovakia, or Italy—brought the virus to Limburg. This one adult could have died from AIDS with little notice. . . . He could have transmitted the virus to his wife and offspring. His infected wife (or girlfriend) could have given birth in a Swedish barrack to a

child who was HIV infected but seemingly healthy. Unsterilized needles and syringes could have spread the virus from child to child.

The truly strange thing about this story, of course, is that not all of the children died. Only a third did. The others did what today would seem almost impossible. They defeated HIV, purged it from their bodies, and went on to live healthy lives. In other words, the strains of HIV that were circulating back in the 1950s were a lot different from the strains of HIV that circulate today. They were every bit as contagious. But they were weak enough that most people—even small children—were able to fight them off and survive them. The HIV epidemic tipped in the early 1980s, in short, not just because of the enormous changes in sexual behavior in the gay communities that made it possible for the virus to spread rapidly. It also tipped because HIV itself changed. For one reason or another, the virus became a lot deadlier. Once it infected you, you stayed infected. It stuck.

This idea of the importance of stickiness in tipping has enormous implications for the way we regard social epidemics as well. We tend to spend a lot of time thinking about how to make messages more contagious—how to reach as many people as possible with our products or ideas. But the hard part of communication is often figuring out how to make sure a message doesn't go in one ear and out the other. Stickiness means that a message makes an impact. You can't get it out of your head. It sticks in your memory. When Winston filter-tip cigarettes were introduced in the spring of 1954, for example, the company came up with the slogan "Winston tastes good like a cigarette should." At the time, the ungrammatical and somehow provocative use of "like" instead of "as" created a minor sensation. It was the kind of phrase that people talked about, like the famous Wendy's tag line from 1984 "Where's the beef?" In his history of the cigarette industry, Richard Kluger writes that the marketers at R. J. Reynolds, which sells Winston, were "de-

lighted with the attention" and "made the offending slogan the lyric of a bouncy little jingle on television and radio, and wryly defended their syntax as a colloquialism rather than bad grammar." Within months of its introduction, on the strength of that catchy phrase, Winston tipped, racing past Parliament, Kent, and L&M into second place, behind Viceroy, in the American cigarette market. Within a few years, it was the bestselling brand in the country. To this day, if you say to most Americans "Winston tastes good," they can finish the phrase, "like a cigarette should." That's a classically sticky advertising line, and stickiness is a critical component in tipping. Unless you remember what I tell you, why would you ever change your behavior or buy my product or go to see my movie?

The Stickiness Factor says that there are   20 specific ways of making a contagious message memorable; there are relatively simple changes in the presentation and structuring of information that can make a big difference in how much of an impact it makes.

3.

Every time someone in Baltimore comes to a public clinic for treatment of syphilis or gonorrhea, John Zenilman plugs his or her address into his computer, so that the case shows up as a little black star on a map of the city. It's rather like a medical version of the maps police departments put up on their walls, with pins marking where crimes have occurred. On Zenilman's map the neighborhoods of East and West Baltimore, on either side of the downtown core, tend to be thick with black stars. From those two spots, the cases radiate outward along the two central roadways that happen to cut through both neighborhoods. In the summer, when the incidence of sexually transmitted disease is highest, the clusters of black stars on the roads leading out of East and West Baltimore become thick with cases. The disease is on the move. But in the winter months, the map changes. When the weather turns cold, and the people of East and West Baltimore are much more likely to stay at home, away from the bars and clubs and street corners where sexual transactions are made, the stars in each neighborhood fade away.

The seasonal effect on the number of cases is so strong that it is not hard to imagine that a long, hard winter in Baltimore could be enough to slow or lessen substantially—at least for the season—the growth of the syphilis epidemic.

Epidemics, Zenilman's map demonstrates, are strongly influenced by their situation—by the circumstances and conditions and particulars of the environments in which they operate. This much is obvious. What is interesting, though, is how far this principle can be extended. It isn't just prosaic factors like the weather that influence behavior. Even the smallest and subtlest and most unexpected of factors can affect the way we act. One of the most infamous incidents in New York City history, for example, was the 1964 stabbing death of a young Queens woman by the name of Kitty Genovese. Genovese was chased by her assailant and attacked three times on the street, over the course of half an hour, as thirty-eight of her neighbors watched from their windows. During that time, however, none of the thirty-eight witnesses called the police. The case provoked rounds of self-recrimination. It became symbolic of the cold and dehumanizing effects of urban life. Abe Rosenthal, who would later become editor of the *New York Times,* wrote in a book about the case:

> Nobody can say why the thirty-eight did not lift the phone while Miss Genovese was being attacked, since they cannot say themselves. It can be assumed, however, that their apathy was indeed one of the big-city variety. It is almost a matter of psychological survival, if one is surrounded and pressed by millions of people, to prevent them from constantly imping-ing on you, and the only way to do this is to ignore them as often as possible. Indifference to one's neighbor and his troubles is a conditioned reflex in life in New York as it is in other big cities.

This is the kind of environmental explanation that makes intuitive sense to us. The anonymity and alienation of big-city life makes people hard and unfeeling. The truth about Genovese, however, turns out to be a little more complicated—and more interesting. Two New York City psychologists—Bibb Latane of Columbia University and John Darley of New York University—subsequently conducted a series of studies to try to understand what they dubbed the "bystander problem." They staged emergencies of one kind or another in different situations in order to see who would come and help. What they found, surprisingly, was that the one factor above all else that predicted helping behavior was how many witnesses there were to the event.

In one experiment, for example, Latane and Darley had a student alone in a room stage an epileptic fit. When there was just one person next door, listening, that person rushed to the student's aid 85 percent of the time. But when subjects thought that there were four others also overhearing the seizure, they came to the student's aid only 31 percent of the time. In another experiment, people who saw smoke seeping out from under a doorway would report it 75 percent of the time when they were on their own, but the incident would be reported only 38 percent of the time when they were in a group. When people are in a group, in other words, responsibility for acting is diffused. They assume that someone else will make the call, or they assume that because no one else is acting, the apparent problem—the seizure-like sounds from the other room, the smoke from the door—isn't really a problem. In the case of Kitty Genovese, then, social psychologists like Latane and Darley argue, the lesson is not that no one called despite the fact that thirty-eight people heard her scream; it's that no one called *because* thirty-eight people heard her scream. Ironically, had she been attacked on a lonely street with just one witness, she might have lived.

25   The key to getting people to change their behavior, in other words, to care about their neighbor in distress, sometimes lies with the smallest details of their immediate situation. The Power of Context says that human beings are a lot more sensitive to their environment than they may seem.

4.

The three rules of the Tipping Point—the Law of the Few, the Stickiness Factor, the Power of Context—offer a way of making sense of epidemics. They provide us with direction for how to go about reaching a Tipping Point. How do these three rules help us understand teenage smoking, for example, or the phenomenon of word-of-mouth, or crime, or the rise of a best-seller? The answers may surprise you.

READING AND THINKING

1. What does Gladwell identify as causes of the 1996 Baltimore syphilis epidemic? What point does he make about each of these contributing causes? Would any of these causes alone have been sufficient to start the epidemic? Explain.

2. What three causes does Gladwell identify for the tipping point? Provide an example of each of these types of causal explanation.

3. What connections does Gladwell make between physical/medical epidemics, such as syphilis, HIV, and the flu, on one hand, and social epidemics on the other? What is a social epidemic?

THINKING AND WRITING

1. Write a summary of Gladwell's essay. Be sure to include the three types of reasons he offers for an event or situation to tip and become an epidemic. Include one example of each category of explanation for such a tipping point.

2. Write an essay in which you explain the different causes of a social event, such as the rise of teenage smoking or the popularity of a bestselling book or popular movie.

3. Write an essay in which you explain the reasons for the emergence of a new trend, such as the use of cell phones for instant messaging or a new form of music.

Thomas Jefferson

Thomas Jefferson (1743–1826) is one of America's founding fathers. He had a seat in the Virginia legislature in 1769, was elected Virginia's governor in 1779, served as the nation's first secretary of state (1790–1793), was Washington's vice president (1779–1801), and then became president in 1801. He wrote both books and political pamphlets.

DECLARATION OF INDEPENDENCE

Jefferson wrote the "Declaration of Independence" in 1776. It was a document that had been conceived in committee, and it was later worked out and approved in committee, but Jefferson's hand composed it. You will see that his style—the shapes of his sentences, the repetitive patterns in his appeals—contribute to the document's effectiveness. There is a reasonable persona behind the document, a patient, enumerating mind that can forge a revolutionary document without rancor. He declares with equanimity and reasonable force.

1   When in the course of human events, it becomes necessary for one people to dissolve the political bands which have connected them with another, and to assume among the powers of the earth, the separate and equal station to which the Laws of Nature and of Nature's God entitle them, a decent respect to the opinions of mankind requires that they should declare the causes which impel them to the separation.

We hold these truths to be self-evident, that all men are created equal, that they are endowed by their Creator with certain unalienable rights, that among these are life, liberty and the pursuit of happiness. That to secure these rights, governments are instituted among men, deriving their just powers from the consent of the governed. That whenever any form of government becomes destructive of these ends, it is the right of the people to alter or to abolish it, and to institute new government, laying its foundation on such principles and organizing its powers in such form, as to them shall seem most likely to effect their safety and happiness. Prudence, indeed, will dictate that governments long established should not be changed for light and transient causes; and accordingly all experience hath shown, that mankind are more disposed to suffer, while evils are sufferable, than to right themselves by abolishing the forms to which they are accustomed. But when a long train of abuses and usurpations, pursuing invariably the same object, evinces a design to reduce them under absolute despotism, it is their right, it is their duty, to throw off such government, and to provide new guards for their future security. Such has been the patient sufferance of these Colonies; and such is now the necessity which constrains them to alter their former systems of government. This history of the present King of Great Britain is a history of repeated injuries and usurpations, all having in direct object the establishment of an absolute tyranny over these States. To prove this, let facts be submitted to a candid world.

He has refused his assent to laws, the most wholesome and necessary for the public good.

He has forbidden his Governors to pass laws of immediate and pressing importance, unless suspended in their operation till his assent should be obtained; and when so suspended, he has utterly neglected to attend to them.

He has refused to pass other laws for the 5 accommodation of large districts of people, unless those people would relinquish the right of representation in the legislature, a right inestimable to them and formidable to tyrants only.

He has called together legislative bodies at places unusual, uncomfortable, and distant from the depository of their public records, for the sole purpose of fatiguing them into compliance with his measures.

He has dissolved representative houses repeatedly, for opposing with manly firmness his invasions on the rights of people.

He has refused for a long time, after such dissolutions, to cause others to be elected; whereby the legislative powers, incapable of annihilation, have returned to the people at large for their exercise; the State remaining in the meantime exposed to all the dangers of invasion from without and convulsions within.

He has endeavoured to prevent the population of these states; for that purpose obstructing the laws for naturalization of foreigners; refusing to pass others to encourage their migration hither, and raising the conditions of new appropriations of lands.

10 He has obstructed the administration of justice, by refusing his assent to laws for establishing judiciary powers.

He has made judges dependent on his will alone, for the tenure of their offices, and the amount and payment of their salaries.

He has erected a multitude of new offices, and sent hither swarms of officers to harass our people, and eat out their substance.

He has kept among us, in times of peace, standing armies without the consent of our legislatures.

He has affected to render the military independent of and superior to the civil power.

15 He has combined with others to subject us to a jurisdiction foreign to our constitution, and unacknowledged by our laws; giving his assent to their acts of pretended legislation:

For quartering large bodies of troops among us:

For protecting them, by a mock trial, from punishment for any murders which they should commit on the inhabitants of these States:

For cutting off our trade with all parts of the world:

For imposing taxes on us without our consent:

For depriving us in many cases of the ben- 20 efits of trial by jury:

For transporting us beyond seas to be tried for pretended offences:

For abolishing the free system of English laws in a neighbouring Province, establishing therein an arbitrary government, and enlarging its boundaries so as to render it at once an example and fit instrument for introducing the same absolute rule into these Colonies:

For taking away our Charters, abolishing our most valuable laws, and altering fundamentally the forms of our governments:

For suspending our own legislatures, and declaring themselves invested with power to legislate for us in all cases whatsoever.

He has abdicated government here, by de- 25 claring us out of his protection and waging war against us.

He has plundered our seas, ravaged our coasts, burnt our towns, and destroyed the lives of our people.

He is at this time transporting large armies of foreign mercenaries to complete the works of death, desolation and tyranny, already begun with circumstances of cruelty and perfidy scarcely paralleled in the most barbarous ages, and totally unworthy the head of a civilized nation.

He has constrained our fellow citizens taken captive on the high seas to bear arms against their country, to become the executioners of their friends and brethren, or to fall themselves by their hands.

He has excited domestic insurrections amongst us, and has endeavoured to bring on the inhabitants of our frontiers, the merciless Indian savages, whose known rule of warfare, is an undistinguished destruction of all ages, sexes, and conditions.

In every stage of these oppressions we 30 have petitioned for redress in the most humble terms: our repeated petitions have been answered only by repeated injury. A prince whose character is thus marked by every act which may define a tyrant is unfit to be the ruler of a free people.

Nor have we been wanting in attention to our British brethren. We have warned them from time to time of attempts by their legislature to extend an unwarrantable jurisdiction over us. We have reminded them of the circumstances of our emigration and settlement here. We have appealed to their native justice and magnanimity, and we have conjured them by the ties of our common kindred to disavow these usurpations, which would inevitably interrupt our connections and correspondence. They too have been deaf to the voice of justice and of consanguinity. We must, therefore, acquiesce in the necessity, which denounces our separation, and hold them, as we hold the rest of mankind, enemies in war, in peace friends.

We, therefore, the Representatives of the United States of America, in General Congress assembled, appealing to the Supreme Judge of the world for the rectitude of our intentions, do, in the name, and by authority of the good people of these Colonies, solemnly publish and declare, That these United Colonies are, and of right ought to be, Free and Independent States; that they are absolved from all allegiance to the British Crown, and that all political connection between them and the state of Great Britain, is and ought to be totally dissolved; and that as Free and Independent States, they have full power to levy war, conclude peace, contract alliances, establish commerce, and to do all other acts and things which Independent States may of right do. And for the support of this declaration, with a firm reliance on the protection of Divine Providence, we mutually pledge to each other our lives, our fortunes, and our sacred honor.

READING AND THINKING

1. Study the eloquent first sentence of the "Declaration." We do not know the meaning of that sentence until we come to its end; it is therefore a periodic sentence, one that suspends us until the very end. Why does Jefferson use such a sentence at the outset?

2. Look up words that interest you in the first sentence, and think about how and why Jefferson uses commas within the sentence.

3. The second paragraph lays out the logic of the document in two parts. The pivotal word between the two parts is *but*. What happens in the first part? In the second?

4. The "so-called Facts," the history of England's abuses, are outlined in paragraphs 3–29. What can you, today's reader, say about those "facts"? Can you confirm them? What assumptions has Jefferson made about his audience?

5. In paragraphs 30 and 31, Jefferson sums up and characterizes the grievances he has outlined. How well do you think Jefferson accounts for his evidence? Is he reasonable? Is his language balanced and rational or is it inflammatory and challenging? Explain.

THINKING AND WRITING

1. Break the first sentence apart into its elements. Rewrite it in your own style, making two or three sentences if necessary. Explain which version is more effective.

2. Consider the very last phrase of the "Declaration": "our sacred honor." In a brief email to one of your classmates, explain what you think Jefferson gains by using that phrase. Explain too why you think the phrase comes last in that series: "we mutually pledge to each other our lives, our fortunes and our sacred honor."

3. Select three grievances that you have against a person or institution. State those grievances in the same parallel form that Jefferson used in the "Declaration."

4. Write a short paragraph characterizing the ethos inherent in this document. Consider the effectiveness of Jefferson's use of "we."

Jamaica Kincaid (b. 1949)

Jamaica Kincaid was born and raised on the island of Antigua, a former British colony. She immigrated to the United States, where she joined the staff of *Ingenue* magazine and became a contributor to and staff writer for *The New Yorker,* served on the Harvard faculty, and won distinction for her books, which include *Annie John* (1985), *A Small Place* (1988), *Lucy* (1990), and *My Brother* (1997). In 2000, she published *Talk Stories,* a collection of profiles, originally written for *The New Yorker.*

ON SEEING ENGLAND FOR THE FIRST TIME

In "On Seeing England for the First Time," Kincaid reveals the difference between the England she inherited and the England she found in reality. She describes the influence England has had on her all her life and how she feels about that influence. The title of the essay refers to the literal trip Kincaid took to England for the first time as an adult and to the metaphorical understanding she arrives at through taking that trip and reflecting on England's influence on her.

1   When I saw England for the first time, I was a child in school sitting at a desk. The England I was looking at was laid out on a map gently, beautifully, delicately, a very special jewel; it lay on a bed of sky blue—the background of the map—its yellow form mysterious, because though it looked like a leg of mutton, it could not really look like anything so familiar as a leg of mutton because it was England—with shadings of pink and green, unlike any shadings of pink and green I had seen before, squiggly veins of red running in every direction. England was a special jewel all right, and only special people got to wear it. The people who got to wear England were English people. They wore it well and they wore it everywhere: in jungles, in deserts, on plains, on top of the highest mountains, on all the oceans, on all the seas, in places where they were not welcome, in places they should not have been. When my teacher had pinned this map up on the blackboard, she said, "This is England"—and she said it with authority, seriousness, and adoration, and we all sat up. It was as if she had said, "This is Jerusalem, the place you will go to when you die but only if you have been good." We understood then—we were meant to understand then—that England was to be our source of myth and the source from which we got our sense of reality, our sense of what was meaningful, our sense of what was meaningless—and much about our own lives and much about the very idea of us headed that last list.

At the time I was a child sitting at my desk seeing England for the first time, I was already very familiar with the greatness of it. Each morning before I left for school, I ate a breakfast of half a grapefruit, and egg, bread and butter and a slice of cheese, and a cup of cocoa; or half a grapefruit, a bowl of oat porridge, bread and butter and a slice of cheese, and a cup of cocoa. The can of cocoa was often left on the table in front of me. It had written on it the name of the company, the year the company was established, and the words "Made in England." Those words, "Made in England," were written on the box the oats came in too. They would also have been written on the box the shoes I was wearing came in; a bolt of gray linen cloth lying on the shelf of a store from which my mother had bought three yards to make the uniform that I was wearing had written along its edge those three words. The shoes I wore were made in England; so were my socks and cotton undergarments and the satin ribbons I wore tied at the end of two plaits of my hair. My father, who might have sat next to me at breakfast, was a carpenter and cabinet maker. The shoes he wore to work would have been made in England, as were his khaki shirt and trousers, his underpants and undershirt, his socks and brown felt hat. Felt was not the proper material from which a hat that was expected to provide shade from the hot sun should be made, but my father must have seen and admired a picture of an Englishman wearing such a hat in England, and this picture that he saw must have been so compelling that it caused him to wear the wrong hat for a hot climate most of his long life. And this hat—a brown felt hat—became so central to his character that it was the first thing he put on in the morning as he stepped out of bed and the last thing he took off before he stepped back into bed at night. As we sat at breakfast a car might go by. The car, a Hillman or a Zephyr, was made in England. The very idea of the meal itself, breakfast, and its substantial quality and quantity was an idea from England; we somehow knew that in England they began the day with this meal called breakfast and a proper breakfast was a big breakfast. No one I knew liked eating so much food so early in the day; it made us feel sleepy, tired. But this breakfast business was Made in England like almost everything else that surrounded us, the exceptions being the sea, the sky, and the air we breathed.

At the time I saw this map—seeing England for the first time—I did not say to myself, "Ah, so that's what it looks like," because there was no longing in me to put a shape to those three words that ran through every part of my life, no matter how small; for me to have had such a longing would have meant that I lived in a certain atmosphere, an atmosphere in which those three words were felt as a burden. But I did not live in such an atmosphere. My father's brown felt hat would develop a hole in its crown, the lining would separate from the hat itself, and six weeks before he thought that he could not be seen wearing it—he was a very vain man—he would order another hat from England. And my mother taught me to eat my food in the English way: the knife in the right hand, the fork in the left, my elbows held still close to my side, the food carefully balanced on my fork and then brought up to my mouth. When I had finally mastered it, I overheard her saying to a friend, "Did you see how nicely she can eat?" But I knew then that I enjoyed my food more when I ate it with my bare hands, and I continued to do so when she wasn't looking. And when my teacher showed us the map, she asked us to study it carefully, because no test we would ever take would be complete without this statement: "Draw a map of England."

I did not know then that the statement "Draw a map of England" was something far worse than a declaration of war, for in fact a flat-out declaration of war would have put me on alert, and again in fact, there was no need for war—I had long ago been conquered. I did not know then that this statement was part of a process that would result in my erasure, not my physical erasure, but my erasure all the same. I did not know then that this statement was meant to make me feel in awe and small whenever I heard the word "England": awe at its existence, small because I was not from it. I did not know very much of anything then— certainly not what a blessing it was that I was unable to draw a map of England correctly.

After that there were many times of see- 5 ing England for the first time. I saw England in history. I knew the names of all the kings of England. I knew the names of their children, their wives, their disappointments, their triumphs, the names of people who betrayed them; I knew the dates on which they were born and the dates they died. I knew their conquests and was made to feel glad I figured in them; I knew their defeats. I knew the details of the year 1066 (the Battle of Hastings, the end of the reign of the Anglo-Saxon kings) before I knew the details of the year 1832 (the year slavery was abolished). It wasn't as bad as I make it sound now; it was worse. I did like so much hearing again and again how Alfred the Great, traveling in disguise, had been left to watch cakes, and because he wasn't used to this the cakes got burned, and Alfred burned his hands pulling them out of the fire, and the woman who had left him to watch the cakes screamed at him. I loved King Alfred. My grandfather was named after him; his son, my uncle, was named after King Alfred; my brother is named after King Alfred. And so there are three people in my family named after a man they have never met, a man who died over ten centuries ago. The first view I got of England then was not unlike the first view received by the person who named my grandfather.

This view, though—the naming of the kings, their deeds, their disappointments—was the vivid view, the forceful view. There were other views, subtler ones, softer, almost not there—but these were the ones that made the most lasting impression on me, these were the ones that made me really feel like nothing. "When morning touched the sky" was one phrase, for no morning touched the sky where I lived. The mornings where I lived came on abruptly, with a shock of heat and loud noises. "Evening approaches" was another, but the evenings where I lived did not approach; in fact, I had no evening—I had night and I had day and they came and went in a mechanical way: on, off; on, off. And then there were gentle mountains and low blue skies and moors over which people took walks for nothing but pleasure, when where I lived a walk was an act of labor, a burden, something only death or the automobile could relieve. And there were things that a small turn of a head could convey—entire worlds, whole lives would depend on this thing, a certain turn of a head. Everyday life could be quite tiring, more tiring than anything I was told not to do. I was told not to gossip, but they

did that all the time. And they ate so much food, violating another of those rules they taught me: do not indulge in gluttony. And the foods they ate actually: if only sometime I could eat cold cuts after theater, cold cuts of lamb and mint sauce, and Yorkshire pudding and scones, and clotted cream, and sausages that came from up-country (imagine, "up-country"). And having troubling thoughts at twilight, a good time to have troubling thoughts, apparently; and servants who stole and left in the middle of a crisis, who were born with a limp or some other kind of deformity, not nourished properly in their mother's womb (that last part I figured out for myself; the point was, oh to have an untrustworthy servant); and wonderful cobbled streets onto which solid front doors opened; and people whose eyes were blue and who had fair skins and who smelled only of lavender, or sometimes sweet pea or primrose. And those flowers with those names: delphiniums, foxgloves, tulips, daffodils, floribunda, peonies; in bloom, a striking display, being cut and placed in large glass bowls, crystal, decorating rooms so large twenty families the size of mine could fit in comfortably but used only for passing through. And the weather was so remarkable because the rain fell gently always, only occasionally in deep gusts, and it colored the air various shades of gray, each an appealing shade for a dress to be worn when a portrait was being painted; and when it rained at twilight, wonderful things happened: people bumped into each other unexpectedly and that would lead to all sorts of turns of events—a plot, the mere weather caused plots. I saw that people rushed: they rushed to catch trains, they rushed toward each other and away from each other; they rushed and rushed and rushed. That word: rushed! I did not know what it was to do that. It was too hot to do that, and so I came to envy people who would rush, even though it had no meaning to me to do such a thing. But there they are again. They loved their children; their children were sent to their own rooms as a punishment, rooms larger than my entire house. They were special, everything about them said so, even their clothes; their clothes rustled, swished, soothed. The world was theirs, not mine; everything told me so.

If now as I speak of all this I give the impression of someone on the outside looking in, nose pressed up against a glass window, that is wrong. My nose was pressed up against a glass window all right, but there was an iron vise at the back of my neck forcing my head to stay in place. To avert my gaze was to fall back into something from which I had been rescued, a hole filled with nothing, and that was the word for everything about me, nothing. The reality of my life was conquests, subjugation, humiliation, enforced amnesia. I was forced to forget. Just for instance, this: I lived in a part of St. John's, Antigua, called Ovals. Ovals was made up of five streets, each of them named after a famous English seaman—to be quite frank, an officially sanctioned criminal: Rodney Street (after George Rodney), Nelson Street (after Horatio Nelson), Drake Street (after Francis Drake), Hood Street, and Hawkins Street (after John Hawkins). But John Hawkins was knighted after a trip he made to Africa, opening up a new trade, the slave trade. He was then entitled to wear as his crest a Negro bound with a cord. Every single person living on Hawkins Street was descended from a slave. John Hawkins's ship, the one in which he transported the people he had bought and kidnapped, was called *The Jesus*. He later became the treasurer of the Royal Navy and rear admiral.

Again, the reality of my life, the life I led at the time I was being shown these views of England for the first time, for the second time, for the one-hundred-millionth time, was this: the sun shone with what sometimes seemed to be a deliberate cruelty; we

must have done something to deserve that. My dresses did not rustle in the evening air as I strolled to the theater (I had no evening, I had no theater; my dresses were made of a cheap cotton, the weave of which would give way after not too many washings). I got up in the morning, I did my chores (fetched water from the public pipe for my mother, swept the yard), I washed myself, I went to a woman to have my hair combed freshly every day (because before we were allowed into our classroom our teachers would inspect us, and children who had not bathed that day, or had dirt under their fingernails, or whose hair had not been combed anew that day, might not be allowed to attend class). I ate that breakfast. I walked to school. At school we gathered in an auditorium and sang a hymn, "All Things Bright and Beautiful," and looking down on us as we sang were portraits of the Queen of England and her husband; they wore jewels and medals and they smiled. I was a Brownie. At each meeting we would form a little group around a flagpole, and after raising the Union Jack, we would say, "I promise to do my best, to do my duty to God and the Queen, to help other people every day and obey the scouts' law."

Who were these people and why had I never seen them, I mean really seen them, in the place where they lived? I had never been to England. No one I knew had ever been to England, or I should say, no one I knew had ever been and returned to tell me about it. All the people I knew who had gone to England had stayed there. Sometimes they left behind them their small children, never to see them again. England! I had seen England's representatives. I had seen the governor general at the public grounds at a ceremony celebrating the Queen's birthday. I had seen an old princess and I had seen a young princess. They had both been extremely not beautiful, but who of us would have told them that? I had never seen England, really seen it, I had only met a representative, seen a picture, read books, memorized its history. I had never set foot, my own foot, in it.

10   The space between the idea of something and its reality is always wide and deep and dark. The longer they are kept apart—idea of thing, reality of thing—the wider the width, the deeper the depth, the thicker and darker the darkness. This space starts out empty, there is nothing in it, but it rapidly becomes filled up with obsession or desire or hatred or love— sometimes all of these things, sometimes some of these things, sometimes only one of these things. The existence of the world as I came to know it was a result of this: idea of thing over here, reality of thing way, way over there. There was Christopher Columbus, an unlikable man, an unpleasant man, a liar (and so, of course, a thief) surrounded by maps and schemes and plans, and there was the reality on the other side of that width, that depth, that darkness. He became obsessed, he became filled with de- sire, the hatred came later, love was never a part of it. Eventually, his idea met the longed- for reality. That the idea of something and its reality are often two completely different things is something no one ever remembers; and so when they meet and find that they are not compatible, the weaker of the two, idea or reality, dies. That idea Christopher Columbus had was more powerful than the reality he met, and so the reality he met died.

And so finally, when I was a grown-up woman, the mother of two children, the wife of someone, a person who resides in a powerful country that takes up more than its fair share of a continent, the owner of a house with many rooms in it and of two automobiles, with the desire and will (which I very much act upon) to take from the world more than I give back to it, more than I deserve, more than I need, fi- nally then, I saw England, the real England, not a picture, not a painting, not through a story in a book, but England, for the first time. In me, the space between the idea of it and its reality had become filled with hatred, and so when at last I saw it I wanted to take it into my hands and tear it into little pieces and then crumble it up as if it were clay, child's clay. That was impossible, and so I could only in- dulge in not-favorable opinions.

There were monuments everywhere; they commemorated victories, battles fought be- tween them and the people who lived across the sea from them, all vile people, fought over which of them would have dominion over the people who looked like me. The monuments were useless to them now, people sat on them and ate their lunch. They were like markers on an old useless trail, like a piece of old string tied to a finger to jog the memory, like old dec- oration in an old house, dirty, useless, in the way. Their skins were so pale, it made them look so fragile, so weak, so ugly. What if I had the power to simply banish them from their land, send boat after boatload of them on a voy- age that in fact had no destination, force them to live in a place where the sun's presence was a constant? This would rid them of their pale complexion and make them look more like me, make them look more like the people I love and treasure and hold dear, and more like the peo- ple who occupy the near and far reaches of my imagination, my history, my geography, and re- duce them and everything they have ever known to figurines as evidence that I was in di- vine favor, what if all this was in my power? Could I resist it? No one ever has.

And they were rude, they were rude to each other. They didn't like each other very much. They didn't like each other in the way they didn't like me, and it occurred to me that their dislike for me was one of the few things they agreed on.

I was on a train in England with a friend, an English woman. Before we were in Eng- land she liked me very much. In England she didn't like me at all. She didn't like the claim I said I had on England, she didn't like the views I had of England. I didn't like England, she didn't like England, but she didn't like me not liking it too. She said, "I want to show you my England, I want to show you the England that I know and love." I had told her many times before that I knew England and I didn't want to love it anyway. She no longer lived in England; it was her own country, but it had not been kind to her, so she left. On the train, the conductor was rude to her; she asked something, and he responded in a rude way. She became ashamed. She was ashamed at the way he treated her; she was ashamed at the way he behaved. "This is the new England," she said. But I liked the conductor being rude; his behavior seemed quite appropriate. Earlier this had happened: we had gone to a store to buy a shirt for my husband; it was meant to be a special present, a special shirt to wear on special occasions. This was a store where the Prince of Wales has his shirts made, but the shirts sold in this store are beautiful all the same. I found a shirt I thought my husband would like and I wanted to buy him a tie to go with it. When I couldn't decide which one to choose, the salesman showed me a new set. He was very pleased with these, he said, because they bore the crest of the Prince of Wales, and the Prince of Wales had never allowed his crest to decorate an article of clothing before. There was something in the way he said it; his tone was slavish, reverential, awed. It made me feel angry; I wanted to hit him. I didn't do that. I said, my husband and I hate princes, my husband would never wear anything that had a prince's anything on it. My friend stiffened. The salesman stiffened. They both drew themselves in, away from me. My friend told me that the prince was a symbol of her Englishness, and I could see that I had caused offense. I looked at her. She was an English person, the sort of English person I used to know at home, the sort who was nobody in England but somebody when they came to live among the people like me. There were many people I could have seen England with; that I was seeing it with this particular person, a person who reminded me of the peo-ple who showed me England long ago as I sat in church or at my desk, made me feel silent and afraid, for I wondered if, all these years of our friendship, I had had a friend or had been in the thrall of a racial memory.

I went to Bath—we, my friend and I, did 15 this, but though we were together, I was no longer with her. The landscape was almost as familiar as my own hand, but I had never been in this place before, so how could that be again? And the streets of Bath were familiar, too, but I had never walked on them before. It was all those years of reading, starting with Roman Britain. Why did I have to know about Roman Britain? It was of no real use to me, a person living on a hot, drought-ridden island, and it is of no use to me now, and yet my head is filled with this nonsense, Roman Britain. In Bath, I drank tea in a room I had read about in a novel written in the eighteenth century. In this very same room, young women wearing those dresses that rustled and so on danced and flirted and sometimes disgraced them-selves with young men, soldiers, sailors, who were on their way to Bristol or someplace like that, so many places like that where so many adventures, the outcome of which was not good for me, began. Bristol, England. A sentence that began "That night the ship sailed from Bristol, England" would end not so good for me. And then I was driving through the coun-tryside in an English motorcar, on narrow winding roads, and they were so familiar, though I had never been on them before; and through little villages the name of which I somehow knew so well though I had never been there before. And the countryside did have all those hedges and hedges, fields hedged in. I was marveling at all the toil of it, the planting of the hedges to begin with and then the care of it, all that clipping, year after year of clipping, and I wondered at the lives of the people who would have to do this, because wherever I see and feel the hands that hold up the world, I see and feel myself and all the peo-ple who look like me. And I said, "Those hedges" and my friend said that someone, a woman named Mrs. Rothchild, worried that the hedges weren't being taken care of properly; the farmers couldn't afford or find the help to keep up the hedges, and often they replaced them with wire fencing. I might have said to that, well if Mrs. Rothchild doesn't like the wire fencing, why doesn't she take care of the hedges herself, but I didn't. And then in those fields that were now hemmed in by wire fencing that a privileged woman didn't like was planted a vile yellow flowering bush that produced an oil, and my friend said that Mrs. Rothchild didn't like this either; it ruined the English countryside, it ruined the traditional look of the English countryside.

It was not at that moment that I wished every sentence, everything I knew, that began with England would end with "and then it all died; we don't know how, it just all died." At that moment, I was thinking, who are these people who forced me to think of them all the time, who forced me to think that the world I knew was incomplete, or without substance, or did not measure up because it was not England; that I was incomplete, or without substance, and did not measure up because I was not English. Who were these people? The person sitting next to me couldn't give me a clue; no one person could. In any case, if I had said to her, I find England ugly, I hate England; the weather is like a jail sentence, the English are a very ugly people, the food in England is like a jail sentence, the hair of English people is so straight, so dead looking, the English have an unbearable smell so different from the smell of people I know, real people of course, she would have said that I was a person full of prejudice. Apart from the fact that it is I—that is, the people who look like me—who made her aware of the unpleasantness of such a thing, the idea of such a thing, preju-

dice, she would have been only partly right, sort of right: I may be capable of prejudice, but my prejudices have no weight to them, my prejudices have no force behind them, my prejudices remain opinions, my prejudices remain my personal opinion. And a great feeling of rage and disappointment came over me as I looked at England, my head full of personal opinions that could not have public, my public, approval. The people I come from are powerless to do evil on grand scale.

The moment I wished every sentence, everything I knew, that began with England would end with "and then it all died; we don't know how, it just all died" was when I saw the white cliffs of Dover. I had sung hymns and recited poems that were about a longing to see the white cliffs of Dover again. At the time I sang the hymns and recited the poems, I could really long to see them again because I had never seen them at all, nor had anyone around me at the time. But there we were, groups of people longing for something we had never seen. And so there they were, the white cliffs, but they were not that pearly majestic thing I used to sing about, that thing that created such a feeling in these people that when they died in the place where I lived they had themselves buried facing a direction that would allow them to see the white cliffs of Dover when they were resurrected, as surely they would be. The white cliffs of Dover, when finally I saw them, were cliffs, but they were not white; you would only call them that if the word "white" meant something special to you; they were dirty and they were steep; they were so steep, the correct height from which all my views of England, starting with the map before me in my classroom and ending with the trip I had just taken, should jump and die and disappear forever.

READING AND THINKING

1. What does England mean for Kincaid? To what extent is her view of England a product of her early education?

2. What does the phrase "made in England" come to mean in the essay? With what does Kincaid contrast things "made in England"? Why does the phrase "Draw a map of England" resonate so powerfully in her memory?

3. What contrasts does Kincaid draw between England and her Caribbean island home? What point does she make through these contrasts?

4. What ironies does Kincaid point up in her discussion of street names in St. John's, Antigua? What are the purpose and effect of her mention of Christopher Columbus?

THINKING AND WRITING

1. Describe the various views of England Kincaid presents. Explain what she says and implies about the "white cliffs of Dover."

2. Explain what Kincaid means by "the space between the idea of something and its reality" as it applies to England as she knows it. To what extent have you yourself experienced this gap between an idea of something and its reality?

3. Identify and explain the significance of her father's felt hat and of one other object that Kincaid gives symbolic treatment.

4. Tell a story or describe a scene about a place that has been significant in your life.

Michael Lewis (b. 1960)

Michael Lewis was born and raised in New Orleans and graduated from the Isidore Newman School there. Lewis received a Bachelor's degree in art history from Princeton University and a Master's Degree in economics from the London School of Economics. He worked as a bond salesman at Salomon Brothers in London, an experience he described in his first book, *Liar's Poker: Rising through the Wreckage on Wall Street* (1985). While at Salomon Brothers, Lewis worked nights and weekends as a journalist, a job that continues to this day, with pieces for magazines like *The New Republic*. His book, *Moneyball: The Art of Winning an Unfair Game* (2003), from which "The Curse of Talent" is taken, was a bestseller, read alike by business people and baseball fans.

THE CURSE OF TALENT

In "The Curse of Talent," from *Moneyball*, a book about the quest for and the secret of success in baseball, Lewis describes the struggles of star athlete Billy Beane, who later became the manager of the Oakland A's. Lewis considers how an athlete can have too much talent and the effects that mega talent can have on an athletic career, in this case the career of Billy Beane as a professional baseball player.

Whom the gods wish to destroy they first call promising.

—Cyril Connolly, *Enemies of Promise*

1   The first thing they always did was run you. When big league scouts road-tested a group of elite amateur prospects, foot speed was the first item they checked off their lists. The scouts actually carried around checklists. "Tools" is what they called the talents they were checking for in a kid. There were five tools: the abilities to run, throw, field, hit, and hit with power. A guy who could run had "wheels"; a guy with a strong arm had "a hose." Scouts spoke the language of auto mechanics. You could be forgiven, if you listened to them, for thinking they were discussing sports cars and not young men.

On this late spring day in San Diego several big league teams were putting a group of prospects through their paces. If the feeling in the air was a bit more tense than it used to be, that was because it was 1980. The risks in drafting baseball players had just risen. A few years earlier, professional baseball players had been granted free agency by a court of law, and, after about two seconds of foot-shuffling, baseball owners put prices on players that defied the old commonsensical notions of what a baseball player should be paid. Inside of four years, the average big league salary had nearly tripled, from about $52,000 to almost $150,000 a year. The new owner of the New York Yankees, George Steinbrenner, had paid $10 million for the entire team in 1973; in 1975, he paid $3.75 million for baseball's first modern free agent, Catfish Hunter. A few years ago no one thought twice about bad calls on prospects. But what used to be a thousand-dollar mistake was rapidly becoming a million-dollar one.

Anyway, the first thing they always did was run you. Five young men stretch and canter on the outfield crabgrass: Darnell Coles. Cecil Espy. Erik Erickson. Garry Harris. Billy Beane. They're still boys, really; all of them have had to produce letters from their mothers saying that it is okay for them to be here. No one outside their hometowns would ever have heard of them, but to the scouts they already feel like household names. All five are legitimate first-round picks, among the thirty or so most promising prospects in the country. They've been culled from the nation's richest trove of baseball talent, Southern California, and invited to the baseball field at San Diego's Herbert Hoover High to answer a question: who is the best of the best?

As the boys get loose, a few scouts chitchat on the infield grass. In the outfield Pat Gillick, the general manager of the Toronto Blue Jays, stands with a stopwatch in the palm of his hand. Clustered around Gillick are five or six more scouts, each with his own stopwatch. One of them paces off sixty yards and marks the finish line with his foot. The boys line up along the left field foul line. To their left is the outfield wall off which Ted Williams, as a high school player, smacked opposite field doubles. Herbert Hoover High is Ted Williams's alma mater. The fact means nothing to the boys. They are indifferent to their surroundings. Numb. During the past few months they have been so thoroughly examined by so many older men that they don't even think about where they are performing, or for whom. They feel more like sports cars being taken out for a spin than they do like young men being tested. Paul Weaver, the Padres scout, is here. He's struck by the kids' cool. Weaver has seen new kids panic when they work out for scouts. Mark McLemore, the same Mark McLemore who will one day be a $3-million-a-year outfielder for the Seattle Mariners, will vomit on the field before one of Weaver's workouts. These kids aren't like that. They've all been too good for too long.

5   Darnell Coles. Cecil Espy. Erik Erickson. Garry Harris. Billy Beane. One of the scouts turns to another and says: *I'll take the three black kids [Coles, Harris, Espy]. They'll dust the white kids. And Espy will dust everyone, even Coles.* Coles is a sprinter who has already signed a football scholarship to play wide receiver at UCLA. That's how fast Espy is: the scouts are certain that even Coles can't keep up with him.

Gillick drops his hand. Five born athletes lift up and push off. They're at full tilt after just a few steps. It's all over inside of seven seconds. Billy Beane has made all the others look slow. Espy finished second, three full strides behind him.

And as straightforward as it seems—what ambiguity could there possibly be in a sixty-yard dash?—Gillick is troubled. He hollers at one of the scouts to walk off the track again, and make certain that the distance is exactly sixty yards. Then he tells the five boys to return to the starting line. The boys don't understand; they run you first but they usually only run you once. They think maybe Gillick wants to test their endurance, but that's not what's on Gillick's mind. Gillick's job is to believe what he sees and disbelieve what he doesn't and yet he cannot bring himself to believe what he's just seen. Just for starters, he doesn't believe that Billy Beane outran Cecil Espy and Darnell Coles, fair and square. Nor does he believe the time on his stopwatch. It reads 6.4 seconds—you'd expect that from a sprinter, not a big kid like this one.

Not quite understanding why they are being asked to do it, the boys walk back to the starting line, and run their race all over again. Nothing important changes. "Billy just flat-out smoked 'em all," says Paul Weaver.

When he was a young man Billy Beane could beat anyone at anything. He was so naturally superior to whomever he happened to be playing against, in whatever sport they happened to be playing, that he appeared to be in a different, easier game. By the time he was a sophomore in high school, Billy was the quarterback on the football team and the high scorer on the basketball team. He found talents in himself almost before his body was ready to exploit them: he could dunk a basketball before his hands were big enough to palm it.

10   Billy's father, no athlete himself, had taught his son baseball from manuals. A career naval officer, he'd spend nine months on end at sea. When he was home, in the family's naval housing, he was intent on teaching his

son something. He taught him how to pitch: pitching was something you could study and learn. Whatever the season he'd take his son and his dog-eared baseball books to empty Little League diamonds. These sessions weren't simple fun. Billy's father was a perfectionist. He ran their pitching drills with military efficiency and boot camp intensity.

Billy still felt lucky. He knew that he wanted to play catch every day, and that every day, his father would play catch with him.

By the time Billy was fourteen, he was six inches taller than his father and doing things that his father's books failed to describe. As a freshman in high school he was brought up by his coach, over the angry objections of the older players, to pitch the last varsity game of the season. He threw a shutout with ten strikeouts, and went two for four at the plate. As a fifteen-year-old sophomore, he hit over .500 in one of the toughest high school baseball leagues in the country. By his junior year he was six foot four, 180 pounds and still growing, and his high school diamond was infested with major league scouts, who watched him hit over .500 again. In the first big game after Billy had come to the scouts' attention, Billy pitched a two-hitter, stole four bases, and hit three triples. Twenty-two years later the triples would remain a California schoolboy record, but it was the way he'd hit them that stuck in the mind. The ballpark that day had no fences; it was just an endless hot tundra in the San Diego suburbs. After Billy hit the first triple over the heads of the opposing outfielders, the outfielders played him deeper. When he hit it over their heads the second time, the outfielders moved back again, and played him roughly where the parking lot would have been outside a big league stadium. Whereupon Billy hit it over their heads a third time. The crowd had actually laughed the last time he'd done it. That's how it was with Billy when he played anything, but especially when he played baseball: blink and

you might miss something you'd never see again.

He encouraged strong feelings in the older men who were paid to imagine what kind of pro ballplayer a young man might become. The boy had a body you could dream on. Ramrod-straight and lean but not so lean you couldn't imagine him filling out. And that face! Beneath an unruly mop of dark brown hair the boy had the sharp features the scouts loved. Some of the scouts still believed they could tell by the structure of a young man's face not only his character but his future in pro ball. They had a phrase they used: "the Good Face." Billy had the Good Face.

Billy's coach, Sam Blalock, didn't know what to make of the scouts. "I've got this first-round draft pick," he says, "and fifteen and twenty scouts showing up every time we *scrimmage*. And I didn't know what to do. I'd never played pro ball." Twenty years later Sam Blalock would be selected by his peers as the best high school baseball coach in the country. His teams at Rancho Bernardo High School in San Diego would produce so many big league prospects that the school would come to be known, in baseball circles, as "The Factory." But in 1979 Blalock was only a few years into his job, and he was still in awe of Major League Baseball, and its many representatives who turned up at his practices. Each and every one of them, it seemed, wanted to get to know Billy Beane personally. It got so that Billy would run from practice straight to some friend's house to avoid their incessant phone calls to his home. With the scouts, Billy was cool. With his coaches, Billy was cool. The only one who ever got to Billy where he lived was an English teacher who yanked him out of class one day and told him he was too bright to get by on his athletic gifts and his charm. For her, Billy wanted to be better than he was. For the scouts—well, the scouts he could take or leave.

What Sam Blalock now thinks he should have done is to herd the scouts into a corner   15 and tell them to just sit there until such time as they were called upon. What he did, instead, was whatever they wanted him to do; and what they wanted him to do was trot his star out for inspection. They'd ask to see Billy run. Sam would have Billy run sprints for them. They'd ask to see Billy throw and Billy would proceed to the outfield and fire rockets to Sam at the plate. They'd want to see Billy hit and Sam would throw batting practice with no one there but Billy and the scouts. ("Me throwing, Billy hitting, and twenty big league scouts in the outfield shagging flies," recalls Blalock.) Each time the scouts saw Billy they saw only what they wanted to see: a future big league star.

As for Billy—Sam just let him be. Baseball, to Blalock's way of thinking, at least at the beginning of his career, was more of an individual than a team sport, and more of an instinctive athletic event than a learned skill. Handed an athlete of Billy's gifts, Blalock assumed, a coach should just let him loose. "I was young and a little bit scared," Blalock says, "and I didn't want to screw him up." He'd later change his mind about what baseball was, but he'd never change his mind about Billy's talent. Twenty-two years later, after more than sixty of his players, and two of his nephews, had been drafted to play pro baseball, Blalock would say that he had yet to see another athlete of Billy's caliber.

They all missed the clues. They didn't notice, for instance, that Billy's batting average collapsed from over .500 in his junior year to just over .300 in his senior year. It was hard to say why. Maybe it was the pressure of the scouts. Maybe it was that the other teams found different ways to pitch to him, and Billy failed to adapt. Or maybe it was plain bad luck. The point is: no one even noticed the drop-off. "I never looked at a single statistic of Billy's," admits one of the scouts. "It wouldn't have crossed my mind. Billy was a five-tool guy. He had it all." Roger Jongewaard, the Mets' head scout, says, "You have to under-

stand: we don't just look at performance. We were looking at talent." But in Billy's case, talent was a mask. Things went so well for him so often that no one ever needed to worry about how he behaved when they didn't go well. Blalock worried, though. Blalock lived with it. The moment Billy failed, he went looking for something to break. One time after Billy struck out, he whacked his aluminum bat against a wall with such violence that he bent it at a right angle. The next time he came to the plate he was still so furious with himself that he insisted on hitting with the crooked bat. Another time he threw such a tantrum that Blalock tossed him off the team. "You have some guys that when they strike out and come back to the bench all the other guys move down to the other end of the bench," says Blalock. "That was Billy."

When things did not go well for Billy on the playing field, a wall came down between him and his talent, and he didn't know any other way to get through the wall than to try to smash a hole in it. It wasn't merely that he didn't like to fail; it was as if he didn't know how to fail.

The scouts never considered this. By the end of Billy's senior year the only question they had about Billy was: Can I get him? And as the 1980 major league draft approached, they were given reason to think not. The first bad sign was that the head scout from the New York Mets, Roger Jongewaard, took a more than usual interest in Billy. The Mets held the first overall pick in the 1980 draft, and so Billy was theirs for the taking. Word was that the Mets had winnowed their short list to two players, Billy and a Los Angeles high school player named Darryl Strawberry. Word also was that Jongewaard preferred Billy to Strawberry. (He wasn't alone.) "There are good guys and there are premium guys," says Jongewaard. "And Billy was a premium premium guy. He had the size, the speed, the arm, the whole package. He could play other sports. He was a true athlete. And then, on top of all that, he had good grades in school and he was going with all the prettiest girls. He had charm. He could have been anything."

20   The other bad sign was that Billy kept saying he didn't want to play pro baseball. He wanted to go to college. Specifically, he wanted to attend Stanford University on a joint baseball and football scholarship. He was at least as interested in the school as the sports. The baseball recruiter from the University of Southern California had tried to talk Billy out of Stanford. "They'll make you take a whole week off for final exams," he'd said. To which Billy had replied, "That's the idea, isn't it?" A few of the scouts had tried to point out that Billy didn't actually play football—he'd quit after his sophomore year in high school, to avoid an injury that might end his baseball career. Stanford didn't care. The university was in the market for a quarterback to succeed its current star, a sophomore named John Elway. The baseball team didn't have the pull that the football team had with the Stanford admissions office, and so the baseball coach asked the football coach to have a look at Billy. A few hours on the practice field and the football coach endorsed Billy Beane as the man to take over after John Elway left. All Billy had to do was get his B in math. The Stanford athletic department would take care of the rest. And it had.

By the day of the draft every big league scout had pretty much written off Billy as unobtainable. "Billy just scared a lot of people away," recalls scout Paul Weaver. "No one thought he was going to sign." It was insane for a team to waste its only first round draft choice on a kid who didn't want to play.

The only one who refused to be scared off was Roger Jongewaard. The Mets had three first-round picks in the 1980 draft and so, Jongewaard figured, the front office might be willing to risk one of them on a player who might not sign. Plus there was this other thing. In the months leading up to the draft the Mets front office had allowed themselves to become part of a strange experiment. *Sports Illustrated* had asked the Mets' general manager, Frank Cashen, if one of the magazine's reporters could follow the team as it decided who would become the first overall draft pick in the country. The Mets had shown the magazine their short list of prospects, and the magazine had said it would be convenient, journalistically, if the team selected Darryl Strawberry.

Strawberry was just a great story: a poor kid from the inner-city of Los Angeles who didn't know he was about to become rich and famous. Jongewaard, who preferred Billy to Strawberry, argued against letting the magazine become involved at all because, as he put it later, "we'd be creating a monster. It'd cost us a lot of money." The club overruled him. The Mets front office felt that the benefits of the national publicity outweighed the costs of raising Darryl Strawberry's expectations, or even of picking the wrong guy. The Mets took Strawberry with the first pick and paid him a then fantastic signing bonus of $210,000. The Blue Jays took Garry Harris with the second pick of the draft. Darnell Coles went to the Mariners with the sixth pick, and Cecil Espy to the White Sox with the eighth pick. With their second first-round draft pick, the twenty-third overall, the Mets let Roger Jongewaard do what he wanted, and Jongewaard selected Billy Beane.

Jongewaard had seen kids say they were going to college only to change their minds the minute the money hit the table. But in the weeks following the draft he had laid a hundred grand in front of Billy's parents and it had done nothing to improve the tone of the discussion. He began to worry that Billy was serious. To the chagrin of Billy's mother, who was intent on her son going to Stanford, Jongewaard planted himself in the Beane household. That didn't work either. "I wasn't getting the vibes I would like," Jongewaard now says. "And so I took Billy to see the big club."

25   It was 1980. The Beane family was military middle class. Billy had hardly been outside of San Diego, much less to New York City. To him the New York Mets were not so much a baseball team as a remote idea. But that summer, when the Mets came to San Diego to play the Padres, Jongewaard escorted Billy into the visitors' clubhouse. There Billy found waiting for him a Mets uniform with his name on the back, and a receiving party of players: Lee Mazzilli, Mookie Wilson, Wally Backman. The players knew who he was; they came up to him and joked about how they needed him to hurry up and get his ass to the big leagues. Even the Mets' manager, Joe Torre, took an interest. "I think that's what turned Billy," says Jongewaard. "He met the big league team and he thought: I can play with these guys." "It was such a sacred place," says Billy, "and it was closed off to so many people. And I was inside. It became real."

The decision was Billy's to make. A year or so earlier, Billy's father had sat him down at a table and challenged him to arm-wrestle. The gesture struck Billy as strange, unlike his father. His father was intense but never physically aggressive. Father and son wrestled: Billy won. Afterward, his father told Billy that if he was man enough to beat his father in arm-wrestling, he was man enough to make his own decisions in life. The offer from the Mets was Billy's first big life decision. Billy told Roger Jongewaard he'd sign.

What happened next was odd. Years later Billy couldn't be sure if he dreamed it, or it actually happened. After he told the Mets he planned to sign their contract, but before he'd actually done it, he changed his mind. When he told his father that he was having second thoughts, that he wasn't sure he wanted to play pro ball, his father said, "You made your decision, you're signing."

In any case, Billy took the $125,000 offered by the Mets. He appeased his mother (and his conscience) by telling her (and himself) he would attend classes at Stanford during the off-season. Stanford disagreed. When the admissions office learned that Billy wouldn't be playing sports for Stanford, they told him that he was no longer welcome in Stanford's classrooms. "Dear Mrs. Beane," read the letter from the Stanford dean of admissions, Fred A. Hargadon, "we are withdrawing Billy's admission . . . I do wish him every success, both with his professional career in baseball and with his alternate plans for continuing his education."

Just like that, a life changed. One day Billy Beane could have been anything; the next he was just another minor league baseball player, and not even a rich one. On the advice of a family friend, Billy's parents invested on their son's behalf his entire $125,000 bonus in a real estate partnership that promptly went bust. It was many years before Billy's mother would speak to Roger Jongewaard.

READING AND THINKING

1. Why do you think Lewis begins his essay the way he does—with a story about running? Is this an effective opening? Why or why not? Explain.

2. What are the tools that baseball scouts most value in a young prospective baseball player like Billy Beane?

3. How much emphasis does Lewis put on the financial side of baseball—on money? What do you learn from this piece about baseball and money?

4. Why do you think Billy Beane changes his mind and chooses to skip attending Stanford University to sign a contract to play professional baseball with the New York Mets? What are the consequences of that decision, as far as you can tell from this selection?

THINKING AND WRITING

1. Explain why the professional baseball scouts, with all their years of experience, "missed the clues" to Billy Beane's shortcomings.

2. Explain why Billy failed to live up to his incredible promise as a professional baseball prospect.

3. Explain the significance of the conclusion of "The Curse of Talent." Is this an effective ending to the piece? Why or why not?

Michael Paterniti

Michael Paterniti is a young journalist who lives in Maine with his wife and son. He won the 1998 National Magazine Award for his article "Driving Mr. Albert," first published in *Harper's Magazine*. The book *Driving Mr. Albert: A Trip Across America with Einstein's Brain* (2005) has been translated in 20 countries. His work has also appeared in the *New York Times Magazine, Details, Esquire,* and *GQ.* A former executive editor of *Outside,* he is now a writer-at-large.

THE MOST DANGEROUS BEAUTY

In "The Most Dangerous Beauty," Paterniti tells us the story of an illustrated medical book that reveals the secrets of the human body in a most beautiful way, but the book also harbors other secrets about WWII and the Nazis. Paterniti gives us this intriguing story through an unnamed narrator (presumably himself) who tells us how a 58-year-old professor (who teaches medical illustration) from the Midwest had dealt, over many years, with this complicated tale of beauty and destruction.

1 Beneath this black roof, on a well-clipped block, in a small midwestern town on the Wabash River, a professor wakes in the dark, confused at first by an outline under the sheets, this limp figure beside him in bed. From some primordial haze slowly comes recognition, then language: *bed, sheets, wife . . . Andrea.* He kisses her and rises. He is 58 years old, and he wakes every morning at this ungodly hour, in his finely appointed brick house with exploding beds of lilies, phlox and begonias. After three heart attacks, he goes now to cardiac rehab. Wearing shiny blue Adidas sweats, he drives off in the family's Nissan. Once at the medical center, he walks briskly on the treadmill, works the cross-trainer machine and then does some light lifting. It's a standing joke that if he's not there at 6 A.M. sharp, the staff should just put on ties and go straight to the funeral home. After his workout, as he drives to his house, the town glows in a flood of new light; the river bubbles in its brown banks as the flies rise; the lawns are almost too bright, green with beauty and rancor.

He feels better for this visit, more alive, as if it's a daily penance ensuring him another day on earth, another chance to breathe in the smell of cut grass before a spasm of summer lightning. He takes Lopressor, Altace and aspirin to thin his thick blood. Even now fragments accumulate, arteries begin to clog, his cardiac muscle weakens, slows, speeds again to make up time. There is so little time.

He wears his silvered hair neatly parted. A creature of habit, he's worn the same style of round tortoiseshell glasses for thirty years. He drinks a cup of chai every afternoon of his well-plotted life at a café near his office at Purdue University, where he teaches medical illustration. He is a humble, somewhat conservative man, a Roman Catholic whose joy for the most simple things can be overwhelming, inexplicable. After his third heart attack, when they jammed tubes into him and he was pretty sure it was over, he became insistent. "Just tell me I'm going to mow the lawn again!" he said to his doctor. "Tell me I'm going to mow the lawn!"

These were nearly his last words.

If this man can be oversensitive and a bit 5 obsessive, if he has an exact recall of the little injustices that have been done unto him—he keeps old hurtful letters on file—he knows he must unburden himself now, make peace with those in his life: wife, children, friends, colleagues. And with the vanished ghosts that roam the rooms of his memory: mother, father, brother.

And what of Pernkopf? What of Batke?

He can't fathom where to begin with the Book, now forever out of print, effectively banned. When considering it, he often conjures the language of some illicit affair: rapture, consumption, shame. And if he was betrayed by that lover, does it lessen all those days he spent in love? Ah, the Book, the nearly unbearable perfection of its paintings, and then, weltering behind it, armies clashing across the face of Europe, 6 million spectral Jews. Under pressure, history splits in two: the winners and the losers, the righteous and the evil.

It is not like this man to act impulsively, to yield control, to risk missing cardiac rehab, to wander 7,000 miles from his dear doctor, but he does. He packs a bag with some old journals, drives from West Lafayette to Indianapolis and gets on a plane. He travels eight hours in coach, through spasms of lightning, wearing his Adidas jumpsuit, hair neatly parted. Fragments accumulate; arteries begin to clog. He drinks some wine; he pores through his journals, these copiously recorded memories of a sabbatical he took twenty-three years ago, when he went on a pilgrimage to find the Book's greatest artist, when he still worshiped—yes, really, that's the word—the Book's achievement. He naps, wakes, reads his decades-old handwriting again. If he were to die on this plane, in a hotel lobby in Vienna, in the echoing halls of the Institute searching for some truth, will he have been cleansed? After all, he didn't do the killing or throw the bodies from the window. He didn't spew the hate that incited a hemicycle of fanatics.

No, his sin, if that indeed is what it is, was more quotidian: He found beauty in something dangerous. There are days when he can't remember how it began, and nights when he can't sleep, remembering.

10   A cloudy afternoon, Vienna, 1957. A man sits and smokes, a body laid before him. A creature of habit, he wears a white lab coat and a white polyester turtleneck, no matter what the weather. He is small, with a crooked nose and skewed chin that give him the appearance of a beat-up bantamweight. He has a lot of nervous energy, except when he sits like this. When he sits like this, he seems almost dead, a snake in the heat of day. Before him lies a nameless cadaver that was brought up from the basement of the Institute, from the formaldehyde pools of torsos and limbs, then perfectly prepared like this: an incision, a saw to the breastbone, the rib cage drawn open, the heart removed. He stares at this open body, looks down at the floor, stares some more.

In his right hand, he holds a Habico-Kolinsky, one with long sable hairs, his brush of choice. On the rag paper before him, he has sketched some rough lines, has plotted his colors. And now, after this prolonged stillness, he bursts from his chair. He paints across the entire canvas, maniacally, almost chaotically. He lays in washes of color, gradually building the glazes. His hand darts back and forth. He goes at the bronchus and then the thoracic duct. With his tongue, he licks the brush and lifts off pigment to show phantasmic light on this internal landscape. He flicks turquoise here and there to make the fascia appear real. What he does is highly intricate, but at this speed it's like running on a tightrope. He is in deep space, underwater, gravityless. He works in a fever, shaking and levitating. Weeks pass, and still he stands before this painting, this body.

What is his desire? To be a rich man, to paint what he chooses, to hang in museums, to make love to beautiful women, but he is on the wrong side of history. And yet he isn't a demagogue or a war criminal. He is merely a trained fine artist who must paint dead bodies for the money—and that's what he will do, for nearly five decades of his life: brains, veins, viscera, vaginas. Perhaps his sin is quotidian, too: In 1933 he says yes to a job because he's hungry, and so sells his soul, joining Pernkopf's army of artists, which soon becomes part of Hitler's army. Now a silver light pours thickly through the tall glass windows. He lifts pigment, then swabs his brush over the *Aquarellfarben* cake. He expertly paints in the ascending aorta and pulmonary trunk, giving them ocher and purple colors. He creates this astral penumbra of arteries and air pipes, galaxies within the body. For one moment, he does it so well he vanquishes memory. It has always been just him and the canvas. And as certain as he will be forgotten, with each painting he believes he won't. He is the righteous one, the butcher's son made king.

The dead have no color. His power is that he gives them color.

They don't know now to treat him, this unusual specimen, this volcanic event. He shakes and levitates in his temporary palsy. It is the summer between seventh and eighth grades, 1957. Far away, in another world, an unknown man named Franz Batke paints in Vienna while this unknown boy, David Williams, has some sort of infection. His body has burst with huge open sores on his face, back and chest. The shots put him into a high fever that brings on convulsions. He is a supernova; he could be cursed.

15   Outside, the Michigan sun burns, it rains lugubriously, and then there is bright light on the panes again. The floor shines menacingly. There is no explanation for this suffering. No treatment that the doctors can find. Inside him a cell has split in two. He is a boy who, by some internal chemical flood of testosterone and disease, is fast becoming something else, a different animal.

In the fall, he is released from his hospital cell. He lifts weights and runs the sand dunes by the lake to build his body back. He dreams of being the middleweight champion of the world, the kid from Muskegon, Michigan, hitting someone so hard that he separates the guy from his body. If only he could convert his rage to power and skill, it might happen. After school he takes a football and runs through the cornstalks in the backyard, pretending each stalk is a tackler. It is twilight now, and the boy has been running through these cornstalks for hours, for days. His shirt is streaked with blood from where he's been stabbed by the stalks, the scabs broken open, releasing pustulants from the body. When he heals, his skin will be runneled and pocked. He will always live a word away from that good-looking upperclassman, the one in the locker room who, before everyone, called him Frankenstein. It will take him decades to understand these scars and what has happened to him. What has happened to him?

Years later, after crossing an ocean in search of something he can't put a name to, he finds himself in a room with the old man, who smokes so many cigarettes it seems he is on fire. They talk about the thing they both loved most: art. Sitting in that studio in Innsbruck, David Williams, the would-be middleweight champion of the world from Muskegon, Michigan, who speaks in faltering German, feels immediately at home with this Austrian, Franz Batke, who speaks no English and who, unbeknownst to him, is a former Nazi. How has this happened? Because they speak only of art. Williams will write in his journal, "I am truly beginning to see this man as a genius." After all, among the scarred carapaces of lost civilizations, among the ugly ruins and tormented dreams of history's fanatics, some beauty must rise, mustn't it?

Mustn't it?

The cell has split in two. There is no diagnosis, no explanation. Clouds cover the city, hyena shaped, turning on themselves. The tanks are rolling, and the people come out of their houses, clutching bouquets to pledge allegiance to their invaders, without fully understanding. They throw flowers and sing. They are thin already, engraved by rib cages and dark rings beneath their eyes. It is not easy to understand. Their euphoria is blinding.

20   On this morning, Eduard Pernkopf rises at 4 A.M. He is a short, stout man with gray-blue eyes, dour and phlegmatic, though not entirely humorless. He wears round glasses and diligently reads his well-thumbed Schopenhauer. He has a scar on his left cheek from a duel he once fought. It is hard to imagine this particular fellow in a duel. And it is equally hard to imagine what moves inside him—ambition, zealotry, some canted idealism? Or is it just sickness? He has thyroid problems and crippling headaches. A blood clot is moving slowly toward his brain. When his first wife dies of tuberculosis at 27, he pens a symphony dedicated to her titled *The Pleasure and Pain of Man*. He marries her sister. He smokes exactly fifteen cigarettes a day. He comes to care about only two things: the Book and the Party.

The Book begins as a lab manual while Pernkopf is teaching at the Anatomy Institute in Vienna. He needs a dissection guide to help students better identify the organs and vessels of the body, but he finds other anatomy texts outdated or unsatisfactory, and he is a maniacal perfectionist. He soon has what seems like an impractical dream: to map the entire human body. And this dream is what leads to his life's work: an epic eponymous four-volume, seven-book anatomical atlas, an unrelenting performance spanning thirty years of eighteen-hour workdays. Here our mortality is delivered in Technicolor, in 800 paintings that illuminate the gooey, viscous innards of our own machine, organized by regions: the Chest and Pectoral Limb; the Abdomen, Pelvis and Pelvic Limb; the Neck; and the Topographical and Stratigraphical Anatomy of the Head.

The group he recruits to paint comprises fine artists, some of whom have trained for years and are known as *akademische Maler*. At this time—the early 1930s—there is no work in Vienna. People scrounge for crumbs.

Beggars line the streets. On Fridays shop-keepers leave small plates of pennies out for the poor. A rich person is someone who owns a bicycle, and the artists take their jobs willingly, thankfully. Perhaps in another place and time, they'd be famous for their watercolors of Viennese parks or Austrian landscapes. But here they draw the cold interiors of the human body.

Pernkopf oversees these men and women: four, seven, nine, then eleven artists in all. Perhaps he is dimly aware that this moment may never repeat itself. Never again will social conditions warrant that so many talented fine artists gather together to detail the body, and never again will the art of medical illustration veer so close to that of fine art itself. The book will coincide with the discovery and refinement of four-color separation: All anatomical works before it will seem to be from Kansas, while *Pernkopf's Anatomy* will seem to hail from Oz.

For his part, Pernkopf directs the dissections and preparations of the cadavers for painting. These preparations can be exacting, hour upon hour spent pinning back skin on a forearm, scraping fascia from a bone, sawing skulls open to reveal a fine minutiae of arteries, the skein of veins beneath the dura. But he learns quickly; the better the preparation—the more fresh and vivid the viscera—the better the painting.

He is driven by ideas of accuracy and clarity. He stresses again and again: The paintings must look like living tissue, even *more* alive than living tissue, if such a thing is possible. He strikes a deal with a publisher named Urban & Schwarzenberg, which after seeing the early work is convinced that Pernkopf's book may one day be mentioned in the same breath as da Vinci's sketches of the body, Vesalius's *Fabrica* or Sobotta's *Atlas der Anatomice des Menschen*.

Meanwhile, the cell has split. The Jewish diaspora of the late nineteenth century—one bringing thousands from southern Poland

and western Ukraine to Vienna—has also now projected Jews into the highest reaches of society, causing deep-seated rancor. Anti-Semitism becomes commonplace. Even at the institute, competing anatomical schools rise under one roof to segregate the Jews from their Austrian detractors, a student army of National Socialists. Passing in the halls, students come to blows.

For Pernkopf this violence is as it should be. From the moment he enrolls as a student at the University of Vienna, in 1907, at 18, he joins a nationalistic German fraternity, which becomes the foundation for his later fervency as a National Socialist, including his belief that Jews have corrupted German culture. Shortly after secretly joining the Nazi Party in 1933—which is against the law in Austria at the time—he joins the Sturmabteilung, or Brown Shirts, the underground uniformed army of Nazis. And then he waits.

Months, then years, pass. Life worsens. The Institute is only a microcosm of Vienna itself, of Austria as a whole, of this entrenched hatred pushing up through the dirt of society. On March 12, 1938, Hitler enters the country uncontested, in an open limousine. He speaks from the balcony of the town hall in Linz to crazed flower-throwing crowds and claims his beloved birthplace, Austria, as his own—a blank-check Nazi annexation known as the Anschluss. In Vienna, where Hitler once made watercolors of Gothic buildings, flags bearing swastikas are unfurled. Some feel a rush of hope; others, like Sigmund Freud, who lives only four blocks from the Institute, pack to leave.

And so, on this morning, Pernkopf readies himself for the most important speech of his life. It is 4 A.M., the time he usually reserves for writing the words that accompany the paintings in his atlas. He writes in shorthand, striving to find the right intonations and arpeggios, giving words to some echo he hears in his head. Later his wife will type the loose pages, and then he will stand in the hemicycle

at the Institute before a room packed with medical-school staff, pledging allegiance to Adolf Hitler, in his storm trooper's uniform, a swastika on his left elbow. He will call for "racial hygiene" and the "eliminating of the unfit and defective." He will call for the "discouragement of breeding by individuals who do not belong together properly, whose races clash." He will call for sterilization and "the control of marriage." And finally he will praise Hitler for being a man who has found "a new way of looking at the world," as someone "in whom the legend of history has blossomed."

The speech becomes an overt declaration of war within the university. Jewish students will soon be thrown from the third floor of the Anatomy Institute to a courtyard below, and 153 Jewish faculty members will be purged—some will eventually be sent to concentration camps; others will flee. In this milieu of bloodlust, the bodies of those tried and guillotined after the Anschluss—more than 1,000 in all, mostly political opponents, patriots, Communists and petty criminals, among them eight Jews—will be stacked like cordwood behind the Institute, to be used as preparations for Pernkopf's sacred atlas. From the legend of these human limbs, his temple rises.

His favorite gift as a kid is a chemistry set with which he relentlessly experiments. And the boy obsessively draws. He draws humans and animals. He does crude landscapes in watercolor. When he holds a brush in his hand, when he puts that brush to paper, he becomes invisible. He cannot be seen. He has no history, no scars.

He becomes the first in the Williams family to graduate from high school, then goes to community college. In his freshman biology class, he sketches a frog, the insides of a frog, with amazing accuracy and clarity. When his instructor sees it, she tells him about universities where one can learn to draw the insides of frogs—and other animals, including humans.

David, the artist, may be an enigma to his factory-working parents, but his younger brother, Greg, is an aberration. While David is short, stocky and a loner, Greg is tall, angular and outgoing. As David has his art and science, Greg toys with the idea of becoming a priest.

If the brothers dwell in alternative realities, they unconsciously remain each other's lodestars, each other's partial reason for hope. For they have the same goal: to escape the blue-collar drudgery of gray Muskegon and a house that has slowly gone from Norman Rockwell portrait to Ingmar Bergman film, mother listing into alcoholism and mental illness, father burdened by some deeply hidden guilt from his own unspoken past. Each son is searching for some kind of euphoria to obliterate the pain of growing up in this house. At the age of 20, David abruptly moves to Hamburg to live with a woman he met when she was visiting the States and who loves him, his scarred self, something he once thought impossible. Greg finds theater and opera, then men and drugs.

35   Years pass. Greg moves to Detroit, New York City. David splits with the woman in Hamburg, returns home, is accepted into the University of Cincinnati's medical-illustration program, meets his wife, a schoolteacher, after being set up in a Muskegon bar. Shortly after they marry, he encounters the Book for the first time.

He remembers the exact particle reality of that moment. At the university, he lives in an almost obsessive world in which people spend a hundred hours drawing a horse hock or the tendons of a human arm, in thrall to brush on paper. One of his professors has purchased *Pernkopf's Anatomy,* a mythic work Williams has heard defined as pure genius, and he goes to the professor's office to see it.

The books are enormous, with blank green cloth covers. Inside could be almost anything—Monet's water lilies, pornography, the detailed mechanics of a car—but when he opens it, when the binding cracks and the dry-cleaned scent of new pages and ink wafts up to his nostrils, there appear before him thousands of thick, glossy sheets; these wild colors, these glowing human bodies!

It is an electric moment, a pinnacle of which a life may contain not more than a handful. But it is more than just the bright frisson of discovery, the wordless awe before some greater fluency. If this is a book with emanations, with a life of its own, then perhaps what startles him most is the glint of self-recognition that he finds in its pages: While he sees the timeless past in the trenches and deep spaces of the body, he also, oddly—and he can't yet put words to this—sees his own future.

What he doesn't know yet, flipping through these pages, is that twelve years from now, as an associate professor, he will take a sabbatical and go in search of the Book, that he will find its last living artist, Franz Batke, who will take him under his wing, impart his lost techniques. He doesn't yet know that he will return again to Batke just before the old man dies—and learn what he'd rather not know about him. That he will write an academic paper about the Book for an obscure journal of medical illustration, in which he'll praise *Pernkopf's Anatomy* as "the standard by which all other illustrated anatomic works are measured." It will briefly help his academic career and bring him a measure of fame. But with it comes a backlash. He will lose friends, question himself and be judged guilty of Pernkopf's crimes by mere association; he will refuse to talk about the Book, curse the day he first saw it.

40   If this is indeed a Book with emanations, as he will come to believe, perhaps even his heart attacks can be blamed on it– Pernkopf, in white lab coat, reaching from the grave for one last cadaver.

The book is blindingly beautiful, an exaltation, a paean and a eulogy all at once. Page after page, the human body unfolds itself, and with each page the invisible becomes visible, some deeper secret reveals itself. What is it?

Here is an eardrum, whole, detached from the vestibulocochlear organ and floating in space. It appears as a strange watered planet. Here is a seemingly glass liver through which appears a glass stomach and then glass kidneys, all in a glass body, an utterly transparent figure, us, glittering. Here is a skull wrapped in red arterial yarn, and here a cranium packaged in the bright colors of the holiday season. There are eyes that look out, irises in bottomless depth, a disembodied gaze that is the gaze of poetry itself. There is an unpeeled penis, a pulsating liver the color of a blood orange, a brigade of soulful brains, levitating.

And then there are the drawings of dead people—cadavers, faces half intact, half dissected, skin drawn back in folds from the thoracic cavity, heads half shelled, showing brain. Consider Erich Lepier's watercolor of the neck. In nearly black-and-white-photographic detail, the dead man seems to be sleeping; the intact skin of his neck is supple, his lips are parted, his eyes half closed. His head is shaved, and he has a mustache. Even the fine hairs of his nose are visible. Inside him a superficial layer of the neck's fascia comes in two strange shades of color: a bluish pearlescent and a translucent olive green. The acoustic meatus, pathway to the inner ear, is visible, as is the mastoid process. Every changing texture is felt, every wrinkle recorded. Half of this dead man is in exact decay and half of him seems alive. The painting is its own kind of pornography, half violation and half wonder.

Or consider Batke's watercolor of the thoracic cavity after the removal of the heart. It is like gazing on a psychedelic tree of life: arteries, veins, bronchus, extending like complex branches inside their bizarre terrarium. Batke employs all the colors of the rainbow, these interwoven lines of yellow, blue, orange, purple, but invented and mixed by him, all

these appear as new colors. The bronchus, which rises in the background, is striped and Seuss-like in white and umber. Although the painting's concern is the minute sorting and scoring of these air and blood tunnels, it still captures an undulating energy, fireworks, the finely rendered thrum of the body. The painting nearly takes wing from the page.

Page by page, *Pernkopf's Anatomy* is stunning, bombastic, surreal, the bone-and-muscle evidence, the animal reality of who we are beneath the skin. And yet, as incomprehensible and terrifying as these landscapes can be, as deep as our denial that life is first and finally a biological process, hinging even now on an unknown blood clot orbiting toward the brain, on a weak heart, on the give of a vein wall, the Book brings its own reassurance. Lepier's detached eyes, like spectacular submersibles, Batke's precisely wrought otherworldly vaginas, Schrott's abstract, almost miraculous muscles/ducts/lymph nodes, Karl Endtresser's bizarre spinal configurations—all of these slavishly striving for the thing itself while being regarded, through Pernkopf's eyes and those of the artists, as beautiful, nearly spiritual objects.

So what can be said about this Book? That its intentions are good? That it is a masterpiece? That each painting contains its own genius? And what if a number of these paintings have been signed with swastikas, what then? Is it possible that only Nazis and their myriad obsessions with the body could have yielded such a surprising text?

And what of the dead stacked like cordwood at the Institute, their body parts pulled down by pitchfork? Do the secrets revealed in the Book count less than the secrets kept by it? Does its beauty diminish with these facts or the political beliefs of its general and foot soldiers? In a righteous world, perhaps it should, but does it?

Shortly after the Anschluss, after thousands of Austrians have been conscripted for the front lines of a war against the world, after more and more Austrians have died of starvation, the euphoria fades, the master race begins to devour itself. And yet Eduard Pernkopf ascends, his name a *Hakenkreuz* and a haunted house.

He is first and foremost a scientist, believing, mimicking, the racial politics of the Third Reich. Well received by the powers in Berlin, he is first named dean of the medical school, then *Rektor Magnificus,* or president, of the University of Vienna. Shortly after the Anschluss—March 12, 1938—he issues a letter to all university staff: "To clarify whether you are of Aryan or non-Aryan descent, you are asked to bring your parents' and grandparents' birth certificates to the dean's office. . . . Married individuals must also bring the documents of their wives."

50   Under his presidency, medical experiments are conducted on the unfit and retarded; children are euthanized. Somewhere in his building is the severed head of the Austrian general, the patriot Wilhelm Zehner who, in the first days of the Anschluss, either committed suicide in political protest against the Nazis or was murdered by the Gestapo. Among the more than 1,000 guillotined bodies Pernkopf claims for himself from the district court, he searches for the best, the youngest, the finest specimens of muscle and skin. He opens the bodies like walnuts, discards what won't serve him. Those he decides to keep go to the formaldehyde pools in the Institute's basement, a kind of Brueghelian hell.

So who is Pernkopf? If he's taciturn with his painters, it is because he maintains the utmost professionalism. A dreamer, an intellect, a lover of music, he is in the workshop early in the morning and late at night: He is simply an overwhelming presence. The Book becomes both his great unwritten symphony and, slowly, his madness. Whether or not he encourages them, some of his artists now sign their work to show their Nazi allegiance:

Lepier follows his name with a swastika, Endtresser fashions the double S of his name as an SS lightning bolt, and Batke seems to do the same with the number 44 when he dates his paintings from 1944.

But even before the American bombs fall on the Institute—mistaking it for a factory, leveling half the building—even before the lot of these men are left scattered on the wrong side of history, half anesthetized by the past and half consumed by it, there is this one last moment in which they believe they are the righteous ones. These paintings of the human body belong to the highest expression of their Nazi idealism, but they exceed even that classification. If they save human lives—which they do every time a surgeon uses them to heal the body—each one is an act of salvation.

There was no note, but nonetheless he knows. He knows from a conversation they had the last time his brother, Greg, came from New York City to West Lafayette, when they sat on the front stoop drinking beers. They talked about everything, and Greg mentioned how he believed hedonism was the highest possible expression of self and that to die in an act of euphoria was the only way to really live. In context it was not alarming, nor really surprising. In retrospect it explained everything.

When he learned of his brother's suicide, David Williams drove four hours to Muskegon, straight to his parents' house. His mother was sitting in the living room shaking her head, and his father refused to believe the body was Greg's, since there hadn't been a positive identification. Someone had to go to New York to identify the body. "You work with dead bodies all the time," his father said, maybe a little cruelly. "You can do this."

The next morning, the elder son flew to La   55
Guardia, then took a bus and walked to the morgue at Bellevue to see the younger son. The waiting room was crowded with people there to identify family members who had

been shot, knifed, beaten or killed by gang members. A very large black man in a uniform, an officer of some sort, brought him into a room with a curtained window. He asked twice if David Williams was ready, and the second time Williams feebly answered, "Yes." When the curtain parted, there was his brother, still tall and angular, lying on a metal dissecting table, in severe rigor mortis, with the back of his head resting on a wooden block, exactly like a cadaver in a gross-anatomy lab. But this was his brother—and there was no longer anything beautiful about him, only a pallid mask where his face had been, a lifeless slab in place of his animated body.

If his brother's death left no mark on the greater world, the rest of those dark days in 1978 are part of David Williams's personal history: how he fell into the arms of the large black man who carried him from the room; how he refused to sign a piece of paper that said his brother was found with needle marks on his arm; how he went to the YMCA to pick up his brother's belongings; and how, when he arrived back in Muskegon, his parents were in denial about their son's sexuality and about his suicide, an act that meant he could not be buried, according to Catholic rite, with the other generations of Williamses at St. Mary's Cemetery.

And it's part of history, too, that his brother, the person whose life most closely tracked his own, ended in the cold, unconsecrated ground of Muskegon, among the graves of factory workers, back in this place they both tried so hard to escape.

Not long after, on sabbatical, David Williams goes to see Franz Batke. He is nervous; he doesn't know what to expect. He leaves his family behind in Munich and drives to Innsbruck. He thinks it is no coincidence that shortly after falling in love with his wife, he first saw the Book, and now, shortly after his brother's death, he arrives in Innsbruck to visit the dying old man who is the last living vestige of the Book itself. But what is it that draws him here? He is looking for answers, yes, or perhaps merely reasons to live. And even if Batke's paintings hadn't changed his life—as they have—it is not so strange that a young man suffering loss might seek counsel from an old man who knows a great deal about loss.

What he finds is that Batke is a hermit living in a cell in self-imposed exile. Batke has come to Innsbruck from Vienna, leaving behind his wife, because Vienna represents the past to him, haunting him even now, defeating him, and after more than fifty years with his wife, he is not sure whether or not he still loves her. And he has come here because he has been offered work by Werner Platzer, the man who after the war and Pernkopf's death brought the last books of the atlas to fruition. Platzer, who is hard driving with frantic dashes of intellect and craziness, has promised his friend Batke pay and living quarters in return for paintings to fill a new book on vaginal surgery.

So Batke lives in two rooms at Innsbruck's [60] Institute of Anatomy, where Platzer is the new director. The old man never leaves, never goes out to take the air. Students bring him his food and sundries. Usually, he drinks ice water all day while he works. At night he has trouble sleeping, due to a bad cough, ominous and deep, which worries even him. Against his doctor's orders, he continues to smoke cigarettes. If he is smoking himself to death, the cigarettes may also be what keeps him alive for two more years.

At first he is mistrustful of David Williams, thinking the American scholar has been sent to spy by the publisher or by someone else looking to profit from him. But slowly Batke realizes that the professor is here for seemingly no reason other than to watch him paint—and to be taught. It dawns on him that, even if he has been remembered by only this one American, he has still achieved a certain kind of immortality. Though they can barely communicate, they become closer and closer. They don't discuss politics, only art. And at the end of each day, Williams records another entry in his journal.

"Herr Batke fixes lunch—scrambled eggs and small pieces of pork and wurst. I continue to work on the vein—he says to paint the middle valve first and then add the dark and light *dichweiß*. He wants me to stop using such small choppy strokes."

And "Even in German, I understand him: 'Loosen up. It's no big deal.' I feel it finally beginning to happen. . . . I actually enjoy it physically—the way the paint floats around. I really think this way of painting can suit me. He also demonstrates a vein. He can still do it at 77 years old. He works for two and a half hours on a very small section."

Under Batke's eye, the body becomes beautiful again for David Williams. After the shock of seeing his brother as a cadaver, he perhaps retrieves some small part of Greg with each new painting. And yet, for all of the gemütlichkeit, for all the warmth David Williams feels toward the master, Batke himself seems broken. He has been stranded on the wrong side of history, and now he never leaves the Institute.

65   Night after night, they sit up talking. Batke shows so many little kindnesses, serves food, cakes, wine. One day when David Williams's family comes to visit, he has presents for the children, charms the American's wife.

So how does one quantify the joy he feels when Batke speaks to him as a friend and mentor—as a father really—when Batke tells him that he, David Williams, might be the only artist with the ability to paint like the old man himself, someone to carry on the mythic tradition handed down by Pernkopf? Or how does one share what it meant that last day in Innsbruck, to see Batke come downstairs and step outside for the first time in years, to stand in a downpour of sunlight, just to say good-bye?

Isn't there something to be said for these moments? Aren't they a part of this man and this Book's history, too?

The tanks are rolling, and the people come out of their houses, clutching bouquets to pledge allegiance to their liberators. They throw flowers and sing. After landing at Omaha Beach, the Allied Army sweeps across France, liberating Paris, and breaches the Siegfried Line near Aachen. Hitler flees to his underground bunker and commits suicide with his mistress, Eva Braun, and the Third Reich implodes.

When American troops arrive in Vienna, they arrest Eduard Pernkopf and Franz Batke. Both are removed to prison camps, where they are placed in what is called a de-Nazification program, one in which prisoners are subjected to hard labor and a history lesson in the truth: movies showing the reality of the concentration camps, among other horrors of the war. Pernkopf, who is 57 now, who has lived with visions of grandeur, is lost and broken. Still, he has visitors sneak in his work, at which he continues to toil during his three-year stay.

Meanwhile, at the university, the members of the old regime have been imprisoned or removed, and the school issues a letter to those still-living former Jewish faculty members now scattered about the world, inviting them back. Of hundreds, only one returns, a man named Hans Hoff, whose wartime travels have taken him from New York City to Baghdad. Well regarded before the Anschluss, he is put in charge of the Neurological Institute. When released from prison, Pernkopf is barred from teaching at his own beloved Anatomical Institute but somehow finagles two light-filled rooms under Hoff's roof to finish his Book. The atlas is all he has left—and all that keeps him alive.   70

In these tattered postwar times, with jobs scarce again, he is able to regather his former artists and then add two more. He works his eighteen-hour days, remaining wholly un-sympathetic to those who can't keep up. Among his painters, disillusionment and internecine squabbles are now pandemic. Batke and Lepier represent opposite extremes, the improvisational versus the mathematical, and both work to fill the Book with their own work in order to bring more glory to it.

In 1952, Pernkopf publishes *Der Hals (The Neck),* but time is short. A blood clot in his brain causes a stroke, and he dies on April 17, 1955, before the completion of his last two books. Werner Platzer, who is regarded by many as Pernkopf's scientific son, finishes those.

Despite Pernkopf's long fall from grace, his burial turns out the entire faculty. He is celebrated by fellow professors as a perfectionist, a stirring teacher and the impresario of what many increasingly regard as the world's greatest anatomy book. Some of those present are former Nazis and some are not, but all who have lived through the war now seem to bear their own burdens, secrets and sins, and clearly they regard Pernkopf as one of their own. So they commend him to Heaven.

The Jew, Hans Hoff, is there, too, in a black suit. But what passes through his mind, what he says to himself as Pernkopf is lowered to the grave, is lost now in the ash of all unspoken things. Perhaps to stand there in the first place, on Viennese soil again, he has already begun the difficulty of forgetting. Or perhaps he marks the moment indelibly, unapologetically. Creator, destroyer—let him lie beneath the burnt grass and dying blossoms of his own history now.

75   One day, during the height of the debate over *Pernkopf's Anatomy,* a close acquaintance, a kind Jewish woman, approaches David Williams and says sharply, "Why would you want to be remembered for your association with this book, of all books?" He has no answer. Another time, in England, while giving a lecture at Cambridge on the atlas, he is confused when a Jewish woman breaks down in tears and is helped from the room, pained by how this man, this American, has found beauty in the ugliest of books. What sickness moves inside of him?

And there is more. He receives a letter from a distinguished academic, challenging his paper for its whitewash of history. "Have you not been struck by the fact, Mr. Williams, when visiting cemeteries in small Austrian towns, how many innocent young men lost their lives on the eastern or western front, but these originators of the Nazi mentality survived?" he writes. "As convenient as it seems to be, one cannot separate a man's professional work from his spiritual being."

Meanwhile, an oral surgeon at Columbia Presbyterian Medical Center in New York City, Howard Israel, has referred to *Pernkopf's Anatomy* before every new surgery of his career. When he finds out about its past, he feels deeply betrayed. He researches the Book with another Jewish doctor, William Seidelman, asserting in a medical journal that cadavers from concentration camps may have been used in the making of the atlas. Their evidence: the appearance of roughly shaved heads and circumcised penises. When Williams is asked about this by a reporter from *The Jerusalem Report,* he disputes the fact, saying that when he asked Batke if death-camp cadavers were used in the Book, the old man became enraged and denied it vehemently. Even famed Nazi hunter Simon Wiesenthal examined the records, and his conclusions seem to bolster Williams's side. The two doctors, however, take a dimmer view of Williams as one of the Book's greatest defenders.

Williams is not alone in his view of the Book. Following the publication of his paper, the two most prestigious American medical journals review *Pernkopf's Anatomy* and declare it in "a class of its own" and "a classic among atlases," with illustrations that "are truly works of art." Nonetheless, Williams increasingly feels isolated, doubtful. How could beauty have made him half blind? Is he, as it appears to some, a Nazi apologist? On public radio, he is asked how it feels to be the one benefiting from a Nazi text, and he fumbles for an answer.

He loses friends; he loses sleep; his heart begins to hurt. He meets several times with the local rabbi, who tells him that his sin may be one of perspective. He must imagine the unimaginable when it comes to the Holocaust, must feel the grief of that woman at Cambridge, assuming she may be like so many who lost mothers and fathers, sisters and brothers, children and spouses, in the ovens and dark chambers of places like Dachau, Auschwitz and Buchenwald. How hard could it be to see that, for some, the Book is not a metaphor for beauty or salvation or transfiguration, that it's not the highest expression of what saves David Williams from Muskegon, Michigan, or, in some complicated way, brings Greg back? No, for that woman at Cambridge, the Book is nothing but a dirty crime scene, violated bodies that might include her brethren. The artists are no better than vultures over their carrion. What affliction or hubris has kept that from him?

80   Three heart attacks and several angioplasties later, he is a different man, one who still lies awake at night thinking about the Book, but thinking about it from the point of view of that woman who broke down at Cambridge. He doesn't speak about *Pernkopf's Anatomy* for years, though he follows developments from afar. Under pressure, the University of Vienna launches and concludes an investigation into *Pernkopf's Anatomy,* claiming, in November 1998, that circumstantial evidence suggests Jewish cadavers were probably not used in the making of the atlas. Reviewing the hundreds of pages of findings, Williams is left unconvinced, believes the university administration has obscured the results to protect its reputation.

From some primordial haze slowly comes recognition. It is the spring of 2002, and in West Lafayette he now prepares to return to Vienna, to Munich. He packs his bags, and when he is briefly overcome with doubt, his wife says, "You are *Pernkopf's Anatomy*. A big part of that Book is who you are." So he travels eight hours in coach, through spasms of lightning. But this time he arrives aggrieved, angry, skeptical, confused, searching for truth—more, perhaps, as a Jew would. He has come to avenge the naïveté of his younger self and to make his final good-byes to the paintings, for he is sure he will never see them again in this lifetime, nor perhaps ever have the desire.

In bright sun, beneath a heavy roof, the Institute occupies half a city block along the trolley routes and shops of Ringstrasse. The first time he came to Vienna, the weather was bad—rain, thick clouds rolling over themselves—and somehow the city seemed cold, less receiving, left him empty and alone. This time he feels more resolute. Somewhere in the locked rooms and forgotten closets, among the thousand cadavers used by a new generation of anatomy students, he hopes, is a more clear answer to the past.

He meets with professor after professor. He is unfailingly polite, phrases sensitive declarations of fact as questions in his midwestern lilt. A few he meets are defensive; most, quite the opposite. A gentle old man, a former president of the university who knew Pernkopf, serves him tea and cakes. Later, he finds out that the old man was an SS officer. Many records, including those of the identities of a number of cadavers, were destroyed by those American bombs that brought down half the Institute. Others were tampered with by those looking to obscure their crimes, so exactness is elusive. Rather than thinking there's a cover-up here, David Williams begins to feel pity for these people, relentlessly driven back to an increasingly untraceable past.

One professor leads him through the Institute on a tour: They stand on the spot where guillotined bodies once were piled in ten-foot-high drifts and taken down for Eduard Pernkopf's use by pitchfork. They stand in the hemicycle, where Pernkopf headily praised Hitler and called on his colleagues to lead a new age of medical experimentation, a period that would come to include the sterilization of the retarded and the euthanasia of nearly 800 defective children. They go to the basement of the Institute, a dark, dank, spooky place, to look upon the formaldehyde pools that once held Pernkopf's cadavers. An attendant opens the lid on one of the pools, activates a hydraulic lift, and suddenly several bodies, bloated and pale, each one donated for use in the school today, appear from the depths on metal trays.

85   Somehow, on his last visit he failed to mark all these spots, or perhaps unconsciously didn't entirely want to or feel he needed to. Now he does, shaking his head, grimacing.

Finally, he dines with a young historian, Daniela Angetter, the woman charged with investigating much of the University of Vienna's Nazi legacy. Her world is one of chilling medical experiments and severed heads, and she wears her work with a gaunt hauntedness and weary eyes. Allergic to protein and lactose, she eats potato chips at dinner while her husband, a plumber, eats blood sausage. "This has been horrible for me, to see dead bodies," she says. "I'm a historian, and to think that people were executed because they were starving and stole a pig and ate it. Would I have been strong enough to stand up? If you didn't conform to the party, you were executed. I've stayed awake many nights thinking about these things."

Sitting there, moved by this young woman, believing her, David Williams comes to realize this: All these people are run down by ghosts, too. He is not alone in his confusion. After illustrious postwar careers, former

SS officers serve afternoon tea; a new generation born thirty years after the war pores over the past, making amends for its grandparents. Even now, on a sunny spring day in 2002, on the eve of the anniversary marking fifty-seven years since the fall of Nazi Germany, students carry urns bearing the last discovered remains of victims at the university during Pernkopf's reign; the government calls for calm in the streets of Austria's capital, deploying 1,500 police officers to ensure that neo-Nazi demonstrators don't rampage in the Heldenplatz, the square where Hitler addressed hundreds of thousands of euphoric Austrians in 1938.

Here is an entire country living the events of the war over and over and over again. Later, in Munich, Williams spends an afternoon with his friend Michael Urban, the erudite 63-year-old grandson of Eduard Urban, the man who first struck a deal in 1933 with Pernkopf to publish his atlas. Having inherited his grandfather's company, Urban sold it to a company that decided to cease publication of the Book. He believes it to be a troubled masterpiece, one that should continue in print with a foreword detailing the most harrowing events of its creation. Now, while the German quietly listens, the American attempts to put into words something that has troubled him, continues to trouble him on this trip: He wonders if, by being friends with Franz Batke, by seeing the magnificence in *Pernkopf's Anatomy,* he is doomed. And yet he feels that to reject both fully is a sin of its own: betrayal.

"David, there's nothing wrong with you," says Urban. "We are moving on two planes: the principal, everyday plane and then one made up of these overwhelming feelings and emotions. When we try to talk about this, we move into a wordless dimension." Here he pauses, runs a tapered finger over his furrowed brow, smiles weakly. "My father was at one of these mass rallies, the Goebbels speech at the Sports Palace in 1943, and he said his arm was up in a Nazi salute before he knew what he was doing. It was hysteria. It's inconceivable what people did to one another during the war. But you must remember: People endure."

90   The next day, he goes to see the original paintings. He is wary, excited and nervous. Urban has arranged for the paintings to be delivered to the downtown offices of the publishing house. And he has also arranged for Werner Platzer, the man who finished the atlas after Pernkopf's death, to come to Munich to lead Williams through nineteen oversize black binders stuffed with 800 original pieces of art.

Platzer operates three cups of coffee ahead of the world. He doesn't eat; he doesn't pee. He just sits with the paintings, providing long discourses on each. And Williams sits with him, a student again, savoring every moment, but this time questioning too. He asks Platzer why he thinks the Book is out of print, and Platzer shakes his head, incensed. "It's too good," he says. "The Book is too good." When Williams paints to a painting that many feel is that of a Jewish cadaver with a shaved head, Platzer explodes. "What does a Jew look like?" he says. "Tell me. It is absurd. I wish you Americans ate what we ate then: nothing. Three days a week, I might not eat. I looked like this man here. Absolute nonsense."

Williams sits before him, unblinking, and presses his concerns. He believes the swastikas and SS symbols have been removed from some of the originals, as they were removed from subsequent printings of the Book, so a laborious hour is spent trying to locate the paintings in question. In the end, he discovers the symbols have been erased, and he seems troubled, angry.

And yet, when he comes upon a Batke painting of the inner ear, he holds it up and stares for a long time. "It's just so alive," he says softly, passing a hand lightly over it.

When he sees another, of the chest, he says, "I'd give anything to have that hanging on my wall." The two men look at the Lepiers and Dietzes, Endtressers and Schrotts. They marvel at the near psychedelic colors and intricate brushwork. With each painting—with each proliferation of arteries, with each gravityless organ—the body becomes that exalted place again.

The viewing takes seven hours, and in the end he feels it all over and over: joy, curiosity, shame, awe. In person, in full color, the paintings still shimmer and mesmerize. They still emanate.

But this time in their presence, he is not 95 exactly euphoric. If he feels a deep sense of fulfillment in seeing these paintings one last time, he also feels a strange sadness. When it is over, when the sun dips below a building and a streetlight blinks on in the window, he is almost trembling. He pulls out a handkerchief, removes his glasses and wipes his face. His hair is slightly disheveled. He exhales, looks once at the oversize binders against the wall, presses his lips tightly together and then turns his back and leaves the room.

The old man sits and smokes, a bottle of beer set before him. He has a crooked nose and a skewed chin. Night pours through the windows of his cell. Sitting across from him is the American, fellow exile and good friend now, who has remembered him, who has made a pilgrimage to record a way of painting that will be forever lost with his death. It is 1980, and they have spent months together now, eating, drinking, laughing. There is so little time. Though they don't speak fluently to each other, they have formed a bond through painting. And now they are a little drunk, and their conversation veers from art to the war.

The old man suddenly rises and disappears for a moment, then returns with a small cardboard box that makes a jingling sound. It is dust covered and full of medals, including an Iron Cross he won for valor on the Russian front, where he was shot in the groin. He passes the medal to the American, who feels its weight in his hand, turns it in the light, admires it. The old man, who trusts the young man now, who is being a little vain and showy, sad and funny, mentions that he is still proud to have worn his Brown Shirt uniform. He says the Americans blew it, joining the war on the wrong side, and accuses the Jews of forcing the Americans to enter the war against the Germans rather than with them. He chides his guest for this. He describes his imprisonment and his days being de-Nazified. And David Williams, the American professor, listens, nods and later writes in his journal. "The evening seems like a dream to me . . . perhaps it's the beer. This man who I have admired for so long—I should say his work—there is no doubt in my mind that as a painter he is a *genius*!!—this man reveals himself as a common Nazi, a Jew hater, a Brown Shirt. . . . Is it possible that all makers of great works of art are ultimately exposed as thus?"

And ever after, he will wonder: Who is this old man, this last living vestige of the Book? And what secret has he found after his life as a vulture at the side of carrion? It appears there is no secret. The Nazis have lost, and he is dying on the wrong side of history. The mouth is made for food, the penis for the vagina, the heart made to beat. Until it simply ceases. Death is no salvation. The only thing left is to paint.

On the wall above David Williams's desk at home today in Indiana hangs a painting by Franz Batke, near an old portrait of Eduard Pernkopf. Sometimes, at the end of the day, after mowing the lawn, he spends a minute gazing at them. But if asked why the pictures are there, David Williams shakes his head; he can't say why. But he doesn't take them down.

READING AND THINKING

1. Why does Paterniti frame this complex tale with a story about the proximity of death? What does that hint of death in the beginning have to do with the "Book," capital B?

2. The body of the essay begins years earlier in 1957. Who is the man who "sits and smokes" and then paints in a frenzy?

3. Who, in the next scene, is David Williams? Why does Paterniti place the two men side-by-side using the language that he does to describe them?

4. The next scene introduces the third character in this drama, the man responsible for the Book. Why does Paterniti place Williams between these two men?

5. How would you characterize Williams's relationship with Batke?

THINKING AND WRITING

1. How much does Paterniti reveal about his "sin" in the essay's lengthy beginning? What does Paterniti gain by invoking sin in that context? Explain, citing evidence from the beginning.

2. What is the "glint of self-recognition" that Williams finds in *Pernkopf's Anatomy* the first time he looks into its pages? Explain the significance of the moment of recognition. Might it have something to do with the "sin"? Explain.

3. When Paterniti begins one section of his essay, "The book is blindingly beautiful," he himself becomes a medical illustrator. Explain how, in that section, he repaints the paintings for us with language.

4. Explain how Williams's life's work is colored by his association with Batke. Assess the value and the costs of working with Batke.

5. Should *Pernkopf's Anatomy* be in wide use now, republished to reveal once again its beauty—republished to save lives? Explain in a brief essay.

Walker Percy (1916–1990)

Walker Percy was a physician before he became a writer. His first novel, *The Moviegoer,* won the National Book Award for fiction in 1962. His other novels include *Love in the Ruins* and *The Thanatos Syndrome.* He also published two books of essays. "The Loss of the Creature" comes from the first of those books, *The Message in the Bottle: How Queer Man Is, How Queer Language Is, and What One Has to Do with the Other.* The title suggests Percy's lingering preoccupation with language.

THE LOSS OF THE CREATURE

In "The Loss of the Creature," Walker Percy's discussion of language is often intertwined with his discussion of perception. As you read the essay, try to keep separate the places where he discusses language, per se, and those places where he discusses the role of language in perception. A subtle essay, "The Loss of the Creature" is lengthy as well, but rewarding in its insights. After you have read the essay, you may find yourself encountering creatures lost and found in your everyday life.

1   Every explorer names his island Formosa, beautiful. To him it is beautiful because, being first, he has access to it and can see it for what it is. But to no one else is it ever as beautiful—except the rare man who manages to recover it, who knows that it has to be recovered.

Garcia López de Cárdenas discovered the Grand Canyon and was amazed at the sight. It can be imagined: One crosses miles of desert, breaks through the mesquite, and there it is at one's feet. Later the government set the place aside as a national park, hoping to pass along to millions the experience of Cárdenas. Does not one see the same sight from the Bright Angel Lodge that Cárdenas saw?

The assumption is that the Grand Canyon is a remarkably interesting and beautiful place and that if it had a certain value P for Cárdenas, the same value P may be transmitted to any number of sightseers—just as Banting's discovery of insulin can be transmitted to any number of diabetics. A counterinfluence is at work, however, and it would be nearer the truth to say that if the place is seen by a million sightseers, a single sightseer does not receive the value P but a millionth part of value P.

It is assumed that since the Grand Canyon has the fixed interest value P, tours can be organized for any number of people. A man in Boston decides to spend his vacation at the Grand Canyon. He visits his travel bureau, looks at the folder, signs up for a two-week tour. He and his family take the tour, see the Grand Canyon, and return to Boston. May we say that this man has seen the Grand Canyon? Possibly he has. But it is more likely that what he has done is the one sure way not to see the canyon.

Why is it almost impossible to gaze directly at the Grand Canyon under these circumstances and see it for what it is—as one picks up a strange object from one's back yard and gazes directly at it? It is almost impossible because the Grand Canyon, the thing as it is, has been appropriated by the symbolic complex which has already been formed in the sightseer's mind. Seeing the canyon under approved circumstances is seeing the symbolic complex head on. The thing is no longer the thing as it confronted the Spaniard; it is rather that which has already been formulated—by picture postcard, geography book, tourist folders, and the words *Grand Canyon.* As a result of this preformulation, the source of the sightseer's pleasure undergoes a shift. Where the wonder and delight of the Spaniard arose from his penetration of the thing itself, from a progressive discovery of depths, patterns, colors, shadows, etc., now the sightseer measures his satisfaction *by the degree to which the canyon conforms to the preformed complex*. If it does so, if it looks just like the postcard, he is pleased; he might even say, "Why it is every bit as beautiful as a picture postcard!" He feels he has not been cheated. But if it does not conform, if the colors are somber, he will not be able to see it directly; he will only be conscious of the disparity between what it is and what it is supposed to be. He will say later that he was unlucky in not being there at the right time. The highest point, the term of the sightseer's satisfaction, is not the sovereign discovery of the thing before him; it is rather the measuring up of the thing to the criterion of the preformed symbolic complex.

Seeing the canyon is made even more difficult by what the sightseer does when the moment arrives, when sovereign knower confronts the thing to be known. Instead of looking at it, he photographs it. There is no confrontation at all. At the end of forty years of preformulation and with the Grand Canyon yawning at his feet, what does he do? He waives his right of seeing and knowing and records symbols for the next forty years. For him there is no present; there is only the past of what has been formulated and seen and the future of what has been formulated and not seen. The present is surrendered to the past and the future.

The sightseer may be aware that something is wrong. He may simply be bored; or he may be conscious of the difficulty: that the great thing yawning at his feet somehow eludes him. The harder he looks at it, the less he can see. It eludes everybody. The tourist cannot see it; the bellboy at the Bright Angel Lodge cannot see it: for him it is only one side of the space he lives in, like one wall of a room; to the ranger it is a tissue of everyday signs relevant to his own prospects—the blue haze down there means that he will probably get rained on during the donkey ride.

How can the sightseer recover the Grand Canyon? He can recover it in any number of ways, all sharing in common the stratagem of avoiding the approved confrontation of the tour and the Park Service.

It may be recovered by leaving the beaten track. The tourist leaves the tour, camps in the back country. He arises before dawn and approaches the South Rim through a wild terrain where there are no trails and no railed-in lookout points. In other words, he sees the canyon by avoiding all the facilities for seeing the canyon. If the benevolent Park Service hears about this fellow and thinks he has a good idea and places the following notice in the Bright Angel Lodge: *Consult ranger for information on getting off the beaten track*—the end result will only be the closing of another access to the canyon.

It may be recovered by a dialectical movement which brings one back to the beaten track but at a level above it. For example, after a lifetime of avoiding the beaten track and guided tours, a man may deliberately seek out the most beaten track of all, the most commonplace tour imaginable: he may visit the canyon by a Greyhound tour in the company of a party from Terre Haute—just as a man who has lived in New York all his life may visit the Statue of Liberty. (Such dialectical savorings of the familiar as the familiar are, of course, a favorite stratagem of *The New Yorker* magazine.) The thing is recovered from familiarity by means of an exercise in familiarity. Our complex friend stands behind his fellow tourists at the Bright Angel Lodge and sees the canyon through them and their predicament, their picture taking and busy disregard. In a sense, he exploits his fellow tourists; he stands on their shoulders to see the canyon.

Such a man is far more advanced in the dialectic than the sightseer who is trying to

10

get off the beaten track—getting up at dawn and approaching the canyon through the mesquite. This stratagem is, in fact, for our complex man the weariest, most beaten track of all.

It may be recovered as a consequence of a breakdown of the symbolic machinery by which the experts present the experience to the consumer. A family visits the canyon in the usual way. But shortly after their arrival, the park is closed by an outbreak of typhus in the south. They have the canyon to themselves. What do they mean when they tell the home folks of their good luck: "We had the whole place to ourselves"? How does one see the thing better when the others are absent? Is looking like sucking: the more lookers, the less there is to see? They could hardly answer, but by saying this they testify to a state of affairs which is considerably more complex than the simple statement of the schoolbook about the Spaniard and the millions who followed him. It is a state in which there is a complex distribution of sovereignty, of zoning.

It may be recovered in a time of national disaster. The Bright Angel Lodge is converted into a rest home, a function that has nothing to do with the canyon a few yards away. A wounded man is brought in. He regains consciousness; there outside his window is the canyon.

The most extreme case of access by privilege conferred by disaster is the Huxleyan novel of the adventures of the surviving remnant after the great wars of the twentieth century. An expedition from Australia lands in Southern California and heads east. They stumble across the Bright Angel Lodge, now fallen into ruins. The trails are grown over, the guard rails fallen away, the dime telescope at Battleship Point rusted. But there is the canyon, exposed at last. Exposed by what? By the decay of those facilities which were designed to help the sightseer.

15   This dialectic of sightseeing cannot be taken into account by planners, for the object of the dialectic is nothing other than the subversion of the efforts of the planners.

The dialectic is not known to objective theorists, psychologists, and the like. Yet it is quite well known in the fantasy-consciousness of the popular arts. The devices by which the museum exhibit, the Grand Canyon, the ordinary thing, is recovered have long since been stumbled upon. A movie shows a man visiting the Grand Canyon. But the movie maker knows something the planner does not know. He knows that one cannot take the sight frontally. The canyon must be approached by the stratagems we have mentioned: the Inside Track, the Familiar Revisited, the Accidental Encounter. Who is the stranger at the Bright Angel Lodge? Is he the ordinary tourist from Terre Haute that he makes himself out to be? He is not. He has another objective in mind, to revenge his wronged brother, counterespionage, etc. By virtue of the fact that he has other fish to fry, he may take a stroll along the rim after supper and then we can see the canyon through him. The movie accomplishes its purpose by concealing it. Overtly the characters (the American family marooned by typhus) and we the onlookers experience pity for the sufferers, and the family experience anxiety for themselves; covertly and in truth they are the happiest of people and we are happy for them through them, for we have the canyon to ourselves. The movie cashes in on the recovery of sovereignty through disaster. Not only is the canyon now accessible to the remnant: the members of the remnant are now accessible to each other, a whole new ensemble of relations becomes possible—friendship, love, hatred, clandestine sexual adventures. In a movie when a man sits next to a woman on a bus, it is necessary either that the bus break down or that the woman lose her memory. (The question occurs to one: Do you imagine there are sightseers who see sights just as they are supposed to? A family who live in Terre Haute, who decide to take the canyon tour, who go there, see it, enjoy it immensely, and go home content? A family who are entirely innocent of all the barriers, zones, losses of sovereignty I have been talking about? Wouldn't most people be sorry if Battleship Point fell into the canyon, carrying all one's fellow passengers to their death, leaving one alone on the South Rim? I cannot answer this. Perhaps there are such people. Certainly a great many American families would swear they had no such problems, that they came, saw, and went away happy. Yet it is just these families who would be happiest if they had gotten the Inside Track and been among the surviving remnant.)

It is now apparent that as between the many measures which may be taken to overcome the opacity, the boredom, of the direct confrontation of the thing or creature in its citadel of symbolic investiture, some are less authentic than others. That is to say, some stratagems obviously serve other purposes than that of providing access to being—for example, various unconscious motivations which it is not necessary to go into here.

Let us take an example in which the recovery of being is ambiguous, where it may under the same circumstances contain both authentic and unauthentic components. An American couple, we will say, drives down into Mexico. They see the usual sights and have a fair time of it. Yet they are never without the sense of missing something. Although Taxco and Cuernavaca are interesting and picturesque as advertised, they fall short of "it." What do they couple have in mind by "it"? What do they really hope for? What sort of experience could they have in Mexico so that upon their return, they would feel that "it" had happened? We have a clue: Their hope has something to do with their own role as tourists in a foreign country and the way in which they conceive this role. It has something to do with other American tourists. Certainly they feel that they are very far from "it" when, after traveling five thousand miles,

they arrive at the plaza in Guanajuato only to find themselves surrounded by a dozen other couples from the Midwest.

Already we may distinguish authentic and unauthentic elements. First, we see the problem the couple faces and we understand their efforts to surmount it. The problem is to find an "unspoiled" place. "Unspoiled" does not mean only that a place is left physically intact; it means also that it is not encrusted by renown and by the familiar (as in Taxco), that it has not been discovered by others. We understand that the couple really want to get at the place and enjoy it. Yet at the same time we wonder if there is not something wrong in their dislike of their compatriots. Does access to the place require the exclusion of others?

Let us see what happens.   20

The couple decide to drive from Guanajuato to Mexico City. On the way they get lost. After hours on a rocky mountain road, they find themselves in a tiny valley not even marked on the map. There they discover an Indian village. Some sort of religious festival is going on. It is apparently a corn dance in supplication of the rain god.

The couple know at once that this is "it." They are entranced. They spend several days in the village, observing the Indians and being themselves observed with friendly curiosity.

Now may we not say that the sightseers have at last come face to face with an authentic sight, a sight which is charming, quaint, picturesque, unspoiled, and that they see the sight and come away rewarded? Possibly this may occur. Yet it is more likely that what happens is a far cry indeed from an immediate encounter with being, that the experience, while masquerading as such, is in truth a rather desperate impersonation. I use the word *desperate* advisedly to signify an actual loss of hope.

The clue to the spuriousness of their enjoyment of the village and the festival is a certain restiveness in the sightseers themselves. It is given expression by their repeated exclamations that "this is too good to be true," and by their anxiety that it may not prove to be so perfect, and finally by their downright relief at leaving the valley and having the experience in the bag, so to speak—that is, safely embalmed in memory and movie film.

25   What is the source of their anxiety during the visit? Does it not mean that the couple are looking at the place with a certain standard of performance in mind? Are they like Fabre, who gazed at the world about him with wonder, letting it be what it is; or are they not like the overanxious mother who sees her child as one performing, now doing badly, now doing well? The village is their child and their love for it is an anxious love because they are afraid that at any moment it might fail them.

We have another clue in their subsequent remark to an ethnologist friend. "How we wished you had been there with us! What a perfect goldmine of folkways! Every minute we would say to each other, if only you were here! You must return with us." This surely testifies to a generosity of spirit, a willingness to share their experience with others, not at all like their feelings toward their fellow Iowans on the plaza at Guanajuato!

I am afraid this is not the case at all. It is true that they longed for their ethnologist friend, but it was for an entirely different reason. They wanted him, not to share the experience, but to certify their experience as genuine.

"This is it" and "Now we are really living" do not necessarily refer to the sovereign encounter of the person with the sight that enlivens the mind and gladdens the heart. It means that now at last we are having the acceptable experience. The present experience is always measured by a prototype, the "it" of their dreams. "Now I am really living" means that now I am filling the role of sightseer and the sight is living up to the prototype of sights. The quaint and picturesque village is measured by a Platonic ideal of the Quaint and Picturesque.

Hence their anxiety during the encounter. For at any minute something could go wrong. A fellow Iowan might emerge from a 'dobe hut; the chief might show them his Sears catalog. (If the failures are "wrong" enough, as these are, they might still be turned to account as rueful conversation pieces. "There we were expecting the chief to bring us a churinga and he shows up with a Sears catalog!") They have snatched victory from disaster, but their experience always runs the danger of failure.

30   They need the ethnologist to certify their experience as genuine. This is borne out by their behavior when the three of them return for the next corn dance. During the dance, the couple do not watch the goings-on; instead they watch the ethnologist! Their highest hope is that their friend should find the dance interesting. And if he should show signs of true absorption, an interest in the goings-on so powerful that he becomes oblivious to his friends—then their cup is full. "Didn't we tell you?" they say at last. What they want from him is not ethnological explanations; all they want is his approval.

What has taken place is a radical loss of sovereignty over that which is as much theirs as it is the ethnologist's. The fault does not lie with the ethnologist. He has no wish to stake a claim to the village; in fact, he desires the opposite: he will bore his friends to death by telling them about the village and the meaning of the folkways. A degree of sovereignty has been surrendered by the couple. It is the nature of the loss, moreover, that they are not aware of the loss, beyond a certain uneasiness. (Even if they read this and admitted it, it would be very difficult for them to bridge the gap in their confrontation of the world. Their consciousness, so that with the onset of the first direct enjoyment, their higher consciousness pounces and certifies: "Now you are doing it! Now you are really living!" and, in certifying the experience, sets it at nought.)

Their basic placement in the world is such that they recognize a priority of title of the expert over his particular department of being. The whole horizon of being staked out by "them," the experts. The highest satisfaction of the sightseer (not merely the tourist but any layman seer of sights) is that his sight should be certified as genuine. The worst of this impoverishment is that there is no sense of impoverishment. The surrender of title is so complete that it never even occurs to one to reassert title. A poor man may envy the rich man, but the sightseer does not envy the expert. It is due altogether to the eager surrender of sovereignty by the layman so that he may take up the role not of the person but of the consumer.

I do not refer only to the special relation of layman to theorist. I refer to the general situation in which sovereignty is surrendered to a class of privileged knowers, whether these be theorists or artists. A reader may surrender sovereignty over that which has been written about, just as a consumer may surrender sovereignty over a thing which has been theorized about. The consumer is content to receive an experience just as it has been presented to him by theorists and planners. The reader may also be content to judge life by whether it has or has not been formulated by those who know and write about life. A young man goes to France. He too has a fair time of it, sees the sights, enjoys the food. On his last day, in fact as he sits in a restaurant in Le Havre waiting for his boat, something happens. A group of French students in the restaurant get into an impassioned argument over a recent play. A riot takes place. Madame le concierge joins in, swinging her mop at the rioters. Our young American is transported. This is "it." And he had almost left France without seeing "it"!

But the young man's delight is ambiguous. On the one hand, it is a pleasure for him to encounter the same Gallic temperament he had heard about from Puccini and Rolland. But on the other hand, the source of his pleasure testifies to a certain alienation. For the young man is actually barred from a direct encounter with anything French excepting only that which has been set forth, authenticated by Puccini and Rolland—those who know. If he had encountered the restaurant scene without reading Hemingway, without knowing that the performance was so typically, charmingly French, he would not have been delighted. He would only have been anxious at seeing those things get so out of hand. The source of his delight is the sanction of those who know.

This loss of sovereignty is not a marginal process, as might appear from my example of estranged sightseers. It is a generalized surrender of the horizon to those experts within whose competence a particular segment of the horizon is thought to lie. Kwakuitls are surrendered to Franz Boas; decaying Southern mansions are surrendered to Faulkner and Tennessee Williams. So that, although it is by no means the intention of the expert to expropriate sovereignty—in fact he would not even know what sovereignty meant in this context—the danger of theory and consumption is a seduction and deprivation of the consumer.

In the New Mexico desert, natives occasionally come across strange-looking artifacts which have fallen from the skies and which are stenciled: *Return to U.S. Experimental Project, Alamogordo. Reward.* The finder returns the object and is rewarded. He knows nothing of the nature of the object he has found and does not care to know. The sole role of the native, the highest role he can play, is that of finder and returner of the mysterious equipment.

The same is true of the laymen's relation to *natural* objects in the modern technical society. No matter what the object or event is, whether it is a star, a swallow, a Kwakuitl, a "psychological phenomenon," the layman who confronts it does not confront it as a sovereign person, as Crusoe confronts a seashell he finds on the beach. The highest role he can conceive himself as playing is to be able to recognize the title of the object, to return it to the appropriate expert and have it certified as a genuine find. He does not even permit himself to see the thing—as Gerard Hopkins could see a rock or a cloud or a field. If anyone asks him why he doesn't look, he may reply that he didn't take that subject in college (or he hasn't read Faulkner).

This loss of sovereignty extends even to oneself. There is the neurotic who asks nothing more of his doctor than that his symptoms should prove interesting. When all else fails, the poor fellow has nothing to offer but his own neurosis. But even this is sufficient if only the doctor will show interest when he says, "Last night I had a curious sort of dream; perhaps it will be significant to one who knows about such things. It seems I was standing in a sort of alley—" (I have nothing else to offer you but my own unhappiness. Please say that it, at least, measures up, that it is a *proper* sort of unhappiness.)

II

A young Falkland Islander walking along a beach and spying a dead dogfish and going to work on it with his jackknife has, in a fashion wholly unprovided in modern educational theory, a great advantage over the Scarsdale high-school pupil who finds the dogfish on his laboratory desk. Similarly the citizen of Huxley's *Brave New World* who stumbles across a volume of Shakespeare in some vine-grown ruins and squats on a potsherd to read it is in a fairer way of getting at a sonnet than the Harvard sophomore taking English Poetry II.

40   The educator whose business it is to teach students biology or poetry is unaware of a whole ensemble of relations which exist between the student and the dogfish and between the student and the Shakespeare sonnet. To put it bluntly: A student who has the desire to get at a dogfish or a Shakespeare sonnet may have the greatest difficulty in salvaging the creature itself from the educational package in which it is presented. The great difficulty is that he is not aware that there is a difficulty; surely, he thinks, in such a fine classroom, with such a fine textbook, the sonnet must come across! What's wrong with me?

The sonnet and the dogfish are obscured by the two different processes. The sonnet is obscured by the symbolic package which is formulated not by the sonnet itself but by the media through which the sonnet is transmitted, the media which the educators believe for some reason to be transparent. The new textbook, the type, the smell of the page, the classroom, the aluminum windows and the winter sky, the personality of Miss Hawkins—these media which are supposed to transmit the sonnet may only succeed in transmitting themselves. It is only the hardiest and cleverest of students who can salvage the sonnet from this many-tissued package. It is only the rarest student who knows that the sonnet must be salvaged from the package. (The educator is well aware that something is wrong, that there is a fatal gap between the student's learning and the student's life: the student reads the poem, appears to understand it, and gives all the answers. But what does he recall if he should happen to read a Shakespeare sonnet twenty years later? Does he recall the poem or does he recall the smell of the page and the smell of Miss Hawkins?)

One might object, pointing out that Huxley's citizen reading his sonnet in the ruins and the Falkland Islander looking at his dogfish on the beach also receive them in a certain package. Yes, but the difference lies in the fundamental placement of the student in the world, a placement which makes it possible to extract the thing from the package. The pupil at Scarsdale High sees himself placed as a consumer receiving an experience-package; but the Falkland Islander exploring his dogfish is a person exercising the sovereign right of a person in his lordship and mastery of creation. He too could use an instructor and a book and a technique, but he would use them as his subordinates, just as he uses his jackknife. The biology student does not use his scalpel as an instrument, he uses it as a magic wand! Since it is a "scientific instrument," it should do "scientific things."

The dogfish is concealed in the same symbolic package as the sonnet. But the dogfish suffers an additional loss. As a consequence of this double deprivation, the Sarah Lawrence student who scores A in zoology is apt to know very little about a dogfish. She is twice removed from the dogfish, once by the symbolic complex by which the dogfish is concealed, once again by the spoliation of the dogfish by theory which renders it invisible. Through no fault of zoology instructors, it is nevertheless a fact that the zoology laboratory at Sarah Lawrence College is one of the few places in the world where it is all but impossible to see a dogfish.

The dogfish, the tree, the seashell, the American Negro, the dream, are rendered invisible by a shift of reality from concrete thing to theory which Whitehead has called the fallacy of misplaced concreteness. It is the mistaking of an idea, a principle, an abstraction, for the real. As a consequence of the shift, the "specimen" is seen as less real than the theory of the specimen. As Kierkegaard said, once a person is seen as a specimen of a race or a species, at that very moment he ceases to be an individual. Then there are no more individuals but only specimens.

45   To illustrate: A student enters a laboratory which, in the pragmatic view, offers the students the optimum conditions under which an educational experience may be had. In the existential view, however—that view of the student in which he is regarded not as a receptacle of experience but as a knowing being whose peculiar property it is to see himself as being in a certain situation—the modern laboratory could not have been more effectively designed to conceal the dogfish forever.

The student comes to his desk. On it, neatly arranged by his instructor, he finds his laboratory manual, a dissecting board, instruments, and a mimeographed list:

Exercise 22: Materials
   1 dissecting board
   1 scalpel
   1 forceps
   1 probe
   1 bottle india ink and syringe
   1 specimen of *Squalus acanthias*

The clue of the situation in which the student finds himself is to be found in the last item: 1 specimen of *Squalus acanthias*.

The phrase *specimen of* expresses in the most succinct way imaginable the radical character of the loss of being which has occurred under his very nose. To refer to the dogfish, the unique concrete existence before him, as a "specimen of *Squalus acanthias*" reveals by its grammar the spoliation of the dogfish by the theoretical method. This phrase, *specimen of,* example of, instance of, indicates the ontological status of the individual creature in the eyes of the theorist. The dogfish itself is seen as a rather shabby expression on an ideal reality, the species *Squalus acanthias*. The result is the radical devaluation of the individual dogfish. (The *reductio ad absurdum* of Whitehead's shift is Toynbee's employment of it in his historical method. If a gram of NaCl is referred to by the chemist as a "sample of" NaCl, one may think of it as such and not much is missed by the oversight of the act of being of this particular pinch of salt, but when the Jews and the Jewish religion are understood as—in Toynbee's favorite phrase—a "classical example of" such and such a kind of *Voelkerwanderung,* we begin to suspect that something is being left out.)

If we look into the ways in which the student can recover the dogfish (or the sonnet), we will see that they have in common the stratagem of avoiding the educator's direct presentation of the object as a lesson to be learned and restoring access to sonnet and dogfish as being to be known, reasserting the sovereignty of knower over known.   50

In truth, the biography of scientists and poets is usually the story of the discovery of the indirect approach, the circumvention of the educator's presentation—the young man who was sent to the *Technikum* and on his way fell into the habit of loitering in book stores and reading poetry; or the young man dutifully attending law school who on the way became curious about the comings and goings of ants. One remembers the scene in *The Heart Is a Lonely Hunter* where the girl hides in the bushes to hear the Capehart in the big house play Beethoven. Perhaps she was the lucky one after all. Think of the unhappy souls inside, who see the record, worry about scratches, and most of all worry about whether they are *getting it,* whether they are bona fide music lovers. What is the best way to hear Beethoven: sitting in a proper silence around the Capehart or eavesdropping from an azalea bush?

However it may come about, we notice two traits of the second situation: (1) an openness of the thing before one—instead of being an exercise to be learned according to an approved mode, it is a garden of delights which beckons to one; (2) a sovereignty of the knower—instead of being a consumer of a prepared experience, I am a sovereign wayfarer, a wanderer in the neighborhood of being who stumbles into the garden.

One can think of two sorts of circumstances through which the thing may be restored to the person. (There is always, of course, the direct recovery: A student may simply be strong enough, brave enough, clever enough to take the dogfish and the sonnet by storm, to wrest control of it from the educators and the educational package.) First by ordeal: The Bomb falls; when the young man recovers consciousness in the shambles of the biology laboratory, there not ten inches from his nose lies the dogfish. Now all at once he can see it directly without let, just as the exile or the prisoner or the sick man sees the sparrow at his window in all its inexhaustibility; just as the commuter who has had a heart attack sees his own hand for the first time. In these cases, the simulacrum of everydayness and of consumption has been destroyed by disaster; in the case of the bomb,

literally destroyed. Secondly, by apprenticeship to a great man: one day a great biologist walks into the laboratory; he stops in front of our student's desk; he leans over, picks up the dogfish, and, ignoring instruments and procedure, probes with a broken fingernail into the little carcass. "Now here is a curious business," he says, ignoring also the proper jargon of the speciality. "Look here how this little duct reverses its direction and drops into the pelvis. Now if you would look into a coelacanth, you would see that it—"And all at once the student can see. The technician and the sophomore who loves his textbooks are always offended by the genuine research man because the latter is usually a little vague and always humble before the thing; he doesn't have much use for the equipment or the jargon. Whereas the technician is never vague and never humble before the thing; he holds the thing disposed of by the principle, the formula, the textbook outline; and he thinks a great deal of equipment and jargon.

But since neither of these methods of recovering the dogfish is pedagogically feasible—perhaps the great man even less so than the Bomb—I wish to propose the following educational technique which should prove equally effective for Harvard and Shreveport High School. I propose that English poetry and biology should be taught as usual, but that at irregular intervals, poetry students should find dogfishes on their desks and biology students should find Shakespeare sonnets on their dissection boards. I am serious in declaring that a Sarah Lawrence English major who began poking about in a dogfish with a bobby pin would learn more in thirty minutes than a biology major in a whole semester; and that the latter upon reading on her dissecting board

That time of year Thou may'st in me behold
When yellow leaves, or none, or few, do hang
Upon those boughs which shake against the cold—
Bare ruin'd choirs where late the sweet birds sang

might catch fire at the beauty of it.

55   The situation of the tourist at the Grand Canyon and the biology student are special cases of a predicament in which everyone finds himself in a modern technical society—a society, that is, in which there is a division between expert and layman, planner and consumer, in which experts and planners take special measures to teach and edify the consumer. The measures taken are measures appropriate to the consumer: the expert and the planner *know* and *plan,* but the consumer *needs* and *experiences.*

There is a double deprivation. First, the thing is lost through its packaging. The very means by which the thing is presented for consumption, the very techniques by which the thing is made available as an item of need-satisfaction, these very means operate to remove the thing from the sovereignty of the knower. A loss of title occurs. The measures which the museum curator takes the present the thing to the public are self-liquidating. The upshot of the curator's efforts are not that everyone can see the exhibit but that no one can see it. The curator protests: why are they so different? Why do they even deface the exhibit? Don't they know it is theirs? But it is not theirs. It is his, the curator's. By the most exclusive sort of zoning, the museum exhibit, the park oak tree, is part of an ensemble, a package, which is almost impenetrable to them. The archaeologist who puts his find in a museum so that everyone can see it accomplishes the reverse of his expectations. The result of his action is that no one can see it now but the archaeologist. He would have done better to keep it in his pocket and show it now and then to strangers.

The tourist who carves his initials in a public place, which is theoretically "his" in the first place, has good reasons for doing so, reasons which the exhibitor and planner know nothing about. He does so because in his role of consumer of an experience (a "recreational experience" to satisfy a "recreational need") he knows that he is disinher-ited. He is deprived of his title over being. He knows very well that he is in a very special sort of zone in which his only rights are the rights of a consumer. He moves like a ghost through schoolroom, city streets, trains, parks, movies. He carves his initials as a last desperate measure to escape his ghostly role of consumer. He is saying in effect: I am not a ghost after all; I am a sovereign person. And he establishes title the only way remaining to him, by staking his claim over one square inch of wood or stone.

Does this mean that we should get rid of museums? No, but it means that the sightseer should be prepared to enter into a struggle to recover sight from a museum.

The second loss is the spoliation of the thing, the tree, the rock, the swallow, by the layman's misunderstanding of scientific theory. He believes that the thing is *disposed of* by theory, that it stands in the Platonic relation of being a *specimen* of such and such an underlying principle. In the transmission of scientific theory from theorist to layman, the expectation of the theorist is reversed. Instead of marvels of the universe being made available to the public, the universe is disposed of by theory. The loss of sovereignty takes this form: as a result of the science of botany, trees are not made available to every man. On the contrary. The tree loses its proper density and mystery as a concrete existent and, as merely another *specimen* of a species, becomes itself nugatory.

Does this mean that there is no use in tak- 60 ing biology at Harvard and Shreveport High? No, but it means that the student should know what a fight he has on his hands to rescue the specimen from the educational package. The educator is only partly to blame. For there is nothing the educator can do to provide for this need of the student. Everything the educator does only succeeds in becoming, for the student, part of the educational package. The highest role of the educator is the maieutic role of Socrates: to help the student come to himself not as a consumer of experience but as a sovereign individual.

The thing is twice lost to the consumer. First, sovereignty is lost: it is theirs, not his. Second, it is radically devalued by theory. This is a loss which has been brought about by science but through no fault of the scientist and through no fault of scientific theory. The loss has come about as a consequence of the seduction of the layman by science. The layman will be seduced as long as he regards beings as consumer items to be experienced rather than prizes to be won, and as long as he waives his sovereign rights as a person and accepts his role of consumer as the highest estate to which the layman can aspire.

As Mounier said, the person is not something one can study and provide for; he is something one struggles for. But unless he also struggles for himself, unless he knows that there is a struggle, he is going to be just what the planners think he is.

READING AND THINKING

1. Percy devotes some seventeen paragraphs to the story of the Grand Canyon. Through careful analysis (with pencil in hand), break that story down into its component parts. Mark the breaks. Note in the margin what develops in each section.

2. As you analyze the logical ordering of those early paragraphs, consider what Percy means by these terms: preformed symbolic complex, sovereignty, seeing and knowing, recovery, authenticity. Trace their importance throughout the essay.

3. Are you willing to concede that you are one of those who has unknowingly given up your sovereignty, a victim, if you will, of your loss of sovereignty? Explain to yourself why or why not.

4. In part II of the essay, Percy moves directly into the domain of education—presumably the source of our blighted perceptions. How effective do you find Percy's examples of the dogfish and the sonnet? Do those examples ring true of your own experiences in college?

5. What does Percy mean about extracting the thing itself (the dogfish, the poem, the Grand Canyon) from the "symbolic package"? What is the fundamental requirement of a proper education: to create the package or to nullify its effect—or is there another way to think about this complex matter?

THINKING AND WRITING

1. Throughout the essay, Percy makes a number of assumptions about the way we see, the way we are constrained by what we know and have learned. Select one of those assumptions and question it, analyze it in terms of your own experience, and make some informed judgment about the assumption itself.

2. In one or two succinct paragraphs identify what Percy believes that we perceivers have lost. In two additional paragraphs outline Percy's plan for recovery. Finally, respond to Percy in an essay that develops your own ideas about seeing and knowing, loss and recovery. Let the essay reveal what you consider to be a proper education, an antidote to the loss of sovereignty.

Plato (ca. 427–347 B.C.E.)

Plato, along with Aristotle, is the most revered of the Greek philosophers, and the most widely read. A student of Socrates, Plato cast his philosophy into the form of dialogues between Socrates and other interlocutors, or speakers. Many of his dialogues do not resolve the questions they raise, but rather suggest the limits of knowledge. Plato's most famous work, *The Republic,* is an attempt to define the ideal state, based on the idea of the Good, which, for Plato, existed as an independent and eternal reality.

THE ALLEGORY OF THE CAVE

In "The Allegory of the Cave," excerpted from *The Republic,* Plato describes the state of knowledge (or ignorance) in which human beings find themselves. Plato explains humanity's lack of true knowledge through Socrates, who uses an analogy to convey Plato's central idea, a distinction between true knowledge of reality and the illusion of appearances.

1 And now, I said, let me show in a figure how far our nature is enlightened or unenlightened: Behold! human beings living in an underground den, which has a mouth open toward the light and reaching all along the den; here they have been from their childhood, and have their legs and necks chained so that they cannot move, and can only see before them, being prevented by the chains from turning round their heads. Above and behind them a fire is blazing at a distance, and between the fire and the prisoners there is a raised way; and you will see, if you look, a low wall built along the way, like the screen which marionette players have in front of them, over which they show the puppets.

I see.

And do you see, I said, men passing along the wall carrying all sorts of vessels, and statues and figures of animals made of wood and stone and various materials, which appear over the wall? Some of them are talking, others silent.

You have shown me a strange image, and they are strange prisoners.

5 Like ourselves, I replied; and they see only their own shadows, or the shadows of one another, which the fire throws on the opposite wall of the cave?

True, he said; how could they see anything but the shadows if they were never allowed to move their heads?

And of the objects which are being carried in like manner they would only see the shadows?

Yes, he said.

And if they were able to converse with one another, would they not suppose that they were naming what was actually before them?

Very true.   10

And suppose further that the prison had an echo which came from the other side, would they not be sure to fancy when one of the passers-by spoke that the voice which they heard came from the passing shadow?

No question, he replied.

To them, I said, the truth would be literally nothing but the shadows of the images.

That is certain.

And now look again, and see what will   15 naturally follow if the prisoners are released and disabused of their error. At first, when any of them is liberated and compelled suddenly to stand up and turn his neck round and walk and look toward the light, he will suffer sharp pains; the glare will distress him and he will be unable to see the realities of which in his former state he had seen the shadows; and then conceive some one saying to him, that what he saw before was an illusion, but that now, when he is approaching nearer to being and his eye is turned toward more real existence, he has a clearer vision—what will be his reply? And you may further imagine that his instructor is pointing to the objects as they pass and requiring him to name them—will he not be perplexed? Will he not fancy that the shadows which he formerly saw are truer than the objects which are now shown to him?

Far truer.

And if he is compelled to look straight at the light, will he not have a pain in his eyes which will make him turn away to take refuge in the objects of vision which he can see, and which he will conceive to be in reality clearer than the things which are now being shown to him?

True, he said.

And suppose once more, that he is reluctantly dragged up a steep and rugged ascent, and held fast until he is forced into the presence of the sun himself, is he not likely to be pained and irritated? When he approaches the light his eyes will be dazzled and he will not be able to see anything at all of what are now called realities.

20   Not all in a moment, he said.

He will require to grow accustomed to the sight of the upper world. And first he will see the shadows best, next the reflections of men and other objects in the water, and then the objects themselves; then he will gaze upon the light of the moon and the stars and the spangled heaven; and he will see the sky and the stars by night better than the sun or the light of the sun by day?

Certainly.

Last of all he will be able to see the sun, and not mere reflections of him in the water, but he will see him in his own proper place, and not in other; and he will contemplate him as he is.

Certainly.

He will then proceed to argue that this is 25 he who gives the season and the years, and is the guardian of all that is in the visible world, and in a certain way the cause of all things which he and his fellows have been accustomed to behold?

Clearly, he said, he would first see the sun and then reason about him.

And when he remembered his old habitation, and the wisdom of the den and his fellow-prisoners, do you not suppose that he would felicitate himself on the change, and pity them?

Certainly, he would.

And if they were in the habit of conferring honors among themselves on those who were quickest to observe the passing shadows and to remark which of them went before, and which followed after, and which were together; and who were therefore best able to draw conclusions as to the future, do you think that he would care for such honors and glories, or envy the possessors of them? Would he not say with Homer,

Better to be the poor servant of a poor master,

and to endure anything, rather than think as they do and live after their manner?

Yes, he said, I think that he would rather 30 suffer anything than entertain these false notions and live in this miserable manner.

Imagine once more, I said, such an one coming suddenly out of the sun to be replaced in his old situation; would he not be certain to have his eyes full of darkness?

To be sure, he said.

And if there were a contest, and he had to compete in measuring the shadows with the prisoners who had never moved out of the den, while his sight was still weak, and before his eyes had become steady (and the time which would be needed to acquire this new habit of sight might be very considerable) would he not be ridiculous? Men would say of him that up he went and down he came without his eyes; and that it was better not even to think of ascending; and if any one tried to loose another and lead him up to the light, let them only catch the offender, and they would put him to death.

No question, he said.

35   This entire allegory, I said, you may now append, dear Glaucon, to the previous argument; the prison-house is the world of sight, the light of the fire is the sun, and you will not misapprehend me if you interpret the journey upwards to be the ascent of the soul into the intellectual world according to my poor belief, which, at your desire, I have expressed—whether rightly or wrongly God knows. But, whether true or false, my opinion is that in the world of knowledge the idea of good appears last of all, and is seen only with an effort; and, when seen, is also inferred to be the universal author of all things beautiful and right, parent of light and of the lord of light in this visible world, and the immediate source of reason and truth in the intellectual; and that this is the power upon which he who would act rationally either in public or private life must have his eye fixed.

I agree, he said, as far as I am able to understand you.

Moreover, I said, you must not wonder that those who attain to this beatific vision are unwilling to descend to human affairs; for their souls are ever hastening into the upper world where they desire to dwell; which desire of theirs is very natural, if our allegory may be trusted.

Yes, very natural.

And is there anything surprising in one who passes from divine contemplations to the evil state of man, misbehaving himself in a ridiculous manner; if, while his eyes are blinking and before he has become accustomed to the surrounding darkness, he is compelled to fight in courts of law, or in other places, about the images or the shadows of images of justice, and is endeavoring to meet the conceptions of those who have never yet seen absolute justice?

Anything but surprising, he replied.   40

Any one who has common sense will remember that the bewilderments of the eyes are of two kinds, and arise from two causes, either from coming out of the light or from going into the light, which is true of the mind's eye, quite as much as of the bodily eye; and he who remembers this when he sees any one whose vision is perplexed and weak, will not be too ready to laugh; he will first ask whether that soul of man has come out of the brighter life, and is unable to see because unaccustomed to the dark, or having turned from darkness to the day is dazzled by excess of light. And he will count the one happy in his condition and state of being, and he will pity the other; or, if he have a mind to laugh at the soul which comes from below into the light, there will be more reason in this than in the laugh which greets him who returns from above out of the light into the den.

That, he said, is a very just distinction.

READING AND THINKING

1. What is the effect of the dialogue structure of question and answer that Plato uses in this selection?

2. Explain the symbolic significance of shadows and light. What do light and darkness represent?

3. Explain the significance of the journey metaphor that Socrates uses. What is the goal of the journey, and why is it important?

4. To what extent might Plato's allegory of the cave be given a religious interpretation? Explain.

THINKING AND WRITING

1. Analyze Plato's "Allegory of the Cave." Explain, in a few paragraphs, what the various elements represent.

2. Discuss Plato's notion of "absolutes"—absolute justice, absolute goodness, and absolute truth, for example.

3. Develop an application of Plato's allegory of knowledge and ignorance to a contemporary issue or to the problem of understanding something complex and mysterious—whether religious, scientific, or philosophical.

Jonathan Swift (1667–1745)

Jonathan Swift was born in Dublin of English parents, and he received his education in Ireland. He is best known for his satirical attacks on various forms of injustice. Swift always wrote for the betterment of mankind, but his sometimes savage pen led to misunderstanding about his aims. His best-known works include *The Tale of a Tub, Gulliver's Travels,* and "A Modest Proposal."

A MODEST PROPOSAL

"A Modest Proposal" is a satirical attack on Ireland's failure to feed and care for its indigent population, the poor who could not fend for themselves. Satire blends humor and wit to instigate change. Swift is also ironic: he suggests one thing but really asks us to see and understand another. Writing tongue-in-cheek, he expects us to pay attention to double meaning. Swift's "Proposal" causes repulsion by the surface proposal (eating children), but we are moved to action by the cause that necessitates it (hunger).

For Preventing the Children of Poor People in Ireland from Being a Burden to Their Parents or Country, and for Making Them Beneficial to the Public

1 It is a melancholy object to those who walk through this great town or travel in the country, when they see the streets, the roads, and cabin doors, crowded with beggars of the female sex, followed by three, four, or six children, all in rags and importuning every passenger for an alms. These mothers, instead of being able to work for their honest livelihood, are forced to employ all their time in strolling to beg sustenance for their helpless infants, who, as they grow up, either turn thieves for want of work, or leave their dear native country to fight for the Pretender in Spain, or sell themselves to the Barbados.

I think it is agreed by all parties that this prodigious number of children in the arms, or on the backs, or at the heels of their mothers, and frequently of their fathers, is in the present deplorable state of the kingdom a very great additional grievance; and therefore whoever could find out a fair, cheap, and easy method of making these children sound, useful members of the commonwealth would deserve so well of the public as to have his statue set up for a preserver of the nation.

But my intention is very far from being confined to provide only for the children of professed beggars; it is of a much greater extent, and shall take in the whole number of infants at a certain age who are born of parents in effect as little able to support them as those who demand our charity in the streets.

As to my own part, having turned my thoughts for many years upon this important subject, and maturely weighed the several schemes of other projectors, I have always found them grossly mistaken in their computation. It is true, a child just dropped from its dam may be supported by her milk for a solar year, with little other nourishment; at most not above the value of two shillings, which the mother may certainly get, or the value in scraps, by her lawful occupation of begging; and it is exactly at one year that I propose to provide for them in such a manner as instead of being a charge upon their parents or the parish, or wanting food and raiment for the rest of their lives, they shall on the contrary contribute to the feeding, and partly to the clothing, of many thousands.

There is likewise another great advan- 5 tage in my scheme, that it will prevent those voluntary abortions, and that horrid practice of women murdering their bastard children, alas, too frequent among us, sacrificing the poor innocent babes, I doubt, more to avoid the expense than the shame, which would move tears and pity in the most savage and inhuman breast.

The number of souls in this kingdom being usually reckoned one million and a half, of these I calculate there may be about two hundred thousand couples whose wives are breeders; from which number I subtract thirty thousand couples who are able to maintain their own children, although I apprehend there cannot be so many under the present distress of the kingdom; but this being granted, there will remain an hundred and seventy thousand breeders. I again subtract fifty thousand for those women who miscarry, or whose children die by accident or disease within the year. There only remain an hundred and twenty thousand children of poor parents annually born. The question therefore is, how this number shall be reared and provided for, which, as I have already said, under the present situation of affairs, is utterly impossible by all the methods hitherto proposed. For we can neither employ them in handicraft or agriculture; we neither build houses (I mean in the country) nor cultivate land. They can very seldom pick up a livelihood stealing till they arrive at six years old, except where they are of towardly parts, although I confess they learn the rudiments much earlier, during which time they can however be looked upon only as probationers, as I have been informed by a principal gentleman in the country of Cavan, who protested to me that he never knew above one or two instances under the age of six, even in a part of the kingdom so renowned for the quickest proficiency in that art.

I am assured by our merchants that a boy or a girl before twelve years old is no salable commodity; and even when they come to this age they will not yield above three pounds, or three pounds and half a crown at most on the Exchange; which cannot turn to account either to the parents or the kingdom, the charge of nutriment and rags having been at least four times that value.

I shall now therefore humbly propose my own thoughts, which I hope will not be liable to the least objection.

I have been assured by a very knowing American of my acquaintance in London, that a young healthy child well nursed is at a year old a most delicious, nourishing, and wholesome food, whether stewed, roasted, baked, or boiled; and I make no doubt that it will equally serve in a fricassee or a ragout.

I do therefore humbly offer it to public consideration that of the hundred and twenty thousand children, already computed, twenty thousand may be reserved for breed, whereof only one fourth part to be males, which is more than we allow to sheep, black cattle, or swine; and my reason is that these children are seldom the fruits of marriage, a circumstance not much regarded by our savages, therefore one male will be sufficient to serve four females. That the remaining hundred thousand may at a year old be offered in sale to the persons of quality and fortune through the kingdom, always advising the mother to let them suck plentifully in the last month, so as to render them plump and fat for a good table. A child will make two dishes at an entertainment for friends; and when the family dines alone, the fore or hind quarter will make a reasonable dish, and seasoned with a little pepper or salt will be very good boiled on the fourth day, especially in winter.

I have reckoned upon a medium that a child just born will weigh twelve pounds, and in a solar year if tolerably nursed increaseth to twenty-eight pounds.

I grant this food will be somewhat dear, and therefore very proper for landlords, who, as they have already devoured most of the parents, seem to have the best title to the children.

10

Infant's flesh will be in season throughout the year, but more plentiful in March, and a little before and after. For we are told by a grave author, an eminent French physician, that fish being a prolific diet, there are more children born in Roman Catholic countries about nine months after Lent than at any other season; therefore, reckoning a year after Lent, the markets will be more glutted than usual, because the number of popish infants is at least three to one in this kingdom; and therefore it will have one other collateral advantage, by lessening the number of Papists among us.

I have already computed the charge of nursing a beggar's child (in which list I reckon all cottagers, laborers, and four-fifths of the farmers) to be about two shillings per annum, rags included; and I believe no gentleman would repine to give ten shillings for the carcass of a good fat child, which, as I have said, will make four dishes of excellent nutritive meat, when he hath only some particular friend or his own family to dine with him. Thus the squire will learn to be a good landlord, and grow people among the tenants; the mother will have eight shillings net profit, and be fit for work till she produces another child.

15 Those who are more thrifty (as I must confess the times require) may flay the carcass; the skin of which artificially dressed will make admirable gloves for ladies, and summer boots for fine gentlemen.

As to our city of Dublin, shambles may be appointed for this purpose in the most convenient parts of it, and butchers we may be assured will not be wanting; although I rather recommend buying the children alive, and dressing them hot from the knife as we do roasting pigs.

A very worthy person, a true lover of his country, and whose virtues I highly esteem, was lately pleased in discoursing on this matter to offer a refinement upon my scheme. He said that many gentlemen of his kingdom, having of late destroyed their deer, he conceived that the want of venison might be well supplied by the bodies of young lads and maidens, not exceeding fourteen years of age nor under twelve, so great a number of both sexes in every county being now ready to starve for want of work and service; and these to be disposed of by their parents, if alive, or otherwise by their nearest relations. But with due deference to so excellent a friend and so deserving a patriot, I cannot be altogether in his sentiments; for as to the males, my American acquaintance assured me from frequent experience that their flesh was generally tough and lean, like that of our schoolboys, by continual exercise, and their taste disagreeable; and to fatten them would not answer the charge. Then as to the females, it would, I think with humble submission, be a loss to the public, because they soon would become breeders themselves; and besides, it is not improbable that some scrupulous people might be apt to censure such a practice (although indeed very unjustly) as a little bordering upon cruelty; which, I confess, hath always been with me the strongest objection against any project, how well soever intended.

But in order to justify my friend, he confessed that this expedient was put into his head by the famous Psalmanazar, a native of the island Formosa, who came from thence to London above twenty years ago, and in conversation told my friend that in his country when any young person happened to be put to death, the executioner sold the carcass to persons of quality as a prime dainty; and that in his time the body of a plump girl of fifteen, who was crucified for an attempt to poison the emperor, was sold to his Imperial Majesty's prime minister of state, and other great mandarins of the court, in joints from the gibbet, at four hundred crowns. Neither indeed can I deny that if the same use were made of several plump young girls in this town, who without one single groat to their fortunes cannot stir abroad without a chair, and appear at the playhouse and assemblies in foreign fineries which they never will pay for, the kingdom would not be the worse.

Some persons of a desponding spirit are in great concern about that vast number of poor people who are aged, diseased, or maimed, and I have been desired to employ my thoughts what course may be taken to ease the nation of so grievous an encumbrance. But I am not in the least pain upon that matter, because it is very well known that they are every day dying and rotting by cold and famine, and filth and vermin, as fast as can be reasonably expected. And as to the younger laborers, they are now in almost as hopeful a condition. They cannot get work, and consequently pine away for want of nourishment to a degree that if any time they are accidentally hired to common labor, they have not strength to perform it; and thus the country and themselves are happily delivered from the evils to come.

20   I have too long digressed, and therefore shall return to my subject. I think the advantages by the proposal which I have made are obvious and many, as well as of the highest importance.

For first, as I have already observed, it would greatly lessen the number of Papists, with whom we are yearly overrun, being the principal breeders of the nation as well as our most dangerous enemies; and who stay at home on purpose to deliver the kingdom to the Pretender, hoping to take their advantage by the absence of so many good Protestants, who have chosen rather to leave their country than to stay at home and pay tithes against their conscience to an Episcopal curate.

Secondly, the poorer tenants will have something valuable of their own, which by law may be made liable to distress, and help to pay their landlord's rent, their corn and cattle being already seized and money a thing unknown.

Thirdly, whereas the maintenance of an hundred thousand children, from two years old and upwards, cannot be computed at less than ten shillings a piece per annum, the nation's stock will be thereby increased fifty thousand pounds per annum, besides the profit of a new dish introduced to the tables of all gentlemen of fortune in the kingdom who have any refinement in taste. And the money will circulate among ourselves, the goods being entirely of our own growth and manufacture.

Fourthly, the constant breeders, besides the gain of eight shillings sterling per annum by the sale of their children, will be rid of the charge of maintaining them after the first year.

Fifthly, this food would likewise bring great custom to taverns, where the vintners will certainly be so prudent as to procure the best recipes for dressing it to perfection, and consequently have their houses frequented by all the fine gentlemen, who justly value themselves upon their knowledge in good eating; and a skillful cook, who understands how to oblige his guests, will contrive to make it as expensive as they please.

Sixthly, this would be a great inducement to marriage, which all wise nations have either encouraged by rewards or enforced by laws and penalties. It would increase the care and tenderness of mothers toward their children, when they were sure of a settlement for life to the poor babes, provided in some sort by the public, to their annual profit instead of expense. We should see an honest emulation among the married women, which of them could bring the fattest child to the market. Men would become as fond of their wives during the time of their pregnancy as they are now of their mares in foal, their cows in calf, or sows when they are ready to farrow; nor offer to beat or kick them (as is too frequent a practice) for fear of a miscarriage.

Many other advantages might be enumerated. For instance, the addition of some thousand carcasses in our exportation of barreled beef, the propagation of swine's flesh, and improvements in the art of making good bacon, so much wanted among us by the great destruction of pigs, too frequent at our tables, which are no way comparable in taste or magnificence to a well-grown, fat, yearling child, which roasted whole will make a considerable figure at a lord mayor's feast or any other public entertainment. But this and many others I omit, being studious of brevity.

Supposing that one thousand families in this city would be constant customers for infants' flesh, besides others who might have it at merry meetings, particularly weddings and christenings, I compute that Dublin would take off annually about twenty thousand carcasses, and the rest of the kingdom (where probably they will be sold somewhat cheaper) the remaining eighty thousand.

I can think of no one objection that will possibly be raised against this proposal, unless it should be urged that the number of people will be thereby much lessened in the kingdom. This I freely own, and it was indeed one principal design in offering it to the world. I desire the reader will observe, that I calculate my remedy for this one individual kingdom of Ireland and for no other that ever was, is, or I think ever can be upon earth. Therefore let no man talk to me of other expedients: of taxing our absentees at five shillings a pound: of using neither clothes nor household furniture except what is of our own growth and manufacture: of utterly rejecting the materials and instruments that promote foreign luxury: of curing the expensiveness of pride, vanity, idleness, and gaming in our women: of introducing a vein of parsimony, prudence, and temperance: of learning to love our country, in the want of which we differ even from Laplanders and the inhabitants of Topinamboo: of quitting our animosities and factions, nor acting any longer like the Jews, who were murdering one another at the very moment their city was taken: of being a little cautious not to sell our country and conscience for nothing: of teaching landlords to have at least one degree of mercy toward

their tenants: lastly, of putting a spirit of honesty, industry, and skill into our shopkeepers; who, if a resolution could now be taken to buy only our native goods, would immediately unite to cheat and exact upon us in the price, the measure, and the goodness, nor could ever yet be brought to make one fair proposal of just dealing, though often and earnestly invited to it.

Therefore I repeat, let no man talk to me 30 of these and the like expedients, till he hath at least some glimpse of hope that there will ever be some hearty and sincere attempt to put them in practice.

But as to myself, having been wearied out for many years with offering vain, idle, visionary thoughts, and at length utterly despairing of success, I fortunately fell upon this proposal, which, as it is wholly new, so it hath something solid and real, of no expense and little trouble, full in our own power, and whereby we can incur no danger in disobliging England. For this kind of commodity will not bear exportation, the flesh being of too tender a consistence to admit a long continuance in salt, although perhaps I could name a country which would be glad to eat up our whole nation without it.

After all, I am not so violently bent upon my own opinion as to reject any offer proposed by wise men, which shall be found equally innocent, cheap, easy, and effectual. But before something of that kind shall be advanced in contradiction to my scheme, and offering a better, I desire the author or authors will be pleased maturely to consider two points. First, as things now stand, how they will be able to find food and raiment for an hundred thousand useless mouths and backs. And secondly, there being a round million of creatures in human figure throughout this kingdom, whose sole subsistence put into a common stock would leave them in debt two millions of pounds sterling, adding those who are beggars by profession to the bulk of farmers, cottagers, and laborers, with their wives and children who are beggars in effect; I desire those politicians who dislike my overture, and may perhaps be so bold to attempt an answer, that they will first ask the parents of these mortals whether they would not at this day think it a great happiness to have been sold for food at a year old in this manner I prescribe, and thereby have avoided such a perpetual scene of misfortunes as they have since gone through by the oppression of landlords, the impossibility of paying rent without money or trade, the want of common sustenance, with neither house nor clothes to cover them from the inclemencies of the weather, and the most inevitable prospect of entailing the like or greater miseries upon their breed forever.

I profess, in the sincerity of my heart, that I have not the least personal interest in endeavoring to promote this necessary work, having no other motive than the public good of my country, by advancing our trade, providing for infants, relieving the poor, and giving some pleasure to the rich. I have no children by which I can propose to get a single penny; the youngest being nine years old, and my wife past childbearing.

READING AND THINKING

1. The first six paragraphs of this proposal identify a number of problems in Swift's Ireland. Make a list of these problems in the order that Swift identifies them.

2. What particular use does Swift make of the unnamed American in paragraph 9? Of the American in paragraph 17?

3. What is the effect of Swift's numerical calculations and his tone of voice? Do these aspects of his work appeal more to pathos, ethos, or logos?

THINKING AND WRITING

1. Return to paragraph 9 and recall your initial reaction to what Swift says. In a paragraph, explain how that paragraph influences your sense of the writer's character (ethos)?

2. Reread paragraph 4 and identify how Swift both disguises and foreshadows his proposal. Find two other examples of double meaning in the proposal.

3. Classify Swift's satire. Is it gentle, biting, or some combination of the two? Justify your claim with evidence from the proposal itself.

Paul Theroux (b. 1941)

Paul Theroux was born in Medford, Massachusetts, and graduated from the University of Massachusetts at Amherst. Theroux joined the Peace Corps and taught in Malawi, Africa. After being expelled from both Malawi and the Peace Corps, he moved to Uganda, where he taught at Makerere University, and where he published the first of his 28 novels. A prolific writer, Theroux has published fifteen books of nonfiction, among them the highly regarded books recounting his epic train journeys, *The Great Railway Bazaar, Riding the Iron Rooster, Dark Star Safari,* and *The Old Patagonian Express.* An author of many volumes of short stories, as well as a few children's books, Theroux has taught at the University of Singapore and the University of Virginia, and he holds honorary doctorates from a number of American universities, including Tufts University in the town of his birth.

BEING A MAN

In "Being a Man," Theroux expresses his dissatisfaction with being expected to live up to an image of manhood that he detests. In the course of criticizing various aspects of the male mystique, Theroux raises questions about what it means to be a man in America today.

1   There is a pathetic sentence in the chapter "Fetishism" in Dr. Norman Cameron's book *Personality Development and Psychopathology.* It goes, "Fetishists are nearly always men; and their commonest fetish is a woman's shoe." I cannot read that sentence without thinking that it is just one more awful thing about being a man—and perhaps it is an important thing to know about us.

I have always disliked being a man. The whole idea of manhood in America is pitiful, in my opinion. This version of masculinity is a little like having to wear an ill-fitting coat for one's entire life (by contrast, I imagine femininity to be an oppressive sense of nakedness). Even the expression "Be a man!" strikes me as insulting and abusive. It means: Be stupid, be unfeeling, obedient, soldierly and stop thinking. Man means "manly"—how can one think about men without considering the terrible ambition of manliness? And yet it is part of every man's life. It is a hideous and crippling lie; it not only insists on difference and connives at superiority, it is also by its very nature destructive—emotionally damaging and socially harmful.

The youth who is subverted, as most are, into believing in the masculine ideal is effectively separated from women and he spends the rest of his life finding women a riddle and a nuisance. Of course, there is a female version of this male affliction. It begins with mothers encouraging little girls to say (to other adults) "Do you like my new dress?" In a sense, little girls are traditionally urged to please adults with a kind of coquettishness, while boys are enjoined to behave like monkeys toward each other. The nine-year-old coquette proceeds to become womanish in a subtle power game in which she learns to be sexually indispensable, socially decorative and always alert to a man's sense of inadequacy.

Femininity—being lady-like—implies needing a man as witness and seducer; but masculinity celebrates the exclusive company of men. That is why it is so grotesque; and that is also why there is no manliness without inadequacy—because it denies men the natural friendship of women.

It is very hard to imagine any concept of 5 manliness that does not belittle women, and it begins very early. At an age when I wanted to meet girls—let's say the treacherous years of thirteen to sixteen—I was told to take up a sport, get more fresh air, join the Boy Scouts, and I was urged not to read so much. It was the 1950s and if you asked too many questions about sex you were sent to camp—boy's camp, of course: the nightmare. Nothing is more unnatural or prison-like than a boy's camp, but if it were not for them we would have no Elks' Lodges, no pool rooms, no boxing matches, no Marines.

And perhaps no sports as we know them. Everyone is aware of how few in number are the athletes who behave like gentlemen. Just as high school basketball teaches you how to be a poor loser, the manly attitude toward sports seems to be little more than a recipe for creating bad marriages, social misfits, moral degenerates, sadists, latent rapists and just plain louts. I regard high school sports as a drug far worse than marijuana, and it is the reason that the average tennis champion, say, is a pathetic oaf.

Any objective study would find the quest for manliness essentially rightwing, puritanical, cowardly, neurotic and fueled largely by a fear of women. It is also certainly philistine. There is no book-hater like a Little League coach. But indeed all the creative arts are obnoxious to the manly ideal, because at their best the arts are pursued by uncompetitive and essentially solitary people. It makes it very hard for a creative youngster, for any boy who expresses the desire to be alone seems to be saying that there is something wrong with him.

It ought to be clear by now that I have something of an objection to the way we turn boys into men. It does not surprise me that when the President of the United States has his customary weekend off he dresses like a cowboy—it is both a measure of his insecurity and his willingness to please. In many ways, American culture does little more for a man than prepare him for modeling clothes in the L.L. Bean catalog. I take this as a personal insult because for many years I found it impossible to admit to myself that I wanted to be a writer. It was my guilty secret, because being a writer was incompatible with being a man.

There are people who might deny this, but that is because the American writer, typically, has been so at pains to prove his manliness that we have come to see literariness and manliness as mingled qualities. But first there was a fear that writing was not a manly profession—indeed, not a profession at all. (The paradox in American letters is that it has always been easier for a woman to write and for a man to be published.) Growing up, I had thought of sports as wasteful and humiliating, and the idea of manliness was a bore. My wanting to become a writer was not a flight from that oppressive roleplaying, but I quickly saw that it was at odds with it. Everything in stereotyped manliness goes against the life of the mind. The Hemingway personality is too tedious to go into here, and in any case his exertions are well known, but certainly it was not until this aberrant behavior was examined by feminists in the 1960s that any male writer dared question the pugnacity in Hemingway's fiction. All the bullfighting and arm wrestling and elephant shooting diminished Hemingway as a writer, but it is consistent with a prevailing attitude in American writing: one cannot be a male writer without first proving that one is a man.

It is normal in America for a man to be dismissive or even somewhat apologetic about being a writer. Various factors make it easier. There is a heartiness about journalism that makes it acceptable—journalism is the manliest form of American writing and, therefore, the profession the most independent-minded women seek (yes, it is an illusion, but that is my point). Fiction-writing is equated with a kind of dispirited failure and is only manly when it produces wealth—money is masculinity. So is drinking. Being a drunkard is another

10

assertion, if misplaced, of manliness. The American male writer is traditionally proud of his heavy drinking. But we are also a very literal-minded people. A man proves his manhood in America in old-fashioned ways. He kills lions, like Hemingway; or he hunts ducks, like Nathanael West; or he makes pronouncements like, "A man should carry enough knife to defend himself with," as James Jones once said to a *Life* interviewer. Or he says he can drink you under the table. But even tiny drunken William Faulkner loved to mount a horse and go fox hunting, and Jack Kerouac roistered up and down Manhattan in a lumberjack shirt (and spent every night of *The Subterraneans* with his mother in Queens). And we are familiar with the lengths to which Norman Mailer is prepared, in his endearing way, to prove that he is just as much a monster as the next man.

When the novelist John Irving was revealed as a wrestler, people took him to be a very serious writer; and even a bubble reputation like Eric (*Love Story*) Segal's was enhanced by the news that he ran the marathon in a respectable time. How surprised we would be if Joyce Carol Oates were revealed as a sumo wrestler or Joan Didion active in pumping iron. "Lives in New York City with her three children" is the typical woman writer's biographical note, for just as the male writer must prove he has achieved a sort of muscular manhood, the woman writer—or rather her publicists—must prove her motherhood.

There would be no point in saying any of this if it were not generally accepted that to be a man is somehow—even now in feminist-influenced America—a privilege. It is on the contrary an unmerciful and punishing burden. Being a man is bad enough; being manly is appalling (in this sense, women's lib has done much more for men than for women). It is the sinister silliness of men's fashions, and a clubby attitude in the arts. It is the subversion of good students. It is the so-called Dress Code of the Ritz-Carlton Hotel in Boston, and it is the institutionalized cheating in college sports. It is the most primitive insecurity.

And this is also why men often object to feminism but are afraid to explain why: of course women have a justified grievance, but most men believe—and with reason—that their lives are just as bad.

READING AND THINKING

1. In his opening paragraph Theroux says that it is an "awful thing" to be a man. Do you agree with him? Why or why not?

2. What aspects of the cult of manliness does Theroux object to? Why? Why is he so hard on sports? On dressing like a cowboy?

3. What image of femininity does Theroux present as a counterpoint to the masculine ideal he criticizes?

4. How does Theroux describe the relationship between being a "man" and being a writer? What is the significance of his references to Ernest Hemingway, William Faulkner, and Norman Mailer?

THINKING AND WRITING

1. Evaluate the evidence Theroux uses to support his claim that being a man is a "punishing burden." Consider the extent to which his argument is convincing.

2. Analyze the cultural values embodied in the image of manliness that Theroux criticizes. Consider the extent to which these values affect the way men think of themselves.

3. Define, in a paragraph, masculinity. Then, in another paragraph, define femininity. Consider the relationship between the two gender images in your pair of paragraphs.

4. Discuss the use of humor in Theroux's essay. Explain what humor contributes to the essay's tone and whether it aids or impedes Theroux's argument.

Sojourner Truth (ca. 1797–1883)

Sojourner Truth was born a slave in upstate New York with the given name of Isabella. When slavery was abolished in the state, she worked for a time with a Quaker family. In 1843, announcing that she had received messages from heaven, she took on the name Sojourner Truth and began a career as an itinerant preacher. She advocated the abolishment of slavery and the advancement of women's rights. She was a striking physical presence and an effective speaker and commanded an intense following. Her memoirs were published as *Narratives of Sojourner Truth* (1875).

AIN'T I A WOMAN

In "Ain't I a Woman," a speech made at a women's rights convention in 1851, Sojourner Truth refutes the arguments that women are inferior to men. Her speech makes effective use of questions, particularly the refrain, "Ain't I a woman?"

1   Well, children, where there is so much racket there must be something out of kilter. I think that 'twixt the negroes of the South and the women at the North, all talking about rights, the white men will be in a fix pretty soon. But what's all this here talking about?

That man over there says that women need to be helped into carriages, and lifted over ditches, and to have the best place everywhere. Nobody ever helps me into carriages, or over mud-puddles, or gives me any best place! And ain't I a woman? Look at me! Look at my arm! I have ploughed and planted, and gathered into barns, and no man could head me! And ain't I a woman? I could work as much and eat as much as a man—when I could get it—and bear the lash as well! And ain't I a woman? I have borne thirteen children, and seen most all sold off to slavery, and when I cried out with my mother's grief, none but Jesus heard me! And ain't I a woman?

Then they talk about this thing in the head; what's this they call it? [member of audience whispers, "intellect"] That's it, honey. What's that got to do with women's rights or negroes' rights? If my cup won't hold but a pint, and yours holds a quart, wouldn't you be mean not to let me have my little half measure full?

Then that little man in black there, he says women can't have as much rights as men, 'cause Christ wasn't a woman! Where did your Christ come from? Where did your Christ come from? From God and a woman! Man had nothing to do with Him.

If the first woman God ever made was 5 strong enough to turn the world upside down all alone, these women together ought to be able to turn it back, and get it right side up again! And now they is asking to do it, the men better let them.

Obliged to you for hearing me, and now old Sojourner ain't got nothing more to say.

READING AND THINKING

1. How does Truth begin her speech? Why does she suggest that the "white man will be in a fix"? What does she mean?

2. Why does she refer to Jesus and his birth? With what effect?

3. How would you characterize the tone of the speech?

THINKING AND WRITING

1. Translate Sojourner Truth's speech into standard English, a more formal and grammatically correct English. What is gained or lost in your "translation"?

2. Analyze the speech, identifying each of its key points and how Sojourner Truth makes each point.

Lawrence Weschler (b. 1952)

Lawrence Weschler is the author of twelve books, including *Mr. Wilson's Cabinet of Wonder: A Natural History of Amazement* (1995) (short-listed for both the Pulitzer Prize and the National Book Critics Circle Award) and *Vermeer in Bosnia: Cultural Comedies and Political Tragedies* (2004). Weschler, who for more than twenty years was a staff writer at *The New Yorker,* is now director of the New York Humanities Institute at New York University, where he has been a fellow since 1991. He is a two-time winner of the George Polk Award (for Cultural Reporting, 1988, and Magazine Reporting, 1992). He is also a recipient of the Lannan Literary Award.

VERMEER IN BOSNIA

"Vermeer in Bosnia" challenges us to think in unusual ways about the prosecution of war criminals. Weschler takes us to the scene of the trials in the Hague, but he also takes us across the city to the museum where many of Vermeer's paintings hang. With the help of those paintings and a few well-chosen written texts, he calls on us to see justice in a fresh way. He encourages us to re-envision racial stereotypes and deep-seated blood wars so that we can imagine that individuals, rather than groups, might be the most serious perpetrators of the greatest atrocities—the people we should hold singularly accountable. His reinvention of causal possibilities makes us reconsider the narrow frame from which we sometimes try to make sense of the world we inhabit.

1   I happened to be in The Hague a while back, sitting in on the preliminary hearings of the Yugoslav War Crimes Tribunal—specifically, those related to the case of Dusko Tadic, the only one of more than forty accused war criminals whom the Tribunal had actually been able to get its hands on up to that point. While there, I had occasion to talk with some of the principal figures involved in this unprecedented judicial undertaking.

At one point, for instance, I was having lunch with Antonio Cassese, a distinguished Italian jurist who has been serving for the past two years as the president of the court (the head of its international panel of eleven judges). He'd been rehearsing for me some of the more gruesome stories that have crossed his desk—maybe not the most gruesome but just the sort of thing he has to contend with every day and which perhaps accounts for the sense of urgency he brings to his mission. The story, for instance, of a soccer player. As Cassese recounted, "Famous guy, a Muslim. When he was captured, they said, 'Aren't you So-and-So?' He admitted he was. So they broke both his legs, handcuffed him to a radiator, and forced him to watch as they repeatedly raped his wife and two daughters and then slit their throats. After that, he begged to be killed himself, but his tormentors must have realized that the cruelest thing they could possibly do to him now would simply be to set him free, which they did. Somehow, this man was able to make his way to some U. N. investigators, and told them about his ordeal—a few days after which, he committed suicide." Or, for instance, as Cassese went on, "some of the tales about Tadic himself, how, in addition to the various rapes and murders he's accused of, he is alleged to have supervised the torture and torments of a particular group of Muslim prisoners, at one point forcing one of his charges to emasculate another—*with his teeth.* The one fellow died, and the guy who bit him went mad."

Stories like that: one judge's daily fare. And, at one point, I asked judge Cassese how, regularly obliged to gaze into such an appalling abyss, he had kept from going mad himself. His face brightened. "Ah," he said with a smile. "You see, as often as possible I make my way over to the Mauritshuis museum, in the center of town, so as to spend a little time with the Vermeers."

Sitting there over lunch with Cassese, I'd been struck by the perfect aptness of his impulse. I, too, had been spending time with the Vermeers at the Mauritshuis, and at the Rijksmuseum, in Amsterdam, as well. For Vermeer's paintings, almost uniquely in the history of art, radiate "a centeredness, a peacefulness, a serenity" (as Cassese put it), a sufficiency, a sense of perfectly equipoised grace. In his exquisite *Study of Vermeer,* Edward Snow has deployed as epigraph a line from Andrew Forge's essay "Painting and the Struggle for the Whole Self," which reads, "In ways that I do not pretend to understand fully, painting deals with the only issues that seem to me to count in our benighted time— freedom, autonomy, fairness, love." And I've often found myself agreeing with Snow's implication that somehow these issues may be more richly and fully addressed in Vermeer than anywhere else.

5   But that afternoon with Cassese I had a sudden further intuition as to the true extent of Vermeer's achievement—something I hadn't fully grasped before. For, of course, when Vermeer was painting those images, which for us have become the very emblem of peacefulness and serenity, *all Europe was Bosnia* (or had only just recently ceased to be): awash in incredibly vicious wars of religious persecution and proto-nationalist formation, wars of an at-that-time unprecedented violence and cruelty, replete with sieges and famines and massacres and mass rapes, unspeakable tortures and wholesale devastation. To be sure, the sense of Holland during Vermeer's lifetime which we are usually given—that of the country's so-called Golden Age—is one of becalmed, burgherlike

efficiency; but that Holland, to the extent that it ever existed, was of relatively recent provenance, and even then under a continual threat of being overwhelmed once again.

Jan Vermeer was born in 1632, sixteen years before the end of the Thirty Years' War, which virtually shredded neighboring Germany and repeatedly tore into the Netherlands as well. Between 1652 and 1674, England and the United Provinces of the Netherlands went to war three times, and though most of the fighting was confined to sea battles, the wars were not without their consequences for the Dutch mainland: Vermeer's Delft, in particular, suffered terrible devastation in 1654, when some eighty thousand pounds of gunpowder in the town's arsenal accidentally exploded, killing hundreds, including Vermeer's great contemporary, the painter Carel Fabritius. (By the conclusion of those wars, the Dutch had ended up ceding New Amsterdam to the British, who quickly changed its name to New York.) These were years of terrible religious conflict throughout Europe—the climaxes of both the Reformation and the Counter-Reformation and their various splintering progeny. And though the Dutch achieved an enviable atmosphere of tolerance during this period, Holland was regularly overrun with refugees from religious conflicts elsewhere. (Vermeer himself, incidentally, was a convert to Catholicism, which was a distinctly minority creed in the Dutch context.) Finally, in 1672, the Dutch fell under the murderous assault of France's Louis XIV and were subjected to a series of campaigns that lasted until 1678. In fact, the ensuing devastation of the Dutch economy and Vermeer's own resulting bankruptcy may have constituted a proximate cause of the painter's early death, by stroke, in 1675: he was only forty-two.

Another preliminary session of the Tribunal was scheduled for late in the afternoon of the day I had lunch with Judge Cassese, and, following our conversation, I decided to spend the intervening hours at the Mauritshuis. On the taxi ride out, as I looked through a Vermeer catalogue, I began to realize that, in fact, the pressure of all that violence (remembered, imagined, foreseen) is what those paintings are all about. Of course, not directly—in fact, quite the opposite: the literary critic Harry Berger, in his essays on Vermeer, frequently invokes the notion of the "conspicuous exclusion" of themes that are saturatingly present but only as *felt absence*—themes that are being held at bay, but conspicuously so. It's almost as if Vermeer can be seen, amid the horrors of his age, to have been asserting or *inventing* the very idea of peace. But Hobbes's state of nature, or state of war (Hobbes: 1588–1679; Vermeer: 1632–75), is everywhere adumbrated around the edges of Vermeer's achievement. That's what the roaring lions carved into the chair posts are all about—those and also the maps on the wall. The maps generally portray the Netherlands, but the whole point is that during Vermeer's lifetime the political and geographic dispensation of the Netherlands, the distribution of its Protestants and Catholics, the grim legacy of its only just recently departed Spanish overlords, and the still current threats posed by its English and French neighbors—all these matters were still actively, and sometimes bloodily, being contested. When soldiers visit young girls in Vermeer's paintings, where does one think they have been off soldiering—and why, one wonders, does the country need all those civic guards? When pregnant young women are standing still, bathed in the window light, intently reading those letters, where is one invited to imagine the letters are coming from?

Or consider the magisterial *View of Delft*—as I now did, having arrived at the Mauritshuis and taken a seat before the magnificent canvas up on the second floor. It is an image of unalloyed civic peace and quiet. But it is also the image of a town only just emerging from a downpour, the earth in the foreground still saturated with moisture, the walls of the town bejeweled with wet, the dark clouds breaking up at last, and the sunlight breaking through, though not just anywhere: a shaft of fresh, clean light gets lavished on one spire in particular, that of the radiantly blond Nieuwe Kerk, in whose interior, as any contemporary of Vermeer's would doubtless have known, stands the mausoleum of William the Silent, one of the heroes of the wars of Dutch independence, assassinated in Delft at the end of the previous century by a French Catholic fanatic.

I found myself being reminded of a moment in my own life, over twenty-five years ago. I was in college and Nixon had just invaded Cambodia and we were, of course, all up in arms; the college had convened as a committee of the whole in the dining commons—the students, the professors, the administrators—what were we going to do? How were we going to respond? Our distinguished American history professor got up and declared this moment *the* crisis of American history. Not to be outdone, our eminent new-age classicist got up and declared it the crisis of *universal* history. And we all nodded our fervent concurrence. But then our visiting religious historian from England—a tall, lanky lay-Catholic theologian, as it happened, with something of the physical bearing of Abraham Lincoln—got up and suggested mildly, "We really ought to have a little modesty in our crises. I suspect," he went on, "that the people during the Black Plague must have thought they were in for a bit of a scrape."

Having momentarily lanced our fervor, he went on to allegorize, deploying the story of Jesus on the Waters (from Matthew 8:23–27). "Jesus," he reminded us, "needed to get across the Sea of Galilee with his disciples, so they all boarded a small boat, whereupon Jesus quickly fell into a nap. Presently a storm kicked up, and the disciples, increasingly

10

edgy, finally woke Jesus up. He told them not to worry, everything would be all right, whereupon he fell back into his nap. The storm meanwhile grew more and more intense, winds slashing the ever-higher waves. The increasingly anxious disciples woke Jesus once again, who once again told them not to worry and again fell back asleep. And still the storm worsened, now tossing the little boat violently all to and fro. The disciples, beside themselves with terror, awoke Jesus one more time, who now said, 'Oh ye of little faith'—that's where that phrase comes from—and then proceeded to pronounce, 'Peace!' Whereupon the storm instantaneously subsided and calm returned to the water." Our historian waited a few moments as we endeavored to worry out the glancing relevance of this story. "It seems to me," he finally concluded, "that what that story is trying to tell us is simply that in times of storm, we mustn't allow the storm to enter ourselves, rather we have to find peace inside ourselves and then breathe it out."

And it now seemed to me, sitting among the Vermeers that afternoon at the Mauritshuis, that that was precisely what the Master of Delft had been about in his life's work: at a tremendously turbulent juncture in the history of his continent, he had been finding—and, yes, inventing—a zone filled with peace, a small room, an intimate vision . . . and then breathing it out.

It's one of the great things about great works of art that they can bear—and, indeed, that they invite—a superplenitude of possible readings, some of them contradictory. One of the most idiosyncratic responses to Vermeer I have ever encountered was that of the Afrikaner poet and painter Breyten Breytenbach during a walk we took one morning through the galleries of New York's Metropolitan Museum. Breytenbach, who was a clandestine antiapartheid activist, had only recently emerged from seven years of incarceration in the monochrome dungeons of the apartheid regime, and most of his comments that morning had to do with the lusciousness of all the colors in the paintings we were passing. For the most part though, we were silent, moving at a fairly even pace from room to room—that is, until we came to Vermeer's painting of the young girl in the deep-blue skirt standing by a window, her hand poised on a silver pitcher, the window light spreading evenly across a map on the wall behind her. Here Breytenbach stopped cold for many moments, utterly absorbed. "Huh," he said finally, pointing to the gallery's caption giving the date of the painting: circa 1664–65. "It's hard to believe how from all that serenity emerge the *Boere*. Look." He jabbed a finger at the little boats delicately daubed on the painted map's painted coastline. *"That's them leaving right now!"* (And, indeed, Cape Town had been founded by the Dutch East India Company only a decade earlier, and would soon start filling up with some of the Huguenots who had flooded into Holland following a fresh upsurge of repression back in France.)

Edward Snow, for his part, makes quite a convincing case that Vermeer's art is above all about sexuality and as such provides one of the most profound explorations of the wellsprings of the erotic in the entire Western tradition. It is about female reserve and autonomy and self-sufficiency in the face of the male gaze, Snow suggests, or even in the seeming absence of such a gaze.

In this context, the pièce de résistance in his argument is a brilliantly sustained twenty-page close reading of Vermeer's magnificent (though uncannily diminutive) *Head of a Young Girl*—sometimes referred to, alternatively, as *The Girl in a Turban* or *The Girl with a Pearl* (at the Mauritshuis, it happens to face *The View of Delft,* just across the room). Snow's approach to this overexposed and by now almost depleted image is to ask, Has the girl just turned toward us or is she just about to turn away? Looked at with this question in mind, it does seem that such immanence, one way or the other, is of its essence. As Snow points out, if we momentarily blot out the face itself, everything else conspires to make us expect a simple profile of a head—so that afterward, as we allow ourselves to look again on the face unobstructed, the girl does seem to have only just now turned to face us. But if we look for a moment at the pendant of cloth cascading down from the knot at the top of her turban, it seems at first as if that pendant ought to fall behind her far shoulder; in fact it falls far forward, provoking a visual torsion precisely opposite to that of the one we'd surmised earlier: no, on second thought, she seems to be pulling away. The answer is that she's actually doing both. This is a woman who has just turned toward us and is already about to look away: and the melancholy of the moment, with its impending sense of loss, is transferred from her eyes to the tearlike pearl dangling from her ear. *It's an entire movie in a single frozen image.* (One is in turn reminded of the obverse instance of Chris Marker's ravishing short film from 1962, *La Jetée,* a Vermeer-saturated romance made up entirely of still shots unfurling evenly, hypnotically, one after the next, with the sole exception of a single moving-picture sequence: the woman asleep in bed, her eyes closed, her eyes opening to gaze up at us, and then closing once again. A sequence that passes so quickly—in the blink, we say, of an eye—that it's only moments later that we even register its having been a moving-picture sequence at all.)

15   The girl's lips are parted in a sudden intake of breath—much, we suddenly notice, as are our own as we gaze back upon her. And in fact an astonishing transmutation has occurred. In the moment of painting, it was Vermeer who'd been looking at the girl and registering the imminent turning-away of her attention (the speculation among some critics that Vermeer's model for this image may have

been his daughter renders the conceit all the more poignant); subsequently, it was, of course, the painted image that would stay frozen in time, eternally attentive, while it was he as artist who'd eventually be the one turning away; and, still later, it would be Vermeer himself who, through the girl's gaze, would remain faithful, whereas it would be we viewers, casually wandering through the museum and tarrying before the image for a few, breath-inheld moments, who would be the ones eventually turning away. *The Head of a Young Girl* thus becomes a picture about presence and eternity, or, at any rate, posterity.

But this is only because it is first and foremost a painting about intersubjectivity: about the autonomy, the independent agency, dignity, and self-sufficiency of the Other, in whose eyes we in turn are likewise autonomous, self-sufficient, suffuse with individual dignity and potential agency. And here is where we come full circle: because if Vermeer's work can be said to be one extended invention—or assertion—of a certain concept of peace-filledness, this is precisely how he's doing it, by imagining or asserting the possibility of such an autonomous, inhabited sense of selfhood.

The scale of Vermeer's achievement becomes even clearer if, like me, you have a chance to walk among some of the genre pieces by Vermeer's Dutch contemporaries, also scattered about the Mauritshuis (it was getting late now and I wanted to make it back for the final session of the preliminary Tadic hearing, but I did tarry for a few minutes longer in some of the museum's adjoining rooms).

For many years, Vermeer's works were themselves seen primarily as instances of these sorts of moralizing genre images. The Metropolitan's *Girl Asleep* was thus cast as yet another castigating allegory of feminine sloth and drunkenness, while Berlin's *Woman Putting on Pearls* was folded into the tradition of vanity motifs. The Frick's *Officer and*

Laughing Girl was assigned to the tradition of vaguely unsavory prostitution images (as, naturally, was Dresden's *Procuress,* from earlier in Vermeer's career); conversely, the Louvre's *Lacemaker* was seen in the context of more positively tinged illustrations of industriousness, and the Rijksmuseum's *Milkmaid* was cast as yet another prototypically Dutch celebration of the domestic virtues. All of which misses the essential point, because in each of these instances and in virtually every other one of his paintings, Vermeer deploys the conventional iconography precisely so as to upend it. No, his paintings all but cry out, this person is not to be seen as merely a type, a trope, an allegory. If she is standing in for anything, she is standing in for the condition of being a unique individual human being, worthy of our own unique individual response. (Which is more than can be said, generally, for the men in Vermeer's paintings, who do seem, hovering there beside the women, to stand in for the condition of being somewhat oafishly de trop.)

Or so, anyway, I found myself thinking in the taxi as I returned to the Tribunal—of that and of the way in which the entire Yugoslavian debacle has been taking place in a context wherein the Other, even one's own neighbor, is suddenly being experienced no longer as a subject like oneself but as an instance, a type, a vile expletive, a Serb, a Croat, a Turk, and, as such, preordained for an ages-old, inevitable fate. (Note that such a construction has to be as assiduously "invented" as its obverse: people who've been living in relative peace for decades have to be goaded into seeing one another, once again, in this manner.) No wonder that Cassese flees to Vermeer for surcease.

20   A Dutch journalist named Alfred van Cleef recently published a remarkable book, *De Verloren Wereld van de Familie Berberovic (The Lost World of the Berberovic Family),* in which he traces the downward

spiral of the last five years in Yugoslavia through the shattered prism of one Bosnian family's experience. Early in his narrative, he recounts how the war came came to the Berberovic family's village, how for many months its members had been picking up the increasingly strident harangues welling out from the Belgrade and Zagreb television stations but hadn't worried because theirs was a peaceful village, where Serbs and Croats and Muslims lived equably together, with a high degree of intermarriage, and so forth. Then the war was just two valleys over, but still they didn't worry, and then it was in the very next valley, but, even so, no one could imagine its actually intruding into their quiet lives. But one day a car suddenly careered into the village's central square, four young men in militia uniforms leaping out, purposefully crossing the square, seeming to single out a particular house and cornering its occupant, whereupon the leader of the militiamen calmly leveled a gun at the young man and blew him away. The militiamen hustled back to their car and sped off. As van Cleef subsequently recounted the incident for me, "They left behind them a village almost evenly divided. Those under fifty years of age had been horrified by the seeming randomness of the act, while those over fifty realized, with perhaps even greater horror, that the young man who'd just been killed was the son of a man who, back during the partisan struggles of the Second World War, happened to have killed the uncle of the kid who'd just done the killing. And the older villagers immediately realized, with absolute clarity, that if this was now possible everything was going to be possible."

David Rieff tells a story about visiting a recent battlefield at one point during the war in the company of a small band of fellow journalists: Muslim corpses strewn across the muddy meadow, a Serb soldier grimly standing guard. "'So,' we asked the soldier, this young kid," Rieff recalls, "'What happened here?' At which point the soldier took a drag on his cigarette and began, 'Well, in 1385 . . .'"

Yugoslavia today has been turned back into one of those places where people not only seem incapable of forgetting the past but barely seem capable of thinking about anything else: the Serbs and Croats and Muslims now appear to be so deeply mired in a poisonous legacy of grievances, extending back fifty years, two hundred years—indeed, all the way back to the fourteenth century—that it's almost as if the living had been transformed into pale, wraithlike shades haunting the ghosts of the long-dead rather than the other way around.

Which is to say that we're back in the moral universe of epic poetry: the Iliad, Beowulf, the Chanson de Roland, the Mahabharata, and, of course, *Finnegans Wake*—a modernist recasting of the entire epic tradition, composed during the thirties by James Joyce, who once characterized history as "two bloody Irishmen in a bloody fight over bloody nothing." Not so much over bloody nothing, perhaps, as vengeance for vengeance for vengeance for who-any-longer-knows-what? That's the heart of the epic tradition: those twinned themes of the relentless maw of vengeance and the ludicrous incommensurability of its first causes recur time and again, from one culture to the next. It's worth remembering how, also during the thirties, when the great Harvard classicist Milman Parry was trying to crack the Homeric code—to determine just how the ancient Greek bards were able to improvise such incredibly long poems, and what mnemonic devices they had devised to assist them—he scoured the world for places where such oral epic traditions were still alive, and the place he finally settled on as perfect for his purposes was Yugoslavia (see his disciple Albert Lord's seminal account in *The Singer of Tales*).

Vermeer was not a painter in the epic tradition: on the contrary, his life's work can be seen, within its historical moment, as a

heroic, extended attempt to steer his (and his viewers') way clear of such a depersonalizing approach to experiencing one's fellow human beings. It was a project, I now realized, as I took my seat in the visitors' gallery facing the Tribunal's glassed-in hearing room, not all that dissimilar from that of the Tribunal itself.

The day before, I'd spoken with Richard Goldstone, the eminent South African jurist who has been serving as the Yugoslav Tribunal's lead prosecutor. (He is serving the same role on the Tribunal that has been established to prosecute the war criminals in Rwanda.) I'd asked him how he envisioned the mission of the Tribunal, and he'd described it as nothing less than a breaking of the historic cycle of vengeance-inspired ethnic mayhem. He does not believe in the inevitability of such violence. "For the great majority of their histories, the Croats and Serbs and Muslims, and the Tutsis and Hutus, have lived in relative peace with one another—and they were all doing that relatively nicely once again until just recently," he told me. "Such interethnic violence usually gets stoked by specific individuals intent on immediate political or material advantage, who then call forth the legacies of earlier and previously unaddressed grievances. But the guilt for the violence that results does not adhere to the entire group. Specific individuals bear the major share of the responsibility, and it is they, not the group as a whole, who need to be held to account, through a fair and meticulously detailed presentation and evaluation of evidence, precisely so that the next time around no one will be able to claim that all Serbs did this, or all Croats or all Hutus—so that people are able to see how it is specific individuals in their communities who are continually endeavoring to manipulate them in that fashion. I really believe that this is the only way the cycle can be broken."

The preliminary hearings now resumed. Tadic was seated in a sort of aquarium of bulletproof glass, a panoply of high-tech gadgetry arrayed all around him and around the various lawyers and judges: instantaneous-translation devices, video cameras and monitors, computerized evidence screens, and so forth.

Inventing peace: I found myself thinking of Vermeer with his camera obscura—an empty box fronted by a lens through which the chaos of the world might be drawn in and tamed back to a kind of sublime order. And I found myself thinking of these people here with their legal chamber, the improbably calm site for a similar effort at transmutation.

I looked up at the TV monitor: the automated camera was evidently scanning the room. It caught the prosecutors in their flow-ing robes shuffling papers, the judges, the defense table, and now Tadic himself. The camera lingered on him—a handsome young man, improbably dapper in a navy-blue jacket and a gleaming white open-collared dress shirt—and then zeroed in for a closer shot of his face.

There he was, not some symbol or trope or a stand-in for anybody other than himself: a quite specific individual, in all his sublime self-sufficiency; a man of whom, as it happened, terrible, terrible allegations had been made, and who was now going to have to face those allegations, stripped of any rationales except his own autonomous free agency.

For a startling split second, he looked up 30 at the camera. And then he looked away.

READING AND THINKING

1. Why does Weschler tell two stories of horror in his beginning? How does the judge keep from "going mad himself" as he is "obliged to gaze" into such horror?

2. Why does Weschler himself find the judge's answer perfectly apt?

3. Near the middle of the essay, Weschler turns to Vermeer's painting *Head of a Young Girl* and tells us that in this "almost depleted image" the girl simultaneously turns away from us and toward us. What use does he make of this observation in the ending of the essay?

4. To what extent does this essay depend on the power of images and the well-crafted story to develop its ideas?

THINKING AND WRITING

1. In a brief paragraph explain what use Weschler makes of Edward Snow's ideas in this essay.

2. What does Weschler figure out about Vermeer's paintings that informs his ideas about Bosnia and war crimes? Explain in one or two paragraphs.

3. Explain in a paragraph why Weschler contrasts Vermeer with the epic tradition in literature. Why is Vermeer's effort to "steer his (and his viewers') way clear of . . . a depersonalizing approach to experiencing one's fellow human beings" so central to Weschler's thinking?

4. To what extent is this essay an attempt to absolve ethnic groups of heinous crimes so that we begin to hold individuals responsible for their own misdeeds? In one or two paragraphs, explain the larger consequences of such thinking.

Mary Wollstonecraft (1759–1797)

Mary Wollstonecraft was born in London to a well-established family, whose fortune was wasted by her father. She was a radical feminist centuries before the idea of radical feminism became popular. Like many women of her era, Wollstonecraft worked as a seamstress and governess. In her twenties she became part of a circle of radical English artists and thinkers. Her publication, in 1790, of "A Vindication of the Rights of Man," a defense of the French Revolution, earned her a measure of fame. More controversial was her "A Vindication of the Rights of Women" (1792), which prompted one critic to refer to her as a "hyena in petticoats." Wollstonecraft died of complications related to the birth of her second child, Mary Shelley, author of *Frankenstein* and wife of the English poet Percy Bysshe Shelley.

A VINDICATION OF THE RIGHTS OF WOMEN

In "A Vindication of the Rights of Women," Mary Wollstonecraft provides a revolutionary examination of the status of women in eighteenth-century society. A polemic encouraging women to believe in their strength and spirit, Wollstonecraft's "Vindication" is a defense of women's rights. She presents an image of woman as an equal vessel rather than a man's weaker vessel, and one who should develop her character as a human being on an equal footing with a man.

1   My own sex, I hope, will excuse me, if I treat them like rational creatures, instead of flattering their *fascinating* graces, and viewing them as if they were in a state of perpetual childhood, unable to stand alone. I earnestly wish to point out in what true dignity and human happiness consists—I wish to persuade women to endeavor to acquire strength, both of mind and body, and to convince them that the soft phrases, susceptibility of heart, delicacy of sentiment, and refinement of taste, are almost synonymous with epithets of weakness, and that those beings who are only the objects of pity and that kind of love, which has been termed its sister, will soon become objects of contempt.

Dismissing, then, those pretty feminine phrases, which the men condescendingly use to soften our slavish dependence, and despising that weak elegancy of mind, exquisite sensibility, and sweet docility of manners, supposed to be the sexual characteristics of the weaker vessel, I wish to show that elegance is inferior to virtue, that the first object of laudable ambition is to obtain a character as a human being, regardless of the distinction of sex; and that secondary views should be brought to this simple touchstone.

This is a rough sketch of my plan: and I should express my conviction with the energetic emotions that I feel whenever I think of the subject, the dictates of experience and reflection will be felt by some of my readers. Animated by this important object, I shall disdain to cull my phrases or polish my style; I aim at being useful, and sincerity will render me unaffected; for, wishing rather to persuade by force of my arguments, than dazzle by the elegance of my language, I shall not waste my time in rounding periods, or in fabricating the turgid bombast of artificial feelings, which, coming from the head, never reach the heart. I shall be employed about things, not words! and, anxious to render my sex more respectable members of society, I shall try to avoid that flowery diction which has slided from essays to novels, and from novels into familiar letters and conversation.

These pretty superlatives, dropping glibly from the tongue, vitiate the taste, and create a kind of sickly delicacy that runs away from simple unadorned truth; and a deluge of false sentiments and overstitched feelings, stifling the natural emotions of the heart, render the domestic pleasures insipid, that ought to sweeten the exercise of those severe duties, which educate a rational and immortal being for a nobler field of action.

5   The education of women has, of late, been more attended to than formerly; yet they are still reckoned by a frivolous sex, and ridiculed or pitied by the writers who endeavor by satire or instruction to improve them. It is acknowledged that they spend many of the first years of their lives in acquiring a smattering of accomplishments: meanwhile strength of body and mind are sacrificed to libertine notions of beauty, to the desire of establishing themselves—the only way women can rise in the world—by marriage. And this desire making mere animals of them, when they marry they act as such children may be expected to act—they dress; they paint, and nickname God's creatures. Surely these weak beings are only fit for a seraglio!—Can they be expected to govern a family with judgment, or take care of the poor babes whom they bring into the world?

If then it can be fairly deduced from the present conduct of the sex, from the prevalent fondness for pleasure which takes place of ambition, and those nobler passions that open and enlarge the soul; that the instruction which women have hitherto received has only tended, with the constitution of civil society, to render them insignificant objects of desire—mere propagators of fools!—if it can be proved that in aiming to accomplish them, without cultivating their understandings, they are taken out of their sphere of duties, and made ridiculous and useless when the short-lived bloom of beauty is over,* I presume that *rational* men will excuse me for endeavoring to persuade them to become more masculine and respectable.

Indeed the word masculine is only a bugbear: there is little reason to fear that women will acquire too much courage or fortitude; for their apparent inferiority with respect to bodily strength, must render them in some degree, dependent on men in the various relations of life; but why should it be increased by prejudices that give a sex to virtue, and confound simple truths with sensual reveries?

Women are, in fact, so much degraded by mistaken motions of female excellence, that I do not mean to add a paradox when I assert, that this artificial weakness produces a propensity to tyrannize, and gives birth to cunning, the natural opponent of strength, which leads them to play off those contemptible infantile airs that undermine esteem even whilst they excite desire. Let men become more chaste and modest, and if women do not grow wiser in the same ratio, it will be clear that they have weaker understandings. It seems scarcely necessary to say, that I now speak of the sex in general. Many individuals have more sense than their male relatives; and, as nothing preponderates where there is a constant struggle for an equilibrium, without it has naturally more gravity, some women govern their husbands without degrading themselves, because intellect will always govern.

---

*A lively writer, I cannot recollect his name, asks what business women turned of forty have to do in the world?

READING AND THINKING

1. How would you characterize the tone of Wollstonecraft's opening sentence? How does she employ irony and cliché there and elsewhere in the passage? With what effects?

2. What argument does Wollstonecraft make about the intelligence of women and the wisdom of men? How does she use the conventional wisdom about women's intelligence to undermine traditional views of women's role as homemakers and raisers of children rather than as social and cultural influencers and leaders?

3. Why does Wollstonecraft urge the abandonment of conventional and customary descriptions of women, and of language such as "delicacy of sentiment" and "refinement of taste" when describing them?

4. What is the main idea of Wollstonecraft's piece, and where is it most directly and forcefully stated?

THINKING AND WRITING

1. Summarize in one paragraph the gist of Wollstonecraft's argument. Provide a clear statement of her main idea, along with a few sentences that identify the kinds of reasons she offers to support it.

2. Discuss the issue of physical strength as an apparent aspect of women's inferiority to men. To what extent do you think this remains an issue in gender relations? Why do you think Wollstonecraft brings it up?

3. Write an essay in which you consider the extent to which women at the beginning of the twenty-first century have achieved equality with men. Explain how women's status has changed since the time of Wollstonecraft, and consider ways in which the status of women has remained much the same.

FINDING EVIDENCE AND DOCUMENTING SOURCES

Good writing not only uses the English language effectively, but also incorporates evidence appropriately. Consider your everyday conversations with friends, family, or other students. Even in these informal situations, most of us use a variety of techniques to support our assertions. If you want to convince your friends to try a new restaurant, you might tell them that the restaurant was positively reviewed by the local newspaper. You might also point to the ways in which the testimony of others or personal experience corroborates your claim. Similarly, a strong written argument is comprised of both claims and evidence.

WHAT IS EVIDENCE?

Any outside source that enables you to write more critically and thoroughly about your topic of research, and assists you in persuading your audience of your argument, can be considered evidence. Evidence includes a wide range of materials; it can be either written or visual. Remember that you can find evidence from your reading, your observation, and your own experiences. As you develop your idea, or account for your evidence, you may look to traditional forms of evidence, such as books, journals, magazines, newspapers, and electronic sources (such as websites, discussion forums, and online books and magazines). You might also, however, turn to nontraditional items as sources. Billboards and signs, even song lyrics and video games, can be used as evidence. The controversies that shape the world around us are reflected not only in written works, art, music, and film, but also in the clothes that people wear, bumper stickers, and children's toys. Your idea about a particular topic will be expressed best to your audience if you provide a wealth of evidence and support. Allow yourself to be creative as you look for evidence to help you develop a perspective about a particular topic.

As you conduct research, you'll want to distinguish between primary and secondary sources. Primary sources can be generally defined as original work. For example, in the humanities, a primary source is a document, such as a letter, diary, or literary work. In the social sciences, primary sources include measurements and experiments. Some other examples of primary sources include interviews, memos, manuscripts, memoirs, autobiographies, and records collected by a government agency. Primary sources allow you to get as close to original ideas as possible and, consequently, to develop your own interpretation of an idea without being influenced by someone else's analysis. If you want to write an essay that explains Thomas Jefferson's ideas about slavery, reading his correspondence, diaries, and speeches will allow you to interpret his views more accurately. Similarly, if you are trying to determine your point of view regarding homelessness, you might examine statistics that tell you how many people are homeless, their ages, and their genders. Along with finding out what others think about a source or sources, it is a good idea to review that evidence yourself.

A secondary source interprets, examines, or analyzes a primary source or sources. Encyclopedias, textbooks, and dictionaries are examples of secondary sources. Other examples of secondary sources include a review of a film or novel, a journal article that explains the results of a scientific survey, or a book that examines the letters and poems of a poet. Secondary sources are useful in several ways. If you are unfamiliar with your topic, secondary sources can provide you with a summary of the evidence. You might be interested in writing an essay about candy, for example. An encyclopedia will tell you the history of candy and might inspire you to write about a more specific aspect of candy. Secondary sources also allow you to study other people's perspectives about an idea. Studying the body of evidence about prayer in school, for example, requires a consideration of how both those opposed to and for prayer in school understand the United States Constitution. A good essay interprets all of the views about a controversial issue for the audience, and that requires an examination of secondary sources. Knowing whether the evidence you are studying is primary or secondary will enable you to understand and use the source in the most effective way.

THE USES OF EVIDENCE

Since evidence can be found in such a wide range of places, you might assume that adding it to your paper is as simple as opening up any book, picking out a quote or fact that seems to support your argument, and inserting it into your paper. Using evidence, however, and more importantly, using it *well,* requires thought and effort. Following are some of the most basic ways in which evidence is used, although evidence can be used in many ways and you can adapt or create your own methods for successfully using evidence. Many writers decide on a thesis or main idea and then find evidence that either confirms or challenges that idea. By engaging in a dialogue with the evidence, the writer proves his or her point. Another more sophisticated way of using evidence requires the writer to think of a research topic but refrain from forming an opinion about the issue at hand until reviewing a significant number of sources. For example, a student might decide that she wants to write about global warming. Instead of beginning her research paper with a perspective in mind, such as "global warming is caused by pollution," the student gathers information about global warming with the aim of formulating her main idea based on her consideration of the evidence. The paper is then written *because of* the evidence; the evidence does not support the paper's thesis, but *drives* it.

USING EVIDENCE AS SUPPORT

One of the most common uses of evidence is to support your argument. Supporting evidence can come from a variety of places. You might point to the ways in which statistics, charts, graphs, photographs, government documents, or websites confirm your assertions. For an idea to be convincing, it must be defended. As a reader, you probably often ask yourself, "How does the author know this?" Your audience will ask the same of you as a writer, and you must be prepared to explain how you have arrived at your conclusions. One of the best ways to convince your audience of your point of view is to appeal to sources that corroborate your main idea.

Consider a controversial issue—for example, same-sex marriages should be legalized. Clearly, there are many people who disagree with this statement. Consequently, a writer will not convince a skeptical audience that they are correct by beginning and ending their argument with this idea. If, however, the writer adds that statistics, expert testimony, and legal precedents support the notion that same-sex marriages are a good idea, the writer stands a better chance of changing the minds of those who disagree.

As you integrate sources into your paper, remember to make strong, unambiguous connections between the topic you are exploring and the evidence. While you may know how specific statistics, facts, or testimonies support your perspective, the audience does not. A convincing essay includes explicit statements that clearly state the relationship between the evidence and the main idea.

USING EVIDENCE TO ADDRESS COUNTERCLAIMS

Most issues that are worth arguing about are controversial; there is an abundance of evidence that supports different points of view. There are many views, for example, of the relationship between the media and teenage violence. A plethora of scientific studies demonstrates that the media causes teens to behave in violent ways. Similarly, there is much evidence that shows that the media and teen violence are unconnected. A good essay evaluates and explains both supporting evidence and the sources that disagree with your main idea.

Consequently, an essay whose main idea is that the media causes teens to commit violent acts should evaluate and comment on the sources that disagree. By addressing other viewpoints in a respectful way, you demonstrate to your audience that you are a well-informed, credible author.

USING EVIDENCE TO ADD DEPTH AND COLOR

Evidence can also be used to add depth and color to a paper. The best papers are those that include detailed and engaging sources. There are several other ways in which you can use evidence to flesh out your papers. Remember that evidence is not confined to the work of a famous author. What is appropriate evidence depends on the subject of your essay. You would not, for example, consult Charles Dickens's *Oliver Twist* if you were writing about your grandfather's experience as an orphan. On the contrary, you would interview your grandfather and use his words to explain the experience of living in an orphanage to your audience. If you are the president of a recycling group and decide to write about the benefits of recycling, your personal experiences are invaluable to your essay. Using personal narratives and interviews is most effective when you include several detailed memories. If, for example, a student is writing a personal narrative about his or her childhood, specific examples from the past will make it more interesting. You might explain to the readers that you spent the first three years of your life living in India, but without details about your daily life and important events, what could be an exciting narrative is just a fact about your childhood.

Another technique is to use narrative cases or examples that implicitly make your point. You might describe someone's personal experience or write in detail about a specific event as a means of supporting your main idea. A paper about migrant farm workers might be improved by adding a narrative paragraph about an individual's or family's experience. Cases or firsthand accounts provide opportunities for the writer to appeal to the reader's emotions and to fully engage the reader in the essay.

USING EVIDENCE TO BEGIN YOUR ESSAY

Evidence can also be a great way to begin your essay. As a reader, you are probably drawn to books and articles that start with an exciting plot twist or event. Similarly, as a writer you can use evidence to grab the reader's attention and to develop a framework for your paper. As mentioned earlier, using a case or example that supports your main idea is an excellent way to begin your paper.

You might also use the beginning of your essay to summarize your evidence and explain how you arrived at your main idea. If you are using evidence to drive your paper, the introduction is an opportunity to tell your audience that the sources you examined led you to adopt a certain point of view about your topic.

WHERE TO FIND EVIDENCE

It may be overwhelming to begin looking for evidence, but it's actually all around you. To help focus your search, though, you might want to consider looking on the Internet and searching at the library. But remember that you can use a range of materials—like texts, photographs, artworks, advertisements—as evidence, as this book has shown you to do, as long as you provide enough critical thought to show your mind has been working through the evidence.

FINDING EVIDENCE ONLINE

The Internet is one place to find information about a wide range of topics. You may be very familiar with the Internet and how to use it, but if not, there are several places you can go for help. Most schools have computer centers that provide orientation courses which teach students how to log on to the Internet, send e-mails, and access websites. If your school does not provide such services, the local public library is another place that usually offers free Internet orientation courses.

Once you access the Internet, you can begin using it to search for evidence. Most students find that the best way to locate information online is to use a search engine. Some of the most popular search engines are Yahoo!, Google, Ask, and Lycos. Each of these search engines allows you to enter any search term. If you wanted to find information about the Hershey company using Google, for example, you would type "Hershey" into the text entry box and then click on "Google Search." The result is a list of URLs—everything from Hershey's website to personal home pages devoted to the benefits of eating chocolate will find their way into your list. The most effective searches are those that use specific search terms and employ the most appropriate search engine for your topic of research. You might think about narrowing your search by including dates, important names, or even specific places in the text entry box. A good place to find out more about search engines and their uses is Search Engine Watch.com (http://www.searchenginewatch.com/). This website provides information about specific search engines and their limitations. While the Internet can provide you with good evidence for your paper, there are several other places you can look for and find good evidence.

FINDING EVIDENCE AT THE LIBRARY

Libraries contain novels, magazines, newspapers, dictionaries, encyclopedias, journals, films, music, and a wide range of other materials. Entering a library can be overwhelming, but there are a few general rules that apply to most libraries. Usually, the best way to start researching your topic is to consult the library's catalog. Many libraries have online catalogs that can be searched using computer terminals. Some universities even have online catalogs that you can access from your home computer, which makes researching even easier.

In most cases, the catalog provides several different search options. If you have a particular book in mind, you might search for it using the title or the author as a keyword. If not, you might do a subject search to compile a list of books that fit your research interests. During your search you will notice that each book is identified by a call number. Write the complete call number down and then consult a map of the library to find your book.

Most libraries have separate electronic indexes for periodicals. Some popular indexes include *InfoTrac, Expanded Academic ASAP,* and *Lexis-Nexis.* Many of these indexes include the full text of the article, which makes researching much simpler. If the index does not include the full article, however, you will need to consult the library's general catalog as well. Once you have compiled a list of articles you are interested in reading, search the library catalog to find the call number for the periodical in which the article appears.

Most libraries also provide their patrons with many opportunities to improve their understanding of the library. There are usually a variety of orientation classes that provide instruction on everything from finding books to searching electronic indexes. Another option is to consult the librarian at the help desk. If you understand how your library works, conducting research will be more efficient and profitable.

FINDING EVIDENCE ALL AROUND YOU

Good researchers know that evidence is everywhere. You might read an article in a magazine or an editorial in your school newspaper that sheds new light on your topic of research. Many writers reference television commercials, sculptures, or photographs when making an argument. As mentioned earlier, it is important to be flexible as you gather evidence about your topic. A body of evidence is determined by the subject, and it is not limited to books, articles, and the Internet. Consequently, an essay might point to images, objects, or personal experience as a way to convey, as well as support or disprove, the main idea. Once you choose a research topic, you can examine the world around you through the lens of your subject. You might find your best evidence in the most unlikely of places.

EVALUATING SOURCES

This appendix has focused on the importance of being flexible when gathering evidence. Such a view might suggest that any and all evidence is appropriate for any essay. On the contrary, while the kind of evidence you use can be varied, you must always evaluate the appropriateness and content of your sources. As you examine your sources, you should ensure that the topic each source relates to somehow addresses the question you are asking. Evaluating sources also requires that you determine whether a source is credible or biased, which shapes how you interpret and use the source. By evaluating your sources, you ensure that you understand and effectively use the evidence you gather.

DOES IT ADDRESS MY RESEARCH QUESTION?

Many writers get discouraged when they begin researching because there is simply too much information. As you research and write, the focus of your paper might change, and a source might lose its relevancy. If you get frustrated, keep in mind that researching is a process, and it takes time to decide which sources will be most relevant and how to focus your ideas.

As you read through books, you might find that only one chapter is applicable to your topic. Do not feel that a source should be ignored simply because only part of it is useful. There are several ways to determine whether a source addresses your topic and what specific parts of it pertain to your research question. Before you read an entire book, peruse the table of contents. Look for keywords that indicate whether a specific chapter contains information that is relevant to your topic. If the book has an index, inspect it as well. There is often no need to read a book cover to cover. The table of contents and the index are like maps to a book; consulting them can save you time and make your research process more efficient.

Journal articles are often prefaced by abstracts. Before diving into the article, skim the abstract and look for signs that the article is relevant. If the article does not have an abstract, examine the section heads, or read the topic sentence of each paragraph.

HOW RELIABLE IS THE INFORMATION?

While finding evidence is important, of equal value is deciding whether that evidence is credible. Certainly, you may use evidence that is not credible or that is biased, as we will discuss later. When you examine your body of evidence, however, a source's credibility can determine how it can be interpreted and used in your essay.

THE AUTHOR

To establish the reliability of the source you are using, begin by examining the author's credibility. A dependable author addresses the reader in a respectful way. They also use specific evidence to support their assertions, and they explain how and from where they obtained their information. Credible authors also address potential counterclaims to their assertions. Notice that the rules for good writing also apply to sources.

There are several techniques you can use to find out more about an author who is not well known. Check the jacket of the book first; a brief biography of the author often appears on the front or back. The preface is another place where authors list credentials. You can also search for information about the author on the Internet. University and college professors as well as popular novelists and political writers often have their own Web pages. As you delve deeper into the research process, you might notice that all of the articles and books you are reading refer to a particular author. The frequent reference of an author by other sources is another good indication that the author is credible. Finally, reviews often include information about an author's profession, education, and previous work.

As you examine authors' credentials, assess how well their past experiences prepared them to write about their topic. A reliable author often has an educational background that is closely related to the subject matter. If the author's previous or current job is related to his research, that is another good indication that the author is knowledgeable about the topic. Also review the author's publishing record; a history of well-received work suggests that the author is credible.

THE PUBLICATION

Another way to determine the reliability of your sources is to evaluate the publication in which the information appears. Generally, books that are published by academic presses are dependable. Some examples of academic presses are Yale University Press, Cambridge University Press, and Chicago University Press. Commercial presses also publish well-researched texts, but keep in mind that these publishers are more focused on profits than academic presses are. Some examples of commercial presses with strong reputations are HarperCollins; Farrar, Straus and Giroux; and Random House. Similarly, academic journals are usually more credible than popular magazines. Academic journals are often refereed; they only publish work that has been recommended by reviewers. When evaluating a popular magazine, consider the reputation of the magazine, the length of the article, and the credibility of the author. Magazines such as the *Atlantic Monthly, Harper's Weekly, The New Yorker,* and *The Economist* are more respected than magazines like *US Weekly, Esquire,* and *Mademoiselle.* Newspapers also have varying reputations, and you should assess each newspaper article by examining the content and the author's credibility. Newspapers like the *New York Times,* the *Washington Post,* and the *Los Angeles Times* have stronger reputations than newspapers like *USA Today.* Do not dismiss a newspaper, however, simply because it is not nationally recognized. Your local newspaper and school newspaper, for example, are often good sources of information if you are writing about an issue that affects your city or college.

THE WEBSITE

When evaluating a website's reliability, examine the site's content, its timeliness, and its author. Does the author back her claims by pointing to specific and relevant evidence? Has the site been updated recently and are the links active? Often the author of a website is not listed, so it is difficult to determine the author's credentials. If an author is listed, follow the rules mentioned earlier to evaluate the author's reliability. Also ask yourself if the sponsors of the site are well respected and if they have a specific agenda in mind. While many websites might appear to be informative, in many cases they are simply marketing tools. Take care to determine whether a website is informational or an advertisement. If the website documents its sources through citations and active links to other sites, that is another good indication that the site is credible.

VISUAL SOURCES

You should also evaluate the visual sources you use. In many cases, you can assess a visual source's credibility by following many of the same rules you do for written sources. Although visual sources do not have authors, the name of the individual who created the visual is often listed. Photographs in newspapers and magazines, for example, are usually credited to a particular person. Similarly, paintings and sculptures are usually credited to an artist. Like information about authors, information about photographers and artists can also be found on the Internet and in written reviews. Researching an artist or photographer's past work and career history will also help you evaluate his reliability and even his purpose or motivation. Where a visual is published is also a good way to determine whether it is credible. Photographs that appear in reputable newspapers and magazines, for example, are more reliable than photographs that appear in the *National Enquirer*. While a photograph of an alien from the *National Enquirer* might be a perfectly appropriate source to include in an essay that explains why people believe in UFOs, it is important to recognize and explain to your audience that the photograph is probably biased.

RECOGNIZING BIAS

Biases can be difficult to recognize because many sources argue a certain point of view. While it is often a challenge to determine whether an author is biased, doing so ensures that you understand the source in an appropriate way. There are several distinctions between an author who is dedicated to proving a point and an author who is biased. Often, one can identify a bias by examining the author's tone. Authors who personally attack others or use prejudicial language are biased. Authors with a bias also use incorrect or unverifiable evidence to make their point. Finally, authors with a bias usually ignore or disparage counterclaims and counterarguments.

WHERE DOES MY EVIDENCE STAND?

Once you have decided which sources are credible and which ones are biased, you can evaluate where your evidence stands. It is important not only to examine each source individually, but also collectively. At this point, it is essential that you make connections between each source. If you are using the evidence to drive your paper, to lead you to an expression of an idea for your own essay, studying the evidence as a whole allows you to form that idea.

As you review your sources as a body of evidence, imagine that they are engaging in a dialogue with one another. What kind of conversation would these sources have and how can you contribute to it? Another way to establish connections between your sources is to ask specific questions. Some examples are:

- How do sources with competing views address their opponents?
- What kind of evidence does each source use to support its main point and why?
- Are some sources more interesting or persuasive than others? Why?
- What do biased sources tell you that credible sources do not?
- Are there certain ideas, facts, solutions, or themes that all of your sources refer to?

The more questions you ask to establish relationships between each of your sources, the better able you will be to view them as a collective body of evidence.

WHAT DOES MY EVIDENCE HELP ME DO?

Once you have assessed where your evidence stands and decided on the main idea or ideas your essay will address, you can begin thinking about how to best use each source. Some sources are better than others for supporting a particular point. Consider an essay about the benefits of Internet dating, for example. A writer gathers a variety of evidence, including statistics about how many people use Internet dating services, interviews from people who have used Internet dating services, and websites for specific services. Each source will help the writer support a different point. The writer might use statistics, for example, to explain how widespread the Internet dating phenomenon is. Interviews from those who have used Internet dating services allow the writer to find out what individual participants did and did not like about the process. Finally, although a website for a specific Internet dating service is clearly biased, by studying a specific site, the writer can better understand how participants use the Internet to date. The writer would not, however, use statistics about how many people use Internet dating services to prove the point that participants enjoy Internet dating. While each source supports the writer's main idea, they are not interchangeable. Some sources are better for establishing the issue's background, while others can explain a specific person or group's opinion about a topic. Remember to ask of each source, "What can this evidence help me do?"

INTEGRATING SOURCES AND AVOIDING PLAGIARISM

To integrate sources into your paper, you can either paraphrase or directly quote an author. In both cases, it is important to use the author's ideas to support your point, not to make it. If you are paraphrasing, first introduce the author and then summarize her ideas. Follow this discussion with an explanation of how the source relates to your argument. If you directly quote an author, then follow the quote with a discussion of how it is connected to your main ideas. Without explanation, the quote's intended purpose is lost on the audience.

Deciding whether you should paraphrase or directly quote a source can be difficult. In general, you should only directly quote a source when preserving the author's language is important. There are many famous quotes, such as "To be or not to be, that is the question," from Shakespeare's *Hamlet*. In this case, the author's wording is essential—only this phrasing can convey the idea in the most powerful way. It is more difficult to determine whether you should directly quote a source when it is less well known. In most cases, however, you can paraphrase the author's wording and convey the same information, being sure to give credit to the author in your discussion. Quotations can be distracting, and many authors fall into the trap of using direct quotes to convey their main idea. Consequently, you should try to paraphrase in most cases rather than relying on direct quotes from your sources.

It is essential that you document your sources as you integrate them into your paper. If you present another author's ideas as your own, you are committing plagiarism. Plagiarism is a serious offense that can result in expulsion from your college or university. Certainly, you do not have to document every fact that you include in your paper. There are many facts that are considered general information. Some examples are statements like, "Our solar system is comprised of nine planets," or "Abraham Lincoln was the sixteenth president." Facts that are not well known, however, and that cannot be found in several sources, must be documented. Furthermore, if you include the opinion, assertion, or conclusions of another author in your paper, you must cite the source from which it came. Suppose, for example, that you are writing a paper about school vouchers and you find the following quote:

> Today 63% of all black students attend predominantly nonwhite schools. Public education is also increasingly economically segregated. A voucher system may not foster the ethnic diversity of a Benetton ad, but by diluting the distinction between public and private schools, it would add much needed equality to American education.
>
> Shapiro, Walter. "Pick a School, Any School." <u>Time</u> 3 Sept 1990: 70–72.

Below is an example of plagiarism. The writer uses too many of the same words and phrases as the author of the source:

> Public education is actually increasingly economically segregated. So a voucher system may not foster ethnic diversity, but it will dilute the distinction between public and private schools. This will add much needed equality to American education.

To avoid plagiarizing, you might decide to paraphrase the author, in which case you should use your own words to convey the author's ideas:

> According to Walter Shapiro, the argument that public education ensures that students attend schools with diverse students is erroneous. In fact, Shapiro asserts, public school populations usually comprise students of the same race and economic

background. Consequently, school vouchers might actually increase racial and economic diversity in education by offering minorities and the underprivileged the opportunity to attend the school of their choice (Shapiro 72).

Alternatively, you might decide that you do not want to lose the author's wording and want to quote directly from the source. If so, you can introduce the author and include the page number on which the quote appeared.

Walter Shapiro argues that, "A voucher system may not foster the ethnic diversity of a Benetton ad, but by diluting the distinction between public and private schools, it would add much needed equality to American education" (72).

DOCUMENTING SOURCES

As you add evidence to your paper, you will need to document it. There are several reasons for documenting your sources. Documenting evidence allows other researchers who are interested in your topic to locate the same sources. Documentation also demonstrates to your reader that your evidence is verifiable; by documenting your sources, you give yourself credibility as a writer. Finally, documenting your sources protects you against charges of plagiarism.

Each discipline has its own set of documentation guidelines. The Modern Language Association (MLA) style is often used in the humanities and requires that you document your evidence both within the paper by using parenthetical references and in a list of Works Cited at the end of your paper.

PARENTHETICAL REFERENCES IN THE TEXT

A parenthetical reference tells readers what sources you used in your writing and how you used them, as well as guides readers to the appropriate entry in the works cited list at the end of the paper. In general, then, a parenthetical reference should provide the reader with just enough information so that the source can easily be located in the works cited list.

When you are citing a work by one or more authors. A typical parenthetical reference includes the author's last name and the page number:

(Lasch 14)

If you introduce the author in the sentence, you need only include the page number in parentheses:

According to Rachel Carson, while humans may be at the top of the food chain, our existence is dependent on the health of the environment (149).

When you are citing a work without a listed author. List the title of the source and the page number.

> Many contend that the Food and Drug Administration does not possess enough re-sources to adequately inspect imported produce ("Fresh Produce, the Downside" 14A).

When you are citing an indirect source. When you quote someone who is not the author of the book or article, you are using an indirect source. Indicate that the source you are citing is quoted in another source by abbreviating the word "quoted."

> Describing feminism's contemporary ideology Susan Stein argued that, "feminism today is whatever any woman who calls herself a feminist says it is" (qtd. in Echols 264).

When you are citing an electronic source. If an electronic source does not have a page number, but uses paragraphs, sections, or screen numbers, write the abbreviation *par., sec.,* or the word *screen* and the corresponding number in your citation. Place a comma after the last name of the author.

> The program aims to teach low-income families how to use various software and computer technology (Hammill, par. 2).

If there are no divisions of any kind in the electronic source, simply list the last name of the author.

> At the end of 1991 over 4,000,000 people were connected to the Internet (Cerf).

MLA LIST OF WORKS CITED

Three of the most common documents used as evidence are books, journal articles, and websites.

A book with one author

Bellah, Robert N. Habits of the Heart: Individualism and Commitment in

American Life. Berkeley: U of California P, 1985.

Author's name   City of   Publisher's name,   Year of   Title of the book
in reverse   publication   abbreviated   publication

Paton, Alan. Cry, the Beloved Country. New York: Scribner's, 1948.

Article in a journal with continuous pagination throughout the annual volume

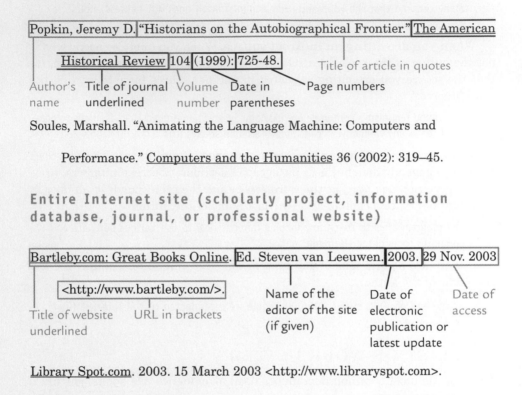

Popkin, Jeremy D. "Historians on the Autobiographical Frontier." The American

Historical Review 104 (1999): 725-48.

Author's name | Title of journal underlined | Volume number | Date in parentheses | Page numbers | Title of article in quotes

Soules, Marshall. "Animating the Language Machine: Computers and

Performance." Computers and the Humanities 36 (2002): 319–45.

Entire Internet site (scholarly project, information database, journal, or professional website)

Bartleby.com: Great Books Online. Ed. Steven van Leeuwen. 2003. 29 Nov. 2003

<http://www.bartleby.com/>.

Title of website underlined | URL in brackets | Name of the editor of the site (if given) | Date of electronic publication or latest update | Date of access

Library Spot.com. 2003. 15 March 2003 <http://www.libraryspot.com>.

BOOKS

A book with two or three authors

Duany, Andres, Elizabeth Plater-Zyberk, and Jeff Speck. Suburban Nation: The

Rise of Sprawl and the Decline of the American Dream. New York: North

Point, 2000.

Names appear as they do on title page

Reverse only the first name and separate names using commas

A book with more than three authors

McCartney, Paul, et al. The Beatles Anthology. San Francisco: Chronicle, 2000.

First name   Followed by
listed on the   et al.
title page

More than one work by the same author(s)

Weinberg, Steven. Dreams of a Final Theory. New York: Pantheon, 1992.

--- Facing Up: Science and Its Cultural Adversaries. Cambridge: Harvard UP,

2001.

In place of the author's name,
three hyphens and a period

A book with an editor

Dickinson, Emily. Collected Poems of Emily Dickinson. Ed. Mabel Loomis Todd

and T. W. Higginson. New York: Avenel, 1982.   Editor   Name of
                                                abbreviated   editors

A work in a series

Hock, Ronald F. and Edward N. O'Neil, ed. The Chreia in Ancient Rhetoric.

Texts and Trans. 27. Atlanta: Scholars, 1986.

Title of   Number in
the series   the series

An anthology

McNamara, Peter and Margaret Winch, ed. Alien Shores: An Anthology of

Australian Science Fiction. North Adelaide, Austral.: Aphelion, 1994.

Name of editor or compiler

A selection from an anthology

Ruskin, John. "The Lamp of Beauty." The Theory of Decorative Art: An Anthology

of European and American Writings 1750-1940. Ed. Isabelle Frank. New

York: Yale UP, 2000. 42-46.

Author of	Page numbers	Title of the part	Name of the editor,
the part of	of the cited	of the book	translator, or
the book	piece	being cited	compiler of the book
being cited			

A reference work

Unger, Rhoda K., ed. Handbook of the Psychology of Women and Gender. New

York: Wiley, 2001.

Editor or compiler
of reference book

Article in a reference work

Crawford, Mary. "Gender and Language." Handbook of the Psychology of Women

and Gender. Rhoda K. Unger, ed. New York: Wiley, 2001.

Author of article	Title of article	Title of book
in reverse	in quotes	underlined

A translation

Kundera, Milan. <u>The Unbearable Lightness of Being.</u> Trans. Michael Henry

Heim. New York: Harper, 1984.

Translator
abbreviated

Name of
translator

PERIODICALS

The entry for an article in a periodical, like that for a book, has three main divisions:

Author's name. "Title of the article." Publication information.

Article in a journal that paginates issues separately

Gardner, Martin. "A Quarter Century of Recreational Mathematics." Scientific

American 279. 2 (1998): 68-76. —— Page numbers

Author of
article

Volume
number,
followed by a
period

Issue number

Year of
publication in
parentheses,
followed by a colon

Title of article
in quotes

Title of
journal

Article in a monthly or bimonthly magazine

Lapham, Lewis. "Hazards of New Fortune: Harper's Magazine, Then and Now."

Harper's Magazine June 2000: 57-83. —— Page numbers

Title of magazine

Month of
publication

Year of publication
followed by a colon

Article in a weekly magazine (unsigned/signed)

Soukup, Elise. "Lights! Camera! Incision!: The Brave New World of Surgery on

the Internet." <u>Newsweek</u>. 14 Aug. 2006: 34. ⟵ Page number

Date of publication,
month abbreviated

Article in a newspaper

Wilkinson, Sean McCormack. "Security Posts Filled." <u>New York Times</u>

Title of article   Title of newspaper
in quotes   underlined

26 Nov. 2003: A12+.

Date abbreviated   If the article does not appear on
followed by a colon   consecutive pages, write the first
                        page number and follow with a
                        "+"

Review

Fields, Suzanne. "No Black-and-White Answers in Murray's <u>The Bell Curve</u>."

Rev. of <u>The Bell Curve</u> by Charles Murray and Richard J. Herrnstein.

<u>Insight on the News</u> 21 Nov. 1993: 40.

                Title of book   Author(s) of book   Title of review
                being reviewed   Date   being reviewed   in quotes
                underlined   abbreviated Page number
Review   followed by
abbreviated   Publication   colon
               in which
               the review
               appears

ONLINE SOURCES

Personal website

Boucicaut, J. R. Home page. 9 Oct. 2001. 14 Sept. 2003 <http://www.geocites.com/

Colosseum/8019/>.

Name of creator   Title of site, or   Date of the   Date of   URL in
of website   if no title   last update   access   brackets
                   "Home page"

Entire online book

Lewis, Sinclair. Babbitt. 1922. Bartleby.com: Great Books Online. Ed. Steven van

Leeuwen. 2003. 10 Oct. 2003 <http://www.bartleby.com/162/>.

Author's   Title of   Original   Title of   URL in   Editor of
name   book   publication   Internet site   brackets   site
                                            date of   underlined
            Date of   print version
            electronic   Date of
            publication   access

Article in a scholarly journal

Darby, Paul. "Africa, the FIFA Presidency, and the Governance of World Football:

1974, 1998, and 2002." Africa Today 50.1 (2003). Project Muse. 20 Oct. 2003

<http://muse. jhu.edu/journals/africa_today/toc/at50.1html>.

                                                                              Date of
URL within   Title of   Volume number   Issue   Year of   access
the   journal   followed by   number   publication
database   underlined   period   in   Name of
                                                         parentheses   database
                                                                              underlined

Article in an online reference book or encyclopedia

"Levi-Strauss, Claude." Encyclopædia Britannica. 2003. Encyclopædia Britannica

Premium Service. 28 Nov. 2000 <http://www.britannica.com/eb/article?eu=49112>.

Title of article in quotes

Name of electronic service

Title of online reference

Date of access

Date of the last update or electronic publication date

URL in brackets

Article in an online newspaper

Becker, Elizabeth. "Drug Industry Seeks to Sway Prices Overseas." New York

Times on the Web 27 Nov. 2003. 28 Nov. 2003 <http://www.nytimes.com/

2003/11/27/business/worldbusiness/27TRAD.html>.

Title of online newspaper underlined

Publication date

Date of access

Title of article in quotes

URL

Article in an online magazine

Soros, George. "The Bubble of American Supremacy." Atlantic Online December 2003.

28 Dec. 2003 <http://www.theatlantic.com/issues/2003/12/soros.htm>.

Date of access

URL of the article

Title of online magazine

Publication date

Work from a library subscription service

McNeill, J. "Historical Perspectives on Global Ecology." <u>World Futures</u> April-June

2003: 263-75. Expanded Academic ASAP. Gale Group. Bergen County

Cooperative Lib. System, NJ. 20 Oct. 2003 <http://www.galegroup.com/>.

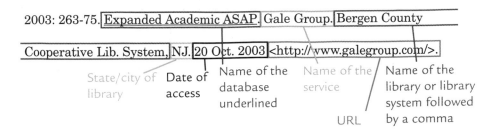

State/city of library   Date of access   Name of the database underlined   Name of the service   Name of the library or library system followed by a comma

URL

Material accessed through an online service

This citation is formatted the same as a work from a library subscription service (see example above).

Posting to a discussion list

Insaaci, Gemi. "Flow Around a Ship." Online posting. 20 Dec. 2003. CFD Online

Main Discussion Forum. 27 Nov. 2003 <http://www.cfd-online.com/

Forum/main.cgi?read =29211>.

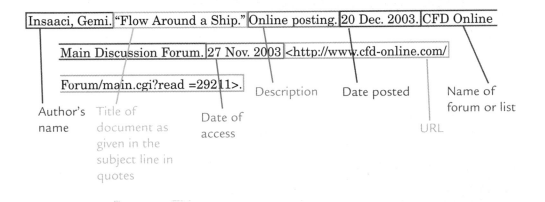

Author's name   Title of document as given in the subject line in quotes   Date of access   Description   Date posted   Name of forum or list

URL

Electronic mail

Nichols, Mona. "Re: Martha Stewart." E-mail to Elena M. Past. 20 July 2003.

Name of writer   Title of message, if any   Description of message that includes the recipient   Date of message

A synchronous communication

Harvey, Jon. Online discussion of how to create the ideal academic community.

7 Feb. 1996. PennMoo. 25 July 2003 <telnet:// www.english.upenn.edu/

~afilreis/103/pennmoo-exchange.html>.

Name of   Forum for the   Date of   URL   Description
the speaker   communication   access   of the event

Date of event

OTHER NONPRINT SOURCES

Material accessed on a CD-ROM, DVD, diskette, or magnetic tape

"Figure-Ground Contrast." Comp21: Composition in the 21st Century. CD-ROM.

Boston: Wadsworth, 2005.

Part of the   Title of source   Type of source
work you are   underlined
citing in
quotes

Painting, sculpture, or photograph on an electronic source

Munch, Edvard. The Scream. 1893. Comp21: Composition in the 21st Century.

CD-ROM. Boston: Wadsworth, 2005.

Artist's   Title of work   Date of work,   Title and type of electronic source
name   of art   if available   (if source is a website, use date of
                                                  access and URL)

An advertisement on an electronic source

Allen Edmonds Shoes. Advertisement. Comp21: Composition in the 21st

Century. CD-ROM. Boston: Wadsworth, 2005.

Name of product
or company being
advertised

Descriptive label
of advertisement
always included

Title and type of electronic source
(if source is a website, use date of
access and URL)

A film clip on an electronic source

The Price of Freedom. Comp21: Composition in the 21st Century. CD-ROM.

Boston: Wadsworth, 2005.

Title of film clip, preceded
by director, if available

Title and type of electronic source (if source
is a website, use date of access and URL)

An advertisement

Ford Explorer. Advertisement. Time 15 July 2002: 20-21.

Name of product or
company being advertised

Publication information (if
on television, use name of
network and the broadcast
date)

Page numbers
in publication

A painting, sculpture, or photograph

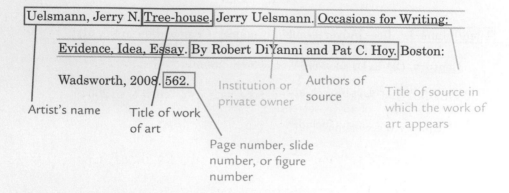

Uelsmann, Jerry N. Tree-house. Jerry Uelsmann. Occasions for Writing: Evidence, Idea, Essay. By Robert DiYanni and Pat C. Hoy. Boston: Wadsworth, 2008. 562.

- Artist's name
- Title of work of art
- Page number, slide number, or figure number
- Institution or private owner
- Authors of source
- Title of source in which the work of art appears

A film or video recording

Pakula, Alan J., dir. All the President's Men. Warner Bros., 1976.

- Director
- Title underlined
- Distributor
- Year of release

A television or radio program

"Firestorm." Narr. Charles Wooley. 60 Minutes. CBS. WCBS, New York. 23 Nov. 2003.

- Title of episode
- Broadcast date
- Narrator or director
- Title of program
- Name of the network
- Call letters and city of the local station

A letter

L'Engle, Madeleine. Letter to the author. 10 June 2003.

- Author of letter
- The kind of letter
- Date the letter was written

An interview

Friedman, Stephanie. Personal interview. 20 July 2003.

- Name of the person interviewed
- The kind of interview
- Date of interview

SAMPLE WORKS CITED PAGE

Works Cited

Bowman, Darcia Harris. "States Target School Vending Machines to Curb Child

    Obesity." <u>Education Week</u> 1 Oct. 2003: 1. <u>Academic Search Premier</u>.

    EBSCO. U of Texas at Austin, Perry-Castaneda Lib. 3 Mar. 2004

    <http://www.epnet.com>.

Chen, Chunming and William H. Dietz, ed. <u>Obesity in Childhood and</u>

    <u>Adolescence</u>. Philadelphia: Lippincott, 2002.

Drummond, Jon W. "Man vs. Machine: School Vending Machines Are in the

    Crosshairs of the Obesity Debate." <u>Restaurants and Institutions</u> 113.25

    (2003): 63-66.

Fairburn, Christopher G. and Kelly D. Brownell, ed. <u>Eating Disorders and</u>

    <u>Obesity: A Comprehensive Handbook</u>. 2nd ed. New York: Guilford, 2002.

Goode, Erica. "The Gorge-Yourself Environment." <u>New York Times</u> 22 July 2003:

    F1. <u>InfoTrac College Edition</u>. University of Texas at Austin, Perry-

    Castaneda Lib. 22 Dec. 2003 <http://www.infotrac.thomsonlearning.com/>.

Goodnough, Abby. "Schools Cut Down on Fat and Sweets in Menus." <u>New York</u>

    <u>Times</u>. 25 June 2003: B1.

<u>The Center for Health and Health Care in Schools</u>. Ed. Virginia Robinson. The

    Center for Health and Health Care in Schools. 26 Mar 2004. 5 Apr. 2004

    <http://www.healthinschools.org/home.asp>.

CREDITS

These pages constitute an extension of the copyright page. We have made every effort to trace the ownership of all copyrighted material and to secure permission from copyright holders. In the event of any question arising as to the use of any material, we will be pleased to make the necessary corrections in future printings. Thanks are due to the following authors, publishers, and agents for permission to use the material indicatcd.

TEXT

Virginia Woolf, "Death of the Moth" from *The Death of the Moth and Other Essays* by Virginia Woolf. Copyright 1942 by Harcourt, Inc. and renewed © 1970 by Marjorie T. Parsons, Executrix. Reprinted by permission of the publisher; "Portrait of a Londoner" from *A Room of One's Own* by Virginia Woolf. Copyright 1929 by Harcourt, Inc. and renewed © 1957 by Leonard Woolf. Reprinted by permission of the publisher.

Paul Zweig "Child of Two Cultures" by Paul Zweig. Copyright © 1982 by Paul Zweig. Originally appeared in the *New York Times Book Review,* February 28, 1982. Reprinted by permission of Georges Borchardt, Inc., for the author.

Ann Zwinger, "A Desert World" from *Testimony: Writers of the West Speak on Behalf of Utah Wilderness.* Compiled by Stephen Trimble and Terry Tempest Williams. Publishers Group West, Milkweed Edition, 1996.

VISUAL

p. xxii © 2004 Estate of Pablo Picasso/Artists' Rights Society (ARS), New York

p. 12 © Christie's Images/CORBIS

p. 66 © Thomas Roma, Brooklyn, NY. From "Show and Tell"

p. 67 © Ralph A. Clevenger/CORBIS

p. 70 top © Kevin Carter/Corbis Sygma

p. 70 bottom © Dan Heller, www.danheller.com

p. 72 © Bruno Barbey/Magnum Photos

p. 77 © Stephen Loy

p. 80 Photographed by Charles Hopkins. Courtesy of DaimlerChrysler Corporation

p. 81 © AP/Wide World Photos/Ken Lambert

p. 88 © Steven Lunetta Photography 2006

p. 97 top © Free Agents Limited/Corbis

p. 97 bottom © Matthias Weinrich

p. 103 © Estate of Guy Bourdin/Art + Commerce

p. 104 © Estate of Duane Hanson/Milwaukee Art Museum/VAGA, New York, NY

p. 112 © National Geographic/Getty Images

p. 113 top © Hubert Stadler/CORBIS

p. 113 bottom © 1969 Joseph Beuys. Image used by permission of Staatliche Museen Kassel. Image © 2006 Artist Rights Society (ARS), New York/VG Bild-Kunst, Bonn.

p. 121 © Estate of Duane Hanson. Licensed by VAGA, New York. NY. Image provided courtesy of the Estate of Duane Hanson.

p. 122 © Estate of Duane Hanson. Licensed by VAGA, New York. NY. Image provided courtesy of the Estate of Duane Hanson.

p. 123 © Estate of Duane Hanson. Licensed by VAGA, New York. NY. Image provided courtesy of the Estate of Duane Hanson.

p. 135 © Tina Fineberg/AP Photo

p. 542 left © 2006 Giraudon/Art Resource, NY/Artists Rights Society (ARS), New York/ADAGP, Paris

p. 542 right © Steven Lunetta Photography, 2006

p. 555 © Andy Warhol Foundation/CORBIS

p. 562 Copyright © 1982 Jerry Uelsmann.

p. 563 Copyright © 1982 Jerry Uelsmann.

p. 566 © Luc Novovith/AP Photo

p. 573 ©2005 China Photos/Getty Images

p. 574 © SHAUN BEST/Reuters/Corbis

p. 575 © Marianne Barcellona/Getty Images

p. 582 left © Bruce Davidson/Magnum Photos

p. 582 right © Bruce Davidson/Magnum Photos

p. 591 © Photo by Alex Wong/Time & Life Pictures/Getty Images

p. 592 © New York Daily News, 1999

p. 597 © Burt Glinn/Magnum Photos

p. 598 © Harry Gruyaert/Magnum Photos

p. 599 © David Turnley/CORBIS

p. 608 © 2006 Digital Image © The Museum of Modern Art/Licensed by SCALA/Art Resource, NY/Salvador Dali, Gala-Salvador Dali Foundation/Artists Rights Society (ARS), New York

p. 609 top p. 609, top © Digital Image © The Museum of Modern Art/Licensed by SCALA/Art Resource, NY

p. 609 middle © Asahachi Kono. Collection of Dennis Reed, Courtesy of the Boston University Art Gallery.

p. 609 bottom © Archivo Iconografico, S.A./CORBIS

p. 622 © Keith Carter

p. 623 © Kirk Anderson. www.kirkcartoons.com

p. 631 © 2006 Banque d'Images, ADAGP/Art Resource, NY/C. Herscovici, Brussels/Artists Rights Society (ARS), New York

p. 632 © Photothéque R. Magritte-ADAGP/Art Resource, NY/C. Herscovici, Brussels/Artists Rights Society (ARS), New York

p. 641 top © Bruce Gilden/Magnum Photos

p. 642 bottom © Thomas Hoepker/Magnum Photos

p. 652 top © CHAPLIN/UNITED ARTISTS/THE KOBAL COLLECTION

p. 652 bottom © 20TH CENTURY FOX/THE KOBAL COLLECTION/PAPPE, ALAN

p. 653 © WARNER BROS/THE KOBAL COLLECTION

p. 661 © Best of Latin America, Cagle Cartoons, El Universal, Mexico City

p. 669 © Sherwin Crasto/Reuters/Corbis

p. 670 © Najlah Feanny/CORBIS SABA

p. 671 Courtesy www.adbusters.org

p. 677 © Scott Leigh

INDEX OF VISUALS
AND READINGS